THE HISTORY OF THE
UNIVERSITY OF OXFORD

VOLUME III

Henry VIII is portrayed in the initial letter of a
mortmain licence granted to Cardinal Wolsey for the
endowment of Cardinal College, 10 May 1526.
Christ Church Archives F2.

THE HISTORY
OF THE
UNIVERSITY OF OXFORD

GENERAL EDITOR · T. H. ASTON

VOLUME III

The Collegiate University

EDITED BY
James McConica

CLARENDON PRESS · OXFORD
1986

Oxford University Press, Walton Street, Oxford OX2 6DP

Oxford New York Toronto
Delhi Bombay Calcutta Madras Karachi
Kuala Lumpur Singapore Hong Kong Tokyo
Nairobi Dar es Salaam Cape Town
Melbourne Auckland

and associated companies in
Beirut Berlin Ibadan Nicosia

Oxford is a trade mark of Oxford University Press

Published in the United States
by Oxford University Press, New York

British Library Cataloguing in Publication Data

The History of the University of Oxford.
Vol. 3: The collegiate university
1. University of Oxford—History
I. McConica, James
378.425'74'09   LF509
ISBN 0-19-951013-X

Library of Congress Cataloging in Publication Data
(Revised for vol. 3)
Main entry under title:
The History of the University of Oxford.
Contents: v. 1. The early Oxford schools/edited by
J. I. Catto —   — v. 3. The collegiate university/
edited by James McConica.
1. University of Oxford—History—Collected works.
I. Aston, T. H. (Trevor Henry)
LF508.H57   1984   378.425'74   83–17303

Set by Joshua Associates Limited, Oxford
Printed in Great Britain
at the University Printing House, Oxford
by David Stanford
Printer to the University

General Preface

I T is to be doubted if any private institutions have been so fortunate in attracting the attention of antiquarians and historians as have the university and colleges of Oxford. As early as the beginning of the fourteenth century Henry Harclay compiled his *historiola*, and in the next century John Rous assembled facts relating to the history of Oxford as well as his important list of colleges and academical halls. From the sixteenth century we have for instance Miles Windsor, 'antiquae historiae Artifex' (Brian Twyne) and author of the brief *Academiarum totius Europae catalogus* (1586 etc.). Later we have an increasingly rich assemblage of works and collections on the university and its colleges. To select but a few from the scholars and artists who directed at least some of their attention this way: Brian Twyne, indefatigable antiquarian and archivist of both Corpus Christi College and the university and collector of much other information on town and gown, who wrote the first, if short, history of the university, his *Antiquitatis academiae oxoniensis apologia* (1608), not least for propagandist purposes in relation to the relative antiquity of Oxford and Cambridge; David Loggan, in the tradition of John Bereblock (1566) and Ralph Agas (1578), the most outstanding draughtsman ever to tackle both university and colleges, who published in 1675 his beautifully executed engravings which are an invaluable architectural presentation; Anthony Wood who compiled the first large-scale history; John Gutch who finely edited and expanded Wood's work in the late eighteenth century; and Rudolph Ackermann, in whose history (1814) various artists depicted not only the exterior but also the interior of university and college buildings, not to mention academic robes and founders of colleges.

In the last century or so the pace has quickened. For instance we have the first attempt to survey the history of all colleges in the unpretentious but none the less useful series of College Histories (1898–1903), not to mention other particular studies. More recently in the third volume of the *Victoria History of the County of Oxford* (1954) we have short studies of the history of the university and each of the colleges by various hands. Much more important have been the publications of the Oxford Historical Society beginning in 1884. Some of these have been monographs of a high standard, but the majority have been of source material bearing on the history of the university and its colleges and of institutions in the town or the town itself with all of which they had the closest connections. Of the society's contributors one stands paramount, H. E. Salter, responsible alone or in collaboration for no less than thirty-five volumes. Then there is the relevant material in the Oxfordshire Record Society which began publication in 1919. Besides all this must be mentioned Strickland Gibson's *Statuta antiqua* (1931), a most masterly achievement even though subsequent work on the earliest volume of statutes, Registrum A, by himself and more prominently Graham Pollard, has altered the dating of many statutes and changed our understanding of the make-up of the volume as a whole; John Griffiths's edition of the Laudian code, with subsequent amendments, published in 1888; and the royal commission's edition, albeit far from definitive, of the *Statutes of the Colleges of Oxford* (1853). The result is that all the pre-1500 records of the university and much of later date are now available in scholarly print. In addition, on the side of biographical studies vital for social no less than personal and intellectual history, we have following on Foster's heroic if imperfect eight volumes covering the period 1500 to 1886 A. B. Emden's superb four volumes to 1540 not to mention sundry college registers.

But not surprisingly historians have recoiled from the monumental task of essaying an up-to-date version of Wood's history, save for Sir Henry Maxwell Lyte (1886) for the earlier centuries and Hastings Rashdall in the third volume of his *The Universities of Europe in the Middle Ages* (1895), subsequently (1936) and admirably edited by F. M. Powicke and A. B. Emden. It took an amateur, Sir Charles Mallet, boldly to attempt the overall task in his three-volumed *History of the University of Oxford* (1924–7). For one man this was in many ways a remarkable achievement, but it is no discredit to Mallet to observe that it did not really meet the need. Nor, in fact, could that need be met by a single person or even by a small number, though V. H. H. Green published an interesting short history in 1974. After all, by about 1966–7 there had been published, according to E. H. Cordeaux's and D. H. Merry's *Bibliography of Printed Works relating to the University of Oxford* (1968), no less than 8,868 items, some slight of course but more or less all requiring at least some attention. And in addition to these specifically relating to the university are countless others which have at least something to say of relevance to its history and character: many biographies, literary output, ephemera and other material. And yet the very richness of the collections, published and unpublished, primary and secondary, the vital role of Oxford over the centuries, the importance of its institutional and social no less than its intellectual history and so on required and posed the challenge for a truly comprehensive treatment on the grand scale. It was Lord Bullock who, towards the end of 1966, saw the need, pointed to the wealth of available material and to the fact that no individual scholar could undertake the necessary research for the authoritative account that was possible and required; it would have to be a co-operative effort. He took note of the fact also that the university was engaged on an extensive series of reforms which was a particularly appropriate time 'to put these reforms into a proper historical perspective [which] would be a declaration of confidence in ourselves as heirs of a great tradition which could not fail to make its impact at home and abroad' (memorandum to hebdomadal council, 17 October 1966, hebdomadal council papers, vol. 255, pages 279–80). The work was envisaged as a comprehensive history covering such aspects as the intellectual, the institutional, the social, the economic and the architectural character of the university in relation to national life and also its international role, with material on the colleges being included wherever this was relevant to the history of the university as such. Though to be launched by the university itself, the new History was in no way thought of as an 'official' one. Rather was it to be as scholarly and objective as possible and by no means to be written exclusively by scholars in Oxford.

It was Lord Bullock too who not only chaired the committee of inquiry into the proposal for a new and ambitious history but who steered it and its report through many discussions. Thus it was that the Project for the History of the University was launched in October 1968, among the most ambitious research projects in the humanities that the university has ever sponsored.

That the Project ever really materialized was, however, due not only to Lord Bullock's insight and skill as a negotiator, but to the financial generosity of various bodies. First, of course, the university itself. Then the university's higher studies fund. Thirdly the Nuffield Foundation with most handsome and continuing support. And finally, signalling the comprehensiveness at which the Project was aiming, the generality of the colleges which responded most warmly to the request for assistance. For this financial support we are deeply grateful. Beyond this we are indebted to bodies and persons who have supported the Project in various other ways. The colleges again, for instance, in the readiness with which they have given us access to their archives; and numerous individuals who will be thanked personally in the usual way in the editorial prefaces and chapters of the several volumes. Lastly we are deeply indebted to the Oxford University Press for shouldering the burden of publishing the new History. The new History will thus not only be co-operative in the sense that it is the work of many hands; it will also be so in the wide support on which it is founded.

T. H. A.

Preface

THE third volume of the History of the University of Oxford is planned to run from the end of the middle ages to the end of the Tudor period. The starting point is marked by the resumption of record evidence in the series of university registers which is broken in the fifteenth century. Institutionally, the dissolution of the religious houses is an obvious dividing line from volume two. However, the division is not neat. The dissolution as such, along with the last years of the monks and friars in Oxford, is treated in the second volume of this series as marking the end of the 'middle ages'. On the other hand the story of the rise of the undergraduate college, perhaps the dominant phenomenon of this crucial century in Oxford's history, cannot be explained satisfactorily without reference to the great undergraduate foundation in the previous century, so the opening chapter begins with a discussion of Magdalen College. At the close of the volume the foundation of the Bodleian Library would form a natural conclusion to the Elizabethan age but, by a general editorial decision at an early stage, it was agreed that the actual foundation should open the volume succeeding this one. Somewhat later it was also decided that the chapter on the finances of the university would be taken to the year 1640. Apart from those decisions responsibility for the organization of this volume is mine alone.

Within the limits imposed by collective authorship I have tried to construct a plan that would form, as far as possible, a unified study rather than a collection of specialist essays. As a framework it is intended that the narrative account of the public life of the university should be set forth in the two complementary chapters on the relations between the university and the Tudor state. The chapter on reformation controversies which somewhat overlaps them is meant to enlarge on aspects of the reformation in Oxford that could not be dealt with adequately from the stand-point of the university's response to public policy. The university's studies and intellectual life are discussed mainly in chapter 4 in connection with the teaching of the faculties but the first and last chapters contain important additional information, especially with respect to the arts faculty, in relation to the growth of collegiate teaching. The burden of the remaining chapters should be sufficiently clear from each title.

One of the aims of this History is to show the social relations of Oxford in each succeeding age. The fragmentary legacy of Tudor records made it abundantly clear that nothing in the way of a statistical study could be attempted. At the same time something had to be said about those social changes which have attracted so much attention from historians and caused the term 'educational revolution' to be applied to this century in particular. I have explained my approach in chapter 10, hoping to avoid generalization that may be both superficial and impressionistic, and instead to describe the membership of the college which set the pattern for the other foundations of the century, Corpus Christi. For the financing of investigation into the membership of Corpus Christi College from its foundation to the end of the reign of Elizabeth I, I am chiefly indebted to the Canada Council and its successor institution, the Social Sciences and Humanities Research Council of Canada, which was more than generous in encouraging this study.

As the investigation of the history of Tudor Oxford proceeded we were deprived by death at the height of his powers of J. P. Cooper of Trinity College. I am particularly grateful to Dr Gerald Aylmer, master of St Peter's College, for his generous and unhesitating response to my invitation to take up Dr Cooper's task. I must also record sadly the deaths of Canon Greenslade, who had virtually completed his study of the faculty of theology, and of N. R. Ker whose contribution had only just been completed when his life was so tragically cut short. There are other scholars less directly but very intimately involved in the creation of this volume who did not live to see its appearance, and I must mention in particular the late W. A. Pantin, A. B. Emden and R. W. Hunt. Our debts to them will be understood by any who have laboured in these fields.

Compared to the medieval centuries the history of Oxford under the Tudors is a fairly recent study and to some degree those involved in the preparation of this volume have had the task of writing what should aim to be a standard history largely from original and almost unexplored sources. All are indebted however to the volumes in the two series of the Oxford Historical Society, and to the recent discussions associated with the names of J. H. Hexter, Mark Curtis, Lawrence Stone, Christopher Hill, Joan Simon and the many others whose works are recorded in these pages and who have conducted the vigorous recent debate about the role of the university in Tudor and Stuart England. I should like to add my personal debt to the Shelby Cullom Davis Center for Historical Studies at Princeton University for a rewarding semester in that international seminar.

The work of individuals is, as I hope, sufficiently acknowledged where appropriate in these pages but I should like to make special acknowledgement here of some whose contributions were made on many occasions and over a long period of time: W. T. Mitchell and Ruth Vyse of the Oxford University Archives, and Dr Gregor Duncan who, in addition to his own part of this history, did much editorial work on the volume as a whole, as did Charles Everitt. J. S. G. Simmons read much in typescript and all the proofs; Susan McConnel typed most of the manuscript and Humaira Ahmed typed the final sections of chapter 10. All of the contributors to this volume helped the editor's task by their willingness to pool their knowledge and by their patience through many unforeseen delays. Mr Julian Munby prepared the maps of Oxford in 1500 and of the central university zone *c*.1500, as well as the plans of the library arrangements on page 622. Dr John Blair prepared the map of Oxford in 1578 by re-drawing to scale the original map of Agas.

The archives of all of the Oxford colleges founded prior to the reign of Elizabeth I have been consulted at some time by one or another of our authors, assisted almost invariably by the synopses of their holdings prepared by Malcolm Underwood. Since my own study has concentrated on the role of the colleges I have laid them under particularly heavy contribution and I would like especially to thank the warden and fellows of New College, the president and fellows of Magdalen College, the principal and fellows of Brasenose College, the president and fellows of Corpus Christi College, the governing body of Christ Church, the president and fellows of St John's College and the president and fellows of Trinity College for free access to their muniments over many years. To this I must add my gratitude to those assistants in college archives who have been unfailingly courteous and helpful, especially Mrs Parry Jones, Mrs Christine Butler, Mr Robin Pedell, Mrs June Wells, Mrs Caroline Dalton and Mrs Francis McDonald. As for my colleagues at All Souls College, I can say only that without their friendship and support nothing at all could have been achieved.

All Souls College   JAMES McCONICA

Contents

List of Plates   xv

List of Maps and Plan   xvii

Abbreviations   xviii

1   The Rise of the Undergraduate College   JAMES McCONICA   1

2   Oxford Town and Oxford University ·   CARL I. HAMMER, JR.   69

3   Oxford and the Tudor State from the
    Accession of Henry VIII to the
    Death of Mary   CLAIRE CROSS   117

4   Studies and Faculties
    Introduction   JAMES McCONICA   151

4.1 The Faculty of Arts   J. M. FLETCHER   157

     Appendix: Music in the Faculty of Arts   JOHN CALDWELL   201

4.2 The Faculty of Medicine   GILLIAN LEWIS   213

4.3 The Faculty of Law   JOHN BARTON   257

     Appendix: The King's Readers   JOHN BARTON   285

4.4 The Faculty of Theology   S. L. GREENSLADE   295

4.5 Public Lectures and Professorial Chairs   G. D. DUNCAN   335

5   Reformation Controversies   JENNIFER LOACH   363

6   Elizabethan Oxford: State, Church
    and University   PENRY WILLIAMS   397

7   The Provision of Books   N. R. KER   441

     Appendices: I   Lincoln College Election
                       Lists   N. R. KER   479
                   II Merton College Inven-
                       tory 1556   N. R. KER   487
                   III Books at Christ Church
                       1562–1602   N. R. KER   498

8   The Economics and Finances of the
    Colleges and University
    c 1530–1640   G. E. AYLMER   521

     Appendices: I   The Property of Balliol
                       College c 1500–c 1640   G. D. DUNCAN   559

II   An Introduction to the
Accounts of Corpus
Christi College   G. D. DUNCAN   574

9   The Physical Setting: New Building and
Adaptation   JOHN NEWMAN   597

Appendix: The Goods of George Holland
and Thomas Key   JOHN NEWMAN   633

10   Elizabethan Oxford: The Collegiate
Society   JAMES McCONICA   645

Index   733

List of Plates

Frontispiece Manuscript portrait of Henry VIII

Between pp. 392 and 393

I	(a) Magdalen College (b) Brasenose College
II	(a) Corpus Christi College (b) Christ Church
III	(a) Trinity College (b) St. John's College
IV	New College hall
V	Domestic plate: a college mazer
VI	A pre-reformation chalice
VII	Elizabethan communion plate: chalice and paten
VIII	Elizabethan communion plate: flagon
IX	College furnishings: a study
X	College expansion: a cockloft
XI	Merton College library: Elizabethan book stalls
XII	(a) A donated library book: Christ Church
	(b) A borrowable library book: Lincoln College
XIII	Library catalogue: Corpus Christi College
XIV	(a) A Hebrew manuscript at Corpus Christi College
	(b) A Greek book from Grocyn's library at Corpus Christi College
XV	(a) Memorial brass to John Claymond
	(b) A portrait monument of Sir Henry Savile
XVI	(a) Portrait of John Rainolds (b) A portrait monument of Laurence Humfrey
XVII	(a) John Case *Speculum moralium quaestionum*
	(b) Notebook of Randolph Cholmondeley
XVIII	Emblems of authority: Elizabethan university staves
XIX	Details of the staff belonging to the Faculty of Theology (a) head (b) footknop
XX	University records (a) matriculation register (b) subscription register
XXI	University records (a) chancellor's register (b) register of congregation
XXII	College records (a) *libri magni* of Corpus Christi College (b) admissions register of Corpus Christi College
XXIII	Plan of All Souls College
XXIV	Map of an All Souls College Northamptonshire estate

Acknowledgements

Acknowledgement is gratefully made to the Dean and Chapter of Christ Church for permission to publish the frontispiece and plate XIIa; to the Curators of the Bodleian Library for plates Ia and b, IIa and b, IIIa and b and XVIIa and b, and for the photographs for these and the frontispiece and plates XIIa and b, XIII, XIVa and b, XXa and b, XXIa and b, XXIIa and b, XXIII and XXIV; to the Warden and Fellows of New College for plate IV; to the Warden and Fellows of All Souls College for plates V, VIII, X, XXIII and XXIV; to the President and Fellows of Corpus Christi College for plates VI, VII, XIII, XIVa and b, XVa, XVIa and XXIIa and b; to the President and Fellows of St. John's College for plate IX; to the Warden and Fellows of Merton College for plates XI and XVb; to the Rector and Fellows of Lincoln College for plate XIIb; to the President and Fellows of Magdalen College for plate XVIb; to the Visitors of the Ashmolean Museum for plates XVIII and XIXa and b, and for the photographs for these and plates VI and VII; to the Keeper of the University Archives for plates XXa and b and XXIa and b; and to Mr. J. W. Thomas of Thomas-Photos, Oxford for the photographs for plates IV, V, VIII, IX, X, XVb and XVIa and b.

Maps

1   Oxford in 1500   xxii–xxiii
2   The central university zone *c* 1500   8
3   Oxford in 1578   642–3

Plan

Library furniture: A–B, *Merton College Library*, as
fitted with stalls from 1589: A, plan (after Clark), B,
end bay in south range; and C, *Duke Humfrey's
Library*, showing medieval lectern and Bodley's stalls
of 1598–9.   622

Abbreviations

APC	*Acts of the Privy Council of England* (32 vols 1890–1907)
BL	British Library, London
Bodl.	Bodleian Library, Oxford
BRUC	A. B. Emden, *A Biographical Register of the University of Cambridge to A.D. 1500* (Cambridge 1963)
BRUO to 1500	A. B. Emden, *A Biographical Register of the University of Oxford to A.D. 1500* (3 vols Oxford 1957–9)
BRUO 1501–40	A. B. Emden, *A Biographical Register of the University of Oxford A.D. 1501–1540* (Oxford 1974)
Cal. Cl. Rolls	*Calendar of the Close Rolls preserved in the Public Record Office, 1485–1509* (2 vols 1955–63)
Cal. Pat. Rolls	*Calendar of the Patent Rolls preserved in the Public Record Office, 1485–1509, 1547–78* (19 vols 1914–82 in progress)
Cal. SP Dom.	*Calendar of State Papers, Domestic Series, preserved in the Public Record Office, 1547–1704* (89 vols London etc. 1856–1924)
Cal. SP Foreign	*Calendar of State Papers, Foreign Series, preserved in the Public Record Office, 1547–89* (25 vols in 28 London etc. 1851–1950)
Cal. SP Venetian	*Calendar of State Papers and Manuscripts relating to English Affairs, existing in the Archives and Collections of Venice, and other Libraries of Northern Italy* (38 vols in 40 1864–1940)
c.c. invents	OUA Chancellor's Court Inventories, Hyp./B/10–19 (the inventories are arranged alphabetically according to surname)
Dean's Register of Oriel	*The Dean's Register of Oriel, 1446–1661*, ed. G. C. Richards and H. E. Salter (OHS lxxxiv 1926)
DNB	*Dictionary of National Biography* (22 vols 1885–1901, repr. 1921–2)
Epist. acad. ed. Anstey	*Epistolae academicae oxon*. ed. H. Anstey (2 vols OHS xxxv–xxxvi 1898)
Epist. acad. 1508–96	*Epistolae academicae 1508–1596*, ed. W. T. Mitchell (OHS new ser. xxvi 1980)

Foster, *Alumni*

Joseph Foster, *Alumni oxonienses: the members of the University of Oxford 1500–1714: their parentage, birthplace and year of birth, with a record of their degrees; being the matriculation register of the university arranged, revised, and annotated* (4 vols Oxford and London 1891–2)

Foxe, *Acts and Monuments*

John Foxe, *Actes and Monuments of these latter and perillous dayes touching matters of the Church* (1563)

L & P Henry VIII

Letters and Papers, Foreign and Domestic, of the Reign of Henry VIII, preserved in the Public Record Office, the British Museum and elsewhere in England (21 vols in 33 1862–1910; new edn of vol. i in 3 pts 1920; vol. of addenda in 2 pts 1929–32)

Laudian Code

Statutes of the University of Oxford codified in the year 1636, ed. John Griffiths with an introduction on the history of the Laudian Code by C. L. Shadwell (Oxford 1888)

Macray, *Reg. Magdalen*

W. D. Macray, *A Register of the members of St Mary Magdalen College, Oxford from the foundation of the college* (new ser. 8 vols 1894–1915)

OCA

Oxford City Archives

OHS

Oxford Historical Society

Original Letters

Original Letters relative to the English Reformation, ed. Hastings Robinson (Parker Soc., 1 vol. in 2 1846–7)

OUA

Oxford University Archives

PRO

Public Record Office, London

Reg. ann. mert. 1483–1521

Registrum annalium collegii mertonensis 1483–1521, ed. H. E. Salter (OHS lxxvi 1923)

Reg. ann. mert. 1521–67

Registrum annalium collegii mertonensis 1521–1567, ed. John M. Fletcher (OHS new ser. xxiii 1974)

Reg. ann. mert. 1567–1603

Registrum annalium collegii mertonensis 1567–1603, ed. John M. Fletcher (OHS new ser. xxiv 1976)

Reg. Canc. 1506–14

OUA Chancellor's Register 1506–14, Register 7, Hyp./A/3

Reg. Canc. 1527–43

OUA Chancellor's Register 1527–43, Register EEE, Hyp./A/4

Reg. Canc. 1545–1661

OUA Chancellor's Register 1545–1661, Register GG, Hyp./A/5

Reg. Canc. 1556–61

OUA Chancellor's Register 1556–61, Register HHH, Hyp./A/6.

Reg. Cong. 1505–17	OUA Register of Congregation and Convocation 1505–1517, NEP/*Supra*/Register G
Reg. Cong. 1518–35	OUA Register of Congregation and Convocation 1518–1535, NEP/*Supra*/Register H
Reg. Cong. 1535–63	OUA Register of Congregation and Convocation 1535–1563, NEP/*Supra*/Register I
Reg. Cong. 1564–82	OUA Register of Congregation and Convocation 1564–1582, NEP/*Supra*/Register KK
Reg. Cong. 1582–95	OUA Register of Congregation and Convocation 1582–1595, NEP/*Supra*/Register L
Reg. Cong. 1592–1606	OUA Register of Congregation and Convocation 1592–1606, NEP/*Supra*/Register M
Reg. Univ. ed. Boase	*Register of the University of Oxford* i, ed. C. W. Boase (OHS i 1885)
Reg. Univ. ed. Clark	*Register of the University of Oxford* ii, ed. Andrew Clark (4 pts OHS x–xii, xiv 1887–9; cited by number of part)
SCO	*Statutes of the Colleges of Oxford* (3 vols Royal Commission 1853)
Statuta	*Statuta antiqua universitatis oxoniensis*, ed. Strickland Gibson (Oxford 1931)
Statutes of the Realm	*The Statutes of the Realm from original records and authentic manuscripts* (11 vols in 12 1810–28)
STC	A. W. Pollard, G. R. Redgrave *et al.*, *A Short-Title Catalogue of Books printed in England Scotland and Ireland and of English Books Printed Abroad 1475–1640* (1946)
Valor	*Valor ecclesiasticus temp. Henr. VIII auctoritate regis institutus* (6 vols Record Commission 1810–34)
VCH Oxon. iii	*The Victoria History of the County of Oxford* iii, ed. H. E. Salter and Mary D. Lobel (1954)
VCH Oxon. iv.	*The Victoria History of the County of Oxford* iv, ed. A. Crossley (Oxford 1979)
VCH Oxon. v	*A History of the County of Oxford v: Bullingdon Hundred*, ed. Mary D. Lobel (1957)
VCH Oxon. vi	*A History of the County of Oxford vi: Ploughley Hundred*, ed. Mary D. Lobel (1959)
Wood, *Athenae*	Anthony à Wood, *Athenae oxonienses*, ed. Philip Bliss (4 vols 1813–20)
Wood, *Fasti*	Anthony à Wood, *Fasti oxonienses*, ed. Philip Bliss (1815)

Wood, *History and Antiquities*

Anthony à Wood, *History and Antiquities of the University of Oxford*, ed. John Gutch (2 vols in 3 Oxford 1792–6)

Wood, *History and Antiquities of the Colleges and Halls*

Anthony à Wood, *History and Antiquities of the Colleges and Halls in the University of Oxford* (Oxford 1786)

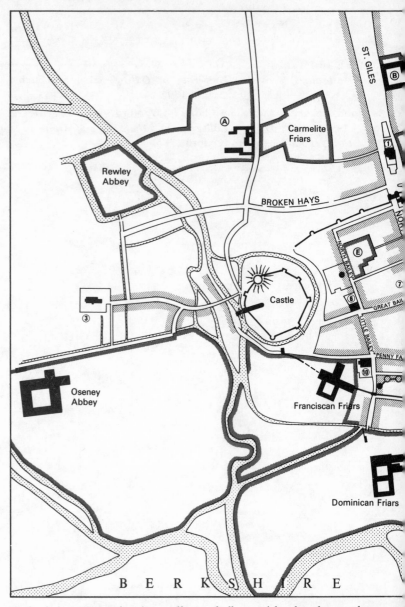

Oxford in 1500, showing colleges, halls, parish churches and monast
precincts. The halls are those occurring in *Registrum Cancelarii 1498–15*
(OHS new ser. xxvii 1980). Of fifty-eight halls mapped here many we
grouped together as halls with annexes or shared a principal. They form
some thirty-three separate institutions, several of which were virtually colle
satellites. A further seven had no recorded principal in these years.

Churches	Colleges
1 St Mary Magdalen	A Gloucester College
2 St Cross	B St Bernard's College
3 St Thomas	C Durham College
4 St Michael at the Northgate	D Balliol College

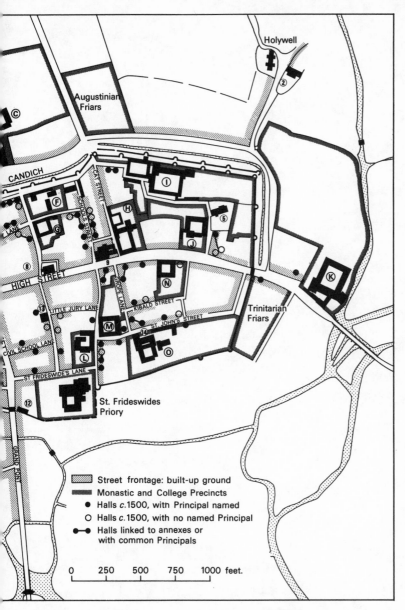

Holywell

Augustinian
Friars

CANDICH

CAT STREET

SCHOOLS STREET

LANE

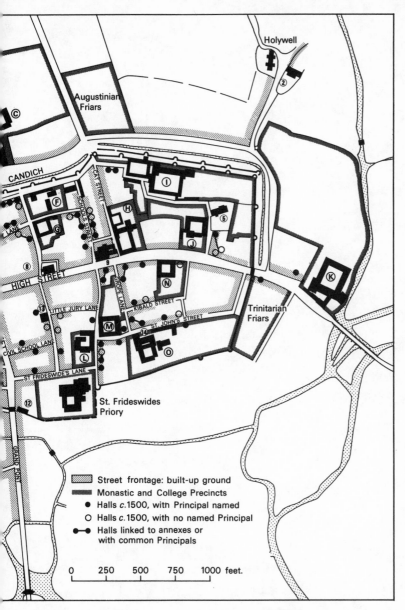

HIGH STREET

LITTLE JURY LANE

GROPE LANE

KIBALD STREET

ST JOHN'S STREET

CIVIL SCHOOL LANE

ST FRIDESWIDE'S LANE

St. Frideswides
Priory

Trinitarian
Friars

GRAND PONT

Street frontage: built-up ground
Monastic and College Precincts
● Halls c.1500, with Principal named
○ Halls c.1500, with no named Principal
●—● Halls linked to annexes or
    with common Principals

0   250   500   750   1000 feet.

Churches		Colleges	
5	St Peter in the East	E	St Mary's College
6	St Peter in the Bailey	F	Exeter College
7	St Martin	G	Lincoln College
8	All Saints	H	All Soul's College
9	St Mary the Virgin	I	New College
10	St Ebbe	J	The Queen's College
11	St Aldate	K	Magdalen College
12	St Michael at the Southgate	L	Canterbury College
13	St Edward	M	Oriel College
14	St John	N	University College
		O	Merton College

I

The Rise of the Undergraduate College

JAMES McCONICA

WHEN Anthony Wood introduced his history of the colleges and halls in the university of Oxford, he began with 'some observations . . . very proper for strangers to know'. These were intended to acquaint the ignorant with the most notable features of Oxford's collegiate societies—their modest beginnings, their government by statute, their provision for 'foundation-men', commoners and servitors— and they concluded with this remarkable verdict:

. . . all the Colleges are very fairly built of stone, out of quarries near Oxford (the worst of them is as good as some Universities in foreign countries) and have belonging to them all conveniences that are fit for human life. If you except the Colleges and Halls, the City of Oxford, in relation to building, is a very inconsiderable place, and no better than an ordinary Market Town. And so be they were quite gone (which God forbid it should come to pass) it would be one of the beggarliest places in England, it being not accommodated with a public road through, traffick in, or an eminent river by, it.[1]

The place that Wood described with such loving partiality as being rescued from the commonplace only by a crown of opulent collegiate buildings did not exist a century before he wrote; in the early years of the reign of Elizabeth I Oxford still wore the aspect of a medieval market town, whose churches were its principal adornment. Its transformation in the century before 1668 was a consequence of changes which were already under way before the Reformation, which were greatly accelerated in the course of the century and whose effects it is the chief business of this volume to describe. At the centre of all these changes—notably, the disappearance of the religious orders, the resort to the university of increasing numbers of laymen, the vast enlargement of royal authority and the expansion of the curriculum—was the secular college, which in the Tudor period replaced the medieval hall as the typical home of the undergraduate. The resulting growth of the colleges in size and influence, and their physical supplanting or absorption of the medieval halls made

[1] Anthony Wood, *History and Antiquities of the Colleges and Halls* [2].

Oxford take on, socially and architecturally, the face we know today. In the five successive foundations of the century from that of Brasenose (1512) to St John's College (1557) we can trace the evolution of this essentially medieval institution, in which the adaptability of medieval statutory provisions and a continuity with the past are equally marked. Among the Tudor foundations the most spectacular by far was Wolsey's Cardinal College and its royal successor, Christ Church. Jesus College, which received its letters patent of foundation in 1571, had to wait until the next century to get properly under way, and until 1622 to receive its statutes.[1] Its story, therefore, will be dealt with more appropriately in the following volume. In the statutes of the foundations up to the end of the reign of Mary Tudor, however, we have the best continuous record of slowly changing attitudes about the nature of the university itself.

LATE MEDIEVAL ANTECEDENTS

Although the first foundation of the sixteenth century was Brasenose College, the story really begins in the previous century with Magdalen College, so that some account of the medieval background is necessary.[2] As is well known, the vast majority of the scholars of the medieval university lived in halls or lodgings, scattered about the town, and belonging to townsmen, religious houses or colleges. The university at first confined itself to controlling rents, and insisted, with varying degrees of success, that every scholar be enrolled with some regent master engaged in lecturing. By the early fifteenth century the university and crown were together insisting that all scholars live in academic halls under the government of principals —often regent masters—who were held responsible by the university for the conduct of scholars in their charge; about 1450 there were some seventy halls, and scholars were forbidden to lodge with a townsman. Colleges for the most part were reserved for a small minority of graduates to enable them to remain at the university during the long years required to qualify in the higher faculties of law, theology and medicine. It was the creation of New College, in 1379, that provided Oxford with an entirely new conception, both in scale—Wykeham provided for a warden with seventy fellows or scholars—and in the composition of the foundation, since the

---

[1] See J. N. L. Baker, *Jesus College, Oxford 1571–1971* (Oxford 1971); the statutes of 1622 were closely derived from those of Brasenose: cf. *VCH Oxon.* iii. 265.

[2] The chapter by Dr A. B. Cobban on colleges and halls *c* 1380–*c* 1500 in the second volume of this History will discuss these developments in detail. See also J. R. L. Highfield, 'The early colleges' in J. I. Catto (ed.), *The Early Oxford Schools* (History of the University of Oxford i Oxford 1984). On halls see below p. 52 n. 2.

scholars of New College were to be non-graduate and between fifteen and twenty years of age, having spent at least one year at Winchester College, the founder's grammar school.[1] This use of the endowed collegiate foundation rather than the hall as a suitable home for undergraduate members of the university had been anticipated at Cambridge in the royal college of the King's Hall, which became an endowed society in 1337, and which from the first provided for a sizeable undergraduate element on the revenues of the foundation. It seems entirely likely that the King's Hall at Cambridge was one of the English models for the college William of Wykeham founded in Oxford.[2]

The presence in college of undergraduates sharing the common life with more senior members raised the issue of teaching arrangements. The halls provided lectures which supplemented the public lectures of the university, and 'repetitions' in the afternoons, when the students were made to expound the morning's lecture. Similarly, within the monastic colleges, where young monks prepared for the study of theology and were restrained from going about the town, there grew up well-developed systems of college lectures and college tuition.[3] For the undergraduate members of his new foundation, William of Wykeham provided something similar through a salaried tutorial system, in which the more senior scholars were to act as *informatores* to the juniors during their first three years. The deans, who were five in number (two artists, a civilian, a canonist, and a theologian) selected these tutors who were entitled to payments for each pupil, and they also supervised the regular college disputations which were held in all faculties. As usual, all scholars were expected in addition to attend the university lectures and exercises.[4]

Magdalen College

The next critical event in provision for undergraduates at secular colleges in Oxford came during the second half of the fifteenth century, with the foundation of Magdalen College by William of

[1] A. B. Cobban, *The King's Hall within the University of Cambridge in the Later Middle Ages* (Cambridge 1969), 46–8; R. L. Storey, 'The foundation and the medieval college 1379–1530', in John Buxton and Penry Williams (eds), *New College Oxford 1379–1979* (Oxford 1979), 6–7; *VCH Oxon*. iii. 155–6.

[2] Cobban, *King's Hall*, 64–5.

[3] *The Letter Book of Robert Joseph*, ed. H. Aveling and W. A. Pantin (OHS new ser. xix 1967), xxi; *Chapters of the English Black Monks 1215–1540*, ed. W. A. Pantin (3 vols. Camden Society 3rd ser. xlv, xlvii, liv 1931–7), ii. 55, 75; iii. 31.

[4] *VCH Oxon*. iii. 156; the system is described more fully by Cobban, 'Colleges and Halls'. The term 'scholar' here applied indifferently to both graduate and undergraduate members supported on the foundation. They would have to be between 15 and 20 years of age to be eligible for election. Only after two years of probation were they eligible for election as fellows (*in veros socios*): SCO i. pt 5 (New College), pp. 7, 16.

Waynflete. Magdalen, indeed, is important in several respects, and foreshadows the developments of the next century in its comprehensive system of college teaching, in the provision for endowed lectureships open to the university at large, in the marked emphasis on aspects of the arts curriculum (notably grammar and moral philosophy) which were inextricably associated with humanism, and in the provision for undergraduate commoners.

The founder of Magdalen College, who was bishop of Winchester and chancellor of England, had come from the Lincolnshire village from which he took his name, and began his career as Master of the school at Winchester and provost of Eton. He modelled his Oxford society closely on that of his eminent predecessor in the see of Winchester, William of Wykeham. This emulation is evident in the size of his foundation, which provided for a president and seventy scholars, in the fact that (as at All Souls) long sections of the statutes are copied word for word from those of New College, and in Waynflete's decision that only fellows and former fellows of New College or his own foundation should be eligible for the office of president.

Despite these outward resemblances, which were carried over into the architectural plan, Waynflete's statutes demonstrate genuine originality. The source of his innovations must be a matter of conjecture. It is tempting to attribute his concern for grammar teaching and the liberal studies to his experience as a schoolmaster, while his decision to provide for public teaching in the university may owe something to observation of conditions in Oxford itself, since his full foundation had functioned for some twenty years before it received its first statutes. These were granted on the accession of the second president, Richard Mayew, a fellow of New College, in 1480.

Like New College, Magdalen College was meant to fortify the secular clergy: all MAs except those studying civil law or medicine were to proceed to the priesthood within a year of completing their regency.[1] As a society, it was primarily designed to carry its undergraduates through the arts course, again like New College. But whereas all seventy scholars at New College were on an equal footing, at Magdalen they fell into two categories, forty who were clerks directed to the priesthood, and thirty more (with half stipend, and hence called 'Demyes' in the statutes) who were to study grammar, logic and sophistry.[2] There was no provision for the demies to move into the ranks of the full scholars, nor did they have a voice in the election of the president. They could be accepted at the age of twelve, and remain on the foundation up to the age of twenty-five.

[1] *Statutes of the Colleges of Oxford* (3 vols Royal Commission 1853) ii. pt 8 (Magdalen), 34.   [2] Ibid. 6.

They were to be selected from the poor in parishes or places where the college had possessions, and were to be well-grounded in Latin grammar before being allowed to study logic and sophistry.[1] Two or three of the demies, moreover, were to devote themselves to the pursuit of grammar and poetry and the other humanities ('alias artes humanitatis') both for their own profit and in order that they might be able to instruct others. How Waynflete envisaged their future is not clear. Certainly some were likely to become school-masters; perhaps others would enter the priesthood, lacking degrees in theology, although well-grounded in Latin grammar, logic and sophistry. In the history of collegiate societies at Oxford and Cambridge, however, their place remains anomalous: they most nearly resemble the undergraduate scholars of medieval Balliol and Exeter colleges.

Among the full scholars or fellows, the study of theology was to be supported by natural and moral philosophy. These supplanted civil and canon law in Wykeham's college, and show Waynflete's sympathy with training in the arts—in this case, the *quadrivium*—against the professional faculties. In the same way, whereas twenty of the scholars at New College were to be jurists, only two or three of those at Magdalen were to study civil or canon law, and the same number, medicine.[2] Again, the civilian and the canonist among the five deans at New College were dropped at Magdalen, where two of the three deans were chosen from MAs of senior standing, and the third from the theologians. The artists supervised the lectures and disputations especially of the sophists and logicians, and the theo-logian, the same exercises in theology.[3] The most conspicuous teaching innovation, however, was Waynflete's foundation of three lectureships in the two philosophies and theology. These were to serve the needs not only of members of Magdalen College, but of scholars in the university at large, both secular and religious. The lecturers were to be well paid, over and above their other stipends from the college, and their work clearly helped to remedy the defects of the regency system.[4]

In the comprehensiveness of his teaching programme, too, Wayn-flete emulated and built upon the precedent of New College. The sound formation in grammar came from a 'feeder' school, his version of Winchester College being a school within Magdalen College itself, which soon gained a reputation as a distinguished centre for the new methods of teaching Latin.[5] As at New College, 100s was set aside

[1] Ibid. 16.   [2] Ibid. 6.   [3] Ibid. 24.
[4] Ibid. 47; on the regency system, see below J. M. Fletcher, 185–7.
[5] R. S. Stainer, *Magdalen School* (OHS new ser. iii. 1940), 55 f.

annually for the instruction of the new arrivals in logic and sophistry during their first three or four years by tutors termed as at New College, *informatores*.[1] Senior fellows, under the supervision of a dean, would take responsibility for this teaching of the juniors at a rate of 6s 8d a head per annum, over and above other emoluments, and any of the fellows was bound to accept the office if chosen to do it.[2] At the higher levels of the arts course there were weekly disputations, where the more advanced were again to instruct their juniors. The deans in arts were to regulate the holding of the disputations; instruction and the solution of disputed questions were the responsibility of the lecturers.[3] A parallel arrangement existed for the theologians. And during the summer vacation each year, bachelors in arts were to lecture cursorily at least three times a week in the presence of all the MAs and scholars in arts, on some useful and important subject. Those suggested in the statutes were all in natural philosophy: the *De sphaera, Algorismus*, or the *De motu planetarum*.[4]

Waynflete's further provisions indicate that, like Wykeham, he intended that each of his scholars should keep the full number of terms and exercises provided by the university for his faculty, subject to the judgement of the president, and senior officers and fellows of the college. If they judged a bachelor to be adequately prepared, he must incept MA within a year; equally, all MAs, after completion of their necessary regency must enter the faculty of theology and adhere strictly to those studies, except in vacation. In the eighth year at the latest after completing their regency in arts they were to qualify as bachelor in theology; after no more than a further eight years, as doctor. Once again, all decisions about the aptness of a candidate to oppose or incept were to be made by the appropriate officers of the college, and again, a scholar might only avail himself of the customary graces of the university to alter or shorten his course, if these officers gave him the licence so to petition. Since the registers of the university abound in evidence that the statutory programme in all faculties was by now heavily and routinely qualified by the granting of such graces, the practical effect of these regulations, as at New College and elsewhere, was to place

[1] On the earlier history of the tutorial system, see Cobban, 'Colleges and Halls'.

[2] *SCO* ii. pt 8, 78.

[3] Ibid. 34–5.

[4] Ibid. 35; the interval was that between the feast of the Translation of St Thomas the Martyr, 7 July, and the Assumption of the Blessed Virgin, 15 August. The first two were among the works in 1409 to be heard *lectionatim* in college or hall before determination; *Statuta*, 200. The treatise *De motu planetarum* is evidently the *Theoretica planetarum*, an anonymous and synoptic treatise on celestial mechanics which completed the *corpus astronomicum* in common use.

the supervision of all degrees effectively in the hands of the college authorities. In this Waynflete was not only following the precedent set at New College, but was echoing like provisions in the statutes of most colleges since those of Oriel in 1329.[1] The evolution of such supervision, with that of intra-mural teaching, gave the colleges the opportunity to develop a comparatively flexible and reliable alternative to the regency system of the university proper, when by the end of the fifteenth century that system was in serious decline.[2]

It remained for college teaching to be made available to those who were not, as scholars or fellows, actual members of the foundation, and this step too was taken at Magdalen College, in the first place through the provision of public lectures freely available to all members of the university. A second innovation, which had dramatic implications, was Waynflete's provision for undergraduate commoners. 'Commoners' were those—not maintained on the revenues of the foundation—who paid to live in the college society and share its common table; they were often graduates, whose payment for room and board is recorded sporadically in the accounts of many medieval colleges.[3] Waynflete's innovation at Oxford was to open the college by design to the sons of noble or distinguished personages up to the number of twenty to be admitted at the discretion of the president to lodgings and commons at their own charge. They were to be under the guardianship and government of a *creditor*, vulgarly called a 'creanser'. The setting of this provision,[4] and the passing mention it receives in Waynflete's statutes, make it fairly clear that we should see it more in light of a late medieval prelate's magnificence and hospitality, and of his acute awareness of the importance of the support the great could give—Magdalen's guests are sons of 'friends of the college'—than as an academic innovation; but the idea was not lost upon Waynflete's successors.

Brasenose College

The first to follow in Waynflete's footsteps were William Smith and Richard Sutton, co-founders of Brasenose College, who obtained a charter for 'The King's Haule and Colledge of Brasennose in Oxford'—*vulgariter nuncupatum*—in January 1512. Their foundation is seen usually as a step back to the small, clerical society of Lincoln College, rather than forward to the humanistic Corpus

---

[1] *SCO* i. pt 3, 14, where the assent of the provost and majority of fellows was required for inception.

[2] See Fletcher, below 186.

[3] See Cobban, 'Colleges and Halls'.

[4] The innovation is introduced in a conventional statute against the introduction of strangers at the college's expense; *SCO* ii. pt 8, 60.

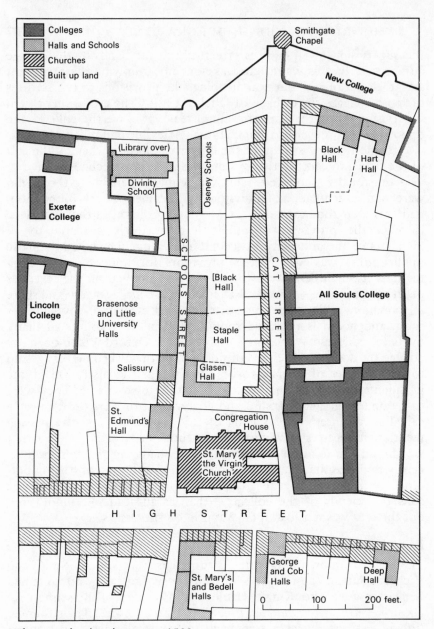

The central university zone *c* 1500

Next to the university church of St Mary the Virgin was the greatest concentration of halls and schools in Schools Street, including the group of halls that was to become Brasenose College. Cat Street was still the centre of the book trade. Only All Souls College and University College had buildings fronting onto the High Street, where the number of shops standing in front of houses and halls demonstrates the vitality of commercial life in this part of the town.

Christi College, which was its near contemporary. The college's historian himself stresses the contrast, gloomily conceding that at Brasenose, 'the Scholars and Fellows are still to mumble the dry bones of scholastic philosophy and to turn their backs upon the new ideas which were about to regenerate a decadent civilization.'[1] If we look closely, however, we find that Brasenose was neither so unreconstructed, nor Corpus so entirely forward-looking, as this suggests.

To begin with, the partnership of an eminent bishop and a simple layman was entirely unprecedented, and leads us immediately to the world of urbane and lettered piety which sprang up around London and the royal court in the fifteenth century. Sir Richard Sutton, Bishop Smith's collaborator, was of an ancient gentry line in the county palatine of Cheshire,[2] the younger son of Sir William Sutton, who was hereditary master of the well-endowed hospital of Burton Lazar's in Leicestershire.[3] Sir Richard was a governor of the Inner Temple, a member of the privy council to Henry VII and steward of the Brigittine monastery of Syon where, as an unmarried man, he had chambers, and where he paid for the publication of their magisterial spiritual treatise *The Orchard of Syon* in 1519.[4] Syon monastery was the chief devotional nursery of the reforming circle led by the Lady Margaret Beaufort, countess of Richmond and Derby and mother of the king. The co-founder of Brasenose, Bishop William Smith, whose great-niece Anne was a nun of the Brigittine house, had probably been educated in the Lady Margaret's household. He rose rapidly in the royal administration after the new dynasty had been established.[5] An able and energetic prelate, he was made bishop of Coventry and Lichfield in 1493 and translated to the see of Lincoln in 1496. In 1501 he become lord president of the council of Wales, and he had long been in the council of Prince Arthur. From 1 November 1500, when he succeeded Cardinal Morton in the post, until August 1503, he was chancellor of Oxford, during which time the prince visited the university. Smith amassed a very considerable estate, and showed himself from the first keenly interested in promoting education. In Lichfield he refounded

[1] I. S. Leadam, 'The early years of the college', in *Brasenose College Quatercentenary Monographs* (2 vols in 3, OHS lii–liv 1909) ii. no. 1, 24.

[2] Ralph Churton, *The Lives of William Smyth Bishop of Lincoln and Sir Richard Sutton Knight* . . . (Oxford 1800), 405 ff; I. S. Leadam in *DNB*.

[3] John Nichols, *The History and Antiquities of the County of Leicester* (4 vols 1795), ii. pt 1, 276; its yearly value at the dissolution was £265 10s 2½d, cf *The Victoria History of the County of Leicester*, ii., ed. W. G. Hoskins and R. A. McKinley (1954), 36–8.

[4] Phyllis Hodgson, '*The Orchard of Syon* and the English mystical tradition', *Proceedings of the British Academy* (1964), 229–49.

[5] I. S. Leadam in *DNB*; Churton, *Lives*, 13.

the derelict hospital of St John as an almshouse and free grammar school; in 1507 he founded a fellowship at Oriel College, established a free school at Farnworth in Lancashire, and generously endowed Lincoln College (of which, like Oriel, he was visitor as bishop of Lincoln). In 1510 he aided the endowment of St John's College, Cambridge, by assisting in the suppression there of the priory of St John.[1] In his career and that of Sutton there is no hint of apprehensive conservatism; rather, they appear to have been a part of the same world that brought about the refoundation of Godshouse, Cambridge, as Christ's College in 1505. This latter was the first such venture by the Lady Margaret and John Fisher, then bishop of Rochester and chancellor of Cambridge University, and the statutes of Brasenose bear comparison with the new statutes of the Lady Margaret for Christ's in Cambridge or with those of Magdalen College, Oxford, far more readily than they do with the scheme of Richard Fleming for Lincoln.[2]

The initiative in founding Brasenose seems to have been taken by Sutton, who obtained the lease of Brasenose Hall and Little University Hall from University College in October 1508; the next year on 1 June, he and Smith together laid the foundation stone of the new building. Of the college's first statutes we know nothing, since the only document of that time to survive is the patent of foundation, dated 15 January 1512, which provided for a principal and sixty or more scholars, depending on resources.[3] They were to study sophistry, logic, and philosophy, and afterwards theology; the echo of the charter of Christ's College, Cambridge, with its sixty members dedicated to similar studies,[4] is worthy of remark, the more so since the first surviving statutes at Brasenose provided only for a principal and twelve scholar-fellows.[5] These statutes were the work of Bishop Smith's executors between 1514 and 1519, a revision presumably of his lost originals. The final revision by Sutton in 1522 added provision for as many undergraduate scholars as the college could house.[6]

There are several indications that a society, partly undergraduate,

[1] DNB; Vivian Green, The Commonwealth of Lincoln College 1427-1977 (Oxford 1979), 72-4.

[2] Ibid. 5-6. Cf the groundless assertion of R. W. Jeffery that Smith's foundation was made 'more than likely . . . with the intention of raising a bulwark against the spread of heresy in the University': Brasenose Monographs, ii. no. 10, 5.

[3] SCO ii. pt 9 (Brasenose), p. iii; 'ad numerum sexaginta scholarium et ultra.'

[4] 1 May 1505; Documents Relating to the University and Colleges of Cambridge (3 vols Royal Commission 1852), iii. 148. The latter statutes, like those of Brasenose, envisaged fewer members; cf H. Rackham, Early Statutes of Christ's College (Cambridge 1927).

[5] Brasenose College Archives (hereafter BNCA) MS A 2.1, fo 1.

[6] SCO ii. pt 9, 12.

and more on the scale of Magdalen College or Christ's College, Cambridge, was always in view if and when the money could be raised. The most important of these is the building itself, which was completed by 1518, and designed to accommodate some eighty occupants.[1] The statute *De numero scholarium*, both in Sutton's version and in the earlier version by Smith's executors, looks forward to benefactions to maintain scholars, graduate or undergraduate, which would increase their number. The visitation of the college by John Longland in September 1530 revealed, besides the principal, six fellows, five probationer fellows, two referred to as *quidam scolares* (accused of gambling for money and neglecting their books), and eleven others, four MAs and seven BAs, a total of twenty-four.[2] No undergraduate was mentioned, although of the twenty-four scholars in the college, three were not yet bachelors when the visitation was held. Five years later the *Valor ecclesiasticus* listed nine fellows; the *Valor* of 1547[3] mentioned the principal and fourteen fellows, and 'lx pore Scholers and other', for whom, however, there was no allowance for commons, and it is likely that the phrase simply recalled the words of the charter.[4]

The next list to provide useful information about the composition of Brasenose College is that of 1549, the first of a series in the vice-principal's register.[5] This, a *Catalogus scholasticorum et ministrorum*, consists of twenty-two names, beginning with the principal and senior fellows. Eight of the names are of commoners, and these were all of the traditional variety—graduates of the university who were renting rooms. Three years later, however, a census of colleges and halls made by the vice-chancellor shows a marked change in the make-up of the collegiate society at Brasenose. In a list of seventy men, forty-five were undergraduates.[6] Only three of these—Richard Barnes, Patrick Sacheverell, and Edmund Parkynson—were future fellows of Brasenose. Two (Birch, Elys) were bible clerks, not known to have taken degrees. Three more (Robert Eston, Thomas Atkyns, Humfrey Hall) were future fellows of Exeter, Merton, and All Souls Colleges, respectively. Five others on the list are known to have

---

[1] John Newman, 'The Physical Setting', below 606.

[2] *Visitations in the Diocese of Lincoln 1517–1531*, ed. A. Hamilton Thompson (3 vols Lincoln Record Society xxxiii, xxxv, xxxvii 1940, 1944, 1947) iii. 51–5.

[3] Following 37 Henry VIII, c. 4; *Brasenose Monographs* ii. no. 9, app. 2.

[4] Leadam, 'Early years', 159–62; Lady de Villiers, 'Brasenose College' in *VCH Oxon.* iii. 209.

[5] BNCA, Registrum A, MS A1. 1, fo 88.

[6] The list from Reg. Canc. 1545–1661, Hyp. /A/5, fo 68^V is printed in *Reg. Univ.* ed. Boase, xxiii. The last two names before the butler and cook are also of servants; Hardyng was a manciple the same year, and Boldwyn does not appear elsewhere in the records. The heading *subgraduati* found in Boase does not appear in the manuscript.

taken degrees,[1] five are known only by surname, and the rest appear to be 'gentlemen commoners' in the accepted sense—men who paid for a place in the college, who held no degree on arrival, and who for the most part cannot be traced in subsequent degree lists. The one exception is Mathew Smyth, a servant to the principal, who was the only member of this group to come from the college's recruitment area in Lancashire. The others come from a wide range of counties, including Yorkshire, Dorset, Durham, Kent, and London, but there is a conspicuous concentration around the Welsh borders, Herefordshire, Worcestershire, and Gloucestershire, and Wales itself. All told, these undergraduate commoners seem to have constituted about 40 per cent of the membership of Brasenose College in 1552.

It is tempting to imagine that it was the university's initiative in conducting a general census of the colleges and halls that elicited the names of these Brasenose undergraduates for the first time, and to suppose that—although present—they had been ignored previously in the official catalogue of college membership. This may be true, and if it is, the allusion to the sixty 'pore scholers' in the *Valor* of 1547 would gain added meaning. However, the college's record of its own membership had already begun to take note of undergraduates in 1551. Some of them appear in the census of 1552; in 1553–4, the *Catalogus omnium studentium nostri collegii* included the names of many more such undergraduate commoners.[2] Brasenose College continued to draw up similar comprehensive lists periodically for the next twenty-five years, and the constitution of the college's population of undergraduate commoners can be studied in the printed register.[3] By the early seventeenth century more than one hundred and fifty persons battled each week, of whom more than half were undergraduates.[4]

One significant detail in the statutes was taken directly from Magdalen College: provision of rooms for the sons of noblemen and influential persons. In the chapter by Smith's executors dealing with the admission of outsiders into the college, the terms follow those of Waynflete exactly, with the difference that Brasenose provided for six, rather than Magdalen's twenty.[5] Even the term 'creansers' is taken over, and the men in question were to be lodged in the upper

---

[1] Wm. Constantine, Salop, BA, BCL, DCL; Lewis Evans ('Lewes'), Flint, BA, MA, supplicated BTh; Michael Coles, Worcs. BA; Bryan Tyson, Mx BA; Richard Thatcher, Kent, BA.

[2] BNCA Registrum A, MS A1.1 fo 91; 9 *magistri*, 4 *domini*, 6 servants, and 48 others in the initial list, to which 13 more were added during the year.

[3] *Brasenose College Register 1509–1909* (2 vols OHS lv 1909).

[4] Lady de Villiers in *VCH Oxon*. iii. 209.

[5] BNCA MS A2.1, fo 23^V 'De extraneis non introducendis ad onus collegii.'

and lower chambers next the hall.[1] They were to be commoners, paid for by their family or by friends. Sutton's statutes, however, brought them directly on to the foundation, and they therefore appear in his regulations for the admission of scholars who were not fellows: the sons and relations of nobles and magnates were to be exempt from the prohibition that scholars should have no more than twelve marks a year by way of income.[2] Sutton explicitly stated, moreover, that by 'sons' he meant heirs with a patrimony worth forty pounds a year. Each was to have a tutor ('creanser' is dropped) —the principal or a fellow of the college—who was to take responsibility for his expenses and fines. What is more, the principal or vice-principal was empowered to dispense them from the statutes, when observance was inconvenient for them.[3]

Whatever their precise importance in Sutton's conception of the college, the noble scholars were meant to be part of that larger undergraduate population which the principal and vice-principal were directed by his statutes to admit to the foundation according to the capacity of the college to house them, each to be of honest character and apt for study, and to have a tutor from among the members (not necessarily the fellows) of the college who would be responsible for his expenses and fines.[4] The college responded as benefactors appeared. What provision was made to teach these men?

Responsibility for the education of the scholars fell, of course, upon the fellows. These were to be natives of the diocese of Coventry and Lichfield, with a preference in favour of those born in the counties of Lancashire and Cheshire.[5] They were to be bachelors of arts, and to have weekly disputations in the chapel on problems of natural and (during Lent) moral philosophy as they proceeded to the MA. Masters of arts studying theology were likewise to dispute in chapel once a week on theological questions. After their first year of regency they were to be admitted to theological lectures, and after the third, to dispute in the Schools, when all the bachelors of the college were to be present. Responsibility for the enforcement of the statutes in these as in all matters fell on the principal, vice-principal, and six senior fellows, who were also to decide when a master was fit to enter the exercises in his faculty.[6]

Although the statutes of Smith's executors lacked any specific

[1] Ibid. fo 26^V 'De dispositione camerarum'.
[2] SCO ii. pt 9, 12. This entire chapter (viii) is added by Sutton.
[3] Ibid.
[4] Ibid.
[5] Leadam, 'Early years', 16; there were difficulties in interpreting the statutes; see de Villiers in VCH Oxon. iii. 208.
[6] Chapter 16: De disputationibus; SCO ii. pt 9, 20-2.

provision for the recruitment of undergraduates, it is apparent that they foresaw the arrival of undergraduate members, since four pounds a year were to be set aside to pay a lecturer to teach them.[1] Sutton's more elaborate arrangements insisted that the lector be chosen from among the fellows, and that he have responsibility for seeing that the undergraduate members were prepared in logic and sophistry, through lectures given by himself or his deputies; any bachelor, whether a fellow or not, could be asked to assist in this teaching. The scholars were to study for three years in sophistry and logic before supplicating for the bachelor's degree, and each bachelor a further three years in philosophy before inception.[2] With responsibility for teaching went the power of discipline. The lector was to punish offenders for lateness, absence, or unruly behaviour, and along with the principal and vice-principal he was responsible for deciding whether any member of the college might present himself for a degree; penalty for doing so without such approval was expulsion, *ipso facto*. The graces recording the college's fulfilment of this provision are regularly enrolled from the start of the first vice-principal's register, in 1539.[3]

A more vivid picture of the ordinary functioning of the system comes, perhaps inevitably, from an account of its partial neglect, in the visitation of Bishop Longland in 1530.[4] A probationer fellow, Thomas Tippyng, elected the previous year, testified that the bachelors deputed by the lector, William Sutton, to read in the hall, were negligent at all times—during lectures, during *sophismata in dubiis*, and during repetitions—because they tolerated inattentiveness among the undergraduates. Sutton, who was further accused of making little progress in his own studies, was also responsible, it seems, for distributing books to the scholars.[5]

Payments to the *lector scolarium in aula* were recorded regularly in the bursar's rolls of account, and there we find glimpses of other teaching arrangements. In 1536 Brasenose College paid 3s 2½d in contribution to the first half-year's stipend of the new public reader in theology, Richard Smith. In 1551 this payment was made to the public reader in philosophy, the readership that replaced it.[6] By the end of the seventh decade, the hall lectureship too was described as

[1] BNCA MS A2.1, fo 27 *De nostro informatore logicorum et sophisticarum*.

[2] *SCO* ii. pt 9, 15–17; chapter 11: *De electione lectoris, et eius officio*; all scholars were also to attend in the Parvise; cf Fletcher, 169 below.

[3] BNCA MS A1.1.

[4] Note 2 p. 11 above; de Villiers in *VCH Oxon*. iii. 208–9.

[5] *Visitations*, ed. Hamilton Thompson iii. 52–3.

[6] BNCA bursar's rolls 5, fo 23; bursar's rolls 11 (no foliation); cf G. D. Duncan, 343 below. See Leadam, 'Early years', app. 1, p. 183, for payments in 1545–6.

a 'public readership',[1] perhaps reflecting a new attitude both to the office and to the college's contribution to teaching in the university. The designation goes back at least to 1560, when annual lists of the officers of the college were first entered at the end of the vice-principal's register.[2] Richard Barnes was the first *publicus praelector* so listed, and some of his successors were called *publicus aulae praelector, aulae praelector*, or simply *praelector*.[3]

The new title was quite likely taken over from the first important addition to the provision for teaching. In 1555 Sir John Port, a fellow, left two hundred pounds to provide readers in natural philosophy and humanity; they too received four pounds per annum, and were to read three times a week during term—the humanity reader in the vacation also. The reader in natural philosophy was to reply every Friday at the bachelors' disputations, and the humanity reader to hear repetitions every Saturday.[4] They were functioning at least from the early 1560s;[5] in 1572 they were joined by a public lecturer in Greek,[6] and from that time the four public readers, each paid four pounds per annum, appear together.

One further and early addition to the resources of Brasenose College must be mentioned. In 1538 John Claymond, president of Corpus Christi College and former president of Magdalen, gave the college the first endowment designed to support undergraduates on the foundation; six scholars were to be elected by the president, vice-president, and humanity reader at Corpus Christi College. They were to be maintained for three years after their determination as bachelors, or until they took their MA, and during their tenure they were to hear the humanity and Greek readers at Corpus Christi College.[7]

Claymond's benefaction recalls in the first place the inadequate maintenance for scholars at Brasenose—he foresaw their disappearance unless some help were provided—and it helped to promote that enlargement of the college which the founders envisaged in their statutes. It also associated Brasenose in some degree with the humanist teaching at Bishop Richard Fox's new foundation. Claymond may even have been returning a favour; the arms of Sir Richard

---

[1] BNCA bursar's rolls 13 (no foliation), 1569 'publicus lector dialectices in aula'.

[2] BNCA MS A1.1, fo 102^V.

[3] Ibid. fo 104^V.

[4] *Brasenose Monographs* i. no. 4, 15.

[5] There is no payment in 1557, the first complete roll after 1555; payment only to the reader in dialectic is recorded in 1561 in a damaged roll; the first entry in the surviving records is in 1562 (BNCA, bursar's rolls 12).

[6] *Brasenose Monographs* i. no. 4, 19; a position endowed by Richard Harpur, Esq. of Swarkestone, Derbyshire, a justice of common pleas, not apparently a Brasenose man.

[7] Ibid. 12–14.

Sutton were included in the cornice of the president's chamber over the gateway of Corpus, perhaps to commemorate some benefaction to Fox's new college.[1]

The foundation and early history of Brasenose College epitomize the world of late medieval Oxford, and also show the potential for adaptation of a fairly conventional collegiate society. It was designed to promote the Christian faith and the welfare of church and state, like the foundations of Waynflete, the Lady Margaret, and so many others. Although it too was probably intended to be chiefly a society of future priests, its clerical character was actually less emphatic than was that of Magdalen College or the Lady Margaret's foundations at Cambridge. Brasenose, too, had a comprehensive internal teaching system, more conventional and less grand than that at Magdalen, so that despite the familiarity of its founders with the circle of the Lady Margaret, John Fisher, and Richard Fox, its undergraduate teaching more closely resembled that done in the halls. It may indeed have been taken over from the teaching of Brasenose Hall, with which its history is continuous. Both Smith and Sutton apparently had kinsmen who had been principals of Brasenose Hall in the previous century. The last principal but two was a benefactor of the new college; his successor was a fellow on the new foundation, and Matthew Smith, the last principal of Brasenose Hall, became the first principal of Brasenose College.[2] In 1514 he was spoken of as 'Principal of the College and Hall of Brasen Nose', and Sutton's statutes referred to it under both titles, as we have seen.[3]

These connections illustrate another feature of the transition from the late medieval to the collegiate university of the sixteenth century. There is no sharp line to be drawn between the 'vanishing' world of the medieval hall and the world of the Tudor university. Brasenose Hall, whose history reached back to the late thirteenth century, had already absorbed four adjacent halls in the course of time. The new foundation eventually absorbed five more.[4] Such expansion of the site explains the rapid enlargement of accommodation in the course of the century, even if annexation did not always involve suppression. In addition to these adjacent tenements, Brasenose hired halls opposite the college in Schools Street—Black Hall and Glasen Hall, and in 1556 Staple Hall, the last on a perpetual lease from Lincoln College. Annexes like these were sublet to senior

---

[1] Churton, *Lives of Smyth and Sutton*, 440.
[2] De Villiers in *VCH Oxon*. iii. 208.
[3] J. Buchan, *Brasenose College* (1898), 14.
[4] F. Madan, 'The site of the college', in *Brasenose Monographs* i. no. 1; Leadam, 'Early years', 10–11. Newman, p. 606 and McConica, p. 694 below.

members of the college or university, to cope with the problem of discipline.[1]

We have seen like adaptation in the teaching of the college. The statutes of Smith and Sutton are a deceptive guide to the real nature of the society, which soon opened itself to undergraduate commoners as well as scholars, which showed a slow but striking increase in numbers, and which, by the end of the century, boasted four public readerships in disciplines—dialectic, humanity, Greek, and natural philosophy—that summed up admirably this blend of the traditional and the new.

THE FOUNDATIONS OF FOX AND WOLSEY

Corpus Christi College

In 1501 the see once held by Wykeham and Waynflete was again occupied by a royal administrator of immense energy and initiative who founded a college at Oxford of notable importance in the history of the university at large. Richard Fox was born about 1448 near Grantham, in Lincolnshire. According to his biographer Thomas Greenway, who was president of Corpus Christi College from 1562 to 1568, Fox had been a commoner of Magdalen College, and we know that he matriculated subsequently at Louvain in canon law, and later studied at Paris. Like his episcopal colleague William Smith, the founder of Brasenose, he built his career under the new dynasty. In 1485 he became royal secretary, in 1487 keeper of the privy seal, and thereafter he served the crown repeatedly on diplomatic missions. He was chancellor of Cambridge (1498–1500) and master of Pembroke College there (1507–18) while he established his own foundation at Oxford. Although it is important not to exaggerate their novelty, his college, and that of Wolsey with which it was closely linked, unquestionably introduced a new era in the university. Since Corpus Christi College also served as a model for later Tudor foundations, it has been chosen for detailed study in this volume.[2]

Fox's first idea was purely conventional. This was to establish a house of studies for the Benedictine monks of St Swithin at Winchester which would have had the same relationship as that of Durham College to St Cuthbert's at Durham, and of Canterbury College to Christ Church at Canterbury. He obtained a royal licence for this purpose in the spring of 1513, but his intention to endow

[1] Leadam, 'Early years', 41–2.
[2] See Chapter 10 for discussion of the college's government and discipline, and of its membership. On the college economy see G. E. Aylmer. and G. D. Duncan, pp. 575–85.

Oxford with a college of some sort was clearly known to the university in 1511.[1] Tradition credits Hugh Oldham, bishop of Exeter, with the influence that dissuaded Fox from making a further investment in monastic education, and persuaded him to devote his resources instead to the improvement chiefly of the secular clergy.[2] He apparently began to acquire property from Merton College for the site as early as 1511, and in November 1516 he obtained a royal licence to establish a college consisting of a president and thirty scholars, more or less, endowed with lands in mortmain to the annual value of £350.[3] The charter of foundation was issued on 1 March 1517, and the statutes in June. These original statutes provided for a president, twenty fellows, and an equal number of undergraduate 'disciples' —discipuli—with two priests, two clerks not yet ordained to the priesthood, and two choristers.[4] Fox did not intend that his society should be further enlarged, and its special character rested upon a kind of planned intimacy that was reflected both in the living and the teaching arrangements. To this was joined a severe discipline, and an aim that was taken directly from the world of pious humanism associated with the court circles of the Lady Margaret and the queen, and Fox's episcopal associates, Smith, Tunstall, Warham, and Fisher.

Fox's preface to his statutes, written with a humanistic turn of phrase that could not be maintained through the traditional terminology of such enactments,[5] deemed his college a beehive whose

---

[1] *Epist. acad. 1508-96*, no. 27, where he is thanked, 'non solum inanimatos nobiscum spendidissime coniungi facies, verum etiam vivos edificabis lapides'. On the foundation see Thomas Fowler, *The History of Corpus Christi College* (OHS xxv 1893), J. G. Milne, *The Early History of Corpus Christi College Oxford* (Oxford 1946), and *Letters of Richard Fox 1486-1527*, ed. P. S. and H. M. Allen (Oxford 1929).

[2] This much-repeated anecdote seems to rest on the authority of Holinshed; the idea was widely current, however. Oldham, the founder of Manchester Grammar School, contributed 6,000 marks to the foundation of Corpus; he was also a life-long friend of William Smith; see Fowler, 29-31.

[3] Fowler, 407; *SCO* ii. pt 10, pp. iii-vii, where the patent roll cited should be 8 Hen. VIII.

[4] The official text of the original statutes of 1517, signed by Fox, is Bodl. MS Laud misc. 621, hereafter cited as 'MS Laud'. It is paginated. Originally only four ministers of the chapel were provided for, the two choristers being added; MS Laud, p. 1. Although Fowler acknowledges the 1517 statutes, he invariably cites the 1528 revision printed in *SCO* ii, attributing its provisions to 1517. I am grateful to Dr G. D. Duncan who assisted me in the collation of the two texts. The manuscript, a fair copy, is heavily annotated in places with marginal and interlinear notes. Many of these were followed in 1528, and it is clear that the manuscript was used in the preparation of the revision at the end of Fox's life. However, the 1528 version contains material that does not appear in the original, and the original contains annotations that were not adopted in 1528. The English version of the 1517 statutes by G. R. M. Ward, *The Foundation Statutes of Bishop Fox for Corpus Christi College* (1843), sometimes follows the original text, sometimes the revisions, without any indication. Where the two versions are the same, I cite the printed Latin text for convenience.

[5] Hence the warning about un-Ciceronian *barbara vocabula*; *SCO* ii. pt 10, 2.

scholars, like industrious bees, would make wax to the honour of God, and sweet honey for their own profit and that of all Christians. The rhetoric of the statutes, which reappears usually at the beginning of each chapter as a prologue to perfectly conventional phraseology, was certainly intended to inform their provisions with the ideals of the new humanist and rhetorical educational programme. No doubt they were also meant to engage the enthusiasm of the hearers while they were also instructed, when the statutes were formally read aloud each year.[1]

The president was to be in priest's orders and a graduate in theology,[2] with a mandate for strict supervision of every aspect of the material, intellectual, and moral order of the society. He was to be 'feared like a Prince',[3] and to remain in office for life unless disabled or guilty of some gross misconduct. He was to be assisted by a vice-president chosen from the seven senior fellows,[4] who was to function generally as his deputy. Two deans, chosen by the president and seven seniors from the more mature and discreet, were to watch and take notice of the conversation and conduct of all the others, and to enforce discipline. One was to be an MA with responsibility for the studies of the artists: to moderate their disputations, to send them to their lectures, and to be present at the readings and disputations of the sophists and logicians at least thrice weekly. The other dean, who was to hold a degree in theology or at least be a scholar, had similar responsibilities for the theologians. After 1528 the second decanal office fell automatically to the vice-president.[5]

The location of the college estates determined its local constituency, which broadly imitated that of the university as a whole. Places were awarded to men born in one or another of eleven counties or dioceses,[6] commemorating in a general way the stages of Fox's episcopal career and his debt to Hugh Oldham, bishop of Exeter; otherwise they served the interests of the counties whence the college drew its revenues.[7] The fellows were to be elected to two probationary years from among those who could satisfy the regional requirements, who

---

[1] Ibid. 101.

[2] MS Laud p. 2; in 1528 Fox added the proviso that he should be neither a bishop nor a religious, and that he might be on the point of qualifying in theology; *SCO* ii. pt 10, 2.

[3] Ibid. Discipline is discussed in the last chapter, pp. 652 ff. below.

[4] So in 1517; the seven seniors take a much larger part in 1528, replacing the 'majority of those present' in most provisions.

[5] *SCO* ii. pt 10, 15; cf MS Laud p. 16, line 20 ff.

[6] They were the dioceses of Winchester (5), Durham (1), Bath and Wells (2), Exeter (2), in each of which Fox had been bishop, and the counties of Wiltshire (1), Gloucester (2), Kent (2), Bedfordshire (1) and Oxford or Berkshire (1) in which counties the college held lands and rents. Two were added for the county of Lincoln and one for Lancaster, where Fox and Oldham respectively were born.

[7] I cannot reconcile the views of Milne, *Early History of Corpus*, 3, with the wording

were bachelors of arts and not yet masters nor admitted to incept, and who were not yet past their twentieth year.[1] During their probationary period they were known as 'scholars'. Fox also provided that no one was to be elected either a fellow or scholar who was illegitimate or who was not so well grounded in grammar and the Latin poets, orators, and historians as to be able to compose verse and dictate letters extempore.[2] The candidate must also have the first clerical tonsure and, apart from his youth, be free from any canonical impediment to priestly orders (a consideration which accounts also for the insistence on legitimacy). A scholar was to be scrutinized closely during his probationary years, and might be expelled at the end of either the first or second if he was found deficient in the desired qualities of intellect, character, or morals. Election to full fellowship at the end of the second year was by open vote of the assembled body of graduate fellows, presided over by the president or vice-president in the chapel. The newly elected fellow would enter into a bond for one hundred pounds, payable to the president and scholars of the college if he defaulted on his obligations.[3]

Since the twenty undergraduates or disciples were intended to succeed their seniors, the rules for their qualification were the same, including the requirement of first clerical tonsure. The standard of proficiency in Latin was scarcely mitigated, and prospective disciples were expected to be initiated in logic, or at least to have sufficient grammar to allow them to undertake such study along with that of humane letters—a concession that seems to make allowances for youth.[4] They were also to be instructed in plainsong, to be between the ages of twelve and seventeen years,[5] and possessed of an annual income not exceeding five marks. They might remain to the age of twenty-four unless they were promoted to a higher category of fellowship, or disqualified by increment of income, provided that they observed the requirements of the statutes. If they qualified as MAs, however, they might remain until an appropriate place in the fellowship fell vacant. They were elected by the president, vice-president, and other officers of the college, with the readers in theology, Greek and humanity, who convened the candidates in the chapel and examined them then and there in plainsong and Latin letters.

of the statutes either in 1517 or 1528: MS Laud, p. 19, *SCO* ii. pt 10, 17–18. The phrase 'in quibus iam habent terras et redditus' is, moreover, part of an addition to the 1517 text.

[1] MS Laud, 19; 'twenty three' in 1528.   [2] Ibid. 21.

[3] Ibid. 32; *SCO* ii. pt 10, 30–1.

[4] MS Laud, 34; provision was made in 1528 for remedial training in *bonis literis*, but until they reached the desired standard, such candidates would be allowed their commons only, without stipend or clothing money: *SCO* ii. pt 10, 31–2.

[5] Raised in 1528 to nineteen years: ibid.

This close attention to detail in the screening and admission of members to the college, of which only the main lines can be indicated, is a typical feature of Fox's statutes. They are much more carefully constructed than are those of Brasenose, and in their general conception reflect the traditions of New College and Magdalen, erecting a society in which undergraduate members, half the total foundation, are integral to the design. When we turn to the provisions for teaching them, we find like precision.

The best-known feature of Fox's college, his provision for three public lecturers, was a direct imitation of Waynflete's foundation at Magdalen College; but where Waynflete endowed the public teaching of the *quadrivium* and theology, Fox's lecturers proclaimed the curriculum of the humanist reformers. They were to teach humanity, Greek, and in a markedly new way sacred theology. The authors they were to expound confirm the intellectual patrimony suggested by the titles of their lectureships.[1] The reader in humanity lectured on the authors of Latin eloquence—Cicero and Quintilian—the historians Sallust, Valerius Maximus, and Suetonius, along with Pliny for natural history, lecturing on those for an hour on Mondays, Wednesdays, and Fridays throughout the teaching year, beginning at 8 a.m. On Tuesdays, Thursdays, and Saturdays the authors were to be Virgil, Ovid, Lucan, Juvenal, Terence, or Plautus. On feast days in the afternoon he was also (at an hour to be assigned by the president and seniors) publicly to read and explain Horace or Persius.[2] Moreover, three times a week during the ordinary terms, and on four occasions of his own choosing during vacations, he was to read privately, Valla's *Elegantiae*, Aulus Gellius's *Noctes Atticae,* and the *Miscellanea* of the famous Italian poet and philologist, Angelo Poliziano, or some such author.[3]

Fox's chair in Greek narrowly anticipated the first permanent provision at Cambridge.[4] He alluded to the decree of the council of

---

[1] *Lector seu professor artium humanitatis, Lector Graecorum Graecaeque linguae, Lector sacrae theologiae*, all were to be 'botanists (*herbarii*)' in his garden of bees. *SCO* ii. pt 10, 48 ff.

[2] MS Laud p. 52; this last provision was omitted in 1528 but no alteration was indicated in MS Laud.

[3] In 1528, these lectures were confined to the vacations; *SCO* ii. pt 10, 49.

[4] Fox's establishment of a public lectureship in a college was not matched at Cambridge until Fisher's statutes for St John's College of 1530. The first regular provision for Greek teaching at Cambridge came however, with the appointment of Richard Croke in 1518. In the same (Michaelmas) term, John Clement began his tenure of Wolsey's humanity lecture in Oxford, almost certainly teaching Greek, at least in part. Before this time there is sporadic evidence of Greek teaching at both universities, with the first known course of lectures at Oxford sponsored officially in the Christmas vacation, 1512. Erasmus began lecturing at Cambridge through John Fisher's initiative in the autumn of 1511, and (while spending most of the next year in London) retained this position until his departure

Vienne which, two centuries earlier, had directed the teaching of
Greek at Oxford,[1] and he insisted that those who had the obligation
to support a Greek lecturer at their own charge should not now stand
excused from their duty.[2] The Greek lecture was to begin at 10 a.m.,
on the same general terms as those of the reader in humanity. On
Mondays, Wednesdays, and Fridays, Greek grammar was taught along
with the speeches of Isocrates, Lucian, or Philostratus; on Tuesdays,
Thursdays, and Saturdays, the lecturer was to read the poets and
rhetoricians: Aristophanes, Theocritus, Euripides, Sophocles, Pindar,
Hesiod, or another of the *antiquissimi Graeci poetae*, with something
of Demosthenes, Thucydides, Aristotle (presumably the *Rhetoric*
or *Poetics*), Theophrastus, or Plutarch; on feasts he would provide
Homer's epigrams or something of the 'divine Plato' or a Greek
theologian.[3] Like his Latinist counterpart he was also to lecture three
times a week during the ordinary year, and on four occasions of his
own choosing during the vacations, on Greek grammar and rhetoric.[4]

All members of the college below the degree of bachelor of theology—even the masters of arts—were bound to attend the public
lectures in Greek and Latin, and the Greek lecturer was obliged to
examine these auditors in the evening for half an hour, as often as he
should lecture.[5] Negligence, or refusal to undergo examination, or
neglect of lectures were all punished by loss of commons.

The third reader, in theology, was not concerned with undergraduate teaching but he should be discussed briefly here, since the
furthering of theology was the essential object of the foundation.[6]
He was to lecture, not on the *Sentences* but on some part of scripture,
the Old and New Testaments in alternate years. In his interpretation
he was to use the ancient doctors of the church, both Latin and
Greek.[7] All the theologians except the doctors were bound to attend.
Like the other readers, he was to encourage his auditors to question
him after his lectures, which were scheduled for 2 p.m., subject

early in 1514. For the teaching of Greek at Corpus see below, pp. 25-7. See also, Cobban,
King's Hall, 82-3; A. Tilley, 'Greek studies in England in the early sixteenth century',
English Historical Review, liii (1938) 221-9, 438-56.

[1] Hastings Rashdall, *The Universities of Europe in the Middle Ages* (2 vols, Oxford
1895), new edn by F. M. Powicke and A. B. Emden (3 vols, Oxford 1936), i. 566 note,
iii. 161, 162 note.
[2] *SCO* ii. pt 10, 49.
[3] MS Laud p. 52; provision for feasts omitted 1528.
[4] Ibid. p. 52; as with the humanity lectures, reduced in 1528 to vacations.
[5] *SCO* ii. pt 10, 49-50.
[6] Ibid. 50.
[7] Jerome, Augustine, Ambrose, Origen, Hilary, Chrysostom, John Damascene 'et alios
eius generis', *not* Nicholas of Lyra or Hugh of Vienne, who are far behind them both in time
and doctrine; *SCO* ii. pt 10, 50-1.

(like the others) to the judgement of the president and senior fellows. Only public acts of the university could take precedence over these public lectures. The readers were to be chosen from the fellows and scholars of Corpus, with an additional stipend of £5 beyond their ordinary emoluments for the readers in Greek and humanity, and £6 13s 8d for the reader in theology.[1]

The regulations for the public lecturers were only part of the detailed provision for college teaching.[2] Theologians who were not yet doctors were expected to attend two further lectures daily, one at 7 a.m. in the theology school, which was the Lady Margaret lecture, the other at 9 a.m. at Magdalen College.[3] This would continue until they reached perfect proficiency, as determined by testing in the college. Bachelors of arts were expected daily to attend the two philosophy lectures at Magdalen College, coming and going in a body[4] as far as their attendance at the humanity and Greek lectures would permit. To forestall idleness during the summer, they were also to read lectures three times a week in the presence of all save the graduates in theology, on the De sphaera, Algorismus, or De motu planetarum—a provision taken directly from the statutes of Magdalen College.[5] In the shorter vacations the dean of arts would choose one to discourse to his peers and the undergraduates on some poet, orator, or historian.

Responsibility for undergraduate instruction fell on one or two fellows[6] chosen by the president and dean of arts to serve for a year. Their wide authority over the sophists and logicians extended to the use of flogging, a penalty that first appeared in the statutes of Brasenose College.[7] They were to teach by constant lecturing, and by vigilant attention to the undergraduate rehearsal of what had been read. Sophisms were to be heard before noon, and if necessary in the afternoon after the midday meal; variations were heard after supper. All undergraduates who had studied sophistry and logic for six months were also bound to attend the exercises in parviso.[8] No fellow might decline this considerable addition to his responsibilities

---

[1] MS Laud p. 55; increased slightly in 1528; cf SCO ii (10), 51. Fox allowed the election of a public reader from outside the college, if a willing candidate was found who was markedly more competent, provided he was born in England, Greece, or Italy beyond the Po; ibid. 53.

[2] Ibid. 54 ff., 'De caeteris lecturis legendis et audiendis'.

[3] Statuta, 302, ll. 21-2.

[4] At 6 a.m. and 1 p.m. respectively; cf SCO ii. pt 8, 47.

[5] Ibid. pt 10, 57; see above, p. 6.

[6] 'secundum numerum audientium', SCO ii. pt 10, 56; the original provision for one only (MS Laud, p. 60) echoed the conventional medieval 'logic lecturer'.

[7] SCO ii. pt 10, 56; see below, pp. 654-5.

[8] On these elementary dialectical disputations see J. M. Fletcher, p. 169.

at risk of perjury in violation of his oath; in 1528 instruction of his pupils in Porphyry and Aristotle, first in Latin and then in Greek, was added to his duties.[1] For these duties he was paid over and above his ordinary stipend according to the number of pupils he taught; neglect of his duties was punished by fines or abatement of commons. During holidays undergraduates were to use the time in composing verses and epistles according to the rules of eloquence, and their compositions were to be shown to the reader in humanity for correction.

Apart from the lectures, the chief scholastic activity of the college was disputation. These exercises were held twice weekly for both artists and theologians from the first Sunday of October to the first Sunday of August, except during the three weeks of Christmas, Easter, and Pentecost. All bachelors of arts were to dispute in turn in hall on Wednesdays and Fridays, on questions posted in public three days earlier. Wednesdays were given to logic, except during the 'vespers' exercises,[2] when the questions discussed that week in the university were also to be discussed in the college and when any bachelor of the college was to take part in the Austin disputations,[3] his questions were likewise to replace those in logic on the preceding Wednesday. The Friday disputations dealt with natural philosophy and metaphysics, except during Lent, when they were devoted to moral philosophy.[4] These exercises were to be attended by all the bachelors of arts and the ministers of the chapel, as well as the masters and doctors for at least the greater part of an hour, since the senior members of the college had responsibility to instruct the bachelors and junior members,[5] and the dean of arts was to preside over the whole.[6] It seems reasonable to suppose that the more senior of the *discipuli* would have been in the audience at these occasions.

After three years or at most four in sophistry and logic, every undergraduate was to proceed BA within six months of satisfying the college that he was adequately prepared to do so.[7] In 1528 a clause was added requiring him at the request of the president to expound a book of some Latin poet, orator, or historian on which he might have heard lectures.[8] Bachelors of arts had also to lecture on Greek logic or philosophy with similar regulations for their proceeding to the master's degree. They might not use any grace or dispensation from the university except from the hearing of ordinary

[1] *SCO* ii. pt 10, 56.
[2] *Statuta*, xcvii–xcviii.   [3] Ibid. lxxxvi.
[4] *SCO* ii. pt 10, 57–9.   [5] Ibid. 58.
[6] The theologians held like sessions once a week; ibid. 58–9.
[7] The decision to fall to a committee of senior members; ibid. 59.
[8] Ibid.

lectures or the requirement of reading a book in the Schools. Thus the college maintained a stringent control over the fulfilment of the university's statutory regulations and, what is more, insisted that any member who sought a degree in the faculty of arts without the prior approval of the college was *ipso facto* expelled for life.[1] Indeed, the whole apparatus of teaching at Corpus was supported with a mass of rules and penalties unlike anything seen earlier, and little leeway was allowed even in time of pestilence. If the plague forced the college to remove from Oxford, the scholars were meant if possible to settle close to the refugees from Magdalen so they would still have access to their lectures.[2]

The archives of Corpus Christi College allow us to see something of the way in which these regulations were put into practice.[3] The Greek reader was the first to be appointed.[4] Edward Wotton (BA 1514) appears in the first surviving college accounts for 1521/2 under the heading for readers in Greek and logic at the statutory stipend of £5.[5] Accompanying him as lecturers were Richard Curwen (BA 1519), Edward Martin (BA December 1520) and David Edwards (BA December 1522). The number of pupils in each term is specified for the college lecturers and they appear to have been paid at the rate of 1s 3d per pupil per term. In the next surviving account, for 1526/7, Wotton was paid £10 for four terms, suggesting that he might have delivered both the Greek and Latin (humanity) public lectures. The other two lectures were again paid at the rate of 1s 3d per pupil per term.[6] Wotton, whose tenure of the readership in Greek lasted until 1527/8, was a master of arts and fellow of Magdalen. Fox constituted him a *socius compar* to secure his services for his own foundation. After Wotton left Oxford for Padua, where he took a DM, he was succeeded as reader in Greek at Corpus by John Donne of Exeter diocese (BA 1526, MA 1528), who was paid only £2 in his

---

[1] Ibid. 62; a marked intensification of the regulations at Magdalen, ibid. pt 8, 37.

[2] Ibid. 55; concerning the heightened corporate discipline, see chapter 10.

[3] I am greatly indebted to Dr C. S. Knighton who extracted and assembled the relevant data from the Libri Magni, recording payments to the college readers and lecturers. The first Liber Magnus gives the names of public readers and their stipends, then the names of the lecturers and the numbers of pupils taught each term. From 1534 on the names of the pupils also are given until 1588-9. The names of those attending on the public readers are never given, but those lectures were compulsory in the college and open to the rest of the university.

[4] Although the term 'reader' and 'lecturer' are interchangeable, for the sake of clarity I shall confine the former here and elsewhere to public as opposed to intramural college lecturers.

[5] Corpus Christi College Archives Libri Magni i. fo 3. His appointment would seem to have coincided with Fox's letter of 2 January 1521, contrary to Emden's suggested date of 1524. He presumably left for Italy at the end of 1521/2 for further study; see *Letters of Richard Fox 1486-1527*, no. 74, 126-7.

[6] Corpus Christi College Archives LM i. fo 11; Fowler, *Corpus Christi*, 371.

first year.[1] The first regular reader in humanity seems to have been James Curthorpe (Courthope) of Kent, who held the post from 1538/9 until the first term of 1546/7. He was paid at the rate of £5 6s 8d until 1542/3, when he and his colleague in Greek, who by then was George Etheridge (BA 1539, MA 1543, BM 1545), later the regius professor of Greek at Christ Church,[2] were both paid at the statutory rate of £5. This and like irregularities suggest that in these first years the college was still feeling its way. No reader in theology was appointed, perhaps because by an addition to the statutes in 1528, the vice-president, who was necessarily a senior fellow and theologian, was given all the duties assigned to the dean of theology, and may have performed the functions of reader as well.[3]

This information from the accounts may shed further light on the relations between the foundations of Fox and Wolsey. Both of these prominent ecclesiastics were thoroughly familiar with the needs and wishes of the university, and the tradition of their collaboration in providing public lectures at Oxford goes back to the mid-sixteenth century.[4] The story of Wolsey's lectures is told in another part of this volume,[5] but it should be said here that they are first heard of in Michaelmas term 1518, when John Clement began to lecture in humanity.[6] By May the next year Thomas Brinknell was lecturing in theology.[7] In March 1520 Clement was succeeded by Thomas Lupset (also an accomplished Grecian) who in turn was succeeded by Vives in 1523. Of these, Lupset, Vives, and Clement can all be connected closely with Corpus, at least as having delivered their lectures there.[8] It seems not unlikely therefore that Fox made no ordinary appointment of a humanity reader in this period because his scholars were so well served by distinguished readers paid by Wolsey. In May 1524 Vives returned to Flanders to marry; in the next Liber Magnus (1525/6, the second to survive) Nicholas Udall appears as a lecturer for four terms at the annual stipend of £2. In 1527/8 he lectured for one and a half terms at the same rate of payment; for the intervening period we have no information. He had been admitted BA as recently as 1524/5, but his appearance in the college accounts just at the time Vives left Oxford suggests, in light of his later scholarly distinction, that he might have functioned for

[1] Corpus Christ College Archives LM i. fo 36.

[2] See below, p. 355.

[3] SCO ii. pt 10, 13; there is no corresponding insertion in MS Laud. Since the theologians were served not only by Wolsey's reader but by lectures at Magdalen College and the Lady Margaret professor, economy with respect to Fox's third readership would be understandable.

[4] Fowler, op. cit. 88.   [5] See G. D. Duncan, pp. 337–41.

[6] Epist. acad. 1508–96, 83–4.   [7] Ibid. 91.

[8] See Duncan, pp. 338–9.

two years or so as Vives' successor in the university and as first public reader in humanity at Corpus, perhaps at first as deputy to Wotton.[1] He was paid at the same rate as Wotton's youthful successor in the Greek readership, John Donne. As it happens, it was Donne who had completed Udall's terms as lecturer in 1527/8.

The accounts are also informative about the actual procedures in undergraduate teaching. In 1528 Fox added to his statutes a requirement that lectures in Greek be given to the undergraduates.[2] The next year, in 1529/30, a college lecturer was paid for the first time for teaching seven of his ten pupils in the third term in Greek.[3] From 1534/5 the accounts regularly list the names of the pupils as well as the lecturers,[4] and specify the subject of the lectures, so that it is possible to follow the progress of the *discipuli*. In 1534/5 for example William Chedsey of Somerset (BA 1530, MA 1534), who had already served as lecturer in logic since 1532, taught four men 'in logica graeca'[5] and seven others in Latin logic for the first two terms. Subsequently Hugh Good, also of Somerset (BA 1534, MA 1537), took the Grecians during the last two terms of the year, along with those reading Latin. The two lecturers were paid at the rate of 1s 3d for those reading Latin, and 1s 8d for each of the pupils reading Greek. The system appears to have been well established by the early years of Elizabeth, when in 1559/60, for example, we find eight new arrivals being taken in their first classes in Latin logic by William Phelps, again a man from Somerset (BA 1558, MA 1562). He took them again in the first term the following year, after which they were passed on to another lecturer for three terms of Greek logic, while Phelps took on another group of freshmen. It would be misleading to give the impression that absolute regularity was always observed; in some years only Latin instruction is given (1558/9), in some years only Greek (1540/1). By the 1560s, moreover, lecturers to undergraduates were being paid a flat stipend of ten shillings a term, regardless of the number of pupils, so that it becomes more difficult to be certain which classes were given in Greek. Until mid-century it was common for an undergraduate to do two or three years of Greek; thereafter the normal limit was three terms. Of the 259 pupils listed by name in the years from 1534 to 1588, 56—or approximately one-fifth—went on to become lecturers in their turn, and 21 to be public readers of the college.

[1] See above, p. 25 n. 6.

[2] See above, p. 24.

[3] Corpus Christi College Archives LM 1, fo 64ᵛ.

[4] This practice stops in 1588–9.

[5] Corpus Christi College Archives LM 1, fo 122; in the first accounts the top form is usually said to read Greek; from 1535/6 usually 'Aristotle in Greek'.

More must be said of the significance of Corpus Christi College in the life of Tudor Oxford.[1] For the present we confine our attention to the specific theme of the growth of the secular undergraduate college. It will be seen that Fox's foundation added nothing in principle to the conception of William Waynflete. Corpus had a comprehensive system of college teaching, together with endowed lectureships open to the university at large, but it also showed an emphasis on the new curriculum which amounted to a dramatic advance on the statutes of Magdalen College. In that respect Fox's society was a compliment to the achievement of Waynflete's college and school. The warden of New College and the president of Magdalen College presided over the inception of Corpus; indeed, by Fox's statutes, they were to arbitrate along with the chancellor of the university in any dispute between a president of Corpus and his college.[2] The first president of Corpus was none other than the president of Magdalen, John Claymond; the first reader in Greek was a fellow there, and among the founder's fellows Magdalen supplied so many of exceptional talent, like Reginald Pole, as to make it clear that Fox intended the distinction of Waynflete's foundation should be carried over to his own. The place of undergraduate commoners paralleled their place at Magdalen since in revising his statutes Fox also provided for from four to six sons of nobles or lawyers to live in the college, at the discretion of the president, under a tutor and at their own expense.[3] It cannot be said, however, that commoners played a large part in Fox's design which was meant once again to fortify the secular clergy of the realm.[4] Every fellow on obtaining his MA was expected to be ordained to the priesthood within a year of completing his necessary regency.[5] The study of theology was to be supported not only by natural and moral philosophy but by Latin and Greek philology, and for the better comprehension of sacred scripture by knowledge as well of the Greek and Latin doctors of the church. In place of an associated school there was a requirement in *bonae literae* and an entrance examination that was entirely new,

---

[1] See below, chapter 10.

[2] Fowler, *Corpus Christi*, 56; *SCO* ii. pt 10, 8.

[3] The provision at the end of the statute *De extraneis non introducendis*, ibid. 80, does not appear in 1517, or in MS Laud as an interpolation. It is integral to the text of the three official copies of 1527/8 now in the college archives: A/4/1/1, A/4/1/1A, and A/4/1/1B. All are signed by Fox; the first is also sealed; the first two have the oath of supremacy inside the cover and were evidently in ordinary use in the college, cf *SCO* ii. pt 10, 100. Milne's assertion, *Early History of Corpus*, 5, that this clause 'is added in a considerably later hand to the official copy in the Archives' appears to be groundless.

[4] For another view, see Milne, *Early History of Corpus*, 4 ff.

[5] *SCO* ii. pt 10, 62; in 1528 the one fellow permitted to study medicine is alone excepted.

although it is clear that in many cases the college was prepared to supply deficiencies in Latin before actually admitting promising pupils as undergraduate members.[1] What distinguished Fox's foundation from Magdalen, apart from this emphasis on the humanistic formation of its divines, was its intimacy and concentration. A small society it was, and meant to grow no larger, in which each undergraduate was paired with a fellow-tutor, where every aspect of the daily life was regulated to an unprecedented degree, where systematic secret delation was the foundation of discipline, and penalties for misconduct were precise and often severe—this was a society unlikely to welcome the more casual association of gentlemen commoners, and the evidence suggests that they were not, indeed, numerous.[2]

Cardinal College

Wolsey's occasional provision of lectures[3] was soon abandoned in favour of a much grander scheme. By 1524-5 he was planning his most magnificent creation in the form of Cardinal College, intended, predictably, to surpass the noble foundations of Wykeham and Waynflete and—intentionally or not—certain to cast Fox's provision for new studies at Corpus Christi College quite into the shade.

It is tempting to think that so novel a conception as Cardinal College was inspired by a foreign university, but the evidence does not confirm this. The nearest foundation likely to have stimulated Wolsey was the trilingual college at Louvain, about which both Fox and Wolsey were certainly well-informed,[4] but Wolsey's scheme was far grander, and it was not trilingual. It seems like so much else that he did, to have surpassed all precedent in scale, but in its nature to have been composed entirely of traditional elements, skilfully adapted to meet new conditions. Once again Magdalen College, where Wolsey had been bursar, seems to have been the starting-point, even architecturally,[5] and to that it is most logical to add his experience of the university's needs and demands over the years, and his dealings

---

[1] See below, p. 668 n. 5.

[2] See chapter 10, p. 669.

[3] See above, pp. 26-7 and Duncan, pp. 337-41.

[4] The *collegium trilingue* was founded by Jérôme de Busleiden in 1517, consisting of eight scholars and three professors in Latin, Greek and Hebrew. The scholars were to attend lectures in the faculty of arts during the week, and to study with the professors—who were otherwise to lecture publicly to the university—on Sundays and feast days; the whole was to be grafted on to an existing college. See H. de Vocht, *History of the Foundation and the Rise of the Collegium Trilingue Lovaniense 1517-1550, part 1: the foundation* (Louvain 1951).

[5] See John Newman, p. 613 below.

not only with Fox but with the entire humanist circle, not least with Erasmus, whose patron in part he was.[1]

While the six public professorships in Cardinal College[2] quite plainly show the influence of the humanistic programme, they none the less preserve the traditional structure of the schools, with chairs in the three higher faculties of theology, canon law, civil law, and medicine, and (for the artists) in philosophy and humanity. The influence of the new learning is predictably most obvious in humanity, with two lectures daily, one on Latin authors and the other on Greek, and in philosophy, whose professor was to lecture on the works of Aristotle and occasionally on Plato. The rhetorical declamation was also written into the programme, since the public professors were to set themes each week and to examine their students on them at the end.[3] All professors were to be available for questioning by their pupils, including those in law and medicine for practical professional advice. Arrangements like these seem to imply the complete revision of the university's statutes that Wolsey also undertook, and suggest that he meant to redirect the activity of the entire university.[4] This is also suggested by the constitution of the college of electors for his public professors,[5] which for the first time recognized the growing importance of the heads of the secular colleges, and as Maxwell Lyte pointed out, completely ignored the monastic element in the university.[6] By its scale alone his college was bound to make a strong impact, since it surpassed the largest of the previous foundations by a third, providing for a hundred fellows who were secular canons, with thirteen chaplains, twelve clerks, sixteen choristers, and a teacher of music, besides a large staff of servants. The sixty senior canons were to be bachelors of arts and to proceed to their MA degrees before going on to one of the superior faculties; all were eventually to seek ordination as priests. Four were to be chosen as college lecturers in sophistry, logic, philosophy, and humanity, to teach the juniors. These, the forty petty canons, who were to be chosen from grammar schools to be established by Wolsey in different parts of England, were to be at

---

[1] Erasmus's dedicatory letter to a new edition of translations from Plutarch in 1517 carried news of the death of Busleiden; *Opus epistolarum Des. Erasmi Roterodami*, ed. P. S. Allen et al. (12 vols Oxford 1906–58) iii. no. 658, pp. 52–4.

[2] For the details of Wolsey's scheme, see G. D. Duncan, pp. 339–41.

[3] Ibid. p. 341.

[4] Cf *Epist. acad. 1508–96*, pp. 376–7 (note to no. 78).

[5] Duncan, p. 340.

[6] H. C. Maxwell Lyte, *A History of the University of Oxford* (1886), 452. Wolsey also intended to build schools suitable to the dignity of his professors; *Epist. acad. 1508–96*, no. 136; E. Mullaly, 'Wolsey's proposed reform of the Oxford University statutes: a recently discovered text', *Bodleian Library Record* x no. 1 (1978), 22–6.

least fifteen years of age at entry, and until they reached the age of twenty were to be placed under the direction of tutors chosen from the senior canons. They were to leave at the age of twenty-five, or after their fifth year in the college, unless they had by then been promoted senior canon.

This splendid conception which underlay the design of the successor foundation of Christ Church was matched by remarkable endowment. Apart from his resort to papal and royal power to obtain both endowment and the right to hold lands in mortmain to the clear annual value of £2,000, Wolsey sought stone from Caen, negotiated for the purchase of books in Rome and Venice, and arranged for the transcription of the Greek manuscripts which had belonged to Cardinal Bessarion and to the late Cardinal Domenico Grimani. It was to have been an affair of international importance.[1]

None the less, Wolsey's college grew in the local soil from native roots. His public professors gave a permanent establishment to the lectureships he had been providing occasionally, at the university's insistent demand. Whether or not they were so badly needed for instruction in the traditional curriculum as the university claimed,[2] they certainly allowed the implantation of new authors and new approaches to established texts. Except in scale, the college to which they were attached essentially resembled Magdalen, but with the senior fellowships—as at Corpus—open to the juniors. The fellow-canons recalled the former priory of Austin Canons which had been dissolved to make way for Wolsey's scheme. The statute allowing twenty sons of noble or wealthy persons to lodge and study under the supervision of 'creansers' was virtually copied from Waynflete's constitutions.[3] The extirpation of heresy was added to otherwise conventional aims;[4] the general organization of teaching followed the lines worked out at Corpus. Petty canons were to be admitted after a general examination in hall in the presence of officers of the college, and the elaborate provision for their tuition was a chief innovation in Wolsey's statutes. The disciplinary arrangements also resembled those at Corpus; like Fox's president, the dean of Cardinal College was to be feared *tamquam princeps*,[5] and he was assisted in

---

[1] See Maxwell Lyte, 449–50. Report of Lorenzo Orio from London in the Sanuto Diaries, vol. xl, for 23 December 1525; cf *Cal. S.P. Venice* iii. 515. Cardinal Grimani, who was a patron of Erasmus in Rome with Cardinal Riario, had died in 1525.

[2] See the remarks of W. T. Mitchell in *Epist. acad. 1508–96*, p. xxxii.

[3] Where Magdalen's noble commoners were to be 'filii nobilium et valentium personarum' those at Cardinal College were 'filii procerum sive nobilium ac opulentarum personarum'; *SCO* ii. pt 11, 103, cf pt 8, 60.

[4] Patent of foundation, 17 Henry VIII; ibid. pt 11, 4.

[5] *SCO* ii. pt 11, 14; chapter 10 below, p. 654.

the control of his large society of young men by the sub-dean and four censors; the latter had the tasks of deans in other colleges and most importantly, responsibility for the instruction of the junior members.[1] At Cardinal College, for the first time, it was envisaged that every discipline taught in the university would be taught within the college, including medicine. The balance between regard for tradition and enthusiasm for the new studies is perhaps best summed up in Wolsey's instruction that the public professor of theology teach the canonical books of the Old and New Testaments 'as intelligibly, lucidly and elegantly as he can', while he was also to instruct in the 'subtle scholastic questions of Scotus', lest ignorance of scholastic learning, so necessary 'for the understanding of divine philosophy and the confutation of heresy', advance imperceptibly.[2] Such respect for established philosophical tradition was to remain a persistent element in Oxford throughout the Tudor period, and beyond.

THE SUCCESSOR FOUNDATIONS

Christ Church

The building of Cardinal College began in January 1525. By the time Wolsey fell from power at the end of 1529, enough of the vast quadrangle had been completed to leave an enduring monument to a collegiate plan unprecedented at either university. Eighteen canons were named in the foundation charter, and two public readers are known to have been appointed, Nicholas de Burgo in theology and Mattheus Calphurnius in Greek.[3] The short life of the new foundation had been marked, ironically, by the introduction of the Lutheran heresy into the university,[4] and with the fall of Wolsey the future of the dean and canons was precarious. It was not until almost twenty years later that Wolsey's original conception was taken up again; in the interval, the life of the society was barely preserved by the modest foundation of 'King Henry VIII College' in 1532, and was complicated by the erection of the diocese of Oxford with its cathedral at Oseney in 1542. King Henry VIII College was without any express educational purpose. In 1545 both the college and the cathedral foundation were surrendered to the crown, and on 4 November 1546 a charter of foundation was issued by letters patent to a corporation

---

[1] Waynflete's three deans were supplemented with a fourth, a second theologian, who was to have had the duty of supervising the lawyers and students in medicine; *SCO* ii. pt 11, 15.

[2] Ibid. 127.

[3] See Duncan, p. 341.

[4] See J. Loach, pp. 363 ff.

called, 'the cathedral church of Christ in Oxford' of which Richard Cox was named dean, with eight canons, of whom four had previously been canons of the cathedral of Oseney, and one, of King Henry VIII College. This patent, however, established the ecclesiastical corporation only and did not lay down the foundation of the academic college.[1] The discovery of a set of draft statutes drawn up for 'Christ churche of kyng Henry theightes ffundacion' belies the tradition that the death of the king on 28 January 1547 entirely prevented the preparation of statutes, and helps to explain why the college came into being as it did.[2] Although these statutes are difficult to date and never came into force, they show an important stage of official thinking about the successor foundation to Wolsey's great scheme, and require attention here.

The draft statutes, which are unsigned, closely resemble those of other cathedrals of new foundation; as the editor of those for Peterborough Cathedral remarked, that foundation was likewise, 'placed on a collegiate basis, following as far as possible the precedent set by Wolsey in his foundation of Cardinal College, Oxford, and his college of Ipswich'.[3] These Henrician statutes provide for a dean, with 8 canons of the first order, 40 canons of the second order, and 20 *discipuli* eligible for promotion to the rank of canons or permanent fellows. The canons of the first order, who were to be masters of arts or graduates in theology,[4] had no precedent in Wolsey's scheme, and were evidently meant to form the chapter of the cathedral or Church (as the college is always designated); they owned

[1] On these changes see H. L. Thompson, *Christ Church* (1900), ch. 1 and app. B, pp. 272–80 on the documents relating to the foundation; *VCH Oxon.* iii. 234–5; and the account by J. E. A. Dawson, 'The early career of Christopher Goodman and his place in the development of English protestant thought' (Durham PhD thesis 1978) and eadem, 'The foundation of Christ Church, Oxford and Trinity College, Cambridge in 1546', *Bulletin of the Institute of Historical Research*, vol. lvii (1984), pp. 208–15.

[2] Christ Church Archives (hereafter CCA) MS D.P. vi. b. i. fos 157–96. They were correctly identified by Mr Malcolm Underwood in an early survey of collegiate archives in Oxford for the History of the University, having come to the Christ Church archives from the dean's study; cf. the report of G. D. Duncan and J. K. McConica in *Archives* xv no. 66 (1981), 101. They have the appearance of a complete draft text prepared for circulation and comment, fairly written, and in places are heavily annotated in various hands. The interlinear and marginal annotations however, are generally disregarded by the later Edwardian code (see below, p. 37), suggesting that Cox was not their author.

[3] *Peterborough Local Administration*, ed. W. T. Mellows (2 vols Northamptonshire Record Society xiii–xiv 1947, 1941) ii. I am greatly indebted to Dr C. S. Knighton for advice about the contemporary foundations. It seems likely that the statutes under consideration were drawn up in the interval between late January 1546, when the royal grant authorizing the erection of a new cathedral church was stopped, and the issuing of the letters patent the following November; see Dawson, 'The foundation of Christ Church', *Bulletin of the Institute of Historical Research*, vol. lvii, p. 211.

[4] CCA MS D.P. vi. b. i, fo 162; the provision about masters of arts was subsequently deleted.

the property and had a role, for example, in the election of the public professors and in custody of valuables, and the four senior among them were to hear the annual accounts with the dean and auditor. The permanent canons of the second order were to be bachelors of arts without impediment for priestly orders, and without any certain annual income beyond eight marks; they thus closely resemble Wolsey's canons of the first order.[1] The size envisaged was smaller than Wolsey's, with a total of sixty-eight on the college foundation in addition to the dean and three public readers, as opposed to Wolsey's hundred students and six public readers. In 1540 five regius chairs had been established in Oxford to be supported by the new cathedral foundation of Westminster, and the three readerships named in the draft statutes of Christ Church are the same three—in theology, Hebrew, and Greek—whose support had been transferred from Westminster to the new royal foundation at Oxford in the latter half of 1546.[2]

The undergraduates at Christ Church, according to these same draft statutes, were to be recruited from pupils 'in our grammar school' who were more than fifteen years of age and under twenty-five.[3] Their instruction was to be in the hands of five domestic lecturers chosen from the second order of canons,[4] two in dialectic, a third in rhetoric, a fourth in natural philosophy or mathematics, and the fifth in moral philosophy. Domestic lectures would begin at 6 a.m. immediately after mass, when authors prescribed by the dean or other authorized persons were to be expounded. It is clear that the chief responsibility for beginners would fall on the lecturers in logic, who were in the event the first to be appointed (in 1547), and they were to be present at every disputation or other exercise. Canons of the second order were to attend the daily public lectures in Greek, as indeed were all in the college to the extent that their other duties permitted it. With regard to the other public lectures, in Hebrew, civil law, medicine, and theology, all canons of the second order and *discipuli* were to attend those in their own faculty, and others as the dean determined. The lecture in Hebrew was mandatory for theologians. Once again, the auditors were to be able to respond to themes set by their professors.[5] As in other sections of these statutes the form and phraseology of Wolsey's provisions for Cardinal College were followed closely here. The oath to be sworn by

[1] *SCO* ii. pt 11, 20.
[2] See Duncan, p. 345.
[3] CCA MS D.P. vi. b. i. fo 162^V: it appears that a school attached to the foundation is meant. This section is one of the most heavily over-written.
[4] Ibid. fo 163.
[5] Ibid. fos 163^{r-v}, 169^V-70^V, 173^{r-v}.

the public professors, too, was virtually identical to that demanded of Wolsey's public readers, and so were their duties to their pupils. None the less some differences are worthy of note. Apart from the dissimilar composition of the college, there were shifts in the provision for the domestic lectures which seem to indicate a new notion of curriculum—though this is impossible to prove since no text is mentioned: 'sophistry' is dropped and instead there are two lecturers in dialectic. Little can be said about a change from 'humanity' to 'rhetoric', but there were now to be two readers in philosophy, and the reader in natural philosophy was made specifically responsible for the teaching of mathematics. Indeed, along with the public chair in Hebrew, a specific chapter on mathematics is the most conspicuous addition to Wolsey's conception: one of the ablest and most apt of those in the second order of canons was to be chosen by the dean and censors of arts to teach the *discipuli* and all the bachelors daily, or at least on alternate days throughout the year.[1] Arithmetic, geometry, the *De sphaera* or cosmography was to be assigned as his subject, 'so that our scholars may be able to acquire a taste for mathematics'.[2]

The first surviving accounts to reveal the composition of the newly founded college in practice are weekly summaries of battels and commons which begin on 14 January 1547.[3] These show a full complement of over one hundred men on the foundation, and an internal organization different from either Cardinal College or the scheme in the draft statutes. At the head was the dean, followed by a sub-dean and seven canons, but in place of the forty canons of the second order and twenty *discipuli*, there followed then five ranks of names, totalling exactly one hundred. Comparison with a treasurers' account which survives for the three quarters of the year ending with Michaelmas term, 1547,[4] enables us to identify these ranks or categories as students or canons of the superior class (*studentes sive canonicos superioris classis*), students or canons of the inferior class, 'bachelor students (*bacularibus studentes*)', logicians (*logicionariis*

---

[1] Ibid. fo 166ᵛ, 'De lectionibus mathematicis'. The relation of this provision to that for the five domestic lecturers above is not entirely clear. In the clause providing that one should lecture in 'philosophia naturalis seu mathematica' the second provision is struck out in the MS (fo 163).

[2] 'Ut matheseorum gustum aliquem scholastici nostri capere possint'; ibid. fo 166ᵛ. It should be remembered that as it was then understood, 'mathematics' included astronomy and astrology.

[3] CCA MS x (1) c. 1, the so-called 'Buttery Books'; the next surviving is for 1553–6 (MS x (1) c. 3). Daily battels begin 1575; quarterly accounts in 1695.

[4] CCA MS iii. c. 4, account of Alexander Belsyer, Thomas Daye, John Marten, and Richard Master, clerks, treasurers; fos 28–33 contain a list of payments to named members of the college for stipends, wages, and exhibitions covering three quarters of the year ending at Michaelmas 1547, for 179 men in all.

studentes) and grammarians (*grammaticis studentes*). In addition on the cathedral side there were vicars and clerks serving in choir, sacristans, eight choristers, seventeen other officers and ministers, and twenty-four almsmen. The three public readers were Smith, Harding, and Etheridge (in theology, Hebrew, and Greek respectively),[1] and the following offices were also named: sub-dean, three treasurers, a censor in theology, two censors in philosophy, two lectors in logic, and a cantor.[2]

Another highly stratified organization was set out in full with some retrospective adjustment in the first folios of a register recording elections and periodic lists of members receiving payment from the date of foundation to 1619. The first entry shows members elected from 1547 to 1550[3] with their age and county of origin. After eight canons and the three public readers, there are twenty *theologi*, elected between 1547 and 1549, twenty *philosophi primi vicenarii*, all elected in 1547 except two in 1546 and one in 1548, twenty *philosophi secundi vicenarii* whose elections dates range from 1547 to 1550, and the names of thirty undergraduates admitted in the same years. Clearly the initial organization had been clarified and consolidated. The *theologi* were all MAs in the theology faculty, and the canons were all graduates in theology. The philosophers were divided into two years, the top year composed of twenty MAs or senior bachelors, the lower year of BAs or men in the year of their determination; in the former rank, there were seven MAs and thirteen bachelors, in the latter, ten bachelors and ten undergraduates in their final year. A list of all those receiving stipends on 1 October 1550 confirms this organization and denotes the undergraduate members as *discipuli*.[4] By 1552 we find an establishment consisting of a dean, eight canons, three public readers (Martyr, Bruerne, and Lawrence), seventeen *theologi*, nineteen *philosophi primi vicenarii*, sixteen *philosophi secundi vicenarii*, and forty-two *discipuli* now also divided into two years, eighteen in the higher, twenty-four in the lower. The list of officers for that year includes a sub-dean, three treasurers, two 'censors or lectors' in natural and moral philosophy, two readers in dialectic, one in rhetoric and one in

---

[1] See below, pp. 352-7.

[2] A Disbursement Book surviving for 1548 (CCA MS xii. b. i. fo 6[v]) confirms the censors in arts and readers in logic, but makes no mention of the censor in theology; no further Disbursement Book survives until 1577-8 (CCA MS xii. b. 20), by which time the establishment was much more complicated.

[3] CCA MS D & C i. b. i. fos 1-3. The notarial date is 12 March 1549/50; some elections are dated '1550'.

[4] Ibid. fos 3[v]-4. This inscription appears to be in a different but contemporary hand.

mathematics.[1] The constitution of Edwardian Christ Church was now complete.[2]

That constitution was almost certainly the work of Richard Cox, dean of the cathedral, almoner to the king and commissioner for the survey of Oxford college lands.[3] The alteration from the Henrician modification of Wolsey's statutes to the form we have just described took place after 1547 and not later than 1550, when the first elections register was prepared. In the same collection of collegiate statutes which contained the Henrician draft for Christ Church there is a second set signed by the Edwardian visitors, dating therefore from about 1549.[4] This too seems to have lacked official confirmation, and the quest for statutes at Christ Church went on throughout the sixteenth century.[5] The most puzzling feature of the Edwardian statutes is the disappearance of all chapters dealing with the number, qualifications, teaching, and election of the three collegiate regius professors or public readers; they also have new chapters on a number of practical matters not dealt with in the Henrician draft. Nevertheless, the three public readers in theology, Greek, and Hebrew were included in the opening account of the constitution of the college, an account that otherwise follows the evidence in the register just described with remarkable fidelity. There can be little doubt that the statutes signed by the Edwardian visitors were the effective constitution of Cox's cathedral and college. There were to be a dean, eight canons, twenty *theologi*, forty *philosophi*, and forty *discipuli*, in addition to the public readers, and the provision for ministers in the church and for servants to the college is also close to that actually recorded in the Edwardian accounts.[6] The three censors in the Edwardian statutes were to supervise studies in dialectic, philosophy and, in place of humanity, mathematics.[7] The eight canons were to be of English birth, masters of arts or theologians, and elected from among the *theologi* of the Church. The *theologi* were masters of arts, eligible in every way for the priesthood, and to be elected from the *philosophi* by the dean

[1] Ibid. fo 7[v].

[2] The first *lector graecus* in the surviving accounts appears in 1569; ibid. fo 41.

[3] *L & P Henry VIII* xxi. pt 1, 148 (77); cf. the commission for Cambridge, ibid. 68; I owe this reference to Dr J. E. A. Dawson.

[4] CCA MS D.P. vi. b. i. fos 115-56[v], signed by Dudley as earl of Warwick, Henry Holbeach as bishop of Lincoln, Richard Cox, and Simon Heynes, dean of Exeter.

[5] In his preamble, the king recited that of the Henrician statutes and then, by his commissaries, did 'publish, decree and promulgate' what follows. In the same archives, in CCA MS D & C i. b. 2, two letters were copied, one of 1556 from Stephen Gardiner, the second from Leicester of 1581, both adverting to statutes yet to come from their respective queens, 'indented according to the foundacyon'; pp. 289, 288.

[6] CCA MS D.P. vi. b. i. fos 115[v]-16.

[7] Ibid. fo 117.

and a majority of canons. The *philosophi* in turn were to be elected from the best of the *discipuli* between the ages of eighteen and twenty-four years.[1]

Allowing for the alterations in the various ranks of fellows, this pattern of election to each rank from the best of the rank below followed the procedure in the Henrician statutes. The undergraduate membership, however, was doubled and the recruitment greatly widened. In the Henrician draft there were to be twenty such boys from whom the canons of the second order were to be chosen.[2] They were to be elected from the best of those in the grammar school of the foundation between the ages of fifteen and twenty-five years, with preference given to those born in places whence the revenues of the foundation were chiefly drawn. However, if there were no suitable candidates, then others were to be chosen from 'our other schools'. In the Edwardian version, the upper age of eligibility was reduced to twenty years, and the number of boys was increased to forty.[3] A provision that they were to be the sons of poor men was added, and they were to be elected (with like reference to the revenues of the foundation) from 'our schools' of Canterbury, Chester, Westminster, Rochester, and Winchester.[4] The election of all ranks was to be made twice a year within eight days of Michaelmas and of Easter.[5]

Among the domestic lecturers, the Henrician reader in rhetoric was dropped, and an independent place was accorded to the reader in mathematics, a provision which seems to have been to some extent foreshadowed in the chapter *De lectionibus mathematicis* in the earlier version.[6] The chapter on studies and the hearing of lectures omitted the Henrician provision that undergraduates and BAs, prior to admission, were to attend the daily public lectures in Greek. In the regulations for disputations and exercises, undergraduates hearing mathematical lectures were to join those in dialectic for the daily two-hour disputations (9 a.m.–11 a.m., or 3 p.m.–5 p.m.).[7] The provisions concerning examination also show increased

---

[1] CCA MS D.P. vi. b. i. fo 120^{r-v}.

[2] Ibid. fo 162^V.

[3] The register of the college at foundation, CCA D & C i. b. i. (above, p. 36), which ascribes ages to all listed, shows that the average age of the *theologi* was 29, with a range of 43–20 and a median age of 28. The *philosophi primi vicenarii* averaged 22.5 years, with a range from 40 to 18, and a median age of 20; the *philosophi secundi vicenarii* averaged 18 years, and the 10 last in precedence in the total catalogue of 90, averaged 16.6 years, the youngest of them being 13 years old.

[4] CCA MS D.P. vi, b. i. fos 120^V–21: if the best there come from places where the Church has income.

[5] Ibid. fo 121.

[6] Above, p. 35 n. 1.

[7] CCA MS D.P. vi. b. i. fo 122^V.

sophistication. An important innovation in the Henrician statutes was the chapter on examinations, by which the public readers were to examine their hearers privately on each of their lectures.[1] In the Edwardian version only the public reader of Hebrew was left with this task; the auditors of the other public readers were to be examined by the domestic readers in the same subjects. In both sets of statutes, on every day when a lecture was held, the hearers were to be examined for an hour (or at least half an hour) as designated by the dean.[2] Of the other new clauses, the most important for the present theme is the introduction of the scrutiny, not mentioned in the Henrician statutes or those of Cardinal College, but now adapted from the statutes of Corpus Christi College.[3] Like the earlier draft statutes, the Edwardian code includes provision on the usual terms for up to twenty sons of men of prominence or nobles, no canon to be tutor to more than two, no *theologus* to more than one. As in Wolsey's statutes, all restrictions were to be waived for kings of England and their eldest sons, who were always to be received with the highest honours.[4] Nothing further was said about commoners.

A vivid impression of the functioning of the system comes from an entry in the register for 5 October 1550 recording that the sub-dean, with the consent of the dean, had convened the two censors in arts to examine the juniors, 'according to the statute of the same house' which decreed that at the end of his second year each junior member was to be examined for his proficiency in studies and morals.[5] Only one *bene profecit* was awarded among the twelve young scholars whose names then follow, and that went to Herbert Westfaling, the future bishop of Hereford.[6] This examination co-incided with the annual election of new members, held in 1550 on 7 October. Those elections are recorded again in 1551, 1552, 1553 (September), in December 1554, and in 1555.[7] No other examination of juniors is recorded, but it is to be presumed from the steady promotion through the ranks that they continued, since many names disappear from the records, and promotion was quite evidently not automatic.[8] Beyond making clear the responsibility of the sub-dean and the censors for the scholastic progress of the juniors, the Edwardian statutes say nothing about such an examination pro-cedure, which may have been required by some decree of the chapter

---

[1] Ibid. fo. 166^V.   [2] Ibid. fos 124, 166^V-7.   [3] Ibid. fo 130^V; see chapter 10.
[4] *SCO* ii. pt 11, 140; MS D. P. vi. b. i. fos 146^V, 189^V.
[5] CCA MS D & C i. b. i. fo 17^V.
[6] He was admitted in 1547 at the age of 15; ibid. fo 2.
[7] Ibid. fos 18–22; the next recorded (fo 23) is for 1561.
[8] Lists of membership continue to record stipends, for 1 Oct. 1550, 1551, 1552, 1561, 1563 (Dec.), 1564, and 1566; ibid. fos 3^V-7^V, 23^V-4^V, 25^V-6^V, 27^V-8^V, 30^V-1.

that does not survive. The statutes did provide, in a clause taken over from the Henrician statutes, that all *discipuli* wishing to remain in the Church must be examined by the dean and censors after two years, and removed if they show no aptitude for their studies.[1] Those judged diligent and apt, however, were to be allowed to remain for up to five years, unless in the meantime by their merit they were promoted to the number of the *philosophi*; the examination procedure may be implicit in this last clause.

Another entry in the same register as that recording the examinations and elections shows that in 1550 pupils were assigned to tutors in a systematic way, with the tutors being selected from the canons, *theologi*, and senior *philosophi*.[2] Among the canons, only Tresham, who was senior, Peter Martyr, who was second, and Etheridge, the public reader in Greek, took no pupils. This list completes the evidence for a highly organized and individual teaching system at the college in the very first years of its foundation.

This vigour must have been due above all to the zeal of the new dean, now also chancellor of the university, Richard Cox. He seems to have used his authority and the resources of Christ Church to organize the teaching of the university around the college in a way which probably reflected Wolsey's original vision. According to Wood, many public disputations were moved to the hall of Christ Church.[3] This is apparently confirmed in part by John ab Ulmis, a Swiss student of medicine, in a letter of 5 November 1550[4] in which he describes disputations for the MAs on Mondays and Wednesdays, for the higher faculties on Thursdays, and for bachelors on Fridays and Saturdays. These were presided over by the appropriate professor at Christ Church: Peter Martyr for the theologians, Thomas Francis in medicine, and Weston in civil law. According to John ab Ulmis, 'all these disputations take place in public, and may be heard and attended by anyone'.[5] Scholastic activity was certainly intense even for a commoner. Conrad ab Ulmis, living at Broadgates Hall, an annexe for commoners at Christ Church, left a similar account in a letter written a few months later.[6]

He wrote:

[1] CCA MS D.P. vi. b. i. fo 131^V-2.

[2] 'Nomina tutorum et pupillorum quibus tutores prospicere oportet ut recte instituantur et bonis moribus educantur ad Dei gloriam et ad huius ecclesiae commodum Anno domini 1550'; CCA MS D & C i. b. i. fo 60^V ff.

[3] Wood, *History and Antiquities*, ii. 113.

[4] *Original Letters*, 419, to Rodolph Gualter.

[5] It is not clear, however, that these disputations necessarily displaced those in the schools; his further account of teaching in other colleges suggests that his knowledge of the university at large was not very accurate.

[6] 1 March 1552; *Original Letters* 460, to John Wolfius.

I devote the hour from six to seven in the morning to Aristotle's Politics, from which I seem to receive a twofold advantage, both a knowledge of Greek and an acquaintance with moral philosophy. The seventh hour I employ upon the first book of the Digests or Pandects of the Roman law, and the eighth in the reconsideration of this lecture. At nine I attend the lecture of that most eminent and learned divine, Peter Martyr. The tenth hour I devote to the rules of Dialectics of Philip Melanchthon, *de locis argumentorum*. Immediately after dinner [at 11 a.m.] I read Cicero's Offices, a truly golden book, from which I derive no less than a twofold enjoyment, both from the purity of the language and the knowledge of philosophy. From one to three I exercise my pen, chiefly in writing letters, wherein as far as possible, I imitate Cicero, who is considered to have abundantly supplied us with all instructions relating to purity of style. At three I learn the Institutes of civil law, which I so read aloud as to commit them to memory. At four are read privately, in a certain hall in which we live, the rules of law, which I hear, and learn by rote as I do the Institutes. After supper the time is spent in various discourse; for either sitting in our chamber, or walking up and down some part of the college, we exercise ourselves in dialectical questions.

Even if we accept that the youthful writer spared no pains to give his Swiss preceptor a favourable impression of his devotion to study, this suggests a busy schedule for a commoner. Not surprisingly, his studies, which seem to have blended law and theology with the common diet of humanistic rhetoric of the day, diverge widely from the pattern laid down in the Edwardian statutes for members on the foundation. By these, every member of the Church was bound to attend the public lectures, according to their degree and order. The domestic lectures in mathematics, dialectic, natural and moral philosophy were given at 6 a.m., and the readers were bound before beginning to examine their hearers on the preceding day's lectures. After some initial instruction in sophistry, it can be presumed,[1] the dean chose those thought capable of benefiting to attend the mathematical and dialectic lectures; in due course, they would be promoted to the lectures in philosophy. Disputations for the logicians and mathematicians were held daily for two hours, either from 9 a.m. to 11 a.m., or in the afternoon from 3 to 5. These were supervised by one of the readers in dialectic, and by a censor. The remaining regulations discussed the work of the graduates and theologians.[2] Since in all other matters the surviving records of Edwardian Christ Church seem to confirm the provisions of the Edwardian statutes, we may assume that this teaching too was put into operation and enforced.

Cox's Christ Church was the culmination of the evolution in

[1] See below, p. 169
[2] CCA MS D.P. vi. b. i. fos 122^V–3^V.

undergraduate collegiate instruction which had begun at New College. Although the details of its story are obscure, it is clear that there was a rapid development in the design of the college from the time the Henrician statutes were drafted to the moment, in January 1547, when the new foundation actually began to function. This was the final result at Oxford of a sudden change in royal policy between the time the chantries act received the royal assent on 23 December 1545,[1] and the end of January 1546, when the king apparently decided not only to leave the endowments of the universities alone, but to found a new college at each which would support the new learning and enlarge royal control over Oxford and Cambridge at the same time. At Oxford it also solved the difficulties remaining after the fall of Wolsey and the suspension of his revolutionary aim virtually to reorganize the university around his new foundation. The king was generous. Wolsey's college had been granted the right to hold lands in mortmain to the clear annual value of £2,000.[2] The new foundation was to have a yearly income of £2,200, and Trinity College, Cambridge, £1,640.[3] Although the plans for Cardinal College underlay it, the royal foundation of Christ Church developed Wolsey's grand design and the tentative Henrician modification to take in the full resources of the reformed and humanistic curriculum, a new emphasis on mathematics as an undergraduate subject, and an altogether more sophisticated system of instruction. Numbers were increased to restore the scale of Wolsey's creation, and a completely new system of classes adopted, in which both the BAs and the undergraduates were divided into years of roughly equal numbers, with rigorous annual examination, promotion, and elimination, in accord with the most recent humanistic practice.

Trinity and St John's Colleges

The last important Tudor foundations at Oxford were both established in the reign of Mary by catholic laymen: Trinity College by Sir Thomas Pope in 1555, and St John's College by Sir Thomas

[1] The universities and their colleges were specifically included; C. E. Mallet, *A History of the University of Oxford* (3 vols, 1924–7) ii. 79; *Victoria History of the Counties of England, Cambridge and the Isle of Ely*, ed. J. P. C. Roach, ii (1959), 462. Cf. Dawson, 'The foundation of Christ Church', pp. 209–11.

[2] Maxwell Lyte, *History of the University of Oxford*, 442.

[3] Dawson, p. 211. Henry's generosity was of lands surrendered by Westminster and other cathedral foundations when they were released from the obligation to maintain readers and pupils at Oxford and Cambridge; much of this property was used to endow Christ Church and Trinity College, Cambridge. C. S. Knighton, 'Economics and economies of a royal peculiar: Westminster Abbey 1540-1640', in R. O'Day and F. Heal (eds), *Princes and Paupers in the English Church 1500-1800* (Leicester 1981), 45–64.

White in 1557.[1] In their statutes provision was made for the first time for numbers of undergraduate commoners as well as scholars to form an integral part of the collegiate society.

Sir Thomas Pope, who was the elder son of a yeoman farmer of Deddington in north Oxfordshire,[2] attended school at Banbury and subsequently at Eton College, was articled to Richard Croke, comptroller of the hanaper, and from that start made his way to a lucrative career through the chancery. He was a friend of Sir Thomas More, whom he visited in the tower shortly before his execution, and he lived as a clerk in the house of More's successor as chancellor, Sir Thomas Audley, who became his patron.[3] He was made clerk of briefs in star chamber in 1532, and by 1536 was sufficiently prominent to be appointed first treasurer of the new court of augmentations. As one of Audley's executors, he was involved in completing his Cambridge foundation of Magdalene College, which occupied the site of Buckingham College, the dissolved Benedictine house.

On 20 February 1555 Pope acquired the buildings and part of the site of Durham College, Oxford, the house of studies of Benedictines of Durham Priory, for his own memorial and benefaction.[4]

Pope's college, dedicated to the holy Trinity, had an establishment of twelve fellows and twelve scholars.[5] The founder wished them to serve the glory and honour of God, the public benefit of the country, and the growth of orthodox faith and the Christian religion. All

[1] The best account of Trinity is that by H. E. D. Blakiston, *Trinity College* (1898); he also wrote the chapter on Trinity in *VCH Oxon.* iii. 238–51. For St John's and its predecessor, St Bernard's College, see W. H. Stevenson and H. E. Salter, *The Early History of St John's College Oxford* (OHS new ser i 1939). Statutes of Trinity are printed in *SCO* iv; for those of St John's see *SCO* iii. pt 12, and Stevenson and Salter ch. 11 and app. 26. For the Elizabethan foundation of Jesus College, see pp. 2, 64.

[2] His mother came from Witney and his Oxfordshire origins were reflected in the constitution of the college; *SCO* iv (Trinity), 18.

[3] *DNB*; Blakiston, *Trinity College*, ch. 2.

[4] At the dissolution, Durham College and its endowment was granted to the new dean and chapter of Durham, but the college was again surrendered to the crown in 1546. In December of that year half of its garden and grove was included in the grant of St Bernard's College to the dean and chapter of Christ Church, from whom Sir Thomas White acquired that property for his own foundation of St John's College on 11 December 1554; see *VCH Oxon.* iii. 238; Stevenson and Salter, 113. Pope made his purchase from Dr George Owen of Godstow and William Martyn of Oxford, to whom the site and derelict buildings of Durham College had been granted by the crown on 3 February 1553. For the Cistercian foundation of St Bernard's College, see the first part of Stevenson and Salter, 3–110.

[5] The letters patent of 8 March 1555 authorized a college consisting of a president, twelve fellows and eight scholars, with a 'Jhesus scolehouse' at Hook Norton, Oxon. or thereabouts; the college was established by charter of erection dated 28 March 1555. The original members were admitted on 30 May 1556; the statutes are dated 1 May 1556. Four additional scholars were added in September 1557, after Pope decided there were enough grammar schools in the towns near Hook Norton and Deddington, and abandoned his 'Jhesus scolehouse'; *VCH Oxon.* iii. 243; Blakiston, 52–4.

fellows were to study philosophy and theology, at least four of them being priests, and all masters of arts in the college were obliged to be ordained as priests before the end of their fourth year after taking that degree; indeed, Pope's foundation would provide for them until they completed their doctorates in theology.[1] Despite this traditional and designedly clerical objective, the statutes of Trinity provided its undergraduates, only some of whom intended a clerical career, with studies that characteristically blended humanistic learning with the older scholastic disciplines in logic and disputation. The provision of college lecturers was predictably much simpler than that at Christ Church—a logic lecturer divided all the teaching duties with a lecturer in humanity[2]—but the statutes nevertheless shared the intention of that splendid royal foundation to provide a complete and comprehensive programme of instruction within the walls of the college.[3] They repeat the conventional insistence that university exercises be attended and university requirements be fulfilled, but they also envisage a degeneration of the ordinary lectures of the regent masters to the point of virtual uselessness.[4] The scholars on the foundation and the commoners were to be taught together, studying authors as traditional as Porphyry and as humanistic as Plato, Quintilian, Titus Livius, and Rudolph Agricola; the study of Greek was clearly regarded as desirable but improbable.[5]

Commoners and battelers[6] might be added to the foundation up to the number of twenty, according to the statutes, and they were to form an ordinary part of the establishment at Trinity alongside the scholars, at table as well as in the classroom; this was the final stage in the recent evolution of the undergraduate college. For the first time as well, the social distinctions were made explicit. At the high table with the president sat the vice-president, two doctors or

[1] SCO iv (Trinity College), 7, 26, 46–7. Scholars were to take the BA after completing an extra assignment in Latin authors; fellows were to have taken the BA, apparently, cf. ch. 16 'De tempore assumendi gradus', ibid. 46. But the chapters on elections are silent on academic qualifications for a fellowship.

[2] SCO iv (Trinity College), 17 (no part numbers in vol. iv); the computi bursariorum (vol. i. 1556–1600) in the college archives (uncatalogued) show their respective payments of 40s and 26s 8d continuing through the century; no hiring of additional lecturers is recorded.

[3] Ibid., chs 14–16, pp. 40–8; cf. the account of Blakiston, 60–4. The total value of Pope's endowment was only £226 11s 8d: Blakiston, 55.

[4] SCO iv (Trinity College), 46.

[5] Ibid. 44.

[6] Ibid. 29. 'Battelers' were usually associated with commoners but as having inferior rank; some menial service seems to have been part of their lot in return for 'commons'; for the 'battels' over and above that they would pay. Their precise status is as unclear as is the origin of the term 'battel' in its distinctively Oxford use. One can only repeat the verdict of the Oxford English Dictionary that, 'the etymology . . . has been the subject of abundant conjecture'. Cf C. L. Shadwell, Registrum Orielense (2 vols, 1893–1902) i. pp. vii–viii.

bachelors of theology, and commoners who were the sons of lords or knights ('fellow-commoners'). At the first table on the east side of the hall sat the rest of the fellows with fellow-commoners of inferior birth; below them sat the scholars, some of whom acted as waiters.[1] Commoners must have played a considerable part in the life of the college. There were already seventeen of them in 1565, and between ten and twenty-five were admitted annually, staying from one to three years, so that the statutory limit must often have been exceeded. Each commoner was connected with a fellow who acted as his tutor, and who gave a bond of £10 to the college for each pupil's commons and room rent. In 1579 it was decreed that commoners and battelers should pay 40s and 30s each by way of caution money, and a register of these payments is the only record of such admissions until the regular registers begin in 1648.[2] They were undoubtedly of more gentle birth than the members on the foundation, and their conspicuous presence in Trinity College introduces a new dimension in the history of the secular collegiate foundation, as it foreshadows the social stratification of early Jacobean Oxford.[3] At St John's College their role in the economy of the foundation was even more important than it was at Trinity.

Sir Thomas White was a rich merchant and former lord mayor of London, whose college was named after St John the Baptist, the patron of his company, the Merchant Taylors. His was the most conspicuous of all the many benefactions to higher education made by the mercantile community, and his loyalty to the towns important in his career left an indelible mark on his creation.[4] After extensive work on the former conventual buildings of St Bernard's College, the foundation was celebrated on the patronal feast, 24 June 1557. It seems that the original statutes (now lost) were taken almost verbatim from those of Corpus Christi College, so that the members of St John's College were directed to the study of theology and the arts.[5] For the next several years Sir Thomas effectively directed the college by personal rule, and produced two further codes of statutes, in 1562 and again in 1566. He died on 12 February 1567.[6]

[1] SCO iv (Trinity College), 28–9; Blakiston, 62–4. See also James McConica, 'Scholars and commoners in renaissance Oxford', in Lawrence Stone (ed.), The University in Society (2 vols, Princeton 1975), i. 156, 160–2. [2] Blakiston, 83–4.

[3] More than 60 per cent of the commoners were sons of gentlemen and above, compared to some 25 per cent among the scholars and fellows; McConica, 'Scholars and commoners', 161. See also below, pp. 47–8.

[4] Stevenson and Salter, Early History of St John's, 116–17.

[5] On the complex history of the statutes of St John's and the potentially generous but muddled endowment, see Stevenson and Salter, chs 1: 'The Foundation of the College', and 3: '1567–1572'.

[6] Stevenson and Salter, Early History of St John's, 121–9, and 144 ff. In app. 26 the

White ordained a college of fifty fellows who, unlike those at Corpus, upon whose statutes his own continued to be modelled, were of one class. There was therefore no distinction between fellows and *discipuli*; instead, the newly elected were expected to undergo a two-year probationary period, extended in 1566 to three years. In the final version all these fellowships were reserved, six for founder's kin, and the rest for scholars to be elected from towns with which White had had important connections: one from Tonbridge school, two each from Reading (his native town), Coventry, and Bristol, and the rest, thirty-seven, from Merchant Taylors School.[1] The college elected none of these except the founder's kin. Scholars from the towns were ordinarily chosen by the mayor and his council. At Merchant Taylors, the president and two fellows of the college were to be present each year on St Barnabas's day when the election was held, but the actual choice was in the hands of the president of the company, aided by examiners appointed by himself. All candidates were to be over thirteen and under twenty years of age.[2] In chapter 16 of the statutes, which was original to him, White stated that he aimed at 'the increase of the orthodox faith and of the Christian profession in so far as it is weakened by the damage of time and the malice of men' and to help theology, 'much afflicted of late as we see with sorrow and grief'.[3] All fellows were to be ordained to the priesthood within three years of completing their necessary regency,[4] including the twelve who were permitted to study civil and canon law.[5] The college officers were the same as at Corpus, with the difference that the lecturerships were domestic, not public, and were in the disciplines of rhetoric, Greek, and dialectic; they were elected annually. Otherwise the teaching arrangements exactly correspond to those at Fox's foundation.[6]

For a quarter of a century St John's was unable to complete the founder's design owing to poverty, having an incomplete endowment that at the time of White's death was about £230 a year in place of the £500 or so which was needed; in the five and a half years following

---

text printed in *SCO* iii is corrected clause by clause. These emendations are assumed in the following references to the printed text.

[1] See McConica, 'Scholars and commoners', 164–8.
[2] Stevenson and Salter, 147; *SCO* iii. pt 9, 116.
[3] Stevenson and Salter, 146.
[4] As opposed to one at Corpus; *SCO* iii. pt 9, 61.
[5] Another departure from Fox's scheme, and a return to New College practice; ibid. 36–9; one might study medicine, who was excused from orders.
[6] Ibid. 49 ff. The lecturers in Greek and rhetoric are actually ordered to read 'publice'; the few variations from the Corpus statute c. 21 are noted in Stevenson and Salter, 452–3. For the succession of lecturers from 1557, ibid. 321.

the death of the founder, only four new members were admitted.[1] In these circumstances the commoners seem to have been indispensable. White's statutes provided for up to sixteen *convictores*; at the end of his life he had wished the number reduced to twelve.[2] Nevertheless, in the earliest surviving bursars' accounts we find that in 1569 they numbered 53; at Lady Day 1571 there were 57. By 1578 the number had fallen to about twenty, and it seems to have remained under thirty for the next ten years.[3] The reason for such numbers of commoners is not far to seek. In 1569 the income from their battels actually exceeded that from rents and quitrents,[4] and although the actual profit from battels does not appear to have been great, commoners contributed to the college income in other ways as well. On 18 March 1568 it was decided that all commoners should henceforth pay an entrance fee according to rank, ranging from 20s for the heir of an earl, to 6s 8d for the heir of a gentleman, and a minimum of 5s for all others.[5] Their tutors received stipends which were settled by private arrangement, and which were of undoubted importance in augmenting their meagre college allowances. Moreover, on 28 November 1578 the college officers agreed that every commoner should pay 12d quarterly to the servants of the house, 7d to the manciple, 5d to the cook, and 4d to the butler.[6] In 1582 they were ordered to pay 40s caution money to the bursar. Finally, on 23 November 1580 the college instituted a lecture in moral and natural philosophy which was to be paid for by 'the rente which the commoners doe paie for their chambers'.[7] Since they were not part of the foundation, the commoners were not part of the legal corporation of the college, and here as elsewhere the records of their presence tend therefore to be casual: an entry concerning benefactions in the college register, a surviving list of cautions. But the practical absorption of the commoners into the life of the college is clear once more from the dining arrangements: the son of a peer could expect to sit at the president's table, and others at the high table, masters' table, or bachelors' table, according to their wealth and rank.[8]

These arrangements for commoners at Trinity and St John's

[1] Stevenson and Salter, 129–30, 141, 151, 163, 170 f.
[2] *SCO* iii. pt 9, 75–6, 80; Stevenson and Salter, 421–2.
[3] Stevenson and Salter, 169–70, 303–4, 308.   [4] Ibid. 168.
[5] Ibid. 163, who note that no such payment is recorded after Michaelmas 1570. In the light of usual collegiate practice with such accidental sources of income, one may perhaps differ with their conclusion that 'probably' the fee was repealed; cf G. E. Aylmer, below, pp. 527–8.
[6] St John's College Archives Register 1557–91, fo 169[V]; not noted in Stevenson and Salter.
[7] Ibid. fos 212[V], 189[V].
[8] Ibid. 273, 303. See also ch. 10.

Colleges no doubt reflect the practical experience of the earlier foundations in the 1540s and early 1550s, and especially the organization of life at Christ Church (although no record survives to show the emergence of commoners at Christ Church with any exactitude).[1] The experience of Brasenose suggests some parallels.[2] The question of numbers is pursued in another part of this volume,[3] but from the point of view of statute and theory, the development of the secular college into a mingled lay and clerical society, where the supervision and teaching of undergraduate scholars and commoners occupied an ever-increasing part of the time and energy of the college fellows, was finally achieved with the foundations of Pope and White. At the same time, the undergraduate hall characteristic of the middle ages was supplanted and to a considerable degree swallowed up by these expanding collegiate foundations.[4] There remained only one further stage in the transition from the medieval to the modern undergraduate university, and that was the incorporation of the undergraduate commoner into the university itself.

MATRICULATION AND THE COLLEGIATE UNIVERSITY

The problem of the undergraduate living in the town, beyond the reach of university authority and discipline was very familiar. The medieval university as such kept no comprehensive record of its members. Early statutes required all scholars to be on the rolls of a regent master,[5] and the rolls were read thrice yearly at the beginning of term. None of these rolls has survived. By the fifteenth century, the university had made the principals of the halls responsible for their scholars, but without the obligation to keep a register of them. There was, however, continued indiscipline and frequent disruption of the peace,[6] so that about the year 1410 the university decreed that scholars who were attached to no society—'chamberdeacons' —should reside in a college or hall, under penalty of imprisonment or banishment. Townsmen were forbidden to take them as lodgers

---

[1] The 'Matricula Aedis Christi' or 'Dean's Entry Book' in the college archives is cited confidently by Thompson, *Christ Church*, and others as showing 'Hye Commoners' and 'Second Commoners' in the college from 1553. This collection is an eighteenth century compilation by an unknown hand, and its lists cannot be verified from any surviving earlier record. The archivist, Mr E. G. W. Bill, has told me that it is highly unlikely there should have been any losses or dispersals from the college records during or after the eighteenth century, and that in the seventeenth century, undergraduates are not described by status but according to the amount of fees paid.

[2] Above, p. 12.
[3] See below, pp. 152–6.
[4] See below, pp. 51–5.
[5] *Statuta*, 60–1.
[6] C. I. Hammer, Jr. 'Patterns of homicide in a medieval university town: fourteenth-century Oxford', *Past & Present*, lxxviii (1978), 3–23.

except by permission of the chancellor. This decree was reinforced by a royal ordinance of 1420, declaring that within a month of arrival at the university scholars and their servants were to take an oath to observe the statutes, to be under the government of a principal, and not to lodge with a townsman.[1]

On 11 August 1552 the deputy vice-chancellor, Richard Marshall, apparently acting on his own initiative, revived the ordinance of 1420 and entered it in his register along with the names of scholars in the various colleges and halls, partly to conduct a census, partly to ensure that all of them took the oath to observe the statutes.[2] This is the first list of those in residence. Within a year of Marshall's survey Edward VI had died, to be succeeded by Mary and the catholic restoration in Oxford.[3] After the accession of Elizabeth, the persistent presence in the university of adherents to the old religion undoubtedly lent fresh urgency to the familiar problem of unregistered students, and on 16 July 1562 the bedell of civil law summoned all scholars living with townsmen to report to the vice-chancellor at St Mary's church to state the name of the tutor under whom they had placed themselves.[4] Almost one hundred names were then recorded, but such expedients were casual.

With the new statutes of 1565—the *nova statuta*—came the statute which first instituted, in theory at least, the keeping of a register of matriculation by the university.[5] It was to be divided into heads for each college and hall, with details of the name, age, place of origin, and status of each member, scholar, servant, or other priviledged person. All these, if at least sixteen years of age, were to take an oath in the presence of the chancellor to observe the university's statutes. Heads of houses and halls were to see that all new arrivals were presented for this ceremony within a week of admission. Scholars attached to no college or hall were to be placed under the supervision of some master or tutor who was such a member, and matriculation fees were charged according to social rank varying from 13s 4d for the son of a prince, duke, or marquis to 4d for a commoner—*plebei filius*. This enactment was only casually

---

[1] *The Register of Congregation 1448-1463*, ed. W. A. Pantin and W. T. Mitchell (OHS new ser. xxii 1972), p. xxx; *Statuta*, pp. lxxxii, 208 (1410), 226-7 (1420); Rashdall, *Universities*, i. 216. For the successive statutes about matriculation see *Reg. Univ.* ed. Clark i. 162-9. Cf Elizabeth Russell, 'The influx of commoners into the University of Oxford before 1581: an optical illusion?', *English Historical Review*, xcii (1977), 731 ff.

[2] Reg. Canc. 1545-1661, fo 68 f. printed in *Reg. Univ.* ed. Boase, pp. xxi–xxv. For numbers in this return, see below, p. 153.

[3] See Loach, pp. 375-83.

[4] Reg. Canc. 1545-1661, fos 89ᵛ–90ᵛ; printed in *Reg. Univ.* ed. Clark ii. 5-9.

[5] *Statuta*, 378 f. The matriculation statute is 391-5; in December 1564 and February 1565 committees were established to consider the problem; *Reg. Univ.* ed. Clark i. 163.

administered. The first list, of Christ Church, is dated 1565, but in most cases the listings do not begin until 1572 and for the next ten years remain very imperfect.[1]

The problem continued to be discussed in the following years, and on 14 December 1579 all students living with townsmen were ordered to move into colleges and halls.[2] The next February the oath of supremacy which all were bound to observe, was introduced into the statutes and on 27 June 1580 convocation again decreed that all scholars still living in the town must be brought into a hall or college.[3] This time, however, important provisions were added: in future, permission to supplicate for graces and promotion to any degree was made contingent not only on membership of one of the recognized houses, but also on the entry into the matriculation book of the name of the candidate and his hall or college; this information was now to be entered in addition in the register with every grace. Those proposing the graces were to be members of the candidates' own houses, who presumbly could vouch for them.[4] It was this provision that finally completed the process of assimilation; henceforth all seeking degrees and graces were to be matriculated, and all matriculands were to be members of colleges or halls, with petitions moved in almost every instance by one of the college deans. The protestant, undergraduate, collegiate university was now an accomplished fact. The dominance of the colleges was reflected as much in the government of the Elizabethan university as it was in the university's provision for undergraduate lodging and instruction. The day of the 'chamberdeacon' had come to an end. The few surviving independent halls more closely resembled the colleges in their size and organization (though not in their lack of endowment) than they did their often small and transitory medieval predecessors. The undergraduate living privately in lodgings in town could only qualify for recognition by the university if he did so as a member of and with the permission of one of these recognized bodies. It was also in this way, quite incidentally, that the colleges and halls acquired virtual control over admission to the university, which simply registered the names of those they were willing to sponsor.[5]

In June 1581, one year after the last decree, copies of Edmund

[1] *Reg. Univ.* ed. Clark ii. 9.

[2] Ibid. i. 166; a survey of recusants had been ordered by the privy council in November 1577; cf Russell, 'The influx of commoners', pp. 733-4.

[3] Clark, i. 166; *Statuta*, 416-17, 419. The Act of Supremacy (1559) had provided that the oath be taken by all taking orders or degrees in the universities; 1 Eliz. I c.1 xii.

[4] *Reg. Univ.* ed. Clark i. 166-7.

[5] The matriculation registers, OUA Matriculation Register 1564-1614, SP/1/Register P, and Matriculation Register 1615-47, SP/2/Register PP are described in *Reg. Univ.* ed. Clark i. pp. viii-x.

Campion's *Decem rationes* were left in each man's place at the university Act, a gesture of impudent defiance that further intensified the fear of secret popery. The next autumn a new statute of matriculation tightened the arrangements by combining subscription to the statutes of the university and to the religious settlement.[1] Written in English, it insisted that the matriculand subscribe both to the articles of religion and to the royal supremacy, and that matriculation take place within a week of admission to any hall or college for those aged 16 or more. Moreover, all tutors were to purge themselves of suspicion of popery before 'the nativitye of Christ next insuinge' if they wished to keep their pupils.[2] At the same time there was an energetic search for unregistered undergraduates that brought the total of matriculands that year to over 800.[3] The problem of the unmatriculated commoner, however, continued to haunt the authorities.[4]

THE MEDIEVAL HALLS AND COLLEGES

At the beginning of this chapter the place of the academic hall in the medieval university was emphasized, both as the typical home of the undergraduate, and for its part in the history of intra-mural teaching through the lecture system. By the early years of the sixteenth century, despite the fall in numbers after the fourteenth-century

[1] 14 November 1581: Reg. Cong. 1564–82, fos 340 f. *Statuta*, 421–3; *Reg. Univ.* ed. Clark i. 167–9. For the Subscription Books see ibid. i. vi–vii, now OUA Subscription Register 1581–1615, SP/38/Register Ab.

[2] *Reg. Univ.* ed. Clark i. 167; the vice-chancellor was to enforce the statute against all persons who received students into their houses; ibid. 168.

[3] Mallet, *University of Oxford*, ii. 122.

[4] On 25 January 1583, Leicester as chancellor wrote to convocation protesting that scholars continued to live in the town unmatriculated, with no university tutor to answer for them. After the threat of Spanish invasion in 1588 there were further measures to eradicate the Catholic presence. In January 1589 promotion to BA and MA was made conditional on the candidate's ability to recite the articles of faith and religion by heart and to give an account of them in a scriptural sense. Similar requirements were made of those requesting any grace whatsoever, although these were also liable to interrogation in congregation concerning their purely academic disciplines; *Reg. Univ.* ed Clark i. 169. Shortly after, in a reversal of previous policy, the privy council decided to resort to terror. Four catholics arrested in Oxford—two seminary priests and two laymen—were tried before the vice-chancellor after interrogation in London, condemned to death and executed in Oxford on 5 July 1589. APC xvii. 205, 329; *Unpublished Documents Relating to the English Martyrs*, ed. J. H. Pollen and W. MacMahon (2 vols, Catholic Record Society v 1908, xxi 1919) i. 168–9. On 10 December 1594 Buckhurst as chancellor, 'being advertised by some' of the defects and abuses in religious conformity at Oxford, urged the university to enforce the existing laws so that 'the universitie may be purged from all Jesuits, Seminaries and notorious recusants which have secretly crept in amongest you and may happelie lye still lurking there in corners', and urged that 'no iustly suspected person or knowen papist' should be allowed to have the tuition of young scholars. Reg. Cong. 1582–95, fo 272^{r-v}; I owe this reference to Dr C. M. J. F. Swan.

pestilence and in spite of the chronic vulnerability of these unen-
dowed institutions to the vagaries of time, it would seem that the
number of halls was not dramatically lower than in the time of
John Rous, c 1440–50.[1] The chancellor's register of the day shows
that in 1505 there were some fifty-two in use.[2] The rapid disappearance of the halls seemingly begins after that date; in 1513 the
number had already dwindled to eighteen.[3] In the interval only one
college—Brasenose—had been founded, so appropriation by new
collegiate foundations cannot explain this; perhaps fresh visitations
of the plague and the rise in prices were partly to blame. In 1523 the
university referred anxiously to the effect of high prices on the
halls, and in 1526 Dr John London asserted that there were not
seventy scholars left in them.[4] In 1537, in the last of the lists entered
in the chancellors' registers each September when the principals gave
security, only eight halls were named.[5] Fifteen years later, the first
census of the university showed the numbers attached to the eight
remaining halls as follows: Broadgates, 41; St Mary, 23; St Alban,
38; Magdalen, 35; Hart, 45; White, 20; New Inn, 49; St Edmund,
9. It is clear that while the number of independent halls had greatly
diminished, some of them were now as large as the smaller colleges.[6]
The record of the university's visitation of the halls in 1580/1 following the new disciplinary decrees would tend to confirm this, except
that for five of them—Hart, St Mary, St Alban, Magdalen, and
St Edmund—only the names of those absent are listed, owing perhaps to the suspicion that those who had evaded the visitation were
likely also to be those who were reluctant to take the oath. In the
remaining halls the numbers in 1580/1 were: Broadgates, the principal, 12 'jurors', 31 absent; New Inn, principal, 3 jurors, one absent;
Gloucester (much suspected as a papist stronghold), principal,

[1] T. H. Aston, 'Oxford's medieval alumni', Past & Present, lxxiv (1977), 19–20; idem,
'The date of John Rous's list of the colleges and academical halls of Oxford', Oxoniensia,
xlii (1977), 226–36.

[2] Reg. Canc. 1498–1506, 184–5. I am here following A. B. Emden, 'Oxford academical
halls in the later middle ages', in J. J. G. Alexander and M. T. Gibson (eds), Medieval Learning and Literature: essays presented to Richard William Hunt (Oxford 1976), 357; hereafter cited as Emden, 'Halls'.

[3] Ibid. 357; Reg. Canc. 1506–14, fo 199.

[4] Emden, 'Halls', 358; Epist acad. 1508–96, 145–6, 148–51. In the last of the lists for
1514 only twelve halls were mentioned; ibid. 384.

[5] Emden, 'Halls', 358; Reg. Canc. 1527–43, fo 373. The list is as follows: Magdalen,
St Mary, Hart, Alban, Peckwater's Inn or Vine Hall (same principal), White Hall or Lawrence
Hall (same principal), Broadgates, Edward. Of these the following regularly took lawyers
as principals: Edward, Broadgates, White and Lawrence, Peckwater and Vine Hall. In
January 1538 Ottwell Toppyng, a fellow of Queen's, offered himself as principal of
St Edmund Hall, vacant since 1533; fo 375[V]; cf A. B. Emden, An Oxford Hall in Medieval
Times (Oxford 1927), 239, 280.

[6] On the census of 1552 see below, p. 153.

13 jurors and 16 absent. The count at New Inn Hall confirms the decline in the study of civil law, but the other two halls, with totals of 44 and 30 respectively, were substantial houses.[1]

The story is more complex than a simple supplanting of halls by endowed colleges. In the foundation of Brasenose College we have already traced a continuous evolution from an agglomeration of halls into a college which, in its first years, was actually described as a 'hall'. The late medieval halls, like the colleges, were managed by manciples and were accustomed to provide tutorial supervision, although this may have been more common in the legal halls, where there were graduates available. In September 1551, for example, a former manciple of Hart Hall claimed the sum of 26s from one of the hall's tutors for unpaid commons and battels owed by a pupil, William Jakman. The tutor, Pascoe, was to pay in full for the first five weeks, and to try to persuade Jakman's friends to pay the rest.[2] In 1531 one Thomas Laton, a student, was to pay 3s 4d to the principal of White Hall, a legal inn, as a term's fees for lectures and rooms for himself and his pupil.[3] In 1533 we know there were Christmas plays at Broadgates Hall, because a scholar named John More had to pay the manciple the balance of a sum advanced to buy costumes for the entertainment, which was meant to be covered by a collection among the students.[4] In many respects, therefore, life in an early Tudor hall must have been much like that in a college.

It is also possible to discover evidence of colleges making use of halls to supplement their own accommodation. On 20 July 1548 Mr Mann, the principal of White Hall, complained that one of his scholars, a Thomas Wysse, had been removed from the hall by his tutor Thomas Ponsonby, a fellow of New College, and had been transferred without authority to St Mary's College. It was decided that the boy should be returned, and that the tutor not attempt to transfer him again without a letter from the boy's father to the vice-chancellor.[5] Some 'lost' halls were entirely taken over in this fashion, as Vine Hall was by New College,[6] disappeared from the annual payment of sureties in the vice-chancellor's court, yet nevertheless

[1] OUA NEP/*supra*/45, fos 11–19. The first fascicule of this manuscript, all of which is devoted to materials on halls, came directly to Brian Twyne from the registrar, according to an inscription made at the time of binding in 1913. It is quite likely that the sheets surviving for the visitation represent only a part of the original record. The later visitation articles, discussed below, appear under the name of Hovenden; see p. 54 n. 4.

[2] Reg. Canc. 1545–1661, fo 53^V.   [3] Reg. Canc. 1527–43, fo 179^V.

[4] Ibid. 257^V.

[5] Reg. Canc. 1545–1661 fo 29^V. St Mary's was not formally dissolved and lingered on as a secular hall; R. W. Jeffrey, 'A forgotten college of Oxford', *The Brazen Nose* iv no. 6 (1927), 260–88.

[6] Reg. Canc. 1527–43, fo 26^V.

retained much of their earlier character. Many fellows took up the principalships of halls that were owned by their colleges, since they could do so and still retain their fellowships. The examples are numerous. In addition to Vine Hall, New College took over Trillock's Inn; Merton, St Alban's Hall; Exeter, Great Black Hall and Hart Hall; Balliol, Burnell's Inn, and Oriel, Great Bedell Hall.[1]

The most striking evidence of the adoption of collegiate practices in the surviving independent halls comes from Elizabethan visitation records in the university archives. In 1575 New Inn Hall was so visited, and questions were asked not only about the giving of the law lecture, but about lectures in logic and humanity. Inquiries were also made about discipline: about prayers in hall, the maintenance of an order for attending church, and the locking of gates at night.[2] In 1580/1 and again in 1582/3, further visitations were conducted as part of the university's effort to regulate life outside the colleges, especially with respect to the religious settlement. It was expected that there would be morning prayer, grace at meals, resort to the local parish church every sabbath and feast day in both morning and evening, that all those aged sixteen years and older would receive communion three times a year, all attend the public sermons with their principal, that there would be weekly catechism in hall, and that all those who refused to go to church, or to communicate, would be identified along with their alternative places of worship. Apart from these and like provisions to do with religion, the halls were expected not only to have lectures, disputations, and repetitions in logic, but the rhetorical exercise of declamations as well.[3] There was a further inquiry as to whether any lecture was given in rhetoric or Greek, or ought to be so given 'by the auncient orders of your house'. Predictably, each scholar was to have a tutor, but this article also attempted to ensure that tutors did their work conscientiously, so that the scholars would remain in their rooms usefully occupied, and 'stand not idle at the gates of there houses nor walke the streetes or resorte to tavernes, but studiouslie imploye the tyme to the certaine increase of learninge and vertue'.[4]

---

[1] Emden, 'Halls', 360-1.

[2] OUA NEP/*supra*/45, fo 6.

[3] Ibid. fo 15^{r-v}. For evidence of halls having libraries of their own see T. H. Aston, G. D. Duncan, and T. A. R. Evans, 'The medieval alumni of the University of Cambridge', *Past & Present*, lxxxvi (February 1980), 17 n. 22.

[4] Ibid. fo 16. A further visitation was held in 1582/3 by the new vice-chancellor, Robert Hovenden, warden of All Souls. This was more specifically concerned with discipline and less with studies; ibid. fos 21-30^v. All of these records, with the accompanying injunctions, are additional evidence of the university's apprehension about unattached students in these years. For the relation between these documents see the comments of W. T. Mitchell in the typed transcripts in OUA, the use of which I wish here gratefully to acknowledge.

It can be seen, therefore, that while collegiate life became much more the norm for the Tudor undergraduate than heretofore, some of the medieval halls survived by a process of adaptation. Sometimes they were taken over by the colleges if they were not actually pulled down to make way for them. Sometimes they survived by amalgamation, and it must not be forgotten that the eight still in existence at the end of the century matriculated a large proportion of the undergraduate entry.[1] At the same time, those surviving halls were more complex than their medieval predecessors, and their teaching had responded to the new interests to the extent of providing tutorial supervision, regular exercises in declamation, and perhaps also occasional lectures in Greek and rhetoric. Since, lacking any form of endowment, they left few records of their own, we are dependent chiefly on the university's archives for what we know of them, and it seems unlikely that we shall learn much more.

At the colleges of medieval foundation the growth of organized teaching in the new subjects can be traced in the accounts. At New College a reader in Greek appears first in 1537/8 with the annual stipend of £5. Greek was taught each year along with dialectic by two readers lecturing in hall and in 1542/3 these lecturers were joined by a lecturer in civil law. In 1552/3 a lecturer in philosophy was added. Thereafter the full complement of college lectures embraced dialectic, Greek, civil law, and philosophy; in 1553/4 an additional senior lecturer in civil law was added.[2]

The arrangements at Magdalen College had been more complicated since the time of foundation.[3] The *liber computi* at the turn of the sixteenth century shows payments to the statutory public readers in theology, moral, and natural philosophy. The first was paid £10 annually, the latter two £6 13s 4d each. The grammar master was paid the same salary as the public reader in theology, a measure of the importance attached to his position, and the two college lecturers in logic were paid £5 each. In 1520 an assistant schoolmaster was added at half the salary of his superior. Lectures in Greek appeared first in 1539, when two masters, Michael Drome and John Armstrong, were paid the sum of 46s 8d for *lectura greca*. Like New College, Magdalen thus conformed to the injunctions of the Cromwellian

---

[1] Of 139 matriculants recorded in 1590, 66 or 48 per cent matriculated from the halls, including three of Dr Case's pupils. In 1595, with an identical entry (139) it was 24 per cent. For figures based on decennial averages see Lawrence Stone, 'The size and composition of the Oxford student body 1580–1909', in *University in Society*, i. 34.

[2] New College Archives bursars' rolls, 7490, 7493, 7495, 7496, 7498, 7500, 7501, 7503, 7506, 7508, 7518, 7520, 7522, 7523, 7525, 7526, 7528, 7529, 7530, 7533, 7540, 7548, 7557.

[3] See above, p. 4 f.

visitation in 1535.[1] Drome, who had come to Canterbury College from Cambridge, was one of those suspected of Lutheran sympathies at the time of the Garrett affair, and had been admitted a fellow of Magdalen in 1531 (BA 1527, MA 1531, BTh 1540). Armstrong, who had been admitted a fellow in 1534 (BA 1533, MA 1538) carried on as sole lecturer the following year at the stipend of 40s, and was apparently reading medicine at the same time.[2] In 1565 there was a further expansion at Magdalen. A lecture in Greek grammar was introduced in the fourth term for which the existing Greek lecturer, Nicholas Balguay, was paid an additional 10s above his regular 40s stipend. It seems likely that this teaching was done at the grammar school, because in subsequent accounts the stipend is raised to 40s for 'Greek in school'. Balguay, who was elected a demy in 1559 (BA 1560, MA 1564) was allowed a special grant of 41s in 1566 to buy books for his library, and the next year resigned his fellowship to become the schoolmaster at the grammar school, a post he held until 1583.[3]

The year 1565 saw the institution of two additional lectureships at Magdalen. The first was in Hebrew, for which Thomas Kingsmill was paid 15s in the final term of 1564/5. Kingsmill was a strong protestant who had been elected demy in 1558 (BA 1559, MA 1564). From 1563 to 1565 he had held the readership in natural philosophy, and in 1564 was admitted to the study of civil law. He held the Hebrew lectureship until 1569 when he resigned to take up the regius chair.[4] The second new post was in rhetoric, and the first holder another strong protestant, a former chorister named Thomas Turner, who had been elected demy in 1555 (BA 1560, MA 1565).[5] From this time forward these various lectureships continued to provide Magdalen College with a range of teaching unequalled in Oxford outside of Christ Church, a provision that in this last phase must be seen as part of the achievement of Laurence Humfrey, newly elected president in 1561.

Thus far we have dealt with the two medieval foundations where undergraduates had always played a large part in the collegiate life. Among the others, financial need was probably a more powerful inducement to open their doors to junior members than was the

[1] See Duncan below, p. 342. For what follows, Magdalen College Archives *Libri computi* for 1490–1510, 1510–30, 1530–42, 1543–59, 1559–80, 1586–1605.

[2] On Drome or Drumme and Armstrong see Macray, *Reg. Magdalen*, ii. 17, 19, 55, 66, and 74 respectively. The records at New College unfortunately only rarely name the fellow receiving the stipend.

[3] Macray, *Reg. Magdalen*, ii. 149–50; Foster, *Alumni*.

[4] See Duncan below, p. 357; on Kingsmill, Macray, *Reg. Magdalen*, ii. 148–9; Foster, *Alumni*.

[5] On Turner see Macray, *Reg. Magdalen*, ii. 36, 38, 155.

desire to emulate the ideals exemplified in the statutes of Fox and Wolsey and their successors. Of the early medieval foundations Balliol College attracts immediate interest since its statutes were revised in 1507 by Richard Fox under a commission granted by Pope Julius II.[1] Fox's new order replaced the rather confused democracy of the medieval college with a more disciplined and stratified society nearer to his own ideals. All government was put in the hands of ten seniors (who were to be at least BAs) formerly called 'scholars' but now to be known as fellows, and these were to share responsibility for teaching the juniors, the scholars, whose numbers were reduced from twenty-two to ten. Fox thus introduced at Balliol the same parity and association between seniors and juniors that a decade later was to characterize his own foundation, and in doing so, actually diminished the undergraduate element on the foundation.[2] Each of the undergraduates was to be nominated by a fellow who supervised his education and was made responsible in the usual fashion of tutors for his purse and conduct. The census of 1552 revealed twenty-nine residents, eight of them MAs, six BAs, and four matriculated servants with eleven undergraduates.[3] There were no arrangements for intramural lectures, however, until 1571, when they were ordered to be established in Greek, logic, and rhetoric.[4] These posts were filled annually until 1599, when a lectureship in theology (really a catechetical post) was added to them.[5] In 1571 provision was made also that commoners of the college, who were permitted under Fox's statutes,[6] should find approved sureties for the payment of their debts at the time of admission. While each fellow was held responsible for the finances of his scholars, the bursars at first were made answerable for the battels of the commoners and, in return, were allowed to take profit from the charges for battels. In 1587 it was further decided that each

---

[1] H. W. C. Davis, *A History of Balliol College* (1899, rev. by R. H. C. Davis and Richard Hunt, Oxford 1963), 57 ff.

[2] See above, p. 18; Davis, *History of Balliol*, 59–60.

[3] Ibid. 79; the list *Reg. Univ.* ed. Boase, p. xxiii, which is cited, shows one doctor, six MAs, six BAs, and thirteen others, apart from four servants named by office.

[4] Balliol College Archives Balliol College Register 1514–1682, p. 128; R. W. Hunt in *VCH Oxon.* iii. 83. Revenues from the rectory of Fillingham, Lincolnshire, which was annexed to the mastership of the college were to be used to pay college lecturers in Greek, dialectic, and rhetoric, for which the sum of £8 was to be set aside annually. The bursars' accounts in the archives show the first payment made in 1572 at the rate of 10s per reader per term, but only in philosophy (fos 9ᵛ, 13). Annual elections to all three posts are recorded in the Register from October 1575 along with those of the college officers: pp. 140, 143, 145, etc. See also A. Kenny, 'Reform and reaction in Elizabethan Balliol 1559–1588', in John Prest (ed.), *Balliol Studies* (1982), 27.

[5] Hunt, *VCH Oxon.* iii.

[6] *SCO* i. pt 1 (Balliol), 20 'De extraneis ad convictum et cohabitationem recipiendis'.

commoner was to have a tutor, and was to perform the same exercises and disputations as the scholars; at this point the bursars were relieved of their former responsibility for the insolvency of commoners. The university census of 1572 showed a considerable expansion of the college: in a total population of sixty-five, forty-six were undergraduates, of whom eight were scholars and nine were servitors, leaving a further twenty-nine who were presumably undergraduate commoners.[1] Their room-rents had so augmented the college's revenues that the allowance for the commons of the fellows and scholars was increased.[2] It is quite certain that the private income of the fellows too was greatly enlarged by tutorial fees, but these by their very nature left no trace in the college records.

Another early foundation, Exeter College (1314), received new statutes and a new lease of life at its virtual re-foundation in 1566 by Sir William Petre. Petre was a Devonian who had come up to the college in 1520 as a commoner. In due course he rose high in the Tudor state, surviving successive changes in religion without loss to his personal fortune. His statutes, like those of Fox at Balliol, extinguished the rather chaotic democracy of young men to set up a much stricter regime, and introduced a new rank of commoners and battelers subordinate to the scholars.[3] Studies were organized under the supervision of a sub-rector, dean, and lector. The sub-rector was to preside at the disputations in theology, while the dean was to preside at the classical and philosophical disputations of the bachelors, to lecture on logic to the undergraduates, and to hear their logical exercises. For this he could expect a fee of 8d a quarter from each commoner and batteler who attended his lectures. He might also appoint a deputy, and the rector's accounts from 1566 show payments of 13s 4d to 'bachelors for assisting the dean in hearing the disputations of scholars'.[4] The literary aspects of the arts curriculum were to be covered with the assistance of the lector. Among the orders at the end of Petre's statutes we discover that a scholar was to be elected each year as lector with the office of reading something of Cicero, Livy, Quintilian, or another classical Latin or Greek author. During the long vacation he was to lecture on arithmetic, geometry, and cosmography at least four days a week. His stipend was to be 26s 8d, and we find this recorded annually in the rector's accounts from 1566.[5] The college register for the

[1] Davis, *History of Balliol*, 83–4, 89; *Reg. Univ.* ed. Clark, ii. 30–1.   [2] Ibid. 89–90.
[3] R. W. Southern in *VCH Oxon.* iii. 109–10; Petre finally raised the number of fellows by eight to twenty-two; C. W. Boase, *Register of the Rectors, Fellows, and other members . . . of Exeter College, Oxford* (OHS xxviii 1894), lxxxiv.
[4] Exeter College Archives A. ii. 9 (not foliated); Boase, *Register of Exeter*, lxxxix.
[5] Exeter College Archives A. i. 1 (vellum; not foliated).

same period[1] shows the annual election of officers with the addition from 1588 of a *moderator philosophiae in sacello* who was the catechist. By this time Exeter had surpassed even Balliol in its appetite for undergraduate members; in the census of 1572 there were ninety-one members of the college besides the fellows, of whom more than sixty were undergraduates; in 1612 there were one hundred and eighty three.[2] Between 1580 and 1605 inclusive, the college elected forty-six fellows, some sixty percent of them being from the West Country, and in the same period no fewer than five hundred and eighty undergraduates were matriculated.[3] So eager was the college to recruit new members that fellows and rectors alike, and even an enterprising head butler, added rooms and cocklofts to accommodate this profitable overflow.[4]

The story is much the same at the other medieval foundations. Queen's College began the century with its medieval complement of fellows studying theology, some chaplains, and a number of graduate commoners in rented rooms. In 1552 there were about a dozen undergraduates who were not on the foundation; by 1560 they were twenty; by 1570, forty; by 1581, seventy; by 1612, there were one hundred and ninety-four such commoners, and these were now under the supervision of tutors.[5] After the Cromwellian visitation of 1535 the college had apparently responded to its recommendations by establishing lectureships in grammar, logic, and theology, the first two presumably for the 'poor boys' or choristers on the foundation, but perhaps also for the undergraduate commoners.[6] Lectures in Greek are recorded in 1563/4, although there is no subsequent reference in the college accounts until 1581/2. A catechist was appointed in 1583, and a lecturer in rhetoric the next year.[7] At University College, where graduate commoners were also a familiar part of the medieval establishment, there was a slow rise in undergraduate membership during the century, and in 1583 the college established a teaching organization consisting of a dean (who had general supervision of the scholars) and four lecturers: in theology (a catechist), Greek, philosphy, and logic.[8] At Lincoln College, an

---

[1] Exeter College Archives Register 1540–1619, A. i. 5.

[2] Southern, *VCH Oxon.* iii. 110; Boase, *Register of Exeter*, xcvi–vii.

[3] J. K. McConica, 'Scholars and commoners', 168.

[4] Southern, op. cit. 116.

[5] R. H. Hodgkin, *Six Centuries of an Oxford College* (Oxford 1949), 57–8, 71–2, and in *VCH Oxon.* iii. 134; J. R. Magrath, *The Queen's College, Oxford* (2 vols 1921), i. 181–2, 194–5.

[6] Magrath i. 184–5, but see Duncan below, p. 343.

[7] Magrath i. 200 note 1, 214 note 1; Hodgkin, *Six Centuries*, 66; *VCH Oxon.* iii. 134.

[8] W. Carr, *University College* (1902), 91; A. Oswald in *VCH Oxon.* iii. 65; the Bursar's Rolls in the college archives show payments for the Greek and logic lecture in 1583/4.

increase in undergraduate membership was under way by the accession of Elizabeth I, and a Greek lectureship was instituted in 1573; otherwise the college was provided with lectures in logic and philosophy.[1] Oriel seems to have experimented briefly in mid-century with the election of scholars—*scholastici*—who were designated to succeed to fellowship, but this was contrary to the statutes and reproved by the visitor. Graduate commoners were familiar there as elsewhere, but undergraduates seem to have been uncommon until the later decades of the century.[2] In the census of 1572 there seem to have been fifteen senior members, with four BAs, three servants (including the cook) and twenty others, most of whom were gentlemen commoners, among them Walter Raleigh.[3] For internal teaching a logic lecturer was established in 1591 and in 1585 a catechist; a Greek lecture was at last decreed in 1624.[4] Despite the indications in the register there is no trace of payments to these officials in the college accounts; however, the stipends may have come from payments by the auditors as and when there was a demand for such lectures. In this respect, the situation at Oriel resembles that at Queen's and at Balliol, where payments are entered only in 1572, the year following the establishment of the lectureships.[5]

Among the early medieval foundations, however, it was Merton that left record of the most impressive response to the new studies and teaching methods. Despite a resolute conservatism in most other matters, the fellows of Merton had greater resources to meet their needs than did the members of other early foundations.[6] The college register also preserved a unique account of college business, including much detail unavailable in other Oxford foundations over such a long period. There are frequent references to determinations and disputations in college and in the university. References to variations too are particularly numerous, and give the titles of the questions considered by members of the college, while the newer rhetorical exercise of declamation is recorded at Merton first in 1560.[7] A lecturer in grammar was appointed in 1559,[8] in 1565 a lecturer in Greek at

---

[1] A catechist was mentioned in 1561; Vivian Green, *The Commonwealth of Lincoln College 1427–1977* (Oxford 1979), 145–6.

[2] D. W. Rannie, *Oriel College* (1900), 72–6; C. L. Shadwell, *Registrum Orielense* (2 vols, 1893–1902), i. 51 ff.

[3] *Reg. Univ.* ed. Clark ii. 39–40; some were exhibitioners: see C. L. Shadwell, *Registrum Orielense*, i. pp. viii–ix, 40–4.

[4] Rannie, *Oriel College*, 93; *Dean's Register of Oriel*, 182, 201, 257.

[5] See above, p. 57, n. 4.

[6] In the valuation of 1592 to pay the cost of the Queen's visit, Merton ranked sixth in income with St Johns, after New College, Magdalen, and All Souls among the medieval foundations, but ahead of all the others; *Reg. ann. mert. 1567–1603*, 287, xxii.

[7] *Reg. ann. mert. 1521–1567*, 122 (without topic).   [8] Ibid. 192.

a stipend of 26s 8d[1] and another in rhetoric at about the same time.[2] In addition the Linacre lectureships had been under way since 1550.[3] The college also required incepting masters and others to give intramural lectures for the instruction of juniors and the conditions imposed give a glimpse of the works required which we would very much like to have for other colleges: the cosmography of Heinrich Glareanus along with Horace in 1536;[4] two of the orations of Isocrates in Greek and Lefèvre d'Étaples's introduction to the *Ethics* of Aristotle in 1539,[5] Valerius Maximus in 1548.[6] From 1572 to 1576 Johann Drusius, the Flemish Hebraist and biblical scholar, lectured in Hebrew at the annual stipend of 40s, at least for the first two of those years; in 1574 Leicester, on the strength of his teaching at Merton and Magdalen, recommended that the university hire Drusius to teach Syriac.[7] In 1595 a certain Italian—'Italo cuidam'— was paid an honorarium of 6s 8d for some months teaching of Italian and Spanish.[8] The surviving bursars' accounts suggest that from early in the reign of Edward VI the subjects of 'humanity' and physics were added to the college lectures in philosophy, and confirm the regular payment of the other college lecturers already mentioned.[9]

Were these lectures intended for undergraduates? The question raises an issue that applies as well to the other medieval foundations which were adding to their teaching in these years. Apart from New College and Magdalen which had for a long time set the pace in organized undergraduate instruction, the growth of the system of lectures and disputations was associated in the older colleges with the marked rise in their undergraduate population. The further

[1] Ibid. 251; the lecturer was Thomas Bodley.

[2] Ibid. 261.

[3] Merton College Archives MCR 3901. See Gillian Lewis below, p. 221 and J. M. Fletcher, 'Linacre's lands and lectureships', in F. Maddison, M. Pelling, and C. Webster (eds), *Essays on the Life and Work of Thomas Linacre c. 1460-1524* (Oxford 1977), 144 f.

[4] *Reg. ann. mert. 1521-1567*, 68. Glareanus published *De Geographia liber unus* with Faber in Basle in 1527, an introductory work dedicated to John à Lasko which was frequently reprinted, eventually in Cologne in 1581 in the *Theoricae novae planetarum* of G. Purbachius (Peurbach). See O. F. Fritzsche, *Glarean: sein Leben und seine Schriften* (Frauenfeld 1890), 91-3.

[5] *Reg. ann. mert. 1521-1567*, 77; *Artificialis introductio per modum Epitomatis in decem libros Ethicorum Aristotelis adiectis elucidata commentariis* (Paris, 1502); likewise frequently reprinted. See E. F. Rice Jr, *The Prefatory Epistles of Jacques Lefèvre d'Étaples and Related Texts* (NY & London 1972), 101, 540-1.

[6] *Reg. ann. mert. 1521-1567*, 140.

[7] Reg. Cong. 1564-82, fo 177[V], 25 October 1574; cf. Mark Curtis, *Oxford and Cambridge in Transition 1558-1642* (Oxford 1959), 141-2. The exhibition was paid, however, in 1575 and 1576 as well; *Reg. ann. mert. 1567-1603*, 43, 54, 64, 66, 75, 87.

[8] *Reg. ann. mert. 1567-1603*, 317.

[9] Merton College Archives MCR 3897, 3898, 3900, 3901, 3936, 3957; I am indebted for these references to Dr John Fletcher.

appointment of catechists confirms a recognized responsibility for undergraduates, even in a society of theologians like Queen's. The same thing applied at University College, at Lincoln, where the increase dated from the 1560s, and at Oriel.

The experience of Merton was rather different. Since the fourteenth century Merton had had an undergraduate component from the benefaction of a former fellow, John de Wylliot. His nine exhibitioners, called 'portionists', were to study logic especially, under the supervision of a bachelor fellow who was elected annually as their principal.[1] By the time of Elizabeth these boys were allocated to MAs as servants, were instructed in religion by a catechist, and no doubt instructed in the fundamentals of the arts curriculum, although the arrangements for teaching them seem to be obscure. Some entries in the register may bear on this. In May 1586 all of the regents were dispensed from their ordinary lectures during the next year, provided some of them instructed the portionists either privately or publicly 'in cognitione spherae vel arithmeticae'.[2] Again, in 1553 and 1554 at the beginning of the reign of Mary Tudor, a *praelector scholasticorum* was elected among the college officers along with a president (*praeses*) but this arrangement, whatever it signified, did not continue.[3] The occasional commoners too are recorded in the register, but in general it does not seem that at Merton College there was any significant reception of undergraduate membership beyond that already provided by the portionists.

This supposition is confirmed by the record of matriculation. If we add up the number of matriculations from 1585 to 1600 for colleges of medieval foundation, excluding New College and Magdalen, we obtain a total of 1,453.[4] These were apportioned among the colleges in diminishing order as follows: Exeter 352; Queen's 284; Balliol 201; Oriel 196; University 182; Lincoln 123; Merton 97; All Souls 18. It may be seen that whereas Exeter College matriculated almost a quarter of the whole, Merton's share was under 7 per cent, and that of All Souls, one percent. In 1592 the various colleges were assessed for the cost of the royal visit according to the rentals from their foundation endowments.[5] If we plot the subsidy rating of each college against that for All Souls, which at

---

[1] *Reg. ann. mert. 1483-1521*, xii–xiv; B. W. Henderson, *Merton College* (1899), 54–6.

[2] *Reg. ann. mert. 1567-1603*, 209.

[3] *Reg. ann. mert. 1521-1567*, 152-4.

[4] This figure is taken from *Reg. Univ.* ed. Clark ii, table B; the incompleteness of the record must be remembered, but if it affected the colleges more or less equally, the comparison is still informative.

[5] See *Reg. ann. mert. 1567-1603*, xxii, 287; and Aylmer below, p. 523.

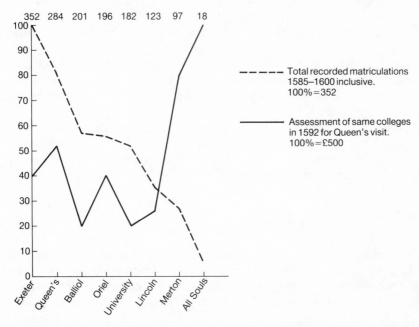

Numbers of matriculations compared to estimated wealth of the medieval foundations in Elizabethan Oxford

£500 was the highest of those now under consideration, and compare this with their matriculations expressed as percentages of Exeter's total (352), we arrive at an admittedly crude but nevertheless suggestive result: see graph.

Allowing for the fact that by 1592 when the ratings were made, the income of some of the poorer foundations might already have been augmented notably by donations or purchase of new properties, we find evidence for the supposition that the incentive to attract undergraduates was closely related to the endowment wealth of the foundation. At All Souls College, where only eighteen matriculations are recorded in the last fifteen years of the century, the *computus* and expense rolls from 1555 show that throughout the period the college continued with its medieval arrangements. There was a rector of theology, a lecturer in natural philosophy, and from 1559 to 1560, a lecturer also in civil law. In 1567–8 a Mr Dennie was paid £4, like the other two lecturers, to teach Greek, and this payment was repeated in 1572–3, but not subsequently.[1] The lawyers and

[1] Bodl. MSS D.D. All Souls c. 283; Charles Trice Martin, *Catalogue of the Archives in the Muniment Room of All Souls' College* (1877) p. 405. From 1577–80 there is a £4

theologians at All Souls were well provided but the space available in the college was extremely restricted, the forty fellows being distributed among sixteen chambers. The lawyers, in their very small faculty, are not likely to have attracted many pupils, and such as they did take may well have been placed at one of the legist halls which were combined to found Jesus College, an event in which fellows of All Souls played a conspicuous part. None of the recorded matriculants was a lawyer, and none went beyond the MA. Apart from the occasional founder's kin, it seems likely that all were clerks or servants of the college. Since these conditions prevailed for at least another century, they determined that this college, alone among its fellows at Oxford and Cambridge, should retain its medieval constitution as a society of graduates.[1]

CONCLUSION

Elizabethan Oxford was dramatically different from the Oxford of Chaucer's clerk, not only in the changes imposed by the reformation and the establishment of a national church, but also in the internal life of the university itself. Both Oxford and Cambridge became recognizable to us as universities made up almost entirely of powerful and well-endowed societies of masters, with undergraduate scholars and commoners housed in colleges; they became collegiate universities, attractive alike and in growing numbers to the future clergy and laity of the realm. One of the aims of this chapter has been to show that this development rested on a comprehensive system of collegiate undergraduate teaching which evolved with remarkable rapidity in the new foundations of the first half of the sixteenth century. These teaching arrangements in turn rested upon medieval experience, especially the precedent set by William of Waynflete's Magdalen College. Although the founders of the early Tudor colleges brought in the new studies—most notably, the teaching of Greek to undergraduates—they did so chiefly with the medieval method of the lecture. Dialectic and disputations also

payment to a lecturer 'in artibus', but this appears to be the lecturer in philosophy, who resumes in 1580–1.

[1] Thomas Denton, who matriculated *armigeri filius* of Bucks. in 1589 and took no degree may have been of the founder's kin. On the foundation of Jesus College see *VCH Oxon.* iii. 264 f; E. G. Hardy, *Jesus College* (1899), J. N. L. Baker, *Jesus College, Oxford 1571–1971* (Oxford 1971). David Lewes, the first principal, John Lloyd, William Aubrey, regius professor of civil law in 1553, Robert Lougher, regius professor in 1577, all among the founding fellows, were likewise all DCL and fellows of All Souls College. On the non-resident *servientes* at All Souls and Matthew Parker's abortive scheme for scholarships tied to Canterbury School, see Montagu Burrows, *Worthies of All Souls* (1874), 115–16.

continued to be prized, so that the teaching of these renaissance foundations shows an unstudied blend of old and new. Examination of undergraduate candidates by the collegiate body is another mark of novelty, as is sequential teaching of classes and the comprehensive and systematic nature of the curriculum. These developments reached their apogee in Edwardian Christ Church, where the large population of junior members was apparently regulated, taught, and examined annually in classes of twenty or so. Despite the growing complexity and sophistication of intra-mural undergraduate (and graduate) teaching, there is no evidence in the statutes of these foundations that university lecturing was being supplanted; quite the contrary, it was customary to state that members must fulfil all of their statutory obligations to the university in addition to those enacted by the college. However, the decision as to whether or not the regulations had been met rested with the colleges, whether of medieval or modern foundation. Fox's revised statutes for Balliol College in 1507 serve for all: a bachelor proceeding to the MA was permitted to approach the university only if a majority of all the fellows who were masters of arts agreed in secret consultation that he was worthy of the degree.[1] In practice the decision seems to have been left to a senior committee—the master of Balliol with the appropriate dean and three senior fellows—and the Balliol register usually states simply that the candidate was licensed by the college to proceed to the degree.[2] Such control was not new; it first appears in the statutes of Oriel College. With the growth of collegiate authority over the undergraduate population, however, it meant that the colleges not only effectively controlled admission to the university[3] but the awarding of degrees as well.

With the Marian foundations of Trinity and St John's undergraduate commoners were fully and explicitly incorporated into the life of the collegiate society, and this final stage throws into relief another of the features of the Tudor university, the replacement by the undergraduate of the old graduate commoner, usually a lawyer or theologian hiring a room on a casual basis in a college glad to have the income. The appearance of the undergraduate commoner on a large scale was the most conspicuous influence in the transformation

---

[1] SCO i. pt 1, 17.

[2] At Exeter a few of the entries likewise specify the approval of the rector, sub-rector, and a 'majority of the fellows'. There is an unusually full and explicit account of the order of events in the Merton register for 3 May 1583: one Richard Fisher who on 24 March had received permission from eight seniors to supplicate for his MA and to be admitted to the number of masters of arts at Merton, reappears with this entry: 'dominus Richardus Fisher admissus in numerum magistrorum istius domus, et postero die presentatus est congregationi ibique creatus est magister incipiens in universitate'; Reg. ann. mert. 1567–1603, 157–8.

[3] Above, p. 50.

of the Tudor college, and more will be said about this in a later chapter.[1] His appearance was linked to the evolution of the office of the college tutor. Alongside the senior fellow responsible for the welfare and tuition of a junior on the foundation there emerged the college fellow who, in addition to his ordinary statutory duties, took private employment on a contract with the parents or guardian of a young commoner, to be responsible for his finances, general welfare, and finally, tuition. Little has as yet been said about this, partly because the full development of the tutorial relationship came in the later decades of the century, but also because that method of teaching followed upon the provision of college lectures and disputations designed originally to teach the undergraduates who were maintained on the foundation. This part of the story has hitherto been almost entirely overlooked. There is evidence, as we have seen, that undergraduate commoners too were expected to attend the lectures and disputations which were the backbone of college teaching, and which were by no means abandoned as archaic with the appearance of the printed book and college tutor. Indeed, it was to the provision of lectures and the careful supervision of the regular exercises of disputation and declamation that the colleges devoted their money and attention as they strove to cope with the new studies. The halls and colleges of medieval foundation in their turn emulated the provision for teaching in the newly founded colleges as they strove to attract the lucrative custom of the commoners. Thus one by one, whether their original statutes had provided for undergraduate membership or not, they acquired a large undergraduate component with the exception only of two, Merton and, most notably, All Souls.

While the evolutionary nature of this development deserves more attention than it has hitherto received, we have also seen that the foundation of Corpus Christi College brought with it a commitment to humane studies and a degree of discipline which set an entirely new style. Unfortunately, none of Fox's surviving correspondence allows us to trace the evolution of his collegiate plan, although we have seen that some aspects of it were anticipated in his new statutes for Balliol College.[2] His many connections with the humanist circle, and his long experience with educational foundations make it certain that his innovations were well understood and deliberate. Erasmus hailed his Oxford college as a great advance for humane literature

[1] See chapter 10 for this and the emergence of the private tutor; also on the tutorial system, Lawrence Stone in *University in Society*, i. 25–6, and Curtis, *Oxford and Cambridge in Transition*, 78–81.

[2] See above, p. 57.

and classical studies.[1] However, the best evidence that Fox and his allies meant to disturb the established order comes from a letter of Thomas More.

At the end of March 1518, More wrote to the university of Oxford from the court at Abingdon, explaining his concern at persistent reports in London that a body of scholars in the university, through hatred of Greek or misguided and destructive mischief, had formed themselves into a party called 'Trojans', to oppose the study and ridicule all who took it up.[2] The letter had been provoked by a further report that one of this party had quite recently used the occasion of a Lenten sermon to the university to attack all Greek learning, good Latin, and indeed, the liberal arts. In the body of the letter he defended the place of secular learning in sacred studies and concluded by alluding to the happier state of affairs in Cambridge, to the determination of Oxford's chancellor, Archbishop Warham, of Wolsey and of the king that Oxford's system of studies should not go to ruin, and to the lavish endowments enjoyed by so many colleges to support scholars in the study of the liberal arts. In its tone, structure, and general style, the letter has the form and impact of a classical declamation; it was no routine piece of official correspondence.[3]

More's letter reveals dissension within the university that left no trace in the official records. It was also written at a critical moment for the new studies. Fox's charter of foundation and statutes had been issued one year before and his college was just struggling to life. Moreover, sometime early in 1518—not later than early May —the university waited on the king at Abingdon, and subsequently entertained the queen and cardinal at Oxford.[4] As they delightedly reported to their chancellor, Wolsey planned to found lectures in

[1] Epp. 965, 990 in *Opus epistolarum Erasmi*, iii. There is also the evidence supplied by Fox's books; *BRUO to 1500*, ii. 171–9. The addition of Claymond's Greek and Hebrew manuscripts to the important humanistic Latin and Greek texts given by Fox justified Erasmus's compliment to the 'trilinguis bibliotheca' in his letter to Claymond (ep. 990); see B. C. Barker-Benfield, *Trilinguis bibliothecae spectaculum: some Manuscripts of Corpus Christi College, Oxford, Displayed to the Double Crown Club, Saturday, 1 July 1978* (privately printed for the Double Crown Club 1978), p. 1.

[2] *The Correspondence of Sir Thomas More*, ed. E. F. Rogers (Princeton 1947), no. 60, pp. 112–20. For a modern critical text and translation see *Defenses of Erasmian Humanism: letters to Dorp, Oxford, Lee and a monk with a new Latin text and translation of the history of Richard III*, ed. Daniel Kinney (Collected Works of Saint Thomas More xv New Haven, forthcoming).

[3] The account of the episode by Erasmus a year later is silent about More's letter, but expands on the concern of the king. Erasmus was writing to give public support to Petrus Mosellanus at the Leipzig disputation between Eck, Karlstadt, and Luther; *Opus epistolarum Erasmi*, iii. ep. 948 from Louvain, 22 April 1519. The allusion to Cambridge would sting the university's pride; on the rather similar provision for Greek studies there see p. 21 n. 4 above.   [4] *Epist. acad. 1508–96*, no. 63.

the humanities at his own expense, and to provide the lecturers with an ample salary;[1] under the circumstances, the university was considering submitting all statutes to the cardinal for reform of the curriculum.[2] Wolsey's lectures are first heard of in Michaelmas Term, 1518, when John Clement, proficient in both Greek and Latin, began to lecture in Humanity.[3] It is therefore certain that Wolsey's final arrangements were being made just at the time More wrote his letter, and that More knew of them. His intervention points to the highly placed and distinguished circle at court which undoubtedly supported these initiatives, and whose religious and intellectual concerns Fox's foundation reflected.

The evolution of the medieval college into the Elizabethan undergraduate college has been related in terms of the arrangements for teaching, which are a certain guide to the changing conceptions of patrons and founders, as they are to the efforts of the medieval foundations to adapt to the new educational tastes. They are less certain as a guide to the actual performance of their sponsors' expectations, particularly with respect to studies, and this matter will be taken up in a later chapter.[4] Outside Oxford a like development can be discovered only at Cambridge. At Paris and Louvain, for example, where colleges were also well established, the resemblances are superficial. In both these universities as elsewhere abroad, the colleges were much more closely linked with the faculties and government of the university, and run by them.[5] In such a perspective, it was the distinctly casual association between the collegiate foundations and the faculties in England that gave the colleges the freedom to shape their own destinies in the critical years following the reformation.

---

[1] 'quotidianas quasdam bonarum litterarum lectiones'; ibid., p. 75.

[2] As they did, against Warham's advice, on 1 June 1518; ibid. nos. 64–5. Although the letters are undated, we know that by mid-April 1518 Wolsey had left the vicinity, so it is likely that his visit to Oxford with the queen took place about the time More's letter was written; *L & P Henry VIII*, ii. pt 2, 1276 (4125).

[3] See above, p. 26. From 1516/17 William Latimer, another able Grecian, had been living at Canterbury College, well-placed to report to this circle on the progress of Greek studies and the activities of its opponents. *Canterbury College Documents and History*, ed. W. A. Pantin (3 vols, OHS ser. vi–viii 1947–50), ii. 256–9.

[4] See Chapter 10.

[5] A. B. Cobban, *The Medieval Universities: their Development and Organization* (1947), 129 ff. H. de Vocht, *History of the Foundation and the Rise of the Collegium Trilingue Lovaniense 1517–1550*, i; M. Reulos, 'L'université et les collèges, *Bulletin de l'association Guillaume Budé*, 3 ser. no. 2 (1953), 33–42.

2

Oxford Town and Oxford University

CARL I. HAMMER, JR.

THE URBAN COMMUNITY

From Saxon times until the fourteenth century Oxford was a major centre of industry and trade.[1] It was a central crossroads, and the site of an important royal castle. Beaumont Palace was just outside its walls, and the royal manor at Woodstock, a popular hunting lodge, was only a few miles away. Taken together, these circumstances account for the prominent role played by the town in the political history of high medieval England. By the standards of the time, therefore, the early *studium* at Oxford took root and grew in a significantly urban environment, but this was not so surely the case by the fifteenth and sixteenth centuries. That the university's growth caused the economic decline of the town remains only an assertion, and an unlikely one, in spite of its perennial popularity.[2] On the other hand, by the early sixteenth century the close economic dependence of the town upon the university is evident, and one can easily trace the symbiotic relationship between the burghal host and the academic guest.

The Borough

By modern standards the late medieval and early modern borough of Oxford was a small place. Within the walls it covered an area of 90 acres which was divided into four segments, known as wards, by the major north–south, east–west streets intersecting at Carfax. In the

[1] The economic history of the town is dealt with in the fourth volume of *VCH Oxon.* There is a good account of Saxon Oxford by E. M. Jope, 'Saxon Oxford and its region', in D. B. Harden (ed.), *Dark Age Britain* (1956), 234–58. For Oxford's location see maps 39 and 62 in *A New Historical Geography of England*, ed. H. C. Darby (Cambridge 1973), 175, 289.

[2] The case was put most forcefully by J. R. Green in his essay, 'The early history of Oxford', where it is asserted that the university reduced the borough to 'a cluster of lodging houses': J. R. Green, *Stray Studies from England and Italy* (1876), esp. 332–3. The tone of the assertion, if not the particulars, was adopted by later historians: see notably Hastings Rashdall, *The Universities of Europe in the Middle Ages* (2 vols Oxford 1895), new edn by F. M. Powicke and A. B. Emden (3 vols Oxford 1936), esp. iii, 79–113.

early sixteenth century Oxford had within the walls nine separate parishes of varying size. Outside the walls to the south was a built-up area along Grandpont leading towards Abingdon. To the east, across the Cherwell River was the parish of St Clement's in Bullingdon Hundred.[1] To the west lay the important suburban parish of St Thomas which was closely tied to Oseney Abbey, the great foundation of Austin Canons.[2] In the north-east was Merton's manor of Holywell which formed the eastern limit to the most important suburban area, the parish of St Mary Magdalen in the Hundred-outside-the-Northgate.[3] Finally, at the northern edge of St Mary Magdalen was the small, semi-rural parish of St Giles.

Within this framework university growth was largely restricted to the eastern part of the town and, later, to the suburban areas in the north. Although some important halls such as New Inn Hall were in the western wards, the majority were in the two eastern wards as were the schools.[4] Of the colleges within the walls, none founded before Cardinal College (1525) was located west of the Turl (St Mildred's Lane), nor west of Oriel to the south of the High Street. No Tudor college was sited west of the line formed by the modern St Aldate's–Cornmarket–Magdalen St–St Giles. Balliol was located at an early date (by 1284) in the northern suburb but was not joined there until the mid-sixteenth century by the two Marian foundations, St John's and Trinity. The eastern section of the town (particularly from St Mary's onwards) accordingly formed a virtual *pagus academicus* as it still does today.

The size of the urban community can only be guessed at. The sources for estimating total population in our period are the poll tax of 1377, the lay subsidies of 1523–5 and 1543–4 and the incomplete chantry certificates of 1545/7.[5] None of these is a true census, but they do allow one to arrive at a rough figure. Russell

[1] *VCH Oxon.* v. 258–66.

[2] Oseney Abbey employed about two-fifths of those assessed in the parish by wages for the 1523 subsidy.

[3] See H. M. Cam's essay, 'The hundred outside the northgate of Oxford' reprinted in her *Liberties and Communities in Medieval England* (Cambridge 1944), 107–23.

[4] See W. A. Pantin, 'The halls and schools of medieval Oxford' in *Oxford Studies Presented to Daniel Callus* (OHS new ser. xvi 1964), esp. 98–9, and the map between 36 and 37 in *VCH Oxon.* iii.

[5] J. C. Russell summarizes the information from the poll tax of 1377 in *British Medieval Population* (Albuquerque 1948), 142. The schedule of the subsidy for 1523 is printed in *Oxford City Documents*, ed. J. E. Thorold Rogers (OHS xviii 1891), 53–75. The original rolls for April 1524 and February 1525 are PRO E.179/161/174, 182. The schedules dated April and October 1524 for St Clement's are PRO E. 179/161/169, 183. The two schedules for 1543–4 are printed in *Surveys and Tokens*, ed. H. E. Salter (OHS lxxv 1923), 139–62. The chantry certificates are printed in *The Chantry Certificates and the Edwardian Inventories of Church Goods for Oxfordshire*, ed. R. Graham (Oxford Record Society i 1919), 12–16.

put the late fourteenth-century population (1377) at about 3,500. By using the subsidies for 1523-5 to supply information for the parishes missing from the chantry certificates, one arrives at a total non-privileged population in the mid-sixteenth century (1547) of about 5,500–6,000.[1] The largest parish was the suburban St Mary Magdalen with about 855 communicants in 1547, or perhaps 1,250 to 1,300 residents. Within the walls, St Martin's had about 1,000 residents, while St Michael's Northgate had as few as 200 communicants or 300 residents. Suburban parishes (apart from St Mary Magdalen) tended to be small, with Holywell and St Giles' containing about 75 and 120 persons respectively.

This population was highly mobile. Almost three-quarters of the assessed wage earners (journeymen and labourers) who made up about one-third of the taxable municipal population in 1523–5 probably stayed in Oxford for at most one year.[2] Oxford was also a poor place with perhaps two-thirds of the entire population below the level of exemption from the subsidy. Nor were the plutocrats of local society particularly rich by early Tudor standards.[3]

In 1523–5 the wealth of the urban community was centred west of the area of greatest academic concentration. The two central parishes of All Saints and St Martin's were the most generally prosperous while the small north-central and western parishes of St Michael's Northgate and St Peter in the Bailey seem to have been 'blue-collar' neighbourhoods, as was St Peter in the East. The large suburban parish of St Mary Magdalen contained very marked economic extremes as did St Ebbe's in the south-west.

The early prosperity of Oxford seems to have been based primarily on cloth manufacture, and specifically, on weaving, but by the early fourteenth century the craft was virtually extinct. A textile 'renaissance' may have occurred in the later fourteenth century, but it did not last far into the fifteenth century. Only two weavers survived when the fullers were incorporated into their guild in 1439, and the situation remained unchanged in the sixteenth century.[4] The

[1] For further information see my 'Some social and institutional aspects of town–gown relations in late medieval and Tudor Oxford' (Toronto PhD thesis 1974), 111–15; a copy has been deposited at the Bodleian Library, Oxford. The privileged population is dealt with in the following section.

[2] See my 'The mobility of skilled-labour in late medieval England: some Oxford evidence', *Vierteljahrsschrift für Sozial-und Wirtschaftsgeschichte* lxiii (1976), 194–210.

[3] Only one assessment, that of John Traves of St Mary Magdalen in 1525, exceeded £100.

[4] See E. M. Carus-Wilson's articles, 'An industrial revolution of the thirteenth century', *Economic History Review*, xi (1941) and 'The English cloth industry in the late twelfth and early thirteenth centuries', *Economic History Review* xiv (1944), reprinted in her *Medieval Merchant Venturers* (1954). There were about thirty weavers in 1380: A. R. Bridbury, *Economic Growth; England in the Later Middle Ages* (1962); *Cal. Pat. Rolls, 1436–41*, 347.

secondary leather trades, particularly those of the cordwainer or shoemaker and glover, were on a small scale but enjoyed considerable prosperity throughout the fifteenth and sixteenth centuries, while primary production tanning seems (like weaving and fulling) to have moved out of the town in the later middle ages.[1] In contrast to the cordwainers and glovers, there were large numbers of tailors, many of whom were also engaged in distributive trade though only a few of them were very prosperous. In 1380/1 there were about forty master tailors, and a like number in 1523-5, when they formed the largest single occupational group. By 1586 the master members of the tailors' guild had increased to about seventy-five in number, and the journeymen totalled 196.[2] The distributive trades were neither large nor specialized, but they enjoyed a steady prosperity. In 1572 the mercers (including grocers) and drapers formed Oxford's first mercantile company which oversaw a variety of specialities. Particularly in the later sixteenth century the relative importance of the drapers and mercers in the local economy seems to have been great.[3] Finally, the building trades, especially those of carpenter and mason, had a large number of practitioners as a result of collegiate building activities, but the influence of both trades was reduced by the high degree of mobility and the modest wealth of their members.[4]

The most striking aspect of Oxford's economy throughout our period, but especially in the early sixteenth century, was the strength of the victualling trades, particularly the brewers. In 1523-5 the brewers, the whitebakers, brownbakers, butchers, fishmongers, vintners and innkeepers, accounted for about half the total assessed wealth of the town, and their per-capita assessments were well above average though not quite so high as those of the smaller group in the distributive trades. The brewers alone, however, had the highest individual assessments in the town with the possible exception of the small group of important chandlers. This was the result of a process of concentration which had removed the brewing industry from the fragmented 'cottage' stage of the fourteenth century and which had reduced the number of those who brewed for sale to about twenty by the early fifteenth century. This, combined with the large, transient academic market, gave brewing in Oxford an

---

[1] Hammer, 'Town–gown relations', 156-60.

[2] Multiple occupations and changes of occupation were common in all trades except those related to building, the leather crafts and blacksmithing: *Oxford City Documents*, 421; Bodl. MS Morrell 6, fos 35-6^V.

[3] OCA A.5.5. fos 163^V-75; G.5.4. fos 1-10^V. By 1584/5 they had displaced the victuallers in their domination of the Oxford Town Council.

[4] See E. A. Gee, 'Oxford masons, 1370-1530', *Architectural Journal* cix (1952), 54-131; E. A. Gee, 'Oxford carpenters, 1370-1530', *Oxoniensia* xvii/xviii (1952/3), 112-84.

industrial character which it seems to have lacked in most other towns.[1]

The lack of industrial specialization, together with the importance of the victualling trades, the university-oriented building trades and the secondary trades such as tailoring, glove- and shoemaking which would have found a ready market among academic consumers, all lead to the conclusion that the late medieval and Tudor economy was based largely upon supplying goods and services to the university. Indeed, this was one point upon which town and gown themselves were in complete agreement.[2] From an economic point of view, Oxford was a university town.

The political community of the town was formed by the ancient guild merchant whose membership comprised the freemen of the town or, to use a local term, the *hanasters*.[3] This was the body which acquired the fee-farm of Oxford in 1199 and which, through its officers, administered the franchise into modern times. The constitutional organs of this group seem to have reached some degree of maturity between the mid-fifteenth and mid-sixteenth centuries and were ratified by a royal charter of incorporation at the relatively late date of 1605. The most important officers elected by the freemen were the mayor, the chief executive officer elected yearly from among a group of five aldermen, the two bailiffs to whom the administration of the fee-farm was entrusted and who had judicial functions as well, and the two chamberlains who administered the financial affairs of the guild itself.

By the early sixteenth century all these officers as well as past incumbents were grouped into a kind of upper or mayor's council of varying size. Below them was a common council of fixed size, twenty-four in all, which first appears in 1518/19 but which probably had some sort of existence from at least the mid-fifteenth century. Chamberlains were recruited from this lower group, and a regular *cursus honorum* leading from chamberlain through bailiff

[1] The assize lists, 1311–50, are printed in *Mediaeval Archives of the University of Oxford*, ed. H. E. Salter (2 vols OHS lxx, lxxiii 1920–1), ii. 184–265. See also *Oxford City Documents*, 417 (1380/1) and *Registrum cancellarii oxoniensis, 1434–1469*, ed. H. E. Salter (2 vols OHS xciii–iv 1932), i. 9–10, 149 (1434, 1447). Alan D. Dyer has noted a similar situation in his *The City of Worcester in the sixteenth century* (Leicester 1973), 139–40. An early sixteenth-century (1506?) account book from the brewers' trade survives as Bodl. MS Top. Oxon. c 235; it is especially interesting for the list of academic customers which it supplies, but the interpretation of this document is still uncertain.

[2] See the municipal petitions and rejoinders printed in *Selections from the Records of the City of Oxford . . . [1509–1583]*, ed. W. H. Turner (Oxford and London 1880), esp. 88, 113.

[3] The subject of town government is discussed in detail in my 'Anatomy of an oligarchy; the Oxford town council in the fifteenth and sixteenth centuries', *The Journal of British Studies*, xviii (1978), 1–27.

and alderman (assistant) to mayor had emerged before the early sixteenth century when it can be traced in detail.

The elastic nature of the mayor's council meant that the total membership of local government was quite large. While local government was certainly not democratic, there is no evidence that in the fifteenth and sixteenth centuries it was more oligarchic than in, say, the thirteenth; indeed, there is good evidence that the opposite was true. An analysis of surviving fifteenth and sixteenth century council lists shows that, while there is a definite correlation as regards wealth, age, and position, the council as a whole reached far down into and accurately reflected the composition of at least the taxable community. Moreover, there was a rapid turn over in the personnel of local government which ensured some share of authority for the able and the willing. In sum, by Tudor standards, the urban community of the borough was a modest, relatively homogeneous and open body.

Privileged Persons

Besides the freemen, 'foreigners' (non-freemen) and 'scholars', both teachers and students, there was a fourth group resident in Oxford which, while it did not participate in the academic life of the university, nevertheless, enjoyed its privileges. These were the persons who served the academic community directly. In 1459 an agreement between the university and the town defined them as:

> . . . every dailly continuell servaunt to eny of [the scholars] bifore rehersed belonging, the Styward of the Universite and feed men of the same Universite with their menyalle men, also alle Bedells with their dailly servauntz and their housholdes, alle Stacioners, alle bokebynders, lympnours, wryters, pargemeners, barbours, the bellerynger of the Universite with alle their houshold, alle catours, manciples, spencers, cokes, lavenders, pouere childrene of scolers or clerkes within the procincte [sic] of the said Universite, also alle other servauntz takyng clothing or hyre by the yere, half yere, or quarter of the yere, takyng atte leste for the yere vi s. viii d., for the half yere iii s. iiii d., and the quarter xxd. of eny doctour, Maister, graduat, Scoler or Clerc withoute fraude or malengyne, also alle common caryers, bryngers of scolers to the Universite or their money, letter or eny especiall message to eny scoler or clerk, or feccher of eny Scoler or clerk fro the Universite for the tyme of such fecchyng or bryngyng or abiding in the Universite for that entent; . . .[1]

But, in essence, this was only an elaboration of the corresponding clause of the *reformatio pacis* made between the town and university by Edward I in 1290, and this group can be paralleled at all

---

[1] *Mediaeval Archives*, i. 245.

European universities.[1] We fortunately possess an assessment of the privileged persons made for the subsidy granted in 1522 which allows us to examine them in a way comparable to the non-privileged community.[2] The list contains 111 assessments or about one-fifth of the total number assessed in the town, divided almost equally between goods (55) and wage (56) assessments. We find there that the range of wealth in the privileged community was more limited than for their burghal counterparts, but that within this narrower range, the privileged persons were slightly better off.

Among the privileged persons the bedells—the senior servants of the faculties—were by far the most well-to-do. Throughout our period they numbered six: three esquire (superior or armigerous) bedells for each of the three faculties of theology, civil law and arts, and their servants, the three yeomen (inferior) bedells.[3] The goods' assessments for the three esquire bedells, £30, £20 and £18, fall within the ranges established for such prosperous municipal occupations as those of vintner and mercer-grocer, and even two of the yeomen bedells were assessed at a healthy £10. The magnificent probate inventory of 1533 for the esquire bedell of law, Edward Standishe, confirms this impression of solid prosperity.[4]

From the early fifteenth century onwards we can establish a reasonably complete list of bedells.[5] Although literacy was essential for holders of the office, it was only from the late fifteenth century that a few names of university men appear, and it is not until about 1590 onwards that all the esquire bedells (though not the yeomen bedells) were graduates. From the 1450s to the 1530s there is evidence that the crown tried to use the positions for purposes of patronage—additional evidence for their desirability—but, surprisingly, it was not until the turn of the century with the influence of Lady Margaret that these attempts met with success.[6] It seems

[1] *Munimenta academica or documents illustrative of academical life and studies at Oxford*, ed. Henry Anstey (2 vols Rolls Series l 1868) i. 46–56; see *Mediaeval Archives* i. 88–94 for an *inspeximus* of 1315. Of course, this group was common to all medieval universities: cf. A. B. Cobban, *The Medieval Universities: their development and organization* (1975), 53–4, for the origins of the privileged persons.

[2] The schedule, dated 5 February 1524, is printed in *Oxford City Documents*, 55–9. Only one assessment, that of the esquire bedell of theology, Richard Wootton, reaches £30, but if we disregard the highest goods' assessments for the town, those of £40 and above, the average goods' assessment for the privileged persons, £5 9s 6d, is somewhat higher than that for the townsmen, £5 3s 5d (1523/4) and £4 19s 10d (1525).

[3] See *Statuta*, pp. lxxvii–lxxviii, and *Reg. Univ.* ed. Clark i. 256–61. The canonists were served by the bedells for theology and the medical faculty by those of the artists.

[4] Reg. Canc. 1527–43, fos 307ᵛ–10ᵛ.

[5] See the printed lists in *Reg. canc. 1434–69* i. pp. xlv–xlvii, and *Reg. Univ.* ed. Clark i. 256–61. The gaps for the first 30–40 years of the sixteenth century can be filled from the chancellors' registers OUA Hyp. A 2, 3 and 4.

[6] See *Epist. acad.* ed. Anstey i. 334–6; ii. 464–5, 524, 603–4, 665–6. The successful

that some yeomen bedells were recruited from among the other *privilegiati*, but, oddly enough, there is little evidence that townsmen tried to obtain these potentially lucrative posts.[1]

There was a fair degree of mobility of a 'careerist' sort within the bedellships. Among the yeomen bedells in the first half of the sixteenth century this followed the course, arts to law to theology, and the period from the mid-fifteenth to the mid-sixteenth century saw a number of transfers from yeoman to esquire bedell, though no particular pattern is discernible. Transfers within the esquire bedellships were unknown. The esquire bedellship of arts, especially desirable because of the large number of graduates with their customary fees, was relatively resistant to mobility from within, and was the particular object of trafficking.[2] Like other privileged persons, bedells engaged simultaneously in other occupations and offices, particularly in the victualling trades such as brewing, and their privileged status and peculiar duties do not seem to have segregated them socially or economically from the larger urban community.[3]

Of all the trades carried on in Oxford, none was more clearly a result of the university's presence than the book trade. It is also, with the exception of the building trades, the best studied local occupation. Moreover, the chance survival of John Thorne's account-book for 1520 allows a more intimate glimpse into its daily round than is possible for other local trades.[4]

The most striking thing about the social composition of the trade

candidates were: Thomas Pantrey, esquire bedell of arts (1500–33), and Richard Wootton, esquire bedell of theology (1501–40): *Registrum cancellarii 1498–1506*, ed. W. T. Mitchell (OHS new ser. xxvii 1979–80), 92; *Epist. acad.* ed. Anstey ii. 667–8.

[1] Richard Pate, for example, occurs as manciple at Exeter College (1504) and St Mary's Hall (1506) before becoming yeoman bedell of arts by 1507 at the earliest (*Reg. canc. 1498–1506*, 67, 165). An example of a townsman becoming a bedell is that of the draper, James Edmonds, who was a member of the common council when elected yeoman bedell of arts in 1522: Reg. Cong. 1518–35, fo 77ᵛ; OCA, A.5.3. fo 364. The lack of townsmen seems to be connected to the peculiar status of the bedells which precluded their being both privileged persons and freemen; see below, p. 86.

[2] The abortive Edwardian statutes sought to combat this by: forbidding bribes, making the offices life-long, equalizing fees (primarily 'culets' at graduation) for the esquire bedells, and abolishing two of the yeoman bedellships: *Statuta*, 351–2.

[3] For example, Richard Wootton was the master of the brewers' guild in 1527: Reg. Canc. 1527–43, fo 37ᵛ. William Bulcombe, esquire bedel of law, gave up his position about 1500 to trade as a woollen draper and innkeeper. Within four years of his last appearance as a bedell (1499) he was elected mayor of Oxford (1503): see my 'Town and gown in Tudor Oxford: a note and two documents', *Oxoniensia* xxxix (1975), 77–84, and *BRUO to 1500* i. 302.

[4] The account book of Thorne or 'Dorne' was printed by Falconer Madan in C. R. L. Fletcher (ed.) *Collectanea* i (OHS v 1885), 71–177, and in M. Burrows (ed.), *Collectanea*, ii (OHS xvi 1890), 453–78. Thorne's will, dated 21 September 1545, is Bodl. MS Wills Oxon. fos 179, 285ᵛ. See my 'Some new information on John Thorne and Joseph Barnes of Oxford', *The Library*, 6th ser. i (1979), 367–8.

at the time of the subsidy was its domination by 'Douchemen'. Half of the assessments, and all of the more important ones, in 1524 were levied on this group of foreigners. This situation seems to have arisen only in the very late fifteenth century,[1] and persisted until the latter part of the sixteenth century. Of the four privileged booksellers assessed in 1567, all were foreign born, and only from about the 1580s onwards were Englishmen in the majority.[2] In part, the 'problem' tended to solve itself. Richard Garbrand, the son of the important alien bookseller, Garbrand Harkes, began his career in 1573 as a native, while Harkes also trained a second 'son', his apprentice, Joseph Barnes of Long Wittenham (Berks.), who was to revive printing in Oxford in 1585 after a hiatus of more than half a century.[3]

Like the bedells, the members of the book trade had outside interests, especially the sale of ale and wine.[4] The 'Dutchman' William Howberghe was a member of the brewers' guild in 1524, and in 1554, two years after becoming a freeman, Garbrand Harkes took an apprentice as a mercer.[5] His contemporary, the stationer Henry Millward, had earlier dabbled in the trade of haberdashery, and Millward held, moreover, the triple mancipleship of All Souls, Trinity and Broadgates Hall in 1570.[6] But the influence of the book trade on the local community was not only economic, for its numbers supplied the core of the (continental) protestant cell around Harmon Men in the late 1530s and also the most notorious recusant of Elizabethan Oxford, Roland Jenkes, who is associated with the infamous 'black assizes' of 1577.[7]

Aside from personal servants, whose total numbers are difficult to assess, the largest group of privileged persons was that of the common servants of the colleges and halls. The 'essential' common servants retained by a small college such as Exeter in 1535 were a manciple, cook, barber (who usually doubled as porter) and

[1] See J. Johnson and S. Gibson, *Print and Privilege at Oxford to the year 1700* (Oxford Bibliographical Society vii 1946), 3.

[2] PRO E. 179/162/330.

[3] OCA A.5.3. fo 96; Johnson and Gibson, *Print and Privilege*, 6–8; Harry Carter, *A History of the Oxford University Press* i (Oxford 1975), 17–24.

[4] See *Reg. Univ.* ed. Clark i. 320–2. This does not necessarily indicate (as Clark supposed) that the book trade was unprofitable.

[5] OUA WPβ/B/34/b; OCA A.5.3. fos 231^V, 74.

[6] OCA A.5.3. fos 229, 55^V, 56; *Reg. Univ.* ed. Clark i. 262 (Reg. canc. 1545-1661, fo. 66); OUA Chancellor's Court Act Book 1566-78, Hyp./A/8 fo 150. He occurs as manciple of All Souls already in 1563: OUA Chancellor's Court Act Book 1561-6, Hyp./A/7 fo 97.

[7] See the documents from 1539 in *L & P Henry VIII* xiii pt 1, 811; xiii pt 2, app. 19; xiv pt 1, 684. The affair is discussed in G. R. Elton, *Policy and Police; the enforcement of the reformation in the age of Thomas Cromwell* (Cambridge 1972), 98-9. For Jenks see *APC: 1575-1577*, 347, 368-9, 392; see also *APC: 1581-1582*, 34-5 for 28 April 1581.

a laundress. Most foundations had a like list, although a large and wealthy college such as Magdalen or the abortive Wolseian foundation of Cardinal College might have very elaborate provision for servants.[1] The monastic colleges seem to have been comparable in this regard to a small college such as Exeter, while the small halls probably did not retain more than a cook on a regular basis and perhaps a manciple.[2] Altogether the common servants in the 1520s and 1530s probably numbered about 150, somewhat more than half of whom (81) were assessed in 1524. There is no solid evidence that their numbers were substantially higher in the mid-fifteenth or late sixteenth centuries although the plethora of small halls in the earlier period would suggest that the proportion of manciples and cooks from the labour-intensive halls was probably higher at that time, while the proportion of menial servants such as kitchen-knaves was probably greater in the late-Elizabethan Oxford made up of colleges and a few larger halls.

The manciple was the most important entrepreneurial figure amongst the *privilegiati*. The main task of the manciple in both the colleges and halls was to purchase provisions and to supervise their distribution. At All Souls, whose statutes of 1443 were very influential, the manciple (*mancipium sive dispensator*), assisted by the cook, was to purchase provisions weekly (*singulis septimanis*) under the supervision of the bursars and seneschall and to superintend the distribution of food and drink (*dispensatio panis et potus*) at refections. He was to have under him a butler (*subdispensator*) who was to attend regularly in the pantry and buttery (*in panetria et botellaria*) to serve the scholars of the college.[3] In return, the manciple received a statutory salary (in colleges) or fixed fees (in halls) and, depending upon the type and prosperity of the foundation, collegiate allowances for commons and livery.[4] Extra money could be earned

[1] For Exeter see *Valor* ii 268-9; for Magdalen and Cardinal College see ibid. 287, and *SCO* ii. pt 11 (Cardinal College), 51-3, 91-101. The statutes of All Souls (1443) were very influential in this regard because the statutes of New College lacked provisions for servants. At All Souls the statutory servants were: manciple, sub-manciple, head cook, two assistant cooks, a barber-janitor, a groom and a laundress: *SCO* i. pt 7 (All Souls), 58-9.

[2] For the monastic colleges see *Canterbury College*, ed. W. A. Pantin (3 vols OHS new ser. vi-viii 1941-4) ii. 257-61 (1521/2, 1528/9); 'Some Durham College rolls', ed. N. E. D. Blakiston, in M. Burrows (ed.) *Collectanea*, iii (OHS xxxii 1896), 67-70 (1541/2). In the halls the barber and laundress would be employed casually, not on a salary. See H. E. Salter, 'An Oxford hall in 1424', in H. W. C. Davis (ed.), *Essays in History Presented to Reginald Poole* (Oxford 1927), 421-35; *Statuta*, 583-5; A. B. Emden, *An Oxford Hall in Medieval Times* (Oxford 1927), 197 ff.

[3] *SCO* i. pt 7 (All Souls), 58-9.

[4] These allowances would excede the actual salary. According to the *Valor* ii. 287, the manciple of Magdalen received £2 per annum in salary but 8d per week or £1 14s 8d per annum in commons plus 16s per annum for livery.

from the medieval equivalent of the 'tuck shop', battels—that is, snacks beyond commons which were supplied from the buttery.[1] However, there are indications that the real financial attraction of the office was the supplying of victuals which seems to have been treated as a kind of 'farm', allowing a profit on the difference between the institutional allocations for commons and the actual costs of the victuals supplied.[2] Moreover, peculation was the occupational disorder of the manciple.[3] It is clear, therefore, that the office of manciple could be attractive financially. This is confirmed by an examination of the persons who were manciples in the fifteenth and sixteenth centuries.

Mancipleships were subject to a high degree of mobility, and, as we have noted above with the stationer Henry Millward, several could be held at the same time.[4] Obviously, the duties of the manciple made the position attractive to victuallers. At the turn of the sixteenth century two manciples, Thomas Peperell of Gloucester College and John Rodgers of Exeter, occur on the brewers' *rota*; in 1556 University College acquired the affluent white-baker John Lewis as its manciple.[5] Conversely a mancipleship could be a convenient spring-board into municipal life, and manciples seem to have been particularly adept at snatching up the widows of prosperous townsmen. This is what the manciple of All Souls, Richard Busterd, did when sometime between 1456 and 1466 he married Joan, the widow of William White, a prominent Oxford baker.[6] By July 1528 Richard Gunter, who occurs as manciple of Gloucester College in the 1524 subsidy, had married another Joan, the widow of William

---

[1] See Rashdall, *Universities* iii. 402.

[2] For example, according to the All Souls computus and expense rolls for 1445/6, the first extant year, the manciple John Page, was paid £111 13s for the commons of the fellows and battels of the bursars and the clerk of the works; by 1584/5 this amount was almost £500: Bodl. MS D.D. All Souls College c. 276, 284. Dr A. B. Emden informed me that this was still the practice at St Edmund Hall in this century.

[3] See the regulations in *Statuta*, 153, 182–3, 583–4, and in Reg. Canc. 1545–1661 fo 355 (undated but between 1545 and 1547). In 1581 the vice-chancellor, Arthur Yeldard, tried to stop what seems to have been an active market in mancipleships (as well as the offices of butler and cook), not unlike the earlier trafficking in bedellships. All new manciples were to swear that they had obtained their offices 'sine conventione vel emptione': OUA, Chancellor's Court Act Book 1578–82, Hyp. A/12, *sub* 31 March 1581.

[4] This argues against A. B. Cobban's conclusion that the high turnover of personnel at the King's Hall, Cambridge, necessarily entailed inexperience in the new staff: *The King's Hall within the University of Cambridge in the later Middle Ages* (Cambridge 1969), 237. For examples see Hammer, 'Town–gown relations', 239–44.

[5] *Reg. canc. 1498–1506*, 103–4, 129. Reg. Canc. 1545–1661, fo. 262. Lewis had been admitted a freeman as a baker in 1538: *Records of Oxford*, 156.

[6] Bodl. MS D.D. All Souls, c. 276–7; cf *Reg. canc. 1434–69* i. 242, 312–13. William White's will was proved in May 1456 and Joan Busterd's in March 1466: *Liber albus civitatis oxoniensis; abstract of wills, deeds and enrolments contained in the white book of the city of Oxford*, ed. W. P. Ellis and H. E. Salter (Oxford 1909), 76–7.

Reve, a brewer and member of the common council; at his death in 1553 Gunter was an alderman of Oxford and held numerous lands and tenements in Oxford and elsewhere including a manor at Whitnel, Somerset.[1]

Finally, a mancipleship seems to have been a welcome source of additional income to a number of Oxford's more prosperous citizenry such as the mercer George Mondy, who was manciple of St John's in 1567, and the tailor and draper John Philips, who became manciple at Lincoln College in 1571. Both men enjoyed solid careers as officers of town and guild, and in neither case did the assumption of privileged status represent a repudiation of municipal authority or guild control.[2]

Many manciples were little men about whom we know virtually nothing, but there was great potential in the office which linked the internal academic and external municipal economies. As an entrée into new markets, as a spring-board into municipal life and as a supplement to normal income, the office of manciple played a prominent role in the economic and social life of the town.

Unlike the manciples, cooks and barbers exercised skilled, manual occupations which made their post incompatible with casual occupation by townsmen and others. The cooks, who formed the largest single group in the 1524 subsidy (35), were often charged, as we have seen, with accompanying the manciple on his buying trips and with the care of the kitchen utensils, besides the preparation of food.[3] At a large foundation there was a head cook who had his various assistants and kitchen knaves. The duties of the barber were more varied. Besides shaving and providing medical attention for the inhabitants of the college or hall, the barber, from the Queen's College statutes (1340) onwards, was entrusted with the office of janitor or porter, and the All Souls statutes specified that he was to assist the other college servants at refections. In 1517 the Corpus statutes also charged the barber with the preparation or procurement of candles.[4] The salaries of the cooks and more particularly the barbers were considerably below those of the manciple, but the cooks at most colleges and halls were allowed to keep the drippings as perquisites of their office, a source of additional income.[5]

[1] Reg. Canc. 1527–43, fo 68[V]; cf OUA WPβ/B/34/b; PRO Probate 11/36.

[2] PRO E 179/162/330; Reg. Canc. 1545–1661, fo 92[V] (cf *Reg. Univ.* ed Clark i. 288); see below, pp. 85–6 ff.

[3] SCO i. pt 7 (All Souls), 58–9. In the halls the manciple was responsible for cleaning the mugs (*Statuta*, 584). At Magdalen the cook had the 'curam et onus custodiae' of all college dishes, *SCO* ii. pt 8 (Magdalen), 91.

[4] *SCO* i. pt 4 (Queen's), 31–2; pt 7 (All Souls), 58–9; ii. pt 10 (Corpus Christi), 39–40.

[5] The *Valor* shows the wages of the head cook varying between £1 and £1 6s 8d with only New College and Magdalen having highly paid ones receiving £3 6s 8d and £3 13s 4d

Occasionally the cook, as the more essential figure, also occupied the office of manciple, and like the manciples the cooks moved freely among institutions although this was not so generally the case with barbers.[1]

Cooks and barbers could also supplement their incomes by keeping ale-houses and selling wines, and links between the cooks and baking, both white and brown bread ('horse-loaves'), seem to have been common.[2] The steady advancement of the late sixteenth century alderman William Furness, a white-baker and former cook of Christ Church, illustrates the opportunities for social mobility open to members of the trade.[3] While some barbers may have baked horse-loaves, side occupations in general seem to have been less common for them, and the most important one was chandlery as indicated by the Corpus statutes.[4]

The barbers and the cooks were unique among the privileged persons in that both were organized into guilds under university supervision. The barbers' guild, which seems to have included all barbers, surgeons and makers of 'singing bread' in the town (and not just privileged persons), possessed the oldest surviving ordinances, confirmed by the university's chancellor in 1348, for any occupation in Oxford. In 1484 the ordinances were re-confirmed, and in 1499 the 'hurers' or cappers were incorporated into the guild.[5] Between 1505 and 1529 we can trace numerous admissions of barbers and the enforcement of guild regulations in the registers of the chancellor's court, but after about 1530 these references cease, and the association of the guild with the town seems to have become close, possibly under the influence of the large number of freemen barbers who had no academic connections.[6]

respectively, where they outranked even the manciple (*Valor* ii. 264, 287). The wages of college barbers varied between 8s (University) and £1 13s 4d (Merton and Magdalen): *Valor* ii. 228, 233, 287.

[1] Barber-manciples were also not unknown. See Reg. Chanc. 1527–43, fos 193, 198, 375, and for Robert Jerman, *Oxford City Documents*, 57. Unlike the manciples, the cooks moved from college to college as well as between colleges and halls, but they seldom or never held more than one position at a time.

[2] See the lists of vintners' and ale-house licenses in *Reg. Univ.* ed. Clark i. 323–7, and Reg. Canc. 1556–61, fo 164, for details on the activities of college cooks as bakers for their foundations.

[3] Generally these important cook-bakers seem to have given up their former trade and devoted themselves exclusively to baking as they progressed in the municipal hierarchy.

[4] As early as 1495/6 we find John Camney, a 'stager' or senior member of the barbers' guild occurring as a chandler: *Munimenta civitatis Oxonie*, ed. H. E. Salter (OHS lxxi 1917), 234; Bodl. MS D.D. Par. Oxf. St Peter in the East, a.1. fo 17.

[5] *Munimenta civitatis*, 109–17, 234–7; *Epist. acad.* ed. Anstey ii. 495.

[6] *Reg. canc. 1498–1506*; Reg. Canc. 1506–14; Reg. Canc. 1527–43, passim. The admission evidently included an oath to observe the privileges and customs of the university which

The cooks' guild seems to have been restricted to privileged persons. In 1463 it was functioning under the governance of two wardens, one elected by the collegiate cooks (*coci collegiati*) and the other by the aularian cooks (*coci aulares*).[1] Although a number of privileged cooks became freemen of the town in the mid-sixteenth century, the guild was combating this tendency by the 1570s, and the strong institutional connections of the privileged cooks kept the guild firmly under university control.[2] On 8 April 1534, when the town council appointed a committee to examine the ordinances to be made for the 'common wele' of the various crafts, we find the barbers and cappers, but not the cooks, on the list.[3] Cooks such as William Furness, referred to above, who established themselves in new occupations and who progressed in the municipal hierarchy, seem eventually to have abandoned their old occupation and its guild.

Besides these main groups of privileged persons, various sources, such as statutes, assessments and court records, supply us with details relating to a number of other privileged persons. For example, musicians from Magdalen and Christ Church occur regularly, often in contexts which lead into the larger community of Oxford. These might be only 'familiar' such as Richard Ball, 'singingman' of Magdalen, whose brother Edward and nephew Gregory were occupied as freemen glovers in Oxford until their deaths in 1571.[4] But they might also be more 'institutional'. The organist at Christ Church, Bartholomew Lant, became a freeman in 1546 and sat on the Common Council from 1549 to 1585 when he retired at the age of 72. In 1556 his good relations with the town government secured him a grant of fishing rights from the 'tayle of the myll to Osney mede poynt' for 13*s* 4*d*; two years later, in 1558, he was granted a university licence to sell wines.[5]

indicates that admission to the guild included admission as a privileged person: for example Reg. Chanc. 1506–14, fo 28 for 1507. In 1551 the town council sealed the ordinances of the guild, and in 1580 it authorized the barbers (with the bakers) to draw up new ordinances for confirmation; *Records of Oxford*, ed. Turner, 210, 409.

[1] *Reg. canc. 1434–69* ii. 118. Non-academic cooks maintained stalls in the market: *Munimenta civitatis*, 124, 192.

[2] Between the mid 1530s and mid 1560s perhaps as many as fifteen cooks became freemen, but they were always a small minority within the guild. In 1567 only three of the twenty-two academic cooks were freemen; in 1577 none. See OUA Chancellor's Court Act Book 1566–78, Hyp./A/8 fo 293.

[3] OCA A.5.5. fo 367^V; cf *Oxford Council Acts, 1583–1626*, ed. H. E. Salter (OHS lxxxvii 1928), xii. The persons mentioned indicate that the administrative year is 1533/4.

[4] Bodl. MS Wills Oxon. 185, fo 108; *Records of Oxford*, 267, 315 ('Edmund').

[5] *Reg. Univ.* ed. Clark ii. 13; PRO E. 179/162/330, 344; OCA, A.5.3. fo 225; *Records of Oxford*, 186, 201; *Council Acts*, 21; Reg. Canc. 1556–61, fo 173^V. Another 'singingman' of Christ Church, the later bedell, John Woodson, was also a 'fysher', taking an apprentice in 1570 (OCA A.4.1. fo 50^V; A.5.3. fo 128^V; *Reg. Univ.* ed. Clark i. 323).

From the early sixteenth century onwards we can trace members of the building trades such as masons, carpenters, slatters and plumbers who were on retainers from various colleges and were thus considered privileged, as were the lesser college employees such as gardeners and grooms.[1] One additional group which deserves mention is that of the university carriers. Although 'alle common caryers' serving the university were considered privileged by the mid-fifteenth century at the latest, the first surviving licence is a *plenam vehendi potestatem* granted by congregation in 1492 to the northern carrier (*ad partes aquilonares*).[2] In 1509 a monopoly to London was also established by congregation. Moreover, New College maintained its own carrier to ensure regular communications with its 'daughter' foundation at Winchester.[3]

Finally, the extensive properties of the colleges created a group of administrators such as rent collectors, stewards and bailiffs, many of whom had local connections.[4] As early as 1498, Edward Mortimer, chamberlain of the city in 1502/03, occurs as a rent collector for Magdalen,[5] but the office seems to have acquired an enhanced significance in the 1570s and 1580s. Of the seven such persons assessed by the university for the subsidy in 1577, four, the rent collectors Richard Hanson (BNC), Giles Swete (St John's), John Wayte (Corpus) and the *clericus computi* or steward of Corpus, Morris Vaughan, are all familiar from town sources as tradesmen and local officials.[6] And these men, particularly Wayte and Swete, have an additional interest for us because they lead us to a final topic, that of changes in the legal status of Oxford residents.

The foregoing discussion has provided several examples of privileged persons becoming freemen of the town and of freemen acquiring privileged status, but an examination of this topic must begin rather with the durable institution of scholars' servants (*servientes scolarium*).

The *reformatio pacis* of 1290 had provided that all servants (*familiae et servientes*) of scholars (*cleric[orum]*), as well as others wearing academic livery (*qui sunt de robis ipsorum clericorum*) were to enjoy

---

[1] See, for example, the 1556 contract of the Oxford plumber, Robert Munson, with All Souls: Reg. Canc. 1545–1661, fo 92; *Reg. Univ.* ed. Clark i. 288. Eustace Hore, gardener of New College was elected a freeman and 'hearde and keeper' of Portmeadow in 1586: OCA A.5.3. fo 22ᵛ; *Council Acts*, 25.   [2] *Epist. acad.* ed. Anstey, ii. 611.

[3] *Reg. Univ.* ed. Clark i. 315. Thomas Angell, who occurs as New College's carrier in 1581, is designated as the college's carrier to Winchester in the assessment of 1600 see: PRO E. 179/163/393.

[4] The *Valor* also shows that collection of rents in Oxford was often done by college fellows, for example at Merton, University, All Souls, Lincoln and Oriel: *Valor* ii. 224, 232, 234, 239, 242.

[5] *Reg. canc. 1498-1506*, 32, 157.   [6] PRO E. 179/162/336, 340.

the privileges of the university, but the regularization of the status of personal servants was not finally achieved until the fifteenth century beginning with the statutes of Henry V in 1420.[1] Then, in January 1459, convocation authorized the chancellor and the bishop of Exeter to look more closely into the matter of privileged status, an investigation which was concluded in the next month with the indenture quoted at the beginning of the previous section, an agreement confirmed three days later by letters patent.[2] This indenture established the criteria by which a legitimate scholar's servant might claim his privileged status. He must be a 'dailly continuell servaunt' and receive a wage or livery to the amount of 6s 8d computed on a yearly basis. Finally, 'fraude or malengyne' must be absent from the relationship.

From 1461 onwards enrolments of scholars' servants occur regularly in the chancellors' registers, often incorporating the elements specified in the indenture, and in the 1460s a fixed procedure emerged for admission by the chancellor (or his deputy) to privileged status including an oath to the university. Indeed, the terms of the indenture (including the level of the salary!) and the forms of admission persisted well into the sixteenth century, and only ended with the end of the institution itself.[3] The chancellor's register from the 1460s contains 35 enrolments or acknowledgements of 32 different scholars' servants, 23 of them in the four years from 1466 to 1469. When the chancellor's registers resume in 1498, the first two contain 235 enrolments up to 1515 with as many as 23 in 1504 alone. The first years of the next register from 1527 to 1529 also contain substantial numbers of enrolments but they drop off rapidly in the 1530s.[4]

In 1524 fourteen liveried servants (servientes de roba), including two laundresses, were assessed for the subsidy.[5] These included such prosperous men as Robert Huckvall (£10), who occurs as town clerk in the following year, and the tailor, James Collinson (£13), a former

---

[1] Munimenta academica, i. 52; Statuta, 226-7.

[2] The Register of Congregation, 1448-1463, ed. W. A. Pantin and W. T. Mitchell (OHS new ser. xxii 1972), 336-7; Mediaeval Archives i. 243-7; cf. Reg. canc. 1434-1469 i. xxxi-xxxiii.

[3] Four enrolments before 1461 are preserved, but the forms vary. In late 1461 Thomas Sharpe was certified as a scholar's servant 'secundum exigenciam composicionis nuper facte inter universitatem et villanos [sic] Oxonie': ibid. ii. 67. In December 1527 there is a reference to the indenture of 1459; Reg. Canc. 1527-43, fo 261, and in October 1552, after nearly a century of inflation, a servant was still hired according to form for 6s 8d yearly 'aut unam robam': Reg. Canc. 1545-1661, fo 81.

[4] The last is in 1537. The quality of the register deteriorates in the 1530s, but the total of seven admissions between 1552 and 1563 recorded in the next register shows that this is not a sufficient explanation.

[5] Thorold Rogers thought that they were 'persons engaged as makers of academical costume' (Oxford City Documents, 54).

master of the guild who may also have become a bedell later in the decade.[1] In fact a careful investigation of all the persons admitted as scholars' servants will show that a large number of them, perhaps a majority, could not have been legitimate servants, since they can be shown to have exercised other trades in the community. In essence then the position of scholar's servant seems commonly to have been a convenient fiction by which a townsman or other person could gain privileged status, in order, for example, to practice a trade free of guild restrictions or to enjoy the jurisdiction of the chancellor's court.[2] As such it was opposed by the town government. In December 1527 a by-law was enacted forbidding anyone of the bailiff's rank or above from becoming either a scholar's servant taking 'yerly wages [or] lyverry' or a rent collector for an 'abby' or college on pain of a severe fine.[3] This ordinance, with its restrictions, would not of itself have been sufficient to end the practice, but the increasing unattractiveness of privileged status during the troubles of the 'thirties', which we shall examine shortly, seems to have effected what legal measures failed to do. In the later sixteenth century townsmen wishing to acquire privileged status for one reason or another seem to have turned rather to the other alternative named in the ordinance of 1527, that of the socially more restricted collegiate rent collector.

Naturally this fluidity of legal status, which operated in both directions, was not without its complications. In the later sixteenth century two lists were drawn up by the town in connection with disputes before the privy council.[4] They sought to show that priviledged persons must be freemen of the town in order to carry on a trade, and to this end they listed a number of examples reaching back to the early part of the century. Essentially they only confirm an impression which we have already derived piecemeal from other primary sources, that privileged persons, particularly in the earlier sixteenth century, were often made free and became prominent in municipal life. For example the lists contain the names of six early

[1] See *Records of Oxford*, 31; OCA A.5.3. fos 365^{v}–70 (and see also G. Pollard, 'The medieval town clerks of Oxford', *Oxoniensia* xxxi (1966), 43–76, which goes to 1522/6), Reg. Canc. 1506–14, fo 105; Bodl. MS Morrell 9, fo 12; for Collinson's will see Reg. Canc. 1545–1661, fos 57$^{\text{r–v}}$.

[2] Between 1498 and 1537 I have identified 105 persons practising 37 different trades who were enrolled or occur as scholars' servants. The largest single group is that of the tailors (19). In the early sixteenth century 21 servants are identified as coming from outside Oxford, mainly from the surrounding countryside. The position of laundress seems to have been the female counterpart to the male scholar's servant. For examples, see below in the sections on industrial organization and the chancellor's court.

[3] *Records of Oxford*, 57. Interestingly, of the members of the town council who passed the act, two aldermen, four other members of the mayor's council, two common councillors and two other town officials had all been scholars' servants.

[4] Edited in Hammer, 'Town and gown in Tudor Oxford', 79–84; cf p. 76 n. 3.

sixteenth-century aldermen, and three from later in the century.[1] But like the account of the scholars' servants, these lists also raise the question of double legal status.

In his Ford's lectures on medieval Oxford, Dr H. E. Salter stated that it was impossible for a person to be both a freeman and a privileged person.[2] While it is true that there are two relatively late university statutes to this effect (dating from 1565 and 1576), which were later incorporated into the Laudian code (1636), there is no evidence that they were enforced, and there was never at any time a municipal by-law which forbade *all* freemen from acquiring *any* privileged status.[3] Rather the problems seem to have centred on the excessive use of rival franchises; only for the bedells is there consistent evidence that the university forbade dual status.[4] For the rest, neither town nor gown seems to have been greatly concerned. In October 1591 Randall Potter, a former chamberlain, was excused 'uppon his earnest peticion' from attendance at the town council 'by reason of his office in Christ Church'.[5] Peaceful accommodation of this sort seems to have characterized the relations between the two communities—in sharp contrast to the constitutional inflexibility which we must now examine.

POLITICS AND PRIVILEGE

The Medieval Growth of University Privilege

In the roughly one-hundred and fifty years from the early thirteenth to the mid-fourteenth century the university, as a body, acquired an impressive number of privileges, primarily from the crown, of which a considerable number touched on its relations with the town.[6]

---

[1] The legendary John Bereford, mayor of Oxford during the St Scholastica Day riot of 1355, seems to have followed this route: see 'Poems relating to the riot between town and gown on St Scholastica's day and two following days', ed. H. Furneaux, in *Collectanea* iii. 171. Occasionally, we have direct information on motivation. For example, the 'singingman' John Woodson, became a freeman in 1566 to gain access to municipal common pasture and waters: see the depositions of Richard Edges on 23 June 1580 and of John Wayte and Thomas Smith on 21 and 22 June for details, OUA Chancellor's Court Depositions, 1578–84, Hyp/B/2 under name and date.

[2] H. E. Salter, *Medieval Oxford* (OHS c 1936), 55.

[3] Reg. Cong. 1564–82, fo 12^V (cf *Statuta*, 393), 207^V; *Laudian Code*, esp. 27–8.

[4] The two rent collectors John Wayte and Giles Swete were disenfranchised in 1578 and 1583 respectively, not for becoming privileged persons, but, rather, for removing cases from the town courts to the university: *Records of Oxford*, 397; *Council Acts* 5. John Broke, esquire bedell of law, for example, became a freeman and a brewer in October 1551 and was expelled from his bedellship in the following September. Evidently he was allowed to serve out the administrative year: OCA A.5.3. fo 231; Reg. Cong. 1535–63, fo 133; cf *Reg. Univ.* ed. Clark i. 258.   [5] *Council Acts*, 67.

[6] The most complete (though not always reliable) account is found in P. Kibre, *Scholarly Privileges in the Middle Ages* (Cambridge Mass. 1962). See also J. F. Willard, *The*

Under Henry III and the three Edwards several important urban franchises were gradually delegated by the king to the university, franchises which normally would be or had been the concern of borough government alone. By this process the crown hoped to secure an equitable situation for a large and influential body which was effectively excluded from participation in local political life. The main areas affected were such daily concerns as housing, provisioning, public safety and debt jurisdiction, and, although the situation appears at first sight to have been highly unusual, the theory was the same as in other royal boroughs. The difference was that public authority in Oxford, rather than being the monopoly of one body (normally the guild merchant) was divided between two sets of royal officers, those of the borough and those of the university.[1]

The *locus classicus* of this development is the great charter of 27 June 1355, issued after the famous riot beginning on St Scholastica's Day (10 February) in that year.[2] By this charter the chancellor acquired sole custody of such central activities as the assizes of bread, ale and wine and the assay of weights and measures. To be sure, this was not done without preparation. For example as early as 1248 the chancellor and proctors or their deputies had acquired the right to attend the assize of bread and ale (*temptacio panis et cervisie*) conducted by municipal officers, and in 1324 attendance was converted by letters patent into joint custody.[3] But although the way had been prepared and although the bailiffs received some financial compensation for this and other losses to their income against the fee-farm, the real impact on the borough, both politically and financially, was clearly large as is evidenced by the running disputes which followed each redelegation of franchise jurisdiction.[4] Protection

Royal Authority and the Early English Universities (Philadelphia 1902). Two early sixteenth-century summaries of university privileges, one in Latin, the other in English, provide an excellent overview *Mediaeval Archives* i. 352-70. Finally, the chapter in Rashdall on 'The university and the town' should be consulted: Rashdall, *Universities*, iii. 79-113.

[1] On local officials as royal agents see E. T. Meyer's chapter, 'Boroughs' in J. F. Willard, W. A. Morris and W. H. Dunham (eds), *The English Government at Work, 1327-1336* (3 vols Cambridge Mass. 1950) iii. 105-41, and also C. R. Young, *The English Borough and Royal Administration, 1130-1307* (Durham N.C. 1961).

[2] A fine description of these events is given in W. A. Pantin, *Oxford Life in Oxford Archives* (Oxford 1972), 99-104. The relevant documents are printed in *Mediaeval Archives* i. 148-61, and in *Royal Letters Addressed to Oxford*, ed. O. Ogle (Oxford 1892), 62-4. A diminished group of privileges was restored to the town on 26 July 1355.

[3] *Mediaeval Archives* i. 19-21, 107-8. The arrangements, especially for the assay, were disputed by the town, but matters were settled by a composition in 1348: ibid. 143-6. In 1356 the university's privileges were extended to include the Northgate hundred as well: ibid. 161-6.

[4] See the remarks in M. D. Lobel, 'Some aspects of the crown's influence on the development of the borough of Oxford up to 1307', *Beiträge zur Wirtschafts- und Sozialgeschichte: Festschrift für Hektor Ammann* (Wiesbaden 1965), 65-83.

for the academic community had been secured at the cost of local constitutional stability even though the effects of this were clearly not so catastrophic or wide-ranging as has often been supposed.

On the whole the later fourteenth and fifteenth centuries saw little constitutional change in Oxford.[1] However, the early sixteenth century seems to have been a period of renewed municipal vigour, coinciding with (possibly caused by) the ineffective exercise of academic privilege.

In the midst of their troubles in 1514, the university made its first approaches to a new patron, their diocesan, the bishop of Lincoln, Thomas Wolsey.[2] Nine years later this relationship was crowned by a new royal charter of privileges obtained by Wolsey, the last of the major grants to the university in the medieval tradition.

Although the charter and the accompanying confirmation of older privileges in the form of letters patent are dated 1 April 1523, there is some confusion as to the actual date of their reception in Oxford; in fact Wolsey seems to have withheld the charter for five years.[3] His reasons for doing this are not entirely clear; possibly, he wished to combine the formal presentation of the charter with the promulgation of a reformed set of statutes, a much more difficult problem which was not solved until more than a century later by Laud.[4] In any case on 14 July 1528 John Higden, dean of Wolsey's new foundation, Cardinal College, appeared before congregation, and the

[1] The main exception to this was the grant of 1406 which gave the chancellor power to appoint a lay steward to try privileged persons accused of treason, insurrection, felony or mayhem in Oxfordshire and Berkshire: *Mediaeval Archives* i. 231-4.

[2] Evidently university officials were unsure of the extent of their privileges due to the poor order of the archives, see Bodl. MS 282, fos 1, 2, 3[V]. This was clearly the occasion for the drafting of the summaries mentioned above in n. 6 p. 56. The letter thanking Wolsey for defending university privileges against the town is dated 26 June 1514: ibid. fo 17[V].

[3] *L & P Henry VIII* iii pt 2, 2925-6. The text is printed in *Mediaeval Archives* i. 255-72. Anthony Wood (*History and Antiquities* ii. 23) thought that it was taken directly to Oxford, and he was followed by C. E. Mallet (*A History of the University of Oxford* (3 vols 1924-7) i. 437, note 2) who relied upon documents misdated by Turner (*Records of Oxford*, 35-41). H. C. Maxwell Lyte, however, gave a proper account: *A History of the University of Oxford: from the earliest times to the year 1530* (1886), 428-9. In early 1528 the university wrote to both Wolsey and John Longland requesting that their privileges— which, they understood, had been confirmed—be returned so that they could ward off attacks on their authority by the town: Bodl. MS 282, fos 87[V], 88. Two years earlier 'ad mandatum dicti reverendissimi cardinalis' congregation had voted to surrender up to Wolsey two papal charters 'et tertium [munimentum] quo dominus rex Hen. viii eandem universitatem [sic] donavit', but since no details are provided, it is impossible to say whether this is the 1510 confirmation of privileges or one of the 1523 documents; probably the former, however: Reg. Cong. 1518-35, fo 155.

[4] Reform of the statutes was a continuing concern in this period. There are indications that Wolsey was planning to visit Oxford during Lent of 1527, and the statutes seem to have been part of the agenda: Bodl. MS 282, fos 76[V]-77. See the letter from Longland to Wolsey in *L & P Henry, VIII* iv. pt 3, 5189, dated there to 20 January 1529.

scribe read out the provisions of the new charter which were much more extensive than the university had dared to hope (*multo maiora et ampliora . . . quam ipsa academia . . . optare sit ausa*).[1] The document was then conveyed (significantly), not to the university archives, but to Cardinal College for safekeeping.

The terms of 'Wolsey's charter' have generated almost as much heat among modern historians as they did among contemporaries.[2] However, a close examination of the text itself shows that the charter, for all its legal verbosity, was in fact a modest document. First, with regard to such matters as the chancellor being a justice of the peace, the charter merely codified customs of long-standing and clarified controversial points. As we shall see the same is true of the clauses regulating the commercial rights of privileged persons and the university's authority over guilds.[3] Secondly, it is obvious that a privilege such as prohibition of appeal from the university would work as much against scholars as against townsmen.[4] Thirdly, and most important, a large number of privileges seem designed not so much to increase the university's powers *per se* as its income. Indeed the Crown was prepared to secure these new revenues at its own expense by conferring forfeitures of felons' goods, deodand and treasure-trove on the university. Finally, the fact that a privilege was granted was no guarantee that it would be put into effect. The university gaol for example existed only on paper. In sum the content of Wolsey's charter hardly bears comparison with an important document such as the grant of 1355. It seems rather to have aimed at the regularization and confirmation of established custom and the acquisition of new sources of income. Moreover, its success even here is questionable, for the charter at first brought more trouble than benefit to the university.

The municipal authorities seized upon the charter as an occasion for attacking the entire fabric of university privilege which had been built up during the preceding three centuries.[5] This became easier as Wolsey's position grew less secure. In May 1529 the town council

---

[1] Reg. Cong. 1518-35, fo 200. The wording of the entry implies that the charter of 1523 had not been promulgated formally before this. Higdon also returned the 'privilegia antiqua' which probably refers to the surrender of 1526, above (n. 3, p. 88).

[2] Mallet, for example, saw the charter as primarily directed against the town, raising 'the authority of the Chancellor and his officials to a height not touched before': *History of the University* i. 436-7.

[3] See *Reg. canc. 1434-69* i. pp. xxiii-xxv. Moreover, a provision such as the exclusion of royal purveyors with their rights of pre-emption in the market has a distinctly *ad hoc* aspect, being tied to the completion of Cardinal College.

[4] In 1537 the principal of Peckwater Inn declared that any statute preventing appeal contrary to common law was 'not worth a eere': Reg. Canc. 1527-43, fo 392[V].

[5] See *Records of Oxford*, 35-113 passim; Bodl. MS 282, fo 94[V].

rejected Wolsey's request that the dispute be submitted to the arbitration of the university's high steward, Sir Thomas More, and the first session of the 'reformation parliament' in 1529, following Wolsey's indictment for *praemunire* in October, saw the attempted introduction of a private bill on behalf of the mayor and 'corporation' of Oxford to protect them against the jurisdiction of the university which had been made 'more arbitrary' by Wolsey's charter.[1] In this new situation of heightened insecurity the real beneficiary of Wolsey's charter was to be neither the university, nor even the town, but rather the increasingly vociferous third party in local affairs, the crown.

Cromwellian Reform

The local crisis of town and gown in Oxford coincided neatly with a rather larger crisis, that of the king's 'great matter'. This latter problem indirectly provided the impetus towards the solution of the former. With Wolsey removed from the scene, the university turned again of necessity to its ageing chancellor, the scholarly archbishop of Canterbury, William Warham, who for some years had been forced into the background by Wolsey's vigorous university policies. On 3 February 1530 Warham wrote to the university expressing his joy at not having resigned his office as he had often thought of doing; he then requested a unanimous opinion from the university on the validity of Henry's marriage.[2] Shortly thereafter the king himself wrote to the university, but the matter did not proceed smoothly for the 'youth' of the university, the artists, were delaying a (to the king) satisfactory solution. This, in Henry's words, would 'stir up a hornets' nest' (*irritare crabrones*) before it was finally settled. After centuries of royal benevolence the university had been found wanting when asked to perform a simple favour. If the university was to set a satisfactory course in the storms and stresses of the new decade, a new helmsman was wanted. This person was Thomas Cromwell, a man already well acquainted with Oxford from his days in Wolsey's service, and for him the local tensions in Oxford proved to be the means to establish effective control.[3]

In Oxford, as in the nation, the years 1530 and 1531 were the 'years without policy', but this changed radically in 1532 with

[1] *Records of Oxford*, 63–4; Bodl. MS 282, fo 93. For the bill see *L & P Henry VIII* iv pt 3, 6046 (text in *Records of Oxford*, 37–41, where it is incorrectly dated to 1523). Cf S. E. Lehmberg, *The Reformation Parliament, 1529–1536* (Cambridge 1970), 96.

[2] For this and the following: Bodl. MS 282, fos 100, 104–6ᵛ.

[3] For Cromwell's role in the foundation of Cardinal College see G. R. Elton, *The Tudor Revolution in Government; administrative changes in the reign of Henry VIII* (Cambridge 1953), 86, 88–9.

Cromwell's entry into the inner circle of the king's council, a body which had already taken some interest in Oxford affairs.[1] Cromwell set out to establish control over the local situation in Oxford by the time-honoured device of the submission of royal privileges by both town and university. By the end of September 1532 both bodies had submitted all their disputes to the king's award, and by the end of February 1533, after some second thoughts, both had also submitted their charters.[2] The disputes between town and gown arising from Wolsey's charter had provided Cromwell with the means to strip the university of its defences—its muniments.

Moreover, Cromwell was in a position to encourage the town on a selective basis against the university in order to remind the latter of its vulnerability. And this was the easier since the 1530s saw the rise of a 'Cromwellian' party in local government, evidently headed by an old associate of John London, Alderman William Frere, who had also been involved in the foundation of Cardinal College.[3] Following the submission of the charters, Cromwell revived the notion of transferring the night-watch from the university to the town, but a more significant development centred on the market franchises. In December 1533 the commissary had discommoned the mayor, aldermen and twenty other burgesses for their inspection and marketing of butchers' weights.[4] The town sent a bill of complaint to London, and found strong support with Cromwell. Indeed, not only was the university to reinstate the discommoned townsmen, but it was also to forbid scholars to engage in trade as did freemen (*more civium*) without municipal consent, a clear

[1] The phrase is Elton's; see his *England under the Tudors* (1955), 122-6. Bodl. MS 282, fo 93.

[2] See *L & P Henry VIII* v. 1330, 1332, 1343; *Records of Oxford*, 111. Convocation had adopted 'contingency plans' on this matter in January of either 1531 or 1532: Bodl. MS 282, fo 122ᵛ; there is no entry in Reg. Cong. 1518-35. In January 1533 the town and the university had tried without success to prevent submission of their charters by a proposal for local negotiations: *L & P Henry VIII* vi. 20, 21. The university evidently submitted before the town did: ibid. 183.

[3] The other two key men were Aldermen John Pye and William Banister, both former yeomen of the guard, who were on crown retainers in this period; see *L & P Henry VIII* xiii pt 1, 1342; Elton, *Tudor Revolution*, 82; OUA WPβ/B/34/b. William Frere had been enrolled as a scholar's servant to John London in 1512: Reg. Chanc. 1506-14, fo 158. He collected rents for St Frideswide's and Cardinal College in 1525 and helped to arrange the takeover of Balliol property for building of Cardinal College in 1529: A. Wood, *Survey of the Antiquities of the City of Oxford*, ed. A. Clark (3 vols OHS xv, xvii, xxxvii 1889-99) iii. 29; ed. H. E. Salter (OHS lxiv 1913), 96-7. A letter from Frere to Cromwell in 1535 survives: PRO SP 1/98, fos 170-1ᵛ; *L & P Henry VIII* ix. 720. All three were active in the enforcement of the reformation and in the dissolution later in the decade in association with Frere's former 'master' John London; see for example *L & P Henry VIII* viii. 967; ix. 720; x. 647, 903; xiii. pt 1, 1335; xiii. pt 2, 775; cf Elton, *Policy and Police*, 93-100.

[4] *L & P Henry VIII*, vi. 457; vii. 890; cf. Bodl. MS 282, fo 55ᵛ (1522). *Records of Oxford*, 117-18. 'Discommoning' was an academic trade boycott.

contradiction, as the university pointed out, of their privileges.[1] Not since the thirteenth century had the university suffered such a rebuke, and their helplessness was revealed.[2]

However, the university soon had an opportunity to redeem itself. In late May 1534 Henry again made a request to the university, this time to deliver an opinion on the powers of the bishop of Rome in England. Now, with the privileges in London, the town pressing hard, and the unsympathetic Cromwell in charge, the university knew its duty; the bishop of Rome had no powers in England beyond those of any foreign bishop, that is, in effect, none.[3] Cromwell's policy had been vindicated. In two years he had converted the university into a willing agent: he had fashioned the town–gown disputes of the past into an instrument of policy. In doing so he had also prepared the way for such vital academic reforms as the visitation of 1535.

What had happened to the disputed privileges in the meantime? Throughout the 1530s Cromwell seems to have retained them in order to preserve the leverage afforded by the (consequently) unstable situation. However, with Cromwell's fall, the privy council, which had been a participant in these events since the late 1520s, emerged from its enforced tutelage as a body willing and able to bring about a final settlement.[4] In early 1541 it directed a letter to the town ordering it to send an authorized person next term to hear council's decree on the dispute with the university.[5] The town appointed a special committee headed by their high steward, Charles Brandon, the duke of Suffolk, but apparently matters were again delayed, for it was not until December 1542 that the town posted a bond to abide by the award rendered by a select committee of the council.[6] This committee included both the town's high steward, Brandon, and the newly elected (7 November) high steward of the

[1] *Records of Oxford*, 117-18; *L & P Henry VIII*, vii. 617, 619. In early 1534 Cromwell wrote to the university that 'the King is informed of your usurpations and ungentle demeanor towards the inhabitants of Oxford, at which I cannot but marvel, ye being men of learning': *L & P Henry VIII*, vii. 618.

[2] In 1262 the university had incurred the royal wrath by excommunicating the bailiffs who had arrested some clerks accused of mayhem: *Cal. Cl. Rolls. 1261-64*, 106-7.

[3] Bodl. MS 282, fos 127ᵛ, 128; *Statuta*, 335-7.

[4] The university seems to have received a temporary commission in 1533 to exercise its 'old', i.e. pre-Wolseian, privileges until a final settlement: *L & P Henry VIII* vi. 266, 274; there seems to be an undated copy in the University Archives: WPβ/B/20. See above, n. 1, p. 91.

[5] *L & P Henry VIII* xvi. 445.

[6] *Records of Oxford*, 161, 168. The office of high steward of the town was itself, evidently, a Cromwellian innovation, designed to provide a patron-watchdog counterpart to the chancellor and high steward of the university. Brandon seems to have been the first high steward, and the earliest reference is in October 1535 in William Frere's letter to Cromwell referred to in n. 3, p. 91 (the calendar in *L & P Henry VIII* omits 'Hyy' from the title).

university, John Russell, who had also just become the lord privy seal.[1] Hence the corporate role of the privy council was as much a natural outgrowth of the individual roles of its personnel as it was a function of administrative change.

On 23 May 1543 the mayor and commissary appeared before council, and as a sign of the times Cromwell's old partisan William Frere was berated as 'a great stirrer of this garboil'; he was to attend on council until dismissed, and in the meantime a decree based upon the charter of 1355 was drafted and approved.[2] The university was restored to these 'traditional' privileges until the town could disprove them by law, but like the commission of 1533 this decree could only have been intended as an interim measure. Before a final solution could be reached, something would have to be done about the prime source of contention, Wolsey's charter.[3] At this point Henry himself finally intervened. In July 1543 he restored and confirmed to the university *all* the privileges granted by him and his predecessors, but in the same month the university's commissary, William Tresham, posted a £1,000 bond that the university would produce an obligation not to draw any benefit from Wolsey's charter.[4] Thus the contentious charter became a dead letter, and Henry was spared the embarrassment of repeal. Edward VI and Mary then simply omitted it from their confirmations of university privileges in 1547 and 1555 respectively.[5] However, in July 1566 shortly before Elizabeth's first visit to Oxford, the university scribe conveniently discovered the exemplar of the charter in the hanaper of the chancery in London. The university petitioned for its confirmation along with the other privileges. This was done in January 1567, and in 1571 the charter was included in parliament's act of incorporation for the university.[6] After almost a quarter of a century the charter had returned, and not without some consequences for the town as we shall see presently.

[1] See Bodl. MS 282, fo 129[V].

[2] *APC 1542-47*, 137; *L & P Henry VIII* xviii. pt 1, 583, 594.

[3] The university may even have considered a petition to the king and parliament for repeal; OUA WPβ/B/18; *Records of Oxford*, 170-2, but this seems to have been only a draft even though from Turner onwards it has been considered as equivalent to an actual act of repeal: ibid. xi.

[4] For the charter see *L & P Henry VIII* xviii. pt 1, 538, which is dated 10 July, while the copy in the university archives, WPβ/L/5/a, is dated 16 July. The bond is printed in *Records of Oxford*, 172, from Twyne. The copy in the university archives is WPβ/B/8. The wording of the bond precludes the possibility that the charter had been repealed or revoked, and the register of congregation for 1543 merely records that, 'Hic annus memorabilis erat [pro] privilegiorum nostrorum restitutione': Reg. Cong. 1535–63, fo 97.

[5] *Mediaeval Archives*, i. 272-3.

[6] Reg. Cong. 1564–82, fo 31[V]; *Calendar of the Manuscripts of the . . . Marquis of Salisbury* (24 vols Historical Manuscripts Commission 1883–1976) i. 339; *Mediaeval Archives*, 273-4.

In 1543 Henry had intervened at the last minute to bring about a settlement, but the negotiations over the charter after Cromwell's fall nevertheless mark the final step in the emergence of the privy council as a body ready and able to deal with town–gown disputes on a regular basis.[1] Particularly from the 1570s onwards the council was obliged to intervene repeatedly in local affairs, and on the whole its decisions seem to have been fair, even conciliatory.[2] In 1578 when the university claimed jurisdiction, under dubious circumstances, of a case pending in the mayor's court, it was not only scolded by its chancellor, Leicester, but also received a letter from the council warning it to be careful, or 'they maie not loke for that favor at their Lordships' hands that by their good dealings otherwise they might deserve'.[3] In 1596 when the town had a commission of oyer and terminer to try a townsman accused of murdering a privileged person, the council wrote saying that, though justice might be served, 'nevertheless because in lyke cases as ys not unknowne unto us how matters are often carried with favour' the case should rather go before the justices of the assize.[4]

For the first time both corporations had a standing body which could anticipate problems and arbitrate differences. Moreover, the prestige and composition of the privy council (as in 1543) gave both parties confidence in its decisions, a confidence which was not abused. The medieval pattern of sporadic, direct intervention by the sovereign in reaction to crisis (for example a riot), with all its undesirable side-effects, had yielded here, as elsewhere, to regular institutional supervision. As Wolsey's charter marked the end of one tradition of town–gown relations, so the events of the 1530s, dominated by Thomas Cromwell, marked the beginning of a new era, an era when the constitutional and political relations between borough and university were directly conditioned by their respective relations with the crown.

THE UNIVERSITY AND URBAN SOCIETY

The University and Industrial Organization

We have seen above that the local economy was rather simple with no particular specialization in production as opposed to distribution.

[1] Only three years later the privy council was again involved in local affairs: APC 1542-7, 375-6, 521-2; L & P Henry VIII xxi. pt 1, 573, 1472.
[2] Since the university's legal position was clearly the stronger one, it generally got the better of the settlements. See, for example, the award of May 1575: APC 1571-75, 376-86; Records of Oxford, 365-74.
[3] Ibid. 380-1, 396-7; APC 1577-78, 264-5.
[4] APC 1595-96, 350-1.

On the other hand, industrial organization was extremely complex. Oxford had guilds which were royal, municipal, mercantile, industrial, masters', journeymen's, amalgamated and particular—in short all the forms found elsewhere in Tudor England.[1] In addition, the presence of the university prompted the growth of two other types of guild structures. The first were the guilds built essentially around privileged persons, those of the cooks and of the barbers and cappers which we have already discussed. The second were the guilds composed of persons not necessarily privileged but whose activities were none the less regulated by the university. These were the two (later three) victualling guilds of the brewers and bakers (white and brown) and the craft guilds of the tailors and (briefly) the skinners.

The university's control of the brewers' and bakers' guilds was clearly a consequence of its exclusive assize jurisdiction acquired in 1355. At least, this is the context in which we first encounter a form of internal organization. In 1434 both the brewers and the bakers were sworn to certain ordinances before the commissary, and at the same time there appear *scrutatores*, that is, officers charged with supervision.[2] Although this does not prove the existence of guilds, the evidence from the 1450s and 1460s indicates that corporate bodies of some sort existed by then, and probably earlier. Apparently by the middle third of the fifteenth century bodies of brewers and bakers were formed, either spontaneously or from without, to supervise the activities of their members, and in this capacity they acted as administrative organs of the university just as they did for borough governments elsewhere.[3]

Early sixteenth-century evidence allows us to describe these groups more precisely. For example in 1513 we find the brewers, headed by a master and two wardens, holding their own 'courte' or meeting to enact new regulations, regulations which then received the commissary's seal and which were enrolled in the chancellor's register 'at the specyall request and desyre off all the seyd bruerese'.[4]

---

[1] There is a good survey of guild history with bibliography in Sylvia Thrupp's contribution to M. M. Postan, E. E. Rich and E. Miller (eds), *The Cambridge Economic History of Europe* iii (Cambridge 1963), 230–80, 624–34. Two studies of special interest for our topic are: E. F. Meyer, 'The English craft guilds and borough governments of the later middle ages', in *The University of Colorado Studies* xvi/xvii (1929/30), 323–78, 350–426, and D. M. Palliser, 'The trade gilds of Tudor York' in P. Clark and P. Slack (eds), *Crisis and Order in English Towns, 1500–1700* (1972), 86–116.

[2] *Reg. canc. 1434–69* i. 8–10; cf 51 (1439).

[3] Wardens—always guild officers in these documents—occur for the brewers in 1462: ibid. ii. 93. The bakers comprised an 'artificium' by 1451 and had a common fund by 1462: ibid. i. 236; ii. 93. See Meyer, 'English craft gilds', esp. xvii. 418. An important aspect of the regulation of the brewers was maintenance of a 'rota' or fixed rotation schedule for brewing in a continuous cycle in order to ensure a steady supply of ale.

[4] Reg. Canc. 1506–14, fos 197^V–8; cf *Records of Oxford*, 10.

In May 1524 the brewers' ordinances, sealed by the chancellor in 1521, were ratified by the vice chancellor (commissary), proctors and congregation.[1] Similarly, the relations between the bakers and the university were close. New bakers were admitted to the guild in the presence of the chancellor (*coram cancellario*) as was George Cokerel in August 1499.[2] He was presented to all the bakers (*omn[es] pistor[es]*) by a (the?) warden of the guild and was sworn to obey the master and all the regulations of the craft (*omnia statuta et ordinaciones artificii*). He then paid an entry fee and was admitted both to the occupation and to the guild (*inter pistores et in societatem seu fraternitatem*) by the commissary. Even though during the next few years the bakers' guild split into two distinct bodies, composed respectively of white- and brown-bakers with separate officers, the university's authority over them remained as before.[3] Therefore by the mid-1520s the control of the university over both the important victualling trades was still uncontested.

We can fix a precise date for the affiliation between the university and the tailors' guild, as we cannot for the brewers and bakers. Although the tailors' craft was an object of academical legislation as early as the mid-fourteenth century, the origins of the guild seem to be independent of the university, possibly in the form of a confraternity dedicated to St John the Baptist, the patron saint of tailors.[4] However in March 1491 at the petition of the master and *procuratores* of the guild, a formal alliance between the tailors and the university was established. This was directed against suburban tailors outside the town's jurisdiction who refused to contribute to the obligations of the guild. The university was to enforce the monopoly of the guild within its precincts in return for a share of the fines, a retainer to the proctors, observance of the statutes on academical costume and the election of a regent master as chaplain of the guild.[5]

---

[1] OUA WPβ/B/34/b. The town had participated in the drafting of the 'composition' of 1521, and the mayor was to share in the fines levied against rebellious brewers after 1524. Neither act created a guild as is implied in the document, but there were several important new provisions, particularly the one limiting the membership to twenty.

[2] *Reg. canc. 1498–1506*, 38.

[3] Masters of the white-bakers and brown-bakers were elected in December 1508 and November 1509 respectively: Reg. Canc. 1506–14, fos 75, 103.

[4] For regulations concerning the price and cut of academical costume see *Statuta*, 97, 158. We know that the eve of the feast of the nativity of St John the Baptist (23 June) was an important day for the tailors by the early fourteenth century: see Salter in *Medieval Oxford*, 62–3, *Oxford City Documents*, 165–6. The administrative year of the guild ended on this day: Bodl. MSS Morrell 6 and 9 passim, and there was a formal connection between the craft-guild and the confraternity and chantry of St John the Baptist in St Martin's church: *Liber Albus*, nos. 217, 241 [by 1459]; Wood, *City of Oxford* ii. 84.

[5] *Statuta*, 298–9; *Epist. acad.* ed. Anstey ii. 594–6. The proctors' accounts for 1492/3 record 3s 4d received 'de arte scissoria pro annuali pensione': *Mediaeval Archives* ii. 346.

From this position the university quickly increased its influence over the guild: a new agreement (*compositio*) was sealed in 1513, and the surviving accounts of the guild between 1510/11 and 1526/7 provide numerous examples of close co-operation between the two bodies.[1] Only during the troubled mayoralties of the vintner and white-baker John Haynes, and of the ex-bedell and draper William Bulcombe, in 1515/16 and 1516/17, is there any evidence of municipal interference in this arrangement.[2] In 1529 a new *compositio* was approved which extended university protection of the guild. This provided a remedy against the numerous tailors who, as scholars' servants, had sought to circumvent the guild through privileged status. The composition also marks the arrival of Wolsey's charter, for it was enacted by authority of the new privileges (*virtute novorum privilegiorum*). This was of prime importance, since the events described in the preceding section were to alter fundamentally the dominant relationship which the university had established with these important crafts.[3]

The importance of Wolsey's charter for guild regulation is tied to statutory legislation on this subject. A parliamentary statute of 1504, allegedly reviving an earlier statute of 1437, provided that guild ordinances must be approved by certain important royal officials.[4] The effect of Wolsey's charter was to create an exception to this rule. It empowered the chancellor, his commissary or deputy, with the consent (*ex assensu*) of congregation to make 'corporaciones, statuta et ordinaciones' binding upon all inhabitants of the town engaged in the sale of merchandise as well as upon victuallers and also glovers, cordwainers and chandlers sojourning in Oxford (*ibidem*

[1] By 1502 the commissary was intervening in internal matters to effect a 'meliorem ordinem inter ipsos', and at about the same time new members were being admitted 'coram Cancellario' as were the bakers: *Reg. canc. 1498-1506*, 112; for example ibid. 159 (1503). For the composition see Reg. Canc. 1506-14, fo 222^V. It is undated but probably originates before June 1513 and certainly before May 1514: Bodl. MS Morrell 9, fo 9, Reg. Canc. 1506-14, fo 218^V. The guild's account rolls for fifteen years between 1510/11 and 1526/7 are Bodl. MS Morrell 9, fos 4-27. Not all of George Hester's datings there are reliable however.

[2] See the account rolls for 1516/17 and 1517/18: Bodl. MS Morrell 9, fos 17, 12. The period 1515-17 was a disturbed one generally: Maxwell Lyte, *History of the University*, 424-7; Mallett, *History of the University* i. 411-12.

[3] Reg. Canc. 1527-43, fo 178; *Records of Oxford*, 85. There are indications that about 1528 the unimportant craft of the skinners or furriers had also received a 'corporation' from the university, the purpose of which was, like that of the tailors, to protect the occupation against 'foreign' competition. Nothing more is known about this guild: *Records of Oxford*, 74, 58, 84-5.

[4] *Statutes of the Realm* ii. 298-9 (1437), 652-3 (1504). See S. Kramer, *The English Craft Gilds and the Government* (New York 1905), esp. 45 and 61 ff, where the effect of these statutes is discounted; also W. S. Holdsworth, *A History of English Law* (16 vols, 1922-66) ix (3rd edn 1944), 58.

commorantes) and selling their goods (*res suas venales*) on an irregular basis (*enormiter*), any previous statute to the contrary notwithstanding.[1] Accordingly, the charter harmonized established practice with the statute of 1504 by placing the chancellor and congregation on an equal footing with the royal officials named in the latter.

With the controversy over Wolsey's charter the town government, which of course included members of these guilds, began a campaign to wrest from the university the control of all the guilds discussed above. Particularly, under William Flemming, mayor in 1528/9 and his successor Michael Hethe, the town began to contest academic authority by means of the freemen's oaths which had been taken by most members of the guilds and also by petitions to the crown, claiming that the university had exceeded its authority in these matters. At the same time the town government and its officers were establishing alternative organizations and encouraging actions to be taken independent of the university.[2] This culminated in an *omnibus* ordinance of 1534 which provided for the examination of 'the actes, ordynaunces and statutes that shalbe made for the common wele' of eighteen separate occupations including the white- and brown-bakers, the brewers and the tailors.[3] However, in spite of this vigorous activity there is no solid evidence that the town gained control of the guilds of bakers and brewers, and there is positive evidence that the university continued to regulate the crafts.[4] On the other hand there are strong indications that the tailors' guild was removed from the university's control in this period. The last reference in the chancellor's register occurs in May 1530 and the guild accounts for 1553/4, when the series resumes, give the mayor a prominence earlier enjoyed by officials of the university.[5]

Reliable information can be gained again in the 1570s. The prospect

---

[1] *Mediaeval Archives* i. 266. It could, perhaps, be argued that congregation's approval of the brewers' ordinances in 1524 (see above) shows that the charter was being applied before its formal promulgation in 1528.

[2] For example, Flemming forbade brewers and bakers from observing university ordinances on pain of prosecution for perjury: *Records of Oxford*, 61, an edict which certainly had some effect on the white-bakers: see Reg. Canc. 1527–43, fos 130[V], 131[V]. See also *Records of Oxford*, 74, 85, 87–8, 102, 107. The question of the university's powers to create a true corporation also arose, and the university seems to have been wary of claiming such authority: for example, *Records of Oxford*, 101. Part of the problem arose from the loose contemporary use of the word '[in-]corporation' with regard to craft guilds: Palliser, 'Trade gilds', 88.

[3] OCA A.5.5. fo 367[V], printed in *Council Acts*, xii. For the date see n. 3, p. 82.

[4] On 7 October 1534 the town did authorize 'a ordynaunce' to be 'devysed by lernyd Counsell under the Town seale' for the brewers and bakers: *Records of Oxford*, 120. It is clear, however, that control of the assizes remained with the university: for example Reg. Canc. 1527–43 fos 379[V] (brewers), 175 (white-bakers), 16[V] (brown-bakers).

[5] Ibid. fo 147[V] (cf *Records of Oxford*, 85); Bodl. MS Morrell 9, fo 29.

of parliamentary incorporation of the university in June 1571, which as we have seen also confirmed Wolsey's charter, touched off a flurry of municipal activity in order to pre-empt the anticipated actions of the university. In January and February 1571 ordinances for the tailors' and brewers' guilds were approved by the town council and forwarded to the justices of the assize for confirmation. At the same time the white-bakers were empowered to draft an incorporation for themselves to be inspected by the mayor and council.[1]

While the university had evidently yielded up its control over the tailors some time before, the brewers (and bakers) were quite a different matter, for in their case control of the guild was equivalent to control of the assize. Hence 1571 and 1572 saw a number of attempts by the university to obtain a repeal of the municipal brewers' corporation and the acceptance of a new incorporation from it.[2] The dispute was finally taken up by the privy council and a comprehensive settlement in May 1575, which cited Wolsey's charter, ordered that the 'said newe booke or divise', that is the municipal ordinances, ought to be 'brought and cancelled' before the chancellor or commissary 'without delaie'. Thus the municipal corporation was quashed although local ambitions remained alive.[3] On the other hand, the victorious university was also unable to have its way completely. Although it continued to regulate the brewers' and bakers' occupations, its control over the contentious guild of the brewers, indeed the existence of the guild itself, was in a kind of limbo due to municipal opposition.[4] Neither party got full satisfaction, and when the wayward tailors again courted the university in 1604 to gain protection, as in 1529, against privileged persons occupying as tailors, the composition had the full approval of the town-government and offenders were to be tried, not in the chancellor's court, but before the guild officers themselves.[5] Clearly the constitutional crisis of the 1530s had diminished the university's authority over the guilds, and hence over industrial activity.

[1] The exemplification of the act of incorporation is dated 9 June 1571: *Mediaeval Archives* i. 274. For related municipal activities see: Bodl. MS Morrell 18, fos 2–4; OCA A.5.5. fos 130–6, 138–47; *Records of Oxford*, 333–5. The fate of the white-bakers' incorporation is unknown.

[2] OUA WPβ/B/32, 33; Reg. Cong. 1564–82, fos 104^V, 114^V, 126^V, 131 ff; OCA P.5.1. fo 107^V; *Records of Oxford*, 347.

[3] Ibid. 365–74, esp. 373. See the resolutions of the town council, 1580–4, regarding the brewers and bakers: ibid. 409; OCA A.5.5. fo 224^V; *Council Acts*, 8.

[4] All the relevant information on control of the occupation is collected in *Reg. Univ.* ed. Clark i. 327–42. For the guild see, for example: Reg. Cong. 1582–95, fos 285 (1585); 263^V (1594); and *Council Acts*, 16, 40.

[5] OCA A.4.1. fo 192; *Council Acts*, 161. The university copy is OUA WPβ/P/7/3.

The Chancellor's Court and the Town

One of the central institutions governing relations between the town and university was the chancellor's court. Although its procedure was very much like that of a church court, particularly an archdeacon's court, the breadth of its jurisdiction made it unique.[1] Throughout the later middle ages and Tudor period the university tried to ensure that the procedure of the court would be simple and swift and such as would encourage summary rather than plenary procedure whenever possible. By comparison with, for example, the two local courts and their interminable delays (essoins), this efficiency clearly made the chancellor's court an attractive place for a plaintiff to bring suit.[2] Likewise arbitration played an important role in the court long after it had disappeared from ecclesiastical courts.[3] Finally, the court could be extremely flexible with regard to the law applied in any particular case. In 1464 the commissary chose to settle the disputed possession of a horse 'secundum ius regni', that is common law, and not according to the 'statuta [of the university] vel iura civilia vel municipalia'.[4] According to circumstance a case could be tried by canon, civil or common law, university statute, municipal (Oxford) or foreign custom. It is not difficult, therefore, to see why so many townsmen occur in the records of the court.[5]

The active commercial relations between local merchants and the academic community meant that townsmen commonly collected debts in the court from privileged persons. In August 1513 Mayor John Broke successfully sued John Godfrey for £3 17s 8d for ale

---

[1] As early as 1244 the chancellor had received jurisdiction over 'causes of clerks' arising from loans, rental agreements and contracts of moveables in the city and suburbs, thereby clearly setting the chancellor's court apart from a church court: *Cal. Pat. Rolls, 1232–47,* 424; Willard, *Royal Authority,* 16. Only in 1346 did the chancellor receive archdiaconal powers over privileged persons: *Munimenta academica* i. 148–52; cf. *Reg. canc. 1434–69* i. xv–xvii. See esp. Holdsworth, *History of English Law* i. (7th edn ed. A. L. Goodhart, H. G. Hanbury and S. B. Chrimes 1956) 165–76, and *Reg. canc. 1434–69* i. xv–xxvii. Two good accounts of ecclesiastical courts in this period are: B. L. Woodcock, *Medieval Ecclesiastical Courts in the Diocese of Canterbury* (Oxford 1952), and R. A. Houlbrooke, *Church Courts and the People during the English Reformation* (Oxford 1979).

[2] *Statuta,* 127, 215, 332, 365. For the municipal courts see *Medieval Oxford,* 54–5. However, the later sixteenth-century municipal court records indicate a simpler procedure: OCA L.5.7. and by 1528 the mayor's sergeant was holding a court for 'convencion/s/' involving less than 6s. *Records of Oxford,* 57.

[3] Woodcock, *Ecclesiastical Courts,* 59; Houlbrooke, *Church Courts,* 59; *Reg. canc. 1434–69* i. xxv–xxvi.

[4] *Reg. canc. 1434–69* ii. 142; cf *Mediaeval Archives* i. 222, 227, 229, 354.

[5] For example, if one compares the town council list of 1469/70 (*Munimenta civitatis,* 229–30) with the index to Salter's edition of the fifteenth-century chancellor's register (*Reg. canc. 1434–69*) which includes administrative acts as well, all of the names except two will be found.

supplied to the latter as manciple of New Inn Hall, and in July 1562 the bailiff John Hartley sued William Langley for clothes and robes (*pro pannis et aliis robis sibi necessariis*). Moreover, councilman Richard Gomersall even found it necessary in 1585 to proceed in the court against his fellow councilman Richard Bellingham in an action for debt of £3 2s 0d, since Bellingham was a graduate and hence privileged.[1] This last case is a tribute to the fluidity of legal status which we have discussed above.

Aside from the numerous suits which were brought by reason of one party's privileged status (*ratione personae*), there is evidence that from the early fifteenth century the university was claiming jurisdiction over all victualling debts, regardless of the personal status of the parties.[2] Between 1503 and 1514 general licences (*generale decretum*) to cite debtors were granted to a number of prominent Oxford victuallers, and in 1527 we even find the outgoing mayor Michael Hethe collecting 2s 8d for ale from a fellow councilman John Rede.[3] However, such actions become rare after 1530 and Christopher Hawkins, a freeman brewer with university connections who died in 1560, is almost unique in collecting debts for ale in the court after this date.[4] This is also true of the actions brought by victuallers from outside Oxford against their local customers, something which gave the late medieval chancellor's court the look of a kind of 'pie-powder' court.[5]

Although the chancellor's court never needed to use the legal fiction of perjury to obtain jurisdiction over debts as did ecclesiastical courts, nevertheless persons involved in suits did use two other legal fictions, the ceding of debt (*cessio debiti*) and the previously discussed scholar's servant, to obtain jurisdiction *ratione personae*.

Already in the first half of the fourteenth century it was a custom of the university that a debt ceded to a scholar for his support (*ad suam sustentationem*) was collectable in the court, provided that the cession was an act of free charity (*per viam elemosine, sponte, pure,*

[1] Reg. Canc. 1506–14, fo 198; Chanc. Court Act Book, Hyp/A/7 fo 39ᵛ; Chanc. Court Act Book, 1584–5, Hyp/A/14, *sub* 12 Feb. 1585; cf. *Council Acts*, 13.

[2] See the town's petition of *c* 1429: *Munimenta civitatis*, 194–5, 197.

[3] For example, licences were granted to the brewer Robert Denham in 1507: Reg. Canc. 1506–14, fo 5ᵛ, the baker John Adams, also in 1507: ibid. fo 4, and the butcher William Goodbody in 1511: ibid. fo 131. for Hethe see Reg. Canc. 1527–43, fo 29ᵛ.

[4] For an instance of his using the court in November 1549 see Reg. Canc. 1545–1661, fo 38ᵛ. He was father-in-law of both the bedell John Broke (ibid. fo 1ᵛ) and a medical student David Sherbroke (see Hawkin's will: Bodl. MS Wills Oxon. 183, fos 360ᵛ–1).

[5] For example in 1465 Robert Darlyngton, a London fishmonger, claimed more than £20 from John Ketyl, 'tabernarius sive piscarius', for fish supplied: *Reg. canc. 1434–69* ii. 163–4, and in 1502 John Repe, a Bristol merchant, successfully sued John Blackborn of Oxford for 26s 8d owed on a tun of wine: *Reg. canc. 1498–1506*, 143, 145.

sine aliqua condicione).[1] For example in 1442 a mercer of London ceded by a written act (*litteram donacionis*) £6 2s owed him by an Oxford man, and in 1514 Richard Langley, a local grocer, ceded a debt owed to him by another Oxford man to Mr Thomas Gilborn.[2] Clearly these are examples of 'fraudulent' use of the device although we lack information on the exact details of the transactions. In any case the practice does not seem to have been used by townsmen after the 1520s.

While the *cessio debiti* was a plaintiff's fiction, that of the scholar's servant seems to have been used most often by actual or potential defendants. In 1461 the fuller John Weste became a scholar's servant, and in the following month David Gilys of Oxford was inhibited from vexing Weste in any other court; in 1510, two days after being admitted as a servant, the beer brewer Martin Williamson obtained an injunction from being sued elsewhere than in the chancellor's court.[3] Likewise cases already begun in local courts could be removed by the half-seal of the university. According to an early sixteenth-century municipal petition this practice of removing 'action [s] personall' begun before the mayor and bailiffs was regularly employed by the university under the guise of the scholar's servant 'to the utter destruction of your farmours of your sayd towne'.[4] The exact purpose of these actions is obscure although they probably served as a delaying tactic. Obviously their frequency declined as scholar's servants became fewer.

As indicated in the previous section, the guilds under university control made extensive use of the chancellor's court. Thus in 1502 Robert Dyer of Crampound admitted a debt of 4s 6d to the wardens of the tailor's guild on behalf of his servant Letitia. In the same year a baker's servant was convicted of rebelliousness against the masters of the guild and of other infractions. Nine years later twelve brewers, including Alderman Richard Gibbes, sought security against John Traves's removal of a guild dispute from the court.[5] Thus the guilds

---

[1] See the accounts by H. E. Salter in *Munimenta civitatis*, xxiv–xxvi, and *Reg. canc. 1434–69* i xxxiii–xxxv; also *Statuta*, 90, *Reg. canc. 1434–69* i. 28 (1438).

[2] Ibid. i. 65; Reg. Canc. 1506–14, fo 216.

[3] *Reg canc. 1434–69* ii. 43, 48; Reg. Canc. 1506–14, fos 123[r–v].

[4] For examples of cases transferred see: *Reg. canc. 1498–1506*, 41, 101–2; Reg. Canc. 1527–43, fos 140[v], 144[v]. *Records of Oxford*, 17–8. The petition is so worded that the scholars' servants appear to be the innocent (involuntary) victims of academic machinations. The production of the half-seal in local courts can be measured only in the later sixteenth century when the institution of scholar's servant was in decline. Between 1577 and 1586 seventeen cases were removed from the hustings court and eight from the mayor's court for all privileged persons: OCA L.5.7. fos 52[v]–258[v], 317[v]–409 passim. The practice was forbidden between freemen by the Town Council in 1576: *Records of Oxford*, 379; see p. 86 n. 4.

[5] *Reg canc. 1498–1506*, 140, 150; Traves was brewing in his house contrary to custom Reg. Canc. 1506–14, fo 135.

used the court both to conduct external business and to enforce internal discipline. However, after the 1530s only the cooks seem, as a body, to have used the court consistently though infrequently.[1]

In this discussion we have focused only upon 'instance' jurisdiction, particularly regarding suits arising from various commercial transactions, but on the basis of even this limited selection it is clear that the university's court served interests beyond those of the academic community, something also attested to by the participation of prominent townsmen as arbiters in numerous suits.[2] On the other hand in a number of matters—victualling debts, *cessio debiti*, scholar's servant, guild business—it is equally certain that the conflicts of the early sixteenth century removed or reduced the occurrence of several important types of actions in the court, and, although there is no way to compare the frequency of suits in say the mid-fifteenth and late sixteenth centuries, the records of the later sixteenth century have a much more pronounced 'academic' flavour about them.[3] Nevertheless the relatively high volume of business between non-privileged persons in the fifteenth and early sixteenth centuries, and the continued jurisdiction over suits by and against privileged persons, still allow one to call the chancellor's court Oxford's third municipal court.

Public Safety and Health

Just as it was the scene of much institutional conflict, so also did medieval Oxford experience a high level of personal violence.[4] Naturally the university concerned itself with this problem at a variety of levels. As early as the thirteenth century the chancellor had acquired some authority over breaches of the peace where one party was privileged; by the early fifteenth century his jurisdiction was exclusive.[5] Moreover, the agreement with the town in 1459 had provided that, even in breaches of the peace where neither party was privileged, jurisdiction still pertained to the university if its officers

[1] OUA Chanc. Court Act Book, Hyp/A/8, fos 282, 284, 292–3 (1573–4); cf Reg. Cong. 1564–82, fo 177ᵛ.

[2] When, for example, the brewer John Traves was sued by his servant John Kyng (evidently for back wages) in 1498 the judgement was to be rendered by four arbiters, all former bailiffs of the town: *Reg. canc. 1498–1506*, 32. Suits involving moral offences and defamation have been excluded here although the latter, in particular, are numerous in the later sixteenth century. Both types involved townsmen.

[3] At the same time local alternatives may have become more attractive (see p. 100 n. 2).

[4] See my 'Patterns of homicide in a medieval university town: fourteenth-century Oxford', *Past and Present* lxxviii (1978), where it is argued that, given the peculiar demographic structure of the academic population, the university's contribution to homicidal violence was not disproportionate even though it was substantial.

[5] See *Mediaeval Archives* i. 20, 226–30; *Munimenta academica* i. 49–50, 53–4; cf *Reg. canc. 1434–69* i. xxiii–xxv.

made the arrest, and Edward III's charter of 1355 had authorized the chancellor to incarcerate and otherwise to punish both scholars and laymen bearing arms contrary to university statute and to confiscate their weapons.[1] The most important consequence of this latter power was the important statute of *c* 1410, 'Cum effrenata', which set down a detailed tariff of fines for various offences and which met with determined opposition from the town when republished in 1432.[2]

Besides these judicial and legislative powers the university had executive powers as well. Although it always depended upon the municipal officials and the sheriff for prison facilities, it controlled a police force in the form of the night-watch under the supervision of the proctors.[3] Their accounts from the fifteenth century show that this was an expensive burden for the university; income from fines and forfeitures generally ran well below expenses, and in about 1530 the university complained to the crown of its 'great charges for nyght wacchys' towards which the town contributed nothing.[4] Of course the town was reluctant to subsidize what it felt to be an encroachment on its functions, but on several occasions it did try to gain control of the watch from the university.[5]

In the fourteenth century the university also received powers for enforcing the repair and cleansing of the streets, powers which were to be backed according to the 1355 charter by ecclesiastical punishments (*per censuras ecclesiasticas*). In 1461 Edward IV authorized the assessment of fines although actual execution was left to the bailiffs, the university levying the fines only when the municipal officials proved to be negligent.[6]

From the early sixteenth century there are continuous administrative records of academic involvement in urban sanitation. For example in 1501 and 1503 prohibitions were issued against persons who allowed pigs to wander loose in the town and who littered the

[1] *Mediaeval Archives* i. 243-7, 154-5.

[2] *Statuta*, 204-9, 242-3; *Epist. acad.* ed. Anstey i. 108-10; cf *Reg. canc. 1434-69* i. xix-xx.

[3] Wolsey's charter proposed to remedy the lack of a gaol, but it had no effect: *Mediaeval Archives* i. 258. For an authorization to the proctors to execute the watch in 1566/7 see OUA, Chanc. Court Act Book, Hyp/A/7, fo 169^V.

[4] The proctors' accounts (1464/5-1496/7) are printed in *Mediaeval Archives* ii. 272-358. For example, in the first surviving year, 1464/5, £3 was spent 'pro expensis factis ad custodiam pacis in nocturnis vigiliis' but only 9s was received 'de pecuniis levatis de diversis personis propter transgressionem pacis'. Allegedly the majority of malefactors were townsmen: *Records of Oxford*, 89; see p. 103 n. 4.

[5] See the references in p. 91 n. 4, and the 1609 letter of Brian Twyne printed in *Council Acts*, p. li.

[6] *Mediaeval Archives* i. 120 (cf 137-8), 155, 250. See the extracts from the municipal views of frankpledge, 1405-1516, printed by H. E. Salter in *Medieval Oxford*, 146-53.

streets with refuse.[1] Indeed it is not until the 1530s, crucial years as we have seen, that we can trace any municipal involvement in these activities, and as late as 1578 convocation still thought it necessary to authorize its own scavengers for the benefit of the townsmen (*oppidanorum*) as well as of the scholars (*academicorum*), even though the town council had enacted a similar measure less than two weeks before.[2] The university scavengers were to be paid by assessment of the colleges and the privileged persons. Thus, in the field of municipal hygiene as in that of public safety, the university was willing to assume the financial burdens of its privileges in measures which would equally benefit the non-privileged population.

Religious Life and Education

The effect of the university or, more precisely, of the colleges on the parochial structure of Oxford was profound.[3] In the thirteenth century Merton college acquired the rectories of St John the Baptist and St Peter in the East with the chapels of St Cross and Wolvercote; the former church, St John the Baptist, was soon absorbed into the college with the building of the chapel, and its parish was added to St Peters.[4] In 1326 Edward II granted to Oriel College the rectory of St Mary the Virgin, and in the same year the bishop of Lincoln acquired the advowsons of All Saints, St Michael's Northgate and St Mildred's.[5] The latter was suppressed in 1429 to supply a site for Lincoln College, and the now enlarged parish of St Michael's and that of All Saints were then appropriated to the new foundation which supplied them with curates. Finally, the parish church of St Michael's Southgate was pulled down to make way for Cardinal College. Thus the colleges were directly involved in the disappearance of three medieval parishes, and were rectors of four important parishes while serving a fifth, St Cross (Merton), as a chapel.[6] Moreover, following the reformation, the double foundation of Christ Church acquired, in succession to Oseney, the control of the suburban livings of St Mary Magdalen and St Thomas's as well as retaining the chapel at

---

[1] *Reg. canc. 1498–1506*, 97–8, 170. The order of 1503 was issued 'ad instancias burgensium' who complained of the dangers to health 'hoc tempore pestis' (29 July).

[2] *Records of Oxford*, 109, 132, 162, 285, 429; *Statuta*, 412, 414; OCA A.5.5. fo 210[V] (printed in part but misdated in *Records of Oxford*, 398).

[3] For the following see especially the chapter, 'The churches of Oxford' in Salter's *Medieval Oxford*, 113–31.

[4] *VCH Oxon*. iii. 95, 100.

[5] *Oriel College Records*, ed. C. L. Shadwell and H. E. Salter (OHS lxxv 1926), 82–8; *VCH Oxon*. iii. 163.

[6] St John the Baptist, St Mildred's, St Michael's Southgate and St Peter in the East (Merton), All Saints (Lincoln), St Michael's Northgate (Lincoln), St Mary the Virgin (Oriel) respectively.

Binsey from St Frideswide's.[1] Finally, in 1573 St John's College acquired the vicarage of St Giles.[2] Hence from the early fifteenth century the colleges controlled all the parishes in the eastern wards, the areas of greatest academic concentration, and in the course of the sixteenth century all of the important suburban parishes passed into collegiate patronage.

However, even though the institutional influence of the university was very great, its impact on the parochial life of the town should not be thought of in terms of patronage alone. Oxford parishes were not particularly lucrative, but their location made them attractive to university men.[3] At least we cannot otherwise explain the high educational level of Oxford's clergy. Of thirteen incumbents listed in a dispute in 1407, twelve can be found in Emden's *Biographical Register* and all but one of the persons holding livings in Oxford at the time of the clerical subsidies of 1523/26 were graduates at the time of their institution.[4] In the later sixteenth century no one without at least an MA was presented to an Oxford living. Moreover, there is little indication that non-residence was an important problem in city livings, and even Oxford's lower clergy such as the curates, chaplains and chantry priests were remarkably well educated.[5] Compared with the normal educational standards elsewhere, Oxford's clergy was exceptionally learned, and the church-wardens' presentments of 1520, the episcopal visitation of 1540 and the chantry certificates all likewise indicate that their moral standards were equally high.[6] There can be little doubt therefore that in this area the presence of the university had not only a profound, but also a beneficial, effect on the religious life of the town.

This conclusion is strengthened by an examination of the city lectureships in Oxford.[7] Although there are some odd notices indicat-

[1] Had Wolsey completed his foundation, the influence of Cardinal College in this regard would have been even greater.

[2] *VCH Oxon.* iii. 255.

[3] *Valor* ii. 174-6, 223, 240-1, 243. Cf D. M. Barratt, 'The condition of the parish clergy between the reformation and 1660, with special reference to the dioceses of Oxford, Worcester and Gloucester', Oxford DPhil thesis 1950, esp. 192.

[4] Wood, *City of Oxford* iii. 98-9. *A Subsidy Collected in the Diocese of Lincoln in 1526*, ed. H. E. Salter (OHS lxiii 1909), xv-xvi, 277-8. See Wood, *City of Oxford* iii. 73-100, for institutions to c 1540.

[5] M. Bowker, *The Secular Clergy in the Diocese of Lincoln, 1495-1520* (Cambridge 1968), 193-213, esp. 207; Barratt, 'Parish Clergy', 49-50.

[6] For example in 1560 two-thirds of the incumbents in the diocese had no degree: ibid. 86-7. 'Churchwardens' Presentments, 1502', ed. H. E. Salter, *Oxfordshire Archaeological Society Report* lxx (1925), 75-117, esp. 112-17; 'A Visitation of Oxfordshire in 1540', ed. H. E. Salter, ibid. lxxv (1930), 289-307, esp. 300-2; *Chantry Certificates*, 13-16, 50-2.

[7] See Salter's remarks in *Council Acts*, xxviii-xxxii, and P. S. Seaver, *The Puritan Lectureships: the politics of religious dissent, 1560-1662* (1970), esp. 92-3, 112-14.

ing municipal support for preaching in the mid-sixteenth century, regular efforts to this end are not evident until the 1570s.[1] However, these innovations, funded by voluntary contributions, seem to have fallen on barren ground, and efforts to revive them in the early 1580s proved unsuccessful; only in August 1585 was a real solution hit upon: municipal funding.[2] Two preachers were to be appointed to deliver sermons at St Martin's (always considered the 'city' church) on Sundays and 'holidays' in return for a combined salary of £10 *per annum*; five months later the 'holiday' sermons were dropped and the stipend raised to 20 marks (£13 6s 8d). A new and (possibly) moderately 'puritan' group coming into power in local government in the late 1570s and early 1580s had finally achieved institutional stability in corporate worship.[3]

The men who held the post for the balance of the century had impressive qualifications, and apparently held moderate views. Five of the early lecturers are found in the *DNB* and one, John Prime, is of special interest as an Oxford native, the son of a Holywell fletcher.[4] A scholar at Winchester and New College, Prime belongs with the other somewhat older 'Oxford' divines, John Garbrand *alias* Harkes and Bishop John Underhill, also Oxford natives and distinguished churchmen.

Recently Seaver has alleged that the Oxford lectureships were developed 'to take advantage of [the] considerable resources of preaching talent at the university'.[5] As a statement of intent this is at best speculative, but it is certainly an accurate description of the practice by which the intellectual resources of the university were mobilized for the edification of the town.[6]

A final institutional connection between town and gown in the area of religion was the confraternity or guild of St Thomas the Martyr in the church of St Mary the Virgin.[7] This association dates

[1] OCA P.5.1. fo 33; *Records of Oxford*, 349, 376, 405-6, 411.

[2] Ibid. 419-20, 431; *Council Acts*, 17-81 (cf ibid. 360, for the key-keepers' accounts for 1585/6). This order is not noted by Salter or Seaver who take the amended version five months later (23-4) to be the initial one.

[3] Hammer, 'Town-gown relations', 452-5. The apothecary William Levins seems to have been a key figure.

[4] See the short biographical sketches in *Council Acts*, xxviii-xxxii, with some additional material from Seaver, *Puritan Lectureships*, 112-13. Those included in the *DNB* are: Miles Smith, John Prime, John Favour, Richard Field and Francis Mason. Prime's father was not a 'butcher' as given in the *DNB* following Wood.

[5] *Puritan Lectureships*, 92.

[6] According to the town council in 1582 their purpose was that 'all estates and degrees within this Cytie' might 'understande and learne theire duties towards God and obeydience to all lawfull magistrates and superiors': *Records of Oxford*, 419.

[7] This subject is dealt with in detail in my article, 'The town-gown confraternity of St Thomas the Martyr in Oxford', *Mediaeval Studies* xxxix (1977), 466-76.

from the later fourteenth century and was formed to support a chantry priest saying morning mass at St Thomas' altar for the benefit of all scholars and other strangers (*alii extranei*) spending the night in Oxford.[1] The original founders of the chantry some years earlier seem to have typified the close connections between the academic and municipal communities which we have already discussed, and the aims of the confraternity reflect this.[2]

The same is true of the membership. Two account rolls for 1483/4 and 1530/1 survive for the guild, providing the names of a large number of brothers and sisters, either newly joined or in arrears on their obligations.[3] In both accounts the membership is composed of a mixture of scholars, *privilegiati* and townsmen and encompasses a broad social range. For example the 1483/4 accounts contain the names of Richard Bernys, president of Magdalen College, John Weston, yeoman bedell of theology, and the fishmonger and ex-bailiff Nicholas Croke and his wife. From the accounts of the troubled year 1530/1 we learn that even the commissary John Cottisford and the alderman John Austin were both members, and hence bound to attend the annual feast (*convivium*), in the words of the statutes 'for the nourishment of love' (*propter amoris nutrimentum*). The confraternity of St Thomas was not the only one which bound together members of the university and the town, nor did it ever achieve the importance of the combined Cambridge guild of Corpus Christi and St Mary which founded a college.[4] Moreover, it may have been in decline at the time of its dissolution.[5] But it was clearly an important historical link between the late medieval town and university, for it allowed members of both communities to mingle with one another on an equal footing.

Although the purpose of a university is to educate, it is notoriously difficult to trace its effects in this area, and this is as true with regard to the local community as it is to the nation as a whole. Therefore,

---

[1] *Oriel Records*, 420-2; see ibid. 422-3.

[2] The founders included three townsmen (and one wife), a privileged person and a scholar. Unlike the other two Oxford confraternities for which guild certificates survive, those of the Blessed Virgin Mary in All Saints' and St Ebbe's churches, the confraternity of St Thomas was not a benefit society: see PRO C.47/45/389, 390.

[3] Bodl. MS Rolls Oxon. 14 (1483/4); Bodl. MS D.D.Par.Oxf. St Mary the Virgin, e.1.(R) (1530/1).

[4] Rashdall, *Universities* iii. 310-2. See, for example, the wills of the bedell Robert Keynsham (1431) and the alderman Richard Hewes (1488), which refer to the confraternity of St Catherine in St Thomas' church: *Munimenta civitatis*, 200; Bodl. MS Wills Berks. 1, fos 289c-99ᵛ.

[5] There were thirty-five new members in 1483/4 but only four in 1530/1. See *Chantry Certificates*, 7-9, 15, 50, where the chantry and confraternity (like the parish church of St Thomas) have been renamed for St Nicholas.

with one exception, we must be content with a few exemplary sketches in place of systematic analysis.

Neither the town government nor individual townsmen seem to have concerned themselves much with grammar education in the fifteenth and sixteenth centuries, either in the form of municipal funding or of private bequests.[1] Only in the late 1570s do the records of local government reveal activity in this field, and even then they display little determination or success.[2] The explanation for this mediocre record is undoubtedly to be sought in the fact that the university and its colleges provided excellent facilities which made parallel municipal efforts superfluous. Throughout the middle ages Oxford was a centre for grammar teaching, and the foundation of Magdalen College School in 1478-80 had a profound influence, since Waynflete did not limit enrolment to members of the foundation. In 1550, when the Edwardian university commissioners threatened to suppress the foundation, the mayor and town council joined the college in its appeal to the king, pointing to 'our childrene' brought up 'in good learninge' at the school, 'little or nothinge at the chardge of theyre parents'.[3] Unfortunately we know very little about the identities of these Oxford schoolboys.

Reliable information on this point is provided only by the matriculation records of a school not in Oxford itself, Winchester College, which regularly received Oxford scholars because of New College properties in the town.[4] Two Oxford names occur in the original list of 1393 and for the fifteenth and sixteenth centuries about eighty-seven Oxford boys, or roughly one in every two years, were admitted. However, within this span the years 1475 to 1549 saw

---

[1] Accordingly, our information, particularly on elementary or petty schools, is haphazard. For example, in 1453 John Martyn alias Clerke alias Scolemaster occurs as an 'informator parvulorum' in the parish of St Michael's Northgate: *Reg canc. 1434–69* i. 324; *BRUO to 1500*. On 26 January 1580 John Langley, a chandler, deposed that about forty years before, 'when [he] was about xii yeres old, he [had gone] to schole with' a certain King who was clerk at St Ebbe's: OUA Chanc. Court Depositions, Hyp/B/2, under name and date. For another example from the same year and for general information on the topic see N. Orme, *English Schools in the Middle Ages* (1973), esp. 233 (misdated to 1579).

[2] See the unsuccessful approach to John Case in 1576: *Records of Oxford*, 378, and the leasing of the schoolhouse in the courtyard of the old Gild Hall: *Oxford City Properties*, ed. H. E. Salter (OHS lxxxiii 1925), 148–9; *Records of Oxford*, 427; *Council Acts*, 23, 54, 117.

[3] R. S. Stanier, *Magdalen School; a history of Magdalen College School, Oxford* (OHS new ser. iii 1940; 2nd edn Oxford 1958), 85–9 (text misdated in *Records of Oxford*, 196–7; cf ibid. 191). On grammar education in medieval Oxford see M. D. Lobel's contribution to *VCH Oxon.* iii. 40–3, and R. W. Hunt, 'Oxford grammar masters in the middle ages' in *Oxford Studies Presented to Daniel Callus*, 163–93.

[4] T. F. Kirby, *Winchester Scholars; a List of the Wardens, Fellows and Scholars of St. Mary College of Winchester, near Winchester, commonly called Winchester College* (London and Winchester 1888). Kirby's information should be checked whenever possible against *BRUO*.

a sharp decline which was reversed only in the second half of the sixteenth century.[1] Since the fluctuation coincides almost exactly with the foundation and early hey-day of Magdalen School, it strongly suggests that both institutions drew from a common and relatively small pool of local boys.[2]

The identities of many Winchester scholars can be established. They include the offspring of such fifteenth- and sixteenth-century families as Offord, Kent, Woodward, Hulle, Williams and Frere, but the original foundationers of 1393, William Stapelford and William Sherborne, were probably the sons of a saddler and a tailor respectively, who occur with their wives in the poll tax of 1380/1, and we have already pointed to the mid-sixteenth-century fletcher's son, John Prime. These examples indicate that the less affluent— if not destitute—levels of Oxford society also benefited from the opportunities afforded by the foundation.[3]

Because of the Winchester records we are relatively well-informed about local boys at New College. This is not the case at other colleges, much less for non collegiate scholars. For the middle ages the best one can do in this regard is to try various approaches such as searching Emden's *Biographical Register* for the names of prominent Oxford families. This method recovers some early local scholars such as the Eus in the early fourteenth century, but it cannot give an accurate overview.[4] The same is true of the odd information provided by the chancellor's registers. From them we learn, for example, that a former manciple of All Souls, the freeman white-baker Richard Busterd, had a son, William, who was a fellow of All Souls; in 1508 the later alderman Michael Hethe had a son at Beef Hall where he (the father) owed 40s for his son's board (*pro mensa filii sui*).[5] But these references are very sparse.

Throughout our period wills are probably the best single source of information because they immediately establish firm genealogical links. They are particularly useful for the sixteenth century when

---

[1] I have some reservations about the six Oxford admissions in 1503/4.

[2] See Stanier, *Magdalen School*, 90 ff, who traces a decline in the second half of the sixteenth century.

[3] *Oxford City Documents*, 30, 24. For Magdalen School see the tailor's son, Thomas Cooper, who became a fellow of the college (1539), master of the school (1549-51, 1559-67), and subsequently bishop of Lincoln (1571-84) and then of Winchester (1584-94). I cannot identify his father (*BRUO*).

[4] For example, Nicholas and Roger Eu, sons of John and grandsons of Philip Eu, both mayors of Oxford: *BRUO to 1500* under 'Ew'. The Eus were related to another important Oxford family, the Wormenhales, and two sons of Alderman Andrew Wormenhale (d. 1342), John and Thomas, were attracted, rather, to Cambridge by their kinsman, John de Eu (Oo) at Ely: *BRUC*; *BRUO to 1500*: *A Cartulary of the Hospital of St. John the Baptist*, ed. H. E. Salter (3 vols OHS lxvi, lxviii, lxix. 1914-16) ii. 178-80.

[5] *Reg canc. 1498-1506*, 54; Reg. Canc. 1506-14, fo. 76.

testamentary evidence becomes plentiful, and their value is in no way diminished by the later appearance of the matriculation lists.[1] As an example of this sort of evidence we may cite the 1550 will of Elizabeth Snowe, the widow of the brewer, John Snowe. From the will we learn that she had had two sons, Oliver and Gregory, by a previous marriage to a man named Stonyng, presumably also a local brewer. Both sons were fellows of Magdalen College early in the century, taking advanced degrees in theology and civil law respectively.[2] Another such example occurs in 1571 when the puritan draper Nicholas Gibberd left £5 to his son Nicholas, 'at his proceading fourth Bacheler'. Before the year was out young Gibberd, a former demy, then scholar at Magdalen, had taken his MB and had settled down to practice in Oxford.[3] Taken together this sort of evidence indicates that a university education for a local boy was not unusual. I have been able to trace Oxford boys in all the faculties and at virtually all the colleges. Indeed at one college, St John's, at least two boys, William and Edward Bridgman, had a kind of proprietary right, since their mother, Mary, Tudor Oxford's most prominent businesswoman, was a sister of the founder Sir Thomas White.[4] But although the evidence is instructive, even highly suggestive, it does not answer the basic question of frequency. Thus we shall never know, for example, whether an Oxford native was more likely to study at the university than was his counterpart from Gloucester or Northampton.

Medieval Oxford's most famous student (as opposed to its most famous scholar) was surely Chaucer's 'poore scolar', 'hende Nicholas', from the Miller's Tale.[5] Although he was a bit disreputable, Nicholas, who was certainly not 'poore' in any pecuniary sense, does not quite correspond to the portrait drawn only a few years later by congregation in the statute of 1410 dealing with his kind. There we read of persons living in the manner of scholars outside halls in diverse places and without the discipline of a principal (*in forma scolarium extra aulas ac sine principalibus in locis diversis*)

[1] On the basis of the matriculation lists from Michaelmas 1580 to Michaelmas 1585 (*Reg. Univ.* ed. Clark ii. 94-116), I have been able to identify fewer than five local residents with any degree of confidence.

[2] Bodl. MS Wills Oxon. 180, fos 28-9, cf *Reg. canc. 1498-1506*, 251, where as 'relicta Stonyng' she (Elizabeth) occurs in the brewers' rota in 1501 with her future husband, John Snowe; *BRUO to 1500*.

[3] Bodl. MS Wills Oxon. fos 185, 142^r-v (cf OUA Chanc. Court Depositions, Hyp/B/2 under 4 February 1580). *Reg. Univ.* ed. Clark ii. 16, 45; iii. 11; Foster *Alumni*.

[4] W. H. Stevenson and H. E. Salter, *The Early History of St John's College* (OHS new ser. i 1939), 393.

[5] On Oxford students in literature see S. F. Hulton, *The Clerk of Oxford in Fiction* (1909). J. A. W. Bennett discusses the historical setting of the 'Miller's Tale' in his *Chaucer at Oxford and at Cambridge* (Oxford 1974), 26-57.

known by the abhorrent name (*nephando nomine*) of 'Chamburde-kenys' who sleep by day and haunt taverns by night, bent upon various crimes and destructive of the peace of the university.[1] In consequence scholars were to dwell only in halls or colleges, taking commons there, and incorrigible elements were to be banned *ut membra putrida*. Moreover, townsmen were forbidden to accept scholars as lodgers or boarders except by the chancellor's permission for good reason (*ex causa racionabili*).

That should have ended the matter, and indeed there is no surviving fifteenth-century evidence to the contrary. However, in the sixteenth century there is a series of records, both legislative and administrative, which indicates that the 'chamberdeacon' or 'poor scholar' was not yet extinct. In 1511 the commissary reissued the fifteenth-century ordinances, and in the following year the register contains details of a number of scholars living in the town. At the end of August 1512, the heads, principals, all doctors and the proctors gathered in St Mary the Virgin and ordered the poor scholars called chamberdeacons (*pauperibus scolaribus qui vocantur 'chamberdekyns'*) there assembled to remove themselves to a college or hall. This proved unworkable, however, and sureties for their good behaviour were produced instead.[2]

Neither the eighteen 'poor scholars' nor their ten landlords scattered about the town in 1512 were very distinguished. The same seems to be true of the eighty-nine students in private lodgings (*in domibus laicorum sive oppidanorum habitantibus*) in July 1562, for whom, unfortunately, the names of only twelve landlords are included.[3] However convocation's decision in December 1579, that the scholar lodgers were a great inconvenience to the university and that the older statutes should be enforced, produced a large number of landlords in the chancellor's court in early 1580 and 1581. The occupations of these thirty-seven landlords, who included a few *privilegiati*, were modest with tailoring being the most important single trade. As in 1512 and 1562 they were spread about the town. Only three were on the town council at the time, including two new common councillors, and only a small minority, ten, were even assessed for the subsidy of May 1581.[4] Therefore throughout the

---

[1] *Statuta*, 208–9; cf ibid. 226–7 (1420).

[2] Reg. Canc. 1506–14, fos 155ᵛ, 165–72 passim.

[3] Reg. Canc. 1545–1661, fos 89ᵛ–90ᵛ (*Reg. Univ.* ed. Clark, ii. 5–9).

[4] Reg. Cong. 1564–82, fo 292; Chanc. Court Act Book, Hyp/A/12, under 19 February and 4 March 1580; 3, 10, 17 February and 10 March 1581. In six cases the number of lodgers is given; they total twenty-four or four per landlord. See the town council list of 1580/1 and the tax assessment of 20 May 1581 for information on the landlords: OCA A.5.5. fos 226–7ᵛ; PRO E.179/162/347.

sixteenth century both groups, poor scholars and their landlords, seem to have been marginal, the one academically, the other economically. For a tailor like William Tidyman, the opportunity to lodge four scholars as he was doing in February 1581, probably represented a significant contribution to his existence.

But not all lodgers were students. Some were old graduates attracted back to the fringes of academic life.[1] Moreover, a variety of contacts between town and gown must have resulted from the diverse number of graduates, including a large group of physicians, who maintained households in Oxford and who can be traced in the later sixteenth century subsidies assessed by the university.[2] Of these many can be attributed to the common denominator of marriage which made collegiate life impossible and which is attested to by the widows' names in the tax lists. Among this group of academic marriages we can identify a number of local wives. Indeed this phenomenon can apparently be traced back to the fourteenth century, and Alderman John Clerk's will in 1484 mentions his son-in-law, John Eggecombe, probably a graduate, who played an important role in municipal life until his death in the early sixteenth century.[3] William Pawe (freeman 1539), an Exeter BA, and the medical student Thomas Tatam (freeman 1551), were also amongst those drawn into local life through marriage.[4]

The available pool of young bachelors must have often been an advantage to townsmen. In his will of 1570, the fishmonger Richard Ivery granted to William Colsell MA the lease of his house on the condition, among others, that Colsell would marry Ivery's 'natural daughter' Elizabeth, which he did in July 1570.[5] Moreover, the university community was not only a convenient source of husbands, but a good one as well, and this is reflected at the upper levels of local society. Alderman Thomas Williams's daughter Anne was married to the distinguished Latinist and physician Roger Marbecke, who was briefly provost of Oriel; in September 1579 Mary Noble, daughter of the mercer William Noble, who became an alderman that same autumn, married Dr Thomas Glasier, the rector of Exeter.[6] This

---

[1] See, for example, the wayward exploits of John Dolber MA in 1527 with his landlord's wife with her husband's connivance: Reg. Canc. 1527–43, fos 207ᵛ–8; *BRUO to 1500*.

[2] See the assessment lists from 1567 to 1600: PRO E. 179/162/330, 336, 344; 163/358, 374, 393.

[3] See *Liber Albus*, no. 3, for Robert de Crashall MA (*BRUO to 1500*, under 'Cressale'). For Eggecombe see *Liber Albus*, no. 256 and *BRUO to 1500*.

[4] Pawe was the son-in-law of the brewer, Thomas Mondy: Bodl. MS Wills Oxon. 178, fos 172–3; Tatam was the son-in-law of Alderman Richard Whittington: ibid. 185, fos 544ʳ⁻ᵛ.   [5] Ibid. fo 12; Wood, *City of Oxford*, iii. 229.

[6] Bodl. MS Wills Oxon. 186, fos 113–14; MS D.D.Par.Oxf. St Martin's b.1. fo 9 (cf fo 4).

is good evidence of the generally friendly relations which must have prevailed between the upper levels of town and academic society as they did at a lower level.[1]

Although we have touched on many points in our examination of Oxford life, we have not yet exhausted the topic of town-gown relations. For example we have only mentioned in passing the very large subject of academic ownership of urban property which was accentuated in the early sixteenth century by trans-fers of religious lands to, especially, the cathedral college, Christ Church. However the groundwork for such a study has been laid by Dr H. E. Salter in his monumental *Survey of Oxford* and other works.[2]

As a result of these transfers, many townsmen had academic land-lords, as did the impoverished alderman Nicholas Todde at his death in 1579.[3] Moreover, the agricultural lands owned by the colleges, espe-cially those near Oxford, were an attraction to a community which was markedly rural in character. Often these rural properties seem to have been leased to servants of the foundation, an additional attraction to privileged status.[4] Thus we have before us one more of the factors which subtly conditioned relations between the two communities.

If we try to characterize these relations in general, we may begin by saying that they were both more extensive and more complex than a simple account of constitutional conflict such as Rashdall's would suggest. Certainly the *corporate* relations between the two bodies were not always harmonious: the disputes surrounding Wolsey's charter make this point rather forcibly. But we should not forget that these were exceptional events, and they too yielded in the sixteenth century to regular supervision and control by the privy council. In general the odd constitutional arrangements

[1] For example, on 29 September 1568 Margaret Reade *alias* Tyler confessed 'se habuisse rem et carnaliter cognovisse' Robert Greneway, scholar of Gloucester Hall, in the house of Roland Thornbury in St Mary Magdalen parish, on Saturday 25 September, between seven and eight o'clock in the evening (OUA Chanc. Court Act Book, Hyp/A/8, fo 64).

[2] H. E. Salter, *Survey of Oxford*, ed. W. A. Pantin and W. T. Mitchell (2 vols OHS new ser. xiv 1960 xx 1969). For a model of topographical exposition see W. A. Pantin's essay, 'Before Wolsey' in H. R. Trevor-Roper (ed.), *Essays in British History presented to Sir Keith Feiling* (1965), 28-59.

[3] Todde asked that his 'very good frendes and land lordes', the provost and fellows of Oriel College, allow his daughters to hold his house as he had heretofore: Bodl. MS Wills Oxon. 186, fos 83^v-4.

[4] See, for example, the 1454 lease by All Souls of a 'pratum . . . vocatum Astonseyte iacens iuxta Oxon' for £5 6s 8d per annum to the former and current manciples, John Page and Richard Busterd: Bodl. MS D.D. All Souls College c. 117, no. 4.

in the borough seem to have functioned remarkably well.[1] The university provided essential services to the town through the administration of local franchises such as the assize of bread and ale, the enforcement of sanitary provisions and the night watch and through supervision of local guilds and commercial activity. Even when these activities were resented as excessive, it would not be easy to prove that they were either corrupt or despotic, nor did contemporaries often claim them to be so. Moreover, townsmen were not slow, as we have seen, to avail themselves of the university's most visible franchise, its court, when it was to their advantage, even resorting to the fiction of scholar's servant to do so.

To be sure, some of these public activities changed or ceased in the sixteenth century under the impact of the conflicts of the 1530s, but the highly integrated nature of economic and social life persisted throughout our period. The university continued to be a major local employer and consumer of goods and services in spite of increased collegiate autarchy, and frequent changes in status ('inter-corporate mobility') and even double status often make it impossible to delineate groupings and allegiances with confidence. Indeed the privileged persons lived precisely on the borderline of the two corporations, enjoying a distinct constitutional status but pursuing economic activities and possessed of a manner of life which united them to the borough and frequently drew them into municipal life. Contacts between townsmen and scholars as lodgers and neighbours occurred daily, and intermarriage between *privilegiati*, scholars and local women, a phenomenon which probably increased in the sixteenth century, cemented the numerous bonds between them. Thus a varied web of relationships, including kinship as well as commerce, connected the members of the two communities.

This fact is exemplified by the history of the confraternity of St Thomas, and when it disappeared during the reformation, a new, albeit very different, religious institution, the city lectureship, arose as an embodiment of the generally beneficent effect of the university on the town's life. This positive influence was complemented by university involvement in local education and even (as we have just noted) in public safety and health. In fact it is difficult to find any area of daily activity, from the purchase of a loaf of bread to the hearing of a sermon, where an Oxford resident would not have been conscious of the university's presence: the relationship between town and gown affected all spheres of local life. At the beginning of this chapter we characterized this relationship as one of 'symbiosis'. Like

---

[1] At Cambridge there was even an early Elizabethan proposal for a joint incorporation of the town and university: PRO S.P.12/75, fos 170[r–v]!

all metaphors this one has its limitations, but with its emphasis on mutuality it surely approximates more closely to the truth (at least as we have been able to recover it) than does Rashdall's famous notion that the burghers of fifteenth-century Oxford lived 'almost as the helots or subjects of a conquering people'.[1]

---

[1] Rashdall, *Universities* iii. 106.

3

Oxford and the Tudor State from the Accession of Henry VIII to the Death of Mary

CLAIRE CROSS

CONTRARY to some older opinions the early Tudor period did not initiate a complete alteration in the relationship between the university of Oxford and the state; it constituted, rather, a time when trends begun in former centuries underwent a very noticeable development. The university's reliance upon the state, already of long standing, increased rapidly with the growth in its traditional need for protection, especially against the assertiveness of the town, and in its desire for further patronage, particularly to enable it to pursue new academic interests. The university looked to the state and the state's servants for this protection, and found it to a probably unprecedented degree. It accepted this beneficence, however, at a price. Oxford continued to supply servants for the state as it had always done, but now to a much greater extent than before, the state expected in return the university's active and unqualified support for state policies. In three successive reigns the university had to acknowledge and justify at least three dramatic changes in religious allegiance with the result that by the death of Mary the state and the university had reached a measure of inter-dependence not previously experienced.

Oxford in the early sixteenth century remained in theory the self-governing institution it had been in the high middle ages. The chancellor chosen by the regent masters presided over congregation, which consisted of the teaching masters—the 'necessary regents'—only, and the larger convocation, which included both the regents and the more senior non-regents. The chancellor usually presided over congregation through his commissary; *regentes ad placitum* (as opposed to 'necessary regents') taught but did not attend. All non-regents were to go to meetings of convocation if summoned. Convocation alone could promulgate statutes, but congregation had the

authority to deal with a large amount of administrative and minor
legislative business; it elected the proctors and bedells, granted graces
and dispensations, interpreted statutes and supervised the organization of studies in the university in general. The two proctors, who
held office for a year, were responsible for good order within the
university and for the day-to-day execution of congregation's decisions. The most significant departure from earlier procedure had
come about in the late fifteenth century when the university began
to appoint non-resident chancellors for prolonged periods, the
chancellor's place in the university being taken by commissaries,
or vice-chancellors, again elected by congregation. Power within the
university seemed to be passing to this quite small group of junior
masters, often not more than twenty in number, who met in the
congregation house adjoining St Mary's church.[1]

The practice of university government, nevertheless, in the first
part of Henry VIII's reign in many details belied appearances. In the
most important respect, the chancellor, though absent, continued
to be a very real force within the university. Congregation in 1506
had offered the chancellorship to William Warham, archbishop of
Canterbury, and he retained the office for over a quarter of a century
until his death in 1532, taking the keenest personal interest in the
university's affairs throughout that time. By contrast, the commissaries who deputized for the chancellor seem elusive and transitory figures, despite most, though by no means invariably all,
being heads of colleges or halls. Compared with the chancellor the
commissaries do not appear to have exercised much influence in
their own right, the internal business of the university being handled
not by one individual but rather by a series of committees answerable to congregation.

Through the fortunate survival of the university's letter-book some
flesh can be put back on the bare bones of the university's formal
structure. Kept systematically from 1508 until about 1530 this
register contains some letters addressed to the university in addition
to the many letters it dispatched year by year. Congregation
obviously could not compose its letters as a body and it delegated
this task to its registrars, three from 1508 to 1524 being fellows of
New College followed in their turn by a further three fellows of
Merton. These men wrote the letters in which the university con-
ciliated its chancellor, secured new patronage or aid in defence
of its privileges, sought reform of its statutes and begged for
financial assistance. From the information revealed by the letter-

[1] *Statuta*, xxi–xxxix, lxxiv; W. A. Pantin, *Oxford Life in Oxford Archives* (Oxford
1972), 21–2, 24–7; and cf Fletcher, p. 164.

book it is possible to reconstruct a fairly coherent picture of university policy in the years before the reformation.[1]

Although he did not reside in Oxford, Warham's frequent letters to the university show that he had no doubts that the office of chancellor conferred on him very real powers, and until 1514 at least he wielded considerable influence over the university. From the moment in 1509 when the scribes begin to record the receipt of letters, Warham assumed a prominent place, initiating an enquiry into the keeping of the university's chests and making suggestions for the better administration of its meagre finances. With the accession of a new monarch congregation thought a fresh confirmation of the university's privileges desirable and approached the chancellor to procure this: it proved to be a much more delicate enterprise than the university had expected, and it was still soliciting his help over three years later to retrieve papal and royal charters from London. Warham from the start interested himself in a scheme for reforming the statutes, though it is doubtful whether he or the university quite understood the magnitude of the task. Warham's concern seems to have been primarily moral: he was uneasy over the possibility that when students on admission to degrees swore to maintain the university statutes they might unintentionally perjure themselves, since no one knew exactly what the statutes prescribed. Consequently in 1514 he proposed that the university should select certain men to examine the statutes, reduce them to order and clarify those which were obscure, and in February of that year convocation duly set up such a committee, but it made little progress, and three years later the university asked Richard FitzJames and Dr John Young to take over the responsibility for the codification. In 1514 Warham also intervened in a matter which periodically surfaced in the early sixteenth century, disorders associated with the annual election of proctors. He had heard that unsuitable men had gained office by bribing regents to return to the university merely to vote in the elections, and strongly advised convocation to pass new statutes making residence in the university henceforth a requirement for voting.[2]

Between 1509 and 1514 the university approached several other highly placed churchmen besides Warham to further its interests, congregation approving the sending of letters to Edmund Audley, bishop of Salisbury, Thomas Ruthall, bishop of Durham, Richard FitzJames, bishop of London and Richard Fox, bishop of Winchester, among others, all of whom with some reason it looked upon as its

[1] *Epist. acad. 1508–96.*
[2] Ibid. nos. 3, 4, 5, 9, 30, 35, 36, 58, 63; *Statuta*, xlvi–xlvii.

patrons, still however according its chancellor due precedence as its chief defender. Then in 1514 the situation altered abruptly when the university suddenly realized that a far greater minister than the chancellor, Warham, was in the ascendant at court. The news that Cambridge had all but stolen a march on Oxford by offering Thomas Wolsey its chancellorship in May 1514 focused Oxford's attention upon him, apparently for the first time. In June Oxford sent him a letter thanking him profusely for refusing the honour proffered by Cambridge out of love for his own university and begging his protection in its perennial disputes with the town. Wolsey responded graciously to these overtures, and the university saw at once where its main advantage lay; to Warham's undisguised chagrin it to all intents and purposes demoted him and elevated Wolsey to the position of being its chief sponsor, acting indeed from this time onwards as if he were its chancellor in all but name. With almost indecent haste the university began making all possible outward expressions of gratitude to Wolsey, first conferring a doctorate of theology upon him and, a little later, in recognition of his help in restoring its liberties, ordaining special prayers throughout the university for his good estate during life, and the well being of his soul after death.[1]

All through the early sixteenth century senior members in Oxford showed themselves single-minded in their efforts to procure ever closer relations with the great men at court. They had already seen that from that direction—and it seemed from that direction alone—substantial gains might accrue to the university. Through Bishop Fisher and his influence with Lady Margaret Beaufort, Cambridge had obtained the new colleges of Christ's and St John's, and Oxford together with Cambridge had received a lectureship in theology. In November 1517 Bishop Fox of Winchester, following Fisher's lead, acquired a royal licence to found his college of Corpus Christi at Oxford to advance the study of theology, philosophy, and the arts. The university had not long to wait before its expectations of Wolsey's largesse materialized. Early in 1518 when the king had brought the court to Abingdon, Queen Catherine and Wolsey paid a visit to Oxford, and while the queen went to reverence the relics at St Frideswide's the cardinal gave congregation notice of his intention to endow new university lectureships. Sir Thomas More, who had also come to Abingdon in the royal entourage, took the opportunity of lending his support to the study of Greek at his old university, insisting on the necessity of a liberal education for the proper cultivation of theology. In the persons of Wolsey and More

[1] L & P Henry VIII i. no. 5121; Epist. acad. 1508–96, nos. 39, 45, 49; Statuta, 331.

the state had now thrown its weight behind the 'new learning' against the old academic conservatism. More, like Fisher, believed that a revival of classical learning at the universities would lead to a renewal of piety in the church: Wolsey's attitude may have been somewhat more secular. He gave more emphasis to the need for the universities to provide a supply of well trained diplomats and administrators for the state. Whatever the motivation for patronage, the universities stood to benefit: it seems quite likely that more than a quarter of the four hundred or so men Wolsey took into his household had studied at Oxford.[1]

Wolsey's offer to found six lectureships placed the university yet more firmly in the cardinal's camp. He had at the same time expressed a desire to reform the statutes relating to the arts faculty, and the university, without waiting for a reply from Warham, who warned that it would be depriving itself of all authority, at once conferred upon Wolsey the fullest powers to revise, repeal and supplement its statutes. As congregation subsequently explained to the bishop of Lincoln who had suggested this compliance with the cardinal's wishes, it had now gained a skilled pilot to steer the university through stormy seas and a patron known to have great influence with the king. Despite several letters from the university to Wolsey direct, and to the bishops of Lincoln and Exeter to solicit their aid in bringing their master's attention to the undertaking, he had little more success than Warham in completing the codification of the statutes. In 1524 he sent to Oxford for scholars to help him in the scheme; three years later the university forwarded him a book containing its statutes and he promised to turn to the business as soon as he could free himself from matters of greater moment, but the whole enterprise came to nothing on the cardinal's fall in 1529.[2]

In the matter of the defence of its privileges against the townsmen the university achieved considerably more tangible benefits from its protector. After much negotiation in 1523 the king, at Wolsey's request, confirmed to the university all the privileges recently in dispute between the university and the town. Now the university was fully secured in its rights against the assertions of the townsmen, its chancellor recognized as a justice of the peace, and its revenues to some extent augmented by a royal grant of felons' goods. It replied again with a statute providing for additional prayers to be said for

---

[1] *Epist. acad. 1508-96*, nos. 1, 63; *L & P Henry VIII* ii. no. 4042.

[2] *Epist. acad. 1508-96*, nos. 63, 64, 67, 76, 83, 93, 94; *Statuta*, xlvii-xlix; E. Mullally, 'Wolsey's proposed reform of the Oxford university statutes: a recently discovered text', *Bodleian Library Record* x no. 1 (1978), 22-7.

Wolsey on account of all the good works he had done or intended to do for the university community.[1]

Undoubtedly Wolsey's greatest benefaction to Oxford was his magnificent college planned on an unprecedented scale. News of the cardinal's design for a college reached Oxford in 1523, although Wolsey did not obtain a papal bull until the following year to dissolve St Frideswide's and other smaller monastic houses in order to establish a college for some two hundred scholars and servants with an annual revenue of £2,000. By 1525 the building work had begun and Wolsey persuaded John Higden, then president of Magdalen, to be the head of his new college. Clearly the creation of a college of this size could not but affect the existing structure of the university, and the foundation of new colleges in the early sixteenth century, of which Cardinal College was by far the most opulent, brought about a significant change in the balance of power in the university. More and more, college heads and college teaching were growing in importance at the expense both of central university administration and university teaching. Wolsey further encouraged this development by linking the six new public lectureships with his college and associating the masters of other colleges in the selection of his lecturers. The extent of the cardinal's benefactions stretched even the university's powers of description, and with pardonable exaggeration it assured Wolsey that it looked upon him not just as the founder of a college but of the university itself.[2]

Patronage, however, even patronage so enthusiastically welcomed as that of Wolsey, brought obligations in its train. The university recognized itself to be overwhelmingly in the cardinal's debt, and the only recompense the masters and scholars could make besides their prayers was a constant exhibition of obedience. The promise of munificent grants and then the grants themselves greatly reinforced Wolsey's control over the university. When in 1522 trouble again occurred over the election of proctors he immediately made his wishes plain, and ordered the university to leave the election to him: it had little choice but to comply and sent an apologetic note to its chancellor to say that it dared not resist the cardinal's command. By this date Warham felt himself quite outclassed as a patron by Wolsey, as he acknowledged with some bitterness. The university now turned to him only in technical matters of disputed jurisdiction or perfunctorily sought his help to add to that of the cardinal when petitioning

[1] *L & P Henry VIII* iii. nos. 2925, 2926; *Statuta*, 335; and see above Hammer, 'Oxford town and Oxford university'.

[2] *Epist. acad. 1508–96*, nos. 125, 129: *L & P Henry VIII* iv. no. 2736; and see above McConica, 'The rise of the undergraduate college', 26.

for relief from royal taxation. Yet even he still expected some return for his goodwill. The university seems to have been totally unprepared for the violence of Warham's recriminations when late in 1522 it failed to appoint his candidate to a vacant under-bedellship. Convocation on receipt of his missives hastily assembled to reverse its decision, and presented his servant to the office. Intervention of this kind by men who were also royal ministers had become increasingly common before the major changes of the 1530s.[1]

Requests for appointments to offices in return for favours received had been addressed to the university from time immemorial and had usually been respected. Of equal antiquity was the university's duty to protect true religion against heresy. With the emergence of Lutheranism on the continent the English government once more called upon the university to take up its traditional role. In 1521 the king summoned theologians from both Oxford and Cambridge to a conference to consider Luther's schism and after this Wolsey went on to commission certain Oxford scholars to write a joint defence of catholic orthodoxy. The collaborative work he proposed never materialized, though he thought sufficiently highly of Dr Powell's treatise on the papacy and the seven sacraments to authorize its separate publication.[2]

In all his dealings with the university Wolsey had clearly regarded Oxford as a haven of orthodoxy. Consequently his consternation knew no bounds when evidence appeared early in 1528 that Lutheranism had not only penetrated the university but found its most ready welcome in his own college. Although the works of Luther almost certainly did not arouse as much sympathetic interest among Oxford academics as among the group of theologians from several colleges at Cambridge which met at the White Horse Inn, by late in 1527 a somewhat similar cell of reforming intellectuals had come into being at Oxford. The university heads subsequently tried to fix the greater part of the blame for the reception of heresy at Oxford on John Clarke, a Cambridge master who had only recently been attracted to Oxford to join Cardinal College: in his chambers there he had been reading 'Paul's epistles to young men and those who were of two, three or four years standing.' Yet when Thomas Garrett, the curate of Honey Lane in London, arrived in Oxford at Christmas 1527 with copies of Tyndale's translation of the New Testament, part of *Unio dissidentium*, a collection of passages drawn from the Bible and the fathers to support the reformers' cause, and other Lutheran books he had little difficulty

[1] *Epist. acad. 1508-96*, nos. 98, 99, 100, 102, 106, 110, 111.
[2] Ibid. nos. 87, 89.

in selling his wares in the university at large and not only in Cardinal College. On Wolsey's instruction the commissary dispatched men to arrest Garrett, and he uncovered some twenty-two suspected Lutherans, the larger number admittedly from Cardinal College, but also some from Corpus Christi and Magdalen, from some of the halls and from several of the monastic colleges. Even as the search proceeded, in Lent 1528 Dr Rowham, a monk from Bury St Edmunds had the temerity to preach in St Peter's, Oxford, against the sequestration of clergy who maintained Luther's opinions, encouraging the reformers to stand firm with the text, 'Do not fear those who kill the body . . .'. The combined strength of Wolsey, the chancellor and the university heads, however, soon broke what outward resistance remained. The heretics in Cardinal College were imprisoned in their own college, and Clark, his brother, Bailey and Sumner all probably died during the epidemic of the plague later in the year: others conformed, and some escaped, Frith to the continent, Cox to the north of England, while Bettes and Taverner returned to Cambridge. By the autumn of 1528 protestantism seemed to have been eradicated, and during his last months in power Wolsey could take heart that the university was again so solidly orthodox that nothing could seriously corrupt its members.[1]

The university had scarcely overcome the Lutheran crisis before it had to face an even worse blow when towards the end of 1529 its much lauded patron lost the king's favour. The preferring of charges of *praemunire* against Wolsey threw all his benefactions into jeopardy, and the university feared it might be about to be deprived not only of his college, now half built, but also of his lectureships. It desperately wanted the king to step into Wolsey's place, yet it no longer enjoyed special access to the chief royal ministers. Now perforce Oxford turned back to its chancellor, and Warham rather pathetically seized the chance of being of service again, but he could not extend the sort of protection the university needed. Lack of clear direction from court may partially account for the university's singularly ill-advised behaviour at this critical juncture. Given an opportunity of demonstrating a greater compliance with demands over the royal divorce than Cambridge was showing, Oxford chose to go out of its way to invite the king's displeasure.[2]

Warham first wrote to Oxford in February 1530 asking for a unanimous opinion on the validity of the king's marriage, and in the

[1] *L & P Henry*, iv. nos. 3962, 3963, 3999, 4004, 4074, 4125, 4150, 4690; *Epist. acad. 1508-96*, nos. 153, 155, 157, 158, 159, 160, 165; Foxe, *Acts and Monuments* v. 4–5, 421–9; John Strype, *Ecclesiastical Memorials* (3 vols 1721) i. pt 1, 569–70, 581–2.
[2] *Epist. acad. 1508-96*, nos. 184, 187 (b).

same month Henry canvassed Cambridge on the subject. The senior members of Cambridge divided fairly evenly on the issue, but after some opposition Gardiner persuaded them to consign the discussion to a committee of theologians, and convocation then without inordinate delay on 9 March produced the required decision that divine and natural law alike prohibited marriage to a deceased brother's wife. Mid-March came, and to Warham's alarm Oxford continued in deadlock. Believing that the regents and non-regents in the arts were obstructing any conclusion he exhorted the heads and rulers of the university to take action. Early the following month, when still nothing had happened, the king wrote himself, ordering the 'youth' of the university, that is the regent masters, to give up their claim to be associated with the theologians in the discussions. The king's agents, led by the bishop of Lincoln, did their best to get convocation to hand over the matter to a committee of theologians as had been done at Cambridge, but the arts faculty still fought against a committee of a higher (though much smaller) faculty being allowed to make a pronouncement in the name of the whole university. Only after further consultations with the heads of houses, and further manipulation of the theologians, did the royal officers get the committee to decide for the king, and convocation to approve the decision in the university's name on 8 April.[1]

In the many letters which passed between the king, his servants and the university in February, March and April 1530 the reasons for the resistance of so many arts regents are made to appear exclusively constitutional, the unwillingness of the young masters to delegate their powers to senior members of higher faculties or to be governed by the heads of their houses. The extent to which this opposition to the king's wishes cloaked a belief in the legality of his marriage and support for Catherine of Aragon must remain in doubt for lack of evidence, though at Cambridge, which gave way earlier, Gardiner did admit the existence of a considerable party hostile to Cranmer's book justifying the dissolution of the king's marriage, and it seems more than probable that considerable numbers at Oxford held a similar view. Whatever the true reasons behind this show of independence by the regent masters may have been, their obstruction of the king's will had the effect of bringing upon the university a closer royal supervision than ever before. The king and the chancellor required the heads of colleges to impose discipline, and this marked a further step in the growth of the authority of the colleges as against the university, though still not embodied in any formal

[1] *L & P Henry VIII* iv. nos. 6218, 6247, 6259, 6306, 6308, 6320, app. 254; *Epist. acad. 1508-96*, nos. 187 (b), 194, 197 (a), 197 (b).

constitutional change. The king had forced the university to recognize that its members were as much his subjects as any other inhabitants of the realm, a lesson hardly but quickly learnt. When for a second time in 1530 Henry consulted the university on another theological issue, though in this case one more congenial to the majority, convocation without demur permitted the matter to be given over to a committee of theologians and returned an immediate reply, denouncing anew the opinions for which Wyclif had been condemned more that a century earlier.[1]

The university's dependence upon the crown, which Henry VIII had gone to such lengths to emphasize during the debates over his marriage, was again brought home on Warham's death when the king instructed the regents to elect the bishop of Lincoln as his successor. Longland had been well acquainted with Oxford's affairs for many years, having frequently acted as an intermediary between the university and Wolsey, and more recently as a manager of the discussions on the king's marriage. Congregation submissively appointed him chancellor, first for two years, and then, when further directed, for life. Longland outlived the king by barely four months, and throughout his time as chancellor employed William Tresham, a former university scribe, as commissary for the unprecedented period of fifteen years instead of continuing Warham's practice of changing commissaries every three or four years. This must have helped to fasten even more firmly the state's grip upon the university.[2]

In this way the king and his advisors displayed much skill in bridling the university which at a crucial time might otherwise have made a stand for the pope. Few senior members, particularly after the heresy proceedings of 1528, seem to have felt much spontaneous interest in religious change. The reluctance of the regents in 1530 to agree to the annulment of the king's marriage could be construed in part as an indirect demonstration of loyalty to the papacy, and as the decade proceeded some conservatives openly voiced their support for the pope in the university. As late as 1533 Dr London took measures against one who had written 'detestable heresies against the bishop of Rome', with the bishop of Winchester taking pride in the fact 'that this our university was so clear from all these new fashions and heresies'. Early in 1534 Cromwell received a report about a monk of Canterbury College who had been about to spread the Nun of Kent's allegations, and of the hostility of the warden of that college to the king's cause. With some justification a young radical in March could assert that there were many underminers of the truth

[1] L & P Henry VIII iv. nos. 6247, 6456; Epist. acad. 1508–96, nos. 202, 203.
[2] BL Add. MS 32091, fo 132; Epist. acad. 1508–96, no. 210.

in Oxford alienating men's minds in sermons. He did not believe they would dare to speak out against the king's ordinances, but thought they would do nothing to advance them. The king's case had to be presented with great care if another confrontation were to be avoided. In April 1534 the commissary began to prepare the way for the rejection of papal supremacy, selecting preachers on whom he could rely to support the king, and both he and the chancellor intervened in the election of proctors to ensure that men were chosen sympathetic to 'the king's great cause'. Consequently when in May the king at last formally ordered the university to consider the power and primacy of the bishop of Rome he encountered little public opposition, no constitutional wranglings, or undue delay. Within a month of the receipt of the royal command, the university on 27 June 1534 returned the acceptable verdict that the bishop of Rome possessed no more authority in the English church than any foreign bishop, and appended to its decree a list of members of colleges who had individually subscribed to the judgement.[1]

The outward docility of the university during the years of the most momentous reformation changes can partly be attributed to its vulnerability to attack not only from the crown but also from the local townspeople. Wolsey's disgrace had emboldened the town to try to get the withdrawal of his charter, and Cromwell used the town's renewed aggressiveness to obtain unquestioning compliance from the university. As a last resort the university in 1532 surrendered all its privileges to the crown and in the next year Cromwell brought the town to do the same, so gaining temporary control over both warring parties. With all its charters in his hands the king claimed throughout the decade that no act of the university was valid without his express consent. He interfered in person over the appointment to an esquire bedell's place, and Cranmer at one stage asserted in his name that nominations to university offices made without royal approval had no legal force. At the exact time that the university was receiving instructions from the king concerning its elections, Cromwell was upbraiding it for its usurpations and harsh behaviour towards the inhabitants of the town. It is scarcely surprising that senior members concluded that the university's very survival depended upon its obedience to the state.[2]

The most palpable intrusion of the state into the university's affairs occurred in 1535 with the royal visitation of Oxford and

[1] BL Add. MS 32091, fo 132; *Epist. acad. 1508-96*, no. 210; *L & P Henry VIII* vii. nos. 101, 146, 303, 308, 565, 891.

[2] *L & P Henry VIII* v. no. 1344; vi. nos. 183, 758, 868; vii. nos. 148, 507, 524, 565, 618.

Cambridge. The visitation had both political and economic purposes in that the government wished to enforce the subscription to the royal supremacy throughout the university in addition to enquiring into the extent of the endowments of all colleges whether secular or religious. Cromwell also had plans for educational reform and succeeded in inspiring his visitors with a vision of academic renewal which would enable the universities to accommodate themselves to the requirements of a new age. The commissioners, Richard Layton and John Tregonwell, arrived in Oxford early in September 1535 and went from college to college on their mission of demanding obedience to the government's policies from all members of the university. One of their first achievements seems to have been a declaration from the president and fellows of Corpus Christi College that henceforth they would refuse to acknowledge any foreign prince and would never consent to treat for the re-establishment of papal supremacy. Their emphasis, at least in their report to Cromwell, was in favour of educational change. In the richer colleges the visitors created a number of public lectures which they probably intended should supplement or even displace the lectures by the regent masters. They told Cromwell that Magdalen already had one lecture in theology and two in philosophy, and that they themselves had set up lectures in Greek and Latin at both New College and All Souls. Corpus Christi, through Fox's provision, already had lectures in Greek and Latin open to all, and they inaugurated similar public lectures at Merton and Queen's. None of the other colleges, they thought, had sufficient revenues to finance lectures so they enjoined, upon penalty, the scholars of these houses to attend a minimum of one public lecture a day.[1]

Throughout their inspection the visitors scornfully dismissed scholasticism and scholastic writers and they seem actively to have encouraged the spoliation of old libraries, describing with approval how on their second appearance at New College they saw the quadrangle 'full of the leaves of Duns'. Their attack on scholasticism, nevertheless, had its constructive as well as its destructive side, and their desire to stimulate the 'new learning' seems to have won fairly wide recognition in the colleges. At a time when scholars were more and more depending upon their college libraries and the central university library was falling into disuse, colleges began devoting their own funds in an unprecedented way to book buying and in the fifteen or so years after 1535 many acquired humanist editions of the Greek and Latin fathers, some medicine, law and history. The fellows of Magdalen in particular quickly grasped the import of the

[1] *L & P Henry VIII* ix. nos. 306, 350, 351.

visitation. They confessed to Cromwell while his commissioners were still in action, that formerly their youth had been brought up very corruptly for lack of the Greek tongue, and so blindly instructed in the principles of logic that they derived no benefit from it; but now at last Oxford, which had hitherto been regarded as a place which maintained no learning nor profited the public weal, would be in a position to produce men who could serve the prince and the community. One other innovation introduced by the visitors affected the faculty of law as drastically as the rejection of scholasticism had the arts faculty: wherever they came upon canon law lectures they substituted a civil law lecture in colleges, inns and halls, so abolishing the independent study of canon law throughout the university.[1]

On the completion of its visitation the university of Cambridge received two sets of injunctions, one from Cromwell on the king's behalf, and one from the visitors, and these can help explain less well-documented events at Oxford. Cromwell required Cambridge solemnly to renounce the pope's jurisdiction under their common seal and to confirm the king's supremacy. As at Oxford certain Cambridge colleges had to establish, at their own expense, daily public lectures in Greek and Latin. He prohibited any lectures on the doctors who had written commentaries on the *Sentences*, and allowed in theology only lectures on the New and Old Testament. Taking religious matters further he expressly stated that all students might study the scriptures privately and attend lectures on them, while forbidding public lectures on canon law or the conferment of degrees in the subject. Laying down the reading of the arts students in some detail he condemned the frivolous questions and obscure glosses of Scotus and other schoolmen. He also ordered the university to abolish all ceremonies which hindered learning and all college statutes repugnant to the injunctions to which in future all deans and presidents must swear on their promotion. It seems very likely that Cromwell sent similar injunctions to Oxford which have not been preserved.[2]

The dissolution of the monasteries which began soon after the visitation of the universities probably did not cause quite the destruction the more apprehensive feared. Although the state annexed the monastic colleges it took no land from any of the secular colleges at either university. The disappearance of the monastic colleges may

---

[1] Ibid. nos. 312, 350, 351; *Oxford College Libraries in 1556: guide to an exhibition held in 1956* (Oxford 1956) and N. R. Ker, 'Oxford College libraries in the sixteenth century', *Bodleian Library Record* vi (1957–61), 459–515; *Letters relating to the Suppression of the Monasteries*, ed. T. Wright (Camden Society xxvi 1843), 70–2.

[2] *L & P Henry VIII* ix. nos. 615, 664.

well have been felt more acutely at Oxford since the number of monks and friars in residence there had always been greater than at Cambridge. Seven hundred and fifty students from religious houses are known to have studied at Oxford between 1500 and 1540, and whereas not all the monastic students withdrew from the university immediately, the closure of the monastic colleges has traditionally been considered as one reason for the decline in student numbers in the mid-century. Cambridge, however, seems to have been rather more vocal than Oxford concerning its losses; seeing the opportunities offered by the vacant monastic sites it repeatedly petitioned the king to convert one of the dissolved houses in the town into a new college.[1]

In the earlier part of Henry VIII's reign Oxford had secured an immense advantage over Cambridge by obtaining Wolsey as its chief patron; in the 1530s when the king's leading minister became chancellor of Cambridge the situation was reversed, and Cambridge gained the supremacy over its academic rival. Lack of formal connections with Oxford, however, did not prevent Cromwell from intervening continuously from 1532 on the king's behalf in university affairs in a largely successful attempt to impose civil order during a period of very rapid change, bringing the disturbances between the university and town to an at least temporary conclusion, and keeping a close watch on university appointments to curb academic unrest. Yet even after 1536 when he accepted Longland's offer of the high stewardship he never displayed the personal affection for the university that Wolsey had shown. Oxford nevertheless acquired something from Cromwell's influence besides the pacification with the town. In 1536 both universities were freed from the payment of first fruits and tenths on condition that they established a university lecturer in theology to be called Henry VIII's lecturer, at the common expense of the colleges. In December convocation complied and worked out a proportional levy from the individual colleges sufficient to raise an annual stipend of 20 marks.[2]

On the whole, however, from the fragments of information which remain Cromwell seems to have been driving the university rather faster along the paths of reform, particularly religious reform, than many senior fellows felt inclined to go, and throughout his ascendancy evidence concerning papal sympathizers at Oxford, suspected in 1534, continued to emerge. In 1535 Robert Croft, a priest of New College, in addition to having in his possession a book, *Enchiridion*

---

[1] *BRUO 1501–40*, p. xxiv; *L & P Henry VIII* xiii. pt 2, nos. 496, 593, 760.
[2] *L & P Henry VIII* x. nos. 804; *Statuta*, 337–40; and see G. D. Duncan, 'Public lectures and professorial chairs', below pp. 342–3.

adversus Lutheranos, was said to have spoken treasonable words in disparagement of the king's measures against the usurped power of the bishop of Rome. The following year Dr London, the warden of New College, believing that the secretary had come to hear of him as a defender of 'papistical purgatory', thought that he might be made to forfeit his college headship; a year later he was still striving to clear his name. Even at Cardinal College, now known as The King's College, some Romanism lingered on, and in 1538 one of the chaplains, John Hatley, accused another, Henry Spicer, of upholding praying to images, of saying he felt sorry for the monks 'because they go down so fast', and, most dangerously, of supporting the cause of Fisher and More. In the same year also an Oxford clerk accused Dr Richard Smith, principal of Alban Hall, of having transgressed the statute abolishing the bishop of Rome's usurped power both in his own hall and in sermons and lectures in the university at large. Again in 1538, Cranmer wrote to Cromwell with a wealth of detail on the religious divisions he had uncovered at Corpus Christi, describing how one of the deans, Mr Chedsey, had said that if he saw a scholar with a New Testament he would burn it, how another fellow had maintained that the study of scripture subverted good order, and yet other fellows still favoured the pope and had spoken against the 'new learning'. Yet again in 1539 news reached Cromwell of a book defending the papal supremacy which had been traced back to a fellow of Queen's.[1]

Religious conservatism obviously persisted in the university in some strength, but the very bitterness of these accusations and counter-accusations demonstrates the existence of two parties in the disputes, the 'new Christians', as their enemies derisively labelled them, and the catholics: protestantism was once more beginning to take root in some colleges. In 1535 John Emerson could assert against Croft of New College that scripture was above the church, and not *vice versa*, and that the king was the head of their congregation and under him the archbishop of Canterbury. Robert Huick of Merton claimed in 1537 to have 'discerned the truth of the gospel' five years previously, he acknowledged the doctrine of justification by faith alone, and wanted to pass on these verities to others in the university. Even at Corpus Christi Marven and Marshall had been spreading protestant beliefs, only to be condemned as heretics by their brethren. In Lent 1539 an Oxford bookseller admitted that at least twenty fellows and scholars of Corpus Christi, Canterbury College, Oriel, Alban Hall, All Souls, King's and Magdalen besides

[1] *L & P Henry VIII* viii. nos. 799; xi. no. 118; xii. pt 2, no. 429; xiii. pt 1, nos. 529, 845, 905, 1257; xiii. pt 2, nos. 308, 561; xiv. pt 1, no. 525; addenda, no. 1085.

some townspeople had eaten flesh, which the authorities (including the chancellor) thought showed advanced protestant leanings. On Cromwell's execution the Oxford reformers received a sudden check; and the fact that these protestant sympathizers felt it prudent to keep quiet or remove themselves for the remainder of the reign probably indicates their relative numerical weakness.[1]

In contrast with the storms of the 1530s the last years of Henry VIII's reign proved something of an Indian summer in the university's history. Pressure from the government for religious change died away while those two areas of vital concern to the university, its privileges and its public teaching, thrown into question by Wolsey's loss of power, at last received a settlement. After much vacillation the king had allowed Wolsey's college to continue in a much depleted form and with a greatly reduced endowment throughout the 1530s, but both the college and the lectureships the cardinal had established seemed still in a precarious state. In 1540 the crown improved the situation a little by imposing upon the newly erected bishopric of Westminster the obligation of maintaining five readerships at each university. Then in 1546 King's College became Christ Church on the transfer to it of the cathedral of the Oxford diocese and the crown once more attached these five readerships, or regius chairs, now financed by the exchequer, to the college. So by the time of Henry's death, both the cardinal's lectureships and his college were legally secure, and his college, indeed, with annual revenues of over £1,000 survived on a scale not altogether disproportionate to his original intentions.[2]

Peace similarly descended upon the university in its disputes with the town. After the prolonged verbal battles of the previous decade with appeals and counter-appeals from both town and university to Cromwell, the privy council finally issued a decree to end the disputes, and in 1543 the king restored the university's privileges in accordance with the charter of Edward III. The university once more enjoyed its former safeguards against encroachment from the town. This protection, however, in no way heralded any diminution in royal control over the university: on the contrary, it increased yet further. In 1541 Henry VIII had returned to the matter of the election of proctors which he considered every year gave occasion for strife, debate and variance, and commanded that in future no one should meddle in the voting but the chancellor, his commissary, the

[1] *L & P Henry VIII* viii. no. 799; xii. pt 1, no. 212; xiii. pt 2, no. 561; xiv. pt 1, no. 684; xiv. pt 2, no. 71; cf Loach, 'Reformation controversies', 367–8 below.
[2] *L & P Henry VIII* xvi. no. 333; xxi. pt 2, nos. 476 (9), 648 (25); Christ Church Archives D.P. vi b i fos 13^V–19^V.

doctors and the masters of colleges, and allowed only masters of arts of at least eight years' standing to be nominated for the office. This order provides yet more evidence that under state pressure real power in the university was being removed from the regent masters and given into the hands of the masters of colleges and the doctors.[1]

The final year of the reign gave the university fresh cause to reflect on the might and capricious purpose of the king it likened to an English Octavius. In January 1546 the vice-chancellors of Oxford and Cambridge received a commission to view the statutes and ordinances of every college in order to produce a valuation of their lands and other possessions. Both universities contrived to send back a return within a month: from the Oxford valuation New College and Magdalen with annual revenues in the region of £800 appear as easily the two wealthiest colleges in the absence of the yet more wealthy Christ Church, presumably not included as it was still in process of refoundation. No other college had an income of as much as £500 a year and most existed on very much less. In later life Archbishop Parker recalled how he as vice-chancellor of Cambridge had taken his university's valuation in person to Hampton Court where the king seemed surprised that 'so many persons [were] so honestly maintained in living by little land and rent' and went on to remark to his lords, who the academics feared were planning to seize their property in a new dissolution, 'that pity it were these lands should be altered to make them worse'. So the state preserved the universities and their colleges in their endowments, though it extended this protection as the senior members more and more came to realize, only in the expectation of unquestioning obedience.[2]

After the relatively placid intermission of the last six years of Henry's VIII's reign the accession of Edward VI introduced into Oxford a new period of radical change. Bishop Longland opportunely died in May 1547, and Richard Cox, dean of Christ Church and tutor to the young king, succeeded him as chancellor. The way now lay open not only for more direct state intervention in the university but also for the dominance within Oxford of the richest, royal foundation. Cox soon revealed himself to be a committed protestant and co-operated closely with Cranmer in the uphill task of transforming Oxford into a protestant university. In 1547 the undertaking must have seemed a daunting one, but the archbishop soon discovered a new source of assistance from continental protestant scholars who, after the promulgation of the *Interim* by the emperor, readily accepted

---

[1] *L & P Henry VIII* xvi. no. 752; xviii. pt 1, nos. 583, 981 (71); *APC* i. 137–8.
[2] *L & P Henry VIII* xxi. pt 1, nos. 68, 148 (77), 244, 299; J. Lamb, *A Collection of . . . Documents from the MS Library of Corpus Christi College . . . Cambridge* (1838), 60.

Cranmer's invitation to seek refuge in England. Peter Martyr, among the first to arrive, landed in England in December 1547 and early in 1548, on the deprivation of the conservative Dr Richard Smith, accepted the offer of the regius chair of theology at Oxford. In Martyr the university found itself provided with one of the most illustrious as well as one of the most controversial figures of the continental reformation. At first he had to contend almost single-handed with a throng of adversaries among the senior members, and his confrontations with them seem to have been far more bitter than anything experienced by the more pacific Bucer who did not come to fill the regius chair at Cambridge until the autumn of 1549. Fairly soon, however, as Oxford afforded a haven to other foreign prote-stant scholars, Martyr gained allies. In 1548 Andrew Croariensis and Augustine Bernher both joined the university as did a frequent correspondent of Bullinger, John ab Ulmis, who with Cox's aid eventually obtained a scholarship at Christ Church. John Rodolph Stumphius who reached Oxford the next year also acquired a bursary there. Ab Ulmis brought over two of his cousins, Henry and Conrad, for a year, while Christopher Froschover, the nephew of the printer, spent rather longer in the university. Alexander Schmutz, nephew of Bernher, studied in Oxford from 1549 till the end of the reign and gained the state pension relinquished by ab Ulmis. In all, at least eleven Swiss students of varying degrees of seniority attended Oxford in the Edwardian period. In addition to broadening the horizons of a somewhat insular university they gave Martyr the moral support he needed so much.[1]

Immediately on his appointment to his professorship in the spring of 1548 Martyr began disseminating his unambiguous protestant beliefs, lecturing first on the epistle to the Corinthians. Besides his public lectures he also sometimes preached in St Mary's and gave private lectures and sermons in Italian in his own house, attracting at the time the admiration of Dr Cole of New College, and Sidall and Curtop of Christ Church, and winning the devoted friendship of Parkhurst, then a fellow of Merton. These scholars, however, in no sense represented the general attitude of the senior members of the university, who complied only reluctantly with the religious innova-tions. Owen Oglethorpe, president of Magdalen, in November 1548 felt it incumbent on him to assure Protector Somerset of his zeal for true religion, asserting that he had not only accepted the new English

[1] C. H. Smyth, *Cranmer and the Reformation under Edward VI* (1926), 108–25, 133–8; Strype, *Memorials* ii. pt 1, 63–4. *Original Letters* 360–1, 377–468, 488, 719–27; J. E. A. Dawson, 'The early career of Christopher Goodman and his place in the development of English protestant thought' (Durham PhD. thesis 1978), 63–98.

communion service but had willingly administered it himself and caused it to be used in his college as the fellows could attest. This new service, in fact, created much uneasiness among many members of the university and the moment that Martyr gave notice of his intention of expounding the nature of Christ's presence in the eucharist, matters came to a head. Less than twenty-four hours before his course was due to begin his opponents posted up bills in English on church doors advertising a public disputation on the sacrament of the altar the next day, so that when the regius professor appeared to lecture the schools were crammed with a restive audience of students and townspeople. Martyr refused to be deflected from his prepared script by the uproar, even when a servant of the ousted Dr Smith in his master's name challenged him to a disputation. The lecture over, to avoid further disorder, the vice-chancellor, Richard Cox, called Martyr, Smith and some of their rival supporters to his house to arrange for a formal academic disputation which he fixed for early in May 1549, in the meanwhile informing the council of all the circumstances. By May, Smith had fled the university, but Dr Tresham and Dr Chedsey presented themselves in his place. So seriously did the government regard the state of affairs that, in an attempt to remove some of the heat from the situation, it decreed that the disputation might only be held under the supervision of the royal visitors.[1]

The crown had published the commission for a further royal visitation of Oxford and Cambridge in November 1548, and in May 1549 the visitors appeared almost simultaneously in each university. The main reasons for the visitation seem to have been to give a formal outward recognition to protestantism, to purge the universities and colleges of any traces of catholicism, and to give a fresh impetus to syllabus reform, in particular to encourage the study of civil law, still considered as a most suitable field of study for future servants of the state. Again, more information about the visitors' actions is available for Cambridge than for Oxford, and the proceedings at Oxford can only be reconstructed hypothetically with reference to Cambridge. The Cambridge visitors, led by Thomas Goodrich, bishop of Ely, and Nicholas Ridley, bishop of Rochester, arrived in the university on 6 May and went immediately to King's College chapel where they gave notice of their commission before the assembled masters and scholars, and all present took an oath against the bishop of Rome. John Cheke, one of the commissioners, then read out the new statutes sent from the king, and the bishop of

---

[1] PRO SP 10/5, no. 12; J. Strype, *Cranmer* (2 vols Oxford 1812), i. 283–6; Strype, *Memorials* ii. pt 1, 324–5; Smyth, *Cranmer*, 118–19; cf Loach, pp. 369 ff. below.

Ely concluded the session by exhorting them all to obey the king, renounce papistry, and to bring in bills of matters in the university and the colleges needing reform. In the following days the commissioners patiently visited each college in turn: they seem to have found few reminders of Roman rites, though at Jesus they had to order the pulling down of six altars and the removal of certain images. The inspection continued from 7 May until 19 June and then on Corpus Christi day, a day obviously selected with care, the visitors presided over a formal disputation in the philosophy schools. They chose for debate two of the most burning theological issues of the day, that transubstantiation had no scriptural justification and that the supper of Christ should be seen not as an oblation but only as a commemoration and thanksgiving. The bishop of Ely himself intervened in the disputation when the defenders of the conclusions seemed hard pressed, and on succeeding days the visitors took further opportunities of reinforcing these key protestant tenets. They did not leave the university till early in July.[1]

In the course of their visitation the commissioners at Cambridge made known the government's plans for the amalgamation of Clare and Trinity Hall to create one college of civil law, but the proposal caused an unexpected breach among the visitors in addition to provoking resistance within the colleges concerned. Reasons of state seemed to be at odds with spreading of the gospel, and Ridley informed Somerset that he considered it 'a very sore thing, a great scandal . . . and a dangerous example to the world . . . to take a college founded for the study of God's word and to apply it to the use of students in man's laws'. The government, nevertheless, persisted in its scheme for a college of civil law, to be called Edward College, but Ridley's stand together with the protests of the two halls ultimately frustrated the venture.[2]

The visitation of Oxford seems to have followed very much the general pattern of that at Cambridge, beginning with a formal meeting of the visitors and the university on 24 May in St Mary's church where Peter Martyr preached the opening sermon. After this the visitors went on to investigate the individual colleges, and their inspection seems again to have stimulated some colleges to add to their college libraries: Merton alone sold plate to the value of over £70 in order to buy books. May 28 marked the climax of the visitation when the disputation on the eucharist, postponed by Cox until the royal visitors could attend, finally took place. In the formal academic exercises which lasted until 1 June Martyr defended against

Tresham, Chedsey and Morgan the main proposition that the sacrament of thanksgiving contained no element of the medieval doctrine of the transubstantiation of the bread and wine into the body and blood of Christ, Cox interjecting arguments in favour of the protestant side, as Ridley had done at Cambridge. Although the outcome of the disputation seemed inconclusive, so that later both sides could claim victory, the presence of the visitors at least prevented further public disturbances, and the occasion served the purposes of protestant propaganda with the council's authorization of the printing of Martyr's version of the debates. In addition to their religious preoccupations, the visitors also attempted to make better provision for the study of civil law, suggesting that the arts fellows from All Souls should be transferred to New College, and the civilians from New College moved to All Souls, so that All Souls could become a civil law college. The proposal seems to have been received without enthusiasm and then quietly dropped, though without exciting the anguished representations Cambridge had made against the amalgamation of Trinity Hall and Clare. The final solemn act of the Oxford visitors happened on 4 June when Holbeach, the bishop of Lincoln, Cox, Morrison and Nevinson, sitting in St Mary's, presented the university with new statutes.[1]

The government had not designed these statutes to be permanent, looking on them merely as a temporary expedient until the long-delayed codification of the old statutes could be accomplished, a reform now all the more urgent since the religious complexion of the university had been so radically altered. Like the injunctions of the Henrician visitors the Edwardian statutes stressed the reordering of teaching within the university, fixing times of lectures in the arts and in Greek and Hebrew, setting out which books should be read, regulating the necessary disputations in the faculties of arts, law and theology, and ensuring that college teaching should not encroach upon the public lectures and exercises of the university. In this respect they seem to have been doing little more than supporting the attempt to revitalize the public teaching of the university begun earlier in the century when first the Lady Margaret and later Wolsey had instituted new university lectureships. Constitutionally the statutes, although they laid down rules concerning the election of the chancellor and vice-chancellor, the proctors, bedels and other university officers, introduced no particularly new developments. They were important rather because they abrogated all statutes with popish implications and for the first time formally associated the

---

[1] Wood, *History and Antiquities* ii. 92–106; Foxe, *Acts and Monuments* vi. 197–305; Smyth, *Cranmer*, 118–19; *VCH Oxon.* iii. 19–20; *Oxford College Libraries*, 17.

university with protestantism. From henceforth fellows and scholars had to attend the protestant communion service at the beginning of each term and regularly frequent protestant prayers in their college chapels. The visitors subsequently amplified the statutes by sending down glosses on certain technical points, such as listing by title the books to be studied in the arts and civil law courses, and added further injunctions which generally tightened up the procedure necessary for admission to degrees.[1]

Acting as the instrument of the central government, first the visitors and, after their departure, Cox as chancellor, did all they could to advance the protestant party in the university. The public disputation before the visitors had neither silenced the conservatives nor quelled the opposition to Martyr. Private religious disputations continued to be held in the colleges; at one in Christ Church, Cox tried to refute the existence of purgatory and condemned the practice of praying for the dead. Still the conservatives would not admit defeat. Without Martyr's knowledge, certain bachelors of theology conspired together to stage a fresh disputation on transubstantiation, this time under the friendly moderation of Dr Chedsey to ensure victory for the catholic side, and the vice-chancellor only foiled the plot at the last moment by forbidding any disputations in theology without the authorization of the regius professor. All these tribulations Martyr related at length to Bucer in Cambridge. Bucer himself paid a short visit to his friend in July 1550 a few months before he died, and read a lecture in Christ Church on the text, 'Consecrate them, O Father, in the truth . . .'. In January 1551 Martyr gained fresh promotion and official recognition when a canonry at Christ Church fell vacant, though his removal there with his wife, a former nun (with Cox's wife, the first woman to live openly in an Oxford college), offended the susceptibilities of the catholics even further. Conscious of the obstacles facing the protestants in Oxford the government in other ways also lent its weight to encouraging protestants both in the university as a whole and in the colleges. In 1550 the king tried, though without success, to persuade Oriel to elect as its provost the doctrinaire William Turner, a subsequent exile who ended his life an eccentric and vehemently anti-catholic Elizabethan dean of Wells. With New College the privy council acted rather more circumspectly at first in October 1551 only prohibiting the fellows from choosing a new warden without royal licence, but then in the new year allowing a commission to look into objections against Dr Cole. The commissioners used their powers to displace Cole who was succeeded

[1] *Statuta*, 341–55, 355–60.

by Ralph Skinner, a former member of the college and a committed protestant.[1]

Other Oxford conservatives in addition to Cole came under increasingly severe government pressure in 1551. Early in the year the privy council called Dr Chedsey before it to account for his seditious preaching in Oxford at the beginning of Lent and eventually imprisoned him in the Marshalsea. A few months later it sent to the Fleet Dr Morwent, the president of Corpus and certain of the fellows suspected of using ceremonies on Corpus Christi day other than those prescribed in the new book of common prayer, nominating a temporary warden of the college during Morwen's detention. Before the end of 1551 it also summoned the former commissary, Dr Tresham, now merely a prebendary of Christ Church, to London to explain his position in relation to the religious changes. It may well be that the government's concern over the amount of conservatism among some senior members of the university led to its decision to renew the commission to visit the university in the autumn of 1551. Yet not even these measures sufficed to crush the opposition, and Somerset's disgrace precipitated catholic riots in Oxford and mass was again celebrated there, the proceedings, according to the Swiss student, Stumphius, ending in drunken orgies. Northumberland's government in consequence in its turn never felt able to relax its supervision over Oxford throughout the remainder of the reign, though it obtained a major triumph in 1552 when it prevailed upon Owen Oglethorpe to resign from the presidency of Magdalen in favour of the king's candidate, the convinced protestant, Walter Haddon.[2]

Edward VI did not live long enough for the policy of his protestant governments towards the university to have much chance of making a lasting impression, though there are indications of protestantism beginning to take root. Cox certainly fostered protestantism at Christ Church; in addition to Haddon, Bentham and Bickley actively proselytized at Magdalen which also included John Foxe among its fellows; at this time Harding at New College proclaimed himself an ardent protestant while William Cole and Jewel led the protestants at Corpus. Compared with Cambridge, however, the acceptance of protestantism seems to have been slow. In the short

[1] Strype, *Cranmer* i. 359–60; Strype, *Memorials* ii. pt 1, 326, 383; PRO SP 10/11, no. 14; *APC* iii. 63–4, 139, 204; G. D. Duncan, 'The heads of houses and religious change in Tudor Oxford 1547–1558', *Oxoniensia* xlv (1980), 226–34; G. C. Gorham, *Gleanings of a Few Scattered Ears during the Period of the Reformation in England* (1857), 80–92, 123–6, 140–2, 151–6, 168–83; *Original Letters* 490–5.

[2] *APC* iii. 237, 287, 305, 307, 371, 384, 429–30; iv. 106, 112; Smyth, *Cranmer*, 273; PRO SP 10/14, no. 58.

term there can be little doubt that state policy affected numbers in the university quite dramatically. The successive religious alterations combined with the spoliation of the church by both Henrician and Edwardian governments meant that the church no longer appeared to offer the safe and lucrative career to university graduates it had formerly done. The government's efforts to attract students to study civil law had no demonstrable result, and it seems that in Edward's reign the number of students at Oxford may have reached its lowest ebb for the entire century. When a census was taken of the university in 1552 only Christ Church, Magdalen and New College returned the names of a hundred or more fellows and scholars. Brasenose, All Souls and Corpus had over fifty members; the remaining seven colleges each contained between twenty-five and thirty-five fellows and scholars. Of the halls which had once specialized in the study of law there were now only eight, and most of these had only a handful of students. The total which the census gives of just over a thousand masters and scholars in colleges and halls may perhaps be an under-estimate of the total number of members of the university in 1552 since it does not take account of students living in the town who did not belong to any college or hall. The numbers of these unattached students because of the innovations in religion and the ensuing colle-giate religious tests may actually have been rising. The evidence nevertheless suggests a real decline in comparison with the decade of the 1520s before there had been any reformation changes, when a record figure of some fifty-five students a year were being admitted to the degree of BA, which probably indicates an annual entry of about two hundred and twenty students to the university.[1]

If in these ways the fortunes of the university reached their nadir in the sixteenth century in the reign of Edward VI, the succession of Mary contributed to a pronounced recovery. By the mid-century English governments fully understood the importance of the two universities in effecting and consolidating religious change: within a month of obtaining the crown Mary ordered the chancellors of Oxford and Cambridge and the heads of colleges to readopt their ancient statutes and put aside any ordinances provided by visitors since her father's death. In doing so the universities would set an example and instruct the rest of her subjects in the knowledge and fear of God and in their duty to the queen. Since the ancient statutes of both the universities and colleges contained abundant directions relating to the observance of the rites and ceremonies of the old

---

[1] *Reg. Univ.* ed. Boase, pp. xxi–xxv; Lawrence Stone (ed.), *The University in Society* (2 vols Princeton 1975) i. 91–2; E. Russell, 'The influx of commoners to the university of Oxford before 1581; an optical illusion?', *English Historical Review* xcii (1977), 721–45.

religion the queen by this command made it possible for the conservatives in Oxford to resume catholic practice even before parliament had met to change the law on the religious settlement. Wood records how Peter Martyr, as he and his band of foreign protestants were leaving the university to return to the continent, heard the bell at Corpus ringing for mass, and, sighing, said, 'that bell would destroy all the doctrine in that college which he before had through his and Jewel's labours planted therein'.[1]

In order to re-create Oxford as a bastion of catholic orthodoxy Mary's advisers realized that the reimposition of the statutes on their own would not suffice. The university needed strengthening financially, and again within less than a year of her accession, in May 1554 Mary made a most important benefaction to Oxford. After reciting how the university had been so afflicted by the wrongs of the times that it lay almost uncultivated, with no means to sustain its dignity, its public schools wasted, its treasury plundered, its ornaments carried off, and its revenues reduced almost to nothing, the queen announced her desire of raising the university up so that once more it might be able to defend the orthodox faith against heretics: with this intent she granted the university in perpetuity the rectories of South Petherwyn and Trenaunte in Cornwall, Syston in Leicestershire and Holm Cultram and Newton Arlocke in Cumberland. These rectories produced an annual income of £131 19s, not in itself a particularly large sum but one nevertheless which tripled the university's yearly revenue. Until this time the university had been seriously underendowed when compared to some of its colleges, and the fairly recent institution of university lectureships had done little to improve its general financial position. Attempts by Warham and later Wolsey to reform the antiquated system of university chests had achieved almost nothing, and mismanagement combined with inflation had meant that in some years the university had not been able to pay its servants: in 1551 there was said to be less than £15 in the chests, and Cox as chancellor maintained that the university had an income of only £5, whereas Cambridge enjoyed almost ten times as much. This new grant, therefore, completely altered the university's financial position. Rather later, in 1556, Cardinal Pole specified precisely how Oxford should make use of Mary's gift: part of the money had to go on masses for the queen and her parents, the rest on fees for university officials, on rebuilding the schools (on which £100 annually had to be spent until their reconstruction was completed), on entertainment of official visitors and on defending its privileges. This gift, made when the university was particularly week

[1] PRO SP 11/1, no. 11; Wood, *History and Antiquities* ii. 117-22; cf Loach, p. 375 below.

contributed very much to the recovery not only of its finances but also of its morale. The university responded with a fervent acknowledgement of its gratitude to the queen.[1]

This new financial support must have been all the more welcome since the confidence of some of the senior and junior members of the university had undergone a severe testing from the moment of Mary's accession. Unlike the foreign protestants who experienced little difficulty in leaving Oxford for the continent very soon after Mary became queen, the English members of the university who had committed themselves to protestantism had no obvious place of retreat. In the many colleges which had a bishop as visitor episcopal visitations began early in the reign, and Gardiner in particular, in his capacity as bishop of Winchester visitor of Magdalen, New College and Corpus, carried out his duties with alacrity. The convenient fact that under Edward VI senior members of the colleges had set aside their ancient statutes provided the bishop's officials with more than adequate grounds for evicting obstinate protestants. By these means a near purge took place in the autumn of 1553 at both New College and Magdalen. The visitors expelled the recently appointed warden of New College, Ralph Skinner, procured the resignation of Walter Haddon, the new president of Magdalen, restoring Oglethorpe to office, and then went on to exclude the dean, Thomas Bentham, and perhaps as many as twelve or thirteen other members of the college. At Corpus some of the conservative faction brought out the vestments and ornaments they had hidden in Edward's reign; on the news of the visitors' arrival Jewel gave up his fellowship, though he did not yet leave the university. Christ Church, where on Cox's departure Tresham regained his lost authority, Exeter, where the rector, William More, was deprived, and Merton were other colleges which lost a number of protestants who preferred exile to conformity.[2]

The majority of the university, however, whether willingly or reluctantly quickly returned to catholic observance, and the government soon took steps to use Oxford as a setting for a demonstration of the heinousness of academic heresy. In March 1554 the privy council sent Cranmer, Latimer and Ridley, imprisoned in the Tower since early in the previous autumn, from London to the university for their trial. The government obviously saw this as a way of publicly reversing the results of the disputations which had been

[1] *Cal. Pat. Rolls Philip & Mary* i. 165–6; I. G. Philip, 'Queen Mary Tudor's benefaction to the university', *Bodleian Library Record* v (1954), 27–37; *Statuta*, 362; PRO SP 11/4, no. 15.

[2] Foxe vi. 566; Strype, *Memorials* ii. pt 1, 81, 220–1; Duncan, 'Heads of houses'; Dawson, 'Early career of Christopher Goodman', 17–21.

staged in the presence of the royal visitors at Oxford and Cambridge in the former reign. It called upon catholic doctors from Cambridge to go to Oxford to join William Tresham, Richard Smith (now once again in possession of the lectureship in theology he had had to vacate for Martyr), William Chedsey and others in a formal disputation on the nature of the mass with Cranmer, Latimer and Ridley. It was held before the assembled university, the mayor and other representatives of the town 'so as their erroneous opinions being by the word of God justly and truly convinced, the residue of our subjects may be thereby the better established in the true catholic faith'. From 14 April until 18 April 1554 the three protestants in turn debated with their catholic opponents 'Whether the natural body of Christ be really in the sacrament, after the words spoken by the priest, or no? Whether in the sacrament, after the words of consecration, any other substance do remain than the substance of the body and blood of Christ? Whether the mass be a sacrifice propitiatory for the sins of the quick and the dead?' After frequently appealing to the auditory, and on occasion translating sections of the Latin disputations into English for their benefit, Weston, the prolocutor, claimed that the truth of the propositions had been amply demonstrated. On 20 April he required Cranmer, Ridley and Latimer to subscribe to the articles, and on their refusal, pronounced each man separately to be a heretic.[1]

Apart from this academic judgement no final action could be taken against the three prisoners until in December 1554 Parliament brought back the medieval laws which provided the death penalty for heresy. Consequently Ridley and Latimer stayed in prison in Oxford for a further nineteen months after the disputation and Cranmer for almost two years. Then in September 1555 the pope gave James Brooks, bishop of Gloucester, authority to investigate charges that Cranmer had broken the canon law and repudiated papal supremacy. Brooks also had powers to enquire into the opinions Ridley and Latimer had maintained at the academic disputation, and on their refusal either to subscribe the articles they had rejected over a year and half ago, or to recognize the pope, he condemned them as heretics for the second time, and in St Mary's on 15 October supervised their degradation from their clerical orders. On 16 October 1555 they died at the stake in the ditch over against Balliol, Dr Smith preaching a sermon on the text, 'If I yield my body to the fire to be burnt and have not charity, I shall gain nothing thereby.' Cranmer's ordeal lasted even longer since, as he had been appointed

---

[1] *APC* iv. 406; Foxe, *Acts and Monuments* vi. 440-535; Reg. Cong. 1535-63, fos 8 ff, 142-43; D. M. Loades, *The Oxford Martyrs* (1970), 128-37.

by the pope to the see of Canterbury, his degradation could not be performed for a further eighty days until his condemnation had been expressly sanctioned by Rome. Part of this period of waiting he spent out of prison in the more lenient custody of Dr Marshall, the dean of Christ Church, until early in 1556 on the receipt of the pope's commission he was sent back to Bocardo. This alternation of harsh and gentle treatment seems to have sapped Cranmer's wavering resolution, and he signed a series of more and more abject recantations fully acknowledging the sovereignty of the pope. Despite his surrender the queen still determined that he should die. On 15 February Bishops Thirlby and Bonner carried out his solemn degradation in the choir of Christ Church and on 21 March, a foul and rainy day, he too came to his burning. Because of the weather the formal proceedings took place in St Mary's where Dr Cole preached on Cranmer's belated conversion. The congregation then waited for the former archbishop to make a public confession of his heresy, but instead of the expected last submission Cranmer, finding strength in his extremity, withdrew all his recantations, renounced the pope and asserted that his beliefs continued to be those which he had set down in his book against the bishop of Winchester. He promised that his hand which had offended, writing contrary to his heart, should be the first part of his body to suffer in the fire. So Cranmer at the eleventh hour in addition to Latimer and Ridley died a martyr for his faith.[1]

The effect upon the university of this treatment of the leading academic protestants, far more harsh than anything Oxford conservatives had endured under Edward VI, seems to have been twofold. The resolute deaths of the martyrs may have encouraged a tiny minority to remain steadfast in their protestantism, and have actually won over others from catholicism, as was certainly the case with Julius Palmer, while the persecution doubtless dragooned a majority into conformity. Over the two years of trials the university itself had clearly been demonstrated to be no place for confessing protestants, and those who had not already left in the early months of the reign withdrew either to more obscure parts of England or overseas. Of approximately 137 university men who went into exile on the continent at least 51, and probably 60, had received their education at Oxford: of 341 known academics who became protestants before 1559, 163 had studied at Oxford compared with 178 at Cambridge, which after the suppression of the monasteries, may well have been approaching Oxford in size. Protestants indeed formed a very small minority

[1] Foxe, *Acts and Monuments* viii. 80–90; Loades, *Oxford Martyrs*, 192–233.

at Oxford, but one which seems not to have been so very much smaller than the minority at Cambridge.[1]

The Marian persecution, however, had consequences other than confirming a band of protestants in opposition. Outside the university as well as within, these strong measures taken to restore catholicism evoked a positive and not merely a negative response. The state itself, perhaps at Pole's prompting, in direct imitation of Cranmer's actions in the previous reign, made a somewhat tardy attempt to reinforce the actual content of catholic teaching at Oxford by placing two Spanish theologians in the university, the friars Peter de Soto and John de Garcia, the latter of whom also held the regius chair of theology. De Soto's readings, it was said, restored the university to the condition of orthodoxy it had enjoyed before Peter Martyr had begun his heretical lectures. No less significantly, some lay concern over the condition of university teaching seems to have been aroused. In the spring and early summer of 1555 two London merchants, Sir Thomas Pope and Sir Thomas White, obtained licences from the crown to establish new colleges in Oxford, dedicated to the Holy Trinity and to St John the Baptist, and Pope in the following year created the nucleus of his college library by presenting Trinity with a hundred books. In the statutes of their respective colleges the two men recorded their common purpose of promoting the orthodox faith and good learning; they also incidentally did what the university of Cambridge had for years begged Henry VIII to do, and made use of the derelict sites of former monastic colleges (in these instances Durham College and St Bernard's College) for their new foundations.[2]

These changes, considerable as they were, did not satisfy Pole, who believed it was necessary to do even more to impose strict orthodoxy upon the universities. Just over a year after he had entered England as papal legate he put in hand plans for legatine visitations of both Oxford and Cambridge in the spring and summer of 1556. The visitation of Cambridge came first, perhaps because until March Oxford's theologians were still engaged in the final proceedings against Cranmer. From the very detailed diary kept by John Mere, registrar of Cambridge, which Matthew Parker took

[1] Foxe, *Acts and Monuments* viii. 206; the figure for university protestants who went into exile is drawn from an analysis of C. H. Garrett, *The Marian Exiles* (Cambridge 1938); I owe the figures of university protestants to Dr J. Fines who has allowed me to use his as yet unpublished 'Register of early British protestants 1520-1558'; J. B. Mullinger, *The University of Cambridge from the royal injunctions of 1535 to the accession of Charles I* (Cambridge 1884), 49; L. Stone, 'The educational revolution in England 1560-1640', *Past and Present* xxviii (1964), 47-51; *University in Society* i. 91-2.

[3] *Cal. Pat. Rolls Philip & Mary* ii. 90-1, 322-3; Strype, *Memorials* iii. pt 1, 475-6; *Oxford College Libraries*.

pains to preserve for posterity, it is clear that Pole and his adjutants deliberately designed the visitations to reverse everything the Edwardian visitors had done and to invigorate catholicism in all possible ways. Arriving in Cambridge in early January they first assisted at mass in King's College chapel before adjourning to the university church to open heresy investigations into the teaching of the dead continental reformers, Bucer and Fagius. While waiting for the outcome of the trial they went from college to college hearing mass, examining the chapel furnishings, looking into the execution of ancient statutes and searching for prohibited books. On 6 February they interrupted their perambulations to preside over the exhumation of the bodies of Bucer and Fagius which were then burnt in the Market Square. After final ceremonies which culminated in the rehallowing of Great St Mary's and a solemn procession and mass at which the corporation joined with the university, the visitors publicly read to the heads of houses a letter from Pole and, on 15 February, presented the university with new statutes.[1]

The legatine visitation of the university of Oxford, entrusted to James Brooks, bishop of Gloucester, Nicholas Ormanet, the pope's datary, Robert Morwent, president of Corpus Christi, Henry Cole, provost of Eton, William Wright, archdeacon of Oxford and others, did not begin till late July. If, as was possible, Cranmer's public recantation and submission to the catholic church had been intended as a triumphant prelude to the visitation, his final espousal of protestantism had thwarted the government's scheme. The university nevertheless had been given a salutary and very recent warning of the fate of heretics. Although again much less is known about the legatine visitation of Oxford than that of Cambridge, a copy of the articles Pole delivered to the visitors has survived. His schedule of enquiries covered thirty distinct topics. He expected his visitors to enquire whether foundation statutes were observed and to examine any new statutes made during the time of schism, to find out whether the ordinary lectures were properly delivered, and all masses, anniversaries, processions, and other divine offices performed in the university and in the individual colleges. He then wanted them to scrutinize the election of university officers, and to assess whether they carried out their administrative duties efficiently, and also whether college officers were similarly conscientiously educating the young. He wished the visitors to look into the university's finances and to discover whether any property had been alienated. He showed particular interest in books, both those dispersed in the time of schism and heretical books publicly or privately retained in the

[1] Lamb, *Collection of Documents*, 184–236.

university. Pole shared with earlier reformers concern that the university disputations and exercises should be correctly kept, and degrees conferred according to the statutes, but in addition to a very marked emphasis on the search for heretics displayed an even greater attachment to discipline than they had done, asking for information about students who did not frequent the schools or engage in study but wasted their time in idleness and games or embroiled themselves in disputes with the townspeople. In the penultimate section of his articles he enquired whether there were as many students in the university as formerly and if, as he implied, there had been a falling off in numbers, asked for reasons for the decline.[1]

Pole's visitors almost certainly progressed round the Oxford colleges as their Cambridge colleagues had done, though there is no detailed record of their itinerary. Three colleges, however, Merton, All Souls and Brasenose, still retain inventories of their libraries presented to the visitors at this time. The vice-chancellor in a letter to the cardinal in November 1556 referred more generally to the abuses the visitors had detected in particular colleges and houses together with the injunctions they had supplied for their redress, so that good order and obedience might be restored. Unlike Cambridge no foreign protestant leaders had been buried in Oxford in Edward's reign, but the visitors still sought ways by which all continental protestant influences could be eliminated. All Oxford could offer was the body of the inoffensive wife of Peter Martyr. The visitors failed to procure enough evidence to justify a posthumous sentence of heresy against her, but because she had broken vows of celibacy to marry, they ordered her corpse to be taken from consecrated ground and thrown on a dunghill. By such actions they hoped to discredit protestantism in Oxford yet further and advance the cause of catholicism.[2]

Ever since Cox had relinquished the chancellorship late in 1552, Oxford had had Sir John Mason as its chancellor, whereas Cambridge in the person of Stephen Gardiner from the beginning of Mary's reign had received the attentions of an ecclesiastic far more involved in the process of catholic restoration. In the autumn of 1556 the tables were turned. Mason resigned and Oxford elected Pole to replace him. The new chancellor immediately granted a commission to Thomas Reynolds, his commissary, to review the existing statutes, to make reforms and, if necessary, to devise new regulations. In the interim, like the Edwardian commissioners, he gave the university

[1] Bodl. MS Twyne vii. fos 155-7.
[2] Cal. SP Dom. Addenda vi. 446-7; Oxford College Libraries; Foxe, Acts and Monuments viii. 296-7.

provisional statutes to be in force until the codification could be completed. Pole's statutes closely echo the matters he had brought to the notice of his visitors earlier in the year. He stressed the commissary's responsibility for seeing that the statutes were observed to the letter, the university purged of heretics and heretical influences and unprofitable students and loose-livers chastised. Like so many in government before him, he also considered the problem of the election of proctors, ordaining that no one under the age of twenty-five and of less than two years' standing as a master of arts could hold office, and emphasized the need for those chosen to be grave and learned. He introduced rules concerning the management of the university's revenues and in particular the expenditure of the queen's gift. All his statutes relating to the behaviour of the vice-chancellor, the proctors and bedels placed a special emphasis on discipline, and in addition entrusted the bedels with the new task of keeping a record of all the students in every faculty. He forbade students to live in private houses contrary to the statutes, and ordered all those over twelve to enrol in a college or hall. This statute directly affected the heads of houses since Pole regarded them as personally answerable for their pupils' spiritual and academic welfare. His statutes ended as they began with an overriding concern for religious orthodoxy: he commanded all lecturers, both in the university and in the colleges to teach nothing contrary to the catholic faith and when, as in philosophy, they had to discuss matters which reflected upon religion, to follow the opinions of those who differed least from catholic truth.[1]

Late in November 1556 the commissary assured Pole that little by little the chancellor would see a new face of the university, as well in life as in learning, and it does seem that Mary's last years marked a slow improvement in Oxford's prosperity. Through the queen's generosity the university for the first time had adequate funds to repair its public buildings; some stability seemed to be returning to academic studies after the religious turmoil of the reign of Edward VI and the early years of Mary; above all there were some signs of an increase of students proceeding long enough at the university to qualify as regent masters in arts. From less than twenty bachelors determining annually in 1554 and 1555 the numbers began to approach thirty a year, that is about as many as there had been in the first decade of the sixteenth century, though still not much more than half as many as had determined in the 1520s. By 1558 Oxford had been re-established as a catholic university governed by a catholic chancellor and catholic heads of houses, but as the previous half century had shown, the university was at the mercy of

[1] *Statuta*, 363–75.

the monarch and successive royal governments. On Mary's death those who had eyes to see must have resigned themselves to yet more violent reversals of academic policy.[1]

From 1509 to 1558 there had been no formal changes in the university's constitution. Yet even in the early years of the century the theoretically self-governing corporation of regent masters had long been accustomed to turn to its chancellor and other government servants for sponsorship of new educational developments and much needed new endowments, as it had continued to appeal to the state for the defence of its privileges, especially against the ambitions of the townsmen. Well before the reformation in times of academic unrest the government had looked to the chancellor, his commissary and to the heads of houses to impose order. This state direction appeared all the more pronounced when Henry VIII began intervening in the choice of university officers. With the religious changes at the time of the reformation the interdependence of the university and the state grew to a very considerable extent. Royal servants and then the crown itself probably gave more to the university than ever before, but undoubtedly asked for more in return. The university at the state's behest within one generation had to renounce Lutheran heresy, support the king's divorce, recognise the royal supremacy and accept the contradictory injunctions of the Henrician, Edwardian and Marian visitors. In the middle ages the university had been beholden to the state for protection, and more than ever in the sixteenth century this protection remained vital for the university's very existence; but the state's expectations of the university had now increased immensely. By the accession of Elizabeth the university had become a highly important adjunct to the state, the supporter of its policies, and a chief source of supply of its servants, and of clerics for its church. To a quite unprecedented degree Oxford and Cambridge had capitulated to state control.

---

[1] *Cal. SP Dom. Addenda* vi. 446-7; Wood, *History and Antiquities* ii. 135-8; *University in Society* i. 91.

4

Studies and Faculties
Introduction

JAMES McCONICA

THE statutory curriculum was the rule and foundation of the university's scholastic programme, but it was never meant to be a restrictive account. The first statutes may indeed have appeared in rather a haphazard fashion whenever a serious question arose about the 'custom of Paris' which the masters at Oxford thought generally to follow. By the fourteenth century these accumulating rules and regulations had been gathered together and were passed on from chancellor to chancellor in Registrum A, the oldest official register of the university.[1]

The power to legislate for the university lay originally with the whole body of masters, the 'universitas', but in time the younger body of regent masters achieved their own right to make enactments on minor matters and routine business.[2] The habit of proceeding largely by unwritten custom had its disadvantages and seems already by the early fourteenth century to have created some anxiety about the text and substance of the 'statutes, privileges and customs' which all took an oath to obey. So acute was the concern about incurring the penalties of perjury that in 1479 Pope Sixtus IV granted the university's chancellor the authority to absolve any member of the university on request.[3] From that time until the time of Laud the need to reform the statutes was a perennial preoccupation of the university's senior members. It greets us as one of the first matters of business before the university at the beginning of our period.[4]

Wolsey's promise and failure to solve the problem left the university singularly vulnerable to royal initiatives and these Oxford experienced under each successive monarch. There were visitations

[1] *Statuta antiqua universitatis Oxoniensis*, ed. Strickland Gibson (Oxford 1931), x, xlii–iv. This collection is referred to hereafter and throughout this volume as *Statuta*.

[2] Ibid. xxi–ii. See Claire Cross, 'Oxford and the Tudor state from the accession of Henry VIII to the death of Mary', p. 118 above.

[3] *Statuta*, xiv.

[4] Cross, 'Oxford and the Tudor state', 119.

under Henry VIII in 1535, in 1549 under Edward VI, in 1556 under cardinal Pole, newly elected chancellor, and in 1559 under Elizabeth.[1] On these or related occasions the statutes were examined in part and injunctions were issued of which the most enduring were those announced in February 1565 by the earl of Leicester, chancellor of the university, and which entered the history of the university as the 'new statutes'—the *Nova statuta*.[2] These were evidently intended to be provisional and the plan to undertake a general revision was not forgotten. Each Tudor decade saw some fresh initiative blunted by the very scale of the undertaking. It was not until 1629, after several more failures, that the successive chancellorships of the earl of Pembroke and of William Laud were able to muster the sustained effort needed to carry the task through to completion, and the new 'Laudian' code was received by convocation in 1634.[3]

It will be seen therefore that the 'statutory curriculum' of the Tudor university is in many ways a very hypothetical concept. When this is not as clearly understood by modern scholars as it was by contemporaries they may bring to its study any number of inappropriate notions ranging from its limitations and supposed rigidity to the clandestine alienation of college teaching from it. Prescriptions in the statutes were minimal: the decree that arithmetic should be studied from Gemma Frisius did not mean from that author only. In what follows the teaching of each faculty will be examined in turn. In the matter of the arts curriculum, however, there is further discussion in chapter 10 of the teaching within the colleges since with the growth of the undergraduate college, we have in this instance to deal with the most important institutional change in the Tudor university.

How large a university was it and what was the relative importance of the several faculties? With this question we are confronted by very difficult issues; our estimate can be only approximate.

The most searching examination of the population of the medieval universities in England has estimated that in the late fourteenth century Cambridge had a population of some 700 members compared to some 1,500 at Oxford.[4] Within a century, however, partly through the rapid accumulation of new foundations, the numbers at Cambridge rose to about 1,300 and those at Oxford much less, perhaps to 1,700 in all.

---

[1] See Penry Williams, 'Elizabethan Oxford: state, church and university', p. 403 below.
[2] *Statuta*, liii.
[3] Finally ratified June 1636. Ibid. lviii–lxvii.
[4] T. H. Aston, 'Oxford's medieval alumni', *Past and Present* lxxiv (1977), 3–40; T. H. Aston, G. D. Duncan and T. A. R. Evans, 'The medieval alumni of the university of Cambridge', *Past and Present* lxxxvi (1980), 9–86.

In August 1552 Richard Marshall, deputy to the vice-chancellor, instituted a census of all residents of the colleges and halls in Oxford. His reasons for this are unknown but it is of a piece with the growing concern about order in the university.[1] The total number in that census was only 1,015 and this figure appears to include the chief college servants. That this was not the whole picture we can be certain; what is not clear is just how many more were resident in the town. In July 1562 the inferior bedell of civil law summoned all students living in houses of the laity to appear before the vice-chancellor and state the tutor in whose charge they were; the number recorded was eighty-nine. If we allow for a large proportion who did not report (and there is no reason to think that such a summons would be widely disregarded) and raise the hypothetical number of town dwellers to 150 or 175 we arrive at a total population between 1,165 and 1,190 members. From this we should deduct some thirty names as belonging to cooks, manciples and other servants; a figure of perhaps 1,150 as a maximum would appear to be reasonable.[2] It is clear that the university's population had dropped sharply and the most obvious cause for this is the effect of the reformation.

Almost 800 religious are known to have studied at Oxford from the beginning of the sixteenth century to the final suppression of the monasteries in 1540.[3] Their disappearance altered drastically not only the size but the whole character of the university's life and population. It may also be presumed that the shock to the regular clergy was at first very considerable, especially with the abolition of the study of canon law. And apart from these changes related to the reformation it was already clear that the number of halls was dwindling in the late middle ages, although this was to some extent compensated for by the growth and amalgamation of surviving halls and by their incorporation into collegiate foundations.[4]

With the appearance of A. B. Emden's final biographical study of the university's alumni from 1501 to 1540 it became possible to say something of the nature of the university in the last medieval decades. Since, however, the story of the religious houses in those years is assigned to the second volume in this history it will be appropriate here to confine our remarks to some very general

[1] *Reg. Univ.* ed. Boase, xxi–xxv.

[2] The servants listed by office are included in the official total; in certain instances, as at Corpus and Brasenose, it is possible to show that other servants are included in the tally by their surnames. It should be added that the heading 'subgraduati' was taken by Boase from Wood and has no authority in the original manuscript.

[3] *BRUO 1501–40*, introduction xxi.

[4] For a discussion of the fate of the halls see James McConica, 'The rise of the undergraduate college', pp. 51 ff. above.

observations.[1] Emden's register contains the names of some 7,000 alumni, perhaps a third of all members who passed through Oxford during the period. It is heavily weighted in favour of those who took degrees, quite obviously, and also to those connected with colleges whose records were well preserved; it is not a random sample. As it is it suggests that the university was heavily English in make up like its medieval predecessor, and that within the English counties it drew most heavily on those from the south. There was a small but steady exchange with Cambridge but contacts with the continental universities seem to have decreased. However, contact in the form of foreign scholars coming to Oxford actually increased; they outnumbered those going abroad to study. Post-graduate study shows up sharply in such a group, of course, with almost forty per cent entering the higher faculties. Theology remained the largest single faculty but if the lawyers—canonists and civilians—are taken together they outnumber the theologians by a third. Almost all of the lawyers were seculars; almost half of the theologians were regulars. If we reckon that a high proportion of those graduating in either or both of canon and civil law were essentially canonists we are prepared for the comparative fate of the two faculties of law and theology after the reformation. In the decade after 1530, when the tensions of the royal divorce and the break with Rome took their full toll, the proportion of the known alumni who went on to graduate study dropped from almost 40 per cent to just half that figure.

A later estimate of the numbers in the university came from an account of the royal visit in 1566. The source is one Richard Stevens who appears otherwise to be unknown.[2] However, the rest of his account accords with information from other sources, and appended to the text of the queen's speech is an estimate of the number of 'students' and servants in the university: 1,764 and seventy-eight respectively. If by *studentes* we understand all senior and junior members this would indicate an increase of some 600 in fifteen years. In favour of such an increase would be the filling of the seventy-five or so places established in the 1550s at St John's and Trinity colleges where (as in so many other colleges as well) there were also increasing numbers of commoners. The Stephens figures

[1] For what follows I am indebted to an unpublished analysis of the Emden register by Mr T. H. Aston, general editor of the history of the university.

[2] 'A brief rehearsall of all such things as were done in the university of Oxford during the Queen's Majesty's abode there this exhibited by Richard Stephens as an extract drawn out of a longer treatise made by Mr Neale reader of Hebrew at Oxford', in *Elizabethan Oxford: reprints of rare tracts*, ed. Charles Plummer (OHS viii 1887); see Williams, 'Elizabethan Oxford', p. 397 n. 1 below.

would advance the influx into the Elizabethan university to the decade before the royal visit,[1] which is not in itself unreasonable. The increase seems too abrupt to accept without supporting evidence and since we know nothing of the background to this estimate it must be treated with scepticism. Nevertheless, it was drawn up at a time when careful estimates were being made of the relative ability of the colleges to pay for the visit, and at the very least it supports other indications that a growing population of commoners in the town brought a new prosperity to the Elizabethan university. If the recent estimate of some 400–50 annual admissions is accurate, and if most matriculants stayed at least three years with many on the foundation going on for four years or more, a figure of some 2,000 members in the last Elizabethan decades would not be out of the question.[2]

To turn to the faculties, how did they fare in the post-reformation years? There was calamity among the lawyers, not only because of the abolition of canon law but in light of the uncertain future of the ecclesiastical courts at large. Royal attempts to encourage the study of civil law met a wall of indifference; by the end of the century there were more legist fellowships in the colleges than there were lawyers to fill them.[3] In the five years from 1581 to 1585 only 4 per cent of the degrees awarded in arts and law (thirty-three out of 787) went to lawyers; in the period from 1591 to 1595 the figure dropped to 2.6 per cent.[4]

The faculty of medicine, never large, was smaller even than law. Small as it was, however, it had a surprisingly active membership, and it was never in danger of extinction although it may from time to time have dropped from sight. There were 177 degrees awarded over the century.[5] In the years from 1591 to 1595 ten took degrees: two bachelors, eight who qualified both for the BM and DM and three more who were licensed to practise without degrees.[6] It is by the quality of their work that judgement of these men must be made.

---

[1] This would include the last years of Mary's reign, which is quite probable. Attempts to examine the collegiate population in the years 1553–8 run up against the frequent disappearance of buttery books and like records during those years. Where I have been able to trace it, however, I have found the membership of the foundations in the Marian years full.

[2] See Lawrence Stone, 'The size and composition of the Oxford student body 1580–1910', in L. Stone, *The University in Society* (2 vols Princeton 1975) i. 91 (table 1A). William Harrison estimated a population at the two universities of 3,000; see *The Description of England*, ed. G. Edelen (Ithaca, New York 1968), 70.

[3] See John Barton, 'The faculty of law', p. 277 below.

[4] James McConica, 'The social relations of Tudor Oxford', *Transactions of the Royal Historical Society*, 5th ser. xxvii (1977), 118.

[5] See Gillian Lewis, 'The faculty of medicine', p. 250 below.

[6] McConica, 'The social relations of Tudor Oxford', 121.

If law declined dramatically and medicine maintained a tenuous existence, theology flourished in the Elizabethan university. Like law it was heavily endowed with college fellowships and unlike law it soon found candidates to fill them. In the years from 1581 to 1585 more than 11 per cent of the men presenting themselves for degrees in arts went on to a degree in the faculty of theology; in the years from 1591 to 1595 the percentage dropped slightly to 10.8. All told the higher faculties drew on some 12 per cent of the arts graduates in the last decade of the sixteenth century and, as can be seen, most of them were in theology.[1] In the same decades from 1580 to the beginning of the seventeenth century it is estimated that the proportion of freshmen who persevered in the university to take their bachelors' degrees rose from 26 per cent to 44 per cent.[2] More than any other statistic this one indicates the growing demand not simply for a taste of the academy's offerings but for a university qualification as such.

[1] McConica, 'The social relations of Tudor Oxford', 120–1.
[2] Stone, 'The size and composition of the Oxford student body 1580–1910', 95 (table 4).

4.1

The Faculty of Arts

J. M. FLETCHER

DESPITE a certain tendency, derived from the pioneering work of Rashdall and Denifle, to exaggerate the common features of the universities of northern Europe in the later middle ages, historians are nevertheless entitled to assume that behind the structure and curriculum of most of these universities at the close of the fifteenth century, there lies some adherence to common traditions derived from the medieval university of Paris. During the sixteenth century much of this common tradition was rejected; supporters of educational reform obtained their policies from the arguments of renaissance scholars such as Erasmus, Melanchthon and Vives, and criticized especially the traditional curriculum and teaching methods. Protestant and some catholic religious reformers expressed doubts about the value of certain medieval authorities used in the teaching of theology. Finally, in many European states, change was imposed on the universities by local secular power which insisted on constitutional alterations affecting the internal organization and the independence of the universities. By the close of the sixteenth century many of the common characteristics of the earlier northern universities had either been modified or had disappeared; the foundation of reformed universities, especially in the territories of the empire controlled by Lutherans, introduced new institutions to northern Europe having somewhat tenuous links with their medieval precursors. The history of the Oxford faculty of arts in the Tudor period must be considered against this background.

THE FACULTY OF ARTS IN ITS EUROPEAN SETTING

A comparative examination of the northern faculties of arts in this century shows clearly the significant feature of the history of the Oxford faculty: the absence of any serious attempt to modify its structure or curriculum by radical statutory change. Many continental universities at this time revised their statutory regulations drastically; the university of Basle, for instance, received new statutes in 1532 and 1539, its faculty of arts new regulations in 1540, 1544, 1551 and 1591.[1] At Tübingen, new statutes for the faculty received in 1536 prescribed a different course of study from that of the 1477 and 1505 statutes; Greek and Hebrew were taught but such medieval authorities as Petrus Hispanus were abandoned.[2] The Ingolstadt statutes issued as early as 1519/20 discarded much of the old curriculum: they spoke of 'lengthy and useless logical commentaries', rejected the Grammar of Alexander in favour of that of Aventinus and accepted the new programme of Eck (*cursus eckianus*) in logic and philosophy. The study of grammar was highly recommended; older translations of Greek works were to be withdrawn. The programme contained in the writings of John Eck was of very recent formulation: his *Bursa Pavonis* had been printed in 1507 and his *In summulas Petri hispani* in 1516. Eck attempted uneasily to combine aspects of medieval logic with newer humanist concepts and styles.[3] His commentaries on Aristotle, also adopted in these statutes, were described as having still to appear (*ubi tandem in lucem venerint*). Yet these new regulations at Ingolstadt, even though they introduced the most recent work into the faculty curriculum, had only a short life. By 1535, the cursus eckianus was itself replaced by the *Dialectics* of John Cesarius.[4] In Scotland, the university of Glasgow was virtually refounded in 1573 and received a new constitution, the *nova erectio*, in 1577. The amount of logic taught in the faculty of arts was greatly reduced while the time given to rhetoric was increased. Classical literature and the Greek language were introduced into the curriculum.[5] In such ways, most northern universities accepted the criticism of renaissance scholars, abandoned the intensive study of logic and most of the works of the medieval logicians, introduced classical literature and Greek, and used declamations in addition to the traditional disputations.

In contrast to this ferment of activity on the continent and in

[1] These are noted and discussed in E. Bonjour, *Die Universität Basel* (Basel 1960). They introduced classical authors and Greek into the curriculum and made the use of the declamation compulsory.

[2] The statutes for Tübingen are found in R. Roth, *Urkunden zur Geschichte der Universität Tübingen aus den Jahren 1476–1550* (Tübingen 1877).

[3] The Eckian 'programme' is discussed more fully in T. Heath, 'Logical grammar, grammatical logic, and humanism in three German universities', *Studies in the Renaissance* xviii (1971), 55-9.

[4] The statutes are printed in K. Prantl, *Geschichte der Ludwig-Maximilians-Universität in Ingolstadt, Landshut, München* (2 vols, Munich 1872).

[5] The changes are discussed in J. Durkan and J. Kirk, *The University of Glasgow 1451–1577* (Glasgow 1977).

Scotland, the Oxford faculty, at least in its statutory legislation, appears to have remained surprisingly unmoved by contemporary criticism. Neither the legislation of Edward VI in 1549 nor the *nova statuta* of 1564–5 seriously altered the structure or curriculum of the faculty. Certain gestures were made to the renaissance interest in grammar, rhetoric and Greek, but these, as will be discussed below, did little more than modify the traditional programme. Even the Laudian statutes received by the university in 1636, which were to govern Oxford until the nineteenth century, retained much of the medieval curriculum in arts. In their piecemeal legislation during the Tudor period and in the early seventeenth century, the masters of the university appear more concerned to enforce and strengthen the old statutes than to introduce any important innovations: modifications are accompanied by phrases that emphasize the validity of the old statutes and their continuing relevance to the contemporary situation.[1] Of course, the demand for change could not be entirely ignored; the wording of the statutes, as we shall note later, often concealed a practice that had changed considerably from that of the middle ages. It is, however, remarkable that no new radical code of statutes was imposed on the Oxford faculty of arts during the Tudor period, and this in itself was one of the reasons for some of the peculiarities shown by the university at the end of the sixteenth century.

The reasons for the reluctance of the Oxford faculty to accept fundamental changes in its curriculum are perhaps not difficult to understand. Certainly an attempt was made at the beginning of the Tudor period to introduce renaissance studies at Oxford: the foundation of Corpus Christi College, with its fine library of classical texts and provision for at least some humanistic studies, and the ambitious plans of Cardinal Wolsey, seemed to foreshadow a bright future for the reformers' programme. What is more, a scheme directed by London humanists of the court and other influential political figures did attempt to insinuate aspects of the new learning into both Oxford and Cambridge, although this programme lost much of its impetus with the involvement of its principal supporters in the political turmoil of the English reformation, often on the losing side.[2] Humanists in search of patronage were drawn to the capital; this may have diverted their energies from the need to reform the two universities. But perhaps of more importance were the results

---

[1] For example, 'reliquis academiae statutis . . . in robore et vigore suo . . . permanentibus', 'vetera statuta observabunt', or 'tempore solito, statuto veteri praescripto'.

[2] See J. M. Fletcher, 'Linacre's lands and lectureships', in F. Maddison, M. Pelling and C. Webster (eds), *Linacre Studies: essays on the life and work of Thomas Linacre c 1460–1524* (Oxford 1977).

of the historical development of the university of Oxford in the late medieval period. Then, in such arts subjects as logic and natural philosophy, the university made major contributions to European culture; Oxford masters claimed that supremacy in arts had migrated from the banks of the Seine to the banks of the Isis. Moreover, the faculty adhered to a type of philosophical outlook derived from Duns Scotus that was out of favour in continental arts universities for most of the late fourteenth and fifteenth centuries. It continued an exceptionally long arts course with a very complicated series of academic exercises, unlike its continental counterparts; it relied for its teaching of logic mostly on the works produced by its own alumni, and rejected such authors as Marsilius von Inghen, Petrus Hispanus and Buridan who found favour in the universities of Scotland and northern Europe. Especially in its organization of the arts curriculum, Oxford seemed by the close of the fifteenth century to be drawing away from the practice of other universities. Perhaps the Oxford masters, proud of their own past, were suspicious of the value of many of the changes urged on them by renaissance scholars, influenced by mainly continental reformers. Some modern educationalists, now less convinced of the value of an exclusively classical training and more sympathetic to the medieval university, may consider that these suspicions were at least partly justified.

THE REFORMATION AND THE FACULTY OF ARTS

The university of Oxford could not escape the impact of the English reformation. The disappearance of the monks and friars from the university, the closure of their colleges and houses, the attack on the study of canon law, the several official visitations of the university, and the removal of suspect 'Roman' material from the curriculum and the libraries meant that the Elizabethan university was very different both visually and in its intellectual tone from that of the reign of Henry VII. These changes actually served to strengthen the faculty of arts. The disappearance of canon lawyers, and the impact this had also on civil lawyers with whom they were closely associated, weakened the faculty that had earlier challenged in numbers and had been most hostile to the faculty of arts. The removal of the religious orders left the faculty of theology controlled by those who had previously studied in the faculty of arts and who were most likely to be sympathetic to its claims.[1] Medical students remained few in number. The predominance of the faculty of arts within the late

---

[1] Religious had frequently proceeded directly to the study of theology or law after completing an arts training in their own schools.

Tudor university must have been emphasized by these changes. The artists kept their privileged position should they themselves wish to study in a higher faculty: sixteenth-century legislation on the length of the course in law, medicine and theology always reduced the time required for those holding the MA degree.[1] Perhaps because of the dominance of the artists, there does not seem to be any serious inter-faculty dispute in the Elizabethan university. It is interesting to see, however, some trace of the survival of rivalry between the lawyers and artists: it was stated in 1589 that no student of civil law or medicine normally was to qualify without the MA degree; lawyers and artists were ordered in 1556 to live in separate halls so that the two subjects should remain distinct;[3] a statute of 1578 reasserted the medieval privileges of the masters against those bachelors of law who had not previously incepted in arts.[4] The loss of students by the higher faculties removed from the university a large group of older men. The Elizabethan university, with its considerable body of young, active arts students was in this respect even more of an under-graduate university than was that of an earlier date.

Effect on curriculum

The faculty of arts also escaped the suspicions of religious reformers and the worst rigours of state intervention. Attacks on the set texts used by the university were to be especially serious in the faculties of theology and canon law; the works of Peter Lombard and the decretals originating from papal legislation could have no place in a reformed university. Criticism of the texts used in the faculty of arts, by contrast, stemmed rather from humanist than religious reformers.[5] Although medieval commentaries might be suspect as having been produced in an era dominated by the authority of the church, sixteenth-century scholars were reluctant to abandon all such texts; the work of John Holywood (Johannes de Sacro Bosco), for example, was still prescribed as the set text in astronomy by the statute of 1564–5.[6] Many texts used were Greek classics, the works of Aristotle, Euclid and Ptolemy, for instance, and no taint of

---

[1] See, for example, the *nova statuta*: for law *Statuta*, 380, for medicine ibid. 378–9, for theology ibid. 380: 'antiqua statuta observabunt'. The 1549 statutes (ibid. 345) reduce the course for the BCL degree by one year for those holding the BA degree only.

[2] *Statuta*, 441.

[3] Ibid. 372.   [4] Ibid. 411.

[5] The royal injunctions for Cambridge university, discussed in J. B. Mullinger, *The University of Cambridge from the Earliest Times to the Royal Injunctions of 1535* (Cambridge 1873), 630–1, forbid the study of Scotus, Burley, Trombet, Bricot and Brulifer. I would suspect that this unusually detailed edict was inspired by the humanist sympathizers at court rather than by the king's government itself.

[6] *Statuta*, 390.

Romanism was attached to these. Indeed most late sixteenth-century supporters of university reform in northern Europe wished, not to supplant the classical authors in the curriculum, but rather to 'revive' them with the techniques of humanist philology and historical understanding, so that, even in such greatly altered universities as Basle, the works of Aristotle, especially on physics, metaphysics, ethics and politics, retained their place. It could also perhaps be argued that the English government was prepared to tolerate debate in the faculty of arts over philosophical and scientific problems that it could not accept in the faculty of theology. Political pressure to modify the curriculum of the faculty does not appear to be a major factor to be considered during the Tudor period.

Numbers

We have suggested that a reduction in the numbers of students in the faculties of theology and law gave the artists an even greater predominance in the university. With the absence of matriculation records before 1565, we can only make an estimate of the number of admissions to the university. However, it is possible for certain years to give figures of those granted a certain status in arts. For 1449–50 fifty admissions to the BA degree, thirty-eight to determination, twenty-six to the licence, and thirty-two to inception were recorded. For 1450–1 only the figure of sixty-three admissions to the BA degree was given.[1] For the early sixteenth century, in the period probably from May 1530 to March 1531 fifty-two students were admitted to the BA and twenty-two to the MA degree.[2] In the act (*comitia*) of March 1529, nineteen inceptors were admitted, and in July 1529, fourteen.[3] Forty students determined in 1528, fifteen in 1529, forty-three in 1530 and thirty-seven in 1531.[4] No other faculty could approach such totals; in March 1529 the nineteen inceptors in arts were accompanied by two in canon law, one in civil law, and one in theology. During the disturbed reigns of Edward VI and Mary, thirty-six determiners were recorded in 1547, twenty-nine in 1548, and forty-four in 1554.[5] The more settled conditions of Elizabethan England give us, probably from April to December of 1569, fifty-three inceptions and eighty-two admissions. From November 1571 to April 1572 there are forty-one inceptions and eighty-five admissions. In 1571 one hundred and fourteen students

[1] *The register of Congregation 1448–1463*, ed. W. A. Pantin and W. T. Mitchell (OHS new ser. xxii 1972), 2–7, 16–17.
[2] Reg. Cong. 1518–35, fos 229[V]–30.
[3] Ibid. fos 209, 217[V].
[4] Ibid. fos 189, 206, 226[V], 245.
[5] Reg. Cong. 1535–63, fos 113[V], 116, 140.

determined, in 1582 one hundred and twenty-one. In a single act in July 1581 seventy-five students incepted in arts.[1]

This increase in the numbers of arts students and graduates must have caused serious problems to the university and faculty: Lawrence Stone has described the period 1560–1629 as witnessing 'by far the fastest increase in the output of graduates in the whole history of the university'.[2] While questions concerning the support of these students, the provision of accommodation for them, and the areas and social classes they came from are not our concern here, such an increase did pose problems affecting the curriculum. How could the university insist on even a modified regency system (in which most graduates were required to teach for a number of years after receiving their MA degree), when such a large number of graduates would produce intolerable demands on the available resources for maintenance? Would it be possible to teach such students by the traditional lecture and disputation methods when the schools available had been satisfactory only for a much smaller number of students? We know that it was stated in 1574 that if all masters attended congregation there would not be room for them,[3] so how could the traditional democratic constitution of the university be maintained? The force of such pressures for change in the structure and curriculum of the faculty of arts, especially in the later years of Elizabeth's reign, is evident.

THE FACULTY IN THE UNIVERSITY

The role of the faculty of arts in the legislative body of the medieval university, congregation, is not entirely clear, but there is a strong case for arguing that the constitution gave to the faculty power to veto all legislation, even when it was accepted by the three other faculties. There is some dispute about the extent of this authority, but if the veto was absolute, it did make the Oxford artists the strongest faculty group of any northern university, including Paris, where legislative supremacy lay with the majority decision of the faculties although in fact it proved difficult there to oppose the wishes of the faculty of arts. The Oxford constitution inherited by the sixteenth-century university therefore placed permanent power in the hands of the young regent masters in arts. Since these masters also held most of the elective offices and the faculty of arts also

[1] Reg. Cong. 1564–82, fos 89–89^V, 109^V–10, 104, 348–348^V, 336.
[2] Lawrence Stone, 'The size and composition of the Oxford student body 1580–1909', in Lawrence Stone (ed.), *The University in Society* (2 vols Princeton 1975) i. 21. A fuller discussion of this subject may be found here.
[3] Reg. Cong. 1564–82, fo 174.

provided the university proctors from among its regent masters, the dominance of the artists was apparent. By the close of the fifteenth century, another feature of the medieval constitution had fallen into abeyance. The 'black congregation', the assembly of the artists called before the meeting of congregation, was no longer summoned. Its functions were perhaps carried out by the artists' representatives, the proctors, who prepared the agenda for congregation and generally supervised its operations,[1] but, in any case, there must have seemed little need for a previous meeting of the artists when their authority within congregation was so dominant. To senior members of the university, and especially to those concerned to maintain good relations with a government anxious to ensure a submissive and peaceful Oxford, the power of such younger, more turbulent, masters could be an embarrassment. Henry VIII had complained in strong terms of the insistence of the artists on their legal rights; in 1530 the masters refused to allow the doctors and other senior members alone to give the university's opinion on the divorce question, claiming that their consent was also necessary. The king accused them of failing to defer to the views of 'the vertuous, wise, sadde and profound lerned men' and required the university to reduce the younger masters 'unto good ordre and conformitie'.[2] In 1570 the new statutes for the university of Cambridge had placed control in the hands of the vice-chancellor and the heads of houses, the so called *caput*, to stifle doctrinal conflict.[3] At Oxford, the chancellor attempted to set up a committee consisting of the vice-chancellor, the doctors, the heads of houses and the proctors to consider first what motions should be brought before congregation.[4] Increasingly, during the reign of Elizabeth, it became usual for congregation itself to establish committees to deal with particular aspects of business. This is probably how the hebdomadal council, the weekly meeting of the vice-chancellor and heads of houses to discuss university business, formally accepted by the university in 1631,[5] originated. It is perhaps significant that the proctors were not represented on the council although they were the elected representatives of the largest group within the university. The medieval, democratic constitution was in this way destroyed, and, until the nineteenth century, control was exercised by the more conservative element at Oxford, easily influenced by political pressure. It was probably in a last effort to reassert

[1] *Statuta*, 67, 108, etc.

[2] W. A. Pantin, *Oxford Life in Oxford Archives* (Oxford 1972), 26–7.

[3] *Documents relating to the University and Colleges of Cambridge* (3 vols Royal Commission 1852) i. 478–9.

[4] Reg. Cong. 1564–82, fo 93[v].

[5] *Statuta*, 570; Pantin, loc. cit.

the authority of the artists that the proctors attempted in 1570 and 1600 to revive the *congregatio nigra*.[1] The Tudor state did not look kindly on reassertions of medieval academic independence; the 1600 attempt did not succeed and the black congregation of 1570 was, in fact, the last to be held.

Undergraduate studies—length of the course

As in the medieval university, the arts student was required to complete a set time in study, attend various lectures and perform various exercises before proceeding to the lower degree, that of bachelor of arts. The Edwardian statutes and the Laudian statutes repeat the medieval requirement of four years of study for the degree.[2] One modification to the traditional length was made in 1591, when the sons of certain noblemen were allowed to request the BA degree after three years.[3] These were the statutory requirements, but the practice of the faculty can best be found by a careful examination of the supplications for graces presented by students applying for degrees. These usually state the time spent in study, or expected to be spent in study, by individuals. For the 1520s they indicate that for the majority of students there was a tendency to allow the course to be shortened by one year. By the 1570s, however, the registers show that this flexibility was no longer maintained; most students then offered the statutory four years in study for the lower degree.

Individual students could depart from these regulations for a variety of acceptable reasons. Personal problems, illness, poverty, an offer of an appointment requiring the possession of the degree or family troubles away from the university were difficulties which generally found the university sympathetic and ready to dispense the students from a part of the statutory course. Some unexplained dispensations allowed students to proceed to the lower degree after only one year.[4] Occasionally the university attempted to ensure that the years offered had in fact been spent properly at Oxford.[5] Sometimes students seeking dispensation were required to perform further exercises to compensate for the reduction in time granted.[6] Other students were allowed to shorten their BA course only if they then lengthened

[1] Reg. Cong. 1564–82, fo 94ᵛ; Reg. Cong. 1595–1606, fo 45. These events are discussed in *Statuta*, p. xxxiv.

[2] *Statuta*, 344. *Laudian Code*, 45.

[3] *Statuta*, 443.

[4] For examples, see ibid. 1535–63, fo 112ᵛ.

[5] For examples, see ibid. 1518–35, fos 108ᵛ, 109ᵛ, 152.

[6] For an example, see ibid. 1535–63, fo 156ᵛ: Philip Collinson offers one and a quarter years only for his lower degree. Two masters are appointed to dispute against him on account of this short period of study.

their programme for the master's degree.[1] The Tudor registers also show that the practice of recording time spent in study during vacations, common in the graces of earlier years of the sixteenth century, had apparently ceased by the reign of Elizabeth.

The mass of detailed material in these registers is still to be properly analysed in conjunction with such other evidence as that presented by college records. However, certain general conclusions appear clear. There is no serious reduction in the length of the BA degree course for the majority of students. The comparative figures for those taking the higher and lower degrees in arts, show that many students were content to retire from the university with just the BA degree. In the last twenty years of the century, for example, an average of seventy students each year incepted in arts, but the average number admitted annually to the lower degree was well over one hundred.[2] Detailed information on the background of students taking the higher degree would probably show that the availability of financial support in enabling such students to remain at the university after obtaining the BA degree was crucial. It is here that the winning of a college fellowship could exercise an important influence on a student's academic career.

Lectures

The Tudor university preserved formally the medieval opinion that knowledge was best imparted to the junior student by the lectures of his seniors, the bachelors and masters. Since both bachelors and masters were required to lecture, their obligations to the university will be fully considered when the course for the MA degree and the burdens of regency are discussed. Then also we shall examine the role of the Tudor public lecturer in Greek. Here we may discuss the more general characteristics of the lectures as they affected the undergraduate.

The medieval emphasis on the importance of lectures came from the impossibility of supplying all students with copies of the set texts. At the beginning of the Tudor period, hand-written books were prohibitively expensive: manuscripts purchased by Richard Fitzjames and subsequently given to Merton College after 1494 cost him such sums as 10s, 27s, 13s 4d and 6s 8d.[3] At about the same time, Merton College was paying a carpenter 6d per day, a plumber 4d per day and a stone mason 6d per day.[4] A student of moderate

[1] See ibid. fo 204, for a student offering one year for the BA degree and expected to offer five years for the mastership.   [2] Stone, 'Size and composition', 94.
[3] F. M. Powicke, *The Medieval Books of Merton College* (Oxford 1931), 225–30.
[4] The payments for the first years of Henry VII's reign are taken from Merton College Record 4009, subwardens' accounts.

means had little possibility of buying the set texts for even the lower degree in arts. Since the use of the university and college libraries was generally restricted to graduates and college fellows, the undergraduate could not obtain access to books in that way. Printed books that began to appear in Oxford in some numbers in the early years of the century did not at first cater completely for this need. Although much cheaper than manuscripts, the more important texts were still sold at a price beyond the reach of many students, especially when bound.[1] During the sixteenth century, the activity of the printing presses produced a large number of editions of pamphlets and books, often designed especially to cater for the academic market, and by the close of the Tudor period, individual masters possessed considerable libraries. David Tolley, a master of arts and a medical and classical scholar, who was a student of Christ Church, possessed two hundred and seventy eight books listed in the inventory of his possessions in 1558; Robert Barnes, a master of arts and doctor of medicine, gave Merton College Library forty-eight books in 1594.[2] If masters could accumulate such large collections, we may assume that students of lesser means now had some access to discarded copies, outdated editions and such material on sale in Oxford. Further research is necessary before we can be more certain of the printed material available to junior arts undergraduates, but the lecturer in the Tudor period was certainly no longer the sole source of information that he had been for most students in the preceding century.

Nor was the university itself the only teaching institution in Tudor Oxford. In the early fifteenth century, the colleges had played a minor role in the daily life of the university. During the late fifteenth and sixteenth centuries, new and splendid institutions had come to rival the older Merton and New Colleges. After the reformation, the movement was resumed with the foundation of Trinity College, St John's College and Jesus College. Such buildings inevitably competed with existing structures for space within the city, and college expansion was often at the expense of the older halls. In 1444 there were sixty-nine halls; by 1553 eight only remained. In and around the old medieval centre of the city, by the close of the Tudor period, the amount of accommodation available outside the colleges was considerably reduced. Other factors, the financial requirements of

---

[1] The prices of books on sale in Oxford in the early sixteenth century can best be seen in F. Madan, 'The daily ledger of John Dorne, 1520', C. R. L. Fletcher (ed.), *Collectanea*, i (OHS v 1885). A bound copy of Euclid's *Geometria* (item 1263) cost 5s; a bound copy of Faber's commentary on the *Ethics* (item 1390) cost 1s 8d. Many other works, such as *Sophistria Oxonie*, however, cost less than 1s.

[2] These and other details of book possession are given in *BRUO 1501–40*, App. B.

the colleges, the belief held by both politicians and academics that better discipline could be exercised when students were housed within established institutions, and finally, the demands by parents, especially of wealthy students, for a more personal relationship with a tutor who could provide a broader range of cultural education than that expected by the university statutes, encouraged undergraduates to move into the colleges. At the close of the fifteenth century the junior arts student, with certain notable exceptions, did not greatly concern the college authorities. By the time of the civil war, the modern college with its small teaching staff and larger undergraduate body is the typical Oxford institution. The exact nature of this development is not yet completely understood, and the evidence for it is examined elsewhere. It did mean, however, that the late Tudor college was increasingly concerned with the teaching of arts undergraduates. Indeed, the new foundation of Trinity College expressly provided full instruction within its walls, anticipating that the existing official ordinary lectures of the masters might at some time be of no value.[1] As college tutors became increasingly confident in their handling of younger students, and as the supply of printed texts that students could borrow or purchase grew, ordinary lectures could no longer be regarded as the essential source of academic information. However, there was no real substitute for the traditional exercises required for the lower degree.

Exercises

Exercises in the Tudor university were organized in the medieval manner. The 'opponent' (*opponens*) proposed the subject of debate and was answered by the 'respondent' (*respondens*). Students in the audience were sometimes allowed to participate as 'arguers' (*arguentes*). Occasionally we have reference to a 'replicator' whose task seems to have been to sum up the entire debate and say a few words of praise or blame to the participants. The position of opponent was generally taken by a senior person, often the teacher himself. The replicator too was a well-qualified academic. Participants were generally informed personally by the faculty bedels of their roles, and the date, place and subject of the disputation were usually announced by proclamation or by the posting of such information in a prominent place. The start of such exercises was generally marked by the tolling of a church bell. Academic exercises were regarded as occasions of some excitement. They provided the opportunity not only for the cut and thrust of normal debate but also for the intelligent student to equal and perhaps outwit his seniors and

[1] *SCO* iv (Trinity College) 46.

colleagues. They also attracted the unruly elements of academic society, and were carefully regulated by the university administration.

In parviso. The exercises required of students working for the lower degree were modified in detail but not in principle during the sixteenth century. The junior arts student performed most of his disputations among his colleagues, as in the medieval period, and these exercises were known as disputations *in parviso*. The origins of the term are obscure, but they may refer to an original meeting place, or metaphorically to the 'entrance' that the student was now making on his career as a disputant. During the Tudor period, these exercises appear to have taken place in the public schools,[1] and by 1584 the students formally processed to the schools led by the three yeoman bedells.[2] What actually took place *in parviso* is very obscure. Apparently, at some stage, after completing one or a series of exercises, the student obtained an officially recognized status and was known as a 'general sophister' (*sophista generalis*). The exercise or exercises performed to obtain this status were known as a *creacio generalis* and could be repeated. The brief Edwardian statutes seem to expect from a student *in parviso* two responsions.[3] They require students who have completed two years of study to respond in descending order of seniority on Thursdays, Fridays and Saturdays from one until three in the afternoon. Three questions, in mathematics, dialectic and in natural or moral philosophy were to be debated. Moderators were to preside over the disputations and allow four students, apart from the principal disputant, to propose arguments against the respondent. The use of notes was forbidden; proper academic dress had to be worn. The selected respondent was not allowed to avoid his responsibilities.[4]

The Elizabethan statutes seem to expect of students only one exercise *in parviso*, but allow students to replace the Lenten exercise, discussed below, by another if they so wish.[5] By 1607 these exercises were apparently much neglected. The statutes of this date speak of the status of the general sophister being obtained only after the completion of six terms at the university and the performance of at least one opposition. This status was to be retained for four terms before the BA degree could be obtained, and during this time the student was required to attend exercises *in parviso* and oppose there at least once.[6] Finally, the Laudian statutes gave a detailed description of these exercises. We must here note that this description, repeated

---

[1] Reg. Cong. 1518–35, fo 313. [2] *Statuta*, 435.
[3] Ibid. 344. [4] Ibid. 346–7, 357.
[5] Ibid. 405–6. [6] Ibid. 485–6.

by Andrew Clark in his influential discussion of the practice of the Elizabethan faculty,[1] differs in detail from that given, however sketchily, by the Tudor statutes. His view, therefore, cannot be accepted as a totally reliable description of the exercises *in parviso* in the sixteenth century.

Frequently in the early years of the century, students record in their graces the performance of an exercise known as a 'variation' (*variatio*). This seems to be an exercise performed by one person only in which he presents various arguments for and against a set thesis. Such variations were almost certainly made *in parviso*, since the Laudian statutes refer to disputations *in parviso* as those 'once known as variations'.[2] No fixed number of such exercises seems to have been required; different students offer two, three, four, five or six.[3] Applications show that performances of some exercises *in parviso* were required throughout the Tudor period. The few students who apply for the lower degree without having apparently performed at lease one exercise are usually instructed by the university to become general sophisters before admission. Only rarely is this requirement relaxed, as when, for example, lack of time or the absence of a disputing colleague prevent the exercise taking place. Then the university usually insists on alternative disputations being performed.

Responsions in determination. The second group of exercises required of the junior arts student was associated with his role in the Lenten determination exercises. These are fully discussed below; here we are concerned only with the obligation imposed on undergraduates that they should then respond to the determining bachelors. The number of times that a junior student had to respond is not clear. The Elizabethan statutes indicate that two 'responsions', each lasting for at least one hour, are expected, but allow students to replace one of these by a responsion *in parviso*. The Laudian statutes repeat this requirement.[4] Entries in the registers of congregation show that most students at the end of the century respond once only to the determining bachelors. Sometimes a shortage of bachelors prevented students from making even this single responsion,[5] but this was an unusual situation and most appear to have complied with the official regulations.

[1] *Reg. Univ.* ed. Clark i. 21–3.
[2] *Laudian Code*, 46: 'quas etiam alio nomine variationes olim dictas fuisse constat'.
[3] Reg. Cong. 1518–35, fos 219 (3 and 4), 218ᵛ (6), 297 (5), 299 (2).
[4] *Statuta*, 406. *Laudian Code*, 49.
[5] For an example, see Reg. Cong. 1564–82, fo 160.

The bachelor's degree

When the student or his master was satisfied that the time spent in study, the attendance at lectures and the performance of disputations had been completed satisfactorily, an application was made for the award of the degree. By the later Tudor period, it had become usual for this to be done in the form of a request to congregation for a grace to proceed; a statute of 1563 required the presence of a representative from the candidate's college when any dispensation for him was being discussed.[1] After approval of his application, the student was required to make a formal circuit of the schools so that all masters could know of his plans and object if they wished. By the reign of Elizabeth, dispensations from the circuit were regularly granted, after inclement weather for example. This did not necessarily mean that the medieval procedure designed to inform all masters of a candidate's intention to take his degree and so allow them to oppose any unsuitable applicant was now abandoned. There is evidence in college registers that fellows formally approved all applications for degrees and so ensured that their college would not be shamed by the presentation of an inadequate candidate. The statutes of New College, for example, provide for the examination of all applicants for the lower degree by a committee consisting of the warden, sub-warden, two deans, the bursars and six senior fellows.[2] A formal deposition, or statement of the ability of the candidate, does not seem to have been required by the university.[3] After 1576 students were required to make a formal subscription to the thirty-nine articles in the presence of the proctors.[4] The final stage, admission, when the student obtained his degree, is not clearly described in the statutes,[5] perhaps reflecting the greater university interest in the higher degree. The student, now a bachelor had (according to the statutes of 1601) paid the registrar of the university 6d for noting his grace, 6d for recording his admission and 10d for entering details of his formal acceptance of the degree from the university.[6]

Contents of the course

The student had completed a long four-year course to obtain the bachelor's degree. We have considered the technical details of this

---

[1] *Statuta*, 377. The procedure is fully discussed in *Reg. Univ.* ed. Clark i. 27–42.

[2] *SCO* i. pt 5 (New College) 49.

[3] I cannot trace the evidence on which Clark (*Reg. Univ.* i. 47) bases his discussion of an elaborate deposition for this degree.

[4] *Statuta*, 409.

[5] Clark's evidence is taken from the 1634 statutes.

[6] *Statuta*, 458.

programme of study; we must now attempt to evaluate the content of this course. As the supply and variety of printed texts increased and the role of the individual tutor became more important, so the differences between the academic training of each student must have become more pronounced. We cannot here consider the value and interest of such individual learning. We are now concerned only with the official texts prescribed by the statutes, which attempted to give to all students a basic knowledge considered valuable by the university. We are given the most comprehensive lists of prescribed texts only as late as the early years of Elizabeth's reign. Until then, formal instruction in the faculty of arts was circumscribed by the medieval regulations, although the Edwardian statutes of 1549 did mention in a very perfunctory manner that philosophy should be taught from Aristotle, Pliny or Plato, mathematics from Mela, Pliny, Strabo or Ptolemy, and dialectic and rhetoric from Aristotle, Cicero, Quintilian or Hermogenes.[1] It is not made clear whether students for the lower or higher degree in arts, or both, were to study such subjects, and the additions to these statutes add texts not noted in the main body. These regulations appear to have been hastily drawn up, lack coherence, were never entered in the official statute book of the university and probably were never fully implemented.

The Elizabethan statutes. The Elizabethan statutes preserved the ancient division of knowledge into the seven liberal arts at a time when such a separation had been seriously modified at Cambridge and totally abandoned in most other European universities. The first list of prescribed texts, of 1564–5, required in grammar the study of Priscian or Thomas Linacre, in rhetoric Aristotle or Cicero, in logic Porphyry, Aristotle or the topics of Boethius, in arithmetic Boethius, Tunstall or Gemma Frisius, in geometry Euclid or the *Perspectiva* of Vitellius and for astronomy Johannes de Sacro Bosco, the *Theoricae planetarum* or the *Almagest* or other work of Ptolemy; music is omitted here.[2] The second list of the same date named for grammar Linacre, Virgil, Horace or part of Cicero's Letters, for rhetoric the *Praeceptiones* or *Orationes* of Cicero, or Aristotle's *Rhetoric*, for logic the *Institutiones* of Porphyry or some work by Aristotle, for arithmetic Boethius or Gemma Frisius, for music Boethius, for geometry Euclid, for astronomy the *De sphera* of Orentius or the *Astronomia* of Johannes de Sacro Bosco.[3] These two lists enable us to judge what Oxford academic opinion at the close of the Tudor period thought were the essential areas of knowledge that should be studied for the lower degree.

[1] *Statuta*, 344, 358.
[2] Ibid. 378. For a discussion of music see the annexe to this chapter.
[3] Ibid. 389–90.

The faculties of arts at the two English universities had a long tradition of contact, with students and masters moving from one to the other frequently during the later middle ages. Although there were differences of detail and emphasis in their curricula, before the sixteenth century they were broadly similar. The new code of statutes at Cambridge in 1570, however, shows how far the medieval traditions had been abandoned there by that time. The studies of the faculty were stated in general terms rather than in the rigid, traditional form still used at Oxford. For the lower degree, rhetoric, dialectic and philosophy were required; for the master's degree, philosophy, optics, astronomy and Greek. The link with the medieval curriculum of seven arts and three philosophies was tenuous: neither grammar nor music was as much as mentioned, nor were the cursory lectures of the bachelor. Indeed, at Cambridge, the medieval regency system that survived so long at Oxford, at least in the formal prescriptions of statute, seems to have been abandoned entirely in the early sixteenth century. On the other hand, in many respects the programme at Cambridge was nearer to that of Oxford than it was to those of continental and Scottish universities: it retained the medieval faculty structure, the long, seven-year course for the MA degree, and the disputation system. On balance, it would seem that Cambridge was affected earlier than was Oxford by movements on the continent, or at least, that its response to these was more speedily reflected in the formal provisions of its statutes.[1]

The retention of the concept of the seven liberal arts and the continued reliance on many traditional authorities indicate that the medieval curriculum had been by no means abandoned. Subjects like history and geography were not mentioned, neither were modern languages and vernacular literature. The set texts in grammar and rhetoric did not include the less familiar works of Roman literature. In contrast to this programme of studies were the courses recommended by other contemporary educationalists and those prescribed by other universities. Sir Humphrey Gilbert's tractate *Queen Elizabeth's Academy* put forward plans for an institution to produce men of action able to serve the state in a variety of ways. Gilbert argued that a knowledge of history, geography and modern languages is essential for the educated man. He also stressed the value of the vernacular and the importance of acquiring ability in the proper use of written and spoken English.[2] At about the same date, the

[1] A more detailed comparison of the Oxford, Cambridge and German faculties is made in J. M. Fletcher, 'Change and resistance to change: a consideration of the development of English and German universities during the sixteenth century', *History of Universities* i (1981), 1–36.

[2] Gilbert's plans are briefly discussed in W. H. Woodward, *Studies in Education during*

statutes of Glasgow university provided for instruction in both geography and history.[1] On the continent, the 'conservative' university of Ingolstadt in 1573 provided, in arts, lectures on dialectic, the *Epistolae* of Cicero, the *Orationes* of Cicero, the *Organon* of Aristotle, mathematics, Latin poetry, Greek grammar and literature, elementary works on physics, and Latin grammar, as well as on the more advanced works of Aristotle which were intended for students for the higher degree.[2] The 'progressive' university of Wittenberg had already in 1545 ten lectureships: one in dialectic and rhetoric, one in elementary physics, two in mathematics, two in Latin literature, one in Latin grammar, one in advanced physics, one in Hebrew and one in Greek grammar and literature which was also to provide instruction in Aristotle's *Ethics*. In 1571 an official lecturer in the French language was appointed by the elector of Saxony, and by 1606 it was noted that in both universities in the elector's domains, Wittenberg and Leipzig, the teaching of history (*lectio historiarum*) had been introduced.[3] The movement away from the medieval structure of the arts course and a greater readiness to adopt new subjects is more evidently seen outside England than at Oxford.

The actual texts recommended in Elizabethan Oxford were often the older authorities. Only in the field of grammar and rhetoric had the new, humanistic texts ousted the earlier books. In logic the traditional introductory work of Porphyry, the basic text of the medieval schools, was preserved as were the writings of Aristotle. There was no mention of such renaissance material as that produced by, for example, Agricola or Melanchthon. For arithmetic the older Boethius was supplemented by the sixteenth-century work of Tunstall, author of the *De arte supputandi*, published in 1522, and of Gemma Frisius who died in 1555. The older authorities, Euclid, Vitellius, John of Holywood, Ptolemy and the *Theorica planetarum* still determined the study of geometry and astronomy, with only the later Orentius added. Many continental universities, on the contrary, deliberately required the use of more recent material. The lengthy and important arrangements made for the universities of Wittenberg and Leipzig in 1606, for example, named the works of Melanchthon, Valla, Linacre, Cardinal Adrianus and Peurbach as

---

the Age of the Renaissance 1400–1600 (Cambridge 1906), 302–6, and in K. Charlton, *Education in Renaissance England* (1965), 156–7. Gilbert's 'Queen Elizabethes Achademy' is edited in *Queen Elizabethes Achademy, A Book of Precedence etc*, ed. F. J. Furnivall (EETS extra ser. viii 1869).

[1] Durkan and Kirk, *University of Glasgow*, 315.
[2] Prantl, *Geschichte der Ludwig–Maximilians–Universität*, ii. 292–4.
[3] W. Friedensburg, *Urkundenbuch der Universität Wittenberg* (2 vols Magdeburg 1926–7) i. 267–8, 674.

texts to be used but also suggested the use of commentaries by Liblerus and Heilandus for the teaching of Aristotle, if necessary.[1] The student for the lower degree in such universities would by official policy be compelled to study a selection of more recent works as well as some of the older authorities.

It is interesting to notice at Oxford the lack of interest in the study of music; there is no reference to any set book in the earlier list, and the later mentions only the writings of Boethius. The Elizabethan registers of congregation indicate that lectures in music were no longer regarded as of great importance. Although by the statutes of 1564-5 two terms in the study of music were required, this lecture was frequently cancelled for lack of those wishing to attend.[2] Such famous renaissance scholars as Vittorino, Agricola, Sadoleto and Melanchthon had argued for the importance of its place in education, but it seems that music was coming to be regarded as valuable for its social and recreational benefits rather than for its academic qualities. It is perhaps significant that, at Ingolstadt, the 1573 arrangement of lectures in arts, in the only reference to the place of music in the curriculum, allocates one hour each day for 'solatium et exercitium musicae', but allows 'alia honesta recreatio' to be taken at this time if required.[3]

The Elizabethan student, therefore, if the statutory evidence alone is considered, worked towards the lower degree in arts through a curriculum that was in many respects essentially medieval. The pressure for change seems, at Oxford, to have been strongly resisted, and we must suspect that many of the senior members of the faculty of arts were not as greatly impressed by the arguments and achievements of humanist scholars as later historians have been. No one could doubt that in the fields of literature, classical studies and rhetoric, such scholars made substantial contributions. In other areas of study, and especially in the speculative natural sciences, they may have delayed progress. In their belief in the value of literature, their view of the importance of 'polished' writing and speech, their emphasis on the acquisition of social graces which they believed necessary for the success of the 'civic humanist', and in their consequent denigration of the carefully organized course in logic which formed the basis of the Oxford medieval arts training, they distracted students from an interest in those texts written in the practical, less-stylish Latin of the schools. Many Oxford masters apparently believed that, outside the realm of grammar and rhetoric, humanists could not yet offer material suitable for academic study that could

---

[1] Ibid. 672-4.
[2] For an example, see Reg. Cong. 1535-63, fo 205.
[3] Prantl, ii. 293.

replace the traditional texts. Indeed, if the wording of statutes alone is considered, the Edwardian reformers were able to insist on the study of more 'humanistic' authors than did those of Elizabeth's reign: the requirement that students in arts should read Pliny and Quintilian is embodied in the earlier code but not in the *nova statuta*.[1] These, and other peculiarities in the Edwardian legislation must lead us to suspect that it originated rather from humanists influential at court than from the initiatives of masters familiar with the practice and requirements of the Oxford faculty of arts.

Study of logic. The arrangement and wording of the Elizabethan statutes do conceal, however, a very real and radical change in the character of studies for the lower degree in arts. During the late medieval period, Oxford logicians had erected on the traditional foundation of the established works of Priscian, Porphyry, Boethius and Aristotle a superstructure of 'sophistry'. They divided the study of elementary logic into a number of separate but related sections under such headings as 'obligations', 'suppositions', 'consequences' and 'insolubles'. Each section was extensively treated by various Oxford logicians so that, by the middle of the fifteenth century, a considerable number of major works and shorter tractates and summaries were available for the guidance of the junior student who could obtain access to them. It was this 'sophistry' which especially aroused the anger and hostility of renaissance scholars: Italians such as Salutati attacked the 'barbaric Britons' whose names were as convoluted as their thoughts, while northerners such as Erasmus and More mocked the barbarous studies of the sophisters and dialecticians. This attack was successful. The process by which these medieval tractates were withdrawn from general use at Oxford is not yet properly understood, but it is perhaps significant that the *Libellus sophistarum ad usum oxoniensium* was last printed in 1530, after the publication of six earlier editions. Texts from these numerous publications survived into Elizabethan Oxford, and we know that individuals then owned these books.[2] There is little evidence, however, for such studies being extensively pursued throughout the faculty and, with the cessation in the printing of the essential texts and the destruction of many manuscript books during the century, little material of this sort can have survived.

During Elizabeth's reign, individuals and the university expressed their hostility to the sophistry of the medieval schools. John Argall, writing in 1605 asserted that he had abandoned all involved (*involuti*)

[1] *Statuta*, 344.
[2] See J. McConica, 'Humanism and Aristotle in Tudor Oxford', *English Historical Review* xciv (1979), 295-7.

books 'with their thorny and intricate questions and quiddities'; he particularly mentions Dorbellus, Scotus, Hispanus, Iavellus, Egidius, Lambertus and Tartaretus, as authors to be avoided.[1] One hundred years earlier, this would have been a list of some of the recommended texts in the arts course of most northern universities. The university itself acted to exclude such 'medieval' aspects of logic from the course; it declared in 1556 that students were disturbed by empty and sophistical disputations,[2] and in 1586 decreed that 'sterile and empty questions dissenting from ancient and true philosophy should be removed and excluded from the schools'.[3] This reference to 'ancient and true philosophy' seems to indicate where the interests of Oxford logicians lay: namely in a closer attention to Aristotelian logic rather than to the development of this logic by medieval scholars. In 1562 a student was required to support the arguments of Aristotle in his disputations, and in 1574 John Barebone was compelled to maintain Aristotle's opinion in three questions.[4] A further instance of the university's defence of Aristotle came in 1586, when a statute noted that the use of different authors in the schools produced conflict; henceforth the views of Aristotle and his supporters only were to be debated by the bachelors in their determination exercises.[5] The Laudian statutes support this respect for Aristotle 'whose authority is supreme'.[6] Some of these references are to studies for the higher degree in arts, but they indicate an attitude to the study of logic that was particularly relevant to the undergraduates for whom this was an important part of the course.

If the university spoke so highly of the Aristotelian system, it is not unexpected to find that its attitude to his critics was not sympathetic. These later strong assertions of the continuing value of his views were probably produced by the need to counter criticisms of Aristotle by Petrus Ramus of Paris. In most European faculties of arts, Ramist views produced conflict between his opponents and supporters: the university of Heidelberg, for example, feared the reintroduction of *factiones* that had earlier accompanied the quarrels between realists and nominalists; the university noted that the philosophy of Aristotle had been respected for two thousand years 'and should still be maintained' (*und noch dofur gehalten wurt*).[7] The same fear of *factiones* probably encouraged Oxford to take a

[1] I. Thomas, 'Medieval aftermath: Oxford logic and logicians of the seventeenth century', in *Oxford Studies Presented to Daniel Callus* (OHS new ser. xvi 1964), 299–300.
[2] *Statuta*, 374. [3] Ibid. 437.
[4] Reg. Cong. 1535–63, fo 207; Reg. Cong. 1564–82, fo 169^V.
[5] *Statuta*, 437. [6] *Laudian Code*, 55.
[7] E. Winkelmann, *Urkundenbuch der Universität Heidelberg* (2 vols Heidelberg 1886) i. 311–12.

strong line against the introduction of Ramist concepts in its official teaching programme. When John Argall, who himself incepted at Oxford in 1565, published his influential book on logic in 1605, he recommended no Ramist works to his readers.[1] Such an official defence of Aristotle must make us cautious in accepting the view that Ramus was well received at Oxford.[2] Of course, Ramus was read by individual masters and his attitude to Aristotle was discussed with students by masters in their lectures; his works appear in private library collections.[3] These were, however, the interests of individuals and cannot be equated with the official attitude of the university clearly expressed in its legislation. Just as the dominance of the scholastic curriculum in the middle ages did not prevent individuals studying classical works and the conservative character of eighteenth-century Oxford did not mean that no one read recent 'enlightened' material, so the official support of Aristotle in the Elizabethan university did not mean that Ramus was ignored by all masters. But to describe medieval Oxford as 'humanist' or eighteenth-century Oxford as 'enlightened' would be quite as misleading as to describe late sixteenth-century Oxford as 'Ramist'.

The work of recent scholars has emphasized the importance of the continued study of the works of Aristotle in moulding the intellectual climate of the late sixteenth and early seventeenth centuries.[4] The evidence for this of the statutes and registers of congregation at Oxford is further supplemented by the survival of the texts of lectures given by masters at the university.[5] Although such lecturers frequently read the works of Aristotle in the original Greek, it was not possible for them to ignore entirely earlier commentators. Works by Scotus, who had taught at Oxford, Aquinas and others appear side by side with more recent Aristotelian commentaries by such scholars as the Italian Zabarella. Thomas Savile, for example, presented in 1591 to Merton College the books he had recently purchased

[1] Thomas, 'Medieval aftermath' 301.

[2] Mark H. Curtis, Oxford and Cambridge in Transition (Oxford 1959), 250 note 73.

[3] Ibid. 119, 253, and W. S. Howell, Logic and Rhetoric in England 1500–1700 (Princeton 1956), 189–93. McConica discusses in 'Humanism and Aristotle' the discriminating use by Rainolds of Ramist material.

[4] See, for the general background, the stimulating essay by C. B. Schmitt, 'Philosophy and science in sixteenth-century universities: some preliminary comments', in J. E. Murdoch and E. D. Sylla (eds), The Cultural Context of Medieval Learning (Dordrecht 1975) and, for England, W. T. Costello, The Scholastic Curriculum at Early Seventeenth-Century Cambridge (Cambridge, Mass. 1958); L. Jardine, 'The place of dialectic teaching in sixteenth-century Cambridge', Studies in the Renaissance xxi (1974); L. Jardine, 'Humanism and dialectic in sixteenth-century Cambridge: a preliminary investigation', in R. R. Bolgar (ed.), Classical Influences on European Culture AD 1500–1700 (Cambridge 1976), and McConica, 'Humanism and Aristotle'.

[5] Ibid. 304–9.

for the college in Germany and Italy: they include works by Aquinas and Zabarella.[1] In this way, Oxford masters of the Elizabethan period maintained a connection with at least some of the major medieval commentators on Aristotle. Their attitude to such earlier authorities may have been critical, but they did not ignore them completely.

Limitations of the statutes. To conclude this brief discussion of the studies at Oxford for the bachelor's degree in arts, it must be emphasized that the evidence considered has been largely drawn from the official requirements as set out in the statutes. There is ample evidence to show that such a picture is incomplete. The university itself was prepared to sanction departures from its statutory curriculum. In 1527 Anthony Frobysher was required to lecture on the logic of Melanchthon, presumably as a bachelor, for the benefit of the junior students.[2] There are also some interesting references to lectures on classical texts: Lucan, Sallust, Quintilian and Cicero.[3] However, such lectures were usually associated with students working for grammar degrees or leaving for teaching appointments. Indeed, in one important reference, a student in the 1520s definitely stated that it was his intention to leave the university so that he could obtain a literary education.[4] Such statements indicate that while lectures on classical authors could be given and heard at Oxford, the university had no intention of abandoning its logical and philosophical studies. There was certainly no desire to see the introduction of a curriculum based almost exclusively on the reading of texts of classical literature and history, such as appears to have been advocated by some of the more extreme humanists of the early sixteenth century.

However, there is no doubt that such an education was demanded by certain students, especially those wealthy students who did not intend to pursue a long academic course or to take even the lower degree in arts, although, as we have already noted the course for the BA degree was shortened for sons of the nobility in 1593. For such students, a programme of education based, for example, on the principles advocated by Guarino da Verona, and designed to produce a cultured aristocrat, able to involve himself in civil, political and social life, was particularly desirable. Such a student would be perhaps more aware of the imperfections of the official course for the BA degree than its virtues. Partly in response to the demand from

[1] *Reg. ann. mert. 1567–1603*, 273–4.
[2] Reg. Cong. 1518–35, fo 168.
[3] Ibid. fos 68, 81[V]. Reg. Cong. 1535–63, fos 52[V], 64.
[4] Reg. Cong. 1518–35, fo 141.

such students and their guardians for an alternative, less traditional course, the college tutorial system evolved at Oxford. Catalogues of the libraries of individual masters as well as the records of purchases for college libraries in the Elizabethan period clearly show that modern works and modern editions of classical writers were obtained in some quantity.[1] Individual masters and colleges were certainly not unaware of contemporary work in such fields that had received little formal recognition by the university in its statutes.

Such a situation did, however, pose problems and produce tensions that were not yet fully apparent at the close of the reign of Elizabeth. If new subjects, such as Greek and Latin literature were being studied, even if only informally, the older view of the unity of studies for the lower degree could hardly be maintained. Whereas it was possible to consider such studies as astronomy, music, speculative grammar, geometry and arithmetic as all closely associated with logic and permeated by concepts arising from basic logical premises, it was difficult to see how subjects such as literature, history, geography, and modern languages, which interested the non-academic sons of the gentry, bore any relation to the study of logic. By the close of the sixteenth century there are strong signs in northern Europe of the disintegration of the ancient faculty of arts into a series of specialist departments each with its own particular lecturer concentrating only on that subject. At Oxford, as we shall argue below, there seems to have been resistance to this development, but the same tendencies that had produced the situation in northern Europe were also at this date at work in Oxford. Equally significant was the strange situation at the end of the century where an influential body of Oxford students was following a course that had little connection with that prescribed by the statutes. Eventually this was to produce among a wider student body a neglect of the official curriculum, its set texts, lectures and exercises, and only a formal adherence to the statutory regulations. Eighteenth-century Oxford was to present such a picture, but the roots of this later situation can be found in the Tudor period.

It would be wrong, however, to dismiss the course for the lower degree at this date as a hotch-potch of conflicting concepts. Although the late Tudor study of logic has been strongly criticized,[2] in the Elizabethan period it still preserved something of value inherited from the earlier studies of the faculty. Oxford masters still read Aristotle, provided lectures on him, and held his works in high esteem. The ability to reason and argue was still considered as of

---

[1] See, for example, the index of books in *Reg. ann. mert. 1567–1603*.
[2] Thomas, 'Medieval aftermath'.

great importance; disputations continued to be exciting events, frequently performed before such important visitors to the university as the queen herself. The study of the elementary Aristotelian and other texts also provided an introduction to scientific and mathematical subjects. On the other hand, a reading of Greek and Latin texts, together with works in grammar and rhetoric gave to the student some awareness of the virtues of a 'literary' education. It could perhaps be argued that such a course endeavoured to combine much of the best of both the medieval and the humanist views of the character of higher education. The Oxford arts course as a whole certainly provided a valuable introduction for those considering further academic study. The late sixteenth century was preoccupied with theological controversy, especially in England where the Roman Catholic opponents of the Anglican church were joined by critics from within the European protestant community. Scholars on all sides relied in presenting their arguments on a basis of rational thought and general knowledge. The Oxford arts course provided both the necessary training in logic and philosophy, and the textual knowledge of Greek and Latin that was required for further study in theology.

THE MASTER OF ARTS DEGREE

That the university regarded the acquisition of the BA degree as simply one stage towards the mastership, is shown when, in the sixteenth century, most applicants for the lower degree were automatically required to determine during the Lent following their admission. Determination was well established at the close of the medieval period as an important part of the arts programme. During the exercises held annually in Lent, the newly admitted bachelor was required to occupy one of the schools normally used by a master, and there to hold disputations with junior students. The unusual feature of these exercises was that the bachelor presided, resolving or 'determining' the argument, acting, in fact, as the master did in the normal, 'ordinary', disputations of the faculty. Determination provided an opportunity for both junior students and bachelors to perform exercises. We have already discussed the role of the undergraduate, now we must consider the importance of determination for the bachelor, the principal disputant.

Determination

The student was already a bachelor before he began his determination. For those who for personal reasons had to be content with only the lower degree, the need to determine was an extra and unnecessary burden. Accordingly, the university found it necessary to grant dispensations to individuals freeing them from their obligation. Students alleged poverty, illness, absence on important business, and the need to take work in a school or parish as reasons for requesting such dispensations. Members of Queen's College often postponed their determination; this was probably the outcome of some college practice unknown to us. Such dispensations were given to individuals, but there is no sign of any general attempt to reduce the importance or necessity of determination. On the contrary, many sixteenth-century statutes re-order and strengthen the procedure at determination, and in 1506 the earlier practice of registering the names of those determining was reasserted.[1] The payments made by students at determination to the bedels, the *collectores*, the proctors, the vicar of St Mary's, the junior bedels in theology and law, and others, were listed in 1601–2; they amounted to the sum of 5s 2d.[2]

The procedure during determination remained unchanged over the century; some details, however, were vague and had to be modified by legislation. All those about to determine were expected to present themselves on the Saturday before Ash Wednesday for examination by officials or *collectores*, appointed to supervise the exercises. This day, known as Egg Saturday, from the Latin *festum ovorum*, was apparently also a time of celebration, for bachelors were, after 1590, allowed to substitute a money payment '*decem drachmas bonae et legalis monetae Angliae*' for the feast they normally gave on that day.[3] No student was allowed to proceed with his determination, except by special dispensation, unless he presented himself on Egg Saturday.[4] The examination of students was closely regulated by the statute of 1597,[5] which also formally stated that henceforth all applicants for the BA degree would be required to determine in the following Lent. On Egg Saturday, the prospective determiners were to dispute with the senior bachelors on logical and ethical material to prove their competence. The senior bachelors were then required to give their opinion of the determiners' ability and religious faith to the proctors on oath, and the support of nine bachelors was essential if a determiner was to be allowed to proceed further. At this time also the *collectores* were appointed. Before 1586, the proctors had chosen these temporary officials, but after this date the election was made by those bachelors about to determine. Measures were taken to ensure that the election was conducted in a responsible

[1] *Statuta*, 321–2.   [2] Ibid. 469.
[3] Ibid. 441–2, 451.   [4] Ibid. 423.
[5] Ibid. 454–5.

and orderly fashion. The *collectores* then divided the determiners into the groups (*classes*) in which they were to proceed through the schools. For this work, the *collectores* received a payment of not more than 12*d* from each determiner.[1] The title given to them suggests that the *collectores* were originally also responsible for collecting other payments due at this time. After 1601, such payments were to be made on the day before Egg Saturday since the proctors were too preoccupied on that day to attend to such matters.[2]

The disputations proper began with a formal ceremony on Ash Wednesday where the determining bachelors disputed with the masters, so reversing the role they were about to take. During the next few weeks, the bachelors disputed with junior students in the schools for which each had, after 1586, paid a hiring fee of 4*s*.[3] Determiners were not allowed to alter the group or school to which they had been allocated, they were to leave their schools 'after the ceasing of the bell', and they were not to have more than one scholar disputing with them each day. The number of disputations expected from each determining bachelor was not clearly indicated, but by the time of the Laudian Statutes it was two.[4] The exercises were to take place during the afternoons on Monday, Tuesday, Wednesday or Thursday, and on Friday mornings. If a congregation was held during an afternoon, then the exercises were to be transferred to the morning. Disputations were to be in logic except on Fridays, when 'Morall, Rhetoricke or Grammer' was to be debated.[5] The wording of this reference to the Friday exercises is significant as the medieval statutes[6] had allocated grammar only to this day, especially requiring exercises on the speculative grammar of the *modistae*. Humanistic influence seems here to have modified slightly the character of the determination exercises. As we have earlier noted, attempts were made to exclude from these exercises authors supporting views contrary to those of Aristotle. Regulations were passed to ensure discipline and decency during determination; all regent masters and bachelors were required to be present throughout the exercises to ensure proper respect for them.[7] The Laudian statutes could assert that the university and the faculty of arts obtained much honour and benefit from these exercises.[8]

The complexity and importance of determination is reflected in the large number of references to the exercises in the registers of

---

[1] Ibid. 435–6.   [2] Ibid. 457–8.
[3] Ibid. 436.   [4] *Laudian Code*, 54.
[5] *Statuta*, 406.   [6] Ibid. 202.
[7] Ibid. 436–7.   [8] *Laudian Code*, 50.

congregation. Frequently, because of illness, absence on necessary business, the danger of plague at Oxford, or the need to visit a relation or patron, students had to request dispensations from the statutory regulations. The strict rules regarding dress and the grouping of candidates were sometimes relaxed for individuals. Registers of the early years of the century often note the performance at determination of an exercise 'beyond form' (*preter formam*).[1] This appears to be an extra disputation to that normally required of determiners. We also find references to the puzzling *determinatio pro aliis*.[2] This may be a determination where a richer student undertakes to cover the expenses of poorer candidates, but this whole subject is very obscure. Sometimes the exact subject of a student's determination exercise is given: the logic of Porphyry, or Aristotle for example.[3] Such graces simply modified a procedure which in its essential features remained unaltered from the fifteenth until the seventeenth century.

Length of the course

In preparation for the higher degree, the bachelor was expected to study for a further period of three years after obtaining the lower degree, that is for a period of seven years altogether for the mastership. During the sixteenth century these traditional requirements were not seriously altered. In 1556, for one year, bachelors of two years standing were allowed to 'incept', and the sons of noblemen were later allowed to obtain dispensations for time,[4] but the Laudian statutes retain the early requirement of three years for the general body of students.[5] Nor does an examination of the Tudor registers of congregation show that there was any movement away from those requirements: in fact, the Elizabethan registers appear to show less flexibility here than those of the earlier period and a greater readiness to adhere to the exact letter of the statutes. Some students offer more years than is required, a few less; some seem to be compensating for a shorter BA course by offering a longer course for the mastership. Such cases, however, are not statistically significant. Some students were allowed, for particular reasons, to shorten their course. The university considered benevolently those requests coming from students who urgently needed the degree: to obtain a benefice, a college fellowship or a teaching post, for example. Such students had usually completed their exercises and were requesting

[1] For an example, see Reg. Cong. 1535–63, fo 94ᵛ: 'bis subeat provinciam disputandi quam vocant praeterformam'.

[2] Reg. Cong. 1518–35, fos 161ᵛ, 164.   [3] Reg. Cong. 1535–63, fo 51.

[4] *Statuta*, 362, 420.   [5] *Laudian Code*, 50.

simply a dispensation for a short period of time. But these grants do not indicate any general movement away from the statutes.

Modification of the regency system

During these years prior to inception, the bachelor attended lectures on the texts set by the faculty and given by the regent masters. It is here that we do see a significant move away from the practice of the medieval university. Early universities fashioned after the organization of Paris recruited their teaching staff from their own graduates. When he obtained the MA degree, the new master promised to remain at the university for some time, approximately two years at Oxford, and give lectures for the benefit of the arts students. During this time he was known as a 'necessary regent' and his lectures covering the compulsory set texts were known as 'ordinary' lectures. Such a system had marked advantages: it provided a changing, fresh body of lecturers who made no financial demands on the university. For the masters themselves, however, the system had obvious disadvantages. It lengthened considerably the time for which the student was bound to be present at the university, a serious drain on the resources of those not intending to study further. It also inhibited the recruitment of really well-qualified lecturers who could only be retained if promised a regular salary and a secure status. By the beginning of the sixteenth century, most northern 'arts' universities had modified or abandoned the medieval system, replacing the necessary regents by lecturers who drew their salaries often from stipends allocated to them by the local secular authority. This practice was approved by humanists who saw in this alliance of state and university an opportunity of employment for themselves and a means whereby a powerful group of salaried lecturers could reform and reshape the medieval curriculum.

Oxford strongly resisted the total abandonment of the medieval system. However, the repeated warnings in the statutes against the avoidance by students and masters of their obligations suggest that it was breaking down. The Edwardian statutes required lecturers in arts to read on five days of each week unless the celebration of a religious feast prevented this.[1] In 1556, and again in 1576, attempts were made to act against scholars and masters who did not attend lectures or give them.[2] Lecturers were expected to read daily except when excused by the custom of the university, but were allowed a free day on Thursdays if no feast day occurred in that particular week.[3] Fines for failing to lecture were imposed in 1567.[4] The

---

[1] *Statuta*, 343.   [2] Ibid. 369, 407.   [3] Ibid. 372–3.   [4] Ibid. 398.

statutes alone seem to indicate that, as the century progressed, both students and masters were reluctant to complete here their statutory duties.

The Tudor registers show how far this process had gone. Not only was the university now prepared to dispense individuals from attendance at and performance of lectures for a variety of reasons—illness, poverty, absence abroad, or employment outside Oxford, for instance—but it also gave wholesale dispensations to groups of regent masters. Regularly, regents were excused their lecturing duties as soon as a new degree ceremony provided a fresh supply of masters. Often immediately after such a ceremony, dispensations would be granted to most masters; only a few were required to remain to lecture. The university appears to have been moving gradually towards the system that seems to have been established by the late 1550s. Then we find mention of masters 'deputed to lecture';[1] the earlier requirement that all masters should lecture after obtaining their degrees was now formally abandoned. The names of certain of the lecturers were occasionally recorded;[2] they were apparently chosen by a committee at each degree ceremony, were punished if they refused the responsibility, and were each paid a salary of four marks.[3] Measures were taken to ensure that nine masters were chosen to lecture so that the arts course could be adequately covered.[4] By 1562, the vice-chancellor and the proctors were made responsible for choosing the public lecturers and for paying to them the money claimed from those masters now excused their regency. However, the university still reserved the right to require their lectures from such dispensed masters if those originally chosen were unable to perform.[5] In 1564 it was the senior bedel of the faculty who collected 6s 8d from each master dispensed and who paid this money to the public lecturers.[6]

The university in this way abandoned the medieval regency system without resort to statutory change. This produced problems: the fiction, for example, that all masters attending congregation were in fact regents who lectured had to be maintained by allowing those reading a short lecture, or a few lectures, to consider this as satisfying the statutory requirements.[7] Even the Laudian statutes still speak of the two years period of necessary regency, although this had long since lost its significance.[8] Indeed, in view of the increase in the

[1] Reg. Cong. 1535–63, fo 168^V.
[2] Ibid. fo 193: 'lectores publici' in four subjects.
[3] Ibid. fo 198.   [4] Ibid. fo 199.
[5] Ibid. fo 200.   [6] Ibid. fo 211^V.
[7] For examples, see ibid. fo 5^V; Reg. Cong. 1518–35, fo 189^V.
[8] For example, *Laudian Code*, 88.

number of those taking the MA degree during the reign of Elizabeth, the university would have been unable to find suitable accommodation if all masters had decided to complete their two years of necessary regency as lecturers. There is, however, some evidence to suggest that the abandonment of regency was less complete than the graces in the registers of congregation appear to indicate. Although the university no longer insisted on the traditional period of necessary regency, some colleges continued to expect their fellows to respect the old statutes. Merton College, which provided a regular supply of candidates for the MA degree, still expected at least some formal lectures to be given by its graduates. The college register for the reign of Elizabeth shows that fellows were very careful to obtain permission from the warden or his deputy if they wished to omit even a small part of their duties as regents. On the other hand, the college appears prepared to grant general dispensations from the second year of regency.[1] Oriel College, however, in 1565 ceased to impose the usual conditions on candidates for the MA degree,[2] requiring that the traditional period of regency should be observed. Before the evidence of the graces can be fully accepted, we need to know more of the extent of the continued college 'use' of the older regency system. Certainly the university registers suggest that students were reluctant to attend such lectures. Several dispensations granted to masters note that few or no hearers attend.[3] The music lecture, as we have earlier noted, seems to have been particularly unpopular and was frequently cancelled.[4] The earlier unique importance of the 'ordinary' lecture was also now threatened by other developments. We have already noted that with the supply of books to Oxford, the regent lecturer was no longer the sole source of information; as well, rival lecturers were appearing.

Public and college lecturerships

Support for public lecturerships by benefactors commenced in the late fifteenth and sixteenth centuries. The higher faculties and those subjects such as Greek and Hebrew not normally taught in the medieval university were first to benefit from this patronage, but the faculty of arts was not to be unaffected for long. Sir Henry Savile in 1619 established two lecturerships in geometry and astronomy, subjects long associated with the faculty.[5] More serious because more

---

[1] For examples, see *Reg. ann. mert. 1567-1603*, 24 (Fleetwood excused his lectures for the first three *dies legibiles* of term); ibid. 28 (three fellows excused their second year of regency), etc.   [2] *Deans' Register of Oriel*, 153.

[3] For examples, see Reg. Cong. 1518-35, fos 71, 144, 189^V, 295^V, 302^V, etc.

[4] For an example, see Reg. Cong. 1535-63, fo 205.

[5] *Statuta*, 528.

pervasive was the challenge of the college teacher. The growth of collegiate instruction is considered in detail elsewhere, but we may mention here that, by the close of the Tudor period, colleges were providing instruction for their members in many arts subjects, and indeed in certain subjects, such as modern languages, ignored by the statutory curriculum. The dean's register at Oriel shows that lectures were given in college; there was a note of a *praelector et moderator logicus* in 1591.[1] At Merton, there were references to lecturers in rhetoric, grammar, dialectic, Greek and Hebrew appointed and paid by the college; a teacher of Spanish and Italian was also mentioned.[2] Lectures were also given on the *Ethics*, the *Politics*, the *Sphera* and on arithmetic.[3] At Trinity College, as has been mentioned already,[4] the statutes regulated in full the studies of the arts student. Lectures on arts subjects during term and during the long vacation were pre-scribed, and the possibility of lectures in classical subjects and Greek was mentioned. The founder's statutes speak as if he expected that the usefulness of the ordinary lectures of the faculty of arts would diminish.

Lectures and disputations

Cursory lectures. The bachelor was, by statute, expected to deliver a certain number of lectures for the benefit of undergraduates in arts. The character of these lectures at the close of the medieval period is obscure, but it seems that they were generally of the type known as 'cursory', that is they contained simply a brief exposition of the text, with a minimum of commentary; in contrast, the master's lecture posed problems and questions related to the text. Such cursory lectures would be those most easily replaced by the pamphlet and booklet material that was becoming available at the beginning of the Tudor period, and there are signs in the earliest surviving registers that these lectures were losing their significance. They were not mentioned in the Edwardian statutes, but the *nova statuta* of 1564–5 expected bachelors to give their lectures in the manner required by the statutes.[5] By 1579 a statute noted that bachelors are expected to deliver cursory lectures on at least two books of logic, one from the old logic and the other from the new logic or both from the new logic, and on one book of natural philosophy. For his lectures in natural philosophy, the bachelor could choose either four books of the *De caelo et mundo*, four of the *Meteora*, two of the *De generatione*

---

[1] *Deans' Register of Oriel*, 144, 201.
[2] *Reg. ann. mert. 1567–1603*, 15, 43, 61, 79, 317, 342 *inter alia*.
[3] Ibid. 96, 209.   [4] See p. 168 above.
[5] *Statuta*, 378.

et corruptione, the *De sensu et sensato* with the *De memoria et reminiscentia* and the *De somno et vigilia*, or the *De motu animalium* with two books of the less-important Aristotelian texts known as the *Minutae naturales*. The statute noted that bachelors had been in the habit of reading different books or not all of the listed books; in future the statute was to be enforced.[1] Yet only five years later the traditional practice was abandoned. The statute of 1584, noting that cursory lectures 'haue bin diuers times read very vnprofitably', henceforth required the bachelors to deliver six formal (sollemne) lectures, three in moral philosophy and three in natural philosophy, 'out of Aristotle', between one and two o'clock during term time.[2] With some additional safeguards, the Laudian statutes incorporated this change in procedure.[3]

The registers of congregation show that many bachelors had to be reminded that lectures must be given.[4] When texts on which they lectured are named in the registers, they are those that we would expect: the *Perihermenias*, the *Elenchi*, the *Predicamenta*, the *Topica*, the *De sensu et sensato*, Porphyry, the *De somno et vigilia*; that is those texts which a junior student would expect to study.[5] Sometimes dispensations allowed the bachelor to reduce the number of lectures given or occasionally apparently to omit them altogether.[6] There is also a significant number of graces permitting bachelors to give their lectures away from the schools; many of these noted that the lectures would be given in college.[7] Occasionally a candidate stated frankly why he preferred to use his college accommodation: William Haynes of Oriel declared he would have a better attendance, *maiorem habebit frequentiam*; another bachelor said that he could not be sure of an audience in the schools.[8] Other dispensations suggest that 'private lectures' (*legendo privatim*) were more profitable than cursory lectures; it also seems to have been difficult to attract an audience after midday.[9] We must not assume that these movements were necessarily part of an encroachment by the colleges on the territory of university teaching, for, although the exact position of the bachelor in the medieval university is obscure, at Oxford he was then expected to undertake some teaching in his college or

[1] Ibid. 415–16. Cf the medieval regulations, 32.
[2] Ibid. 431. *Reg. Univ.* ed. Clark, i. 78, indicates wrongly that the change occurred in 1634.
[3] *Laudian Code*, 58.
[4] For examples, see Reg. Cong. 1535–63, fo 151^V; Reg. Cong. 1564–82, fo 194.
[5] Reg. Cong. 1518–35, fos 65^V, 100, 100^V; Reg. Cong. 1535–63, fo 75.
[6] Reg. Cong. 1518–35, fos 87, 100.
[7] Ibid. fo 126^V (Magdalen); fo 287^V (Corpus Christi).
[8] Ibid. fo 181^V, Reg. Cong. 1535–63 fo 185.
[9] Ibid. fos 201^V, 208^V, 75^V.

hall. There seems an attempt in the sixteenth century to reduce overall the teaching load of the bachelor and to divide this reduced load
of six formal lectures so that some were given in the schools and
some in the colleges. This would have brought with it a partial solution to the problem of providing accommodation for so many lecturers. However, for some at least of the bachelors, the best response
to their lectures was to be found in their colleges, not in the university schools.

Austin disputations. As well as attending and giving lectures, the
bachelor was required to perform various academic exercises with
both his fellow students and with the masters. These were the
'Austin' disputations and the 'ordinary' disputations. The Austin
disputations, or *disputationes apud Augustinenses*, had their origin
in the medieval university and received their title because they were
originally performed in the convent of the Augustinian friars.
Following the dissolution of the friary, the disputations were transferred to St Mary's Church and this venue was confirmed by the
statute of 1564–5;[1] attempts to rename the exercises *disputationes
Marianae* were not successful, and by the reign of Elizabeth the
traditional name was again regularly in use. The exercises followed
the normal pattern, with bachelors taking part as both respondents
and opponents, probably under the supervision of a master or
masters.

The sixteenth-century statutes and registers of congregation
provide us with interesting details of these exercises. By the Edwardian statutes, the disputations were allocated to Fridays from nine
until eleven and to Saturdays from eight until ten. Bachelors in their
second year acted as respondents in descending order of seniority
to opponents also acting 'in their own order'. Four students, if
required by the supervisor of the exercise, could raise arguments
against the respondent. Arrangements for giving notice of the
disputations and to prevent avoidance of the obligation to perform
were also made.[2] Later evidence from the statutes is not of great
value, but the Laudian statutes[3] do give a detailed account of the
Austin exercises and probably reflect something of the practice
of the reign of Elizabeth. Here each bachelor, after his determination, was required to oppose or respond once every year on Saturdays in the school of natural philosophy between one and three,
after being given due notice by the *collectores* in charge of the
exercises. Those refusing to dispute were to be punished. Normally,
the senior disputant was to have the choice of taking the position

---

[1] *Statuta*, 385.   [2] Ibid. 347–8.
[3] *Laudian Code*, 55–7.

of respondent or opponent, but noblemen were to have precedence. If the number of Saturdays was not sufficient, other days were to be allocated for the exercise. A notice of the subject to be debated was to be fixed on the doors of the schools by the respondent three days before the exercise and the supervisor informed seven days earlier. The disputations were to be supervised by two masters appointed annually by the proctors, but the actual naming of bachelors to dispute when individuals do not themselves volunteer is to be in the hands of two bachelors, nominated by the supervisors and known as *collectores*. The Laudian statutes, therefore, required an annual disputation from each bachelor after his determination, that is a total of two if the bachelor had followed the normal course. The vague Edwardian statutes seem to require one opposition and two responsions[1] and the Elizabethan statutes at least one responsion or opposition.[2] However, it is clear from the graces in the registers of congregation that only one opposition or responsion was usually offered throughout the Tudor period; very few candidates mention that they have performed more. Clark's note, based on the Laudian evidence, that an annual exercise was required in the Elizabethan period does not seem to be consistent with the evidence of the registers. In the early Tudor period there is some mention of regent masters participating in these exercises as replicators:[3] this duty does not seem to have been required by the Laudian statutes and perhaps disappeared at the end of our period as concepts of regency changed.

The graces supply evidence of the detailed arrangements for these exercises. The day allocated, which seems already in Elizabeth's reign to have been Saturday, had frequently to be supplemented by other days when the numbers of disputants rose.[4] Disputations were often cancelled or postponed when bachelors, schools or supervisors were not available:[5] the position of respondent and opponent could be interchanged.[6] Some intriguing references suggest that the bachelors were divided into groups for these exercises as well as for determination; we have mention of a *classis* and a *3a forma*.[7] The importance of the Austin exercises was emphasized for one candidate; Hugh Weston refused to respond there after being warned and, as a result, in 1575 was rejected when he came to apply for his MA degree.[8]

Ordinary disputations. The bachelor was also expected to dispute with the masters in the 'ordinary' disputations of the faculty. The

[1] *Statuta*, 344.   [2] Ibid. 378.
[3] See Reg. Cong. 1518–35, fo 302ᵛ, and *Deans' Register of Oriel*, 119.
[4] See, for example, Reg. Cong. 1564–82, fo 168ᵛ for a general dispensation of 1574.
[5] Reg. Cong. 1518–35, fos 74ᵛ, 91, 127.   [6] Ibid. fos 121, 266ᵛ.
[7] Ibid. fos 243ᵛ, 277ᵛ.   [8] Reg. Cong. 1564–82, fo 195ᵛ.

terminology used to describe these exercises in the sixteenth century has produced some confusion among historians.[1] The ordinary disputations of the faculty were, in the Laudian statutes, the *disputationes quodlibeticae*, but they were certainly not known by that name in the medieval or early Tudor university. There were spectacular disputations in the northern medieval universities, often involving the entire teaching staff of the university and given on special occasions usually by a specially appointed master known as the *quodlibetarius*;[2] they must not be confused with the normal exercises required for the master's degree. In the medieval and early Tudor registers at Oxford, care was taken to keep the two distinct.[3] At some time in the middle of the sixteenth century, the ancient 'quodlibets' disappeared and their name was appropriated by the ordinary exercises of the faculty. By 1576 these disputations were officially known as 'quodlibets',[4] the name they were given later in the Laudian statutes.

The medieval statutes are not clear about the number of exercises expected of the bachelor; the same confusion remains in the sixteenth century. The Edwardian statutes seem to expect the bachelor to dispute three times against a master, but in 1564–5 one responsion only was mentioned.[5] This single responsion was also that required by the Laudian statutes.[6] Occasionally, in the registers, students noted that they had performed more than one responsion in the quodlibetical exercises,[7] but usually only the single responsion required by the Elizabethan statutes was offered. In this respect the later Tudor registers show a far greater uniformity than those of an earlier date where a variety of responsions was recorded.

The masters against whom the bachelors disputed were supplied in the medieval and early Tudor university from the necessary regents. After obtaining the master's degree, a new graduate was required to dispute on each of the next forty consecutive *dies disputabiles*, days set apart for the ordinary disputations. Early registers show that the university was concerned to ensure that this obligation was maintained. It seems that, as with determination, Fridays in the medieval university were set apart for grammatical disputations.

The sixteenth century saw many changes in this uncomplicated

---

[1] See, for example, the very confused account in J. Lawson, *Mediaeval Education and the Reformation* (London 1967), 38–9.

[2] See the full discussion in G. Kaufmann, *Geschichte der deutschen Universitäten* (2 vols Stuttgart 1888–96) ii. 381–95.

[3] See, for example, Richard Martyn's grace in 1533 mentioning responsions in quodlibets *and* formal disputations, Reg. Cong. 1518–35, fo 293ᵛ.

[4] *Statuta*, 406.   [5] Ibid. 344, 378.

[6] *Laudian Code*, 57.

[7] For an example, see Reg. Cong. 1564–82, fo 37: two responsions.

system. By the Edwardian statutes, a college or group of colleges was expected to supply disputants, both masters and bachelors, when formally summoned. Disputations took place on Mondays, Tuesdays, and Wednesdays, except on certain feast days, from one until three. Masters were expected to dispute in order of seniority during the two years following their inception; three theses at least were to be debated at each disputation. Arrangements for the prior publication of the theses, control of the exercises and for the formal procession to the schools were also made.[1] It would seem that by this date the earlier allocation of Fridays for grammatical disputations had been abandoned. These arrangements could not have been followed for long. The Elizabethan statutes speak of the disputations now being held at 10 a.m.; references in the contemporary registers show that this time in fact was kept.[2] Otherwise there are not many details of the quodlibets in the registers, but it is probable that the arrangements later recorded in the Laudian statutes were then already being followed. Here the statutes clearly stated that the old system was no longer in operation. Quodlibets were to take place now on every *dies disputabilis* when congregations were not held. Two regent masters in reverse order of seniority were to dispute on each day in the schools, one acting as supervisor the other as opponent.[3]

It would appear, therefore, that the masters disputing at the close of the Tudor period were drawn from the ranks of those selected to lecture and those required by their college to perform at least part of the old obligations of regency. It is clear, however, from the registers that disputations were still held and that each bachelor was expected to respond at least once to the masters. The medieval disputation still retained something of its earlier importance.

The declamation

During the sixteenth century an important addition was made to the methods used to prepare students for the MA degree. Renaissance educationalists were concerned to introduce into the universities one of the standard teaching devices of the orators of ancient Rome, the declamation. Following Quintilian, accepted by Erasmus as the model for all educational reformers, humanists saw the declamation as giving to the student an opportunity to practice prose composition based on the use of standard, classical authorities, and to deliver elegant Latin speeches. The reformed schools and universities of sixteenth-century northern Europe introduced the use of the

---

[1] *Statuta*, 347-9, 356, 359, 360.
[2] Ibid. 378; Reg. Cong. 1564-82, fo 19.   [3] *Laudian Code*, 82.

declamation as a teaching tool to supplement the older disputation. At Oxford the declamation was first formally brought into the curriculum by the Edwardian statutes; bachelors were required to declaim twice on Fridays, from two until three. On alternate weeks they were required to speak for and against a given theme with the most junior bachelor beginning; two masters were to supervise the declamation.[1] However, there is no mention of the declamation in the Elizabethan statutes and it does not appear in the Laudian statutes as part of the programme of work for the mastership. Instead, by these statutes, both undergraduates and bachelors were expected to participate in declamations in their 'halls', the former orally and the latter with written *themata*; these arrangements appear in the section headed *Statuta aularia*.[2] Between the middle of the sixteenth century and the date of the Laudian statutes, responsibility for organizing declamations had apparently passed from the university to the colleges and halls.

Internal evidence from the colleges certainly shows that declamations were organized there during the Elizabethan period. As late as 1586, the dean of Oriel College raised the question of whether he could order bachelors to declaim. During the next year, one bachelor refused to perform a declamation and suggested that he was supported by his colleagues.[3] It would appear that declamations at Oriel were considered a novelty in 1586 and were resisted by the bachelors. At Merton College, however, bachelors were instructed to declaim each week as early as 1560; in later years there are further indications that declamations had been given.[4] We have a few isolated references to the university insisting on declamations being performed. In 1560 Robert Borlis had to declaim twice in St Mary's Church before he was allowed to proceed to the mastership. Edward Danse in 1567 was also required to declaim there before he could obtain the MA degree.[5] Such references may indicate that a formal requirement concerning declamations was known to the university.

Contents of the course

The exact allocation of the texts studied to the lower and higher degree course in arts is not always clear. As we have noted, several students studied for a short period for the BA degree and then for a longer period for the mastership, and vice versa. It is probable that the faculty regarded its set texts, as a whole, as essential for the

---

[1] *Statuta*, 344, 348, 359.
[2] *Laudian Code*, 50, 270.
[3] *Dean's Register of Oriel*, 187, 191.
[4] *Reg. ann. mert. 1521–67*, 198, 254, 262. *Reg. ann. mert. 1567–1603*, 96.
[5] Reg. Cong. 1535–63, fo 192; Reg. Cong. 1564–82, fo 45.

higher degree, and may not have been unduly concerned about whether or not individual texts were studied before or after the BA degree was taken. The essential studies for the mastership seem to have been those associated with the three philosophies: moral, metaphysical and natural. The texts used were the Aristotelian works: the *Ethics* and the *Politics*, the *Metaphysics* and the *Physics*. These texts retained their authority because they had not been replaced by any comparable works, although since medieval times details of the Aristotelian system, especially in natural philosophy, had been challenged. It was not until the end of the seventeenth century that contemporary work could rival the coherence of thought of the great philosopher. The Aristotelian texts were also valuable as set works to study since they provided a base from which a thoughtful student could set out to explore the lesser but significant detailed writings of the sixteenth century: modern works on geography, mathematics, history, politics and cosmography could be related easily to the Aristotelian corpus from which, in fact, many such recent authors had drawn part of their inspiration; new commentaries on Aristotle were readily received.[1] Nor were these studies unrelated to contemporary affairs and contemporary concerns: problems such as the relationship between the heart and the brain and between melancholy and ability, whether the movement of the heavens was perpetual, whether sight was derived from internal or external forces, whether women should receive education, the good or bad nature of the appearance of comets, whether land should be inherited, the role of dreams, whether the English were stronger than the Spaniards, and the relationship of contemporary figures to those of the past,[2] were debated with obvious relevance to the contemporary Elizabethan situation.

Perhaps of most importance to contemporaries was the function of a complete education in arts as preparation for the study of theology. Especially in the course for the MA degree we see the student approaching such subjects as ethics, natural science and metaphysics that were clearly related to the theological studies of that date. Controversies of the sixteenth century between protestants and catholics touched on many topics that would have been partly discussed in the later stages of the arts course at Oxford: the moral value of good works, the position of man in the cosmos, the relationship between God, man and the universe, the scientific problems

---

[1] See, for example, the various lists of books purchased for Merton College Library in the reign of Elizabeth in *Reg. ann. mert. 1567–1603*.

[2] Many titles of theses disputed may be found in Clark and in *Reg. ann. mert. 1521–67* and *1567–1603*.

presented by the different views of the nature of the eucharist. Academic theologians were well aware of the value of these studies of the artists; as we have already noted, a master's degree in arts was usually taken by students in the faculty of theology, and the disappearance of the religious orders had meant that in the Elizabethan university such a degree was in most cases obtained at Oxford itself.

The quality of the theological argument produced in England in the late sixteenth and early seventeenth centuries owes much to the excellence of the instruction in the Oxford faculty of arts. Nor were these virtues of value only to the theologian: an awareness of the fundamental problems of science, ethics and politics was and still is of value to every man. When compared with the outlook of the highly specialized modern graduate, the breadth of the Elizabethan master's knowledge, his obvious articulateness, his command of written Latin and the vernacular may perhaps be envied.

Public lecturership in Greek

An important modification to the arts curriculum, introduced by intervention from the state probably under pressure from humanists at court, was the institution of a public lecturership in Greek by Henry VIII. The confused Edwardian statutes seem to expect bachelors of arts to attend this lecture, but they also indicate that attendance was not compulsory.[1] The regulations of 1576 definitely require attendance, since they provide for the punishment of bachelors not present at the daily Greek lecture;[2] from the wording of the *nova statuta* it would appear that four lectures in fact were given each week during term time.[3] Whether this one lecturership succeeded in modifying radically the medieval arts curriculum is, as we have noted, very doubtful. Perhaps it may be seen as one step in a movement that did not proceed much further. Many later humanists, particularly those actively involved on the protestant side, were more concerned to see the study of Greek as an aid to the proper understanding of the New Testament and the early fathers, rather than as giving the linguistic skills that would enable the student to read the great classics of Greek literature. We must suspect that, at Oxford, many of the more serious students of Greek intended to make use of their knowledge later in the faculty of theology. The royal lectures, however, did provide an instruction which meant that many of the traditional Aristotelian texts could now be studied in the original rather than from inadequate translations.

[1] *Statuta*, 344, 358.   [2] Ibid. 408.
[3] Ibid. 381.

Inception and the act

Having completed his course for the MA degree, the bachelor formally supplicated for permission to proceed. If his grace was granted, the candidate was required to make a formal circuit of the schools. This had originally been done to inform each master of the applicant's intentions, so that any objection to him could be made, and to invite masters to the degree festivities. By the close of the Tudor period, the *circuitus* had become a formality and dispensations from it, for the occurrence of bad weather, or the candidate's late arrival, for example, were frequently granted.[1] The bachelor had then to produce a number of masters who would testify to his ability, that is, make the so-called 'deposition' before he was presented to the vice-chancellor to receive his licence to proceed to the final ceremony. The university usually insisted that all licensed bachelors should take their degrees at the next ceremony, or act,[2] but occasionally exemptions from this were granted. At this stage, the student's name was formally registered by the university.

The degree ceremony was divided into two parts; vespers preceded the *comitia* or act. During both days, formal disputations among those chosen from the candidates, now known as inceptors, and from the masters took place, with an increasing element of comedy, formalized in the Laudian statutes by the role of the *terrae filius*, to enliven the proceedings. At the end of the disputations in the act, the candidates formally incepted; that is they received the master's insignia from the vice-chancellor and were admitted into the ranks of the Oxford masters of arts. By the Edwardian statutes, the date of the act was established as the final Tuesday in June, but this was altered in 1566 to the Monday following 7 July.[3] Although much of the medieval procedure was now retained only as a formality, the act with its lively disputations and often witty comedy remained still the important and respected climax of the Oxford academic year.

As we have already noted, the new master, now a necessary regent, was traditionally expected to remain at the university and provide lectures and disputations for the benefit of arts students. We have discussed the radical changes that were made in the concept of necessary regency during the Tudor period. While regency was expected from the newly created master, he was also required to attend congregation and so play his part in the administration of the university. Dispensations were frequently granted, however, especially

[1] Reg. Cong. 1564–82, fos 7, 7^V.   [2] See *Statuta*, 376 (1561).
[3] Ibid. 343, 396.

to those who found that attendance clashed with teaching duties in their colleges. The ending of the earlier regency system during Elizabeth's reign, in practice if not by statute, inevitably meant that congregation would be dominated by those masters willing and able to remain at the university, that is, by college fellows. However, this would still produce an assembly controlled by the younger, more active, university teachers and in this respect congregation at the close of the Tudor period still retained something of the youthful flavour of its medieval counterpart.

CONCLUSIONS

From this brief survey of an important period in the history of the Oxford faculty of arts, certain tentative conclusions may be drawn. It does seem that the artists by the close of the Tudor period formed an even more powerful body within the university than they had done before the reformation. Challenges to their constitutional power were coming, however, from outside forces concerned at the radicalism of the younger masters. The faculty had retained much of its medieval structure and traditions, disregarding much of its earlier concern with sophistry, but taking little from the humanist reformers except in the few fields, such as the study of Greek, grammar and rhetoric, where their authority was considered better than that of earlier writers. Declamations had been introduced, but had not ousted disputations as the principal instrument of teaching. Slowly and reluctantly, the faculty had accepted some kind of formal public lecturing system similar to that used in the higher faculties and in most other northern universities.

Yet for all its strength within the university, the Oxford faculty of arts was, when considered in its European context, a pale shadow of its late medieval counterpart. Whereas the faculty at the close of the fifteenth century could point to numerous continental universities, where the set texts used by the artists included many written by earlier Oxford masters, and to its own studies which to a great extent utilized material produced by Oxford alumni in the recent past, the artists at the close of Elizabeth's reign could claim no such scholarly dominance. Many of the Oxford works that were common currency in the late medieval university had been discredited and even lost in England; when they had been printed, the books had not been published in England and were no longer always readily available at the close of the sixteenth century. Oxford masters lecturing in the faculty of arts during Elizabeth's reign quoted for the most part from contemporary works by continental scholars printed abroad. No Elizabethan equivalent of Scotus, Ockham or Burley dominated the studies of the artists of the continent. In the area of logic, which in the late medieval period was greatly influenced by Oxford masters, the major controversialist of the Tudor period came from Paris. If the author of the *Philobiblon* could claim at the close of the fourteenth century that Minerva had migrated from the Seine to the banks of the Isis, Paris could perhaps claim her revenge in the sixteenth century.

If study at a reformed northern university is seen as the type of education required by those moving into academic life at this date, then this education could not be obtained by resort to the official Oxford curriculum. Englishmen wishing for such an education who did not desire to travel abroad were forced to rely on instruction provided to their tastes and requirements by the colleges. We may suggest that one reason for the strong development of college tutorial teaching, which from the sixteenth century was to be a unique feature of the Oxford system, was the refusal of the faculty of arts to provide the type of education required particularly by the active, dynamic and richer classes of the late sixteenth century. When this college education in turn, in the eighteenth century, ceased to provide for the requirements of a different social group, English students seeking a modern education were compelled to travel to Scotland or abroad. This development made necessary that reform of the Oxford faculty, during the nineteenth century, by which many of the medieval as well as the renaissance aspects of the curriculum were finally discarded.

Appendix

Music in the Faculty of Arts

JOHN CALDWELL*

THE basis of instruction in music at Oxford during the Tudor period is summed up by the entry in the statutes of 1431, according to which candidates who wished to incept in arts and philosophy (that is, in effect, those proceeding to the master's degree) should have studied 'music for the period of a year, namely Boethius'.[1] The precise point during the seven-year arts course (four years for BA, three more for MA) at which music would be studied is not specified, but there is perhaps a presumption that it should be during the last three. The Edwardian code of 1549, however, recommended the study of the *quadrivium* in the first year of the university course, specifying arithmetic, geometry and astronomy only, though it is unlikely that music was intended to be excluded.[2] The Elizabethan statutes of 1564/5 include music among the subjects required for the BA, the course for which incorporated two terms devoted to music.[3] Again Boethius is specified. They also prescribe the observance of the 'old statutes', which may or may not imply that music would have been further studied by bachelors proceeding to the masters' degree.

It is surprising how tenaciously the *De institutione musica* of Boethius, an obscure and difficult book of little significance to the practice of music even when it was written, should have kept its place in the statutes, even down to the middle of the nineteenth century. It is, of course, a very reasonably compendious and authoritative digest of music as a mathematical discipline, needing only the prior study of arithmetic (preferably in Boethius's own work on the subject) to make it comprehensible as such. Boethius had leant heavily on Greek authors—in particular Nicomachus and Ptolemy—

* I am grateful to Dr F. W. Sternfeld for his advice and encouragement, and to Mr A. Wathey for many helpful revisions in the preparation of this essay.
[1] 'musicam per terminum anni, videlicet Boecii': *Statuta*, 234.
[2] *Statuta*, 344.
[3] 'Duos [terminos] demum musicae': *Statuta*, 390.

and he is the outstanding figure in the transmission of Greek musical science to the medieval west.[1] His nearest rival for this distinction, Martianus Capella, had relied on Aristides Quintilianus, and his work on music, a section of his *De nuptiis Mercurii et Philologiae*, was much shorter; while such authors as Cassiodorus, Isidorus and Augustine had left only highly abbreviated or otherwise incomplete treatments of the subject. Medieval theorists adopted some of Boethius's terminology (in particular on the modes) in their vocabulary of practical music, and held up his work as a whole as a model of *musica speculativa*.

Speculative music may be defined as that whole area of investigation, also called *theorica musica*, in which the sonorous constituents of music were analysed, provided with their numerical values, and allotted their place in the total scheme; and in which analogies between this audible music and the harmonies of the human soul and of the heavens were pursued. Opposed to it is *practica musica*, the practice of music, and the literature which gave instruction in it. The boundary between the two might not always be sharply drawn, but there is a clear distinction between the analytical approach of speculative music and the synthetic character of practical music. It is important to remember that in Boethius's three-fold division into *musica mundana* (of the spheres), *humana* (of the soul—'quisquis in sese ipsum descendit [eam] intellegit') and *instrumentalis*, all three are treated in a speculative fashion. The third, which is to be understood to include vocal as well as instrumental music in our sense,[2] is dealt with as an analytical study of aural phenomena.

Speculative music is a legitimate subject, and the logical precursor to the study of practical music; but it did not stand still, even in the middle ages, and the laconic equation of music and Boethius in the university statutes suggests an ossification of the syllabus. The extent to which the subject was actually studied in the lectures, disputations and other exercises of the arts faculty during the Tudor period is

[1] The *De institutione* survived in the form of supplication for the B Mus prescribed in the Laudian Code; see below for the origin of this form. For the dependence on Nicomachus see U. Pizzani, 'Studi sulle fonti de "De institutione musica" di Boezio', *Sacris Erudiri* xvi (1965), 5–164; C. Bower, 'Boethius and Nicomachus: an essay concerning the sources of the *De institutione musica*', *Vivarium* xvi (1978), 1–45. Boethius as a writer on arithmetic and music is considered by Henry Chadwick, *Boethius: the Consolations of Music, Logic, Theology and Philosophy* (Oxford 1981(, 71–101; and by the present writer in Margaret Gibson (ed), *Boethius: his Life, Thought and Influence* (Oxford 1981), 135–54.

[2] Boethius, *De institutione musica*, ed. G. Friedlein (Leipzig 1867), 187–9. This and two other chapters are translated in Oliver Strunk, *Source Readings in Music History* (New York 1950), 79–86. A number of medieval and renaissance writers, however, equated *musica humana* with vocal music and *musica instrumentalis* with instrumental music in our sense. For the later development of Boethian thought see Alison White, 'Boethius in the medieval quadrivium' in Gibson, *Boethius*, 162–205.

difficult to determine. It is possible that Boethius was supplemented both by digests of and glosses on his work, as well as by more independently conceived speculative writings, and even by some works of a practical nature. Some idea of the intellectual range of an exceptionally learned and cultured musician of the later sixteenth century can be gained from the impressive list of writers given at the end of Thomas Morley's *A Plaine and Easie Introduction to Practicall Musicke* published in London in 1597. Apart from Boethius he cites Aristoxenus, Ptolemy, Guido of Arezzo (all three from quotations by Franchino Gafurius, whose *Theorica musicae* appeared in Milan in 1492, followed by his *Practica musicae* in 1496), the eleventh-century Byzantine writer Michael Psellus (probably from an edition of 1557), Franco of Cologne (thirteenth century), Robertus de Haulo (or de Handlo, whose work is dated 1326) and the *Quattuor principalia musicae* (1351). His more recent authorities include Gafurius himself, Zacconi, Zarlino and Henricus Loritus Glareanus, whose *Dodecachordon* (1547) is a landmark in the development of modal theory, as well as a host of lesser figures. No doubt all this would have been right outside the capacity of the average sixteenth-century university man, whether undergraduate or master; yet we should not assume too readily for lack of evidence that reading in music was confined to what was prescribed. Apart from the works listed by Morley there was available a small selection of books in English on practical music prior to his own monumental contribution.

Yet although the potential for musical learning was considerable it seems probable, so far as the arts course itself was concerned, that the statutes were more often honoured in the breach than in the observance, and that candidates could get by with the merest smattering of the subject. Copies of theoretical works would have been scarce, even in the sixteenth century, and personal ownership by an undergraduate a great rarity. This is amply confirmed, particularly as to manuscripts, by a study of the holdings of college libraries and of personal inventories in the sixteenth century.[1] No doubt the materials are not as complete as one might wish—the personal inventories in particular are confined to senior members and privileged persons, and to scholars who had died in residence or whose books were forfeited to pay outstanding debts—yet the overwhelming impression is that the mathematical arts in general and

[1] See F. M. Powicke, *The Medieval Books of Merton College* (Oxford 1931); N. R. Ker, *Records of All Souls College, Library, 1437–1600* (Oxford 1971); idem. 'Oxford college libraries in the sixteenth century', *Bodleian Library Record* vi (1957–61), 459–515; *BRUO 1501–40*, app. B. I have also used the transcripts of personal inventories listing books made by Walter Mitchell and kept in the university archives. See also p. 204 n. 7 below.

music in particular were the Cinderella of the Tudor libraries. Of the books given in 1439 by Duke Humfrey for the use of lecturers in the 'seven arts and three philosophies' only three remained to be incorporated into the Bodleian in the seventeenth century.[1] Glosses on Boethius from the medieval libraries of Merton and All Souls are still extant;[2] but these represent a minute proportion of substantial holdings. Occasionally an individually owned manuscript copy of Boethius can be descried: Edmund Burton, fellow of Balliol (inventory of effects, 4 March 1529) owned an 'Ars metrica (i.e. *Arithmetica*) et musica Boetii' and one Bysley (1543): 'quinque libri musices', an obvious reference to Boethius.[3] Around 1500 John Tucke, scholar, and later fellow of New College, made a collection of theoretical writings (now BL Add. MS 10336);[4] it includes works by Johannes de Muris and John Hothby, and an epitome of the *Quattuor principalia*, as well as notes by Tucke himself. The same collection was copied in 1526 by William Chell(e) of Hereford Cathedral (Oxford BMus 1524).[5] But the majority of extant fifteenth- and sixteenth-century manuscripts of musical theory, in Oxford and elsewhere, have no demonstrable connection with the medieval or the Tudor university.

The works of Boethius were printed in Venice in 1491–2 and in 1498–9, and in Basle in 1546 and 1570. There was also a separate edition of the *De arithmetica* printed at Augsburg in 1488, but no separate edition of any part of the *De musica* before 1652, when Meibom included in his *Antiquae musicae auctores septem* an extract incorporating variant readings submitted by John Selden.[6] The fifteenth- and sixteenth-century editions appear to have been great rarities in Oxford.[7] Roger Charnoke (All Souls 1577) possessed

---

[1] *Munimenta academica or documents illustrative of academical life and studies at Oxford*, ed. Henry Anstey (2 vols Rolls series 1 1868) i. 327. A comprehensive survey is to be found in M. Masi, 'Manuscripts containing the *De musica* of Boethius', *Manuscripta* xv (1971), 89–95.

[2] Powicke, 158 (no. 522), now Bodl. MSS Digby 190–1. There is a lengthy commentary on Boethius in the English MS Bodley 77 (15th century) of unknown provenance, occupying fos 1–93. Ker, *Records of All Souls College Library*, 22, 38, 47, 59, 65, 133 (item 572, now MS 90, given in 1457 by John Dryelle). Both colleges possessed the two books on arithmetic.

[3] *BRUO 1501–40*, app. B.

[4] See Andrew G. Watson, *Catalogue of Dated and Datable Manuscripts c 700–1600 The British Library* (2 vols 1979) i. 28.

[5] Now Lambeth Palace Library MS 466. For Chell(e) see *BRUO 1501–40*, 115.

[6] For the bibliography see Luca Obertello, *Severino Boezio* (2 vols Genoa 1974) i. 13–14, 16. The *Opera* of 1523 and 1536 did not include the books on the arts or the *De consolatione philosophiae*. In the Basle editions of 1546 and 1570, the books on arithmetic and music were edited by the notable theorist Henricus Loritus Glareanus.

[7] Merton possessed 'boethij opera' in 1556 (inventory prepared for the Marian commissioners, Merton College Record 4277, fo 9^v), probably a reference to the copy of the

'Boethius cum commento' and Nicolas Clifton (1578) 'Boethius cum triplici commento', both valued at 6d; but at that price they are more likely to refer to the *Consolation of Philosophy*, which was often printed with commentaries, than to any edition of the complete works. Richard Secoll, BA (fellow of New College, inventory 1577) possessed 'Boetius', worth 8d, while T. Tatham (Merton 1585) owned a 'Boetii arithmetica', which was probably a sixteenth-century reprint with commentary of the Paris edition of 1521 or else the excerpts made by Johannes de Muris printed in Vienne in 1515, rather than the rare *princeps* of 1488. But these are mere pinpricks among the surviving book-lists of the later sixteenth century, and it is more significant that Robert Dowe (BCL, fellow of All Souls 1588), a musician whose own copies of sixteenth-century polyphonic music are still in the Christ Church library (see below), in a substantial collection possessed no books specifically on music—though he did own the works of Ptolemy valued at 13s.

In the circumstances one might have expected lecturing to fill the needs of undergraduates. A 'lectorum ordinarium designatio' of 1563, nominating lectures in the three philosophies and seven arts, does indeed include the names of three lecturers on music: Robert Leche (or Lyche), John Reve (or Ryve) and John Foux, of whom Leche and Reve were masters and Foux a bachelor of arts.[1] But lecturing was on the decline in the sixteenth century, and dispensations from lecturing on music in particular were frequent: mostly on account of the smallness of the audience ('propter paucitatem auditorum' or some such phrase), but also on one occasion owing to the lack of suitable books[2]—a reason which tends to confirm the view already expressed.

The balance between speculative and practical music was redressed

---

1546 edition which is still in the college library. But the All Souls records do not reveal any copies (Ker, *Records of All Souls College Library*), and neither does the 1589 shelf-list of Corpus Christi College (MS 416, edited in J. R. Liddell, 'The library of Corpus Christi College, Oxford, in the sixteenth century', *The Library* 4th ser. xviii (1937–8), 385–416), though it does include the *Harmonics* of Cleonides (Venice 1497), a manuscript of Ptolemy (MS 100) and the *Arithmetic* and *Consolation* of Boethius. But the All Souls archives are damaged and incomplete, and the Corpus Christi list omits books currently in circulation among the fellows. Corpus and Magdalen at least have long possessed early editions of the *Opera*; these and some others may reflect private or institutional ownership in Oxford in the sixteenth century. The various copies owned by the Bodleian cannot be connected with the Tudor university. The materials for a further study of the question may be found in Sears Jayne, *Library Catalogues of the English Renaissance* (Berkeley and Los Angeles 1956); some additional relevant documents are found in the exhibition catalogue prepared by N. R. Ker, *Oxford College Libraries in 1556* (Oxford 1956), items 1–9.

[1] *Reg. Univ.* ed. Clark i. 97.
[2] Ibid. 100: 'libri ad eam lectionem idonei difficulter inveniuntur' (dispensation to Matthew Gwyn, February 1583).

both in Cambridge and in Oxford by the institution of degrees in music: the BMus and DMus. In medieval Paris there is no doubt that both speculative and practical music were included in the study of music as a liberal art, and the same may have been true of Oxford in the thirteenth and fourteenth centuries. But it is difficult to believe that the study of practical music could ever have been a compulsory part of the course for everyone taking the degrees in arts, and it may have been in recognition of the practical ability of a few that degrees in music were first granted. It is not known exactly when this was, but there is little doubt that Cambridge was first in the field. A Cambridge statute of c 1456 contains a reference to the baccalaureate in music, and it is argued from the wording of the statute in question (which is about caution money) that music was already by then 'a separate faculty . . . with its own personnel'.[1] In 1461-2 Thomas St Just, who in December 1463 was nominated as warden of the King's Hall, Cambridge, was admitted as DMus.[2] On 22 February 1464 Henry Abyndon (or Abyngdon), who was succentor of Wells Cathedral from 1447 to 1497 and master of the children of the chapel royal from 1455 to 1478, was admitted as bachelor of music, and given leave to 'incept' in music on condition that he resided in Cambridge for a year.[3] Inception here refers to the degree of doctor, as in the faculties of law, medicine and theology.

The first name to be associated with an Oxford degree in music is that of Robert Wydow, BMus by 1479.[4] Wydow had been a scholar of Eton and King's College, Cambridge, where he took the degree of master of grammar in 1467/8; in 1497 he succeeded Abyndon as succentor of Wells. He was a rich and widely travelled cleric, but there is no evidence that he was a composer.

The earliest surviving supplication for an Oxford musical degree, dated 16 February 1506/7, is that of Richard Ede for the BMus. The details are interesting: the subject had been studied externally for a lengthy period; a further requirement was made that a mass and antiphon be composed, and performed on the day of admission; and the request was 'to be admitted to the reading of (i.e. to lecture on) any book of the music of Boethius, notwithstanding any statute to

---

[1] N. C. Carpenter, *Music in the Medieval and Renaissance Universities* (Oklahoma 1958), 197. Much of my otherwise unacknowledged information comes from Dr Carpenter's excellent chapters on Oxford.

[2] *BRUC*, 503. On St Just see A. B. Cobban, *The King's Hall Within the University of Cambridge in the Later Middle Ages* (Cambridge 1969), 286-7.

[3] '. . . possit admitti ad incipiendum in eadem sic quod continuet hic ante admissionem per annum', *BRUC*, 1; on the chapel royal and Abyndon see Cobban, 60-2; *Grace Book A . . . 1454-1488*, ed. Stanley M. Leathes (Cambridge 1897), 45.

[4] For Wydow, see *BRUC*, 654-5, *BRUO to 1500* iii. 2106-7.

the contrary.'[1] The university was incapable of defining the status he sought except in terms of its obsolescent arts course, even though his qualifications were purely practical. But its formula set the pattern for future admissions, and a number of distinguished composers supplicated for the degree, particularly towards the end of the period: Nathaniel Giles (1585), John Bull and John Munday (1586), Thomas Morley and John Dowland (1588), Giles Farnaby (1592), Francis Pilkington (1595), Richard Nicholson (1595/6), Robert Jones (1597) and Thomas Weelkes (1602).[2] In 1510 'Hugo Haston', presumably the composer Hugh Aston, supplicated for the BMus, having incepted in arts in 1507.[3]

The doctorate was awarded more sparingly, but in 1511 Robert Fayrfax incorporated from Cambridge and several more musicians, not all of equal merit, had been granted the degree by 1600: Robert Perrot (1515), John Gwyneth (1531, after some hesitation), John Marbecke (1550), John Sheppard (1554)[4] and Robert Stevenson (1596, BMus 1587); in addition Tye (1548) and Bull (1592) incorporated from Cambridge.[5]

Mention of Perrott and Sheppard reminds us of the important part played by the colleges in the musical life of the university, particularly before the reformation and during the revival of the Latin rite under Mary. Many of the colleges had statutes which included provision for choristers, and the largest of them—Magdalen, New College and Christ Church in particular—cultivated polyphonic music widely.[6] Perrott, who was a scholar of King's in 1506–9 and held a Cambridge BMus (1507), was *informator choristarum* at Magdalen from *circa* 1510 to 1535, and acted as organist from 1530 to 1548.[7] Sheppard, *informator* in 1542–3 and from 1545 to 1548,

[1] 'Eodem die supplicat Dominus Ricardus Ede, canonicus regularis et scolaris musice, quatenus studium 10 annorum extra universitatem in musica sibi sufficiat ut admittatur ad lecturam alicuius libri musices Boecii, non obstante quocunque statuto in oppositum. Hic est concessa, conditionata quod componat missam unam cum antiphona ante diem admissionis que eodem die admissionis sue solenniter cantetur': *Statuta*, p. xciii.

[2] Foster, *Alumni*, 567, 208, 1045, 1034, 418, 485, 1164, 1071; *The New Grove Dictionary of Music and Musicians*, ed. S. Sadie (20 vols 1980) ix 703; Foster, *Alumni*, 1593.

[3] Aston was a member of the household chapel of Margaret, dowager countess of Richmond 1507–?, and *informator choristarum* at the collegiate church of St Mary in the Newarke, Leicester 1525–48: F. Ll. Harrison, *Music in Medieval Britain* (1958; 4th edn Buren 1980), 29–30; Nick Sandon, 'The Henrician partbooks at Peterhouse, Cambridge', *Proceedings of the Royal Musical Association* ciii (1976–7), 139.

[4] Wood remarks that although he supplicated, there is no record of his admission or inception. See also *The New Grove* xvii. 249.

[5] *BRUC*, 222; *BRUO 1501–40*, 442, 253–4; Foster, *Alumni*, 1345, 1421; J. A. Venn, *Alumni cantabrigienses* (10 vols Cambridge 1922–54) iv. 283; Foster, *Alumni*, 208.

[6] Much information on this subject can be gained from the pages of Harrison, *Music in Medieval Britain* and Carpenter, *Music in the Medieval and Renaissance Universities*.

[7] *BRUO 1501–40*, 442.

was one of the most distinguished composers of his day.[1] Preston, who held the office only in 1543–4 (and possibly also in 1544–5), was also a distinguished composer, if he can be credited with the considerable body of organ music ascribed to Thomas Preston.[2] The organ played a large part in the late medieval liturgy, and the accounts of New College contain references to the building of organs and of both New College and Magdalen to their repair.[3]

Much of this activity came to a halt with the reformation, though the records of Christ Church, Oxford's cathedral from 1546, include the names of the members of a choir, at least until 1578.[4] Secular music, naturally, was cultivated widely both before and after the reformation, both in the form of private recreation (for which a good deal of documentary evidence survives)[5] and in the form of of public entertainments. There are records of liturgical drama from before the reformation, but not all the references to plays from that

[1] *The New Grove* xvii. 249–51.

[2] On Preston see D. Mateer, 'Further light on Preston and White', *Musical Times* cxv (1974), 1074. Preston moved to Trinity, Cambridge (1548–52, 1554–9) and was also organist at Windsor in 1558–9, when he was deprived of his office for his Roman Catholicism. For his organ music see *Early Tudor Organ Music i: music for the office*, ed. John Caldwell (Early English Church Music vi 1966) and especially *Early Tudor Organ Music ii: music for the mass*, ed. Denis Stevens (Early English Church Music x 1969); for the music of Sheppard see *Collected Works*, ed. D. Chadd and N. Sandon (Early English Church Music xvii–xviii, 1976–7) and further volumes yet to appear. On the church music of the Tudor period see Harrison, H. Benham, *Latin Church Music in England 1460–1475* (1977); P. le Huray, *Music and the Reformation in England 1549–1600* (1967).

[3] P. R. Hale, *'Music and musicians'* in John Buxton and Penry Williams (eds), *New College Oxford 1379–1979* (Oxford 1979), 268; New College Archives Bursars' Rolls, 7410, 7443, 7448, passim; Magdalen College Archives Libri Computi i (1481–88), ii (1490–1510), and Bursary Book, 1477–86, passim. Information kindly supplied by Mr R. Woodley.

[4] Numbers fluctated in this period between 7 and 8 *pueri musici*, and between 8 and 10 *clerici*. The chapter act book makes no mention of the choir after 1578: Christ Church Archives Cathedral Act Book A, passim.

[5] Several of the inventories already mentioned (see above note 6) include instruments and music: Allen (Balliol College 1561) 'Item a gytterne the brydge beyng off'; William Battbrantes (Christ Church 1571) 'iiij singing bookes iiijd'; Nicolas Clifton (1578) 'Item a payre of virginalls vjs. 8d.'; Giles Dewhurst (MA, Christ Church 1577) 'Item a lute'; Robert Dowe (BCL, fellow of All Souls 1588) 'Item his songe bookes vjs. viijd.' (see below); John Dunnet (scholar of University College 1570) 'Item a lute iijs. iiijd.'; Robert Hert (MA, St John's 1570) 'Item a payre of virgynalles, xxs.'; Henrie Huchenson (BA, fellow of St John's 1573) 'A lutinge booke'; Richard Ludbye, priest (Gloucester College 1567) 'A virginall booke jd.'; Thomas Pope (MA, student of Gloucester Hall) 'Item a cytterne and a olde lute vjs.'; James Raynoldes (MA, fellow of Exeter 1577) 'Item a payre of virginalles xxs.' and 'Item a lute viijs.'; William Smalewode (MA, Gloucester College) 'Item a payre of virginalles xxs.' and 'Item a payre of clarecolles [i.e. a clavichord] iiijs.'; John Symson (MA, fellow of Exeter 1577) 'Item iij lutes iij li.' and 'Item a luting boke iiijs.'; and Christopher Tillyard (BA, 1598) '5 Singinge bookes 12d'. Inventories not containing book-lists have not been examined. Richard Ludbye's virginal book may have resembled the present Christ Church MS 371, a small oblong folio of the 1560s, written on printed music paper and in its original parchment wrapper, containing a miscellany of vocal transcriptions, bits of liturgical organ music and other oddments.

time will necessarily have been to sacred drama: in 1512/13 Magdalen College paid 6d to one Petrus Pyper 'pro pypying in interludio nocte Sancte Iohannis' and to a John Tabourner 'pro lusione in interludio Octavis Epiphanie'.[1] This was probably not John Taverner, the composer, who was instructor of the choirsters and organist at Cardinal College from 1526 to 1530.[2] A play called *De puerorum in musicis institutione* by Nicolas Grimald was acted in Oxford during the 1540s, reminding us both of the use of choirboys in secular drama and of the importance to musical education of the song schools and grammar schools.[3] Richard Edwards (MA 1547) master of the children of the chapel royal from 1561, had his *Palaemon and Arcyte*, a play with music, performed before the queen during her visit to Oxford in 1566.[4] During the same visit she heard the *Te Deum* sung with instrumental accompaniment in Christ Church.[5] There are records of plays with music by William Gager (*Dido* 1583, *Ulysses redux* 1591/2) at Christ Church and of the anonymous *Narcissus* at St John's in 1603.[6] These entertainments, as in London, appear to have taken up some of the surplus time and energy left to the choral establishment with the curtailment of services at the reformation.

Elizabeth's visit to Oxford in 1592 seems to have been a more scholarly affair: she was entertained to 'a Lecture in Musick, with the practice thereof by instrument, in the Common Schools', and the usual lectures in the arts (with a Mr Pelling as lecturer in music) were continued during her visit.[7]

Another side of Oxford's musical life can be seen in the music-copying activities of Thomas Mulliner and Robert Dowe. Mulliner was scholar of Corpus Christi College in and before 1564, and *modulator organorum* from 3 March of that year, though it is not certain that he is to be identified with the Londoner who copied the important manuscript of keyboard now in the British Library, Add. MS 30513. Thomas Mulliner the copyist's London associations are clear: his composers are nearly all Londoners by birth or by adoption, and his ownership of the book was testified to by John

[1] Macray, *Reg. Magdalen* i. 68.

[2] *BRUO 1501-40*, 557; for Taverner see *The New Grove* xviii. 598-600.

[3] Carpenter, *Music in the Medieval and Renaissance Universities*, 174. See also G. E. P. Arkwright, 'Elizabethan choirboy plays and their music', *Proceedings of the Musical Association* xl (1914), 127-8; F. W. Sternfeld, 'Music in the schools of the reformation', *Musica disciplina* ii (1948), 99-122.

[4] *BRUO 1501-40*, 186-7.

[5] *Elizabethan Oxford: reprints of rare tracts*, ed. C. Plummer (OHS viii 1886), 199.

[6] Bodl. MS Rawl. Poet 212, fos 67-82ᵛ, reversed. Information kindly supplied by Dr F. W. Sternfeld.

[7] *Elizabethan Oxford*, ed. Plummer, 178.

Heywood, Queen Mary's virginalist, who left England in 1558.[1] Robert Dowe is more easily pinpointed. He was a fellow of All Souls and a BCL, and, as we have seen, his 'songe bookes' was valued at 6s 8d on his death in 1588. These are almost certainly to be identified with the fine set now in the Christ Church Library, MSS 984–8, which belonged to him and are probably in his hand. He is certainly author of the distichs on various composers in the manuscript, for example on William Mundy ('Dies lunae'):

> Ut lucem solis sequitur lux proxima lunae,
> Sic tu post Birdum Munde secunde venis.

The books, which were not completed until 1586 or later, contain a fine collection of sacred, secular and instrumental music, formed partly it would seem out of antiquarian interest (there is a good deal of Latin church music), but also no doubt with a view to performance.

Few other extant manuscripts of the period can be identified with university men; but the 'Forrest-Heyther' part-books of Tudor masses (now Bodl. MS Mus. Sch. e. 376–81) seem to have been begun at Cardinal College during Taverner's stay there, and were continued by William Forrest, petty canon of Oseney Cathedral, till its dissolution in 1545.[2] The books were finally completed later in the century by John Baldwin, gentleman of the chapel royal and 'singing man of Windsor', whose own part-books, quite fortuitously it seems, are numbered consecutively with those of Dowe in the Christ Church Library: MSS 979–83 (both sets were the gift of Dean Aldrich). The 'Forrest-Heyther' part-books themselves were acquired by William Heather, founder of Oxford's chair of music, and given by him to the music school in 1627.[3]

Though Oxford as a musical centre during the reign of Elizabeth exhibits neither the intellectual ascendancy of the thirteenth and fourteenth centuries, nor the unceasing practical activity in the

---

[1] Foster, *Alumni*, 1044. The manuscript is edited in *The Mulliner Book*, ed. Denis Stevens (Musica britannica i 1951, 2nd edn 1954). The oft-repeated assertion, originating in a note in the manuscript by John Stafford Smith, that Mulliner succeeded Redford as almoner and master of the children at St Paul's in 1547 cannot be verified; if true it was a short appointment, for Sebastian Westcote held that post from 1 February 1553 until his death in 1582 (*The New Grove* xx. 371–2). It is also known that Philip ap Rhys took over Redford's duties as organist at St Paul's, perhaps from 1547, and that he was still playing there in 1559: J. Caldwell, *English Keyboard Music Before the Nineteenth Century* (Oxford 1973), 31–2. It is not unlikely that Mulliner was a younger man than such an appointment would imply, and that he can be identified with the organist of Corpus Christi.

[2] See J. D. Bergsagel, 'The date and provenance of the Forrest-Heyther collection of Tudor masses', *Music and Letters* xliv (1963). For Forest, see *BRUO 1501–40*, 209–10.

[3] F. Madan, *A Summary Catalogue of Western Manuscripts in the Bodleian Library* v (1905), 210.

colleges from the earliest part of the Tudor period, nor even the picture of quiet domestic music-making characteristic of the seventeenth century, the university nevertheless through its degrees in music attracted the attention of the wider musical world. Composers of the stature of Bull, Morley, Dowland, Weelkes, John Daniel (1604) and Thomas Tomkins (1607) supplicated for the degree of BMus in the prime of their successful lives, and proudly advertised their distinction on the title-pages of their publications. When Morley with his *Plaine and Easie Introduction* (1597), or Dowland with his translation of Ornithoparcus's *Micrologus* (1609), took in hand the instruction of the public in practical music it must have seemed to many that these works represented the epitome of Oxford scholarship, even though their authors had never studied there.[1] This is particularly the case with Morley's book, a mine of curious learning and neither plain nor easy in content. Another link with the outside world was through the Gresham professorship of music, John Bull being the first holder (1597): though a Cambridge nominee and a doctor of its university he had incorporated at Oxford and no doubt the lustre of his name reflected on both. Nearer home, and perhaps more akin to Oxford's real nature, were an anonymous work, *The Praise of Musicke* (Oxford 1586), and John Case's *Apologia musices* (Oxford 1588). Case, a doctor of medicine and a former scholar of St John's and chorister of Christ Church, referred in his own *Sphaera civitatis* (Oxford 1588) to a book which can only be *The Praise of Musicke* as a 'doctum libellum nuper Oxonii natum et impressum' (a learned book lately written and printed at Oxford) —which makes it clear that Case himself was not its author.[2] The *Praise of Musicke* (a copy of which, valued at 2*d*, was owned by 'Sir Parkin' of Christ Church, who died in 1588) is in large part a justification for the use of music in the church. As for Case's

---

[1] A work by an actual Oxford student however was William Bathe's *A briefe introduction to the true arte of musicke* (Abel Jeffes 1584). No copy of the printed edition survives but the work has been edited from Aberdeen University Library MS 28 by C. Hill (Colorado 1979). Bathe's second book, a revision of the first part only of his original publication entitled *A briefe introduction to the skill of song*, was published by Thomas Este, probably in 1597; see B. Rainbow in *The Musical Times* cxxiii (1982), 243–7, and the letter from Hill in the same, 530–1. Bathe, whose Oxford college is unknown, was born in Dublin in 1564, became a Jesuit in 1596 and died in Spain in 1614. Wood, *Athenae* ii. 146.

[2] J. W. Binns, 'John Case and *The Praise of Musick*', *Music and Letters* lv (1974), 444–53, with other evidence. The title of Thomas Watson's 'A gratification unto Master John Case, for his learned booke, lately made in the praise of Musicke', set by William Byrd as a six-part madrigal and printed by Thomas East (as Este then spelled his name) in 1589, evidently rests upon a misapprehension: the references in the poem are too consistently to the English book to admit of the conjecture that its title is a paraphrasing reference to the *Apologia*. A reconstruction of Byrd's setting, of which only three voices survive, is provided by P. Brett in *The Byrd Edition*, ed. P. Brett (xvi 1976) with identification of allusions to the book.

own work, the *Sphaera civitatis* is a lengthy commentary on Aristotle's *Politics* in which the discussion of music arises out of the philosopher's treatment of its usefulness in the state. The *Apologia*, published later in the same year, has been described as 'the definitive discussion of musical theory in Elizabethan England'.[1] It is concerned not with the practice of music—which is alluded to only in general and anachronistic terms—but with its good effect on the mind, particularly in the contemplation of things divine. Its character resembles that of Tinctoris's treatises, *Complexus effectuum musices* (1472-5) and *De inventione et usu musicae* (1480-7).[2] There is no evidence of direct influence: but these were the common concerns of renaissance musical philosophers, for whom a moral justification for the art was a *sine qua non*. Case's book (unlike *The Praise of Musick*) is philosophical rather than theological in tone, addressed to that wide and international audience which was diverse in religious stance but united in its appreciation of a defence based on human reason and supported by classical rather than biblical or patristic allusions.

The Tudor period saw the decline of music as an integral part of the arts syllabus and the emergence of a system recognizing practical skill, above all in composition. In the definitive regulations of the Laudian code, revised in the nineteenth and twentieth centuries to take account of changing conditions, the BMus and DMus were the university's sole means of rewarding musical ability until the establishment of the honour school in 1951.

[1] Binns, 447.
[2] I owe this dating of the *De inventione* to Mr R. Woodley.

4.2

The Faculty of Medicine

GILLIAN LEWIS

THE TRADITIONAL ASSOCIATION OF MEDICINE
WITH THE ARTS

WHEN Andrew Clark was working on the university's registers in
the 1880s he noticed that the faculty of medicine had no bedell
of its own, but had to rely upon the services of the bedell in arts.
He took this, rightly, as a sign of the weakness of the faculty of
medicine in the affairs of the university. But he might with equal
justice have remarked that a composite faculty of medicine and arts
was commonplace in many continental universities,[1] and that there
was, in Oxford as elsewhere, something appropriate in this recognition of a traditional association between medicine and the seven
liberal arts.

Indeed, the inclusion of medicine among the studies thought
appropriate to the schools had followed on the reception there of
the philosophy of Aristotle, and had early taken the form of Averroist
commentary upon the medical classical texts available. It was in the
context of Aristotle's writings upon natural philosophy that the
student in arts first encountered biological and physiological questions, and it was in this philosophical spirit that much academic
medicine was studied and taught.

No doubt many of those who persisted with their reading in
medicine did so because they were determined to master a corpus
of technical lore which would stand them in good stead as practising
physicians. But others with no such intention may have read medical
texts out of mere interest and curiosity. Among these, no doubt,
from the late fifteenth century on, were some readers whose interest
in Hippocrates and Galen, Dioscorides and Celsus was reinforced by
the humanist respect for these writers as contributors to the wisdom
of classical antiquity, whose texts were to be rescued from a barbarous

---

[1] C. B. Schmitt, 'Science in the Italian universities in the sixteenth and early seventeenth
centuries' in M. Crosland (ed.), *The Emergence of Science in Western Europe* (1975),
36–9.

and distorting transmission. What was more, this humanist fashion enjoyed a vogue with influential patrons; the scholar might find that a smattering of the more elegant kind of medical learning, conceived in the spirit of *literae humaniores*, would be useful to him in his pursuit of worldly success.

If, then, for whatever reason, the curiosity of a scholar in arts had been aroused by what Aristotle or Pliny had had to say about the natural world, what would he do next? He might turn to the study of the earth and the stars, like Thomas Pope of Gloucester Hall, who left at his death in 1578 books on astronomy and cosmography, some instruments and a globe. Or, like William Mitchell of the Queen's College, whose interests lay mainly in theology, he might turn to the study of living things, and buy books on botany and medicine. Jerome Reynolds, a theologian, possessed among his biblical commentaries and patristics, Hippocrates, a herbal, Dryander's recent book on anatomy, and a five-volume Galen valued at the unusually high figure of £3 6s 8d. James Reynolds of Exeter had in his rooms not only virginals and a lute, six pictures and a looking glass, but one hundred manuscript books and more than two hundred printed books on logic, rhetoric, arithmetic, astronomy, natural philosophy and medicine.[1]

Just as university men at this time prided themselves upon the breadth of their humane learning, so cultivated clergymen and lay-men, and masters of arts who had no thought of becoming doctors of physic included in their reading the better-known passages from the standard texts of classical medicine. Some of these men, like Thomas Claymond, had a far deeper and more extensive familiarity with this literature than many physicians. It would be a mistake to suppose that the serious study of medicine in sixteenth-century Oxford was confined to those who sought the university's formal recognition of such study and supplicated for a medical degree.

Among all the branches of philosophy taught in early sixteenth-century Oxford *philosophia naturalis* was strong. Several colleges appointed philosophy lecturers whose interests were in cosmology, astronomy and mathematics, and there are traces in university and college records of a widespread concern with these subjects and with natural history. Whether a man turned to medicine, or to mathematics

[1] Chanc. Court Inv. See also in OUA the typed transcripts of these inventories containing book-lists and of book-lists extracted from wills and inventories. Examples of such libraries could be multiplied. For instance, Thomas Carpenter of All Souls (d. 1577) owned books by Ruel and Mattioli, and recent medical works by Montano, Wecker and Fuchs. Fuchs figured also in the library of Edward Higgins of Brasenose, alongside *Piers Plowman*, and Machiavelli's *Prince*. *BRUO 1501–40*, app. B consists of further lists of books owned by Oxford men.

(or to both), rather than to the law or theology depended, no doubt, in part upon his abilities and upon the way he saw his future prospects in the world; but it may have depended also on the turn which the teaching of philosophy had lately taken in his college.

THE COLLEGES

Richard Fox, the founder of Corpus Christi College, Oxford, did not approve of masters of arts who lingered in the universities when they should have been serving their fellow-men in the wider world. 'Long continuance in an University' was a sign either of 'lack of friends or of lack of learning'; 'it was a sacrilege for a man to tarry longer there than he had a mind to profit'.[1] Reading in one of the higher sciences, however (theology, law or medicine), gave one a legitimate reason to remain, and a college fellowship, for some people at least, made this possible.

It is clear from the statutes of colleges that the intention of their founders had been above all to promote the study of theology in order to help provide a learned clergy for the English church. Only two of the colleges founded before 1500, New College and Magdalen, mentioned medicine in their statutes: each (having made more generous provision for law students) allowed two (or, in the case of Magdalen three) scholars at any one time to read medicine, with the permission of the warden (or president) and fellows. These scholars were still expected to take orders before or upon the expiry of their fellowship, and this the medical fellows of Magdalen and New College continued to do (although not invariably) until late in the sixteenth century. All Souls, Merton and Oriel had no specific statutory provision for medical fellows but had long allowed one or two of their number to devote their time to medical study and to proceed if they wished to a medical degree. In the sixteenth century this tradition continued, intermittently at All Souls, steadily at Oriel, and with great vigour at Merton. Exeter produced medical men at fairly short intervals, and at Christ Church the tradition developed strongly; Balliol, Queen's, Brasenose, Trinity and the halls each had the occasional student of medicine. The first college expressly to set aside a fellowship for a medical scholar, and to exempt him by statute from the obligation to take orders was Corpus Christi, founded in 1517; the second—and the only other—was St John's.[2] In the

---

[1] Wood, *History and Antiquities of the Colleges and Halls*, 383.

[2] *SCO* ii. pt 10 (Corpus Christi), 62; iii. pt 12 (St John's), 37. The statutes of Cardinal College permitted the study of medicine and provided for a public lecturer in the subject, ibid. ii. 11, 73, 128-32. The Henrician statutes of Christ Church continue to allude to medicine in the same terms.

event, not all the *deputati medicinae* of Corpus, nor the *medici* of
St John's persisted with their medical studies, while some of their
contemporary fellows, although they were not so designated, did.
The setting aside of particular fellowships for medical men seems not
to have worked very well; on the other hand it was possible for
medical studies to flourish in a college, briefly or continuously, without any such express provision. The Cambridge experience was
similar; the colleges with a strong (if intermittent) medical tradition
were Trinity, King's, Peterhouse and St John's; the small foundation
of Gonville and Caius did produce a few men who went on to
become doctors of medicine, but it never developed the strong
humanist medical complexion (with frequent dissections, lectures
and debates, and provision for three years' study in Padua, Bologna,
Montpellier or Paris) which had been intended by John Caius.[1]

Although it proved difficult to ensure, by endowment or by pre-
scription, what turn the studies in a given college would take, it was
possible at least to facilitate and encourage legal or medical or
literary studies by bequeathing books to a college library, or by
encouraging a particular scholar to stay. Colleges occasionally offered
informal hospitality to a favoured individual, as Merton did to Henry
Briggs the mathematician when he first came to Oxford, and as
St John's did to its benefactor Sir William Paddy in his retirement.

It was a chancy business. From time to time the guttering flame
of medical studies was in danger, in any one college, of flickering
and going out. By the same token, however, the appearance of a
single new scholar devoted to Galen and Hippocrates could light it
up once more. The presence in 1504 of one Andrew Alazard, doctor
of physic of the university of Montpellier is a case in point. Because
of his desire to be incorporated in the faculty of medicine, he 'did
at the command of the Chancellor and Proctors read publicly the
Treatis of Avicen de Pulsibus, and made excellent Tables on them
extempore; . . . During the time of his abode here he was a
commoner of St. Alban's Hall, where reading divers admirable
lectures, was [not only] frequented by the learneder sort of the
University, and by all those also that were students in Medicine, but
was the chief instrument of making that Hall flourish'.[2]

[1] M. Pelling and C. Webster, 'Medical practitioners' in C. Webster (ed.), *Health, Medicine and Mortality in the Sixteenth Century* (Cambridge 1979), 202.
[2] Wood, *History and Antiquities* ii. 662–3; *Reg. ann. mert. 1483–1521*, 300–1.

Statutes

The pre-1350 statutes of the university of Oxford (like those of most other medieval universities) provided for a doctor's degree in medicine.[1]

The master of arts was required to have studied medicine for at least six years before he could supplicate for this degree. During this time he was to have taken part, as opponent and respondent, in the medical disputations in the schools.

He was also to have lectured publicly on two medical texts, one on theory, the other on practice. The texts prescribed were standard ones set in almost all fourteenth-century university statutes, namely the *Aphorisms* of Hippocrates or the *Liber Tegni* of Galen (for theory), and the *Liber Febrium* of Isaac, the *Antidotarium* of Nicolas or the *De regimine acutorum* of Hippocrates (for practice).

He was not allowed to lecture until he had completed the first four years of his medical studies; it was the formal granting of this 'admission to read the *Aphorisms*' which came to be seen as the equivalent of a bachelor's degree and eventually to be referred to as such.

These early statutes contained also a 'form according to which practitioners of medicine may be admitted' which seems to have been the basis of the university's custom of granting licences to practise medicine or surgery. The statute had been concerned originally with controlling the practice of medicine in the town of Oxford and its vicinity, but by the sixteenth century licences granted by the university were regarded as some kind of seal of approval conferring on their holders the right to practice anywhere in England.

The statutes of 1549 made heavier demands than their predecessors. Six years, not four, were to elapse before 'admission to read' (the bachelor's degree) could be granted, and a further five years, not two, before inception as doctor. Attendance at one or more dissections was required at some stage in this long process, while candidates for the licence to practise had to provide evidence that they had performed two dissections and effected three cures.[2]

Such requirements must have been difficult to fulfil. There is no reference anywhere in the surviving records of the university at this time to arrangements for public anatomical dissection; it is possible, of course, that something of the kind did occur, but it cannot have

---

[1] *Statuta*, 40–2.

[2] *Statuta*, 346; the Edwardian regulations do not distinguish between those with and without arts degrees.

been on any regular or frequent basis. The only way in which an applicant for the licence could have had an opportunity to 'effect three cures' was under the aegis of an established practitioner in Oxford or elsewhere. Such an opportunity would have been a private one, which the student would have to arrange for himself. In no European university at that time, with the exception of Padua, was any official (as distinct from informal) provision made for clinical instruction.

The *nova statuta* of 1564/5 seem tacitly to recognize that the aspirations expressed in the statutes of 1549 had proved unrealistic. All reference to anatomy is dropped. The years of study required before 'admission to read' are reduced from six to three (although they are left at six for candidates who are not masters of arts). Bachelors need not now wait five years, but only four, before becoming eligible to supplicate for their doctor's degree.[1]

The aim of the drafters of the statutes in 1549 and in 1564 seems to be clear: they were concerned to ensure that the university granted its licences and its degrees in medicine only to those who had spent a reasonable number of years in serious medical study. The statutes continued to prescribe a minimum of ten years for someone who was not MA, but settled upon seven years as an acceptable figure for someone who was. In the event these statutory provisions were almost always fulfilled. Dispensations and exceptions were certainly not unusual, but in almost every case the reason for departing from the statutes is set out, usually it is a reason which does not conflict with the statutes' clear intention and sense. Some masters of arts, for example, were admitted to the bachelor's degree less than four years after they took their MA, but not before they had completed four years of medical study.[2]

All this is precisely comparable with the statutory requirements of other European medical schools at that time, while the university's actual practice in the matter compares favourably with all but the most rigorous and exacting of these. The traditional demands made by all universities of candidates for degrees, namely some years of study, public lectures on set texts and participation in disputations, remained standard at Oxford as elsewhere. In medicine this was the case despite the dramatic innovations that had taken place in the actual teaching of many medical schools in the wake of humanist

---

[1] *Statuta*, 379.

[2] This is based upon claims made by candidates for degrees, and upon the intervals between supplication for the lower and higher degree, Reg. Cong. 1518-35, 1535-63, 1564-82, passim. It differs from the view advanced in *Reg. Univ.* ed. Clark i. 123, and by Arnold Chaplin, 'The history of medical education in the universities of Oxford and Cambridge, 1500-1830', *Proceedings of the Royal Society of Medicine* xiii (1920), 85.

critical attitudes, which had brought an enlargement in the number of accessible classical texts, and a new interest in anatomy, botany and the extension and refinement of the pharmacopoea. Rarely do the statutes of sixteenth-century medical faculties afford more than a glimpse of such changes.

In the *nova statuta* there is one such glimpse: the substitution for the old fourteenth-century canon of set texts of a range of separate treatises by Galen, all of which had recent humanist editions.[1] This reflected a change which was by 1564 long established in Oxford. The revolution in Galenic studies which had occurred in Linacre's day had not passed Oxford by; the registers of congregation make it clear that some bachelors had been required as early as the 1520s to lecture on the new fangled texts.[2]

Once a candidate had supplicated for the degree of doctor of medicine and had had his supplication approved, he had still to 'incept in reality' before he was entitled to style himself doctor. Further formal disputations, and the payment of fees were involved here. The university discovered that it had to urge candidates to take this final step. No doubt many of them felt that they had secured enough recognition of their standing through the approval of their supplication; a special journey to Oxford for inception and the payment of fees may not have seemed worth the trouble.

There was the additional consideration, early in the century at least, that efforts might be made to hold a new doctor to his obligation (as a regent master in the faculty of medicine) to lecture for a further two years in the schools, and to dispute there on at least some of the forty *dies disputabiles* (days set aside for exercises) which followed his inception. It was already proving difficult in 1500 to hold doctors to this obligation. After the establishment of the king's reader in medicine attempts to do so were rarely made. Regency in medicine was never formally abolished; it simply faded away.

Provision of teaching in medicine

The disappearance of regency and the frequent dispensing of bachelors (for whatever good reason) from their lecturing duties were serious matters, for upon these conventions alone had depended the pattern whereby one generation of students of medicine instructed the next. Apart from this system (which had intermittently been at risk in Oxford, anyway, because the numbers proceeding in medicine

[1] *Statuta*, 379.
[2] Reg. Cong. 1518–35 fos 142, 177, 189^V, 194, 202, 228^V.

were so small) the university had made no formal provision for
public teaching; traditionally, universities never did.

Nor was Oxford unusually vulnerable in this respect. Late in the
fifteenth century even the celebrated university of medicine of
Montpellier found that regency no longer worked. Lectures had
become few and irregular. A remedy was found in the establishment
by the French crown of four salaried readerships.[1] Such posts had
long ensured continuity in teaching at several Italian universities and
they were beginning to be imitated in Germany at this time.[2] It was
clear that Oxford too needed something of the kind.

The idea of some provision of 'public' lectures by specially
designated lecturers was not completely unfamiliar at Oxford. The
public lecturerships in the humanities established by Waynflete at
Magdalen and by Fox at Corpus Christi were novel in the sense that
the lectures were open to all members of the faculty of arts irrespec-
tive of college or hall. Wolsey on his visit as chancellor in 1518
announced his intention of founding more public lecturerships of
this kind.[3] A detailed scheme appeared in the statutes for his proposed
Cardinal College. It included a reader in medicine who was to lecture
for a full hour once a week upon 'Hippocrates, Avicenna or a book
by some other famous medical author' having announced his theme
publicly in advance. Questioners who had attended his lecture might
call on him afterwards, when he would spend at least an hour answer-
ing their enquiries 'more in terms of the practical side of the art
than the speculative'.[4] The fall of Wolsey and the changes which
came over his college meant that this scheme never materialized.

The nearest the university had to a 'public' reader of physic in the
1520s was Thomas Mosgroff, a Merton man who had held a college
lecturership in astronomy in 1517, who was not only licensed to
practise medicine, but had taken his MD and was personal physician
to Edward Stafford, duke of Buckingham. In 1523 he was said to be
'about to read the public lecture in medicine within Corpus Christi
College'[5] where he was, perhaps, a 'Wolsey' lecturer in the same sense
as Lupset and Vives had been.[6] It is possible, however, that his
association with Wolsey's scheme was tenuous, as was that of Kratzer
whose name is often included in this context.[7]

[1] Archives départementales de l'Hérault: Privilèges de l'Université, G 1277, fo 75[V].

[2] John M. Fletcher, 'Linacre's lands and lectureships', in Francis Maddison, Margaret
Pelling and Charles Webster (eds), *Essays on the Life and Work of Thomas Linacre c. 1460–
1524* (Oxford 1977), 114–17.

[3] H. C. Maxwell Lyte, *A History of the University of Oxford . . . to 1530* (Oxford
1886), 438; *Epist. acad. 1508–96*, 75.

[4] *SCO* ii. pt 11 (Cardinal College), 128, 130–1.

[5] Reg. Cong. 1518–35, fo 101.   [6] See Duncan below, 338.

[7] The tradition of describing Mosgroff as such, along with Vives, Lupset and Kratzer,

Once or twice in living memory there had been a lecture, or a series of lectures in medicine in the university, which had attracted an eager audience; one such, as we have seen, was the series given by Alazard in 1504. Tradition (unsupported, however, by contemporary evidence), has it that Linacre gave a public lecture in Oxford in 1510.[1] But in general the university suffered—as Linacre observed —from a 'lack of instruction' in medicine, because of the decay of regency and because no one had founded there any 'substanciall or perpetual lecture'. This Linacre proposed to remedy.

The Linacre lecturers

Linacre had studied at Padua in the 1490s. At that time the medical teaching was in the hands of four *ordinarii* or salaried professors who lectured daily in the mornings, and of an indefinite number of *extraordinarii*, also doctors of the faculty, who lectured in the afternoons; in addition there was a chance to attend (for a fee) the private teaching of these and perhaps other physicians. Theoretical medicine was covered in a series of lectures designed to last three years, a scheme which was also followed by one of the professors of practical medicine; the third professor covered practical medicine at a different pace, and the fourth taught anatomy and surgery.[2]

Linacre's debt to the Paduan model is noticeable in the scheme he drew up for his proposed lecturerships at Oxford. The junior of the two lecturers was to deal with the theory of medicine, going systematically through Galen's treatises on the temperaments, the natural faculties and the humours. To the senior lecturer was allocated the more technically demanding task of commenting on the wide variety of topics dealt with in the literature of practical medicine.

His will setting out these intentions is dated 18 October 1524, but his executors ran into difficulties and the scheme was hawked around various colleges in the university before Merton agreed to take it on. It was not until 1550 that the first lecturers were appointed.[3]

Merton (like St John's College, Cambridge, which administered Linacre's similar benefaction at the other university) proved careful

goes back at least to Thomas Twyne, himself a fellow of Corpus later in the century, and donor of a considerable collection of books, medical and other, to its library. Corpus Christi College Archives MS 280 fo 215. I am grateful to Dr G. D. Duncan for this reference and for elucidation on this point.

[1] Wood, *Athenae* i. 43.

[2] C. B. Schmitt, 'Thomas Linacre and Italy', in *Essays on Linacre*, 42–68.

[3] Fletcher, 'Linacre's lands and lectureships' in ibid. 107–97. I am grateful to Dr Fletcher and to Mr C. A. Upton for pointing out that the Merton College Bursar's Accounts have an earlier date than does the register of the college for the appointment of the earliest Linacre lecturers, Robert Barnes and Thomas Symonds.

in its trusteeship of the endowment, taking trouble to find genuine medical scholars for the posts. The senior one was held for the extraordinarily long period of fifty-four years by one Robert Barnes, a leading practitioner of medicine in the town, who kept up a close association with the university and with Merton, his old college. He was a friend of the noted mathematician James Whitehead who bequeathed to Henry Billingsley his manuscript notes on the *Elements* of Euclid.[1] Barnes himself had an interest in mathematics, astronomy, astrology and cosmography, as the titles of books in his library reveal; he left his copy of Copernicus to Merton. His catholic tastes ran from John of Jandun *On the Soul*, Walter Burley on the *Physics* of Aristotle, Reuchlin's *Elements of Hebrew*, and the works of Plato to a *Defence of Astrology against Pico*, Cardano *Concerning Subtlety*, Agrippa *On the Vanity of the Sciences* and Fernel *On the Hidden Causes of Things*. He possessed also a copy of the great work of Dioscorides on plants, and the commentaries of Lonicerus and Tragus upon it as well as the work of Charles Estienne on *The Dissection of the Human Body*, Jacques Houllier on surgery, Valerius Cordus on *The Composition of Remedies* and Guillaume Rondelet on the treatment of disease.[2] He gave to the library of St John's College his handsome copy (in an Oxford binding of about 1540) of the famous 1538 Greek edition of the works of Galen printed in Basle.[3] He owned at least one late medieval medical manuscript, a version of the *Isagogue* of Ibn Husain (Johannitius) which also contained some 'questions upon Galen'. This he left to Merton together with a large number of other books.[4]

Barnes figures also among the Oxford physicians whose *consilia*, or written-up case-notes, are cited by the anonymous compiler of a large folio notebook full of medical recipes and jottings put together in Oxford in the late sixteenth century. Its author may have been John Woolton, fellow of All Souls, MB and MD in 1599.[5] Barnes, like the other Oxford practitioners who also figure in its pages—Case, Edwards, Slythurst, Withington and Bayley—emerges as someone whose clinical advice and prescriptions were carefully copied down at first hand or from the notebooks of earlier students. It seems likely that Barnes was a prominent and active figure in Oxford medicine for the whole of the second half of the century. As

[1] Wood, *Athenae* i. 43.

[2] *BRUO 1501–40*, app. B, 714–15.

[3] *Oxford College Libraries in 1556: guide to an exhibition held in 1956* (Oxford 1956), 507.

[4] Merton College MS 0. 1. 10; F. M. Powicke, *The Medieval Books of Merton College* (Oxford 1931), 245; Merton College Library, card-index of donors.

[5] BL Sloane MS 249.

senior Linacre lecturer his responsibility was for the teaching of practical medicine. Since he was also a practitioner in Oxford he almost certainly took on privately a succession of students for a kind of informal clinical training; but no evidence has come to light to establish this probability beyond doubt. In such informal associations students might learn something of surgery, too, for physicians were often in the habit of working closely with some surgeon they could trust.[1]

Linacre had been under no illusion that he could by his endowment create Padua in Oxford, and secure for his lecturerships men already distinguished as medical scholars. But he had stipulated that the incumbents should be 'masters of arts at least', and this Merton was able to fulfil. The college elected as junior Linacre lecturers a succession of its own younger fellows, most of whom had already gone some way with their own medical studies at the time. Thomas Jessop (1565–8) was only a beginner when he was elected, but he went on to take his MB, his licence to practise, and his MD; he later left to the college his copies of the 1561–2 Basle edition of the *Works* of Galen, Fuch's edition of Galen's *De temperamentis* in a Paris printing of 1554, the *Consultationes* of J. B. Montanus and the great *Historia generalis plantarum* published in Lyons in 1587, among other books. His predecessor Roger Gifford (1561–3), who was later president of the London College of Physicians, left about forty books to Merton, a collection which included some botany, anatomy and controversial medical works which had been up-to-date in the 1560s. James Whitehead held the post between 1572 and 1576, and was succeeded by John Chambre (1576–8), Greek lecturer of the college, who was, according to Anthony Wood 'much respected as a scholar, and . . . said to have instructed Sir Henry Savile in mathematics.'[2]

The assiduity of the lecturers, and even their presence in Oxford during much of their tenure becomes rather more doubtful after 1583. For the preceding thirty years, however, they had almost certainly between them contributed very respectably to the teaching of a succession of medical students.

---

[1] Dr George Owen was associated in 1533 with one Thomas Byrde, licensed in 1537 to practice surgery; Reg. Cong. 1535–63, fo 24. If this Thomas Byrde is to be identified either with his namesake the secular chaplain who had been admitted BCL in June 1520 (Reg. Cong. 1518–35, fo 42^V) or with the one (ibid., fo 38) who became BTh in 1520 after twelve years' study in logic, philosophy and theology, he may be an example in support of Wood's contention that the religious troubles of the 1530s drove some clergy into 'sordid professions' like surgery; Wood, *History and Antiquities* i. 62.

[2] G. C. Brodrick, *Memorials of Merton College* (OHS iv 1885), 269.

The setting up of the regius chair of medicine

The king's commissioners in 1536 spoke disparagingly of 'the blind leading the blind' in Oxford medical studies. Their letter (which appears above the names of Thomas Cromwell and William Petre)

hereby strictly lays down and orders . . . that no-one in future is to be admitted to practise nor to any medical degree whatsoever unless he has been judged and approved competent and worthy in the estimation and by the vote of the common and public praelector in medical matters now in existence in the University.[1]

The praelector is then named as one John Warner. This is puzzling. What was the standing of this post? Had the earlier lecturership held by Mosgroff in 1523/4 somehow staggered on? If so who had its incumbents in the interval been? Was Warner their successor? Who paid him? It was not until 1540 that the crown made financial provision (from the revenues of the new cathedral church at Westminster) for the professorship newly established in physic, as for the professorships in Greek, Hebrew, theology and civil law. The first named incumbent of this new post was John Warner. In 1546 the arrangement (although not the incumbent) was changed: with the establishment of the diocese of Oxford with Christ Church as its cathedral, responsibility for the payment of the professors of Greek, Hebrew and theology was assigned to Christ Church, while the salaries of the professors of medicine and of civil law were laid to the charge of the court of augmentations.[2]

Almost certainly the king's letter of 1536 did little more than put the weight of royal command behind established practice when it placed responsibility for testifying to the learning and worthiness of candidates in medicine upon the shoulders of a solitary public lecturer in that art; alone he was to carry the old burdens of the regent-masters.

Had the crown good cause to worry about the learning and worthiness of the candidates admitted to medical degrees before 1536? It seems not: they had included John Chambre, a founding member of the London College of Physicians, and several others later fellows of that college, such as John Burges, Thomas Gwyn, John Warner himself and George Owen, a royal physician who presided at the birth of the future King Edward VI. Others included David Tolley and

[1] Reg. Cong. 1535–63, fly-leaf recto; another copy, lacking the signature of Petre, is Bodl. Tanner MS 338, fo 25. The text is printed by H. E. Salter in *Munimenta civitatis oxoniensis* (OHS lxxi 1917), 249–50.

[2] F. Donald Logan, 'The origins of the so-called regius professorships: an aspect of the renaissance in Oxford and Cambridge', D. Baker (ed.), *Renaissance and Renewal in Christian History (Studies in Church History xiv, 1977)*, 275 note 17 and app.

John Dotyn, owners of large medical libraries, Humphrey Bluett and Thomas Lee, who later practised medicine in Oxford, John Edwards, some of whose remedies survive in the British Library in Sloane MS 249, and John Mason, later privy councillor and chancellor of the university. The register of congregation for the 1520s does not give the impression that the blind are leading the blind. Despite the small numbers of candidates and the decay of regency, an effort was clearly being made to observe both the letter and the spirit of the statutes.

Something a little odd may have occurred briefly between 1528 and 1535: several men whose names do not occur in the records of any college or hall, and who are not described as masters of arts were admitted to practise, and in one or two cases also as bachelors of medicine. Who were they? Anthony Wood believed that the complaints which had provoked the crown's letter of 1536 had arisen 'because divers scholars, upon a foresight of the ruin of the Clergy, had and did now betake themselves to Physic, who as yet raw and inexpert would adventure to practise, to the utter undoing of many'.[1] Were these obscure men such persons? Who was Henry Fortey, secular chaplain, or William Herleis, priest, or John Lassellis, priest, or John Johnson or Leonard Dulse?[2] Perhaps, like Robert Borwen 'skilled in the art of aromatics'[3] some of them were not clerks but empirics. It is impossible to be sure. In any case the phenomenon does not recur; after 1536 almost all those admitted to medical degrees or licensed to practise were (apart from a few highly recommended foreigners) Oxford MAs with clear affiliation to a college or a hall.

The duties of the regius professor

After 1546, by custom rather than by statute, the duties of the public lecturer (or king's reader) in physic came to be three: to guarantee to the university the fitness of candidates, to take part in the exercises in the schools, and regularly to lecture to the students in medicine.

There was no statutory instruction for the professor to follow in testing or testifying to the learning and worthiness of a candidate; it was left to his discretion. Since the faculty was small, and since candidates from outside were rare, all the parties concerned would usually be well acquainted. A college or hall would testify to the truth of a candidate's claim to be a master of arts and to have studied medicine for a number of years while in residence. Some candidates

---

[1] Wood, *History and Antiquities* i. 62.
[2] Reg. Cong. 1518–35, fos 36, 271, 266, 228[V].
[3] Ibid. fo 289.

had been away for an interval of anything between two and eleven years; in such cases it seems likely that the testimony of some established physician, in London or elsewhere, would be invoked, but no document of such a kind has come to light, and it may be that the professor would simply have to take a candidate's assertion on trust. There is no evidence of any formal examination or interrogation of candidates having taken place; for an assurance of the candidate's worthiness the university seems to have been content to rely upon the sufficiency of the professor's word. Professor Thomas Clayton in 1618 went into great detail about one Bernard Wright, who sought a licence to practise surgery. He had 'ascertained Wright's competence by many conferences' he declared for the benefit of congregation and 'had seen him dealing with many patients with good skill, rare judgement and dexterity' and he knew that Wright had 'dissected many bodies for anatomy'.[1] Anthony Aylworth in 1596 had been more laconic in his report (although not necessarily in his scrutiny of the candidate) writing tersely 'I am well content that Mr. Chenell should practise physic'.[2]

Disputations in physic took place at two levels: unofficially within colleges, and officially in the schools. Candidates for degrees were required by statute to have taken part as opponent and as respondent in the public exercises. It was not unusual for a candidate to seek from congregation dispensation from a part of this requirement, or permission to adduce as a substitute for it his participation in the *pro forma* exercises of another candidate, where he was standing in because no doctor of medicine was available at the time.[3] It is not clear whether or not participation in mere college exercises was ever allowed to count towards a candidate's statutory requirement; probably it was not. Nevertheless the college exercises are likely to have been at least as useful as the relatively infrequent university ones (scheduled for the fourth and sixth Thursdays of term, no more often), and may well have been as well attended. An abbreviated summary of one such disputation survives in a manuscript now in the Royal College of Physicians.[4] It is contained in a notebook ascribed (but without certain basis) to Thomas Cogan, who is here recorded as debating with John Jackman, another Oriel man, whether or not medicine can prolong life, and whether theology is the medicine of the soul as physic is the medicine of the body. Major and minor premises are challenged and there is some terminological discussion about the material and proximate causes of innate heat. The notebook also contains a discussion of the stock question 'Are contraries

[1] *Reg. Univ.* ed. Clark i. 124.   [2] Ibid.
[3] OUA Register L, fos 280, 244, 260, 261, 268[V].   [4] Royal College of Physicians MS 201.

cured by contraries?' long used as a way of examining the fundamental assumptions of Galenic medicine. Distinctions are drawn between *curatio* (putting right something that has gone wrong) and *conservatio* (preserving a situation where all is well), between *morbus* (a condition marked by failure of 'coction' of the humours, or by their imbalance, or by both), and *intemperia* (a situation where such an imbalance is just beginning to be perceptible), and of both from *inanitio* (a situation where the natural processes are simply failing and dying away).[1] Such formal logical discourse and such refinement of terminology were the very stuff of the disputations over which the regius professor was expected to preside. At their weakest such exercises could be set-piece answers to *loci communes*— literally commonplaces of medical lore, learned off more or less by rote, or passed from hand to hand, or dressed up for a graduation ceremony in shabby rhetorical finery. The questions debated by incepting doctors at vespers and *comitia*[2] were more often than not light-hearted in spirit, and designed as displays of virtuosity, like the ones with which the queen was regaled on her visit to Oxford in 1592: 'Enchantments, demons and charms cannot cure diseases', and 'For the King's Evil no medicine has more power than the virtuous touch of a Prince'. Behind both of these, perhaps, there was a serious purpose; but many of the questions debated on these occasions in the 1580s and 1590s must have been chosen partly to amuse a lay audience. Is love akin to madness? Can an old man be rejuvenated? When the topics chosen over the whole period 1583–1610 are considered, however, it becomes clear that the prevailing tone was a serious one, and that an overwhelming number of the questions debated were in matters of therapeutics; there is much less on pathology, and scarcely one on the physiology of the body in health. The preoccupations of the Oxford medical school were with the rationale of practical medicine. This was by no means unusual at the time. The titles of the Paris theses over the same period give a remarkably similar impression.[3] The duty of the professor in all this, at Oxford, was to preside; presumably also, if he wished, he could have a hand in the choice of topics debated. There is no idiosyncrasy in the *Quaestiones* which remain, however, which would allow one to see in any of them the hand of a particular regius professor.

Lectures were formal, both in the sense that they were ceremonial

---

[1] Ibid. fos 263–9ᵛ.

[2] Clark i. 232, 194, 190.

[3] H. T. Baron, *Quaestionum medicarum, quae circa medicinae theoriam et praxim, ante duo saecula, in scolis facultatis medicinae parisiensis agitatae sunt et discussae, series chronologica; cum doctorum praesidium, et baccalaureorum propugnantium nominibus* (Paris 1752).

occasions which started with a procession led by the bedell, the lecturer and after him the auditors joining from their colleges and halls and walking together to the schools, and also in the sense that they are predictably structured commentaries upon familiar treatises of Hippocrates and Galen. There was scope, however, within this formula, for a lecturer to digress and to give his discourse whatever complexion he pleased. The notebook ascribed to Thomas Cogan includes lecture-notes in which various ailments are described and treatment suggested. 'Dr. Bayly' (either the Regius Professor Walter Bayley or his kinsman Henry Bayley) is mentioned repeatedly in the margin, especially in the section dealing with botanical simples.[1] Paracelsus is cited in passing on two occasions.[2] None of the sixteenth-century regius professors nor the Linacre lecturers published works which have the appearance of being based on their lectures, unlike the doctors of many other medical faculties. As a result we are as much in the dark about the content of Oxford medical lectures of this period as we are about their frequency.

According to the statutes of 1549 the professor was to lecture between seven and eight in the morning every Monday, Tuesday, Wednesday and Thursday in term (feast days excepted);[3] by the time of the Laudian code the requirement had been reduced to twice a week.[4] There are hints that in the interval it had been difficult to hold the professors even to that. Leicester, as chancellor, in 1583 had heard that 'the Queen's Readers of Greek and Hebrue are plainly said to read seldome or never, the Physic, Law and Divinity Readers few times and very negligently when they do read'.[5]

In 1578 complaint had been made in congregation that there had been 'some intermission in the public lectures and anatomies necessary for the students in surgery'.[6] The reference to students in surgery is surprising—does it refer to the scholars in medicine, or to a class of local surgeons' apprentices? Such provision by university medical faculties was by no means unknown elsewhere,[7] but the precise significance of the Oxford allusion is obscure. In 1590, once more, the physic lecturer, like the others, was admonished to lecture at least once a week in term.[8] The assiduity or otherwise of

---

[1] Royal College of Physicians MS 201, fos 106–262[V].

[2] Ibid. fos 122[V], 138.

[3] *Statuta*, 343–4.

[4] *Laudian Code* tit. IV, sect. I § 16, 39.

[5] Wood, *History and Antiquities*, 200. Leicester had also complained in 1576, Reg. Cong. 1564–82, fos 223[V]–4[V].

[6] Ibid. 272. The reference to anatomies is unique.

[7] For example, in Montpellier, where the lectures to the surgeons' apprentices were highly popular with the medical students, perhaps because they were in the vernacular.

[8] OUA Book of John Bell, Bedell in Arts 1605–1638, S P 34, fo 4.

the lecturers cannot now be discovered beyond doubt. However, it became common at least from 1560 for candidates to claim and for the register of congregation to record, that they had been 'assiduous auditors' at 'the lectures of the professor', or 'at the public lectures'.[1]

It seems likely that the professor was free to please himself a good deal of the time about whether or not to linger in his country property or with his patrons and patients elsewhere, but that when a batch of scholars presented themselves, and medical studies in Oxford spontaneously revived, the professor was to be found in his doctoral chair, lecturing, demonstrating the bones, presiding at disputations and examining, more or less as the statutes required.

Sixteenth-century incumbents of the regius chair of medicine. John Warner was not named by William Bullein, alongside the Oxford men Chambre, Huicke, Clement, Bartlett, Fryer, Edwardes, Phaer, Owen, Masters, Geynes and Caldwell, as a 'physician of credit' in his day.[2] His contemporaries seem rather to have regarded him as 'a great intruder into ecclesiastical livings'[3] and a university figure, rather than as a medical man proper. He was to be warden of All Souls from 1536 to 1560 (with an intermission under Mary), and was vice-chancellor in 1554 and 1559–60. He had taken holy orders in 1537 and from that time on had sought and obtained preferment through the good offices of his friends Sir John Mason and Sir William Parr, becoming, among other things, archdeacon of Ely, canon of St Paul's, dean of Winchester and chaplain to the king.[4]

During all this time, or at least from before 1535 until 1554, he was public lecturer, and then (in effect) king's reader in medicine at Oxford, resident ostensibly, but in practice an intermittent absentee. As early as 1535, in October, he had asked congregation to dispense him from the regency obligation he had incurred by his recent inception as doctor. Exemption was granted to him, and to all the other regents, too.[5] In his case, at least one of the responsibilities of regency, that of testifying to the fitness of candidates, was restored to him, in his capacity as public praelector, by the king's letter of the following March; it may be, however, that he still felt himself dispensed from any obligation to lecture, and that there was for a time no formal provision for medical teaching in the university. No medical graduations or licensings took place in the years 1539–41,

---

[1] Reg. Cong. 1564–82 fos 13, 111, 269^V, 296, 298, 316^V, 321^V; Reg. Cong. 1582–95, fos 29^V, 43^V, 59, 84, 90, 97^V, 115^V, 121^V, 172, 204.

[2] *The Government of Health* (London 1558).

[3] White Kennett: BL Lansdowne MS 981, fo 22.

[4] *BRUO 1501–40*, 607–8.

[5] Reg. Cong. 1535–63, fo 8.

with the exception of a licence to practise surgery granted to one Felix Pontanus, a foreigner settled in the town.[1] By 1544 there had been ten admissions 'to read the *Aphorisms* of Hippocrates' (that is, to the bachelor's degree) in two years. In 1546 Thomas Edowe was able to claim that he had attended medical lectures,[2] presumably those of Warner.

It was in 1546 also that Dr Cox, that indefatigable busybody, took it into his head to pursue a bright idea (which he attributed to the king in person) that all the civil lawyers in Oxford should be herded into one college, and all the 'Physicians and Chirurgians' into another.[3] Warner's reaction to this proposal is unknown, but in Oxford in general there was little support for it, and indeed some active opposition. The scheme (which had a Cambridge counterpart)[4] was briefly revived by the Edwardian visitors (of whom Cox was one) in 1549, but lapsed soon afterwards.

Warner may have had a role in the drafting of the innovatory medical clauses in the 1549 statutes, which tried to extend the period of required medical study, and to lay down conditions about anatomical dissections and the effecting of cures. Certainly he had been a member of the committee which the university had set up in 1545 to look into the question of requirements for degrees.[5]

No doctorate in medicine was awarded between that of John Tucker in 1538 and those of Edmund Crispin and Thomas Hewes in 1549.[6] This reflected in part the turbulence of those years, and in part also the small number studying medicine. It may also, perhaps, have reflected Warner's reluctance to recommend for the higher degree candidates who were not yet, in his view, duly qualified.

There is testimony to Warner's interest in medical learning in the handful of books (no doubt part of a much larger library) which he gave to the library of his college, All Souls, where they joined a considerable collection of medical books given by earlier fellows.[7] All Souls had in the closing years of the fifteenth century a succession of fellows involved in medicine, several of them overlapping in their time there. Warner's gift comprised Mondino's commentary on Mesue, printed at Lyon in 1525, a Venetian edition (1508) of *Liber Rasis ad Almansorem* bound up with the *Opus medicinae* of

[1] Reg. Cong. 1535–63, fo 59ᵛ.   [2] Ibid. fo 109.
[3] Cox to Paget, 29 October 1546; Wood, *History and Antiquities* ii. 81, 99.
[4] See John Barton, 'The Faculty of Law', 272 below.   [5] Reg. Cong. 1535–63, fo 103.
[6] Ibid. fo 103.
[7] William Goldwin's 1492 bequest of ten medical books, Nicholas Halswell's 1528 bequest of two, John Racour's three medical manuscripts and one printed book, and Richard Bartlett's single medical manuscript. N. R. Ker, *Records of All Souls College Library, 1437–1600* (Oxford 1971), 105, 107, 108, 123, 125.

Galeatius of St Sophia (Hagenau 1533), Euclid's *Elements* (Basle 1537), and the 1542 Basle edition of the *De natura stirpium* of Leonhard Fuchs.[1]

Warner's concern with medicine may have been fading in the late 1540s, for although he remained titular incumbent until 1554 he performed none of the duties after June 1550, when he sought and obtained leave of absence 'to go beyond sea for the study of languages, manners and good letters' in attendance upon 'the King's Councillor John Mason, ambassador in France'. He was allowed to keep 'the lecture in the medical art he has from the King in the University of Oxford' but 'to exercise it by deputy'.[2]

The deputy designated was Thomas Francis, of Brasenose and Christ Church, a master of arts of six years' standing, and an ex-proctor. Wood has it that Francis had first 'applied his studies to the theological faculty, but the encouragement thereof in those days being but little, transferred himself to the school of the physicians'.[3] Francis himself claimed in 1552 when he supplicated for his doctorate, that he had studied medicine for eight years, and had responded six times publicly in the schools.[4] John ab Ulmis (Johan Ulmer), the protestant *émigré*, had heard him do this: in a letter to Rudolph Gualter written at the King's College (Christ Church) on 5 November 1550 he speaks of the disputations in medicine which take place there every alternate Thursday afternoon, presided over by 'Thomas Francis, a man of distinguished learning, and formerly an intimate friend and companion of yours when you resided here'. He describes thus 'our lectures on physic, and the study of medicine':

In the morning . . . immediately after morning prayer, namely from six to seven o'clock, are read the eight books of Aristotle on Physics; from seven to eight the commonplaces of Galen upon diseased parts . . . and from ten to eleven Galen's treatise upon natural qualities. These subjects occupy us until dinner-time: but at twelve o'clock some questions in natural and moral philosophy are proposed for our discussion.[5]

Three weeks later he writes:

From three in the afternoon to four [is read] the same author [Galen] upon simple remedies. The professors of medicine lecture very learnedly accurately and intelligently; they are also very courteous and take the greatest pleasure in the progress of their pupils.[6]

---

[1] Ibid. 109, 164.

[2] *Cal. Pat. Rolls 1549–1551*, 300 (2 June 1550).   [3] Wood, *Fasti* i. 143–9.

[4] Reg. Cong. 1535–63, fo 129. He did not incept, however, until July 1555; ibid. fo 154[v].   [5] *Original Letters* 419.

[6] Ibid. 424. I am grateful to Professor J. K. McConica for drawing my attention to these letters.

Who were the other lecturers? If the lectures took place within Christ Church, even if they were open to members of other colleges, then it is possible that they were given by college men whose identity is uncertain. Alternatively what ab Ulmis describes may well have been the earliest courses of lectures given by the newly elected Linacre lecturers, Robert Barnes and Thomas Symonds. Although they were paid by Merton, their lectures were not intended to be available to members of that college only.

Thomas Francis continued to act as deputy to the busy and pre-occupied John Warner until May 1554, when Warner at last resigned the chair upon becoming vice-chancellor. One of the last candidates to be admitted bachelor of physic while Warner was still nominally responsible was one Simon Ludford, about whom there was a first-class row. Allegations were made that he should never have been admitted, since he was 'a man utterly unlearned';[1] the 'great sclaunder' about all this provoked the chancellor, Sir John Mason, to write a letter of reprimand to the university. It may be that Ludford was less unworthy than his enemies maintained;[2] from the start, however, there is a hint of disagreement in the congregation register: Ludford sought admission 'on condition he is presented by Master Francis, Master Walby or Master Barnes' but was granted it 'on condition he is presented by Master Walby or Master Barnes' only;[3] did Francis withhold his consent? One cannot be sure; Francis may simply have been absent at the time.

Despite his protestant beliefs, which must have been common knowledge, Francis stayed in Oxford, and in office, throughout the reign of Mary. These were good years for medical studies in the

[1] The London College of Physicians had rejected Ludford's application for a licence in 1552–3. When John Caius, then president, heard of his admission as bachelor at Oxford he was scandalized and wrote to the vice-chancellor a letter which reprimanded the university, and which was read out in congregation. The university took offence at this interference. It had in any case just received the supplication of David Lawton, a candidate also rejected by the London College, and said by it to be quite ignorant of Latin. He was admitted bachelor of physic in November 1555 to the further fury of John Caius and the college. An angry letter from them was read out in convocation by order of Cardinal Pole's commissioners, and in January 1556 Dr Francis and three others were delegated to write a formal reply. The matter ended inconclusively with suspicion and resentment on both sides. Reg. Cong. 1535–63, fos 143^V, 144, 156, 157; *Eighth Report of the Royal Commission on Historical Manuscripts* (3 pts 1881) pt 1 sec. 1: the manuscripts of the College of Physicians i. 1518–1572; Sir George Clark, *A History of the Royal College of Physicians of London* (2 vols Oxford 1964–6) i. 112–14.

[2] He was a Franciscan with some experience in pharmacy, who later studied in Cambridge. He incepted MD at Oxford in 1560, stating that he was now licensed by the London college to practise medicine; he was elected a fellow of that college in 1563. Its library still possesses his copy of Avicenna and of the *De dissectione partium corporis humanae* of Charles Estienne. Clark, *Royal College* i. 112–14; Reg. Cong. 1535–63, fo 190; library of the royal college of physicians.

[3] Reg. Cong. 1535–63, fo 139.

university. Many of the men who were later to be pillars of the Elizabethan medical establishment were at Oxford between 1554 and 1558. The number seeking medical degrees and licences was, in these years, higher than ever before.[1]

Francis himself did not get round to taking his bachelor's degree until 1554, but then followed it within a year with the doctorate.[2] He was admitted to the one and incepted for the other in the company of Richard Masters and Richard Caldwell, later to be his friends and neighbours in the city of London and his colleagues in the college of physicians. Francis was one of those who defended the university's good name in 1556 when the college accused it of admitting a second unworthy applicant, one David Lawton, alleged to be an unlearned coppersmith.[3] He was also one of the three representatives on the committee appointed by Pole's commissioners in 1556 to look over the medical sections in the proposed new statutes.[4] In 1558 a convocation ordered Drs Francis, Caldwell, Aubrey, Wright, Masters, Slythurst and Hargrave to report on the same matter;[5] their report does not survive, but it seems likely that they reported in the sense later adopted in the *nova statuta* of 1564/5. If this is the case, then Francis should share the credit for the realistic shortening of the years of required study which was there introduced. He should perhaps also be credited with the tightening up in the practice of congregation which is noticeable from 1564. The formula used by candidates began to include an explicit statement that the approval of the professor had been secured. Candidates of high quality were admitted during the tenure of Thomas Francis, which was no doubt partly a matter of luck, but may also have reflected his determination to take seriously this part of his duties.

---

[1] Seven people were given permission to incept as MD, and one (Thomas Huyck) to incorporate from Cambridge. Apart from Francis himself, and Ludford, they were: Masters, Caldwell, Symmynges, Howell, Good and Gifford, all to be fellows of the London college. Among those later well known who were admitted MB in these years were Coveney, Tatham, Hall (John), Edwards (John), Wotton (Henry), Trever, Withington and Bayley (Walter). Ibid. fos 148–200[V]. An odd case was that of Thomas Godwin, fellow of Magdalen, a zealous reformer who was deprived of the headmastership of Magdalen College School, Brackley, under Mary, and was soon afterwards admitted bachelor of physic with no previous declared study of medicine; after Elizabeth's accession he reverted to a clerical career, becoming in the end bishop of Bath and Wells. Rather similar is the case of Thomas Cooper, another protestant fellow of Magdalen and tutor to Philip Sidney, who practised medicine during the reign of Mary but later went back to his interrupted clerical career, becoming dean of Christ Church, vice-chancellor of the university and eventually bishop successively of Lincoln and of Winchester. William Smith, also admitted MB in these years, deserves notice for the expertise in music, geometry and astrology as well as in medicine which is ascribed to him in his epitaph in Merton. *Wood's History of the City of Oxford*, ed. A. Clark (3 vols OHS xv 1889, xvii 1890, xxxvii 1899) iii. 139.

[2] Reg. Cong. 1535–63, fos 148, 154.   [3] Ibid. fo 157.
[4] Ibid. fo 163.   [5] Ibid. fo 171.

That he fulfilled it with some imagination and flexibility is indicated by the admission in 1559 of the unorthodox but remarkable Thomas Phaer. Phaer, who may have attended one or other of the English universities as a young man, never took his MA but practised for many years as a lawyer at Lincoln's Inn. During this time he became interested in medicine, and learned in its literature. In his supplication in 1559 he says that he has 'twenty years of medical study' behind him, and that he was conducted 'various experiements upon poisons and their antidotes and written a book about the ailments of infants, and about the plague'. These qualifications were thought to be sufficient not only to admit him to read and to practise, but to allow him to incept two months later, and to be dispensed from the obligations of regency (an indication, incidentally, that these had, formally at least, not lapsed with the establishment of a public professor).[1] In 1560 Francis did not stand in the way of the inception of Simon Ludford, who had by now managed to convince even the London College that he was respectable. In the same year George James, who had earlier been Linacre lecturer, was admitted to read and to practise with the unusual formula 'since he has the support of the majority of the medical men'.[2]

In 1561 Francis relinquished the regius chair, and within a year had settled in Silver Street, the 'Harley Street' of London, taking his turn as president of the College of Physicians in 1568, and without difficulty clearing himself of the implausible slander of one Elisaeus Bomelius, a foreign practitioner, that he was 'ignorant both of astronomy and Latin'.[3] He died in 1574.

His successor in the regius chair was Walter Bayley (1561–83), a Wykehamist whose fellowship at New College had just expired. He had been bachelor of medicine since 1556 and was to take his doctorate in 1563.[4] His intellectual interests can be inferred from the three little books he wrote, and from what is known of the contents of his library. He wrote *A Briefe Treatise concerning the preservation of the eiesight* (London 1586, reprinted 1616), *A Short Discourse of the three kinds of Peppers in common use, and certaine special medicines made of the same* (London 1588), and *A Briefe Discours of certain Bathes or medicinall Waters in the Countie of Warwicke*

---

[1] Reg. Cong. 1535–63, fos 177, 180ᵛ, 181, 182ᵛ. *The Regiment of Life whereunto is added a treatys of the Pestilence with the booke of children newly corrected and enlarged* (1545). The 1553 edition of *The Boke of Children* has been reprinted with some commentary by A. V. Neale and H. R. E. Wallis (Edinburgh 1955).

[2] Reg. Cong. 1535–63, fo 192.

[3] *Cal. SP Dom, 1547–1580*, 292, 304.

[4] Reg. Cong. 1535–63, fos 163, 200ᵛ, 202ᵛ; L. G. H. Horton-Smith, *Dr. Walter Bailey, or Bayley c. 1529–1592: physician to Queen Elizabeth* (St Alban's 1952).

neare unto a village called Newnam Regis (London 1587). The first two are no more than conceits, which he wrote as New Year greetings for his friends; the third is more substantial and interesting. It is a report in the approved continental style upon a medicinal spring which had a reputation for promoting healing. Bayley distinguishes between those cures which rest upon hearsay alone, and those which he is himself able to attest. He describes tests made upon distilled samples of the water—the hot-iron test for limestone, the black dye test for alum, the heating of the sediment to test for the presence of nitre and various salts. All these tests appear—and in the same order—in Gesner's book *The Treasure of Euonymus* which had made available to English-speaking readers Falloppio's earlier work on spa waters and medicinal springs.[1] Bayley's interest in distillation, and in mineral and botanical *materia medica* was characteristic of medical fashion all over Europe in his generation and the one before.[2] It is not surprising to find among the books he bequeathed to New College 'Matthiolus commentaries vpon Dioscorides of the best edicon wch I haue . . . my Fuchsius herball in folio . . . all my bookes of Gesnerus de quadrupedibus de avibus de aquatilibus de oviparis et reptilibus . . . ' as well as 'One of my Galenes workes in greek of Basils printe bounde in three volumes . . . definitiones medicae Gorraei . . . Theatrum Galeni in folio . . . Brasavolus in aphorismos Hippocratis . . . and in libris hyppoc. de ratione victus in morbis acutis.' a choice selection.[3] To his son-in-law and successor Anthony Aylworth he left 'Twentie of my physicke and philosophie books not bequeathed, to be chosen by himself. And my skeliton of bones in Oxford'.[4]

Bayley was a rich and successful physician, with property in Dorset and in London as well as in and around Oxford. He had friends and patrons among the great. At Buxton, a house built by the Earl of Shrewsbury, there was 'written in the glasse windowes R. Leycester misquoting the famous line "Tempora mutantur" and "Hoc tantum scio quod nihil scio, Doctor Bayley." '[5] Whoever scratched this in the glass clearly intended to suggest that Dr Bayley knew how to keep his mouth shut, as was wise in a physician moving in political circles. Elias Ashmole had a story, compromised perhaps by hindsight,

[1] Allen G. Debus, *The English Paracelsians* (London 1965), 161.

[2] Ibid. passim; Robert Multhauf, 'Medical chemistry and the Paracelsians', *Bulletin of the History of Medicine* xxviii (1954), 101–26, and 'The significance of distillation in renaissance medical chemistry', ibid. xxx (1956), 329–46.

[3] D'Arcy Power, 'Dr. Walter Bayley and his works, 1529–1592', in W. Osler (ed.), *Medical Chirurgicall Transactions* (1907), 460 ff.

[4] Ibid.

[5] *Calendar of the MSS of the Marquis of Bath at Longleat, Wilts* (3 vols Historical Manuscripts Commission 1904–8) ii. 20–2: Harley Papers (Buxton 1573–82).

but indicative of Bayley's reputation, that he had refused to make up a potion for Amy Robsart, Leicester's wife, ostensibly on the grounds that she 'had small need of physic', but really 'misdoubting lest, if they had poisoned her under the name of his potion, he might have been hanged for a colour of their sin'.[1] He prospered, however, enough to become in the 1580s one of the physicians to the queen.

What time did he have for Oxford and for the duties of the regius professor? There are no complaints of his absence during term, and a succession of applicants for degrees during his tenure testifies that they have been assiduous listeners at his lectures. Presumably also he used his 'skeliton of bones' for anatomical demonstrations. From the combined evidence of his books, his writings and his successful practice it seems reasonable to conclude that for the Oxford students in medicine he was a shrewd, up-to-date and practical guide, well-placed to help their prospects after they left the university.

His son-in-law Anthony Aylworth, who followed him as professor from 1582 to 1597, was altogether more obscure. Bayley stepped down from the regius chair just at the moment when Aylworth's fellowship at New College expired, and just before Aylworth's marriage and his well-timed supplication for the licence to practise and for the doctor's degree.[2] It was perhaps through Bayley's good offices that Aylworth too secured the style 'physician to the Queen', in his case almost certainly honorific only, since he seems never to have practised at court or in the city of London. He was never a fellow of the College of Physicians (perhaps for this reason). No imputations by contemporaries upon his learning or upon his professional competence have come to light, but neither, on the other hand, has any positive evidence about his attainments. There is only the epitaph in New College Chapel, put up by his son. In the hyperbolic way of such things it declares:

Here lies Hippocrates, here Avicenna lies. The bones of Dioscorides are here, the bones of Galen . . .

It goes on with a greater air of truth:

He was straightforward in his life, so that one might say that no-one had more of art and less of artfulness than he.[3]

Bartholomew Warner was professor between 1597 and 1612. Originally a Lincoln College man, he had married the step-daughter of John Case in 1583, thus denying himself any further chance of

---

[1] Horton-Smith, *Walter Bailey*.

[2] Reg. Cong. 1535–63, fo 49. He had been admitted bachelor of medicine in 1577. Reg. Cong. 1564–82, fo 236.

[3] Wood, *History and Antiquities*, 203.

a fellowship. In 1585, under the aegis of St John's, he was admitted bachelor of medicine, having been allowed earlier to testify to the suitability of another candidate, since there was (surprisingly, at this date) neither a doctor nor a bachelor of medicine to be found in Oxford at that time.[1] In 1594 he became doctor of medicine, and in 1597 professor in Aylworth's stead. His uneventful and apparently undistinguished tenure lasted until 1612, but even after this he continued to live in Oxford, standing in as senior Linacre lecturer for two years between 1617 and 1619. He has left in the records little trace of his career.

Had the establishment of the regius professorship been a success? In one sense it had: the allocation to one named individual of the responsibility for certifying the worthiness of degree candidates had clearly been an improvement on the older system of relying upon the word of elusive or non-existent regents in medicine. It cannot be claimed, however, that the problem of providing lectures adequately to cover the whole medical syllabus had been solved either by the establishment of the regius chair, or of the Linacre lecturerships, or even of the two together. However hard-working the single professor, however competent and diligent the Linacre lecturers, between them they could not hope to offer the Oxford student anything like the variety and specialized scope of the lectures he would have had available to him in a handful of the more fortunate of the continental faculties. In Montpellier, for example, four 'regius professors', with the help of two or three more regent masters worked hard to provide, week in, week out, between October and March, some four or five lectures every day (Sunday and feast days apart). Two or three official dissections took place each winter (as well as many private autopsies, some the result of clandestine body-snatching). In the summer term the younger masters lectured and the professors took students on botanical expeditions.[2] The story was similar at Basle, and in several north Italian universities.[3] In Paris the sheer size of the faculty, and the fact that any of its doctors who still lived in Paris could be, and sometimes were, called upon to teach, ensured an active institutional life. In such universities the student could hope to hear, in the course of three or four years, lectures on all three parts of the traditional medical syllabus (the 'things natural', or physiology, the 'things non-natural', or environment and diet, and the 'things outside nature', or malady and its treatment), let alone learn many tips to remember about diagnosis and

[1] Reg. Cong. 1582–95, fos 59, 280V.
[2] L. Legré, *La Botanique en Provence au XVIe siècle* (Marseilles 1899-1901), passim.
[3] Schmitt, 'Science in the Italian universities', passim.

clinical care. The lectures of particular masters might be famous for their expert discussion of anatomy (like those of Falloppio or of Fabrizio), or (like those of Montanus, Crato, Fuchs, Rondelet or Platter) for their knowledgeability about the many subtle variations in human malady and of the methods and remedies to be attempted in its cure.

Oxford graduates there were who could have talked to their juniors in this way. They probably did so, but in the privacy of their rich physicians' houses in Silver Street or in the parish of St Olave's in the city of London, in the households of great noblemen, in the bishop's palace at Exeter, in the privacy of colleges and halls, and not in formal lectures open to all students of medicine. It was a pity that no means was found (or even tried, perhaps) of attracting back to Oxford, even for part of the year, such accomplished medical scholars as Chambre, Linacre, Clement, Wotton, Recorde, Edrych, Caldwell, Forster or Matthew Gwynn. Neither the Linacre lecturerships nor the regius chair had the prestige to secure for Oxford the teaching services of any physician who had once left and established himself in the mainstream of English medical life. Nor did these posts, it seems, act as stepping-stones by which an up-and-coming university man might cross over into richer pastures. Their incumbents seem either to have been well supplied with influential friends already, or never to have acquired any worth mentioning. The salaried Oxford posts, even the regius professorship itself, failed to gain the prestige which several continental faculties, in a more competitive world perhaps, managed to acquire for their own comparable lecturerships. At Oxford, stipendiary provision had not proved strong enough to counteract the magnetic pull of London, nor to transform into a lecture-centred public faculty the informal collegiate and private medical studies of Oxford.

INFORMAL MEDICAL STUDIES

Evidence about the existence and character of informal medical studies comes mostly from passing reference in the later writings of Oxford medical men, and from notebooks they compiled during their time at the university.

George Edrych tells us that when in his youth he had 'taken his place among the physicians' and was 'laying the foundations of practical art', he was much encouraged and helped by 'the great physicians Master Owen, Master Clement and Master Fryer, whom I held in the utmost honour. They were men famed for their consumate knowledge of Greek . . . men of repute in every sense . . . and they showed me much kindness when I was teaching Greek in the university at that time'.[1] Owen is known to have worked in close association with Thomas Byrde, an Oxford surgeon.[2] Thomas Arscott, a bachelor of medicine licensed to practise, was on good terms with at least one Oxford apothecary in 1538.[3] Thomas Lee, fellow of Magdalen until his marriage in 1536 (or thereabouts) lived in the High Street, practised medicine, and had some responsibility for the inmates of the hospital of St John.[4] Did he ever take students with him on his clinical visits or did Nicholas Gibberd, who left a row of medical books to Magdalen and who was only one of a succession of fellows of that college who had charge of the almshouse founded by Claymond?[5] John Edwards, a fellow of Corpus Christi in the 1530s, copied out dozens of remedies which figure, alongside *consilia* and recipes for medicines ascribed to Drs Bayley, Bust, Case, Dewe, Dotyn, Slythurst, and Withington in the large compilation usually thought to have been put together by John Woolton in the 1580s or 1590s.[6] An anonymous Oxford physician's notebook of much the same period mentions the *consilia* and remedies of Drs Gibbard and Paddy as well as those of Mr Garbrand and Mr Norris.[7] It was evidently a well-established custom at Oxford as in other universities for medical students to copy out and to pass from hand to hand remedies and tips and clinical lore of this kind. Similar again is the rather scrappy little notebook of William Withy, which sets out to list alphabetically 'the ways to chuse of simples and medicines the best' but which peters out at L and M and is followed by 'four ways of purging, according to the method of Galen' all set out in little tables—hardly a work of serious medical scholarship, or, indeed anything but the jottings of a mere beginner in the art.[8] William Lant left a notebook which contained (apart from an inventory of his books) 'little orations' on metaphysical and medical themes—perhaps exercises set him by a college tutor?[9] Michael Lapworth, in supplicating for his degree in 1571 said that he had performed 'private as well as public exercises',[10] while Fabian Nipho, a distinguished foreigner

---

[1] George Edrych, *In libros aliquot Pauli aeginetae, hypomnemata quaedam seu observationes medicamentorum, quae haec aetate in usu sunt per Georgium Edrychum medicum pro iuvenum studijs ad praxim medicam, collecta* (1588), sig. Aiv.

[2] p. 223 n. 1 above.   [3] *BRUO 1501–40*, 14.

[4] Ibid. 348; *A Cartulary of the Hospital of St. John the Baptist*, ed. H. E. Salter (3 vols OHS lxvi, lxviii, lxix 1914–16) i. 192, iii. 304.

[5] R. T. Gunther, 'The row of books of Nicholas Gibbard of Oxford', *Annals of Medical History* iii (1921), 324–6.

[6] BL Sloane MS 249.   [7] Bodl. Rawlinson MS A 369.

[8] Bodl. MS Corpus Christi 265 F, fos 272^V-87^V.

[9] Bodl. Rawlinson MS D 213.

[10] Reg. Cong. 1564–82, fo 100. He later practised as a physician in Coventry: Reg. Chanc. 1545–1661, fo 245.

recommended to congregation by Leicester as one who was 'famose for his skill in physik, philosophy and other learnings' was said to be glad to help by 'readinge, publique or privat'.[1] John Delaber had taken a doctorate at Basle before returning to Oxford where he remained from 1581 to 1593 as principal of Gloucester Hall,[2] over-lapping there with the celebrated Thomas Allen; between them they could have furnished students with first-class tuition in medicine; it is tantalizing not to know whether or not they did so. Henry Bust, fellow of Magdalen in the 1560s and 1570s married and stayed on as a practitioner in the town. He was (with Matthew Gwynn) one of those named by the university in 1597 to advise on the lectures at Gresham College.[3] In 1602 he had a student, one John James, stay-ing in his house to recover his health—such private lodgings were not uncommon in Oxford at this time. From 1605 to 1617 Bust was Linacre lecturer. If Oxford students did have opportunities to watch physicians at work, or to learn from them in private, it is likely to have been with just such local practitioners as Bust.

Nor was there any shortage of medical literature in Oxford. Apart from the older manuscripts in college libraries and in private hands, many of which had survived the dispersal or destruction of allegedly popish or magical works during the religious troubles, either remain-ing undisturbed, or finding their way into the collections of such men as Thomas Allen, there were many hundreds of more recent printed books on medicine in Oxford. Their presence can be inferred from the titles in college library catalogues and in wills and inven-tories, and in part demonstrated from the scores of extant volumes in sixteenth-century Oxford bindings. It is clear beyond doubt that copies existed in Oxford of most of the medical classics in recent scholarly editions, of contemporary works in anatomy, botany and *materia medica*, of books on the dioagnosis and treatment of disease as well as textbooks, epitomes and vernacular manuals of health. Astrological and chemical medicine were both well represented, and there was a large number of books on medical practice, especially of the schools of Montanus and Fuchs. Places of publication included Venice, Rome, Lyons, Paris, Basle, Zurich, Frankfurt, Louvain and Antwerp, and dates of printing ranged from the late fifteenth to the early seventeenth century, those published between 1540 and 1590 outnumbering the earlier ones by about two to one.[4] A lively market in new and second-hand books existed in Oxford.[5] It was also

[1] Reg. Cong. 1564–82, fo 344.
[2] *Reg. Univ.* ed. Clark i. 287.   [3] Ibid. 232–3.
[4] N. R. Ker, 'The provision of books' below; *Oxford College Libraries; BRUO 1501-40,* app. B; Chanc. Court Inv. (typed transcripts).
[5] *Oxford College Libraries;* N. R. Ker, below.

common practice for scholars to give away or to bequeath their books to kinsmen or to younger colleagues. In 1583, for example, William Marshall left to 'Mr. William Dunne . . . doctor of phisick and late felowe of Exeter Colledge, all such my printed phisicke bookes as shal best lyke him to take his choyce therof . . .'. He also left 'to Mr. Michael Lapworth phicicion now dwellynge in Coventry, a booke of practise of his profession in wrytten hand'.[1] Richard Slythurst and John Case both left to colleagues the choice of books for themselves and the task of sharing out the remainder among poor students.[2] John Jackman left such of his books as his executors should think fit to the library of Oriel College; the rest were to go to a certain Anthony Bruer provided that he was studying physic during the next ten years.[3]

In both Oxford and Cambridge at this time it is clear that there was in existence a considerable amount of medical literature, much of it recently printed, and much of it controversial; far from reflecting a narrow concentration on the works of Galen and Hippocrates, the library lists and inventories reveal an enterprising and eclectic interest in astrological, humanist and Paracelsian medicine alike. As far as their books at least were concerned the medical readers of the English universities were not entirely cut off from the mainstream of contemporary medical thought.

THE WRITINGS OF OXFORD MEDICAL MEN

In the sixteenth century there were three more or less distinct audiences for medical publications. The first was an international public of professional scholars, familiar with recent editions of the medical classics, readers of extended commentaries, of controversy and of specialized treatises. The second was the public of medical students and would-be practitioners, surgeons, apothecaries and the like, customers for the vade-mecum and the textbook, who purchased epitomes, digests, summaries and handy expositions in the form of tables. The third was the general public, the laity, hypochondriacal and curious, at once deferential towards and mistrustful of experts, purchasers of vernacular aids to self-diagnosis, lists of handy medicines, manuals on how to maintain good health. Oxford men in their medical writings catered with some success for the third public, and even, to a limited extent for the second; but between them all they produced little that was of any interest to the first, or which was anything but ephemeral in its value.

[1] Reg. Chanc. 1545–1661, fo 245.
[2] Ibid. fos 253, 181.   [3] Ibid. fo 182.

Exceptions should be made for the work of Linacre,[1] for the contributions of the 'four Britons' to the Aldine edition of Galen,[2] for Edward Wotton's *De differentiis animalium*,[3] for the medical asides and assumptions in the Aristotelian commentaries of John Case,[4] for Matthew Gwynn's contribution to the debate on *aurum potabile*,[5] and for the painstaking collation of manuscripts, Greek and Latin, in Italy and in England, that went into Theodore Goulston's edition of nine of Galen's shorter works.[6] Apart from the *Hypomnemata in libros aliquot Pauli aeginetae* of George Edrych (which were, he said, 'collecta pro iuvenum studiis ad praxim medicam'), this is the sum total of the known works in Latin of all the Oxford medical graduates of the century. Nor does there seem to be warrant for giving Oxford, as such, much of the credit for what they published; for by the time they wrote most of these authors (with the distinguished exception of John Case) had lived and worked elsewhere, and their books were printed in London, or abroad. It is true that Oxford had provided the early, and perhaps the formative part of their education; this was the case, or partly so, for Linacre, Wotton, David Edwards, even Clement and Lupset and Robert Recorde; but all had soon moved on.

The limitations of London as a centre in the European book-trade may help to explain the paucity of English scholarly publication in Latin. London printers were relatively rarely called upon to venture their resources upon large works aimed at the international learned market—this was true in theology and in law as well as in medicine. An Oxford scholar who had ready a manuscript of this kind was well advised to seek abroad for a printer. Such was the case with Linacre and with Wotton early in the sixteenth century, and even with Harvey and with Fludd early in the seventeenth.

Small vernacular textbooks, and English translations of foreign works, however, the London printers would risk. They were prepared to publish also short and popular treatises on the plague, on the pox, and on eye conditions, or collections of remedies for common complaints, coughs, toothache, rashes, fevers and the ailments of women or children. There was a great demand for books which would save you apothecaries' bills by telling you how to dose

[1] Giles Barber, 'Thomas Linacre: a bibliographical survey of his works', in *Essays on Linacre*, 290–336; Richard J. Durling, 'Linacre and medical humanism', ibid. 76–106.

[2] Durling, loc. cit.   [3] (Paris 1552).

[4] C. B. Schmitt, 'John Case on art and nature', *Annals of Science* xxxiii (1976), 546–9.

[5] *In assertorem chymicae, sed verae medicinae desertorem, Fra. Anthonium, Matthaei Gwynn philiatri in medicorum londinensium collegio quarti censoris regestarij succincta adversaria* (London 1611).

[6] Theodore Goulston, *Claudii Galeni Pergameni opuscula varia* (1640).

yourself at home. Physicians were expected to be able to plan for a regimen which would stave off sickness and prolong life. The great might retain a personal physician to make such a plan for them on the basis of their horoscope and the pattern of their life, but the not-so-great had to make do with generalized advice on diet, sleep, exercise and so on, as set out in cheap printed dietaries or regimens of health. Oxford medical men contributed to all these genres.[1] This seems to have been what was expected of them and what they felt competent to produce. Not that it took much learning or special expertise. Many of the most successful and remarkable medical books published in sixteenth-century England were written by men whose formal medical studies were non-existent or very brief. Some of these were simply cultivated gentlemen,[2] others bookish surgeons;[3] others were university men, but ones whose medical studies had never been official; yet others had pursued their medical studies in universities other than Oxford.[4] The only one of the five Oxford regius professors with medical writings to his credit (as far as the surviving evidence allows one to judge) was Walter Bayley. Not one of the Linacre lecturers—not even Barnes—has left a medical treatise in manuscript or in print. George Owen had to his credit *A meet diet for the new ague* (1558), Richard Forster *Ephemerides meteorographicae* (1575), Thomas Cogan *The Haven of Health* (1584), Richard Caldwell *Tables of Surgerie* (posthumously published in 1585), Roger Marbeck *A Defence of Tobacco* (1602). Peter Turner the elder, who qualifies as an Oxford man only by virtue of the doctorate which the university gave him on the strength of his Cambridge and Heidelberg degrees, and by the fact that he was, briefly, a Linacre lecturer in the early seventeenth century, showed in his *Opinion of Peter Turner . . . concerning Amulets or Plague Cakes* (1603), the approved scepticism of the liberal Galenist towards the more fanciful claims of magic.

Some manuscript medical writings survive from sixteenth-century Oxford, or from the hands of Oxford medical men of this time. One or two are attributable, several are not. They include chapter-headings for a proposed book on 'the root Mecoaran' by Thomas Twyne,[5] Richard Caldwell's unfinished translation of Horatius Morus on

---

[1] K. F. Russell, 'A check-list of medical books published in England before 1600', *Bulletin of the History of Medicine* xxi (1947), 922–57.

[2] For example Sir Thomas Elyot and William Vaughan.

[3] For example William Clowes and Thomas Gale.

[4] For example Mark Ridley, Timothy Bright or William Gilbert. A valuable recent discussion is that of Paul Slack, 'Vernacular medical literature', in *Health, Medicine and Mortality*, 237–73.

[5] Bodl. Corpus Christi MS 265 F, fos 220–4^V.

surgery, preliminary versions of Walter Bayley's two publications on the eyes and on the baths at Newnham Regis, John Chambre's *Confutation of Astrological Demonology*,[1] the student notebook said to have been compiled by Thomas Cogan,[2] a book of remedies and memoranda belonging to an unnamed Oxford physician of the 1590s[3] and the large and miscellaneous collections of John Woolton referred to above.[4] Better known are the voluminous notebooks of Richard Napier early in the following century. Even the extraordinary writings of Simon Forman could perhaps cast further oblique light on the English medical world of his day, and upon the activities and beliefs of the Oxford men within it.

ACCESSIBILITY AT OXFORD OF MEDICAL FASHIONS OF THE DAY

The preoccupations of all these miscellaneous writings reveal as clearly as do the contents of the private libraries that Oxford medical men in the sixteenth century were aware of and interested in the medical fashions of their own generation. One such was anatomy. No record has come to light of anatomical dissections being held in public or in private in Oxford in the early part of the century, and yet there must have been some interest in the matter, if no more than a bookish one, for David Edwards, at Corpus between 1517 and 1525, was able not long after his departure to produce a well-informed and deservedly celebrated textbook on the subject; admittedly he had spent the interval between 1525 and 1528 in Italy, where he could more easily have attended such dissections.[5]

The statutes of 1549 require a candidate for the medical licence and for a medical degree to have 'made' at least two anatomies. Whether or not this means that he was to have participated in the actual dissection, or (as is much more likely) simply to have attended and watched, it is a remarkable requirement, and a novel one in Oxford. Perhaps it was not a realistic demand; probably it did not reflect current practice, but merely expressed a pious hope. In the *nova statuta* of 1564 all specific reference to anatomy is dropped. Was this an oversight? If it was, it was one that was not remedied. Interest in anatomy was high in the 1560s among at least some of the Oxford fellows of the London College of Physicians and it seems

[1] Wood, *Fasti* i. 181, 193; *Athenae* i. 744.
[2] Royal College of Physicians MS 201.
[3] Bodl. Rawlinson MSS A369, 370.
[4] BL Sloane MS 249.
[5] A. Rook and M. Newbold, 'David Edwardes: his activities at Cambridge', *Medical History* xix (1975), 389–92.

likely that anatomical demonstrations of some kind did take place in Oxford at this time. In 1578 convocation complained that the 'lectures and anatomies' hitherto available for surgeons in Oxford (itself an interesting hint that some formal tuition was offered by physicians not only to medical students but also to apprentice surgeons as was a common practice on the continent) had lately been interrupted, and should forthwith be resumed; it asked the vice-chancellor and the professor of physic to set this in train. The outcome is unknown. Walter Bayley certainly regarded the teaching of anatomy as part of his duties; the skeleton he bequeathed to his successor was presumably used for this purpose. Anatomical notes (of an elementary kind) survive in more than one of the manuscript notebooks kept by Oxford students.[1] At least three colleges bought copies of the De humani corporis fabrica of Vesalius soon after its publication in 1543, and their libraries contain a fair sprinkling of books on anatomy, although since some of these may have come to them by later bequest, it is not certain that they were all available to students in the sixteenth century.[2] Individuals had the odd anatomical book, Charles Estienne, Dryander and so on, in their possession, but not even the owners of considerable medical libraries, Barnes, Symonds, Tolley, Glover, Paddy, Goulston seem to have taken trouble to build up a specialist collection in the subject. Several men who had studied medicine at Oxford later showed some serious intereest in the teaching of anatomy, although it cannot be claimed that the university, or even their respective colleges, can take any of the credit for this. Richard Caldwell of Brasenose and Christ Church, who took his doctorate in 1555 and who was to be an active fellow of the London College after 1559 and its president in 1570 was associated with his patron Lord Lumley in the setting up of the Lumleian lecturership offered first to the Company of Barber-Surgeons (who failed to accept it) and then to the College of Physicians.[3] He made a translation into English under the title Tables of Surgerie of a Latin version by the Florentine Horatius Morus of the surgical works of Jean Tagault. Five hundred copies of the book were presented by his executors after his death to the Company of Barber-Surgeons for their apprentices' use. The first Lumleian lecturer was another Oxford medical graduate, Richard Forster, who is reputed to have lectured in London (to very small audiences) on Wednesdays and Fridays from 10 to 11 a.m. and to have covered the whole of

[1] Bodl. Corpus Christi MS 263 F, fos 128–9; Ashmole MS 1500.

[2] Oxford College Libraries; N. R. Ker, 'The provision of books', below, 449.

[3] Clark, Royal College i. 150; F. W. Steer, 'Lord Lumley's benefaction to the College of Physicians', Medical History ii (1958), 298–305.

anatomy in a six-year course. If he was as thorough and as slow as this it is perhaps not surprising that his audiences were small. Nevertheless they may well have missed something worthwhile: William Clowes the surgeon, whose views are worthy of respect in such a matter, regarded him as a sound lecturer.[1] He was an accomplished mathematician and the author of a book dealing with the application of astronomical tables to diagnosis and prognosis.[2] He was also a friend of Matthew Gwynn and moved, therefore, in intellectually lively circles in London at the turn of the century. John Banister, the celebrated surgeon, who perhaps did more than any other individual to popularize anatomy and to improve the teaching of surgeons, seems to have studied medicine at Oxford around 1573, when he obtained the university's licence to practise medicine;[3] it was only five years later that he published his *History of Man, sucked from the sap of the most approved Anatomists, in nine books*, which relies heavily on passages translated from the works of various French and German surgeons. He enjoyed the friendship and respect of members of the College of Physicians, among them several Oxford men, but it was to Caius College, Cambridge (not to Christ Church) that he left his ivory and boxwood anatomical figurines when he died.[4] Thomas Hall, a surgeon's son, and himself later a fellow of the college of physicians, had been the first beneficiary of an arrangement whereby the Company of Barber-Surgeons maintained a scholar at each of the universities. In 1560 they ordained that 'Thomas Hall shall have an exhibicyon of fortie shillings by the yere and yerely towards his studye (in Mawdelyn Coledge) in the unyversitie for Surgery annexinge physycke therunto, and thereby hereafter to perfet his other brethren beynge of this mystery . . . by Readynge lectures unto them in the common hall and otherwyse by his councell, conynge and knowledge'.[5] He studied in Oxford for at least four years, becoming master of arts in 1568, bachelor of medicine in 1572 and returning to incept as doctor in 1582, having meanwhile been 'granted by the [Barber-Surgeons'] Company to Desect Thanatomies private or publicke for the terme of Tenne yeres'.[6]

All this may be evidence that in the medical studies of Oxford anatomy did play some part well before the founding of the Tomlins

---

[1] Steer, loc. cit. and William Clowes, *Prooved Practice* (1591); Clark, *Royal College* i. 51.

[2] *Ephemerides meteorographicae ad annum 1575* (1575).

[3] Reg. Cong. 1564–82, fo 149.

[4] D'Arcy Power, 'The education of a surgeon under Thomas Vicary', *British Journal of Surgery* viii (1921), 247–9.

[5] J. F. South, *Memorials of the Craft of Surgery in England* (1886), 149–50.

[6] Ibid. 135.

readership early in the following century.[1] But perhaps it reveals also that anatomy did not play very much of a part; or rather, that it did not go beyond an elementary introduction to the subject. Oxford cannot claim to have nurtured, in the sixteenth century, a single anatomist of European repute. Of most of the other medical schools of Europe the same thing could be said; and although Cambridge rightly claims William Harvey as its own, it was almost certainly in Padua that the foundations of his later distinction in anatomy were laid. At this time neither Oxford nor Cambridge was a centre of anatomical study in the sense that this could be said of Padua, Bologna, Rome, Paris, Montpellier or Basle.

On the face of it, it would seem that the same could be said about botany. But to argue from published works alone might well be misleading. William Turner, one of the few Englishmen of the century whose printed work reveals him to have been outstanding both as an erudite commentator upon Dioscorides, and an excellent field-botanist, wrote in 1551 that 'there have bene in England, and there are now also certain learned men whych have as muche knowledge in herbes, yea and more than diverse Italianes and Germanes whych have set furth in prynte Herballes and bokes of simples. I mean of Dr. Clement, Dr. Wendy and Dr. Owen, Dr. Wotton and Maister Falconer. Yet hath none of al these set furth any thyng.'[2] Why was it, incidentally, that English scholars in medicine and natural history published so much less than their continental counterparts? Perhaps we assume too readily that they lacked the inclination, or the application; could it have been partly also, as suggested above, that London printers were less willing to take on large manuscripts in Latin which would have needed to be printed in folio, perhaps, or which would have had, in England, too small a market to be worth the publishing cost? Whatever the reason, none of the learned men mentioned by Turner in this passage did 'set forth' a book of the kind he had in mind, except Edward Wotton, and the manuscript of his great work *De differentiis animalium* might never have seen the light if his friend (and Oxford contemporary) Sir John Mason had not taken it with him as a favour, when he went as ambassador to France, and found in Paris a printer willing to take it on.[3] Three out of the five

[1] *Laudian Code* tit. IV sect. I § 15. 39 and 258–61. The body is to be dissected by a skilful surgeon in advance of the actual demonstration by the reader. On the first day the liver, spleen and belly are to be commented upon and shown, on the second day the heart and lungs; the reader is to lecture on the skeleton every Michaelmas Term; the audience is to consist of all the students of medicine and all the surgeons in the university. It seems likely that these instructions reflect closely the intermittent sixteenth-century practice at Oxford.

[2] Charles E. Raven, *English Naturalists from Neckham to Ray: a study in the making of the modern world* (Cambridge 1947), 69.

[3] Edward Wotton, *De differentiis animalium libri decem* (Paris 1552), dedicatory letter.

men named by Turner were, or, had been, Oxford men. Clement had stayed there only briefly, lecturing in Greek at Corpus in the 1520s, but Wotton's connection with Magdalen had been longer, and Owen had held a fellowship at Merton. It is likely that his help and his learning were available there to his juniors, as George Edrych indeed recalls.[1]

There are other glimpses, too, of botanical concerns. Richard Bartlett had a garden in London which William Turner saw.[2] All Souls in 1556 had a Ruellius *De natura stirpium* of 1537 and a Dioscorides of 1543.[3] Merton in the 1540s, in a spate of buying books for its library, acquired in the list Ruel, Fuchs, Vesalius.[4] John Dotyn left to Exeter in 1561 (among his other books) two editions of Dioscorides (Paris 1516 and Strasbourg 1529), Brunfels's book on plants (Strasbourg 1534) the letters of Manardus (1535) and Fuchsius *Historia stirpium* (Basle 1542).[5] Examples of this kind, or reference simply to 'my herbal' could be multiplied from almost all the inventories and library lists and bequests of the other Oxford men. Tragus, Dodonaeus, Clusius, even the bulky *Historia generalis plantarum* (Lyons 1586) are to be found. The writer of the notebook ascribed to Thomas Cogan was busy in the 1570s identifying in his margins the botanical ingredients in composite medicines.[6] Was it at Oxford that a beginning had been made in the botanical learning of the North Welshmen, Thomas Williams, rector of Trefriw, who wrote a 'prettye large Herbal in Latine, Welsh and Englishe . . . giving an Account of Herbs and their Physical vertues'[7] and Humphrey Llwyd of Denbigh, who became librarian to Lord Lumley?[8]

As was only to be expected, scholars whose interest in medicine was a part of their wider concern with philosophical questions about the workings of nature, were often attracted also to astronomy, to astrology, to alchemy and to natural magic. The works of Cardano were widely popular among them, as were those of Agrippa of Nettesheim, and Fernel *On the Hidden Causes of Things*. Among the effects of Thomas Bolte when he died were a mortar and pestle, three gold weights, scissors, a small brass pan, and copies of the *De arcanis* of Mizaldus and the *De subtilitate* of Cardano.[9] Thomas Charnock

[1] Above, pp. 238–9.   [2] Raven, 97.
[3] Ker, *Records of All Souls*, 146.
[4] *Oxford College Libraries* nos. 80, 77, 85.
[5] *BRUO 1501–40*, app. B, 719–20.
[6] Royal College of Physicians MS 201, fos 147–262.
[7] BL Lansdowne MS 983, fo 103.
[8] BL Lansdowne MS 981, fo 70; Humphrey Llwyd, *The Treasuri of Helth contaynyng many profytable medicines gathered out of Hippocratiis Galen and Avicen in Englyshe by Humfre Lloyd who hath added the causes and sygnes of every dysease, with the Aphorismes of Hippocraties* (1558).   [9] Chanc. Court Inv. (typed transcripts).

the alchemist, who tells us in his *De lapide philosophorum processus* that he 'travelled all the realm of England over, for to attain unto the secrets of this science', tells us also that he lived and studied in Oxford for some time.[1] Lansdowne MS 703 in the British Library is a dialogue between himself and 'an Oxfordman well learned' on the subject of alchemy. Timothy Willis, who had rather a stormy career as a fellow of St John's in the early 1580s, was the author of a book on transmutation.[2] Chemical medicine is represented among the Goulston books by Guinterius, Quercetanus, Severinus and the *Theatrum chymicum*; but this was only to be expected, for Goulston's library was still being added to after 1600, and by that time such critics, expositors and popularizers of Paracelsian medicine and of the 'chemical philosophy' in general were of long-standing, and to be found on the shelves of the most prudishly traditional of learned Galenists. Guinterius had been one of the earliest humanist Galenic writers to look fairly and seriously at the substance behind the bombast and polemic in Paracelsus, and his *De medicina veteri et nova* had helped to make it possible for Galenic physicians to understand something of Paracelsian pathology and therapy even if they did not accept it. In any case the encyclopedic humanists, represented *par excellence* by the eclectic Gesner, and deeply versed in classical, Arab and vernacular medical traditions, were at much the same time exploring the use of chemically prepared medicines to enlarge the pharmacopoeia. Both Guinterius and Gesner were present on Oxford men's shelves; indeed the world of Gesner, of Fuchs, of Ruel, or Manardus, of da Monte, of Crato and the Montpellier clinicians (in short the world of John Caius) at second-hand at least, was theirs also.

CONCLUSION

Andrew Clark remarked that 'the number of persons proceeding to degrees [in medicine] was very small' in comparison with the numbers in theology and law. 'The faculty' he believed 'would probably have become extinct altogether but for the endowment of a professor and the existence of fellowships in medicine at some colleges.'

Furthermore 'The faculty of Medicine had already lost touch with the requirements of professional study' and 'real students of medicine

[1] BL Sloane MS 2640, fo. 1.

[2] Timothy Willis, *The Search of Causes Containing a Theophysicall investigation of the possibilitie of transmutatorie Alchemie* (1616). He also wrote *Propositiones tentationum: sive propaedeumata de vitis et faecunditate compositorum naturalium: quae sunt elementa chymica* (1615).

recognized that Oxford gave no opportunities for medical study, and sought elsewhere the instruction they could not receive at home'.[1]

Was he right?

That the faculty of medicine as such was weak, cannot be denied. There was little sign of a body of medical men defending their interests as a group against the rival claims of regent masters in arts, or of predatory theologians; but such inter-faculty rivalry was in any case in Oxford at this time fleeting and not of much significance. And the university took care always to have a couple of doctors of medicine alongside the doctors of theology and of civil law on those committees it was continually setting up to review the statutes or to enquire into the conduct of the exercises in the schools. Was the faculty ever in danger of becoming extinct? Here Clark is misleading: so long as the university in its statutes offered degrees and licences in medicine, and so long as these qualifications carried (rightly or wrongly) some weight in the outside world, scholars who intended to practise and practitioners with some claim to scholarship would come forward to supplicate for them; and the university would then (as it did) use its own discretion about the extent to which the statutory requirements had been fulfilled, grant the necessary dispensations and award the degree. There had long been a statutory provision that a master of arts could testify to the suitability of a candidate if no bachelor or doctor of medicine was to be found;[2] the university had long lived with a shortage of these. Technically, therefore, it did not matter if the 'faculty' from time to time did not exist.

The number of persons proceeding to degrees was certainly smaller in physic than in theology, although the lawyers, for good historical reasons, were scarcely more numerous than the physicians. But is 177 in the century so very small a number, especially when it is recalled that these were not scattered evenly over the hundred years but were clustered in the 1520s and 1530s and more thickly still between 1540 and 1585? In the time of Walter Bayley and of Anthony Aylworth no fewer than ninety-two licences and degrees in medicine were sought. Licences in surgery were very rarely issued, and seem to have been intended to apply to Oxford and its locality alone. Only three are recorded in the century, to Thomas Byrde in 1537, to Felix Pontanus in 1540 and to Joachim Wolphe in 1573.[3] Licences in medicine, however, were issued in large numbers, usually in conjunction with the bachelor's degree. Even those few (twenty in all) which were given without the MB went to men at least nine of whom were masters of arts, six of them of Oxford itself. It would be

---

[1] *Reg. Univ.* ed. Clark i. 123.   [2] *Statuta*, 42.
[3] Reg. Cong. 1535–63, fos 24, 59^V; KK, fo 149.

incorrect to suppose that the university handed out its licences to unlearned practitioners, or even that such people bothered to seek a university licence at all. They had no need. It was possible to practise the healing arts as physician or surgeon, or indeed as apothecary where the physicians and surgeons were not too thick upon the ground, without a licence from a university and in many places without permission from the local authorities, municipal or ecclesiastical, despite claims they might intermittently make to the contrary. Attempts were made by several different bodies to protect the different and exclusive standing of physicians, surgeons and apothecaries, but none of these schemes met with complete success, not even the bold monopolistic assertions of the London college of physicians within the confines of the city.[1] Prudent scholars who thought that they might one day want to practise medicine can be seen seeking the university's licence in the course of their medical studies. It is striking that almost all the licences granted by the university of Oxford went to masters of arts who had completed four years' study of medicine and who were applying for 'admission to read the *Aphorisms* of Hippocrates' the formula used for the bachelor's degree. All but twenty-nine of the one hundred and seventy-seven men to whom an Oxford MB or MD was granted were Oxford MAs, and most of the remaining twenty-nine were graduates of other universities. The picture at Cambridge was broadly similar, although the proportion of licences granted to persons with (as far as we know) no university education was much higher than at Oxford—thirty-eight out of ninety-eight as against eighteen out of two hundred.[2]

The London college of physicians not only made it clear (by granting exemption from most of its entrance tests to bachelors of medicine from Oxford and Cambridge) that it respected academic medicine in general, but that it was prepared to regard as adequate the educational background provided by the English universities in particular.[3] Furthermore, the London college expected that an applicant who had been granted its licence, and who was engaged in practice for four years with a view to seeking election as a fellow would take the degree of doctor of medicine just before or just after his election, as befitted his professional standing. This custom (it was never a formal requirement, but it did usually obtain) no doubt helped to swell the numbers of those who bothered to go to the trouble and expense of seeking their MD. In Cambridge (where the bachelor's degree in medicine was little used), it was normal for those

[1] Webster (ed.), *Health, Medicine and Mortality*, 165–88.
[2] Ibid. 192–5.   [3] Clark, *Royal College* i. 98–100.

seeking a medical degree to go straight for the MD.[1] In Oxford it was
more usual to take the MB first. Rather more than half the 177
men who did so never bothered to proceed to the MD, and those
who did so might delay for up to twelve years before doing so.
However, forty out of the forty-seven Oxford men who became
fellows of the college of physicians took their MD shortly before
or shortly after their election.[2] When it is recalled that by no means
all those scholars who were interested in medicine took medical
degrees (and even when allowance is made for those who came back
to take them after an absence), it is plain that in the 1560s, 1570s
and 1580s there was a sizeable handful of students at any one
time engaged upon medical reading. That such small numbers were
adequate for the formation of little groups of like-minded men
is attested by the reminiscences and the later friendships of several
of them. If medicine remained the study of a minority, it was by
no means a negligible one.

Was the danger, perhaps, less of the total extinction of medical
studies than of wavering standards in the awarding of degrees? Theoretically, this might have been so. The royal visitors had seen it as
a real danger in 1535 when they spoke of 'the blind leading the
blind'. The university in fact had taken care throughout the century
to award its medical degrees almost invariably to masters of arts,
usually of the statutory minimum years of standing, who claimed
that they had spent these years in medical study, or more specifically that they had fulfilled the requirements of the statutes. But
had they done so? Who was to say? After 1535, the answer was clear
enough: it was the responsibility of the professor. As we have seen, it
is impossible to be certain just how rigorous each of the professors
was in performing this duty, but apart from one or two odd incidents in the early years, there were no scandals, and the degrees did
go to people who were serious students of medicine well-known in
the university, attested (in effect) by college or hall. The appointment of one man responsible for safeguarding, in this respect, the
university's good name, had clearly been a step forward, and in this
respect Clark was right to see the establishment of the professorship
as important. He was right, too, in seeing as important the willingness of colleges to allow some of their fellows to pursue medical
studies, sometimes for many years; but the 'medical fellowships'
proper seem to have played an insignificant part, and not always
to have been reserved, in any case, for bona fide students of medicine.

[1] Webster (ed.), *Health, Medicine and Mortality*, 195.
[2] Reg. Cong. 1505–17, 1518–35, 1535–63, 1564–82, 1582–95, 1595–1606; passim;
W. Munk, *Roll of the Royal College of Physicians* (1878), passim.

That the faculty of medicine 'had lost sight of the requirements of professional study' we have already seen to be untrue. The general public, although it often took its custom elsewhere, acquiesced in the view which enabled the university-accredited physician 'to claim a dignified position in society, dress according to his rank, and establish his right to charge high fees, and to dominate all inferior groups within the medical profession'.[1] In their licences and degrees the universities were dispensing a commodity valuable to its purchasers. The public and the profession alike assumed at this time that clinical training was best acquired under the private guidance of a mature practitioner. Sydenham was later to argue that an apprenticeship of this kind was worth far more than any amount of bookish lore and that it should indeed take its place. Such a view was not widely held among the élite of the Tudor medical profession; they still had respected seriously the learning of the schools.

What of Andrew Clark's statement that 'real students of medicine recognized that Oxford gave no opportunities for medical study, and sought elsewhere the instruction they could not receive at home'? This is to over-state the case. There were, as we have seen, ample opportunities of a kind. It must be admitted that the Oxford student of medicine (even in one of the more active and lively moments in medical studies there) was unlikely to have the chance to hear in a single day a succession of good technical lectures, let alone to hear them daily, week in, week out, as he might in a few of the continental faculties. Nor would he have the chance to join the circle of some celebrated doctor, like da Monte, or, later, Fabrizio or Falloppio in Padua, Fernel in Paris, Rondelet or Joubert or du Laurens in Montpellier, Erastus in Heidelberg or Felix Platter in Basle. Nor could Oxford offer the stimulus of metropolitan life, or of a large and lively medical student population from many different lands. In comparison with the larger and more combative faculties, to which more travellers came, the whole tone of her medical studies must have been muted and low-key. But to say that Oxford gave 'no opportunities for medical study' is clearly untrue. 'Real' students of medicine there derived most of their knowledge and many of their insights from their own reading and reflection, as 'real' students of any bookish science always do. The Oxford student of medicine was likely to be more or less self-taught, relying on whatever books lay to hand; and this in turn depended on his luck. Could he afford to buy books of his own? It is plain that some students could. Had he inherited part of the working library of a kinsman? This too was not unknown. Was his college well supplied? Some had medical

[1] *Health, Medicine and Mortality*, 189.

manuscripts of Serapion, Rhazes, Avicenna, Galen's so-called *Tegni* and the precepts of the *schola salernitana*; it would be wrong to think that these all disappeared or fell into disuse; Merton in 1564 still kept its Avicenna chained, and Mesue at least enjoyed among the *avant-garde* a revival and a vogue. Although the university's own provision of books was inadequate and sparse until Sir Thomas Bodley's library got into its stride, and although few colleges bought new books regularly and in a systematic way, the collections grew at random, with sudden spates of purchase, and a succession of bequests. And in this context, medicine did well. If Corpus in mid-century still lacked the needed books, and if Dotyn's bequest to Exeter in 1561 was the earliest substantial medical legacy, things were a little rosier at Merton and at Magdalen, at New College and All Souls.[1] And later in the century and early in the next there was a rich harvest of legacies and gifts. Notable among these were the bequests to Merton of Jessop, Barnes and Gifford, and especially Theodor Goulston; Jackman's gift to Oriel, John Baylie's to New College, and above all the munificent eight-hundred book library of Paddy which came to St John's. By the 1620s Oxford colleges, between them, were abundantly (if patchily) supplied with books.

Andrew Clark was right in pointing out that several scholars later celebrated had abandoned Oxford in favour of study elsewhere. Early in the century Clement and Lupset, Rose, Fryer and Wotton had followed the example of Linacre in the 1490s by seeking in Venice and in Padua an opportunity to pursue in medicine the kind of humanist scholarship they had encountered in letters and in philosophy. It was natural for them to gravitate to Italy for this purpose, for while it is true that they would not have found such opportunities in Oxford, they would scarcely have found them, at this date, in Paris either, nor even in Montpellier, nor in the kingdoms of Spain, nor in all Germany. Ten or fifteen years later the picture was transformed. Ruel and Fuchs, Gesner, Sylvius and Guinter, Rabelais, Schyron, Rondelet, Laguna were in their different cities renewing the literature of medicine and natural history. Oxford was a recipient of all this activity, through books, but herself produced no home-bred and home-based contributors to it; she had no Gesner, no Guinter, and later, no Libavius to discriminate among the writings of physicians new and old, and to establish careful criteria for the eclectic acceptance of novelty. The best she could do was to produce thoughtful and well-read students who followed these controversies and fashions at second hand.

The exodus of the able was a striking feature of the 1520s, but it

[1] N. R. Ker, 'The provision of books', below.

did not persist. Indeed, the number of Oxford scholars in the century who pursued their medical studies abroad is remarkably small—after the early ones named above (in whose number should be included John Chambre who went to Italy in 1503), only nine names can be found. Andrew Boorde travelled widely but owed most, he tells us, to his time in Montpellier. Edmund Crispin went away, with permission, in 1543, probably to Italy. Humphrey Hall went to Padua in the early 1560s, John Delaber and Thomas Doyley to Basle in the following decade. John Sherwood, oddly, incorporated in 1596 on the strength of his MD from the obscure faculty at Rheims. John Nowell, John Osborne and William Paddy each took a doctorate in medicine at Leiden in the 1580s, although it is by no means certain that any of them had studied there for any length of time.

The number then was small—some seventeen individuals out of about one hundred and seventy—and the chronological pattern clear: a batch of humanist émigrés in the 1520s, all going to Italy, then nothing but the rare individual travelling more widely in Switzerland and France, perhaps with the encouragement and help of some private patron, and then, in the 1580s a brief flurry, no more, of registrations at the fashionable faculty at Leyden. The picture is similar in all respects to the one presented by the records of the whereabouts of Cambridge men. Nor did many Englishmen later prominent in the college of physicians seek their medical education exclusively on the continent, without having attended either of the English universities; a momentary flutter of anxiety about such a possibility is discernible in the College of Physicians in the 1590s, but it all came to nothing. In the early seventeenth century, all but a tiny minority of the academically accredited physicians in England were Oxford and Cambridge graduates, as they had always been. Foreigners there were in the highest ranks of the medical profession; and some (but not all) of these had incorporated MD, as a matter of courtesy, perhaps, or a precaution, at Oxford or Cambridge. But foreign students of medicine had always been rare at either place; compared with the leading continental faculties the composition of the student body had been local in the extreme, scarcely a Scot or an Irishman to be seen, let alone an alien minority of French or German speakers. Apart from a couple of foreign surgeons and the occasional visitor, Welshmen were the most exotic part of the medical scene.

The vitality of a centre of study is an elusive thing. In the following century Oxford medicine grew livelier and the pace accelerated although the numbers grew little and the institutional framework remained unchanged. The Tomlins readership in anatomy, although it was a new endowment, was held in plurality with the regius chair and seems to have made very little difference. Thomas Clayton would no doubt have contributed as much to anatomical studies without its special stipend. The botanic garden played no part for some time in medical instruction; its role was not comparable to that of the garden at Montpellier nor to that of the *jardin des plantes* in Paris. Although St John's benefited greatly from the munificent benefaction of Paddy to its library, and although the Bodleian early began to build up a comprehensive collection of medical books, facilities for medical study underwent no dramatic change. The colleges remained much as they were. If Oxford medicine did develop a new momentum (which it slowly but surely did) this was to a large extent a reflection of what was happening both socially and intellectually in the country and in Europe at large. And on this reckoning, sixteenth-century Oxford medicine, too, had been a faithful, if a pale, reflection of the demands within the profession and of the international academic medicine of its day.

4·3

The Faculty of Law

JOHN BARTON

THE ABOLITION OF CANON LAW

FOR the lawyers of the university, the most important consequence of the reformation was that courses ceased to be given in the canon law. It is perhaps debatable whether it be strictly correct to say that it was abolished, for contemporaries appear to have thought that the study was merely suspended. The *Corpus juris canonici* could hardly be applied in its entirety in a country which had rejected the supremacy of the pope. The immediate solution was to leave the church to be governed by so much of the former law as was neither detrimental to the prerogative nor contrary to common law or statute.[1] The clergy had excellent reason to know that it was not by any means easy to determine in advance of the fact what actions were detrimental to the prerogative, or contrary to common law or statute. This was intended, however, merely as a temporary expedient. The act of submission empowered the king to appoint a commission of thirty-two members, sixteen from the two houses of parliament and sixteen from the clergy, who were to make a collection of those canons which were to be continued in force, and to present it to the king for confirmation.[2] The same power was again conferred upon the king, in substantially the same terms, in 1536, but the collection was to be prepared and confirmed within three years.[3] In 1544 the king was empowered to appoint a similar commission at any time during his life. The terms of this act were somewhat more ambitious, for what was now envisaged was not a mere collection of existing materials, but a code for the English church.[4] The project did not drop with the death of the king. The statutes which Edward VI's visitors made for the university in 1549 provide that the law professor is to lecture upon the pandects, the code or upon the ecclesiastical laws of the realm which are to be promulgated, and

---

[1] *Statutes of the Realm* iii. 25 Hen. VIII, ch. 19 section 7.
[2] Ibid. sections 1 and 2.   [3] Ibid. 27 Hen. VIII, ch. 15.
[4] Ibid. 35 Hen VIII, ch. 16.

upon no others,[1] and in the same year yet a fourth statute was passed for the appointment of yet another commission of thirty-two members to codify the ecclesiastical law. Their powers were rather more limited. They were to make no canons contrary to existing common or statute law,[2] which meant in effect that their code would require parliamentary confirmation. In the middle ages, it had been the custom both of the spiritual and of the secular power to claim, as against the other, a wider competence in theory than was ordinarily insisted upon in practice,[3] and what ecclesiastical legislation was properly to be deemed contrary to the common law was a question to which there were so many answers which could be supported by authority that it could hardly be determined which was to be deemed correct. In the event, the king died before parliament could reach a decision,[4] and though in the first parliament of Elizabeth I it was proposed that yet another commission of thirty-two members should be appointed, the proposal was dropped.

The proposal that the ecclesiastical jurisdiction should be settled by legislation had been first put forward in the submission of the clergy,[5] and at the beginning of the reign of Edward VI convocation petitioned the parliament that the codification of the ecclesiastical law might be taken in hand again, so that ecclesiastical judges might act 'without danger and peril'.[6] It had not escaped notice in other quarters, however, that the transfer of the ecclesiastical supremacy from the pope to the king might prove a formidable accession to the king's prerogative. In 1547 Gardiner wrote to the protector to excuse himself for refusing to comply with the royal injunctions of that year upon the ground that they were contrary to statute. He agreed that to anyone guided merely by the light of reason it might seem strange to argue that to obey the royal commands would be to incur the pains of *praemunire* for encroaching upon the royal

[1] *Statuta*, 344, lines 2–3.

[2] *Statutes of the Realm* iv pt 1, 3 and 4 Edw. VI, ch. 11, section 5. The legislation of Henry VIII upon this subject is an interesting example of what the late Sir Courtenay Ilbert termed 'diplomatic drafting'. It is carefully provided that *convocation* is to make no canons contrary either to common or to statute law, and that no such canons are to be applied in the ecclesiastical courts, but this restriction does not extend to the canons which are to be approved by the king's commissioners.

[3] On the ecclesiastical practice see *St. German's Doctor and Student*, ed. T. F. T. Plucknett and J. L. Barton (Selden Society xci 1974) dialogue 1, ch. 32, 172; for the practice of the secular courts see R. H. Helmholz, 'The writ of prohibition to court Christian before 1500', *Mediaeval Studies* xliii (1981).

[4] J. C. Spalding, 'The reformatio legum ecclesiasticarum of 1552 and the furthering of discipline in England', *Church History* xxxix (1970), 162–71.

[5] For the attempts at codification under Henry VIII, see F. D. Logan, 'The Henrician canons', *Bulletin of the Institute of Historical Research* xlvii (1974) 99.

[6] R. W. Dixon, *The History of the Church of England from the Abolition of the Roman Jurisdiction* (6 vols 1878–1902) ii. 468, where the text of the petition is given in full.

authority, but he was obliged to take it that this was the law of England. In the previous reign he had broached this question in parliament with Lord Audley, then lord chancellor. Lord Audley had advised him to consult the act of supremacy, where he would see that the king's supremacy was confined to matters spiritual, and reminded him that by another act the spiritual law could not override common law or statute. Without these restrictions the king and the bishops together might have ordered the law as they pleased, but he and his party would make sure of those liberties which the law of the land gave them by making sure that the bishops should never be free of the threat of a *praemunire*.[1]

This uncertainty was not wholly to the disadvantage of the crown. It had been lately discovered that the whole clerical order was guilty of a collective *praemunire* in submitting to Wolsey's legatine authority, and the knowledge that another such discovery was always possible would serve as a powerful disincentive to clerical independence. Moreover, it was by systematically exploiting popular anticlericalism that Henry VIII was enabled to repudiate the pope and retain his throne. The clergy that the plain man loved least were the ecclesiastical judges whose duty it was to exact his tithes and oblations and to correct his religious and moral lapses. It is no coincidence that the attack on the church in the reformation parliament opened with a supplication against the ordinaries. The settlement of the ecclesiastical law was a matter of secondary importance, for which it was not worth running any major political risk. It is significant that this was one of the problems raised by the new ecclesiastical settlement which the prudent Elizabeth thought it wiser to leave alone. This was to have serious consequences at the end of the century, when the common lawyers launched their attack on the ecclesiastical jurisdiction. Its immediate consequence was to leave the university with no approved text of ecclesiastical law, upon which public instruction might be given.

Since ecclesiastical practice was the most obvious use which a university-trained lawyer could find for his qualifications, this was a serious deficiency. It was probably made good to some extent by private tuition. Elizabethan Oxford did produce one canonist of real distinction in Henry Swinburne,[2] who spent the greater part of his undergraduate career in Hart Hall, which was officially a hall of artists. Another member of the hall in his time was John Langford,

[1] *The Letters of Stephen Gardiner*, ed. J. A. Müller (Cambridge 1933), 392.

[2] For his life and work see J. D. M. Derrett, *Henry Swinburne, ?1551–1624, Civil Lawyer of York* (Borthwick Papers xliv York 1973) and for his legal attainments H. Coing, *Das Schrifttum der englischen Civilians und die kontinentale Rechtsliteratur* (*Ius Commune* v) 36–7.

DCL, a former fellow of All Souls and an advocate.[1] A senior member of a hall received no stipend, and had to pay for his commons. Langford would have no reason to enter himself at Hart Hall, unless he were proposing to earn fees by taking pupils. Swinburne seems to have been conscious that he was not altogether an ordinary student, for when he supplicated for the BCL in 1580 he stated that he had spent four years *in utriusque iuris studio*. A puzzled registrar thereupon put him down as a scholar of the faculty of arts supplicating for the BA. An attempt was made to correct the error, and the registrar, by now completely demoralized, struck out *alicuius libri logices* and substituted *cuiuscunque iuris institutorum*.[2] By the end of the century students of the ecclesiastical law, like students of the common law, were learning their profession by attending on the courts and making their own notes of decisions, and it seems to have been accepted that it was necessary for them to pursue their studies outside the university. In 1609 Archbishop Bancroft suspended his predecessor's ruling that any legist of All Souls who practised for more than two years in any court outside the university was to forfeit his fellowship: '. . . forasmuch as I find, by conference with some of the principal doctors of the arches . . . that the said restraint is more prejudicial to the students in the profession of your house, than I suppose was ever intended by my predecessor.'[3]

As the last generation of legists who had received an early training in both laws died or left the university, and their immediate pupils followed them, it was probably becoming progressively more difficult to find satisfactory instruction in canon law, though interest in the subject continued, at least in certain quarters. In 1575 Vigelius (whose *Iuris civilis totius methodus absolutissimus* enjoyed a certain vogue among students in the Oxford faculty if we may judge from the inventories of the effects of deceased or absconding scholars) published from Basle a *Liber de causis matrimonialibus* which was intended as a specimen of the same method applied to the canon law. This in itself would be unremarkable, but it is dedicated to the archbishop of York in an epistle in which the author states that the book had been composed at the suggestion of Richard Percy. Percy was to take his doctorate from Christ Church three years later, and was subsequently commissary to the archbishop of York for twenty years.[4] It is interesting that this cadet of a powerful northern family should take the opportunity of encouraging a distinguished author to produce an introduction to the canon law. Percy had apparently

---

[1] *Reg. Univ.* ed. Clark ii. 29, 35. For Langford's career see Foster, *Alumni, sub nom.*

[2] Reg. Cong. 1564–82, fo 299[v].   [3] *SCO* i. pt. 7 (All Souls) 108.

[4] Wood, *Fasti, sub anno* 1578.

convinced Vigelius that this work might gain him that fame and profit which had hitherto eluded him, but the author's expectations of English patronage appear to have been disappointed, for when the complete *Methodus iuris pontificii* appeared in 1577 it was dedicated to the estates of the Holy Roman Empire in an epistle which contains a harrowing account of the author's undeserved suffering and unrequited merits. In the last years of our period, the influence of Professor Albericus Gentilis was probably somewhat unfortunate. He was by far the most distinguished scholar to hold the chair during the century, and in the civil law he began his career, at least, as a staunch conservative. His condemnation of the French elegant school was so comprehensive and so uncompromising as to lead some to suggest that it must have been meant ironically.[1] Upon popes and papal authority, however, his opinions were very much those which might have been expected of a refugee from the inquisition. That he should have wished to see the commentaries of the canon law committed to the flames was understandable, but he suffered from a graver fault than this: granted that the canon law remained at least partially in force in England, he saw no reason to respect the authority of popish commentators upon the canonical texts. To argue, for example, that texts which the canonists themselves accept as authoritative show that a marriage celebrated between children without the consent of their parents is invalid, and that the opposite conclusion can be supported only by the inept or interested reasoning characteristic of a former age of superstition[2] is open, and with more justice,[3] to the same reproach which he had levelled against the authors of the elegant school. It may be possible to go behind the doctrines of the commentators to the canon law of an earlier and purer age, as it may be possible to go behind the revised texts which Justinian's compilers have left us to the law of classical Rome. It is, however, the doctrines of the commentators which are applied in practice, as it is Justinian's compilations rather than the opinions of the jurists who have been laid under contribution, which are to be taken to have the force of law, and if to seek for historical explanations

[1] G. Astuti, *Mos Italicus e Mos Gallicus nei Dialoghi 'De iuris interpretibus' di Alberico Gentili* (Bologna 1937), 1–7.

[2] *Disputationum de nuptiis libri septem*, lib. 4, chs 4–9 (ed. Hanoviae 1614). The fullest account both of Gentilis's life and of his opinions is now Diego Panizza, *Alberico Gentili, giurista ideologo nell'Inghilterra elisabettiana* (Padova 1981) whose author seems to have been the first of Gentilis's biographers to peruse systematically the fourteen volumes of Gentilis's manuscript remains in the Bodleian Library.

[3] The jurists of the humanist school were more concerned to reconstruct the law of Justinian than that of classical Rome, and their antiquarian tendencies are very easily exaggerated. See, upon this, E. H. Troje, *Graeca Leguntur* (Forschungen zur neueren Privatrechtsgechichte xviii 1971).

of discrepancies between texts which are to be treated as parts of a
code be an activity more proper for the philologist than for the
jurist, to attempt to reconstruct the uncorrupted canon law is a task
for the ecclesiastical historian.

THE REGIUS CHAIR

The first king's professor of civil law, Dr John Story, was excused
his necessary regency in 1538 upon the ground that he was then
delivering the ordinary course in civil law.[1] There is a certain irony
in this entry. Under the thirteenth-century statutes which were still
in force unaltered, the regular delivery of ordinary courses was
theoretically secured by requiring every doctor to remain in the
university for the year of his inception and for the year following as
a necessary, that is, a compulsory regent. The regent doctor was so
called because he ruled over a school, and the delivery of ordinary
lectures was the principal duty of a regent. For rather more than
a century past, however, the *ordinaria* in the two laws had become in
practice the responsibility of the principals of the schools of civil
and canon law,[2] and by the beginning of the sixteenth century this
practice was so well settled that the university could make a formal
offer of the *cathedra* of civil law to a former member who had
incepted at Bologna.[3] The obligations of regency had become merely
ceremonial. The principal of the school was not necessarily the occupant of the *cathedra*. At this date, the principal of the school of civil
law was William Warham, who was also master of the rolls.[4] He was
a doctor of civil law, but it is unlikely that he lectured in person.
So when Dr London attempted to obtain some compensation for the
last principal of the school of canon law he was at pains to stress
that the amount involved would not be large, for the income of his
post had been greatly reduced by his expenses, among them, the
school-rent of his reader.[5] Another of the former principal's claims
upon the royal benevolence is that he paid his predecessor forty
pounds for the office, which seems a high price for an almost value-
less honour. The generosity of Dr London's intention may perhaps
excuse the faults of his reasoning, for he was faced with the task of
arguing simultaneously that the compensation would be no great

[1] Reg. Cong. 1535–63, fo 34[v].

[2] See the previous volume.

[3] *Epist. Acad.* ed. Anstey ii, 658. He declined the offer, and succeeded Warham as
master of the rolls.

[4] *Registrum cancellarii oxoniensis, 1434–1469*, ed. H. E. Salter (2 vols OHS xciii–xciv
1932) 406.

[5] *L. & P. Henry VIII* xi. 430 no. 1184.

burden upon the royal coffers, and that it would be a grave injustice to refuse it. According to the letter of the university statutes, however, the purchaser of a principalship forfeited his school, and was to be fined the same sum which he had paid for it.[1] This statute had apparently fallen so completely into desuetude that it was no longer even thought prudent for those who ignored it to maintain a certain discretion. It is very possible that Warham retained the tenancy of the civil law school, which can hardly have been of any very significant financial advantage to him, because this entitled him to exercise a certain control over the standard of instruction provided, and if he were to part with it his successor might dispose of the school to the highest bidder. One consequence of making the readership in civil law a crown appointment was to give the king this right of supervision. In 1546 the university thought it advisable to ask the king's permission to provide Dr Story with a deputy.[2] The decisive reason for the change, however, was probably that in the later years of Henry VIII the diminution in the number of civilians rendered a civil law chair remunerated only by lecture-fees a somewhat unattractive appointment for an able man.

Thus at the date of Story's appointment a professorial system of teaching had long existed *de facto*. The reader of the ordinary course in civil law was required to lecture upon the *Digestum vetus*[3] and the *Code*[4] in alternate years.[5] The other parts of the *Corpus iuris civilis* were in theory to be lectured upon 'cursorily', by bachelors reading for the doctorate. The Edwardian statutes required merely that the professor should lecture upon some part of the *Code* or *Digest*,[6] and under Elizabeth he was apparently left at liberty to choose what texts he pleased, for the new statutes of 1564 require him to lecture upon four days in every week.[7]

There had been a time at the end of the fifteenth and the beginning of the sixteenth century when it must have seemed to contemporaries that the principalship of the school of one or other law at Oxford was becoming a regular stage upon the road to the woolsack.[8] After the reformation a legist could not aspire so high as this. The offices of lord chancellor and master of the rolls had been captured by the common lawyers, and what they had once obtained

[1] *Statuta*, 79, lines 19–30.

[2] *L. & P. Henry VIII* xxi. pt 1, 473 no. 40 (in a list of documents signed by stamp).

[3] The first of the three parts into which the *Digest* was customarily divided, which ended with title 2 of book 24.

[4] In medieval academic practice, the first nine books of Justinian's twelve.

[5] *Statuta*, 133, lines 5–6.   [6] Ibid. 344, lines 2–4.

[7] Ibid. 381, lines 28–32.

[8] Of Wolsey's five immediate predecessors three, John Russell, John Morton and William Warham were former principals.

they were likely to keep. The new professorship, however, like the old principalship, seems to have been treated by its holders as a stage in their careers rather than as an office which they would expect to hold for the rest of their lives.

Dr Story was first appointed under the sign manual with a salary of forty pounds a year, but in consideration of his service as a military judge at the siege of Boulogne the king granted him the lecture by patent for his life, joining Robert Weston with him for his relief[1] (perhaps at the suggestion of the university).[2] Story, who was firmly attached to the old faith and was eventually to die for it,[3] went abroad at the beginning of the reign of Edward VI. He was re-appointed in 1553 at the beginning of Mary's reign jointly with William Aubrey. Robert Weston entered parliament as member for Exeter in the same year so that it is possible that he was not reappointed, not because he was out of favour with the new sovereign, but because he did not greatly desire to be.[4] Story seems to have been much occupied outside the university and eventually resigned in Aubrey's favour, though he continued to be paid as professor until 1557. Aubrey's academic duties did not prevent him from acting as Judge-Advocate to the English contingent at the siege of St Quentin in that year. A Dr William Mowse, or Mosse, of Cambridge is said to have delivered the lecture for a time.[5] It is clear that Aubrey would have needed a deputy. Since he was to be a particular favourite of Queen Elizabeth, his resignation in the second year of her reign is a sign not that times had changed to his detriment, but that his prospects outside the university were better than his prospects within it.[6] His successor, John Griffith, who held the chair from 1559 to 1566, may have been intended as a stop-gap, for he was not appointed for life like his predecessor and his successor but during the queen's pleasure.[7] He became a man of local importance in his native Wales: he was MP for Carnarvon in 1571, sheriff of the county in 1582–3 and sheriff of Anglesey in 1587,[8] but he did not attain to any national distinction. Robert Lougher, his

[1] Cal. Pat. Rolls (Philip and Mary), 1553–1554, 395.

[2] Page 263 n. 2.

[3] For his life, see the app.

[4] Academically at least, he was rather junior to serve as professor, for he was not admitted doctor until 1556.

[5] Wood, History and Antiquities ii. pt 2, 857. Wood states that Mowse 'succeeded an. 1554, about the latter end of the year, but whether in his own right, or that of Dr. Aubrey, I am uncertain'. Since Aubrey continued to draw his stipend, and Mowse was not paid by the crown, it seems more probable that Mowse was a deputy.

[6] For his subsequent career, see the app.

[7] Foedera, ed. T. Rymer (20 vols 1727–35) xv. 503.

[8] See the app.

successor, held the chair for eleven years. Like his two immediate predecessors he was principal of New Inn Hall, which he left in 1571 to become one of the original fellows of Jesus College. He returned to the hall in 1575 after his successor, Dr Felix Lewes, had been deprived for non-residence. That he was at this time chancellor of the diocese of Exeter, archdeacon of Totnes and rector of no less than three parishes in Devon is not in itself sufficient to convict him of the same offence as Lewes, for it would have been possible to discharge the duties of all these appointments *in absentia*, according to the somewhat relaxed standards of the age. It would on the other hand be surprising if his duties as member of parliament for Pembroke and as master in chancery[1] did not take him away from Oxford upon occasion. Upon his resignation in 1577 Lougher was succeeded by Griffith Lloyd[2] who held the chair for nine years and died in office in 1586, shortly after his election as member of parliament for the county of Cardigan. He may have been somewhat older than his predecessors for he had been chaplain of New College in 1564, and subsequently migrated to All Souls, from which he took his BCL in 1572. He was admitted doctor in 1576. According to Wood:[3]

One Francis James LL.D.,[4] Fellow of the said College[5] and Brother to Dr. James Bishop of Durham (afterwards one of the Masters of Chancery, and Chancellor of Wells) had a patent to succeed him, but never made use of it.

The chair was granted to Albericus Gentilis for his life, with reversion to Dr James after his death or resignation. Gentilis had been Lloyd's deputy,[6] but had left Oxford in the spring of 1586, apparently with the intention of making his career in Germany.[7] Lloyd died on 26 November, and his post was not filled until the following 8 June. No doubt some time would be necessary to induce Dr James to refrain from pressing his claim, but Gentilis may already have succeeded in irritating the godly faction within the university. In 1594, in the course of an increasingly acrimonious correspondence with John Rainolds upon the lawfulness of stage-plays, he mentions that he knows Rainolds to be one of those who had argued that he was disqualified for the chair by the Italian

[1] He was appointed in 1574.
[2] *Cal. Pat. Rolls (Elizabeth), 1563–1566*, 387 no. 2155.
[3] Wood, *History and Antiquities* ii. pt 2, 857.
[4] For James see B. P. Levack, *The Civil Lawyers in England, 1603–1641* (Oxford 1973), 243.   [5] All Souls.
[6] MS d'Orville 612, fo 200, cited by D. Panizzi, *Alberico Gentili, giurista ideologo nell'-Inghilterra elisabettiana*, 50, n. 71.
[7] D. Panizza, op. cit. 50–2.

levity of his character which manifested itself in vainglory and adulation.[1]

He held it for twenty-one years, a longer period than any of his predecessors, and died in office in 1608. The godly faction thought no better of him after his appointment than before, and pursued him with an acrimony which seems in 1593 to have brought him to the point of contemplating resignation.[2] His last years were spent in practice before the court of admiralty, where he held a standing retainer from the king of Spain to argue the causes of Spanish subjects.[3] His successor, Dr John Budden, was recommended to King James as having read the civil law lecture since the departure of Dr Gentilis.[4] Gentilis's lectures were being read by a deputy as early as 1590,[5] but this deputy can hardly have been Budden, who had turned to the law from arts, and had accumulated the degrees in 1602.

In the period covered by this volume, Gentilis is the only professor who could be described as a professional scholar, and the only one to leave behind him any considerable body of published work. We have very little material for judging the attainments of his predecessors. There was no great market in England for scholarly works on the civil law, and for the professor who hoped to go on to employments of greater distinction and greater profit outside the university such glory among his peers as he might gain by publication was hardly worth the effort required to obtain it. Indeed, Gentilis himself turned progressively to what we should describe as questions of international law and political theory, which, in an age which still believed in the law of nature, were not distinct subjects. Gentilis commended Griffith Lloyd as a sound conservative. He observes in the *De iuris interpretibus* that he is not so widely read as he could wish in the literature of the elegant school, for his teaching duties have the first call upon his time, and his pupils, thanks to the beneficent influence of Professor Griffith Lloyd, desire solid and genuine legal knowledge rather than the delicate pages of the moderns.[6] A written argument which Aubrey prepared for use in the great cause upon the validity of the clandestine marriage between Lady Katherine Grey and Edward Seymour earl of Hertford which survives among the Tanner manuscripts in the Bodleian Library

[1] D. Panizza, op. cit. 51 and n. 74.   [2] Ibid. 76 and n. 75.

[3] A collection of his arguments in these causes was published posthumously in 1613 under the title of *Advocationes hispanicae* and was reprinted in 1921 by the Carnegie Endowment for International Peace.

[4] *Cal. SP Dom. (James I), 1603–1610*, 489, no. 48.

[5] Wood, *History and Antiquities* ii. pt 1, 242.

[6] *De Iuris interpretibus dialogi sex*, ed. G. Astuti (Turin 1937), at p. 7

shows him to have been an accomplished canonist.[1] For the rest, we can say only that a professor would have reason not to perform his duties in a manner so manifestly insufficient as to prejudice the continuance of that royal favour upon which his future career would depend.

THE STATUTORY SYLLABUS

When our period opens, the doctor *ordinarie legens* was supposed to read his ordinary course upon every legible day during term. According to the statutes, the other courses in the legal faculties were to be provided by bachelors who wished to proceed to the doctorate, and were required to qualify themselves by teaching their juniors. The student of the civil law who had attended *ordinaria* for six years (or for four, if he had previously completed his regency in arts) might be presented for the licence to lecture upon the *Institutes*. When he had completed this course, he was eligible to be licensed *ad volumina*, and must then deliver a course of one year's duration upon each of the two extraordinary parts of the *Digest*.[2] He was then required to read a further course, either upon one of the three extraordinary books of the *Code*[3] or upon one *collatio* of the *Authenticum*,[4] and would finally be entitled to incept, after he had opposed and responded at least once in every school of the decretists and had deputized for every master reading ordinary lectures in his faculty.[5] Before the canonist could be presented for the baccalaureate he must have studied the civil law for three years and the *Decretum* for two years, and have heard the *Decretals complete*. If he then wished to proceed to the doctorate his burden of lecturing was not so heavy as that imposed upon the civilian. He must lecture *extraordinarie* either upon two or three *causae* of the *Decretum*, or alternatively upon one of its three *tractatus, De symonia, De consecratione*, or *De penitentia*, and also upon one book of the *Decretals*, though he was obliged like the civilian to deputize for every master reading *ordinarie* in his faculty. He was also required, however, to attend lectures on the *Decretum* for a further year, to hear the *Decretals complete* a second time, and to attend Bible lectures for two years.[6]

The statutory form had remained substantially unchanged since

---

[1] Bodl. Tanner MS 193.

[2] The *Infortiatum* (from title 3 of book 24 to the end of book 38), and the *Digestum novum* (books 39–50).

[3] Books 10–12.

[4] The *Authenticum* was a collection of constitutions issued after the promulgation of the *Code*, in a Latin version. It was traditionally divided into nine *collationes*.

[5] *Statuta*, 43–5.

[6] *Statuta*, 46–7.

the early years of the fourteenth century. It was, however, within the powers of congregation to grant a member of the university who had not completed the form required by the statutes a 'grace' to proceed to his degree upon such evidence of his sufficiency as might be thought acceptable, and by the beginning of our period, and indeed long before, the actual practice of the two legal faculties had ceased to correspond even approximately to that envisaged by the statutes. Generalization, however, is very difficult. Between 1530 and 1535 the shortest period of study offered for the baccalaureate in either law is two years for the BCL.[1] The longest is the sixteen years in both laws which Donatus Ream, the reader in canon law at New Inn Hall, offered for the BCnL.[2] It is possible that Donatus Ream was proposing to look for an appointment elsewhere. There were still many purposes for which a period of legal study was essential but a degree was not indispensable, and a candidate might supplicate not at the earliest moment at which he thought the degree which he asked was likely to be granted, but when he had reached a stage of his career at which it would be an embarrassment not to have it. In 1534 Hugh Hollande offers three years of study in the university and the fact that he is a bishop's official as his form for the BCnL.[3] Almost the only general conclusion which the registers unequivocally support is that by the early years of the sixteenth century it was no longer thought necessary to insist that the canonist should have studied the civil law for a certain minimum period. Canonists frequently claim to have studied only in their own faculty, but there is no instance in which a grace is made conditional upon attendance at civil law lectures. On the other hand, a canonist's grace may be conditioned upon his lecturing upon the title *De actionibus* of the *Institutes*,[4] so that it was perhaps assumed that the canonist who did not attend civil law *ordinaria* would receive the necessary grounding in the subject in his hall. A candidate for the baccalaureate in either faculty is frequently required to lecture or to dispute. Ordinarily, though not quite invariably, the candidate who states that he has already delivered lectures will escape. Seniority by itself is no protection. In 1531 John Massey, who had studied the civil law for two and a half years and had read an extraordinary lecture publicly in a hall

---

[1] Reg. Cong. 1518–35, fo 242ᵛ.

[2] Ibid. fo 275.   [3] Ibid. fo 306ᵛ.

[4] See the graces of Henry Gambon (8 February 1531/2, ibid. 262), George Robyns (June 1532, ibid. fo 272) and David Powel (28 April 1532, ibid. fo 268). Powel may have been a special case. He had already supplicated on 17 April, when he had been assigned the title *De appellationibus*, presumably in the *Decretals* though this is not stated. His fate was perhaps intended as a warning that the candidate who supplicated a second time in the hope of getting rid of a condition of his grace might find his last state worse than his first.

of the same faculty, received his grace for the BCL without conditions.[1] Earlier in the same year John Cryse BCL, who had studied both laws for twelve years, was required to lecture upon two distinctions of the *Decretum* for his BCnL.[2] Lecturing conditions may have served incidentally to provide instruction for junior members of the faculty, but they seem to have been imposed primarily to ensure that the candidate did not receive his degree too easily. In 1532 no fewer than nine candidates were required to lecture on the title *De actionibus* of the *Institutes*. It is hardly probable that there was a genuine educational need for so large a number of courses upon the same portion of the same text.

The bachelor who wished to proceed to the doctorate was still at liberty to read for his form in the old manner, and some few did. In 1527 John Farre, who as a fellow of New College was forbidden either to ask or to make use of a dispensation from any part of his statutory course, asked leave to vary the time and place of his lectures. Leave was granted upon condition that he lectured for a quarter of an hour at the least.[3] Congregation appears to assume that if a bachelor does deliver his statutory cursories they will prove 'wall lectures'. Indeed in 1523, George Wever received a grace for the BCL conditional upon his lecturing upon *one title* of the *Institutes* before he proceeded to the doctorate.[4] It was apparently quite conceivable that a civilian might be admitted to the doctorate without delivering any lectures at all. We have no evidence so specific as this for the canonists, but there is no good reason to think that they were held any more strictly to the requirements of the statutes. It is usual in both faculties for the candidate for the doctorate to state that he has delivered lectures: teaching was an obvious means by which the senior canonist or legist who remained in residence might support himself. They do not state that they have completed their statutory form, or even that the lectures which they have delivered were statutory lectures. We may suspect, indeed, that they usually were not. Hall lectures were paid. The statutes say nothing of payment for cursories.

AULARIAN INSTRUCTION

The decline of the statutory cursory and extraordinary courses, like the decay of necessary regency, began well before our period. The reason apparently was that as the halls began to provide tuition for their own members to supplement the ordinary courses, the

---

[1] Ibid. fo 255^V.   [2] Ibid. fo 245^V.
[3] Ibid. fo 168.   [4] Ibid. fo 109^V.

bachelors lost their auditors. Aularian instruction was not regulated by statute, so that we have very little evidence of the manner in which it was organized. According to Cardinal Pole's injunctions of 1556, which were designed to re-establish the ancient discipline, the students in legist halls were to have a morning lecture on the *Institutes*, which the juniors were to be obliged to attend, and upon at least three days in every week they were also to attend a repetition of it after dinner. Over dinner all the students were to exercise themselves in case-putting: a practice which may have been borrowed from the inns of court.[1] The students of one year's standing and above who would be attending the professor's lectures were to take their turns to dispute.[2] The ancient discipline was perhaps not altogether so systematic. We do hear of case-putting in halls in February 1527/8,[3] but the duties of the hall lecturer and the professor were not so clearly distinguished. Hall lectures might be delivered upon the *Code* and *Digest*.[4]

RECRUITMENT AND CAREERS

By tradition, the faculty of civil law had been as clerical a faculty as that of canon law, and though it was perhaps not strictly necessary that a civilian who proposed to serve the king should be in orders it had been both customary and desirable. The services of a cleric might be rewarded with benefices, at no expense to the royal coffers. After the breach with Rome to employ clerics in the great offices of state would have been too offensive to that anti-clerical sentiment upon which the king was obliged to rely for support, and in the new conciliar courts the civilians usually served in a subordinate capacity. The formidable Dr Roland Lee, president of the council of Wales and of the Marches, was an exception.[5] It was becoming the practice for masterships in chancery to be given to civilians. Indeed, at the beginning of the reign of Edward VI the earl of Southampton lost the chancellorship after certain 'students of the common law' had complained by petition that he was in the habit of delegating his judicial duties to subordinates who were civilians not learned in the common law. Though this was the pretext rather than the cause of his removal, it shows that the civilians by this date were more

---

[1] See W. R. Prest, *The Inns of Court under Elizabeth I and the Early Stuarts, 1590–1640* (1972), 117.

[2] *Statuta*, 372, lines 16–32.

[3] Reg. Cong. 1518–35, fo 186 (the graces of Eustace and Trubody). It is not clear why these two candidates should have mentioned case-putting expressly. It was certainly not usual to do so.

[4] Ibid. fo 196.   [5] For his life, see *DNB, sub nom.*

prominent in the chancery than their rivals thought proper.[1] The reorganized court of admiralty provided more employment than it had formerly done. The limited degree of advancement which the professed civilian might hope for was, however, a deterrent to the ambitious, and the new opportunities of subordinate employment were not so numerous as to make the faculty very attractive to those who would be content with a competence but wished to be secure of it. The most obvious reason for taking a degree in either law, rather than in arts, had been that the legal graduate might supplement his income by practice in one or other of the ecclesiastical courts which covered the country, and would have better opportunities of making himself useful to his bishop. The legist or canonist who left the university without a doctorate had had a reasonable prospect of ending his days as a pluralist upon a modest but comfortable scale.[2] Edward VI's professor of civil law at Cambridge, the learned Sir Thomas Smith, in an inaugural lecture which was intended to give his auditors the rosiest possible view of the prospects of the legal graduate principally stressed the opportunities of diplomatic employment, and the value of a legal degree as a qualification for the more desirable benefices in the church.[3] The king did not require a very large number of ambassadors, and in the reign of Edward VI the future of the ecclesiastical jurisdiction was sufficiently uncertain to entitle contemporaries to doubt whether a degree in law would remain a qualification for ecclesiastical preferment for very much longer.[4]

ATTEMPTS AT GOVERNMENTAL ENCOURAGEMENT: THE PROPOSED LEGIST COLLEGE

How far the law faculty had decayed in the last years of Henry VIII it is difficult to be sure. In 1544 and again in 1545 there are only four admissions to the BCL and none to the doctorate.[5] There is a solitary inception in 1546.[6] In 1547 two candidates are *admissi*

---

[1] APC 1547-50, 48. The ill feeling continued. See The History of the Chancery, relating to the Judicial Power of that Court and the Rights of the Masters (1726), 36 for the complaint of a senior Master under Philip and Mary, that the civilians who are now appointed to the court know nothing of the forms of the writs for which they are nominally responsible.

[2] I am indebted for this information to Dr Gregor Duncan, who has been kind enough to communicate to me the results of his investigations of the careers of bachelors in the period immediately preceding the reformation.

[3] J. B. Mullinger, The University of Cambridge from the Earliest Times to the Royal Injunctions of 1535 (Cambridge 1873), 131 ff.

[4] See R. A. Houlbrooke, Church Courts and the People during the English Reformation (Oxford 1979), esp. 8-20.

[5] Reg. Cong. 1535-63, fos 98^V, 104^V.

[6] Ibid. fo 110.

in legibus.[1] There is then nothing at all until 1552. In this year, however, a justly incensed university finally dismissed its registrar for gross neglect of the duties of his office. One of the charges held proved against him was that he had omitted to register any of the degrees which had been conferred in the previous year.[2] Any argument, therefore, which is founded merely upon the silence of the registers is more than ordinarily hazardous, but the faculty was sufficiently decayed for the government to be anxious that the visitors of 1549 should take steps to encourage it. The course suggested was that they should establish a college of legists, which was to be formed by transferring the legists of New College to All Souls, and the artists of All Souls to New College. They were also to consider founding a medical college, to which the existing medical fellowships might be attached.[3] Similar instructions were given to the visitors of the university of Cambridge.[4] Henry VIII's visitors had been considering this proposal when their commission lapsed by the demise of the crown.[5] It had aroused vigorous opposition then, and on this second occasion the opposition proved strong enough to defeat it, for the protector's position was not so strong that he could override opposition in the manner of the old king.[6] The visitors did, however, provide the faculty with its first new syllabus of studies since the fourteenth century, which is set out in the statutes of 1549.

THE EDWARDIAN STATUTES

The candidate for the degree of bachelor of civil law was now required to spend his first year in attendance at lectures upon the *Institutes* in his hall or college. For a further five years, he must attend the professor's lectures. During this time he must dispute publicly three times, and declaim twice upon legal questions. Bachelors of arts might take the degree after four years, upon performing the same exercises. The bachelor who wished to proceed to the doctorate must

[1] Reg. Cong. 1535–63, fo 114^V.

[2] Ibid. fo 130^V. The folios which should contain the graces and admissions between 1549 and 1551 have been torn out of the register, perhaps to hinder investigation. At Cambridge, however, where the registers are complete, there were only eight admissions to the baccalaureate and one to the doctorate between 1544 and 1551.

[3] *Foedera* xv. 183.

[4] The material part of the commission is set out in J. B. Mullinger, *The University of Cambridge from the Royal Injunctions of 1535 to the Accession of Charles I* (Cambridge 1884), 133, note 2.

[5] *L. & P. Henry VIII*, xxi. pt 2, 147 no. 321.

[6] For the fate of the proposal at Cambridge see Mullinger, *Cambridge from the Royal Injunctions*, 133–8 and M. Dewar, *Sir Thomas Smith, a Tudor intellectual in office* (1964), 40–2. The opposition at Oxford is not so well documented, but it evidently proved successful.

attend lectures for a further three years, and dispute and respond twice. A master of arts might take the doctorate after five years' study, performing the same exercises as a bachelor of civil law. After inception the new-made doctor was required to devote himself to the study of the laws of England, and it was provided that at every *comitia* one of the disputants was to determine the question comparatively, explaining the differences between the civil law, the ecclesiastical law and the law of England.[1] The obligatory disputations and declamations seem to have been envisaged very much as minimum requirements. Disputations were to be held in the faculty three times in every term. The doctors were to preside in their turns though bachelors of three years' standing and Masters of Arts might also do so. On each occasion New College was to provide four disputants, and the other societies of legists two.[2] According to the 'interpretations or emendations or additions', New College was to provide two disputants, All Souls two, and the other societies one.[3] Declamations were to take place weekly, and two bachelors were to declaim on each occasion.[4]

THE QUESTION OF THE MARIAN STATUTES

The Edwardian code was revoked at the beginning of Mary's reign, and the masters newly created in 1553 were required to swear that they would observe the ancient statutes of the university.[5] This was necessarily an interim measure. The Edwardian statutes might be unacceptable, but it was more than a century since the practice of the university had much resembled that prescribed by the old statutes, and to require that they should now be strictly followed would have been neither very practical nor particularly desirable. A committee was appointed to prepare new statutes[6] and may have completed at least a part of its work, for in 1558 we find Thomas Powell praying, after a full description of his merits and industry, that if through absence or illness he have not fully completed the form of the new statutes in attendance at ordinary lectures or otherwise this may be graciously pardoned him.[7] This explicit reference to the

---

[1] *Statuta*, 345, line 29–346, line 11.

[2] *Statuta*, 348, lines 3–12.

[3] *Statuta*, 359, lines 12–17. This is presumably a consequence of the abandonment of the plan for a legist college, though under the terms of the visitors' commission it was All Souls rather than New College which was to become a purely legal foundation.

[4] *Statuta* 348, lines 26–9.

[5] Reg. Cong. 1535–63, fo 138[V].

[6] Ibid. fo 136[V].

[7] '. . . ut si formam novorum statutorum vel propter absentiam vel egritudinem minus impleuerit in ordinariis lectionibus frequentandis, id gratiose ei condonetur.' Ibid. fo 174[V].

new statutes appears to be unique, but a number of other candidates of this year pray in rather similar terms to be excused any irregularities of which they may have been guilty. By November, however, the university was appointing a committee to draft a letter of congratulation to Elizabeth upon her succession to the throne,[1] and if the new statutes in truth existed they appear to be lost.

THE NOVA STATUTA OF 1564

It is perhaps a debatable question what statutes should be deemed to have been in force in the early years of the reign of Elizabeth I. In practice the candidate ordinarily states merely that he has completed a certain period of study, and if the university be unwilling to grant him his grace *simpliciter*, he is commonly let off with a disputation or two. These conditions are not taken over-seriously. In 1559 two candidates asked leave to dispute privately because they could find no one to preside over their public disputations. They were thereupon required to read an ordinary lecture and to provide a gallon of wine for the regents.[2] The shortest period of study required in practice for the baccalaureate seems to have been four years. A new official syllabus was finally introduced in 1564 by the *nova statuta* which remained 'new' until they were replaced by the Laudian code in the following century. The candidate for the BCL was now required to attend the professor's lectures for five years, or for three if he were a master of arts. During this period he must dispute once *pro forma* in the theological school for one hour upon two questions. The senior was to respond and the juniors, provided that there were not more than three of them, were to oppose.[3] The bachelor who wished to proceed to the doctorate was required to attend lectures for a further four years and to deliver either six lectures upon a legal subject of his own choosing, or six cursory lectures upon one of the three titles *De iudiciis, De probationibus* or *De re iudicata*.[4] All legist fellows of colleges and all bachelors of civil law residing at their own cost in colleges or halls with the exception of principals of halls, were to take part in their turns in the faculty disputations. These were now to take place once only in every alternate term. Three were to

[1] Reg. Cong. 1535–63, fo 178^V.

[2] Ibid. fos 189^V, 190^V. Disputing conditions seem to have been most popular in 1559–60, when they are attached to more than three-quarters of the graces.

[3] *Statuta*, 380, 379 (many of the requirements in the statutes for the legal faculty are incorporated by reference from the statutes for the medical faculty, which are upon the previous page).

[4] *Statuta*, 380.

dispute on each occasion, the senior responding and the two juniors opposing. These disputations, however, were not to count *pro forma*.[1] Congregation was to have no power to dispense a bachelor from his disputation or a doctor from his lectures.[2]

If we compare these statutes with the Edwardian code, they are at once more conservative and less optimistic. In accordance with older tradition only the master of arts receives any allowance of time in consideration of his previous studies. The useless cursory lectures are revived. The programme of exercises envisaged by the statutes of 1549 has apparently been found altogether too ambitious. Only a single formal disputation is now required of the bachelor. Not only are the faculty disputations far less frequent, the student who is reading for the baccalaureate need not take part in them unless he be a foundation fellow. Of all the degrees which the university offers the baccalaureate in civil law is the most easily gained.

The Elizabethan practice

It was to remain so until the examination system was reformed in the nineteenth century. By the beginning of the eighteenth century it had come to be accepted that the faculty of civil law served as a comfortable refuge for the student with a distaste for intellectual exertion, who felt that to complete the exercises required for a degree in arts would demand an unreasonable amount of effort.[3] There is a suggestive incident as early as 1573. Edward Prise, who had studied for his statutory five years, supplicated that he might be admitted BCL after he had completed his form. He received his grace upon condition that he obtained the consent of the professor.[4] Twelve days later he supplicated again, stating that he had completed the whole of his statutory form, and received his grace *simpliciter*.[5] It would seem that he decided upon reflection that to complete his form was a lesser ordeal than to face the professor. Occasionally a candidate who has completed his form is required to obtain the professor's consent before he takes his degree.[6] This is not strictly regular. The university still maintained that a candidate who had done all that the statutes required of him was in strictness not obliged to ask a grace at all,[7] so that to impose a condition on his

---

[1] *Statuta*, 384, line 35–385, line 5.
[2] *Statuta*, 380, line 15; 379, lines 22–3; 380, line 22; 379, lines 37–40.
[3] See Humphrey Prideaux's suggestions for reform in C. Wordsworth, *Social Life at the English Universities in the Eighteenth Century* (Cambridge 1874), 556.
[4] Reg. Cong. 1564–82, fo 146 (the grace has been cancelled).
[5] Ibid. fo 147[V].
[6] See, for example, the grace of William Wytthey for the BCL, ibid. fo 265[V].
[7] *Statuta*, 378, lines 1–3.

grace was a questionable course. It is perhaps a sign that congregation was aware that the statutory exercises for the BCL were not a very exacting test of attainment, and was willing to do its best to discourage candidates of whose sufficiency there was any serious doubt. For the doctorate we have a hint of another requirement. In 1566 Dr White appealed to convocation. It was the immemorial custom for the doctors of civil law in the university to meet together to consider the merits of the candidates for inception in their faculty. His colleagues had held a meeting to consider the merits of Edward Mericke, archdeacon of Bangor, without notice to him.[1] There is no record of any decision, but Mericke's inception was certainly postponed to the following year.[2]

AULARIAN INSTRUCTION AND PRIVATE TUITION

Mericke had obtained what was at this period the common form of grace, that three bachelors might depose for him in lieu of doctors because of the paucity of doctors in the university.[3] Dr White complains that the 'college' of doctors of civil law has met without him. Any undergraduate member of the faculty let alone its senior resident doctor would have been aware that *tres faciunt collegium*,[4] and that to speak of a 'college' of less than three members is a contradiction in terms. It would seem, therefore, that a doctor who is absent from the university for some purposes may be deemed present for others, and that the form of *supplicat* which comes into use towards the end of the century, which states that the resident doctors are too busy to perform this duty,[5] is nearer to the truth whether or not it be literally exact. It was not, apparently, anticipated that there would be any difficulty in finding a doctor in the university if he might hope to receive a fee when found. A statute of 1594 provided that if the professor declined to preside over a disputation *pro forma* the disputants should be at liberty to ask any other doctor of the faculty to moderate, and he should receive the fee for their presentation.[6] It was not thought necessary to provide what should be done if there were no doctor to be had.

That statements in the registers about the paucity or the absence of doctors are to be taken in a special sense is a matter of some importance when we turn to the very difficult question what other

---

[1] Reg. Cong. 1564–82, fo 30^V. [2] Ibid. fo 47^V.
[3] Ibid. fo 29^V. [4] *Digest*, 50.16.85.
[5] See, for example, Reg. Cong. 1595–1606, fo 79^V.
[6] *Statuta*, 452. It is possible, however, that we owe this statute to the godly faction, and that it is intended to suggest that Gentilis was likely to neglect his duties, rather than to serve any practical need.

instruction, in addition to the professor's statutory lectures, was available to the Elizabethan legist. By the end of our period the decline in the number of those who proposed to make the civil law their career had led to the disappearance of the traditional exercises in the legist halls. By the later years of the sixteenth century there were more legist fellowships in the colleges than there were intending civil lawyers to fill them. The future Mr Justice Whitelocke had resolved to become a common lawyer before he arrived at the university. Thanks to the tolerant attitude of the fellows of St John's he was able to hold a civil law fellowship at that college while studying at his Inn of Court.[1] This tolerance may not have been wholly disinterested for the law fellowships at St John's served primarily to enable those fellows who felt no vocation for the clerical life to postpone the moment when they would be obliged either to take orders or to leave the college,[2] and the future judge would not have been the only person inconvenienced by a pedantic insistence upon the letter of the founder's statutes. The legists of All Souls did not find it so easy to betake themselves to the study of the common law because of the unaccommodating attitude of their visitor,[3] but it is significant that even at All Souls it was thought an adequate sanction for a failure to deliver those lectures on the *Institutes* which were still required by the college statutes, though no longer by those of the university, that the defaulter should be deemed a canonist and required to take holy orders.[4] If it were difficult to find serious students to fill the endowed fellowships in the subject, the number of serious students studying in halls at their own cost would hardly be large enough to enable a principal to assemble enough of them under one roof to keep up the traditional exercises. When Dr Lewes was deprived of his principalship of New Inn Hall in 1575 the members of the hall were asked whether he had read any law lecture either personally or by deputy during the previous twelve months, but they were also asked whether he had read any lecture of logic or humanity during the same period. Though they answered in the negative to both interrogatories the ground of deprivation stated in the sentence was that Dr Lewes had absented himself from Oxford for more than a month during term without the leave of the vice-chancellor.[5] What instruction the principal of a legist hall could be held bound to provide, and how far

[1] *The Liber famelicus of Sir James Whitelocke* (Camden Society lxx 1858), 13–15.

[2] W. H. Stevenson and H. E. Salter, *The Early History of St. John's College* (OHS new ser. i. 1939), 249.

[3] *SCO*, i. pt 7 (All Souls) 119.   [4] Ibid. 91.

[5] OUA NEP *supra* 45, fo 6, fo 10. From fo 11^V of the same file it appears that New Inn Hall had five members (of whom one was absent) at the visitation of 1580.

it was reasonable to punish him for not providing it, seem to have been delicate questions which were better avoided if it were clear that he was liable to be deprived upon some less controversial ground. There are two distinct sets of articles for use in the visitation of halls which bear the name of Dr Hovenden, vice-chancellor in 1583. One contains a special interrogatory for 'houses appointed for law' in which the members of the house are asked whether the daily lecture, the weekly disputation, and the case-putting over dinner are regularly kept up. The second set is virtually identical to the first save that studies are dealt with in a single interrogatory which does not mention the law, and which appears to assume that the principal will provide instruction in arts.[1] This was the form which Dr Hoveden's successors used. It is tempting to conjecture that it was in 1583 that the university authorities were finally obliged to acknowledge that it was useless to contend that any principal was under a duty even to treat the maintenance of the old exercises as an ideal to which he should aspire, let alone to maintain them in practice.

To abandon the traditional exercises was not necessarily to abandon the study of the law. There was nothing to prevent a student from making private arrangements or his tutor from making them on his behalf. Thus we are told that John Budden, who was to succeed Gentilis as professor, migrated from Trinity College to Gloucester Hall after his BA 'for the sake, and at the request of Mr Thomas Allen'.[2] Mr Thomas Allen was well known in his day as a discriminating patron of promising young scholars, and could be trusted to ensure that a *protégé* of his was not neglected. Indeed, to migrate to a hall was the natural course for any senior member of the university who wished to turn to the law and whose college statutes did not provide for legal study.[3] Private arrangements unhappily leave no trace upon public records, but since the responsibility for making them was upon the student himself or upon the tutor to whom his parents had entrusted him, it would have been

---

[1] OUA NEP *supra* 45, fo 16; fo 21.

[2] Wood, *Athenae* ii. 282–3. For Thomas Allen see ibid. i. 76–8.

[3] A 'Mr. Tycheborne' of Gloucester Hall, who was presumably a master of arts, whose goods were seized in 1569, and William Smallwood MA of the same hall, who died in 1572, both possessed extensive collections of legal works: in the case of the latter, exclusively of works upon the canon law. William Stocker MA, commoner of Broadgates Hall, who seems to have died at about the same period, had the commentaries of Hebereda on the *Clementines* and of Dominicus de Sancto Geminiano on the *Sext*, in addition to a glossed *Corpus iuris canonici*. The inventories of books which were made by order of the chancellor's court have been collected by the industry of the keeper of the archives, but since a scholar's goods were inventoried only if he died in the university, or absconded from it leaving his debts unpaid, the sample is somewhat biased in favour of senior men and non-studying students.

entirely possible for a legist residing in a hall to lead a very idle life if he chose to do so.[1] Those colleges which had law fellowships also had law lecturers,[2] and the system of compulsory exercises had not been allowed to fall into disuse, though it is impossible from surviving records to determine the degree of zeal with which it was kept up. Though there would be instruction available in a college for the legist who desired to study his subject it is questionable whether the pressure upon a legist who did not would be very severe. Among Gentilis's minor works there are two orations which he delivered at the *comitia* when pupils of his were admitted to the doctorate, which were published together in 1607 under the title of *Laudes Academiae Perusinae et Oxoniensis*. The university of Perugia where Gentilis had taken his degree is commended for its admirably systematic lecture-courses and the rigour of its examinations. Oxford is praised for the excellent discipline of its colleges, and the licenciate, one Ezo Tiarda, a German,[3] is congratulated upon receiving his degree from a university superior in point of antiquity to any in his native country. Those features of the academic life of Oxford which are not thought to afford any scope for encomium are perhaps as significant as those mentioned.

THE FACULTY AND THE PROFESSION

It was self-evident that the civil law approached more nearly to the rational ideal of the law of nature than did any other positive system. A man who was wholly ignorant of it could hardly deserve the character of an accomplished gentleman. Even the unworldly Latimer held that grammar, logic, rhetoric and the civil law (in addition of course to the word of God) would be an ideal syllabus of studies to qualify the sons of the aristocracy to serve their God and their king as they should.[4] There was no need for a gentleman to enter the faculty of civil law, however, in order to obtain that knowledge of the subject which was proper for his station. At the end of the seventeenth century it was very usual for an undergraduate reading the arts course to be taken through the *Institutes* as part of his grounding in moral and political philosophy,[5] but for a student who was not proposing to qualify himself for doctors' commons to prefer

---

[1] According to Nicholas Fitzherbert, the halls of his time were distinguished from the colleges principally by more expensive living and slacker discipline: *Elizabethan Oxford*, ed. C. Plummer (OHS viii 1886), 16.

[2] *SCO* i pt 7, 89; Hastings Rashdall and Robert S. Rait, *New College* (1901), 139; Stevenson and Salter, *Early History of St. John's*, 253.

[3] He was admitted in 1603.

[4] Mark H. Curtis, *Oxford and Cambridge in Transition, 1558–1642* (Oxford 1959), 69.

[5] *The Flemings in Oxford*, ed. J. R. Magrath (OHS xliv 1903, lxxii 1913) ii. 256,

law to arts would be taken as evidence of a distaste for study. When
Gentilis in his early years at Oxford was obliged to make ends meet
by taking private pupils, he was tutor to Anthony Sherley and the
two Paulet brothers.[1] Sherley took a degree in arts from All Souls,
and became an extremely colourful and consistently unsuccessful
adventurer.[2] The social position of the Paulet brothers made it
unnecessary for them to take degrees at all, though the elder, who
was to attain a certain celebrity as a particulary oppressive governor
of Jersey,[3] may have been created master of arts in middle life.[4]
Sherley at least had progressed well beyond the elements of the
subject, for he is the addressee of a letter upon the proper method of
solving antinomies in the *Digest* which gives an admirably concise
and lucid account of Gentilis's views upon textual interpretation,
but which would not have been very suitable fare for a student of
the *Institutes*.[5] Robert Beale, who was clerk of the council under
Elizabeth, and who had a considerable reputation both as a civilian
and as a canonist, wrote upon one occasion to Whitgift that '. . .
by the space of twenty-six years and upwards he has been a student
of the civil laws, and long sith could have taken a degree if he had
thought (as some do) that the substance of learning consisteth more
in form and title than in matter'.[6]

The tone is perhaps slightly defensive but the suggestion that to
proceed to a degree would be a little vulgar is unmistakable. Sir William
Petre, the second founder of Exeter College, was a legist of the old
school[7] who at the time of the reformation was not yet irrevocably
committed to a clerical career. He served as secretary of state to
every monarch from Henry VIII to Elizabeth I inclusive, and instead
of ending his days in one of the better-endowed bishoprics became
the founder of a substantial family.[8] He made no provision for legist

257. Cf. T. Wood, *Some Thoughts concerning the Study of the Laws of England in the
Two Universities* (1708), 4: '. . . young Men think themselves obliged to read an *Institute*
of the Imperial Law, and a Comment upon the Title *De Regulis Juris*, and then to study
Grotius and *Puffendorff*.'

[1] For Sherley see Gentilis, *Lectionum et epistularum quae ad ius civile pertinent* (Lib. II
1583) book 1, 13. For the Paulets, see book 3 ch. 1. I have not had access to the third
book, which was published (with the other two) in London in 1584, but the relevant
passage is quoted in G. Speranza, *Alberico Gentili* (Rome 1876), 99 n. 25.

[2] For his life, see *DNB*. He has sometimes been confused with the poet.

[3] *DNB*, in the life of their father, Amyas Paulet.

[4] Foster, *Alumni, sub nom.*

[5] Gentilis, *Lectionum et Epistularum* Lib. II book 1, ch. 13.

[6] Cited from his life in the *DNB*.

[7] He took the baccalaureate in both laws in 1526, became principal of Peckwater Inn
about 1527, and in 1529 was appointed an additional proctor for the king in his matrimonial cause with Catherine of Aragon. He took his doctorate (in civil law) in 1533.

[8] He acted as Cromwell's vice-gerent when Cromwell was the king's vicar-general, and

fellowships but he did provide that if any fellow upon his foundation wished to travel abroad to study civil law or medicine, he should be entitled to leave of absence as of course.[1] He too seems to have been of opinion that a knowledge of the civil law was valuable, but that to enrol in the faculty at Oxford was not necessarily the best way to obtain it.

THE CAREERS OF CIVILIANS

The doctorate was a necessary qualification for membership of doctors' commons. Of the forty-nine doctors whose admissions are regularly recorded between 1571 and the end of the reign of Elizabeth[2] thirty-five became advocates of the court of arches.[3] Another four held judicial appointments in the ecclesiastical courts,[4] and two more were episcopal vicars-general.[5] Of the remaining eight, three may be described as mere clerics. Robert Salisbury of Jesus[6] was a country clergyman, Isaac Upton of Magdalen[7] a canon of Wells, and John Favour of New College a north-country divine noted for his charities,[8] who may have become a legist because the faculty which a fellow of New College was required to enter depended upon seniority of election rather than upon his personal choice. Giles Lawrence of All Souls, the regius professor of Greek,[9] also probably took his degrees in the faculty because he had been elected to a legist fellowship. Gabriel Harvey, MA of Cambridge, should perhaps be classified as another academic, since he aspired unsuccessfully to become master of Trinity Hall.[10] His motives for taking his degree was considered for appointment as dean of the arches, but, perhaps wisely, preferred to make his career in the royal administration rather than in the ecclesiastical courts. For his life, see F. G. Emmison, *A Tudor Secretary* (1961).

[1] C. W. Boase, *Register of . . . Exeter College, Oxford* (OHS xxvii 1894), p. xciv.

[2] It is difficult to give precise figures, first, because not every admission is duly registered, and secondly, because it is not wholly clear how many of those registered should be included. I have ignored incorporations *ad eundem*, but have included all those who appear to have stood in the act, even if they received their graces largely upon the strength of studies pursued elsewhere.

[3] For lists of the members of doctors' commons, and of known advocates who were not members, see G. D. Squibb, *Doctors' Commons* (Oxford 1977), apps. 3 and 4.

[4] Richard Percy of Christ Church, admitted 1578; William Merick of New College, admitted 1582; Zachary Babington of Merton, who accumulated the degrees in 1599. The fourth was William Wilkinson of Cambridge, who is perhaps a doubtful case, but appears to have been admitted rather than incorporated doctor in 1593.

[5] William Jones (Bath and Wells), admitted 1574, and John Daye of Magdalen, his successor, admitted 1579.

[6] Admitted 1578.   [7] Admitted 1583.

[8] Admitted 1592. See Wood, *Athenae* ii. 353–4.

[9] Admitted 1578.

[10] Admitted 1585. See C. Crawley, *Trinity Hall* (Cambridge 1976), 64–7.

at Oxford rather than at Cambridge where he had studied and had indeed obtained his grace are not very obvious. Francis Betts of New College who was admitted in 1592, died the year after taking his degree. Edward Spurway of All Souls received permission to substitute a lecture for his *responsio in vesperiis*, because his deafness made it impossible for him to dispute.[1] Whatever career he had in view, it can hardly have been that of advocate or judge. There seems to be nothing further known of Robert Whitmore who took his doctorate in 1575.

The newly admitted advocate was no more certain to gain a living by his profession than was the newly admitted barrister.[2] Not by any means all of our advocates were able to support themselves by the law, but it seems clear that the majority of those who proceeded to the doctorate took the degree as a professional qualification. Half of the remainder were apparently legist fellows who would take the degree if they wished to remain in the university since they were obliged either to proceed in the faculty or to give up their fellowships. Under Elizabeth, as at an earlier time, the majority of those who took the BCL proceeded no further. From 1571, when we have the help of Clark's edition of the university registers, to the end of the reign there were 107 of them. New College and All Souls between them contributed fifty-one to the total and a further twenty came from St John's. Fourteen took the degree from halls or are not known to have been of any college. The baccalaureate does not seem to have been valued as a preparation for the study of the common law for only eight bachelors at most entered an inn of court, and one of them, Sir Ralph Winwood, was an honorary member of Gray's inn, not a practitioner. The bachelor was not qualified for admission as an advocate of the arches, though he might hold a judicial appointment in the ecclesiastical courts and practice there in any other capacity, but for some forms of practice at least the degree was ornamental rather than useful. Francis Clarke, a proctor who acted for the university, supplicated for the BCL in 1594 because after thirty-five years of practice and (by his own account) forty years of study he was proposing to publish a book and thought that the degree would look well upon his title-page.[3] There were bachelors who intended to make the law their profession. Henry Swinburne was one. A doctorate was not a necessary qualification for practice in the northern province in any capacity.

---

[1] *Reg. Univ.* ed. Clark i. 121.

[2] Upon the prospects of the civilian in the latter part of the century see B. Levack, *Civil Lawyers in England*, 51–7.

[3] *Reg. Univ.* ed. Clark i. 114.

The circumstance that nothing is discoverable of the majority of of bachelors save their names and their degrees strongly suggests, however, that relatively few of them took the degree as a preparation for the practice of the law. There is too much reason to suspect that a fair proportion of those who were not obliged as foundation fellows to enter the faculty as a condition of receiving their emoluments, were already attracted to it because a baccalaureate in civil law was a degree much more easily obtained than a baccalaureate in arts.

Appendix

The King's Readers

JOHN BARTON

1. *John Story*, 1541?–1550, 1553–1557?

John Story was an undergraduate of Hinksey Hall. He was admitted
BCL in 1531, and became principal of Broadgates Hall in 1537. In
1538 he was admitted doctor, and dispensed from necessary regency
because he was reading the ordinary course in civil law. He was at
first appointed under the sign manual, at a salary of forty pounds
a year, but on 28 February 1546, in consideration of the good
service which he had rendered at the siege of Boulogne in the administration of martial law under the Lord Marshal, the king granted him
the lecture by patent for his life, joining Robert Weston with him for
his relief. Weston had already been delivering the lecture as his
deputy in 1544.[1] Story refrained from taking out his patent in order
to save the fees of the seal, or so it was subsequently alleged,[2] but
this grant was revoked in Council in the following November, and
the lecture regranted to Story alone.[3]

Story's known religious opinions rendered him somewhat suspect
to the government of Edward VI, but his stipend was finally confirmed to him in November 1548.[4] On 21 November, however,
in the debate on the act of uniformity, his observations in the
commons, where he sat as member for Hendon in Wiltshire, earned
him the distinction of being the first member to be committed
to prison by order of the house.[5] He was finally released, upon making
his submission, on 2 March following, but subsequently left the
country and like many other English exiles lived at Louvain for the
remainder of Edward's reign. His salary ceased to be paid after

For the information in those notes marked with an asterisk, I am indebted to Dr G. D.
Duncan
    [1] Reg. Cong. 1535–63, fo 100.*
    [2] *Cal. Pat. Rolls (Philip and Mary)*, 1553–4, 395.
    [3] PRO E 323/3, rot. 91.*
    [4] *APC* ii. 229.
    [5] H. Hallam, *The Constitutional History of England* (2 vols 1827, 7th edn 3 vols 1854)
i. 271. For the dates of his confinement see Emden in *BRUO 1501–40*.

Michaelmas 1550.[1] He returned upon Mary's accession, and in 1553 was reappointed to the chair jointly with William Aubrey,[2] in whose favour he subsequently resigned.[3] He was, however, still drawing his salary in the early months of 1557.[4]

He was appointed one of the queen's commissioners for the reform of the university, and chancellor of the diocese of London, in which latter capacity he earned himself a place in *Foxe's Book of Martyrs*.[5] He was returned to Elizabeth's first parliament, where he is said to have expressed his regret that he and his companions had '. . . laboured only about the young and little twigs, whereas they should have struck at the root', by which he was understood to mean that he regretted that they had not proceeded against the queen when it would still have been possible to do so. He was committed to the Fleet, but was apparently released soon afterwards. He was subsequently committed to the Marshalsea, from which he escaped. With the help of the Spanish ambassador, he again left the country and returned to Louvain, where he entered the service of the king of Spain, and is said to have been responsible for establishing the inquisition at Antwerp. The duke of Alva gave him a commission to search for heretical books aboard English vessels entering Flemish ports, which led to his kidnapping by three English merchants, who hoisted sail while he was searching the hold of a ship which they had hired to bring him home. In 1571 he was indicted for treason. refused to plead to the indictment on the ground that he was a subject of the king of Spain, was condemned for want of answer and hanged, drawn and quartered.

To his own party he was a martyr to his faith—he was beatified in 1886—and to his opponents a cruel persecutor and a traitor to his sovereign, who had finally received his just deserts. Contemporary accounts of his character and behaviour therefore differ very widely. There is a full bibliography appended to A. F. Pollard's account of his life in the *Dictionary of National Biography*.

2.   *Robert Weston*, 1546, 1550–1553

Robert Weston entered All Souls in 1536 and was admitted BCL in 1538, and by 1544 he was reading the civil law lecture as Story's

[1] The last payment accounted for by the treasurer of the court of augmentations is in PRO E 323/6, rot. 22/24.*

[2] Page 285 n. 2 above.

[3] Ibid.: *Cal. Pat. Rolls Elizabeth I, 1558–60*, 57; *Foedera* xv. 503. The date of his resignation is unfortunately not stated.

[4] PRO E 405/499, 507, fo 75^V, 510.*

[5] See especially the brief tract, written to celebrate his capture and execution, which bears the separate and significant title, *The cursed Life and bloody End of Dr. Story, a cruel Persecutor of Christ in his Members*.

deputy.[1] In 1546 he succeeded Story as principal of Broadgates Hall, and in the same year became joint holder of the chair for a few months.[2] He was paid as professor from 1550 until Story's reappointment in 1553,[3] though he seems never to have received a formal appointment. In 1553 he entered parliament as member for Exeter. In 1556 he received a grace to incept in both laws,[4] was duly admitted, and entered doctors' commons. He became dean of the arches in 1560. In 1566 he was so unhappy as to be appointed lord chancellor of Ireland, and so unwise as to conduct himself in that office in such a manner as to convince the queen that he was indispensable. After long and vainly begging for leave to resign, he died at Dublin, still in office, in 1578. For his life, see the *Dictionary of National Biography*.

3. *William Aubrey, 1553–1559.*

William Aubrey was born in 1529, entered All Souls in 1547, was admitted BCL in 1549 according to Wood,[5] and became principal of New Inn Hall in 1550. In 1554 he was admitted DCL and entered doctors' commons. He was appointed to the chair jointly with Story in 1553,[6] and resigned in favour of John Griffith in 1559.[7] His professorial duties did not prevent him from serving as judge-advocate to the English expedition against St Quentin, and a Dr William Mowse, or Mosse, of Cambridge seems to have delivered the lecture for him.[8] He became a master in chancery while he still held the chair, and retained this office until 1590, when he resigned it upon appointment as master of requests in ordinary. He was auditor and vicar-general in spirituals to Archbishop Grindal of Canterbury, chancellor to Archbishop Whitgift, and a member of the council of the marches of Wales. He died in 1595, and was buried in St Paul's.

In the cause of the clandestine marriage between Lady Katherine Grey and Edward Seymour earl of Hertford he acted for the earl. Among the Tanner manuscripts in the Bodleian library there is a Latin argument which he prepared in this case, which shows him to have been a learned canonist, accompanied by an English paper of

---

[1] Reg. Cong. 1535–63, fo 100.   [2] Above, p. 285 n. 1.

[3] PRO E 323/7, rot. 24/25, 8, rot. 39/40[V].*

[4] Reg. Cong. 1535–63, fo 158.

[5] *Fasti, sub anno.* I have found no entry of his admission in the register, which is, however, so negligently kept at this period that an omission means very little. Wood may have had documentary evidence which has not survived, or which has escaped my own investigations.

[6] Page 285 n. 2 above.   [7] *Foedera* xv. 503.

[8] *History and Antiquities* ii. pt 2, 857. Wood is uncertain whether he were not professor in his own right, but since he was not paid as professor, it seems more likely that he was a deputy, paid by the incumbent.

advice to the earl, which shows him to have had an excellent grasp of forensic tactics.[1] His great-grandson, John Aubrey of the *Brief Lives*, was told by 'Mr. Shuter the proctor' that he finally appealed the cause to Rome.[2] If this were in truth the case the appeal must have been very discreetly managed, for he remained high in favour with Elizabeth, who was accustomed to call him her 'little doctor'.[3] She would certainly have used very different language to anyone suspected of invoking the authority of the pope to establish the marriage of the heir to the Somerset claim to the English throne. In his later years, he suffered the embarrassment of being required to sit as judge upon a petition by which the son of his former client attempted to establish his legitimacy.[4] He remained secretly attached to the church of Rome, and asked for a priest on his death-bed, or so John Aubrey heard from his cousin John Madock.[5]

4. *John Griffith*, 1559–1566

John Griffith was elected to All Souls in 1548, and admitted BCL in 1552. He was appointed to the chair during the queen's pleasure in 1559, Aubrey resigning in his favour.[6] In 1561 he became principal of New Inn Hall, and was admitted doctor in 1562. He entered doctors' commons in 1564, and his successor was appointed in 1566. He was elected to parliament by the borough of Carnarvon in 1571, and served as sheriff of Carnarvonshire in 1582–3, and of Anglesey in 1587,[7] but seems to have taken little part in national as distinct from local affairs.

5. *Robert Lougher*, 1566–1577.

Robert Lougher, of All Souls, was admitted BCL in 1558. In 1564 he became principal of New Inn Hall. He was admitted doctor in 1565, and appointed to the chair in 1566.[8] In 1571 he left New Inn Hall to become one of the original fellows of Jesus College, but returned as principal when Dr Lewes was deprived for non-residence in 1575. He acquired three rectories in Devonshire between 1561 and 1563, and in 1562 became archdeacon of Totnes. In 1572 he entered parliament as member for Pembroke. In 1574 he was appointed a master in chancery. In May 1577 he became official of the consistory and vicar-general in spirituals to the archbishop of York, and on 4 May in the same year he resigned his chair in favour of

[1] Bodl. Tanner MS 193.
[2] John Aubrey, *Brief Lives*, ed. A. Clark (2 vols Oxford 1898) i. 57, *in margine*.
[3] Ibid. 58.   [4] *Cal. SP Dom. 1591–1594*, 121, 282.
[5] *Brief Lives* i. 60.   [6] *Foedera* xv. 503.
[7] There is an account of his life in the *Dictionary of Welsh Biography*.
[8] *Cal. Pat. Rolls (Elizabeth I), 1563–1566*, 387, no. 2155.

Griffith Lloyd.[1] He continued principal of New Inn Hall until 1580, which suggests that it was not thought necessary to proceed against absentee principals in every case. He died in 1585.[2] He seems to have been a man of consequence, and well thought of, but has left nothing behind him.

6. *Griffith Lloyd*, 1577–1586.

Griffith, or Griffin, Lloyd seems to have turned to the law from theology, for he was chaplain of New College in 1564. He was subsequently elected to All Souls, from which he took his BCL in 1572. He was elected principal of Jesus College in the same year. He was admitted doctor in 1576, and became queen's reader in 1577. He entered parliament as member for the county of Cardigan in 1586, but died that year in doctors' commons. Gentilis commends him as a supporter of the old, sound learning,[3] which is to his credit, for since he was not merely the compatriot but the brother-in-law of his predecessor,[4] the uncharitable might be tempted to suspect that he did not obtain the succession wholly by his own merits.

7. *Albericus Gentilis*, 1587–1608.

Albericus Gentilis, the last and by far the most distinguished of the professors appointed during the period covered by the present volume, was born in San Ginesio in the march of Ancona in 1552. In 1572 he obtained his doctorate from the university of Perugia at the early age of twenty. For the next three years he served as *praetor* of Ascoli, where his father had settled. The family returned to San Ginesio in 1575, where Albericus was employed to revise the muncipal statutes. After completing his task in 1577, he announced that he wished to retire from municipal affairs to devote himself to study. In 1579 he was obliged to leave San Ginesio to avoid the attentions of the inquisition. His father and his younger brother Scipio may have left before him. His mother, with her daughter and four other sons, remained behind. After a short stay in Austrian territory, the three refugees found it necessary to move on, and arrived in London in 1580. As a protestant refugee, Albericus found a patron in the earl of Leicester, who recommended him to the university. He was given rooms in New Inn Hall, and incorporated *ad eundem* on 6 March 1580/1, together with John Hotman the younger.[5] He remained in Oxford for six years, during which he

[1] Ibid.
[2] For his life, see the *Dictionary of National Biography*.
[3] *De iuris interpretibus dialogi sex*, 7.
[4] E. G. Hardy, *Jesus College* (London 1899), 19.
[5] Wood, *Fasti, sub anno*.

published, in 1582, his *De iuris interpretibus dialogi sex*, and in 1585, his *De legationibus libri tres*. He had decided to write a systematic work upon the legal status of ambassadors after he and John Hotman had been called upon to advise the privy council in the case of the Spanish ambassador, Mendoza, who was discovered to have been plotting against the queen. In 1586 he left England for Germany, partly, perhaps, because his prospects at Oxford were necessarily limited until the chair should fall vacant, and partly because he had already contrived sufficiently to annoy the godly faction to make his chance of the succession doubtful when it should do so. Griffith Lloyd died in November of the same year, but Gentilis was not appointed until the following June. The chair was then granted to him for his life, with reversion after his death to Dr James of All Souls.[1] According to Wood, Dr James had obtained a patent to succeed Lloyd, 'but never made use of it'.[2] Since Dr James, understandably in the circumstances, did not think it necessary to pay the fees of the seal his patent is not enrolled and we do not know its date. It is thus uncertain whether he were chosen upon the assumption that Gentilis had left England for good, or whether the godly faction had found a rival candidate.[3]

Gentilis's success did not endear him to his opponents, and he was subsequently involved in an acrimonious controversy with John Rainolds of Corpus upon the lawfulness of stage-plays, the pretext for which was the publication in 1593 of his observations upon the two titles of the code, *De maleficis et mathematicis* and *De professoribus et medicis*, in the latter of which he maintained dramatic performances to be lawful, an opinion which Rainolds had already denied in a correspondence with William Gager of Christ Church, who was probably indebted to Gentilis for his explanation of that clause of the praetor's edict which (in its Justinianic form) declared actors to be infamous. Rainolds took particular exception to two of Gentilis's arguments. In discussing Deuteronomy 22.5, 'The woman shall not wear that which pertaineth unto a man, neither shall a man put on a woman's garment, for all that do so are abomination

---

[1] PRO C 66/1287, m. 10–11.*

[2] *History and Antiquities* ii. pt 2, 857.

[3] D. Panizza, *Alberico Gentili, giurista ideologo nell' Inghilterra Elisabettiana* (Padova 1981) at p. 50, inclines to hold that Lloyd's state of health was already such that the question of his successor was under discussion when Gentilis left Oxford, and that his reason for leaving was that he thought that his opponents would prove powerful enough to prevent his appointment. This, however, is an inference from the circumstance that Gentilis was delivering the statutory course, Lloyd being *impeditus*. In Elizabethan Oxford ill-health was not the only or even the most usual impediment which might cause a professor to confide the delivery of his lectures to a deputy, and the circumstance that Lloyd was elected to parliament very shortly before his death would suggest that it was unexpected.

unto the Lord thy God'—a text which caused some difficulty in an age when female parts were taken by men—Gentilis had observed that upon a question of morals, as distinct from faith, he did not give great weight to the authority of theologians. He had met the argument that it was indecorous for a player to act the part of an immoral character by distinguishing, as he had done elsewhere, between the doing of evil to attain a good end, which is unlawful, and the 'abuse' of evil: the employment of means ordinarily evil in such circumstances that they lose their evil nature. To represent an immoral character in order to inculcate a moral lesson is as legiti- mate as the 'officious lie' of the physician to his patient. Rainolds contended that matters of human conduct were the proper concern of the theologian, but that in any event a professor of the civil law, which was pagan in origin and contained much that was morally objectionable, was of all persons the worst qualified to form an opinion upon them. The doctrine of the 'abuse' of evil was a sophism which might serve to legitimate any iniquity. The good fame of the university must suffer severely if it should come to be known that these were the doctrines which studious youth would be likely to imbibe there. Neither party was at any pains to keep the argument private, and some members of the godly faction took care to have Rainolds's admonitions copied and transmitted to Toby Matthew, then bishop of Durham, who was Gentilis's principal surviving patron, to whom the work which had given rise to this correspon- dence was dedicated: a circumstance which, according to Rainolds, was an aggravation of the offence. Gentilis's appointment had been opposed, according to his own account, merely upon the ground that he was an Italian, with those faults of character which are inevitable in one who has had the misfortune to be born a foreigner. He was now represented not merely as an Italian, but as a macchia- vellian and an atheist, or so he asserted in the draft of a speech announcing his intention to resign his chair and devote himself to practice. The speech was never delivered. Toby Matthew stood by his friend, and it would seem that pressure from above was brought to bear, if not to end the dispute, at least to induce the disputants to refrain from abusing one another in public, for the two last printed contributions to the controversy, Gentilis's two short treatises *De actoribus et spectatoribus fabularum non notandis*, and *De abusu mendacii*, and Rainolds's *The Overthrow of Stage-Plays*, which was an edited version of his correspondence with Gager and Gentilis, were not published until 1599, and not even then in England.[1]

It is thus somewhat difficult to determine what proportion of

[1] For an account of this dispute see D. Panizza, *Alberico Gentili*, 55–78.

Gentilis's energies were devoted to the duties of his chair, since the godly party was always alert for any ground of complaint. His lectures were being read by a deputy in 1590, and the chancellor, Sir Christopher Hatton, was informed that '. . . the Law Reader being absent, he that ys deputed for him applyeth himself aboute hys owne buysiness in London, and elsewhere, doth not discharge that duity as your Statutes doe requyre,' an allegation which the vice-chancellor denied.[1] So Rainolds in 1594, in a final admonition to Gentilis to reform his manners and excesses, admonished him to lecture more frequently and with greater diligence.[2] In his last years he held a standing retainer in the admiralty court for the king of Spain, which appears to have obliged him to move to London. His successor, Dr Budden, was recommended to King James as having read the civil law lecture since the departure of Dr Gentilis.[3] He died in 1608 in London, where he was buried.

His published works are concerned less with the technical part of the civil law than with 'jurisprudence', which he took in the Justinianic sense of the knowledge of things divine and human, and of the just and the unjust; a subject upon which his opinions necessarily brought him into collision with the godly party, for while he was perfectly orthodox in holding that no merely human authority could override the law of God, he was also of opinion that upon questions of morals as distinct from faith the final word might properly lie with the jurists and the temporal power, rather than with the theologians and the church. The first edition of his most famous work, *De iure belli*, appeared in three separate parts in 1589, and the final version was published at Hanau in 1598. A new edition by Professor Holland appeared at Oxford in 1877, and the work was again reprinted in 1933, in the series of *Classics of International Law* published by the Carnegie Endowment for International Peace. They had already reprinted in 1931 his *Advocationes hispanicae*, a posthumous collection of his arguments in Spanish causes, which had appeared in 1613. He also found time to contribute to a number of contemporary political and theological controversies. There is a summary account of his views in Van der Molen's *Alberico Gentili and the Development of International Law, his Life, Work, and Times* (2nd edn Leyden 1968), 197–267. His position as a civilian is treated in more detail in G. Astuti, *Mos Italicus e Mos Gallicus nei dialoghi 'De iuris interpretibus' di A. Gentili* (Bologna 1937). The most recent, and in many ways the fullest account of his ideas, which

[1] Wood, *History and Antiquities* ii. pt 1, 242.
[2] D. Panizza, op. cit., 73, n. 37.
[3] *Cal. SP Dom. James I, 1603–1610*, 489, no. 48.

has been drawn upon extensively in the preceding brief summary, is Diego Panizza's *Alberico Gentili, Giurista Ideologo nell'Inghilterra Elisabettiana* (Padova 1981), which also contains a full bibliography of his works.

4·4

The Faculty of Theology

S. L. GREENSLADE*

COMPOSITION AND TEACHING OF THE FACULTY

CHANGE dominates the history of the faculty of theology during the century of the reformation, yet there was continuity as well, of purpose and of structure. The faculty retained its ceremonial privileges; the senior *theologus* was still *cancellarius natus*.[1] Fox's 'bee-hive' of Corpus Christi College, however humanistic, was founded 'solely or principally for the sake of theology', even if the language of its statutes is less glowing than that of Queen's (1341), where the 'heavenly breath (*spiraculum*)' of the theology faculty is likened to the tree of life planted in the paradise-garden of the church militant.[2] Reformation or no, the Tudor university was still, above all else, to serve religion through theological study and the training of clergy, and the theology faculty, concerned with higher degrees only, continued to conduct this training more or less under the old forms at a time when the growth of colleges transformed undergraduate teaching.

The faculty comprised doctors, bachelors and other students, the latter MAs in the secular colleges and halls, or monks and friars who came under special rules. By university regulations resident MAs were obliged after their necessary regency to enter one of the higher faculties. College statutes usually prescribed how many fellows might enter law or medicine; in most colleges masters of arts, or all but two or three of them, were meant to study theology, although at Magdalen two or three of its forty fellows might pursue law and two or three medicine, while at St John's a quarter of the fellows might

* This text is substantially that left by the late Canon S. L. Greenslade at his death and I have tried to keep alterations to a minimum, supplying footnotes from indications in his typescript. I have also added the discussion of the size and composition of the faculty and the section on Greek scholarship—J.M.

[1] The senior doctor of the faculty had the right to act in a vacancy until a new chancellor of the university was appointed: *Statuta*, lxxiv. The term *theologus* will be used as a technical term to indicate a member of the theology faculty, and not simply a 'theologian'.

[2] *SCO* i. pt 4 (Queen's), 5.

choose law and one medicine. Other special cases were New College with twenty lawyers and two students each of medicine and astronomy out of its seventy fellows, and All Souls, with sixteen jurists out of forty. Of Christ Church's hundred members, the twenty senior were styled *theologi* and so they mostly were in fact; most of the rest were not yet MAs. In addition, many college statutes ordered their theologians to proceed BTh and even DTh in due course as a condition of retaining their fellowships.[1] In 1549 the Edwardian visitors reaffirmed this general tradition.[2] Monks and friars presumably lived in the houses of their orders. They were exempt from taking the arts degree, and in accordance with a long-standing agreement with the university,[3] they pursued an arts course partly in their houses of origin and partly in Oxford, where they then became students of theology or canon law. From 1500 to the dissolution, they accounted for a substantial proportion of admissions to the degree of BTh.

The Course of Study

Under the statutes operative until 1549, a master of arts aspiring to the baccalaureate in theology had to spend seven more years in residence, for three of them attending lectures on the Bible; those who were not MAs took nine years over this course. In his fifth year an MA could be admitted to oppose in a formal disputation, and in the seventh he might respond. These were his degree exercises *pro forma*, mentioned in his grace, his conditions of admission entered in the register of congregation. Provided he secured proper depositions testifying to his character and learning and paid the necessary fees, he was then admitted to lecture on a book of the *Sentences* of Peter Lombard (the phrase generally used for admission as a bachelor of theology), on condition that he preached a Latin sermon to the clergy (*ad clerum*) within a year. Four more years were required for the doctorate.[4] The bachelor must lecture, first on the *Sentences*, then on a book of the Bible (his *introitus biblie*) while continuing to attend lectures and disputations; he also had to perform eight responsions and preach a Latin sermon normally at St Mary's, the university church. With further depositions regarding his learning and character from three doctors of theology he could then be licensed for the degree, but strictly became doctor only by incepting at the act (*comitia*), a ceremonial occasion which (with

[1] *SCO* i. pt 4 (Queen's), 5; pt 5 (New College), 3–4; pt 7 (All Souls), 12; ii. pt 8 (Magdalen), 6, cf 36–7; pt 11 (Cardinal College), 11–12, 78; iii. pt 12 (St John's), 37.

[2] *Statuta*, 358.

[3] Ibid. cxiii–cxviii.

[4] Ibid. 48–51.

the vespers immediately preceding) included his last two disputations.[1]

These regulations were modified as the century progressed. The Edwardian statutes of 1549 provided that candidates for the BTh who were already masters of arts were to attend the theology and Hebrew lectures for five years, during which time they must twice dispute against a bachelor, respond twice, and preach a Latin and an English sermon at the university church. Men who entered Oxford aged 24 years or more might proceed BTh without an arts degree after seven years devoted wholly to theological study. To attain the doctorate, the bachelor had to reside for four further years, attending lectures daily, disputing twice, responding once, and preaching at St Mary's twice in Latin and once in English. The Edwardian code was provisional. The 'new statutes' (*nova statuta*) of 1564/5 restored the seven years of study traditional for MAs and required nine from others.[2] These Elizabethan statutes rather vaguely confirmed the old, though they substituted six public lectures in Latin on some part of the scriptures for the eight responsions. It was bluntly stated that wherever the statutes read 'book of the *Sentences*' they were to be understood as 'book of the Holy Scripture'. Minor changes were made later in the century, with explanations and definitions which suggest a need to check increasing laxity,[3] but the general effect was to retain the medieval forms of the curriculum with some changes in substance. While these were the regulations, so readily were candidates excused from them that the actual working of the faculty has to be studied from the graces and dispensations in the registers, from college muniments, contemporary theological literature and from many miscellaneous sources.[4]

Size and Composition

No faculty roll is known to survive from this period, nor do any of the bedel of theology's 'catalogues' of students obliged to attend professorial lectures.[5] Had the registers of congregation been kept more consistently we should know how many supplicated for and achieved the degrees of BTh and DTh, and their graces would show how long they had actually been *theologi*. We could also see what dispensations from statutory residence or from statutory exercises were granted. However, the graces for the early decades

[1] Ibid. 50–1, 179, and index under theology, faculty of.
[2] Ibid. 345, 356–60 (1549), 380–4 (1564/5).
[3] Ibid. 427 (1583), 445 (1592); *Reg. Univ.* ed. Clark i. 135–6, 139–45.
[4] For Strickland Gibson's comments upon laxity in the faculty see *Statuta*, cxx–cxxi.
[5] Ibid. 408, lines 19 ff. See also the discussion of numbers in the introduction to this chapter, pp. 152–6.

of the century are irregular and are not so informative as to allow comprehensive estimates of the length of time spent by individuals in the faculty.

In some secular colleges, the status of *theologus* was formally granted, though in others it may simply have been assumed for all MAs except those destined for law and medicine. At Oriel, in order to secure adequate collegiate teaching in arts, detailed conditions for obtaining the college's licence to incept as MA were laid down, imposing the duty to lecture every term during regency, no matter what dispensation the university granted, and to dispute in college every term for those two years. The books to be lectured on might be explicitly allocated to particular inceptors.[1] Such MAs were normally licensed to *study* theology four years later, but there was an intermediate stage, usually after two years, when they might be dispensed from lecturing and allowed to *attend* theology lectures, though still required to participate in the college's arts disputations.[2] They would thus attend the statutory biblical lectures for three years (their third to fifth as MAs) and then oppose and respond sufficiently to qualify for the BTh seven years from inception as MA (*post gradum*), as required by the university statutes. Some of the licences define the controlled period of arts teaching as four years (still in 1553) but from 1565 the licences are granted unconditionally and admissions to study theology are not recorded in the dean's register of Oriel after that date. At Merton, where the grace for inception specifies college duties for the two years of regency only, fellows nevertheless were not usually deputed to study theology until four years from inception.[3] At Brasenose, masters of arts studying theology were admitted to theological lectures after the first year of regency.[4] The status or seniority of a *theologus* as such might thus vary widely from college to college.

Members of religious orders, unlike seculars, were virtually all enrolled in the faculty, and the minority who took further degrees in law were almost invariably graduates in theology. It is, however, very difficult to determine how much of their work was actually done in Oxford. They were not for the most part expected to graduate in arts, but they were nevertheless required to pursue the study of arts for a number of years and perform the appropriate exercises. The statutes required eight years in arts, and nine in theology before they could be admitted to lecture on the *Sentences*,

---

[1] For example, *Dean's Register of Oriel*, 18 (1508), 29 (1511) and passim.

[2] For example, the case of Ware and Stephyns, ibid. 30–1 (1512).

[3] *Reg. ann. mert. 1483–1521*, 466 (1517); *Reg. ann. mert. 1521–67*, 65–6 (1535).

[4] I. S. Leadam, 'The early years of the college', in *Brasenose College Quatercentenary Monographs* (2 vols in 3 OHS lii–liv 1909) ii. no. 1, 23.

a total of seventeen years of study.[1] In the early fifteenth century the Benedictines and 'possessioner' religious (in effect, all who were not mendicants) were given further concessions.[2] The graces in the register of congregation from 1518 to 1535[3] show that both monks and mendicants were allowed to claim years spent elsewhere in the study of theology, in their monasteries or conventual *studia*, towards a degree. The graces are insufficiently specific, however, to allow any estimate of average attendance in the Oxford Schools for the religious, or, as a result, to make any reliable estimate of the total number likely to have been in active attendance in the faculty at any given time. What does seem most likely is that each case was judged independently, and that the grace as recorded was usually a conventional phrase chiefly indicating the approval of the faculty.

An examination of the surviving graces for all theologians known to have been studying between 1520 and 1529 yields a total of 96 monks and 52 friars.[4] Of these, 11 monks and 8 friars claimed studies elsewhere—sometimes specifying Cambridge, or their religious houses, or 'abroad'. It cannot be assumed, however, that the remainder studied entirely in Oxford, since among them, only 3 monks and one friar explicitly stated that they did so.

Even more marked and important than the variety of *studia* which these findings hint at is the considerable variation in the length of time revealed in the graces of regulars and seculars alike. In both groups there is a wide distribution of from seven to sixteen years offered in the petition, according to the common and uninformative formula, 'in logic, philosophy and theology'. Among the 96 monks, the majority offered periods which clustered around eight to ten years, while the majority of the 52 friars and 170 seculars offered periods of study clustering around ten to fourteen years. There are complications, however, in drawing conclusions from these figures. Among the seculars, 22 petitioned more than once, and some of these double or treble supplications show that the times mentioned in graces cannot necessarily be taken as years already spent in study. The form in the grace was always that the time specified 'should be sufficient', and sometimes this apparently referred to years of study still to be completed. Thus some supplicants petitioned to lecture on the *Sentences* immediately after graduating in arts, offering a certain period, and then, after a lapse approximating to the period of time

---

[1] See *The Register of Congregation 1448-1463*, ed. W. A. Pantin and W. T. Mitchell (OHS new ser. xxii 1972), pp. xxxiv–xxxvi; the libraries of the monastic colleges, Canterbury and Durham, had substantial sections of arts books; ibid. xxxv.

[2] Ibid. xxxvi. [3] Reg. Cong. 1518–35.

[4] Extracted from the register by Mr Charles Everitt, to whom I am very grateful for the analysis that follows, as I am to Mr W. T. Mitchell for his comments.

mentioned, petitioned again citing a similar, or slightly longer, period. In other cases, the first petition occurs about half-way between the dates of graduation in arts and the date of the second petition. It cannot be assumed therefore that when only one grace survives for a given individual, it comes at the end of his period of study.

In the registers of congregation in addition to the graces, there are recorded a number of admissions to opponency and to lecture on the *Sentences*. Not all members of the faculty for whom there are graces were actually recorded as having been admitted to the bachelor's degree, and likewise, there are records of the admission of some regulars and seculars for whom no grace survives in the register. Only 57 seculars with graces are recorded as having been admitted subsequently, representing 33 per cent of all who are registered as having petitioned. The proportions are higher for the regulars: 63 monks (66 per cent of the total with graces) and 30 friars (60 per cent of the total with graces) are recorded as having been admitted. There are 8 monks, 4 friars and 29 seculars for whom there are records of admission but no graces. It is therefore amply clear that we cannot assume that we have a complete account of the business of the faculty in the surviving records. Other variations show that despite the formal regulations, the time claimed for admission to read the *Sentences* was not time spent only in the faculty after graduation in arts, nor was it the entire period spent studying arts and theology, but most commonly included a part of the period spent in arts, with the whole of the time spent in study after graduation. Moreover, according to the statutes the bachelor had to lecture for three years after his admission before petitioning to incept in theology. Although this interval seems to have been observed by most, it should be noted that at least 4 seculars and 3 regulars petitioned to incept in the same years as their petition for the BTh, again showing that the statutes provide an unreliable guide to the actual practice of petition and admission. A smaller proportion of monks compared to friars and seculars appear in the registers as petitioning or being admitted to incept (16 per cent compared with 25 per cent and 22 per cent respectively).

Some further impression of the work and character of the faculty in the decade 1520 to 1529 can be gained from looking at individual careers. Among the seculars, circumstance led one to prominence in medicine. William Freman of Oriel College, who had qualified in arts and studied at Paris, was admitted to the faculty of theology in April 1520, but two years later resigned his fellowship to marry. The next year he qualified as a bachelor of medicine, and in February

1528 incepted as DM; in 1529 he was elected a fellow of the London College of Physicians, and was eventually president in 1545 and 1546. He had before him, moreover, the example of Thomas Mosgroff of Merton, who was lecturer in astronomy there in 1517, scholar of theology in 1519, MD 1523, BTh 1524, public reader in medicine in 1523–4, and who was beneficed from 1524 besides being the duke of Buckingham's physician. John Throwley OSB, moved from theology to a career in medicine as a consequence of the reformation. He supplicated from Canterbury College for his BTh in 1524[1] and was admitted four years later. He was chancellor of Christ Church cathedral priory in Canterbury until the dissolution in 1540, and then in 1545 he was awarded the BM and admitted to practice.

Another *theologus* whose career was drastically altered by the reformation was Walter Buckler, a fellow of Merton. He was admitted as a scholar in theology in 1527 and received his BTh in June 1534. By that time he had been principal of St Alban Hall, a student in Paris, and in 1530 a canon *primi ordinis* of Cardinal College. He was subsequently a canon of King Henry VIII College from 1535 to 1544, but seems never to have taken priest's orders. He returned to the continent to study in Paris and in Padua, and was brought to the attention of Thomas Cromwell; by 1544 he was secretary to Katherine Parr. He was employed on diplomatic missions to the landgrave of Hesse and the duke of Saxony in 1545, and knighted at the accession of Edward VI. He eventually married Katherine, the widow of Sir Edward Tame of Fairford manor, Gloucestershire, where he died some seven years later in 1553. Openness towards careers in other professions was characteristic of the faculty at all times, however, not simply during periods of confessional stress. Edward Cradock, Margaret professor from 1565 to 1597, was an eminent alchemist; Edward Gunter, the distinguished mathematician, was formerly *theologus* and BTh in 1615.[2]

Others among the seculars were future bishops. John Holyman, a Wykehamist and fellow of New College (BTh 1526, DTh 1530) had a career in a number of university offices, and received his first living from New College in 1526. He was consecrated bishop of Bristol during Mary's reign in November 1554, the papal provision being

---

[1] Throwley's grace is typical, and is included for illustrative purposes: 'Eodem die [29 July] supplicat d. Ioannes Throwley, monacus ordinis sancti Benedicti, quatenus studium octo annorum cum 6 magnis vacacionibus in logicis, philosophicis et theologicis sufficiat ei, ut admittatur ad opponendum in novis scolis, qua opposicione habita una cum responsione, possit admitti ad lecturas libri Sentenciarum. Hec gratia est concessa et condicionate quod bis replicet in novis scolis ante gradum et quod predicet sermonem ad quem tenetur per se et non per alium.' I have used the typed transcripts of Reg. Cong. 1518–35, fo 554.

[2] Emden, *BRUO 1501–40* for these careers. For Cradock and Gunter, *DNB* and (for Gunter) R. T. Gunther, *Early Science in Oxford* (2 vols OHS lxxvii–lxxviii 1923) i. 113 ff.

granted the following year. He had been an opponent of the royal divorce, and according to Foxe, took part in the trials of Cranmer, Latimer and Ridley. At his death in 1558, he left a total sum of £30 to New College, and to Winchester College, his former school, the works of Augustine, Jerome, Cyprian, Cyril, Tertullian and Irenaeus, 'or as many as may be found of theym', and a *Historia ecclesiastica tripartita in uno volumine*.

The career of George Browne OSA, another future bishop, was quite different. He was younger than Holyman, apparently, and supplicated for his BTh in 1532 after ten years of study. In 1534 he was incorporated DTh, probably of a foreign university, since a contemporary note reveals a close link with Cromwell, who may therefore have encouraged his studies abroad. He was prior of the London convent by 1532, and remained in that office until his promotion as archbishop of Dublin in 1536. He was also appointed by Cromwell, his London neighbour, prior provincial of the English province. It was he who made the first public announcement of the marriage of Henry VIII to Anne Boleyn at St Paul's Cross on Easter Day 1533, and he was commissioned with Dr John Hilsey OP to carry out a general visitation of all mendicant houses and administer the new oath of succession in 1534. He was deprived of his see by Queen Mary on account of marriage, but decided to conform and obtained a bull of absolution from Cardinal Pole as papal legate in 1555. He died the following year, before he could be faced with the need to adjust his commitments once again.

It might be added that many of the doctors among the seculars ended up in perfectly ordinary livings, as did Nicholas Cartwright (BTh 1523, DTh 1536), who was lecturer in philosophy at Magdalen College, and took part in the debate in 1549 between Peter Martyr and William Chedsey on Martyr's side. He died simply as vicar of Nuneaton in Warwickshire.[1]

Notable careers on the other hand could be won by the bachelors in the faculty. John Bekynsawe (supp. BTh 1529), a Wykehamist who vacated his fellowship at New College when he married abroad, held an exhibition from the king and also lectured in Greek at Paris. Although he to some degree maintained connections with the Pole and More circles, he wrote the *De supremo et absoluto regis imperio* (1546) in support of the royal cause. John Helyar, one of the founder's nominees to Corpus Christi College (BTh 1532), took no further degrees, but he was apparently taken into Wolsey's patronage on account of his exceptional proficiency in the biblical tongues.

---

[1] Emden's statement, *BRUO 1501–40*, 105–6 that he was probably Lady Margaret professor is wrong; see Macray, *Reg. Magdalen* i. 145–7.

He studied abroad for several years, and is credited with commentaries and scholia on classical authors, and a translation of St John Chrysostom. John Ramsey alias Bowle (BTh 1522) an Augustinian canon, was *prior studentium* at their college of St Mary's in 1528, and prior of Merton Priory, Surrey at the time of the dissolution. He owned a considerable library, as the surviving volumes seem to indicate, and was recipient of the dedication of Thomas Paynell's English version of Erasmus's *Comparation of a Vyrgin and a Martyr* (1537). By 1545 he was chaplain to Thomas Cranmer, archbishop of Canterbury. None the less, despite these examples, it is generally apparent that the most conspicuous careers were those of the doctors in the faculty.

The members of religious orders in the pre-Reformation faculty of theology included Benedictines, Franciscans, Cistercians and Dominicans, with smaller numbers of Carmelites, Austin Canons and Austin Friars. The remainder were made up of occasional recruits from orders unprovided with local houses of study: Carthusians, Cluniacs, Bonhommes. Because of the reformation, the subsequent careers of these men are little different from those of the seculars who were their contemporaries. Edmund Baskerville OFM, who was warden of Greyfriars at the dissolution, had a representative and successful career in the national church, having proceeded DTh in 1532. He was dispensed to hold a benefice in 1538, became a canon of Hereford Cathedral, and eventually chancellor of the diocese. When he died in 1567, he left the works of St Jerome and of Origen with other of his books to the cathedral library. William Bennett (BTh 1529, DTh 1535), a Benedictine of Durham College, had a like if less successful career. He was a canon and prebendary of Durham, and vicar of Aycliffe, county Durham, until his death in 1583, and gave the Froben edition of St Jerome's letters to Durham Cathedral Priory.

Not all ex-religious were so fortunate. Robert Ferrer (BTh 1533) sometime Austin canon at St Mary's College, was one of those suspected of Lutheran sympathies in 1528. He seemed well launched in a career as a chaplain both to Cranmer and to Edward, duke of Somerset. In September 1548 he was consecrecrated bishop of St Davids, but with the fall of Somerset the next year, he became embroiled with his cathedral chapter and was eventually prosecuted under a *praemunire*, to be deprived of his see in March 1554. He was imprisoned until the accession of Queen Mary, when his fortunes declined still further. Tried before Stephen Gardiner and condemned for breach of his monastic vows, he was sent for further examination to his former diocese, when he was condemned for heresy by his successor as bishop and by a former member of his defiant cathedral chapter. On 30 March 1555 he was burnt at the stake at Carmarthen.

Although the members of the faculty in the 1520s predictably found varied and sometimes very significant parts to play in the post-reformation church, it is clear that Oxford's reputation as an international *studium* had already drastically waned from its medieval peak. Only three foreign names are found registered in the decade. Antonio Papudo, a Portuguese Franciscan, took his BTh degree in 1527, whereafter he presumably returned to his province. The other two men are better known, and both were in Wolsey's circle in the university. Nicholas de Burgo was an Italian Franciscan, who apparently came to the Oxford convent of his order about 1517, and took a DTh in 1524. He was recruited by Wolsey as professor of theology at Cardinal College, and is the one holder of a chair there who can be shown to have drawn his stipend after Wolsey's fall. He was apparently deeply involved in the problems of the royal divorce, and in 1531 left Oxford for the London convent of his order and thence returned to Italy. John de Coloribus, a Walloon Dominican, had come to Oxford earlier after studies in Paris, where he had deserted the convent and incurred heavy penalties from his religious province. Despite this, he seems to have been welcomed in Oxford, where he earned both the BTh (1511) and DTh (1522). He was granted letters of denization in 1527, and like de Burgo, was selected by Wolsey as a learned counsel both against Luther and in the problems of the royal divorce.

If Oxford rarely appealed to foreign theologians, many Oxford graduates studied abroad. We have already mentioned Walter Buckler, George Browne, John Bekynsawe and William Freman; to these names should be added those of two distinguished scholars who were members in this decade; Robert Wakefield, regius praelector of Hebrew at King Henry VIII College, who had studied at Louvain and Tübingen, and William Latimer, from an earlier generation, the distinguished Grecian who had studied at Ferrara and Padua, and who was back in Oxford in this decade renting rooms at Canterbury College. No precise account of the foreign universities visited is possible, since the graces frequently refer simply to 'study abroad', but it is clear from those reported, that Paris and Louvain were by far the most attractive of the foreign universities to Oxford theologians. However, Turin, Cologne, Rome and Bologna all appear in the graces, almost always as places where the DTh has been taken before incorporation at Oxford.

Within England, Cambridge was frequented by virtually as many as are known to have studied in foreign universities, and the Cambridge men of course included some notables, like Richard Cox and Robert Wakefield, both of whom began there. Some are said simply to have studied 'elsewhere', and since all of these are religious, it is tempting to see in this a reference to their own monasteries or other *studia*. One Benedictine, Richard Glowceter (BTh 1520) of Evesham Abbey, identified his abbey as a place of study outside Oxford in petitioning for a grace, as did the Dominican friar, John Raynolds (BTh 1526) of the Exeter convent. Three secular *theologi* were fellows of de Vaux College, Salisbury.[1]

Although the conventional and laconic phraseology of the graces makes it impossible to form anything like an exact impression of the numbers in residence at any one time, or of the regularity with which *theologi* resided in the university, it is clear that throughout the century, very few stayed on to become doctors, and indeed, that few stayed beyond the bachelor's degree. In 1535 two Benedictines could find no one to whom to respond; in 1537 and 1538 two monks no one to oppose. In 1549 a decree begins: 'Since there are so few bachelors of theology';[2] in 1573 there was a 'great dearth of bachelors in theology', and in 1576 the faculty allowed MA *theologi* instead of holders of the BTh to depone on behalf of new candidates for the degree of BTh.[3] Doctors were even scarcer: a statute of 1551 starts: 'Since very few doctors reside these days . . .'.[4] In 1554 there were not three holders of the DTh to oppose Henry Walsh for his BTh; in 1565 the Margaret professor mentions a 'remarkable scarcity of doctors'.[5]

What did the faculty offer? To answer this question, we must look first at its teaching strength. The system of necessary regency in the arts faculty, whereby MAs gave the standard lectures for the two years after their inception, had almost broken down by 1500. So a few regent masters were selected and paid to give them, and the rest were dispensed annually *en bloc* from lecturing. It is probable, therefore, that unless such men were required for special university or college duties, they could rank immediately as *theologi*; the normal BTh grace from the 1550s, seven years *post gradum susceptum*, implies this.[6] Meanwhile teaching inside colleges developed rapidly.[7] At Christ Church, for example, the censor in theology was

---

[1] William Kyngman, William Mortymer and Hugh Martyn.
[2] *Statuta*, 360: 'Cum paucissimi sint baccalaurei theologiae. . . .'
[3] *Reg. Univ.* ed. Clark i. 136.
[4] *Statuta*, 361: 'Quoniam perpauci admodum doctores his diebus in academia resident ...'.
[5] *Reg. Univ.* ed. Clark i. 134 note; 142.
[6] On necessary regency see J. M. Fletcher, pp. 185–7 above; Salter's discussion in *Reg. ann. mert. 1483–1521*, xxi–xxii is misleading.
[7] See James McConica, 'The rise of the undergraduate college', pp. 1–68 above.

instructed in 1549 to note absences from lectures and disputations, both public and private, and to threaten penalties.[1] In October 1550 he and another censor reported on the young men, naming and classifying twelve. Of these undergraduates only Herbert Westfaling, later Margaret professor and bishop of Hereford, secured a *bene progressus*. In 1550 William Whittingham, then an MA theologus, later DTh and dean of Durham, was allowed up to three years leave to study abroad; on return he must lecture diligently on the epistle to the Galatians in Christ Church hall.[2]

Once the friars had gone, the professors became particularly important in theology, where incepting doctors were usually dispensed at once from lecturing. With royal assistance, the university provided them. There had been foreshadowings and precedents. On the continent lecturers (*professores*) had sometimes been paid in ways which amounted to regular support by the university acting corporately, practices which must have been known to visiting English scholars. In 1432–3 Oxford pleaded with the duke of Bedford to fulfil his expressed intention to provide permanent maintenance for masters giving ordinary lectures on the arts and philosophies, and pressed the duke of Gloucester to support them in this plea. Though the arts were its main concern, reference to 'other faculties' was included.[3] Nothing came of this.

In 1481–2, when the bishop of Salisbury persuaded Edward IV to found a chantry at Windsor, the university was to have the presentation, always preferring a learned theologian, who would, as they hoped, be available to reside for three terms teaching in Oxford. The king was thanked for having actually established a permanent theological lecture without cost to the audience. This also lapsed.[4] Then the Lady Margaret lecturership in theology was established, provisionally in 1497, finally in 1502–3.[5]

Another line of contribution was the provision of college lectures open to the university. Following Waynflete's provision in the Magdalen College statutes of 1480 for college lecturers who should lecture publicly in philosophy and theology to all scholars without fee from them, Bishop Fox included three public lectures in Greek, Latin and theology in his plan for Corpus Christi College

---

[1] Christ Church Archives MS D.P. vi. b. i. fo 117^{r-v}; MS D & C i.b.2, p. 88.

[2] Christ Church Archives MS D & C i.b.1, fo 17^{v} (Westfaling); MS D & C i.b.2, p. 88 (Whittingham).

[3] *Epistolae academicae Oxon*, ed. H. Anstey (2 vols. OHS xxxv, xxxvi 1898), i. letters 65, 66, 72: 'quarumlibet aliarum facultatum', 81, 82, 95.

[4] *Epist. acad.* ed. Anstey ii, letters 302, 304.

[5] Ibid. no. 486 (1497), *Statuta*, 300–10 (1502), and see app.

(1517).[1] Cardinal Wolsey paid for a number of lectures in the next few years before founding his Cardinal College, in whose statutes (revised in 1527) he referred not only to the domestic professors of the college but also to the six public professors whom he had appointed for the common advantage of all students.[2] Evidence of such lectures is to be found in the university's correspondence with Archbishop Warham, then chancellor, and with Wolsey. Amid expressions of fulsome gratitude, the university frequently hinted that Wolsey should make statutory provision for lectures,[3] something which he often said he had under consideration. But Cardinal College meant a change of plan and he had gone no further before his fall and death. Henry VIII and Cromwell continued his work. In 1536 each university was ordered, in return for tax concessions, to maintain a public lecturer in any such science or tongue as the King assigned. Oxford assessed its colleges to make up a stipend of twenty marks for a theology lecturer (Richard Smith), an arrangement which lasted for some years beyond the definitive foundation of regius chairs of theology, Hebrew and Greek in the early 1540s. To these last, with the Lady Margaret chair, canonries at Christ Church were eventually attached.[4]

Wolsey had bidden his professor of theology, attached to Cardinal College, to lecture publicly every day on which a university lecture might be held (*dies legibilis*) either on the Bible or—since some scholastic erudition was necessary against heresy—on Scotus. Or he was to lecture in alternate terms on the Bible and Scotus. Each lecture should later be reviewed by one of the audience, when the professor should allow questions.[5] Subsequently the regius professor of theology lectured on four days a week. From the time of Wolsey to Laud the hour of 9 a.m. was reserved for him alone, so that anyone in the university might attend. The Margaret professor was originally to lecture each *dies legibilis* at 7 a.m. on whatever theological subjects the chancellor and doctors thought proper.[6] Convocation in 1576 was content with three lectures a week from him, and Laud with two, ordering him to alternate with the regius professor in expounding the Bible at 9 a.m. The Hebrew professor's stint was five lectures a week at 8 a.m. reduced to four in 1565 and by Laud to two—in the

[1] SCO ii. pt 8 (Magdalen), 47-9; pt 10 (Corpus Christi 1527), 48-54; Bodl. MS Laud misc. 621 (Corpus Christi 1517), pp. 51-5.

[2] Cardinal College was to have had six public (i.e. university) professors including one in theology; SCO, ii. pt 11 (Cardinal College), 72-4, 127.

[3] Epist. acad. 1508-96, nos. 83, 93, 94, 130.

[4] See G. D. Duncan, below, for a full account of Wolsey's lecturers. King Henry VIII's lectures and the foundation of the regius chairs. [5] SCO ii. pt 11, 127.

[6] The first of these was Edmund Wylsford; see G. D. Duncan, p. 350 below on the Lady Margaret chair.

afternoon. The Greek professor was to lecture four times a week during term, and this also was reduced by Laud to two.[1]

Further lectures were given by bachelors working for the doctorate. Under the old statutes they lectured on the Bible and the *Sentences*; under those of 1565 they gave six public lectures on some part of scripture or expounded *cursorie* one of the Epistles: Galatians, I or II Timothy, Titus, I or II Peter.[2] These were exercises which might or might not provide useful instruction. They did not amount to a systematic curriculum and they were frequently dispensed with, in whole or in part.[3] College lecturers soon became essential to the system to supplement the public lectures. By its statutes (1480) Magdalen's lecturers in theology and philosophy gave lectures open to the university, an innovation as we have seen; Corpus sent its theologians to them. Corpus itself had a lecturer in theology, and although theology lecturers as such were not appointed, the vice-president, it seems, undertook this duty. Finally, the King Henry VIII lecturer was supported by college contributions under the arrangements of 1536.[4]

Besides lectures, disputations had long been organized by the faculty as exercises for theologians who must eventually dispute formally for their degrees. Lincoln (statutes 1480) made all its *theologi* frequent them for most of full term. In 1504 Merton required all its MAs deputed to theology to attend them.[5] Rules of 1549 were adopted by the 1565 statutes and again, with slight changes, were reaffirmed in 1583: in 1549 disputations were to be held fortnightly in term on Thursdays from 1 to 3 p.m. The 1565 statutes reduced this to once a term; but by 1581 ten a year were customary, and this was confirmed by statutes in 1583. From 1549 the matter for discussion was to be difficulties in the interpretation of scripture.[6]

The university supplied the regius professor as moderator, presiding and summing up, while colleges, singly or by groups, were obliged to send bachelors of theology or senior masters of arts as disputants. The senior among them responded to two questions, while the two

[1] Lady Margaret professor; *Statuta*, 407; *Laudian Code*, tit. iv, sectio i: 17, pp. 39–40; Hebrew professor, *Statuta*, 343, 381–2; *Laudian Code*, tit. iv, sectio i: 13, p. 38; Greek professor; *Statuta*, 343, 381–2; *Laudian Code*, tit. iv, sectio 12, p. 38.

[2] *Statuta*, 49–50, 381.

[3] *Reg. Univ.* ed. Clark, i. 140–2.

[4] Thomas Fowler, *The History of Corpus Christi College* (OHS xxv 1893), 58; and see p. 306 n. 5.

[5] SCO i. pt 6 (Lincoln), 17–18; *Reg. ann mert. 1483–1521*, 293.

[6] *Statuta*, 347 (1549); 383 (1565); 427 (1583); *Reg. Univ.* ed. Clark i. 109 for a summary of the provisions of 1583; *Statuta*, 348: 'Themata dubia sacrae scripturae loca sint vel ex illis ducantur.'

next in seniority opposed (1565) and others joined in by order of seniority. Respondents had to give 14 days' notice of their questions, indicating whether they would affirm or deny; they had half an hour for their opening speech, opponents a quarter. Fines were to be levied upon those whose negligence caused a disputation not to be held. Termly disputations were not to be reckoned *pro forma*. All MAs of four years' standing were obliged in 1565 to take a turn in these proceedings unless they were formally students of law or medicine, as were all graduate students of theology living in colleges at their own expense or in halls.[1]

Most colleges were also bound to arrange theological disputations for their own men. The Lincoln statutes go into detail: weekly disputations were to be held on some theological question with two principles or starting points, which were to be attacked on three or four matters or points with good and lively arguments, for as long as the sub-rector or his appointee thought fit.[2] The very similar ordinances of Corpus, Cardinal and St John's colleges, obliged doctors, bachelors and *theologi* to take part in the weekly disputation moderated by the lecturer or dean of theology, or at Cardinal College, by a senior canon. After such practice candidates for theology degrees should have been ready for their *pro forma* disputations.

How effective was this traditional system? Was it preserved by conservatism alone? The year 1515 may have seen an attempt at revolution when all the masters present in congregation on 20 April, dispensed themselves to proceed BTh after only ten years in arts and theology, and thereupon to incept DTh immediately. Presumably this excluded all *pro forma* exercises for BTh, leaving three years for attendance at lectures and private study. This move was soon quashed by the commissary and proctors, but not before some had taken advantage of it.[3] Tyndale, who was MA that year, never proceeded BTh. Rather, he poured scorn on the system by which 'no man shall look on the scripture, until he be noselled in heathen learning eight or nine years, and armed with false principles; with which he is clean shut out of the understanding of the Scripture'.[4] There was nothing here of Colet's influence! New life however did come from Erasmianism, which attracted monks as well as seculars,[5]

---

[1] *Statuta*, 384. [2] *SCO* i. pt 6, 18.

[3] *Statuta*, cxx; this episode should be understood in the light of the growing concern of the university with the confused and anachronistic state of the statutes, by which those who swore to keep them were almost certain to break their vows or perjure themselves; cf *Statuta*, xlv.

[4] *The Practice of Prelates*, from William Tyndale, *Expositions and Notes on Sundry Portions of the Holy Scriptures, together with The Practice of Prelates*, ed. Henry Walter (Parker Society 1849), 291.

[5] J. K. McConica, *English Humanists and Reformation Politics* (Oxford 1965), 61-3,

while Lutheranism and Calvinism changed the attitude to scripture. The old system could be effective in training clergy provided it was backed by college tuition, as was increasingly the case. The awarding of degrees could be fair, despite the lack of examinations, provided deponents were conscientious. It was a form of what now would be termed continuous assessment. Under pressure of controversy on vital issues the opportunity offered by fellowships could stimulate genuine research. After seven years in arts and perhaps a regency, *theologi* were mature men, many of whom must have taken their work with full seriousness. The recorded theses of disputations at vespers and *comitia* are substantial.[1] It is by their subsequent publications that we must judge the interests and ability of Oxford theologians, since so many left the university for office in the church. Before we come to these, and to evidence of advanced study within the university, certain other responsibilities of the faculty need brief mention.

As we have seen, it was the regius professor's duty to moderate the *pro forma* disputations for BTh, though other doctors might participate. Resident doctors of theology, even if dispensed from lecturing, could be summoned to moderate at the vespers of an inceptor or to act as respondent in the *comitia*, though a shortage of doctors was the cause cited for many dispensations.[2] In addition, some members of the faculty, especially the few doctors, were active in convocation and congregation and their committees, in which theologians naturally predominated when their own affairs were discussed. Even a committee of the vice-chancellor, proctors and ten others on disputations in general, constituted in 1591, included two doctors of theology and four MA *theologi* who became doctors. Such committee work was a partial check to the constitutional predominance of the masters of arts.[5]

and on Robert Joseph OSB, monk of Evesham, ibid. 94–8; *The Letter Book of Robert Joseph*, ed. W. A. Pantin and H. Aveling (OHS new ser xix 1967), pp. xxviii–xxxv.

[1] *Reg. Univ.* ed. Clark i. 194–217 (for the years 1576–1622). Queen Elizabeth's visit in 1566 furnishes an interesting but untypical example of a 'show' theological disputation, with Bishop Jewel moderating; see *Elizabethan Oxford*, ed. Charles Plummer (OHS viii 1887), 109 ff. Among the participants were such distinguished doctors as Laurence Humfrey, James Calfhill and Herbert Westfaling. A few serious disputations were published, in some cases worked up: examples are Peter Martyr's on the eucharist ([1550] STC 24665); John Rainolds's *Sex Theses de sacra scriptura et ecclesia* (1580; STC 20624); George Abbot's *Quaestiones sex* (1598; STC 36); and John Howson's *Exore dimissa* (Oxford 1602; STC 13886), a vespers thesis which started a considerable controversy.

[2] See, for example, *Statuta*, 383 (1564/5), 437 (1586); *Reg. Univ.* ed. Clark i. 134, 143. That regular university disputations came to be neglected is indicated by Hatton's reproof as chancellor in July 1590: 'Where there ought alwaies to be in every Terme, certeine sett disputations in Divinitie, the most of them, as I have byn informed, have byn thys yeare omitted.' Wood, *History and Antiquities* ii. 242.

[3] *Statuta*, 444, and for other instances from 1564 to 1594, 396–453.

Although after the departure of the friars, there may have been no homiletic instruction except by example, a theologian had to preach a Latin sermon *ad clerum* for his BTh within a year of admission, although postponement or other dispensation was easily obtained.[1] Resident theologians had all to take their turn with university sermons at St Mary's, Christ Church and St Peter's in the East. This duty fell upon 'everye student in devinitye beinge minister whether he be of Colledge or Hawle' (1584).[2] Should a doctor or bachelor indicate the desire to preach, because of his rank others must yield their turn to him.[3] The elaborate system, controlled by the chancellor through his commissary, is set out in some detail in the *nova statuta* of 1565.[4] Preaching and other clerical duty in colleges was not the concern of the faculty as such, and colleges had their chaplains to take services. The part of fellows in orders and of the faculty in the religious instruction of undergraduates will be noticed later. The licence to preach *per Angliam* was granted by the university, not the faculty. It is likely that individual members were consulted since it was given at discretion, and not on condition of any degree, until 1584. Then rules were introduced: the candidate was to be an MA who had disputed once (and so was of some years' standing) and who had preached four university sermons.[5]

In 1580 additional university sermons were instituted, such as the Latin sermons at the beginning of each term, the three at Christ Church on Good Friday, Easter Monday and Tuesday with one at St Peter's in the East on Easter Day, all four to be repeated as a memory exercise by someone appointed to do this on Low Sunday at St Mary's.[6]

The Paul's Cross sermons in London were almost an obligation. A medieval institution, these sermons were an important means of influencing opinion throughout the reformation period and up to 1633. The sermon of the Oxford Lutheran Thomas Gerrard (Garrett) in 1540 led, through Bishop Gardiner's objections, to his execution that year. In 1541 Richard Smith, regius professor of theology at Oxford, preached against protestant doctrine, only to recant (temporarily) his papistical books when he preached again in 1547; the books were burned during the sermon. Jewel's Challenge sermon, in both forms, was preached there; Sampson, dean of Christ Church,

---

[1] *Reg. Univ.* ed. Clark i. 137–8.
[2] *Statuta*, 431.
[3] Ibid. 354 (1549).
[4] Ibid. 382–3; for earlier practice see the rules of 1431 in ibid. 236–8.
[5] Ibid. 430; *Reg. Univ.* ed. Clark i. 130–2, and the table in ii. 411, column xv.
[6] Bodl. MS. Top. Oxon. fo 53 is a transcript of such a set preached by four theologians in 1596.

and Humfrey, president of Magdalen College, managed to slip in a protest against vestments (1565) and John Oxenbridge commented next year on the parlous state of Oxford where there were said to be not past five or six preachers except 'strawberry preachers' (Latimer's term for non-residents).

Paul's Cross preachers were appointed by the bishop of London and were expected to accept the invitation. But it would prove expensive. In 1595 Thomas Martin of Scrope Hall, Holborn, in a charming letter transcribed in the register of convocation, offered hospitality to Oxford preachers at Paul's Cross.[1] A few weeks later Richard Bancroft, bishop of London, wrote chiding the university for the excuses made, reminding them that he could have used compulsion, but preferred courtesy. The vice-chancellor should summon 'all the preachers of the university' and warn them. Bancroft persuaded Chancellor Buckhurst to write more sternly: if preachers did not accept, they would be compelled. Laud, when bishop of London, simply gave orders: 'you are appointed' . . . 'I require and charge you not to fail' . . . 'send acceptance to my chaplain.'[2]

Recognizing this quasi-obligation, the university worked it into its degree system. A Paul's Cross sermon could count *pro forma* for the doctorate in theology in place of one at Oxford: it might be offered as such by the candidate or demanded from him. Many instances of such graces or dispensations occur in the years 1535–42 and there are some later ones in the register of the university from 1571.[3]

Another theological lecture was instituted by Sir Francis Walsingham in 1586. Persistent Jesuit teaching abroad was to be countered by more lectures at Oxford: he hoped John Rainolds would give them. And so he decreed 'that the common places of the Scripture, the Principles of Religion, and matters of controversye might be handled and expounded, like as at Rheimes and other places beyond the seas.' According to Wood, Rainolds lectured in the theology school thrice weekly in full term, had constantly a 'great auditory', and, 'was held by those of his party to have done great good'. When Walsingham died in 1590, the earl of Essex maintained the lectures which Rainolds resumed, but how long they continued is apparently not known. The stipend was £20 per annum.[4]

[1] Reg. Cong. 1595–1606, fo 7.

[2] Millar Maclure, *The Paul's Cross Sermons 1534–1642* (Toronto 1958), 13.

[3] *Reg. Univ.* ed. Clark i. 137. Much information is to be found in Maclure, but he appears not to know of the connection with the degree or the 1595 correspondence.

[4] Wood, *History and Antiquities*, ii. 226–8; Fowler, *Corpus Christi College* 160, using the Fulman manuscripts at Corpus Christi College. Wood used Reg. Cong. 1582–95; see fo 286[r–v]. His personal view was that the puritanism of the lecturers left little of the genuine Church of England visible.

In the same year 1586, the Oxford city fathers founded two (later four) lecturerships or sermons at St Martin's Church, Carfax. This was the city church. Though appointed by the city, the lecturers were most often Oxford graduates, frequently resident fellows of colleges, the most eminent being Richard Field. Another, Giles Widdowes, is interesting for his controversy with Prynne. H. E. Salter concluded that until Thomas Baylie in 1620, there is no clear evidence from the list that city and university differed ecclesiastically.[1] Swaddon, Field, Francis Mason and Corbett, all of whom rose high, were not strongly Calvinistic, and opposed presbyterianism. With Baylie and others later on, the city came to prefer puritanism.[2]

In London the Gresham lectures also concerned Oxford. Founded to implement Sir Thomas Gresham's will, they were operative from 1597 when his widow died. His house became Gresham College. Lecturers in theology and other subjects were to be appointed, some by the mayor and aldermen, others by the Mercers' Company. Both bodies asked Oxford and Cambridge to nominate two to each faculty and for theology, Oxford, in a committee of convocation on 14 February 1597, chose Dr Richard Latewarr of St John's and Mr Robert Abbott, later regius professor of theology at Oxford and bishop of Salisbury. George Abbott, the future archbishop of Canterbury, held the office a little later.[3] In 1597 all three were just completing their doctorates in theology, Latewarr on a neutral, Christological thesis, Robert Abbott on the thorny issue of election and predestination, and George Abbott on Rome and papal authority.

SCHOLARSHIP

How the Bible was studied in Oxford early in the century has largely to be conjectured from humanist and reforming criticism. Presumably most theological students were instructed in the defence of orthodoxy from scripture. Though Colet's lectures on St Paul, 1497–1504, had opened up a fresh approach to the epistles, he and his circle left Oxford, so that Bishop Fox's instructions to his theology reader (1517) probably mark a new beginning. He must lecture on the Old and New Testaments in alternate years, interpreting them profoundly as the ancient doctors did—Jerome, Augustine, Ambrose, Origen, Hilary, Chrysostom, Damascenus—not like Hugh of Vienne or Lyra.[4]

[1] H. E. Salter, *Oxford Council Acts 1583–1626* (OHS lxxxvii 1928), xxxii.

[2] For an account of the city lectures see ibid. xxviii–xxxii; also P. S. Seaver, *The Puritan Lectureships: the politics of religious dissent 1560–1662* (Stanford 1970), 92 ff.

[3] See John Ward, *The Lives of the Professors of Gresham College* (1740).

[4] *SCO* ii. pt 10, 50–1, as in original statutes, Bodl. MS Laud misc. 621, p. 54.

Reformation influences were quickly added. While Dorne's book sales in 1520—reflecting both traditional theology and the impact of Erasmus—include a little Luther, it is nothing to what Thomas Garrett[1] was privately selling in Oxford in 1528: Luther on Genesis, Exodus, Psalms, Jonah, Habakkuk, Galatians Co(rinthians? Colossians?), Melanchthon on Genesis, Proverbs, Johns, Romans, Corinthians, Colossians; Oecolampadius on Isaiah and other prophets, Romans, I John; Bugenhagen on Deuteronomy, Samuel, Psalms, Galatians; Lambert on Canticles, several prophets and Luke; Brentz on Job, Bucer on Ephesians, Hegendorff on Luke and Hebrews, to mention only the biblical commentaries. Anthony Dalaber pictures for us the scholars who in 1527–8 frequented John Clarke's lectures and disputations at Cardinal College whenever they could. Clarke read St Paul to them, and sent Dalaber every week to absentees, 'to know what doubts they had in any place of the Scripture; that by me, for him, they might have the true understanding of the same'.[2]

Catholic and protestant alike must now study the Bible assiduously, if only for controversial ends, since no major party denied its ultimate authority. It was the attitude that differed, reformers professing to ground doctrine directly in scripture alone and challenging tradition from it as a base, their opponents championing the church's right to determine correct exegesis: so More against Luther and Tyndale. The reformers seemed victorious when the theology professors had all to lecture on the Bible, and the bachelor of theology was licensed to lecture on the Pauline epistles instead of the *Sentences*. In 1550 Oriel College in giving graces to four candidates said that they were to read a book of the *Sentences* or, as the king's new ordinances say, an epistle of St Paul.[3]

Serious biblical study required the original languages. By this time Greek was available through the faculty of arts, although not without a preliminary struggle, for it was denounced from the university pulpit—as Erasmus and More relate.[4] But More helped to defeat the 'Trojans', Oxford theologians took to Greek and, conversely, regius professors of Greek turned their talents to biblical and patristic studies. Giles Lawrence, a fellow of All Souls and doctor of laws who

[1] Garrett, or Gerard, of Lincolnshire was admitted *discipulus* of Corpus Christi College in 1517 at the age of 19, and became a fellow of Magdalen College about 1519. In a letter of 1528 to Wolsey he described himself then as 'of Cardinallis College in Oxford'; BA 1518, MA 1524. As curate of All Hallows Honey Lane in London he brought to Oxford in Lent 1527 two fardels of Lutheran and like books for sale; see *BRUO 1501–40*.

[2] Foxe, *Acts and Monuments* v. 427, and the catalogue of Richard Bayfield's forbidden books (1531) in iv. 682–3.   [3] *Dean's Register of Oriel*, 131.

[4] *Opus epistolarum Des. Erasmi roterodami*, ed. P. S. Allen *et al.* (12 vols. Oxford 1906–58) iii. 456–7 (letter 948); *The Correspondence of Sir Thomas More*, ed. E. F. Rogers (Princeton 1947) 111–20 (letter 60).

held the chair from 1551 to 1553 and again from 1559 to 1585, was instrumental in the revision of the Bishops' Bible.[1] The most scholarly of the Tudor regius professors, John Harmar, a fellow of New College (BA 1577, MA 1582, BTh 1605) who held the chair from 1585 to 1590, was warden of Winchester College from 1596 to 1613. He was also a translator of the New Testament in 1604, having begun his publishing career with an edition of some of the works of Chrysostom in 1586.[2] His *Eclogue sententiarum et similitudinum familiarium Ioanne Chrysostomo desumpta: sive Isagoge ad linguam Grecam* (1622) was a brief (seventy page) work intended for the future clergy, with a column of *sententiae* of Chrysostom in Greek on each page facing a like column in Latin, and it included at the end an index of Greek words. This work may shed a little light on the actual practice of the university in teaching Greek to the *theologi* and future clergy in the arts faculty, since it seems that in general, little if any distinction was made between the authors of classical Greek and the biblical tongue. It is likely that the Greek fathers were the intermediaries. A second work by Harmar, *Lexicon Graeco-Latinum novum*, was an edition of Scapula's abridgement of Estienne's great five volume *Thesarus graecae linguae* (1572), and appeared in London in 1637. Harmar's addition was a *Lexicon etymologicum linguae graecae*, dedicated to Laud as archbishop of Canterbury.

Among the early holders of the regius chair in theology, Peter Martyr (1548–63) was unquestionably the most learned. It is not until we get to his successor, Lawrence Humfrey (BA, MA 1552; BTh, DTh 1562), who held the chair from 1560 to 1589, that we find an English regius professor of real erudition.[3] His successor, Thomas Holland (BA 1571, MA 1576, BTh 1582, DTh 1585) was chaplain to the earl of Leicester in the Netherlands in 1585, and one of those who helped to prepare the authorized version of the Bible.

A search among the library inventories for sixteenth century Oxford might reveal something more of the progress of Greek learning among ordinary members of the faculty, if it were not that their careers almost invariably removed them from the university before they died. One large inventory does survive for William Mitchell, BTh 1596, a fellow of Queen's who died in 1599. Among the 245 books left among his effects, there are enough in Greek to suggest that a *theologus* of no particular reputation or distinction might be expected, by the 1590s, to have a practised command of the language.

---

[1] Discipulus Corpus Christi College 1539; suppl. DCL 1556; tutor to the children of Sir Arthur Darby during the reign of Mary; see below, pp. 355, 316.

[2] See below, p. 355.

[3] See below, p. 354.

Apart from the Greek grammars of Johannes Ceporinus and Nicolaus Clenardus (along with three Hebrew grammars) he had two Greek New Testaments, one of them in Beza's edition, Greek editions of Aristotle's *Physics* and *Ethics*, and a number of works in both Greek and Latin: Isocrates, Herodian, Homer, and Aesop; his inventory also included a Hebrew Genesis.[1]

Though Hebrew was not new to Tudor Oxford, there was now more provision for it, although not quite in the trilingual colleges that Erasmus desired, for neither Corpus nor Cardinal College had a Hebrew lecturer on its establishment. However, King Henry sent to Oxford (*c* 1529) the distinguished Cambridge Hebraist Robert Wakefield, who had taught at Busleiden's college in Louvain and had succeeded Reuchlin at Tübingen. His *Oratio de . . . utilitate trium linguarum* [?1528] was the first book printed in England to include words in (woodcut) Hebrew characters.[2]

John Sheprey (Shepreve) of Corpus was the first regius professor of Hebrew but died at a young age in 1542, the year he was dispensed from statutes affecting the manner of interpreting the Bible. He was allowed, on the surprising plea that otherwise few would willingly attend, to lecture on the Hebrew text of Genesis and other books provided he did it in a pious and catholic way.[3]

The regius chair, founded *c* 1540–2, secured regular lectures on the Hebrew language and the Old Testament, and these the *theologi* were obliged to attend for part of their course.[4] Thomas Harding, its second holder, is best known as Jewel's antagonist. Richard Bruerne, appointed in 1547, was commended by Cox to Peter Martyr as an excellent Hebraist, and was called by Leland, 'Hebraei radius chori'. John Harding, first appointed in 1591, worked on the authorized version, as did Richard Kilbye (BA 1578, MA 1582, BTh and DTh 1596), whose scholarship Casaubon praised highly.[5] Sometimes we hear of college lecturers, especially at Magdalen, and there were other assistants such as the protestant refugees Isaac de Cardenas, who taught Hebrew in Oxford in mid-century, and John Drusius (Driessche) of Louvain, who studied Hebrew with Chevalier at Cambridge and came to Oxford in 1572. Merton hired him to read the Hebrew lecture in their common refectory; Laurence Humfrey requested him to

[1] Taken from the typed transcripts of his will from OUA Chanc. Court. Inv.

[2] *DNB; STC* 24955; *BRUO 1501–40*, 599–600. On the whole question of Hebrew studies see G. Lloyd Jones, *The Discovery of Hebrew in Tudor England: a third language* (Manchester 1983) which appeared too late to be incorporated here.

[3] On Sheprey see *DNB, BRUO 1501–40*, 513, and G. D. Duncan, p. 356 below.

[4] *Statuta* 345, 356 (1549), 408 (1576).

[5] For Harding and Bruerne see p. 357 below; for Kilbye, *DNB* and Vivian Green, *The Commonwealth of Lincoln College 1427–1977* (Oxford 1979), 155–6 and index under name. He was made professor of Hebrew in 1610.

lecture at Magdalen on Hebrew, Chaldee or Syriac, and the chancellor asked the university to augment what those colleges paid him because his knowledge of Syriac also was needed. Others were the Polish scholar Philip Ferdinand, teaching Hebrew privately in several colleges and halls in 1596, and Sixtus Amama from Franeker in Friesland, sojourning at Exeter College around 1615.[1]

Inventories suggest that Oxford *theologi* frequently possessed Hebrew books as the century advanced and they show what textbooks were in use: Münster and Pagninus are common. Richard Clyff (MA Christ Church, d. 1566), for example, had a Hebrew Bible, Hebrew and Chaldee dictionaries, separate texts of Genesis, Psalms, Proverbs and Hosea in Hebrew, a *Grammatica chaldaica* with other elementary Hebrew books and a large number of biblical commentaries.[2] The Bodleian catalogue of 1605 already contains several Hebrew and Polyglot Bibles, copies of almost all the available Hebrew grammars, including those of David and Moses Kimchi, Reuchlin, Münster, Bertram and Martinius, together with Münster's Aramaic grammar and dictionary and Tremellius's Aramaic and Syriac grammars, and various Hebrew dictionaries. Rabbinic works include complete sets of the Talmud and commentaries by Kimchi, Rashi, Levi ben Gershon, Abarbanel and others, with 'quite a disproportionate number of minor cabalistic works'. Kilbye left valuable rabbinic texts to Lincoln College.[3]

Knowledge of Hebrew thus became fairly common, and some excelled, for the standards of the day. Tyndale was a good Hebraist (perhaps not while at Oxford) as was Philpot, both before the chair was founded. So, later, were the catholic scholars Campion, Gregory Martin and Worthington. Nicholas Fuller is of some interest as a philologist. Oxford men tried their hand at Hebrew verse: three of them, including Bodley, whose knowledge Drusius commended contributed to the multilingual poems appended to Lawrence Humfrey's *Vita Juelli* (1573). More important, Roth stresses the *Conference* between John Rainolds and John Hart in 1584 as demonstrating how Oxford scholarship was using such rabbinic writers as Rashi, Ibn Daud and Ibn Ezra.[4] The Oxford press was using Hebrew type in 1588 (or

[1] *Reg. Univ.* ed. Clark, i. 369, 377, 398, 277, and note 4 below.

[2] Reg. Chanc. 1545–1661, fo 207[v].

[3] The draft inventory of Kilbye is in Chanc. Court. Inv. The Bodleian analysis is from David Daiches, *The King James Version of the English Bible* (Chicago [1941]), 165–6. On Hebrew books in college libraries see, *Oxford College Libraries in 1556: guide to an exhibition held in 1956* (Oxford 1956), 18.

[4] Cecil Roth, 'Jews in Oxford after 1290', *Oxoniensia* xv (1950), 63–80; Cecil Roth, 'Sir Thomas Bodley—Hebraist', *Bodleian Library Record* viii pt 5 (1966), 242–51; A. R. Bonner and P. James, 'Two letters in Hebrew addressed to Sir Thomas Bodley', *Bodleian Library Record* viii pt 5 (1971), 258–62.

1591) well before Cambridge's 1632, though Professor Thorne complained in 1603 of inadequate facilities for printing Hebrew. Incepting doctors at the turn of the century liked to argue the necessity of working from the *Hebraica veritas* (so in 1594, 1597, 1599, 1602) and John Rainolds's *Advice on the Study of Divinity* (published posthumously in 1613) emphasized the same principle.[1] Thomas Pye DTh was reckoned an eminent Orientalist; Thomas Holland used the Talmud and introduced it into his sermons; Sebastian Benefield quoted Hebrew and argued from the *hiphil* verb even in his 'country sermons' on Amos, besides often telling his village congregation how Drusius differed from other commentators.[2]

What biblical lectures that made use of every contemporary resource might mean, was displayed in Oxford by Peter Martyr. His teaching was not compartmentalized, with separate lectures (as today) on dogmatic theology, patristic doctrine, ethics, liturgy, and history, but comprehensive and overwhelmingly thorough. Yet this was not austerely academic, nor was it an impartial introduction to theology. 'I chose I Corinthians,' he explained, 'because it treats of many different matters of present controversies and so can heal the Church now.' Some, he knows, will think him prolix, but those who teach contrary to Paul must be described and the controversies explained, and he must include the exegesis of the fathers. John ab Ulmis attended these lectures and wrote about them to Gualter. Jewel was there with pen and ink: Humfrey marvelled to see how fast his fingers flew. Seeking to be perfected by Martyr, Humfrey says, Jewel observed his art, copied out his sermons and lectures, was his notary in the tumultuous disputation in the theology school and became most intimate with him.[3]

It was Peter Martyr's lectures on Corinthians in 1548-9 which set off the great eucharistic debate of the 1550s, while those on Romans

---

[1] On the use of Hebrew type, see F. Madan, *Oxford Books* (3 vols Oxford 1895-1931) ii. 35 (no. 159), 45 (no. 230). The first appearance was in the *Funebria nobilissimi . . . D. Henrici Untoni*, printed by Barnes in 1596 (*STC* 24520) and containing 105 poems, including one in Hebrew. However, in a tribute to James I printed in 1603, a Hebrew poem by the regius professor was omitted for lack of type (*STC* 19019). *Reg. Univ.* ed. Clark ii. 197 (1594), 199 (1597), 201 (1599), 202 (1602); Rainolds's *Advice* (*STC* 20611) sig. A5[r-v]. Rainolds said that when he was first an MA he began the study of Hebrew, but gave it up; the next year, perceiving the use of it he took it up again and persevered.

[2] Pye matriculated at Balliol 1577, DTh 1588: *DNB*; Wood, *Athenae* ii. 59-60; Thomas Holland (Balliol) MA 1575, DTh 1584, was appointed regius professor of theology in 1589, and was one of those appointed to prepare the Old Testament for the authorized version; his funeral sermon in St Mary's (26 March 1612) was preached by Richard Kilbye: *DNB*; Sebastian Benefield, of Corpus Christi College, was made reader in rhetoric there in 1599, DTh 1608. In 1613 he became Lady Margaret professor (resigned 1626), and he wrote a commentary on the prophet Amos: *STC* 1861-1866; *DNB*.

[3] *Ioannis Iuelli angli, . . . vita & mors* (1573; *STC* 13963), 40-1.

in 1550 developed the protestant position on other central doctrines —strictly from scripture, as he believed. The printed forms are expansions, but the lectures were long, each set delivered almost daily throughout the academic year. And they were immensely influential, not only in encouraging learning and stimulating controversy, but also in their religious impact. Bartholomew Green saw the light of the gospel through attending them, Julius Palmer was converted when he read the commentary on I Corinthians (published in 1551) which he borrowed from another Magdalen man. Both Green and Palmer were executed in 1556.[1]

The controversial aspect of Martyr's lectures is considered elsewhere; here their method is relevant. Apart from the Marian interlude, the principle was accepted that lectures in theology would start from the Bible, that exegesis would range widely and contain much history of doctrine, while doctrinal conclusions must be proved from scripture. Proof of this general characterization is found in the principles laid down by, for example, Chaderton at Cambridge and Humfrey and Rainolds at Oxford, though these relate only partially to lecturing. Chaderton insisted on the broad learning required for biblical study: Hebrew and Greek, rhetoric and logic, deep knowledge of Greek and Roman history, commentaries old and new.[2] Rainolds wanted study in the original tongues with commentaries on the chief parts: St John and Romans as the sum of the New Testament, Isaiah and the Psalms of the Old. For the rest, especially the harder places, he would use Calvin and Peter Martyr, who had written best on most of the Old Testament.[3] English scholars were little concerned at this time to produce new biblical texts or even commentaries, though some of these were published; rather, they endeavoured to absorb continental scholarship.

Since theological controversy on crucial issues dominated the century, learning was perforce harnessed to it. Even sermons and devotional writings, in which Oxford men were active ('silver-tongued' Henry Smith among them) usually promoted some particular tradition of piety. Nor were the successive English Bibles occasioned by disinterested erudition, though they required the genuine scholarship which Oxford and Cambridge men contributed,

[1] For Martyr's eucharistic theology see J. C. McLelland, *The Visible Words of God* (London and Edinburgh 1957). The printed versions are *STC* 24672-3, 24665 (an English version of 24673). Foxe, *Acts and Monuments* vii. 731, viii. 206. Two Bartholomew Greens are listed in *Reg. Univ.* ed. Boase, 212, 224, where the martyr 'Bartlet' Green, BA (1530-56) is wrongly credited with the MA (1558) of the Magdalen College man; the martyr was of London, not Warwick. Cf Macray, *Reg. Magdalen* ii. 144.

[2] Printed in H. C. Porter, *Puritanism in Tudor England* (1970), 195-7.

[3] Mark H. Curtis, *Oxford and Cambridge in Transition, 1558-1642* (Oxford 1959), 206-7; cf p. 316 n. 2.

whether at home or abroad. Tyndale had left Oxford and benefited from Cambridge before he made the fundamental English version of the New Testament (1525) and much of the Old. Coverdale was a Cambridge man. Parkhurst, Jewel's tutor at Merton, made him compare Coverdale with Tyndale, a glimpse of college biblical study.[1] Taverner came from Cambridge to Cardinal College and made some original contributions in his revision of Coverdale (1539). Some Oxford men, though more from Cambridge, were among the men 'learned in Hebrew, Greek, Latin and English' appointed by Canterbury Convocation in 1542 to examine the Great Bible.[2] William Cole and other Oxford scholars met at the printer Froschover's house in Zurich (Froschover also came to Oxford), and William Whittingham of All Souls and Christ Church, led the team which produced the Geneva Bible (1576). Oxford and Cambridge invitably shared the bishops responsible for the Bishops' Bible (1568), rivalling the Genevan version; its New Testament was revised in 1572 in deference to the criticism of Giles Lawrence, regius professor of Greek at Oxford. Oxford helped towards a Welsh Bible through William Salesbury, who published the first Welsh–English dictionary in 1547 and urged his countrymen to petition Henry VIII for a translation, and through Richard Davies, bishop of St David's, who with Salesbury translated the New Testament of 1567.[3]

The Rheims-Douay Bible, too, was largely the work of Oxford men: Gregory Martin, Cardinal Allen, Bristow, Worthington, William Rainolds and Barrett. The authorized version perhaps owed its origin to John Rainolds when president of Corpus. In this version the prophets, a difficult assignment, fell to one Oxford company, the gospels, acts and apocalypse to another, while several Oxford graduates were members of the Westminster company which translated Romans-Jude. These men were not all resident members of the university, though three at least were dispensed from their DTh exercises in order to concentrate on this work.[4] All of this, if not a product of the faculty of theology itself, well illustrates one trend in its scholarship. For other aspects we must turn to patristics and controversial theology.

[1] *Vita Iuelli*, 21.

[2] *Records of the English Bible*, ed. Alfred W. Pollard (Oxford 1911), p. xlv; J. F. Mozley, *Coverdale and his Bibles* (1953), 272 ff.

[3] See Glanmor Williams, *Welsh Reformation Essays* (Cardiff 1967), esp. chs 7, 8. Salesbury had been at St Albans or Broadgates Hall, 'or both' according to Wood; he published his dictionary about the time he left Oxford for legal studies in London. Davies was educated at New Inn Hall and was an exile in Geneva under Mary.

[4] John Harmar and Arthur Lake, both MAs of New College, and Thomas Sanderson of Balliol; *Reg. Univ.* ed. Clark, i. 141; *Translating the New Testament Epistles 1601–1611: a manuscript from King James's Westminster Company*, ed. Ward Allen (Vanderbilt U.P. 1977), xii–xiii, xv.

Patristic study

Patristic study, though as such strictly extra-curricular, was incorporated into biblical lectures and was essential for contemporary controversy. Again English scholars relied on the continent for texts, and commentaries were still uncommon anywhere. They did not need translations from Latin; some perhaps welcomed help with Greek fathers. During this century very few of the greatest works of the greater fathers were printed in England, in the original or in translation, and most of the few publications were ethical or devotional. Meredith Hanmer's (MA 1572, BTh 1581, DTh 1582) translation of the *Ecclesiastical Histories* of Eusebius, Socrates and Evagrius (1577) was a valuable exception: he was chaplain of Corpus Christi College, Oxford. There was one greater exception. John Chrysostom's scriptural method and characteristically Greek theology proved attractive to humanists and reformers. The first Greek book printed in England[1] contained two of his homilies and a few Latin and English versions came out in this decade, mostly moralistic, the translators including the humanist Thomas Lupset and the Oxford Calvinist, Thomas Sampson. Later on John Harmar, while regius professor, published the first Greek book of the Oxford press (1586), six homilies of Chrysostom in Greek, and part of the important sermons *Ad Antiochenos* (1590). This interest culminated in the complete critical edition, published in eight folio volumes between 1610 and 1613, which Sir Henry Savile achieved with Oxford helpers collecting manuscripts and earlier printed editions. Not yet entirely superseded, it is one of the glories of Oxford scholarship.[2]

The *Short-Title Catalogue* alone would give an inadequate impression of English patristic scholarship. It tells us nothing of work done or published abroad in Latin by English catholics. It cannot tell us that John Foxe, who matriculated at Basle in 1556 (the very year in which Flacius Illyricus published there his *Catalogus testium veritatis*) spent two months collating Chrysostom manuscripts for the Froben firm when reduced almost to his last farthing; or that Lawrence Humfrey, a fellow-exile, edited for the same firm an important revision of Erasmus's Origen with a preface in which he, a 'puritan', pleads for the study of the fathers as interpreters of scripture. He would put Chrysostom, Gregory of Nazianzus and Basil side by side with Plato and Aristotle *in scolis ac gymnasiis*. He also

[1] R. Wolfe, 1543: *STC* 14634.
[2] J. Barnes, Oxford: *STC* 14635; G. Bishop and R. Newberie: *STC* 14636; Madan, *Oxford Books* i. 18 (item 5); S. L. Greenslade, 'The printer's copy for the Eton Chrysostom', *Studia patristica* vii (Berlin 1966), 60–4.

translated Cyril of Alexandria's commentary on Isaiah into Latin for Froben (published 1563). Humfrey's *Jesuitismus*, written against Campion in 1582–4, had a special section *De patribus*. With his intimate knowledge of the Jewel–Harding controversy behind him, he shows enormous erudition, with cautions as to the proper use (as he sees it) of the later fathers, and with many references to questions of authenticity. He uses Erasmus's treatise on preaching, the *Ecclesiastes*, and many Erasmian editions which he compares with later ones.[1]

The importance of the fathers in controversy was recognized. Rome was confident in its tradition, its continuity with the Church and the teaching of the fathers. Some reformers hoped to turn this by the principle, *sola scriptura*. Others, equally pledged to the final authority of scripture, challenged the truth of the Roman claim and tried to prove *from* the fathers that Rome demanded many beliefs *de fide*, and imposed many practices, which were unknown to or inconsistent with their teaching: hence, in England, Peter Martyr's lectures and eucharistic disputation and Jewel's Challenge sermon and Apology followed by his laborious controversy with Harding. Catholic theologians grumbled at Jewel's negative use of the fathers and reasonably raised the question of doctrinal development in a Spirit-guided *ecclesia docens*. Minute investigation could not be shirked: nor was it. Besides, this negative shifted to a positive: the church of the fathers, uncorrupted (it seemed) in faith and practice, demonstrated how scriptural teaching could and should be embodied. In time, 'Anglicans' saw here a reply to puritan biblicism as well as to Rome. Thus patristic erudition was indeed cultivated, but found expression in controversial theology rather than in works of pure learning. Foundations for the very detailed knowledge necessary must in most cases have been laid in the university, as was certainly true of Jewel and Hooker. The Marian exiles had further opportunities for study and scholarly contacts abroad, with great consequences for the universities and for English religion when they returned, and before long, catholic exiles at Rome, Louvain and elsewhere were absorbing and transmitting the learning of the counter-reformation.

Some special problems troubled scholars in this field. What fathers had been published; how good were the texts; what works were authentic? A few illustrations must suffice. Peter Martyr stunned his Oxford opponents with two passages from Theodoret's *Dialogues*. 'He's a very obscure author, and nobody but you has a copy,' replied Dr Tresham. Chedsey challenged Cranmer's use, at his trial, of

[1] *Jesuitismi pars prima* (1582; *STC* 13961), *pars secunda* (1584; *STC* 13962).

Hilary: *vero sub mysterio carnem corporis sumimus*! 'What is your edition? We have two, from Basle, and Paris, both reading, *vere'* (which, taken with *sumimus*, certainly affects the theology). When Ridley had *De coena domini* pressed against him as Cyprian's work, he answered, 'Yes, it is.' But it is not, as Erasmus's edition would have told him.[1] Knowledge of Erasmus's editorial work was patchy, scholars often took down older editions from library shelves, everyone made mistakes. Gradually, however, a more accurate picture of the early church emerged from the application of academic scholarship to controversy, while scholarly technique itself benefited from the sharpening of weapons. The years 1610–12 furnish a remarkable instance of team research. The Bodleian library had become a major factor in Oxford scholarship and Thomas James, its first librarian, anti-Roman to the verge of fanaticism, published in 1611 *A Treatise of the Corruption of Scripture, Councels and Fathers by Prelates of the Church of Rome*, part of it sub-titled the *Bastardie of the False Fathers*. Zeal and scholarship combined in his detection of false attributions and false readings. He gathered a band of fifteen dons, fairly young *theologi* approaching bachelor of theology status, and these he set to collate recent 'Roman' editions of Gregory I, Cyprian and Ambrose against 56 manuscripts, of which 23 were already in Bodley and 23 in college libraries.[2] Though they stopped work in 1612, James then and subsequently made ample use of their labours, and it was he who finally revealed the truth about Cyprian's *De coena*: it was written by Arnold, abbot of Bonneval in the mid-twelfth century, as the All Souls manuscript (now MS xix) demonstrated. Benefield made clever rhetorical use of this in his reply to Leech.[3] Numerous catalogues and inventories prove how fast patristic manuscripts and printed books were accumulating in the Bodleian, in college libraries and in private collections.

Older disciplines were not forgotten when Erasmian techniques became familiar, but were combined with them. In the Canterbury convocation debate on the eucharist (1553) Theodoret was discussed at length. Did his words fall into the Aristotelian category

[1] John Kennall DCL, of Christ Church, and William Chedsey DTh, of Corpus Christi College, disagreed violently as to the eucharistic presence in quality and quantity while publicly examining a heretic, William Wood of Kent, in 1558; Foxe, *Acts and Monuments* viii. 567. Concerning Tresham, see Martyr's *Disputatio de sacramento eucharistiae habita publice Oxonii* (1549; *STC* 24673), 11: 'deinde satis obscurus est author, et eum praeter te nemo habet.' On Cranmer's use of Hilary, Foxe, *Acts and Monuments* vi. 461. In Erasmus's *Opera divi Caecilii Cypriani carthaginensis . . . repurgata* (Basel 1520), the 'Sermo de coena Domini' is among the 'opera quae videntur falso ascripta Cypriano', 448–56.
[2] H. Lownes (*STC* 14462–3), see N. R. Ker, 'Thomas James's collation of Gregory, Cyprian, and Ambrose', *Bodleian Library Record* iv pt 1 (1952), 16–30.
[3] S. Benefield, *Doctrinae christianae sex capita* (Oxford 1610; *STC* 1867), app. § 22.

of quality or substance? The prolocutor, Weston, previously Margaret professor at Oxford, tired of discussing one doctor and one word, and asked for short arguments. An order of debate was agreed with respondents and opponents like a formal disputation. The protestant Haddon at once turned to syllogisms. So did John Philpot (then archdeacon of Winchester, fellow of New College 1535–41) when told that, for all his talk of Theodoret, he had not produced one 'argument'. Disputation-form, mingled with humanistic elements, appears on such great occasions as the trials of Cranmer and Ridley at Oxford.[1] Chaderton valued the logic of the arts course and its study of rhetoric to discern proper speech from the figurative and tropical, but Cambridge is said to have been more sympathetic than Oxford to the logic of Ramus.

Controversial Theology and its Impact

Controversy, the course of which is described elsewhere, had in this period an existential quality for theologians: it went to the roots of Christian faith, it determined the kind of church in which they lived and worked. Original contributions to particular points of learning were not sufficient. Whatever their standpoint, traditionalist, humanist, Romanist, Lutheran, Calvinist, they must scrutinize their authorities, compile their common-place books, marshal their arguments, teach, preach and, almost inevitably, engage in literary propaganda, whether Henry, Edward, Mary or Elizabeth reigned. The more eminent shared in the formulation of doctrine, worship and discipline at the centre, in Canterbury convocation, special commissions, and if they were bishops, in parliament.

More particularly, catholic theologians were obliged to re-examine their attitude to scholastic theology and to reconsider, in light of learned criticism, their use of the fathers. As Trent demonstrated, they were also obliged to determine the boundary between orthodoxy and heresy. English protestants were faced with different emphases, sometimes contradictory, within the continental theology upon which they so much depended, especially with the rise of puritanism. While stock answers on familiar themes may have sufficed in examinations, the *quaestiones* do at least show how intrinsically fundamental were the subjects on which university teachers were daily employed. Clark prints those of 1576, and 1581–1622.[2] There was little desire to debate the Trinity, the Atonement or the Person

[1] Fully described in R. W. Dixon, *History of the Church of England* (6 vols 1878–1902) iv. 181 ff. On the fourth day John Harpesfield BTh, fellow of New College 1534–51, was allowed to count his part in the proceedings as his *pro forma* responsion for the DTh, with Weston and Cranmer as opponents.

[2] *Reg. Univ.* ed. Clark i. 194–217.

of Christ. Discussion of the sacraments continued, but by this time
the dominant issues were, first, the authority of scripture, the
church, popes and princes together with the propriety of toleration
and coercion; second, the ministry, where both Roman and presbyterian theories raised questions, and above all, the nexus of faith,
justification, free will and predestination. Of all this discussion, precisely because it was so fundamental to a Christian society, the state
believed it must take cognizance. Neither could theologians ignore
the state.

In their attempts to derive doctrine from scripture alone, protestant theologians soon established their own canons of orthodoxy:
the writings of Luther or Calvin so served, as did agreed articles and
confessions which, ostensibly subject to scripture, controlled its
exegesis. Rainolds has already been quoted on this use of Calvin who
dominated English protestant theology when the Marian exiles
returned. Protestant scholars were not thinking of academic freedom
and purity; they wanted to see the pure and true church established.
The state took steps to direct university teaching towards ecclesiastical unity.

Several methods were available. First, control of worship, which
moulds minds, by directives under Henry VIII, by enforcing the
book of common prayer in its successive forms, by restoring the
mass under Mary. Next, in addition to the dissolution, by commissions entailing statutory changes: Cromwell's in 1535, Edward's of
1549, Pole's in 1556, Elizabeth's in 1559. That of Edward insisted
on biblical teaching. Pole set himself to eradicate heresy: the commissary was to purge the university of it, no one to possess, read, buy
or introduce any book contrary to the right faith; the proctors were
to detect heresy, theology lectures to exhort their audiences to
embrace sound doctrine, philosophy lectures to follow the opinions
least dissident from Christian truth and warn their hearers how weak
is human reason in matters proper to revelation.[1] Spanish friars were
dispatched to set the pattern in teaching: Joannes de Villa Garcia,
theology reader at Magdalen College and regius professor, and
Peter de Soto, who lectured on Albert and Aquinas—both of them,
like Antony Rescius, involved in Cranmer's trial at Oxford.[2]

---

[1] *Statuta*, 364, 368, 373.

[2] Foxe, *Acts and Monuments* vii. 548: 'Master doctor Ridley, as he passed toward
Bocardo, looked up where Master Cranmer did lie . . . but Master Cranmer was busy with
friar Soto and his fellows, disputing together.' For Garcia, ibid. viii. 80–3, 90; he finally
witnessed Cranmer's recantation. A brilliant friar from Valladolid, Garcia was theology
lecturer at Magdalen College and succeeded Peter Martyr as regius professor of theology;
Dixon, 508–9; J. Ridley, *Thomas Cranmer* (Oxford 1962), 387, 395 ff.

Catechesis

But what was heresy? In 1579 the university belatedly revised the old statute *Contra hereticam pravitatem* and listed books suitable to extirpate every heresy and inform young men in true piety.[1] These books were primarily intended for religious instruction in college. Graces were sometimes refused to suspect Romanists, and protestants were not exempt from scrutiny. The quarrelsome but learned Spanish evangelist del Corro, for a time preacher at the Temple and minister to continental protestants in London, became unpopular there and moved under Leicester's patronage to Oxford. There, having attacked the refugee theologian Loyseleur, he was himself accused of deviating towards Pelagianism. Though unfavourable reports came from the Belgian, French and Spanish congregations in London, he was eventually exculpated and taught in Oxford; in 1579 he was catechist to Gloucester, Hart and St Mary's Halls.[2] Leicester initiated statutes (1580) requiring the inhibition of unsound or factious university preachers until they were thoroughly reformed. James I ordered that no one, in pulpit or the schools, be suffered to maintain any doctrine not allowed by the church of England, and directed young theology students to study the books most agreeable to it, not staying long over compendiums and abbreviators, but reading fathers, councils, schoolmen, histories and controversies.[3] Further control was secured by subscription to the thirty-nine articles, required of BAs from 1579 and matriculands from 1581, and by the oath to the royal supremacy.[4]

Artists did not approach theology with blank minds. Together with the theological element in their philosophy, they had received religious instruction in their colleges, where pressure for conformity is again evident. Before the reformation, college worship, university sermons and daily contact with clergy perhaps sufficed, though at Corpus all fellows except doctors had to attend the college's

[1] *Statuta*, 412–13; the books are listed below, p. 327.

[2] For a list of the 'principal notices' found in connection with the religious tests, see *Reg. Univ.* ed. Clark i. 152–7. For Antonio del Corro, also called Corrano, see *DNB*, and Penry Williams below, pp. 417–18. The catechetical methods of his Romans (1574; *STC* 5784–6) are enterprising. For a list of catechists in the Halls in May 1579, see *Reg. Univ.* ed. Clark i. 156.

[3] 1617: *Statuta*, 525–6. The vice-chancellor, the dean of Christ Church, and the two theology professors (Prideaux and Benefield) protested in vain; cf H. R. Trevor-Roper, *Archbishop Laud 1573–1645* (1940), 49. Earlier (1608) Bancroft as chancellor had tried to insist that, 'noe private Tutor or Reader shalbe allowed for the instructinge of youth, but such as shalbe first approved by the Vice Chancellor or some other Divines mentioned herein . . .': Stuart B. Babbage, *Puritanism and Richard Bancroft* (1962), 338.

[4] *Reg. Univ.* ed. Clark i. 5, 47, 151 ff: *Statuta*, 416; for the text of the oath of supremacy, 421.

theology lectures; at Cardinal College the Bible was expounded by dean or canon at dinner, and similarly elsewhere. From 1549 government policy combined with pastoral concern for the growing proportion of undergraduates in colleges, to provide something more systematic. The visitation of All Souls in 1549 required tutors to teach all scholars the catechism within two months of entry; scholars may possess and study the Bible—unhindered by the warden!—and attend the public theology lectures. Similar injunctions were sent to other colleges.[1] Later on, in connection with subscription to the articles, it was decreed that tutors could only be assigned pupils after a head and two theologians had approved their religious sincerity, proper doctrine and moral discretion.[2] The heresy statute of January 1579 laid down general rules. It ordered every head of college or hall to appoint tutors privately and a catechist publicly to give instruction, and provided for terminal examinations in the house (*domi*) by heads or catechists, with professors of theology present to review progress. Books were prescribed for such lectures: for juniors, Nowell's *Greater Catechism* in Latin or Greek, or Calvin's in Latin, Greek or Hebrew, or Hyperius's *Elementa christianae religionis*, or the Heidelberg Catechism.[3] For senior undergraduates might be added to these Bullinger's catechism for adults and Calvin's *Institutes*, or Jewel's *Apology*, or the thirty-nine articles with explanations of commonplaces and evidences from scripture and the fathers. A formidable programme indeed. The catechists were appointed. In May 1579 Alban Hall lacked catechism but promised it within a week; the other halls and their catechists. New College appointed an official catechist in 1580, University in 1583, Oriel in 1585 'to lecture publicly in college to juniors on the rudiments of the Christian faith', and Merton in 1589.[4] In that year the ability to recite the *Articles* from memory and relate them to scripture became a statutory condition of obtaining an arts degree.[5]

Careers

Direction and control had their effect upon the theological climate in Oxford, but it was not a one-way process, for the state was not

---

[1] C. E. Mallett, *A History of the University of Oxford* (3 vols 1924-7) ii. 87; *SCO* i. pt 7 (All Souls), 85–9.

[2] *Statuta*, p. liii, note 4; perhaps never implemented. Cf *Statuta*, 414.

[3] From 1587 the Oxford press frequently published an English adaptation of Ursinus's lectures on the Heidelberg catechism by Henry Parry of Corpus, later DTh and bishop of Worcester, evidently much used by catechists (*STC* 24532–9); *Statuta*, 413.

[4] *Dean's Register of Oriel*, 182; *Reg. ann. mert. 1567–1603*, 249.

[5] *Statuta*, 441. A slightly later example of catechetical lectures is John Day's *Days Dyall*, twelve lectures given in Oriel College chapel and published by Joseph Barnes in 1614 (*STC* 6425).

operating in a vacuum of thought. Sovereign, council and parliament took account of the public opinion which theologians had no small share in forming. Bishops counted in policy and administration, preachers and parsons in daily life, and many members of parliament were knowledgeable and deeply concerned in religious matters. In this reciprocity the function of the theology faculty cannot be sharply distinguished from that of the university as a whole. Nearly all English bishops were graduates of Oxford or Cambridge; even if never technically *theologi*, they had lived among theologians. Some ninety Oxford men held episcopal office during the sixteenth century, and among them were Oldham, Fox, Ruthall, Fitzjames, Warham, Bainbridge, Wolsey, Longland, Stokesley, Lee, Hooper, Bonner, Pole, Cox, Jewel, Parkhurst and Bilson—enough names to indicate their influence, especially before 1559. About twenty Oxford theologians were appointed to sees from 1601 to 1630, among them Francis Godwin of Llandaff and Hereford, Thomas Ravis of Gloucester and London, William James of Durham, George Abbot of London and Canterbury, Miles Smith of Gloucester, Robert Abbot of Salisbury, and Laud.[1]

Holders of other administrative offices are too numerous to mention: suffragan bishops, deans, vicars-general, diocesan chancellors, archdeacons, bishops' chaplains. One position was held by Oxford theologians at critical moments. Hugh Weston DTh, Margaret professor (*c* 1542–*c* 1551), rector of Lincoln and dean of Westminster, was prolocutor of Canterbury convocation in 1553–4: as such he presided over the great eucharistic debate and directed the examination of Cranmer, Ridley and Latimer at Oxford. Nowell was prolocutor in 1563, a year in which this Marian exile's support was particularly valuable to Archbishop Parker. Though schoolmasters must be credited to the arts faculty, many troubled *theologi* went off to teach. Nicholas Udall, headmaster of Eton, translated Erasmus's *Paraphrases of the New Testament* and Peter Martyr on the eucharist,[2]

---

[1] In the course of the century Oxford lost the dominance of episcopal appointments it had enjoyed in the middle ages, with a dramatic change in the 1530s. From 1500 to 1529 the ratio was 26 Oxford to 6 Cambridge appointments; from 1530 to 1539, 3 Oxford to 11 Cambridge, from 1540 to 1547, 5 Oxford to 8 for Cambridge. Under Edward VI Cambridge retained the lead with 11 against 3 for Oxford, but under Mary the position was reversed: Oxford 15, Cambridge 10. In the reign of Elizabeth up to 1580 Cambridge regained a slight lead (23) over Oxford (18). In the period from 1500 to 1580 there were 158 appointments all told (men appointed twice to the same see being counted twice) divided as follows: Oxford 70, Cambridge 69, Oxford and Cambridge 12, of unknown university 2, of no university 5. Up to the end of the reign of Mary, there were 113 appointments: Oxford 52, Cambridge 46, Oxford and Cambridge 8, of unknown university 2, of no university 5. I am indebted to Dr G. D. Duncan for these figures—Ed.

[2] See McConica, *English Humanists*, 240–9.

and there were notable theologians at Magdalen College school.[1] Many graduates with a few years in theology became chaplains or tutors in the houses of the nobility or gentry. A glance at any page of Emden uncovers the accumulations of benefices open to holders of theology or law degrees. The influence of resident parish priests, individually elusive, was locally all-important,[2] while some preachers ranged widely, like Bernard Gilpin of Queen's (BTh 1549) the 'Apostle of the North', and Edmund Bunny of Merton (BTh 1570).[3]

THE EMERGENCE OF OXFORD 'ANGLICANISM'

One can see in retrospect how Oxford theologians gradually moved towards a distinctive 'Anglicanism' which, in line with Elizabeth's own policy, rejected strict confessionalism and allowed hope of comprehension. This was achieved not without a struggle. Under Henry VIII Foxe's stories of energetic protestant groups at Magdalen and Cardinal Colleges are balanced by a mainly catholic faculty of theology, influenced by humanism but still tender to scholasticism. It was easy to find men ready to write against Luther in 1521: Roper and Kington, successively Margaret professors, Brinknell, and John de Coloribus.[4] Edward Powell published his *Propugnaculum* against Luther (1523), John Standish wrote against Robert Barnes. Peter Martyr provoked stormy opposition from the leaders of the faculty: Smith, Weston, Chedsey, Tresham. Apart from Tyndale, however, who did not write in Oxford, and Martyr, who arrived from abroad, few if any books of lasting value came from Oxford theologians in this phase.

It was different when the clash came under Edward and Mary and again when a settlement was needed under Elizabeth. On the one hand there were catholic scholars of great learning and ability whose books, often published abroad, are listed in the annals of reformation debate: Allen, Campion, Feckenham, Nicholas Harpsfield, Martin, Parsons, Sanders, Stapleton, to name but a few.[5] Their influence endured. In the other camp stood scholars who longed for thorough reformation, such as Hooper, Philpot, Jewel (at first), Goodman (the Margaret professor and friend of Knox), Sampson and many other returned exiles. They were followed by the Elizabethan puritans,

---

[1] R. S. Stanier, *Magdalen School* (OHS new ser. iii 1943), ch. 3.

[2] Cf. G. R. Elton, *Policy and Police* (Cambridge 1972), 211 ff.

[3] *DNB*, and see A. G. Dickens, *Lollards and Protestants in the Diocese of York 1509-1558* (Oxford 1959) for these and for Sir Francis Bigod.

[4] *Epist. acad. 1508-96*, 111.

[5] A. F. Allison and D. M. Rogers list them in their *Catalogue of Catholic Books in English Printed Abroad or Secretly in England 1558-1640* (Bognor Regis 1956).

among whom Laurence Humfrey, the president of Magdalen, Laurence Tomson, Walsingham's secretary, and Calfhill, Margaret professor, are noteworthy.

Patrick Collinson has rightly challenged the familiar image of puritan Cambridge and churchy, conservative Oxford, of which the trial by Oxford dons of the Cambridge men, Cranmer, Latimer and Ridley, martyred in the city of Oxford, is an unforgettable symbol;[1] and 'Laudian Oxford' is a commonplace. Beyond doubt the early Lutheran group at Cambridge exercised a more powerful influence upon religion in England then did its Oxford counterpart under Henry VIII. Its Marian exiles were on the whole a more distinguished body, its roll of Calvinist theologians and preachers under Elizabeth contains more famous names. Yet although Oxford had plenty of conservatives in residence, besides the numerous recusants who lost their fellowships, opposition to Laud was strong right up to and during his chancellorship. The principal spiritual and theological source of Laudianism, Lancelot Andrewes, was master of a Cambridge college.

It is not only famous names that count. In promoting religious changes the rank and file were also significant, since pastors and preachers spread over the country after their university formation. From Oxford, where the general trend of theology throughout Elizabeth's reign was firmly Calvinistic, a large number of able men threw themselves vigorously into a puritan campaign, some of them becoming leaders in the demand for a scriptural presbyterian order. To the government they were seditious, to the bishops schismatical. Few of them were technically *theologi* for more than a year or two, if so long; since their object was rapidly to supply a preaching ministry of their own outlook, they mostly went down soon after proceeding MA. It was after they had left Oxford that John Field and Thomas Wilcox drew up the *Admonition to Parliament* of 1572. Edward Gellibrand (Magdalen, MA 1590), in a close touch with Field, was something like general secretary to the *classis* movement, and Richard Parker (University College, vicar of Dedham 1582–90) wrote up as secretary the celebrated minutes of the Dedham *classis*.[2] John Penry of Marprelate fame moved from Cambridge to Oxford for his MA; 'And almost all the leaders in Northamptonshire—the most presbyterian of counties—were bred in either Christ Church or Magdalen.'[3] The methods and experiences of Edmund Snape (Merton, MA 1584, curate of St Peter's Northampton 1586–90,

---

[1] Patrick Collinson, *The Elizabethan Puritan Movement* (1967), 129.
[2] He was BA of University College, January 1570; see Collinson, 438.
[3] Collinson, 129.

deprived) are recorded in the evidence produced at his trial by the high commission in 1591.[1] An important factor in many areas was the local influence and patronage of magnates like Henry, the 'protestant earl' of Huntingdon and his brother, Sir Francis Hastings (a pupil of Laurence Humfrey at Magdalen and a friend of Laurence Tomson) in Leicestershire and the West country.[2]

As long as Robert Dudley, earl of Leicester, and Sir Christopher Hatton were its chancellors (1565–88, 1588–91) Calvinist theology and its preaching exponents received general support within the university itself. Thereafter, other influences began to prevail which need illustration from the workings of the theology faculty as such. To return to the act disputations at inception for the DTh, analysis of the theses published by Clark shows at a glance that the majority are still pointed against Rome; here perhaps stock answers preponderated.[3] Others take up themes from the thirty-nine articles which also may have been treated perfunctorily by the more ordinary candidates, who had nevertheless to give ready and adequate answers to the opponents and who would not relish severe criticism or public mockery from the moderator. The disputations become more significant when they bear on the problems of predestination, reprobation and free will in terms more technical and less ambiguous than those of the articles, when the language of the Lambeth articles of 1595 and the five points of Arminianism show through, or when episcopacy *jure divino* is affirmed. These disputations were serious exercises. Humfrey's influence had worked not only through his Magdalen pupils, but markedly in his forceful moderating of disputations as regius professor; Prideaux, in the same office, took the same opportunities when he later attempted to stem the Laudian tide.

Signs of that tide appear when, instead of so frequently championing Anglican orders against Roman attacks, disputants take up the arguments of Bancroft's Paul's Cross sermon, 1589: the Act theses in 1594, to which Latewarr of St John's responded, included 'Equality of ministers in the Church is not grounded upon divine law'; in 1608 Laud himself, incepting as DTh, argued that only a bishop can confer orders and that he is superior to the presbyter *jure divino*.[4] Such theses were not mere formalities: they could not be publicly argued without immediate controversy, without heated discussion in colleges.

[1] Collinson, 344–5, 347–8.
[2] Cf Claire Cross, *The Puritan Earl: the life of Henry Hastings, the third earl of Huntingdon, 1536–1595* (1966).
[3] *Reg. Univ.* ed. Clark i. 194–217, covering the years 1576–1622; see Loach below, p. 389.
[4] Ibid. 206.

Any temptation to simplify these theological and ecclesiastical cross-currents must be resisted. Anti-Romanism is constant, for after 1558 catholics had no chance of replying inside the university: distinguished ex-Oxford scholars worked in and from such places as Paris and Louvain, Rheims and Douai. With respect to the basic doctrines of scriptural authority, predestination and justification, Calvinism predominated over Arminian tendencies well into the seventeenth century and was accompanied by much puritan dislike of ceremonies. As to the ministry, however, and perhaps to eucharistic doctrine, certainly to the place of sacraments in piety, there were shades of opinion and eventually open conflicts among Calvinistic protestants, conflicts which assisted the formation of Anglicanism.[1]

It had at times seemed probable that as at Cambridge, the Oxford faculty would train enough ministers in a fairly rigid type of protestantism to make a confessional church after a continental pattern likely in England. But its resident Calvinists, though shaken by the vestiarian controversy and persisting with their protests against the imposition of ceremonies and against deprivation for not observing them, would not follow the largely non-resident extremists in pursuing a presbyterian ministry and discipline at the risk of separatism. In 1559–61 eleven Oxford men, including Cox, Jewel, Bentham and Parkhurst, accepted sees, thereby helping to put the Elizabethan settlement into operation. For some of their decisions they found support from the Zurich theologians Bullinger and Gualter, rather against the trend in Geneva.[2] Later, in the crises of the 1580s and 1590s, it was non-residents like Field and Snape who forced the issues (this was less true of Cambridge), while the residents, which means the teachers, perhaps accustoming themselves to the decencies of prayer-book worship, wanted peace and unity. Maybe they were confident in the strength and security of their comparative moderation until Arminianism arrived to threaten, as many believed, the foundations of their theology, with practical consequences for the church going beyond the permitted bounds of academic debate.

An alternative position had been emerging ever since Jewel's *Apology*. Still fundamentally protestant, he encouraged an appeal to the early fathers in the exposition of scripture, thus allowing some weight to tradition. Hooker, attacking puritan biblicism, provided a more balanced theory of authority, with room for reason. Thomas Cooper, who had once approved the 'exercises' when bishop of Lincoln, defended himself against Marprelate in 1589; Richard Field (catechism lecturer at Magdalen Hall 1584, DTh 1596) published

[1] Cf Charles Rives in 1599; *Reg. Univ.* ed. Clark i. 197, 206, 201.
[2] Collinson, 79–81.

in 1606 his magisterial *Of the Church*.[1] Leading Oxford Calvinists allowed that the episcopal order was not wrong *per se* and might well be beneficial (Benefield's lectures do this), and that many cere-monies, being *adiaphora*, might be tolerated for the sake of unity. So Oxford and Cambridge both repudiated the millenary petition of 1603 and took part in the Hampton Court Conference of 1604 where the most eminent Oxford Calvinist, John Rainolds, president of Corpus, and Thomas Sparke (fellow of Magdalen 1569, DTh 1581) were among the few chosen to represent the puritans. Rainolds's attempt to have the Lambeth articles added to the prayer book failed, but in some ways he was conciliatory. Sparke, while sharing puritan disappointment that decisions helpful to them were not implemented, published his *Brotherly Persuasion to Unity* in 1607.[2] Men should conform to the required ceremonies, he said, for the sake of the ministry. Scholars of varying outlooks were soon working together on the authorized version: Andrewes and Chaderton, Ravis, George Abbot and (briefly) Rainolds. But the obstacles to compre-hensiveness and toleration became more formidable as the claims of episcopacy *jure divinio*, intensified by the *Perpetual Government of Christ's Church*[3] of Thomas Bilson (New College, DTh 1581, bishop of Winchester) and by Laud and Montague (the latter Prideaux's *bête-noire*), were increasingly blended with Arminianism. Some Oxford theologians resisted the new trend vigorously, others adopted it with enthusiasm. One such was Laud, tutored by Buckeridge at St John's and living there among other like-minded fellows; later, as president, he could enforce his views, later still he sent orders to 'his' university which he conceived it his duty to 'govern' as chancellor. Others changed gradually, for example, Thomas Jackson, fellow and president of Corpus, whose *Com-mentaries on the Apostles Creed*[4] were influential, and Robert Sanderson, whose experience illuminates the Oxford scene. In a letter to Henry Hammond (fellow of Magdalen, canon of Christ Church) he relates how as a student he had read Calvin's *Institutes*, 'commended to me, as it was generally to all young scholars in those times, as the best and perfectest system of divinity, and fitted to be laid as a ground-work in the study of that profession'.[5] But he read Hooker, to his great profit, and moved away from the harshness of

---

[1] *Of the Church, Five bookes* (1606-10; STC 10856-9).

[2] *A brotherly perswasion to unitie, and uniformitie touching the received, and present ecclesiasticall government* (1607; STC 23019), 5-20.

[3] 1593; STC 3065-7.

[4] 1613 and after: see STC 14308-9, 14311, 14313, 14315-19.

[5] Sanderson's outlook is well summarized from his letters and Isaac Walton's *Life*, in G. R. Cragg, *From Puritanism to the Age of Reason* (Cambridge 1950), 22-30.

Calvin and Beza concerning election and predestination without fully accepting any Arminian system, though working more easily with the Laudians.

In such a climate, academic theology could not but affect the country at large, the sovereign, the parliament and the common man.

4·5

Public Lectures and Professorial Chairs

G. D. DUNCAN*

THE terminology of professorships is intricate, and even Donald Logan's instructive article, which aims at precision, has to employ provisional anachronisms.[1] It is certain that the Latin word 'professor' was long applicable to holders of a doctorate, as in the common designation STP—*sanctae theologiae professor*—meaning doctor of theology. It is equally certain that the Latin word 'lector' or 'praelector' was long the current and official term for the later professor, as for the Lady Margaret's lecture.[2] In the university statutes of 1549 we find, under the heading *lectores publici*: 'Qui prelegerit theologiam, ius civile aut medicinam, aut mathematicam' combined with 'linguarum professores, philosophiae, dialecticae et rethorices'. And, in the section of the statutes entitled *Tempora lectionum*, 'theologicus prelector, philosophicus lector, medicinae lector' and 'dialectices et rethorices prelector' are combined with 'Grecae linguae professor' and 'lector Hebraicus'.[3] Then, in the 1564/5 statutes, we have 'publicos theologiae, medicinae, iuris praelectores, linguae Hebraicae Graecaeque professores' (all five of the 'regius professorships') together under section 10, *Pro publicis praelectoribus*, and in section 11, 'per duos theologiae professores, et per Hebraicae linguae praelectorem' followed by 'unus e theologiae praelectoribus vel Hebraicae linguae professor' and, immediately, 'publicus regius professor theologiae . . . Margaritae . . . hebraicae linguae . . .'.[4]

The crucial distinction is between a college lecturer whose lectures

---

* The notes prepared by the late Dr S. L. Greenslade on the regius professors have proved a valuable starting point for the present writer. The opening section on terminology is almost entirely Dr Greenslade's work.

[1] F. D. Logan, 'The origins of the so-called regius professorships: an aspect of the renaissance in Oxford and Cambridge', in D. Baker (ed.), *Renaissance and Renewal in Christian History* (Studies in Church History xiv 1977), 271–8.

[2] *Statuta*, 300–8.

[3] Ibid. 343–4.

[4] Ibid. 381–2.

are intended solely for the members of his college, and a lecturer whose lectures are open to the whole university, even if he holds a college lecturership or is otherwise paid by a college or other ecclesiastical body. The terms are imprecise. In English as late as 1590 chancellor Hatton's letter to convocation speaks of her majesty's readers of theology, law, physic, Hebrew, and Greek, the Lady Margaret's lecture, the *two* theology readers, the queen's professor and the Lady Margaret's reader—all in one paragraph.[1]

While such inconsistency in statutory and official documents would in itself justify a measure of anachronistic simplification in modern accounts, there is also good early precedent for the modern sense of professor, even 'regius professor'. When Wolsey founded Cardinal College in 1525 he spoke not of 'praelectores' but of 'professores', public and private,[2] and when Peter Martyr's Oxford eucharistic disputation was published in London in 1549 he was described as 'Regium ibidem Theologiae professorem'.[3]

The history of public lectures and professorial chairs in Tudor Oxford really began in the late fifteenth century when the statutes of Magdalen College (1480) provided for three praelectors in theology, and moral and natural philosophy who were to lecture publicly as well as to members of the college.[4] We enter the sixteenth century proper with the foundation of the Lady Margaret's theological lecture in 1497–1502 which provided free instruction for all comers, permanently secured on the revenues of Westminster Abbey. Although the early history of this post is obscure, perhaps because of unrecorded elections, it is reasonable to assume a continuous existence from the date of its foundation ordinance (1502).[5]

The next significant step was taken by Richard Fox in his foundation of Corpus Christi College (1517). He provided three public lectures, in Latin, Greek and theology.[6] But before these lectures got under way they were overshadowed by the plans of another great ecclesiastic, Cardinal Wolsey, to maintain university lectures. The whole question of Wolsey's lectures is shrouded in considerable obscurity: to obtain the clearest possible view it is necessary to dispense with Wood's account and return to the main source, register FF, the university's sixteenth-century letter book.[7] Around May

[1] Wood, *History and Antiquities*, 241–2.

[2] *SCO* ii. pt 11, 122 ff. But the statutes also use 'lector' to mean public professor, e.g. 'lector sacrae theologiae' at ibid. 127.

[3] P. Martyr, *Tractatio de sacramento eucharistiae* . . . (1549; *STC* 24673), title page.

[4] *VCH Oxon* iii. 194; W. A. Pantin, *Oxford Life in Oxford Archives* (Oxford 1972), 37.

[5] For the history of this lecture, see below, pp. 347–50.

[6] *VCH Oxon* iii. 220.

[7] Printed as *Epist. acad. 1508–96.* All references have been checked against the original manuscript, now in Bodl. MS Bodley 282.

1518 the university announced to its chancellor, Archbishop Warham, that Wolsey had decided to found lectures in the university
('quotidianas quasdam bonarum litterarum lectiones') and to pay for
the lecturers out of his own pocket.[1] A little later mention was made
of the six public lectures ('sex lectiones publicas') the cardinal had
provided at his own expense.[2] Lectures are first heard of in Michaelmas term 1518;[3] by May 1519 a theological lecturer had been
appointed,[4] and in July 1519 the university learned of Wolsey's plan
to bring over a new lecturer in rhetoric from Spain.[5] In November of
that year, in connection with the problem of securing attendance at
the lectures, the university referred to those who 'a te institute sunt
lectionum interpretes'.[6] Finally, in March 1520 all newly created
masters supplicated that they might not be bound to lecture for the
greater part of the hour so that they could attend the cardinal's
humanity lectures.[7]

It is therefore clear enough that by 1520 Wolsey was supporting
public lectures in theology and humanity at Oxford, but how firmly
established these lectures were is quite another matter. In 1522 the
university asked the bishops of Lincoln and Exeter to intercede with
the cardinal for the proper endowment of his lectures, so that their
benefits could be perpetually assured to future generations.[8] On the
other hand, there can be no doubts about the quality of the men
Wolsey engaged as his lecturers. The first we hear of is John Clement,
who started lecturing on humanity in Michaelmas term 1518.[9] More
wrote to Erasmus in 1518 that Clement 'lectures at Oxford to an
audience larger than has gathered to any other lecturer . . . Even
those to whom classical literature was almost anathema now show
attachment to him, attend his lectures and gradually modify their
opposition'.[10] Clement had been at St Paul's School under William
Lily whence he joined More's household, acting as tutor to his
children. He probably lectured at Oxford from 1518 to early 1520,
when he left England for medical study on the continent.[11]

Clement's successor at Oxford was the even more illustrious

---

[1] *Epist. acad. 1508–96*, 75. [2] Ibid. 81.
[3] Ibid. 83. [4] Ibid. 91.
[5] Ibid. 94. [6] Ibid. 96.
[7] Reg. Cong. 1518-35, fo 34ᵛ: 'causa est ut possint adesse lecturis humanitatis domini
Cardinalis'.
[8] *Epist. acad. 1508–96*, 117–19.
[9] Ibid. 84 where the university writing to Wolsey describes him as *tuum Clementem*.
[10] Thomas Stapleton, *The Life and Illustrious martyrdom of Sir Thomas More*, trans.
P. E. Hallett and ed. E. E. Reynolds (1966), 91. The Latin text of the letter is to be found
in *Opus epistolarum Des. Erasmi roterodami*, ed. P. S. Allen *et al* (12 vols Oxford 1906-
58) iii. 463.
[11] For Clement, see *BRUO 1501-40*, 121-2.

Thomas Lupset, described as 'lector artis rethorice' in March 1520[1] and said by More in the following April to have taken the place of Clement and to be lecturing on Greek and Latin to large audiences.[2] In 1521 the university thanked Wolsey for sending Lupset to lecture to them.[3] He left Oxford for the continent in 1523 and eventually became a member of Reginald Pole's household at Padua.[4]

The last in this very distinguished line of lecturers was the most celebrated of them all—Juan Luis Vives whom Wolsey sent to Oxford in 1523 and for whose services the university was duly grateful.[5]

Wolsey also paid for a lecture in theology, a post to which Thomas Brinknell was appointed, probably in the first few months of 1519.[6] Brinknell, headmaster of Magdalen College School 1502-8, had taken his DTh in 1508 and was one of the university's delegates at the conference convoked by Wolsey for examining Luther's doctrines.[7]

One further lecturer, Thomas Mosgroff, introduces the most baffling feature of these early lectures. Mosgroff, who took the degrees of MD in 1523 and BTh in 1524, is described in March 1523 as being about to read the public lecture in medicine within Corpus Christi College.[8] It has long been assumed that he was acting as one of Wolsey's public lecturers, an assumption which ultimately rests on a tradition preserved by Brian Twyne that Lupset, Vives, Mosgroff and Nicholas Kratzer were 'Quatuor publici lectores Cardinalitii simul in Collegio Corp. Christi'.[9] Now Twyne was certainly right to designate Lupset and Vives as the cardinal's readers. Moreover, Lupset's link with Corpus is clearly attested by two letters he wrote from the college in March and April 1520 and by his witnessing the admission of a scholar there in 1522,[10] while from Twyne's grandfather, John Twyne, we have the statement that he heard Vives

[1] Reg. Cong. 1518-35, fo 37.

[2] Stapleton, *Life of More*, 40; *Epist. Erasmi* iv. 232; *L & P Henry VIII* iii. pt. 1, 406. George Lily said that Lupset lectured publicly on Cicero's *Philippics*: J. A. Gee, *The Life and Works of Thomas Lupset* (New Haven 1928), 96.

[3] *Epist. acad. 1508-96*, 104. In the same year Lupset was lecturing on Proclus, *De sphaera*: ibid. 108.

[4] For Lupset, see *BRUO 1501-40*, 366-7; Gee, *Life and Works of Lupset*, 87-103.

[5] *Epist. acad. 1508-96*, 156, 159; *L & P Henry VIII* iv. pt 1, 520. For Vives, see *BRUO 1501-40*, 594-6.

[6] *Epist. acad. 1508-96*, 91.

[7] *BRUO to 1500* i. 268.

[8] Reg. Cong. 1518-35, fo 101: 'est lecturus lectionem publicam in medicine infra collegium Corporis Christi.' For Mosgroff's degrees and career, see *BRUO 1501-40*, 406-7.

[9] Thomas Fowler, *The History of Corpus Christi College* (OHS xxv 1893), 87, citing Corpus Christi College MS 280, fo 215 where the entry is in the handwriting of Brian Twyne.

[10] Gee, *Life and Works of Lupset*, 304, 312, 101.

'publice praelegentem' in Corpus.[1] From President Cole (1568–98) comes the college tradition that Vives had rooms in the cloister chambers at Corpus.[2] It is therefore virtually certain that, as Wolsey's readers, Vives and Lupset delivered their lectures in Corpus and lived there. Mosgroff may indeed have delivered the cardinal's medical lecture there, but it is hardly likely that he lived in the college, for he was still a fellow of Merton in 1523. Twyne also claims Nicholas Kratzer, the court astronomer and instrument maker, as one of Wolsey's readers linked with Corpus. That would perhaps be good enough were it not for Kratzer's own testimony that he was sent to Oxford (probably in 1523) to teach astronomical and geographical subjects by the king, whose servant he was.[3] There seems to be no evidence for the claim that he was Wolsey's reader in mathematics,[4] nor can anything be established about a possible connection with Corpus. It has been claimed by Allen and Fowler that these men lectured for both Wolsey and Fox and that for a while Wolsey's readers discharged the duties of Fox's public lecturers.[5] But Fox made no statutory provision for the kind of teaching that Mosgroff and Kratzer could have given and in view of the fact that the college records do not begin until 1521–2 the nature of the Corpus connection of Wolsey's readers must for ever remain obscure.

But whatever the exact nature of the arrangements for Wolsey's first public lecturers, things took on a very different aspect in 1524–5. For Wolsey was then planning his most magnificent benefaction to the university in the form of a splendid new college, Cardinal College.

The statutes promulgated by Wolsey for his new college contained elaborate provisions for public professors, going well beyond anything yet attempted in either of the universities and, as we shall see later, establishing a pattern of thinking on this matter for the rest of the sixteenth century.[6] There were to be six professors covering theology, canon law and philosophy (who must be celibate) and civil law, medicine and humanity (who might be married).[7] The professors of theology and humanity were to have annual stipends of £40, the

[1] J. Twyne, *De rebus albionicis, britannicis atque anglicis, commentariorum libri duo*, ed. Thomas Twyne (1590: STC 24407), 6; cf *BRUO 1501–40*, 582–3.

[2] Fowler, *Corpus Christi College*, 71.

[3] J. D. North, 'Nicolaus Kratzer—the king's astronomer', *Studia Copernicana* xvi (1978), 218–21; cf *BRUO 1501–40*, 333.

[4] Made, for instance, in Wood, *History and Antiquities*, 836–7.

[5] Fowler, *Corpus Christi College*, 87–9; P. S. Allen, 'The early Corpus readerships', *Pelican Record* vii (1903–5), 155–9.

[6] The statutes of Cardinal College are printed in *SCO* ii. pt 11, 11–143 with those concerning public professors at 122–35.

[7] A letter of the university to Wolsey mentions seven lectures: *Epist. acad. 1508–96*, 190.

other professors of £20.[1] Professors were to be elected by a committee consisting of the dean, subdean and other most senior members of Cardinal College, the public professors, the commissary of the university or his vice-gerent, and the heads of New College, Corpus Christi, All Souls, Merton, Lincoln, Queen's, University, Exeter, Balliol and Brasenose, and two censors or masters of the university ('duos censores sive magistros scholarium Universitatis').[2] On election the professors had to swear, *inter alia*, not to interfere in the business of the college. Very elaborate rules and procedures were laid down for fining and ultimately for depriving professors who proved to be negligent or incompetent, the procedure for deprivation involving the citation of the offender before special meetings of the electors convoked by the dean of Cardinal College.

The times and subjects of the lectures to be given by the various professors were laid down in general terms with in some cases the provision that the electors should determine the specific texts.[3] The professor of theology was to lecture from 9 a.m. to 10 a.m. on the Old or New Testaments or on Scotus, the latter being especially needed, the statutes claimed, to confute heresy. Lectures in canon law were to be delivered at 7 a.m. on the *Decretals* and the letters of Gregory and Boniface, interpretation of them following the best traditional commentaries, especially in matters of faith. The professor of civil law, also at 7 a.m. was to lecture on the *Pandects* or the *Code*, the professor of medicine at 2 p.m. on Hippocrates, Avicenna or other distinguished medical writers.

Passing now to humanity, two lectures were to be given daily by the professor. The first, at 8 a.m., was to deal with the works of Cicero, Quintilian, Trapezuntius or some other writer on rhetoric. The second lecture, at 1 p.m., was to be either on the rudiments of Greek or, for more advanced students, on Isocrates, Lucian, Philo-

[1] In addition the professors were to have a room each in college, commons of 2s per week and an annual livery of five measures of cloth at 5s the measure. In a document setting out 'The yerelie charge of my lorde Cardinall his colledge in Oxforde when the nombre therein shalbe fully accomplisshed according to his most gracyous Statutes', which gives the salaries of the six 'Publique Reders' broken down into yearly stipend, weekly commons and livery, the readers of theology and humanity were to receive a total of £33 7s 4d each and the others £20 0s 8d each: PRO SP 1/35, fos 85ᵛ–86 and in *L & P Henry VIII* iv. pt 1, no. 1499 (3). Similar lists are to be found in PRO SP 1/35, fo 116 and in *L & P Henry VIII* iv. pt 1, no. 1499 (15); PRO E 36/102, fo 7 and in *L & P Henry VIII* iv. pt 1, no. 1499 (20).

[2] Note the omission of the provost of Oriel and the president of Magdalen. However, the latter, along with the dean of Cardinal College and the commissary of the university, had to elect in certain cases of disputed elections.

[3] It is clear that Wolsey consulted the 'rectores et presides' of the university about the times and places of the lectures, for they sent him a written report on the subject: *Epist. acad. 1508–96*, 190.

stratus, Homer, Aristophanes, Euripides, Sophocles, Pindar, Hesiod or other Greek writers. The philosophy professor was to lecture at 7 a.m. on the works of Aristotle in natural, moral or metaphysical philosophy, as well as occasionally on Plato.

The statutes also tried to set out the methods to be used in teaching. The lecturers were to set themes at the beginning of each week and examine their students on them at the end of the week. On Sundays and certain feast days each of the professors was to be available in his lecture room for up to an hour to deal with any questions put to him by his pupils. In addition the humanity professor could examine and correct his students' letters and declamations if brought to him and the professors of law and medicine could give practical professional advice if asked to do so.

Wolsey's fall from power in 1529, before his new college had been properly established and its sumptuous buildings completed, dealt a fatal blow to this splendid and ambitious plan for the endowment of comprehensive public teaching in the university. Indeed, there is definite evidence for the appointment of only two public readers in the college. The one full account of expenses to have survived, for the college's fifth year of existence (1529–30), shows that there was then only one public reader—Nicholas de Burgo, who was paid £20 per annum 'pro lectione publica Theologie'.[1] De Burgo was an Italian Franciscan who had probably been in Oxford since c 1517 and took his DTh in 1524. He also acted as praelector in theology at Magdalen College.[2] A further undated and fragmentary account of expenses shows a payment of £10 for the stipend of 'Math Caphurii lectoris publici litterarum humaniorum'.[3] This must refer to Mattheus Calphurnius whom John Caius mentions as having been brought to Oxford from Greece by Wolsey for the sake of Greek letters.[4] Finally, it should be noted that in 1526 Laurence Barber asked Wolsey to appoint him to the new professorship in philosophy at Cardinal College.[5] Unfortunately there is no way of knowing whether Barber was appointed. He was a fellow of All Souls from 1513 until at least 1522, had incepted MA in 1516 and had been made acting proctor by Wolsey in 1522.[6]

[1] PRO E 36/104, fo 9; cf also fo 7 where there is a payment of 52s for a year's commons 'famuli Doctoris Nicolai Lectoris in Theologia'. The account has no formal title, for at least the first folio is missing, but the account starts with commons paid for the 'Primus Terminus Quinti Anni' (fo 3).

[2] *BRUO 1501–40*, 85–6.

[3] PRO SP 1/35, fo 136^V and in *L & P Henry VIII* iv. pt 1, no. 1499 (21).

[4] John Caius, *De pronunciatione grecae & latinae linguae cum scriptione nova libellus* (1574), 10, reprinted in *The Works of John Caius . . .*, ed. E. S. Roberts (Cambridge 1912).

[5] PRO SP 1/39, fo 30 and in *L & P Henry VIII* iv. pt 1, no. 2361.

[6] *BRUO 1501–40*, 23–4.

Although the ten years or so after Wolsey's fall saw nothing to match the cardinal's schemes, they none the less witnessed some solid progress in the provision of public lectures. The successor to Cardinal College, King Henry VIII College, was a much smaller institution in which no attempt was made to emulate Wolsey's elaborate provisions. Its statutes, as printed in 1853, make no mention of readers,[1] though at some stage in the planning of the college there was provision for two, one in theology and one in humanity, at annual stipends of £26 13s 4d each,[2] and Nicholas de Burgo (who had been public professor of theology at Cardinal College) was named reader in theology at the new college in July 1532.[3] Among its twelve canons was Robert Wakefield, whom the king wished to teach Hebrew publicly and freely to all comers 'in nostro Collegio regio'. He had been supported by the king in 1529 as a 'reader in Hebrew', and certainly delivered a lecture at Oxford 'in collegio regio'.[4] Wakefield had earlier lectured on Hebrew at Cambridge and on the continent.[5]

The royal visitors of 1535 showed themselves closely interested in the provision of public lectures. Their most important step was to order the richer colleges to endow seven new ones in Latin and Greek. Magdalen was to support a lecture in Greek grammar, Merton and Queen's a lecture in Latin each, with New College and All Souls each maintaining two lectures in Latin and Greek.[6] College accounts show that in consequence Greek lectures were quickly established at Magdalen, All Souls and New College (though there is no indication of the Latin lectures at the latter two).[7] Elsewhere the evidence is patchy. At Merton there is only a solitary payment of 6s 8d 'pro

---

[1] *SCO* ii. pt 11, 185–210. This is clearly a very corrupt text.

[2] PRO SP 1/35, fo 127 and in *L & P Henry VIII* iv. pt 1, no. 1499 (17). *L & P* assigns this document to Cardinal College, but it is in fact an estimate of the establishment costs of a 'Colledge & almes howse newly to be erected established and founded by the kings Royall maiestie within his vnyuersitie of Oxford'. There can be no doubt that this was King Henry VIII College, for the draft provides for a dean, 12 canons, 8 vicars choral, 8 lay conducts, 8 choristers and others including 13 poor men, an establishment very similar to that set out in the letters patent founding the college: cf *VCH Oxon* iii. 235.

[3] *L & P Henry VIII* v. 519.

[4] Ibid. 309; Robert Wakefield, *Syntagma de hebreorum codicu incorruptione. Item eiusdem oratio Oxonij habita vnacum quibusdam alijs lectu ac annotatu non indignis* (?1530: *STC* 24946), E. i, ii.

[5] *BRUO 1501–40*, 599–600.

[6] *Three Chapters of Letters Relating to the Suppression of Monasteries*, ed. T. Wright (Camden Society xxvi 1843), 70–1.

[7] Magdalen College Archives Liber Computi 1530–42, fos 66, 130[V], 146, 157; Bodl. MSS D.D. All Souls College, c.281: rolls for 1535–6 under various expenses and 'post festum', 1538–9, various expenses; c.282: rolls for 1539–40, fees and stipends, 1540–1, fees and stipends; New College Archives 7493, 7495, 7496, 7498 under 'portio informatorum'.

lectione regis' in the account for March to August 1536 and while at Queen's payments for lectures in grammar and logic start in 1535–6, it is not clear that they followed upon the visitors' activities.[1] In addition to these measures the visitors ordered that no degrees in medicine should be conferred without the approval of John Warner, 'in medicinis doctoris ac publico prelectore medicine in dicta academia'.[2] Nothing is known of the origins of this praelectorship unless it somehow descended from the lecture read by Thomas Mosgroff in 1523, but Warner, fellow of All Souls 1520–36 and warden of the college 1536–56, 1559–65, was named as the first regius professor of medicine in 1540.[3]

In 1536, shortly after the visitation, the two universities were exempted by act of parliament from the payment of first fruits and tenths and in return for this concession the colleges and halls in each university were perpetually at their own expense to support 'one discrete and larned personnage to reade one opyn and publique lectour' on any subject to be chosen by the king, the lecture being called 'Kyng Henry the eight his lecture'.[4] By May 1536 Richard Smith had been made 'praelector theologicae nuper a regia maiestate institutae' at Oxford,[5] but it was not until the following December that arrangements were made for the regular payment of the new lecturer when 'pro certa . . . et iusta limitatione salarii eiusdem prelectoris' the colleges were assessed to produce an annual stipend of £13 6s 8d.[6]

It has hitherto been assumed that this lecturership was extinguished by the foundation in 1540 of the regius professorship of theology of which the first holder was the same Richard Smith.[7] But this is certainly mistaken. College accounts show beyond any doubt that King Henry VIII's lecture in theology continued alongside the newer post until 1546 when it was transformed into a new public praelectorship in philosophy which itself lasted until about 1557.[8] The theological lecture was first held by Richard Smith (1536–42), then briefly by George Cotes, master of Balliol (1542–3) and finally by

[1] Merton College Archives MS 3859 under deliveries for stipends; Queen's College Archives Long Rolls for 1535–6: foreign expenses; 1536–7, 1537–8, 1538–9, 1539–40, 1540–1: under deliveries to servants.

[2] Reg. Cong. 1535–63, fo 1ᵛ, copy of an instrument by Henry VIII dated 22 March 1536 confirming the action of his visitors.

[3] BRUO 1501–40, 607–8.

[4] Statuta, 337–8.

[5] Reg. Cong. 1535–63, fo 14ᵛ.

[6] Statuta, 339–40; Epist. acad. 1508–96, 345–6.

[7] Most recently by Logan, 'Origins of the regius professorships', 274.

[8] The college assessments decreed in 1536 have been traced in the accounts of New College, Queen's College, Corpus Christi College, All Souls College, Exeter College and Magdalen College.

Philip Brode, a secularized Cistercian (1543-6).[1] The praelectorship in philosophy was first held briefly by George Etheridge (1546-7) and then by Robert Warde (1547-57).[2] Etheridge, a fellow of Corpus 1541-5, became regius professor of Greek in 1547, while Warde was a fellow of Merton 1537-58 and retained his praelectorship under Edward VI despite conservative religious views.[3]

We must now consider the culmination of all the developments reviewed above and, in a very real sense, the fruition of Wolsey's schemes of twenty years before—the foundation of the regius professorships in theology, Greek, Hebrew, civil law and medicine. Unfortunately there is no foundation document extant for these posts and no body of statutory provision for the duties of the professors in the university comparable to the detailed regulations laid down by the Lady Margaret and Wolsey for their lectures. Rather, the new lectures emerged in 1540 from the crown's plans for the new cathedral foundation of Westminster. Westminster Cathedral was obliged by its statutes to support praelectors in theology, Greek, Hebrew, civil law and medicine at the two universities with annual stipends of £40 each.[4] Two of the Oxford praelectors were named in 1540—Richard Smith in theology and John Warner in medicine—and in the next few years praelectors in the other subjects were

[1] Magdalen College Archives Liber Computi 1530-42, fos 103ᵛ, 104, 121 (120)ᵛ, 135ᵛ, 150ᵛ, 162ᵛ, 176ᵛ; Liber Computi 1534-59, accounts for 1543, 1545, 1546 under external payments; New College Archives MSS 7493, 7495, 7496, 7498, 7500, 7501, 7503, 7506, 7508 under 'custus necessarii ad extra'; Bodl. MSS D.D. All Souls College c.281, rolls for 1536-7, 1537-8, 1538-9 under 'various expenses', c.282, rolls for 1539-40, 1540-1, 1541-2, 1542-3, 1543-4 under 'fees and stipends', for 1544-5 under 'fees', for 1545-6 under 'fees and stipends'; Queen's College Archives Long Rolls for 1536-7, 1537-8, 1538-9, 1539-40, 1540-1, 1541-2, 1542-3, 1543-4, 1544-5, 1545-6, 1546-7 under 'deliberata servientibus'; Exeter College Archives Rectors' Accounts for 1537-8, 1538-9, 1539-40, 1540-1, 1542-3, 1543-4, 1544-5, 1545-6 under 'expenses'; Corpus Christi College Archives C/1/1/1, fo 146; C/1/1/2, fos 10ᵛ, 37ᵛ, 50ᵛ, 64ᵛ, 77, 91ᵛ, 106ᵛ, 120, 134ᵛ. Bodl. MS D.D. All Souls College c.271, no. 288 is a receipt, dated 13 November 1540 and signed by Richard Smith, for his year's salary from the bursar due at the preceding Michaelmas.

[2] Magdalen College Archives Liber Computi 1543-59, accounts for 1547, 1548, 1549, 1550, 1551, 1552, 1553, 1555; Bodl. MSS D.D. All Souls College c.282, rolls for 1546-7, 1547-8, 1549-50, 1550-1, 1551-2, 1552-3, 1553-4 under 'fees' and 'fees and stipends': the account for 1550-1 says that the lectures were delivered in Merton College; c.283, rolls for 1554-5, 1555-6, 1556-7 under 'fees and stipends': the account for 1556-7 has been annotated in a contemporary hand 'non est vlterius solvend'; New College Archives MSS 7511, 7513, 7514, 7515, 7518, 7520, 7522, 7523, 7525, 7526, 7528 under 'custus necessarii ad extra' and 'custus ad extra'; Exeter College Archives Rectors' Accounts for 1546-7, 1547-8, 1548-9, 1549-50, 1550-1, 1551-2, 1552-3, 1554-5, 1555-6, 1557-8 under expenses; Corpus Christi College Archives C/1/1/3, fos 12ᵛ, 26ᵛ, 37ᵛ, 66, 90, 103, 117ᵛ, 129, 149ᵛ, 159ᵛ, 172.

[3] For Etheridge, see BRUO 1501-40, 194 and for Warde, ibid. 605.

[4] Logan 'Origins of the regius professorships', 275; C. S. Knighton, 'Collegiate foundations, 1540 to 1570, with special reference to St Peter in Westminster' (Cambridge PhD thesis 1975), 302-9.

appointed.[1] The professorships were crown appointments. Richard Smith himself testified to his appointment by Henry VIII,[2] while John Story was made first professor of civil law by signed bill.[3] Later appointments were made by letters patent.[4]

The arrangements for the support of the five professors were altered in 1546 as part of the plans for the foundation of Christ Church.[5] In July of that year the dean and chapter of Westminster granted lands to the crown valued at £400 in order to be released from the obligation of supporting ten professors at Oxford and Cambridge,[6] and an account surviving at Christ Church of 'all charges and receyttes both of Frediswydes and Oseney after theyr dissolution' includes among the wages paid at Michaelmas 1546 £20 each to three readers in Greek, theology and Hebrew. They were John Harpesfield, Richard Smith and Thomas Harding who had all previously been paid as professors by the dean and chapter of Westminster.[7] These payments do not appear in the wages account for 25 March 1546—it is therefore almost certain that the support of these three professors was transferred to Henry's emergent Oxford foundation between July and October 1546, that is some few months before its formal foundation by letters patent on 4 November 1546. The remaining two professors, of medicine and civil law, also retained their places but responsibility for the payment of their salaries was transferred not to Christ Church but to the court of augmentations. John Warner received a payment of £60 at Michaelmas 1547 to cover his salary as medical professor for the preceding year and a half, while John Story was paid £40 for his civil law readership at Michaelmas 1547 for the preceding year.[8]

The translation of three of the regius professors to the new double foundation of college and cathedral, in scale if not in form the true heir of Cardinal College, was accompanied by careful provision for the three readers. These regulations are to be found in a code of

[1] Logan, 'Origins of the regius professorships', 275; L & P Henry VIII xvi. no. 333.

[2] R. Smyth, The assertion and defence of the sacramente of the aulter (1546: STC 22815), dedication to Henry VIII.

[3] Cal. Pat. Rolls. 1553-1554, 395.

[4] For a summary of the evidence see the brief histories of the chairs below.

[5] Logan, 'Origins of the regius professorships', 276-7; H. L. Thompson, Christ Church (1900), 12, 272-5. The best account of the foundation of Christ Church, though by no means the last word on a very complicated subject, is to be found in J. E. A. Dawson, 'The early career of Christopher Goodman and his place in the development of English protestant thought' (Durham PhD thesis 1978).

[6] Knighton, 'Collegiate foundations', 310-11.

[7] Christ Church Archives iii.b.99.

[8] Warner: PRO E 323/3, rot. 89ᵛ where the authority for the payment is given as a letter of the chancellor of the court of augmentations dated 17 October 1546; Story: PRO E 323/3, rot. 91.

statutes for Christ Church given by Henry VIII, hitherto neglected, and recently discovered in the college archives. The code, which has been heavily amended by several hands, was never effective and its provisions for regius professors never operative, but it does give some idea of the thinking behind the transference of the chairs to Christ Church.[1] In so far as they deal with the professors the statutes exhibit considerable reliance on Wolsey's statutes for Cardinal College, often simply copying them word for word. There were to be 'in ecclesia nostra tres publici professores et lectores ex bonis nostris in eum vsum datis', covering theology, Hebrew, and 'lingua greca et artibus humanioribus'.[2] Each was to have a chamber in college and to sit at high table.[3] Vacancies in the chairs were to be filled by election. Here the statute follows Wolsey's verbatim except that the electoral body is much reduced in size, now consisting of the dean of Christ Church, the subdean and the rest of the canons, the professors and heads of Magdalen, New College, Corpus and Oriel. A departure from Wolsey's ideas was the provision that professors were to hold office for three years only, though they could be re-elected after that time. On election the professor had to swear an oath, again virtually identical to that demanded of the cardinal's lecturers.[4] The provisions for fining and depriving a negligent or incompetent professor were lifted bodily from Wolsey's statutes.[5]

On the other hand, there was no attempt to lay down the times and subjects of the professors' lectures, a matter which had been very carefully defined in the statutes of Cardinal College. But the Greek professor had to set themes for his pupils much as Wolsey's professors had to do.[6] All three professors were to examine members of the college who attended their lectures on each lecture.[7] At the end of each week at the time of his lecture the Hebrew professor was to examine his auditors.[8] All the professors were publicly to let their

[1] Christ Church Archives D.P.vi.b.1, 'Draughts of Statutes'. The fifth and last code included in this volume (noticed by Miss Dawson but mistaken for statutes of King Henry VIII's College) is entitled 'Statuta ecclesie cathedralis Regis Henrici octaui vulge vocate Christis churche of kyng Henry theightes fundacion' and is shown to be Henrician statutes for Christ Church by its beginning 'Henricus octauus dei gracia &c . . . necnon ecclesie cathedralis Oxon' vulgo vocate Christ churche of kyng Henry theightes ffundacion verus certus et indubitatus fundator [et?] dotator omnibus et singulis infra scripta lecturis et audituris salutem et graciam . . .', fo 157. The oath required of canons and others admitted to the college provides further proof of its Henrician origin: 'Ego N. promitto et iuro me huius ecclesiae statuta, et nunc edita, et in posterum edenda per illustrissimum Regem Henricum octauum . . .', fo 195. The statutes include fifty chapters and extend over thirty-nine folios; an additional chapter has decrees for almsmen.

[2] Christ Church Archives D.P. vi.b.1, fo 169^V.
[3] Ibid. fos 183, 176.
[4] Ibid. fos 169^V–71^V.
[5] Ibid. fos 173^V–75^V.
[6] Ibid. fo 173^{r-v}.
[7] Ibid. fo 166^V.
[8] Ibid. fo 173^V.

pupils know that they were ready at all times to deal with their questions and analyse their arguments.[1]

The statutes given to Christ Church by the visitors of Edward VI (c 1549) show a dramatic change in the provisions for the three professors.[2] There was no mention whatever of any procedure for electing them, no mention of a three-year term, no oath to be taken by them and no provision for fines and deprivation. Even less was said about their academic duties. The new code, however, clearly fixed their stipends at £40 per annum, consisting of 2s 4d per week commons (which the Henrician code had laid down), a salary of £31 18s 8d payable quarterly and 40s 'pro vestibus quas leveratas vocant'.[3]

The three regius professors provided for in the foundation of Christ Church and the two maintained by the exchequer received further endowments in the course of time, but their successful establishment in the last years of Henry VIII brought to a triumphant conclusion, as far as Tudor Oxford was concerned, the quest for properly endowed university lectures which had begun nearly a century before.[4]

THE LADY MARGARET PROFESSORSHIP 1497–1603

Letters patent of 1 March 1497 empowered Lady Margaret Beaufort to found a perpetual theological lecturership in Oxford to be governed by her statutes and ordinances, and gave her and others power to endow it with property to the annual value of £20.[5] This instrument

[1] Ibid.

[2] These are also contained in Christ Church Archives D.P.vi.b.1, the original code of eighty-four pages signed by the visitors being the fourth item in the volume (fos 115–56^V).

[3] Christ Church Archives D.P.vi.b.1, fos 147^V, 150, 152. It is difficult to know what the professors were paid in the early years, for few Christ Church accounts have survived for 1547–58. Payments of £40 to the three readers for the year ending Michaelmas 1555 are to be found in Bodl. MS Top. Oxon. c.23, fo 39^V and it is quite clear that this was the stipend under Elizabeth: Christ Church Archives xii.b.20–47 (Disbursement Books 1577–1603). The other accounts for 1547–58 probably show only incomplete payments: Christ Church Archives iii.b.99 (£20 each); iii.c.4 (£25 16s each); Bodl. MS Top. Oxon. c.22, fos 100^V (£10 each), 105^V (£25 16s each).

[4] Under Mary there was an attempt to restore the public teaching of scholastic theology at Oxford when in 1555 it was proposed to replace the Hebrew chair with a new lecture in the Sentences to be held by Peter de Soto: Epistolae R. Poli, ed. Quirini 5 vols (Brescia 1744–52) v. 47; Cal. SP Ven. 1555–1556, 226–7. In March 1556 the Venetian ambassador reported that Soto was 'public lecturer in holy writ' at Oxford: ibid. 386. Soto left England later that year: ibid. 589.

[5] Cal. Pat. Rolls, 1494–1509, 79; OUA NEP Pyx E, 4. The foundation ordinance of 1502 mentions only letters patent of 10 December 1496 (Statuta, 300) but these cannot be traced in the Calendar of Patent Rolls. An indenture made in 1506 between the Lady Margaret and Westminster Abbey, dealing inter alia with the foundation of the readership, mentions only the patent of 1 March 1497: BL Lansdowne MS 441, fo 4^V.

implies that the lectureship itself was intended to have an income from which, no doubt, the lecturer would receive his stipend. At any rate that was the arrangement adopted in a hitherto unnoticed (and unfortunately undated) draft of the foundation ordinance of the lecture. The lecturership is erected as a perpetual corporation in accordance with the letters patent. An annual stipend of £13 6s 8d is to be paid to the lecturer from the profits and issues of the lands and tenements given to the lecturership, and the lecturer is to render account of all revenue in excess of his stipend to auditors, the excess to be applied to the maintenance of the endowment.[1]

However, this scheme was later abandoned in favour of one which did not oblige the lecturer to act as custodian of the endowment. By 1502 it had been decided to endow the new post indirectly by means of a grant of lands to Westminster Abbey in return for which the abbot and convent agreed to pay the annual stipend of £13 6s 8d. This arrangement was laid down in the foundation ordinance of 8 September 1502[2] and confirmed in 1503.[3] Although the lecturership was still set up as a perpetual corporation it received no endowment whatever.

The most important provisions of the foundation ordinance deal with the appointment of the lecturer and with his academic duties.[4]

The lecturer is to be elected every two years by all doctors (regulars and seculars), inceptors and bachelors of theology previously regent in arts meeting on the last day of term before the long vacation 'in domo vocata le Assemblehows'. If the votes are equal then the candidate with the vote of the chancellor or his commissary wins the election. The successful candidate is to hold office for two years running from 8 September following the election.[5]

[1] OUA NEP Pyx E, 2b: an undated paper roll.

[2] *Statuta*, 307. The foundation ordinance of 8 September 1502 is printed in full in ibid. 300-8.

[3] The lands in question, the manor of Drayton and other lands and tenements in Middlesex, are listed in the agreement of 1 July 1503 between the abbey and John Roper by which they agreed to pay his stipend of £13 6s 8d in perpetuity; the lecturer may distrain upon the lands to recover arrears of his salary; OUA NEP Pyx E, 3. In March 1506 the abbey had held these lands for three years and more, BL Lansdowne MS 441, fo 6ᵛ; and they were the subject of an inquisition *ad quod damnum* dated 21 July 1502, a few months before the foundation ordinance, *Cal. Cl. Rolls, 1500–1509*, 228.

[4] The lecturer is also bound to say special prayers for the foundress and her relations, *Statuta*, 306-7.

[5] *Statuta*, 303-6 gives full details of the election procedures. The draft foundation ordinance provided for an annual election, OUA NEP Pyx E, 2b. In the final ordinance it is actually stated that the lecturer is to be elected every two years to serve 'pro vno anno integro', *Statuta*, 303. This is clearly a slip in view of the provision for biennial election and of the fact that it later orders the lecturer to be admitted 'pro duobus annis integris', ibid. 304; cf *Laudian Code*, 217 where the error is pointed out. The parallel ordinance for the Lady Margaret professor at Cambridge provides for the lecturer to be elected every two

The lectures are to be given free to all comers in the schools on works of theology thought meet by the chancellor or his commissary acting with the doctors of the university. They are to last an hour, from 7 a.m. to 8 a.m. or at another time fixed by the chancellor or his commissary. Lectures are to begin on the first day of each term and be read on every legible day until the end of each term and are to continue in the long vacation until 8 September. During Lent, however, the lectures are to be suspended so that the lecturer and his audience may more readily attend to preaching. The continuity of lectures throughout the term was clearly a prime consideration of the foundress. The lecturer could not suspend his lectures for more than four days in any one term without proving reasonable cause before the chancellor or his commissary and the majority of the doctors of theology, and obtaining the licence of the chancellor or his commissary. Moreover, even with such authority he could not absent himself from lecturing for more than fourteen days in any one term and during his absence he was obliged to provide a suitable deputy at his own expense.[1]

In the course of the sixteenth century these provisions were modified in various ways. After the dissolution of Westminster Abbey in 1540 payment of the stipend eventually became the responsibility of the crown by means of a decree of the court of augmentations.[2] The salary for half of 1553–4 was converted to the repair of the new schools and the use of the university.[3] In 1563 the stipend of Queen Mary's chaplain in the university was assigned to the Lady Margaret professor to bring his salary up to £20 per annum (still only half that of the regius professors).[4] Henceforth his stipend was to consist of two parts, £13 6s 8d from the crown and £6 13s 4d from the university.[5]

About the lectures themselves there is less to be said.[6] According

years 'pro vno biennio integro', *The Endowments of the University of Cambridge*, ed. J. W. Clark (Cambridge 1904), 61.

[1] *Statuta*, 302–3.

[2] The decree, dated 23 June 1543, is exemplified in OUA NEP Pyx E, 5. For payments made to Hugh Weston, Lady Margaret professor, by the court of augmentations (1542–53), see PRO E 323/2b pt 1, rot. 59; pt 2, rot. 40; pt 3, rot. 96^V; pt 4, rot. 42/43^V; pt 5, rot. 40/41; pt 6, rot. 25/27; pt 7, rot. 26/27^V; pt 8, rot. 41/42^V. Cf *L & P Henry VIII* xix. pt 1, 238, xxi. pt 1, 310.

[3] Reg. Cong. 1535–63, fo 141^V.

[4] *Statuta*, 376.

[5] Payment of the augmented stipend may be traced in the Vice-Chancellor's accounts: OUA WPβ/21/4.

[6] Hugh Weston lectured 'de sacrificio messe' in 1548, probably as Lady Margaret professor: Vivian Green, *The Commonwealth of Lincoln College 1427–1977* (Oxford 1979), 88.

to the Edwardian statutes of 1549 the Lady Margaret professor, like the regius professor, was to lecture for at least four days per week; this was confirmed by the *nova statuta* of 1564/5 but by 1576 had been reduced to at least three days a week.[1] By the time of the Laudian Code (1636) the lecturer's duties had been trimmed still further. In common with the other public professors he was to lecture only twice a week, on Tuesdays and Thursdays at 9 a.m. on any part of Holy Scripture, and he need only lecture for up to three-quarters of an hour.[2]

Although the reformation must have swept away the lecturer's obligation to say special prayers for the souls of the foundress and her family, new religious duties were laid upon him during Elizabeth's reign. The *nova statuta* of 1564/5 obliged him to take his turn in preaching an English sermon on Sundays in full term and placed him second in the list of Latin preachers for Ash Wednesday.[3] In 1567, in return for the increase in his salary decreed four years earlier, he was bound four times a year on the day before the beginning of term to moderate public prayers in St Mary's, and to discharge any of the tasks which used to be the responsibility of the university chaplain.[4] Finally, by an order of 1580 he might be called upon by the vice-chancellor to preach a Latin sermon *ad clerum* on the day before the beginning of each term.[5]

Professors

EDMUND WYLSFORD: MA, DTh 1497, fellow of Oriel College c 1483–1507, provost 1507–16; principal of Bedel Hall 1510–14. Sometime confessor to the Lady Margaret. Probably occupied the chair 1497–1500; died 3 October 1516. *BRUO to 1500*, iii. 2115–16.

JOHN ROPER: MA, BTh by 1493, DTh 1500/1, fellow of Magdalen College 1483, still in 1506; principal of Magdalen Hall 1492–4, of Salissury Hall 1502, St George's Hall 1510 and still in 1512; canon of King Henry VIII college 1532. Occupied the chair in 1500, still in 1508. At the king's command wrote a tractate against Luther in 1521/2; died May 1534. *BRUO to 1500* iii. 1590; Bodl. MS 282, fo 1; Macray, *Reg. Magdalen*, i. 104–5.

JOHN KINGTON: OFM, DTh 1494/5. Praelector in theology at Magdalen College in 1502–3, vacated about 1519: occupied chair before 1530, died 20 January 1536. Wrote against the teachings

---

[1] *Statuta*, 343 (1549), 381 (1564/5), 407 (1576).
[2] *Laudian Code*, 39–40. [3] *Statuta*, 382.
[4] Ibid. 397. [5] Ibid. 418.

of Luther. *BRUO to 1500* ii. 1053; *DNB*; Macray, *Reg. Magdalen*, i. 31–2.

WILLIAM MORTIMER: BA 1511, MA 1514, BTh 1522, DTh 1530, fellow of De Vaux College, Salisbury in 1514, in the service of Catherine of Aragon 1534. Probably occupied the chair 1530–4; he was described as a 'late occupant' 26 January 1534. *L & P Henry VIII* vii. pp. 38–9; *BRUO 1501–40*, 403; *Oxoniensia* xix (1954), 84–5.

RICHARD LORGAN: MA 1523, BTh 1532, DTh 1535, fellow of Oriel College 1520–36; principal of St Mary Hall 1521–30; praelector in theology at Magdalen College 1535–6. In 1535 the president of Magdalen described Lorgan to Thomas Cromwell as 'reder of dyvynyte yn Oxforth by the fundacyon of the king's grandmother': PRO SP 1/100, fo 61 = *L & P Henry VIII*, ix. no. 1120; *BRUO 1501–40*, 362.

HUGH WESTON: BA 1530, MA 1533, BM supp. 1537, BTh 1539, DTh 1540, incorp. at Cambridge 1554–5; fellow of Lincoln College 1531–9, rector 1539–56. Dean of Westminster 1553–6, dean of St George's Chapel, Windsor 1556–7. Occupied chair in 1542–*c*1551; payments to Weston as Lady Margaret professor may be found in the accounts of the Treasurer of the Court of Augmentations, PRO E 323. Died 8 December 1558.

CHRISTOPHER GOODMAN: BA 1541, MA 1544, matric. at university of Basle 1554; senior student of Christ Church 1547–53; chaplain to Sir Henry Sidney, lord deputy of Ireland 1566. Occupied chair *c*1551–3; died 4 June 1603. *BRUO 1501–40*, 241–2; *DNB*; Garrett, *Marian Exiles*, 162–4; PRO E 323/8, rot. 41/42^V; J. E. A. Dawson, 'The early career of Christopher Goodman and his place in the development of English protestant thought' (University of Durham PhD thesis 1978), pp. 13, 51 n. 63.

JOHN SMITH: BA 1529, MA 1533; fellow of Oriel College 1530–50, provost 1550–65; treasurer Chichester cathedral 1555–62. Occupied chair in 1554, died 1576. *BRUO 1501–40*, 522–3; OUA Reg. Cong. 1535–63 fo 141^V; *Reg. Univ.* ed. Boase, 152.

FRANCIS BABINGTON: BA Cantab. 1548–9, MA Cantab. 1552, MA Oxon. 1554, BTh Oxon. 1558, DTh Oxon. 1560; fellow of St John's College Cambridge 1551; fellow All Souls College 1557; master of Balliol College 1559–60, rector of Lincoln College 1560–3; was chaplain to the earl of Leicester and fled abroad 1565. Occupied chair before 1562, died 1569. *DNB*; Venn, *Alumni Cant.* I, i. 62; V. Green, *The Commonwealth of Lincoln College 1427–1977*, 127–9.

HERBERT WESTFALING: BA supp. 1551, MA 1555, BTh 1561, DTh 1566; canon of Christ Church 1562, occupied chair 1562–4. Treasurer of diocese of London 1567, canon of St George's Chapel, Windsor, 1577; bishop of Hereford 1586–1602; died 1 March 1602. *DNB; Reg. Univ.* ed. Boase, 217.

JAMES CALFHILL: BA supp. 1549, MA 1552, BTh 1561, DTh 1566; canon of Christ Church 1560, occupied chair 1564–5; archdeacon of Colchester 1565, bishop of Worcester, nominated 1570 but died before consecration in August 1570. *DNB; Reg. Univ.* ed. Boase, 216.

EDWARD CRADOCKE: BA 1556, MA 1560, BTh 1565, DTh 1566; occupied chair 1565–94. Alchemist. *DNB; Reg. Univ.* ed. Boase, 230.

JOHN WILLIAMS: ?BA supp. 1580. MA 1585, BTh 1594, DTh 1598; fellow of All Souls College 1594, principal of Jesus College 1602–13; occupied chair 1594–1613, died 1613. OUA Reg. Cong. 1582–95, fo 277^V; *Reg. Univ.* ed. Clark, iii. 92, 126.

REGIUS PROFESSOR OF THEOLOGY

Richard Smith was named professor in 1540 (*L & P Henry VIII* xvi. 154), but no statutory provision by the university or foundation document from the crown is extant.

The professor was appointed by the crown (cf R. Smith, *The assertion and defence of the sacramente of the aulter* (1546) dedication to Henry VIII), but no instrument of appointment appears to survive until letters patent of 11 July 1589 granting 'the Office or rome of reading of our divinitye lector' to Thomas Holland for life: PRO C 66/1331, m. 27.

According to statutes and decrees of 1549, 1564/5 and 1576 the professor was to lecture four times a week during term. He alone could lecture at 9 a.m. under the 1549 statutes and only on Holy Scripture (Peter Martyr lectured on Romans from 9 a.m. to 10 a.m. in 1550, *Original Letters* 419), while the 1556 code ordered that he must lecture for one hour at least. In addition he was to moderate at theological disputations (1564/5, 1583). Martyr presided at disputations in 1550, *Original Letters* 420, 481.

The *nova statuta* of 1564/5 provided that he should take his turn in preaching an English sermon on Sundays in full term and put him at the head of a list of Latin preachers for Ash Wednesday. A statute of 1580 ordained that he could be called on to preach in Latin *ad clerum* the day before the beginning of term.

The professor received a stipend of £40 per annum plus certain fees from candidates for degrees in theology.

Sources: Statuta, 343, 344 (1549); 373 (1556); 381, 382, 383 (1564/5); 407 (1576); 418 (1580); 427 (1583); 511–13 (1613: fees). See too, in general, *Reg. Univ.* ed. Clark i. 132 ff, 221–4.

Professors

RICHARD SMITH: BA 1527, MA 1530, BTh 1536, DTh 1536; fellow of Merton College 1528–37, principal of Alban Hall, vacated 1539; canon of Christ Church 1554–9, King Henry VIII's lecturer in theology 1536–42. He occupied the chair from 1540 to 1547, again from 1553 to 1556 (when he disappears from the battels books at Christ Church). He was incorporated at Louvain in 1547, at Paris 1551, at St Andrews 1551. He was public lector in theology at St Mary's College, St Andrews University in 1552 and was there still in 1553. He was chaplain extraordinary to the king and queen in 1554. He was appointed dean at St Peter's, Douai, and royal chaplain by Philip II. In 1562 he was chancellor and professor of theology at the catholic university of Douai. He died on 9 July 1563. *BRUO 1501–40*, 524–6; *DNB; L & P Henry VIII*, xvi, p. 154; Westminster Abbey muniments, *ex. inform.* Dr C. S. Knighton; *ex inform.* Professor J. K. Cameron (St Andrews); Christ Church Archives iii.b.99 (wages); iii.c.4 (expenses); Bodl. MS Top. Oxon. c.22, fos 100^V, 105^V; Bodl. MS Top. Oxon. c.23, fo 39^V.

PETER MARTYR: DTh Padua ?1527, incorporated DTh Oxford 1548; canon of Christ Church 1550–3; professor of theology at Strasbourg 1542–7, again 1554–5; member of a commission to reform church law (England) 1551; professor of Hebrew at Zurich 1556–62. He held the chair in Oxford from 1548 to 1553, first appearing in the battels books at Christ Church in January 1548 (Christ Church Archives x(1)c.1). *DNB sub nomine* Vermigli; *Reg. Univ.* ed. Boase, 214; Le Neve, *Fasti*, ed. Hardy ii. 517.

JUAN DE VILLA GARCIA: BTh Valladolid; incorporated BTh Oxford 1555, DTh 1558; praelector in theology at Magdalen college 1555–7; he occupied the chair from 1556 to 1558. *Reg. Univ.* ed. Boase, 229; Macray, *Reg. Magdalen*, ii. 31, 90; *Cal. SP Foreign 1559–60*, 3; J. Ignacio Tellechea Idigoras, *Inglaterra, Flandres y España (1557–1559) en cartas inéditas de Carranza y otros*, 26, 30, 32.

LAURENCE HUMFREY: BA, MA 1552, BTh 1562, DTh 1562, incorporated at Cambridge DTh 1569; fellow of Magdalen College c 1548–56, president 1561–90; dean of Gloucester 1571–80, of Winchester 1580–90. He occupied the chair from 1560 to 1589, and died on 1 February 1590. *DNB; Reg. Univ.* ed. Boase, 218; OUA Reg. Cong. 1582–95, fo 296; Christ Church Archives D & C i.b.1; xii.b.20–31.

THOMAS HOLLAND: BA 1571, MA 1575, BTh 1582, DTh 1585; fellow of Balliol College 1573, of Exeter College 1592, rector of Exeter 1592–1612. He occupied the chair from 1589 to 1612. He was chaplain to the earl of Leicester in the Netherlands 1585, and helped to prepare the authorized version of the Bible. He died on 17 March 1612. *DNB*; Christ Church Archives xii.b.31–56; PRO C66/1331 m. 27; *Reg. Univ.* ed Boase, 281; ed. Clark, iii. 53.

REGIUS PROFESSOR OF GREEK

John Harpesfield was professor in 1543, and may have been in the post as early as 1541, but no statutory provision by the university or foundation document from the crown is extant.

The professor was appointed by the crown. The earliest evidence concerning the method of appointment is a letter of 27 August 1553 from the privy council ordering the chancellor of the university 'to place George Ethrege in the Greake lecture at Oxforde, to enjoye the same from Michaelmas next commyng with thole fee . . .', *APC, 1552–1554*, 333. Under Elizabeth appointment by letters patent was usual. John Harmar (25 March 1585), Henry Cuffe (20 April 1590) and John Perin (9 February 1597) were all appointed in this way, PRO C 66/1256, m.18; C 66/1340, m.29; C 66/1473, m.3. All were to hold office 'quam diu . . . se bene gesserit'.[1]

According to the statutes of 1549 the professor was to lecture five times per week from 8 a.m. until 9 a.m. on Homer, Demosthenes, Isocrates, Euripides or another of the ancients and on 'artem vna cum proprietate linguae'; this was reduced to four days a week in 1564/5, a provision reinforced in 1576.

The professor received a stipend of £40 per annum.

Sources: Statuta, 343, 344 (1549); 381 (1564/5); 407 (1576).

Professors

JOHN HARPESFIELD: BA 1538, MA 1541, BTh by 1554, DTh 1554; fellow New College 1534–51; chaplain to Edmund Bonner

[1] Harmar succeeded on the death of Giles Lawrence, but Cuffe and Perin were to succeed when their predecessors left office.

while bishop of London; dean of Norwich 1558, deprived by 1560. He occupied the chair from 1543 to 1547, but may have been professor as early as 1541 when he supplicated for dispensation from his necessary regency as a recently created MA 'quia publice prelegit et decanum Wellensem instituit' (OUA Reg. Cong. 1535-63, fo 74). *BRUO 1501-40*, 267-8; N. Harpesfield, *The Life and Death of Sir Thomas More*, ed. R. V. Hitchcock (Early English Text Society 1932), clxxix, citing Westminster Abbey muniments; Christ Church Archives, iii.b.99 (wages); Bodl. MS Top. Oxon. c. 22, fos 100^v, 105^v.

GEORGE ETHERIDGE: BA 1539, MA 1543, BM 1545; fellow Corpus Christi College 1541-5. He occupied the chair in 1547, vacated it by October 1551 and took it up again 1553-9. He first appears in the battels books in January-March 1547 and occurs in the same source throughout Mary's reign until his replacement by Giles Lawrence in April 1559 (Christ Church Archives, x(1)c.1, 3, 5, 6 passim and esp. 6, fo 87^v). *BRUO 1501-40*, 194; *DNB*; Christ Church Archives, iii.c.4; D & C i.b.1, fos 1, 3^v, 4^v; *APC 1552-1554*, 333; *Cal. SP Rome, 1558-1571*, 68.

GILES LAWRENCE: BCL, supp. DCL 1556; adm. Corpus as disc. 19 August 1539 aged 17; fellow All Souls College 1542, still in 1549-50; tutor to the children of Sir Arthur Darcy, resident near the Tower of London in the time of Mary. He first appears in the battels books replacing Etheridge in April 1559 (Christ Church Archives x(1)c.6, fo 87^v). He occupied the chair earlier from 1551 to 1553, then again 1559-85. He had died by 25 March 1585. *BRUO 1501-40*, 343-4; Christ Church Archives D & C i.b.1 fos 4^v, 6; also xii.b.20-7; *APC 1552-1554*, 333; PRO C 66/1256, m. 18.

JOHN HARMAR: BA 1577, MA 1582, BTh 1605; fellow New College *c* 1575. He occupied the chair from 1585 to 1590, was warden of Winchester College 1596-1613, and was one of the translators of the New Testament in 1604. He died 11 October 1613. For his publications see the discussion in the account of the faculty of theology. *DNB; Reg. Univ.* ed. Clark iii. 64; Christ Church Archives xii.b.27-32; PRO C 66/1256, m. 18.

HENRY CUFFE: BA 1581, MA 1589; fellow Trinity College 1583 and later expelled; fellow Merton College 1586; secretary to the earl of Essex *c* 1594. He held the chair from 1590 to 1596, and was executed for his involvement in Essex's rebellion in 1601. A Mr Spensar appears as regius professor of Greek in the Christ Church lists for the third term of 1594-5 during Cuffe's tenure (Christ

Church Archives xii.b.37). *DNB*; Christ Church Archives xii.b. 32–40; PRO C 66/1340 m. 29; *Reg. Univ.* ed. Clarke iii. 90.

JOHN PERIN: BA 1580, MA 1583, BTh 1589, DTh 1596; fellow St John's College 1575–80, prebendary of Christ Church 1600. He occupied the chair from 1597 to 1615 and died 9 May 1615. W. H. Stevenson and H. E. Salter, *The Early History of St John's College, Oxford* (OHS new ser. i. 1939), 250–1; Foster, 1148; PRO C 66/1473 m. 3; Christ Church Archives xii.b.40–59; *Cal. SP Dom. 1598–1601*, 387.

REGIUS PROFESSOR OF HEBREW

John Shepreve was professor *c* 1542 but no statutory provision by the university or foundation document from the crown is extant.

The professor was appointed by the crown. Thomas Kingsmill (1569), John Harding (1591) and William Thorne (1598) were all appointed by letters patent, *Cal. Pat. Rolls, 1566–69*, 341–2; *Foedera* xvi. 337, but whereas Kingsmill was appointed for life, Harding and Thorne were to hold the post *durante bene placito nostro*.

According to the statutes of 1549 the professor was to lecture five times per week between 8 a.m. and 9 a.m. on Holy Scripture only and on grammar and 'linguae proprietatem'. His obligations were reduced to four days per week in 1564/5, reaffirmed in 1576.

In 1555 it was planned to substitute a new lecturership in scholastic theology for the Hebrew professorship 'quae paucos habet, aut nullos potius auditores', *Epistolae R. Poli* v. 47; *Cal. SP Ven. 1555–1556*, 226–7.

The *nova statuta* of 1564/5 ordained that the professor was to take a turn in preaching the English sermon on Sundays in full term and placed him third in the list of Latin preachers for Ash Wednesday.

The professor received a stipend of £40 per annum.

Sources: Statuta, 343, 344 (1549); 381, 382 (1564/5); 407 (1576).

Professors

JOHN SHEPREVE: BA 1530, MA 1533, fellow Corpus Christi College 1530, vacated by 1542. He was given leave by congregation in April 1542 to lecture on the book of Genesis in the Hebrew text provided that 'modo pie et catholice legat'. He died in July 1542. *BRUO 1501–40*, 513–14; *DNB*; J. Shepreve, *Hyppolitus ovidianae phaedrae respondens*, ed. G. Etheridge

(Oxford 1586; *STC* 22405) in Etheridge's preface; Westminster Abbey Muniments *ex inform*. Dr C. S. Knighton.

THOMAS HARDING: BA 1538, MA 1542, BTh 1552, DTh 1554, fellow New College 1536–54, subwarden 1553–4. Occupied chair in 1544, vacated 1547. He was chaplain to Henry Grey, marquis of Dorset *c* 1546; chaplain of John White, bishop of Lincoln 1555; chaplain and confessor of Stephen Gardiner, bishop of Winchester 1555, and was at Louvain by 1561. He took part in a celebrated controversy with bishop Jewel in the 1560s. *BRUO 1501–40*, 265–6; Christ Church Archives iii.b.99 (wages) c.4 (expenses); Bodl. MS Top. Oxon. c. 22, fos 100^v, 105^v; Westminster Abbey Muniments *ex inform*. Dr C. S. Knighton.

RICHARD BRUERNE: BA 1537, MA 1539, BTh supp. 1548, DTh supp. 1555; as BM supp. for DM 1562; fellow of Lincoln College by 1538, vacated 1546; canon of Christ Church 1553–65; fellow of Eton College 1544–61, Provost 1561; canon and prebendary of St George's Chapel, Windsor 1557–65. He occupied the chair 1547–59, first appearing in the battels books in September 1547 (Christ Church Archives x(1)c.1). He died in April 1565. *BRUO 1501–40*, 69; Christ Church Archives, D & C i.b.1, fos 1, 3^v 4^v, 6; Bodl. MS Top. Oxon. c.23, fo 39^v; *APC 1558–1570*, 44; *DNB*.

THOMAS NEALE; BA 1543, MA 1546, BTh 1556; fellow New College 1540–58; canon of Christ Church 1553–65, pensioner of St John's College nominated by the founder 1566, commoner of Hart Hall 1567; chaplain to Edmund Bonner, bishop of London. He occupied the chair from 1559 to 1569 when he resigned. He then moved to Cassington, 6 miles from Oxford and was an occasional conformist. *BRUO 1501–40*, 413–14; *DNB*; *APC 1558–1570*, 44; Christ Church Archives, D & C i.b.1; OUA Reg. Cong. 1564–82, fo 78; *Cal. Pat. Rolls Elizabeth I, 1566–1569*, 341–2; Alan Davidson, 'Roman Catholicism in Oxfordshire from the late Elizabethan period to the Civil War', Bristol PhD thesis, 646–7.

THOMAS KINGSMILL: BA 1560, MA 1565, BTh supp. 1572, fellow Magdalen College 1559–68. He occupied the chair from 1569 to 1591. Richard Hooker was Kingsmill's deputy from 14 July 1579 when Kingsmill was ill. *DNB*; *Cal. Pat. Rolls Elizabeth I, 1566–1569*, 341–2; Macray, *Reg. Magdalen* ii. 148; OUA Reg. Cong. 1564–82, fo 288.

JOHN HARDING: BA 1578, MA 1581, BTh 1592, DTh 1597; fellow of Magdalen College by 1583, president 1608–10;

chaplain to James I 1608. He occupied the chair from 1591 to 1598 and again 1604–10. He died on 5 November 1610. Macray, *Reg. Magdalen* iii. 72–80; *Reg. Univ.* ed. Clark iii. 73.

WILLIAM THORNE: BA 1590, MA 1593, BTh 1600, DTh 1602, fellow New College 1587; dean of Chichester 1601–30. He occupied the chair 1598–1604, and died 13 February 1630. *DNB*; Clark iii. 153–4.

REGIUS PROFESSOR OF CIVIL LAW

John Story was appointed by the crown *c* 1541, but no statutory provision by the university or foundation document from the crown is extant.

The professor was usually appointed by letters patent. Story, the first professor, was appointed by signed bill (*c* 1541) and reappointed for life with Robert Weston by letters patent of 28 February 1546, PRO E 323/3, rot. 91 refers to these letters but they cannot be located in *L & P Henry VIII*, no doubt because Story failed to have them sealed: *Cal. Pat. Rolls, 1553–1554*, 395; cf *L & P Henry VIII* xxi pt i, 473 no. 40. These letters were subsequently revoked by the council and the office regranted to Story alone by council letters of 19 November 1546 (PRO E 323/3, rot. 91 refers to the council's actions, no trace of which is to be found in *APC*). Nevertheless, Weston appeared as sole recipient of the professor's salary for 1550–3, see below under Weston. Story and William Aubrey were appointed for life in survivorship by letters patent (1553), though Story made over his interest in the office to Aubrey, *Cal. Pat. Rolls, 1553–1554*, 395; *Foedera*, ed. T. Rymer (20 vols 1727–35) xv. 503; likewise John Griffith was appointed *durante bene placito nostro* in 1559: ibid. xv. 503, Robert Lougher for life in 1566: *Cal. Pat. Rolls, 1563–1566*, 387; Griffith Lloyd for life in 1577: PRO C 66/1152, m. 17–18; and Albericus Gentilis for life in 1587, though this last patent also granted the reversion of the office to Francis James: PRO C 66/1287, m. 10–11.

According to the statutes of 1549 the professor was to lecture four times a week from 8 a.m. to 9 a.m. on the *Pandects, Code* or ecclesiastical laws of the realm; the provision of four lectures a week was repeated in 1564/5 and 1576. He was also to moderate at disputations in Law (1564/5, 1583, 1594). Robert Weston was reported in November 1550 to be presiding at disputations in Civil Law, *Original Letters* 420. Under Elizabeth the professor lectured at 10 a.m.; Clark i. 95, 113.

The stipend of the professor was £40 per annum.

Sources: Statuta, 343, 344 (1549); 381, 384 (1564/5); 407 (1576); 429 (1583); 452-3 (1594). See too, in general, *Reg. Univ.* ed. Clark i. 113 ff.

Professors

For further information about the occupants of the chair in civil law see John Barton, 'The King's Readers', pp. 285-93 above.

JOHN STORY: BCL 1531, DCL 1538, matriculated Louvain 1564, scholar at Hinksey Hall 1530, still 1532, admitted principal Broadgates Hall 1537. Born about 1510, he was executed 1 June 1571 and beatified 1886. He occupied the chair *c* 1541-50, again 1553, still 1556-7. Payments to Story as professor of civil law occur in the accounts of the treasurer of the court of augmentations for the period Michaelmas 1546 to Michaelmas 1550 (PRO, E 323/3, rot. 91, 4, rot. 38/39, 5, rot 36/37^v, 6, rot. 22/24). Payments were made to Story and William Aubrey 'lectoribus ciuilis lecture apud Oxenford' in issues of the exchequer for fees and annuities 1553-6/7 (PRO, E 405/499, 507, fo. 75^v, 510). At some stage of Mary's reign Story resigned to Aubrey his interest in the appointment of 1553 (*Cal. Pat. Rolls 1553-4*, p. 395; *1558-60*, p. 57; Rymer, *Foedera*, xv. 503). He was a member of parliament in 1547, 1553, 1554, 1555, 1559, chancellor of London and Oxford dioceses temp. Mary; went abroad 1563. *BRUO 1501-40*, 544-5; *DNB*; *APC 1547-50*, 229; Westminster Abbey muniments, *ex inform.* Dr C. S. Knighton.

ROBERT WESTON: BCL 1538, DCL 1556, fellow All Souls College 1536, still 1549-50; principal Broadgates Hall 1546-9. He was born *c* 1515 and died 20 May 1573. He was made joint holder of the chair with John Story by letters patent of 28 February 1546, having lectured for the regius professor in 1544 (OUA, Reg. Cong. 1535-63, fo. 100). These letters were subsequently revoked by the council (probably in connection with the transferring of payments from Westminster to the augmentations) and the office regranted to Story alone by council letters of 19 November 1546 (PRO, E 323/3, rot. 91). Weston appears as sole recipient of payments as professor for the period Michaelmas 1550 to March 1553 (E 323/7, rot. 24/25, 8, rot. 39/40). Cf *The Report of the Royal Commission of 1552*, ed. W. C. Richardson (Morgantown 1974), 81. He was a member of parliament in 1553, 1558, 1559, dean of the arches 1560, official of the court of Canterbury 1560, vicar-general of the bishop of Coventry and Lichfield 1560, dean of St Patrick's, Dublin 1566-73, dean of Wells *in commendam* 1570–3, lord chancellor of Ireland 1567, lord justice of Ireland 1567–8. *BRUO 1501–40*, 618; *DNB*.

WILLIAM AUBREY: BCL by 1554, DCL 1554, fellow All Souls College 1547, still 1549–50, principal New Inn Hall 1550. Born about 1529 and died 23 July 1595. He occupied the chair from 1553 to 1559; see above concerning John Story. He was appointed auditor and vicar-general in spirituals for the province of Canterbury by archbishop Grindal and was chancellor to archbishop Whitgift. He was a member of the council in the marches of Wales, being admitted in 1577, a master in chancery *c* 1555, master of requests 1590, and a member of parliament in 1554, 1558, 1559, 1562 and 1592. *DNB*; *Dictionary of Welsh Biography*, 17; *Cal. Pat. Rolls 1553–4*, 395, ibid. *1558–60*, 57; *Reg. Univ.* ed. Boase. 225; P. Williams, *The Council in the Marches of Wales* (Cardiff 1958), 342–3.

JOHN GRIFFITH: BCL 1552, DCL 1562, fellow All Souls College 1548, principal New Inn Hall 1561–4. He died in 1587, having occupied the chair from 1559 to 1566. He was a member of parliament in 1571. *Dictionary of Welsh Biography*, 293; *Reg. Univ.* ed. Boase, 215; *Cal. Pat. Rolls 1558–60*, 57; *Cal. Pat. Rolls 1563–6*, 387.

ROBERT LOUGHER: BCL 1558, DCL 1565, fellow All Souls College 1553, principal New Inn Hall 1564–70, 1575–80, fellow Jesus College 1571. He died in June 1585, having occupied the chair from 1566 to 1577. He was a member of parliament in 1572, master in chancery 1574 and official of the consistory and vicar-general in spirituals at York, 1577. *DNB*; *Reg. Univ.* ed. Boase, 237; *Cal. Pat. Rolls 1563–6*, 387.

GRIFFITH (GRIFFIN) LLOYD: BCL 1572, DCL 1576, fellow All Souls College by 1572 and principal Jesus College 1572–86. He died 26 November 1586, having occupied the chair from 1577 to 1586. He was chancellor of the bishop of Oxford, and a member of parliament in the year of his death. Wood, *History and Antiquities*, 857; *Cal. Pat. Rolls 1563–6*, 387; PRO, C 66/1152 m. 17–18; *APC 1586–7*, 56; *Reg. Univ.* ed. Boase, 282; *Reg. Univ.* ed. Clark iii. 23; *VCH Oxon.* iii. 278; E. G. Hardy, *Jesus College* (1899), 19.

ALBERICUS GENTILIS: DCL Perugia 1572, incorporated at Oxford 1581. He was born on 14 January 1552 and died 19 June 1608, having occupied the chair at Oxford from 1587 to 1608. The letters patent of 8 June 1587 granting the 'Office or roome of readinge of our Civill lecture' to Gentilis for life also granted the reversion to Francis James, BCL, effective from the death of Gentilis or upon his forfeiting the office for other reasons: PRO, C 66/1287, m.10-11. He accompanied the embassy to the Elector of Saxony in 1586 and was a member of Gray's Inn in 1600. He had a large practice in maritime and civil causes in London from 1590. For further information see John Barton, pp. 261, 265-7 above. *DNB; Reg. Univ.* ed. Clark i. 149, 379.

REGIUS PROFESSOR OF MEDICINE

For an account of this chair and its holders see Gillian Lewis, 'The faculty of medicine', pp. 224–38 above.

5

Reformation Controversies

JENNIFER LOACH*

IN the late 1520s Oxford men were anxious to claim that the university had been free from doctrinal error until the young graduates imported from Cambridge by Cardinal Wolsey brought in the ideas they had picked up in 'little Germany', the Cambridge public house in which Lutheran books were freely circulated and discussed. 'It were a gracious deed', moaned Dr London in 1528, 'if they were tried and purged, and restored again unto their mother, from whence they came, if', he added ominously, 'they be worthy to come thither again.'[1] There was clearly an element of self-justification in this picture of Oxford bathed in religious calm, undivided and undisturbed, for both the accounts of the Oxford bookseller John Dorne and a letter from Archbishop Warham, the chancellor of the university, show that by 1521 books by Luther and Melanchthon were already circulating in Oxford:[2] after the religious tension of the previous century the university was very anxious to prove its orthodoxy. None the less, it seems possible that protestant ideas might have been accorded no more than the academic courtesy of a careful perusal had it not been for the interest shown by many of those in Wolsey's new foundations.

The ringleader of the group was John Clarke, a Cambridge graduate who became one of the first canons of Cardinal College.[3] His disputations and lectures gained a great reputation among the young scholars and graduates, and with a chosen few he read and commented on the Pauline epistles in his rooms in college.[4] Clarke's radical views

* I am grateful to the Reverend Dr T. M. Parker, who generously supplied me with the materials he had assembled for this chapter when ill health forced him to abandon it, to Professor P. M. J. McNair and the Reverend C. M. Dent for their willingness to discuss with me the career of Peter Martyr and the development of protestantism in Oxford respectively, and to them and to Elizabeth Russell for allowing me to read unpublished work, and to Professor J. K. McConica and Mr. P. H. Williams for their advice on various drafts of this chapter.

[1] *L & P Henry VIII* iv. pt 2, 3968.

[2] F. Madan, 'The daily ledger of John Dorne', in C. R. L. Fletcher (ed.), *Collectanea* i (OHS v 1885), index I; *L & P Henry VIII* iii. pt 1, 1193.

[3] *BRUO 1501–40*. [4] Foxe, *Acts and Monuments* v. 426–7.

were shared by a number of his colleagues including Henry Sumner
from King's, William Bettes from Gonville, Thomas Lawney and the
musician John Taverner.[1] Through Thomas Garrett, curate of All
Hallows, Honey Lane, this group acquired from London Tyndale's
first translation of the New Testament and other unorthodox
works.[2] On the pretext of learning Greek and Hebrew Garrett was
able to distribute in the university at least seven copies of *Uniones
dissidentium*, the writings of Hus and the fourteenth-century mystic
John Tauler, and books by Luther, Melanchthon, Oecolampadius
and the French reformer Francis Lambert. In early 1528 the authorities caught up with him. The careful investigations that followed
revealed the full involvement of Cardinal College and the other
recent foundation, Corpus; Anthony Delaber and a Benedictine
colleague at Gloucester College were also implicated.[3]

The authorities, and Wolsey in particular, were understandably
shaken by this episode, but they may have exaggerated its importance. Some of those involved, such as John Frith and Garrett himself, did indeed become protestant martyrs, but the subsequent
careers of most of those questioned were far more ambiguous.
Nicholas Udall of Corpus, for example, was circumspect enough to
find favour as a dramatist and translator at the courts of both
Edward VI and Mary, John Fryer of Cardinal College went on to be
imprisoned for popery in 1561 and the martyrologist Foxe himself
admitted that Michael Drome 'afterwards fell away and forsook the
truth'.[4]

Certainly the attitude of the university in 1530 towards Henry VIII's
attempt to rid himself of his first wife suggests sympathy with the
papal position. When asked to agree to the proposition that by divine
and natural law it was forbidden to marry a dead brother's wife the
university at first stalled, then involved itself in constitutional
wrangles and was finally forced to agree only by the somewhat
dubious process of decreeing that the sentence of a majority of the
faculty of theology was to be taken as that of the whole university.[5]
According to William Forrest's *History of Grisild the Second*, a work
dedicated to Mary Tudor, the king's commissioners were pelted by
the women of Oxford and the opposition to the royal proposition was
led by William Mortimer, the Lady Margaret professor of theology,
by John Moreman, later to be imprisoned by the government of
Edward VI, and by John Holyman, subsequently Marian bishop of

[1] Foxe, *Acts and Monuments* v, 4–5.
[2] Ibid. 421–9.   [3] Ibid. app. 6.
[4] For Udall, see *DNB* and *BRUO 1501–40*. For Fyer and Drome, see Foxe, op. cit.
v. 4–5.
[5] *Records of the Reformation*, ed. N. Pocock (2 vols Oxford 1870) i. 284–93, 528–30.

Bristol.[1] The opposition was defeated, however, and the university as a whole apparently learnt its lesson, for in 1534 it meekly accepted Henry VIII's gloss on the power of the pope.[2]

But submission did not save the university from the new brooms of the 1535 visitors, who abolished the study of canon law and substituted direct study of the Bible for the *Sentences* of Peter Lombard.[3] The impact of the visitation on college libraries was equally decisive, since Richard Layton and his colleagues delighted in the sight of scholastic manuscripts being destroyed and dispersed, reporting with glee the spectacle of New College quadrangle thick with the leaves of medieval texts and a Buckinghamshire gentleman collecting them to use for scarecrows.[4] Over the next few years the process of cutting Oxford off from its religious past went further. The monastic houses were dissolved: Canterbury College, Gloucester College and Durham College, to which the Benedictine abbeys had sent their monks, disappeared, as did the Cistercian institution, St Bernard's. In 1538 the houses of the friars at the universities were suppressed, apparently without any substantial resistance: by this time the friars were few in number and their houses in the city decayed.[5] With the disappearance of the Carmelites, the Augustinians and the Franciscans—the Dominicans were to appear again briefly in the reign of Mary[6]—a notable tradition of theology and philosophy within the university came to an end.

There was, however, increasing opposition to another religious change.[7] In 1536 William Weston of Lincoln College criticized undergraduates for their interest in heretical topics and went on to make 'a most grievous exclamation against the heresy of such as should say there was no purgatory'.[8] Richard Smith of Merton, later regius professor of theology, preached a sermon proving 'that works did justify and not only faith' and prayed for souls in purgatory: the following year Smith was reported to Cromwell for having prayed in Evesham parish church for Henry VIII as 'supreme head of this realm' rather than 'of the church' and for again praying for souls

[1] Bodl. MS Wood empt. 2, ch. 9, printed as W. Forrest, *The History of Griseld the Second*, ed. W. D. Macray (Roxburghe Club 1875). For the last two mentioned see also *L & P Henry VIII* vii. 101.

[2] See Claire Cross, above, 127. Some fellows of Balliol did, however, qualify their acceptance of the royal supremacy; H. W. C. Davis, *A History of Balliol College* (Oxford 1899, revised by R. H. C. Davis and R. Hunt, Oxford 1963), 71.

[3] Claire Cross, above, 129.

[4] *L & P Henry VIII* ix. 350.

[5] See for example Andrew G. Little, *The Grey Friars in Oxford* (OHS xx 1892), 116–24.

[6] See below, 378.

[7] A. Kreider, *English Chantries: the road to dissolution* (Harvard 1979), 164 ff.

[8] *L & P Henry VIII* x. 950.

'that lie in the pains which is purgatory'.[1] There was a disagreeable scene in St Mary Magdalen's in May 1538 when Richard Yakesley, a monk from Thame, commended pilgrimages and the veneration of saints, encouraging his hearers to continue 'to do as they have done in times past'; he also offered to prove the existence of purgatory.[2] The mayor and civic dignitaries were deeply offended by the expression of ideas so contrary to government doctrine. In 1541 the council again had to act, this time against a citizen, John Wilson, who had said that before he died friars and monks would be 'uppe agayn'.[3] The government's final action against purgatory was to threaten the very existence of the university: the 1545 act for the suppression of the chantries enabled the crown to dissolve all colleges, including those in Oxford and Cambridge and the colleges of Eton and Winchester.[4] The reason why the universities were not excluded from the working of the statute may have been financial, or it may have been a desire fundamentally to 'order, alter, change and reform' the colleges of the universities. Fortunately Matthew Parker, then vice-chancellor of Cambridge, and some of his colleagues were quick to make their fears known and in May 1546 Henry promised to look favourably upon the universities. By contrast, the 1547 act—necessitated by Henry VIII's death before the suppression legalized by the 1545 statute had been completed—specifically exempted the universities from its provisions and even withheld from the king the chantries and obits within the colleges.[5] Nevertheless, the anxious months of 1545 and 1546 during which the universities waited to hear whether they would be reprieved must have hardened the distaste for change felt by many academics.

Of course some members of the university were interested in the new ideas, even if they were finally to reject them. Thomas Harding of New College, later a stalwart upholder of the catholic cause, launched one of his pupils, John Lowthe, on a protestant course by lending him Frith's attack on purgatory: Lowthe kept the book for twenty-one days rather than the two for which it had initially been lent.[6] At this time New College seems to have harboured a number of protestants, including John Philpot, the future martyr, and Ralph Skinner, one of the very few members of parliament who openly

[1] *L & P Henry VIII* xii. pt 2, 534.

[2] 'Ibid. xiii. pt 2, 308.

[3] *Selections from the Records of the City of Oxford . . . [1509–1583]*, ed. W. H. Turner (Oxford and London 1880), 163.

[4] Kreider, *English Chantries*, 180–208.

[5] *Statutes of the Realm* I Edw. VI, c. 14.

[6] *Narratives of the days of the Reformation*, ed. J. G. Nichols (Camden Society lxxvii 1859), 55.

opposed the restoration of catholicism in Mary's reign.[1] Brasenose, where John Foxe supposedly shared a room with Alexander Nowell,[2] the author of the catechism most used in the Elizabethan church, appears in the 1530s to have included a number of members interested in continental protestantism,[3] while radicals had not been entirely eliminated from Wolsey's foundation.

In this atmosphere, biblical drama flourished, often propagating reforming ideas.[4] Foxe, who later declared that 'players, printers, preachers . . . be set up of God, as a triple bulwark against the triple crown of the pope', himself wrote *Christus Triumphans*.[5] A more important dramatist was Nicholas Grimald, a Cambridge graduate who, like Foxe, spent some time in the radical atmosphere of Brasenose, and then moved to Christ Church.[6] His *Christus redivivus*, which may have been performed at Brasenose, was, with its omission of any mention of the Virgin Mary or of purgatory, moving towards a more protestant interpretation, while his *Archipropheta*, which was dedicated to Richard Cox and performed at Christ Church in 1546, put Grimald firmly into line with reformed thinking by its choice of John the Baptist as hero,[7] for reformers saw the prophet as the prototype of the protestant preacher: in the contrast, emphasized by Grimald, between the ritualism of the Pharisees' religion and the Baptist's simple message, they saw a parallel with the church of Rome and their own teachings.[8] Grimald also wrote at this time *Christus Nascens*, performed at Merton or Christ Church, and *Protomartyr*.

None the less, Oxford remained conservative. Foxe, who had moved to Magdalen in 1538, was accused by other fellows of belonging to 'a new religion', and abandoned the university. His colleagues Robert Crowley, the writer and printer of protestant polemic, and Thomas Cooper, bishop successively of Lincoln and Winchester

---

[1] *BRUO 1501–40* (*s.n.* Skynner). For Skinner's parliamentary career see J. Loach, 'Opposition to the crown in parliament, 1553-1558' (Oxford DPhil thesis 1974), 299–301. For Protestants in New College in 1534 see *L & P Henry VIII* vii. 146.

[2] J. F. Moxley, *John Foxe and his Booke* (1940), 16. For Nowell's Catechism see below, 388.

[3] Brasenose also contained conservatives reluctant to expunge the pope's name: Reg. Chanc. 1527–43, fo 327^V.

[4] Ruth H. Blackburn, *Biblical Drama Under the Tudors* (The Hague and Paris 1971), 79–81.

[5] The quotation is from Foxe, *Acts and Monuments* vi. 57. The play was printed in Basle in 1556, and in an English translation by John Day in 1579.

[6] Grimald's career is outlined in L. R. Merrill, *Nicholas Grimald, the Judas of the reformation* (Baltimore 1922).

[7] Blackburn, 91. *Christus redivivus* was published in Cologne in 1543.

[8] J. H. King, *English Reformation Literature: the Tudor origins of the protestant tradition* (Princeton 1982), 297–8.

under Elizabeth, went with him.[1] Some sympathizers remained in Magdalen—John Harley, for example, the Edwardian bishop of Hereford whom Mary imprisoned in September 1553 for leaving church at the elevation of the host, was to preach a vehemently protestant sermon at Edward's accession.[2] The college was bitterly divided over religion in 1548 when a priest was attacked in the chapel as he celebrated mass on Whit Sunday. One of the fellows, Thomas Bickley, in Elizabeth's reign to be warden of Merton, 'most unreverently toke away the sacrament and broke it'; the celebrant himself was manhandled and various service books were damaged.[3] Despite incidents such as this, despite the little cells of protestant thinkers in some colleges, visitors believed that 'the Oxford men . . . are still pertinaciously sticking in the mud of popery', declaring that 'the common sort of people is so vnskilful as the Gospel seemes but a fable vnto them'.[4] Radical change could thus be imposed on the university only by means of direct intervention from outside. The government of Edward VI tried to impose such change and called upon foreign protestants for assistance. Martin Bucer was sent to help in Cambridge and Peter Martyr, rather to his own annoyance, to Oxford.

Martyr's impact on Oxford was to be immense. His past history—he had risen to be prior of an Augustinian house in Naples before his conversion—his cosmopolitan breadth of vision and the intensity and ferocity with which he approached the task of improving a university which he believed was infected with 'superstitious and perverse opinions' were to attract English enthusiasts and foreign students alike.[5] Even men like Thomas Harding, whose later career was so different from Martyr's own, were greatly impressed by him. His energy was enormous: in 1548 he replaced Richard Smith in the regius chair of theology, and to the usual lectures and sermons added the task of presiding over theological disputations every week in his own college, Christ Church, and over the similar fortnightly university debates that were instituted after the visitation of 1549.[6] His most influential teaching, however, was done at home. In 1566

[1] PRO SP 10/5 no. 12; J. F. Mozley, *John Foxe and His Book* (1940), 22–5.

[2] H. A. Wilson, *Magdalen College* (Oxford 1899), 87–8.

[3] For Bickley's later career see below, 383.

[4] Peter Martyr in an Oxford sermon quoted by P. M. J. McNair, 'Peter Martyr in England', in J. C. McLelland (ed.), *Peter Martyr Vermigli and Italian Reform* (Waterloo Ontario 1980), 95; see also *Original Letters*, 464 (Stumphius to Bullinger, 28 February 1550).

[5] For Martyr's early life and his Oxford experiences see M. W. Anderson, *Peter Martyr, a reformer in exile (1542 to 1562)* (Nieuwkoop 1975); for foreign students in Oxford see Claire Cross, 'Continental students and the protestant reformation in England in the sixteenth century', in D. Baker (ed.), *Reform and Reformation: England and the Continent c1500–c1750*, (Studies in Church History subsidia 2, Oxford 1979), 44–5.

[6] *Original Letters*, 481 (Martyr to Bullinger, 1 June 1550), 419 (ab Ulmis to Gualter, 5 Nov. 1550).

Harding recalled that he had been present at many private sermons 'which in his house he made in the Italian tongue to Madame Catherine the Nonne of Letz in Lorraine his pretensed wife, to Sylvester the Italian, to Frauncis the Spaniard, to Iulio his man and to me', and John Jewel was also deeply influenced as a graduate student by these 'private lectures and his private sermons, in Italian, at his home'.[1] It was probably in these small and intimate gatherings that Martyr first expounded in England the ideas on purgatory and the real presence that caused so much discussion when set out in his university lectures on the first epistle to the Corinthians.

It was, as McNair has pointed out, 'a cool and courageous thing' for Martyr to begin his Oxford career with lectures in 1549 on the first epistle to the Corinthians, for this involved discussion of three controversial topics: purgatory, clerical celibacy and the nature of the eucharist.[2] In fact, although Richard Smith later took issue with him over celibacy it was not until March 1549 when Martyr reached the crucial verses on the eucharist, I Corinthians 10: 16–17 that hot debate arose.[3] Abandoning the caution he had hitherto displayed, Martyr set out his own views, defended Zwingli and attacked his opponents.[4] Martyr's critics pounced. Smith, who had been attending the lectures, attempted to force him, unprepared, into a public debate. Josias Simler was later to relate how Martyr's enemies 'without his knowledge fastened upon everie Church papers written in the English tongue, that the day following he would dispute openly against the presence of Christ's bodie in the holie supper'. The next time Martyr went to lecture the schools were packed with his opponents. Martyr, who had been intercepted on his way by Smith's servant with a letter challenging him to a public disputation, told his audience that 'he refused not the disputation, but that now he came not hither to dispute, but to reade'; only after the lecture was over did he agree to a debate which, he insisted, should be properly conducted in the presence of judges, moderators and notaries.[5]

This disputation finally took place at the end of May in the

---

[1] T. Harding, *A Reiondre to M. Iewels Replie* (Antwerp 1566), sig CCC 3. For Jewel, see below, 371, 375, 380.

[2] P. M. J. McNair, 'Peter Martyr in England', in J. C. McLelland (ed.), *Peter Martyr Vermigli and Italian Reform*, 99–100.

[3] *Original Letters*, 388 (ab Ulmis to Bullinger, 2 March 1549); Anderson, *Peter Martyr*, 499–506, where Martyr's letter to Cox of 22 August 1559 is printed.

[4] I have followed S. Corda, *Veritas Sacramenti: a Study in Vermigli's Doctrine of the Lord's Supper* (Zurich 1975), section 1 and McNair, 'Peter Martyr in England', in their belief that Martyr had already rejected consubstantiation before his arrival in England, but that he was not at first willing to make this known publicly.

[5] This account is based on J. Simler's funeral oration, printed in *The Common Places of Peter Martyr* (1583), sig Qqv.

presence of those appointed by the crown as visitors of the university.[1] Smith having in the meanwhile fled, Martyr's first opponent was William Tresham, a canon of Christ Church and chaplain to Edmund Bonner, the conservative bishop of London. On the second day Martyr disputed with William Chedsey of Corpus.[2] The third day's debate should have been between Martyr and Tresham but Tresham's servant had failed to bring his books and papers; the president asked if there were anyone present who was willing to fill the place and Morgan Phillips, principal of St Mary Hall, offered himself.[3] Phillips did not produce any original contribution and the debate on both the third and the fourth days, when Chedsey again took part, proceeded along lines similar to those of the earlier two.

The three propositions debated were:

1 In the sacrament of the eucharist, there is no transubstantiation of the bread and wine into the body and blood of Christ.
2 The body and blood of Christ is not carnally and corporeally in the bread and wine; nor, as others say, under the shows of bread and wine.
3 The body and blood of Christ is sacramentally joined to the bread and the wine.[4]

Controversy centred on the question of whether the phrase 'this is my body' was to be interpreted literally or figuratively. Martyr's position was summed up in a quotation from Theodoret: just as Christ has two natures, divine and human, so 'in the sacrament there abydeth the natures of bread and of the bodye'.[5]

In the debate Martyr laid much emphasis on the fact that patristic texts continued to describe the elements as bread and wine even after consecration. This use of the fathers set Martyr a little apart from the usual reformed practice as exemplified at the end of the disputation by Cox's comments on the 'puddle' of the fathers and councils and his assertion that truth could come only 'out of the livelie fountaines of the word of God'.[6] Martyr was certainly critical

---

[1] Manuscript accounts of the disputation are in BL Harleian MS 422, fos 4–31, BL Sloane MS 1576, fos 1–88ᵛ; Bodl. Additional MS C 197 and Bodl. Rawlinson MS D 1326, fos 1ᵛ–23ᵛ. A protestant account was published in London in 1549: *Tractatio de sacramento eucharistiae, habita in universitate Oxoniensi*. The following year Udall (see above, 364) published an English translation, *A discourse or traictise*. I have here used the account in *The Common Places*, 173–250. For discussion of Martyr's part in the debate, see J. C. McLelland, *The Visible Words of God* (London and Edinburgh 1957); Anderson, *Peter Martyr*, and McNair, 'Peter Martyr in England'.
[2] For the subsequent careers of Tresham and Chedsey see below, 375.
[3] *The Common Places*, 210. Morgan Phillips became a religious exile in Elizabeth's reign, dying in 1570 at Douai: *DNB*.
[4] According to Simler, the choice of propositions was largely Martyr's: *The Common Places*, sig. Qq ii.   [5] Ibid. 181.   [6] Ibid. 249.

of what he regarded as the papist habit of collecting 'little sentences out of the writings of the Fathers' in order 'to obscure truth more easily'.[1] However, when Morgan Phillips asked him whether he intended to argue from the scriptures alone, or also from the fathers and councils, Martyr replied that although of course his 'principle or touchstone' was the scriptures and 'the verye censure or judgement of *our* contensyon ought to be deryved onelye from the scriptures themself' he would not reject the fathers or even the councils just because the papists were, as one account of the disputation puts it, 'superstitiouslie' addicted to them.[2] He therefore expounded with great learning the writings of Cyprian, Augustine, Irenaeus, Epiphanius and Theodoret. When Tresham challenged the use of Theodoret on the grounds that the bishop was a Nestorian and 'but an obscure Author' Martyr was able to retort with a quotation against Nestorius taken from Theodoret and with the observation that since the book had been printed at Rome it was 'there to be solde if any man will seke for him'. To this Tresham unwisely retorted that 'it is to farre to Rome and to tedyous a journeye to go to Rome for one suche booke'.[3] Martyr's approach to the fathers, so much more positive than that of many of his colleagues, was something he passed on to Jewel, who was later, in Zurich, to spend his afternoons reading aloud to Martyr from the works of the fathers.[4]

Martyr's defence, assisted only once, and that briefly, by Nicholas Cartwright of Magdalen,[5] was a *tour de force*. Cox's summing up in which he described the Italian as 'worthelie called Peter, for his assured stedfastnes' and 'worthilie called Martyr, for the innumerable testimonies which he manie times uttereth of the truth' was partisan, but in general his chairmanship did not offer Martyr any particular advantage.[6] Catholic accounts of the debate do, however, show that Phillips was somewhat brusquely guided by Cox and Richard Sampson, the bishop of Lincoln, as to the line of attack he could take.[7] None the less Martyr was dissatisfied about his showing, telling Bucer, to whom he sent a transcript of the debate, that 'my strength being small, the matter perplexing, and the adversaries both obstinate and

---

[1] McLelland, *Visible Words*, 267, quoting Martyr's locus on justification in his commentary on the epistle to the Romans (2 vols Basle 1558).

[2] *The Common Places*, 210.

[3] Ibid. 181–2.

[4] Humphrey's *Vita Iuelli* (1573), 89–90, quoted in J. E. Booty, *John Jewel as Apologist of the Church of England* (1963), 112. See also S. L. Greenslade, *The English Reformers and the Fathers of the Church* (Oxford 1960), and J. P. Donnelly, *Calvinism and Scholasticism in Vermigli's Doctrine of Man and Grace* (Leiden 1976), ch. 2.

[5] Cartwright recanted under Mary and in 1554 disputed against Cranmer.

[6] *The Common Places*, 248.

[7] Bodl. Additional MS C 197, fo 28^V.

very audacious, in the compass of four days I was unable to effect more than you can see'.[1] Although a protestant account of the disputations was soon printed and translated into English, Martyr appears to have felt that he had not acquitted himself well and afterwards he always urged his friends to avoid such formal debates. Indeed, it seems probable that it was Martyr's explicit rejection of consubstantiation in his public lectures on Corinthians that influenced contemporaries rather than the set-piece arguments of the disputation. Certainly the Marian martyr Bartlet Green later told Bonner that his views on the eucharist were shaped 'by the Scriptures, and authorities of the doctors, alleged by Peter Martyr in his lectures upon 1 Cor. XI, while he entreated there on that place, "De coena Domini", by the space of a month together.'[2] However, Bernard Gilpin, 'the apostle of the north', first began to question the tenets of catholicism when urged by Chedsey, Weston and Morgan to join them in their attack on Martyr: on reflection he considered that the reformer had the better case.[3]

Perhaps Martyr was just dispirited because despite his efforts and despite the visitation of the university that took place in May and June of 1549, the conservatives remained powerful in Oxford. Among the thirteen heads of colleges, for example, only two positively favoured the government's religious policy.[4] When Somerset's fall encouraged some contemporaries to believe that Henrician catholicism might be restored, conservatives in Oxford revived the mass and other ceremonies.[5] So tense was the atmosphere that Martyr retreated for a time to London.[6] On his return he found things going on 'tolerably quietly' but feared that the resumption of theological disputation, forbidden for a time by royal proclamation, would be 'promotive of tumult rather than of edification'.[7]

This proved to be the case. Martyr's opponents tried to use the public disputations held in September 1550 to make him look foolish. They planned to hold a formal debate on transubstantiation in which Martyr's views would be put foward rather weakly by the opponents and easily overthrown by the respondents. Chedsey was chosen as moderator and Martyr, if he had been allowed to contribute

[1] G. C. Gorham, *Gleanings of a Few Scattered Ears* (1857), 81 (15 June 1549).

[2] Foxe, *Acts and Monuments* vii. 737.

[3] G. Carleton, *The Life of Bernard Gilpin* (1629), 4, 33.

[4] G. D. Duncan, 'The heads of houses and religious change in Tudor Oxford 1547-1558', *Oxoniensia* xlv (1980), 227. The two were Cox and William More of Exeter.

[5] *Original Letters*, 464 (Stumphius to Bullinger, 28 February 1550).

[6] Silmer's Oration in *The Common Places*, sig. Qqv. The Magdalen accounts for this year refer to a charge 'pro expensis in excubiis tempore commotionis', Wilson, *Magdalen College*, 91.

[7] Gorham, *Gleanings*, 126 (Martyr to Bucer, 18 December 1549).

at all, would have spoken 'almost in the night itself, all the hearers being tired and going away'. A great throng of Martyr's critics actually gathered: among those prepared to speak were the chaplain of the conservative Cuthbert Tunstall, bishop of Durham, and Dr Seton, Bishop Stephen Gardiner's chaplain and an upholder of the catholic cause in Cambridge. In the end the vice-chancellor, perhaps fearing a disturbance, refused to allow the debate to proceed.[1]

However, transubstantiation was being superseded as a controversial topic by the problem of justification. Martyr's own lectures on Paul's epistle to the Romans contributed to the debate, but interest was already lively when he began: in March 1550, just before he started, he told Bucer that he had recently been involved in a discussion about merit and 'the different degrees of reward for the blessed'.[2] Thus although the lectures did not appear in print until 1558 and were then obviously modified to take account of Richard Smith's attack in *Diatriba de hominis justificatione edita Oxoniae adversus Pet. Martyrem*, published in Louvain in 1550, it seems likely that Martyr's firm assertion of the theory of predestination and his dismissal of both congruous and condign merit was part of the original lectures.[3] In Oxford he probably concentrated his attack on the theories of justification put forward by the Dutch theologian Albert Pighius, to whom, he later said, Smith had joined himself as Theseus did to Hercules.[4] Martyr was always critical of Pighius, one of those who had espoused the theory of double justification at Ratisbon in 1541. Pighius's theory had gradually, according to Martyr, evolved into the idea that man's works, if carried out in grace, could operate with the merits of Christ, sacramentally bestowed, to produce salvation. Martyr's own view was that although sacraments could 'help, confirm and increase faith', they could not in themselves give grace, which was to be obtained neither directly through the sacraments, nor through works, but by a 'lively' faith which enabled the chosen to apprehend God.[5] He was extremely scornful of the concept of grace as something that could be, as he put it, contained within the sacrament

---

[1] BL Additional MS 19410, fo 20ᵛ (Martyr to Bucer, 20 September 1550); Gorham, 178 (Martyr to Bucer, 6 September 1550); 181–2 (the same, 10 September 1550).

[2] Ibid. 141.

[3] His views on justification are set out as a *locus* in the commentary on Romans 11, subsequently reprinted in *The Common Places*, pt 3, ch. 4. On Martyr's concept of justification see Donnelly, *Calvinism and Scholasticism*. The schoolmen distinguished between congruous merit, which arises simply from a man doing what he can and being 'fittingly' rewarded, and condign merit, which was a claim due for services done in a state of grace, the 'merit of worthiness'. Martyr's discussion of this distinction is in *The Common Places*, pt 3, ch. 4, 153.

[4] Ibid. 147.

[5] Ibid. 135–7.

as if it were a bag and then 'poured out uppon the communicantes and receauers'.[1]

But the centre of theological debate was not only changing its character, it was also moving from the universities to Lambeth, where the ordinal of 1550 and the prayer book and revised ordinal of 1552 were devised. The controversy over vestments that arose in 1550 after Hooper said that he would refuse the bishopric of Gloucester if it obliged him to accept 'superstitious ceremonies' seems to have aroused little interest in Oxford. Martyr later told Thomas Sampson 'when I was at Oxford I would never use those white vestments in the choir, though I was a canon', but this practice was not apparently remarked on at the time.[2] More heat was generated over clerical celibacy, however. The conservative William Forrest accused Cox and Martyr of persecuting priests who did not take wives,[3] and the presence of Martyr's wife within the walls of Christ Church certainly caused offence, the more so because both husband and wife had once taken vows of celibacy. Their home was pelted with stones and Martyr's wife was abused orally and in print before her death in 1553;[4] in the next reign her bones were to be dug up and thrown on the dunghill. The issue of celibacy was of course widely treated in catholic and protestant polemic from the time of Luther onward. Martyr discussed the question in his 1550 lectures on Corinthians,[5] to which Richard Smith replied in De coelibatu sacerdotium and De votis monasticis published in Brussels and Louvain the following year.

Although academic debate had diminished, feelings still ran high in Oxford. This was partly the result of the strong line taken against the conservatives by Northumberland's regime. During Lent 1550 Chedsey was imprisoned for his 'sediciouse preaching' and Tresham was imprisoned in the Fleet in December 1551.[6] In June of that year the president of Corpus, Robert Morwent, and two of the fellows, Welch and Richard Allen, were put in the Fleet for hearing the old service on Corpus Christi day.[7] The election of a head of house also led to government interference at New College and Magdalen,[8] while scholars unsympathetic to reform such as George Etherege lost their posts.[9]

---

[1] The Common Places, pt 4, 107.
[2] McLelland, Visible Words, 60; Anderson, Peter Martyr, 114.
[3] Forrest, Griseld the Second, ch. 7.
[4] Gorham, Gleanings, 154 (Martyr to Bucer, 10 June 1550).
[5] Ibid. 152.   [6] APC iii. 237, 410, 450.
[7] Ibid. 287, 295, 305, 307, 317, 383, 431.
[8] Duncan, 'Heads of houses', 229-30.
[9] Etherege had vacated his post as regius professor of Greek by October 1551 (see G. D. Duncan, p. 355 above).

However, in July 1553 the catholic Mary came to the throne. Within a month Etherege was reinstated, Oglethorpe, who had been forced to resign in 1552, resumed the presidency of Magdalen and Cox was replaced by Richard Marshall as dean of Christ Church.[1] After a brief confinement Peter Martyr left Oxford and England and Richard Smith recovered the regius chair of theology.[2] By March 1554 the crown felt sure enough of the loyalty of the university to send Cranmer, Latimer and Ridley there for what was then expected to be immediate trial. All three were Cambridge men and the choice of university must have been decided by Oxford's greater orthodoxy.

The action against Cranmer, Latimer and Ridley began with formal disputations in April, to which members of the university of Cambridge were invited.[3] The disputations bore a strong resemblance to those of 1549: once again, Chedsey and Tresham defended transubstantiation, producing in evidence many of the same arguments and authorities as before. Only one of the three articles debated—the question of the mass as a sacrifice—touched on a fresh topic and this, as Ridley afterwards complained, was never fully discussed. In particular the debate with Ridley concentrated on the same spatial questions as had been raised in 1549, the reformer arguing that if Christ sat permanently on the right hand of God he could not also be physically present in the sacraments.[4]

Neither side acquitted itself well, the protestants at least to some extent because of the partial behaviour of the prolocutor, Hugh Weston, rector of Lincoln College. Weston was so determined to put his opponents in the wrong that he was trapped into a stupid assertion that *homo* referred only to the male sex.[5] Jewel complained later of the 'grinning and skoffing' of the catholics, as well as of bad scholarship and worse Latin.[6]

The occasion was certainly used to put pressure on those of doubtful opinions. Jewel himself, a notary at the disputation, formally subscribed after the three protestants had been condemned on 20 April 1554 to the tenets of transubstantiation, and agreed that 'the Masse is a Sacrifice propitiatorie for the quicke and dead'.[7] Jewel explained his action as prompted by fear of 'fyer and fagot':[8] in fact, much to the queen's annoyance, a bill to revive the medieval heresy statutes failed in the month of Jewel's subscription and it was

[1] *BRUO 1501–40*.   [2] Ibid.
[3] There is an account in Foxe, *Acts and Monuments* vi. 439–536.
[4] Ibid. 481.   [5] Ibid. 504.
[6] J. Jewel, *The Trve Copies of the Letters betwene the reverend Father in God, Iohn Bisshop of Salisbury and D. Cole* (1560), fos 46, 61ᵛ, 63.
[7] T. Harding, *A Reiondre to M. Iewels Replie* (Antwerp 1566) sig CCCC 1ᵛ.
[8] Jewel, *The Trve Copies*, fo 79ᵛ.

not until early 1555 that the legislation necessary before burnings could take place was enacted. By the time Cranmer and his colleagues came to trial in September 1555, however, the issue was unequivocally one of life and death. Protestants had already been burnt, including Bishop Hooper.

The question most crucial in these trials was that of authority, as both Cranmer and Ridley acknowledged by their refusal to bow to those of their inquisitors who symbolized the power of the pope.[1] Cranmer was in greatest trouble, for he was charged with having led Henry VIII and his subjects away from the Roman obedience and with having refused to recognize the papal authority now restored by Queen Mary.[2] Once again the three questions debated in April 1554 were set out, and Ridley was then able to declare his belief that Christ 'made one perfect sacrifice for the sins of the whole world, neither can any man reiterate that sacrifice of his'.[3] Pole's commissioner, John White, bishop of Lincoln and formerly warden of Winchester College, made a moving plea for the unity of the church, echoing Weston's words at the opening of the 1554 disputations,[4] and James Brooks, bishop of Gloucester and formerly master of Balliol, produced an elegant defence of the claims of the church rather than those of individual conscience in matters of authority.[5] It was to no avail. Although White conducted the examination of Ridley and Latimer with some sympathy, telling the former that 'it is no strange country whither I exhort you to return. You were once one of us; you have taken degrees in the school', neither could be moved.[6] They were condemned, degraded and burnt.

Cranmer's defence was less stalwart. Whereas Ridley when charged with inconsistency had compared himself to Paul, the one-time persecutor of Christ, Cranmer twisted and turned. He said that oaths once taken could not be broken and also that he was under no moral obligation to maintain an oath sworn to the pope. He was evasive about the development of his sacramental thinking and at one point appeared to repudiate the royal supremacy. It was not a convincing performance. His subsequent recantations, although the actions of a man tormented by more subtle doubts and scruples than his fellow prisoners had known, did considerable harm to the protestant cause.[7] Even when he entered St Mary's on 21 March 1556 he seems to have been unsure as to what course to adopt. To Henry Cole, who preached

---

[1] Foxe, *Acts and Monuments* viii. 45; vii. 519–20. The examination and execution of Latimer and Ridley is in ibid. vii. 517–51, that of Cranmer in ibid. viii. 44–90.

[2] Ibid. viii. 58–9.   [3] Ibid. vii. 528.

[4] Ibid. vii. 524; vi. 441–2.   [5] Ibid. vii. 538.

[6] Ibid. vii. 520.

[7] See, for example, *Original Letters*, 173 (Sampson to Bullinger, 6 April 1556).

a sermon pointing out that 'among men nothing is so high, that can promise itself safety on the earth', falls the credit of persuading the former archbishop to courage at the last.[1] Cole told the congregation that Cranmer could not be pardoned, for 'he had been a heretic, from whom, as from an author and only fountain, all heretical and schismatic opinions that so many years have prevailed in England did first rise and spring.' Cranmer, exhorting the people to obey their monarch 'without murmuring or grudging', then finally, to the astonishment of his listeners, repudiated the pope and his own recantation and declared, 'as for the sacrament, I believe as I have taught in my book against the bishop of Winchester, the which my book teacheth so true a doctrine of the sacrament, that it shall stand at the last day before the judgement of God'.[2]

Cranmer's fortitude at the stake was, of course, to pass into protestant mythology, but it appears to have had little impact on contemporary Oxford. Indeed, the only obvious effect of the three burnings was the conversion of Julius Palmer, a fellow of Magdalen who was subsequently burnt at Newbury;[3] in general protestants now regarded Oxford as a lost cause. None the less, Cranmer's death is a blot on the justice of Mary's proceedings. Apologists for the regime were never to provide a satisfactory answer to the question of why Cranmer was condemned to burn despite his recantation.[4] Mary was doubtless correct in regarding him as a prime agent in the establishment of English protestantism, but there was no law whereby her vengeance could be justified.

Oxford could afford to shrug aside the fortitude of the martyrs. It basked in the sovereign's personal favour: as early as August 1553 Mary had written to the university explaining how vital its example was for the country as a whole, and nine months later she provided money for the repair of the public schools, thus enabling the university to defend itself better against heresy.[5] She assisted New College, Magdalen and Brasenose, and made up a deficiency in her father's endowment for Christ Church.[6] Her example was followed, and two new colleges, Trinity and St John's, were founded. Mary's enthusiasm was justified. Oxford became a bastion of orthodoxy: Pole's

---

[1] Foxe, *Acts and Monuments* viii. 85–6. Cole was Warden of New College from 1542 to 1551. In 1554 he became provost of Eton and in 1556 dean of St Paul's. He refused the oath of supremacy in 1559 (*DNB* and *BRUO 1501–40*).

[2] Foxe, *Acts and Monuments* viii. 87–8.

[3] Ibid. 201–19. Thomas Dorman, a stalwart defender of the old faith under Elizabeth (see below, 385) declared in 1565 that 'with mine own eyes I sawe Ridley and Latymer burned': see his *A disprovfe of M. Nowelles reprovfe* (Antwerp 1565), fo 19.

[4] Posed by, for example, Jewel in *The Trve Copies*, fo 74.

[5] BL Add. MS 32091, fos 145–95^V; *Cal. Pat. Rolls, Philip and Mary* i. 165.

[6] Ibid. ii. 60; iii. 276: Christ Church MS i. c. 4, vol. i, I, 449.

injunctions of 1556 convey an impression of great theological serenity, in which the lecturers on philosophy were urged to use patience and care in their efforts to incline the young towards true piety—they were to listen 'benigne' to any of their audience who produced arguments different from their own, and to respond punctiliously to difficulties raised in this way.[1] In 1557 one of the visitors, Fray Bartolomé Carranza de Miranda, declared that he had inspected 'Oxford and its thirteen colleges, examining the doctrine read and taught therein . . . finding it Catholic and correct'.[2] The study of canon law was revived, and provision for its teaching was included in the founder's statutes for St John's.[3] Most dramatic of all as an expression of confidence in the continuance of the restored faith was the re-establishment of a Dominican house in the university; in 1557 Juan de Villa Garcia, a Spanish Dominican who briefly held the chair of theology, took possession of the house, 'albeit with a very few monks'.[4]

Nothing so clearly demonstrates the achievement of Marian Oxford as the prominent part its graduates later played in recusant life. Nearly thirty of the secular and seminary priests ordained after 1559 were the product of Marian Oxford, among them Gregory Martin, James Fenn and Thomas Stapleton; only three or four Cambridge men of the same generation were ordained abroad.[5] At least seven Oxford graduates of Mary's reign went on to join the Jesuits, and Edmund Campion, one of the first scholars of St John's, must have been influenced by the enthusiastic orthodoxy that surrounded him.[6] In 1581 the privy council commented bitterly that 'most of the seminarie Priests which at this present disturbe this Churche have ben heretofore schollers of that Universitie'.[7] It has been suggested that the spirit which created the English mission owed little to the 'bluff and sceptical conservativism of Queen Mary's reign',[8] but the history of Oxford belies this: the complicated subtleties of the Jesuit Jasper Heywood cannot be distinguished from those of Robert Parsons himself,[9] while the vigour of men such as

---

[1] *Statuta*, 363–75, especially 374.

[2] J. Ignacio Tellechea Idigoras, *Fray Bartolomé Carranza y el Cardenal Pole* Pamplona 1977).   [3] Wood, *History and Antiquities* ii. 133.

[4] J. Ignacio Tellechea Idigoras, *Inglaterra, Flandes y España (1557-1559)* (Vitoria 1975), 25–6 (Carranza to Villa Garcia, 19 September 1557); 26–7 (Carranza to Villa Garcia, 26 September 1557). I am grateful to Dr J. R. L. Highfield for this reference.

[5] G. Anstruther, *The Seminary Priests* (2 vols Ware Durham 1969) i.

[6] B. Bassett, *The English Jesuits from Campion to Martindale* (1967), 15.

[7] *APC* xiii. 170.

[8] J. Bossy, *The English Catholic Community, 1570-1850* (1975), 15. For a wider attack on Bossy's view that has appeared since this was written see C. Haigh, 'The continuity of catholicism in the English reformation', *Past and Present* (1981), 37–69.

[9] Heywood matriculated in 1554. For his later views see A. Pritchard, *Catholic Loyalism in Elizabethan England* (1979), 76.

Laurence Vaux was no less than that of subsequent Elizabethan converts.[1]

The catholicism of Marian Oxford was, in any case, more than mere conservativism. The university once more came into contact with reformed catholicism: its chancellor was, after all, Reginald Pole, the friend of Contarini and Morone, and thus an object of suspicion to the reactionary Paul IV.[2] Pole's secretary Nicholas Ormanet was one of the visitors appointed by the chancellor in 1556; another was the Dominican Carranza, who was later, as archbishop of Toledo and primate of Spain, himself a prisoner of the inquisition.[3] The appointment of foreign scholars such as Garcia to positions within the university during Mary's reign has sometimes been seen as a despairing attempt to revive flagging enthusiasm: on the contrary, it was a reflection of the widening of England's cultural horizons which was a consequence of the Spanish marriage. Peter de Soto, the Dominican who succeeded Garcia as professor, had, for example, been Charles V's confessor. From 1549 to 1553 he had held the chair of theology at Dillingen. As supervisor of the German province of his order, he had considerable experience of the problems of restoring catholicism in protestant lands, and he was the author of several controversial works, two of which were directed against the Württemberg reformer John Brenz.[4] The reputation of the Spanish Dominicans has been tarnished by the part they were alleged to have played in the proceedings against Cranmer, but their role was in fact minor and aimed primarily at reconciliation.[5]

By the late 1550s protestantism seemed to have been eliminated in Oxford: indeed in 1560 Jewel was to tell Peter Martyr that the city was 'without learning, without lectures, without any regard to religion'.[6] Why had protestantism succumbed so readily to the Marian reaction? One answer is, of course, that of obedience: members of the university were moved by the same instincts of loyalty and the same desire for advancement as the majority of Mary's subjects. But the government's permissive attitude towards flight was also enormously important; the alternative of exile allowed many fellows to avoid the clash of loyalties that proved so disastrous for Cranmer. Academics were, more than most, flexible about their

---

[1] Lawrence Vaux supplicated for a BTh in 1556. His later career is set out in *DNB*.

[2] D. Fenlon, *Heresy and Obedience in Tridentine Italy: Cardinal Pole and the counter reformation* (Cambridge 1972).

[3] *New Catholic Encyclopaedia* iii. *sub nom.*

[4] Ibid. He was the author of *Assertio catholicae fidei . . .* (Cologne 1555), and *Defensio catholicae confessionis* (Antwerp 1557). He should not be confused with Dominic de Soto.

[5] See, for example, Foxe, viii. 207–8.

[6] *The Zurich Letters*, ed. H. Robinson (Parker Society 1842), 77.

place of residence and they therefore formed a high proportion of the Marian exiles.[1]

In Oxford, moreover, the cause of protestantism had rested on the shoulders of a few men. Chief amongst these was Richard Cox, elected vice-chancellor in May 1547. A product of Eton and King's, Cox had been at Cardinal College briefly in the mid-1520s. In 1530 he returned to his old school and reformed the curriculum on Erasmian lines. In 1544 he became dean of Oseney, Oxford's cathedral and two years later dean of Christ Church which succeeded Oseney as the cathedral church:[2] under his guidance Christ Church became a powerhouse of Edwardian protestantism, attracting men such as Laurence Nowell, William Whittingham, Thomas Randolph and John Pullan, all subsequently Marian exiles.[3] Christopher Goodman and John Jewel also migrated to Christ Church during this period. Christ Church under Cox was a college held up by Protector Somerset as an example to all others,[4] but when Cox left soon after Mary's accession and when the foreign students attracted by Peter Martyr also departed, Christ Church fell into the hands of the conservatives. Martyr's own canonry was bestowed on Richard Bruerne, and at least two radical canons, Thomas Barnard and John Bankes, were subsequently deprived.[5] Martyr's departure in 1553, speeded by his apparent implication in Cranmer's rash publications, was another great blow to protestantism in Oxford. The attraction of his ideas clearly depended to some considerable extent on the intensity of his exposition and the charm of his personality. Jewel, busily transcribing Martyr's sermons, was much influenced by the Italian during his stay in Oxford, and the two men grew even closer when they shared a house in Strasbourg during Mary's reign.[6] On the other hand, left behind in Oxford, two of Martyr's admirers in Christ Church, Henry Sidall and James Courthorpe, had conformed by the late autumn of 1553.[7] Thomas Harding, once considered 'a hearer and admirer of Peter Martyr, and a most active preacher of the gospel', swung violently against reformed ideas. In 1561 he was to be described

[1] C. H. Garrett, *The Marian Exiles* (Cambridge 1938).

[2] This account is based on *DNB, BRUO 1501–40* and J. Fines, *A Biographical Register of Early English Protestants* (Sutton Courtenay 1980). For Oxford's cathedral, see James McConica, 'The rise of the undergraduate college', pp. 32–3 above.

[3] Bodl. MS Wood C8, fos 1ᵛ, 3.

[4] Jane E. A. Dawson, 'The early career of Christopher Goodman and his place in the development of English protestant thought' (Durham DPhil thesis 1978), 24. This contains an interesting account of Christ Church under Cox.

[5] Ibid. 18.

[6] Humphrey declares that Jewel came to regard Martyr as a father: *Vita Iuelli*, 31. See also Anderson, *Peter Martyr*, 528 (Jewel to Martyr, 15 August 1561).

[7] *Zurich Letters*, 45, 147. On Courthorpe, once 'attentus auditor Petri Martyris' see Humphrey, 31.

as a man 'learned in King Edward's time', who had 'preached the truth earnestly, and now [is] stiff in papistry'.[1] In such changes there was perhaps an element of time-serving, but one may also sense the relaxation of men returning to their accustomed modes of thought.

Catholicism was, however, to prove more difficult to eradicate than protestantism had been.[2] Despite the purge of 1559 which forced so many academics into exile, the authorities recognized that a large number of catholics remained in the university.[3] Nicholas Sanders of New College declared that the visitors had avoided asking everyone in his college to subscribe to the oaths of supremacy and uniformity for fear of even more refusals,[4] and the story is confirmed by a letter of Bishop Horn of Winchester informing William Cecil that a thoroughgoing examination would have almost emptied two of the colleges of which he was visitor, New and Corpus.[5] Through-out the 1560s and 1570s a steady stream of Oxford men left for the seminaries of Louvain, Douai and Rheims. When Edmund Campion returned to England on his fatal mission he was accompanied by Robert Parsons, a former fellow of Balliol, by Ralph Sherwin of Exeter College and by Alexander Briant of Hart Hall; it was William Hartley, another St John's man, who laid out Campion's *Decem Rationes* on the seats of St Mary's.[6] Undeterred by Campion's death, ten Oxford men left for Rheims in 1583. Even the execution in Oxford of two seminarists and two laymen in 1589 did not end the traffic.[7] John Jones, a St John's man who shared a lodging with William Laud, left in 1591,[8] and in that decade the college also educated a number of future Benedictines, including Leander Jones, later president of the English congregation of the order.[9] The halls played an important role, providing a refuge for catholics turned out of the colleges and a training ground for the sons of catholic families. Gloucester Hall for example, described in 1577 as 'greatly suspected',

[1] *Cal. SP Dom.* 1601–3, addenda 1547–1565, xi. no. 45.

[2] See C. M. J. F. Swan, 'The introduction of the Elizabethan settlement into the universities of Oxford and Cambridge, with particular reference to the Roman Catholics, 1558–1603' (Cambridge PhD thesis 1955), *passim*. I am most grateful to Dr Swan for making this work available to me.

[3] On the purge, see Williams below, 406.

[4] 'Dr Nicholas Sander's report to Cardinal Moroni', ed. J. H. Pollen, in *Miscellanea* i (Catholic Record Society i 1905), 43.

[5] PRO SP 12/19 no. 56.

[6] E. E. Reynolds, *Campion and Parsons* (1980), 101–3.

[7] Swan, 'Introduction of Elizabethan settlement', 332; A. Davidson, 'Roman Catholicism in Oxfordshire from the late Elizabethan period to the civil war (c 1580–c 1640)' (Bristol DPhil thesis 1970), 453–4. The four who were caught at the Catherine Wheel public house, a well-known meeting place for recusants, were sent to London for interrogation but returned to Oxford for their trials and subsequent deaths: *APC* xvii. 329.

[8] Davidson, 655.

[9] D. Lunn, *The English Benedictines, 1540–1688* (1980), 29–30.

contained at various times James Fenn, the future martyr, who had been expelled from Corpus, George Blackwell, who had left a fellowship at Trinity and was later to become the archpriest, and Christopher Brigshaw who died at Wisbech after thirteen years' imprisonment.[1] The gunpowder-plot conspirator Robert Catesby was educated there, and so was the flower of the catholic aristocracy. Influential senior members included Edmund Rainolds, the moderate brother of the radical John and of the papist William, and Thomas Allen, the mathematician and antiquary.

Allen did not arrive at Gloucester Hall from Trinity until 1570, however, and his career is a reminder of how great is the difficulty of dividing men at this time into 'catholic', 'church catholic' and 'protestant', and of how confused contemporaries themselves seem to have been about precisely where their loyalties lay. Allen was carefully absent at the time of the 1577 visitation; he was said to have been reconciled with Rome on his deathbed, but his whole religious life is clouded in ambiguity.[2] What were Thomas Neale's views in the 1560s, when he was regius professor of Hebrew?[3] Neale had spent a large part of Edward's reign in Paris, and on his return in 1556 became a chaplain to Bishop Bonner, yet he accepted a chair at Elizabeth's accession and was the author of the dialogue presented to the queen on her visit in 1566. Three years later, however, he abandoned the chair and retired, first to Hart Hall and then to Cassington. Some of the catholics of Elizabethan Oxford were, like Neale, products of the Marian reaction, and others were to be converted by the missionary priests, but there is a third group of which Parsons is only the best known, whose views were moulded by the environment in which they lived and the books they read. The influence of catholic or crypto-catholic tutors is of great importance here,[4] as is the ease with which catholic books seem to have circulated. In 1585 Edmund Rainolds admitted receiving seditious literature from abroad, including William Allen's *A True, Sincere and Modest Defence of English Catholiques* (a work later translated into Latin by Reynolds's brother) and a book written by his brother to refute Whitaker's attack on Campion.[5] The halls undoubtedly provided a centre for the distribution of clandestine literature, but many of

---

[1] PRO SP 12/118 no. 37; 'Diocesan returns of recusants for England and Wales, 1577', in *Miscellanea* xii (Catholic Record Society xxii 1921), 101. For members of the college see G. H. Daniel and W. R. Barker, *Worcester College* (Oxford 1900).

[2] I am grateful to Mr M. Foster for allowing me to read his unpublished paper, 'Thomas Allen of Gloucester Hall, Oxford (1540–1632)', now published in *Oxoniensia* xlvi (1981), 99–128.

[3] Davidson, 'Roman Catholicism in Oxfordshire', 647–8.

[4] Ibid. 643.   [5] Ibid. 674–80.

the exiles' arguments were in any case known to those in Oxford because of the contemporary habit of setting out an opponent's argument before attacking it: thus, for instance, Whitaker's *Ad Rationes Decem . . . Responsio*, which was translated into English by William Hubbock of Corpus reiterated all Campion's arguments before replying to them. It is in the light of this background, a background in which catholic apologetic was common knowledge, that the careers of men such as William Spenser of Trinity become more comprehensible.[1] Spenser was a scholar of the college in 1573 and did not leave until 1581, although his sympathies had been known for some years before that; he was neither a product of Marian Oxford nor a Jesuit convert. Oxford in the 1560s and 1570s thus contained both relics of the Marian reaction and men who had chosen catholicism for themselves; in the 1580s men converted by the missionaries were added.

Although both English and continental protestants were aware of the doctrinal deficiencies of Oxford little was done to remedy them. The task perhaps appeared unattractive. Martyr could not be tempted back and few of those who had left Oxford in Mary's reign returned. Cox instead became bishop of Ely and Jewel bishop of Salisbury, Laurence Nowell dean of Lichfield and Whittingham dean of Durham. Only Laurence Humfrey came back, as regius professor of theology and later president of his old college, Magdalen.[2] He was joined in 1561 by another former exile—a Cambridge man —Thomas Sampson, but Sampson was turned out of his position as dean of Christ Church by the queen in 1565.[3] Three years later William Cole became president of Corpus and Thomas Bickley, who had spent Mary's reign in France, was elected warden of Merton.[4] In the first years of the reign, therefore, there was but a handful of men in Oxford who had had direct experience of continental protestantism.

As a result Oxford played only a small part in the controversies of the 1560s about the precise nature of the Elizabethan church. Although Humphrey and Sampson were the leaders of the opposition to the prescribed vestments, this controversy centred on convocation and the London churches and did not trouble the university greatly.[5] James Calfhill, the sub-dean of Christ Church, certainly opposed the

---

[1] J. H. Pollen, *Acts of the English Martyrs* (1891), 273–8.

[2] Humphrey spent his exile in Zurich and Basle (Garrett, *Marian Exiles*, 193–4).

[3] For Sampson's restless travels in Mary's reign, see ibid. 279–81.

[4] Cole, a fellow of Corpus from 1545, was in Zurich by April 1554. He later visited Frankfurt, Basle and Geneva: Garrett, 123. For Bickley see ibid. 90, and above, p. 368.

[5] C. M. Dent, *Protestant Reformers in Elizabethan Oxford* (Oxford 1983), 34–46.

use of the cross in baptism and the wearing of the surplice. Calfhill
was also involved in the debate, led by Sampson and Jewel, over the
silver cross that the queen allowed on the altar of the chapel royal,
and wrote *An Aunswere to the Treatise of the Crosse* in response to
the jibes of John Martial, a former fellow of New College.[1] In 1564
Andrew Kingsmill of All Souls wrote to the archbishop arguing for
permissiveness over the wearing of vestments and he also discussed
the matter with his brother-in-law, Bishop Pilkington.[2] Two years
later Kingsmill and another Oxford man, Ralph Warcupp of Christ
Church, formed part of a delegation sent by the English radicals to
seek support in Geneva; Kingsmill was to remain in Switzerland for
the rest of his life. In one college alone was there considerable
support for Sampson and Humfrey: many fellows of Magdalen
were censured by the visitor's commissary in 1566 for not wearing
the surplice. Humfrey would probably have lost his office, as
Sampson did, if the archbishop had felt on secure enough ground.[3]
Even the *Admonition to the Parliament* of 1572 caused little stir
in Oxford, for Humphrey was not sympathetic to its extremist tone,
its demands for an 'equalitie of ministers' and the abolition of 'all
popish remnants'. The following summer a letter was sent from the
council to the vice-chancellor asking him to apprehend anyone who
urged people to try to alter the forms of service, but little action
seems to have been necessary. It was, after all, in that same year that
five fellows of St John's left for the continent and popery. However,
in the mid-1570s Oxford was pulled briefly into the mainstream of
protestant debate when the quarrels of the Stranger Churches, with
their oddly mixed congregations of narrow precisians and theological
iconoclasts, spilled over into the university. In May 1574 the university granted an MA degree to Franceso Pucci, a Florentine refugee.[4]
The grant was perhaps made in ignorance of the conflict between
Pucci and the French church over doctrines of election—in 1575
the church suspended him from the sacrament—but news soon
filtered through to Humfrey and Pucci shortly left Oxford.[5] In
1576 an even fiercer battle raged over the earl of Leicester's request
that the Spanish refugee Antonio del Corro should be granted a
doctorate. The complicated saga of Corro's relationship with Oxford
has been related elsewhere;[6] what is interesting here is that the

---

[1] London 1565. See also W. P. Haugaard, *Elizabeth and the English Reformation* (Cambridge 1968), 183–200.
[2] Dent, 38–9.   [3] See Dent, ch. 3.
[4] *Reg. Univ.* ed. Clark i. 379.
[5] For Pucci see *Lettere, documenti e testimonianze*, ed. L. Firpo e R. Piattoli (Florence
1955), and L. Firpo, *Gli scritti di Franceso Pucci* (Turin 1957).
[6] See Williams below, 417.

Italian and French churches in London, with which Corro was on bad terms, were able to stir up enough hostility in Oxford to prevent a man recommended by the chancellor from getting his degree. Moreover, though Corro was refused a degree a great enemy of his, the minister of the French church, Peter Villiers, was granted one.

Throughout the first two decades of Elizabeth's reign, then, most of the intellectual talent of the university was involved either in discreet self-preservation or the defence of the 1559 settlement against catholic jibes, not in discussion of further radical alteration of the church. From their places of exile the catholics issued a volley of criticism of the settlement and much of their shot was aimed at former colleagues.[1] The most bitter debate was that between Jewel and Harding, men whose paths had earlier lain together. Jewel reminded Harding of a time when the latter had declared Rome to be like 'the sink of Sodom' and had wished for a voice 'equal with the great Belle of Oseney' to ring in 'the dul eares of the deafe Papists';[2] Harding pointed out the frequency with which Jewel changed course.[3] This debate, which began with Jewel's 'challenge' sermon of 1559 in which he urged the catholics to produce evidence from the primitive church for the doctrine of transubstantiation, for the habit of offering the laity communion in only one kind, for private masses and for services in languages other than the vernacular, drew in most of the Oxford men in exile.[4] The first to respond was Henry Cole; he was followed not only by Harding but also by John Rastell, Dorman and Stapleton, all of them former members of New College.[5] The discussions turned on the interpretation of texts and on their authenticity. Both sides could be shown to have been guilty of bad scholarship; Jewel pointed out, for example, that Cranmer had been criticized at his trial for misreading Hilary but that Richard Smith had earlier made the same error in print.[6] One problem of the debate was the uncertain state of some key texts: Jewel, for instance, had argued that Ignatius spoke of the marriage of St Paul, whereas Harding believed on the evidence of 'auncient copies . . . and specially

[1] P. Milward, *Religious Controversies of the Elizabethan Age* (1978), ch. 1.
[2] *A Replie unto M. Hardinges Answeare* (? 1565), sig. II, i.
[3] *A Reioindre to M. Iewels Replie*, sig. CCC1–CCC2^V.
[4] *The copie of a Sermon pronounced by the Byshop of Salisburie at Paules Crosse* . . . (1560).
[5] Rastell became a fellow in 1547: *Reg. Univ.* ed. Clark i. 228. Dorman, a Wykehamist, was elected to a probationary fellowship at New College, but became a fellow of All Souls in 1554 (*DNB*). Stapleton was a fellow of New College from 1554 to 1559. In 1571 he became professor of controversy at Douai, and in 1590 professor of scripture at Louvain: M. R. O'Connell, *Thomas Stapleton and the Counter Reformation* (Yale 1964).
[6] *The Trve Copies of the letters betwene the reverend Father in God Iohn Bisshop of Salisbury and D. Cole* (1560), fo 63.

. . . that of Maudelen Colleges librarie in Oxford' that the text had been corrupted.[1] The debate encouraged that interest in history that has been described as so characteristic of the English reformation: Harding, in his *Answere* to Jewel, cited and translated Bede, and Thomas Stapleton produced the following year an edition of Bede intended to show 'in how many and weighty pointes the pretended reforurmers . . . have departed from the patern of that sounde and Catholike faith planted first among Englishemen by holy S. Augustin our Apostle'.[2] Later, but on the other side, Meredith Hanmer, a fellow of Corpus, published translations of Eusebius and other historians of the church.

As the 'challenge' controversy indicates, much of the catholic polemic of these years came from the pens of Oxford men and, in particular, from former fellows of New College. At least thirty-three fellows left New College in the first decade of Elizabeth's reign;[3] many of them were close friends, and their communities of exile at Louvain and Douai must have borne a strong resemblance to the common-room they had abandoned.[4] In their controversial work they were much assisted by the fact that one of their number, John Fowler, who had been a fellow from 1555 to 1559, was in 1565 admitted as a stationer at Louvain: before 1577 he published thirty-one controversial and devotional works in English.[5] These works appear to have been avidly read in the exiles' former college—Nicholas Sanders's *The Supper of our Lord* (1565), Dorman's *A disprovfe of M. Nowelles Reprovfe* (December 1565) and other books by Harding, Rastell and Martial were circulating there in 1566.[6] Amongst these New College scholars, with their editions and translations, Sanders stands out.[7] Like the learned Stapleton, Sanders

---

[1] *A Reioindre to M. Iewels Replie against the sacrifice of the Masse* (Louvain 1567), fo 170ᵛ.

[2] *The History of the Church of Englande* (Antwerp 1565), sig. O 4.

[3] Penry Williams, 'From the reformation to the era of reform 1530–1850' in John Buxton and Penry Williams (eds), *New College, 1379–1979* (Oxford 1979), 49. P. McGrath, 'Winchester College and the old religion in the sixteenth century' in R. Custance (ed.), *Winchester College: sixth centenary essays* (Oxford 1982), 45, suggests that this number may be an underestimate.

[4] In 1563, for instance, Nicholas Sanders, Thomas Stapleton and John Martial all shared a lodging at Louvain.

[5] A. C. Southern, *Elizabethan Recusant Prose, 1559–1582* (London and Glasgow 1950), 338–9, 342.

[6] Bodl. MS Top. Oxon. c 354 (a transcript of Bishop Horne's register), fos 27–8. The injunctions issued for the college in that year specifically forbade the introduction or perusal of the works of Harding, Martial, Dorman and 'other schismatics': *Visitation Articles and Injunctions of the period of the Reformation*, ed. W. H. Frere and W. M. Kennedy (3 vols Alcuin Club xiv–xvi 1910) iii. 182.

[7] T. McN. Veech, *Dr. Nicholas Sanders and the English Reformation 1530–1581* (Louvain 1935).

consistently defended the papal supremacy—it was Sanders, for example, who wrote a justification of the bull excommunicating Elizabeth—but unlike most of his colleagues he was prepared actively to ferment rebellion, dying in Ireland during the Fitzgerald rising. However, Sanders's most influential work was the composition of *De origine ac progressu schismatis anglicani*, which went into fifteen editions within ten years of its posthumous publication in 1586.[1] In this book Sanders outlined an interpretation of the reformation in England which was to survive for three centuries among his co-religionists; he also provided much information about Oxford, including the assertion that 'the catholic faith was so advanced in the University . . . that men were found there who by speaking and writing denied openly the ecclesiastical supremacy of King Edward VI'.[2]

In so far as the university was involved in national and international debate about religious matters it was thus forced to concentrate on the conflict with Rome. The Jesuit mission, for instance, brought forth a spate of defences of the established church: Meredith Hanmer of Corpus published in 1581 his *The great bragge and challenge of M. Champion a Iesuite* and *The Iesuites Banner*; Humfrey's *Iesuitismi* appeared in 1582; Rainolds published an account of his conference with the imprisoned seminary priest John Hart in 1584; and four years later Humfrey, in *A view of the Romish Hydra*, argued in favour of severe punishment.[3] Those responsible for discipline within the university shared these preoccupations. From 1573 onward a small number each year of the supplicants for degrees found their theological credentials being examined and found wanting.[4] Arthur Torles and Jonas Meredith, for example, were rejected for the degree of MA on account of *religionis suspicio*—both were from the highly suspect college of St John's. Ralph Swinburn, again from a suspect college, Trinity, was questioned at length in 1575 and was the cause of a great dispute in congregation. In the same year Hugh Weston had his supplication for a BA refused because he was *papismi manifeste convictus*; the degree was finally granted two years later only after Weston had signed a declaration of belief in the articles of the church, in justification by faith alone and in the desirability of a married clergy, and after he had rejected the notion of the mass as a propitiatory

[1] Milward, *Religious Controversies*, 71. The work was published in English by D. Lewis as *The Rise and Fall of the Anglican Schism* (1877).

[2] Lewis, 212.

[3] *A View of the Romish Hydra* (Oxford 1588), 186. Humfrey says (fo 8ᵛ) that the book grew out of some lectures he gave in Oxford.

[4] *Reg. Univ.* ed. Clark i. 152–7.

sacrifice.[1] Only one candidate, Henry West, appears to have come under suspicion for extreme protestant views.[2]

Thus when convocation decided at the end of 1578 that the statute *De inquisitione et cautione facienda contra bereticam pravitatem* should be expanded, the main motive appears to have been the protection of protestantism against the old faith. In future undergraduates were to be fully instructed in the faith, and the books they were to use were carefully prescribed.[3] These included Calvin's catechism of 1542 and the Heidelberg catechism of 1563, written by Zacharias Ursinus and Caspar Olevianus for the reformed church of the Palatinate. The shorter, clearer and more positive Heidelberg catechism was preferred over Calvin's in most of the continental reformed churches, and the frequency with which it was reprinted at Oxford reveals its popularity in England. Alexander Nowell's *Cathecism*, commissioned by convocation in 1562 but not published until 1570, was also prescribed. In this influential work, which went into forty-four editions before 1647,[4] Nowell took a moderate stance on various controversial matters, arguing for instance that although the Scriptures contained all that it was necessary for man to know for his salvation, the decrees of councils and other non-scriptural sources might be helpful in the 'expoundyng of darke places of the word of God' and in the 'orderly stablishyng of the outward gouernance of the church'.[5] While stating firmly that man was justified not by obedience to the Law nor by faith but by Christ alone, Nowell produced cogent arguments in favour of good works as an important manifestation of belief.[6]

Besides these three catechisms, the *Elementa christianae religionis* of Andreas Hyperius, or Gerardus, was prescribed. Hyperius had spent some time in England as the guest of Erasmus's patron Charles Mountjoy before he settled at the university of Marburg, and his writings enjoyed much favour in England. Henry Parry's translation of the *Elementa*, which was a commentary on the Heidelberg catechism, was one of the first books published in Oxford, and it was reprinted four times before Elizabeth's death.[7] Bullinger's catechism

---

[1] *Reg. Univ.* ed. Clark i. 153–5.   [2] Ibid. 152.

[3] Ibid. 155–6.

[4] J. R. Mulder, *The Temple of the Mind* (New York 1969), 107. It is interesting to find an Oxford undergraduate writing at the end of the 1570s to tell his mother that 'on Satterdayes and Sundayes we reade a peace of Mr. Nowelles Catechisme' (Folger Shakespeare Library, Washington, MS 1 a 36).

[5] *A Catechisme*, fos 1^V, 2^V.

[6] Ibid. fo 50^V. Faith, for Nowell, was not the cause but the instrument of justification.

[7] Ortius' oration at Hyperius' funeral, in A. Hyperius, *The practis of preaching*, translated by J. Ludham (1577), sig. B^{b}4. F. Madan, *Oxford Books* (Oxford 1895), 87, 89, 91, 96.

was suggested by convocation as an additional aid to study, together with Calvin's *Institutes,* Jewel's *Apology* and the articles of the church.

Despite this decree, and the evident popularity of the works it prescribed, the chancellor of the university, Leicester, still complained in 1582 of 'secret and lurking Papists amongst you, which seduce your youth and carry them over by flocks to the Seminaries beyond Seas'. He argued that the chief problem was a 'want of instructing' in 'the Principles of Religion';[1] a lecturership in theology was subsequently established at St Mary's,[2] and in 1585 the city, which had in 1579 required all freemen with their wives and families to attend sermons every Sunday and holiday on pain of a fine of 12*d*, set up a weekly lecture at St Martin's.[3] In 1586 Sir Francis Walsingham endowed a lecturership in the university, to which John Rainolds was appointed. Walsingham, like Leicester, argued that 'in our Universities here at home as great care . . . is not had for the advancement of trewe Religion' as the catholics took over the progress of their faith 'in seminaries abroad'. It was agreed that 'the common places of the Scripture, the Principles of Religion and matters of controversye' should 'be handled and expounded like as at Rheimes and other places beyond the seas'.[4]

Well into the 1590s the questions posed for candidates for the degree of doctor of theology show a similar concern for the defence of protestantism against Roman Catholicism rather than for debate between different reformed doctrinal positions. In 1581 the prescribed questions concerned the real presence and whether Christ's flesh was actually chewed in the sacrament; similar questions were set in 1584, 1585 and 1590. The questions chosen by candidates reveal the same preoccupations: in 1581, for example, Robert Hovenden of All Souls debated whether or not the pope could err, whether he was the true head of the universal church and if he were Anti-Christ; John Underhill discussed ubiquity, whether Christ alone was head of the church and if He were the only mediator; and Thomas Sparke considered whether the sacraments should be administered in two kinds, if ministers might take wives and whether the liturgy should be in the vernacular.[5] It is interesting that even Meredith Hanmer chose to defend very basic questions about masses for the dead and the invocation of saints, not more controversial

[1] Wood, *History and Antiquities* 212–13 (21 Jan. 1582).

[2] P. S. Seaver, *The Puritan Lectureships* (Stanford 1970), 112; *Records of the City of Oxford*, 406.

[3] *Oxford Council Acts*, 1583–1626, ed. H. E. Salter (OHS lxxxvii 1928), 23.

[4] Wood, *History and Antiquities* ii. 227–8.

[5] *Reg. Univ.* ed. Clark, i. 195–6.

issues about ornaments or the hierarchy of the church.[1] In the late 1580s and the early 1590s questions about justification were usual: the questions set in 1591 asked, for example, whether works were necessary for salvation and in 1593 the distinction between congruous and condign merit was debated.[2]

However, the university was not entirely untouched by the growing conflict within European Calvinism between the followers of Beza, with their emphasis on the doctrine of a limited atonement, and those who argued that the number of the elect was not necessarily fixed. Franceso Pucci, for example, appeared to deny the doctrine of a specific covenant, arguing instead that men could, by the exercise of reason, decide whether or not to choose salvation.[3] Pucci's stay in Oxford was short, but Antonio del Corro, who held not dissimilar views, was in Oxford intermittently from 1579, when he became a catechist for several halls, until his death in 1591.[4] Like Pucci, Corro emphasized human responsibility: all men were endowed with the possibility of faith.[5] Although he accepted the theory that all men had been chosen (or rejected) before the creation of the world he argued that man was free, even after the fall, to choose sin, and he stressed what he saw as 'the temptation of predestination'.[6] When Rainolds urged Humfrey to resist the move to give Corro a degree he predicted that the Spaniard would 'raise such flames in our university as the Lord doth know, whether these shall be quenched', but in the event Corro's impact on the 'young schollers and wits unripe' about whom Rainolds was so concerned appears to have been negligible.[7] It is nevertheless interesting that Richard Hooker, who had earlier appeared to share the views of his former tutor Rainolds, declared in his Paul's Cross sermon of 1581 that God was 'a permissive and no positive cause of the evil, which the schoolmen called *malum culpae*';[8] Walter Travers, in his great dispute with Hooker in 1586, charged Hooker with teaching 'certain thinges concerning predestination not unlike that wherewith Corranus sometime troubled the church'.[9] Looking back just before the Hampton Court conference, one strict Calvinist declared that doctrine had never been pure since the arrival in the universities of two foreigners, Peter Baro and Corro:[10] for Baro's impact on

[1] *Reg. Univ.* ed. Clark, i. 195. [2] Ibid. 197.

[3] Dent, *Protestant Reformers*, 109–10.

[4] E. Boehmer, *Spanish Reformers of Two Centuries from 1520* (Strassburg 1904), 1–74.

[5] Dent, 185–7.

[6] *A Theological Dialogve* (1575), fos 152^V, 147–8.

[7] Wood, *History and Antiquities* ii. 180–2.

[8] R. Hooker, *Works*, ed. I. Walton, R. W. Church and F. Paget (3 vols Oxford 1888) iii. 592.

[9] Ibid. 567. [10] Bodl. MS 124, fo 57.

Cambridge there is a great deal of evidence, but Oxford in fact seems to have shown little interest in 'Arminianism *avant la lettre*'.[1] Hooker is here of crucial significance, but far more is known about his intellectual development after he went to London in 1581 than about his time at Corpus. None the less, even if much of his most distinctive ideas originated in the 1580s or after, it was at Corpus that he drew to himself two influential pupils, Edwin Sandys, son of the archbishop of York, and George Cranmer. Sandys and Cranmer later helped Hooker with his writings, commenting on and criticizing in great detail book six of the *Laws of Ecclesiastical Polity*,[2] for example, and Sandys took further some of Hooker's theories about the possibility that catholics and even the pope himself might be saved, arguing in his *Europae speculum* that the church of Rome had some good features, such as the beauty of its buildings, and pleading for unity among Christians.[3] Hooker and Sandys were of obvious importance in the development of rational theology, so too was another Corpus man, John Spenser, who was, as president of the college from 1607 to 1614, responsible for the publication of Hooker's later writings.[4] The other Oxford figure of note in this context is Albericus Gentilis, incorporated in 1580 as 'an exile for religion' and later regius professor of civil law.[5] Thus towards the end of the sixteenth century there existed in Oxford a group of men interested in a more eirenical and tolerant attitude in religious matters. None the less, the group was a small one, and it would be an error to believe that the university as a whole slipped imperceptibly from catholicism into Arminianism or Socianianism.

Indeed, recent scholarship has emphasized the role played by Oxford in the puritan movement of Elizabeth's reign. The university certainly produced a number of radical laymen and clergy: over forty puritan ministers in the decade after 1565, for example.[6] Oxford-trained clergymen spread radical ideas in Lancashire and Cheshire, where many Brasenose men had livings, while Queen's produced puritans to preach the gospel in the north-west.[7] Some colleges were, like Brasenose and later Queen's, especially noted for their radical atmosphere: for example at least seventeen Elizabethan

---

[1] I take this phrase from N. R. N. Tyacke, 'Arminianism in England, in religion and politics, 1604 to 1640' (Oxford DPhil thesis 1968), ch. 3.

[2] W. Speed Hill, 'Hooker's *Polity*: the problem of the "three last books" ', *Huntington Library Quarterly* xxxiv (1971), 317–36.

[3] E. Sandys, *Evropae speculum* (Hagae-Comitis 1629), fos 8–9.

[4] *DNB*.

[5] *Reg. Univ.* ed. Clark i. 149. W. K. Jordan, *The Development of Religious Toleration in England* (Gloucester Mass. 1965), 366.

[6] Patrick Collinson, *The Elizabethan Puritan Movement* (1967), 129.

[7] Dent, *Protestant Reformers*, 167–77.

fellows of Magdalen became puritan ministers and every major reform movement of the reign found some support there.[1] Typical of these Oxford-bred puritans is Arthur Wake, who was an undergraduate at Christ Church during the brief period in which Sampson was dean.[2] Wake was a supporter of the *Admonition* (itself in part the work of another Oxford man, John Field) and he preached a sermon in favour of Cartwright at Paul's Cross. He was a rector in the radical county of Northamptonshire until his views led to his deprivation, and he was the author of the first book of discipline for the reformed church of the Channel Islands.[3]

In the late 1580s there was considerable support in the university for the *classis*.[4] Edward Gellibrand of Magdalen sounded out opinion in various colleges and was able to inform Field that he had discovered many who favoured reform, although they were not 'Ministers, but young students'.[5] Gellibrand, John Rainolds and a third man, probably John Walward of Corpus, were censured by Archbishop Whitgift in 1586 for sermons containing criticisms of the existing discipline of the church. Walward was ordered to preach in All Saints in such a way as to 'stirre upp all his hearers to unitie & peace & to obedience & good likeing of the magistrates lawes and orders, and present government of this churche'.[6] Despite this admonishment, it was Gellibrand who was probably responsible the next year for the circulation in Oxford of the English translation of the *Disciplina Ecclesiae*.[7]

By this date John Rainolds was the leader of those within the university who were dissatisfied with the existing state of the church. He was an influential lecturer and tutor whose pupils—Hooker at Corpus, for instance, or Richard Crakanthorpe at Queen's—revered him. The vast range of both his learning and his friendship can be seen in the long list in his will of books and of those to whom they were to be given.[8] The arch-opponent of the 1576 proposal that Corro should be given a degree, a great critic of undergraduate play-acting, a man rebuked by Elizabeth herself in 1592 for running before the laws, Rainolds was for three decades the radical conscience

---

[1] Collinson, 129.

[2] *Reg. Univ.* ed. Clark ii, 12, 252.

[3] Collinson, 149, 143.

[4] W. J. Sheils, *The Puritans in the Diocese of Peterborough, 1558–1610* (Northamptonshire Record Society xxx 1979), 97–8, notes the part played by Oxford clerics in the development of the *classis* in the 1580s: before and after that decade, Cambridge men provided the more radical element.

[5] Dent, *Protestant Reformers*, 132, citing BL Additional MS 38492, fo 80. The letter is quoted in Wood, *History and Antiquities* ii. 225.

[6] Dent, *Protestant Reformers*, 139, citing Dr Williams' Library Morrice MS 'B' ii. fo 103[V].

[7] Collinson, 322–3.   [8] Bodl. MS D 10.

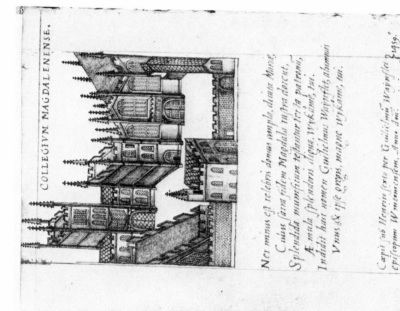

I *a, b.* Magdalen and Brasenose Colleges. The earliest surviving views of Oxford buildings were drawn by John Bereblock, fellow of Exeter College, to illustrate a manuscript topography of the university which was presented to Queen Elizabeth on the occasion of her visit to Oxford in 1566. The text, in the form of a Latin verse dialogue, was by Thomas Neale, regius professor of Hebrew. *Bodleian Library, MS Bodl. 13, fos 8[r], 11[r].*

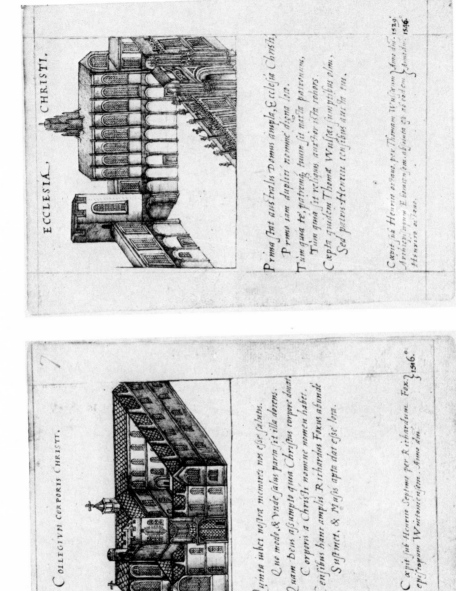

II *a*, *b*. Corpus Christi College and Christ Church. *Bodleian Library, MS Bodl. 13, fos 7, 5ᵛ.*

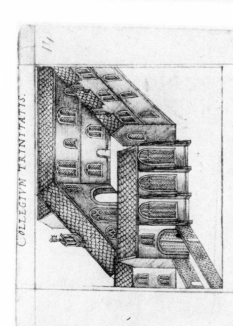

COLLEGIVM TRINITATIS.

Vrbis at egressæ iam muros, proxima sedes
Occurrit Thomæ sumptibus aucta Popi.
Quam sarrisianita truadis tþ nomen habere
Iußit mauratus miles, equesq; Decus.
Huius adhuc teneros fœtus, pia mater adauget
Coniunx, iam digno romuge digna sui.

Cœpit sub Maria Regina per Dñm Thomam Popum 1556°
ordinis equestris militem mauratum. Anno dñi.

COLLEGIVM IOANNIS BAPTISTE.

Cancell.

HAS T. homas Whitus, Londini gloria, raras
Mercator merces donat, emitq; sibi.
Qui Londinensi bis Prætor in urbe, superstes
Vixit adhuc, equitum non mediocre Decus.
Faxit ut ille diu vivat, valeatq; superstes
Nusq; at demum cælitis regna petat.

Cœpit sub Maria Regina per Dñm Thomam White 1557
ordinis equestris militem mauratum. 40 dñi

III a, b. Trinity and St. John's Colleges.   *Bodleian Library, MS Bodl. 13, fos 14, 15ᵛ.*

IV. New College hall, panelling and screen 1533-5. *Thomas-Photos, Oxford*

V. Mazer mounted on silver gilt stem and foot with openwork decoration
incorporating renaissance motifs. It bears London hall marks for 1529.
All Souls College; cf. H. C. Moffatt, *Old Oxford Plate* (1906), 94 and plate xlvii;
Thomas-Photos, Oxford.

VI. Gold chalice (the paten for which also survives) belonging to Richard Fox, part of the plate given to his college by the founder, with London hall marks for 1507. *Corpus Christi College*; cf. Moffatt, *Old Oxford Plate*, 128 and plate lxii.

VII. Chalice and paten in silver gilt bearing London hall marks for 1564. An early
specimen of the Elizabethan form of chalice. The college arms are enamelled in a
shield on the foot of the cover paten.   *All Souls College*; cf. Moffat, *Old Oxford Plate*, 84
and plate xlii; *Thomas-Photos, Oxford.*

VIII. Silver gilt flagon, one of a pair with London hall marks for 1598.
Corpus Christi College; cf. Moffatt, *Old Oxford Plate*, 132 and plate lxiv.

IX. Timberframed study in St. John's College, staircase 4.2, a furnishing which survives from St. Bernard's College. The panel indicates the height and decorative style of these structures within the common chamber; cf. the plans in *VCH Oxon* iii 151.
Thomas-Photos, Oxford.

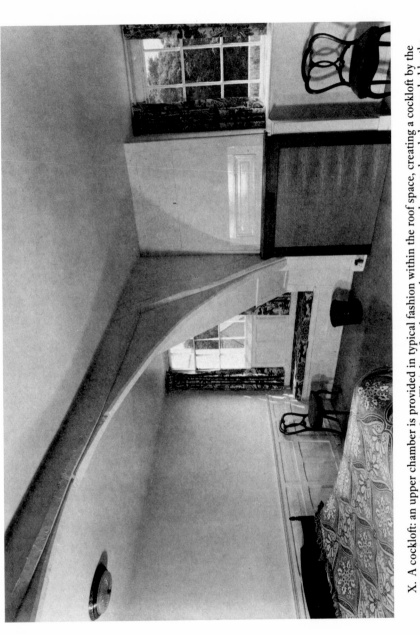

X. A cockloft: an upper chamber is provided in typical fashion within the roof space, creating a cockloft by the addition of a floor and dormer windows. The chamfered centre beam rests on decorated corbels concealed by the floor and was intended originally to be visible from the floor below. A small staircase leads to the cockloft where an adjacent study, also provided with a dormer, now functions as a bathroom.   *All Souls College, staircase V; Thomas-Photos, Oxford.*

XI. The west range of Merton College library, 1589-90, showing the Elizabethan book stalls in relation to the medieval windows and benches; see page 622 below. *Thomas-Photos, Oxford.*

XII *a*. The inscription in this copy of Walter Burley's commentary on the *Ethics* of Aristotle shows William Lambarde's donation to Christ Church library of a book that had once belonged to Laurence Nowell. See N. R. Ker, 'Books at Christ Church 1562–1602' 1578-3, p. 504 below.
Christ Church Library e.6.26.

XII *b* (*right*). This *Speculum morale* (Strasbourg 1476) from the library of a former fellow of Lincoln College was counted in 1550 as a part of the borrowable collection; see N. R. Ker, 'Lincoln College Election Lists' 1.(28), p. 480 below.
Lincoln College Library K.10.4.

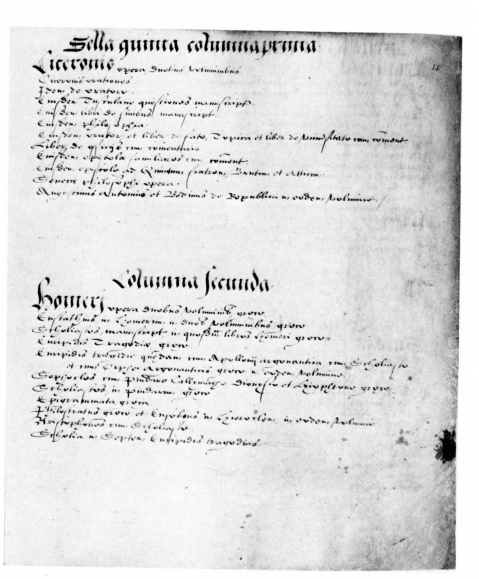

XIII. A page from the 1579 library catalogue of Corpus Christi College, indicating the new arrangements consequent on the introduction of book stalls. *Corpus Christi College Archives*, *D/3/1 fo 4.*

XIV *a*. A Hebrew manuscript of I Samuel and Chronicles with an interlinear Latin version, given to the library of Corpus Christi College by the first president, John Claymond.   *Corpus Christi College Library*, *MS 9 fo 225*.

XIV *b*. A copy of the Greek Lexicon, 'Suidas', originally compiled about the end of the tenth century. It had belonged to William Grocyn and was given to Corpus Christi College by John Claymond. Grocyn's ownership is indicated in the upper right margin. *Corpus Christi College Library*, MS *77 fo 1*.

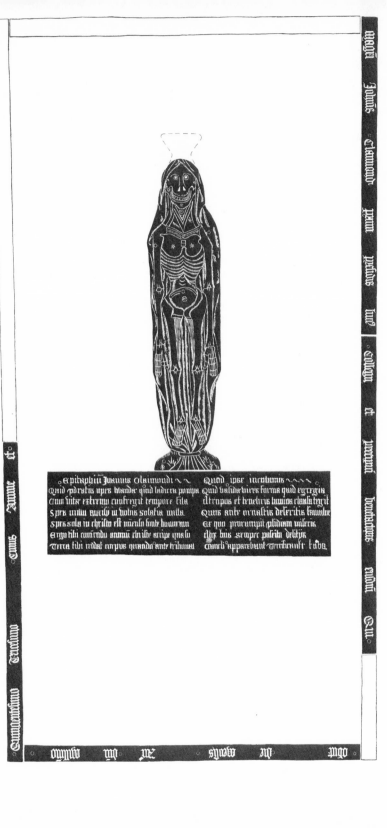

XV *a*, *b*. Funeral monuments: a comparison of (*a*) central portion of the memorial brass to John Claymond, first president of Corpus Christi College, 1517-1537, in the College chapel (*The Oxford Portfolio of Monumental Brasses*, ser. 2, pt. 5 (The Oxford University Archaeological Soc., Oxford, 1955), plate 4; the brass was engraved *c* 1530); and (*b*) the wall monument erected at Merton College for Sir Henry Savile (died 1622). Savile's monument in the Merton ante-chapel shows his bust flanked by figures representing his studies: Chrysostom, Ptolemy, Euclid and Tacitus, while the base paintings show Merton and Eton colleges, Savile having been provost of Eton as well as warden of Merton. *Thomas-Photos, Oxford.*

XVI *a*. John Rainolds, president of Corpus Christi College 1599-1607. Mrs. R. L. Poole, *Catalogue of Portraits in the Possession of the University, Colleges, City and County of Oxford*, ii. *Portraits in the Colleges and Halls* (Oxford Historical Society, lxxxi, 1926), Corpus Christi College, no. 15.

XVI *b (right)*. The funeral monument of Laurence Humfrey, president of Magdalen College 1561-1590, in the college ante-chapel. Mrs. R. L. Poole, *op. cit.*, Magdalen College, no. 20.   *Thomas-Photos, Oxford.*

SPECVLVM MORALIVM

QVAESTIONVM IN VNIVERSAM ETHICEN

Aristotelis, Authore Magistro IOHANNE CASO
Oxoniensi, olim Collegij Diui Io-
hannis Præcursoris
Socio.

SENECA LIB. II. EPIST. XVI. AD LVCILIVM.

¶ Illud ante omnia vide, vtrum in philosophia, an in ipsa vita profeceris: non est philosophia po-
pulare artificium, nec ostentationi paratum; non enim in verbis sed in rebus est.

¶ OXONIAE,

Ex officina Typographica IOSEPHI BARNESII *Celeberrimi*
Academiæ Oxoniensis Typographi,
Anno 1585.

XVII *a*. The title-page of John Case's *Speculum moralium quaestionum* (Oxford 1585),
the first book published by the newly-established press.
Bodleian Library, D.10.20 Linc (2).

XVII *b*. The last page of Randolph Cholmondeley's notebook shows the chief points to be noted in reading any author. The heading reads, 'Haec praecipue spectanda atque annotanda sunt, in sequendo authore aliquo'. See James McConica, 'Elizabethan Oxford: the collegiate society', pp. 710-11 below. *Bodleian Library, MS Lat. misc. e 114 fo 175*.

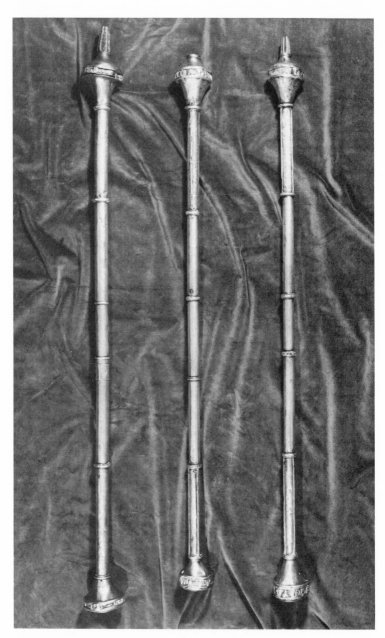

XVIII. Emblems of authority: the old university staves of the three faculties, arts and medicine, civil law, and theology. They date from the late sixteenth century, and their shafts have wooden cores covered with silver. The longest (belonging to the faculty of arts) measures 3 ft. $11\frac{1}{8}$ in., the diameter of the top being $3\frac{3}{8}$ in. The respective mottoes borne by the staves are: 'columna philosophiae scientia et more'; 'columna justitiae aequum et bonum', and 'Ego sum via, veritas et vita'. They vanished before the arrival in 1647 of the parliamentary visitors, who searched for them fruitlessly; see Moffatt, *Old Oxford Plate*, 5. *Ashmolean Museum, Oxford.*

XIX. Details of the staff of the faculty of theology

a (top). the head with the inscription 'veritas et vita' and a flanged and blunt spike;

b (bottom). the footknop (which bears the inscription, 'Ego sum via') is engraved with the university arms. *Ashmolean Museum, Oxford.*

XX. University records

a. The matriculation entry of John Pym, the future parliamentarian, is recorded among others from Broadgates Hall on 18 May 1599, as being from Somerset, the son of an esquire, aged 15.   *OUA Matriculation Register 1564–1614, SP/1 Reg. P, p. 499.*

XX. University records   *OUA Subscription Register 1581–1615, SP/38 Reg. A.b. fo 95ʳ.*

b. Pym's signature on subscription is also shown.

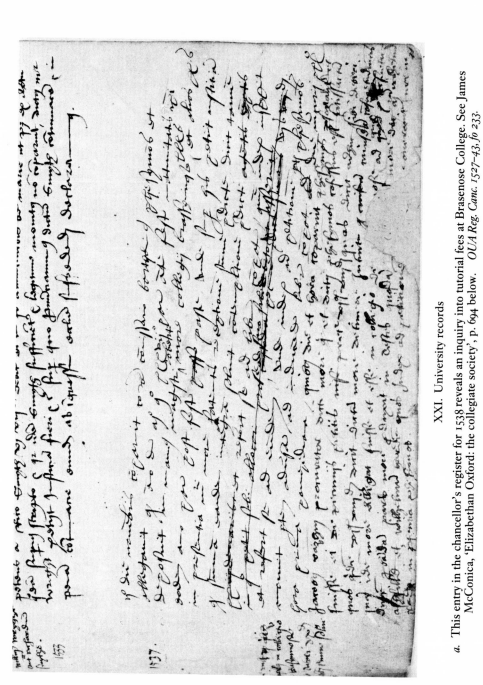

XXI. University records

a. This entry in the chancellor's register for 1538 reveals an inquiry into tutorial fees at Brasenose College. See James McConica, 'Elizabethan Oxford: the collegiate society', p. 694 below.　*OUA Reg. Canc. 1527–43, fo 233.*

XXI. University records

b. The register of congregation records the concern of Chancellor Buckhurst in December 1594 that existing laws be strictly enforced, he 'being advertised by some' of there being in Oxford 'not so generall a reformation and conformitie procured in all things as were greatly to be wished'. See James McConica, 'The Rise of the Undergraduate College', p. 51, n. 4 above.

OUA Reg. Cong. 1582–95. fo 272.

XXII. College records

a. This entry in the *libri magni* of Corpus Christi College for 1534-5 shows a payment of £4 to John Scheprey (Shepreve) for four terms as the college reader in Greek. William Chedsey is paid 13s 4d for having taught four men 'logica graeca' for two terms; in the next two terms the same pupils (their names being given for the first time in this year) continued their Greek instruction with 'D[ominus] Gode'. See James McConica, 'The Rise of the Undergraduate College', p. 27 above.

Corpus Christi College Archives C/1/1/1 fo 122.

XXII. College records

b. This notarized entry in the admissions register of Corpus Christi College shows the admission as fellow on 10 June 1578 of John Spensar (Spenser), bachelor of arts, who was to be president of Corpus from 1607-14. Spenser had received his degree in the previous October. *Corpus Christi College Archives 13/1/3/1.*

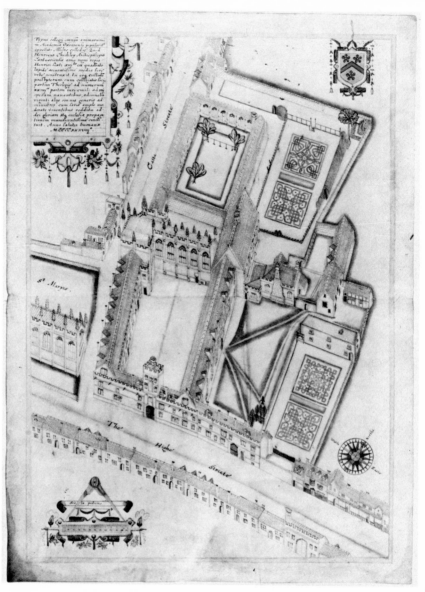

XXIII. The *typus collegii* of All Souls College, the most detailed representation of any Tudor college, is one of nearly a hundred maps on vellum of college properties which were commissioned by Warden Hovenden between 1586 and 1605. In the original quadrangle the medieval hall is set at right angles to the east end of the chapel, and adjoining it are the kitchens and offices. To the north of the chapel is the cloister.

The range on the High Street to the east was the first extension of the original building, initiated by Warden John Warner and completed in 1553. The new warden's lodgings were panelled by Hovenden, the first married warden, who lived in them with his family.   *All Souls College Archives, Hovenden Maps vol. 1, no. 1.*

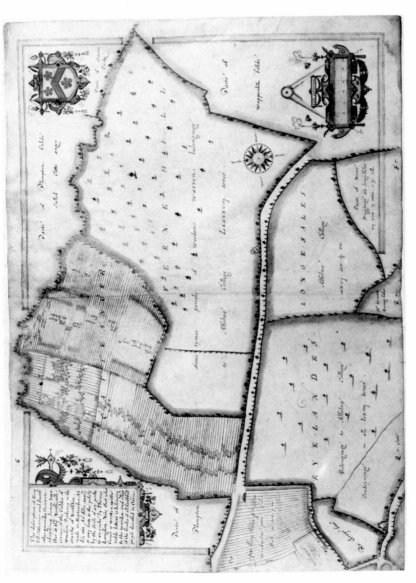

XXIV. Estate map of Weedon, Northants, made in 1594 by Thomas Langdon. The reproduction cannot indicate the fine colouring of the original in this important and luxurious new departure in college record-keeping.   *All Souls College Archives, Hovenden Maps vol. 1, no. 14.*

of the university.[1] He was closely linked with the London puritans, whose desire for improved discipline within the church he shared. Yet his views, unlike theirs, were at length absorbed into the mainstream of the English church. At the Hampton Court conference in 1604 Rainolds accepted the notion of episcopacy, arguing only that members of the laity should be associated with the church hierarchy for various purposes.[2] It was in his lodgings at Corpus, of which he had been elected president in 1599, that much of the translation of the authorized version of the Bible was completed.

Throughout his career Rainolds had in fact been prepared to compromise over what he held to be things indifferent. This moderation sprang in part from his belief that protestants should stand united against the catholic threat: 'I take greater comfort', he told Sir Francis Knollys in 1589, 'in labouring to discover and overthrow the error of Jesuits and papists, enemies of religion, than of ministers of the Gospell and brethren confessing the true faith of Christ'.[3] The bulk of his controversial energies were thus diverted into the fight against catholicism rather than into the task of reforming the established church. From 1580, when *Sex theses*, an attack on the Rheims Testament, was published, Rainolds worked relentlessly on sermons and books meant to refute the teachings of the catholics including his *De Romanae Ecclesiae Idolatria* published in 1596 as a reply to Bellarmine.

For Rainoldes, as for so many Oxford men of his time, Rome still posed an active and urgent challenge. This fact may explain why, despite the influence in Elizabeth's reign of Sampson, Humfrey and Rainolds himself, Oxford did not produce radicals in either the number or quantity of Cambridge.[4] The Marian reaction was more complete and more enduring in Oxford—Leicester, complaining of catholicism in Oxford in 1582 declared that 'the other [university] is untouched with it'[5]—and the energies of protestants in Oxford were therefore expended in combating the lures of Rome rather than in attempts to change the 1559 church settlement.

Throughout the sixteenth century Oxford had been slower to espouse radical religious ideas and faster to return to orthodoxy than

---

[1] *DNB*. For the controversy over play acting, see *Th'ouerthrow of stage-playes, by the way of controversie betwixt D. Gager and D. Rainoldes. Whereunto are added certeine latine laetters betwixt Maister Rainoldes, and D. Gentiles* (Middleburg 1599).

[2] M. Curtis, 'The Hampton Court conference and its aftermath', *History* xlvi (1961), 10.

[3] Folger Shakespeare Library, Washington, MS V.b. 214, fo 57.

[4] For an interpretation of Cambridge puritanism see P. Lake, *Moderate Puritans and the Elizabethan Church* (Cambridge 1982).

[5] Wood, *History and Antiquities* ii. 227–8.

was its sister university. Perhaps one reason for this was a distant memory of Wyclif: the events of the late 1520s and the early 1530s suggest that the university itself was very anxious to repudiate any charge of unorthodoxy. Other reasons for the difference may perhaps be sought in the religious complexion of the surrounding countryside and the links of Oxford with Paris and Louvain.

Although Erasmus had paid a lengthy visit to Cambridge it was in Oxford that his ideas achieved concrete expression with the foundation of Corpus and later Cardinal College. This Erasmian tradition was heightened by the interchange of scholars between Oxford and the *collegium trilinguae* at Louvain, itself a monument to Erasmian ideals.[1] Oxford men went to Louvain for its associations with Erasmus and for the excellence of its language teaching. It was, for instance, via Louvain that Wolsey sent his son Thomas Winter on his journey to Italy, at Louvain that notable Hebrew scholars such as Robert Wakefield received their training and from Louvain by way of Cambridge that the Syriac lecturer John Drusius came to Oxford in 1572. But the faculty of theology at Louvain had been quick to condemn Luther in 1519, and visitors to Louvain seem to have found themselves confirmed in a conservative stance. It was during a stay in Louvain that Thomas Goldwell, later bishop of St Asaph during Mary's reign, declared that he could not accept Henry VIII's breach with Rome, and at much the same time John Helyar, one of the scholars of Corpus nominated by the founder, decided to abandon a promising career at home.[2] Two at least of the Oxford men at Louvain, Gabriel Dunne and Henry Phillips, were instrumental in the arrest of Tyndale, although Phillips was rewarded only by inclusion in the 1539 act of attainder as one who had 'traiterously maintained the pope's headship of the church of England'.[3] So committed to the papal cause had Louvain become that when Stephen Gardiner visited the university on his way back from the diet of Ratisbon he found himself described as 'an excommunicate person and a schismatic' because of his book justifying the break with Rome; he was refused the opportunity of saying mass in the university church.[4] It was to this 'nearest harbour' of the old faith that Nicholas Harpsfield, fellow of New College, Hugh Turnbull of Corpus and various members of the More circle went when they fled from England at Edward's accession.[5] When Elizabeth came to the throne there was again an exodus to Louvain. Morgan Phillips spent some years at

[1] H. de Vocht, *History of the Foundation and the Rise of the Collegium Trilingue Lovaniense, 1517–1550* (Louvain 1950), passim.

[2] *BRUO 1501–40, passim.*   [3] *L & P Henry VIII* xiv. pt 1, 402.

[4] Foxe, *Acts and Monuments* vi. 139–40, 202.

[5] Lewis, *Rise and Fall of the Anglican Schism*, 201.

Louvain before he joined his former pupil William Allen at Douai: indirectly and directly Douai was the product of Oxford and Louvain. The conservative religious stand of Louvain and that of Paris in the 1530s and 1540s was of great significance, for they were the foreign universities most often visited by Oxford scholars. Only a few went, like Tyndale, to Wittenberg or the other German universities. Lawrence Tomson, later Walsingham's secretary, spent some time at the university of Heidelberg in 1567 but thereafter few Oxford men visited this centre of aggressive Calvinism.[1]

Oxford's links were thus with centres of conservativism rather than radicalism. The importance of such links was increased by the religious isolation of the university in the second part of the century: although in the reign of Edward Oxford had been pulled into the mainstream of continental protestant thought, the Marian reaction and the failure of the exiles to return to Oxford meant that for several decades afterwards the university was an observer rather than a creator of radical ideas. Although a trickle of foreign protestant visitors and refugees came to Oxford, few, if any, had a perceptible intellectual impact on the university.

The religious complexion of the areas from which colleges took the majority of their undergraduates—obviously decisive in the case of Exeter, for example, with an intake largely from the conservative south-west—and the atmosphere of the surrounding countryside is clearly also relevant to an explanation of Oxford's greater conservatism. Although Lollardy once flourished in the Thames valley, events in Oxfordshire and Buckinghamshire in 1549 and 1553 suggest a strong attachment to catholicism in those areas.[2] Throughout the reign of Elizabeth a large proportion of the gentry of Oxfordshire remained catholic, ensuring numerous country houses at which a priest could be found; indeed, the county itself produced about thirty secular priests.[3] Even in the city there were public houses such as the Catherine Wheel in which mass was frequently celebrated; one contemporary, complaining of the 'huge garrison and mighty multitude' of catholics in Oxford, declared that they lurked in 'dimme caves, secret closetes, merck clowdie taverns [and] darck mistie victuallinge howses', being 'even on their ale benches' great perverters of the young.[4] In the city and the surrounding countryside there was, therefore, support and refuge readily available for the conservative academic.

---

[1] I. Backus, 'Laurence Tomson (1539–1608) and Elizabethan puritanism', *Journal of Ecclesiastical History* xxviii (1977), 19.

[2] A. Vere Woodman, 'The Buckinghamshire and Oxfordshire rising of 1549', *Oxoniensia* xxii (1957), 78–80.

[3] Davidson, 'Roman Catholicism in Oxfordshire', 453.

[4] Bodl. MS Ashmole 1537, fos 38–9.

Throughout the sixteenth century, with some notable exceptions, the university and its surroundings remained conservative in religion. Yet this was not—in the reign of Elizabeth could not be—an aggressive or outgoing conservativism: during these years there was a distinct lack of confidence about the theological speculations of Oxford men, who seem to have looked to the old faith for comfort rather than for intellectual excitement. Only in the reign of Mary did a large part of the university emerge with confidence from the theological backwater in which it dozed, and the ill success of that venture paralyzed the university for five decades.

6

Elizabethan Oxford:
State, Church and University

PENRY WILLIAMS

ON Saturday 31 August 1566, Queen Elizabeth, who had visited Cambridge two years earlier, came on progress to Oxford.[1] These two state visits reflect the growing attention given by the Tudor dynasty to pageantry and ceremonial and the importance attached by the crown to the role of the universities in national life. The Oxford visit—it almost deserves the name of visitation—was carefully prepared and elaborately executed; it was no mere afternoon passage through cheering crowds. Already, in 1564, the Oxford proctors had gone to Cambridge in order to learn how such occasions might be arranged. Now, three days before the queen's arrival, the earl of Leicester, chancellor of Oxford, and William Cecil, chancellor of Cambridge, came to inspect the university's preparations.

On her arrival at Wolvercote, a few miles north of the centre of Oxford and the margin of the university's liberties, Elizabeth was received by Leicester, who had travelled ahead of her, by the

* Acknowledgements. I should like to thank the Reverend Dr Christopher Dent for drawing my attention to important source material, reading a draft of this chapter, making many helpful suggestions, and allowing me to read his own work in typescript. His book, *Protestant Reformers in Elizabethan Oxford* (Oxford 1983) provides a much fuller account of that subject than is possible here. Dr Simon Adams, Dr G. D. Duncan and Dr Jennifer Loach also read the chapter in draft and I am grateful to them too for many valuable suggestions and references. I am obliged as well to Dr Jane Roscoe for making transcripts and abstracts of various documents.

[1] The original sources for the visit of 1566 are: (a) Bodl. MS Twyne xvii, fo 160 (by Thomas Neale; extensively used by Wood in *History and Antiquities* ii. 154–63); (b) Richard Stephens, 'A Brief Rehearsal . . .'; (c) Bodl. MS Twyne xxi, fo 792 (by Miles Windsor); (d) Nicholas Robinson, 'Of Actes Done at Oxford . . .'; (e) John Bereblock, 'Commentarii de rebus gestis Oxoniae . . .'. The accounts of Stephens and Robinson were printed in J. Nichols, *The Progresses and Public Processions of Queen Elizabeth* (3 vols 1823) i and that of Bereblock in T. Hearne, *Historia vitae et regni Ricardi secundi* etc. (Oxford 1729); all three were reprinted in C. Plummer, *Elizabethan Oxford* (OHS viii 1887). See also E. K. Chambers, *The Elizabethan Stage* (4 vols Oxford 1923) i. 226–8; and Glynne Wickham, *Early English Stages* (3 vols 1959–81) i. app. H; ii. pt 1, 251–2, 263 ff. On progresses and pageantry generally see S. Anglo, *Spectacle, Pageantry and Earl Tudor Policy* (Oxford 1969) and David Bergeron, *English Civic Pageantry* (1971).

vice-chancellor, Dr Kennall of Christ Church, and by three other doctors, eight masters of arts, and three bedells, who surrendered their staves to her. Roger Marbecke, until recently the university's first public orator and later to be the queen's own physician, welcomed her with a Latin speech. The royal party then proceeded southwards to within a mile of Oxford, where, at the city boundary, they were met by the mayor and aldermen in scarlet. Elizabeth was greeted with a speech from the mayor in English. At the north gate of the city, near the site on which Cranmer, Latimer and Ridley had been burned a decade before, she was welcomed by an undergraduate, Robert Deale of New College, with another oration. She then passed through the ranks of scholars, BAs, MAs, and doctors, cheering and calling out 'Vivat Regina', to which she replied 'Gratias ago'. At Carfax the professor of Greek spoke to her for fifteen minutes in Greek; but when the queen began to reply her mules became understandably restive. On entering Christ Church she had to listen to yet another speech, described by one witness as 'somewhat long'. At last, after hearing a *Te Deum* in the cathedral, she was able to retire. This was the beginning of six days of sermons, lectures, disputations, feasts and plays, arduous for the university, the court and the queen.

On Sunday the queen stayed in her rooms, but the official programme continued in her absence: sermons in the morning and the afternoon, followed by a play in Christ Church hall at night. A special door had been cut in the wall of the old deanery to allow the queen to pass directly from her lodgings to the hall without being jostled by the crowd. Inside, the hall had been panelled in gold and painted up to the roof. A stage had been set up in place of the high table, while a throne had been built for the queen at the other end of the hall. Seating was provided on tiered scaffolding for the 'illustrious spectators', while the townspeople and undergraduates watched from the floor. According to John Bereblock the entire hall had been transformed into the grandeur of a Roman palace, so lavishly provided with lamps, torches and candles that it shone as brightly as the day. Plays were performed here on the Sunday, Monday, Wednesday and Thursday nights. Monday's performance was marred, but not interrupted, by the death of three men, killed by the collapse of a wall on the staircase under the weight of the crowd. Sunday's play was in Latin, entitled 'Marcus Geminus'; on Monday and Wednesday the English play 'Palaemon and Arcite' was presented in two parts; and on Thursday there was another Latin production called 'Progne', written by a canon of Christ Church, James Calfhill.[1]

[1] Wickham i. app. H. W. Y. Durand, *'Palaemon and Arcyte, Progne, Marcus Geminus*

After Sunday, the days were filled with the normal business of the university, lectures and disputations, attended by the courtiers and, usually, by the queen herself. On Tuesday from two o'clock until six in the evening she heard disputations in natural and moral philosophy, on such questions as 'whether the moon causes the movement of the tides' and 'princes should be chosen by inheritance, not election'. One of the disputants was the brilliant young fellow of St John's, Edmund Campion, later, as a Jesuit, to be executed for treason. Wednesday afternoon was given over to disputations in civil law, Thursday to physic and divinity, to which the queen is said to have listened with 'very attent care'. On Friday a meeting of convocation was held, at which various dignitaries of the court, from the duke of Norfolk downwards, were given honorary degrees. At the queen's departure from Christ Church after dinner Mr Toby Mathew made a farewell speech. The city fathers took leave of her at Magdalen bridge, the university representatives at Shotover, where proceedings ended with an oration by the public orator. Two things are worth noticing about this prolonged visit. First, the queen's powers of endurance were in no way spared, for she sat through twelve hours of disputations, although she managed to avoid listening to any sermons. Second, with the exception of Christ Church, where she lodged, she visited no colleges, although the earl of Leicester, the Spanish ambassador and various courtiers rode to see New College.

There was a slightly sour aftermath to the visit when the dean and canons of Christ Church complained that their college had alone to bear the entire cost of the queen's stay. This was more, they claimed, than they could afford and contravened a promise made by the chancellor that the expenses would be shared out. Leicester duly wrote to convocation asking the university to help, and, after a committee had deliberated and reported, Christ Church was reimbursed £37 6s 8d —one-third of the total expenses.[1]

Twenty-six years later, in 1592, the queen made a second visit to Oxford. A committee was appointed to make arrangements for the visit and empowered to punish anyone infringing their decrees. Precise and detailed orders were laid down for the queen's reception: the subjects and protagonists of disputations, the names of

---

and the theatre in which they were acted, as described by John Bereblock (1566)', *Publications of the Modern Language Association of America* xx (1905). Bereblock's descriptions of these plays read like the synopses of opera *libretti* in modern theatre programmes and display about the same degree of clarity.

[1] *Report on the Pepys Manuscripts* (Historical Manuscripts Commission 1911), 92; Reg. Cong. 1564–82, fos 36[V], 38.

preachers, the allocation of expenses, the dress of all present, the persons responsible for plays and the provision of suitable verses for public display were all laid down. The keynote is set by the words 'on Monday and every working day during her Majesty's abode the ordinary lectures be diligently read at the time appointed and frequented': the queen was to see the university going about its normal business. The queen arrived on Friday 22 September and left on the following Thursday. As before, she heard several disputations; and this time she attended a sermon on the Sunday, given by the dean of Christ Church. There were two departures from the programme of 1566. The queen and her entourage seem on this occasion to have visited the colleges, where she was—inevitably—received with speeches. Second, a lecture in music was provided in the schools, 'with the practice thereof by instrument'. Perhaps because the only surviving original account was written by a Cambridge man, Philip Stringer, one gets the impression that this visit was less successful than the first, the queen less patient with the *longueurs* of academic life; but even Anthony Wood, who had access to other sources, clearly thought the occasion only a qualified success. Stringer reports that the two plays were both 'but meanly performed', and he describes the queen as often wearied with the long oratory to which she was subjected. Herbert Westfaling, bishop of Hereford, seems to have been especially prolix: according to Wood, when asked by the queen to shorten his sermon, he was unable to 'put himself out of a set methodical speech for fear he should have marred all'. The queen also took advantage of the occasion to reprimand Dr John Rainolds, as a leading puritan, 'for his obstinate preciseness' and then went on to make a speech of her own—some compensation for all the oratory to which she had been subjected. Again, she had a taunt for the puritans: God, she pronounced, should be worshipped as his laws command, 'not after the exquisite searching and examining wits'.[1]

RULING THE UNIVERSITY

Ceremony and ritual were important for binding the communities of England to the monarchy; and the personal appearances of the queen raised the temperature of loyalty. But in the normal running of Oxford's affairs Elizabeth stayed in the background, leaving the

[1] Philip Stringer, *The Grand Reception and Entertainment of Queen Elizabeth* (1623); repr. Plummer, *Elizabethan Oxford*, 245–61; cf also Plummer, 275 ff. Stringer's account can be supplemented from Wood, *History and Antiquities* ii. 248–53. See *Reg. Univ.* ed. Clark ii. 228–32 for the preparations; and BL Cotton MS Faustina C vii, fos 210–13 for the queen's speech.

task of control to the university's own officials and to external delegates. She intervened directly and personally only in matters of
patronage.

Highest of the university's own officers was the chancellor. Until
the middle of the fifteenth century the chancellor was usually a
resident graduate, but the practice then developed of electing a clerical grandee who could act as a friend at court. Although a layman,
Thomas Cromwell, was appointed chancellor of Cambridge in 1533,
Oxford continued to be ruled by clerical chancellors until the election of Sir John Mason, diplomat and privy councillor, in 1552.
Mason resigned in 1556 to make way for Cardinal Pole, but the lay
succession was firmly established under Elizabeth. The earl of
Arundel was chancellor from 1558 to 1559 and Mason was re-elected
in 1559. Five years later Mason resigned for the second time to be
succeeded by the queen's favourite, Robert Dudley, earl of Leicester,
who presided over the university until his death in 1588. His
successor was Sir Christopher Hatton, then lord chancellor of
England. When Hatton died in 1591 there was a contest for the
office between Robert, earl of Essex, and Thomas Sackville, Lord
Buckhurst. Under pressure from the queen the university chose
Buckhurst who remained chancellor until his death in 1608.[1] Thus
throughout Elizabeth's reign the chancellor was a lay grandee,
capable of bringing to bear considerable pressure on the university
but able in exchange to provide patronage and favour. Theoretically elected by convocation, the chancellor had by the reign of
Elizabeth become a royal nominee.

Naturally such men stood aloof from the daily running of the
university. But, as we shall see, they were active in securing places
for their friends, and at intervals they delivered sonorous rebukes
and exhortations to the vice-chancellor, convocation and congregation.[2] The executive and judicial powers of the chancellor over
members of the university and over townsmen were wielded by his
commissary, the vice-chancellor. Originally the vice-chancellor had
been elected by congregation, but under the earl of Leicester the
appointment came into the hands of the chancellor. At first, in 1565,
Leicester allowed congregation to make its own choice and wrote
to approve its election of Dr Kennall, dean of Christ Church, a civil
lawyer. But two years later he censured the university for rejecting
his nominees and ordered the appointment of a divine. After 1570

[1] W. A. Pantin, *Oxford Life in Oxford Archives* (Oxford 1972), 21-3. Curtis, 29. *Calendar of the Manuscripts of the . . . Marquis of Salisbury* (24 vols Historical Manuscripts
Commission 1883-1976) iv. 162, 165. On the office of chancellor see also ch. 3 above.

[2] Below, pp. 423-34, for the intervention of Leicester, Hatton and Buckhurst in university affairs.

the vice-chancellor was invariably nominated by the chancellor, whose power of appointment was officially established by the Laudian statutes of 1636. Under Leicester the vice-chancellor also came to be chosen exclusively from the heads of colleges and the canons of Christ Church.[1]

The vice-chancellor, acting as head of the chancellor's court, had wide powers over members of the university and over the town. His court had jurisdiction in minor criminal and in civil cases. It could punish breaches of the peace and immorality; it dealt with testamentary disputes and offences against university and college regulations; it heard cases of libel and defamation; it enforced the ecclesiastical laws; and, most often of all, it decided suits for debt. It was especially important as the principal, possibly the only, instrument which could eject recusants from halls. Until the reign of Elizabeth the jurisdiction of the court and, indeed, the privileges of the university had rested only upon royal grants by letters patent. Then, in 1571, was carried what Sir Edward Coke called 'this blessed act of parliament' (13 Elizabeth c. 29). The two universities were incorporated, the letters patent to Oxford of 14 Henry VIII were confirmed, and all the privileges, possessions and liberties of both Oxford and Cambridge were ratified. Authority that had once rested upon royal charters was now founded securely upon statute.[2]

The powers of the resident MAs in congregation were gradually eroded by the growing authority of heads within their own colleges and by the use of small committees of senior men to prepare business for congregation and convocation. The college became the focal point for the lives of most members and, as we shall see, the government largely worked through the heads of houses in enforcing its policies. The heads also came to exercise an increasing though informal role within the wider arena of the university. In 1569 Leicester ordered that nothing should go before convocation unless it had been approved by the vice-chancellor, the proctors, heads of houses and doctors; and from 1590 the preparation of business came to rest largely in the hands of the vice-chancellor and the heads.

This development was recognized and deplored at the time. Roger Jones BCL, fellow of New College and registrar of the chancellor's

[1] Pantin, 22–3. *Pepys Manuscripts* 46. For vice-chancellors see Wood, *Fasti* i. For the conflict of 1567 see below, 425.

[2] For the jurisdiction of the chancellor's court see Pantin, ch. 5, see also pp. 100–3 above. For the exercise of that jurisdiction under Elizabeth see Reg. Chanc. 1556–61; OUA Chancellor's Court Act Book 1561–6, Hyp./A/7; Chancellor's Court Act Book 1566–78, Hyp./A/8 and Chancellor's Court Depositions. For comments on 13 Elizabeth c.29: E. Coke, *The Fourth Part of the Institutes* (1797), ch. 44, 227–9; W. Blackstone, *Commentaries on the Laws of England* (4 vols Oxford 1765–9) iii. 83–5.

court, protested in 1597 that the vice-chancellor, heads of colleges and doctors had contrived to get all decisions into their own hands before meetings of convocation and congregation, which were consequently 'of small moment'. They no longer informed congregation of the business to be transacted in convocation. If any man dared to speak in convocation against the vice-chancellor's view he was 'discountenanced for sauciness' and threatened with imprisonment for breach of the peace. The vice-chancellor's power of imprisonment had given him effective control. In Jones's opinion such authority could only be damaging to the university, which would be governed by ageing men using it as 'a stirrup to mount themselves up to preferment'; the vice-chancellor expected to be rewarded with at least a deanery. Young men letting fall a loose word in a sermon would at once be punished by a convention of doctors, who hoped in this way to gain credit for themselves. In any case, age was not the best qualification for government, since the old are 'ruins of men'. Needless to say, such protests were vain. The oligarchy tightened its grip and its power was later formally enshrined in the hebdomadal board established by the Laudian statutes.[1]

Apart from the officers of the university, state and church were able to call upon certain external agencies for the control of Oxford. Occasional visitations had been used by Elizabeth's predecessors in 1535, 1549 and 1556 as instruments for enforcing conformity to religious change and for reforming various aspects of both universities. She herself appointed university visitors in 1559, but little has been recorded of their activities and probably their main role was to enforce the oath of supremacy.[2] The ecclesiastical commissions, especially the high commission in London, occasionally interfered in university affairs; but after a serious rebuff at Cambridge, where the vice-chancellor insisted on the university's independence from the high commission in 1573, it operated only occasionally and discreetly. It summoned John Travers of Magdalen in 1578, Edward Gellibrand of Magdalen and John Walward of Corpus in 1586 and dealt with one or two other cases thereafter; but, compared with its major role in the national enforcement of the religious settlement, it was relatively unimportant in the two universities.[3]

[1] Below, 426; Pantin, 27-8. Wood, *History and Antiquities* ii. 167-8, 199, 212-14, 241-5. Bodl. Wood MS d. 18 (Jones's 'apology'). Jones matriculated from New College as a probationary fellow in 1585 and was probably therefore in his late twenties when he wrote his 'apology'.

[2] Mark H. Curtis, *Oxford and Cambridge in Transition, 1558-1642* (Oxford 1959), 167-9 and 286 note J.

[3] H. C. Porter, *Reformation and Reaction in Tudor Cambridge* (Cambridge 1958), 146-8, 150-63. Curtis, 178-82. *APC* x. 250-4. Below, 419.

The privy council played a much more active role than the high commission and its registers are liberally sprinkled with instructions to the university authorities. Student disorders were to be quelled, investigated and punished.[1] Controversies between town and university were laboriously sifted and settled.[2] Innumerable disputes within and between colleges were heard or referred to commissioners for settlement: for instance in 1575 a suit between the master of Balliol and the principal of Magdalen Hall was sent for arbitration to Dr Humfrey and five others.[3] Instructions were issued for the repair of roads and bridges in the neighbourhood of Oxford.[4] In 1593 plays and players were forbidden within Oxford and Cambridge because of their 'lewd example'.[5] Above all, the privy council watched carefully over the religious life of the university and kept a steady pressure on the authorities to ensure conformity.[6]

College visitors had a critical function within the individual houses. Now that the colleges had achieved dominance within Oxford, control of them brought with it control of the university. Each college had been provided at its foundation with a visitor, who had the power to interpret statutes, to issue injunctions, to deprive heads and fellows, to settle disputes among the members and to carry out formal visitations, investigating the conduct of secular and spiritual business. The queen herself was the visitor at Christ Church; the archbishop of Canterbury at All Souls and Merton; the archbishop of York at Queen's; the bishop of Winchester at New College, Corpus Christi, Magdalen and Trinity; the bishop of Lincoln at Oriel, Lincoln and Brasenose; the bishop of Exeter at Exeter, the earl of Pembroke at Jesus; and the university itself, represented by the chancellor, at University College. The position at Balliol and St John's was slightly complicated. The fellows of Balliol had, in principle, the right to choose their own visitor, but in practice the bishop of Lincoln held that office until 1691, except for a brief period from 1637 to 1643 when Laud was visitor. At St John's the founder's statutes of 1562 appointed the bishop of Winchester, but a new set of statutes, issued in 1566, replaced him by William Roper and Sir William Cordell, master of the rolls. After some dispute between Cordell and the bishop, the office of visitor was assigned to Cordell for his lifetime; after his death in 1581 it reverted to the bishop. Thus, after 1581, all but three colleges were visited by

---

[1] For example, *APC* vii. 114, 118–19; x. 433–4; xvi. 276.
[2] For example, *APC* viii. 376–86; ix. 352–5. Cf. ch. 2.
[3] Ibid. x. 56.
[4] For example ibid. ix. 117, 120–1.
[5] Ibid. xxiv. 427.   [6] Below, 413.

bishops or archbishops, the bishop of Winchester supervising five, the bishop of Lincoln four, the archbishop of Canterbury two, the archbishop of York and the bishop of Exeter one apiece.[1]

ENFORCING RELIGIOUS POLICY

In 1559 earnest protestants viewed the state of Oxford and Cambridge' with alarm and repugnance. In January of that year both universities had endorsed convocation's affirmation of the Romanist doctrines of the mass and papal supremacy. In March, John Jewel lamented to Peter Martyr that ignorance and obstinacy had much increased since Martyr had left Oxford in 1553: religion and good learning were now abandoned. Two months later John Parkhurst warned Bullinger against sending his son to Oxford, for 'it is as yet a den of thieves, and of those who hate the light'; there were, he said, 'few gospellers . . . and many papists'. Jewel confirmed this gloomy pronouncement: only two persons were left at Oxford who thought with him and Bullinger, and they were broken in spirit. No doubt this picture of popish darkness was overdrawn, for a few protestants had remained in Oxford under Mary; but by and large her government had purged the universities speedily and effectively. Protestant fellows had mostly been ejected and catholic services fully restored in the university church and college chapels.[2]

It has been said that the Elizabethan authorities showed moderation in enforcing religious policy upon the universities and aimed at no more than outward conformity and seemly order.[3] They certainly showed moderation and caution in the early years of the reign, but it would be a mistake to suppose that they aimed merely at outward conformity or that the various authorities, civil and ecclesiastical, shared identical aims. Some of them, possibly most of them, regarded the universities as special communities, from which more must be demanded than from the nation as a whole. They were, after all, nurseries of the clergy, and unless the universities showed something more positive than outward conformity, the task of converting England to the protestant faith would be almost impossible.

[1] *VCH Oxon* iii, 69, 119. H. W. C. Davis, *A History of Balliol College* (Oxford 1899, revised by R. H. C. Davis and Richard Hunt, Oxford 1979), ch. iv. W. H. Stevenson and H. E. Salter, *The Early History of St. John's College, Oxford* (OHS new ser. i 1939), 129, 157–62, 227, 479–501. I am grateful to Dr G. D. Duncan for advice on the matter of college visitors.

[2] J. Strype, *Annals of the Reformation* (3 vols 1709; 4 vols Oxford 1824) i. 194–6. H. Gee, *The Elizabethan Clergy and the Settlement of Religion* (Oxford 1898), 3. H. N. Birt, *The Elizabethan Religious Settlement* (1907), 257–8. *The Zurich Letters*, ed. H. Robinson (2 vols Parker Society 1842–5) i. 11–12, 29, 33.

[3] Curtis, *Oxford and Cambridge in Transition*, 167.

The royal visitation of 1559 was the first thrust of the Elizabethan counter-attack. Unfortunately, its records have disappeared and we cannot fully assess its impact. Its intention was the enforcement of the oath of supremacy, and it may well not have been very insistent on further compliance. Two heads of houses, Wright of Balliol and Henshaw of Lincoln, resigned early in the reign without waiting to be dismissed. Three were deprived for religious non-conformity in 1559: Reynolds of Merton, Marshal of Christ Church and Slythurst of Trinity. One other head was ejected that year, Belsyre of St John's, but he was removed by the founder of the college for dishonesty and not for popery. Eley of St John's, who had replaced Belsyre, resigned in 1561, while Dugdale of University, Hodgson of Queen's, Coveney of Magdalen and Butcher of Corpus Christi were either ejected or persuaded to leave in the same year. Within two years of the Elizabethan settlement only one head elected under Mary remained in office: Whyte of New College. The protestant scythe had cut slowly but thoroughly.[1]

However, protestants had little more reason to be pleased with the condition of the university in 1561 than they had been two years earlier. Bishop Horne of Winchester found three of his four colleges —New College, Trinity and Corpus—largely hostile to the Elizabethan church; and probably they were more typical of the rest than was Magdalen, which he found 'conformable'.[2] Even Magdalen caused him trouble, for President Coveney, deprived of office by Horne as visitor, refused to go and appealed to the queen. The earl of Bedford, a strongly protestant courtier, urged Cecil to support Horne. Bedford's correspondent in Oxford, Richard Chambers, insisted that the appeal must be heard and rejected quickly, and that the protestant candidate, Laurence Humfrey, be given full backing. His advice was followed: Coveney's appeal was rejected by two common-law judges in November and Horne wrote to the fellows ordering them to proceed to an election. Many of the fellows were already predisposed towards Humfrey and had been encouraged by Richard Chambers to support him. At the first scrutiny there were five candidates and Humfrey secured 25 out of the 52 votes. On the second round he was elected unanimously. Horne had been able to

---

[1] This account is based mainly upon the histories and records of the colleges concerned, with assistance from Foster and the works of Antony Wood, which need to be treated with scepticism. See Curtis, 168, 286 note J. On the visitation of 1559 see Gee, 130-2, 136. On Belsyre see Stevenson and Salter, 123: Belsyre was probably a papist, but so too was the founder, Thomas White. On Hodgson see *Cal. Pat. Rolls, Elizabeth* ii. 1560-1563, 129-30. On Henshaw, Vivian Green, *The Commonwealth of Lincoln College 1427-1977* (Oxford 1979), 127.

[2] PRO SP 12/19, no. 56.

act at Magdalen because many of the fellows were hostile to Coveney and had appealed to their visitor against him. Elsewhere he was less fortunate.[1]

At New College Thomas Whyte clung to the wardenship in spite of the hostility of the reformers. Chambers wrote of him in September 1561:[2]

> as touching Mr. White of New College there is as yet nothing done, but I trust hereafter upon information given to the higher powers by further authority gotten more shall be done.

But Whyte trimmed his sails successfully and remained as warden until 1573 in spite of further charges of popery. The rest of the fellowship at New College was, however, drastically transformed. The college had long been one of the most learned and devout centres of catholic humanism. Over the past generation it had numbered John and Nicholas Harpsfield, Thomas Harding, Nicholas Sanders and Thomas Stapleton among its fellows. By 1558 both Harpsfield and Harding had left the college for other appointments. But Sanders and Stapleton were still there with a strong catholic following in the college, twenty-four of the fellows refusing to subscribe to the Elizabethan settlement as late as 1561.[3]

The purge of New College began in 1560, when six fellows were expelled and three—Stapleton, Sanders and John Fowler—resigned and went into exile. Within the next two years eleven more were deprived of their fellowships: and in 1564 five men were expelled for absence from the college, having presumably left to go overseas. Four more expulsions were made in 1565-8. Within ten years from the Elizabethan settlement twenty-nine men who had been fellows at the accession of Elizabeth resigned or were removed. In addition, nine fellows elected after 1558 were deprived or fled, four of them before 1568, five after.[4] Even this severe treatment did not turn New College into a protestant community. Horne's visitation of the college in 1566 revealed that the new forms of service were

---

[1] Ibid. nos 55, 55 i, 56. BL Harleian MS 6282, fo. 143. *Reg. Magdalen*, ed. Bloxam iv. 111-14. Horne's visitation of Magdalen College in 1566 suggests that there was little trace of popery in the college: see Magdalen College Archives MS 785.

[2] PRO SP 12/19, no. 55 i.

[3] Bodl. MS Top. Oxon. c. 354: a transcript made in 1901 of the visitation records in Bishop Horne's register. I owe this reference to the Reverend Christopher Dent.

[4] The evidence for these figures is largely based on the manuscript register compiled by Warden Sewell and kept in New College library. See Penry Williams, 'From the reformation to the era of reform 1530-1850' in John Buxton and Penry Williams (eds), *New College Oxford 1379-1979* (Oxford 1979), 48-51. On catholic humanists at New College see J. K. McConica, *English Humanists and Reformation Politics* (Oxford 1965), 44, 52-3, 99-101, 266, 271.

neglected, that twenty-three fellows refused to subscribe to the thirty-nine articles, and that several had not communicated since 1559. As late as 1571 the rood-loft was still standing and work-men were paid for removing it in that year. Not until 1576 do the visitation records suggest that New College had conformed in religion: the charges brought then and later against the college involved neglect of learning, loose living and financial mismanage-ment rather than popery. New College never became an active centre of protestant learning as it had once been of catholic humanism. But from about 1571 it was at least conformist and produced a few protestant preachers of some note.[1] The college has always been regarded as the heaviest sufferer from the Elizabethan settlement; and certainly the expulsions, deprivations and resignations far exceeded those of any other college. But one needs to remember that New College contained far more fellows than most: compared with fourteen or fifteen fellows of Merton at this time its fellowship body of seventy was huge. The real significance of the purge lay in the quality rather than the number of deprived New College catholics.

Horne found Corpus Christi no more conformable than New College. William Butcher had become president in 1559 after the deprivation of his predecessor, William Chedsey, earlier that year. Yet Butcher was thought by the visitor to be thoroughly unfit for the post. Unfortunately for Horne, since the fellows of Corpus refused to enter a complaint against their president, he could not legally act against him. Instead, he thought it best 'to travail with him voluntarily to resign his place', which Butcher finally did in 1561. Butcher's successor, Thomas Greenway, was financially suspect and quarrelled with the fellows. The visitation of 1556 shows the college split into fiercely warring factions, Greenway's enemies accusing him of taking bribes and sleeping with loose women. On Greenway's departure in 1568 the queen recommended William Cole, a strong protestant, who had been exiled in Zurich under Mary. The majority of the fellows preferred their own, less protestant candidate, Harrison, whom they elected. The queen annulled the election, appointed a special commission of visitation under Leicester, the chancellor, and had Cole installed. With the subse-quent expulsion of Harrison's supporters, Corpus seems to have

---

[1] For the records of visitations see New College Archives nos. 3093, 3688; Bodl. MS Top. Oxon. C.354; and *Visitation Articles and Injunctions of the period of the Reforma-tion*, ed. W. H. Frere and W. M. Kennedy (3 vols Alcuin Club xiv–xvi 1910) iii. 131–3, 182–3. Bursars' rolls for 1559–71 record structural changes in the chapel. There is a good description of the visitations in H. Rashdall and R. S. Rait, *New College* (1906), 124 ff. See also Williams in *New College Oxford*, 50–1.

been made securely protestant, becoming in later years distinctly puritan.[1]

In the fourth of Horne's colleges, Trinity, popish influence was long and firmly embedded. The Marian president, Thomas Slythurst, was quickly removed in 1559, but his successor Arthur Yeldard did little to instil protestant practice and belief. True, all the fellows subscribed to the thirty-nine articles in 1566; but four years later Horne harshly reprimanded the president and fellows for keeping popish ornaments and monuments, which he ordered to be destroyed at once. This seems to have been done, and six fellows resigned or were ejected in 1571. Even so, a strong, though discreet, popish element survived at Trinity into the 1580s. As late as 1583 four or five students left Trinity for Rheims: one of them, Richard Blounte, had been chosen as a probationer in Trinity in the face of explicit prohibition by the queen, after he had been ejected by Balliol. It seems that the influence of his aunt, Lady Paulet, a devout catholic and widow of the founder, had secured his admission to Trinity.[2]

In most colleges the establishment of protestantism was frustrated by obstacles similar to those which had confronted Horne. Apart from Magdalen, only Christ Church and Oriel were converted from popery with relative ease. Richard Marshall, the dean of Christ Church, had been deprived in 1559. When his successor George Carew resigned to take the deaneries of Bristol and of Windsor, the students, led by James Calfhill, the vice-dean, and Laurence Humfrey, the regius professor of theology, petitioned Robert Dudley to persuade the queen to appoint Thomas Sampson, a strong puritan, who had gone into exile under Mary. Their wish was granted, Sampson was installed and at once began the destruction of popish monuments, ornaments and missals.[3] At Oriel, Provost Smith had been elected in 1550, survived in office under Mary and bent again to the changes under Elizabeth. The principal Romanists in the college—William Allen, John Hemming and John Herniman—departed from Oxford early in the reign without any apparent fuss. Allen and Herniman, together with Richard Mucklestone, were deprived of their fellowships for absence in 1565. Allen became one of the most active and important of the English catholic exiles,

[1] PRO SP 12/19, no. 56. Thomas Fowler, *The History of Corpus Christi College* (OHS xxv 1893), ch. v. J. Strype, *Life and Acts of Edmund Grindal* (Oxford 1821), 196–7. *Cal. Pat. Rolls, Elizabeth* iv. *1566–1569*, 329. *Pepys Manuscripts*, 88.

[2] H. E. D. Blakiston, *Trinity College* (1898), 73–80. PRO State Papers Domestic Elizabeth, 161/13. Lady Paulet was the daughter of Walter Blount and widow of Sir Thomas Pope, founder of Trinity.

[3] BL Landsowne MSS 5, fo 4; 57, fo 226. H. L. Thompson, *Christ Church* (1900), 19–27. Strype, *Annals* i. 404.

founding the college at Douai in 1568. But his significance lay overseas rather than in Oxford.[1]

Elsewhere progress was much more difficult. The archbishop of
Canterbury himself had to contend with a strong and even violent
catholic element at Merton, where the struggles between factions were intense and dramatic. Thomas Reynolds, warden since
1545, was ejected in 1559; and William Tresham, David de la Hyde,
Anthony Atkins and Robert Dawkes were deprived of their fellowships in 1560 for refusing the oath of supremacy. From a fellowship of fourteen or fifteen members this was a high proportion of
expulsions.[2] Reynolds's successor, James Gervase, stayed for only
two years and resigned in 1561. By then there were two factions
within the college. One, led by William Hall and Roger Gifford, was
popish in sympathy and was supported by at least five other fellows.
Their opponents, headed by James Leech, just outnumbered them,
being eight in all; but they were not united on every issue. Hall was
accused of hiding popish books and monuments and of encouraging
other fellows to follow Romish ways. When James Leech sang an
English psalm, Hall snatched the book out of his hand. Another of
the popish party, Thomas Bynyon, struck one of his colleagues with
a dagger, and John Pott stole a book from the library—very
properly regarded as a most serious offence. In riposte Hall's party
accused Leech of committing buggery with John Pott, who confessed the offence.[3]

In the circumstances the election of Gervase's successor was unlikely to be very peaceful. According to the statutes the senior
fellows were to choose three candidates, from whom the archbishop
as visitor would select the warden. In 1562 the fellows chose no
fewer than five candidates, all of whom were rejected by the archbishop in favour of Mr John Mann, one of his own chaplains. After
Mann had read out his letter of nomination the fellows asked for
three days delay before admitting him. He presented himself at the
gate of the college on 2 April and was refused admission by the vote
of a majority. However, John Broke, the senior fellow, opened the
gate and Mann entered the college. The accounts differ on what
happened next. Wood says that Hall, now sub-warden, gave Mann
a box on the ears, while Strype, whose version is more plausible,
tells us that Hall snatched the statutes out of Mann's hands

[1] *Dean's Register of Oriel*, 147, 153, 155.

[2] G. C. Brodrick, *Memorials of Merton College* (OHS iv 1885), 49–50, 250, 260–1. *Reg.
ann. mert. 1521–67*, 188–9, 197.

[3] *Registrum Matthei Parker, diocesis cantuariensis, A.D. 1559–1575*, ed. E. M. Thompson and W. H. Frere (Canterbury and York Society xxxv, xxxvi, xxxix, 1928, 1933) i.
392–4, 398; ii. 684–717.

and had him carried bodily out of the college. Parker immediately issued a visitation, had Mann installed and got Hall, together with three of his followers, expelled.[1] Bitterness and contention continued to prevail at Merton for several years in spite of the removal of Hall, but it does not seem that the feuds of subsequent years were over religion.[2] Religious conformity had been bought in Merton at the cost of nine expulsions or resignations within five years. More general calm was achieved only with the passage of time.

At Queen's, on the deprivation of Provost Hodgson, Elizabeth, acting on the advice of the archbishops of Canterbury and York, nominated Dr Thomas Francis, regius professor of medicine, as his successor. When Francis and others arrived at the college for his installation, they found a large crowd gathered and the disturbance so great that they feared a violent onslaught. No reverence was shown to the assembled doctors or to the archbishop's letter of appointment. The resistance was such that Francis was only installed with the greatest difficulty.[3]

At St John's, founded by the devoutly catholic Thomas White, twelve fellows were deprived between 1567 and 1574, six of them members of the original foundation, the others appointed by the founder between 1559 and 1567. The most celebrated of them was Edmund Campion, who conformed at the beginning of the reign and even disputed before the queen in 1566. In 1569 he evidently had a change of heart, for he did not take the degree of BTh, to which he was entitled, and in 1570 he left Oxford for good.[4] Exeter was still considered to be strongly papist as late as 1578, in spite of the removal of John Neale, the first perpetual rector, in 1570. An anonymous source claims that it contained only four protestants out of eighty members, 'all the rest secret or open Roman affectionaries', especially one Savage. In May 1578 the privy council ordered the bishop of Exeter, visitor of the college, to issue a commission to the vice-chancellor and others, empowering them to eject unsuitable fellows and to reform abuses. After the death of the bishop in the next month, there was a vacancy in the diocese for a year, during which the bishop of Lincoln was called upon to renew the commission, which had become void, and to end the religious disorders

[1] Brodrick, 50–4. *Reg. ann. mert. 1521–67*, 209–16, 227–8. Wood, *History and Antiquities* ii. *148–51*. PRO SP 12/17 no. 21; 12/21 no. 57; 12/23 no. 31. J. Strype, *Life of Matthew Parker* (Oxford 1821) i. 228–32. *Reg. Parker* ii. 684–95.

[2] *Reg. ann. mert. 1567–1603*, 3, 8, 13, 18, 20. *Reg. Parker*, ii. 473–6, 486–97. Strype, *Annals* iii. 499–503.

[3] PRO SP 12/17, nos 7, 22. J. R. Magrath, *The Queen's College, Oxford* (2 vols Oxford 1921) i. 185–8. Strype, *Grindal*, 92. *Cal. Pat. Rolls, Elizabeth* ii. *1560–1563*, 129–30.

[4] Stevenson and Salter, *St. John's College*, 180–91, 320–41.

of the college. One major difficulty lay in the right of Sir John Petre, the catholic descendant of the great Tudor benefactor of the college, to nominate scholars, a right that he exercised to the limit and beyond, putting into Exeter several strong catholics.[1]

Balliol was deeply riven by religious feuds in the first decade of Elizabeth's reign. William Wright, restored as master under Mary, resigned with three other fellows in 1559; and a fourth followed them in 1560. His successor, Francis Babington, shortly moved to Lincoln. In 1565 the visitor, the bishop of Lincoln, issued a special commission of visitation to Laurence Humfrey, president of Magdalen, Mr Thomas Godwyn and Mr Richard Barber. Their injunctions suggest that the chapel services at Balliol were being conducted in a way far different from that laid down in the prayer book. They had to order that all fellows and scholars resort to chapel at the time of divine service and 'behave themselves in such godly manner that they hinder not the word of God', that morning prayer be said in English, and that the Bible, the communion book, the psalter and the homilies be purchased by the college. However, matters got worse rather than better in the next few years, for in 1568 Robert Parsons became a fellow of Balliol. Once a Calvinist, Parsons was already moving towards Rome. A man of outstanding intellectual ability and an excellent tutor, Parsons wielded great influence in the college and attracted many pupils. He quarrelled bitterly with the master, Adam Squier, whom he charged with peculation, and divided the college into warring factions. Eventually Parsons was forced by his opponents to resign and in 1574 he went to Louvain, joining the Jesuit order in the following year. However, his departure did not stifle catholicism in Balliol, for his followers preserved the tradition and, it was said, on resigning their fellowships handed them on to their own pupils.[2]

The crown did not restrict itself to enforcing uniformity within the colleges. A special commission was sent to Oxford in 1569 for searching out heretical books.[3] In June 1573 the privy council ordered the vice-chancellor to collect suspect literature and to deal with any persons who infringed the religious settlement; and in December that year a special commission of *oyer et terminer* was issued for imposing conformity within the university.[4] The sale of

[1] Strype, *Annals* iv. 196. *APC* x. 221, 295. PRO SP 12/160, no. 56.
[2] Davis, *History of Balliol*, 78. H. Foley, *Records of the English Province of the Society of Jesus* (7 vols 1875–82) vi. 678–80. PRO SP 12/146, no. 10. Balliol College Archives Register i. 108: injunctions of 4 March 1564/5; I am grateful to Mr R. E. Alton for this reference.
[3] *Pepys Manuscripts*, 166.
[4] *APC* viii. 120, 171.

popish literature continued to exercise the privy council for some years. Orders were sent down in 1573 for questioning a bookseller named Jenkes, who was still troubling the authorities as late as 1581.[1]

In 1577 the privy council ordered a religious census to be held in Oxford and elsewhere. Its results show that by then the crown had won substantial success in establishing protestantism within Oxford, although pockets of catholic resistance survived. The vice-chancellor reported that only four colleges contained any recusants: All Souls, Exeter, Balliol and Queen's. To this list we should probably add Trinity. Queen's and Balliol housed only one recusant each, and All Souls only three. Exeter was the least conformist of the colleges: three of its fellows were abroad in catholic cities, and five of its other members were suspect in religion—the names Catesby and Plowden suggest that they came from catholic families. The problem was more serious in the halls, where discipline was less strict, especially in Gloucester Hall and Hart Hall. Since the halls depended for survival upon the fees paid by residents their heads were reluctant to expose or expel men suspect in religion. Recusants in halls could, however, be brought before the chancellor's court. Robert Mowsehurst of Broadgates Hall was prosecuted there in 1567 as a disturber of the peace and 'a great talker against the religion that is now set forth'; and in 1578 proceedings were begun against six members of Hart Hall, including Randall, the principal.[2]

In spite of the success achieved by 1577 the government continued to feel uneasy about the threat of popery, and its anxiety was heightened by the entry of Jesuits and seminary priests into England during the next few years. In October 1581 the chancellor, Robert Dudley, earl of Leicester, warned the university that 'many papists have heretofore and may hereafter lurk among you, and be brought up by corrupt tutors'. He proposed various measures which were immediately adopted in the matriculation statute of that year. No student should be admitted to any college or hall unless he subscribe to the royal supremacy and the articles of religion, as well as being matriculated in proper form. Private tutors should only practise with the consent of the vice-chancellor, the head of his own house and at least two doctors, bachelors of divinity or preachers. Any tutor suspected of popery was to be deprived of his pupils unless he purged

---

[1] Ibid. ix. 347, 354; xiii. 34, 350, 399–400.

[2] Ibid. x. 87–8, 94–5. PRO SP 12/118, no. 37i; 12/119, no. 5i. For All Souls, *Correspondence of Archbishop Parker*, ed. T. T. Perowne (Parker Society 1853), 296–8, 300. For the halls: OUA, Hyp. B.1, 65, 68, 70–1. (I owe these references to the Reverend Christopher Dent.) For a detailed account of religious change in Lincoln College see Green, *Commonwealth of Lincoln College*, 127–45.

himself of the suspicion.[1] But by that date, in spite of Leicester's alarm, the battle against the catholics had been won.

Three general points may be made about the Oxford catholics and their ultimately vain struggle against the government and the church. First, some of them, like Nicholas Sanders and Thomas Stapleton, had been prominent in the Marian reaction; some, like Edmund Campion and Robert Parsons, seem only to have become firm opponents of the church of England during the early years of Elizabeth's reign; while others, like the twelve or fourteen Oxford men led to Rheims by Edward Stranchen in the 1580s, were converted by the missionaries later still. These men often differed among themselves about the role that they should play. Stapleton and Harding, for instance, devoted themselves to scholarly polemic, Saunders, Campion and Parsons to missionary work in the field; but there was no sharp distinction between the groups as such. Indeed, there were some scholars, such as Thomas Neale, regius professor of Hebrew, whose sympathies were catholic but who stayed within the established church. Loyalties and dividing lines were indistinct and uncertain.[2]

Second, while the government proceeded cautiously at both Oxford and Cambridge, its actions were ultimately more drastic at Oxford. Eight Marian heads of Cambridge colleges had ceased to hold office by 1560, but only two had been deprived. Many with distinctly Romanist views were allowed to remain in their lodgings for several years: Baker of King's until 1570; Caius at Gonville and Caius until 1573; Pory of Corpus until his death in 1570; and Perne of Peterhouse until he died in 1589. Pory and Perne, both elected under Mary, were highly influential in Elizabethan Cambridge. Nor did the protestant scythe cut so deeply into the Cambridge fellows as it did at Oxford: certainly no Cambridge college endured losses comparable to those of New College. Cambridge in general seems to have been less ardently Romanist than Oxford at the accession of Elizabeth and to have contributed less to the catholic movement abroad. Perhaps for that reason the government felt that it could deal more leniently with the younger university.[3]

Third, the Oxford catholics never formed a united movement

[1] Wood, *History and Antiquities* ii. 205–10. *Reg. Cong.* 1564–82, fos 338, 340. *Reg. Univ.* ed. Clark i. 167–8. *APC* xiii. 170.

[2] John Bossy, *The English Catholic Community, 1570–1850* (1975), 11–34, argues that there was a clear distinction between the 'conservative' Marian catholics and the 'spiritual enthusiasm' of later converts. For a refutation of this view and a more extended discussion of the problem, see Jennifer Loach, 'Reformation Controversies', 379 ff. above. On Stranchen see J. H. Pollen, *The Acts of the English Martyrs* (1891), 251–4.

[3] John and J. A. Venn, *Alumni cantabrigienses* (6 vols Cambridge 1922–7) i. Porter, *Reformation and Reaction in Tudor Cambridge*, 101–18.

as long as they remained within the university. Separate colleges, like Balliol, might find an influential papist leader such as Robert Parsons. But the battles were fought separately within the colleges and no organization was formed in the university as a whole to combat the encroachments of church and state. Probably this was inevitable, since the catholics were breaking the law and could only survive by clandestine activity within the colleges and halls. To have organized themselves under a leader would have been an invitation to disaster. Only when they left Oxford for the safe ground of Douai, Louvain or Rome could they come together as an open and organized force. The conduct of the Oxford puritans was, as we shall now see, utterly different.[1]

PROTESTANT RESISTANCE

In order to defeat the papists, authority had to call on the support of energetic and devout protestants, who often chafed at the tardy pace of ecclesiastical reform. Early in Elizabeth's reign two men were appointed to headships of colleges who later caused considerable trouble to the authorities: Laurence Humfrey, president of Magdalen, and Thomas Sampson, dean of Christ Church, both of whom entered office in 1561 with powerful support from their colleges, although only Humfrey was elected (Sampson was appointed by the queen at the urging of Lord Robert Dudley). For the next two or three years the authorities concentrated upon the task of erasing the remnants of popery, but as early as 1563 Humfrey and Sampson were protesting at the government's insistence on the wearing of the surplice and the special outdoor dress for the clergy prescribed in the injunctions of 1559. When in 1566 Archbishop Parker eventually issued his 'advertisements' at the command of the queen, Humfrey and Sampson led the opposition, which produced a protest signed by twenty prominent clerics. Humfrey and Sampson asked for more time to consider their position, but were peremptorily told by Parker that they must conform or be deprived; again they asked for more time. Humfrey's colleagues at Magdalen had already supported him by telling Parker that they had left off wearing the surplice of their own accord and not in order to please their president. At the same time both men were appointed to preach at St Paul's Cross, presumably by Grindal, greatly to Parker's fury.[2]

[1] A great deal more information on catholics in Elizabethan Oxford than I have been able to provide is to be found in C. M. J. F. Swan, 'The introduction of the Elizabethan settlement into the universities of Oxford and Cambridge, with particular reference to the Roman Catholics, 1558–1603' (Cambridge PhD thesis 1955).

[2] Patrick Collinson, *The Elizabethan Puritan Movement* (1967), 74. BL Lansdowne MS

The archbishop's commands were being resisted both at Oxford and at Cambridge, and Parker suspected Cecil of complicity, or at any rate lenience, with the dissidents: 'Execution, execution, execution of laws and orders must be the first and the last part of good governance', wrote Parker.[1] Sampson presented the government with a relatively easy target, since his appointment as dean belonged to the crown and in 1565 he was deprived of office—to become master of Wigston Hospital in Leicester under the patronage of the earl of Huntingdon.[2] But Humfrey could only be deprived by the visitor of the college—Bishop Horne of Winchester—after complaint by the fellows; and neither the fellows nor Horne would act. Humfrey therefore survived, to move into a more conformable middle age. The difference in treatment experienced by Humfrey and Sampson shows that the government, however much Parker resolved on securing obedience, was determined to keep within the law. In practice, the government seems to have won a partial victory, since Humfrey's resistance was moderated and there appears to have been a general conformity for some time. Sampson's successor, Thomas Godwin, was evidently a conformist, since he became dean of Canterbury two years later, and *his* successor Thomas Cooper, was frequently under attack from puritans after he had become bishop of Lincoln and then of Winchester. Sampson's loss was compensated to some extent by the election of William Cole as president of Corpus in 1568. Cole had had an impeccable protestant career, having been in exile at Zurich and Geneva; he had also preached to the Merchant Adventurers in Amsterdam, and was the first married president of the college. Unfortunately he was an incompetent—possibly even a corrupt—administrator, and the college was so riven with faction in his time that his religious influence was probably slight. An attempt to remove him was made in 1579 by an appeal to the visitor, which Cole countered by the plea that he should not again be forced into exile: 'What my good Lord, must I then eat mice at Zurich again?'[3]

Apart from Humfrey and Cole, the remaining heads of Oxford houses, after Sampson's removal, seem to have been moderate and obedient men. Nor were the professors—unlike Cartwright in Cambridge—markedly different. But trouble inevitably blew up

---

8, fos 17–18; *Correspondence of Parker*, 239–45; Strype, *Parker* i. 322–45, 367. Evidence that the fellows of Magdalen were refusing to wear the surplice is given in Horne's visitations of 1566: Magdalen College Archives MS 785.

[1] BL Lansdowne MS 8, fo 144.

[2] *Correspondence of Parker*, 243–5. Strype, *Parker* i. 367–75.

[3] Fowler, *Corpus Christi College* 127.

after the publication in 1572 of the puritan *Admonition to Parliament*, written by two Oxford graduates, Field and Wilcox, both based on London. The *Admonition*, which described bishops as drawn out of the 'pope's shop' and their government as 'Antichristian and devilish and contrary to the scriptures', evidently gained some support in Oxford: the privy council wrote to the vice-chancellor complaining of the stir and ordering that all dissident books should be collected by the vice-chancellor. Unfortunately we have no evidence as to the identity of the supporters of Field and Wilcox.[1] But it is clear that Humfrey, erstwhile leader of the puritans, disapproved. He visited the authors of the *Admonition* when they were in prison, to tell them that they 'overshot themselves'. At this stage he considered that the name and the work of a bishop were both 'commendable in Scripture'. A few years later he wrote to Burghley that he hoped to secure favour and countenance from the queen by his obedience.[2]

The limits of Humfrey's conformity were, however, to be defined and tested by the dispute which broke out in the late 1570s over Antonio del Corro, the controversial Spanish divine.[3] Corro had been converted to Lutheran doctrines while a member of the order of Observant Hieronymites in Seville. He had left Spain in 1557 and moved in uneasy exile across Europe, quarrelling with most of the Calvinist churches of Switzerland and France. He was accused of adhering to the heresies of Servetus and of being 'ambitious'. Essentially he favoured an eirenical, tolerant approach to religion and was naturally viewed with suspicion by his fellow-Christians. Having arrived in London in 1567 he was rejected by the refugee churches for his unorthodox views on divine election, but managed to secure, probably through Leicester's influence, a readership in theology at the Inner and Middle Temples. In 1576 he was commended by Leicester to the university of Oxford for the degree of DTh, without having already proceeded BTh. John Rainolds, later to be a leading figure among the Oxford puritans, urged upon Humfrey, who was then vice-chancellor, that a man suspected of heretical views on election and justification should not be allowed into the university. Convocation agreed that Corro be allowed to proceed to the doctorate only if he could first clear himself of heresy, but this he was unable or unwilling to do. Two years later Corro was more fortunate. Leicester recommended him for a lecturership and

---

[1] Collinson, 119. Wood, *History and Antiquities* ii. 172–4. Reg. Cong. 1564–82, fo 148.
[2] BL Landsowne MS 24, fo 52.
[3] Most of what follows on Corro is based on William McFadden, 'The life and works of Antonio del Corro, 1527–91' (Belfast PhD thesis 1953).

convocation, under the leadership of Vice-Chancellor Culpepper, one of Leicester's supporters, lifted its ban. Corro thereafter resided, in reasonable comfort, as *censor theologiae* at Christ Church until 1586. In 1582 charges were brought against him by the French church in London and Leicester ordered that any member of the university with complaints against Corro should bring them to convocation: no one stirred. Yet in spite of this victory Corro was deprived of his lecturership at Christ Church and his teaching posts in two halls four years later. His career shows that a man of decidedly unorthodox opinions could—with powerful backing—survive puritan attacks, but not indefinitely.[1]

By the mid-1570s Humfrey seems to have been largely discredited as a puritan leader, even—perhaps especially—within his own college. He was an autocratic but incompetent administrator, accused of showing more concern for his own finances than for the material well-being of his college. Growing discontent exploded into protest in 1575 when six fellows of Magdalen refused to take part in the election of a dean until certain controversies had been settled. Humfrey reacted vigorously, even dictatorially, by expelling all six of them, though he later relented over three. The expelled fellows, Cole, Powell and Lambard, wrote for advice to Laurence Tomson, an old Magdalen man who was closely tied to Field and acted as an agent of Walsingham. The dispute probably involved an element of personal hostility between Humfrey and the expelled fellows; but there is evidence that religion played its part since one of them mentioned 'too much preciseness in religion [on our part]' as a possible cause of the trouble. The controversy soon spread beyond the walls of Magdalen. Not only were Burghley and Walsingham involved but also, as Tomson disapprovingly noted, the ladies and gentlewomen of the bedchamber at court. Walsingham and Burghley urged Humfrey to be lenient, but the visitor, Bishop Horne, recommended the expulsion of the dissidents. What seemed at first to be a domestic storm soon involved the highest in the land.[2]

By the 1580s Humfrey's rule at Magdalen had become thoroughly discredited among the earnest puritans in Oxford. Serious allegations were made to the visitor by several of his colleagues. Edward Lord, who was to be one of Cartwright's co-defendants in Star Chamber in 1590, complained at the visitation of 1585 that in Magdalen communion was celebrated only two or three times a year, with a poor

[1] McFadden, op. cit., chs. 29–33. Wood, *History and Antiquities* ii. 180–4. Reg. Cong. 1564–82, fos 207, 214, 219, 260ᵛ.

[2] PRO SP 12/103, nos. 65–7, 71–4; 105, nos. 1, 2, 4, 12, 13, 16, 19, 20; 125, no. 38. J. R. Bloxam, *A Register of St Mary Magdalen College* (8 vols Oxford 1853–85) iv. 128. BL Lansdowne MS 24, fo 52.

attendance from the fellows, that disputations in divinity were performed 'dissolutely' and that theology lectures were seldom read. Manners were poor, swearing rife, and commoners showed little respect for the fellows. Furthermore, the college estates had been mismanaged and the president had allowed the woods to go to waste. Lord's charges were echoed by several of his colleagues, notably by Edward Gellibrand, who had been a fellow since 1573 and was by now a leading figure among the Oxford presbyterians. It is significant that Humfrey's puritan opponents charged him with two main deficiencies: failure to maintain religious discipline and instruction; and neglect of the college's endowment. In their eyes the latter was almost as important as the former—not because they were imbued with any 'capitalist spirit' but because they knew very well that a sound financial basis was essential to a nursery of godly preachers. It is impossible to say exactly how far Humfrey was guilty of the charges. But it seems likely that he had been negligent and certain that he no longer carried weight with the reforming protestants in Oxford.[1]

Despite these difficulties puritan agitation revived. But the new activists were much more radical than Humfrey had been, corresponding with the leaders of the London *classis* and attacking the office of bishop.[2] Their most vigorous member was Humfrey's enemy Edward Gellibrand; their most distinguished supporter was John Rainolds, appointed to a theology lecturership in 1586 on the recommendation of Sir Francis Walsingham. Most of the Oxford activists were drawn from Magdalen, Christ Church and Corpus Christi; and the university had strong links with the puritan ministers of Northamptonshire. In 1587 a presbyterian conference was held in Oxford, attended by Rainolds and also by Travers and Chark from other parts of the country. This seems to have been the high point of Oxford religious radicalism. An anonymous letter of 1586 describes heated controversies in the university over sermons preached by Rainolds, 'Walford' (probably Walward) of Corpus, and Gellibrand. The high commission ordered that Gellibrand and Walward be examined by the vice-chancellor and certain doctors, who eventually dismissed them without penalty after some disputation on the topics of non-residence and the authority of bishops. The two men were then summoned before the high commission itself, when Whitgift

---

[1] Magdalen College Archives MS 684. Macray, *Reg. Magdalen* ii. 101–18. The charges of maladministration are borne out by Bishop Cooper's visitation in 1585: Macray, iii. 11–24; Bloxam, *Reg. Magdalen* iii. 131 ff. *Reg. univ.* ed. Clark ii. 37.

[2] A *classis* was an assembly of representatives from a group of churches, usually consisting of a minister and a lay elder from each congregation. See Collinson, *Puritan Movement*, 300–2.

accused Gellibrand of inveighing against the titles of archbishop and
bishop, of impugning the bishop of Winchester and of asserting that
non-residents were worse than Jesuits. Gellibrand denied that his
remarks could be so interpreted. They were nevertheless sentenced
to be bound over in recognizances of £100 each, to refrain from
preaching and to read confessions. The author of the anonymous
letter, evidently a fellow of University College, reports that he and
his colleagues had left off wearing surplices and that when they were
challenged about this, they replied that neither the archbishop nor
the vice-chancellor had authority over them: they would obey only
their visitor, the earl of Leicester. The fellows of Magdalen also seem
to have been refusing to wear the surplice at this time.[1]

But in spite of this evidence of radical spirit the 1587 conference
saw the waning of the movement. Gellibrand had reported to Field
in 1584/5 that although there were many supporters of reform in
Oxford, some had not had time to peruse the book of discipline,
and others were young students 'of whom there is good hope, if
it be not cut off by violent dealing'. He himself left Oxford in 1588
to become minister of the English church at Middelburgh in the
Netherlands.[2] One of his supporters, William Hubbock of Magdalen,
was ejected from his fellowship and imprisoned for an offensive
sermon in 1589.[3] Chancellor Hatton, who succeeded Leicester in
1588, sent down orders that no student of theology should be
allowed to preach unless he subscribed to two articles: that the book
of common prayer contained nothing contrary to the word of God
and that the thirty-nine articles were agreeable to God's word. On
Hatton's death two years later, the puritans evidently hoped that
Essex might succeed him as chancellor.[4] But in spite of considerable
support for Essex, Archbishop Whitgift secured the election of Lord
Buckhurst, who could be relied on to support the episcopal establishment.[5]

In these years the crown managed to detach Magdalen College
from its position at the centre of Oxford puritanism. The manner

[1] BL Additional MS 38492, fo 480. A. Peel, *The Seconde Parte of a Register* (2 vols
Cambridge 1915) ii. no. 193. Dr Williams's Library: Morrice MS B fos 109–10. (I am grate-
ful to the Reverend Christopher Dent for a transcript of this document.) Bloxham, *Reg.
Magdalen* ii. 339–40. On links between Oxford puritans and Northamptonshire see W. J.
Shiels, *The Puritans in the Diocese of Peterborough* (Northants. Record Society xxx 1979),
96–8.

[2] [Richard Bancroft] *Daungerous Positions* (1593), 74–5. Collinson, *Puritan Movement*,
322–3.

[3] Ibid. 405.

[4] Wood, *History and Antiquities* ii. 237–40. Reg. Cong. 1535–63, fo 297. See also ibid.
fo 295[V] and *Statuta*, 440.

[5] Collinson, 428. Below, 423.

of this achievement was distinctly bizarre. After Humfrey's death in 1589 the queen directed that the college elect Dr Bond, one of her chaplains. The majority of the fellows replied that they could not in conscience do so, since they considered him 'light' in behaviour and deficient in administrative skill. Moreover, they had already chosen Ralph Smith, another of the queen's chaplains.[1] Their bland announcement of Smith's election disguised, however, some dramatic events. Magdalen's procedure for the election of a president was complicated. Each fellow nominated two candidates, and the votes were then counted by scrutineers. If any two men secured a clear majority they went on to the next stage; if not, fresh nominations were held until two men had a majority. In the second stage the thirteen seniors made the final choice.[2] The evidence is conflicting about events on the first round, but it seems clear that some of Bond's supporters, fearing that Smith had a majority among the seniors, tried to disrupt the election by tearing up the ballot papers. The vice-chancellor and proctors were called in to restore order and the election proceeded, with eight out of thirteen seniors voting for Smith. Bond's party then accused Smith and his supporters of standing for factious puritanism and argued that the queen's orders should be followed in order to maintain her prerogative, to win her friendship and to silence the puritans. They justified their continued resistance on the ground that some of the seniors had not been properly sworn in before the election. This view was ultimately upheld and Bond emerged as president.[3] He was not to have any easy time in office, for the puritans continued to harass him as much as they could.[4] But with Bond's election Magdalen ceased to be the leading puritan college in the university, a distinction that passed gradually to Corpus Christi.

Although radical presbyterianism seems to have been driven from Oxford in the late 1580s and early 1590s, and although Magdalen ceased to be the driving force behind Oxford puritanism, there remained, in the final years of the century, a group of protestant reformers in Oxford; and while their views were decidedly more moderate than those of Gellibrand, they continued to stir up controversy. Their leader was undoubtedly Dr John Rainolds, who became president of Corpus Christi in 1598. But by then Rainolds was more conciliatory in mood and in doctrine than he had been in the days of the classical movement. At Hampton Court he was spokesman

---

[1] BL Lansdowne MS 59, fo 14.
[2] BL Harleian MS 6282, fo 146.
[3] Ibid. fos 127, 132–3, 146. BL Lansdowne MS 75, fos 22–8.
[4] Magdalen College Archives MS 280, fo 53. BL Harleian MS 6282, fo 121.

for the moderate reformers.[1] Even so, he and his friends were coming to find themselves in difficulties in late Elizabethan Oxford. On 17 November 1602, the queen's accession day, the vice-chancellor, Dr Howson, challenged the puritans with a sermon in defence of ceremonies and feast-days. Attacking the catholics on the one flank for superstitious use of festivals, he criticized puritans on the other both for their excessively strict sabbatarianism and for denying the monarch's right to appoint feast-days. John Sprint, one of the leading Oxford puritans, replied to this with a general attack upon Howson, other university officers and the ceremonies of the church. Howson had Sprint imprisoned, and when his allies, notably Provost Airey and Robert Troutbeck of Queen's, launched a campaign of protest, the vice-chancellor appealed for support to the privy council. Airey, Sprint and Troutbeck were called to London for questioning, and forms of submission drawn up for all three to subscribe. Sprint and Troutbeck duly made public submissions but Airey seems to have avoided doing so, although he had earlier been suspended from preaching. Neither side could claim an unqualified victory: Airey survived largely unscathed, but the conservative forces seem for the moment to have occupied the commanding heights of the university. Howson and several heads of houses moved to the attack by charging the puritans with factiousness and by asking for a commission to proceed against them.[2] Congregation ordered all preachers and ministers to testify that the queen had, under God, the government of all her subjects in matters lay and ecclesiastical; that the book of common prayer and the ordination service contained nothing contrary to the word of God; and that they allowed the articles of religion.[3] When the Millenary Petition was presented in the following year to James I, a semi-official answer was sent to the king from the vice-chancellor, proctors, doctors and several heads of houses, opposing the puritan position.[4]

Oxford, then, was scarcely less puritan than Cambridge in the reign of Elizabeth. Cambridge led the movement, with Thomas Cartwright at its head, in the 1570s, but Humfrey and Sampson were probably more important in the vestiarian controversy of the

[1] Collinson, 455–62.

[2] Wood, *History and Antiquities* ii. 271–8. *Cal. SP Dom. 1601–3*, 290. J. Howson, *A Sermon Preached at St. Maries in Oxford, the 17 Day of November, 1602* (Oxford 1602), *passim*. I am grateful to the Reverend Christopher Dent for helping me to elucidate this complex set of events, see his *Protestant Reformers in Elizabethan Oxford* (Oxford 1983) for a more ample discussion.

[3] Reg. Cong. 1595–1606 fo 153. Wood, *History and Antiquities* ii. 277–8. The entry in the register suggests that these articles were reissued at the start of the reign of James I.

[4] *The Answer of the Vice-Chancellor, Doctors, both Proctors and other Heads of Houses in the University of Oxford ... to the Humble Petition* (Oxford 1603). Collinson, 452.

previous decade than any of the Cambridge puritans; and both universities played a significant role in the classical movement. But Cambridge has gained a reputation as the more puritan university. Partly this may stem from the founding of Emmanuel College. Partly it may be due to the greater savagery with which the controversies were conducted in Cambridge. In the Oxford colleges there were no battles between puritans and their opponents to match the vindictive disputes at St John's, Cambridge. The two greatest Oxford puritans, Humfrey and Rainolds, fairly quickly abandoned their radical stance and adopted more moderate postures. By contrast Cartwright maintained the radical position much longer, although he too conformed in old age. Above all, there was no one in Oxford to compare with John Whitgift, who became master of Trinity in 1567 and hammered the Cambridge puritans relentlessly. With Whitgift setting the tone of controversy, moderation and compromise were impossible.[1]

THE RULE OF LEICESTER

The most influential single figure in Elizabethan Oxford was undoubtedly Robert Dudley, earl of Leicester, chancellor of the university from 1564 until his death in 1588. Vice-chancellors might have a closer, more direct and more intimate authority, but their tenure was brief. In the early part of the reign they usually held office for a three-year period, but after Laurence Humfrey's long reign as vice-chancellor from 1571 to 1576, Leicester decided that in future the post should change hands each year, and so it normally did, except that Dr James of Christ Church held it from 1590 to 1592, Dr Lilley of Balliol from 1593 to 1596 and Dr Ravis of Christ Church from 1596 to 1598.[2] Before his election as chancellor Leicester had had close contact with the university, especially with Christ Church, where he had strongly and successfully backed Thomas Sampson for the deanery. In December 1564 Sir John Mason, chancellor since 1559, resigned, recommending Leicester as his successor. The recommendation was accepted by convocation.[3]

Leicester's reputation as chancellor has not stood high. The catholic polemic *Leycesters Commonwealth* accused him of bringing the university near to destruction.[4] The anonymous author charged

[1] For Cambridge puritanism see Porter, *Reformation and Reaction in Tudor Cambridge*, *passim*; Peter Lake, *Moderate Puritans and the Elizabethan Church* (Cambridge 1982).

[2] Reg. Cong. 1564–82 fo 216^V.

[3] Ibid. fos 6, 6^V.

[4] *Leycesters Commonwealth*, 96–9. This was an anonymous work, now thought to have been written by Charles Arundell, a catholic courtier who had emigrated to Paris. It was first

Leicester with atheism and lamented the dissolution of order, discipline and learning under his rule: 'the public lectures abandoned . . .; the Taverns and ordinary tables frequented; apparel of students grown monstrous . . . '. These words were substantially echoed by Antony Wood writing nearly a century later. Leicester, he claimed, had allowed the university to become 'debauched and very loose', ruling it through a small band of favourites: Dr Walter Bayley of New College, physician to the queen; Dr Martin Culpepper, warden of New College; Mr Thomas Allen, principal of Gloucester Hall; and Mr Arthur Atye, fellow of Merton and ultimately Leicester's personal secretary. Wood—a man of strong prejudices—claimed that Leicester found the university flourishing and left it in disorder.[1] There is certainly much evidence of scandals, slackness and abuses at the time of Leicester's death. But there is also a great deal to suggest that they were rampant at the time he took office.

Whatever one may say of Leicester one cannot charge him with neglecting the university of Oxford. He took a close and continuous interest in its proceedings, issuing general directives, recommending or appointing men to offices, and—more dubiously—securing leases of land for his friends. He visited Oxford at least six times: late in 1565 or early 1566; then with the queen in August 1566; and again in 1569, 1572, 1583 and 1585.[2] His predecessor, Sir John Mason, had left little impression upon the university, but Leicester's election marked the beginning of a long series of letters from the chancellor to convocation, congregation and the university's officers, reprimanding, ordering and advising them about a wide range of affairs. Comparison of the university's registers before 1564 with subsequent volumes shows a sudden intensification of the chancellor's activity under Leicester.[3] His concern with the minutiae of academic life—sermons, disputation and dress—as well as with patronage, is surprisingly detailed. On 8 February 1565 he informed the doctors and proctors that he had received their notes for new statutes, liked them very well, and having discussed

---

printed abroad in 1584 and reprinted, probably in England, in 1641. I have used the edition prepared by F. J. Burgoyne (1904).

[1] Wood, *Annals* ii. 231 ff. Wood's assessment of Leicester is very similar to that in *Leycesters Commonwealth* and may well have been based upon it: for that reason it is even less to be trusted than most of Wood's judgements.

[2] HMC, *Pepys MSS*, 155. I owe the information on Leicester's visits to Dr Simon Adams, who has supplied me with the following references: Bodl. Rawlinson MS D 837, fo 17; PRO, State Papers Domestic Elizabeth (SP 12) 89/6; E. K. Chambers, *The Elizabethan Stage* (Oxford 1923), 129, note 3.

[3] Compare Reg. Cong. 1564–82 with the earlier registers Reg. Cong. 1518–35; Reg. Cong. 1535–63.

them with the vice-chancellor wished them to be promulgated. He intimated that he wanted provision to be made for a sermon at the start of each term and for more frequent disputations. Convocation agreed to the first but postponed deliberation of the second. The *nova statuta* were the fruit of these deliberations. They emphasized the importance of academic exercises, laid down the titles of books for study—mostly those already in use—ordered that an English sermon be preached every Sunday, abolished some obsolete statutes relating to masses, regulated apparel, established a register of matriculation and settled fees for undergraduates according to rank.[1]

Two years later the chancellor wrote in less friendly terms. His recommendation for the post of vice-chancellor had been ignored and convocation had failed to agree on any of the candidates. Leicester reprimanded them for their fickleness, hinted that he would regard Laurence Humfrey as a suitable choice and ordered fresh elections to be held. Convocation duly met and elected Thomas Cooper, dean of Christ Church, later to become bishop of Lincoln and then of Winchester. Leicester offered no opposition to this election and asked Cooper to continue as vice-chancellor in 1568, 1569 and 1570. The chancellor's letter of 17 April 1570 makes it clear that in future he intended to nominate the vice-chancellor, whose election by convocation would henceforth be a formality. In the following year, when Cooper was promoted to the bishopric of Lincoln, Leicester named Humfrey as his successor and ensured his reappointment, perhaps against Humfrey's own wishes, for the next four years.[2]

In 1568 Leicester issued the first of many thunderous complaints about the conduct of the university's affairs when he criticized the disorderly proceedings at the election of proctors. A committee was appointed to look into the matter but its deliberations evidently had little effect, since Leicester remonstrated again about the proctorial elections in 1574: factious dealing had, he claimed, influenced the result—in particular the practice of men long absent from Oxford coming back especially to vote. Another committee was appointed and drew up statutes on the electoral procedures.[3] These do not seem to have solved the problem, for Leicester wrote once more in 1576. He had evidently asked for the previous year's proctors, John Underhill of New College and Henry Savile of Merton, to be re-elected, but had been denied this by convocation, which had allowed his request to be 'overthwarted' by a small faction led by a man newly arrived

[1] Reg. Cong. 1564–82, fo 7ᵛ. *Statuta*, 378–96. *Pepys Manuscripts*, 47.
[2] Reg. Cong. 1564–82, fos 39ᵛ–40, 93, 106, 123ᵛ, 145.
[3] Ibid. fos 63–4ᵛ, 165, 168.

from Cambridge. Convocation gave way before the chancellor's anger and allowed him to nominate the proctors himself for that year only. He duly chose Savile and Underhill; the latter was Leicester's own chaplain and later became, through his influence, rector of Lincoln College. This appears to have seen the end of disputes about proctorial elections during Leicester's term of office.[1]

He had, however, turned his attention before this to the procedures of convocation itself. A committee had been appointed in 1569 to reform the methods of public voting and had produced a draft acceptable to Leicester. Unfortunately the proposals were not acceptable to convocation, which had, in Leicester's word, 'impugned' them. The central issue lay in the proposal that a steering committee, composed of the vice-chancellor, proctors, doctors and heads of colleges, should prepare the agenda of convocation. This had been rejected by members of convocation who desired what Leicester called 'immoderate liberty'. The chancellor ordered convocation to conform to the new proposals and the evidence suggests that it did. Henceforth the larger democracy of convocation was 'guided' by a small oligarchy of senior men.[2]

Twelve years after Leicester took up the office of chancellor he expressed grave concern over general disorders within the university. Convocation had, in October 1576, set up a committee for reforming various matters, especially in connection with the public academic exercises. The committee's proposals were sent to Leicester, who gave them his approval and also ordered the execution of the university's statutes on apparel.[3] Three months later Leicester again wrote to convocation, enclosing the queen's recent proclamation against excessive luxury and ostentation in dress. The chancellor sharply observed that reform of abuses in apparel had often been attempted at Oxford but never to any effect. The officers of the university and the heads of colleges were now to impose effective discipline: in future breaches of the law would bring punishment not only on the offender himself but also upon negligent officials.[4] From this date onward Leicester, pressed by the queen, constantly bombarded the university with reprimands about the disorderly apparel of its members. In 1579 he threatened to remove—or do his best to remove—any head of a house who failed to enforce the laws. Graduates were to wear the dress appropriate to their degrees, all members to cast off 'great ruffs, silks, and velvets, and cuts in hose and

[1] Reg. Cong. 1564–82, fos 209^V–12.

[2] Ibid. fos 26^V, 93^V, 126^V. Above, 402.

[3] Ibid. fos 222^V, 223, 228. Wood, History and Antiquities ii. 185.

[4] Reg. Cong. 1564–82, fo 230^V. P. L. Hughes and James F. Larkin, Tudor Royal Proclamations, ii. The Later Tudors (1553–1587) (New Haven and London 1969), nos. 623, 646.

doublets'. Such things were not seemly for students.[1] A few weeks before his death he was writing to complain of the renewed abuses in dress. He laid the blame upon heads of colleges for their negligence and threatened to visit Oxford soon to see for himself the improvement that he wanted.[2] Death intervened before he could come. The concern with apparel is almost obsessive and indicates the importance attached by the crown and the political élite to the ordering of ranks within society, an ordering which should be— but seldom was—reflected in the dress of its members.

Leicester's concern was not however confined to the dress of university members. In August 1579 he told convocation that he had been informed of great faults in the public exercises of the university, blame for which had been laid upon himself. It greatly grieved him to hear 'what negligence and slackness' were reported in lectures and disputations. These matters, unlike apparel, were the very substance of the university and the abuses must be corrected.[3] In 1583 he sent further letters of reproach about the defects in university statutes and neglect in their observance, following them up with a report that the queen herself had criticized him for these shortcomings. He wished, he said, that members of the university could have heard her words and seen her countenance. One consequence of Leicester's admonition was the passing of the elaborate statute of 1584 which attempted to reform some of these defects. Under the statute all terms were to be fulfilled before graces could be proposed; every bachelor had to read six lectures on Aristotle; every student in theology was to preach according to seniority; speeches in convocation and congregation were to be made in Latin; ministers of religion were forbidden to play football; and common players were excluded from the precincts of the university. Finally, scholars were admonished to behave with modesty, patience and reverence, and were warned not to 'gad up and down the streets'.[4]

Leicester also lamented the failure to eliminate popery. In 1579 he wrote of England generally that 'the papists were never in that jollity they be at this present', and in 1582 that the queen's neglect of their increase endangered her estate. In 1581 he complained to the university authorities that many papists 'lurke among you' and ordered them to ensure that no student be admitted to any hall or colleges without first subscribing to the articles of religion and taking

---

[1] Reg. Cong. 1564–82, fos 261, 288^V, 289, 388. Wood, *History and Antiquities* ii. 207.
[2] Reg. Cong. 1582–95, fos 227^V, 241, 242.
[3] Reg. Cong. 1564–82, fo 289.
[4] Reg. Cong. 1582–95, fos 231^V, 234^V, 236, 241, 242. *Statuta*, 431–4.

the oath of supremacy. His command was duly incorporated by convocation into the matriculation statute of 1581.[1]

If words and statutes could have cured the ills of the university, then all would have been well. Leicester cannot be accused of passively tolerating the abuses of Elizabethan Oxford. But the insistent repetition of his tirades and the repetitions by later chancellors of the same themes suggest that his strictures did little good.

He had a much more direct and visible effect on appointments to positions than on the general conduct of the university. As chancellor he nominated the public orator: Thomas Kingsmill, Arthur Atye and Thomas Smith all owed their tenure of this position to him.[2] Richard Hooker became deputy lecturer in Hebrew at Leicester's recommendation.[3] Thomas Cooper had his support for the post of vice-chancellor in 1568 and probably for the bishopric of Lincoln. As we have seen, Antonio del Corro owed his lectureship to Leicester.[4] His influence was as great within the colleges as it was within the university generally. He supported Sampson for the deanery of Christ Church in 1561, and when Sampson was deprived of that office helped to obtain for him the mastership of Wigston Hospital, Leicester.[5] He probably backed William Cole for the presidency of Corpus Christi; and when Cole was expected to resign in 1579 he intervened on behalf of Mr Barefoot, chaplain to Leicester's brother, the earl of Warwick.[6] Francis Babington, reputedly Leicester's own chaplain, became rector of Lincoln in 1560, only to be deprived for popery three years later. The chancellor's next appointment at Lincoln, John Bridgewater, another of his chaplains, was no more successful, for in 1574 he too was deprived and migrated to Douai.[7] Leicester again intervened very strongly at Lincoln in 1577 when he supported John Underhill, yet another of his chaplains, for the rectorship. This attempt nearly led to failure, since Leicester discovered that the queen and the archbishop were supporting other candidates. He managed to dissuade the other men from standing and then, when the fellows chose someone else, com-

---

[1] Reg. Cong. 1564–82, fo 314. Wood, *History and Antiquities* ii. 205–10. *Statuta*, 420. On Leicester's anxiety about popery see his letters in BL Harleian MS 6992, fo 112, and PRO SP 12/155, nos. 80–1, references that I owe to Dr Simon Adams.

[2] Reg. Cong. 1564–82, fos 15ᵛ, 131, 351.

[3] Ibid. fo 288.

[4] McFadden, 'The life and works of Antonio del Corro', ch. 31. Above, 417.

[5] Claire Cross, 'Patronage in the Elizabethan Church', *Historical Journal* iii (1960), 8.

[6] Fowler, *Corpus Christi*, 124–8, 139.

[7] Green, *Commonwealth of Lincoln College*, 127–38. Evidence connecting Bridgewater to Leicester is in PRO SP 15/27a, no 256, and in BL Lansdowne MS 443, fos 126, 141ᵛ. I am indebted to Dr Adams for these references.

plained that he believed they had wanted Underhill. In spite of the earlier election and after strong resistance from the fellows he got his man chosen.[1] William James, elected master of University College in 1572 and appointed dean of Christ Church in 1584, was certainly Leicester's man and attended him on his deathbed.[2] Finally, although there is no evidence that Martin Culpepper owed to Leicester his election as warden of New College in 1573, he was reputedly one of the chancellor's closest associates within the university. Two principals of Gloucester Hall, Thomas Allen and John Delaber, were certainly among Leicester's protégés.[3]

Probably many fellows of colleges owed their position to the chancellor. One of them, John Harmar, fellow of New College, can speak for them all, and in so doing sum up the nature of the earl's patronage. In dedicating to Leicester his translation of Calvin's *Sermon on the Ten Commandments*, Harmar praised 'your honour's good procurement of her majesty's gracious favour, whereby I first became a scholar in Winchester College, afterward to be removed to the New College of Oxford . . ..' Harmar later became regius professor of Greek through Leicester's influence.[4]

Leicester's patronage was valuable, not only for securing posts within Oxford, but also for helping prominent university men to preferment outside. He persuaded the queen to appoint Willis, the president of St John's, to the vacant deanery of Worcester. Willis was opposed by Archbishop Whitgift, who described him as a man whose skill lay in husbandry rather than in scholarship and whose wife, sister and daughter were of ill repute. 'God forbid', wrote Whitgift to Burghley, 'that such a man should be placed there.' Nevertheless, Leicester's influence prevailed against the archbishop and Willis obtained the deanery, allegedly as a *quid pro quo* for getting Leicester's 'good servant' John Delabere elected principal of Gloucester Hall and for granting leases of college property to Leicester's friends. The knowledge that preferment could be speeded by the government and by courtiers probably helped to make the university susceptible to

[1] The complicated story of Underhill's election is fully told in Green, 139–42.

[2] W. Carr, *University College* (1902), 87–9. On James's connection with Leicester see, for example, *Cal. SP Foreign* xxi. pt 2, 51–4; Bodl. Tanner MS 78, fos 155–6; J. Harrington, *Nugae antiquae* (1779, repr. 2 vols 1804) ii. 268. I am again indebted to Dr Adams for these references.

[3] According to Wood, Leicester secured the right to nominate principals of halls: Wood, *History and Antiquities* iii. 653. I owe this reference to Dr G. D. Duncan. But this is uncertain, since Delabere was named principal of Gloucester Hall by St John's in 1581: Stevenson and Salter, *Early History of St. John's*, 223. Above, 413. In a controversy over the election to the principalship of St Edmund Hall in 1601 it was alleged by Queen's College that they elected the principal and the chancellor 'allowed' their choice: *Cal. SP Dom. 1601–3*, 20–2.

[4] Eleanor Rosenberg, *Leicester, Patron of Letters* (New York 1955), 218.

external influence, as Roger Jones complained. Out of twenty-seven
men who held the office of vice-chancellor under Elizabeth, nine
reached the episcopal bench and five others became deans of
cathedrals: university office was obviously a valuable qualification
for clerical preferment.[1]

The earl of Leicester has generally been considered a great patron
of the puritan cause. Certainly, within Oxford and outside it, many
puritans had reason to be grateful to him: Sampson, Humfrey, Cole
and Kingsmill were among their number. But he also supported
Francis Babington and John Bridgewater, who were papists, Antonio
del Corro, a heretical protestant and Richard Hooker, the greatest
opponent of puritan ideas. Leicester's patronage seems to have been
eclectic, and it may not be naïve to think that he was as much concerned with attracting able scholars to Oxford as with the promotion
of a particular party.[2] In one instance especially his patronage had
lasting, important and beneficial results. Joseph Barnes, the printer,
had been lent £100 by convocation in 1584 to enable him to set up
a press in Oxford, and a petition was soon afterwards sent to the
chancellor asking him to procure from the queen a licence allowing
Barnes to print in the university—at that time regulations governing
the press allowed printing only in London. Evidently the licence was
granted, although it does not survive, and in 1585 Barnes printed
John Case's *Speculum moralium quaestionum*, dedicating it to
Leicester with an encomium on the advantages to the university of
a press 'which by your means our university has lately obtained'.
Although the press was privately owned by Barnes, it marks the true
beginning of the Oxford university press, perhaps Leicester's major
legacy to the university.[3]

In other respects Leicester's patronage was damaging. The colleges
possessed large estates, from which profitable leases could be
extracted. Leicester seems to have requested and obtained several
leases from St John's for himself and for his friends, including his
secretary Arthur Atye.[4] The most notorious college lease obtained
through Leicester's patronage was of Merton's manor of Malden with
Chessington Park. These were leased to the queen for no less than
five thousand years, the queen sub-letting the manors to the earl of
Arundel. It is probable that this highly favourable bargain was wrung

---

[1] *Salisbury Manuscripts* iii. 153. Stevenson and Salter, 223–4, 262. Cf the comments of
Roger Jones cited above, 402–3.

[2] See James McConica, 'Humanism and Aristotle in Tudor Oxford', *EHR* xciv (1979),
299 n. 3.

[3] H. G. Carter, *A History of the Oxford University Press* i (Oxford 1975), 19–22.

[4] Stevenson and Salter, 223 ff, 265. St John's College Archives Vetus Registrum, fos 205–
6; Mun. xiii, no. 19.

out of the college by Leicester, acting through Atye, then a senior fellow of Merton.[1]

During Leicester's chancellorship two parliamentary statutes were enacted which were significant for Oxford and Cambridge. Although it is unlikely that the earl had a hand in either, they may conveniently be mentioned here to round off this account of Leicester's term of office. The first, 13 Elizabeth c. 29, has already been discussed: it put the privileges and jurisdiction of both universities upon a sound and statutory footing.[2] The second, carried in 1576, was designed 'for the better maintenance of learning and the better relief of scholars'; more specifically it was intended to protect college revenues against inflation. Probably designed by Sir Thomas Smith and certainly guided by him through the house of commons, the statute provided that one-third of all rents due to colleges in Oxford, Cambridge, Eton and Winchester should be paid in corn valued at a fixed price.[3]

THE RULE OF HATTON AND BUCKHURST

The earl of Leicester died in August 1588 and his successor, Sir Christopher Hatton, was elected chancellor of the university in September.[4] Hatton was already lord chancellor of England, a man well placed in the favour of the queen and an unrelenting enemy of the puritans. He at once showed every intention of taking his duties at Oxford seriously. On 12 October he asked convocation to send him an account of his new office, especially of its powers, and also a statement of the deficiencies and disorders in the university. A committee was appointed to draw up a suitable reply.[5] In January 1589, possibly in consequence of the committee's answer, Hatton ordered the strict execution of religious tests and then, in August, delivered a long set of injunctions to be read publicly in convocation. His letter did not propose any new decree, but insisted, in some detail, on the strict observation of the existing statutes. Hatton gave special emphasis to the proper execution of all decrees, especially those concerning religion. He suggested a single formula for religious subscription where it was required (although he allowed

[1] *Reg. ann. mert. 1567–1603*, 66–7. On Atye see G. Ungerer, *A Spaniard in Elizabethan England: the correspondence of Antonio Perez* (2 vols 1974) ii. 250–3, 256–8. I am greatly obliged to Dr J. R. L. Highfield for throwing light on this incident and for the references to Ungerer's work. For Merton's later protest against the lease see Bodl. MS Wood 423 (12).

[2] Above, 402.

[3] *Statutes of the Realm* iv. pt 1; 18 Eliz. 1 c. 6. Mary Dewar, *Sir Thomas Smith: a Tudor intellectual in office* (1964), 185–6.

[4] Reg. Cong. 1582–95, fo 293ᵛ.

[5] Ibid. fo 294ᵛ.

the matriculation statute to vary from it). All those required to subscribe—for instance all those taking degrees—must confess that the prayer book contained nothing contrary to the word of God, that its form for administering the sacraments might lawfully be used and that the articles of religion were agreeable to the word of God.[1] Hatton's concern about the university may also have been in part responsible for a parliamentary statute of 1589 'against abuses in elections', although it probably had other promoters as well. An earlier bill had been introduced in 1576, perhaps at the instigation of Sir Thomas Smith, and after passing both houses had been vetoed by the queen. The new bill was successful, although it was amended more than once after its introduction into the house of lords on 17 February 1589. The final act lamented that elections in colleges were often accompanied by gifts and bribes, so that the fittest persons 'are seldom or not all preferred'. It laid down that if any fellow of a college or member of a university received a reward for his vote then his position would become vacant as if he 'were naturally dead'. Men taking bribes to resign their fellowships would be fined double the amount of the bribe. The statute was to be read out at the election of every fellow, as it still is in New College at the present day.[2]

For a few months Hatton's attitude in his dealings with the university was conciliatory, but on 8 July 1590 he ordered the vice-chancellor, Dr Bond of Magdalen, to read out in convocation a searing denunciation of the state of the university: lectures and disputations had been neglected; Hatton's own orders about religious subscription had been ignored; Latin was not spoken in colleges; abuses in dress were as rife as ever. The vice-chancellor, with some courage, refused to read the letter publicly. There is, significantly, no reference to it in the register of convocation; but equally significantly Bond resigned the vice-chancellorship on 16 July, exhausted by the burden imposed on the office by the prevailing disorders. Two days later he wrote to Richard Bancroft, excusing his conduct on the ground that a public reading of Hatton's accusations would have brought disgrace upon him and pointing out the injustice of many of the criticisms. He begged Bancroft to intercede with Hatton on his behalf. Bond's resistance does not seem to have led him into any trouble and his successor brought in certain decrees to satisfy Hatton. The incident shows that the oppressive interference of a chancellor could be effectively resisted and that moderation and conciliation were often the best way to reformation.[3]

[1] Reg. Cong. 1582–95, fos 295[V], 297. Wood, *History and Antiquities* ii. 234–40.

[2] *Statutes of the Realm* iv. pt 2, 31 Eliz. 1 c. 6. *House of Lords Journals* ii. 150, 156, 161, 164. Dewar, *Sir Thomas Smith*, 186.

[3] Reg. Cong. 1582–95, fo 246. Wood, *History and Antiquities* ii. 241–5. BL Harleian

Hatton's rule was in any case brief, for he died in 1591. Two candidates were proposed in convocation as his successor. One, the hope of the puritans, was Robert, earl of Essex, the young favourite of the queen. The other was Thomas Sackville, Lord Buckhurst, an elder statesman, a privy councillor and a man of some literary achievement who had collaborated in *The Mirror for Magistrates* and in *Gorboduc*. Essex's 'agent' at Oxford calculated that the earl could count on 200 out of 280 votes in convocation. But the influence of the queen, working through Dr Bond, was brought to bear against him, and after some disturbances in convocation Buckhurst was elected. He was clearly the candidate not only of the queen but also of the enemies of the puritans.[1]

In his letter of acceptance in January 1592 Buckhurst urged the discovery and punishment of Jesuits and recusants, an order which he repeated in the following April. His most solemn pronouncement to the university came in 1594, when the vice-chancellor read out a letter in which Buckhurst ordered the purge of all Romanists, the observance of rules concerning lectures, disputations and other exercises and the execution of regulations about dress. According to Antony Wood this letter succeeded—where Leicester and Hatton had failed—in bringing about a reform of conduct and discipline. There is no evidence to confirm his assertion, except that Buckhurst is thereafter silent about university affairs; no more cancellarial rebukes are heard in the reign of Elizabeth. But the silence of the chancellor is scarcely evidence that all was well.[2]

Buckhurst's patronage within Oxford was limited and contested. He nominated George Abbot to the mastership of University College in 1597 and John Howson to the vice-chancellorship in 1602. He had had to contend with continuing rivalry from the earl of Essex, who successfully backed Dr Bilson for the bishopric of Worcester in 1596 against Buckhurst's candidate, William James, dean of Christ Church. Later in the same year, after James had been appointed to the deanery of Durham, there was a tense struggle for the deanery of Christ Church. The appointment lay in the hands of the crown, but Buckhurst believed that it should in practice be exercised by the chancellor. His own candidate was Dr Thomas Ravis, against whom Essex had put up Dr Richard Eedes, chaplain to the queen. Buckhurst wrote in desperate terms to Robert Cecil that if Edes were appointed his prestige would be so severely damaged that he would have to

MS 6282, fos 117-20ᵛ. Archbishop Whitgift expressed similar criticisms of the university at this time: John Strype, *Life of John Whitgift* (1718; 3 vols Oxford 1822) i. 609-12.

[1] *Salisbury Manuscripts* iv. 162, 165. Reg. Cong. 1582-95, fos 251-2.
[2] Ibid. fos 252-3, 272. Wood, *History and Antiquities* ii. 258.

resign. In the event Ravis was appointed and Buckhurst's face was saved. But it is a measure of his weakness that he had to appeal so fervently to Cecil: one cannot imagine Leicester doing anything of the kind. Thereafter Buckhurst seems to have been secure, as far as one can tell, from threats to his influence within Oxford.[1]

PATRONAGE AND INFLUENCE

Chancellors were not, of course, the only persons to influence the university and its colleges. The queen herself sometimes intervened directly in matters of patronage. She protested to the president of Magdalen in 1589 against the expulsion of Christopher Wade from his fellowship for absence: he had been sent on a special assignment by the privy council and should be given leave of absence by the college. The royal request was refused and Wade was deprived. She instructed Magdalen to elect Henry Hungerford to a fellowship at their next election in 1593, which they did; and in 1601 she recommended Samuel German, a poor boy from Guildford, to the same college for a scholarship to be followed by a fellowship; again the college complied.[2] Sometimes her demands met resistance. When she ordered the fellows of Magdalen to admit John Ivory, son of her serjeant-at-arms, to the next vacant fellowship, they refused to comply. However, after they had been admonished by their visitor for showing 'an uncommon carelessness of the Queen's Majesty's letters', they gave way and allowed Ivory to be admitted.[3] But royal intervention was not always successful: when the queen asked the university to give a degree to Mr Larke, so that he might become warden of Winchester, her request was refused.[4]

But these royal demands were relatively rare; usually patronage and influence were brought to bear by courtiers and officials rather than by the queen herself. Such intervention was common enough in academic life for a sixteenth-century formulary of petitions to include sample letters to universities and colleges. The book provided standard letters for the chancellor commending a college principal, for a nobleman supporting a candidate to the chancellor, for procuring votes for election to a law fellowship and for the reversion to the office of college butler.[5]

[1] *Salisbury Manuscripts* vi. 194–5, 197.
[2] *APC* xvii. 32, xxiv. 362; xxxii. 29. Cf *Cal. SP Dom. 1595–97*, 496; *1598–1601*, 476, 477. BL Lansdowne MS 15. Macray, *Reg. Magdalen* ii. 163–4; iii. 122, 136.
[3] Macray, iii. 64–7.
[4] *Reg. Univ.* ed. Clark i. 150.
[5] *Catalogue of Manuscripts in the Library . . . of the Inner Temple*, ed. J. Conway Davies (3 vols Oxford 1972) ii. 725–32.

Apart from Leicester, William Cecil, Lord Burghley, wielded the greatest influence in university affairs. Relatively humble men appealed for his help in securing college fellowships: Robert Dowe wanted a position at All Souls, John Lilly at Magdalen and G. Newman at Corpus. Dow was successful but the other two were not.[1] Men of greater stature were also glad of his support. Laurence Humfrey begged Cecil to get him confirmed in his prebend at Christ Church, lamenting that he could not live on the stipend of the Magdalen presidency alone; and Herbert Westfaling thanked Cecil effusively for obtaining for him a prebend at the same house.[2] Colleges as well as individuals were glad of his backing. In 1561 both sides appealed to him in the dispute over the provostship of Queen's: the fellows asked him to help them keep out Dr Francis, while the latter and his supporters wanted him to help them overcome the resistance of the college.[3] The fellows of Merton begged Cecil to act as an intermediary on their behalf in the election of their warden in 1562. Like the fellows of Queen's they failed, even so, to keep out the government's nominee.[4] Christ Church wanted him to secure the appointment of Herbert Westfaling as dean in 1583/4; they too were unsuccessful, since William James was appointed.[5] The failure of such appeals is not so much evidence that Cecil's influence was weak as a sign that he would not oppose the 'official' candidate. He was evidently more help to St John's over a protracted lawsuit, since the college paid him £20 for his services and gave another £10 to his secretary, Henry Maynard, for procuring them.[6] There is no sign that Cecil's influence was resented within the university. The vice-chancellor wrote to him in 1561 acknowledging that although another man (Sir John Mason) might be chancellor in name and dignity, Cecil was their chancellor and patron in deed; the memory of his beneficence would survive as long as Oxford flourished.[7] However, although Cecil's support was always welcome, it seems that his influence in Oxford was at its peak before the appointment of Leicester as chancellor in 1564; thereafter, while he continued to have a voice in university affairs, he took second place to Leicester.

Robert Cecil exercised an influence similar to that of his father.

[1] BL Lansdowne MS 17, nos. 77, 80, 84; 19, nos. 16, 17. Cf ibid. 23, no. 48; 45, no. 60; and *Cal. SP Dom. 1547-80*, 40/59 for other examples.

[2] PRO SP 12/21, nos. 5, 28; 22, no. 1.

[3] Ibid. 17, nos. 7, 22.

[4] Ibid. 21, nos. 28, 57.

[5] BL Lansdowne MS 39, no. 5.

[6] BL Lansdowne MS 29, no. 51; 39, nos. 2, 8; 42, nos. 61, 67, etc. Stevenson and Salter, *Early History of St. John's* 276-7. Cf the role of Burghley's agent Michael Hickes described in A. G. R. Smith, *Servant of the Cecils* (1977), 60-1.

[7] PRO SP 12/20, no. 29.

Edward Kirkham persuaded him to intercede with the dean of Christ Church on behalf of his son for election as a Westminster scholar; the boy was duly elected. Henry Robinson thanked Cecil for help in allowing him to keep the provostship of Queen's after his presentation to the bishopric of Carlisle. The students of Christ Church appealed for Cecil's aid in their protracted dispute with the canons over their allowance of bread.[1] More important was the urgent appeal made to Cecil by the chancellor, Lord Buckhurst, in 1596 when Buckhurst had to enlist Cecil's support against the earl of Essex over the appointment of Dr Ravis as dean of Christ Church.[2] Two years later Archbishop Whitgift asked for Cecil's help in a plan for moving William Cole, president of Corpus, to the deanery of Lincoln so that the then dean, John Rainolds, could rule over Corpus. Cecil was to persuade the queen to bestow the deanery upon Cole. Whitgift stressed the importance of placing Rainolds in Oxford, since he was engaged in writing against the Jesuits. The plan succeeded and the exchange of posts was duly executed. It is remarkable to find Whitgift, arch-enemy of the puritans, supporting Rainolds, who had for some time been intellectually outstanding among Oxford puritans, and it is a tribute to Robert Cecil's influence that his voice had to be sought in a church appointment by the archbishop of Canterbury.[3]

Sir Francis Walsingham also wielded some influence in Oxford. The provost and fellows of Queen's wrote him a fulsome letter of thanks in 1582, assuring him that their successors would call him 'most honourable Walsingham, greatest patron of Queen's College, and singular cultivator of letters'.[4] In 1586 the university itself acknowledged its gratitude to him for defending its privileges.[5] Richard Hakluyt, the great chronicler of English voyages, suggested that Walsingham promote the establishment of two lecturerships in navigation, one in London, the other in Oxford. The London lectureship was eventually set up, but nothing came of the Oxford proposal. Even so, the idea illustrates an interesting link between academic Oxford, the royal court and the world of exploration, for Hakluyt was a student of Christ Church until October 1586.[6] Walsingham's most fruitful contribution to Oxford was his establishment of a divinity lecturership in 1586 and his recommendation that John Rainolds fill it: in this way one of the most impor-

[1] *Salisbury Manuscripts* vii. 170; ix. 13; xiii. 597.
[2] Ibid. vi. 194–5, 197. Above, 433   [3] Ibid. viii. 332.
[4] PRO SP 12/156, no. 31; 176, no. 17.   [5] Ibid. 186 no. 33.
[6] Ibid. 170, no. 1. *The Hakluyt Handbook*, ed. D. B. Quinn (2 vols Hakluyt Society 2nd ser. cxliv–cxlv 1974) i. 290. Kenneth Charlton, *Education in Renaissance England* (1954), 281–2.

tant of Elizabethan theologians and teachers established his academic career.[1]

Many other nobles, courtiers and officials influenced, or tried to influence, appointments and elections at Oxford. Lady Paulet secured the entry of her nephew Richard Blounte into Trinity after he had been rejected by Balliol. Sir John Petre claimed the right— as the descendant of a benefactor—to interfere in the election of scholars at Exeter College.[2] Lord Norris and Sir Francis Knollys, intending to place the puritan leader John Field in a lecturership at Henley, asked for and received a licence from the chancellor for him to preach.[3] One of the most striking attempts to interfere in collegiate elections was made by that otherwise upright puritan nobleman, Henry Hastings, third earl of Huntingdon, who had long been a patron of Magdalen College, having sent his two younger brothers there for a protestant upbringing under Laurence Humfrey. In 1590 the fellows of Magdalen elected a young scholar, John Milling, into a northern fellowship. One of Milling's defeated rivals, Thomas Pullen—then at New College, but not a fellow—complained to the queen's Latin secretary, Sir John Wolley, that Milling was not properly qualified and asked for support. Wolley persuaded Huntingdon to press Pullen's suit on the college, which he evidently did without success. Pullen then, with Wolley's help, procured a royal signet letter for the displacement of Milling and for his own election. The fellows replied that it would be contrary to their statutes to deprive an elected fellow and unjust to eject a young scholar of 'rare and singular towardness'. Huntingdon came back into the fight with another request that Pullen be elected. The president, Dr Bond, replied that this would be totally illegal and insisted that he would resign rather than allow it; he begged Huntingdon to restrain Pullen's 'preposterous humour'. In the end Milling kept his place and Pullen never entered Magdalen. The college had demonstrated its readiness—repeated in 1688—to stand up to royal and aristocratic pressure.[4]

One figure played a smaller part in the affairs of Elizabethan Oxford than he wished or than we might have expected. Robert, second earl of Essex, had outstanding influence at court and was

[1] Wood, *History and Antiquities* ii. 227-8. On Rainolds see McConica, 'Humanism and Aristotle in Tudor Oxford'.

[2] Blakiston, *Trinity College*, 48, 80. Above, 409. *Cal. SP Dom 1581-90*, 160/56.

[3] *Reg. Univ.* ed. Clark i. 149.

[4] The story is told in full in papers contained in an (at present) unnumbered box in the Magdalen College Archives. I am grateful to the late J. P. Cooper for drawing my attention to the papers and supplying me with xerox copies. Some of the letters concerning the dispute are copied in BL Harleian MS 6282, fos 124-5, 134[V]. See also Macray, *Reg. Magdalen* ii. 111.

untiring in his manipulation of the patronage network. He saw himself—and was seen by others—as the political heir to the earl of Leicester and he evidently hoped to play a similar role at Oxford. When, thanks to the intervention of the queen, his rival Buckhurst was chosen to succeed Hutton as chancellor, Essex successfully supported Dr Bilson for the bishopric of Worcester against Buckhurst's candidate, Dr James, but he was defeated over Dr Ravis's appointment as dean of Christ Church, which Buckhurst saw as a test of his own prestige. Thereafter Essex seems to have wielded little influence in Oxford. Henry Robinson wrote to him from Carlisle to say that he would resign the provostship of Queen's when the fellows were ready to elect a successor favourable to Essex. Whether or not Robinson's successor, Henry Airey, was Essex's protégé it is hard to say; but it is as well to remember that Robinson wrote a fulsome letter of thanks to Robert Cecil as well as keeping in touch with Essex. With this one possible exception there is no sign that Essex had any influence over Oxford appointments in the last five years of his life. Nor was the university implicated in the Essex rising. It is true that Henry Savile, warden of Merton, was suspect through his friendship with Essex's secretary Henry Cuffe. But a search of Savile's rooms at Eton revealed nothing seditious and there is no reason to suppose that he was in any way involved. There was, however, a curious aftermath to the rising which suggests that Essex may have had a following among the younger members of the university. In April 1601 Abraham Colfe, a BA of Christ Church, made a passionate oration in Christ Church hall, extolling Essex as a great warrior and a friend to scholarship and attributing his fall to the envy of his rivals. Colfe was instantly sent to London, where, imprisoned in Newgate, he pleaded rather disingenuously that he had meant only to praise Essex's virtue, not to condone his rebellion or grieve at his condemnation. Rather surprisingly Colfe's plea for mercy seems to have been accepted, and three years later he was established as curate of Lewisham.[1]

Courtiers and other outsiders did not confine their interference to appointments and patronage. College leases were regarded as fair game: as President Bond remarked, 'if a lease be of any valor and near expiring, it lyeth in the eye of some great man or other'.[2] Leicester's acquisition of leases for his friends has already been noted.[3] He was not alone in the hunt. The queen herself signified to All Souls that they should let Lewkenor parsonage to John Brooke,

[1] Above, 433. Reg. Cong. 1582-95, fos 251-2. *Salisbury Manuscripts* iv. 162, 165; vi. 194-5, 197; viii. 405; ix. 13; xi. 54, 56-7. *Cal. SP Dom. Elizabeth, 1601-03*, 35-6, 44.
[2] BL Harleian MS 4240, fo 87. [3] Above, 430.

and the privy council required Magdalen to let Basing parsonage to Barnaby Wakefield, yeoman of the queen's chamber. The most notorious dispute over a lease came in 1587 with the queen's request to All Souls that they let their woods in Middlesex to Lady Stafford. The college had already let two of its best manors to Sir Walter Raleigh on highly favourable terms and might have been thought pliable. But this time the warden, Robert Hovenden, resisted. Pressure was brought upon him by Lady Blanche Parry, Lady Cobham, Archbishop Whitgift, Sir Thomas Heneage, Sir Walter Raleigh, Lord Hunsdon and Lord Burghley. He was told that the queen took his refusal 'in very evil part' and was offered a bribe of £100. In spite of all this Hovenden stood firm and Lady Stafford was denied her lease.[1]

It is difficult to measure the extent of outside patronage in Elizabethan Oxford, for our knowledge depends more than in most matters upon the chance survival of evidence; and there were obviously more ramifications of the network than we can now detect. But it seems likely that lay patrons played a much greater part than before in appointments to university posts, in the promotion of university men on the clerical ladder and in the disposal of college property.

THE UNIVERSITY SUBDUED

The religious tensions of the Elizabethan period and the increasingly important role of the universities as nurseries for the upbringing of the clergy made governmental interference in their affairs more necessary and more persistent. The interest of courtiers and landowners in the education of their sons and in the advancement of their protégés exposed both Oxford and Cambridge to the demands of royal and lay patronage. The crown's influence over the university certainly increased, and power within it was concentrated in fewer hands. At Cambridge this centralization of authority was marked by the statutes of 1570, which entrusted the choice of vice-chancellor largely to the heads of colleges, increased the power of the steering committee (the *caput senatus*), confined the election of the *caput* to heads, doctors and senators, and gave heads a right of veto over elections within their own colleges.[2] No such formal

[1] *Salisbury Manuscripts* vii. 523. APC xvi. 287. C. R. L. Fletcher (ed.), *Collectanea* i, (OHS v 1885), 179–247.

[2] C. H. Cooper, *Annals of Cambridge* (5 vols Cambridge 1842) ii. 258–61. Porter, *Reformation and Reaction in Tudor Cambridge*, 164–6. John Lamb, *A Collection . . . Illustrative of the History of the University of Cambridge* (1838), 315–54.

change was made in Elizabethan Oxford. Although several attempts were made to produce a comprehensive set of statutes, the university had to wait until 1636, when the Laudian statutes formally established oligarchic control. But under Elizabeth the tendency in that direction was strong and unequivocal. Royal influence over the election of the chancellor, the chancellor's nomination of the vice-chancellor and his constant interference in university affairs, the effective establishment of a steering committee for convocation, and the influence of crown, chancellor and visitors over the election to headships are evidence enough of that. The impact of the governmental machinery was decisive, even if it was not rapid. Catholicism was gradually purged and puritanism never obtained a permanent hold over the university, its more extreme exponents either departing or moderating their views. The pressures of church and crown destroyed the catholic scholarship of New College and ended Magdalen's pre-eminence among Oxford puritans. But the government's methods were seldom stark and dictatorial, the university never entirely subservient. The crown was careful to observe the legal forms, as the long survival of catholicism demonstrates; and the colleges were sometimes capable of resisting encroachment, as Bond showed at Magdalen and Hovenden at All Souls.

The total effect of interference by monarch, chancellors, courtiers and landowners is not easily assessed. The purge of catholics deprived Oxford of some notable scholars. Patronage probably secured positions for mediocrities who should not have held them. On the other hand, Humfrey, Rainolds, Hooker and Corro—all of them distinguished men—owed much to outside patrons. The university had, however, come to rely upon external support and lay open to state influence. Until the end of the sixteenth century this process was probably not, on balance, seriously damaging. But it held threats of dangerous consequence for the future: the university's independence had been heavily mortgaged; it was not to be redeemed until three centuries had passed.

7

The Provision of Books

N. R. KER

EXISTING books, college records, wills and inventories, and documents relating to the book-trade are the main sources for our knowledge of books in Oxford in the sixteenth century. They reveal what is of course obvious anyway, that the invention of printing and, to a lesser degree, the change of religion, caused vast alterations in the book collections in Oxford, as elsewhere. There has been nothing like it in any other century.

The books are looked at here in seven divisions (A–G): books chained in the libraries of the ten secular colleges founded before 1500; non-library books in the same ten colleges; library and non-library books in five colleges founded in the sixteenth century;[1] books in the colleges maintained in Oxford by the Benedictines; books of the public library of the university; books owed privately by members of the university.

Most of the first and third and some of the study of non-library books will be found differently arranged in my Sandars Lectures.[2] Something is said there and need not be repeated here about accounts, benefactors' books, book-lists, library finance, library furniture and library-keepers. This chapter is mainly concerned with the books themselves and with the changes in the book stock in a period when colleges were faced with a problem that got worse and worse—lack of space in what were still medieval library rooms. The problem was solved at Merton in 1589 by putting the books on horizontal shelves instead of sloping lectern desks, and similarly in other colleges more or less soon thereafter. Until then lack of shelf-room inhibited growth. We can see what three important college libraries possessed in the way of books at certain points in the second half of the century, Merton in 1556, All Souls (with some gaps) in 1575 and Corpus in 1589, but this does not tell us very much about

[1] The history of the collection of books at Jesus College, founded in 1574, is a blank until 1601: see C. J. Fordyce and T. M. Knox, *The Library of Jesus College, Oxford* (Oxford Bibliographical Society v pt 2 1937), 11.

[2] N. R. Ker, 'Oxford and Cambridge libraries in the sixteenth century', *Bodleian Library Record* vi no. 3 (1959), 459–515.

what books were available in these colleges, but only about what books could be fitted into their library rooms. Small books were excluded: their first appearance is at Merton in 1590, after the library had been converted to the new horizontal shelving. For up-to-date reading the books belonging to fellows were important, more important probably than the rather miscellaneous collections of books which belonged to colleges, but they were kept outside the library. Evidence of the extent to which the community was informed about continental thought must be looked for in section (G), therefore, rather than in sections (A)–(D). How much evidence is there? The answer is that we do not know: the inventories and existing books have not yet been explored. The evidence for one important book, Jean Bodin's *De republica*, is however unusually easy to come by. It was surely a much read book in Oxford in the last fifteen years of the century. Not only do three of the four long book-inventories of these years include it, as Curtis noticed,[1] but the 1586 folio edition in Latin was bought immediately by at least two colleges, Magdalen and Corpus.[2] To look further is hardly necessary. A little search among the two dozen copies of sixteenth century editions in Oxford libraries produced at least five copies in contemporary Oxford centrepiece bindings. One of them belonged to 'Gualterus Cheney', who may be identified with the Walter Cheney who matriculated at University College in 1583 aged 18 and took his MA in 1590: it has a good many annotations, probably in his hand.[3]

Where did Oxford colleges and members of the university get their books? In 1535/6 and 1538/9 some of the many books bought by Magdalen came from London and there is one reference to a London bookseller, Raynarde, no doubt Reyner Wolfe.[4] In 1573/4 Queen's bought Foxe's *Acts and Monuments* in London. In 1589 and 1591 Merton made large purchases on the continent, in Italy and at the

---

[1] Mark H. Curtis, *Oxford and Cambridge in Transition, 1558–1642* (Oxford 1959), 137.

[2] 'Solut' pro Bodino de Republ. 15 s' is in the Magdalen accounts for 1586 and 'For Bodine de repub. with Antonius Augustinus 18 s' in the Corpus accounts for 1586. Both copies are still in the libraries concerned.

[3] N. R. Ker, *Fragments of Medieval Manuscripts used as Pastedowns in Oxford Bindings with a survey of Oxford Binding c.1515–1620* (Oxford Bibliographical Society new ser. v 1954; hereafter cited as Ker, *Pastedowns*) records centrepiece ii on the octavo edition (Frankfurt 1591) in Bodl. Vet.D.1. e 305, inscribed 'Gualterus Cheney prec' vi^s vi^d'; centrepiece xi on the octavo 1591 edition at Corpus; centrepiece xiv on the folio 1586 edition at Balliol, inscribed 'Ex dono Philippi Sheffeylde'; centrepiece xvi on the octavo 1579 edition at Oriel; centrepiece xvi on the octavo 1594 edition in the Bodleian, 8° C. 256 Linc. inscribed 'Liber Roberti Whitbie et amicorum vi^s'.

[4] Macray, *Reg. Magdalen* ii. 16–19. The entries about carriage are in Magdalen College Archives Liber Computi 1530–42, fos 92, 132^v (two entries), 133.

Frankfurt fair, recorded in the college register for those years. Other purchases made outside Oxford may have been recorded in now missing accounts. The accounts, though patchy, are numerous enough to show that Oxford colleges dealt as a rule with Oxford booksellers. Not all of them were important buyers, but they are the only buyers whose accounts survive. From the mid-1530s (there is no reference to book buying earlier in the sixteenth century) until the late 1580s we meet with only two names, Evans and Garbrand, save only that in 1549 (?) Merton divided a large order between Evans, Garbrand and Gore[1] and that Corpus paid 10s in 1552/3 'to stoffler for ii bookes of our owne' and bought a book from Gore in 1554/5. Evans died in 1563 and after this Garbrand's is the only name. This is not surprising for the sixties, when Garbrand seems to have been the only Oxford bookseller of importance. But it is surprising later, considering that seven persons were admitted officially as book-sellers in the years 1570-4.[2] Perhaps colleges saw no reason to change their allegiance and perhaps some purchases for which the seller's name is not recorded—the Corpus accounts are particularly uninformative in this respect—did not in fact come from Garbrand. All Souls bought books from Garbrand in 1575/6 and 1587/8, but the five-volume *Concilia generalia* bought in 1586/7 may have come from Pinart, since he did the bindings.[3]

The name Garbrand covers two men, Garbrand Herks who died about 1570 and his son Richard. The son is called Richard Garbrand in full in New College, Queen's, Merton and Christ Church accounts of the 1580s, perhaps to distinguish him from his brother John Garbrand, fellow of New College. Perhaps he (or the binders he employed) was not giving satisfaction in the 1580s: we can only judge by bindings and certainly those with Gibson's rolls XXI and (especially) XXII compare unfavourably with Pinart bindings.[4] For whatever reason Magdalen switched from Garbrand to Joseph Barnes in or before 1589 and did not use Garbrand again until 1596. Merton, as we have seen, got most of their books abroad at this time; they came in sheets and were bound by Pinart. Only a few small orders went to Garbrand.

Written evidence of who supplied books to members of the university is hard to find. There is none or virtually none in Dorne's

---

[1] Ker, 'Oxford and Cambridge libraries', 484.

[2] *Reg. Univ.* ed. Clark i. 321.

[3] N. R. Ker, *Records of All Souls College Library 1437-1600* (Oxford Bibliographical Society new ser. xvi 1971), 33, 142. Sir Edmund Craster, *The History of All Souls College Library*, ed. E. F. Jacob (1971), 55.

[4] Binding references preceded by Gibson are to Strickland Gibson, *Early Oxford Bindings* (Bibliographical Society illustrated monographs x. 1903).

day-book.[1] We know of two books bought from Baltazar (Church-yard), one in 1528, the other in 1531, of one book bought from Henry (Renkens or Mancipull?) stationer in 1531, of books bought from Garbrand in or before 1553, of two books bought 'of Stoffolde', one in 1561 and the other in 1563, of one book bought from Garbrand Herks in 1567, and of forty-four books bought from William Spire, probably in 1588.[2] Here are some new names at least. 'Stoffolde' is of special interest. As Gordon Duff saw, the name conceals Christopher Cavey.[3] Cavey was not admitted bookseller until 1570, but he appears to have been selling second-hand books at a much earlier date.[4] He is known as a binder by 1553 and was using Gibson, roll XII in 1556-7.[5] There is some evidence that he used Ker, centrepieces i and vii.[6] These, with centrepiece xiii, are probably the earliest Oxford centrepieces, used in the mid-sixties if not before then. Fellows of colleges liked them, probably because they were rather cheaper than rolls, but colleges did not use them much on their own books before the nineties. All the books in Oxford bind-ings owned by Toby Mathew and John Rainolds have centrepieces, not rolls: many of Rainolds' have centrepieces i and vii.[7] One of Mathew's with centrepiece i has the date '1565' on the title-page and another with centrepiece vii the date '1566'.[8] Probably Garbrand employed Cavey to bind the books he sold.[9]

[1] See F. Madan, 'The Daily Ledger of John Dorne, 1520', in C. R. L. Fletcher (ed.), *Collectanea* i (OHS v 1885), 77.

[2] Baltazar: (i) see N. R. Ker, *Medieval Libraries of Great Britain* (1941, 2nd edn 1964), 188, 311; (ii) Bodl. Th. 8° T.59, Prudentius (Basle 1527), 8° 'Emptus eram xviii d' Oxonie in officina baltazaris bibliote anno a virgineo partu . . . quinto decimo die mensis Ianuarii.' Henry: John Rylands University Library Manchester Rylands Lat. 176 (J. Felton, Sermones), 'liber Ricardi ewer [Merton College MA 1525] emptus a henrico stacionario anno domini 1531 die fe.9'. 'Stoffolde': see below, p. 468 n. 3. Garbrand: (i) books to the value of 25s 7d which Thomas Symonds had bought, but not paid for, as is recorded in his inventory (below, p. 471 n. 1); (ii) Durham Cathedral, Biblia (Zurich 1543), in a binding with Gibson roll XII, bought 'garbrandi hercanii bibliopole oxon', 8 December 1567. Spire: at the end of the inventory of Edward Higgins (see below, p. 463) is a list of forty-four books which must have been bought very shortly before Higgins died, since the inventory-maker noted that Spire was willing to take them back at the price for which he had sold them.

[3] Strickland Gibson, *Abstracts from the Wills and Testamentary Documents of Binders, Printers and Stationers of Oxford from 1493 to 1638* (Bibliographical Society 1907), 8, 10.   [4] See also above, the payment by Corpus in 1552-3.

[5] Gibson, *Oxford Bindings*, 8; Ker, *Pastedowns*, app. no. cxcviii.

[6] Ibid. 216. All binding references preceded by Ker are to ibid.

[7] Ibid. 267.   [8] Ibid. 146, 216.

[9] For sixteenth-century booksellers and binders in Oxford see especially: *Reg. Univ.* ed. Clark i. 320-1; *Oxford City Documents, financial and judicial 1268-1665*, ed. J. E. Thorold Rogers (OHS xviii 1891), 56; F. Madan, *Oxford Books* (3 vols Oxford 1895-1931) i. 272-6; Gibson, *Wills*; Gibson, *Oxford Bindings*; Ker, *Pastedowns*, pp. xiii, 203-23; Ker, 'Oxford and Cambridge libraries', 497; Ker, *Records of All Souls Library*, 171-2; G. Pollard, 'The names of some English fifteenth-century binders', *The Library*, 5th ser. xxv (1970), 210-11.

A. THE CHAINED LIBRARIES IN COLLEGES FOUNDED
BEFORE 1500

I begin with All Souls College because only there can we see in some detail how what had been a few years before 1500 a collection of manuscripts with a few printed books became by 1576, a collection of printed books, not many of them incunabula, with a few manuscripts.[1] The change was gradual. It is most marked in the 1540s when more than 100 new volumes were bought and, in consequence, about the same number of old volumes were discarded. This process was inevitable in any well-furnished library throughout the sixteenth century, since only a small number of books could be placed on the lectern desks and on shelves above and below the desks. What happened at All Souls was not of course exactly what happened in other colleges. The poorer colleges lagged behind the richer colleges, but not so much that they had not reached the 1540s position by the end of the century. A main difference from college to college is likely to have been in the policy about discards. If an old book was unchained in favour of a new book what did one do with the old book? The obvious choices are: sale, discard or transfer to the collection maintained 'ad usum sociorum', that is to the collection discussed under (B). Individuals with opinions, new brooms and conservationists, may have had great influence in shaping the collections as we know them now, both on occasions in the sixteenth century and at the moment at the turn of the century or after 1600 when the libraries were converted to horizontal shelving and librarians could, if they wished, bring in their non-library books.

Medieval manuscripts are a side-line in the sixteenth century, but an important side-line. We can ask questions, but often there are no satisfactory answers. Why were there so many at Merton, New College, Magdalen, Balliol and Lincoln? Why only a certain number at Oriel and All Souls, a few at Exeter and University College and none at all (from the medieval library) at Queen's? For Balliol the answer may be that the college was not rich, the library a room of some size, and the manuscripts mainly the gift of a great benefactor and above average in quality. There was probably less motive to discard and more motive to preserve than in wealthier colleges with more varied collections. At Lincoln, too, *pietas* may have played a part. The founder and the founder's nephew had been generous benefactors, as was plainly to be seen on the books themselves, with their labels 'Ex dono fundatoris' and 'Ex dono Magistri Roberti

---

[1] See N. R. Ker, *Records of All Souls Library* (Oxford 1971).

Flemmyng'.[1] As for Merton, Mr H. W. Garrod suggested to me that
Warden Fitzjames (warden from 1483 to 1507: Erasmus did not like
him and nor did Garrod) 'kept the place medieval' and that his influence lasted. Probably we should remember with gratitude William
Browne, Robert Barnes, Thomas Symons and William Marshall who
were book-loving fellows of Merton holding positions of authority
on the governing body in the crucial years of the reign of Edward VI.[2]
At Queen's somebody in authority may have said 'Out with these
useless old books'. At All Souls we are in a fair way to knowing what
actually happened. There, almost all the manuscripts of the fathers
and almost all the manuscripts in many other subjects were removed. On the other hand, a certain number of manuscripts judged to
be particularly fine or useful were kept. The selection was not haphazard. In 1576 in the first place, in every sense, came a handsome
and large two-volume twelfth-century Bible, which stood by itself
'in medio dextu', probably a double lectern desk in the central gang-
way of the library.[3] Next, there were four manuscripts of civil law
on the first desk on the law side of the library. They had been in the
library since its foundation and had been brought together deliberately in or about 1513 to form a set of the *Digest* and *Code*: in
1576 they were still together, but now accompanied by two printed
editions, one with apparatus and one without.[4] Thirdly, there were
fifteen and, no doubt, more than fifteen manuscripts which had been
allowed to remain because they had not been or could not be replaced by printed editions. Seven of the fifteen were medical manuscripts and five were legal and the other three were commentaries on
works of Boethius and Aristotle and a commentary on Leviticus.[5]
And, finally, there was a medical manuscript probably given as
recently as 1557.[6] The inventory is damaged and almost certainly
recorded a few more manuscripts. Was MS 18, a twelfth-century
copy of Gregory's *Registrum*, among them? One would like to think
so because this book, given to the college in 1439 by Thomas
Gascoigne and which stood on the fourth desk on the theology side
of the library, *c* 1548, had been put to good use by Francis Milles,
when he was a fellow. The story is told at length by Thomas James,

---

[1] Possibly the Balliol manuscripts had similar labels and nearly all of them were jetti-
soned on rebinding. See the description of MSS 3, 91, 117, 125, 185, 295 in R. A. B.
Mynors, *Catalogue of the Manuscripts of Balliol College, Oxford* (Oxford 1963).

[2] *BRUO 1501–40*; for Browne also, below, p. 471 n. 1, and for Marshall, Ker, 'Oxford
and Cambridge libraries', 505.

[3] All Souls College MS 4.

[4] Ibid. MSS 49–52.

[5] Ibid. MSS 68, 69, 72, 75, 78, 79, Exeter Cathedral MS 2506; All Souls College MSS
59, 60, 62, 164, 182; MSS 84, 90; MS 13.

[6] Pembroke College Oxford MS 2.

how Milles was searching for Bishop Jewel's authority for referring in a sermon at Abingdon to *exercitus sacerdotum* when the reading of the editions was *exitus sacerdotum*; how he 'turned diuerse editions, but still found *exitus*. In the ende, it so pleased God to put into his minde, to seeke it in the *Manuscripts*: and remembring that they had one in the Librarie of good antiquitie, in that Coll. whereof he was then fellow, hee did so; went vp into the *Librarie*, found the words there as Bishop Jewel had reported them: which was no small comfort vnto him'.[1] The incident may have done something to bring back a taste for manuscripts.

The chained collections in college libraries were formed to make a useful collection for reference and reading of the sort of books a college fellow was not likely to have access to otherwise. The principal medieval method of getting these books was the apparently haphazard one of receiving them as gifts. The libraries were largely dependent upon the testamentary dispositions of fellows or former fellows of the college who had become of some standing in the world in or outside the university. This system worked in a way in the middle ages. In the conditions prevailing after 1500 it did not work. Gifts—and there were not so many of them, though those there were may have been larger than before—did not produce what was wanted. Thus Archbishop Warham's gift to All Souls in 1532 of ninety-one volumes of theology had only three books in it worth putting in the library. They were two newly printed books, the Pagninus Bible of 1528 and Bucer on the Psalms of 1529, and a *sexta pars* of the printed Augustine, probably of the Basle 1506 edition.[2] The Bible and Bucer kept their places in 1576 and are still in the library. The Augustine was turned out in 1558-9 and is lost.

[1] T. James, *Corruption of Scripture (1611)*, 78–80. Dr D. M. Barratt tells me that the reading 'exercitus' had been noted by Jewel in his *Answer To Mr. Hardinge's Preface* (1565 edn), 226: 'Ita in manuscriptis, melius quam exitus.' He may have seen it also in the 1504 edition of the *Registrum*. *Exitus* is the reading in 1518, *Rex superbie prope est/ et (quod dici nephas est) sacerdotum est preparatus exitus*, and remained, until it was turned out by the Maurists. Dr Barratt tells me also that the writer of the 'Biographical Memoir of Jewel' thought that the sermon at Abingdon was at the visitation in 1571 (*The Works of John Jewel, Bishop of Salisbury*, ed. John Ayre (2 vols in 4 Parker Society 1845-50) iv. p. xxi) but this seems unlikely. If Jewel had already commented on *exercitus-exitus* in print the fact would have been known to his hearers. More probably he got the right reading from an early edition, saw that it was better, and, after preaching the sermon, learned from his Oxford friends that it had support in the manuscripts. Milles was BA 1559, MA 1562. He appears to have vacated his fellowship before November 1569, a date I owe to Mr John Simmons. The passage he wanted is on fo 58ᵛ of All Souls MS 18: 'Rex superbie propę (sic) est. et quod dici nefas est sacerdotum ei pręparatur exercitus.' In the editions of Milles's time and James's the letter in which it occurs is no 38 of book 4. It is volume 44 in Ewald's edition in the *Monumenta Germaniae historica* and volume 18 in Migne (*Patrologia cursus completus*, ed. J.-P. Migne, series latina (221 vols Paris 1844–64) lxxvii. 741).

[2] Ker, *Records of All Souls Library*, nos 651, 677, 698.

The rest of Warham's gift, many incunabula or near-incunabula and a few manuscripts, would have done nothing to bring the college library up to date. These books were put into the non-library collection, whence seventeen of them found their way back into the library in due course, probably early in the seventeenth century.[1]

That it was necessary to buy books became gradually apparent. What happened and when and what books were bought was the subject of my second Lyell lecture in 1955.[2] Here I give the main facts only. The amounts spent, so far as we know them, are these: over £73 at Magdalen between 1536 and 1550; £30 at Oriel in 1543/4; at least £46 at All Souls between 1544/5 and 1547/8;[3] more than £60 at Merton in or about 1549; some money almost certainly at Balliol, where there are no accounts before 1568. What books did this money buy from the great choice available in the 1540s; new editions of what was well-known already, for example the principal Latin fathers, or editions of works written in the more or less distant past which had been until lately almost or quite unobtainable, for example the Greek fathers in Greek, or works by contemporary writers or writers only recently dead, or something of all three? Our evidence is good for All Souls, all but conclusive for Merton, fair for Magdalen. There is some evidence for Balliol, New College and Oriel. No doubt a first charge on the money of every college was theology and in particular the *opera* of the four great Latin fathers, Augustine, Jerome, Ambrose and Gregory (to whom the chapel at All Souls was dedicated), and after these the *opera* of other Latin fathers and of the Greek fathers in Latin translations or in Greek. Losses in this class of book have been very heavy. Every new edition weakened the chance that a mid-sixteenth century edition would keep its place and reasons for discarding must have been very strong after the great Maurist editions appeared at the end of the seventeenth century. At Balliol a long list of books for which no donor could be found was put into the benefactors' register *c* 1630. It has the merit of giving not simply titles, but also dates and places of printing. We know therefore that Balliol had then and later parted with, among much else, the Basle Augustine of 1543, the Basle Jerome of 1538, the Basle Ambrose of 1549 and the Basle Gregory of 1533. Similarly at Oriel a catalogue of 1653 shows that the college then had the 1529 Augustine, the 1537 Jerome and the 1538 Ambrose: all were

---

[1] Ker, *Records of All Souls Library*, no. 188, the asterisked items.

[2] Ker, 'Oxford and Cambridge Libraries', 479–96.

[3] I could give no figure in 1955. See now, Ker, *Records of All Souls Library*, 117.

discarded. At Magdalen there are no lists, but we know what happened to the college's Jerome of 1516—a gift, not a purchase: it is now in the Bodleian.[1] And Magdalen's Augustine of 1529 is only in Magdalen now through a series of happy chances.[2] All Souls and Merton were conservative colleges, however, and the entries in their inventories can often be matched against the books themselves now on the library shelves. Both colleges were able to contribute much to the patristic as well as to other sections of the exhibition 'Oxford College Libraries in 1556' held in the Bodleian Library in 1956.[3] We do not know what has been lost from New College but the library still has a certain number of patristic and other books which are likely to have been bought in the 1540s.[4]

The evidence suggests that at least three colleges bought, besides a certain amount of patrology, also the works of Galen in Greek or Latin, or both, Homer in Greek, Plato in Greek or in Latin, and works of the twelfth-century theologian Rupert of Deutz; also copies of the *Epistolae medicinales* of Manardus (1540), the *De humani corporis fabrica* of Vesalius (1543), the editions by Crabbe of the councils of the church (1538 and 1551), the statutes of the realm in English (1543), Robert Estienne's Latin *Thesaurus* first published in 1532, Guillaume Budé's *Commentarii linguae graecae* (1529) and *Chiliades adagiorum* of Erasmus.[5] A popularity table of this kind should not be taken too seriously, however. All Souls may have refrained from spending money on the important *De historia stirpium* of Leonhard Fuchs (1542), because members of the college had access to the copy in the lodgings of the warden, John Warner. In due course Warner's Oxford-bound copy came to the college.[6]

The colleges also specialized, as we can see from the books on the shelves and from the inventories. All Souls bought the works of Aristotle in Greek (five volumes) and Latin (two volumes) and ten volumes of the Greek commentators on Aristotle, mostly printed

---

[1] Ker, *Medieval Libraries*, 147, 291.

[2] Macray, *Reg. Magdalen* iii. 9, viii. 14. It is now back in Magdalen; see Ker, *Pastedowns*, nos 158-60.

[3] For Josephus, Irenaeus, Origen, Eusebius, Epiphanius, Gregory Nazianzen, Chrysostom, and John Damascene see *Oxford College Libraries in 1556: guide to an exhibition held in 1956* (Oxford 1956; hereafter referred to as *OCL 1556*), 9-24; for Tertullian, Arnobius, Hilary, Optatus, Jerome, Augustine, Eucherius, and Gregory, ibid. 24-8.

[4] The books in question include Theophylact in Latin (1540), Epiphanius in Latin (1543), Irenaeus (1534), Origen (1536), and Jerome (1526). *Ex libris* inscriptions in various hands, all probably of the second half of the sixteenth century, occur in these and many other books: a common form is 'Liber collegii beatæ marię Winton in Oxon'. One of the writers was John Prime, fellow 1570-91.

[5] *OCL 1556*, nos. 44, 46, 52, 57, 78, 83, 90, 92, 93, 96, 98.

[6] I failed to record it in Ker, *Pastedowns*, 32.

at Venice in the thirties.[1] It bought also a set and perhaps two sets of the Roman civil law and as many as thirty volumes of commentaries on the civil law printed at Lyons and Basle in the thirties and forties.[2] Merton, in contrast, bought no Roman law at all. Its specialities were late medieval and sixteenth-century theology, mainly in Paris and Cologne editions of the thirties and forties, and, to temper the bias towards medievalism, a fine row of scientific books of the same two decades (*OCL 1556* nos. 70–83). Surviving books at Magdalen suggest that the college, which seems to have led the way by buying as early as 1536, laid out money wisely. They include six volumes of history and geography (*OCL 1556* nos. 62–6, 69), Sir Thomas Elyot's Latin-English dictionary (1538: *OCL 1556* no. 95) and probably the *Opera* of Erasmus (1541).[3] The Magdalen copies of Oecumenius and Vesalius were bought in 1544 and 1545 respectively.[4]

Six of the ten old colleges had modernized their library collections by the middle of the century and presumably took pride and pleasure in showing off their new books clad in handsome new Oxford bindings (but how much some of these same books were actually read is another matter).[5] What of the other four colleges? That they are not known to have spent money on buying books at this time is no evidence that they did not do so. If, however, they got their most essential books, the fathers, by gift some time in the second half of the century, we may assume that they had not bought these fathers or anything less essential at an earlier date. And this we do know. In 1567 Sir William Petre gave Exeter College the two greatest Latin fathers, Augustine (1543) and Jerome (1546) in twelve volumes, each bound in a handsome grolieresque style and labelled on the spine with volume number and 'S[IR] W[M] PETRE'S FATHERS'. In 1580 Robert Dighton bequeathed Augustine, Ambrose, Gregory, Jerome and Chrysostom, seventeen volumes in all, to Lincoln College.[6] In 1586 Thomas Browne gave £10 to University College with which a five-volume Augustine (1569) and some other patristic texts were bought, according to the benefactors' book. At Queen's the benefactors' book credits Gregory Bell, fellow 1543–52, with the gift of a six-volume Augustine and of Chrysostom in Latin: the Chrysostom, three volumes, 1546, survives. Later, many *patristica* came in the great gift from Edmund Grindal.

[1] Ker, *Records of All Souls Library*, 59, 146–7 (nos. 1150–63, 1165–7).
[2] Ibid. 89–92, 152–3 (most of nos. 1393–1418).
[3] Ker, *Pastedowns*, nos. 279–80 and footnote.
[4] Ibid. nos. 293a, 374.
[5] In particular, the Merton books bought in 1549 (?) have an unread look about them.
[6] Lincoln College Archives Registrum Medium, fo 7. I owe the reference to Mr Ian Philip.

Some gaps had been closed before Mary died. One large one became obvious after 1558, that there were no books by the reformers. That there never had been any is not certain of course. In 1520, the one year in which we know something about the activities of an Oxford bookseller, John Dorne sold two copies of *'Opera Luteri'* for 3s 10d and 4s.[1] It was perhaps a substantial enough volume to have been placed in a library. On the whole, however, the reformers' books were printed at first in small volumes which would have wasted space in chained libraries. After 1558 suitable editions were available, but there does not seem to have been any rush to get them. Magdalen made a beginning in 1562 by spending £4 12s 6d on six centuries of the Magdeburg Centuriators and seven volumes of biblical commentaries by Calvin, Musculus and Marloratus. In 1563 the college gave £6 13s 4d to a former fellow, John Foxe 'pro libro ad Collegium misso', that is to say the English edition of Foxe's *Acts and Monuments* published that year.[2] Elsewhere our only evidence for the sixties is from Merton which had some free money at this time through the sale of unwanted books from the bequest of Richard Ewer who had died in 1558. The college decided in 1562 that the books should be sold to 'Mr Leche' (fellow 1557–67) 'provided y^t iff there by anye rare boukes emong them y^t we have not in our librarie, those to be inchenyd and other strange bouks to be bowght wth ye money y^t the sayd Mr Euer bouks eldyth'.[3] The final result seems to have been that forty-one books were chained in the library, four in 1564 and thirty-seven in 1565. Some of them still exist and two volumes of Bonaventura on the *Sentences*, the *Summa* of Antoninus, archbishop of Florence, and the sermons of Culmannus, contain evidence that they belonged to Ewer. The 'strange bouks' include, no doubt, Foxe's *Acts and Monuments*, Sleidan, *De statu religionis* and single volumes of biblical commentaries by Bucer, Oecolampadius, Musculus, Gualterus and Borrhaeus.[4]

The largest sum spent by an Oxford college until the very end of the century was the £120 paid by Magdalen in 1571 and 1572 for the library of John Jewel. The purchase of eleven dozen of chains in 1573/4 may indicate its extent: the eighty-two volumes now known to be in Magdalen are certainly not the whole number. Probably the president, Laurence Humfrey, wanted to get Jewel's books for the college and a memorandum in the accounts for 1573/4

[1] Madan, 'Ledger of Dorne', 164.
[2] For the payments at Magdalen in 1561–3, see Macray, *Reg. Magdalen* ii. 35, 77.
[3] College Register 1521–67, fo 349^V; not in printed *Register*.
[4] The lists of books chained in 1564 and 1565 are printed in *Reg. ann. mert. 1521–67*, 242–3, 252–3.

suggests that he and other fellows contributed money. Jewel did not have as much protestant literature as one might have expected and three of the books of this kind were not books he had bought for himself, but books which their authors, Bullinger, Lavater and Peter Martyr, had given to him.[1] Elsewhere, except at Merton, the policy in the seventies and early eighties seems to have been the old one of waiting to see what came. Andrew Kingsmill, ex-fellow of All Souls, left the college in no doubt about what he wanted them to get with his bequest of £5: it was to be spent on works of Calvin and Martyr. The money would have been enough for seven or eight volumes, but in fact the college bought ten, six of Calvin and four of Martyr, in 1576, paying the 27s overplus themselves.[2]

At New College very little was spent on books to judge from the accounts. Of half a dozen specifically named books the only protestant one is 'Illyrici 12ª centuria et glossa Illirici' bought in 1571/2: presumably the first eleven of the Magdeburg centuries were already in the library. Richard Meredyth gave two volumes of Calvin on the major prophets, apparently on vacating his fellowship in 1584.[3] In the end 'wait and see' made Queen's the best of the older college libraries for protestant books, indeed the best in Oxford altogether, except perhaps Corpus: this latter because of the great gift of some 150 volumes from Archbishop Grindal in 1583. One hundred and six or so survive. The payment of £1 for chaining in 1585/6 suggests that many of them were put in the library.[4]

At Merton soon after Bickley became warden the college thought of a means of procuring money with which to buy books. This was a levy on newly elected fellows, to take the place of the customary feast. On the first occasion, 21 March 1572, eight fellows contributed either £3 6s 8d or £2 or £1, and the £11 so obtained was to be spent on books 'quam cito commode fieri poterit'.[5] Forty-two fellows were elected later in the century and their payments produced perhaps

---

[1] Macray, *Reg. Magdalen* ii. 43–4, 197. N. R. Ker, 'The Library of John Jewel', *Bodleian Library Record* ix (1977), 256–64. The rough account for 1573–4 has a heading 'Memoranda' and under it 'Memorandum Mʳ Preses Lilly Bond et alii debent pro libris' (fo 420ᵛ).

[2] Ker, *Records of All Souls Library*, 33, 142. Craster, *History of All Souls Library*, 55.

[3] Listed in the Benefactors' Register at 1584. Dr Hunt suggested to me that a New College fellow sometimes gave a book or two when he vacated his fellowship. The printed *ex dono* labels in these volumes are badly damaged and no date can be read.

[4] There is much evidence in college accounts that chaining cost 2d, 3d, or 4d a book in the sixteenth century. The rates of 2d in 1509/10, 3d in 1574/5 and 4d in 1587/8 at All Souls (Ker, *Records of All Souls Library*, 116, 118, 119) may reflect a rise in prices. On the other hand '3 dossens bookes' were chained at Magdalen in 1575/6 for 6s: they were probably Jewel's. At University College chaining of the Magdeburg Centuriators in 1577/8 cost 4d a book.

[5] *Reg. ann. mert. 1567–1603*, 41.

nearly £100 'ad emendos libros ad bibliothecam'.[1] There is no record of how the money was spent, but the purchases of works of Calvin and Peter Martyr for £8 18s 6d in 1584 were financed from this source no doubt.[2] The fund may have been underspent at first but must have been a welcome means of paying for some of the many books bought after Savile became warden in 1587.

Curtis dated the beginning of a new era in Oxford at about 1575.[3] It is about or a little after the moment when there are hopeful new signs in college accounts. Writing and spelling and sometimes phrasing have tended to be poor for many years: now they improve. At New College the heading 'Custus librariæ' comes back into the account for 1569/70 after a lapse of fifty-one years. Rather more money is spent on the library in the richer colleges. More trouble is taken about attracting gifts: a donor may now expect to have his name recorded in a handsomely written and carefully worded inscription or printed on an *ex dono* label.[4] Binding improves, thanks to the arrival of Dominique Pinart. At the very end of the century Merton is spending money on having the edges of books coloured.[5] Heads of houses were influential no doubt in small and large matters. The libraries at All Souls, Merton and Queen's prospered. They did so partly, at least, because Hovenden at All Souls (1571-1614),[6] Bickley and Savile at Merton (1569-85, 1585-1621), and Robinson at Queen's (1581-99) took an interest in them. Leach, Barnes and Gifford, when they gave books to Merton, will have known that Savile would take care of them and it was no doubt Savile who encouraged Merton to buy the great collection of law books of John Betts in 1599 and to spend considerable sums on buying books from year to year. Robinson probably caused Archbishop Grindal to leave his books to Queen's.[7]

---

[1] Ibid. 99, 122, 172, 184, 211, 215, 254-5, 264, 298, 321. In 1595 and 1597 (316, 329) there were elections, but nothing is said of moneys received.

[2] Ibid. 167, 174.

[3] *Oxford and Cambridge in Transition*; see especially his third chapter, 'Well-born successors to the medieval clerks'.

[4] For finely written and carefully worded inscriptions in books at All Souls see Ker, *Records of All Souls Library* 142 (nos. 965-74), 155 (nos. 1465-6), 169-70 and pl. III. In 1595 and 1596 Magdalen paid 7s 2d and 7s for an expert writer to inscribe books given by President Bond (Macray, *Reg. Magdalen*, iii. 32). Printed labels are found in New College books given by Meredyth (1584?) and John Garbrand (1590); in Queen's College books given by Williams (1596) and Robinson; and in Brasenose College books given by Kyrdebye, Waren (1588) and Foster (1596).

[5] The colouring of edges is a revival at the end of the century of an earlier practice (cf Gibson, *Bindings*, 42, and Ker, 'Oxford and Cambridge libraries', 515).

[6] On Hovenden see Craster, *History of All Souls Library*, 54.

[7] J. R. Magrath, *The Queen's College, Oxford* (2 vols Oxford 1921) i. 211, 238. Ker, 'Oxford and Cambridge libraries', 510.

An obvious point about the last quarter century is that medieval and contemporary catholic theology were received once more. President Humfrey of Magdalen had no use for books of this sort, one supposes, but the purchase of Holcot's commentary on Wisdom in 1587 is one of the first signs of library revival at Magdalen after a long bleak period. After his death in 1589 and the election of President Bond, the *Summa* of Aquinas and two volumes of Bellarmine were quickly obtained and further catholic books were acquired each year.[1] The real revival of the library at Queen's dates only from Robinson's time, but there are signs of interest in it already in 1575: not only were some protestant books bought, but some catholic books were chained. In 1575 also John Ridsdale gave a copy of Denys the Carthusian on Denys the Areopagite (Cologne 1536), at the request of Provost Bousfield;[2] and in this or some other year, according to the benefactors' book, he gave two volumes of Lipomanus on Genesis and Exodus, which have been supplanted by later editions. Robinson himself gave Genebrard on the Psalms and Guilliaud on Matthew while he was provost, and the works of St Bernard after he became bishop of Carlisle in 1599.[3] Finally, 1575 is the year when Bruno the Carthusian on the Psalter (Paris 1524) and the *Confessio Augustiniana* of Jerome Torres SJ were given to University College.[4]

Medieval manuscripts were another new line in the last quarter of the century, two purchases and a trickle of select gifts, chosen probably because of the language they were written in or as beautiful objects or curiosities. Thomas Browne knew better than to offer the sort of manuscripts he possessed to University College in 1583 or, if he offered them, the college knew better than to accept: they may not have been unlike those which University College had rid itself of a dozen years earlier.[5] Merton College chose one manuscript from William Martial's collection in 1583. At least fourteen manuscripts came to the older Oxford colleges at this time or a little earlier than this, and some of them may have been put in the libraries; also some early printed books which were probably in the same class of curiosites.[6]

---

[1] Macray, *Reg. Magdalen*, iii. 26–33. For costly purchases of Aquinas and Tostatus at Magdalen and Merton in the 1590s see Ker, 'Oxford and Cambridge libraries', 513.

[2] Queen's College 71.d.4.

[3] Queen's College 77.c.15, 79.b.2, 68.d.8.

[4] Bodl. Univ. Coll. c.16, and University College H.31.9.

[5] Ker, 'Oxford and Cambridge libraries', 23–4. University College received these manuscripts in the seventeenth century.

[6] The following were given or bought in the reign of Elizabeth (I include acquisitions of the post-1500 colleges, but exclude the manuscripts which came to New College in 1559 from Cardinal Pole's executors as being Marian rather than Elizabethan gifts): given in 1566

B. NON-LIBRARY BOOKS IN COLLEGES FOUNDED
BEFORE 1500

Not much is known about how the older Oxford colleges arranged for the safe keeping and use of their non-library books after the beginning of the sixteenth century. Until then there was no problem: these books were 'distribuendi inter socios' or—to use the common term—'in electione sociorum'. Occasional book elections still took place at Merton in the second decade of the century: we have records of the distribution of large numbers of books in 1508, 1513 and 1519.[1] At All Souls, a list of books for distribution among the fellows must date from a little after 1500, since it contains books which had come to the college after the death of James Goldwell

to Christ Church, Westminster Abbey MS 1, Pentateuch in Hebrew; given in 1566, Corpus Christi College MS 22, Chrysostom on Psalms in Greek (in the chained library in 1589, catalogue no. 242) and MS 110, Aristotle, Metaphysics, in Greek; given in 1566, Trinity College MS 44, Gregory Nazianzen, in Greek; given in 1567, Exeter College MS 47, Psalter; given in 1577, Magdalen College MS 182, Astronomica; given to Merton College in 1583, 'Liber astronomicus manuscriptus', now missing, unless it is Bodl. MS Digby 107; given in 1584, New College MS 65, illustrated apocalypse in French, MS 67, New Testament in English, MS 266, Gower, Confessio Amantis, and MS 276, Geoffrey of Monmouth; given in 1588, Christ Church MS 95, Epistolae Pauli glosatae; given in 1589, Merton College MS 297B, Statuta Angliae; bought in 1591, Merton College MS 304, Euclid, etc., in Greek; given in 1595, Christ Church MS 89, Higden, Polychronicon; given in 1595, Queen's College MS 202, Horace, and MS 314, Silius Italicus; given in 1596, Balliol College MS 1, Bible; given in 1598, St John's College MS 48, Bible, MS 109, Felton, Sermones, MS 193, Bible, MS 196, Psalter and MS 199, Julianus Pomerius; bought in 1598, Magdalen College MS 100, Psalter; given in 1599, Oriel College 77, Bible; given in 1599, Queen's College MS 299, Bible; given in 1600, St John's College MS 29, Bible, and MS 35, Lactantius; given in 1601, Christ Church MS 90, commentary on Daniel, and MS 91, sermons of Nicholas de Aquavilla; St John's College MS 194, Gospels. The gifts to Christ Church of MS 105, Bible, and MS 145, Bible in English, are undated, but before 1601. The gifts to Christ Church in 1601 are something new. Medieval manuscripts of no special distinction are now once more being given a place in college libraries. Examples of early printed books given to colleges at this time are: given in 1584, Balliol College Ar.C.1.9. *Rudimentum novitiorum* (Lübeck 1475), given in 1590, Bodl. Univ. Coll. b.2, Isidore, *Etymologiae* (Strasbourg *c* 1473) and Boethius, *De consolatione philosophiae*, with the commentary of pseudo-Aquinas (Cologne 1476). The Balliol book has lost six of the first seven woodcuts. Someone—a modern hand says Anthony Wood—wrote at the foot of the first page 'Is it not a great shame to y[e] scholars of Ball. Coll. to suffer such a choice book as this to be thus defaced'. In all fairness one should add that men with scissors have defaced some books in most college libraries.

Three more Greek manuscripts with dated inscriptions may be added to this list, the Glasgow Octateuch (Glasgow University, Gen. 322), a Galen in Paris (Bibliotèque nationale Paris Supplement gk. 2168), and a Josephus in Leyden (Gk.16 J). The first two were gifts to Corpus Christi College in October 1563, 'ut orent pro fidelibus defunctis', and the third— I owe my knowledge of it to Dr R. W. Hunt—was a gift to New College at the same time. Perhaps the donor, John Clement, waited for better times in which to send them and better times never came. He was an exile for the sake of religion from 1559 until his death at Malines (Mechelen) in 1572 (see *DNB*). It is extremely unlikely that these books ever reached Corpus and New College.

[1] F. M. Powicke, *The Medieval Books of Merton College* (Oxford 1931), 247–52.

in 1499.[1] At Oriel, MS 58 was given as an election book about 1500 and was in the election of John Stevens (fellow in 1511).[2] At Exeter, MS Bodley 42 was 'de electione Smale', so falls between 1508 and 1516. At New College, MS 210, the *Decretum* of Gratian, was given by Richard Wylleys, warden of Higham Ferrers (1504–23), with the interesting provision that the fellow who had it 'per indenturam' should give it up temporarily to any fellow who was going to carry on his studies in the country for fear of some contagious disease: the implication is that the *Decretum* was less necessary to one remaining in college, because there were other copies to be had there. At Lincoln, Edward Hoppey, formerly a fellow—he had taken his BA in 1527—bequeathed books in 1536 to go in elections of fellows and bachelors: his will shows that the system still had some life in it.[3] But with so many new and important books being printed, the election could only continue to be the flourishing institution it appears to have been in the Middle Ages if it was brought up to date with new books. There is no evidence that this happened. More probably a case was made for not trying to have a college lending library on the old lines, now that books were so much cheaper and more easily available: fellows could afford their own textbooks. Yet, the old books of the election were there, some so old and out of date that they had to be cleared out—large numbers of medieval textbooks at Merton had this fate—but some still of value, although old fashioned, like Goldwell's incunabula at All Souls. And every now and then people gave books which for one reason or another were not suitable as library books, like many of David Pole's and nearly all Warham's at All Souls.[4] Probably these were rules for the use of these books. Some may have been kept in cupboards in a special class of valuable small books. Nearly ninety of Pole's non-library books, many of them octavos, survive at All Souls College.

Evidence for an actual election system continuing in use throughout the sixteenth century is to be found at one college only, Lincoln, where the college registers contain four lists: one of ninety-two books 'in communi Electione sociorum' in 1543; one of thirty-two books 'in communi electione sociorum' entered on 29 February 1568, according to the heading, but the hand looks later; and two in the hand of Edmund Underhill, sub-rector, one dated 1595 of eighteen books brought in by fellows and the other dated 1596 of eighteen books (the same eighteen possibly) 'chosen' by fellows.[5] These

[1] Ker, *Records of All Souls Library*, 99–102, 156–7.
[2] *Dean's Register of Oriel*, 29.
[3] *BRUO 1501–40*, 298, 722.
[4] Ker, *Records of All Souls Library*, 24–33, 134–42.
[5] Lincoln College Archives Registrum Vetus fo 22 (1543), fo 234[V] (1567). Registrum

are not any of them election lists of the medieval kind. Most of the books are standard theology in old editions: to judge from survivors, many in the 1543 list came by bequest from Bishop Edmund Audley in 1524.[1] Only 'Secundum volumen Doleti' in the 1568 list and 'Foxius de consensu platonis cum Arist.' in the 1568, 1595 and 1596 lists are different.[2]

Although so far as I know, the word 'electio' is only used in records later than 1519 (Merton), at one of the older colleges, Lincoln, some evidence for the existence of borrowable books in other colleges is to be found. Thus, Merton decided in 1595 that if any of the (fifty-eight) books given the year before by Robert Barnes duplicated books already in the library they were to be available for loan to fellows.[3] Duplication is much in evidence at New College. It is very remarkable that this college was willing to accept and has piously preserved large numbers of very large law books printed in the late fifteenth century and the early sixteenth century, not only civil law books but also canon law books which came to it in the bequests of Richard Rede in 1575 and Thomas Stempe in 1581. Many of them were duplicates, notably Panormitanus on the *Decretals*.[4] Their only use must have been as borrowable duplicates.

To sum up the evidence: the books kept outside the libraries do not seem to have been cheap textbooks; some may have been valuable books which were not chained in the library because they were small and in the wrong sort of binding;[5] others were duplicates of books already in the library; others were books of secondary interest. Probably many of them turned into library books when, about and soon after 1600, college libraries became less crowded—even unfilled—because new cases with horizontal shelving had been substituted for the old lectern desks. Provision for small unchainable books, unchainable because in parchment covers, may have been made at this time: the existing cupboards at Merton look as if they were part of the 1589 design.

Medium, app. pp. 11, 12 (1595–6). The 1543 list is quite different from and three times as big as the collection 'in communi electione' in 1476 printed by R. Weiss, 'The earliest catalogues of the library of Lincoln College', *Bodleian Quarterly Record* viii (1937), 342–3.

[1] Audley's gifts to Lincoln College are listed in *BRUO to 1500* i. 76. All of them except Rainerius, *Pantheologia*, are probably in the 1543 election list. For the Lincoln lists see app. 1.

[2] Etienne Dolet, *Commentaria linguae latinae* (2 vols Lyons 1536–8, folio). S. Foxius, *De naturae philosophia seu de Platonis et Aristotelis consensione* (Paris 1560, octavo).

[3] *Reg. ann. mert. 1567–1603*, 316; *BRUO 1501–40*, 28, 714.

[4] Ker, 'Oxford and Cambridge libraries', 504.

[5] William Marshall made this point in his will, Reg. Canc. 1545–1661, fo 245: 'all my bokes of diuinitie in bordes of y[e] larger volume' were to go to Merton to be chained in the library. 'Bokes in past' are mentioned later in the will, among bequests to individuals.

C. THE CHAINED LIBRARIES IN COLLEGES
FOUNDED AFTER 1500

The colleges founded in the sixteenth century had to be furnished
with books and, except at Christ Church and Jesus, they received
generous gifts almost at once. Since the time of William of Wykeham
at New College, founders had seen to it that a good many books
could be marked 'ex dono fundatoris'. They were influential people
and their friends contributed. The existing libraries acted as a
pattern. A collection of manuscripts was felt to be desirable by
Smith in 1514 and Fox in 1517 and by White and Pope in 1555.
These manuscripts have survived better than the manuscripts of the
older colleges: librarians did not have to worry so much about which
of them to get rid of in order to make room for new printed books.
At Brasenose and Corpus the founders did not have the same opportunities, of course, as post-dissolution founders. They had to take
what they could get from among the considerable number of manuscripts in private hands. Smith gave a large thirteenth-century Bible
and four other manuscripts to Brasenose.[1] Fox gave at least sixteen
manuscripts to Corpus.[2] Also, by a happy chance, a remarkable
collection of Greek manuscripts became available when William
Grocyn died in 1519. Corpus bought some and John Claymond
bought others and gave them later to his college. Thus Corpus had at
least twenty-five Greek manuscripts within twenty years of the
foundation. No other college had so many.[3] At St John's and Trinity
the foundation books could include manuscripts from dissolved religious houses. White had a particular source through his brother who
had acquired the Augustinian priory of Southwick in Hampshire,
where some of the books were older than one would expect them to
be in a house founded in 1133. Pope's gift of twenty-six manuscripts
included at least nine from religious houses, some handsome patristic
books among them; also a twelfth-century psalter in Greek which
John White, bishop of Winchester, had given to him.[4]

The libraries of two of the sixteenth-century colleges, Brasenose
and Corpus, can be looked at as a whole. Brasenose, like All Souls
and Merton, still has what is presumably its 1556 catalogue, a roll
on which 102 volumes are entered under the heading 'Librorum
nomina in bibliotheca'.[5] Manuscripts are not noticed as such, but

---

[1] BRUO to 1500 iii. 1722.   [2] Ibid., ii. 717.

[3] J. R. Liddell, 'The library of Corpus Christi College, Oxford, in the sixteenth century',
The Library, 4th ser. xviii (1938), 401.

[4] Listed in H. O. Coxe's catalogue of the manuscripts: Catalogus codicum MSS. qui in
collegiis aulisque oxoniensibus hodie asservantur (2 vols Oxford 1852).

[5] Arch. Bibl. 1.

'Biblia in pargamento magno vol.' is the present MS 1, no doubt, and 'Officia Ciceronis' may be MS 7. Apart from these two and perhaps a few others, the books, to judge from their titles and from the survivors, were mostly not very new printed books, some incunabula and some of 1501–20, some classics, a little medicine and a fair amount of medieval theology, contributed in the first place by Smith himself and by John Hafter, vicar of St Mary Magdalen, Oxford, and added to later by John Longland, bishop of Lincoln, and John Booth, archdeacon of Hereford, whose books were also not very new.[1] This collection was improved in the forties by the purchase of some twenty-eight volumes of patristic theology.[2]

The books in the library of Corpus Christi College were a much better collection. Large gifts of Fox and Claymond are set out in Emden's *The Biographical Register of the University of Oxford to A.D. 1500*. The ninety-seven or so printed volumes from the founder made it at once the best library in Oxford for the classics. The newest of them, like the Greek Plutarch of 1517, had probably been bought by Fox specifically for his college. A seven-volume manuscript Bible came from Claymond, who gave also some of the essential patristic texts. Thomas Walsh, who died in 1528, gave others in editions of the 1520s. Corpus did not need to modernize in the forties, therefore, and the fellows of Corpus had to be content to read their fathers in editions older than those at All Souls or Merton. Liddell's conveniently arranged, but incomplete, table[3] shows that by 1556 the library contained just over 300 books, some forty-seven of them manuscripts, from known sources—mostly Fox and Claymond, together with a certain number of printed books and manuscripts, probably not more than sixty in all, of which the provenance is not known. To the total, 360 or so, we should add an unknown number of books which were taken off chains later in the century, for the most part probably in 1577, to make room for the books received on the death of Thomas Greneway. By 1589 when the catalogue was made, Corpus had 478 library books, and, thanks to Greneway, as good a collection of reform literature as was to be found in any Oxford library. Besides gifts there were some purchases, in addition to the Grocyn books already mentioned: five volumes (three titles) in 1554–5, and single volumes in 1561–2, 1573, 1586 and 1588. Between 1589 and 1600 fourteen volumes were bought, thirteen in 1593 and one in 1596.[4] Some of the sixty volumes of

[1] *BRUO to 1500* iii. 1722, ii. 846, 1161; *BRUO 1501–40*, 61 (not listing books).
[2] Probably nos. 51–74, 98–101 of the inventory.
[3] Liddell, 'Library of Corpus Christi', 400–2.
[4] Five of the fourteen are named in the accounts and the other nine are lumped together as 'nine phisicke bookes for the librarie'.

unknown provenance were probably purchases. Their absence from the college accounts, extant for all but eighteen of the eighty years from 1521 to 1600, is not surprising; extraordinary expenses of any size tend not to be paid out of ordinary college revenue. Books were chained in 1551-2 at a cost of 5s, so twenty or thirty books:[1] the date is not near that of any known benefaction. Some of them are probably the existing books printed in the 1530s and 1540s which have no *ex dono* inscriptions in them: to leave bought books unmarked seems to have been a convention in sixteenth-century Oxford. The Greek Eusebius, Josephus and Epiphanius, all printed in 1544, are among the books in question.[2] The college authorities may have felt that they should buy these important books to maintain their Greek collection. The Josephus is still in its contemporary Oxford binding.[3]

Near the end of the century the library at St John's became larger than the library at Corpus and perhaps the largest in Oxford. Until then it was a small, but rather distinguished collection formed almost entirely of the more important and bigger books given by three men, Gabriel Dunne, Henry Cole and Thomas Paynell who, between them, gave at least 260 volumes (64 + 46 + 150) within eight years of the foundation.[4] The gifts of Dunne and Cole include some forty books in Greek. Paynell's gift was partly of law books. Theology was not conspicuous and the first protestant books seem to have arrived at St John's in 1579, twenty-two years after the foundation: the early donors were all catholics. The great increase in the number of books at St John's began in the late nineties when the college built for itself a fine new library room and fitted it with horizontal shelving on the Merton model. Some of the accessions of these years and the contribution made by Sir Thomas Tresham were noticed in my third Sandars lecture.[5]

Trinity, the second foundation of 1555, had four early donors, Thomas Pope, the founder (99 volumes, 3 in Greek), Thomas Slythurst, the first president (17), Thomas Rawe (39) and John Ardern (22).[6] Between them they produced a mainly theo-

---

[1] See above, p. 452 n. 4.

[3] Ker, *Pastedowns*, no. 568.

[5] Ker, 'Oxford and Cambridge libraries', 511-15.

[2] 1589 list, nos. 212, 214, 219.

[4] *BRUO 1501-40*, 720, 717, 728.

[6] The figures for Slythurst, Rawe and Ardern are from the Benefactors' Book. Pope's ninety-nine volumes (excluding service books, but including the twenty-six manuscripts) are listed in an inventory taken on 26 May 1556 and entered on fo 5 of College Register A and—the last six—in an addendum on fo 18 of books 'receyvid from our founder' in June 1588. At least fifty-six of Pope's printed books remained at Trinity. Twenty-seven of them are marked 'Ex grenewech' and fifteen 'Ex hampton cowrt', so they came from two of Henry VIII's libraries: for three of the bindings see H. M. Nixon, 'English book bindings xiv: a binding for King Henry, *c*. 1540', *The Book Collector* iv (1955), 236.

logical and almost exclusively catholic collection which was not much added to before 1600: a few protestant books came from Slithurst.

The library at Christ Church grew differently and in a more interesting way. Here no one donor gave many books, and many people gave a few books or just one. To judge from the dated inscriptions on title-pages a start was made in 1562 by soliciting books or money for books from wealthy friends and a continuing flow of books was secured later by arranging that members of Christ Church proceeding to degrees should give a book or books to the library. These 'degree gifts' were sometimes second-hand books, something off the donor's own or his father's bookshelves, or, more often, new books which might reflect the donor's own interest or the interest of the college. In 1562 ten people gave books in pairs, five books in all. In 1583 a group of five, in 1584 a group of eight and in 1585 a group of nine 'Magistri in facultate Artium incepturi' gave books. Presumably what they gave was, in fact, money to buy the books in which their names are entered. The first priority was as usual the Greek and Latin fathers. Twenty-one out of twenty-four volumes bearing the date of acquisition '1562' and '1563' were patristic. The progress in building up a collection of books in the late seventies and early eighties and the careful inscriptions in the books, which at this time record not simply the year but also the day of acquisition, may be because there was a book-loving dean from 1576 to 1584 in the person of Toby Mathew. The books were on various subjects and reformation theology is only moderately represented: for example the known gifts of 1584 were Quintilian and Plautus (both incunabula), the *Scriptores de chirurgia* and—from the eight 'Magistri'—four volumes of Denys the Carthusian.[1]

One can only learn about the early Christ Church library by taking the books off the shelves and looking at the title-pages. The results of this search are set out in Appendix [3].

D. NON-LIBRARY BOOKS IN COLLEGES FOUNDED AFTER 1500

Probably books were kept outside the libraries in all sixteenth-century colleges, but good evidence for their existence is to be found only at Corpus and St John's. At Corpus the founder laid down conditions for borrowable books that they should be unworthy of the library or duplicates of books already there.[2] Inscriptions in three books show that they were loaned to fellows of the college in the

---

[1] Christ Church e.2.56–7, Orrery o.2.7, Hyp.K.30–3.
[2] Liddell, 'Library of Corpus Christi', 393.

thirties.[1] After the thirties there does not seem to be any written evidence for lending, but evidence that there were books outside the library can be had if we compare the 1589 catalogue with existing books. Corpus was a conservative college, not too busy about ridding itself of 'duplicates', so we still have one volume of Claymond's copy of the *Opera* of Jerome (1516), as well as Greneway's four-volume copy (1565), and the Claymond (1527) and Martial (1529) sets of Ambrose, as well as the Greneway set (1567), the three-volume *Concilia generalia* of 1551 bought in 1554–5, as well as the four-volume *Concilia generalia* of 1567 given by Greneway. Probably the older books were made available for loan when the newer books arrived: no. 258 (Jerome) and no. 263 (Ambrose) in 1589 are likely to be the Greneway copies, like no. 208 (*Concilia*). Besides these duplicates, other books were weeded out to avoid overloading the desks. Thus, three manuscripts given by Fox, MSS 16, 58 and 71, were chained at first, as one can see from the bindings,[2] but they had been taken out of the library before 1589. And some books were never in the library at all; at least eight given by Greneway and still at Corpus are not entered in the 1589 catalogue.

At St John's 'electio' was envisaged in the statutes, but there are no records of it. The books given by Dunne, Cole and Paynell can

---

[1] Liddell, 'Library of Corpus Christi', 394. The inscriptions are in: φ F.4.6, Hieronymus, *Epistolae* (Basle 1597): 'Orate pro anima Iohannis Claymondi aluarii Corporis christi primi presidis qui vsum huius libri dedit M. Sclatero quamdiu manserit in dicto Collegio ut in electione inter socios semper percurrat in qua electione preferantur Iohannes garrattus et Iohannes Claymondus cognati mei dum illic manserint'; φ B.3.9,10, Johannes Duns Scotus, *In sententias Petri Lombardi* (2 vols Venice 1497), with almost the same inscription, but naming William Chedsey instead of Thomas Sclater, and also at the end of the second volume 'M' Kyrtonus librum hunc possidet' and 'Thomas Kyrtonus socius huius collegii 1555'; φ F.3.4, 5, Johannes Chrysostomus, *Homiliae* (2 vols Venice 1503), bought by Claymond in Oxford in 1505 and inscribed in the second volume 'Orate pro anima Ioannis Claimondi primi presidis collegii corporis christi qui hunc librum eodem collegio dedit tradendum per indenturam visibus sociorum sic tamen ut consanguinei sui 'si adsint' aliis preferantur in electione hoc est huius libri possessione. Interea mihi Gregorio Stremero vsum accomodauit 1534'. This last inscription is evidently in Stremer's hand and the other hands are presumably Sclater's and Chedsey's. The word 'electio' is used here in a new sense, temporary possession by a nominated person: Stremer felt it needed explaining. The Chrysostom was taken to bits and used as binding leaves in the seventeenth century. Proctor and Milne reassembled it in 1891: see J. G. Milne, *The Early History of Corpus Christi College, Oxford* (Oxford 1946), 52–3. Milne's chapter on the library (pp. 37–53) is valuable, as is the evidence he prints (pp. 29–33) of quarrels among the fellows in 1536 about teaching 'the youth whye the bushoppe of Rome was expulsed', removing Romanist books from the library, and 'blottinge owte papa' in the library copy of the *Opera* of Gregory the Great.

[2] The mark of chaining at the foot of the front or back cover about the middle on these books and on other books at Corpus and in other Oxford college libraries is important evidence that they were chained before desks were done away with in favour of horizontal shelving. With horizontal shelving such a position for the attachment of the chain is of course impossible. A position at the extreme corner of the lower edge is just practicable, however. See Ker, *Records of All Souls Library*, 173–4.

be distinguished, however, as library or non-library, if they are in their old bindings, as they often are. The library books have a chain-mark at the foot of the back cover, or less commonly, the front cover. The non-library books either have no mark of chaining or a chainmark in a position which only came into use at a later date. All but a few small books of the Dunne and Cole gifts seem to have been chained. On the other hand, many of Paynell's, most but not all of them small, were not chained.

Edward Higgins, fellow of Brasenose, had thirty-three college books in his study when he died in 1588.[1]

E. BOOKS IN THE COLLEGES MAINTAINED IN OXFORD
BY THE BENEDICTINES

Canterbury College, Durham College and Gloucester College had collections of manuscripts in the fifteenth century. Canterbury College still had theirs in 1534 and presumably it was there in the dissolution year. Nothing is known about the collection at Gloucester College in the sixteenth century and nothing directly about the collection at Durham College. We do know, however, that the monks of Durham Cathedral priory acquired and had the use of many printed books: no less than 118 of them survive, with dates of printing up to 1524.[2] Some at least are likely to have been acquired in Oxford by the Durham monks who studied there. Perhaps what happened at Canterbury College is much what happened at Durham College. For Canterbury College we have what looks like full information from a series of inventories over a period of nearly 100 years. They are of 1443, 1459, 1501 (two inventories remarkably different from one another), 1510, 1521, 1524 and 1534 and have been admirably edited by W. A. Pantin.[3] The collection consisted of manuscripts transferred from Christ Church, Canter-bury, on more than one occasion, together with books which had been acquired for Canterbury College itself. The differences between the first five inventories show that the collection was being added to after 1510. It became practically a closed collection after 1521 (inventory F) when 189 volumes were in the library (187 in 1510) and another 134 in the warden's study and in chests in the cubicle of the warden and Dom William Pecham.[4] To the last it seems to

[1] As is noticed in the inventory of his goods; cf p. 471 n. 2.

[2] Ker, *Medieval Libraries*, 61–76, 252–60. At present there are four additions to what is recorded there.

[3] W. A. Pantin, *Canterbury College Oxford* (3 vols OHS new ser. vi–viii 1947–50) i. 1–76, inventories A–H.

[4] The warden's cubicle was a room of some size to judge from the amount of furniture

have been almost entirely a collection of manuscripts. Five books
in the first 1501 inventory are said to be 'impressus' and, to
judge from titles, these may be about all the printed books there
are.[1] In 1521 twelve books, none of much importance, are said
to be 'impressus'.[2] Here then was a sizable collection of manuscripts which was almost completely destroyed at the dissolution.
Some of them were fine twelfth-century books, no doubt: two
civil law books came from the collection of 'Libri Sancti Thome'.[3]
It is sad to think that these books would have had a better chance of
surviving if they had not been transferred from Canterbury to a seat
of learning.

There is something odd about the inventories. Why were there
almost no printed books? We are being misled of course. The 'personal inventories' printed by Pantin show that the Canterbury monks
were using printed books before 1500 and that they had the use
of them in abundance by the end of the first decade of the sixteenth
century.[4] When Dom Richard Stone died at Canterbury in about
1509, twenty-five manuscripts and sixteen printed books were found
in his cubicle. In the previous year a list was taken of the goods 'ad
usum doctoris Holyngborne', warden of Canterbury College, 'evidently made after Holyngborne's death which apparently took place
at Oxford about Easter 1508'. It includes ninety-four books under
sixty-eight titles and, to judge from the titles, most if not all of them
were printed books, including a good deal of standard theology of
which there is no sign at all in the inventories of 1510 and later
years. On the other hand, eight books are probably eight of the eleven
printed books in the warden's study in 1521.[5] May it be that the
inventories of common college property did not extend to books
belonging (in some sense) to individual monks? In that case the eight
books may be books added to the common store in Oxford after
Holyngborne's death, instead of being handed on to the monks or
sent to Canterbury. The list of Holyngborne's books is accompanied
by notes which suggest that the new warden, William Gillingham,

it contained, Pantin i. 62-3, 68-9. Presumably the books in the study were more often used
than those kept inconveniently in chests.

[1] Ibid. pp. 21, 23, 26 (inv. C, nos. 131, 133-4, 184 (the Oxford Lathbury of 1482),
273).

[2] Ibid. pp. 61-2, 105 note 185 (inv. E no. 185 = inv. F no. 184; inv. F nos. 282-5,
289, 294-9).

[3] Ibid. p. 61 (inv. F nos. 260, 262) = p. 24 (inv. C nos. 215, 222). Neither is in inv. A.B.
They are nos. 839, 840 in M. R. James, *Ancient Libraries of Canterbury and Dover* (Cambridge 1903), 84.

[4] Pantin i. pp. 80-95.

[5] Ibid. p. 85 (no. 25) = pp. 61-2 (inv. F. nos. 285-6); pp. 85-6 (nos. 27, 39, 52, 57, 58,
66) = pp. 61-2 (inv. F nos. 282, 297, 299, 298, 284, 294).

sent it to the prior at Canterbury Cathedral priory '. . . many of hys
bokys be yn small volumys save y^t they [are ne]w an rare workys
and therefor we thynke he bowght them'; also '. . . And as for small
bokys may be distribute amonge the yong scolars as ytt schall lyke
your fatherhod to sygne me for to them I thynke them nessessarye'.[1]
I suggest that Holyngborne's big sets went to Canterbury, that his
small books were distributed at Canterbury College, as the new
warden wished, and that a few books of an intermediate kind became
common college property and were put into the warden's study,
where we find them in 1521.

F. BOOKS OF THE PUBLIC LIBRARY OF THE UNIVERSITY

That three hundred or so manuscripts were destroyed when Canterbury College ceased to exist in 1540 is not surprising. What does surprise us is that the large collection of manuscripts belonging to the
university itself and partly at least chained to desks in a splendid
library-room finished as recently as 1488 was allowed to vanish in
the middle of the next century. How could such a thing happen?
Part of the answer must be that the university library ceased to have
an obvious function soon after it was built. It did not attract gifts
and it did not have money to buy books and so it became a closed
and out-of-date collection in the four decades after 1500 during
which printed books took the place of manuscripts in other libraries.
The letters in register F suggest that the university took much
interest in its library during fifty years after Duke Humfrey's first
gift and then about 1490 dropped it in favour of other projects.
From 1490 onwards is an almost complete blank, so far as records of
the library go.[2] Claymond was allowed to borrow a copy of Pliny's
Natural History in 1527.[3] After this there are only the reports of
Leland and Bale—Bale's is not earlier than 1547[4]—and the notice
of the appointment of a committee on 25 January 1556 to arrange

---

[1] Ibid. pp. 87, 88, but *sowe* should be *save*. Enough remains of the letter before *an* to
show that it is *w*. Not more than four letters are missing before *w*. I am indebted to Miss
Anne Oakley for a photograph.

[2] See Anstey's index under the headings *Books* and *Library* in *Epist. acad.*, ed. *Anstey*,
the same situation prevails in *Epist. acad. 1508–96*.

[3] Reg. Canc. 1527–43, fo 261^V. The 'secundo folio' is recorded there as 'quoque in
luminibus accensis', so this is the copy in Duke Humfrey's 1439 list, no. 84, 'Plinius de
naturis rerum 2 fo quoque': Anstey read *quem* for quoque *wrongly*.

[4] John Leland, *De rebus britannicis collectanea*, ed. T. Hearne (6 vols Oxford 1715,
2nd edn 1774) iv. 58, and *Commentarii de scriptoribus britannicis*, ed. A. Hall (2 vols
1709), 334, 336, 432, 437, 443. J. Bale, *Index Britanniae scriptorum*, ed. R. L. Poole and
M. Bateson (1902), 578.

for the sale of the 'subsellia librorum in publica Academiae biblio-teca'.[1]

A library like this was easy game. Because it was largely the collection given to Oxford by Duke Humfrey its destruction is a supreme example of enmity to fifteenth-century Oxford by persons highly placed in the university. Protestant reformers in the reign of Edward VI were not the main destroyers of old books, but in this instance they are to blame. In the next reign, with a catholic queen, Sir Thomas Pope and Sir Thomas White felt very differently. They gave medieval manuscripts to the colleges they founded almost at the same moment as the library desks were for sale in the noble room above the theology school. According to Thomas Walley, as reported by Archbishop Parker, Christ Church bought the 'stalls and desks' of the old university library.[2] Surely they would have been glad to acquire some of the books also, if there had been any books, any time after 6 July 1553, when King Edward died. No doubt the books were removed between Bale's visit and the accession of Mary. The year 1550 is the usually accepted date for this disaster and may well be right. According to Edward Weston the books were burnt. According to Gerard Langbaine, Richard Cox, dean of Christ Church, was the chief villain.[3]

[1] W. D. Macray, *Annals of the Bodleian Library Oxford* (1868; 2nd edn Oxford 1890), 12, from Reg. Cong. 1535–63, fo 157.

[2] Walley was a Christ Church man, student in 1551, BA in 1553, MA in 1556, proctor in 1563, sup. DCL in 1570, according to Foster's *Alumni*. He visited Archbishop Parker, 2 November 1574, and, as Parker noted in Corpus Christi College, Cambridge, MS 423, p. 79 (printed thence by M. R. James, *A Descriptive Catalogue of Manuscripts in the Library of Corpus Christi College, Cambridge* (2 vols Cambridge 1909–12) ii. 326), he 'shewed me that whilest he was Proctor the Librarie of the Diuinitie schoole theare was replenished with old Authors written, and with stalles and Deskes, on both sides Librarie wise, weare taken awaie and solde to Christes Church theare'. We need not doubt the sale to Christ Church, but it looks as if Parker was confused about its date, unless the sale initiated in 1556 hung fire for a surprisingly long time. His note cannot be taken as evidence that the manuscripts were still *in situ* when Walley became a member of Christ Church, let alone when he was proctor.

[3] Weston and Langbaine wrote respectively fifty and ninety years after the event, but they may provide us with real facts. Weston was the great-nephew of Hugh Weston, rector of Lincoln College from 1539 to 1556, who will have been in a good position to know, if not to observe what happened. In the dedicatory letter of his *De triplici hominis officio* (Antwerp 1602), sign b 2[v], Weston says, referring to the medieval school-men, 'Illorum autem et aliorum multorum scripta in Bibliothecam Oxoniensem, veluti in communem thesaurum congesta invidiosa, rudis ac barbara haeresis nupero incendio, at post illud Diocletiani gravissimo devastavit'. Langbaine's reference is in his preface to John Cheke's *The true subject to the Rebel* (1641). He says of the visitation of the university by the commissioners appointed by Edward VI in 1549: 'What other effects that Visitation had, does not well appeare, but (tis said) Richard Coxe who was one of them, did so clearly purge the Vniuersitie-Librarie of all Monuments of superstition, that he left not one booke in it of all those goodly Manuscripts, of which by the munificence of severall Benefactors, that place was very amply furnished.' A bonfire would help to explain why no pastedown has been found which looks as if it might be from a university library book: if the books had been

G. BOOKS OWNED BY MEMBERS OF THE UNIVERSITY

A historian of books in Oxford in the middle ages need not pay special attention to books belonging to members of the university because there is nothing to distinguish them from college books. Nearly all books in colleges were the gifts of individuals and almost any book would be welcome in college, in the *electio*, if not in the library. In the sixteenth century it is different. Many privately owned books are now in a special class. Books were so much commoner and cheaper than they had been that people with only a little money could buy essential textbooks, like the small quartos printed by the short-lived Oxford press in 1517, 1518 and 1519[1] and the six octavos listed in *OCL 1556*:[2] large numbers of books like this were sold by John Dorne in 1520 for less (often much less) than a shilling a volume. It is unlikely that colleges would bother to keep a store of such books or even of books which cost a little more than this; rather, students and junior fellows bought them or got them gratis from their seniors, as indeed they always had to some extent.[3]

To take one class of book as an example. Until the end of the fifteenth century, the works of the major Latin poets and play-wrights were not common in England, except perhaps Ovid's *Meta-morphoses*. There is little sign of them in college libraries for that reason. In the sixteenth century these classical texts were printed in small-format cheap editions. Again there is little sign of them in college libraries, but this time for another reason, because they were too cheap and small. In the year 1520 alone—the one year for which we have this precious information—Dorne sold thirty copies of Virgil and forty-four copies of Terence—not counting 'Vulgaria Terencii' and smaller, but still substantial numbers of copies of Ovid, Lucan, Horace, Martial and Plautus.[4] The selling price of 'Textus

sold for what they would fetch one might expect binders to have got some of them and perhaps also that rather more would have survived in private hands. I owe the references to Weston and Langbaine to marginalia in the hands of Macray and E. W. B. Nicholson respectively at p. 12 of copies of the second edition of Macray's *Annals* in the Bodleian.

[1] *Oxford Books* i. 5–7, 263–5, and cf 12.

[2] *OCL 1556*, 52–3.

[3] There are many instances in wills of the handing on of books to younger men. Thus, John Kitson, fellow of Balliol, left 'unto my scolar Thomas Browne all my bokes' in 1536 and John Pantry, provost of Queen's, left to William Pantry 'scolastico meo . . . all such bokes as ar necessary to him' in 1540 (Reg. Chanc. 1527–43, fos 384ᵛ, 398ᵛ: Thomas Banke, rector of Lincoln College, 1503, left one book to each of the fellows (*Registrum cancellarii 1498–1506*, ed. W. T. Mitchell (OHS new ser. xxvii 1980), 304). See also below, p. 472 concerning Tehy-Morcott. For book-buying by Cambridge undergraduates in the 1570s see Philip Gaskell 'Books bought by Whitgift's pupils in the 1570s', *Transactions of the Cambridge Bibliographical Society* vii (1979), 284–93.

[4] See Madan's index in 'Ledger of Dorne'.

therentii' was 10*d*, but copies 'cum commento'—Dorne sold six in
1520—cost about 1*s* 7*d* as a rule. Virgil sold for 1*s*, 1*s* 2*d* or 1*s* 4*d*,
but one copy 'cum commento' cost probably 4*s*. It alone might have
been bought by or have been a suitable gift to a college.[1] There were
in fact a new folio 'cum commento' editions in the libraries, a 1555
Horace given to All Souls in 1566, a Martial and an Ovid at
Magdalen, a Plautus at All Souls and at Merton,[2] but with the texts
easily available in cheap editions they were not among the more
essential books.

The book-owning members of Oxford university, who they were
and what they owned, are known to us partly through ownership
inscriptions and partly through wills and inventories, nearly all of
which are in the chancellor's register for 1506–14 and 1527–43 and
in the series of inventories which begin in 1558. The inscriptions
of ownership are always of interest, but only a few tell us when,
and even fewer where, a book was acquired and many inscriptions are
in rebound books. An undated or undatable inscription in a rebound
book is generally of little interest for our purpose. Owners like John
Rawe, Francis Babington, Thomas Summaster and Stephen Limiter
who tell us more than their name are to be remembered gratefully,
especially by students of Oxford binding. Rawe was a fellow of Oriel
from 1547 to 1565. Eleven books bear his name and the name is
followed by a date in all but one of them: the dates are between
1550 and 1563. He had early printed books: his Josephus was
printed in 1483; his Ovid in 1497; his Statius in 1498 (bought in
1561 from 'Stoffolde'); his Cicero, *De officiis* in 1509.[3] Babington
had a career in Oxford (including an All Souls fellowship) from at

---

[1] The 1517 Lyons quarto Terence with commentary may be one of those which Dorne
sold at 1*s* 7*d*. A good specimen of it is in Queen's College, Oxford—good because
annotated in a contemporary English hand. The owner used particularly acts 3 and 4 of
Adelphoe, much of which he translated freely into English in the margins, for example
'Hei mihi vtinam hic prope adesset alicubi atque audisset hec' is rendered 'Wold to god*es*
passyon he were here at haund to here thus'. Bodleian books with much contemporary
scribbling and annotation in English hands include a 1520 Virgil (8° K.86 Linc.), and
Bucolics in de Worde's 1514 edition (4° Rawl. 206).

[2] Ker, *Records of All Souls Library*, no. 1205. *OCL 1556*, nos. 106, 50. See app. II:
Merton inventory of 1556, no. 306.

[3] Rawe is not known to have been a benefactor to Oriel, but his Josephus, Ovid, and
Cicero are there now, together with Perottus, *Cornucopia* (Basle 1526), and Arculanus,
Practica (Basle 1540), this last one of many medical books bequeathed by John Jackman in
1600. Rawe's Galen in Latin (Lyons 1560), in a contemporary Oxford binding, and his
Dacquetus (London 1556), bought from 'Stoffolde' in 1562 for 2*d* are in Bodl. (Ashmole
1564 and 8° L. 37 Med.). Other books of his are J. B. Montanus, *In artem parvam Galeni*
(Venice 1554), bought in 1560, and now at Pembroke College, Oxford, in a contemporary
Oxford binding (Ker, *Pastedowns*, no. 719), J. Gropperus, *Capita institutionis ad pietatem*
(Cologne 1553), in Worcester Cathedral; and *In philosophiam M. T. Ciceronis annotationes*
(Basle 1544), now at Urbana in the library of the university of Illinois (Baldwin 1438),
'John Rawe 17 Sept. 1561 I bought this boke of Gyllam': Gyllam is perhaps the surgeon

least 1557 until 1569, when he died as rector of Lincoln College: the dates in many of his books are after 1557.[1] Summaster and Limiter were fellows of All Souls, 1560–77 and 1574–84, respectively:[2] of fourteen books belonging to Summaster seven were acquired between 1565 and 1576. Limiter's seven were acquired in the years 1576 to 1581. All but one are in contemporary Oxford bindings.[3] Mostly they are protestant theology.

Earlier information of this sort is far from plentiful. Examples are: three small books which William Edys, monk of Burton-upon-Trent, obtained in 1514, 1515 and 1517, when, as he tells us, he was a student in Oxford;[4] a Latin Diogenes Laertius of 1524 in a contemporary Oxford binding, which belonged to Christopher Holdsworth in 1533, probably the Christopher Haldesworth who was admitted BGramm at Oxford in 1528;[5] an Aristophanes in Greek (Basle 1532) and a Primasius on the Pauline Epistles (Lyons 1537) both in contemporary Oxford bindings and both owned by William Buckland, monk of Abingdon: Buckland was a member of Gloucester Hall in 1537;[6] a Latin Plato of 1539 in a contemporary Oxford binding: Robert Whitton of Magdalen College bought it in 1548 for 11s 8d and wrote 'Deus philosophorum plato' on the title-page below his name;[7] a copy of Cardanus, *Contradicentium medicorum libri 2* (Lyons 1548) in a contemporary Oxford binding with 'Sum Thome Simondi codex 1550 6s' on the title-page.[8]

who attended Edward Beaumont and witnessed his nuncupative will (below, p. 472 n. 3). The Statius is in the Kepier collection in the library of the university of Newcastle-upon-Tyne.

[1] Most of Babington's books are at Stonyhurst College, Lancashire.

[2] The dates when they appear to have vacated their fellowships were supplied by Mr John Simmons.

[3] For nine of Summaster's books and six of Limiter's see Ker, *Pastedowns*, 268, 265. A fifteenth volume belonging to Summaster in which three octavos are bound together in an Oxford binding (Gibson, roll XII) was lot 2527 in the sale of pre-1641 books from the Phillipps and other collections at Sotheby's, 26 Nov. 1973: (1) J. Foxe, *Syllogisticon* (STC 11249); (2) J. Calvin, *Institutiones christianae religionis* [London] 1576 (STC 4414); (3) Ratramnus, *De corpore et sanguine domini* [Geneva] 1541.

[4] Now at All Souls College. See Ker, *Medieval Libraries*, 15–16, 232.

[5] Now in the Bridgnorth Parochial Library, deposited in the County Library, Shrewsbury: Ker, *Pastedowns*, no. 181.

[6] *BRUO 1501–40*, 80. The Primasius is at Pembroke College, Cambridge: Ker, *Medieval Libraries*, 2, 226. The Aristophanes is in the library of Sir E. Fairfax-Lucy at Charlcote Park, near Stratford-upon-Avon. Its covers bear an Oxford roll, J. Basil Oldham, *English Blind-Stamped Bindings* (Cambridge 1952), HM h. 1: Gibson, *Oxford Bindings*, roll V and also J. Basil Oldham, *Blind Panels of English Binders* (Cambridge 1958), HM 27, 28. It provides welcome evidence that these are panels used by an Oxford binder, as seemed likely for other reasons.

[7] Now at Oriel College: Ker, *Pastedowns*, 193, app. no. lxxxvii. To judge from the notice of him by Macray, *Reg. Magdalen*, ii. 86, Whitton may have been a young man of means.

[8] Bodl. AA 13 Med. Seld. See Ker, *Pastedowns*, no. 533, but I failed to record the inscription. The book is no. 128 in Symonds's inventory: see below, p. 472.

In the absence of dates, bindings provide some evidence. We hardly need it for owners like the two Oxford medical doctors Robert Barnes and John Jackman: that their books are nearly all in Oxford bindings merely confirms what we should expect, that they were acquired in Oxford.[1] For owners who began as students and fellows in Oxford colleges and had a career later outside Oxford—say, David Pole, John Jewel, Bernard Gilpin, Toby Matthew—the binding is a pointer. The books bound in Oxford at the time or a little before the time when the owners were at Oxford,[2] may be the ones they acquired at that time; the books in non-Oxford bindings the ones they acquired after they left Oxford. Alas, most books have been rebound.

It is more pleasing to hold in one's hand the Cicero of 1509 inscribed 'John Rawe 1550' than to read in some inventory 'Officia Ciceronis'. Nevertheless, inventories are by far our best source of information as to what books and how many books members of the university owned in the sixteenth century. They exist in various repositories and notably for our purpose in the university archives. There we find lists of goods of members of the university and privileged persons who died in Oxford.[3] The members of the university are young men who died before they left Oxford for a benefice or other employment and older men who continued to hold a college fellowship for an unusually long time or who came back to Oxford to a position of importance such as a college headship or to reside on retirement in college rooms. The young are numerous. It is specially interesting to know what they had in the way of books.

For the first four decades of the sixteenth century there are forty-eight inventories of members of the university in the chancellor's registers for 1498-1506, 1506-14 and 1527-43: all but three record one or more books other than service books. For the fifth and sixth decades up to the death of Edward VI in July 1553 there

[1] For Barnes's see *BRUO 1501-40*, 714-15. Jackman's are at Oriel.

[2] See the index to Ker, *Pastedowns* for Pole, Gilpin and Matthew, and nos. 376, 601-3, and app. lxxxv for books belonging to Jewel.

[3] Not many of the sixteenth-century inventories of the goods of privileged persons include books. Five manciples have some: Richard Lye manciple of Lincoln College, died 1575, had 92 books; John Lewis, white-baker and manciple of University College, admitted freeman of Oxford in 1538, died 1579, had a strongly catholic collection: the 49 + 25 titles are listed in *BRUO 1501-40*, 725-6; Edward Foster, manciple of Christ Church, died 1584, had 'an English byble a testament and vii other bookes' valued at 10s; Richard Lewis, manciple of University College, died 1590, had 42 books; John Kitchen, manciple of Oriel, died 1593, left books to the value of 21s. Other privileged persons with books are: Robert Jones 'one of the sexteynes', died 1557 (21 books): Nicholas Syckes, butler of Christ Church, died 1562 (42 books); John Mychell, servant to Dr Bayley, died 1572 (10 named books worth 3s 8d and some small books 'nothynge worth'); Richard Lant, singing man at Christ Church, died 1577 ('lawe bookes and grammar bookes' valued at 26s); Thomas Gryme, yeoman bedel of divinity, died 1591 (unspecified books valued at 29s).

are only six inventories and for Mary's reign (1553–8) only three.[1] After that there is a good supply, except at first. For Elizabeth's reign, lists of goods of close on one hundred members of the university are to be found in the collected series of inventories in the university archives.[2] Nearly all of them include books and many of them large numbers of books: in all, something like 6,000 titles are given. Unfortunately for us, the numbers overwhelmed the inventory-makers who more or less abandoned their practice of listing titles of books in 1586: until then only books of very small value had been lumped together at the ends of lists.[3] The longest pre-1586 book list is John Glover's: he had 325 books in 1578. In 1586 itself, titles are given of 357 books of a total value of £19 19s 3d in the inventory of Thomas Tatam, fellow of Merton College, who had also 'a certay[n] company of english bookes' valued at 15s and 'books for master Rape iii s'. In the same year the books of Roger Kiblewhyte and Richard Green were summarily dealt with: 'His study of bookes' £6 13s 4d; 'Item all the books in his studdye xl s'. Lump sums are usual after this. For 1587–1602 there are seventeen lump-sum inventories and seven detailed lists. Of the latter only three lists are long ones, Robert Dowe's and Edward Higgins's in 1588 and William Mitchell's in 1599.

[1] One of these inventories, Bysley's (1543), is the last in Reg. Chanc. 1527–43 and five are in its continuation, Reg. Chanc. 1545–1661 (William Hurdys 1551, William Darbyshire 1551, Edward Beaumont 1552, Thomas Symonds 1553, John Price 1554). Matthew Smith's is among the Oxfordshire wills in the Bodleian. Thomas Burgayne's of 1551 and William Browne's of 1558 are in the Chanc. Court Inv. series (see next note). Browne's will is headless and was at some time put inside the folded sheet containing the inventory of goods of David Tolley, lawyer of St Mary Hall, who also died in 1558. Jayne distinguished it from Tolley's but misdated it c 1600, Sears Jayne, *Library Catalogues of the English Renaissance* (Berkeley and Los Angeles 1956, repr. Godalming 1983), 134. Emden printed the list as part of Tolley's (*BRUO 1501–40*, 740–1, nos. 1–228). The evidence that it is Browne's (*BRUO 1501–40*, 78; died 19 Aug. 1558), comes from the last words, 'Also Mr Smyth of Merton College hathe some the wch Mr. Browne had of Merton College'.

[2] Chanc. Court Inv. The inventories were collected and bound in a single alphabetical series in 1837. Jayne lists fifty-one of sixty-five Elizabethan inventories in which fifteen or more books are named (pp. 110–35) and three of eleven inventories in which less than fifteen books are named (p. 193). He excludes the inventories in which books are valued in a lump sum: L. Powell (1565), J. Dymsdale (1578), R. Kiblewhyte (1586), R. Green (1586), John Reade (1587), R. Highley (1587), W. Lea (1588), F. Arnolde (1589), T. Glazier (1592), T. Belson (1592), S. Lynch (1592), F. Betts (1593), T. Awburie (1595), J. Gowre (1595), G. Holland (1596), R. Jackman (1597), G. Risley (1597), J. Gunter (1598), J. Case (1600), J. Jackman (1600), J. Baylie (1602). So far as I know, the only two Elizabethan members of the university whose inventories are wholly devoid of books are Thomas Palmer of St John's College (1566) and William Pawle BA (1575).

[3] Lump sums of earlier date known to me are in the inventories of Roger Mason, scholar of London College 1510, died 1513, 'Item in bokys' 19s 6d (Reg. Canc. 1506–14, fo 200), of Thomas Burgayne, died 1551, 'xxvi bokes of the cyvell and cannon lawe good and bad xx s', of Lewes Powell, died 1565, 'Item a certen number of bookes by estemacion xl gevon to the liberary of Sanct Johnis Colledge . . . x s', and of John Dymsdale, died 1578, 'Item certen bookes prised at xii s'.

If we consider numbers or priced items of books a pattern emerges.[1] In the first four decades of the sixteenth century young men who had not taken or had only recently taken the degree of MA and who were not yet or had only recently become fellows of colleges, could not expect to have more than a dozen books of their own. Their elders might have two or three dozen. If someone had more it might be because he was a bibliophile or because he had been given books. Among the inventories of the register 1498–1506 John Morcott's stands out. He was young and owned seventy-five books. By good luck we know that he had had bequeathed to him the logic and philosophy books of Robert Tehy, fellow of Magdalen from 1487 until his death in 1506: Morcott survived Tehy for less than two years.[2]

There are so few inventories for the fifth and sixth decades that we cannot say much more than that people had begun to own more books. A young student (of arts?) at Broadgates Hall, William Hurdys, had 39. A twenty-one year old BA of Christ Church, Edward Beaumont, had 117, Matthew Smith, principal of Brasenose, had 74. One of the more senior fellows of Merton, Thomas Symonds, had 131 and an ex-fellow, William Browne, more than 229. A mysterious Master Bysley had 133.[3]

For the sixties evidence is still not abundant. But we can see that in the seventies, if not earlier, someone who had been a fellow of a college for half a dozen years could expect to have a library of about 100 books (and might have considerably more than that) and a young man could easily have as many books as much more senior fellows had had in the thirties. A new position had been reached: one might have too many books. A fellow of Christ Church, William Withy, put the point neatly on a book he gave to his college, probably

[1] Numbers are minimum numbers. Books may have escaped being inventoried for various reasons: thus when both will and inventory exist—which happens only seven times in Reg. Chanc. 1506–14, 1527–43—we can see that specific bequests are not always included in an inventory, not for example in Dewer's (*BRUO 1501–40*, 169). Priced items are the best to add up: there is usually one price per title (not of course per volume). To use them as I have done when large law books are concerned is not very satisfactory, however. The five prices and five titles in Mervyn's list (*BRUO 1501–40*, 729: below, p. 475) represent fifteen or so separate volumes.

[2] *BRUO to 1500* ii. 1301.

[3] Cf above p. 471 n. 1. Beaumont made a nuncupative will, 22 August 1552, in which he bequeathed half his antiquities 'being certain strange coynes in silver' to Laurence Nowell BA and half to '(John) Bridges'. According to the seventeenth-century Christ Church matriculation register he was born in London in 1531. He, Bridges and Nowell were 'Philosophi secundi vicenarii' at Christ Church in 1550. Bridges's name is not in the buttery book beyond 5 October 1552 nor Nowell's beyond 24 December 1554. Emden wondered if Bysley was a bookseller (*BRUO 1501–40*, 95), but his duplicate and triplicate copies of cheap textbooks may have been for convenience in teaching. One at least of Symons's books still exists: see above, p. 469 n. 8.

in the seventies: 'Cum legere non possis quantum habeas sat est habere quantum legas.'[1] 1577 was a plague year: among the young men who died then were William Dawson, elected fellow of Queen's in 1575; William Dayrell elected fellow of Magdalen in 1576; Giles Dewhurst, MA Christ Church in 1574; John Gray, scholar of Oriel; John Marshall of St Alban Hall, MA in 1577; and Thomas Standley of Brasenose, BA in 1575; they had respectively 36 + 66, 29, 45 + 40, 17 + 12, 29 + 6 and 41 books.[2] Senior men begin to have 300 and more books in the later 1570s and 1580s. John Tatam, rector of Lincoln College, had over 900 when he died in 1576. Two hundred and twenty of them are listed in his inventory, and, 'Item a great many of lytell books in parchment to the number of vii hundreth, worth by estimacion vi^s viij^d'. The year 1586 is a good one to remember, the point of time at which members of the university of Oxford commonly had so many books that the inventory-makers gave up listing them individually, save on rare occasions.[3] As a rule after this we can only guess at how many books people had from the total value of the books. Thomas Tatam's 350 were worth £20 in 1586, Higgins's 300 £25 in 1588, Dowe's 300 £29 in 1588, and Mitchell's 250 £30 in 1599. In 1602 Baylie's 476 books—they are not named, but the numbers in each subject are recorded— were worth £25. One wonders how many books Nicholas Bond, president of Magdalen, had when he died in 1607: their value was estimated at £290. But even Bond's library was much smaller than the library of John Rainolds who died in the same year. The inventory-maker counted 2,232 books in all, apart from an unspecified number of 'books unbound', and valued them at £774 10s.[4]

The 6,000 titles in the Elizabethan book inventories have been relatively inaccessible until very recently. They are not in print and cannot be discussed here.[5] One can attempt, however, to make a few points about the Henrician, Edwardian and Marian inventories.[6]

---

[1] 'When you cannot read as many as you have, it is enough to have as many as you can read'; in the Christ Church copy of P. de Crescentiis (Basle 1548).

[2] The figures after the plus signs are the rumps like Dewhurst's forty old books 'worth by estimacion' 2s 6d. Dayrell's inventory is printed in Macray, Reg. Magdalen iii. 61-2: cf Curtis, Oxford and Cambridge in Transition, 100.

[3] Only some twenty-six book-inventories are in Chanc. Court Inv. for the period 1601-1720.   [4] Corpus Christi College MS 352, fo 5.

[5] They have been transcribed by Mr Walter Mitchell. His typescript is in the University Archives. It includes all the book-lists in inventories in Reg. Chanc. 1506-14, 1527-43, 1545-1661 and in Chanc. Court Inv.; also extracts from wills in so far as they relate to books. The period covered is 1506 to 1720.

[6] Twenty-eight book-lists are printed, omitting valuations, in BRUO 1501-40, 715-42, from inventories in Reg. Canc. 1506-14 (8), Reg. Canc. 1527-43 (13), Bodl. Wills Oxon 179 (1), Reg. Canc. 1545-1661 (2) and the Chanc. Court Inv. (4): Bydnell, Haywood, Jackson, Mychegood, Robinson, Rothley, Thomson, Valyn; Burton, Bysley, Cartwright,

The valuations are a useful guide. Most books had little value, as we
should expect. For example, those priced at more than 1s are ten out
of seventy-three in Morcott's inventory, eleven out of thirty in the
inventory of William Thompson, fellow of University College, died
1507, the year he was northern proctor, and twenty-two out of 133
in the inventory of 'Master Bysley' (1543): on the other hand, they
are twenty-two out of thirty in the inventory of Lionel Jackson,
fellow of Balliol College by 1505, died 1512. Many of the cheap
books are small textbooks of logic, philosophy and theology, the
sort of books we do not find at all in college records. Other more
substantial volumes were perhaps low priced because they were in
poor condition or not in demand. Others, more perhaps than we
might expect, are books of value. At least half the inventories
contain titles priced at five shillings or more. The top prices, ten
shillings or more, are mainly for sets, Lyra on the Bible, and the
legal 'Course of Civil', 'Course of Canon', 'Course of Abbot', 'Course
of Jason', 'Course of Barthol', that is to say the *Corpus juris civilis*
and *Corpus juris canonici* and the multi-volume commentaries of
Nicholas de Tudeschis 'abbas Panormitanus' on the canon law and
of Jason Maynus and Bartholus de Saxoferrato on the civil law.[1]
The over-five but under-10s class contains Duns Scotus in two
volumes, Bonaventura in two and Denys the Carthusian in two
(Dorne was selling 'Scotus Nouus in tribus' at 14s in 1520) and also,
in 1529 and later, collected works of the fathers, Gregory, Ambrose
and Origen. The few books young men had were sometimes good
books. Thus, John Robinson, fellow of Balliol who died soon after
he took his MA (1510) had a 12s Lyra and a 5s Duns among his half
dozen, and the young lawyers, Carter, Colles, Mervyn and Purfrey,
none of whom is known to have held a college fellowship, had
weighty and costly law books which probably came to them as

Colles, Griffith, Gryce, Hamlyn, Hodges, Hoppey, Lacy, Mervyn, Wodrofe, Yardeley; Smith;
Price, Symons; Conner, Daye, Tolley + Browne. Short lists from six inventories in Reg.
Canc. 1506–14, 1527–43 are included in *BRUO 1501–40* with the notices of Hartburn,
Hawarden, R. Hunt, Kytson, Purfrey and an abbot of Talley (pp. 271, 275, 305, 336, 467,
556: on p. 467 Purfrey's list stops short of the last three items which are 'Decisiones Rote',
'Dinus super regulis iuris' and 'Nicholaus siculi'). The three law-books in Roger Grene's
inventory, 30 May 1504, are not mentioned on p. 245, but are listed in *Reg. canc. 1498–
1506*, 233. The book-lists of persons recorded in *BRUO to 1500* have not been printed
except Thomas Pety's, 6 Nov. 1503, in *Reg. canc. 1498–1506*, 225. Except for Pety's and
W. Lilborne's they are referred to in the text (95, Balborow; 291, Bryan; 1067, Kyffey;
1301, Morcott; 1537, Quaryndene; 1553, Rawson; 1602, Roxborow; 1863, W. Thomson;
2070, Wood; 2114, Wylcocks).

[1] An example of this sort of book is at St David's University College, Lampeter 21 E,
a five-volume quarto *Corpus juris civilis* (Lyons 1551), in a contemporary Oxford binding
and inscribed 'Jeuons (?) me possidet precium iii^{li} xiii^s'.

gifts. For example, George Mervyn, scholar of New Inn Hall, died 1529, had no other books than 'Corse of Abbat', 'Cowrse of Canon', 'Corse of Jason', 'Cowrse of Civill' and 'Digestum Novum', but these five titles, valued at £4 2s involved a great weight of paper and millions of printed words. The inventories show that copies of great law books were to be found in the studies of young men in halls as well as in college libraries and the collections of elderly lawyers like Richard Rede and Thomas Stempe.

The earlier inventories date from a time when printed books had not altogether taken the place of manuscripts in ordinary use. Most people had some manuscripts, probably, but the inventories are almost no help in distinguishing them. They only once specify that a book is a manuscript[1] and very seldom say 'in pargameno'. Jackson 29 (*BRUO 1501–40*, 723), 'liber vocabularius in pargameno', is a manuscript, no doubt; so too Rothley's 'olde bokes of parcement prec' vi d' are manuscripts. Many titles can apply only to printed books, a few only to manuscripts, for example, Valyn 10 (*BRUO 1501–40*, 742), 'Medulla Grammatice in lingua anglica iiii d'. The twenty-eight law books in the only inventory which gives the medieval form of reference by the opening words of the second leaf, Balborow's of 1514, were presumed by Jayne to be all manuscripts, but two items are certainly printed and perhaps all are printed.[2] That a quite ordinary manuscript might be still worth buying and selling in the thirties and forties is shown by inscriptions in a copy of Felton's sermons which belonged first to Hugh Millyng (died by January 1532), and then to Richard Ewer who bought it from a bookseller in February 1532, and sold it to Leonard Arderne in 1544: perhaps these unprinted sermons had a special interest to Ewer and Arderne because they were by a vicar of St Mary Magdalen, Oxford.[3]

The loss of the register for 1515–26 means that there are no inventories for a crucial dozen years when Erasmus became popular in Oxford and Greek was introduced. Dorne's day book is evidence enough, however, that works of Erasmus and Gaza's Greek grammar sold well in 1520. Erasmus and Greek are to be found in two inventories of 1529, Burton's and Wodrofe's, but not in Gryce's of 1528: Gryce was the oldest of the three by perhaps ten years and not interested, it seems, in new authors and new subjects. Wodrofe, the youngest, had a *Primarium* and *Alphabetum* to give him the rudiments of Hebrew: Dorne had sold one copy of the *Alphabetum*

[1] Roger Grene, died 1504, had a 'Digeste wrytten' (*Reg. canc. 1498-1506*, 233).

[2] Jayne, *Catalogues of the English Renaissance*, 95.

[3] John Rylands University Library Manchester MS Rylands Lat. 176. For Millyng see *BRUO to 1500* ii. 1282, and for Ewer and Arderne *BRUO 1501–40*, 197, 12.

in 1520. In the thirties, Lacy and Hoppey, two youngish fellows of Lincoln College (BA 1524 and 1527) and Thomas Hodges were of Gryce's opinion, to judge from the inventories printed in *BRUO 1501-40*. In 1543 Bysley had the Bible in Greek and some Greek and Hebrew Grammars. In 1552 Beaumont had some Greek and Greek-Latin books, Homer, Pindar, Euripides, Xenophon and works of rhetoricians. For the thirties, forties and fifties, bindings provide rather better evidence than the few and meagre inventories that many people in Oxford were buying printed books in Greek. Fifty-one out of about 830 books in Oxford bindings of *c* 1530-1558 are in Greek or in both Greek and Latin, not counting books which were college property from the first.[1]

In conclusion I add a few words to stress what seem to me main points.

The libraries of the older colleges were medieval rooms designed to hold chained manuscripts on lectern desks and the libraries of the newer colleges were modelled on them. In these conditions we might expect that at any rate by the middle of the century the books which had been in these rooms of the older colleges in the fifteenth century would have been displaced to make room for new books. Inventories and surviving books suggest that there was in fact a great deal of variation from college to college, according to wealth, the chances of benefactions, and probably most important of all, the opinions of people in authority. What we might expect is what we actually find at Queen's: no medieval manuscripts or incunabula until very late in the century, when 'old books' came into fashion once more. But it is not at all what we find at Merton or Balliol. All Souls, which alone of all the college libraries can be studied in detail, falls somewhere between these extremes.

In the 1590s and early in the seventeenth century the old way of keeping library books was abandoned in college after college in favour of horizontal shelving. That the old way lasted so long is perhaps not surprising. The conversion to horizontal shelving was an expensive business hardly possible except in a period of prosperity.

[1] Ker, *Pastedowns* records these Greek or Greek-Latin books: (a) bound before *c* 1530, nos. 69, 71, 96; (b) bound between *c* 1530 and *c* 1558, nos. 52, 53, 61, 111, 163, 178, 195, 200, 204, 207, 208, 239, 244, 248, 267, 270, 271, 275, 278, 281, 293a, 301, 302, 304, 306, 310, 315, 316, 317, 318, 331, 356, 373, 387, 390, 394, 396, 402, 418, 427, 442, 467, 469, 489, 497, 519, 523, 568, 578, 583, 589, 594, 694, 717, 718, 742a, 756, 768, 814, 827, 827b, 852, 866a, app. lvii, lxxxiii, lxxxv, lxxxvi, xc, xci, xciii, ciii, cxxiii, cxlviii, clii, clxvii, ccxxv, cclviii. Some additions can be made, notably Buckland's Aristophanes (above, p. 469. Twenty-seven items are certainly or probably books which have never been in private hands, having been bought new for college libraries: (All Souls) nos. 301, 302, 304, 306, 310, 315-18; (Corpus) nos. 207, 568; (Magdalen) nos. 111, 163, 239, 244, 293a, 373, lxxxiii, lxxxv; (Merton) nos. 387, 390, 394, 396; (New College) nos. 418, 717-18.

In the late middle ages college books were either in the library, or, if not wanted there, 'in electione sociorum'. The election system came to an end during the sixteenth century and most of the books which had been in election were probably discarded. The word itself, but perhaps not quite the thing, continued to be used at Lincoln College for a long time. For other colleges we have no precise information, but the evidence from existing books, shows that some colleges at least took care of quite large numbers of non-library books. It seems likely that some arrangements were made for their use.

Books became cheaper and more plentiful early in the century and most graduate members of the university acquired no doubt at least a few. Private collections continued to be fairly small, however, for a long time. We do not know that any Oxford man who died between 1500 and 1557 left behind him as many as 200 books. In Elizabeth's reign private collections became much larger and even young men commonly possessed the beginnings of a library.

The evidence from inventories for probate is at its best in the 1570s and 1580s. The year 1577 is important: the inventories of that plague year suggest that young men in the 70s might expect to own as many books as much more senior men owned in the 30s. The year 1586 is important too, because the inventories from then on commonly give only a lump-sum valuation of books. People often had so many books, 300 or more, that the task of listing and valuing individual items was no longer practicable. As a result the information to be derived from book titles in inventories—it has still to be studied —is only plentiful for a short time.

Appendix I

Lincoln College Election Lists

N. R. KER

1. Books 'in communi electione sociorum' in 1543, from Registrum Vetus, fos 22 (nos. 1–32), 22^v (nos. 33–81), 23 (nos. 82–112). The title and nos. 1–49 are in one hand. The rest were added in six hands: 50–3; 54–81; 82; 83–90; 91, 92; 93–112.

Libri qui subscribuntur sunt in communi Electione sociorum Collegii Lincoln' et nomina eorum fuerunt intitulata anno domini 1543°

(1)	In primis Cronica Cronicarum 2° fo *in principio*
(2–5)	Diuus Thomas in 4^{or} voluminibus 2° fo 1^e partis libri 1^i *non est sapiencia.* 2° fo 2^i libri *ratione qua.* 2° fo libri primi 2^e partis *sicut enim.* 2° fo 2^i *inferius versus*
(6)	Vincentius in speculo naturali 2° fo *reddit*
(7)*	Hugo Cardinalis 2° fo *Liber generacionis*
(8)	Concordatie biblie 2° fo *he dicte sunt promissiones*
(9)	Hugo Cardinalis 2° *liber generacionis*
(10)	Diuus Thomas Aquinatis 2° fo *minora sub tempora*
(11)*	Epistole d. Hieronimi 2° fo *Cruciatu*
(12)	Homelie Crisostomi 2° fo *abs te*
(13–15)*	Quinquagena d. Augustini in 3^{bus} voluminibus. 2° fo primi *Incipiunt.* 2° fo 2^i *qua republica.* 2° fo 3^i *Corporis*
(16)	Vincentius in speculo morali 2° fo *vitulus sicut vacca*
(17)	Speculum Vincentii naturale 2° fo *reddit*
(18)	Vincentius in speculum doctrinale 2° fo *quo que imperitia*
(19)	Nider in decalogum 2° fo *peccatum*
(20)	Diuus Thomas Aquinatis super Euang' 2° fo *catena*
(21)	Historie noui ac veteris testamenti 2° fo *mundi valde*
(22–4)	Lira in 3^{bus} voluminibus. 2° fo prima *Nolui.* 2° fo 2^i *erat sacerdos* 2° fo 3 *imponitur*
(25)	Calepinus 2° fo *A nemine*
(26)	Plutarchus cum aliis 2° fo *sumptus*

(27)*	Augustinus in ciuitate dei 2° fo *pietatis*
(28)*	Speculum morale 2° fo *Infirmorum visitacio*
(29, 30)	Scotus in 4^m (cancelled) librum sentenciarum 2° fo 1^i *reales* 2° fo 2^i *consequentis*
(31)*	Strabo 2° fo *extollunt*
(32)	Eusebius de preparacione euangelica 2° fo *Intellectualis*
(33)	Titus liuius 2° fo *romanorum*
(34)	Boetius de consolacione philosophie 2° fo *suscepti*
(35)*	Boccatius 2° fo *genuit*
(36)	Virgilius 2° fo *materia*
(37)	Terentius 2° fo *lectionum*
(38–41)	Lira in 4^or voluminibus 2° fo 1 libri (*blank*)
(42)	Aulus gellius 2° fo φopα
(43)	Boetius de consolacione philosophie 2° fo *sis oportet*
(44)	Ethica Aristotelis 2° fo *Aristoteles*
(45)	Novum testamentum grece 2° fo Μαριατ
(46)	Plutarchus de viris illustribus 2° fo *exercebat*
(47–9)*	Blondus flauius in 3^bus voluminibus 2° fo 1^i *illum* 2^i *nulli* 3^i *circuitus*
(50)	Chrisostomus in genesim 2° fo *Venerando*
(51)	Bartholomeus de proprietatibus rerum 2° fo *quid notificent*
(52)	Postillæ maiores in euangelia et epist' 2° fo *Annotationis*
(53)	Petrus barthorius 2° fo materiæ
(54)*	summa predicantium
(55–6)	scotus in duobus
(57)	lincoln'
(58)	biblia scripta
(59)	glosa in paulum
(60–2)*	Antoninus in 3^bus
(63)	Augustinus super gen' (?: *entry cancelled*)
(64)	theologia naturalis
(65–8)*	lira in 4 sine textu
(69)	Thomas in epistolas
(70)*	sermones thesauri
(71–6)	sex libri legales
(77)	scotus super sententias
(78)	bonaventura
(79)	2^a 2^e divi Thomæ
(90)	supplementum cronicarum
(81)	lateburius super trenos

(82)	seneca 2 fo amplissimo	
(83)	concordantiæ maiores	
(84)	Hugo card' in epistolas	ex dono magristri mitchel
(85)	opscula Augustini	
(86)	Homiliarius doctorum	
(87)	sermones Iacobi de Vorag'	ex dono magistri
(88)	hugo cardinalis in psalterium	Iones
(89)	fasciculus temporum	
(90)	donatus super 8 part' orationis	
(91)	Calepinus	
(92)	tartareus super logicam et philosophiam naturalem	

Nomina librorum quos Mr Weston dedit Collegio lincoln'

(93–5)	opera D. Ambrosii 3^bus voluminibus
(96–7)	opera Origenis 2^bus voluminibus
(98)	opera Damasceni uno volu.
(99–102)	opera Alexandri de Ales 4^or voluminibus
(103)	paulina de recta paschæ celebratione
(104–9)	opera pellicani sex voluminibus
(110)	Vignerius
(111–12)	M^r babington dedit collegio duos illos tomos quos edidit Venerabilis beda et in Evang' et in d.pauli omnes Epistolas

2. Books 'in comuni electione Sociorum', 29th February 1568, from Registrum Vetus, fo 234^v.

libri qui subscribuntur sunt in comuni electione Sociorum collegii lincoln' quorum nomina fuerunt asscripta in sequente Albo: vicesimo nono die februar ii Anno 1567

(1)	Ambrosii Calepini lexicon
(2)	Marc' Tull C. de philosophia volumen secundum
(3)	Marc' T.C. tuscul quest.
(4)	Græca grammatica Cęporini
(5)	Maximus Tyrius
(6)	Vergilius cum comento
(7)	Quest. scoti in metaph.
(8)	Primum volumen orationum Cic'
(9)	Tercium volumen orationum Cic'
(10)	Titus Livius
(11)	Plutarchus de vitis illustrium
(12)	Policronicon de etatibus mundi
(13)	Encomie morum eras.
(14)	Boetius de consolat' philosophiæ cum comento

(15)	Boetius de consolat' philosophiæ cum comento
(16)	Epistolę pollitiani
(17)	Julius pollux
(18)	Secundum volumen Doleti
(19)	Foxius de consensu platonis cum Arist.
(20)	Eusebius de evangelica præparatione
(21)	Quodlibeta scoti
(22)	Novum testamentum
(23)	secundus tomus Erasmi paraphrasis
(24)	Guido in terentium
(25-7)	Prima 2ª et 3ª quinquagena divi Augustini
(28)	supplementum chronicarum
(29)	lyra in mathęum
(30)	Philosophiae Ciceronis
(31)	frater Armandus
(32)	martinus de magistris in Ethica Arist

3.   Books returned by fellows in 1595, from Registrum Medium, app. p. 11. The list is in the hand of Edmund Underhill (sub-rector 1596).

1595

Mr Lodington brought in the fourthe and ninethe tome of Austin

Mr Randall	{ Commentar. in prophetas { Commentar. in Esdram, etc.
Mr Burroughes	{ Augustinus in psalmos 5 (?) tom. { De civitate dei
Mr Underhill and Mr Chalfont	{ August. de civitate Dei { 7us tomus operum August. { 2us tomus operum August. { Lira in Psalmos { Opera Cypriani
Mr Vincent and Mr Burton	{ Augustini quęstiones { August. in psalmos { Vincentius Lirinensis
Mr Burbadge	Servius in Virgilium
Mr Godwin	primus et tert. tomus Augustini
Dominus Hartelye	Foxii philosophi
Mr Collarde Dominus Lodgington Sr Norris	} none

4.   Books taken out by fellows in 1596, from Registrum Medium, app. p. 12. In the same hand as 3.

1596

Mr Lodington hathe chosen	4us tom. August. 7 tom. August
Mr Randall	commentar. in Prophetas Mr Goodwin hab.
Mr Underhill	{ Cypriani opera { 8 tomus August.
Mr Burton	{ August. de civitate dei { Lira in psalmos. postill.
Mr Burbadg	{ August. de civitate dei { 9us tomus Augustini { quęstiones Augustini
Mr Collerde	prim. et 2us tomus Augustini
Dominus Hartely	Vincentius Lirin.
Dominus Lodgington	Servius in Virgilium
Mr Chalfont	{ 3us tomus Augustini { Decad. August. in psalter'.
Mr Goodwin	Lira in psalmos
Sr Norris	Foxius in philosophi

Notes on Lincoln College Election Lists:
1543 (List 1)

1   K.10.7 or K.10.6. (H. Schedel), Nuremberg 1493. F. R. Goff, *Incunabula in American Libraries* (New York 1973), S. 307. Both copies rebound.

7 or 9   K.10.17. Hugh of St Cher, *Postilla super Euangelia* (Basle 1482). Goff, H.529. A line of writing has been cut off at the head of fo 1, except for the tails of seven letters, but there can be no doubt that it read 'Hugo cardinalis ex dono edmundi sar' episcopi': compare nos. 13–15, 27, 31, 47–9, 54, 65–6. The form, title and *ex dono*, is more usual before than after 1500. This book can be added, therefore, to the list of Audley's gifts to Lincoln College in *BRUO to 1500*, 76. Oxford binding, with Roger Barnes's rolls, Gibson, *Oxford Binding*, XVII and XXI (Oldham, *English Blind-Stamped Bindings*, RP.c.1. and FL.c.1), as on nos. 28, 31, 54, 60–2 below and on many Lincoln College manuscripts. No. 54 and seven of the manuscripts, Lat. 2, 17, 40, 44, 59, 88, 111, contain inside the covers printed fragments of Sampson Price, *A heavenly proclamation to fly Romish Babylon*, printed by Joseph Barnes in 1614 (Madan, *Oxford Books* i. STC 20331 p. 98). The date of binding of K.10.17 is probably a little later than this, however, since its binding leaves are from an Oxford printed book, which occurs also at one end of K.10.19 (Plato in Greek, Basle 1534): there the sheet at the other end is

from the 1620 edition of Thomas Godwyn's *Romanae historiae anthologia*, printed at Oxford by John Lichfield and James Short (Madan, *Oxford books* i. *STC* 11958 p. 113): Madan knew a title-page but no copy.

11 K.10.5. Strasbourg 1469. Goff, H.162. 'Liber collegii lincoln ex dono episcopi sar' ', not in the same hand or form as other Audley inscriptions. The contemporary binding, with a different pattern of fillets on each cover, but no other ornament, is in a fine state of preservation.

13–15 K.8.26–8. *Gesamtkatalog der Wiegendrücke* (hereafter *GW*) 2908. '1^a quinquagena Aug' ex dono edmundi sar' episcopi' in vol. 1 and similar inscriptions in vols 2 and 3. 'layd in ye librarie 1603' at the head of the first leaf of K.8.26: cf no. 24. Contemporary stamped bindings: each cover bears eight stamps, none of them identifiable in Oldham, *English Blind-Stamped Bindings*. Cf 1568.25–7.

22–4 24 is K.8.15, vol. 3 of Koberger's edition of the Bible with Lyra's commentary (Nuremberg 1486). *GW* 4288: secundo folio *hic ponitur*. Presumably the two missing volumes were of the same edition: *nolui* and *Erit sacerdos* (the first words of the commentary on 1 Ezra) are the secundo folios. The 1487 reprint has the same three secundo folios. K.8.15 is inscribed 'layd in ye librarie 1603', like K.8.26. 'master hans*er*ed' at the end: cf *BRUO 1501–40*, 264. Contemporary stamped binding: Oldham's Binder F.

25 Presumably the Calepinus which Edward Hoppey bequeathed in 1537 to go in election among the fellows: see above, p. 456. Cf 1568.1.

27 K.10.3. Basle 1479. *GW* 2885. 'Augustinus de ciuitate dei cum exposicionibus thome valoies et nicholai treuett ex dono edmundi sar' episcopi'. Rebound.

28 K.10.4. Strasbourg 1476. Goff, V.288. 'Liber Collegii lincolln' Vniuersitatis Oxon 1550'. 'Liber Collegii lyncoln' ex dono edoardi Darby Archidiaconi de Stow': Darby was fellow in 1490 perhaps and still in 1499, died 9 January 1543. Bound as no. 7.

29, 30 The two-volume edition (Nuremberg 1481; Goff, D.380) has the secundo folio *rales* (not *reales*) for the first volume (on books 1–3) and the secundo folio *consequentis* for the second volume (on book 4).

31 MS 114, containing Strabo, *De situ orbis* (secundo folio *extollunt*), and Julius Firmicus, *Astronomia*. A paper manuscript in Italian hands, s.xv. 'Strabo de situ orbis ex dono edmundi sar' episcopi' at the head of fo 1. A label now pasted to fo 1 but formerly on the front cover, is inscribed 'Strabo de scitu orbis / Julius firmicus in astronomia'. The names 'William Weston' and 'Wogan' scribbled on fo 1: cf *BRUO 1501–40*, 618, 635. Bound as no. 7.

32 The edition by U. Zell (Cologne *c* 1473; *GW* 9441) has this secundo folio.

33 The copy once at All Souls College (Ker, *Records of All Souls*

College Library, 48 no. 1066) had this secundo folio. Cf 1568. 10.

35   K.8.2. (1) *De genealogia deorum* (Venice 1472), *GW* 4475. (2) *De montibus* etc. (Venice 1473). *GW* 4482. 'Librum donauit Longlandus episcopus istum'. 'The Colledge book 1550 dominus Saundersone eiusdem socius John Baber in artibus Bacca: eiusdem Collegii socius'. Binding of old boards, rebacked. Notes in an English humanist hand.

John Longland, bishop of Lincoln, died in 1547. His will specifies the books bequeathed to Eton College and to three Oxford colleges, Lincoln, Magdalen and Oriel (cf H. R. Plomer, 'Books mentioned in wills', *Transactions of the Bibliographical Society* vii (1904), 120). None of them is known to exist and it looks as though some catastrophe occurred between probate and despatch. No. 35 and two other books with the same inscription at Lincoln College and sixteen books with the same inscription at Brasenose College (see *BRUO to 1500* ii. 1161–2) are not mentioned in the will and were given in Longland's lifetime, no doubt.

45   MS.Gk.18, given by Audley, and called 'vocabula greca' in the inscription of gift. The secundo folio agrees. The title in the 1543 list is an improvement.

46   Possibly MS 111, an Italian copy on paper, s.xv, which has no known history before the early seventeenth century, when it was rebound by Roger Barnes. The first two leaves are missing. Cf 1568. 11.

47–9   K.8.12, 11, 10 (47) *Decades* (Venice 1483). *GW* 4419. (48) *Roma triumphans* (Brescia 1482). *GW* 4425. (49) *Roma instaurata* (Verona 1482). *GW* 4423. 'Opus blondi flauii Ex dono Edmundi sar' episcopi' in K.8.10 and similar inscriptions in the other two volumes. All rebound.

53   P. Bersuire. Probably the *Morale reductorium*.

54   Probably K.10.1. J. Bromyard, *Summa predicantium* (Nuremberg 1485). Goff, J.261. 'Summa predicantium ex dono edmundi sar' episcopi'. Also inscribed 'Liber Thomæ Arderne': one of this name was fellow of Lincoln College by 1538 (*BRUO 1501–40*, 12). Bound as no. 7.

58   A manuscript Bible.

60–2   Probably K.10.9–11. Antoninus Florentinus, *Chronicon* (3 vols Nuremberg 1484). *GW* 2072. All bound as no. 7.

65–8   Probably K.8.13 and K.8.14 are nos. 65 and 66. Cologne *c* 1485. Goff, N. 136. In K.8.14 Psalms is bound before 1 Chronicles–Job. The inscriptions are '1^a pars Lyre ex dono edmundi sar' episcopi' and '2^a pars Lyre ex dono edmundi sar' episcopi'. Contemporary stamped bindings. K.8.13 has three stamps, (1) fighting dragons as a border stamp (cf Oldham, *English Blind-stamped Bindings*, pl. xxvi (stamp 359; binder C) and Gibson, *Oxford Binding*, stamp 30); (2) beast and bird; (3) small rosette. K.8.14 has

(3) only. Merton College 61 dd.1, vol. 1 of Petrus de Monte, Brixiensis (Padua 1480), has the same three stamps and the name of a contemporary owner, Roger Walle (*BRUO to 1500* iii. 1966: archdeacon of Coventry, died 1488).

70   Probably K.8.17. *Sermones Thesauri novi de sanctis* (of unknown authorship, Strasbourg 1486). Goff, P. 512. 'Liber collegii lincolnii', *c* 1500, on the title-page; also 'Io. Cotsford' (fellow of Lincoln College 1509-19 and rector 1519-39).

83-4   John Michel, fellow of Lincoln College by 1532, MA 1533, vac. 1539: *BRUO 1501-40*, 396.

85-90   John Jonys, fellow of Lincoln College *c* 1530, still in 1535: *BRUO 1501-40*, 322.

93-112   In the sixteenth-century index to Registrum Vetus (Registrum Vetus, fos 25-6^v), the entry relating to the 1543 election list, 'Librorum inventarium qui sunt in electione rectoris et sociorum' (item 22), is followed by 'Libri a Magistro Weston et Magistro Babington promissi sed (?) non extant'. Hugh Weston was fellow of Lincoln College 1532-8 and rector 1539-56, died by April 1559 (*BRUO 1501-40, DNB*). Some of Francis Babington's books are now at Lincoln College, but most of them are at Stonyhurst College, Lancashire. Nos. 111-12, pseudo-Bede on the Gospels and the Pauline Epistles (Paris 1521 and 1522), are at Stonyhurst. Both are inscribed 'Franciscus Babinton s. Theologiæ Bachalaureus venerandum Collegium Lincolln' Oxon hoc libro donauit 1559 Maii 23°'.

110   Perhaps an error for Vigerius. The *Decachordum christianum* of Marcus Vigerius was printed at Hagenau in 1517.

1568 (List 2)

     Nos. 1, 6, 10, 11, 14, 15, 20, 25-7, 28 may be the volumes entered in 1543 as nos. 25 (or 91), 36, 33, 46, 34, 43, 32, 13-15, 80 respectively.

24   The commentary of Guido Juvenalis was printed in 1492 and later.

31   Armandus de Bellovisu. His *Collationes super Psalterium* was printed at Mainz in 1503, at Paris in 1519, and at Lyons in 1525; cf T. Kaeppeli, *Scriptores ordinis praedicatorum medii aevi* i (1970), 122, no. 315. Other works are in incunable editions: *GW* 2500-2505.

Appendix II

Merton College Inventory 1556

N. R. KER

THE inventory of books (Rec. 4277, membranes 8 and 9) is part of a set of inventories of Merton College goods drawn up no doubt in 1556 for the commissioners of Cardinal Pole who visited Oxford that year. It begins with a summary list of 51 service books and some other furnishings under the heading 'Imprimis eorum quæ in choro habentur'. Next comes the heading 'Libri theolog. in biblioth. exist.', and after it 457 unnumbered titles which appear to stand for a total of 529 volumes in print and manuscript.[1] No divisions are shown, but it is possible to detect five main divisions: (a) nos. 1–121: 122 volumes (see no. 45), printed books and (nos. 110–14) manuscripts of theology under 86 titles; (b) nos. 122–283: 163 volumes, all manuscripts, chiefly theology, but with some history, etc. (nos. 243–67), under 141 titles; (c) nos. 284–329: 46 volumes, all printed books, mainly classics, history and medicine, under 39 titles; (d) nos. 330–487: 158 volumes, all manuscripts, philosophy, medicine and other subjects, with two large blocks of theology (nos. 352–95, 409–48), under 155 titles: (e) nos. 488–527: 41 volumes, printed books and (nos. 506–12) manuscripts, mainly science and philosophy, under 38 titles. The grand total of manuscripts seems to be 333 which is only seven more than we can arrive at by taking the collection now at Merton and, so far as we know, there already in 1556 (MSS 1–303, 305–20) and adding to it the seven volumes of Ambrose and Gregory which were transferred to the Bodleian about 1600. The grand total of printed books seems to be 196, but may have been a little more than this in fact, since the maker of the list seems to have failed sometimes to note that works covered by one title were in more than one volume: see the notes to nos. 45, 53, 521. Over 130 of them appear to be still at Merton.

Divisions (b) and (d) are not printed here. Their chief interest is *en bloc*, as evidence that the library contained even in the second

---

[1] My numbering of the items 1–122, 122a, 123–493, 493a, 494–527 is contrived so that the numbers agree with the numbers assigned in *OCL 1556* and in Ker, *Pastedowns* (where, however, the numbers 512, 522, 526, are one behind).

half of the sixteenth century considerably more manuscripts than printed books. Most of the titles are uninformative.

The books are listed on two membranes, each about 475 x 250 mm. Nos. 1–265 are in three columns on the front of the first membrane and nos. 266–527 in four columns on the front of the second membrane. The backs are blank. The entries for printed books fill column 1 (nos. 1–89), part of column 2 (nos. 90–121), part of column 4 (nos. 284–329), part of column 6 (nos. 488–500) and column 7 (nos. 501–27). The condition is good, apart from some fading of the ink. Fading is worst in column 7 and nos. 501–27 at the head of the column—the rest of it is blank—are very faint by ordinary light. Here and elsewhere I was helped by H. W. Garrod.

Entries which are likely to refer to books now at Merton College are marked †.

Imprimis eorum quae in choro habentur

Libri theolog. in biblioth. exist.

1–4	†Veteris test. græ. et hebr. conscripti. vol. 4^{or}
5	Magna biblia stephani
6	†Opera Clementis papæ cum aliis
7	†Opera Tertulliani
8	Concordantiæ bibliæ
9	Novi Test. græ. et lat. volu. 1^{m}
10	Vocabularium in vetus et novum Test. etc.
11–20	August. opera vol. 10
21	Eras. Annotat. in novum Test.
22–6	†Chrysost. opera vol. 5
27–30	†Hierony. opera vol. 4
31	†Opera hilarii
32	†Opera lactantii
33–4	Opera Cyrilli vol. 2
35	†Opera Cypriani
36–7	†Ambrosii opera vol. 2
38–9	†Opera basilii vol. 2
40	H[. . .]ri opera
41	†Chronica Eusebii
42	†Eusebius de euang. preparatione
43	†Eusebius græce
44	†Ecclesiastica hist. eiusdem lat.
45, 45a	†Epiphanius græce et lat.
46	†Arnobii opera aduersus gentes
47	[Le]onis opera

48	Damasceni opera
49	†Albertus magnus in prophetas minores
50	†Esichii opera in leviticum
51	†Eucherii opera
52	†Catena in Genesim
53	†Josephus
54	†Opera Bernardi
55	†Anselmi opera
56–7	†Ruperti opera volum. 2
58	†Caietanus in genesim
59	†Opera Theophylacti
60–1	Opera Bedæ vol. 2
62–3	Faber super Evan. vol. 2
64	†Oecumenius in paulum
65	Petrus in paulum
66–7	†Albertus magnus in evang. volum. 2
68	†Ambros. Ausbertus in Apoca.
69	†Ludolphus de vita Christi
70	Gorrham in paulum
71	†Gorrham in Euang.
72	†Caietanus in Euangelia
73	Catena d. Tho. in Euang.
74	†Haymo in Euang.
75	Homeliæ Nausaæ
76	Catechismus Naus.
77	†Koynigsten in Euan.
78	†Cassia in Euangelia
79	†Haymo in psalmos
80	†Caietanus in psalmos
81	†Catena in psalmos
82	†Iacobus de valentia in psalmos
83	†Sententiæ Theologorum
84	†Elucidarium Ecclesiasticum
85	†Opera victoris
86	†Ioannes maior in Evang.
87	Polyantea
88	†Opera bruni
89	†Isagoge pagnini
90	Platina de vit. pont. cum aliis
91	†Canones concilii Coloniensis
92–4	†Consilia genera. vol. 3
95	Arborei Theosophiæ
96	†Driedonis opera omnia

97–8	†Alberti pighii opera vol. 2
99–104	†Hug. Card. opera vol. 6
105	Epistolæ Aug. solol.
106	†Gabriel Biel super expo. missæ
107–9	†Opera S. Hug. de vict. vol. 3
110	Libellus de virt. morali. cum ali.
111	Moral' excerptae ex orig.
112–13	D. Tho. Quæst. volu. 2
114	Distinc. Mauricii
115	Tertius Tomus Originis
116	†Viues de verit. fid. Christianæ
117	†Eras. de concionandi ratione
118	Quinquag. August.
119	†Eugubinus de perenni philos.
120	Chrys. super Genesin
121	Secunda pars operum Chrys.
	. . .
284	Liber statutorum
285	Suidas græce
286	†Commentaria budæi
287–8	†Promptuarium linguæ latinæ vol. 2
289	†Bibliothe. gesneri
290	†Cælius Rodiginus de lect. antiquar.
291	†Opera laurentii vallæ
292	Isocrates lat.
293	†Comment. in Rhet. Ciceronis
294	Chron. pauli phrygionis
295	†Valerius max.
296–7	Opera plutarch. lat. vol. 2
298	†Calcagnini opera
299	†Dionys. halicarnassi de antiquitatibus romanis græ.
300	Suetonius cum aliis
301–2	†Chro. Sabellii vol. 2
303	Cornelius Tacitus
304	†Alex. de Alex. genial. dierum
305	†Novus orbis per quosdam doctos editus
306	†Plautus cum commentis
307	†Homerus græ. cum commentis
308	Comment. voleterrani
309	†Aristopha. græ. cum comm.
310	Strabo lat.
311	†Opera Arculani medici
312	†Clementini opera med.

313	†Manardi opera medi.
314	†Alex. Tralliani opera med.
315	†Constantini Africani opera med.
316	Horontii protomathesis
317	†AEtii de simplicium medicam. viribus
318–20	†Opera Avicennæ vol. 3
321	†Fuccius de natura stirpium
322	†Ruellius de nat. stirpium
323	Carolus stephanus de dissectione humani corporis
324	Vadius florentinus de chirur
325	†Vesalius de hum. corp. fabrica
326–8	Galeni opera volum. 3
329	†Plinii opera
	. . .
488	†Alkindus de temporum mutationibus
489	†Sphæra mundi per Stephlerum (?)
490	†De iudiciis nativitatum libri tres
491	Prucneri Astronomicon lib. 8
492	Tabulæ ptolomæi.
493	†Ioan de regiomonte de triangulis
493a	†Tractatus aliquot de sphæra.
494	†Euclides
495	†Albertus durerus de variis facultatum instrumentis
496	†Opera luciani græce.
497–9	†Dictionarium Stephani volum. tribus
500	†Arist. et Theophrasti metaphysica
501	Physica Aristo.
502	†Petrus Victorius in Rhet. Arist.
503	†Alex. Acillini opera omnia
504	†Partitiones theolog. Conradi Gesn.
505	Opera medic. eiusdem
506	Trac. de primis philosophantibus cum aliis
507	Textus [. . .] physices
508	Arist. de Animalibus
509	†Boetii opera quædam
510	Logica Algazelis
511	Commenaria in metaph.
512	AEgid. super phys. lib. etc.
513	†Simplicius in eosdem
514	Politica cum commen. Arist.
515	Parva naturalia cum commento
516	†Harmonia mundi
517	†Chiliades Erasmi

518	Polydorus virgil de hist anglo.
519	Plotini opera de philo.
520	Politica cum comment.
521	†Eustratii in Ethic. comment.
522	†Boethii opera
523	†Sceggius in physica Arist.
524	Comment. in lib. posteriorum Arist.
525	†Commenta Donati in Ethica Arist.
526–7	Platonis opera græce et† lat.

Notes on Merton College Inventory 1556

1–4	The Complutensian polyglot (1514–17).
5	The copy now at Merton, Paris 1532 (*OCL 1556*, no. 10), is inscribed 'Liber Roberti Huicci', and may not have come until after Huicke's death in 1581. He was fellow of Merton 1530–7 and fellow of the Royal College of Physicians of London from 1536: *BRUO 1501–40*, 304.
6	Paris 1544. Bound before Gregorius Nazianzenus, *Orationes triginta octo* (in Latin Paris 1532).
7	Paris 1545. *OCL 1556*, no. 24. *Pastedowns*, no. 714.
8	Probably the copy bequeathed by Robert Purvyar, died 1536 (*BRUO 1501–40*, 468). A concordance of 1555 is the earliest now at Merton. Cf *OCL 1556*, no. 11.
11–20	The earliest edition now at Merton is of 1569. Cf *OCL 1556*, no. 31.
21	Cf *OCL 1556*, no. 98.
22–6	Basle 1530. 5 vols Latin. *OCL 1556*, no. 22.
27–30	Paris 1546. 4 vols. *OCL 1556*, no. 30.
31	Paris 1544. *OCL 1556*, no. 27. *Pastedowns*, no. 393.
32	Cologne 1544.
33–4	The earliest edition now at Merton in Greek-Latin, 1638.
35	Paris 1541.
36–7	Basle 1538. 5 vols in 2. Cf *Pastedowns*, 65.
38–9	Basle 1532 in Greek (*Pastedowns*, no. 387) and Basle 1540 in Latin.
40	I cannot read the name which begins with *H* and appears to end *ri*. A copy of Irenaeus would be a likely item in this inventory: cf *OCL 1556*, no. 14.
41	Basle 1536 in Latin.
42	Cologne 1539 in Latin. *OCL 1556*, no. 18.
43	Cologne 1544. *OCL 1556*, no. 18.
44	Basle 1544.
45, 45a	*Contra octaginta haereses*. Basle 1544 (Greek) and 1543 (Latin). The inventory does not make it clear that there are two volumes, but this must be so, since no. 45 is in a contemporary binding (*Pastedowns*, no. 394). *OCL 1556*, nos. 19, 20.

46   Rome 1542. *OCL 1556*, no. 25.

47   The name is hard to read. Garrod read 'Ivonis'. But 'Leonis' seems almost certain in view of the copy at Merton (Cologne 1546, bound up after Hegesippus, Cologne 1544), which is in a contemporary Oxford binding (*Pastedowns*, no. ccxxxviii).

48   The earliest edition now at Merton is Greek–Latin, 1559. Cf *OCL 1556*, no. 23.

49   Cologne 1536. Bound after Radulphus Flaviacensis, *In Leviticum*, Cologne 1536.

50   Hesychius (Basle 1527). Cf *Pastedowns*, 65.

51   Basle 1531. *OCL 1556*, no. 32.

52   The catena on Genesis of L. Lippomanus (Paris 1546).

53   Either Basle 1524 in Latin or Basle 1544 in Greek. Perhaps both were intended. *OCL 1556*, no. 13.

54   Paris 1547.

55   *Opuscula* (Paris 1544). Cf *Pastedowns*, 65.

56–7   Rupert of Deutz (Cologne 1526–7). *OCL 1556*, no. 57.

58   Thomas de Vio, Caietanus, on the Pentateuch (Paris 1539).

59   On the Gospels. Latin (Basle 1541).

60–1   The earliest edition now at Merton is of 1563 (8 vols).

62–3   Jacobus Faber, Stapulensis. The copy at Merton (Cologne 1541) is a single volume in a binding of *c* 1600: it has never been two volumes.

64   Antwerp 1545 in Latin.

65   The catalogue printed in 1800 lists a copy of Peter Lombard on the Pauline Epistles, 'fol. *Par.* 1537', which is not now to be found.

66–7   Hagenau 1504–5.

68   Ambrosius Autpertus (Cologne 1536). The word 'papam' on the title-page was first cancelled and then restored.

69   Ludolphus de Saxonia (Paris 1534).

70   Nicholas de Gorran. The copy now at Merton (*sine loco* 1502) belonged to Robert Purvyar (cf no. 8), and, in view of the chain-mark at the foot, is likely to be the copy bequeathed by William Marshall in 1583.

71   Cologne 1537. *OCL 1556*, no. 58.

72   Thomas de Vio, Caietanus (Paris 1532). Cf *Pastedowns*, 65.

73   No copy now at Merton outside the *Opera omnia* of Aquinas (1588–95).

74   Cologne 1536.

75–6   Fredericus Nausea.

77   Antonius Broickwy (Cologne 1539).

78   Simon de Cassia ([Cologne] 1533).

79   Freiburg im Breisgau 1533.

80   Thomas de Vio, Caietanus (Paris 1532).

81   *Catena aurea super Psalmos*, ed. F. de Puteo (Paris 1529).

82   Jacobus Parez, de Valentia Paris (1518). Contemporary binding:

Oldham, *English Blind-Stamped Bindings*, roll HM.h.16 and ornament B.2.

83 Antonius monachus, Melissa, *Sententiarum tomi tres*, translated by Gesner etc. (Zurich 1546).

84 J. Clichtoveus (Paris 1540).

85 Ricardus de Sancto Victore (Paris 1518).

86 Paris 1529.

87 The copy of D. Nanus, *Polyanthea*, now at Merton (Lyons 1522) was given by William Marshall in 1574.

88 C. Brunus, *De haereticis* and Optatus, *De schismate Donatistarum* (Mainz 1549). *OCL 1556*, no. 29. *Pastedowns*, no. 715.

89 Cologne 1540.

90 The earliest edition now at Merton is of 1572.

91 Cologne 1538. *Pastedowns*, no. ccxxvi.

92-4 Cologne 1538. 2 vols (not 3 vols). *OCL 1556*, no. 91. *Pastedowns*, no. 571.

95 The edition now at Merton, Paris 1540, was given by William Marshall in 1583.

96 The inventory does not note more than one volume, but the entry probably covers the three volumes now in the library: *De ecclesiasticis scripturis et dogmatibus* (Louvain 1543); *De concordia liberi arbitrii et praedestinationis divinae et de gratia et libero arbitrio* (Louvain 1547). *De captivitate et redemptione humani generis* (Louvain 1548). It is not likely that they ever formed one volume.

97-8 (1) *Hierarchia ecclesiastica* (Cologne 1544). (2) *Controversiae* (Cologne 1545); *De libero hominis arbitrio* (Cologne 1542).

99-104 Hugo de S. Caro, *Postilla in Biblia* (5 vols out of 6 *sine anno et loco* but preface dated 1504).

106 Lyons 1527. Many notes.

107-9 Hugo de Sancto Victore (3 vols Paris 1526).

110-14 Presumably manuscripts. 114 is MS 102.

115 Merton has a two-volume Origen of 1530 which bears the name of Richard Wyllanton, fellow of Lincoln College in 1541.

116 Basle 1543.

117 *Ecclesiastes sive de ratio concionandi*. The Merton copy (Basle 1535) is inscribed 'Ex dono Magistri Ioannis Estwycke'. Perhaps he gave it when he ceased to be a fellow in 1546. *Reg. ann. mert. 1521-1567*, 161-2, records a gift of books from him, 22 November 1556.

118 Perhaps a manuscript.

119 Eugubinus Steuchus, *De perenni philosophia* (Lyons 1540).

120-1 Perhaps odd volumes of printed Chrysostom, additonal to nos. 22-6.

284 Eighteen editions of *Statutes of the Realm* are known between 1484 and 1556 (*STC* 9264-79). There is no early edition at Merton now.

285	The earliest edition now at Merton is Greek–Latin, 1619.
286	G. Budeus, *Commentaria linguae graecae* ([Paris] 1529). *OCL 1556*, no. 96.
287–8	T. Trebellius (2 vols Basle 1545).
289	This and 504 are 2 vols Zurich 1548–9. *OCL 1556*, no. 97.
290	L. Caelius Rhodiginus (Basle 1542).
291	Basle 1540.
292	The copy at Merton (Basle 1548) is that given by James Leech in 1589. *OCL 1556*, no. 48.
293	*In omnes de arte rhetorica commentaria* (Basle 1541).
294	Paulus Constantinus, Phrygius (Basle 1534).
295	[Paris] *sine anno*.
296–7	The earliest edition now at Merton is Greek–Latin, 1599–1620.
298	Basle 1544. *OCL 1556*, no. 73.
299	Paris 1546. *OCL 1556*, no. 40. *Pastedowns*, no. 396.
300	No pre-1556 edition now at Merton.
301–2	M. A. Coccius, Sabellicus, *Opera* (2 vols Basle 1538); the first *Pastedowns*, no. 389, the second rebound in Oxford *c* 1600, *Pastedowns*, nos. 909–10.
303	The earliest edition now at Merton is of 1627.
304	Alexander ab Alexandro, *Genialium dierum libri sex* (Paris 1539).
305	*Novus orbis*, ed. S. Grynaeus (Paris 1537). *OCL 1556*, no. 67. *Pastedowns*, no. 388.
306	Probably the copy at Merton (Milan 1500).
307	Basle 1541. *OCL 1556*, no. 46. *Pastedowns*, no. 390.
308	R. Maffeius Volaterranus, *Commentariorum urbanorum libri 38*. There were several editions before 1550. No copy now at Merton.
309	Basle 1547. *OCL 1556*, no. 35.
310	The earliest edition now at Merton is Greek–Latin, 1587.
311	Basle 1540. *OCL 1556*, no. 72.
312	Basle 1535. Bound with Marcellus Empiricus, *De medicamentis* (Basle 1536). *Pastedowns*, no. 387a.
313	J. J. Manardus, *Epistolae medicinales* (Basle 1540). *OCL 1556*, no. 78. Merton has also the copy (Basle 1535) given by Robert Barnes in 1594.
314	(1) *De singularum corporis partium* (Basle 1533) in Latin. (2) J. Mesue, Damascenus, *Curandi artis libri vii* (Basle 1543) in Latin. *Pastedowns*, no. cxvi.
315	Basle 1536.
316	The copy of Orontius Fineus, *Protomathesis*, now at Merton (Paris 1532) was given by Mrs Gulston in 1635.
317	(1) Venice 1534. (2) Alexander Trallianus, *Opera* (Paris 1548).
318–20	Perhaps the edition (Venice 1523) now bound in five volumes.
321	L. Fuchsius, *De historia stirpium* (Basle 1542). *OCL 1556*, no. 77. Old binding with pattern of fillets, almost certainly Oxford work.
322	Paris 1536. *OCL 1556*, no. 80. Same binding as no. 321.

323	The copy now at Merton, Paris 1545 (*Pastedowns*, no. clxxxvi) was given by Robert Barnes in 1594. Cf *OCL 1556*, no. 75.
324	Not identified.
325	Basle 1543. *OCL 1556*, no. 85.
326-8	Merton has now a copy of the Latin Galen (3 vols Pavia 1515–16), given by Mrs Gulston in 1635, and a copy of the Greek Galen (5 vols Venice 1525). Cf *OCL 1556*, nos. 43–4.
329	Basle 1535. Given by Thomas Raynold, warden (1545–59). *OCL 1556*, no. 55.
488	Paris 1540. *OCL 1556*, no. 71. *Pastedowns*, no. ccxxvii.
489	J. Stoefflerus, *In Procli Diadoche sphaeram mundi commentarius*. Merton now has the copy (Tübingen 1534) given by Robert Barnes in 1594. Cf *OCL 1556*, no. 82.
490	J. Schonerus (Nuremberg 1545). *OCL 1556*, no. 81.
491	Julius Firmicus, *Astronomica*, ed. N. Pruckner (Basle 1533).
492	The copy of Ptolemy, *Geographia*, at Merton (Ingolstadt 1533) was given by Mrs Gulston in 1635. Cf *OCL 1556*, no. 61.
493	Nuremberg 1533. *OCL 1556*, no. 79.
493a	*Spheræ tractatus*, ed. L. Gauricus (Venice 1531).
494	Probably the copy of Euclid in Latin (Venice 1505) given by Richard Rawlins, warden 1508–21, died 1535, 'studentibus collegii in geometria et perspectiua concessus', *OCL 1556*, no. 42.
495	A. Dürer: (1) *Institutiones geometricae* (Paris 1532); (2) *De symmetria partium* (Nuremberg 1532); (3) *De varietate figurarum* (Nuremberg 1534). *OCL 1556*, no. 74.
496	Florence 1517. Given by Thomas Raynold, like no. 329.
497-9	Robert Estienne (3 vols Paris 1543). *OCL 1556*, no. 93.
500	(1) Aristoteles et Theophrastus, *In metaphysica*, in Latin and Theophrastus, *In metaphysica*, in Latin (Paris 1515). (2) Antonius Andreae, *Quaestiones super 12 libros Metaphysicae* (Venice 1513). The inscription of gift from Thomas Raynold, as in nos. 329, 496, is on the title-page of (1), but probably covers (2) also. (2) has at the end 'Liber Edwardi Foxe emptus a Magistro Lethar vigilia diue Katherine'.
501	This copy of the Physics is not identifiable.
502	Basle 1549. *Pastedowns*, no. cxviii.
503	A. Achillini (Venice 1545). *OCL 1556*, no. 70.
504	Cf 289.
506-12	Probably manuscripts. 508 is MS 270 or MS 271: the title does not occur earlier in the inventory. 509 is perhaps MS 309, where the last item is Boethius on the Topics. 510, 'Logica Algazelis', cannot be distinguished from 339, 'Logica Algazelis cum aliis': one of these is MS 285 and the other the now missing copy recorded by T. James in *Ecloga Oxonio-Cantabrigiensis* (1600), as no. 98. 512 is probably MS 305.

513	Paris 1544. Latin. *Pastedowns*, no. 711.
514	The copy of the *Politics* in Latin (Paris 1543) was a gift from James Leech in 1589.
516	F. Georgius, Venetus (Paris 1544).
517	*Adagiorum chiliades* (Basle 1541). *OCL 1556*, no. 98.
518	Vergilius. The copy (Basle 1534) has the name 'Antho: Style' on the title-page, crossed through. The binding bears Oldham, *English Blind-Stamped Bindings* roll HE.g.4.
519	The earliest edition now at Merton is Greek–Latin (Basle 1580).
520	Cf 515.
521	Either the Latin translation with preface of J. B. Felicianus (Basle *sine anno*): *Pastedowns*, no. 249, or the Greek text (Venice 1536) or possibly both.
522	Basle 1546. *Pastedowns*, no. 712.
523	J. Schegkius (Basle 1546). *Pastedowns*, no. 398.
524	Perhaps the commentary of Giles of Rome (Colonna) (Venice 1500) which bears the name of Edward Hoppey as owner (*BRUO 1501–40*, 722: recorded in his inventory after death, 26 January 1538).
525	D. Acciaiolus (Paris 1541).
526-7	The Latin Plato is Basle 1546 (*Pastedowns*, no. 397). The copy of the Greek Plato now at Merton (Basle 1534) was given by Robert Barnes in 1594. *OCL 1556*, no. 52.

Appendix III

Books at Christ Church 1562–1602

N. R. KER

ALL but the last two of the 174 volumes listed here contain inscriptions of gifts to Christ Church which are dated or are datable in the reign of Elizabeth I. The earliest date is 1562 and the latest 12 July 1602. I collected most of the inscriptions many years ago when I was looking for Oxford bindings. About twenty are new finds, either on the shelves or as a result of going through a sheaf of notes on donors and owners compiled by W. G. Hiscock.[1] The present list is no doubt an imperfect record of what exists and it is of course an even more imperfect record of what once existed. Many books were discarded as 'duplicates'.[2] The Disbursement Books which begin in in 1577–8 and are complete from then until 1602, are a useful supplement to the inscriptions. They record the purchase of 109 chains over eleven years from 1580–1 to 1590–1,[3] of chains in 1595–6 and 1596–7 at a cost of 10s 6d and of chains in 1601–2 at a cost of about £2.[4] Against this there are sixty-three inscriptions for 1580–90, four for 1596 and 1597 and twenty-three for 1601 and 1602, when a special effort seems to have been made to obtain texts of Aristotle in Latin and commentaries on Aristotle in Latin. Occasionally the Disbursement Books give more specific information which can be compared with what we find or do not find on the shelves. In 1578–9 three volumes of the Statutes at Large and two other common-law books were bought (fo 30ᵛ): one of the volumes of statutes is 1579.9. In 1580–1 three books of Sabellicus given by Mr Copley were clasped (fo 33ᵛ) and a book given by Mr Baldwin

---

[1] I owe my knowledge of these notes to Mr Paul Morgan.

[2] W. G. Hiscock, *A Christ Church Miscellany* (Oxford 1946), 89, refers to sales in 1793 and 1813. In 1793 books were sold *en bloc* to (Peter) Elmsley who paid £277 for them on 21 June and put them up for sale by auction at King's in Covent Garden on 17 July, when 2,577 lots fetched £506 16s 9d. A priced copy of the catalogue of this sale, which included 200 books printed before 1600 is in the Routh collection in the university of Durham. The earliest book in the catalogue seems to be the six-volume Bible with the commentary of Nicholas de Lyra, Strasbourg 1501.

[3] Chains cost 6d or 7d each in 1581–2 and the next few years, and 8d each in 1588–9 and 1589–90.

[4] Perhaps more chains were bought in 1601–2 than were actually used at this time.

was bound (fo 55): two survivors are 1580.1 and 1581.3. On 15 June 1582, 3s 6d was paid for seven chains 'vsed in the librarie on books given at that tyme by the students' and on 30 July 4s for eight chains 'vsed in the librarie on books then given' (fo 49^v): fifteen books with inscriptions dated in 1582 have been found. In 1582-3 there was payment for binding a book given by Mr Hotoman (fo 10^v) and for chains for twelve books given by the dean (fo 66): Hotoman's book and five books from Dean Matthew are 1582.1 and 1583.5-9. In 1583/4 'foure chains from Mr Morreys bookes' were bought (fo 49): no book inscribed as a bequest from Thomas Morey, died 1584, has been found, but his will records a bequest of Calvin on the New Testament in two volumes, Calvin on Isaiah in one volume, and Calvin on Daniel in one volume, 'unto the Librarye of Christ-church to the use of the studentes theire'. In 1586-7 the college paid for carriage and other charges of 'nyne great bookes' given by Lady Burghley (fo 27): eight of them survive (1586.1, 2). In 1592-3 two chains, staples, etc. 'for to fasten in bookes y^t Dr White gave' cost 1s 8d (fo 62): no doubt White gave two books, one of which is 1593.1. In 1597/8 10d was paid 'For a chayne and a staple with the Smithes labo^r in fastening a booke given by Sr Sprint' (fo 41): Sprint's gift has not been found. In 1601/2 Roger Barnes bound 'Alex. Aphrodiseus', now 1601.17, and also other books, probably four in all (fo 6^v), two of which are likely to be 1601.12 and 1601.14, to judge from the bindings.

Inscriptions are in Latin. Usually they are in the form 'ex dono . . .', which is nearly always preceded by either 'Liber ecclesiæ Christi' or 'Liber ædis Christi', the latter a form favoured by Dean Matthew which became common and is usual in 1601.[1] The status of the donor is not expressed by any word or words after his name in 1562.4-12, 1563.2, 1565.3 and 1585.4, but from 1565.2 onwards the fact that he was a member of Christ Church is conveyed by the word 'ibidem' or something to the same effect, for example '. . . ex dono Guilielmi Arnoldi ibidem artium magistri . . .' (1583.1) or '. . . ex dono M^{ri} Guilielmi Watkinsoni S. Theologiæ bachalaurei eiusdem ædis alumni' (1588.3). Only eight post-1567 donors were not members and four of these eight had connections with Christ Church, two through sons (1588.1, n.d.17) and two because they were on the staff (1582.10, 1601.2). The four others are Richard Polsted, John Hotoman, Mr Bourne of Lincoln College, and Lady Burghley (1570.1; 1582.1; 1582.4; 1586.1, 2). On the other hand, in and before 1567 twenty-one out of twenty-four donors have no known connection with Christ Church. These are the people who

[1] Unusual inscriptions are given in full below, in text or notes.

began the library, moved to do so probably by a begging letter from Lord Arundel.[1] More information about them would be welcome. Fulke Greville, Thomas Lucy, Roger North and William Lambarde are well-known names. Thomas Howard, fourth duke of Norfolk, was Arundel's son-in-law. His near contemporary Henry Hastings, third earl of Huntingdon, comes into library history as the founder of the church library in Leicester, which formed the original nucleus of the present town library. Fourteen books in that library are in bindings by the same binder as 1562.1, 3 (vols 2–4, 5.9).[2]

The occasion of a gift or the reason for it is seldom expressed in the standard forms of inscription: 1588.1 was a gift in memory of the donor's son; n.d.11 was a bequest; 1591.1 and several gifts of 1601 were 'in gratiam studiosorum'. We know more only through other sources of information—see, for example, the note to 1582.10 —or from more informative non-standard inscriptions. Seven of these, 1583.4, 1584.2, 1585.1–3, 1602.2, tell us that the gift was on the occasion of inception after taking the degree of MA or DTh.

The inscriptions are dated as a rule. From 1578.1 onwards the day of the month is usually specified as well as the year. Presumably it is the day on which the inscription was written, which may or may not be the day on which the book became part of the library. If a gift was in the form of money with which to buy a book, the conversion will have taken time. Undated inscriptions (n.d.1–23) can mostly be dated approximately through evidence about the donor or evidence from chaining.

Over half the books in this list are in contemporary or near contemporary bindings. It is a good proportion and a credit to the library. Enough remains to show that the books that came in first came ready bound: they are not in Oxford bindings. Later, from 1581 onwards, the majority were Oxford bound. Centrepieces, not rolls, were the common form of ornament on Oxford bindings by this time, except when binders were doing work for the older colleges which had been accustomed to having their bindings decorated with rolls. At Christ Church there could not be any old traditions. The college employed Garbrand and allowed him to put his rather odd roll, Gibson XXII, on a book he bound in 1581 (1581.3). Perhaps it was not admired, since the next book to be bound for

---

[1] Bodl. MS Rawlinson D.264, fo 29. See Ker, 'Oxford and Cambridge libraries', 469.

[2] For the Leicester library see *Parochial Libraries of the Church of England*, ed. N. R. Ker (1959), 86. The books at Leicester bearing the three rolls Oldham, *English Blind-Stamped Bindings*, HM.a.4, HM.a.7 and SW.b.2 are mainly works of the fathers in editions dated between 1544 and 1562. Probably the binder was a leading London craftsman employed by Lord Huntingdon.

Christ Church bears his centrepiece, Ker ix (1582.1). Later the college binder was Roger Barnes. We find his centrepiece, Ker xiv, on 1601.12, 14, 17, and his rolls XVII, XXI on 1602.1 and on two rebindings, 1562.3/5 and 1579.2. These were special orders. The accounts suggest that there were not many of them. The reason why most of the books acquired in 1581 and later are in Oxford bindings is because their donors were Oxford graduates.

The presence of so many books in old bindings means that it is easy to observe changes in the method of chaining books between 1562 and 1602. The books acquired in or before 1581 were chained differently from those acquired in or after 1582. They have a chain mark at the foot of the front cover, or less often and not before 1578, the back cover: the mark is unusually long on some of the books acquired in 1562. The books acquired in or after 1582 have a chain mark on the backcover or less often the front cover, near the foot and close to the foredge: the mark is more conspicuous on the books acquired between 1582 and 1591 than it is later. The evidence from chaining confirms other evidence that most of the books without a date of acquisition are early gifts. n.d.1–4, 6, 8, 12, 13, 16, 18, 20, 21(?), 22 were chained at the foot of the front cover and n.d.5 was chained at the foot of the back cover: the unusually long mark is on n.d.6 and 22. On the other hand, n.d.7, 11, 19, and 23 have the chain mark in the later position.

List of Books with inscriptions, 1562–1602

* indicates a contemporary or near contemporary binding, (*) a rebound book with a chainmark from the old binding showing on a leaf inside.

The aquisitions of each year are arranged and numbered in the order of acquisition, so far as this can be deduced from the inscriptions. Up to and including 1582 my arrangement is for a year beginning on 25 March. I have presumed that the Christ Church year probably began on 1 January, not 25 March, in 1583 (for which I know of no evidence either way) and in 1584: these are the only two years after 1582 in which books were inscribed with dates between 1 January and 24 March. For the bull of Pope Gregory XIII of 24 February 1582 which ordered a reformed calendar and a year beginning on 1 January see *Handbook of Dates for students of English History*, ed. C. R. Cheney (1945), 10, and for possible ambiguity in 1583 and later, *Reg. Magdalen*, ed. Macray iii. 10. Evidence that the Christ Church year began on 1 January in 1584 and 1585 comes from the inscriptions in 1584.2 and 1585.2.

All books are folios, except 1582.11, 1584.5 and n.d. 21. In the notes on bindings, references besides Ker and Gibson as used above, when preceded by Gray and Oldham are to G. J. Gray, *The Earliest Cambridge Stationers and Bookbinders* (Bibliographical Society Illustrated Monographs xiii 1904) and Oldham, *English Blind-Stamped Bindings*, respectively. References to rolls in the form 'HM.a.4' are to Oldham.

1562.1	Thomas (Howard), duke of Norfolk (1536–72) *Cellar I.1.2.3–6. Hieronymus, *Opera* (4 vols Basle 1553).
1562.2, 3	Henry (Hastings), earl of Huntingdon (1535–95)
2	*Orrery D.2.9, 10. Gregorius Nazianzenus, *Opera* (in Greek and Latin; 2 vols Basle 1550).
3	*Cellar I.2.2.1–5. Augustinus, *Opera* (5 vols Paris 1555).
1562.4	Mr Cupledick Cellar G.3.3.6. Epiphanius, *Contra octoaginta haereses* (in Latin; Basle 1560).
1562.5	Mr Fulke Grevil and Mr Topleif *Cellar E.2.8.16. Irenaeus, *Contra haereses* (Basle 1560).
1562.6	Dominus Thomas Haward Cellar E.2.8.20. Eusebius, *Opera* (in Latin; Basle 1549).
1562.7	Mr Thomas Lucye (1532–1600) and Mr Drury Cellar G.3.3.4. Basilius, *Opera* (in Greek; Basle 1551).
1562.8	Mr Roger North (1530–1600) *Cellar G.2.3.1–2. Origines, *Opera* (in Latin; 2 vols Basle 1557).
1562.9	(i) Mr Clement Poston; (ii) John Abel *Nicholson E.4.2 (i) R. Gualterus, *In Marcum* (Zurich 1561) (ii) R. Gualterus, *In Acta apostolorum* (Zurich 1557)
1562.10	Dominus Sheffeld and Mr Thomas Huggens Cellar G.2.3.6.7. Ambrosius, *Opera* (2 vols Basle 1555).
1562.11	Mr Tyrwitt and Mr Sampoll *Cellar H.2.4.2. Epiphanius, *Contra haereses* (in Greek; Basle 1544).

1562.12   Dominus Willoughby
               (*) Aldrich B.1.14. Plato, *Opera* (in Latin; Basle
               1561)

1563.1   Margaret Toye, widow, citizen and bookseller
               of London
               Cellar G.3.3.7. Tertullianus, *Opera* (Basle 1562).

1563.2   Mr P. Worsop
               Aldrich C.2.14. Cicero, *In omnes de arte rhe-
               orica libros commentaria* (Basle 1541).

1565.1: 14 Jan. Richard Bruarn (canon 1553, DTh 1555, died
               April 1565)
               Westminster Abbey, MS.1. Pentateuch (in
               Hebrew). s.xiii

1565.2   Richard Clive, chaplain (by 1564, died 1566)
               Morris B.2.5, 6. *Biblia hebraica Munsteri* (2
               vols Basle 1546).

1565.3   Mr Simon Parett (fellow of Magdalen College
               1541–50, died 1584)
               Orrery n.2.3. O. Brunfels, *Onomasticon medi-
               cinae* (Strasbourg 1534).

1567.1   Henry (Hastings), earl of Huntingdon
               Cellar G.1.3.1, 2. *Concilia generalia* (vols 1, 2
               Cologne 1567).

1567.2   William Lambarde (1536–1601: *DNB*)
               *Cellar H.2.4.5. Theodoretus, *Opera* (in Latin;
               Cologne 1567).

1567.3   Thomas Sampson, 'olim' dean (1561–4)
               Cellar G.1.3.3. *Concilia generalia* (vol 3 Cologne
               1567).

1567.4   Dominus Thomas Wentworth
               Cellar G.1.3.4. *Concilia generalia* (vol 4 Cologne
               1567).

1570.1   Richard Polsted, armiger
               Orrery F.2.11. *Historiae ecclesiasticae scriptores*,
               ed. J. Christopherson (Latin; Cologne 1570).

1571.1, 2   Henry Siddall, prebendary (canon 1547–72, died
               2 May 1572)
      1   Hyp.0.79–86. D. Erasmus, *Opera* (8 vols Basle
               1540).
      2   *Hyp.Q.63. D. Erasmus, *Paraphraseon in novum
               testamentum* (Basle 1556).

1578.1: 13 May   Mr. Richard Colfe, alumnus
*Cellar I.3.2.7. J. Foxe, *Rerum in ecclesia gestarum commentarii* (Basle 1559).

1578.2: 13 May   Richard Colfe, 'magister' (MA 5 May 1575)
*Hyp.Q.43. H. Bullinger, *In Apocalypsim* (Basle 1570).

1578.3   William Lambarde, armiger
*e.6.26. W. Burley, *In Ethica Aristotelis*; etc. (Venice 1500; etc.).

1579.1: 30 Mar.   Stephen Lence alumnus MA (6 July 1576)
(*)Cellar D.2.1.1. W. Lazius, *Commentaria* (Basle [1551]).

1579.2, 3: 30 Mar.   William Watkinson MA (2 May 1578)
2   *e.3.56. A. Trombeta, *In tractatum formalitatum Scoti sententia*; etc. (Venice 1505; etc.).
3   *Hyp.L.30. Theodorus Metochita, *In Aristotelem* (in Latin; Basle 1559).

1579.4: 7 Apr.   Israel Pownall MA (5 May 1578)
e.1.34. Ludolphus de Saxonia, *Vita Christi* (Strasbourg 1483).

1579.5: 9 Apr.   William Wake, MA (22 May 1577)
*Cellar A.2.4.7. C. Sigonius, *De antiquo iure* (Paris 1576).

1579.6: 10 Apr.   Stephen Lence MA (6 July 1576)
(*)Hyp.L.99. Aristoteles, *De animalibus* (in Latin); etc. (Basle 1534; etc.).

1579.7: 6 May   Toby Matthew dean (1576–84)
e.3.7. J. Foxe, *Actes and Monuments* (London 1576).

1579.8: 1 June   Thomas Weltden MA (2 May 1578)
(*)Cellar H.2.4.6. Hilarius, *Opera* (Basle 1550).

1579.9 16 Feb.   *e.6.5. *Statuta Edwardi Sexti* etc. (London 1572).

1579.10–12   John Lawrence, vicar of Rainham, Essex, 'quondam' poor scholar
10   Hyp.P.49. *Monumenta s. patrum orthodoxographa*, ed. J. J. Grynaeus (Basle 1569).
11   Z.T.2.7. M. Flacius, *Ecclesiastica historia, 13ᵃ Centuria* (Basle 1574)
12   Cellar G.3.3.8. *Orthodoxographa* (Basle *sine anno*).

1580.1   Peter Copley MA (22 May 1579)
Orrery X.1.20a. A. Coccius Sabellicus, *Rapsodie historiarum Enneadum* (Paris 1509).

1581.1–3: 19 Mar.   Justinian Baldwin 'olim' alumnus (MA 1573–4)
1   *Nicholson E.4.7, 8. R. Gualterus, *In Epistolas Pauli* (2 vols Zurich 1572).
2   *Nicholson E.4.3, 4. R. Gualterus, *In Lucam* (2 vols Zurich 1573–5).
3   *Nicholson E.4.9. R. Gualterus, *In Epistolam ad Galathas* (Zurich 1576).

1582.1: 23 May   J. Hotomanus (1552–1636)
*Orrery b.2.2. (i) F. Arrianus, *Periplus* (in Latin; Geneva 1577); (ii) *Leges Wisigothorum* (Paris 1579).

1582.2: 3 July   John Hillierd MA (15 June 1580)
*Hyp.L.107. A. Niphus, *In Topica Aristotelis* (in Greek and Latin; Paris 1542).

1582.3: 6 July   Isaac Colfe MA (4 July 1582)
*Nicholson A.2.11. *Biblia* interprete Sebastiano Castalione (Basle 1556).

1582.4: 28 July   Mr Bourne of Lincoln College
*Hyp.K.4. J. Sichardus, *Antidotum contra haereses* (Basle 1528).

1582.5: 31 July   Ecclesię Christi, in qua educatus, et prębendarius factus est hoc amoris, pietatisque suę qualecumque testimonium dedit Thomas Thornton (canon 1568).
Cellar I.1.2.2. Hieronymus, *Opera* (vols 6–9 (in 1) Antwerp 1578–9).

1582.6: 18 Jan.   William Arnold MA (22 June 1579)
Hyp.N.120 M.A. Constantius (S. Gardiner), *Confutatio cavillationum* (Paris 1552).

1582.7: 18 Jan.   John Bentley MA (26 March 1574)
*Hyp.I.2. J. Faber, Stapulensis, *In Evangelia* (Meaux 1522).

1582.8: 18 Jan.   Emmanuel Maxey MA (22 May 1579)
Cellar G.2.4.12 (i) *Epistolae Oecolampadii et Zwingli* ([Strasbourg] 1548); (ii) J. Vadianus, *De eucharistia* (*sine loco* 1536).

1582.9: 18 Jan.   William St Barbe MA (6 July 1579)

*Hyp.I.7. Anselmus, *In Epistolas Pauli* (Cologne 1533).

1582.10: 18 Jan. Sylvester Tennand, janitor
*Hyp.P.19. H. Zanchius, *De tribus Elohim*; etc. (Frankfurt am Main 1573; etc.).

1582.11: 18 Jan. William Watkinson MA (2 May 1578)
*Cellar H.2.5.13. V. Strigelius, *In Psalmos* (Leipzig 1573). 8°.

1582.12: 21 Jan. John Broun MA (22 May 1577)
Aldrich C.2.13. *In omnes M.T. Ciceronis orationes enarrationes* (Lyons 1554).

1582.13: 2 Feb. Richard Edes MA (2 May 1578)
*Cellar C.1.4.2. C. Gesner, *Pandectae* (Zurich 1548).

1582.14: 18 Feb. William Wickham MA (22 June 1579)
*e.2.54. Boethius, *Opera* (Venice 1491–2).

1582.15 Leonard Hutton MA (3 March 1582)
*Cellar D.2.1.15. Appianus, *De bellis civilibus* (Paris 1521).

1583.1: 18 Jan. William Arnold MA (22 June 1579)
*d.2.25. G. Postellus, *De orbis terrae concordia* ([Basle,] *sine loco et anno*).

1583.2, 3: 18 Jan. Thomas Aubrey MA (22 May 1577)
2 Aldrich B.2.15. Titus Livius, *Historiae* (Basle 1531).

3 *Cellar D.2.1.8. Seneca, *Opera* (Basle 1573).

1583.4: 7 July Magistri in artibus incipientes quorum nomina subscripta sunt hunc librum ædi Christi in gratiam studiosorum dono dederunt Anno dom. 1583° Julii 7° videlicet Thomas Denington (?) Joannes King Thomas Craine Thomas Ailwin Thomas Bache
Nicholson E.4.5. R. Gualterus, *In Isaiam* (Zurich 1583).

1583.5–9 29 July Toby Matthew DTh, dean (1576–84)
5 *Arch.Inf.c.2.4. Ptolemaeus, *Geographia* (Strasbourg 1522).

6 *d.3.6. Paulus Constantinus, Phrygius, *Chronicum regum* (Basle 1534).

7 *d.2.21. J. Funccius, *Chronologia* (*sine loco* 1545).

1583.5–9 29 July (*cont.*)

8	Hyp.P.41. O. Epplinus, *Selectiora iudicia* (Königsberg 1560).
9	*Hyp.I.3. M. Flacius, *Clavis scripturae sacrae* (Basle 1567).

1584.1: 6 Jan. Leonard Hutton MA (3 March 1582)
*Orrery o.2.7. *Scriptores de chirurgia* (Zurich 1555).

1584.2 Magistri in facultate Artium anno 1584 incepturi quorum nomina subscripta sunt hunc librum Ecclesiæ Christi dono dederunt Eustachius Kyghtly Thomas Dunscomb Franciscus Godwyn Guilielmus Bust Griffinus Sheppard Christophorus Tappam Johannes Edmonds Richardus Martin (MAs 6 March 1583–4)
*Hyp.K.30–3. Dionysius Carthusianus, *Opera* (4 vols Cologne 1539–43).

1584.3: 25 July William Bust MA (6 March 1583–4)
Y.y.1.67. Aristophanes (Florence 1525).

1584.4,5: 25 July Francis Godwyn, MA (6 March 1583–4)

4	*e.2.56. Quintilianus, *Declamationes* (Parma 1494).
5	Orrery M.4.3. (i) A. Mizaldus, *Cometographia* (Paris 1549). 4° (ii) G. Marstallerus, *Artis divinatricis . . . encomia* etc. (Paris 1549). 4°.

1584.6: 31 Dec Francis Godwin MA (16 March 1583–4)
(*)e.2.57. Plautus (Venice 1499)

1585.1 D. Daniel Bernardus in sacra Theologia ex æde Christi incepturus Anno Domini 1585, hunc librum eidem Ecclesiæ dono dedit. (DTh 2 April 1582)
*Cellar I.1.4.9. P. Viretus, *De vero ministerio* ([Geneva] 1553).

1585.2 Magistri in facultate artium ex æde Christi incepturi Anno Domini 1585 quorum nomina subscripta sunt, hunc librum eidem Ecclesiæ dono dederunt Richardus Thornton Guilielmus Sutton Richardus Braunche Richardus Lloide Guilielmus Coxe Richardus Vaughan Gerardus Williamson Richardus Jones (MAs 10 February 1584–5)

*Cellar G.1.2.8. Sixtus Senensis, *Bibliotheca sancta* (Cologne 1586).

1585.3   D. Martinus Heton in sacra Theologiae ex æde Christi incepturus Anno Domini 1585 hunc librum Ecclesiæ eiusdem studiosis dono dedit (DTh, 4 July 1585)
*Hyp.0.102. J. Rivius, *Opera theologica* (Basle 1562).

1585.4   Miles Smith (BTh 1 February 1585–6)
*Cellar D.2.1.5. J. Bentzius, *Thesaurus elocutionis* (in Greek and Latin; Basle 1581).

1586.1, 2   Lady Burghley
1   *Orrery n.1.3–5 Galen, *Opera* (in Greek; 3 vols Basle 1538).
2   (*)Orrery n.1.6–10. Galen, *Opera* (in Latin; 5 vols Venice 1562–3).

1587.1   John Howson (see 1602.1)
Cellar C.2.4.12. P. Jovius, *Vitae duodecim vicecomitum Mediolani principum* (Paris 1549).

1588.1: 14 June   George Bys[chop] of London, in memory of his son John, 'nuper defunti'.
*d.1.15. J. Zabarella, *Opera* (Lyons 1587).

1588.2: 24 June   Thomas Browne, vicar of Basingstoke, 'quondam' alumnus
Cellar I.3.4.2. J. Damascenus, *Opera* (in Greek and Latin; Basle 1575).

1588.3: 24 June   William Watkinson BTh alumnus (MA 2 May 1578)
*Cellar Jb.1.8. J. Pierius Valerianus, *Hieroglyphica* (Basle 1575).

1588.4   John Howson (see 1602.1)
*MS 95. Epistolae Pauli glosatae. s.xii

1591.1: 28 Apr.   Thomas Grantham, generosus (matriculated 9 May 1589) 'in gratiam studiosorum'
*Hyp.L.60. J. Zabarella, *De rebus naturalibus* (Cologne 1590).

1591.2: 24 Dec.   Christopher Trivett MA (Broadgates Hall, MA 4 June 1584), chaplain 'huius aedis'
*e.5.51. Lambertus de Monte (et al.), *In Aristotelem* (Cologne 1497–8).

1593.1: 15 Aug.   Thomas W[hyte] D[Th] prebendary (1591)
Wake t.1.12. H. Schedel, *Liber cronicarum* (Nuremberg 1493).

1595.1   Samuel Burton MA (15 June 1591), alumnus
*MS 89. R. Higden, Polychronicon s.xiv.

1595.2   William James DTh dean (1584–96)
*Hyp.P.3. Gregorius de Valentia, *De rebus fidei controversis* (Lyons 1591).

1596.1–3   William James DTh 'olim' alumnus and dean (1, 2 dean of Durham)

1   Hyp.L.56. J. Perez de Valentia, *In Psalmos* (Paris 1521).

2   Hyp.L.54. J. B. Folengius, *In Psalterium* (Basle 1549).

3   Cellar A.1.3.5. A. Marloratus, *Novi Testamenti catholica expositio* (Geneva 1593).

1597.1: 7 Apr.   John Oxenbridge MA (17 July 1556), 'olim' alumnus
*Cellar D.2.8.35–6. C. Jansenius, *In Psalmos*, etc. (2 vols Lyons 1586, 1596).

1601.1: 16 June   Humphrey Lynde BA (7 July 1600), 'in gratiam studiosorum'
*Aldrich B.2.5. Thucydides (in Greek; Basle 1540)

1601.2: 20 June   William Gris, seller of wine and keeper 'huius bibliothecæ'
*Hyp.P.23. A. Sadeel, *Opera theologica* ([Geneva] 1567).

1601.3: 5 Oct.   John Best MA (16 April 1594), 'in gratiam studiosorum'
*Hyp.L.112. G. Pachymerius, *In universam fere Aristotelis philosophiam* (Basle 1560).

1601.4, 5: 5 Oct.   William Ballowe MA (13 May 1594) 'in gratiam studiosorum . . . testificandi amoris sui ergo'.

4   *MS.90 Comment. in Danielem. s.xv in.

5   *MS.91 N. de Aquavilla, Sermones; etc. s.xiii ex.–xv

1601.6: 9 Oct.   Jaspar Swyft MA (26 January 1599/1600)
*Hyp.I.85. Aristoteles, *Opera* (vol. 1 in Latin; Venice 1489).

1601.7: 10 Oct.   Griffin Owen MA (20 May 1590), 'in gratiam

studiosorum' Stratford E.2.17. Saxo Grammaticus, *Danorum regum historie* (Paris 1514).

1601.8: 11 Oct.
Andrew Adams BA (25 October 1599)
*Hyp.L.87. Aristoteles, *Ethica* (in Latin) *cum
comment. D. Acciaioli* (Paris 1560).

1601.9: 11 Oct.
Thomas Thornton BA (25 October 1599)
*Hyp.L.70. F. Vicomercatus, *In physica Aristo-
telis* (Venice 1567).

1601.10: 13 Oct.
Edward James alumnus and MA (11 May 1594),
'in gratiam studiosorum'
*Orrery O.2.4. J. Schonerus, *Opera mathematica*
(Nuremberg 1551).

1601.11: 20 Oct.
Abraham Buckley MA (30 June 1596), 'in
gratiam studiosorum'
*Aldrich E.2.5. Aulus Gellius ([Paris] 1536).

1601.12: 27 Oct.
William Negose MA (24 October 1601)
*Hyp.L.104. F. Vicomercatus, *In meteorologica
Aristotelis* (Paris 1556).

1601.13: 7 Nov.
Ferdinand Moorcroft MA (20 June 1601)
*e.6.27. (i) J. Duns Scotus, *In Aristotelis meta-
physica* (Venice 1503); (ii) A. Andreae, *In
Aristotelis metaphysica* (Venice 1491); (iii)
J. Duns Scotus, *Formalitates*, etc. (Venice 1505).

1601.14, 15: 7 Nov.
John Perin DTh (DTh 9 July 1596), regius professor of Greek, (14) 'in gratiam studiosorum'.

14
*Cellar G.2.2.4 Clemens Alexandrinus, *Opera*
([Heidelberg] 1592).

15
Cellar E.2.8.17. Clemens Alexandrinus, *Opera*
(in Latin; [Heidelberg] 1592).

1601.16: 16 Nov.
John Bancroft MA (21 May 1599) alumnus
Hyp.L.95. (i) Aristoteles, *De generatione et
corruptione* (in Latin), *cum comment, Aegidii
Romani, et al.* (Venice 1505) (ii) Aristoteles,
Metheora (in Latin), *cum comment. Caietani
de Tienis* (Venice 1522).

1601.17: 16 Nov.
Simon Juckes MA (20 June 1601)
*Aldrich D.4.17. Alexander Aphrodisaeus *In
Topica Aristotelis* (in Latin; Paris 1542).

1601.18: 16 Dec.
John Lant MA (1579) alumnus
*Orrery O.2.3. G. Bonatus, *De astronomia* (Basle
1550).

1601.19: 24 Dec.   John James BA (25 January 1600)
e.2.55. Geraldus Odonis, *In Ethica Aristotelis* (Venice 1500).

1602.1: 18 May   John Howson STP prebendary (DTh 17 Dec. 1601)
*Cellar B.1.1–4. N. de Tudeschis, *In Decretales* (4 vols [Lyons], N. de Benedictis, 1501).

1602.2: 12 July   William Goodwyn STP (DTh 8 June 1602) 'In gratiam studiosorum AEdis Christi dono dedit cum inceperet Oxonii Anno domini 1602 Julii 12'
*Hyp.P.28. Didacus de Stella, *In Lucam* (Lyons 1592).

1602.3:   Magistri in facultate artium qui inceperunt anno 1602 quorum nomina subscripta sunt hunc librum Ecclesiæ Christi dono dederunt Johan. Jeames. Joh. Hamden. Tho. Thornton. Edvar. Watkin. Tho. Bickerton. Andr. Adams. Norwicus Spackman (MAs 8 June 1602 and (Jeames) 28 June 1602)
*Hyp.I.9. B. Pererius, *In Genesim* (Cologne (1601).

n.d.1–4   Arthur Bedell MA (17 June 1500: BCL 1565)
1   (*)Cellar D.2.1.7. J. Fernelius, *Cosmotheoria*; etc. (Paris 1528; etc.).
2   *Hyp.L.59, Plotinus, *De rebus philosophicis* (in Latin; Solingen 1540).
3   *d.4.16. L. Bellantius, *De astrologica veritate* (Basle 1554)
4   *Hyp.L.106. A. Maioragius, *In quatuor libros Aristotelis de coelo* etc. (Basle 1554).

n.d.5   Mr Laurence Bodley alumnus (MA 9 July 1568)
*Morris A.3.10. Biblia Pagnini (Basle 1564).

n.d.6   Richard Caldwell DM (1555, died 1585)
*Stratford S.H.10.5. G. Budaeus, *Commentarii linguae graecae* (Basle 1530).

n.d.7   *Mr Richard Edes alumnus and proctor (1583)
Orrery g.1.11. Plutarch (in Latin; Basle 1573).

n.d.8   Thomas Godwyn TP 'quondam' dean (1565–7; bishop of Bath and Wells, died 1590) *d.4.2. F. Guicciardinus, *Historiae* (in Latin; Basle 1566).

n.d.9 John Hill BTh (MA 30 May 1555, BTh 12 December 1561)
Aldrich E.2.1. Demosthenes, *Orationes* (Basle 1532).

n.d.10 [John Lawrence] vicar of Rainham 'scholaris [. . .]' (cf 1579.10-12)
Nicholson B.2.4. Testamentum Novum Bezae (in Greek and Latin; [Geneva] 1582).

n.d.11 Stephen Lens 'quondam' alumnus and MA 'ex testamento . . . qui obiit Anno domini 1587 Mart. 12°'
*Cellar A.1.3.6. A. Marloratus, *In Genesim* (Morges 1585).

n.d.12, 13 Mr Thomas Parris MA (21 November 1558)
12 *Hyp.I.84. J. Duns Scotus, *Quodlibeta*, etc. (Nuremberg 1481).

13 (*)Hyp.L.47-8. J. Duns Scotus, *In Sententias P. Lombardi* (2 vols Paris 1513).

n.d.14 William Prichard alumnus and MA (15 June 1588)
MS 105. Biblia. s.xiii

n.d.15 Richard R(?) [. . .], 'ibidem in artibus magister'
Cellar H.2.4.4. Ricardus de Sancto Victore, *Opera* (Paris 1518).

n.d.16 William St Barbe alumnus (MA 6 July 1579)
*d.5.27. Arnobius, *In Psalmos*, etc. (Basle 1522).

n.d.17 Edward Sanders of Flore, Northants.
MS 145. Bible (in English). s.xiv/xv

n.d.18 Dominus Scroope
(*)Cellar G.3.3.5. Athanasius, *Opera* (in Latin; Basle 1556).

n.d.19 Herbert Westphaling (MA 12 July 1555), bishop of Hereford (1585-1602)
*Aldrich E.1.26. A. Ortelius, *Theatrum orbis terrarum* (Antwerp 1575).

n.d.20 William Withye Bachelor of Laws (BCL 12 February 1579)
*Arch. Sup. F.2.8. P. de Crescentiis, *De omnibus agriculturae partibus* (Basle 1548).

n.d.21   Henry Wotton (BA Christ Church 1547–8, fellow of Corpus Christi College 1566, and Greek reader)

(*)Orrery d.4.16. Hermogenes, *Ars rhetorica* (in Greek; Paris 1530). 4⁰.

n.d.22   (*)Arch.Sup. E.1.10. C. Gesner, *Historia animalium* (Zurich 1551)

n.d.23   *Hyp.K.21. H. Bullinger, *Sermones* (Zurich [1577]).

Notes on the List of Books at Christ Church 1560–1602

1562.1	Binding of vol. 4: rolls HM.a.4, HM.a.7, SW.b.2.
1562.2	Binding: rolls HE.k.1 and HM.h.10.
1562.3	Binding of vols 2–4: HM.a.4, HM.a.7, SW.b.2. Vols 1 and 5 were rebound in Oxford in s.xvii in.: the rolls are (1) Gibson XIX, XXV and (5) Gibson XVII, XXI.
1562.5	Binding: rolls HM.a.4, HM.a.7, SW.b.2.
1562.9	Abel's *ex dono* in (ii) is not dated. Presumably he and Poston had the two commentaries bound together. 'John Abells booke 1559' is at the end of (ii). Binding: rolls HM.a.4, HM.a.7, SW.b.2.
1562.11	Binding: rolls HE.k.1 and HM.h.10.
1567.2	Inscribed 'pæccaþ þine leochtfæt. Þilhelm lambheort' on the title-page. For Lambard, 1536–1601, see *DNB*. He also gave 1578.3. Binding: pattern of fillets.
1571.2	Binding: rolls HE.a.10 and HM.a.3.
1578.1	Binding: rolls HE.a.1 and RP.a.1.
1578.2	Binding: Oxford centrepiece (not in Ker, *Pastedowns*).
1578.3	Binding: Cambridge, by Spierinck (Gray, stamps 1, 2). Inscribed 'Laurentii Nouelli 1553'. It is tempting to see here a link between Laurence Nowell of Christ Church and Laurence Nowell, Anglo-Saxonist, cartographer, and friend of Lambarde, and to suppose that Lambarde chose this book as a gift for Christ Church because it had belonged to Nowell when he was at Christ Church. Mrs Retha M. Warnicke has shown recently in her 'Note on a court of requests case of 1571' (*English Language Notes* xi (1974) 250–6) that Lambarde's friend was not, as was supposed, Laurence Nowell, dean of Lichfield (Brasenose *c* 1536; MA 1544, died 1576), but a kinsman. The Christ Church Laurence Nowell is recorded there from 1550 until 24 December 1554. According to the matriculation book compiled in the seventeenth century, but using sixteenth-century material not now known to exist, he was born in Lancashire in 1530. He was BA by August 1552 and had then some interest in 'antiquities', we may presume: see above, p. 472 n. 3. He may have been 'my cozen Lawrence Nowell' to whom Robert Nowell, the Dean's brother, bequeathed

£20, an annuity of £5 and 'as much satteine as will make him a coate and doublet', by will 6 February 1568-9: see *The spending of the money of Robert Nowell*, ed. A. B. Grosart (Manchester 1877), pp. l, li, 76-7.

1579.2   Binding: Oxford, Gibson rolls XVII, XXI (Ker, *Pastedowns*, no. 1182).

1579.3   Binding: centrepiece.

1579.5   Binding: centrepiece.

1579.7   Inscribed 'Hoc pietatis monumentum, testem temporum, lumen veritatis, memoriam vitæ, magistrum mortis. Tobias Matthew S. Theologiæ Professor et AEdis Christi Oxon. Decanus primum et ' perpetuum suæ beneuolentiæ μνημοτυνον eidem Ecclesię D.D. Pridie Nonas Maii 1579 anno R. Sereniss. Elizabethę viges. primo'.

1579.9   Binding: roll FP.f.1. The inscription is 'Liber Ecclesiæ Christi Oxon' ex fundatione R H 8 16 Februarii 1579'. The Disbursement Book for 1578-9, fo 30^V (term 2) has under 'Expenses in the Lawe and iournies' the entry 'To Mr Audito^r for iii law bookes cont' all the statutes at lardge and for th'abridgement and pulton, bowne and boste. liiii^s'.

1579.10   The Christ Church *ex libris* and Lawrence's name have been cut off, but from 'vicarii' to 'scholaris pauperculi 1579' the inscription is the same as in 1579.12. Cf also n.d.10.

1579.11   The inscription ends 'pauperis scholastici 1579'.

1580.1   Disbursement Book, 1580-1, fo 33^V (term 2, 28 February): 3^s paid to Richard Cakebreade for 18 clasps and 8 staples for the library and for 'clasping three bokes of Sabellicus geven by Mr Copley'.

1581.1   Binding: rolls HM.a.3, HM.a.6, and crested roll.

1581.2   Bindings: Oxford, Ker centrepiece xxi and ornament 62.

1581.3   Binding: Oxford, Gibson roll XXII (Ker, *Pastedowns*, no. 1216). Disbursement Book, 1580-1, f. 55 (term 3, 18 April): 2s paid 'To Rich. Garbrand for the bynding of Gualter vpon thepistle at Galatas geven by Mr Baldwin'.

1582.1   Binding: Oxford, Ker centrepiece ix and ornament 68 (Ker, *Pastedowns*, no. 1650). Inscribed 'Collegio AEdis Christi, doctissimisque et ornatissimis Magistris, ceterisque studiosis, optime de re meritis, pignus hoc amicitiæ et obseruantiæ suæ reliquit Jo. Hotomanus Franc.F.LL. Doctor x Kal. Jun. M D LXXXII': according to the *Nouvelle biographie générale*, Jean Hotman (1552-1636) was five years in England in the service of Lord Leicester. Disbursement Book, 1582-3, fo 10^V (term 1): 2s 6d paid 'To Richd Garbrand for binding of Stuckius in Arriani periplum ponti Euxini et maris Erithrei: given to the librarie by D. Hotoman bound in parchment'; 6d paid 24 September 'To Norris for a chaine for the same booke'.

1582.2   Binding: Oxford, Gibson roll XII (Ker, *Pastedowns*, no. 631).

'Joannes Hillierd 15° Junii 1580': this is the day on which Hillierd took his MA. Earlier the property of Richard Verney (BA 1562).

1582.3   Binding: contemporary German pigskin.

1582.4   Binding: contemporary, with two rolls (not in Oldham) and a cornerpiece ornament.

1582.5   I.1.2.2 is the second of two volumes. I.1.2.1, vols 1-5 (in 1), is not inscribed.

1582.6   Arnold's name is also in e.3.57, J. Picus de Mirandola, *Opera* (Bologna 1496), which had belonged earlier to Longolius: 'Christophorus de Longueil Emptus xlv [. . .]'; 'William Arnolde 1579 October'.

1582.7   Binding: London by Reynes, roll AN.b.1 and orn.A.1.

1582.9   Binding: roll TP.1.

1582.10   Binding: Oxford, Ker centrepiece i and ornament 55. Tennand's will is in the T-V volume of Chancellors's Court wills (Hyp.B.34), 26 December 1579. He left 'xx^s to buye a dyvynytye booke for Christchurche liberary' and 'to sixe of suche poore scollers as doe paynfully applye ther bookes wythyn christeschurch v s. a peece'.

1582.11   Binding: Oxford, Ker centrepiece xviii. '1579 Sum liber Gulielmi Watkinsoni ædis Christi Oxon prec' iii^s'.

1582.13   Binding: Oxford, Gibson roll XX and roll IN.2 (Ker, *Pastedowns*, no. ccxxii).
          'Richardi Edes ædis Christi Oxon' Maii 9 1579'.

1582.14   Binding: Oxford, stamped, by the 'G. W. binder' (Oldham, pl. x, stamps 20-2, 24). An earlier inscription of ownership is 'Liber Gulielmi Roswoldi ex Dono Thomae Rowsweldi'.

1582.15   Binding: London, by John Reynes.

1583.1   Binding: roll RC.b.6, strigil roll, and small ornament as centrepiece and cornerpieces.

1583.3   Binding: Oxford, Ker centrepiece xxi and ornament 57.

1583.4   The first name might be Donington, or even Derrington or Dorrington, rather than Denington. According to Foster, Craine became MA on 6 February and the three others on 15 February 1582-3.

1583.5-9 Disbursement book, 1582-3, fo 66 (term 4, 31 August): 7s 'for xii chaynes bought for bookes given by Mr Deane'.

5   Binding: Oxford, Ker centrepiece xxviii, ornament 50 and another ornament.

6   Binding: roll MW.d.3. Earlier inscriptions 'Ornatiss. Viro, D. Ioanni Bourn Equiti Aurato Ser^{mae} Reginæ nostræ Secretario primario. 1556° 10 Iunii' and 'Sum Io.Bourne'. Bourne (1575) was principal secretary of state from August 1553 to March 1558: see *Handbook of British Chronology*, ed. F. M. Powicke, Charles Johnson and W. J. Harte (1939) 2nd edn ed. F. M. Powicke and E. B. Fryde (1961), 111. 'Sum Io. Bourne' is also in a Merton College copy of the *Expositiones antiquae* of Oecumenius

and Aretha, Verona 1532, which belonged to Matthew in 1579 and was given by him to Merton when he was dean of Durham. Other books with Bourne's name in them are among those which Matthew's widow gave to York Minster after his death in 1628. Mr Bernard Barr tells me of VI.G.14 (Adams, S.1391 + M. 1045 + P.413), X.G.1 (Adams, C.2357 + 2381), XII.C.22 (Adams, D.917) and XV.B.1 (Adams, P.1184 + 1190).

7	Binding: centrepiece, gilt. Earlier inscription 'Sum Io. Bourne'.
9	Binding: Oxford, Ker centrepiece i and ornament 35 (Ker, *Pastedowns*, no. 1267).
1584.1	Binding: Oxford (?), Gibson roll XVI.
1584.2	Binding: roll FP.f.6. Earlier inscription 'Ric. Spenseri sum' in vols 2 and 4.
1584.4	Binding: Italian.
1584.6	Earlier inscriptions, 'Magistri Linacri' and 'Th: Godwyn', on the title-page.
1585.1	Binding: Oxford, Ker centrepiece ix and ornament 68.
1585.2	Binding: Oxford, Ker centrepiece ix and ornament 68.
1585.3	Binding: Oxford, Ker centrepiece ix and ornament 68.
1585.4	Binding: Oxford, Ker centrepiece xvi and ornament 62.
1586.1, 2	'Mildreaæ Ceciliæ liber emptus decimo septimo die Septembris Anno domini 1567' in each volume. Disbursement Book, 1586–7, fo 26 (term 2, 7 March): 4s 8d 'For the chardges of nyne great bookes given by ye R.H. the lady burghley, bringing from London'; (13 March) 4s 8d 'for cheynes for the same bookes'.
1	Continental roll bindings. 'MB 1586' on the covers.
1587.1	Disposed of as a duplicate in 1793 and restored by gift in 1910: cf Hiscock, p. 105.
1588.1	Binding: centrepiece resembling Ker xiv. 'Sum ex libris Joannis Bischoppi', so this was a book John had, at Oxford no doubt, shortly before his death.
1588.3	Binding: Oxford, Ker centrepiece ix and ornament 68.
1588.4	Binding: medieval.
1591.1	Binding: centrepiece resembling Ker xiv and 1588.1.
1591.2	Binding: Oxford, Ker centrepiece i and indistinct ornaments.
1593.1	Disbursement Book, 1592–3, f 62 (term 4): 1s 8d 'for 2 chaines, staples, etc' for to fasten in bookes y^t Dr White gave'.
1595.1	Binding: medieval.
1595.2	Binding: Oxford, Ker centrepiece ii and ornament 55.
1597.1/1, 2	Bindings: Oxford, Gibson roll xxii (Ker, *Pastedowns*, no. 1217).
1601.1	Binding: Cambridge, centrepiece.
1601.2	Binding: Oxford, Gibson roll XI. 'RG' is repeated eight times in roundels on the spine in place of the usual hatching. For the donor see Hiscock, *Christ Church Miscellany*, 4.
1601.3	Binding: Oxford (?), centrepiece not in Ker. Earlier inscription 'Sum liber Anto.Martini ex dono Gulielmi Stor anno domini

1583'. William Stor, St Edmund Hall, BA 6 July 1582. Anthony Martin, Corpus Christi College, BA 1584, aged 19.

1601.4,5   William Ballowe gave eighteen medieval manuscripts to the Bodleian Library in 1604 and 1605: see R. Hunt (ed.), *A Summary Catalogue of Western Manuscripts in the Bodleian Library at Oxford* i; *historical introduction and conspects of shelf marks* (Oxford 1953) i.89, 91. For evidence that the two Christ Church manuscripts and five of the Bodleian manuscripts had belonged to the collegiate church of Holy Cross at Crediton in Devon see, 'Mugge-Mason MSS.' in *Bodleian Library Record* ii (1941-9), 91. MSS 90, 91 are in medieval bindings.

1601.6   Binding: contemporary, with stamps of four patterns. An earlier scribble is 'Ihon Tatam procurator Academiæ' (proctor in 1573, rector of Lincoln College, died 1576).

1601.8   Binding: centrepiece resembling 1588.1 and 1591.1.

1601.9   Binding: Oxford, Ker centrepiece i and ornament 50 (Ker, *Pastedowns*, no. 1268). Belonged to [. . .] of Christ Church in 1576, price 6s.

1601.10   Binding: continental roll.

1601.11   Binding: rolls CH.a.1 and RC.b.3.

1601.12   Binding: Oxford, Ker centrepiece xiv and ornament 68 (Ker, *Pastedowns*, no. 1792).

1601.13   Binding: Oxford, roll AN.1.1, Ker ornaments 9, 10, and Oldham stamp 153 (Ker, *Pastedowns*, p. 229, addenda no. ii). Earlier inscriptions 'Possessor huius libri Georgius Doygge' and 'Thomas loudell'.

1601.14   Binding: Oxford, Ker centrepiece xiv and ornament 68.

1601.15   Inscribed 'Hanc Latinam editionem alter benivolentiæ suæ AEdi Christi μνημοτυνον Joh. Perin Theologiæ Doctor et Graecae Linguae Professor Regius dono dedit 7° Nouembris 1601', Cf 1601.14.

1601.16   Earlier inscription 'Johannes Ryge'.

1601.17   Binding: Oxford, Ker, centrepiece xiv and ornament 68 (see Ker, *Pastedowns*, p. 162, note 1). Disbursement Book, 1601-2, fo 6^v (term 1): 2s to Roger Barnes 'for binding Alex Aphrodiseus in fo.'.

1601.18   Binding: Oxford, Gibson rolls VII, XIV (Ker, *Pastedowns*, no. 357).

1602.1   Binding: Oxford, Gibson rolls XVII, XXI over wooden boards. Howson's inscription is in vols 3, 4. All four volumes contain a protestation in the hand of Thomas Hughes 'Clerke' that he did 'detest and abhore the vsurpyd powere of the byshope of Rome nor do I not kepe ne fauere this boke nor no partie therof but onlye to studye thos thynges wis (*sic in vol. 3,*: that *vol. 4*) be not repugnaunt to the Lawes of this realme and statutes'. 'Robert Salusbury' in vols 1, 2 and mottoes 'Sine deo non est Salus' and 'hebb ddu heb ddym'.

1602.2	Binding: Oxford, Ker centrepiece xxii and ornament 62.
1602.3	Binding: Oxford, Ker centrepiece i and ornament 60.
n.d.1	Rebound in changed order. The inscription is on the Fernel, now in last place.
n.d.2	Binding: London, Reynes.
n.d.3	Binding: Oxford, Gibson rolls XIX, XX (Ker, *Pastedowns*, no. 695). 'Christopherus Carieus 1554 die 23° Iulii Oxon' ': he was of Balliol College, MA 1553.
n.d.4	Binding: Oxford, Ker centrepiece xx (Ker, *Pastedowns*, no. 1922).
n.d.5	Binding: Oxford, Gibson roll VII (Ker, *Pastedowns*, no. cvii).
n.d.6	Binding: Oxford, rolls HMd.1, FC.c.1. Caldwell died in 1584 (see *BRUO 1501–40*, 97 and *DNB*), but this book was given in the early sixties, to judge from the long chain mark.
n.d.7	Edes also owned f.6.6, Aeneas Silvius, *Descriptio Asiae et Europae*, *sine loco* 1531: 'Richardi Edes AEdis Christi Oxon' a.d.1575 Maii 13°'.
n.d.8	Binding: Oxford, Gibson rolls VII, XIV (Ker, *Pastedowns*, no. cviii). Disbursement Book, 1590–1, fo 16 (term 2): 6d 'for clasping a book bestowed by the B. of Welles'; 7d 'for a cheyne'; 1s 6d 'to the carryer for bringinge the B. of Welles his booke'.
n.d.10	'Liber Ecclesię Christi [. . .] vicarii de Reynam in [. . .] Ecclesię scholaris [. . .]: cf 1579.10–12.
n.d.11	Binding: centrepiece. For Lence's other gifts see 1579.1.6.
n.d.12	Binding: Oldham stamps 86 (?), 93, 97 and ornament I.3 (Monster Binder). The first leaf contains ironical verses on Scotus and 'Epitome versuum. Magistri 'forte'stomachus eructauit verbum: et nox nocti indicauit scientiam', s.xvi.
n.d.14	A gift to Prichard from his uncle, Dr David Lewes, judge of the Supreme Court of Admiralty (1558–75: *DNB*).
n.d.15	Damaged inscription: 'ibidem in artibus magistri' suggests a date about 1582.
n.d.16	Binding: roll FL.b.3 and ornament B.4 (?)
n.d.17	Given to Sanders by Robert Claye, vicar of Flore, in 1575. Sanders's son, also Edward, was of Christ Church, MA 24 April 1586.
n.d.19	Binding: Oxford, Ker centrepiece vi(a) and ornament 59.
n.d.20	Binding: Oxford, Ker centrepiece xxi and ornament 62. A fragment—two bifolia—of Clement Maidstone's *Directorium sacerdotum*, printed by Caxton in 1489, was in the binding and is now kept as MS 528.
n.d.21	The Disbursement Book for 1591–2, fo 24 (term 2), records that Mr Norris was paid 10d for the 'new bindinge of Hermogenes Rhetoricke torne out of the safe in yᵉ librarie', probably this copy.
n.d.22	The title-page is missing, but evidence for acquisition in the early sixties remains in the form of the chain-mark about three inches long at the foot of the first remaining leaf.

n.d.23   Binding: Oxford, Ker centrepiece ix and ornament 68, as on
            1582.1 (bound by Richard Garbrand), 1585.1–3, 1588.3. Nearly
            all the title-page is missing and any inscription there was, has been
            lost.

8

The Economics and Finances of the Colleges and University *c* 1530–1640

G. E. AYLMER*

THE really interesting and important things that happen in universities are, or certainly should be, to do with the life of the mind. But whether these involve what we call research, or teaching, or informal intellectual contacts, they must presuppose some kind of institutional framework, and this in turn must rest upon a material, economic base. The particular form which this framework and base took in the case of the two ancient English universities was largely dictated by the college system, which from its origins in the thirteenth century had begun to assume a recognizably modern form in Oxford before the end of the fourteenth century. In the year 1500 there were ten colleges; by the start of the Henrician reformation three more had come into existence; in the course of the mid to later sixteenth century another three were added, and in the earlier seven-

* Ideally this chapter should have been based on exhaustive research into the relevant records of all the colleges which were in existence between 1530 and 1640. It was to have been written by the late J. P. Cooper, fellow of Trinity College. At the time of his death in the spring of 1978 John Cooper had collected a great deal of material on three of the colleges in his 'sample': All Souls (where his interest in the accounts and the estate records went back far beyond the inception of the History of the University to his time as a prize fellow around 1950), Corpus Christi and New College; rather less on one another: Magdalen (where again he had a special interest, having been an undergraduate pupil there of the late K. B. McFarlane); a little on two more: Queen's and Wadham (neither of which feature in two 'sample' lists in his notes); and nothing on two others which were on his lists: Merton and St John's. Another note suggests that he had hoped to include Brasenose and Jesus as well. The All Souls accounts and correspondence have been used direct from his notes, cross-checked against the interleaved copy in the Selden End, Bodl. of C. Trice Martin, *Catalogue of the Archives in the Muniment Rooms of All Souls College* (1877). In the case of New College I have benefited from the generosity of Dr Penry Williams in lending me his transcripts of the accounts, and I have completed the run of totals back to the beginning of the sixteenth century. For the completion and reorganization of the notes on the Corpus Christi materials, Dr Gregor D. Duncan is entirely responsible, as he is for the addition of the materials on Balliol; we have divided Christ Church between us. For Merton I have depended on the generous help of Dr John M. Fletcher and his assistant, Dr Christopher Upton, except for the period from 1585 on. I have added the materials for University College, with the kind help of Mr A. D. M. Cox and the use of his transcripts down to 1597;

teenth century a further two, making—by 1640—eighteen in all. At the same time, or to be more accurate over the period from about 1450 to 1600, the number of academic halls fell from between sixty and seventy to only seven or eight. The halls were essentially resident student hostels, either controlled by the university (which the colleges of course were not), or sometimes by a nearby college; and they were without their own endowments or independent governing bodies. Legally a college was a corporation enjoying its privileges by charter from the crown, a hall was a kind of tutorial lodging house, licensed or at least ultimately regulated by the university.

Three different estimates of total university numbers have survived from the early seventeenth century. All in fact come to a total of between two and three thousand people, and the proportion of those in halls, as opposed to colleges, ranges between seventeen and twenty per cent of the total in each of the three enumerations.[1] Although as owners of property, communal living units and even teaching institutions, the colleges had eclipsed the university itself by the later sixteenth century, the university had managed to retain certain residual powers, notably to matriculate students, that is to admit them as members studying for degree courses, and to award degrees. As we shall see, the university operated financially speaking on the sixteenth-century equivalent of a shoestring, but

I am also responsible for all the work based on the archives of the university, where I am much indebted to the help of Miss Ruth Vyse. I am also grateful to the following for their help: Mr J. Bergass, Dr D. M. Barrett, Mr E. G. W. Bill, Mrs Caroline Dalton, Dr M. Griffiths, Dr C. Haigh, Dr Felicity Heal, Mrs V. Jobling, Mr P. A. Johnson, Dr Anne Laurence, Mr I. G. Philip, Mr V. Quinn, Professor C. Russell, Professor L. Stone, Mr J. M. J. Tonks, Mr K. V. Thomas, Dr M. Underwood, Mr D. Vaisey and Mrs June Wells. The help of others is acknowledged in the notes to the chapter.

Although Dr Duncan deserves much of the credit for broadening the basis on which this chapter now rests, and although it incorporates the researches of at least eight other people, I must accept responsibility for its defects. For nine colleges, existing or founded during the period, I have had to rely on printed sources, primary and secondary: wholly so for Exeter, Oriel, Lincoln, Brasenose, Trinity, St John's and Jesus; largely too for Queen's and Wadham. The word 'sample' will not be found in the text of the chapter; however I hope that it is based on a broadly representative selection.

Finally it should be remembered that John Cooper's own primary interest was in the Oxford colleges as one type of early-modern landowner. He saw his chapter of the History as a part of his (sadly uncompleted) life's work: a comparative study of different kinds of landownership from about the fourteenth to eighteenth centuries. I am not an economic historian and I am acutely aware of this chapter's consequent limitations.

[1] *The Life and Times of Anthony Wood*, ed. A. Clark (4 vols OHS xix, xxi, xxvi, xxx 1891–5) iv. 150–1 (printed from Bodl. MSS Twyne 2, fo 80, 21, fos 513, 614; Bodl. MS Tanner 338, fo 28. The last is also printed in [J. Walker] *Oxoniana* (4 vols [1809]) ii. 247–56).

enjoyed a sudden access of additional wealth towards the end of the period.

The wealth of each individual college depended first upon its original endowment, which until the 1520s can be compared to that of a religious house, taking the form of manors, lands, rectories, house property, etc., and then on its subsequent benefactions. The extent of these holdings, the efficiency with which they were managed, the commitments of a college in terms of capital outlay on buildings and their furnishings, and of running costs, that is the expenses of the head, fellows and scholars, determined its fortunes at any given time. In several, perhaps in most, cases their respective founders had provided capital for buildings over and above the endowment, and subsequent building had usually been undertaken as a result of additional benefactions often made for this specific purpose. Yet some colleges managed to build, to alter and to re-equip and refurnish their premises out of savings on their recurrent revenues. Occasionally a subsequent benefaction was so massive as almost to constitute a refoundation, as was the case with Exeter in the 1560s. General appeals to old members for help were as yet unknown, New College in the 1670s being the first such case, although Oriel made an appeal to selected ex-commoners and even ex-fellows as early as 1636.[1]

Although the colleges of the sixteenth and early seventeenth centuries have all survived to distinguish the Oxford scene of today with their physical as well as their academic presence, there was from their beginnings a great disparity in wealth between them. After Queen Elizabeth I's first visit to Oxford in 1566, Christ Church—the royal re-foundation of Thomas Wolsey's Cardinal College and easily the richest single house—complained of having had to bear the entire cost of the royal visit. So when the queen came to Oxford again, in the early 1590s, a scale of contributions was agreed upon, among all the existing colleges, in proportion to their 'old' or un-improved rents and other external revenues.[2] This table continued to be used for other taxation purposes, at so much in the pound, for example to provide poor relief in the early seventeenth century, although it was rapidly becoming less and less realistic as an actual

[1] Gervase Jackson-Stops, 'Gains and Losses: the college buildings, 1404–1750' in John Buxton and Penry Williams (eds), *New College Oxford 1379–1979* (Oxford 1979), 208; *Dean's Register of Oriel*, 284–5.

[2] For versions of this table see OUA Register of Convocation 1615–28, NEP/*Supra*/ Register N (unfoliated at the beginning); OUA WPβ/24/5, fo 49; WPβ/5/1/1; Bodl. MS Tanner 338, fo 27ᵛ; *Collectanea curiosa*, ed. J. Gutch (2 vols Oxford 1781) i. 190–1; *The Diary of Thomas Crosfield, M.A., B.D., fellow of Queen's College, Oxford*, ed. F. S. Boas (1935), 89–90; *Reg. Ann. 1567–1603*, 287.

assessment of college revenues. The table extends from Christ Church at the top with £2,000 per annum down to Jesus at the bottom with £70; the average of all the eighteen colleges in the seventeenth century (two more having been added and Jesus upgraded to £100, the next lowest level) is £431 and the median figure is £260 per annum. By the 1640s, when an anonymous author was writing a defence of the university and the colleges against the threat of spoliation by either the royalists or the parliamentarians in the English civil war, the gross sum was put at more than three times the 1592 total, and the net sum at a little under this.[1]

The difficulty with all such figures is to know what they represent. In all the college accounts extant for the period, it is necessary to make various deductions from the total receipts in order to arrive at meaningful figures of net disposable income. Incomings may be crudely classified under the following heads: rents from property that was let to farm, profits of property under direct management (of which there was very little indeed by the mid-sixteenth century), entry fines from new or renewed leases, capital windfalls from wood sales, and profits (if any) from members not on the foundation, particularly the board and lodging, buttery and tuition charges of commoners. In no single college are there reliable, or at any rate intelligible figures for the last group of items, although room charges appear on the University College accounts from 1519 to 1520 and are already present when the Balliol accounts begin in the 1570s.[2] Moreover, in most colleges a varying proportion, if not the whole of the entry fines on leases went direct as a 'dividend', or windfall profit to the head of the college and the fellows, and so did not appear on the accounts at all. Conversely there are some items which appear year after year on the accounts but which do not represent real payments at all, such as long-standing arrears, 'lost' rents and notional credit balances from preceding years. Basically, however, the rental constitutes the backbone of regular income, or 'ordinary' receipts as they were known at the time. And it is important to remember that many tenancies were held on very long leases, and that they assumed static prices; that is to say, constant money values, as had been the case, apart from short-term fluctuations, during much of the fifteenth century. When prices began to move up again, and the value of money correspondingly to fall, in the course of the sixteenth century there was no immediate, corresponding increase of rents by colleges. This was due partly to the length of the

[1] *Coll. cur.* ed. Gutch i. 191–5 (also from Bodl. MS Tanner 338, fo 203 ff).
[2] University College Archives transcripts of early account rolls by A. D. M. Cox; Balliol College Archives Bursars' Books, I.B.1.

leases, and partly to the fact that, when they did expire and came up for renewal, there was a failure to distinguish the long-term or secular price rise of the period from short-term fluctuations due to such influences as harvest failures, wars, depreciations of the currency by the crown, movements of the foreign exchanges and other temporary alterations in the terms of trade.

Another puzzle is to estimate how much difference to the fortunes of the colleges as landlords was made by the actual terms of leases, as opposed to their duration and the rents required in them. A carelessly drawn lease might lead the owner into liability for excessive costs of maintenance, repairs, improvement, replanting and so on. Likewise a failure to specify carefully all the tenant's necessary liabilities might lead to the deterioration of the property, through over-cropping, under-manuring, indiscriminate felling of trees, or for other reasons, and so to a fall in its capital value. The records of most, if not all, colleges show a striking uniformity in the terms of leases. And the acute financial difficulties of Balliol (which was effectively bankrupt by the 1670s) were due to other kinds of mismanagement than ill-drawn leases. Its misfortunes stemmed rather from prolonged failure to collect arrears of rents and of battels and to poor use of the Blundell bequest, leading to the chronic overstrain of limited resources.[1] University College, whose position was broadly similar measured by resources in relation to commitments in the mid-sixteenth century, was in an altogether healthier state by the second quarter of the seventeenth century; here too the terms of leases do not seem to have made more than a negative difference. While the importance of this aspect of estate management has been rightly emphasized by historians of private landownership in the period, it is hard to argue that the varying fortunes of different colleges at different dates owed much to this factor when almost all leases displayed the same characteristics in matters affecting tenant liability.[2]

[1] See app. 1 to this chapter by G. D. Duncan, p. 566 n. 1.

[2] See Mary E. Finch, *The Wealth of Five Northamptonshire Families 1540–1640* (Northamptonshire Record Society xix 1956); Alan Simpson, *The Wealth of the Gentry 1540–1660: East Anglian studies* (Cambridge 1961); Joan Thirsk (ed.), *The Agrarian History of England and Wales: iv. 1500–1640* (Cambridge 1967); E. Kerridge, *Agrarian Problems in the Sixteenth Century and After* (London and New York 1969), all indexed under 'fines' and 'leases'; Lawrence Stone, *The Crisis of the Aristocracy 1558–1641* (Oxford 1965), indexed under 'leases and leasing policy'. And, more recently, Peter Roebuck, *Yorkshire Baronets 1640–1760: families, estates and fortunes* (Oxford 1980), indexed under 'entry fines'. For Oxford, see *A Cartulary of the Hospital of St. John the Baptist*, ed. H. E. Salter (3 vols OHS lxvi, lxviii, lxix 1914–16) iii. 329–37, and for 'fine books' with tables of house rents 338–78. The editor suggests that at Magdalen College the system of taking fines originated between 1561 and 1591. For a slightly later example on a private estate, see 'Mosley family', ed. Ernest Axon, *Chetham Miscellanies* i (Chetham Society, new ser.

How then was all of this reflected on the outgoings or spending side of college accounts? The costs of food, drink, fuel, lighting, clothing (where provided for foundationers and service staff), furniture and some building materials inflated more or less in step with the general fall in money values. Wages, that is payments to college servants, and any stipendiary payments to the heads and fellows of colleges certainly did not do so. Indeed, college servants, from having been relatively well paid in the fifteenth and earlier sixteenth centuries seem on the whole to have been falling behind by the seventeenth century. Whether they began to recoup themselves by taking perquisites in kind and by accepting gratuities from fellows and students, particularly commoners, or whether they had always pursued these practices, remains obscure.[1] Those who are in a position to match inflation in this way may be presumed to have tried to do so. As with fellows in their capacities as tutors, those in the colleges which had the largest numbers of relatively wealthy commoners may on the whole have done the best.

One reason why it is difficult to generalize about Oxford college finances is that each college had a slightly different way of keeping its accounts. Merton was the most distinctive in this respect, having three successive four-monthly accounts by three different bursars every year and additional accounts by other college officers. The University College accounts had to be approved by the vice-chancellor as well as by the master. In New College the two annually appointed bursars accounted to the warden and 'seniors'. An All Souls memorandum, probably of the late seventeenth century sets out the annual procedure for taking and auditing the accounts in great detail, and much the same system seems to have been in operation earlier.[2] The Corpus method (which is admirably explained in Dr Duncan's appendix two of this chapter) was slightly different again, though nearer to the New College model than to that of its next-door neighbour Merton. Essentially the founders of colleges, or those who drafted their original charters and statutes wanted to guard against

xlvii 1902), no. 4, 58. For Christ Church see below, p. 543 n. 3. John Cooper, and the various assistants who worked with him on this chapter, collected notes in abbreviated form on hundreds of college leases from the late fifteenth to the seventeenth centuries, especially for All Souls, Corpus Christi, Magdalen and New Colleges. I much regret not having been able to make fuller use of them, and am ready to be corrected in my judgement about the significance of leasing policy and the terms of leases (other than rents and duration).

[1] In Balliol fixed termly payments from all commoners to the manciple were prescribed in 1559 and—at a higher rate in 1613, see Balliol College Achives College Register 1514–1682, pp. 84, 197.

[2] All Souls Archives Misc. 346/14 (no date but ends with summary of the accounts for 1696–8).

fraud in the getting and auditing of the revenues from their respective endowments in land and other forms of real property. Hence the prescribed arrangements made very little, if any provision for internal management and accounting on the domestic as opposed to the estate side. An extreme example of this can be well illustrated from the case of University College where the then bursar ran up bills totalling over £500 to the college brewer and of nearly £200 to its baker, with lesser debts making a total of over £700 in all, at a time—in the 1620s and 1630s—when the total annual turnover on the formal college accounts did not exceed £500 and latterly in years when these accounts showed a comfortable surplus. He was still trying to sort things out two decades later.[1] Correspondingly, of course, the profits made by bursars on the domestic account, either personally or on behalf of their college do not appear on any surviving accounts before the restoration.

In some respects more serious, since it relates to the 'external' or estates' side of college revenues, is the failure of bursarial and other normal accounts to include the total income gained from entry fines and wood sales, sometimes also from heriots and manorial court profits. Again this is explained in detail by Dr Duncan in his analysis of the Corpus Christi accounts, but the same would be broadly true elsewhere. The nearest that we have to a comprehensive statement about the disposal of fines, in any single contemporary source, is in a Queen's College document of the 1620s or 1630s. In this the proportions given are as shown in Table 8.1. Renewals of leases at constant rents could only make any sense in economic terms, during a period even of gentle inflation, if entry fines were realistically heavy to compensate for this, and if they were treated as an augmentation of college revenues. So to a considerable extent, as can be seen from this table, the individual heads and fellows were profiting at the expense of their respective foundations. That some of this wealth may ultimately have returned to the colleges in the forms of legacies and benefactions, does not alter that fact.[2] The

---

[1] See A. D. M. Cox, 'The bursar and the beer', *University College Record 1977*, 136–41. For John Elmhirst's accounts as bursar in 1633 and 1635 see University College Archives General Account Book A 'supputationes' 1632-1667, pp. 11-22, 40-54; the college accounts for his other years (1624 and 1629) are missing, like all those for 1597-1632. For his correspondence about his debts see University College Archives, William Smith, transcripts ix. 57-64. For evidence about an allegedly corrupt bursar, namely Robert Parsons (the future Jesuit) in the early 1570s, see Anthony Kenny, 'Reform and reaction in Elizabethan Balliol, 1559-1588', in John Prest (ed.), *Balliol Studies* (1982), esp. 29-31.

[2] There is much material about the Oxford colleges, their members, and other donations to them in the works of W. K. Jordan; see his *Philanthropy in England 1480-1600* (1959), app. table v, 373; *The Charities of London 1480-1660* (1960), 252-67; *The Charities of Rural England 1480-1660* (1961), 59-60, 352, 353, 355-9, 29-30; 'Social

Table 8.1

Amount of fines to go to the colleges and *not* to the head or fellows

All Souls	two-thirds
Brasenose	one-ninth
Corpus Christi	one-fifth
Jesus	three-quarters (*NB* This may be a later addition to the manuscript)
Magdalen	one-quarter
Merton	normally a half
New	„ „ „
Queen's	two-thirds (by a decree of 1628)
Trinity	one-third
Balliol, Lincoln, Oriel	not known

[Christ Church, Exeter, St John's and University, and the newest foundations, Pembroke and Wadham are not mentioned at all.][1]

granting of favourable leases to present or past members of governing bodies, or to their friends, relatives and patrons was more blatantly a malpractice, although whether more damaging is hard to say. Again some of the wealth so diverted from college revenues may have come back to the institutions eventually by indirect means; that is, if those who enjoyed the benefits felt a corresponding sense of obligation and acted upon this either in their lifetimes or on their deathbeds. The case with wood sales may have been rather different.

institutions in Kent 1480–1660 . . .', *Archaeologia cantiana* lxxv (1961), 66–98; *The Social Institutions of Lancashire* (Chetham Society 3rd ser. xi 1962), 35 note, 72, 74; 'The forming of the charitable institutions of the west of England . . . Bristol and Somerset, 1480–1660', *Transactions of the American Philosophical Society*, new ser. l pt 8 (1960), 62 note, 65–7. On the personal wealth of academics see also Rosemary O'Day, *The English Clergy: The emergence and consolidation of a profession 1558–1642* (Leicester 1979), 156; Felicity Heal, *Of Prelates and Princes: a study of the economic and social position of the Tudor episcopate* (Cambridge 1980); Felicity Heal and Rosemary O'Day (eds), *Princes and Paupers in the English Church 1500–1800* (Leicester 1981); and one earlier study, W. C. Costin, 'The inventory of John English, B.C.L., fellow of St. John's College', *Oxoniensia* xi–xii (1946–7). In the most systematic attempt to make such calculations for any Oxford college during this period, Vivian Green reckons the average annual stipend of a fellow in 1607 to have been just on £15, with whatever value is to be set on 'rooms, services and a few minor allowances' to be added on top of this, *The Commonwealth of Lincoln College 1427–1977* (Oxford 1979), 194–8. I am grateful to Dr M. Feingold for information kindly supplied about the very large library of John Rainolds, president of Corpus Christi College, 1598–1607, of which he is preparing an account (based on the contemporary catalogue) for the Oxford Bibliographical Society. More work is needed on unpublished inventories.

[1] Queen's College Archives Provost's Memorandum Book, fos 136, 140. The All Souls figure can be confirmed from the visitor's directive of 1592 (All Souls College Archives I/54), and that for New College from the bishop of Winchester's visitatorial injunction of 1567 (New College Archives 3093, no. 32).

Then as now, because of the length of time which timber takes to mature, it is hard to know whether its yield should be treated as an irregular form of income or as something more like a capital gain. In All Souls the main profits from such sales clearly did not go to individuals, for in 1619 it was ordered that poundage of 5 per cent on these transactions was to be divided equally between whichever fellow actually effected the sale and the bursars, woodwards, etc. In 1636 the 'riding bursar' was to receive £4 for each sale in place of poundage; assuming that he would previously have received 2½ per cent (that is, half of the 5 per cent), then on any sale yielding over £160 the college was the gainer, on any of less than that, the bursar was.[1] Returning to the domestic side of college finances, money earned from tutorial teaching of noble and gentlemen commoners likewise usually went direct into the pockets of individual fellows, and it is therefore wholly absent from college accounts. How much either the tutors or the bursars profited from the non-academic charges on commoners is less clear.[2]

A little light is cast on the difficulties and temptations of bursars by the will of Christopher Gregory, made in 1600. He ended his days as archdeacon of York, having been a demy and then a fellow of Magdalen from the 1560s to the 1580s. Gregory served as bursar there in 1575–6; as this revealing passage shows, he clearly still had something on his conscience a quarter of a century later:

Item whereas I beinge sometime a member and a fellow of the most famous Colledge in Oxford dedicated to the remembrance of Marie Magdalen, and chosen one yeare to be a burser of the said house, I did other waies then I ought to have done (God in the infinitnes of his mercie for Christe his sonne's saike, I beseech him, forgive it me) mispend and misbestow some parte of the Colledge goodes committed unto my trust, for the dischardge of my conscience and in a satisfaction partiall of the said house, I bequeath thereunto the some of tenn poundes to be sent in angell golde with this style, 'Restitutio Christoferi Gregorie olim harum ornatissimarum edium socii et bursarii'. I have often had in mynde to have made this restitacion myselfe but still one thing or other hindred me, haveinge in full resolution att the least in my last will and testament to doe it.[3]

---

[1] All Souls Archives Acta in Capitulis, 1601–1707, fos 50^V, 95.

[2] In 1575 Balliol granted its bursars a flat rate annual allowance of £5, instead of the profits on bread, beer, etc., supplied to commoners, which they had previously enjoyed. In 1582, ten years after the first institution of admission fees for commoners, these were made payable to the bursars, not to the college: Balliol College Archives College Register 1514–1682, pp. 80, 122, 127, 134–5, 150, 225; *SCO* i. pt 1, 28, 32.

[3] Claire Cross (ed.), *York Clergy Wills 1520–1600: I, Minister Clergy* (Borthwick Texts Calendars: Records of the Northern Province 10. University of York, 1984), no. 61, p. 148. On Gregory see also J. R. Bloxam, *A Register of the Presidents, Fellows, Demies . . . of*

The pre-reformation ecclesiastical origins of the older Oxford and Cambridge colleges explain why each foundation had a visitor prescribed in its charter. Just as the medieval chancellors of the universities had been more like modern vice-chancellors, being the active not merely the formal heads of their institutions, so the visitors in some cases took a much more active part than would be the case today in discussions, even in negotiations about college property and about estate and financial management. The fullest evidence of this is to be found in the long series of letters from successive archbishops of Canterbury to the wardens and fellows of All Souls. Many are extremely detailed; among the most outspoken are those from Bancroft, Abbott and Laud. Whether the governing body of All Souls was more often in need of such admonishment than those of other colleges, or whether successive primates (all of whom from 1559 to 1690, except Bancroft, had themselves been heads of either a college or a hall in one or other university) felt a greater sense of responsibility than other visitors may remain an open question. In 1609 the warden received a stinging rebuke from Bancroft about the fraud recently committed by the two bursars; if they had cheated the college of £20 over the cost of coal, what else he asked might they not have done? They should be punished with expulsion or else worse might befall the whole college.[1] Some years later, George Abbott, who had himself been master of University and was to be a benefactor of his own old college, Balliol, wrote as follows:

I have found out of long experience that good husbandry is the very life of any Corporacon & that societies cannot stand without order & frugalitie, and therefore having known that it is too ordinary a custom in some colleges that Bursars when they give over their office doe retaine in their hands part of the publick stock under one pretence or other and so consequently the house hath rather. Papers & Bills of Arrerages then the present use of their Money. I have thought it fitt to require you Mr Warden, the Officers and the rest of the Seniors to call in all such debtts, before the time of your next generall Accounts. & further when your quarterly Accounts doe come, you shall doe well to examine plainly & distinctly, how & in what manner your Bursars do disburse that running stock which you put into their hands at their entering into their office . . . In a word I commend good husbandry in all things as being the true foundacon of your welfare & prosperity . . .[2]

St. Mary Magdalen College . . . Oxford, vol. 4, The Demies, i (Oxford, 1873), 161–2; Foster, Alumni, 602; John Le Neve, Fasti Ecclesiae Anglicanae 1541–1857 (new edn.), iv, York Diocese, comp. Joyce M. Horn and David M. Smith (University of London, Institute of Historical Research, London, 1975), pp. 13, 21.

[1] All Souls Archives I/96.

[2] Ibid. 147, 15 Sept. 1624. There is another version of this letter in Bodl. MS Tanner

And in the last months of his life Abbott was warning them against frivolous expenditure on unnecessarily frequent progresses to visit their properties around the country. Laud returned to earlier themes, forbidding the misuse of the dividends from fines or of the general surplusage on the accounts, and added a more personal note, inveighing against depopulations.[1] There are also examples from Balliol and New College of visitatorial directives about accounts and college finances, suggesting that All Souls was different in degree not in kind as regards the role of the visitor.[2]

Besides inflation, other external events of the sixteenth century naturally affected the colleges. The destruction of the religious orders by Henry VIII and Thomas Cromwell from 1536 to 1540 altered the face of Oxford very considerably; those colleges which were at the same time monasteries or friaries either disappeared altogether or else were absorbed into new, secular foundations. King Henry's, *alias* Cardinal College, later renamed as The Church of Christ, became the cathedral chapter for the new diocese of Oxford. As well as its primacy in wealth, this gave Christ Church the semi-ecclesiastical character that it still retains. But the disappearance of the regulars and of the monastic colleges, and a description of the new foundations as 'secular' should not be allowed to mislead us. All the colleges of Oxford remained, in a much more real sense than is the case today, as much religious as educational establishments. Although not intended by Henry VIII, another difference was soon to affect their governing bodies and so indirectly their economic circumstances. Between 1547 and 1553 and again from 1558/9 onwards the ending of clerical celibacy, coupled with the continued ban on fellows of colleges being married, meant that more of them came to seek college-owned parish livings as matrimonial homes; this put a premium on colleges possessing rectories and advowsons, which were by no means necessarily the most lucrative form of real property considered strictly as investments. Moreover, the heads of colleges—as if to emphasize their distinctness from medieval abbots and priors—were allowed to marry. At first this made little difference to the general pattern of college life. Not all heads took advantage of the possibility, and some of those who did so maintained a second home with their families outside college, even away from Oxford altogether. But in the slightly longer run, say by the early

340, fo 107^V (I have used John Cooper's transcripts of both, preferring the college copy except where the other makes better sense.)

[1] All Souls Archives i. 171, 172–3, 177.
[2] See *The Oxford Deeds of Balliol College*, ed. H. E. Salter (OHS lxiv 1913), 323–4; Balliol College Archives College Register, 1514–1682, p. 134; New College Archives, 3093, 3688.

seventeenth century in most cases, this meant that the majority of the colleges had larger residences, either newly built or much extended, for their respective masters, presidents, principals, provosts and wardens, while the cost of maintaining what was sometimes quite a sizeable household came to be reflected both in the scale of their stipends and in the costs of this building. Then as now the head alone, and not his family, had rights of common table like the fellows.

As will already have become clear, it is always difficult to estimate the true wealth and to assess the fortunes of the various colleges at particular dates. The size of apparent profits and losses on revenue accounts can be misleading even today; certainly before the nineteenth century it is seldom possible to derive a clear view of actual incomings and outgoings of all kinds from any single set of accounts or series of figures. It is, however, clear, from all the surviving accounts so far consulted, that there was no general and sustained increase in revenues before the 1580s or 1590s. There is indeed evidence that some colleges, including Corpus Christi, were having difficulty in making ends meet,[1] whereas from about that time onwards until the 1620s, in most cases into the early 1640s, there was a massive, if irregular increase.

The New College accounts show a broadly similar pattern. In 1578, 1579 and 1580 there was actually a deficit on the revenue-expenditure account, although in other years a small surplus was achieved. Taking an average of nine years between 1574 and 1584, the college was £38 a year in surplus, but this is misleading in that there was an unusually large positive balance in the first accounting year of those being considered. The actual charge and discharge of the two bursars for each year ran from 16 November to the same date in the following year, whereas the revenue-expenditure account ran from Michaelmas to Michaelmas; and for these same nine years the bursars were on average £366 in debt to the college. That is to say, this amount was the average of what they had to pay in to the warden and senior fellows, who then (it appears) had to decide whether to pay the whole such sum over to the bursars for the next

---

[1] In only one year from 1571 to 1587 inclusive was any money laid up in the tower (or college treasury) at Corpus after the annual audit; 'decrements', or payments for the higher costs of diet were apparently having to be met out of the yield from fines. So without these semi-capital windfalls, the college (one of the richest for its size in the university) was not making ends meet on its current account (see app. 2, pp. 581–2). The income of Queen's College appears to have declined, even at constant money values, between the time of the *Valor ecclesiasticus* in 1536 (and the final Henrician survey of 1546/7) and the assessment of the 'old rents' in 1592 (*Valor* ii. 228–31; PRO E. 315/441; *Coll. cur.* ed. Gutch i. 190–1). All Souls, Balliol, Christ Church and New Colleges were all in debt on their revenue–expenditure accounts for parts of the 1570s.

year (whose accounting year had begun on 29 September but who were only effectively in charge from 16 November), or to transfer part of it to the college's reserves. Normally the debt owing by the bursars for the previous year (to Michaelmas) was paid in by January at the latest, and the same amount, or sometimes a slightly smaller sum appears among the amounts charged to the next pair of bursars (for the then current year).[1]

To understand the changes which came about, we need to return to the Tudor state. The proverbial story about Henry VIII being persuaded to spare the endowments of the Oxford and Cambridge colleges on the grounds that they gave good value for money in the cause of education and learning has at least a symbolic truth, whatever the facts may have been.[2] As for the next reign, it remains a matter of dispute whether or not collegiate endowments, like episcopal and capitular ones, would have been under real threat from the continuance of Northumberland's regime in the 1550s, following Somerset's abolition of the chantries at the beginning of Edward VI's reign. Under Mary I two new colleges were founded in Oxford, and— as we shall see—the queen herself was an important benefactor of the university. But the Marian government made no more of a major, concerted attempt to undo the work of 1536–40, and to refound and re-endow regular religious houses, in the universities than it did in the country at large. So in spite of the dramatic changes in doctrine and personnel, the institutional and financial changes were relatively slight. Elizabeth I's early financial difficulties led to what were in theory voluntary, in practice forced exchanges of property between the crown and various religious institutions, normally both to the short- and to the long-term disadvantage of the latter; but fortunately for the colleges as well as for the church in general this policy was not continued and extended.

---

[1] New College Archives 7551, 7553, 7555–7, 7559, 7561, 7563–4. Unfortunately the accounts are missing for 18–19 Elizabeth (1576–7); hence the averaging of nine years' figures over a ten-year span.

[2] Understandably the threat to the universities and colleges from the so-called chantries and colleges act (*The Statutes of the Realm*, ed. A. Luders *et al.* (11 vols 1810–28) iii. 37 Hen. VIII, c. 4 sec. 6) bulks much larger in histories of Cambridge than of Oxford, since it was largely due to the efforts of Sir John Cheke and Dr Thomas Smith that an open attack was staved off. See C. H. Cooper, *Annals of Cambridge* (5 vols Cambridge 1842–1908) i. 430–8; J. B. Mullinger, *The University of Cambridge from the royal injunctions of 1535 to accession of Charles I* (Cambridge 1884), 76–9; *A History of Cambridge and the Isle of Ely* iii, ed. J. P. C. Roach (Victoria History of the Counties of England 1959), 177; Mary Dewar, *Sir Thomas Smith: a Tudor intellectual in office* (1964), 24–5; J. J. Scarisbrick, *Henry VIII* (1968), 519–20. The Oxford equivalent of the Cambridge commission of inquiry produced the document now PRO E 315/441, already cited for college incomes in 1546/7; see *The Chantry Certificates*, ed. Rose Graham (Oxfordshire Record Society i 1919 and Alcuin Club xxiii 1920), pp. viii–ix.

By the beginning of the 1570s concern over the financial situation and prospects of the colleges and of similar foundations began to be reflected in legislation. The surviving parliamentary and academic records do not enable us to be sure whether the initiative came from within the universities or from court and parliamentary circles, although in the most important case of all there are some clues to this. Measures passed in the parliaments of 1571 and 1572 affected the duration and conditions of all future leases to be made by the colleges. Agricultural property was not to be rented for a term of more than three lives or twenty-one years, nor any urban house property for more than forty years.[1] This of course meant that— assuming inflation continued—colleges would be in a position to renew their leases and so in theory to adjust the rents upwards more often than if they had been free to enter into very long leases, of say fifty or even ninety-nine years.[2] The frequency of lease renewals brought financial benefit in the more frequent levying of entry fines. One would expect that, the longer the lease and the lower, or the more 'beneficial' to the tenant the rent, the larger the fine would be, in proportion to the value of the property concerned. But this would assume that the landlord knew its true, or 'rack-rent' value, and how to calculate the fine in relation to this, to the number of 'years' or 'lives' still to run in the lease, and to the actual rent. The size of the fine would likewise be affected by whether the landlord was giving the existing tenant the first option on renewal, or was putting the lease out for bids. In the course of the seventeenth century a number of sophisticated guides were to be published, explaining how to calculate the correct fines on various types of lease.[3] But in the case of the late sixteenth-century colleges things were probably less standardized than this would suggest. It was not merely, as we have seen, that only a proportion (varying from one college to another) of the money from fines ever found its way into the college's coffers, let alone onto its accounts; it is not clear in how many instances bursars and governing bodies were yet making these calculations in a deliberate, rational way. None the less there was clearly an awareness of these problems and of the abuses to which they could give rise. A further act passed in 1576 attempted to close a loophole left by that of 1571. While excessively long leases could be damaging

[1] *Statutes of the Realm* iv. pt 1, 13 Eliz. c. 10 and 14 Eliz. c. 11.

[2] In practice, however, rents were very seldom raised during this period, the need to do so being obviated by the alternative means of increasing college revenues which is described below.

[3] See works cited on p. 525 n. 2 above, and the pioneering article by H. J. Habakkuk, 'The long-term rate of interest and the price of land in the seventeenth century', *Economic History Review*, 2nd ser. v (1952–3), 26–45.

to the interests of colleges, over-frequent renewals of leases could be too. The making of a fresh lease to the same tenant was now prohibited if there were over three years of the existing lease still to run.[1] There seems no doubt that some colleges used spurious 'surrenders' by tenants as a means of getting round this. More frequent, if smaller entry fines and secure continuity of tenure presumably produced mutual advantages for college tenants and individual members of governing bodies; again it was the colleges as institutions which suffered.[2] As we have seen, the gain to the college rather than the head and the fellows might be as much as three-quarters of the yield from fines in one case but as little as one-ninth in another. The difficulties in calculating the actual amounts are explained in detail for Corpus Christi by Dr Duncan (see appendix two). At University College the accounts suddenly begin to record receipts from fines as a separate sub-total on the incomings side in 1572–3, although individual fines or parts of them appeared along with the rents from particular holdings at a much earlier date.

While the levying of entry fines and the duration of leases affected colleges as they did other landlords, there was one requirement peculiar to them. This was the famous corn rent act of 1576, sometimes known simply as the corn act, sometimes as Sir Thomas Smith's act. It specified that in all future leases made by any of the colleges in Oxford or Cambridge and by those of Eton and Winchester one-third of the 'old' or existing rent was to be reserved; this could either be paid in kind, in a combination of wheat and malt barley, the amount of grain due being calculated on the basis of a price of 6s 8d a quarter (or 10d a bushel) for wheat and 5s a quarter (or 7½d a bushel) for malt, or in cash, but the amounts so due were then to be translated into the current market prices for wheat and malt in Oxford, Cambridge, Windsor or Winchester as the case might be.[3] Thus, if we assume a rent in a lease of 10s a year being renewed after 1576, then 6s 8d would be taken in cash and the other 3s 4d reserved; this would be the equivalent, at the prices specified in the act, to two bushels of wheat (=1s 8d) and two and two-thirds bushels of malt (=1s 8d). Since in practice the colleges in all the cases so far studied seem to have taken the reserved third from their tenants in cash and not in kind, we then have to translate these quantities into the current prices in the Oxford market at the time of the renewal of the lease. Let us suppose that the current

---

[1] *Statutes of the Realm* iv. pt 1, 18 Eliz. c. 11.
[2] For spurious surrenders in the case of Balliol, app. 1, 566–8.
[3] *Statutes of the Realm* iv. pt 1, 18 Eliz. c. 6.

prices were then 1s 8d a bushel for wheat and 1s 3d for malt; the two bushels and the two and two-thirds bushels would then be worth 40d plus 40d or 6s 8d. The total 'new' rent would thus be 13s 4d. What was known as the 'increment of corn rent' or more often simply as 'the corn rent' was reckoned as the difference between the whole of the old rent (10s in our example) and the whole of the new rent (13s 4d at the time when the new lease began), or initially 3s 4d. The reserved third was recalculated in market prices each time that the rent fell due. The extent to which this measure served as a hedge against inflation, or as we might say as a form of index linking, can be appreciated from the fact that whereas in the act the price of wheat had been set at 10d a bushel and of malt barley at $7\frac{1}{2}d$ a bushel, the Oxford market prices during the whole period from 1590 to 1660 (as reflected in the Balliol and the Corpus accounts) never fell below 2s 1d and 1s 4d a bushel respectively. And although the corn rents may appear in slightly different ways in the accounts of different colleges, these soon almost all begin to show a striking increase in gross annual receipts. In Corpus Christi this began in the late 1580s; in Balliol from 1590; in All Souls slightly sooner, from the early 1580s; in New College from the late 1580s or early 1590s.

There are two further points to be borne in mind here. First of all, there may have been other reasons independent of the corn rent act why in some cases gross receipts show an upward trend over this particular time span, for example the inclusion of profits from wood sales and/or entry fines, an actual increase of rents in new leases, or the appearance of new sources of income such as room and other charges on commoners. So the accounts and other records of any individual college need careful scrutiny before we can say definitely, or at all exactly, how much difference the corn rent system was making to their fortunes. And in the second place, the requirement of translation into the current market price of the reserved third of the rent on every agricultural property that was leased meant that the increment was subject to short-term fluctuations resulting from good and bad harvests and the consequent falls and rises in the price of grain, as well as to long-term inflationary (and, in theory, also deflationary) trends. Hence we find that the gross revenues of the colleges go up and down from year to year, sometimes by very considerable amounts. The good harvests of the early 1590s tended to produce a downswing after the initial corn rent increases of the 1580s; but the very bad harvests of 1595–7 produced a massive upswing; then there was a further decline again, with several subsequent peaks as well as a general upward trend. From the date of the act to the mid-seventeenth century, the worst harvest years, producing the highest recorded price levels, included for wheat 1586, 1595-7, 1608, 1613, 1617, 1622, 1630, 1637, 1647-9; and for barley 1586, 1590, 1595-7, 1600, 1609, 1612-13, 1614-15, 1622, 1625, 1629-30, 1634, 1637-8, 1647-9. These findings, by historians of agriculture and prices, are broadly reflected in the accounts of colleges, sometimes with a time-lag of a year depending upon their particular accounting methods.[1]

It is a puzzle how any sort of financial control, let alone forward planning, was possible with some of the very steep annual variations between 1590 and 1640. For example in All Souls an increase of over £1,000, or more than 60 per cent, in a single year, was followed by a fall of nearly £700, or some 25 per cent, in the next year. Part of the answer is that the corn rent increment was intended —and by the statute required—to be used only for the commons and diet of those on the foundation of the college, and it would of course have been the food and drink required for the head of the college, the fellows and the scholars which would have been most sensitive to short-term price fluctuations, resulting from the volume and quality of the previous harvest. Whether or not there was much of a time-lag would have depended presumably on the exact annual sequence of the payments of rent in relation to the settling of tradesmen's bills; then surely, as now, a good deal must have rested upon the skill and cool nerves of college bursars. Once more the correspondence between successive visitors and the governing body of All Souls illustrates some of the problems to which the operation of the act gave rise. As early as December 1582 Archbishop Grindal (who, despite his suspension by the queen from his primacy, continued to exercise his visitatorial functions[2]) issued the following injunction about the augmentation of commons:

Whereas the statutes [of the College] . . . allowe but XVI [pence] a weeke ad omne manis for every fellow and probationer, & the said allowance [is] too smale they nowe spend after the rate of 2/8 a master & 2/2 an other fellow the whiche overplus above 16d. runneth in decrements It is thought good that the said fellowes shall keepe the same allowance until the improvement of corne be

[1] W. G. Hoskins, 'Harvest fluctuations and English economic history, 1480-1619', *Agricultural History Review* xii (1964), 28-46; Hoskins, 'Harvest Fluctuations . . . 1620-1759', ibid. xvi (1968), 15-31; C. J. Harrison, 'Grain price analysis and harvest qualities, 1465-1634', ibid. xix (1971), 135-55; P. Bowden, 'Agricultural prices, farm profits, and rents', Thirsk (ed.), *Agrarian History 1500-1640*, together with statistical app. A table 1, esp. 817-21.

[2] *DNB*, under Edmund Grindal; Patrick Collinson, *Archbishop Grindal 1519-1583 the struggle for a reformed church* (1979), 271-2.

so much as is sufficient to bear out & discharge the foresaid overplus of 2/8 and 2/2 & the encrease of corne afterwards to be put to the encrease of commons in this sorte viz. that out of the encrease of corn so much money be subtracted as make the full score of the olde rente & imploied to the comon use of the colledge besides, comons, & the residewe of the same encrease to be imploied for betteringe of the wardens, masters, fellowes & probationers commons in such proportion as heretofore hath bene used & this order his grace taketh to stand with the equitie of the Statute.[1]

The governing body cannot have been very happy with this ruling, for within two years they obtained a professional opinion on the same matter from one of the leading lawyers of the day—the attorney of the duchy of Lancaster, who was also, more materially in this connection, counsel for Cambridge University:

. . . in my poore opinion the employing of the money which was receaved in lieu of the corne part whereof was bestowed to increase of dyet [the] other part about the necessarie affairs of the college is no cause to deprive the Governors & chief rulers of the college for that the intention of the lawe was that . . . the chief rulers of houses of learning should by leasing their possessions not make their private gaine as they used to doe, but that a perpetuall benefitt should redound to the said college & principally to the relief of comons and dyett such porcions or sums of money is ment weekly to be yelded by the fellows and schollers for the same as hath been of auncyent tyme & although that the words of the statute bee that the money should be expended to the relief of comons & diet only, that may be intended to the general benefitt of the colledges: so that the fellows & schollars be with convenience eased in their chardg of diett for if a $\frac{1}{3}$ part of all their possessions be reserved in corne after the rate appointed in the statute & should be wholly employed to the relief of comons that is much more in my simple judgement then manie of the houses can or do *comunibus annis* expend: or els the comons therby may growe to bee to[o] liberall for students, or at the lest the fellows and scholars should be more eased in their dyett then was intended by the words in the statute. viz. & by no fraud be let or sould away from the benefitt of the said colleges doe inforce my conceite herein, & theis words viz. to the use aforesaid, may bee conserned to imploy so much as is convenient to the reliefe of commons & dyett . . . having yeelded my simple opinion (not having the statute at lardge which would give great light to the true understanding of the lawe) . . .[2]

Quite how Brograve could read this into the 1576 act is a mystery, and not surprisingly the use of the corn rent increments was to become a source of trouble with subsequent visitors. An undated paper (but from its context *c* 1600) by the fellows put their viewpoint, along the lines of the opinion quoted above. This clearly failed to satisfy Bancroft, who wrote a strong letter of warning to them in 1609:

[1] All Souls College Archives Letters I/39 A.
[2] Ibid. Liveries 99/243. For John Brograve (*c* 1538–1613), see *DNB*.

. . . there is some question arisen betwixt you concerning a dividend growing by the improvement of corne which you the fellowes challenge (by stat. 18 Eliz.) urging your Warden with danger of deprivation if hee yeelds not unto you: I have therefore upon perusall of the said statute thought good to signifie that I do not find it any such matter of deprivation unto your Warden so long as the corne or money . . . after a competent encrease of commons fit for students is imployed to the common good of the college & not let nor sold away from the profit thereof, but converted to amendment of dyet & other necessary uses of common charge: But doe rather take to bee directly against the intent of the Statute That you should divide any parte of the . . . money amongst yourselves, it being no other than a fraudulent diverting of the same . . . unto privat uses which is a point principally forbidden by the statute. Wherefore I require you Mr Warden that no such division by made But that you content yourselves with a convenient augmentation of diet so that the common and necessary charges of your house may be supported as heretofore they have been: & not in respect of the Wardens withstanding your demaund in this kind, you deny the keeping of courts & necessary defence of your Right by law in refusing to give allowance for that purpose, as I heare you have lately done in a cause of great Importance, whereat I do much mervaile.[1]

The previous fellows' paper, which we may infer was aimed against the warden, had referred to four increases in the cost of commons since the 1576 act, and had complained about the unused surpluses from corn rents in years of very high prices; it looks as if the bursars wanted to be allowed to carry them over for the fellows' benefit in the following years and the warden was opposing this.[2] Whatever the immediate aftermath of this dispute, the very success of the corn rents system evidently continued to make for trouble, as can be seen in an outspoken letter from Bancroft's successor, Archbishop Abbott in 1628:

I am informed that upon your last accomptes there being some remaynder of money which your Warden thought fitt to be carried into your Treasury you have with some strange and extraordinarie renitence [*sic*? remissness] hindered the same and this, when you understood that I had returned this answere unto your notion, that in desiring this division you came too fast upon mee By which chalenge of yours & by your so much insisting upon the Statute of Q.Eliz. I have reason to conjecture that you plead it a right of duty belonging unto you. I may tell you that in the Lord Bancroft's time, when his grace would by [no] means been induced to yeeld any such matter, I was the person that with some labour obteyned of his lordship, that as a favour for encouragement of learning he would condescend to yeeld . . . & in what sort for that particular I have

---

[1] Ibid. 99/260 (a copy).
[2] Ibid. 99/253. It may be significant that Robert Hoveden or Hovenden (1544–1614), warden from 1571 to his death, had been elected after only six years as a fellow but that he was chaplain to Archbishop Parker (see *DNB*); and, for the disputes between the warden and the fellows, see C. Grant Robertson, *All Souls College* (1899), 76–9.

frequently gratified you I appeale unto yourselves . . . you urge that other colleges do make such division at the end of the year; to which I do except as specially knowing that in diverse it is not so; & if in some there bee that done which cannot be justified, it is an ill argument to conclude an use out of an abuse. The Statute of Q.Eliz. prescribeth that the provision of corne should bee imployed for improving of commons: what is this to a divident [?] If you have superfluity of meate are there no prisoners in Oxford? may there not be an Almsbaskett for those that come to the Gate [?] might there not be releefe found for such as want & yet are ashamed to beg ? Remember what the prophet Ezekiel saith concerning fulness of bread, & do not forgett that this example will administer good argument unto such as in Parlament have desired the qualifying of that Statute which as they say pincheth on the Tenant & maketh some students wanton. At this time wheat is sold heere in Kent for $\frac{1}{2}$ the crowne a bushel & malte at 21d., & both of these of the best & if in any such propor-tion your corne rents do arise for this year to come how will these commons be maintained which now you have? & if there be a great decrement, must you fetch this out of the Treasury & abate the college stocke or will you every man of your purses make satisfaccion for that which formerly you had wasted, you think not of these things, nor by what steppes you have mounted to that happines . . . (The founder gave your maintenance *in puram eleemosynam* therefore you should not grudge out of your alms, but to settle the question 2 fellows to attend me at Foorde bring the Statutes, 18 Eliz., Accounts 50 years after the founder's death & the 50 years after that & to informe me out of the books when after the Statute of provision how your Commons at 1st were increased & what was added therunto in 10 years after that & so from 10 years to 10 years unto this present . . . also what wages & liveries your founder left unto you & how it standeth at this day, when the addition hath bene & when & by what authority.[1]

This is the first suggestion that a 'back-lash' had been building up outside academic circles against the effects of the act.[2] Once more the fellows produced an answer, though it is simply a fuller version of their earlier paper.[3]

Whatever the proper uses to which surpluses arising from corn rents might be put, two other aspects of the act operated more smoothly than they might have done. It states that, of the old rent,

---

[1] Ibid. Letters I/156, dated 8 January 1627 [8]; copy in Bodl. MS Tanner 340, fos 110^v-11^r.

[2] The existence of corn rents, or 'the provision act' as it was also sometimes called, was being used as a kind of threat or lever, to try to bully All Souls into leasing all their Middle-sex woodlands to a female favourite of the queen as early as 1587-8. C. R. L. Fletcher, 'All Souls College vs. Lady Jane Stafford, 1587', C. R. L. Fletcher (ed.), *Collectanea* i (OHS v 1885), 179-247. The college's case was weakened by the fact that a similar lease to that desired for Lady Stafford, had been granted to the warden's brother on equally favourable terms as recently as 1580; the college seems to have been saved from defeat by Walsing-ham and Burghley, rather than by its visitor, Archbishop Whitgift.

[3] All Souls College Archives Letters I/157.

one-third 'at the least' is to be reserved, but in practice no college ever seems to have tried to treat more than one-third in this way. The act also specifies payment, of the reserved third, in kind or in money 'at the election of the lessees'; yet a choice in favour of payment in kind never seems to have been exercised. As to the general consequences of the act, a measure of comparison is fortunately available from outside Oxford. Much the most comprehensive financial history of any college in either university is that published in 1935 for one of the very richest, and likewise archivally one of the best endowed, St John's, Cambridge.[1] Both the long-term benefits and the short-term variations arising from the operation of the 1576 act are at least as clear in this work as in the records of any of the Oxford colleges. Certainly, some colleges were much more generously endowed, some enjoyed better financial management than others. But whether any of them would have achieved a stable, let alone a buoyant real income over the period *c* 1580–*c* 1640 without corn rents seems highly doubtful. So is tradition correct in portraying Sir Thomas Smith as the saviour of Oxford and Cambridge?

The earliest known attribution to Smith, who was secretary of state from 1572 until his death in 1577, was by Thomas Fuller in 1655.[2] In 1698 John Strype embroidered this by adding that Smith had already practised the same system (the reserved third of rents) in his capacity as provost of Eton (1547–54).[3] More plausibly, like Fuller, he said that Smith thought the bill would succeed in getting through parliament because grain prices were relatively low that year; and, unlike most of his contemporaries, Smith knew that they would go up again and would continue to do so.[4] This is the more persuasive in that Smith wrote one of the earliest and most thoughtful accounts of the sixteenth-century price inflation.[5] However, in the same year as Fuller published his history of Cambridge (and its origins in 1066!),

[1] Henry Fraser Howard, *An Account of the Finances of the College of St John the Evangelist in the University of Cambridge 1511–1926* (Cambridge 1935).

[2] Thomas Fuller, *The History of the University of Cambridge from the Conquest to the Year 1634* (orig. edn 1655, ed. M. Prickett and T. Wright Cambridge & London 1840), 273–4.

[3] James E. Thorold Rogers, writing in 1887 (*A History of Agriculture and Prices in England from . . . (1259) to . . . (1793) . . .* (7 vols in 8 pts 1866–1902) vi. p. vii) said that Eton and King's College Cambridge were reserving a third of rents, for payments in kind at fixed rates, long before the act of 1576.

[4] [John Strype], *The Life of the Learned Sir Thomas Smith Knight . . .* (1698), 192, 194.

[5] For Sir Thomas Smith (1513–77) see *DNB*; Dewar, *Sir Thomas Smith*, 185 (the reference given by Dewar for Smith's Eton leases (PRO C. 24/40) does not appear to include any example of a third of the rent being reserved in kind); also *A Discourse of the Commonwealth of this Realm of England Attributed to Sir Thomas Smith*, ed. M. Dewar (Charlottesville 1969), ix–xxvi.

a sermon commemorating the sixteenth-century vice-chancellor and master of Peterhouse, Dr Andrew Perne, well known as a side-changer in the religious conflicts of his time, described him as the author and contriver of the act.[1] Certainly Perne, whether or not his general reputation as a turncoat is justified, knew Smith well enough to preach his funeral sermon the year after the act was passed, and he was of sufficient standing to have exercised such influence.[2] Meanwhile, as early as the 1610s Dr Andrew Willett, in compiling a list of protestant charitable works, ascribed the act's authorship, or at least its promotion in parliament, to William Cecil Lord Burghley, lord treasurer and chancellor of Cambridge. And Strype subsequently came to agree with this.[3] But Oxford's most learned, if also most eccentric seventeenth-century historian Anthony Wood was not to be outdone by allowing Cambridge men all the credit. He ascribed both authorship and promotion of the bill to the future provost of Queen's and bishop of Carlisle, Henry Robinson.[4] This seems inherently unlikely, for Robinson was only 23 at the time; he had been elected a fellow of Queen's in 1575 and was appointed principal of St Edmund Hall after the parliamentary session of 1576.[5] It is possible that, even as a young man, he enjoyed some court or parliamentary connection which enabled him to lobby or even to draft a private bill, although Oxford's official lobbyists for that parliament were much more senior.[6] All in all, the likeliest course of events is that the bill originated with Perne and Smith, was pushed by Smith

[1] J. Clerk, alias Clarke, *Two Sermons Preached at Cambridge* (Cambridge 1655), 29 (commemorative sermon on Perne) first cited in John Strype, *Annals of the Reformation* (3 vols 1709; 4 vols 1824) iv. 609 (notes by Thomas Baker, fellow of St John's Cambridge, which were added in manuscript to Strype's original edition). Baker (1656–1740), a non-juror, himself wrote a history of Cambridge which was never published (*DNB*).

[2] For Andrew Perne (1519?–1589) see *DNB*; Cooper, *Annals of Cambridge* ii. 343 (following Strype); C. H. & T. Cooper, *Athenae cantabrigienses* (3 vols Cambridge 1858–1913) ii. 45–50; Mullinger, *Cambridge* ii. 374–80; *VCH Cambridge* iii. 188–9.

[3] Andrew Willett, 'A catalogue of such charitable works' appended to his *Synopsis papismi* (5th edn 1634), 1220, first cited by Strype, in his own manuscript additions to his *Life of Smith* 192, and then in his *Annals* ii. pt 2, 69 again followed by Cooper and by Mullinger. Willett (1562–1621), although not old enough to have known about the passage of the bill at first-hand, was more nearly a contemporary than Fuller or Clerk, and was Perne's godson, so he cannot be disregarded; see *DNB*.

[4] Wood, *History and Antiquities*, ii. pt 1, 178.

[5] For Henry Robinson (1553?–1616) see *DNB*. Curiously Wood makes no mention of the 1576 act in his biography of Robinson, but does say that as provost he restored Queen's College to a flourishing condition after it had previously fallen on hard times (Wood, *Athenae* i. 724–5). More recent historians of Oxford have not followed Wood on the authorship of the act, though this of course is not absolute proof that he was wrong.

[6] OUA WPβ/21/4, W. T. Mitchell's transcript of vice-chancellors' accounts shows that it was normally the vice-chancellor and/or the registrar who made special journeys to London, to solicit on the university's behalf during the sittings of parliament or convocation; I have found no example there or in Reg. Cong. 1564–82 (again in Mr Mitchell's invaluable typed transcripts) of anyone as junior as Robinson being sent to do this. None the less, if Wood

in the commons and enjoyed Burghley's blessing in the lords.[1] The fact that other institutional landlords, such as bishops, cathedral chapters or hospitals were not also included in it may seem surprising; we must, however, remember that the essential purpose of the reserved third of rents was to subsidize common tables, which post-reformation cathedrals and episcopal households did not have. Hence the logical inclusion of the fellows and scholars of Eton and Winchester and the exclusion of other famous schools such as Westminster and St Paul's.[2]

Parliamentary legislation did not have the same consequences in all cases. At All Souls the acts of 1571 and 1572, which prescribed maximum durations for different types of leases, actually led to longer rather than shorter leases. Before that time there had been variations, which subsequently disappeared, some houses and other urban properties which had previously been let for twenty years (and usually renewed after ten) now becoming standardized at forty-year leases, the permitted statutory maximum. For Christ Church, however, the long-term consequences of these measures were almost the reverse of that.

Herein lies the answer to what is otherwise a mystery: of all the Oxford colleges, the richest was also the last one to benefit from the corn rent system proportionately to its total wealth. Christ Church had so many of its holdings, including most of its largest ones, on such very long leases[3] that the 1576 act had made relatively little difference to the financial position even after having been in force for twenty years. So evident had this become that near the end of her long reign, the queen, acting in her capacity as visitor, empowered a special commission to negotiate with the dean and

got his information from the materials left by Brian Twyne (?1574–1644), it would have to be treated with greater respect.

[1] *Journals of the House of Lords* i. 743–7; *Journals of the House of Commons* i. 110–12; *Journals of all the Parliaments during the reign of Queen Elizabeth*, ed. S. D'Ewes (1683), 252–60. I am extremely grateful to Professor G. R. Elton for explaining to me the progress of the 1576 bill through both houses, and for clarifying problems connected with its drafting and status.

[2] As a royal foundation (or, strictly refoundation) Westminster was often bracketed with Eton and Winchester (which of course was not one). See e.g. *Statutes of the Realm* iv. pt 2, 43 Eliz. c. 4; *Stuart Royal Proclamations, i. royal proclamations of King James I 1603–1625* ed. P. Hughes and J. Larkin (Oxford 1973), 118–21 no. 55, where the three schools were first joined with the universities and their colleges in being exempted from the charitable trusts and uses act of 1601, and then included along with them in the proclamation of August 1605 against the misuse of charitable benefactions.

[3] Christ Church Archives D.P.i.b.9 (grants and leases, 1546–55), xx.c.1 (leases, etc. 1553–90), xx.c.2 (register of leases, 1540–92), xx.c.3 (leases, etc. 1597–1639), xx.c.4 (leases, etc. 1635–58), provide the basis for this statement. A fuller study is certainly needed.

chapter's tenants, to try to secure agreements more equitable to the college's interests. This was no ordinary commission of academic or governmental functionaries. Its members included some of the most powerful men in the realm: the archbishop of Canterbury, the lord treasurer, the senior secretary of state (Sir Robert Cecil) and the chancellor of the exchequer (Sir John Fortescue).[1] Despite some evidence of their efforts being reflected in leases made after the turn of the century, it was not until nearer 1630 that corn rents began to make a major difference to Christ Church's total revenues.[2] The difficulties in which Christ Church found itself at the end of the sixteenth century are also illustrated by a squabble between the dean and chapter on the one side and the students (equivalent in other colleges to both fellows and scholars) on the other. At the beginning of 1596 a visitatorial committee, consisting of the lord keeper of the great seal, the archbishop of Canterbury and another privy councillor (the future lord treasurer, Lord Buckhurst) gave a ruling that the nine ounces of wheaten bread allowed daily to each of the students was quite sufficient for them, and cautioned them severely against making any further trouble. But some time later in the same year the students complained to Sir Robert Cecil, who became secretary of state in July, that the dean and chapter had annulled this order and had put them back on to a fixed weekly cash allowance; they accordingly asked that the January order should be continued pending the outcome of the visitation of the college. Presumably at a time of exceptionally high grain prices a fixed quantity of bread would have been preferable to a fixed amount of money.[3]

Economic well-being was naturally affected by other influences besides the maximizing of landed income. Before we turn back to reconsider the spending side and the commitments of different colleges, there is the matter of further benefactions, including what we would nowadays call capital endowments. In addition to the founders of new colleges in the sixteenth and seventeenth centuries —Bishop Fox, Wolsey, Sir Thomas Pope, Sir Thomas White, Dr Hugh Price, Nicholas and Dorothy Wadham, and others—there were those who gave or devised money and property to both new and existing foundations. These included Bishop Oldham at Corpus Christi, Sir William Petre (almost a 're-founder') and the Reverend George Hakewill (£1,200) at Exeter, Warden Savile of Merton (over £2,000 for a new quadrangle), the Reverend Charles Greenwood and

---

[1] Christ Church Archives MS xx.c.3, fo 52, describing the commission and showing it in operation by February 1599/1600.

[2] Ibid. iii.c.1, 5–9, accounts (figures extracted by Dr Duncan).

[3] *Cal. SP Dom. 1595–1597*, 163–4; *Calendar of the Manuscripts of the . . . Marquis of Salisbury* (24 vols HMC 1883–1976), 597–8.

his one-time pupil Sir Simon Bennett at University College; Brasenose received thirty-two benefactions between its foundation and the Civil War.[1] And although Balliol actually lost from the way that the Peter Blundell benefaction was invested and then implemented, it gained from the generosity of its noted Calvinist alumnus, George Abbott, archbishop of Canterbury, whose brother Robert was master in the earlier part of James I's reign. Nor did one function exclude another: Richard Fox was a benefactor of Magdalen, Oxford and Pembroke, Cambridge, as well as the founder of Corpus Christi, Oxford.

It may be asked, how did the colleges spend their money? At a purely formal level this can be readily deduced from the various items on the expenditure side of college accounts. The difficulty lies in being able to tell what particular entries in the accounts actually represent. And it is seldom possible to make direct comparisons between the headings of expenditure in different colleges. Balliol had entries for 'expensae diminutae' and for 'commons'; All Souls—curiously in view of all the correspondence with successive visitors—had no entry for commons as such but a general one called 'promptuarium' (probably meaning store-room), covering almost all supplies. University College had three main headings: payments, the largest and most miscellaneous; commons and battels, the next largest and the most varied in character; and expenses, the smallest, consisting mainly of maintenance items. In Corpus Christi commons was the largest item in the 1520s–30s and in the 1570s, but had been overtaken by 'impensae' in the 1620s; this too was a widely varied category, the literal meaning of payments or expenses covering legal charges and the cost of progresses round the college's properties. Once the colleges had their commons reinforced by corn rents, all but the poorest and least well managed of them were able to branch out, increasing the various allowances to college officers, fellows and staff, spending more on progresses and litigation, although only rarely endowing additional fellowships and scholarships (unless they received special donations for these) and virtually never (save for All Souls under the vigilant eyes of successive primates) themselves giving much to general charitable purposes. In New College expenditure fell into three main categories: commons for fellows, scholars and chaplains, which was in turn divided between the original statutory allocation and the money spent on purchases of supplies for commons over and above this; the maintenance and running costs

---

[1] Mark H. Curtis, *Oxford and Cambridge in Transition, 1558–1642* (Oxford 1959), 282, note B, citing A. J. Butler, 'An account of the benefactions bestowed upon the college', *Brasenose College Quatercentenary Monographs* (2 vols in 3 OHS lii–liv 1909) i.

of other departments, which included the chapel and the stables together with external charges and the costs of litigation; and finally cash payments to the warden, the fellows (who got very little individually, but there could be as many as seventy of them), other staff and college servants. In the 1570s –1580s the first of these headings comprised easily the largest section of expenditure. Whereas in New College the term 'liveries' was used for stipendiary payments to fellows and others, in Merton the same word denoted payments for commons. Expenditure there was itemized under a larger number of separate headings which were not grouped together, although by the 1630s two large categories, of 'table' for fellows, servants and post-masters (the Merton name for scholars), and 'liveries', or allowances in cash, had swallowed up most of the others.[1] In All Souls the 'promptuarium' heading dominated the whole expenditure side of the accounts. In the 1520s it accounted for £200 out of an average annual total of £455; in the 1570s the corresponding figures were £375 and £700, and by the 1630s no less than £1,128 out of £1,835. These ten-year samples from the All Souls accounts show that if we take the 1520s total of expenditure as equal to a 'base-line' or index of 100, then the corresponding figure for the 1570s would be 153.8 and for the 1620s 403.3. That is another way of illustrating the relatively greater buoyancy of college finances in the second half of our period compared to the first.

The historian of English philanthropy in the period 1480–1660, W. K. Jordan, has been severely criticized for failing to take proper account of inflation in his calculations of capital endowments and annual values. This applies especially in his comparison of the late sixteenth and early seventeenth centuries with the first half-century or so covered by his study. According to the now well-known Phelps Brown–Hopkins index of the prices of consumables, if the quarter-century 1451–75 is taken as a base-line average of 100, there was only a very slight increase, of about 10 per cent until the end of the 1510s, but a massive and sustained, if extremely uneven increase to an average of over 615 from the 1520s to the 1630s.[2] Now on this

---

[1] Merton College Archives Bursars' Book, 1585–1633. For all earlier information on Merton I have relied either on printed sources or on material kindly supplied by Dr Chris Upton from his work done in collaboration with Dr John Fletcher.

[2] E. H. Phelps Brown and Sheila V. Hopkins, 'Seven centuries of the prices of consumables, compared with builders' wage rates', *Economica*, new ser. xxiii no. 92 (1956), 296–314, reprinted in E. M. Carus-Wilson (ed.), *Essays in Economic History* (3 vols 1954–62) ii and in P. H. Ramsey (ed.), *The Price Revolution in Sixteenth Century England* (1971). It is of interest that Brown and Hopkins based their more controversial construction of a table (and graph) of real wages largely on Thorold Rogers's use of Oxford college records from the fifteenth to the seventeenth centuries (see 'Seven centuries of building wages', *Economica*, new ser. xxii no. 87 (1955), reprinted in Carus-Wilson (ed.), *Essays* ii).

basis a college would have to have increased its income more than sixfold over the period from the later fifteenth century to the eve of the civil war, or a little over fourfold during the period with which we are concerned in this chapter, that is from the beginning of the reformation under Henry VIII to the early 1640s, simply in order to have kept level in real terms. However, not all costs inflated at the same rate as the Phelps Brown–Hopkins 'basket' of consumables. Fees and wages certainly did not; nor did books and various other manufactured products. Timber probably did; stone, tiles and bricks did not. To give but one example of wage payments: at University College the butler, later renamed the manciple, was receiving an annual fee of two marks (26s 8d) in the later fifteenth century, an and was still receiving this much in the reign of Charles I.

The cost of litigation is not easily classified under either of the modern headings of capital or recurrent expenditure. In the minds of contemporaries in the Tudor and Stuart periods it was generally 'extraordinary' rather than 'ordinary', although there were some cases where law suits dragged on for so long that the charges to which they gave rise became a regular, if varying, item on the college accounts. A perhaps extreme instance is provided by the disputes between All Souls and successive Lords Cromwell over lands which had once belonged to the prior of Launde at Whadborough in Northamptonshire. When the case was due to come up for hearing yet again in the Hilary term of 1598/9, it was said that:

During theis 40 years the college have been in suite for the lands in the Courts of Chancery, the King's Bench, Common Pleas the Exchequer and the Exchequer Chamber & have been delayed by ayde [of] prayer injunctions and such like.

Litigation seems to have continued for at least another twenty years after this, and possibly for longer.[1] Who was the gainer from such a protracted dispute, besides the respective parties' lawyers, is far from clear, though it should be said that the total Whadborough holding amounted to 910 acres, so a large rental was at stake. Nor were lawyers' charges by any means static over this kind of time-span.[2] The limits of what should be thought of as legal costs are not easily defined. If we take account not only of formal charges made by courts and lawyers but also of further payments in the form of retaining fees, gratuities and 'gifts', then this begins to shade off

[1] All Souls Archives W 145/50; part if not the whole of the story can be followed from the rest of MS 145.

[2] See W. R. Prest, 'Counsellors' fees and earnings in the age of Sir Edward Coke', in J. H. Baker (ed.), *Legal Records and the Historian* (1978).

imperceptibly into something more like a 'cost-benefit analysis' of the colleges' place in the entire Elizabethan–Early Stuart patronage system. The crown, the nobility, the episcopate, sometimes influential and wealthy members of the gentry and the mercantile élite used, and needed to use, the colleges in order to place relatives, dependants and clients in them as scholars or fellows. The colleges needed, or felt that they needed, protection and support from the most influential people in the realm, from monarchs and other royalty, their ranking favourites and archbishops downwards, in order to preserve and, if possible, extend their corporate interests. And that takes us outside the proper boundaries of this chapter and into those of other contributors.[1]

Granted then the inadequacy of college accounts, and the lack of any single consolidated index by which we can turn money incomes into real incomes, are there any alternative tests of economic health? When we find from the records that cash reserves were being built up, substantial building work being undertaken, or even (as at Corpus Christi) additional land being brought out of the cumulative surpluses on the current account, then we can surely infer that the institutions concerned, and those members on their foundations, were not doing so badly.

Several, perhaps most of the existing colleges were engaged in building during the period roughly between mid-Elizabethan times and the eve of the Civil War.[2] Much of this took the form of 'cock-lofting', that is adding another top storey to existing buildings, or else converting roof-spaces into sets of rooms.[3] The object of this was generally to give resident fellows more and better accommodation, but it may also have had the effect of freeing other rooms in college for gentlemen commoners, who could be charged rent and on whose hall and buttery accounts bursars no doubt also reckoned to make a profit (whether for themselves or for the college). Balliol, for example, instituted a new category of fellow-commoners from

[1] See in particular chs 2, 3 and 6 above by C. I. Hammer, Claire Cross and Penry Williams respectively.

[2] There was substantial new building, or rebuilding, in the following colleges between the 1550s and around 1640: (in the order of their age by foundation date) University, Merton, Exeter, Oriel (virtually rebuilt 1610–40), New, Lincoln, Corpus Christi, Christ Church, Trinity, St John's, Jesus, Wadham, Pembroke, also Hart Hall and St Edmund Hall. This list is compiled from *City of Oxford* (Royal Commission on Historical Monuments 1939); *VCH Oxon* iii.; Jennifer Sherwood and Nikolaus Pevsner, *Oxfordshire* (Buildings of England series Harmondsworth 1974). For fuller details on both the architectural and financial aspects see John Newman's chapters in this volume and in the fourth volume of the History (forthcoming).

[3] This took place in New College, All Souls, Brasenose, Corpus Christi and Trinity, and probably elsewhere as well. It is interesting that in 1979–81 two colleges (Worcester and St Peter's) have 'cock-lofted' in reverse, to enlarge their respective college libraries upwards.

1610, though there had certainly been commoners of gentry and even nobles as well as more lowly status there in the fifteenth and early sixteenth centuries.[1] Nor were they the first in this field, for Mr V. H. H. Green's spendidly detailed history shows that Lincoln instituted a new category of gentleman-commoner in 1606.[2] But in 1639 two different lists of caution money show respectively four gentlemen to sixty-two ordinary commoners and two to forty-five. There can be little doubt that a college and its individual fellows as tutors reckoned to make something out of those in the grander, more prestigious category, and perhaps hoped that the college would receive a fine piece of silver plate from such students either at the end of their time in Oxford, or later as a benefaction. But, as we have seen, it is much more difficult to know what the colleges made out of having ordinary commoner undergraduates, or indeed in a few cases graduates who were not on the foundation.[3]

Besides physical expansion and growth in numbers, the accumulation of reserves in cash and plate may also be seen as evidence of financial buoyancy. By the time that the first series of University College accounts, so admirably transcribed by Mr Cox, come to an end in 1596 the surplus in the bursar's hands at the end of the year had mounted by fits and starts, from a few pounds or nothing at all some decades earlier, to £127. At All Souls hundreds of pounds were being transferred to the tower in most years by the 1620s and 1630s, in spite or perhaps because of the arguments over the increase of commons to which corn rents had given rise. The same was even more evident at Corpus Christi, but without the attendant disputes. Just after the period with which this chapter is concerned virtually all the Oxford colleges gave, or in theory 'lent', large quantities of silver plate for the royalist war effort in 1642-3. Some colleges advanced sizable sums of money to the king, as well as or instead of plate. In the case of Queen's, although their revenues had increased proportionately less than those of several other colleges since the 1590s, this totalled no less than £2,881 (£1,400 from the provost and £1,481 from the college); even Balliol managed to raise £210.[4]

To compare the absolute wealth of different colleges is one thing; to assess their wealth relative to their size and the scale of their commitments quite another. Thus Corpus Christi, with 'old rents'

[1] See H. W. C. Davis, *A History of Balliol College* (Oxford 1899, revised by R. H. C. Davis and Richard Hunt, Oxford 1979), 30, 80-9, 99-101.

[2] Green, *Lincoln College*, 158-60, 223 n. 1.

[3] Ibid., chs 7 and 9, shows that payments by all categories of undergraduates were growing in this period.

[4] Queen's College Archives Provost N, fo 133[V]; Balliol College Archives Bursars' Books I.E.1, 3-4.

rated at £500 a year and a gross annual income estimated at £1,200 by the 1640s, may in terms of wealth per head of those on the foundation and other necessary expenses (maintenance and furnishing of buildings, etc.) have been 'richer' than Christ Church, with 'old rents' of £2,000 and an estimated gross income fifty years later of £6,000 a year. University College apparently increased its income sixfold, but only enlarged its foundation when the Simon Bennett benefaction became fully operative later in the seventeenth century,[1] whereas New College was bound by its statutes to maintain seventy fellows—no more and no less.[2] By the 1640s All Souls and St John's were reckoned to have the same gross income, likewise Merton and Corpus Christi; such comparisons could be extended. It seems a fair guess that Magdalen and Corpus were the best off, measured by the number of those on the foundation; and by the same criterion Balliol and probably Jesus the worst off.

So, with corn rents, entry fines, wood sales, benefactions and payments by commoners, it looks as if the colleges did on the whole weather the so-called 'price revolution' successfully.

Can the same be said of the university itself? Throughout this period its formal revenues, of which regular accounts were kept, were modest indeed compared to those of the best-endowed colleges, not to say pitifully small. Income on the proctors' accounts was running at the level of £20–£24 a year in the 1560s and 1570s and, apart from a once-for-all windfall of arrears, it never exceeded £40 a year as late as the 1630s.[3] The vice-chancellor's accounts, which progressively became more important than those of the proctors in the course of the sixteenth century, show that the annual income was tripled by Queen Mary I's gift of three rectories, but even then the total was only running at between £150 and £180 a year (except when there were special levies or collections for such events as royal visits) until into the seventeenth century.[4] From the 1620s there was indeed a massive increase, but this was largely due to the special

---

[1] A word of caution is necessary here: the author of the 1640s paper, tabulating college revenues, gives University £600 per annum gross; but the college accounts show that, whereas the apparent gross receipts from all known sources did indeed average £645 a year for the decade 1633–43, the actual net receipts (deducting arrears and other items carried over from previous years) only averaged £491 per annum for the same ten-year period (University College Archives General Account Book A).

[2] There were not always exactly seventy fellows; on occasion more full fellows died or resigned than there were qualified probationers ready to take their places; sometimes too probationers died or left, so that more Winchester scholars then had to be admitted to make up the numbers (New College Library, Warden Sewell's MS book of fellows, from the foundation to c 1890).

[3] OUA WPβ/23/2, proctors' accounts, 1560s to 1770s.

[4] OUA WPβ/21/4, W. T. Mitchell's typescript of the vice-chancellors' accounts, 1547/50–1666.

endowments—mostly tied to particular purposes—which flooded in, following Sir Thomas Bodley's refoundation of the university library.

As with many other historical events which come in chronological sequence, it would be wrong to say that Bodley's great benefaction 'caused' all the others. It certainly did help to bring about the other gifts, in books, manuscripts and cash, to the library, because Bodley himself acted as a kind of unofficial fund-raiser in that respect. His money, together with the further sums which were raised by his executors and by the university itself, was used to complete the re-building of the schools, round what is now the old library quad-rangle. But successive vice-chancellors' accounts were also swollen by endowments for chairs and lecturerships, for a botanical garden and even by one or two legacies for general purposes. As the late W. A. Pantin wrote, 'between 1619 and 1636 eight professorships or lectureships were founded . . . eight chairs in 17 years compares favourably with eight chairs founded between 1660 and 1800'.[1] Unfortunately the university did not invest its capital benefactions as wisely as most of the colleges usually did; some of the legacies were simply merged with income, and others were used to buy pro-perty which at least initially proved unprofitable. Certainly before Laud's time as chancellor, the university's statutes—unlike those of virtually every college—were not drawn with an eye to preserving and, if possible, extending the institution's landed possessions. So the swollen revenue accounts and the large annual surpluses of the 1620s to 1640s are somewhat misleading, even if by the standards of forty, let alone eighty, years earlier they look very impressive.

On top of all this, the building programme and these other achievements, by the end of 1641 the university had amassed the sum of £922 in its chests as a cash reserve. And of this £800 was to be 'lent' to the king for military purposes in 1642.[2] Given the small scale of its financial operations, at any rate until well into the seventeenth century, this may seem a considerable amount. Yet Corpus Christi College alone spent £5,319 on property from 1563 to 1639, and over more or less the same span of time had about another £900 in surpluses deposited in its various chests, an aggregation of over £6,200 in all.[3]

Of course the truth is that the university was largely kept going

[1] W. A. Pantin, *Oxford Life in Oxford Archives* (Oxford 1972), 38.

[2] OUA WPβ/21/2, cista acad: 1545–1668 (unpaginated after the 1580s), July 1642. By 1645 the reserves in the chests were down to 9*s* 1*d*.

[3] Corpus Christi College Archives C. 7/1–2, registers of chests kept in the tower; C. 1/1/1–9, Libri Magni.

financially by sources of income which do not appear in any surviving accounts. There are indeed tables which were drawn up, some of which were given statutory backing by the university at different dates, of the fees which were to be paid by different categories of student, more or less at every stage from entry to final departure. Fees for degrees were scaled according to the wealth and status of the graduand, as well as the type of degree. To put it at its most extreme, sons of peers and gentry receiving doctorates had to pay at the highest rate; poor scholars of plebeian status becoming bachelors at the lowest.[1] Thus the income from this source, which was channelled through the bedells who were entitled to retain a considerable amount for themselves, would vary both with the size of the university and with the social background of its members. So the 'educational revolution', of which Professor Lawrence Stone has written, together with the 'gentrification' of the Oxford student body, as portrayed by Professor Mark Curtis and others,[2] most definitely helped the university not only to survive but also to employ staff who received an income not wholly unrelated to rising costs. Just to illustrate the invisibility of this fee income on the official accounts: an annual revenue of 43s 6d is recorded on the proctors' accounts for 1564, but this was less than the registrar's stipend of 53s 4d, although it exceeds the university clerk's at 32s. In 1580 the rent of the farm of the matriculation fees, the yield from which went to the bedells, brought in the derisory sum of £1 on the vice-chancellor's account, and was producing the same forty-eight years later.[3]

In theory the registers of matriculations and degrees together with the fee tables should make it possible for us to calculate the value of this revenue. In practice this would be extraordinarily laborious and, because of the incompleteness of the evidence, actually impossible of precise attainment. Thus, at the end of our period in 1637–9, according to Professor Stone,[4] the annual average of matriculations was 420: of these thirty were sons of peers, baronets or knights for whom the fees ranged from 13s 4d (for a duke's or

[1] Material on fees is to be found scattered in Boase's and Clark's editions of the first two volumes of the registers. For those promulgated in the winter of 1601–2, see *Statuta*, 458–81 and (in an edited form) *Reg. Univ.* ed. Clark i. 218–25.

[2] See Lawrence Stone, 'The educational revolution in England, 1560–1640', *Past and Present* xxviii (1964), 41–80; Curtis, *Oxford and Cambridge*; and more recently Lawrence Stone, 'The size and composition of the Oxford student body 1580–1910', in Lawrence Stone (ed.), *The University in Society* (2 vols Princeton 1975) i. 3–110.

[3] The accounts of 1580 and 1628 were chosen for detailed study because it so happened that future archbishops were vice-chancellors in both those years. (OUA WPβ/21/4, Toby Mathew's account, 21 Dec. 1580, William Juxon's account, 26 July 1628).

[4] Stone, 'Size and composition', 93 table 2.

a marquis's son) down to 3*s* 4*d* (for a knight's). So, if we assume at a minimum ten entrants paying 6*s* 8*d* and twenty paying 3*s* 4*d*, this would have brought in £6 13*s* 4*d*; then, since forty-nine were the sons of esquires, at 1*s* 8*d* each, this is another £4 1*s* 8*d*: 123 were gentlemen's sons at 1*s* each, which is £6 3*s*; sixty-two more were sons of clergy or doctors, who if their fathers were privileged persons connected with the university or any of the colleges, would pay only 2*d*, otherwise according to status, so at say an average of 6*d* a head, this meant £1 11*s*; finally, 156 were plebeians' sons, which at 4*d* each meant £2 12*s* more. Thus we arrive at a very approximate annual total for these, admittedly peak years of £21. Whatever the margin of error in these calculations, the bedells' rent of £1 suggests a handsome profit.

The same sort of estimates can be attempted with degree fees. Graduands were rated more by income than by fathers' rank, grand compounders being those with over £40 a year from non-academic sources, petty compounders those with over 5*s* a year likewise. Thus, given an average of 203 BAs a year in the 1630s (Stone's figures again),[1] and assuming that 103 of them were rated at below 5*s* a year income, they would only have paid 6*s* 6*d* at admission and then 5*s* 2*d* at determining, or 11*s* 8*d* in all, making a total of £56 6*s* 8*d*; if seventy were petty compounders, at 17*s* 2*d* plus 5*s* 2*d* or £1 2*s* 4*d* in all, their total would be £78 3*s* 4*d*; finally if thirty were grand compounders, at £13 6*s* 8*d* and £10 or £23 6*s* 8*d* apiece in all, they would have brought in no less than £700. So we arrive at a total here from all categories of £888 10*s*. This may well be too high, but even if we put those in the bottom income bracket at 160 out of 203, the petty compounders at thirty and grand ones at only thirteen, that still comes to an annual total of £443 on BA degree fees. While, even if every single one of the 140 proceeding MA paid at the lowest rate, which was 8*s* 7*d* plus 14*s* 7*d*, or 23*s* 2*d* in all, this would still have amounted to another £162 yearly. The nineteen BThs likewise at the lowest rate of £2 would have yielded another £38; and, finally, the seven doctors at £10 17*s* 8*d* each, £76 3*s* 8*d* more, making a 'low' or minimum estimated total here of £619 a year, which is an extraordinarily large 'invisible', or below-the-line addition to the university's official income even in those relatively prosperous times. Looking back to the decades 1520–70, Stone's figures show an average of only thirty-five BAs a year, and, since they are in any case more likely to have been charged at the minimum rate when fees were lower for all grades at all stages, it can be readily appreciated that this form of university income had shown a most enviable elasticity.

[1] Ibid. 94 table 3.

These estimates can to some extent be correlated with such early 'fee books' as have survived. The fullest and most remarkable of these, kept by the senior law bedell from 1618 to 1642 (and then briefly resumed by his successor in 1658–9) shows massive sums changing hands every year, from candidates for every type of degree to the various university officers.[1] Another volume lists the members of colleges and halls paying fees to be examined for the degree of BA between 1608 and 1620; except for one nobleman everyone seems to have paid 2s. The total number approved having been just over 2,250 for twelve years, at an average of 187 or 188 this would represent about £18 15s per annum (not allowing for the odd aristocrat paying at a higher rate).[2] The third volume is concerned with dispensations and graces from 1609 to 1614, and it contains at the end what look like annual totals for each year, set out term by term, which range between £62 and £79 for the five years for which all four termly sub-totals are given. Unfortunately it is not clear whether these are the totals raised altogether from all kinds of graces and dispensations, or the total amounts paid or payable to a particular official.[3] Returning to the first of these three volumes, this is divided into moneys received by the person actually keeping the record, that is Matthew Crosse the esquire bedell of law, the amounts owing by him to the university itself, to the professor of civil law, to the other bedels and to the clerk of the university (the registrar's chief assistant), and, finally, the amounts actually paid by him. Part of this last section shows very considerable sums being paid in the 1630s to successive vice-chancellors, £50 or £60 a year, rising to £90 and even £132 in 1639, solely for proceeders in law, for which there is no corresponding entry in the vice-chancellors' accounts for these years. At the end of Trinity term 1636 Bedell Crosse reckoned up where he stood, calculating the various amounts which he owed to the university, his colleagues and others at a total of £113, and then calculating what was owing to him from different sources and from the university for expenses, this amounting to just under £103. It

[1] OUA WPβ/21/3, officially described as a book of fees, 1618–58/9, but actually 1618–41, with a very few 1658–9 entries in a totally different hand. Before the original numbered foliation, the following description is entered: 'A Booke of all Receipts Payments etc/ wch belong unto me by vertue of/my Office in the Universitie.' Besides other clues as to the book's ownership, in the right-hand column of [fo 178ᵛ] under the heading 'I am to receaue June 29 1636', is the entry 'Accounts for my journey to London 34 *li*.5s.6d.', and the vice-chancellor's account for that year (OUA WPβ/21/4/3, W. T. Mitchell's typescript copy), a payment of this amount is noted under Dr Pinck's extraordinary outgoings, to Matthew Crosse, the senior law bedel, for the delegates' expenses going to Hampton Court in connection with the (archiepiscopal) visitation of the university. Miss Ruth Vyse kindly helped me with this identification.

[2] OUA WPβ/21/1.

[3] OUA SP/63.

would of course be most unwise to conclude from this that Crosse was £10 out of pocket on the academic year 1635/6; the figures are more revealing of the amounts changing hands in fees and like payments, and as such they need—as already suggested—to be put in the context of the university's very modest income even by the early seventeenth century from other sources, as recorded in the vice-chancellors' and the proctors' accounts.[1]

It would be exaggerated to argue that every registrar, bedell and even clerk made his and (if he had one) his family's fortunes during these years. None the less the probable sums passing in fee payments do introduce a kind of 'court–country' dimension to any assessment of the university's place in Tudor and Stuart society. To this must likewise be added whatever payments were made to college fellows and lecturers for giving private tuition, and whatever was given to other college servants in the form of gratuities. A glance at the kind of men who served as successive registrars to the university from the eve of the reformation until the era of the restoration may perhaps provide a pointer to the relative attractiveness of that office. From the 1520s to 1550s we find a succession of men who, discounting temporary fluctuations in their fortunes due to the various changes in the country's official religion, clearly used the post as a stepping-stone, rising to be bishops, vice-chancellors, or at the least heads of colleges or halls.[2] From the 1550s we find longer tenures, ending with death or retirement, only one going on to become head of a hall, and with the first registrar known to have been married dying in office in 1629. The whole span from 1608 to 1737 was covered by two families, the years of a puritan-republican holder of the position (1651–9) alone excepted.[3] The registrar had to be an MA and a notary public, or from 1660 onwards to be

[1] OUA WPβ/21/3.

[2] They were James Turbervile (see *DNB*; *BRUO 1501–40*, 579), William Tresham (*DNB*; *BRUO 1501–40*, 576–7), Robert Taylor (*BRUO 1501–40*, 560), Richard Smyth or Smith (*DNB*; *BRUO 1501–40*, 524–6) and Thomas Kay or Key (*DNB*; 'Caius'; *BRUO 1501–40*, 325–6, 723), who despite being sacked for incompetence recovered sufficiently to end his days as master of University College.

[3] The succession ran as follows: William Standish or Standyssh, 1552–79: Foster, *Alumni* i. 1407; *BRUO, 1501–40*, 534; *Epist. acad. 1508–96*, 402 (note to letter 199) and also pp. xxviii–xxix); Richard Cullen 1579–89: Foster, *Alumni* i. 361; James Hussey or Hussee 1589–1602: Foster, *Alumni* i. 776; Thomas Frederick Kirby, *Winchester Scholars* (1888), 147; Brian P. Levack, *The Civil Lawyers in England, 1603–42* (1973), 241; Maurice Merrick or Meyricke 1602–8: Foster, *Alumni* i. 1006; Kirby, *Winchester Scholars*, 146; OUA WPβ/ 21/2a); Thomas French 1608–29: Foster, *Alumni* i. 535; OUA WPβ/21/2a; John French 1629–51: Foster, *Alumni* i. 534; *The Register of the Visitors of the University of Oxford, from A.D. 1647 to A.D. 1658*, ed. Montagu Burrows (Camden Society new ser. xxix 1881), 526; William Whittingham 1651–9: Foster, *Alumni* i. 1624; Benjamin Cooper 1659–1701: Foster, *Alumni* i. 324; *Register*, ed. Burrows, 149; George Cooper 1701–37: Foster, *Alumni* i. 324.

eligible to become a notary if he was not already one.[1] There would seem little doubt that the office became more attractive as our period progressed, that is to say to remain in, rather than to use as one rung of an upward *cursus honorum*.

By contrast to the colleges, the halls were run on a frankly commercial basis. And it seems likely that only by practising economies of scale, namely by increasing student numbers, could they both provide an adequate education and keep in credit. Such at least seems to be the late A. B. Emden's message in his valuable history of St Edmund Hall, where the most detailed information comes not from the hall's own accounts, of which no regular series survives until the later seventeenth century, but from the records of the then vice-chancellor's visitation conducted in 1613.[2] Only Magdalen Hall is recorded as having had more students than St Edmund's both in 1612 and again in the 1640s. It is noteworthy that, in the 1612 returns of university and college numbers which, however faulty, are the most detailed of the period, three colleges (Queen's, Brasenose and Exeter) are shown as having had more commoners than any of the halls (194, 145 and 134 respectively) and four more colleges (Balliol with 70, Lincoln 60, Trinity 52 and St John's 43) more than any except Magdalen Hall. The fact that all but one of the halls were eventually to be absorbed by the colleges was due primarily to the tremendous advantage that the colleges enjoyed through chartered incorporation and permanent endowments; but successful competition for fee and battel-paying commoners must also have played its part.

So, if we are to try to give a brief and no doubt over-simplified answer to the question of how the university itself kept going through the period of inflation, this must certainly include mention of Queen Mary, Sir Thomas Bodley and his contemporaries and successors, and the educational revolution (due to demographic and other causes, mainly concentrated between about 1570 and 1620). It is indeed a sobering thought that the university of Oxford seems not to have received a single benefaction during the space of forty years or so between Mary Tudor and Bodley, while its library was virtually extinct from the early 1550s to the beginning of the 1600s. The unique collegiate structure of the two ancient English universities thus provided them with sources of economic, as of intellectual strength denied to more unitary institutions. Then as now, however, although the reasons may be different in an utterly changed historical context, this was at the same time a potential source of danger for the university.

[1] C. E. Mallett, *A History of the University of Oxford* (3 vols 1924–7) ii. 336, n. 3.
[2] *VCH Oxon* iii. 327–8.

The economic and financial effects on Oxford and its colleges of the civil wars and interregnum lie beyond the scope of this chapter. Besides parting with virtually all their holdings of silver plate, the colleges' generous cash contributions to the king's cause must in many cases have exhausted their reserves. Then, on top of this, came disruption in the payment of rents (from parts of the country either directly affected by the fighting or under parliamentary control while Oxford was the royalist capital from 1642/3 to 1646), the loss of income from commoner numbers falling off, and in the university's own case from matriculations and graduations drastically diminishing, together with the additional burdens of wartime and post-war taxation, both direct (the weekly pay, then the monthly assessment) and indirect (the excise). The colleges and halls of the two universities, together with those of Eton and Winchester, had enjoyed exemption from the payment of direct taxes since the late fifteenth century or earlier. This seems to have temporarily lapsed in the last years of Henry VIII's reign, but to have been re-established under Edward VI; and a clause granting exemption can be found in all the acts of parliament for subsidies, tenths and fifteenths under Elizabeth, James and Charles I down to 1641. The convocation of the clergy ceased to meet after the spring of 1640, and the long parliament began to tax the clergy together with the laity. The year 1641 saw more massive grants of taxation than any previous year in English history. In some of these the colleges maintained their exemption, but it was left to the discretion of local commissioners and dropped in the act for the grant for the defence of the kingdoms of England and Ireland and for the repayment of debts for which the parliament had made itself responsible; this measure was designed to raise £400,000 in two equal instalments (equivalent in all to a grant of five subsidies). And so far as can be seen the colleges were not singled out for special treatment or exemption in either the parliamentarian or the royalist taxes of 1642/3 to 1644/5.[1] Then in the spring of 1645 the university of Cambridge and its colleges and halls recovered exemption from parliament's monthly assessment and any similar forms of direct taxation.[2] This may have been meant as no more than

[1] Magdalen College Archives, a general grant of exemption by the crown to the colleges, 15 May 1464 (I am grateful to Dr G. L. Harriss for this reference and for other help on this matter); *Enactments in Parliament concerning Oxford and Cambridge*, ed. L. L. Shadwell (4 vols OHS lviii–lxi 1911–12) i. 84–5, 86, 90–1, 95–7, 126; iv. 341–9; *Statutes of the Realm* v. 8, 21, 38, 51–2, 77, 100, 145–67 (for 1625–41); *Journals of the House of Commons* ii. 176 (resolution giving discretion to the commissioners, 15 June 1641).

[2] *Acts and Ordinances of the Interregnum, 1642–1660*, ed. C. H. Firth and R. S. Rait (3 vols 1911) i. 666–7. A petition from the university was brought to the commons by Herbert Palmer, provost of Queen's (Cooper, *Annals of Cambridge* iii, 386); Sir Dudley North and Sir Anthony Irby were appointed by the commons to take the ordinance up to

a temporary respite, while wartime losses were made good, but even better was to follow. Not long after the surrender of Oxford to the parliament's forces—and before the notorious visitation of 1647–8 and the massive purges to which it gave rise—a remarkable concession was won by the two universities and other educational bodies. The assessment ordinance of June 1647 (which was actually to authorize the monthly assessment for a year from the preceding 25 March) gave exemption from payment to the universities, their constituent colleges, houses and halls, the foundations of Westminster, Winchester and Eton, and 'all other free schooles'.[1] In fact the proviso had been agreed as early as 7 April after being referred to a small committee of which John Selden was the first-named member and from which he reported back to the house. And so far as the evidence goes, this remained in operation until the restoration.[2] A cursory inspection of the university's archives for 1648–60 and such figures as there are available for colleges from the same years suggest that, whatever truth there may be in the arguments about their intellectual health under the republic, materially something of a recovery was achieved. As to whether or not college endowments were under a greater threat from either the long parliament or the Barebones in the years 1646–53 than they had been under Henry VIII and Edward VI a century or so earlier, there are too many imponderables in the way of a clear-cut answer. That they were under no greater a threat then than that which they are under today may perhaps be ventured as one conclusion. Cambridge and Oxford and their constituent colleges may come to need as good and effective friends in high places by the late twentieth century as they were fortunate enough to have had in the persons of Smith, Selden and others at times of crisis during the sixteenth and seventeenth centuries.

the lords (*Journals of the House of Commons* iv. 106; *Journals of the House of Lords*, vii. 314).

[1] Presumably this meant schools which had free places for scholars or others, even if they also had fee-paying pupils.

[2] *Journals of the House of Commons* v. 134–5; *Acts and Ordinances*, ed. Firth and Rait i. 984; BL Additional MS 37344 Bulstrode Whitelocke's 'Annals' iv. fo 83ᵛ. On the other hand, an act of the All Souls governing body in 1652 expresses concern lest tenants should try to shift their fiscal obligations on to their collegiate landlords, and directs that in all future leases tenants must covenant not to do so, in respect of the assessment and other levies or contributions (All Souls Archives Acta in Capitulis, 1601–1707, fo 122).

Appendix I

The Property of Balliol College
c 1500–c 1640

G. D. DUNCAN

THROUGHOUT the sixteenth and seventeenth centuries Balliol was reckoned one of the poorest colleges in the university. When in 1536 the colleges were laid under contribution for the stipend of King Henry VIII's lecturer in theology Balliol was assessed at 4s 1d a year, propping up the table along with University College.[1] In 1592 the colleges were ranked for contributions to the expenses of the queen's visit according to the rentals from their ancient endowments (*reditus antiqui*) and Balliol at £100 again brought up the rear with University College.[2] Towards the end of our period in 1643 when the colleges and halls were once more assessed, this time for the fortification of Oxford, Balliol was inevitably given the lowest place among the colleges in company now with University College, Wadham, Jesus and Pembroke.[3]

The sixteenth century had begun badly, not to say disastrously for the college when it was induced to grant one of its most valuable Oxford properties, Burnell's Inn and the Dolphin, to Wolsey who needed it for the site of Cardinal College. Balliol became the victim of the 'dexterite & policie' of the cardinal and his agents who paid nothing for the property but merely made unfulfilled promises of lands or benefices in exchange. In 1535, the college complained that it had lost £10 7s 6d a year as a result of this shady transaction, no mean sum for an institution so slimly endowed.[4]

At the time of the *Valor ecclesiasticus* in 1535 and the survey made for the chantry commissioners in 1546 the college had properties in London and Oxford, Oxfordshire, Bedfordshire, Huntingdonshire and Northumberland.[5] The college's holdings in Oxford itself have been fully described by H. E. Salter in *The Oxford Deeds of*

[1] *Statuta*, 339.
[2] *Reg. ann. mert. 1567-1603*, 287.
[3] *Dean's Register of Oriel*, 299-300.
[4] *Balliol Deeds*, 95-8, 127-35, quotation at 97.
[5] *Valor* ii. 269-70; PRO E 315/441, fos 89-94ᵛ. For the background of the 1546 sur-

Balliol College.[1] They consisted of various tenements in the parishes of St Mary Magdalen, St Giles, St Aldates, St Mary the Virgin, St Peter le Bailey and St Ebbes, plus a few fixed rents. The most important Oxford properties were in the parish of St Mary Magdalen on or near the site of the college. In 1535 all of the Oxford holdings were assessed as bringing in £11 15s 0d a year gross, £11 7s 7¼d de claro, and in 1546 at £10 19s 9d *clare* a year.[2]

In Oxfordshire at Oddington (Otmoor) there was a house with half a virgate of arable and 4½ acres of meadow;[3] at Nethercot (Tackley) a house, the close in which it stood with 30 acres of arable and 3 acres of meadow;[4] at Steeple Aston 12 acres of meadow;[5] in Old Woodstock a farm called Praunces Place and in Wootton near Woodstock three tenements with 2½ yardlands;[6] and at Moreton, near Thame, a messuage of land,[7] assessed at about 22 acres with 1 acre for the house, backside, garden, orchard and close in a terrier of 1663.[8] In 1546 all of this brought in a further £20 2s 9d *clare*.[9] To complete the tally of the Oxfordshire properties, mention should be made of the quarrying rights enjoyed by the college at Heading-ton—they became a source of profit and consequently of dispute in the early seventeenth century when a chancery decree confirmed Balliol's right to a freestone quarry, lately challenged by the lord of the manor. According to the decree the dispute had arisen 'because the getting of stones and vse of the Quarrie was become then of late a matter of more profitt then it was accustomed to be'. Receipts from sales of stone appear in the bursars' accounts for the years 1612–22, reaching a peak of over £15 in 1614–15.[10]

In Huntingdonshire Balliol possessed the rectory of Abbotsley which, according to a terrier of 1621, had 87½ acres, almost all of it arable, and a further 4¾ acres of copyhold land leased with it.[11] In 1535 it was worth £17 9s 5d a year gross, £11 8s 7d de claro.[12]

vey see *Chantry Certificates for Oxfordshire*, ed. Graham, pp. viii–ix; *Oriel College Records*, ed. C. L. Shadwell and H. E. Salter (OHS lxxxv 1926), 424.

[1] *Balliol Deeds, passim.*

[2] *Valor* ii. 269; PRO E 315/441, fo 90ᵛ.

[3] *VCH Oxon.* vi. 280, note 15. An undated terrier of the college's lands at Oddington says that it had just under 30 acres of meadow, pasture and arable in the fields of Odding-ton: Balliol College Archives (hereafter BCA) Lease Book II, unpaginated section at end of volume.   [4] BCA A.21.1.

[5] H. Savage, *Balliofergus* (1668), 34.

[6] BCA F.1.1, A.22.1, A.22.6, A.22.7, A.22.8, A.22.9.

[7] Savage, *Balliofergus*, 85; BCA, A.17.2.

[8] BCA Lease Book II, unpaginated section at end of volume.

[9] PRO E 315/441, fo 91.

[10] BCA A.14.20; BCA Bursars' Books I.B.3, *recepta contingentia*. Cf Savage, *Balliofergus*, 82; BCA Lease Log Book, fo 172ᵛ.

[11] BCA Lease Book II, unpaginated section at end of volume.   [12] *Valor* ii. 269.

Not far from Abbotsley, but in Bedfordshire, the college owned a tenement in Beeston with 6½ acres of arable and 1 acre of leys.[1] The rural property was completed by the rectory of Long Benton in Northumberland (now in Newcastle) with lands in Heugh and Stamfordham worth £16 2s 8d gross in 1546, £15 12s 11¼d net.[2]

The remainder of the college's property at the time of the surveys of 1535 and 1546 lay in London. Here Balliol had several houses in the parish of St Margaret Patens[3] and, most precious of all, the rectory of St Lawrence Jewry with fixed rents from various tenements in the parish.[4] In the survey of 1546 the rectory and the fixed rents were worth £49 a year gross, £28 5s 0d net,[5] while the tenements in St Margaret Patens brought in another £11 0s 8d gross, £10 12s 8d net.[6]

In addition to the property listed in the surveys of 1535 and 1546 Balliol possessed the rectories of Fillingham, Risholm and Brattlesby, all in Lincolnshire.[7] Savage says that they were appropriated to the college, but it is puzzling to find that they are omitted from the two surveys and that no income from them is ever recorded in the bursars' accounts. The college register shows the college presenting to the rectories and granting the advowsons from time to time and the rectories were held by the masters of Balliol at various times in the early sixteenth century.[8] Evidence about the management of the properties is hard to come by. In 1656 and 1658 the college leased 'All y^t their Rectory and Tithes of the Parsonage Rectory and Farme of Rysome' and in the 1630s the lessee of Fillingham was Lord Castleton.[9] Fillingham was clearly the most important of the three and from 1571 until 1616 was annexed to the mastership, the master being bound by oath to hold it during his term of office.[10]

[1] BCA Lease Book I, fo 32; cf BCA E.6.13 & Lease Log Book, p. 107.

[2] BCA E.2.2; PRO E 315/441, fos 91^V-2. In July 1561 the master was sent north 'ad componendas lites et discordias inter vicarium nostrum de Mychelbenton quosdam parochianos & firmarios nostros Rectorie eiusdem' and to recover some college land in Heugh unjustly detained, for which purpose he took six documents from the common chest: BCA Balliol College Register 1514–1682, p. 90.

[3] BCA B.18.11. Cf Balliol Deeds, 319.

[4] St Lawrence Jewry was leased in two parts: the tithes (BCA B.19.2 etc.) and the parsonage house (BCA B.19.3. etc.).

[5] PRO E 315/441, fo 92.   [6] Ibid. fo 92^V.

[7] R. J. Faith, 'Balliol College Property to 1350' (unpublished typescript, History of the University of Oxford), 10; The State of the Church in the Reigns of Elizabeth and James I, ed. C. W. Foster i (Lincoln Record Society xxiii 1926), 332, 337, 346–7.

[8] Savage, Balliofergus, 54; BCA Balliol College Register 1514–1682, pp. 129, 216, 217, 221, 233, 257, 258, 82, 102, 115; BRUO to 1500 iii. under Thomas Sisson, BRUO 1501–40, under George Cotys, William Wryght.

[9] BCA Lease Book I, p. 170; BCA Balliol College Register 1514–1682, p. 327; Savage, Balliofergus, 57–8; BCA E.5.15.

[10] BCA Balliol College Register 1514–1682, p. 128; Savage, Balliofergus, 59–60.

From the revenues of the rectory he was to pay the salaries of three lecturers in Greek, dialectic and rhetoric, an obligation consequent upon his having leased the rectory in February 1571 for 99 years at an annual rent of £22.[1] Fillingham had been valued at £22 in 1535 and at £66 13s 4d (supposed to represent its value when leased) in 1603–4, Risholm at £4 in 1535 and £10 in 1603–4 and Brattlesby at £7 10s 0d in 1535 and £30 in 1603–4.[2]

In the century or so after 1546 Balliol's rental was augmented by the gift and purchase of further properties, mainly for the support of new scholarships and fellowships. We may first, though, deal with acquisitions unconnected with such new foundations. In Oxford itself Balliol obtained from Oriel College in 1553 a lease of a close of pasture next to the college in the parish of St Mary Magdalen for 21 years at a rent of 6s 8d, which the college in turn leased to the master in 1562 and to Robert Richardson, a joiner, in 1563.[3] But this arrangement did not last long for in 1597 we find Oriel itself again letting the property.[4] In 1610 Balliol bought from Elizabeth Allwyn, widow, her lease from Christ Church of the Cardinal's Hat at the north end of the college site. Christ Church renewed the lease to Balliol in 1630 and 1655 and Balliol let out the new property in several parcels.[5] Finally, in 1638 the college bought the George Inn at Woodstock which it let for an annual rent of £10.[6]

But the most significant new properties were all linked to the foundation of additional fellowships and scholarships. In 1556 John Bell, bishop of Worcester, who may have studied arts at Balliol in the 1490s, bequeathed three houses and gardens in Clerkenwell, London. From this property the college was to pay the exhibitions of two scholars born in the diocese of Worcester: Balliol was to have £4 a year from the houses, the scholars the remainder.[7] In 1557 the property was leased for £13 6s 8d a year, reduced in 1563 to £10.[8]

[1] BCA Balliol College Register 1514–1682, pp. 128, 121, 327; VCH Oxon. iii. 83; Savage, Balliofergus, 55.

[2] Valor iv. 133, 129; State of the Church, ed. Foster, i. pp. lix, 356, 359.

[3] Balliol Deeds, 90–1: BCA Balliol College Register 1514–1682, pp. 94, 97.

[4] Oriel College Records, 277.

[5] Balliol Deeds, 73–80. On 30 January 1611 Caleb Morley, fellow, was admitted 'in maius trium tenementorum proxime adiacum Collegio nostro de Baliolo, vna cum Gardino . . . nuperrime a vidua Allen empt' ', at a rent of £14 a year (BCA Balliol College Register 1514–1682, p. 196).

[6] BCA F.10.5. It seems that the college spent £320 on the transaction: BCA F.7.8–10. Of this £100 came from a special fund in the treasury: BCA Bursars' Books I.E.1, p. 2 (20 January 1637–8).

[7] Savage, Balliofergus, 78–9; SCO i. pt 1 (Balliol College), 25–8; Balliol College Library, Andrew Clark's MSS, 'Tables Illustrating the Constitution of Balliol College 1520–1857' ii. fo 21; Davis, History of Balliol, 80–2.

[8] BCA B.23.3, B.23.5.

In 1605 the college received from Sir William Dunch an annual rent charge of £10 issuing from lands in North Morton, Berkshire. Out of this Balliol was to pay £8 a year to one scholar in fulfilment of the wish of Dame Mary Dunch, Sir William's grandmother, and retain the other £2.[1] A similar arrangement was made in 1608 when the college was given a rent charge of £2 10s 0d a year for the support of another scholar (Browne's scholar) issuing from lands in Rotherwick, Hampshire.[2]

Seven years later, in 1615, Balliol used £700 from the executors of Peter Blundell of Tiverton to buy land in Woodstock for the perpetual support of a fellow and scholar.[3] The bursars' accounts show that from 1616 to 1620 £35 a year was received from this new property, and £40 a year from 1621 onwards.[4]

The last endowment of this type in our period was made by Lady Elizabeth Periam, daughter of Sir Nicholas Bacon and sister to Francis Bacon, for the support of one fellowship and two scholarships at Balliol. In July 1620 she caused a property called Borough Farm in Hambleden, Buckinghamshire (1 messuage, 1 dovehouse, 1 garden, 1 orchard, 145 acres of arable, 7 acres of meadow, 10 acres of pasture, 43 acres of wood)[5] to be conveyed to the college.[6] It had already been leased to her for 61 years from Michaelmas 1620 at an annual rent of £50 payable to Balliol[7] and on her death in 1621 her executors granted the remainder of the lease to two Hambleden men who were obliged to pay the rent to the college.[8] Further land for this endowment came to Balliol in 1622, consisting of a tenement at Loseley Row in the parish of Princes Risborough, Buckinghamshire, with a close of 14 acres of pasture and wood ground, another close with 13 acres of arable and 20½ acres of land in the common fields.[9] Again the property had already been leased for 60 years at a rent of £12 payable at the 'Common and vsuall great dyneinge hall' of the college.[10]

All of this meant that as compared with a gross rental of around £115 in 1546,[11] by 1641 the college was receiving about £243 a year (excluding corn rents).[12] If we deduct from this figure the

---

[1] *SCO* i. pt 1, 46; Balliol College Library, Clark's MSS, 'Tables . . .' i. fo 45ᵛ.

[2] BCA D.18.1; Clark's MSS, 'Tables . . .' ii. fo 32.

[3] Savage, *Balliofergus*, 82–4; *SCO* i. pt 1, 51; BCA F.8.82 and annexe. Another £6 6s 8d was spent in connection with this endowment in 1614: BCA F.8.81. Cf Davis, *History of Balliol*, 108–11.

[4] According to Savage in *Balliofergus*, this property was 'set almost at a Rack-rent' to defray the high cost of purchase.

[5] BCA E.12.62.
[6] BCA E.12.66.
[7] BCA E.12.65ᵃ,ᵇ.
[8] BCA E.12.67ᵇ.
[9] BCA E.15.4, E.15.10.
[10] BCA E.15.5. Cf Davis, *Balliol*, 111.
[11] PRO E 315/441, fo 93.
[12] BCA Bursars' Books I.B.3, account for 1640–1.

costs of the scholarships for which most of the new property was given and the outgoings from Abbotsley for which the college always remained responsible (almost all other outgoings were met by the lessees), we reach a net annual rental (excluding corn rents) of about £191, still a substantial improvement upon the net income of £87 in the 1546 survey.[1]

Of course, Balliol's rental income was also increased by the introduction of corn rents. In 1576 an Act was passed 'for the Maintenaunce of the Colledges in the Universityes, and of Winchester and Eaton'. It laid down that in future when leasing any property to which tithe, arable land, meadow or pasture belonged, colleges must reserve at least one-third of the old rent to be paid in corn, the amount of grain due being assessed at the rate of 6s 8d per quarter (10d per bushel) for wheat and 5s per quarter (7½d per bushel) for malt. This corn rent was to be paid in kind or money (at the choice of the lessee),[2] and if rendered in money the amount was to be calculated according to the prices for the best wheat and malt in Oxford market on the market day next before the rent was due. The corn rent thus received was 'to be expended to the use of the Relief of the Commons and Diet of the saide Colledges . . .' and to no other purpose.[3]

Under this act, which did not affect Balliol's important holdings in London and Oxford, corn rents were written into the leases of Oddington, Nethercot, Moreton, Steeple Aston, Old Woodstock, Wootton, Abbotsley and Long Benton between 1588 and 1602.[4] The new leases provided a significant but unstable and unpredictable increase over the old rent. In 1641 the college received an additional £59 from this source.[5]

How was this modest estate run? A comprehensive answer to the question is impossible, but from the many surviving leases and incidental information in the college archives some interesting pointers emerge.

By the time of the Henrician surveys made in 1535 and 1546 all of the property was leased out in one way or another. The college did not indulge in direct exploitation of its agricultural holdings. Thus of the eight Oxfordshire properties listed in the survey of 1546, seven were let by indentures for terms of years and only one at will

[1] PRO E 315/441, fo 93. It is likely that the tenants met some of the charges of about £28 set off against the gross rental in this survey.

[2] Probably paid in money at Balliol.

[3] *Enactments in Parliament* i. 190–1.

[4] BCA A.23.11, A.21.2, A.17.2, A.18.2, E.2.6, F.1.5, A.22.8, E.8.3. A tenement in St Giles with arable land in the open fields attached was converted to corn rent by the lease of 31 October 1595: *Balliol Deeds*, 247.

[5] BCA Bursars' Books I.B.3, account for 1640–1.

from year to year.[1] The rectories in Huntingdonshire and Northumberland were also let by indentures for terms of years as was the house property in St Margaret Patens (by leases made in 1534 and 1544).[2] At St Lawrence Jewry the parsonage house was likewise leased by indenture, but it is unclear how the tithes were managed at that time (though they were certainly leased by indenture from 1549 onwards).[3] On the other hand, of 19 Oxford tenements listed in 1546 only 3 were let by indentures for years, made as recently as 1541 and 1544, while the remaining 15 properties were let at will from year to year.[4]

This discrepancy in leasing arrangements between the Oxford holdings and the rest of the college's property did not survive the sixteenth century and may well have been eliminated quite soon after the survey of 1546. The Oxford leases printed and summarized by H. E. Salter in *The Oxford Deeds of Balliol College* show that by the later part of the sixteenth century the Oxford city properties were being leased in exactly the same way as the other holdings of the college, i.e. by means of indentures for terms of years and not by tenancies at will. Henceforth the college practised on all its properties the system of leases for years or lives, made and renewed for a fine, with a low reserved rent.[5]

Throughout the period, apart from the introduction of corn rents on the rural properties in the 1590s it was rare for a rent to be altered in any way. For almost all of the college's holdings the rents listed in 1546 remained unaltered in successive leases. Any change was usually made for quite definite reasons. Thus, in 1563 the rent of the Clerkenwell tenements was reduced from £13 6s 8d to £10 on renewal of the lease[6] because the tenements needed repairs and the new tenant 'contulit domui nostrae vigintae libras'.[7] Indeed, it was so unusual a thing for a rent to be increased that when the

---

[1] PRO E 315/441, fos 90^V-1. The exception was a tenement at Wootton leased to Roger Horne 'ad voluntatem de anno in annum': ibid., fo 90^V.

[2] Ibid., fos 91^V-2, 92^V.

[3] Ibid., fo 92; BCA B.19.2 (lease of tithes dated 6 May 1549).

[4] PRO E 315/441, fos 89–90, the exceptions being a tenement in St Aldates leased to Stephen Harvey by indenture of 1 December 1541 for 21 years, a garden in St Mary the Virgin leased to John More by indenture dated 1 March 1541 for 20 years and a tenement in St Giles leased to Richard Popyswell by indenture dated 4 November 1544 for 21 years. It is interesting to note that the college statutes of 1507 envisaged leases for one year only which could be negotiated by the bursars: *SCO* i. pt 1, 19.

[5] In several cases the first leases recorded by Salter for particular properties date from the 1550s and 1560s: *Balliol Deeds*, 84, 86, 178, 202, 217, 235, 238. It is worth comparing this with the move away from tenancies at will on customary lands discussed in *Agrarian History 1500–1640*, 684.

[6] BCA B.23.3, B.23.5.

[7] BCA Balliol College Register 1514–1682, p. 98; cf BCA Lease Log Book, p. 76.

compiler of the lease log book[1] found that it had actually happened
to the rent of the parsonage house of St Lawrence Jewry, increased
from £4 to £10 on renewal of the lease in 1637,[2] he was moved to
write a biting comment on the whole system of low reserved rents:
'But in regard that he raised his rent £6 p.a., it was better for the
college, than if he had given £140 fine. I could wish that all our
tenants, who pay candle rents, would do the like. For whereas they
do not pay above the 20th part of the yearly value of their tenements, I could wish that their fines might be (for once) either wholly
remitted, or so abated, that their rents might be raised, to pay the
5th or 6th part of the yearly value to the college, as Mr Neve [the
tenant in question] then did.'[3] This comment was probably made
in the 1670s at the lowest point of Balliol's financial misfortunes,
but the earlier appearance of produce rents (usually a couple of
capons annually), especially on urban leases, may have been a token
response to the dangers of static rents.[4]

The terms of the leases made by the college in the period up to
1640 show a marked difference between those for the country properties (including the rectories of Abbotsley and Long Benton) and
those for the town holdings in London and Oxford. For the country
properties leases for three lives and for 21 years were equally in
vogue while for the urban holdings the lease for 21 years, though by
no means uncommon, was easily outstripped by that for 40 years as
the most frequent, almost the standard form of tenancy.[5] In fact,
this pattern is exactly what might be expected in view of the acts for
collegiate leases passed by parliament in 1571-6. This legislation had
the effect of prohibiting leases of more than 21 years or three lives,
except in the case of urban property where up to 40 years was
allowed, and insisted that a lease could not be renewed until only
3 years or less remained unexpired.[6] It is quite clear that Balliol

[1] This volume, probably started in the 1670s, attempts a summary history of leases
arranged under each property, and is particularly concerned with the ways in which the
college set fines for renewals. The author, who obviously had first-hand experience of estate
administration (such as it was at Balliol), is consistently critical of the efforts of his predecessors, especially in the 1640s and 1650s about which he writes most. The book is pretty
clearly a product of the financial disasters of the 1670s (see note 4 below).

[2] BCA B.19.11, B.19.14.

[3] BCA Lease Log Book, p. 81.

[4] For the financial crisis at Balliol in the 1670s see VCH Oxon. iii. 83-4; Davis, History
of Balliol, 142-5. For produce rents on urban leases see Balliol Deeds, 76, 78, 195, also
BCA B.19.6. For the whole subject of produce rents as one means of coping with the
inflation of our period see Agrarian History 1500-1640, 682-3.

[5] On the country properties in the period to 1640 roughly 11 leases for 3 lives were
granted, 12 for 21 years; cf the comments of Kerridge, Agrarian Problems in the Sixteenth
Century and After, 47. On the urban properties in the same period there were about 25
leases for 21 years, but roughly 63 for 40 years.

[6] For the legislation see Enactments in Parliament i. 176-7, 188-9, 192-3.

obeyed the law so far as the length of leases was concerned (preferring the maximum of 40 years for its urban tenements). On the country holdings the legislation effectively ended the granting of very long terms of years which occurred before the 1570s—63 years at Old Woodstock in 1532, 70 years there in 1560, 31 years at Nethercot in 1563 and 51 years at Long Benton in 1568.[1] On the other hand, the provision for renewals was honoured only in the breach—the college appears to have ignored it. If we look at leases for years of the Oxford properties renewed to the same person (taking 'renewal' to include cases where the old lease was surrendered, clearly a device to circumvent the law[2]), we find them being renewed with anything from twelve to thirty years unexpired.[3] Indeed, it was not unheard of for the college and its tenant to include a specific covenant for renewal in the lease. When Jerome Nash leased Praunces Place at Old Woodstock for three lives in 1589 it was agreed that he could at any time surrender the lease and have a new one for three new lives or twenty-one years on the same terms, as long as on the sealing of the new lease he would give the college plate worth £3 6s 8d and £1 for a breakfast.[4] In 1611 a new lease was made of the rectory of Abbotsley for three lives and the college agreed to confirm or renew it on the same terms within ten years at the request of its tenant and not to make a lease to any other person during the term of the lease. Similar provision was written into leases of Long Benton made in 1589, 1591 and 1602. A forty-year lease of the tenements in St Margaret Patens made in 1602 allowed the lessee to surrender the lease within one year and have another for forty years on the same terms without a fine, as long as it was written out at his expense.[5] The system meant that very often the leases descended in one family for several generations. Thus, at Oddington, the Head family held the lease from the 1550s until 1613 when they lost it by creating a subtenancy without the college's permission.[6] The Tredwells of Nethercot (husbandmen) held the lease of Nethercot from 1563 until 1611.[7] The parsonage house of St Lawrence Jewry

[1] BCA A.21.1, E.2.4, F.1.1, F.1.2. The lease of Old Woodstock was renewed in 1573 for 58 years but this was merely a continuation of the seventy-year lease made in 1560 and therefore fell outside the terms of the legislation: BCA F.1.4.

[2] This is the view of J. Dunbabin, 'College Estates and Wealth 1660–1815' (draft chapter, History of the University of Oxford), 2–3.

[3] *Balliol Deeds*, 75, 84, 85–6, 195, 208, 217, 237, 238. For examples from the country properties see BCA F.1.4–5, E.2.11–12. Some leases were made in reversion: BCA A.18.1, E.2.3, E.2.5, E.8.1, A.22.3, A.22.6–7, B.18.11, B.18.13–14.

[4] BCA F.1.5.

[5] BCA E.8.4, E.2.6–7, E.2.10, B.18.7. See too BCA B.18.21, B.18.24.

[6] BCA A.23.11, A.23.13.

[7] BCA A.21.1–3.

was held by a member of the Neve family, citizens and merchant tailors of London, from 1611 until the 1650s.[1]

The success of such a policy, with low annual rents and fairly frequent renewals, depended on the college having a clear idea of the real annual value of its properties when it came to setting the level of a fine. For the fine was really the only way in which the college could tap the full value of its property.[2] In the end successful management came down to setting realistic fines for renewals.

Unfortunately, we have virtually no evidence for the 'real' value of Balliol's estates, very little systematic evidence about the assessment of fines or even of the size of individual fines—they are not recorded in leases and occur only sporadically in the bursars' accounts and never after 1629. If we simply take the leases of London or country property made after 1572 which happen specifically to mention that a fine was levied (by no means all of such leases) we find that in only two cases can any fine be traced in the bursars' accounts. Nevertheless receipts for the fines paid by named lessees are recorded in eighteen of the accounts between 1587–8 and 1628–9.[3] After 1628–9 no fines appear in the accounts, or at least no receipts are so described. The lease log book, begun in the 1670s, records a fair number of fines from the 1640s and 1650s but its compiler leaves the clear impression that he knew little more about fines set before the civil war than we do and even then had no proper or systematic record of them before him.[4] In addition the college register contains a few stray references to fines.[5] In only one case is a fine actually endorsed on a lease.[6] The fines recorded in the bursars' accounts can usually be assigned to the appropriate lease, for they generally appear in the account for the year in which the lease was made. They are almost always small sums, very much smaller than the fines recorded for the same properties in the 1640s and 1650s. For instance, a fine of £12 10s 0d is recorded for the lease of Abbotsley in 1611, yet in 1642 the lease log book gives a fine of £350. It looks as if either the sums recorded in the bursars' accounts represent all that was left to the college proper after a fellowship dividend, or as if fines rose dramatically between the 1620s and 1640s. The former possibility is lent some support by the

[1] BCA B.19.10–11, B.19.14, B.19.16, Lease Log Book, p. 81.

[2] Cf the comments on rising land values and the heavy increases in rents on private secular estates from the 1570s and 1580s onwards in *Agrarian History 1500–1640*, 690–1.

[3] Those for 1587–8, 1591–2, 1596–7, 1599–1600, 1600–1, 1602–3, 1609–10, 1610–11, 1611–12, 1612–13, 1613–14, 1618–19, 1622–3, 1624–5, 1625–6, 1626–7, 1627–8, 1628–9.

[4] He frequently comments 'no fine expressed'.

[5] BCA Balliol College Register 1514–1682.

[6] BCA A.23.15, lease of Oddington, 1636, £56.

reference in the college register to a fine of £60 paid in 1595 'collegio et sociis'.[1]

For what it is worth the account of the college's policy (or lack of policy) in these matters given by the compiler of the lease log book is a gloomy one. There is a lot to suggest that Balliol found it hard to come by reliable information about the real value of its property. For instance, when the tenant of the parsonage house of St Lawrence Jewry came to the college in 1653 to renew his lease the master and fellows had recourse to one of their number, Thomas Careless 'who was a Londoner born, and therefore, thought to know best the value of the thing'.[2] According to the commentator the result was a fine set too low.[3] In 1662 the writer of the lease log book was informed by the vicar of Abbotsley that the college's estate there was worth £200 a year, though at another time he said it was worth only £160 a year.[4] This happens to be an estate of which the college had a terrier, taken on 30 August 1621, possibly in consequence of a covenant in the lease of 1615 obliging the tenant to deliver within 5 years 'a true and iust terriar and not of all the landes belonging vnto the said Rectory or parsonage'.[5] Of Nethercot (Tackley) only a few miles from Oxford, our writer is driven to note in despair, 'This estate is one of those, whereof we can get noe Terrier, and consequence, noe certain knowledge of it'.[6]

Of course, there were some advantages for the college under this regime. On the whole it ensured an easy life as far as the administration of the estate was concerned—it was left largely to the tenants. They were virtually always made responsible for repairs which the college could view if it wished and for any outgoings from the property (quit rents, heriots and the like), the major exception being the rectory of Abbotsley where the annual outgoings of £5 7s 6d were met by the college and not by the farmer.[7] At Oddington, for example, the tenant had to pay heriot of 6s 8d and all rents and services due to the chief lord and in 1588–9 the bursars' account records a receipt of 6s 8d 'ab Head de Odington pro Heriotts'.[8] At

---

[1] BCA Balliol College Register 1514–1682, p. 170.

[2] BCA Lease Log Book, pp. 81–2.

[3] Ibid., p. 82.

[4] Ibid. p. 100.

[5] The terrier is copied into the back of BCA Lease Book II; BCA E.8.10. In 1620 the lessee of Long Benton covenanted to make at his own cost a terrier in parchment of the college's lands and to deliver it to Balliol within 7 years from the date of his lease: BCA E.2.11.

[6] BCA Lease Log Book, p. 129.

[7] These were regularly paid under the heading 'Indemnitates' in the expenses of the bursars' accounts.

[8] BCA A.23.11.

Moreton the lessee had to pay a quit rent of 8*d* a year to the bailiff of Thame, while the farmers of the tithes of St Lawrence Jewry were responsible for a similar due of 5*s* at Easter payable to the parson of St Mary Magdalen in Milk Street.[1]

On the other hand, there is evidence that Balliol did try to keep some kind of control over subletting and assignment of leases. The tenant of Oddington forfeited his lease when he sublet for seven years in 1613 without the licence he was required to obtain from the college.[2] Leases for Nethercot, Wootton and Abbotsley also stipulated that the lessee could not sublet without the college's licence.[3] In other cases the tenant was not allowed to transfer or assign his indenture without first securing a licence from Balliol.[4] The lease of the tithes of St Lawrence Jewry made in 1563 included such a covenant, but the college agreed to give the farmer a licence in return for 'one doson of eared pewther disshis p'ce sixe shillinges eight pence And the Dyshis havinge the name of the said Edward [the lessee] upon theym'.[5] Three licences to the tenants of the parsonage house of St Lawrence Jewry allowing them to alienate and make over their leases are extant.[6]

The college also imposed restrictions on the felling of timber. The lease of Oddington was forfeited in 1613 partly because the lessee felled two elm trees without the college's permission.[7] The tenants of Nethercot were forbidden to fell ash, oak or elm and were obliged to 'dress and nourish' at least two or three young oak, ash or elm trees every year.[8] At Wootton in 1536 the tenant was not allowed to use any stone or cut any timber without the licence of the college, in 1563 he was not permitted to cut down any trees without Balliol's licence and in 1599 he was not to cut down any oak, ash or elm except for necessary repairs or with the special licence of the college.[9] This restrictive timber policy was sensible, for the college

[1] BCA A.17.2, B.19.2. Cf the comments on repairs and quit rents in *Agrarian History 1500–1640*, 681.

[2] BCA A.23.11, A.23.13.

[3] BCA A.21.1–3, A.22.1, A.22.7, E.8.1.

[4] BCA B.19.4, etc. (St Lawrence Jewry parsonage house).

[5] BCA B.23.22.

[6] BCA B.19.8–9, B.19.13; cf *Balliol Deeds*, 77 for an Oxford example. The instrument by which Ralph Delavale gave and sold his lease of Long Benton to his brother is at BCA E.2.9 (9 August 1591). In 1600 the farmer of the tithes of St Lawrence Jewry sold his lease to trustees for the parishioners for £300 paid to the master of Balliol: BCA B.23.30. These provisions about subletting and assigning are in line with the comments of Kerridge, *Agrarian Problems*, 49, 52.

[7] BCA A.23.13, A.23.21.

[8] BCA A.21.1, etc. According to *Agrarian History 1500–1640*, 677 this was a very unusual provision.

[9] BCA A.22.1, A.22.7, A.22.9.

derived useful income from its timber. In 1610/11 £12 was received 'of Tredwell [tenant] from 14 trees at Nethercott' and £10 from Inatt [tenant of Moreton] 'pro arboribus'. In 1612/13 £4 10s 0d was realized from the sale of trees at Beeston and another £16 at Oddington.[1]

Sporadic references cast fitful light upon other aspects of college estate policy. At Abbotsley the farmer had full power to keep the college's court among its tenants once a year. He was to send the court rolls to the college annually or at least every two years.[2] A clause was written into the lease of Praunces Place at Old Woodstock allowing the master and fellows to have use of rooms in the house at any time of plague or infection in Oxford.[3] The farmers of Long Benton were to provide at their own expense board and lodging for the master or a fellow and their servants for 6 days and nights when they came to oversee the parsonage, and also sufficient food and litter for their horses.[4] In 1588–9 the college spent 5s 9d on 'a Supper for our Tenants of the North'.[5] In 1609–10 and again in 1612–13 it collected money from its tenants for the feudal aids levied on the knighting of Prince Henry and the attainment of 7 years by Princess Elizabeth.[6] The college took advantage of the legal expertise of its tenant at Old Woodstock, Michael Nash, one of the attorneys of the common pleas, who agreed in his leases to give Balliol free legal advice when required. [7]

Balliol differed from Corpus (and presumably from other wealthier colleges) in needing no elaborate system of bailiffs' accounts. For the Oxfordshire properties the leases generally stipulated that the rents should be paid by the tenants at Balliol itself, often in the college hall. This was true also of Long Benton and Abbotsley, where the farmer was responsible for collecting 9s 5d in free rents (included in his annual rent).[8] But the London and Oxford rents were managed somewhat differently. In 1563 the farmer of the tithes of St Lawrence Jewry agreed to collect the college's rents in London (except Clerkenwell) and pay them over to the bursars.[9] Two years earlier the

[1] BCA Bursars' Books I.B.2, *recepta contingentia.*

[2] BCA E.8.1, etc: no such rolls are extant at Balliol.

[3] BCA F.1.5, 1589.

[4] BCA E.2.2, etc.

[5] BCA Bursars' Books I.B.1.

[6] BCA Bursars' Books I.B.2; for these aids see *Select Statutes and other Constitutional Documents Illustrative of the Reigns of Elizabeth and James I,* ed. G. W. Prothero (Oxford 1894; 4th edn 1913), 355–8.

[7] BCA F.1.2, F.1.4, F.1.36.

[8] BCA D.13.8, E.1.61, E.2.5, E.2.6, etc; BCA E.8.1, E.8.3, E.8.6, E.8.9.

[9] BCA B.23.22. This was Edward Broke alias Litle, baker of Oxford. He was described as brewer in 1557 when he and his wife leased a college house in St Mary Magdalen: *Balliol Deeds,* 224.

rent of Clerkenwell had been made payable to the vicar of St Lawrence Jewry for the college 'vppon the fontstone' in the church of St Lawrence Jewry, but in 1563 it was made payable at the college hall in the usual way.[1] The office of collector of rents in London was granted to William Allen alias Hilliard in 1563 for 31 years.[2] Fifteen years later the college temporarily lumped all of its London properties into one lease and made the lessee responsible for the payment of all the rents in the hall.[3] Very soon afterwards the lessee, John Shrawley, citizen and mercer of London, was made collector of the college's rents in London with power to prosecute John Hollingbridge, the late farmer of the tithes of St Lawrence Jewry, for monies received and not yet paid over to the college. This collectorship was to run concurrently with the lease.[4] According to John Atkinson, fellow 1560–9, Hollingbridge had been responsible for the payment of all the London rents (except Clerkenwell), but had consistently kept back from the college 6s 9d a year of the £37 7s 4d due 'by meanes of overseight in the wrytting of his lease'.[5] Finally, in 1614 the college granted to John Royse of Oxford, tailor, for life, the office of bailiff or receiver of its rents within the city and suburbs of London at an annual fee of 6s 8d.[6] There was in addition a collector of rents for Oxford. On 1 December 1583 Augustine Pricket was appointed and in 1596 the college granted the office of receivership of all their farms and rents in the city and suburbs of Oxford for life to Edmund Blith, pewterer of Oxford.[7]

An interesting sidelight is cast on the economics of rent-collecting from small rural properties by a suit in chancery initiated by Balliol against its tenants at Beeston in Bedfordshire some time between 1603 and 1617. The college complained that the tenants were refusing to bring the rent to Oxford but rather bidding the college 'to fetch the said Rent if they will have it', although they knew very well that the cost of sending for the rent to a place more than 60 miles from the college would be more than it was worth.[8]

We may conclude our survey by noting a few other references to estate officials. The *Valor* of 1535 records a payment of 13s 4d from

[1] BCA B.23.3, B.23.5.

[2] BCA Balliol College Register 1514–1682, p. 99.

[3] BCA B.23.23.

[4] BCA B.23.10. Hollingbridge (along with Edward Litle of Oxford) had received a lease of the tithes of St Lawrence Jewry in 1557: BCA Balliol College Register 1514–1682, p. 81. Litle became sole lessee in 1563: BCA B.23.22.

[5] BCA Balliol College Register 1514–1682, pp. 340–1; for Atkinson see Foster, *Alumni*, i. 41.

[6] BCA B.14.6.

[7] BCA Balliol College Register 1514–1682, p. 156; BCA D.12.7.

[8] BCA E.6.13.

the rectory of Abbotsley 'nostro senescallo Thome Chace' and another payment of 13s 4d from Long Benton 'nostro senescallo Johanni Davy annuatim pro suo labore'. It also mentions fees totalling £2 for the general receivers of the college and a payment of £5 'pro dietis generalium receptor' & Ball'.[1] In the 1546 survey the lessee of Abbotsley is allowed 3s 4d for bringing the rent to Oxford and 10s is paid to the collector of the tithes of St Lawrence Jewry. Allowance is also made for the diet of farmers rendering their accounts.[2]

[1] *Valor* ii. 269–70.
[2] PRO 315/441, fos 91^V, 92, 94.

Appendix II

An Introduction to the Accounts of Corpus Christi College

G. D. DUNCAN

THE statutes of the college show that the founder was fully aware of the need for sound estate management.[1] He laid down that the president had to be expert in all matters regarding rents, buildings and the leasing of property. Two chambers were laid aside for financial administration—one for the bursars' treasury (*pro thesauraria dispensatorum*) and another for the reckoning of accounts and allied business conducted by the clerk of accounts. And, in general, he makes clear provision for the running of the college's estates, income and expenditure.

The main instrument for supervision of the estates is the progress. Every year, as soon after Easter as possible, the president and clerk of accounts are to visit those college properties thought to be in need of supervision. During the progress they are to collect money due and arrears and see that any necessary repairs are carried out. Any sums of money they receive are to be handed over to the bursars within two days of their return from progress and recorded in the great indentures (*magnis indenturis*). In addition every year after the harvest (*post autumnum*) another progress may be made by a fellow and the clerk of accounts (or in case of extreme urgency by the president himself). But this second progress may be omitted if it seems likely to be more costly than useful (*quando videbitur praedictis non necessarius sed potius sumptuosus*).[2]

---

[1] The statutes of Corpus Christi College, as revised c. 1528, are printed in *SCO* ii. pt 10 (Corpus Christi College), 1–117. The translation into English by G. R. M. Ward, *The Foundation Statutes of Bishop Fox for Corpus Christi College* (1843) is based upon the original text of 1517 signed by Fox and now Bodl. MS Laud Misc. 621; but see p. 18 n. 4 above.

[2] *SCO* ii (Corpus Christi College), 87–8. The Libri Magni regularly includes expenses of progresses and progress material is to be found scattered throughout the college archives. For example, F/6/1 includes 'Mr President his expenses in riding Bedfordshire progresse with one fellowe the clerke of the landes and two servantes the seaventeenth daie of Aprill 1598'. The expenses come to 45s 8d and the journey, which took a week, covered Newport Pagnell, Sharnbrook, Pertenhall, Bedford, Leighton Buzzard and Heyford. The president's progress to Kent in May 1598 took three weeks and expenses of £9 10s 9d (F/6/2). A document

There are to be two bursars, elected from the fellows, and responsible for receipts and expenditure. All income (*redditus et proventus*) received by them from college property is to be recorded in 'great indentures' drawn up between them and the president (*duae magnae indenturae*) and the sums received deposited in a chest in the treasury. From this chest the bursars may draw sums solely to meet expenditure on commons and other daily requirements (*ad utilitatem collegii et necessitatem et non alios usus*). When the statutes were revised (*c* 1528) a very important gloss was made on this procedure whereby income of the previous year was on no account to be mixed up with that of the current year, but each must be deposited in a separate chest. Current expenses must be met only from the chest containing the previous year's income; nothing must be taken from the current income for current expenses. The bursars are required to keep detailed accounts of all expenditure from the chest in the treasury (each withdrawal to be accounted for in the week in which it occurs) and to write a quarterly 'view' (*visus*) of all expenditure on commons and other establishment costs.

To help the bursars when need arises the statutes institute two loan chests in which are to be maintained respectively 200 and 100 marks. Any sum borrowed from these chests by the bursars is to be entered in their own hands in the great indentures (presumably those between them and the president recording receipts) and in the paper register of the chests. Any sum so borrowed must be restored to the chest at the end of the year before the bursars render their final account.

The entire accounting procedure is drawn together at the November audit in college, notice of which is to be given to the local accountants during the progress after harvest or later. The statutes seem to envisage that the audit would take up to two weeks.[1] First those responsible for the college's various properties (*forinseci receptores, ballivi, firmarii et alii computantes*) are to present their accounts for audit by the president (or vice-president), the deans, four senior fellows and the clerk of accounts. After the audit these

survives from the early seventeenth century entitled 'Placies of intertainement in progresses provided for by leases' which lists the responsibilities of various tenants under their counties, giving references to the lease books and often the date of the lease in question (F/6/2). The Corn Rent Book for 1593–5 includes receipts from the Devon progress of 1595 (rents, heriots, fines), and this, and the books for 1598 and 1599 also include itineraries for progresses into Devon and Hampshire (F/10/1). There are detailed 'Remembraunces of Gloucestershire progresse 1600' in Fb.23.28 and the acts of seniority provide a glimpse of the college planning a progress to Cheltenham in 1599 (B/4/3/1, 9 March 1598-9).

[1] The exposition of the Bible reading in hall at dinner is to be suspended for two weeks at the time of audit: *SCO* ii. pt 10 (Corpus Christi College), 47.

accounts are to be written out in detail on clean parchment and carefully preserved with court rolls and other memoranda.[1] In addition, after this audit, two parchment indentures are to be made setting out all sums received from the college properties, and all expenses of the same for the past year with arrears, one part to remain with the president, the other with the bursars for the coming year. These indentures are to be stored with the accounts.

After the receipts have been audited and recorded in this way and the bursars have repaid any sums borrowed from the loan chests, they are to present a final account of all commons *et aliarum expensarum extrinsecarum* which is to be audited and duly written out in detail. Any surplus for the year must then be placed in a chest kept in the tower for that purpose. The statutes lay down that these surpluses (*pecuniae provenientes de excrescentiis communiarum, et ex redditibus et proventibus collegii, in fine computi dispensatorum*) are to be preserved for expenditure on litigation and for buying new property. This chest is to have a register recording its income and its contents.

To cope with the considerable amount of technical work entailed by all of this the college may, if it wishes, employ a clerk of accounts (*clericus computi*) who must not only be expert in the auditing and writing of accounts, but also in the holding of courts. He may receive a stipend of £2 13s 4d *per annum* and commons at the highest rate.

On the whole the college accounting system, as it is reflected in the extant documents, followed the pattern laid down by the statutes. It is best approached through the general college account, the Liber Magnus, which records annual income and expenditure.[2]

The receipts from the college's properties appear in the Liber Magnus as a series of entries for each property, noting the sum received and the name of the person who paid it over (usually but not always the accountant). This section of the Liber Magnus is really a copy of the statutory great indentures of receipts between the president and the bursars. The indentures were usually drawn up in December after the completion of the annual audit and detail sums received by the bursars for the year ending at the previous Michaelmas. Some of the later indentures contain, as required by statute, notes of sums borrowed by the bursars from the chests, though this information is not transcribed in the Liber Magnus.[3]

---

[1] Fair parchment copies of the bailiffs' accounts were, it seems, only made in the 1520s: see the bailiffs' accounts for Temple Guiting, Corpus Christi College Archives (hereafter CCCA), F.b.6. and for Pertenhall, CCCA E.b.5.

[2] The volumes covering the period 1517–1640 are CCCA C/1/1/1–9.

[3] The great indentures are CCCA C/3/1/1–3, C/3/2/1–7, C/3/3/1–7. For examples of indentures with notes of sums borrowed, see C/3/2/2, 3.

The great indentures are themselves based upon the annual accounts of those responsible for paying over the revenues from the college's properties. These 'bailiffs' accounts', as the period covered by the indentures suggests, run from Michaelmas to Michaelmas.[1] From the late 1520s onwards (probably in accordance with the revised statutes of c 1528) sums delivered by the bailiffs for one year are put in the Liber Magnus for the next. For example, the bailiff of Pertenhall in Bedfordshire delivers £30 10s 0d *super compotum* in his account for the year 1527-8, which sum appears as a receipt in the Liber Magnus for 1528-9.[2] The receipts in the great indentures, when they can be checked against those in the Liber Magnus, accordingly appear in the Liber Magnus for the next and not the current year. It is therefore clear that the college accounts reflect the statutory provision for meeting expenses not from the current year's income but from the previous year's.

It is important to realize that the receipts as set out in the great indentures and the Libri Magni do not cover all of the college's income. Wood sales and fines *are* certainly included at times. Until 1535-6 wood sales are often recorded as separate deliveries under individual properties,[3] and in the Libri Magni for 1536-7, 1538-9 and 1540-1 they are grouped together as one entry, in the last two accounts combined respectively with profits of courts and fines;[4] after that the receipts make no specific reference to them.[5] Fines are mentioned far less frequently in the receipts—once in 1528-9, 1529-30, 1532-3, 1533-4 and 1540-1—after this last day they are not mentioned at all.[6] Now it may be that after 1540-1 wood sales, fines, profits of courts and the like are simply merged into the general deliveries from accounts (without a detailed study of many series of bailiffs' accounts this must remain unclear), but there is good reason to suppose that their absence from the Libri Magni actually indicates that at least some of this revenue was going elsewhere and not being recorded in the general account. Bailiffs' accounts provide useful evidence on this point. Thus in 1541-2 the account for Guiting, Gloucestershire records a delivery *super compotum* of £44 7s 1d and a further delivery of £17 for wood sold. Only the delivery *super compotum* appears in the Liber Magnus. Or

[1] I have examined three series of these accounts for the period 1520-1640: Temple Guiting (CCCA F.b.6), Pertenhall (CCCA E.b.5) and Heyford ad Pontem (CCCA A.o.5).

[2] CCCA E.b.5, bundle for 1529-39.

[3] CCCA C/1/1/1, fos 6^v, 7^v, 19^v, 31^v, 44, 60, 75, 76, 93^{r-v}.

[4] CCCA C/1/1/2, fos 2 (1536-7), 27^v (1538-9), 40 (1540-1).

[5] Though sales of horses are still mentioned: for example, ibid., fos 66^v, 79, 92^v.

[6] CCCA C/1/1/1 fos 31^v (1528-9), 60^v (1529-30), 76 (1532-3), 94 (1533-4); C/1/1/2, fo 40 (1540-1).

again, the account for 1545–6 has a delivery *super compotum* of £48 12*s* 11*d* with a further sum of £10 10*s* 1*d* for wood sold and £6 7*s* 8*d* for profits of the court—neither of the latter two deliveries appears in the Liber Magnus although the first is duly recorded in the receipts.[1] It is the same in the account for 1561–2—deliveries for wood sold and profits of the court do not go through the receipts in the Liber Magnus.[2] A similar picture emerges with regard to fines, as the accounts for Heyford ad Pontem in Oxfordshire show quite clearly. For instance, in 1553–4 the bailiff accounts for £29 9*s* 6*d* delivered *super compotum ad manus* and another £1 13*s* 4*d* for assorted fines—only the delivery *super compotum* appears in the Liber Magnus for 1554–5. The accounts for 1555–6, 1556–7 and 1557–8 together with their respective Libri Magni reveal the same pattern.[3]

It seems therefore that from at least the 1540s (it is difficult to be sure about the earlier period) income from wood sales, fines and probably other estate dues like heriots is either unrecorded or incompletely recorded in the Liber Magnus. Where then did it go and how was it accounted for? President Rainolds, writing in the 1590s and reviewing the history of fines at Corpus, said that before the 1570s there was a chest called the *cista finium* under the control of the president and the bursars into which the president placed receipts for 'fines, heryotts, mony for wood sales, &c' collected, it would appear, on progress and accounted for at his discretion in the 'fine book'.[4] The existence of such a chest is confirmed by the great indenture for 23 December 1567 which alludes to receipts for leases of woods in Milton and Guiting as 'redditus repositi in cista finium . . .'.[5] The 'coffer of fines' was kept in the bursary at that date when £200 comprising fines, heriots, wood sales, old debts, profits of courts and other things was transferred from it to the *cista placitorum*.[6] We may suspect that some such chest had been in existence since at least the 1540s.

We know nothing about the income and expenditure of this chest until 1575 when indentures (accounts) of the chest of fines begin. It is virtually certain that this series of accounts resulted from a reform of the accounting procedure for fines carried out *c* 1574, replacing the former system whereby the president himself entered

[1] CCCA F.b.6, bundle for 1540s.

[2] CCCA F.b.6, bundle for 1560s.

[3] CCCA A.o.5, bundle for 1550–9.

[4] Thomas Fowler, *The History of Corpus Christi College* (OHS xxv 1893), 349–50.

[5] CCCA C/3/1/3: 'Redditus repositi in cista finium quibus dispens' non onerantur, recepti tamen cum eorum supervisio.'

[6] CCCA C/7/1 (Register of the *cista placitorum*), *sub.* 1567.

the sums he had received on progress in the 'fine book'.[1] The indentures for the chest of fines, drawn up between the bursars and the president, record sums received by the bursars 'debitas dicto collegio pro cista finium' and also, in some cases, detail expenses from this fund.[2] The receipts consist mainly of wood sales, fines, profits of courts, tenurial incidents and the like.[3] The sums involved are large and give some idea of how defective the Liber Magnus is as a source for estimating receipts. For instance, the indenture of 6 December 1578 lists total receipts of £212 5s 8d and expenses of £72 17s 11d —the total income recorded in the Liber Magnus for 1578-9 is £518 9s 4d.[4]

From 1587-8 the indentures of the chest of fines are regularly incorporated in the Liber Magnus and the income used to help meet ordinary expenses on commons and other running costs.[5] How the surpluses which must have accrued in the fund were used before this date is unclear, though we have already seen that in 1567 £200 was transferred to the chest of pleas and we shall see later that some of the money in the fine chest may have been used to keep up the value of commons in the 1570s and 1580s before the emergence of corn rents.

The incorporation of the indentures of the chest of fines into the Liber Magnus, while it substantially adds to the account's value as a record of receipts, does not mean that henceforth it records all the money received by the college from its estates. According to President

[1] Fowler, *Corpus*, 350. In this passage Rainolds implies that this reform left the *cista finium* an accounting device or a distinct fund rather than an actual chest.

[2] Indentures for the chest of fines are CCCA C/5/1-2; in addition some indentures for the chest of fines may be found sewn to the ends of the great indentures: CCCA C/3/1/3 (1585), C/3/3/1 (1586, 1591, 1592, 1593, 1594), C/3/3/2 (1600, 1603), C/3/2/2 (1606), C/3/3/4 (1614).

[3] Julian Tonks has analysed the receipts and expenses of the *cista finium* for 1577-9, 1586-99 under the following heads:

Receipts: wood sales, rents of woodland, heriots & perquisites, fines, provisions, arrears, debts.

Expenses: charcoal/carriage, lawsuits, etc.

It is worth noting that the indentures for the chest of fines include some payments for commons.

[4] CCCA C/5/1, indenture for 6 December, 21 Eliz. (1578). The following are the receipts and expenses recorded in the indentures to survive before their incorporation in the Liber Magnus (1587-8):

Date of Indenture	Receipts			Expenses			References
	£	s	d	£	s	d	
1575-6 (29 Nov. 1576)	171	17	5	—			C/5/1
1577-8 (6 Dec. 1578)	212	5	8	72	17	1	C/5/1
1584-5 (18 Dec. 1585)	133	2	3½	46	10	10	C/5/1
1585-6 (17 Dec. 1586)	65	19	2	27	15	6	C/5/1

[5] The Liber Magnus for 1585-6 includes the indenture of the chest of fines for 18 Dec. 1585, but it is simply transcribed and not counted into the general account.

Rainolds, writing in 1599, all fines were applied to the use of the college until about 1580. After that date, when the introduction of corn rents obviated the need to use fines for maintenance of commons, the president and fellows decided that they could reasonably retain a proportion of fines for distribution among themselves.[1] As a result, there can be no doubt that at least in the decade of the 1590s when controversy raged about the division of fines, and probably thereafter, the indentures of the chest of fines record only that proportion of the fines which went to the college. The indenture for 1599 totals the receipts for the chest of fines to £365 13s 9¾d, but adds a section entitled 'Receiptes of fynes—99 for leases' totalling £280 3s 4d which, it notes, were 'divided amongst president & fellows'. While the total of £365 13s 9¾d goes through the Liber Magnus, the £280 3s 4d does not.[2] According to President Rainolds around £500 was received for fines on renewals of leases in the year 1597/8 of which the college received only £50.[3]

In the Liber Magnus for 1584–5 a receipt for corn rent appears for the first time, a new source of income for the college not envisaged in the statutes at all. The beginnings are modest enough, only £15 8s 11d in this first entry. But by the end of the 1590s the college was receiving huge sums from this source—£480 in 1596–7 and £730 in 1597–8. This latter was not the last year in which receipts from corn rent actually exceeded the old rental income from college property.[4]

The expenditure as it is recorded in the Liber Magnus may be dealt with more briefly. The largest single item is the termly expenditure on commons. This is followed by other payments made to members of the foundation and to the college's servants (stipends, vests) and the running costs of the college arranged under several heads.[5] As with the receipts, so with the expenses, the Liber Magnus is by no means a complete record. The college maintained considerable cash reserves in chests kept in the tower. Unfortunately, contrary to the founder's wishes, no annual record of their contents appears to have been kept, though we know that in December 1614 there was c £1,500 in the *cista magna* and in 1621 the 'Colledge estate in moneyes' included about £790 in the tower plus a further £170 in the loan chests.[6] From these reserves in the later sixteenth and early

---

[1] Fowler, *Corpus*, 350–1.

[2] CCCA C/5/1, *indentura acceptorum pro cista finium 1599*.

[3] Fowler, *Corpus*, 345.   [4] See table of Libri Magni receipts appended.

[5] Of course, the headings changed a little over the years, but a typical list would include the following: chapel, pantry, kitchen, stable, *domus dispensatorum*, expenses internal and external, fees, legal costs, riding charges.

[6] *1614*: CCCA C/7/2, 19 Dec. 1614 (after a review by the president and others); *1621*:

seventeenth centuries over £5,300 was spent, mainly in the acquisition of new property.[1] This expenditure is not recorded in the Liber Magnus.[2]

The Liber Magnus ends with a balance.[3] In the first surviving balance (1526-7) the total expenses are deducted from the receipts to produce a *debent* from which are deducted in turn certain payments—to the loan chest, for the *scheda petitio* (carried forward into the next year's receipts)—the remainder being placed in the tower (in accordance with the statutes).[4] Roughly speaking, despite changes in detail, this remained the procedure until the emergence of corn rents in the 1590s.[5] In 1529-30 the *debent* is partly accounted for by the *scheda petitio* but there remains a *debent* of £1 6s 4½d which is unaccounted for, a feature which recurs for much of the sixteenth century.[6]

In 1547-8 the *debent* of £29 5s 8½d is partly allowed to the bursars 'propter annone (?) et victualium caritatem'.[7] This presages a difficulty which seems to have become acute from the middle of the 1560s onwards. In the accounts for 1565-6, 1566-7 and 1567-8 parts of the final *debent* are paid to the president and seniors on account of the dearness of mutton. For instance, in 1566-7 £38 is paid 'presidenti et senioribus per charistia carnis ouillae, vltra consuetam allocationem dictae carnis current' intra collegium ab initio'.[8] In the account for 1570-1 the *debent* is £84 1s 0¾d 'et sic expenderunt ultra omnia allocata' and from 1571-2 there is a long sequence of accounts which show that the bursars were spending the final *debents* (without first putting anything in the tower) together with additional sums from an unidentified source outside the main account itself.[9] Indeed, during

CCCA C/6/1, *onus dispensatorum* for 1621. In the 1570s reserves in the *cista placitorum* had fallen to £8 4s 2d (C/7/1, 29 November 1576).

[1] CCCA C/7/1, 2.

[2] It should also be noted that expenditure was financed from the chest of fines before it was incorporated in the Liber Magnus: see p. 519 n. 4 above. From 1587-8 expenditure from the chest of fines is recorded in the Liber Magnus until 1598-9, corresponding with the surviving indentures of the chest of fines which also record expenditure. After that date none of the indentures records expenditure, but 'deposita e cista finium' reappear in the Libri Magni for 1606/7-1611/12, 1614/15-1616/17, 1620/1, 1623/4-1639/40.

[3] The first account (1521-2) has no such balance: CCCA C/1/1/1, fos 1-6; nor does 1530-1, ibid. fos 43-56. [4] CCCA C/1/1/1, fo 15ᵛ.

[5] The *scheda petitio* disappears after the account for 1570-1.

[6] In 1546-7 the final *debent* was spent on building works at Overton (CCCA C/1/1/3, fo 14).

[7] CCCA C/1/1/3, fo 29; cf ibid. fo 105 (1550-1), C/1/1/4, fos 50ᵛ (1559-60), 67 (1560-1).

[8] CCCA C/1/1/4, fo 130; cf. ibid. fos 118ᵛ (1565-6), 136ᵛ (1567-8).

[9] CCCA C/1/1/5, fo 11. The accounts in question are those for 1571/2-1590/1. Cf Fowler, *Corpus*, 334.

the years 1571–87 (with one exception) no money was laid up in the tower after the audit, a radical break with previous practice. There can be no doubt that during this period the college was unable to meet its running costs from ordinary income, far less maintain a healthy surplus.

The additional sums spent were by no means negligible. For example, in 1573–4 £97 13s 3¼d was spent in addition to the *debent* of £17 16s 9¾d, while in 1585–6 an extra £155 14s 11¾d was spent beyond the *debent* of £40 4s 0½d.[1] Where did the college find such substantial extra sums and for what purpose were they expended? The additional money spent in the first such balance, £26 6s 1d, had been drawn by the bursars from the *cista placitorum* on 7 June 1572.[2] Most unfortunately it is impossible to trace the other additional sums to the cash reserves on account of the gaps in the chest records, but it may be that they were generally met from these reserves.[3] On the other hand, they may have come, at least in part, from the *cista finium*.[4]

The final statements give no indication of the purposes for which these extra sums were spent. However, during the controversy in the 1590s about dividing fines President Rainolds clearly stated that even before the corn rent act of 1576 the college had been forced to support commons with extra expenditure in the face of rising prices. He goes on to imply that the college defrayed 'decrements' from the fines and that when corn rents were introduced they were applied to that purpose, so leaving the fines free for division between the president and fellows. It is a reasonable assumption that the extra sums we have been discussing were indeed payments for 'decrements' in support of commons; only the introduction of corn rents, we may agree with Rainolds, 'supplyed those wants better'.[5]

---

[1] CCCA C/1/1/5, fo 50 (1573–4), C/1/1/6, fo 68^V (1585–6).

[2] CCCA C/1/1/5, fo 26^V, C/7/1, *sub* 1572.

[3] Register of *cista placitorum* is blank 1576–95 (CCCA C/7/1), register of *cista magna* only starts in 1593 (C/7/2), register of loan chest only starts in 1599 (C/7/3).

[4] Cf Fowler, *Corpus*, 334. The appearance of revenue from the chest of fines in the Liber Magnus for 1587–8 onwards may have some bearing on the disappearance of these additional sums: see p. 583 n. 1.

[5] Fowler, *Corpus*, 350–1; quotation at 346. The expenditure on commons in the period 1572–87 fluctuated but did not substantially increase. For almost all of the period the rates remained at 20d, 15d and 14d per week for the three grades of commons (they were actually reduced in 1579–80 and the first term of 1580–1 to 17d, 12d, 10½d). These rates were certainly a good deal higher than those prevalent in the 1520s but by no means unprecedented (see the rates for 1554–5, 1555–6, 1559–60, 1560–1, 1565–6). I owe this information about rates to Dr C. S. Knighton's analysis of the commons accounts in the Libri Magni. According to the statutes the bursars were not to exceed the statutory allowances (on a sliding scale according to corn prices)—if they did they themselves were responsible for the excess unless they could show that it had not occurred by their fault or neglect. In that case they could ask the auditors that the college contribute to financing the overplus.

With the incorporation of receipts from the chest of fines and the emergence of corn rents as a substantial new element in the college's income, the final balances undergo a considerable change and the 'una cum' sums disappear.[1] Receipts from corn rents first occur in the account for 1584–5 in which the sum of £15 8s 11d is recorded under this head. At this early stage the receipts are not accounted for separately in the final balance but are simply lumped together with the ordinary rents. In the account for 1587–8 a change of practice takes place. Although the corn rent (£119 14s 6¾d) is still merged with the ordinary rents (and now also with receipts from the chest of fines), it is later allowed *in toto* to the bursars as one of the sums for which they account out of their receipts. This remains the procedure for the next four years until in the Liber Magnus for 1591–2 we can first see clearly the corn rent being used, albeit marginally, to augment commons, the purpose for which it had been introduced by parliament in 1576.[2] Of the total corn rent of £154 10s 6¾d, £153 18s 6½d is allowed, while the remainder, the tiny sum of 16s 11¾d, is reserved 'pro convictu studentium ampliori'.[3] However, for the next three years all the corn rent is allowed to the bursars as before until in 1595–6 the balance reverts to the method adopted in 1591–2. In this account, of £372 18s 1¾d in all from corn rent only £286 10s 2d is allowed, leaving £86 8s 0d 'quae pars excrescens de reditu frumenti allocatur illis pro ampliori convictu studentium et inhabitantium'.[4]

With the next account, for 1596–7, an important and lasting change in the method of striking the final balance takes place when, for the first time, the corn rent is accounted for separately. The balance is henceforth set out in two parts: (1) receipts from old rents and the chest of fines, from which all ordinary expenditure on commons and the various sections of the Liber Magnus are met, any surplus being put into the tower fund and (2) corn rent, which is generally accounted for by expenditure on decrements and augmentation of commons.[5] Thus in 1596–7 corn rents total £482 16s 11¼d

In the 1528 revision of the statutes it was provided that if the price of corn increased and with it the allowances for commons beyond what the annual revenues with all other expenses could support, the bursars could take a loan to make up the amount from the *cista placitorum* (*SCO* ii (Corpus Christi College), 73–6, 114–15).

[1] They end in the account for 1590–1, no doubt as a result of the incorporation of the chest of fines in 1587–8 and the development of corn rents.

[2] According to 18 Eliz. c. 6 the revenues from corn rent were 'to be expended to the use of the Relief of the Commons and Diett of the saide Colledges . . .': *Enactments in Parliament* i. 191.

[3] CCCA C/1/1/6, fo 128.

[4] Ibid. fo 171[V].

[5] See table of Corn Rents in the Final Balances appended.

of which £414 5s 1¼d is allowed for decrements and the rest 'pro ampliori convictu studentium'.[1] This pattern of accounting for the revenues in two distinct ways remains in effect throughout our period.[2]

It will by now be clear that the Liber Magnus is really a composite account, no doubt made up at or soon after the annual audit. Its value as a guide to the financial affairs of the college therefore depends upon what it includes and what it omits. On the receipts side the main difficulty is that until 1587–8 it records little of the casual income from the estates and even after that date we cannot be sure how seriously the record of the *cista finium* underestimates the revenue from fines—according to one early seventeenth century source the college received only one-fifth of fines.[3] There are other features of the finances to which the Liber Magnus is no guide at all. From 1621 onwards we have a series of records called Onus Dispensatorum independent of the Liber Magnus and appearing to record the financial position which the bursars handed on to their successors.[4] These documents, apart from listing over £400 worth of debts reaching back to 1576, mention loans from the various chests as yet to be repaid by the bursars, receipts for battels and various gifts to the college.[5] In addition to this series there are also the *Indentura arreragiorum* starting in 1614 and summarizing the annual accounts for each property with the detailed arrears of each accountant.[6] As far as expenses are concerned we have already seen that substantial expenditure on property was financed from cash reserves —of this the Liber Magnus has nothing to say. Again, it is quite clear from the registers of the various chests that the bursars relied heavily upon temporary borrowing from them to meet current expenditure.[7] Though these sums were generally repaid after the audit (as required by the statutes) this feature of the college's financial system again leaves no trace in the main account.

With these caveats in mind we may use the Liber Magnus with some confidence to trace the college's incomings (old and corn rent)

[1] CCCA C/1/1/6, fo 182ᵛ.

[2] Except in 1601–6 when three sections occur with the addition of receipts from *grossis pistorum et brasiatorum*, and in 1606–8 when corn rents are merged with ordinary revenue, though still in fact expended specifically on decrements and augmentation of commons.

[3] Queen's College Archives Memorandum Book, fo 140.

[4] CCCA C/6/1.

[5] In 1633 there was an attempt to write off many of the old debts: CCCA C/6/1, *onus dispensatorum* 1633.

[6] CCCA C/4/1/1, C/4/2/1.

[7] For instance, on 27 April 1601 they borrowed £64, repaid 7 December 1601; on 6 August 1607 £88 8s 2d was borrowed for the necessary uses of the college, to be repaid at the final account, repaid 11 December 1607 (CCCA C/7/1).

from its properties and its casual income by way of wood sales, heriots and the like, along with that proportion of the fines which went to the college's account. We may also gain a clear idea of the ordinary running costs. In comparison with Balliol, we are at least fortunate to have at Corpus the subsidiary records to tell us that this is by no means the whole story.

TABLE 1

CORPUS CHRISTI COLLEGE: RECEIPTS IN THE LIBRI MAGNI 1521–1660

	£	s	d	
1521–22	326	7	11½	
1522–26	missing			
1526–27	350	1	10	
1527–28	334	18	11½¹	
1528–29	367	15	0	
1529–30	342	0	1	
1530–31	387	13	3	
1531–32	missing			
1532–33	385	8	3	
1533–34	368	19	6	
1534–35	365	17	11	
1535–36	427	17	0	
1536–37	413	8	11	(includes 37 4 0 pro bosco vendito hoc anno)
1537–38	394	10	4½	
1538–39	436	5	2½	(includes 35 0 11 pro bosco vendito hoc anno et perquisit' curie)
1539–40	448	7	10½	
1540–41	473	17	4	(includes 38 8 11 pro finibus et boscis venditis hoc anno)
1541–42	453	3	11	
1542–43	456	10	10½	
1543–44	443	12	9	
1544–45	443	17	4½	
1545–46	445	16	7	
1546–47	456	4	5	
1547–48	453	3	6	
1548–49	462	19	4½	
1549–50	463	1	7½	

Year	£	s	d	Notes
1550–51	520	16	3	(includes recept. forinsec. of 43 17 8 de cista stauri)
1551–52	466	0	8	
1552–53	missing			
1553–54	486	17	9	
1554–55	490	5	0	
1555–56	486	1	$4\frac{1}{2}$	
1556–57	486	19	9	
1557–58	488	3	$9\frac{1}{2}$	
1558–59	511	10	$6\frac{1}{2}$	
1559–60	533	7	3	billa 1558–59: 45 18 9[2]
1560–61	516	11	$10\frac{1}{2}$	billa 1559–60: 37 12 $3\frac{3}{4}$
1561–62	526	11	$9\frac{1}{2}$[3]	
1562–63	517	12	$8\frac{1}{2}$	
1563–64	missing			
1564–65	492	1	$5\frac{1}{2}$	
1565–66	523	5	$11\frac{1}{2}$	
1566–67	520	10	2	
1567–68	516	3	$9\frac{1}{4}$	billae 1566–67: 2 4 $8\frac{1}{2}$ & 7 8 6[4]
1568–69	524	19	6	billae 1567–68: 1 3 6 & 7 1 2
1569–70	528	3	10	billa 1568–69: 4 6 11
1570–71	528	12	9	no billa for 1569–70
1571–72	527	16	8	billa 1570–71: 0 8 0
1572–73	526	0	$7\frac{1}{2}$	no billa for 1571–72[5]
1573–74	521	18	$7\frac{1}{2}$	
1574–75	521	6	$8\frac{1}{2}$	
1575–76	519	5	1	
1576–77	524	11	$7\frac{1}{2}$	
1577–78	515	4	$1\frac{1}{2}$	
1578–79	518	9	4	
1579–80	515	3	$1\frac{1}{2}$	
1580–81	521	5	$0\frac{1}{2}$	
1581–82	524	0	$10\frac{3}{4}$	
1582–83	518	5	3	
1583–84	475	19	$6\frac{1}{4}$	(Incrementa Redditus Frumentarii occurs for first time in receipts, but no sums filled in)

Table 1 (*cont.*)

	Old Rent £ s d	Cista Finium £ s d	Grossis £ s d	Solut. For. £ s d	Decrem. Comm. £ s d	Total £ s d	Corn Rent £ s d	Total £ s d
1584–85	503 17 3¾	—	—	—	—	—	15 8 1	519 5 4¾
1585–86	504 2 2	—	—	—	—	—	53 12 2	557 14 4
1586–87	470 3 1½	—	—	—	—	—	117 6 7	587 9 8½
1587–88	502 5 1¾	178 8 0[6]	—	—	—	—	119 14 6¼	800 7 8
1588–89	488 4 5	187 5 1½	—	—	—	—	60 9 7½	735 19 2
1589–90	502 4 2¼	138 5 8	—	—	—	—	93 0 10	733 10 8¼
1590–91	497 12 4¾	116 4 2	—	—	—	—	157 3 7¼	771 0 2
1591–92	516 12 0¼	253 4 5	—	—	—	—	154 10 6¼	924 6 11½
1592–93	525 10 8	189 2 10¾	—	—	—	—	100 5 4	814 18 10¾
1593–94	489 4 0	152 5 0¾	—	—	—	—	117 14 1¼	759 3 2
1594–95	522 6 4¾	124 4 1½	—	—	—	—	229 18 10	876 9 4¼
1595–96	548 12 0¾	194 14 1½	—	—	—	—	372 18 1¾	1116 4 4
1596–97	480 8 6¼	161 7 6	—	—	—	641 16 0¼[7]	482 16 11¼	1124 12 11½
1597–98	548 10 4¼	228 17 11¼	—	—	—	777 8 3½	731 16 9½[8]	1509 5 1
1598–99	530 8 10½	292 16 3½	—	—	—	823 5 2	486 0 6¼[9]	1309 5 8¼
1599–1600	546 3 10½	365 13 9¾[10]	29 7 0 e cista placitorum[11]			941 4 8¼	276 2 9	1217 7 5¼
1600–01	544 18 4¼	320 3 11½	—	—	—	865 2 3¾	371 13 9¾	1254 9 5½[12]
1601–02	496 6 2	287 0 10½	17 14 6[14]	60 0 0 e cista placitorum[11]		843 7 0½	383 18 3½[13]	1244 19 10
1602–03	501 11 9	337 15 6	26 10 8	—	—	839 7 3	308 18 7¾	1174 16 6¾
1603–04	533 4 9	294 16 5	26 1 10	—	—	828 1 2	314 18 6¼[15]	1169 1 6¼
1604–05	544 12 7	400 12 2¾	30 5 0	—	—	945 4 9¾	300 7 10	1275 17 7¾
1605–06	541 17 8½	494 18 9¼	27 5 4	—	—	1036 16 5¾	407 19 1	1472 0 10¾
1606–07	511 16 10¾	470 10 10¾	—	—	—	—	383 16 2¼	1366 3 11½[16]
1607–08	516 7 11½	629 16 10¾	—	—	—	—	422 5 2½	1568 10 0¾
1608–09	518 1 8¼	531 13 9½	—	—	—	—	641 9 7	(1691 5 0¾)
1609–10	509 16 11	565 6 8¼	—	—	—	1075 3 7¼	660 2 5¼	1735 6 0½
1610–11	526 16 6¼	451 6 3¼	—	—	—	978 2 9½	404 2 1¾	1382 4 11¼
1611–12	561 3 7	365 18 11½	—	—	—	927 2 6½	450 12 8¾	1377 15 3¼
1612–13	500 8 10¼	470 8 3¾	—	—	—	970 17 2	605 7 3¼	1576 4 5¼
1613–14	missing	—	—	—	—	—	—	—
1614–15	554 1 0¾	604 8 0½	—	—	—	1158 9 1¼	700 3 3½	1858 12 4¾
1615–16	570 7 6½	648 12 5¾	—	—	—	1219 0 0¼	565 11 2	1784 11 2¼
1616–17	559 2 5½	792 1 3	—	—	—	1351 3 8½	625 6 0¼	1976 9 8¾

1619–20	559 17 1½	249 5 5½	—	—	—	809 2 7	497 17 0¾	1306 19 7¾
1620–21	547 6 4¼	433 10 9¼	—	—	—	980 17 1½	414 6 2¼	1395 3 3¾
1621–22	581 19 2	521 11 4¼	—	—	—	1103 10 6¼	373 4 3¼	1476 14 9½
1622–23	598 4 1¼	515 8 6¼	—	—	—	1113 12 7½	776 6 2¼	1889 18 9¾
1623–24	598 11 9¾	670 1 0¼	—	—	—	1268 12 10	857 5 0	2125 17 10
1624–25	587 0 6½	640 4 7½	—	—	—	1227 5 2	629 19 1½	1857 4 3½
1625–26	585 17 11	334 2 1¾	—	—	—	920 0 0¾	653 11 2¼	1573 11 3
1626–27	563 4 8¼	387 6 3¼	—	—	—	950 10 11½	726 13 9½	1677 4 9
1627–28	541 6 2½	450 19 11	—	—	—	992 6 1½	521 13 3½	1513 19 5
1628–29	564 5 6¼	646 16 8¼	—	—	—	1211 2 2½	374 11 1¼	1585 13 3¾
1629–30	548 13 4	512 12 5¼	—	—	—	1061 5 9¼	586 2 8¾	1647 8 6
1630–31	558 6 3½	709 15 5	—	—	—	1268 1 8½	859 4 2	2127 5 10½
1631–32	558 14 3	705 14 10	—	—	—	1264 9 1	990 6 4¼	2254 15 5¼
1632–33	584 16 9	772 3 4¼	—	—	—	1357 0 1¼	710 11 7¼	2067 11 8½
1633–34	574 1 11½	782 19 1¼	—	—	—	1357 1 0¾	768 5 8¾	2125 6 9½
1634–35	572 10 9	855 9 10¼	—	—	—	1428 0 7¼	835 4 6¼	2263 5 1½
1635–36	604 12 8	724 5 11	—	—	—	1328 18 7	732 10 4½	2061 8 11½
1636–37	599 19 11	777 0 11¾	—	—	—	1377 0 10¾	765 4 9	2142 5 7¾
1637–38	597 14 9½	597 9 4½	—	—	—	1195 4 2	899 15 7¼	2094 19 9¼
1638–39	588 16 9	648 1 2½	—	—	—	1236 17 11½	932 0 2	2168 18 1½
1639–40	592 3 10	616 1 8¾	—	—	—	1208 5 6¾	665 8 4¾	1873 13 11½
1640–41	582 8 6¼	741 16 2	—	—	—	1324 4 8¼	622 10 2	1946 14 10¼
1641–42	513 10 9	300 10 9	—	—	—	814 1 6	670 2 1¾	1484 3 7¾
1642–43	409 10 0¾	220 15 5	—	—	—	630 5 5¾	402 1 1¼	1032 6 7
1643–44	324 1 8¼	313 5 4	—	—	—	637 7 0¼	362 11 5¼	999 18 5½
1644–45	155 10 10¾	259 10 11¼[17]	—	—	—	415 1 10	164 0 7¾	652 3 8
1645–46	missing	—	—	—	—	—	+73 1 2¼ arr	
1646–47	282 8 3¾	1314 2 0¾	—	—	—	1596 10 4½	471 17 3¾	2068 7 8¼
1647–48	306 17 5¾	816 11 9¼	—	2 14 0	—	1585 11 4½[19]	616 6 9¼	3029 16 11¼
1648–49[18]	459 8 1½						827 18 9½	
1649–50	384 2 3	1207 11 5¼	—	2 7 0	—	1594 0 8¼	1102 0 8	2696 1 4¼
1650–51	no receipts entered in account							
1651–52	no receipts entered in account							
1652–53	119 2 11½	749 16 2½	29 1 8	3 2 0	—	872 1 2[21]	657 13 2¼[22]	1558 16 0¼
1653–54	581 16 9½	521 14 7	23 9 4	3 3 0	—	1106 14 4½	497 14 1¼	1653 13 3¼
							+25 15 5½ arr	
1654–55	564 4 5¼	640 5 5½	21 11 8	3 4 0	—	1207 13 10¾	328 1 9¾	1557 7 4½
1655–56	528 1 5	884 15 11½	22 17 4	3 5 0	—	1416 2 4½[23]	467 15 10½	1926 15 2¾
							+19 19 7¾ arr	

Table 1 (*cont.*)

	Old Rent £ s d	Cista Finium £ s d	Grossis £ s d	Solut. For. £ s d	Decrem. Comm. £ s d	Total £ s d	Corn Rent £ s d	Total £ s d
1656–57	missing	—	—	—			—	—
1657–58	589 13 10½ +15 8 5 arr	779 16 0¼	31 3 8	3 4 0	4 7 4½[24]	1388 2 3¾[25]	686 3 2½ +20 17 9¼ arr	2130 14 4
1658–59	526 13 4½ +44 13 6½ arr	476 13 2	35 3 2	3 7 0	6 18 3	1051 7 1[26]	760 4 10 +104 6 8½ arr	1958 0 0½
1659–60	552 10 0	471 1 10½	—	4 0 0	—	1023 11 10½[27]	847 5 8½ +68 8 5¾ arr	1943 6 0¾
1660–61	509 10 0¼	484 4 11½	—	—	—	993 14 11¾	782 16 10¾	1776 11 10½

1 Items carried forward into the next year's receipts (*scheda/billa petitionis*) are netted out henceforth where possible.

2 In the accounts for 1559–60, 1560–61 the *billa petitionis* is not distinguished in the receipts (as it had been previously). It has therefore *not* been netted out, but the sums allocated to it in the previous year's account have been noted alongside for reference.

3 In this and succeeding accounts the *billa* is distinguished in the receipts and has therefore been netted out.

4 See note 2.

5 Henceforth the *billae* disappear from the final balance of the accounts and are not mentioned in the receipts.

6 In this account the receipts of the *cista finium* are first incorporated in the *Liber Magnus*.

7 The sums in this first 'total' column = old rent + cista finium which is now balanced separately from corn rent at the end of the account.

8 Including £28 0s 9½d arrears.

9 Including £8 19s 9½d arrears.

10 Now called receipts for fines, wood sales and other profits (punishments, amercements, arrears of rent, perquisites of courts, heriots &c).

11 A receipt simply occurring in the balance and not in the body of the account,

12 Includes £17 13s 4d for one-sixth of a fine, added to the corn rents in the final balance.

13 Including £11 11s 0d arrears.

14 Occurs as receipt only in the final balance; divided among fellows and scholars for augmentation of commons.

15 The bursars had a deficit of £16 15s 0¼d on the corn rent account 'quae summa illis persoluenda est e vectigalib. redit. frument. huius & superio-rum annorum, nondum receptis' (cf arrears in notes 8, 9, 13).

16 This year there is no receipt for *grossis* and the three main sources of income are lumped together, though in fact corn rents are still kept for expenditure on decrements and augmentation of commons.

17 This is the figure given in the balance; in the body of the account arrears of corn rent have been added to it.

18 Uniquely, one account covers two years.

19 Including the solut. for. of £2 14s 0d.

20 This includes both of the figures for corn rent, though in the final balance that for 1648–49 is omitted.

21 Excludes grossis, but includes solut. for.

22 This does not tally with the total in the body of the account (£689 13s 2¼d).

23 Excludes £115 1s 11d carried forward from previous year.

24 *Pro decremaentis commensalium*, added to the corn rent side of the balance.

TABLE 2

Corn Rent in the Libri Magni, 1597–1660: The Final Balances

Account	**Corn Rent***	Decrements	Ampliori Convictu	Grossis	Commons	Bursars of previous year		Surplus/Deficit
	£ s d	£ s d	£ s d	£ s d	£ s d	£ s d	£ s d	£ s d
1596–97	482 16 11¼	414 5 1¼	68 11 10	—	—	—	—	—
1597–98[1]	731 16 9½	359 8 3¾	372 8 5¾	—	—	—	—	—
1598–99	486 0 6¼	352 6 2¾	133 14 3½	—	—	—	—	—
1599–1600[2]	276 2 9	276 2 9	—	—	—	—	—	—
1600–01[3]	389 7 1¾	389 7 1¾	—	—	—	—	—	—
1601–02[4]	383 18 3½	329 0 5¼	54 17 10¼	—	—	—	—	—
1602–03	308 18 7¾	287 15 5½	35 16 6½ [sic]	—	—	—	—	—
1603–04[5]	314 18 6¼	327 15 10¼	—	—	—	—	—	16 15 0¼*d*
1604–05[6]	300 7 10	402 13 4½	—	—	—	—	—	87 12 2½*d*
1605–06[7]	407 19 1	352 6 1¼	—	—	—	—	—	70 6 3¾*s*
1606–07	383 16 2¼ [sic]	378 10 0¾	5 6 1¾	—	—	—	—	—
1607–08	432 18 6½	355 3 3½	77 15 3	—	—	—	—	—
1608–09	652 2 11	399 5 8¾	252 17 2¼	una cum 25*s*	—	—	—	—
1609–10	670 15 9¼	348 1 9½	322 13 11¾	—	—	—	—	—
1610–11[8]	418 5 5¾	376 4 2	42 1 3¾	—	—	—	—	—
1611–12[9]	461 6 0¾ [sic]	433 6 11¼	27 19 2	—	—	—	—	—
1612–13	616 0 7¼	392 5 3½	223 15 3¾	—	—	—	—	—
1613–14	missing	—	—	—	—	—	—	
1614–15	710 16 7½	414 6 3¾	296 10 3¾	—	—	—	—	—
1615–16	576 4 6	475 8 6½	100 15 11½	—	—	—	—	—
1616–17[10]	635 19 4¼	478 4 4	147 1 8¼	—	—	—	—	—
1617–18	621 16 5	512 4 4½	109 12 0½	—	—	—	—	—
1618–19	623 0 8¼	452 15 6½	170 5 1¾	—	—	—	—	—
1619–20[11]	548 10 10¾	398 4 8¼	84 0 10½	66 5 4	—	—	—	—
1620–21[12]	414 6 2¼	351 3 5	63 2 9¼	—	—	—	—	—

Table 2 (*cont.*)

Account	Corn Rent*	Decrements	Ampliori Convictu	Grossis	Commons	Bursars of previous year		Surplus/Deficit
	£ s d	£ s d	£ s d	£ s d	£ s d	£ s d	£ s d	£ s d
1621–22[13]	373 4 $3\frac{1}{4}$	—	373 4 $3\frac{1}{4}$	—	—	—	—	—
1622–23[14]	797 4 $0\frac{1}{4}$	130 16 $2\frac{1}{4}$	509 1 0	44 13 4	14 0 0	255 15 5	55 19 6 (brewhouse)	212 1 5*d*
1623–24[15]	867 18 4	111 18 $10\frac{3}{4}$	492 7 8	41 5 0	4 16 8	—	101 2 $7\frac{1}{4}$	—
	—	—	116 7 6	—	—	—	(*pro parte debiti* 1622)	—
1624–25[16]	652 19 5	?134 10 5	397 11 $8\frac{3}{4}$	35 0 8	44 6 2	—	39 16 $5\frac{1}{4}$ (spices)	—
1625–26[17]	664 4 $6\frac{1}{4}$	37 6 $11\frac{1}{2}$	31 11 $3\frac{1}{4}$	44 1 1	—	—	30 8 $6\frac{1}{2}$ (spices)	—
		—	520 16 8	—	—	—	—	—
1626–27	737 7 $1\frac{1}{2}$ [*sic*]	118 12 8	560 14 $5\frac{3}{4}$	39 17 0	4 16 4	—	13 6 8 (solut' D^ri Jermyn)	
1627–28	532 6 $7\frac{1}{2}$	106 17 3	393 3 $2\frac{1}{2}$	32 6 2	—	—	—	—
1628–29	385 4 $5\frac{1}{4}$	141 15 $11\frac{3}{4}$	258 10 $4\frac{1}{4}$	21 12 $2\frac{1}{2}$	—	—	—	36 14 $1\frac{1}{4}$*d*[17a]
1629–30[18]	596 16 $0\frac{3}{4}$ [*sic*]	227 10 $1\frac{3}{4}$	300 16 2	27 4 2	—	—	46 19 5 (spices)	5 13 $10\frac{1}{4}$*d*
1630–31[19]	869 17 6	157 2 $2\frac{3}{4}$	570 3 4	38 12 0	—	—	35 14 5 (spices)	27 2 $5\frac{1}{4}$*d*
	—	—	45 13 4	—	—	—	22 12 $2\frac{1}{4}$ (*allocata est pro parte debit' e red frum 29 et 30*)	—
1631–32	1000 19 $8\frac{1}{4}$	214 8 $4\frac{1}{2}$	687 2 6	28 3 8	—	—	50 11 3 (spices) 4 0 0 (obsonatori pro cura in cul') 2 10 0 (pro pauper' Lincol' temp' pestis).	14 3 $10\frac{3}{4}$*s* *quae summa soluta est*
1632–33	721 4 $11\frac{1}{4}$	191 0 $11\frac{1}{2}$	487 16 2	31 9 0	2 16 4	—	—	8 2 $5\frac{3}{4}$*s*
1633–34	778 19 $0\frac{3}{4}$	235 5 $5\frac{3}{4}$	504 6 7	31 1 0	—	—	—	8 6 0 *s*
1634–35[20]	845 17 $10\frac{1}{4}$	162 18 10	570 18 11	26 18 8	—	—	—	—
	—	—	85 1 $5\frac{1}{4}$	—	—	—		—
1635–36	743 3 $8\frac{1}{2}$ [*sic*]	184 0 $3\frac{1}{2}$	575 18 2	28 8 8	—	—	—	45 3 $5\frac{1}{4}$*d* *allocand' ex red*

1636–37	775 18 1	212 16 8	522 17 6	26 8 2	—	—	—	13 15 9 *s*
1637–38[21]	899 15 $7\frac{1}{4}$	174 19 $0\frac{1}{2}$	618 17 11	29 18 0	—	—	—	—
	—	—	76 0 $7\frac{3}{4}$	—	—	—	—	—
1638–39[22]	924 13 6 [*sic*]	220 9 $4\frac{1}{2}$	598 15 5	26 2 10	—	—	—	—
	—	—	70 10 0	—	—	—	—	—
	—	—	26 15 10	—	—	—	—	
1639–40	676 1 $8\frac{3}{4}$ [*sic*]	238 5 9	415 10 4	26 3 0	—	—	—	3 17 $4\frac{1}{2}$*d* *allocanda est ex red frum anni sequentis*
1640–41	633 3 6	128 19 $6\frac{3}{4}$	468 14 5	20 2 2	—	—	—	15 7 $4\frac{1}{4}$*s*
1641–42	680 15 $5\frac{3}{4}$	140 12 $7\frac{1}{2}$	514 19 8	17 2 6	—	—	—	8 0 $8\frac{1}{4}$*s*
1642–43	412 14 $5\frac{1}{4}$	91 9 0	421 2 2	23 19 4	—	—	—	123 16 $0\frac{3}{4}$*d*
1643–44[23]	367 18 $1\frac{1}{4}$	60 14 $11\frac{3}{4}$	428 7 8	15 0 0	—	—	—	136 4 $6\frac{1}{2}$*d*
1644–45[24]	164 0 $7\frac{3}{4}$	19 7 —	208 9 —	—	—	—	—	63 16 $8\frac{1}{2}$*d*
	73 1 $2\frac{1}{4}$	—	—	—	—	—	—	—
1645–46	missing	—	—	—	—	—	—	—
1646–47	482 10 $7\frac{3}{4}$ [*sic*]	49 2 $3\frac{1}{4}$	691 9 6	7 3 0	—	—	—	265 4 $1\frac{3}{4}$*d*
1647–48 1648–49 [25]	616 6 $9\frac{1}{4}$	75 11 1	930 18 7	—	—	—	—	390 2 $10\frac{3}{4}$*d* *allocanda est e red frum an 1649*
1649–50	1112 14 0	37 11 $11\frac{1}{4}$	1113 5 5	—	5 15 11	390 2 $10\frac{3}{4}$	—	434 2 2*d* *remanet allocandum dispensatoribus e rec frum 1650*
1650–51	no balance	—	—	—	—	—	—	—
1651–52	no balance	—	—	—	—	—	—	—
1652–53[26]	686 14 $10\frac{1}{4}$	34 0 $8\frac{1}{4}$	535 13 $4\frac{3}{4}$	29 1 8	—	229 18 $0\frac{1}{4}$	27 0 $0\frac{3}{4}$ (to officers & logic lector)	168 18 $11\frac{3}{4}$*d* *allocanda est dis-pens e red frum anno 1653*
1653–54[27]	546 18 $10\frac{1}{2}$	39 19 2	381 19 2	23 9 4	—	168 18 $11\frac{3}{4}$	—	67 7 $9\frac{1}{4}$*d* *allocanda est . . . e red anno 1654*

Table 2 (cont.)

Account	Corn Rent*			Decrements			Ampliori Convictu			Grossis			Commons			Bursars of previous year						Surplus/Deficit		
	£	s	d	£	s	d	£	s	d	£	s	d	£	s	d	£	s	d	£	s	d	£	s	d
1654–55[28]	349	13	5½ [sic]	35	15	9¾	334	9	9¼	21	11	8	–			67	7	9¼	–			109	11	6¼ d allocanda &c
1655–56[29]	510	12	10¼ [sic]	36	4	11	333	6	2½	–			–			109	11	6¾	(?8)12		9¾ (part of new allowance to officers and logic lector)	–		
1656–57	missing			–			–			–			–			–						–		
1657–58[30]	742	12	0	13	19	9¾	681	6	4¾	31	3	8	–			14	11	5½	10	0	0 (part of new allowance to officers)	8	9	4d allocanda &c
1658–59[31]	906	12	11¼	–			856	12	1¾	35	3	2	–			8	9	4	16	10	0 (part of new allowance to officers)	10	1	8½ d allocanda &c
1659–60[32]	930	7	6¼ [sic]	4	16	9¼	1013	1	8	–			–			10	1	8½	–			97	12	7¾ d petunt sibi allocari

* From 1607 to 1608, unless otherwise stated, the figure for corn rent includes £10 13s 4d, an allowance regularly added to it in the balance *pro caristia boum et festis solennioribus.*

[1] The sum entered here and given in the balance for corn rent does not correspond to that entered in the body of the account (£703 16s 0d).

[2] £276 2s 9d: *quae tota illis allocata est pro decrement' in pane, potu, sale, ceteroque convictu & lignis ac carbonibus: praeter 61 10 6 quam summam aliunde persolvi eis oportet.*

[3] In this year the corn rent totals £371 13s 9¾d to which is added in the balance £17 13s 4d for the sixth part of a fine from Bad and Webbe giving a total of £389 7s 1¾d: *quae illis allocata est pro resid' decrem' super' anni & pro decrementis buius anni, in pane, potu, sale, ceteroque convictu, & lignis ac carbonibus praeter 14 4 3¾ e reditu frumentario anni sequentis illis persolvend.'*

⁴ The total for corn rents includes £11 11s 0d arrears; decrements include £289 3s 3½d pro decrementis huius anni and £39 17s 1¾d pro superioris anni decrementis reliquis & alii ad decrementa spectantibus.

⁵ Decrements £327 15s 10¼d: de qua summa subductis 14 13 4 (a Fundatore ad minuendum decrementorum onus allocatis) restant debit' dispensatorib' 16 15 0¼ quae summa illis persolvenda est e vectiqalib' redit' frument' huius & superiorum annorum, nondum receptis. The arithmetic of this balance does not seem to work out.

⁶ Again, £14 3s 4d (a Fundatore &c) is deducted from expenses on decrements to arrive at the debit; nothing is said about method of dealing with the £87 12s 2½d deficit.

⁷ Again, £14 13s 4d deducted from decrements; £70 6s 3¾d: debita dispensatoribus (praeter accepta arreragia & 2 17 6 deinceps accipienda) ob superioris anni decrementa.

⁸ In this account the £10 13s 4d is subtracted from the decrements along with £3 10s pro magistro Audley, but I have added them to the original receipt for corn rent of £404 2s 1¾d.

⁹ Slight discrepancy in the arithmetic.

¹⁰ Although £10 13s 4d has been added to the corn rent as usual, it has been missed out by the auditors in their calculation of the surplus for division.

¹¹ The total for corn rent is made up as follows: corn rent, £497 17s 0¾d; caristia boum, £10 13s 4d; allocat' in billa promi ultra summa expens' in brasinio, £35 17s 6d; pro communiis magistrorum discipulorum, £4 3s 0d; the sum of £66 5s 4d is pro grossis divisis inter socios & scholares and various payments for commons.

¹² No indication of £10 13s 4d being added to corn rent, but the dividend for augmentation of commons is, unusually, said to be vna cum allocatione fundatoris in lib' senesc'.

¹³ Again, £10 13s 4d not added.

¹⁴ Corn rent is supplemented by the standard £10 13s 4d and also £10 4s 6d pro communiis mᵒ discip'; the £509 1s 0d divided is said to be paid in pecuniis; deficit of £212 1s 5d solvenda e red' frum' pro anno futuro.

¹⁵ The two dividends under ampliori convictu are: £492 7s 8d divis' inter studentes omnium ordinum ter' quatuor, £116 7s 6d (= remanet) divisa est inter alumnos omnium ordinum.

¹⁶ Commons payments include Dr Jermyn and M. Gorstelow, famuli, communiis studentium emmissorum tempore parliamenti.

¹⁷ The two dividends under ampliori convictu are: £520 16s 8d allocat' studentibus omnium ordinum pro pane & potu hoc anno, £31 11s 3¾d (= remanet) divisa est pro ampliori convictu.

¹⁷ᵃ Deficit: quae summa allocand' est e Reditu Frum' Anni sequentis.

¹⁸ Deficit allocand' est e reditu frumentario anni sequentis.

¹⁹ The two dividends under ampliori convictu are: £570 3s 4d for augmentation of commons, £45 13s 4d (= part of remanet) divisum inter alumnos; deficit allocand' in toto e red' frum' anni sequentis (deficit made up of debts).

²⁰ The two dividends under ampliori convictu are: £570 18s 11d for augmentation of commons; £85 1s 5¼d (= remanet) divisa est in fine anni inter alumnos.

²¹ £618 17s 11d augmentation of commons, £76 0s 7¾d (= remanet) etiam divisa inter alumnos.

²² £598 15s 5d augmentation of commons, £70 10s 0d (= part of remanet) ulterius divisum inter alumnos, £26 15s 10d (rest of remanet) dividenda est ante exonerationem dispensatorum.

²³ Only £5 6s 8d added pro caristia boum.

²⁴ £73 1s 2¼d is received for part of corn rent due 1643 and *allocata est pro parte expensarum ultra accepta de reditu frumentario ann' ?1642.*

²⁵ This account contains, in the receipts, two sums for corn rents (£616 6s 9¼d 1648, £827 18s 9½d 1649) but only the first, without the addition of £10 13s 4d, is balanced.

²⁶ The figure for corn rents (corn rent £657 13s 2¼d + grossis £29 1s 8d) does not correspond to that in the body of the account (£689 13s 2¼d).

²⁷ Corn rent = corn rent 1653, £497 14s 1¼d + arrears corn rent 1652, £25 15s 5½d + grossis £23 9s 4d.

²⁸ Corn rent = corn rent 1653 and 1654, £328 1s 9½d + grossis 1655, £21 11s 8d.

²⁹ Corn rent = corn rent 1655, £467 15s 10½d + arrears corn rent £19 19s 7¾d + grossis 1656, £22 17s 4d.

³⁰ Corn rent = corn rent 1657, £686 3s 2½d + arrears corn rent £20 17s 9¼d + grossis £31 3s 8d + decrements *commensalium* £4 7s 4½d.

³¹ Corn rent = corn rent 1658, £760 4s 10d + arrears corn rent £104 6s 8½d + grossis £35 3s 2d + *decrem. commensal.* £6 18s 3d.

³² Corn rent = corn rent 1659, £847 5s 8½d + *caristia boum et festis solemnioribus* £10 13s 4d + arrears corn rent £68 8s 5¾d + *solut' forins'* £4 0s 0d.

N.B. [*sic*] indicates that the arithmetic of the original account does not work out, usually by a fraction of a penny.

9
The Physical Setting:
New Building and Adaptation

JOHN NEWMAN

THE Tudor period saw the final domination of the colleges over the Oxford architectural scene. The buildings of the earliest foundations, University College, Balliol, Queen's, Oriel, Exeter, and even Merton, were relatively modest and (apart from Merton's chapel) architecturally unpretentious, with loosely related hall, chapel and residential ranges. The magnificent formal quadrangle of New College in the 1370s first demonstrated that Oxford's academic communities could be housed as splendidly as were the monasteries, Oseney, Rewley and St Frideswide's, which fringed the western edge of the town. In the mid-fifteenth century the new regularity was echoed at All Souls, and, on a more modest scale, at Lincoln and Durham Colleges. At the dawn of the Tudor era a new standard of size and grandeur was reached at Archbishop Wayneflete's foundation outside the walls to the east. Magdalen's main buildings, hall, chapel, founder's tower, and a cloister quadrangle surrounded by two-storeyed chamber ranges, were complete by the mid-1480s; but the college made its full visual impact only after the construction of the chaplains' quadrangle towards the road to the south, and, above all, of the mighty bell tower, completed in 1509.

Three new colleges were built in the early sixteenth century, Brasenose and Corpus in the heart of the town, and Cardinal College, Wolsey's shortlived attempt to outdo Magdalen, breaking through the town walls and replacing the priory of St Frideswide with buildings spectacular in scale and style. During the next decade Oxford's remaining monastic foundations were dissolved and in 1538 the four friaries surrendered. By the middle of the century their buildings had largely been swept away, only the quadrangles of Durham, St Bernard's and Canterbury Colleges surviving to find a new use in the post-reformation university.

The academic halls where the majority of the undergraduates in the medieval university resided and which occupied much of the

street frontages, particularly in the eastern part of the town not
occupied by colleges, were by the late fifteenth century in drastic
decline. The fifty halls listed in 1469 had dropped to half that
number in 1511, and only three years later the number had halved
again, to twelve.[1] This reduction was caused partly by amalgamation
and the enlargement of the remaining halls, and partly by the absorption of halls in the newly founded colleges. But the result was to
leave a considerable number of derelict halls and abandoned sites
reverting to garden grounds. Agas's map of 1578, which records the
town in its most denuded state, shows such open or underdeveloped
areas within the walls;[2] though this was soon to change as the population of both university and town increased sharply in the half-
century from about 1580.

UNIVERSITY BUILDINGS

The buildings of the university itself, as opposed to the colleges, have
always been few. Nevertheless, the last quarter of the fifteenth
century saw what amounted to a thoroughgoing rehabilitation of
those which it did possess, namely its church and its schools. First of
all the theology school, with a new university library over it, was
after long delays finished in 1478–81, thanks to a fund-raising campaign crowned by the gift of 1,000 marks from Thomas Kempe,
bishop of London.[3] Books were transferred to the new library
from the old one over the congregation house on the north side
of the chancel of St Mary's church, thereby freeing the old library
to become the meeting place of congregation instead of the dark
and dank lower chamber which it had hitherto been forced to
use. Both upper and lower rooms in the congregation house, however, were improved with a new set of much enlarged north windows
extending above and below the intermediate floor to light both
storeys. The side walls were raised sixteen inches and a new and
less steeply pitched roof was set up in about 1508. The ceiling of
the upper room was then decorated with gilded bosses bearing
shields of arms.[4]
    The canon law school in Blue Boar Lane in St Edward's parish
to the south-west was already in 1465 said to be in need of rebuilding,

    [1] W. A. Pantin, 'The halls and schools of medieval Oxford', in *Oxford Studies Presented
to Daniel Callus* (OHS new ser. xvi 1964), 34–5.
    [2] *VCH Oxon.* iv. 88; a redrawing of Agas's map to scale, pp. 642–4 below, greatly reduces
the impression of open space conveyed by the eighteenth century version of Agas.
    [3] A series of letters begging funds from well-placed dignitaries in church and state is
printed in *Epist. acad.* ed. Anstey ii. 377–478.
    [4] T. G. Jackson, *The Church of St. Mary the Virgin* (Oxford 1897), 102–4.

and in 1482, as soon as the theology school was finished, attention turned seriously to them. The intention was to erect a two-storey building, the canon law school occupying the lower part, the civil law school the upper.[1] By July 1488 the foundations of a canon law school only were laid and in the following January the university was discussing with the bishop of Lincoln whether to furnish the new canon law school with the disused desks in the old library over the congregation house.[2] It was 'nearly finished' in 1490.[3]

The programme of reconstruction by the university, if it can rightly be called a programme, concluded with the rebuilding of the nave of the university church. The chancel of St Mary the Virgin had been rebuilt in about 1462 at the expense of Walter Lyhart, bishop of Norwich; but it was in the nave that the university acts took place. By 1476 the nave roof was in danger of collapse, and in 1487 money and materials were being collected to repair it; but by the following year complete rebuilding of the nave had been agreed upon. The principal benefactors were Dr Litchfield, archdeacon of Middlesex, and Richard Fitzjames, warden of Merton.[4]

The masonry work of the new nave was complete by 1495, but the roof seems not to have been finished until 1503.[5] A stone pulpit was constructed in 1508 costing £20, in part at any rate the work of a mason, John Fusting, resident in the parish. This too was paid for by donations, from Fitzjames, John Claymond, president of Magdalen, Bishop Audley and Archbishop Morton.[6] The church's function as the setting for the university's ceremonial acts was celebrated in the stained glass which filled the thirty-five lights of the great west window, in which were depicted the apocryphal early history of the university, beginning with Alfred's expulsion of the Danes, and its various scholarly grades and activities.[7]

Thus by 1510 all the university's premises were newly improved, and Schools Street, the heart of its activities, was marked by two splendid new buildings, the theology school at the north end and the nave of St Mary's church at the south.

After that nothing more was done until the middle of the century. The block of schools built at right-angles to the theology school in Schools Street in 1440 by Abbot Hooknorton of Oseney was

---

[1] *Epist. acad.* ed. Anstey ii. 377, 480.   [2] Ibid. 547, 556–7.
[3] Ibid. 571   [4] Ibid. 630–1.
[5] Jackson, *Church of St. Mary*, 112–27.
[6] See ibid. 215 for Fusting's inventory. The pulpit was demolished in the seventeenth century but fragments survive, and Anthony Wood gives armorial details: ibid. 179.
[7] Ibid. app. B. Already by the beginning of the seventeenth century the glass was badly damaged. All that we have today is the text of thirty-two of the descriptive pentameters, published by Brian Twyne in 1608.

modernized in 1557–9 at a cost of £220. Ten three-light and eleven two-light windows were inserted and glazed together with one in the end wall, two new doorcases with battlementing over them were erected, and internally the building was new-floored and three staircases were set up. It was significant of the changed circumstances of post-reformation Oxford that some of the materials came from the demolished canon law school (the site of which had been included in the enlarged boundaries of Christ Church), and that the money needed for the remodelling came not from distinguished ecclesiastical alumni but almost exclusively from heads of colleges.[1] The appearance of the remodelled schools is recorded in Bereblock's woodcut, but what struck visitors was not the building so much as the inscriptions on it, referring to the liberal arts and *virtutes scholasticae: Patientia, Humilitas, Fortitudo, Spes* and *Cautio*.[2] The schools were demolished in the early seventeenth century to make way for Sir Thomas Bodley's schools quadrangle.

THE EARLY TUDOR COLLEGES

Before a detailed account is given of the buildings of the new foundations, Brasenose, Corpus and Cardinal Colleges, it may be well to look at the fabric and fittings of an established college as they were used, remodelled and brought up to date in the decades before the reformation. This can be done for Merton College, thanks to the detailed register kept by Warden Fitzjames and, in somewhat less abundant detail, by his successors.

Richard Fitzjames, fellow of Merton from 1465, university proctor in 1473, and a chaplain to Edward IV, took up the wardenship of Merton in August 1483. His involvement in the new buildings of the university has already been noted. While still warden he was raised to the episcopate, first, in 1497, to the see of Rochester; in 1503 he was translated to Chichester, and, resigning as Warden in 1507, he ended his career as bishop of London. Under this ambitious and largely absentee warden, academic standards at Merton are said to have fallen; but Fitzjames's register shows that he put in hand and liberally fostered an extensive campaign of improvement to the college fabric and amassed plate and other valuables. It is possibly significant that books given by the previous warden were in 1486 ordered to be sold to raise money for the new roodloft.[3]

[1] Pantin, 'Halls and Schools', 94; OUA, NW/3/6.

[2] P. Hentzner, *Itinerarium Germaniae, Galliae, Angliae* (Nuremberg 1612), 143, reporting a visit in 1598; see also N. Chytraeus, *Variorum in Europa itinerum deliciae* (2nd edn Herborn 1599), 598–9. I am indebted to Josephine Turquet for these references.

[3] *Reg. ann. mert. 1483–1521*, passim.

In September 1483, a month after his election, money was allocated for the completion of a new wall, and the building of two new gates was authorized from the road at the west end of the college to the kitchen, for the use of all service vehicles. But soon attention was diverted from the efficient working and maintenance of the college to enhancing the beauty and comfort of its major rooms. The chapel claimed attention first and most continuously. Fitzjames gave generously himself, and numerous gifts, most of them fairly small, came from fellows, ex-fellows and other friends of the college; but a considerable amount of the cost was borne by the college itself. First, on 11 August 1486 the warden and fellows entered into a contract with John Fissher, citizen and joiner of London, who undertook to make a roodloft for £27. He was to take the new roodloft in Magdalen College chapel as the model for the main part, making it 12 feet high, with space for two altars on the nave side. It was, however, to have 'ferre better dorys then ther be in Mawdelyn College aforesaid', and the superstructure—the coving supporting the loft to east and west—was to be modelled on the roodloft in the church of St Mildred Poultry in London, 'or better then it is there'. Fissher was to include in the price 'certeyn ymages in clene tymbre for the space of xxx fote, and eche of them shalbe ii fote long at the lest assise, soche ymages as the seid warden . . . shal name and assigne'. The loft was complete by the patronal feast of St John the Baptist, in June 1488, but gifts for the work were inadequate to pay Fissher's bill, and £2 6s 6d debt was charged against the account of the new organ which was to go on the roodloft.

In March 1488 an organmaker, William Wotton of Oxford, undertook to 'make or cawse to be made a goode and suffycyent payr of organs' for £28. Once again Magdalen College provided the standard, in this instance because Wotton had made (or rather 'promysyd to make') a pair of organs there. Wotton was to set up the organs 'withyn the new rodlofte' by Whitsun 1489. Gifts towards the organ recorded in the *registrum* total only £8, of which £5 came from the warden. In 1489 a precentor had been appointed, and it was decreed that in future matins and vigils on important occasions should be Sarum use. In November 1493 the college undertook the recurrent expense of an organist, John Frampton, whose salary of 6s 8d per quarter was to be raised according to his needs and merits. A little later, musical ambition extended further, for in October 1507 it was agreed to appoint a choirmaster, at a salary of 6s 8d per annum, and to insist that in future all scholars and commoners admitted to Portionists' Hall should be able to sing 'cantus fractus' (pricksong);

but this requirement proved impossible to maintain and in 1519 it was agreed to abandon it.

Meanwhile, in March 1488, the two new altars were dedicated, the southerly one to St Jerome, to whom the warden was especially devoted, the northerly to St Andrew, the saint whom Dr John Martock held in particular honour. The vestments, altar books and plate allocated to the St Jerome altar were provided in large part by Fitzjames; Martock supplied those of the St Andrew altar.

Money was being collected for new choir stalls from 1487, and it seems that they were in position by 1491, when a donation was made towards painting them. The rood screen, loft and doors, and the altars with the figures of St Jerome and St Andrew above were painted by a certain Henry between December 1490 and April 1491, work for which he was paid £15 13s 4d, subscriptions in this instance more than covering the cost.

Next, in 1497, the choir was ceiled with wainscot at a cost of £90. On the raising of money for this the *registrum* is quite explicit: £20 came from John Marshall, bishop of Llandaff, £40 from Thomas Lindley, a former fellow and lector in theology, the remainder being 'provided by the Warden from what he had been able to beg here and there of their charity from various friends of the college'.

The ceiling of the 'nave', i.e. the transept, was delayed until 1517–18. Fitzjames, by this time bishop of London, still came high on the subscription list, though he had resigned the wardenship a decade before.

Besides the embellishment of the fabric of the chapel, a constant supply of vestments, plate and other precious objects flowed in for its use and beautification. Between 1483 and 1520 the following gifts, almost all of them to the chapel, were recorded in the *registrum*: eighteen pairs of vestments, three copes and £110 to buy copes with, 2½ dozen cups and 8 other cups, 3 chalices, 7 basins, 10 bowls, 4 salts, 4 altar-cruets, 2 reliquary tables, 2 thuribles, 2 candelabra, 2 paxes and 2 altar-cloths, together with a gilt cross weighing 220 ounces, a corporal, an incense-boat, a missal, a manual, a reliquary ring, a lenten veil, a ewer, a mazer, a holy water bucket, a set of staves, a chrismatory, a sepulchre cloth and a lectern. Of all this bounty only the lectern remains, no doubt largely because of its size and because it was of brass, not a precious metal. It came to the college in 1504 by the bequest of Dr Martock. The bequest was arranged by Fitzjames, as is shown by his shield of arms engraved on the face of each desk of the lectern. But the encircling inscription 'Orate pro anima Magistri Johannis Martok' is a reminder of what lay behind so much generosity to a community of men in holy orders. Martock left many other gifts to the college, notably £100 to buy copes, and in July 1504 a perpetual obit was decreed, all fellows and future fellows being ordered to pray for his soul. Similarly, the gilt cross listed above was bequeathed to the college by Thomas Kempe, bishop of London. It reached Merton on 11 April 1489, and within three weeks, on 2 May, Kempe's name was added to the list of college benefactors. Later in the same year Fitzjames himself presented a reliquary table enclosing parts of the staff, a tooth and some blood of St John the Baptist, the college's patron saint. On the day on which he made the presentation his parents were added to the 'brethren' of the college, for whom prayers were to be offered. Smaller gifts too were expected to earn similar rewards. In December 1484 the warden procured as a gift from Sir John Leynham a chalice inscribed on the foot 'Oretis pro animabus Iohannis Leynham militis et Margarete uxoris eius'; and in January 1488 a certain William Withers, not a member of the college, gave a white cope bearing the words 'Orate pro anima magistri Willelmi Withers'.

The only example of the foundation of a chantry at Merton during this period is that of Ralph Hamsterley, a former fellow who had been master of University College but chose to spend the last years of his life within the walls of his old college. Dying in August 1518, he left lands at Hensington for a priest to celebrate in chapel continually for his soul. A more typical arrangement was that whereby Simon Mollond, a former fellow who held the college living of St Peter in the East, left £20 to the college for an obit to be said annually for twenty years, and an annual distribution of £1 among the fellows and probationer bachelors.

Fitzjames's role and influence in all this are once again made clear by the fact that on his death in January 1522 the stream of benefactions virtually ceased to flow, never to be restored until the reformation cut off the motive for such gifts altogether. But in his time it was not only the chapel that was refitted and improved. The present boarded ceiling of the western arm of the library, with moulded ribs and carved bosses, cost £27 6s in 1502–3. Fitzjames's arms are on one of the bosses. His arms (and those of the diocese of Rochester) occur also on the so-called Fitzjames gateway, part of the extension of the warden's lodging begun in 1497. The foundation stone was laid on 12 March of that year at 10.20 a.m., the Warden having obtained a horoscope for the building.[1] The gateway itself has a vault with finely carved bosses representing the signs of the

[1] J. Chamber, *Treatise against Judicial Astrology* (1601), 36, quoted in *VCH Oxon.* iii, 102.

zodiac with, in the centre, the Tudor royal arms. The vault carried a room communicating with the hall dais, and beyond that were two further rooms, both with south-facing oriels.[1] The absence of any allusion in the *registrum* to this enlargement of the lodging suggests that it was financed entirely by Fitzjames himself.

During Fitzjames's lifetime the only improvement to the college building which cannot be connected with his initiative is the re-furbishing of the hall under Warden Harper. On 28 January 1512 Harper handed over twenty marks, the gift of William Nele, an ex-fellow, to be spent on embellishing the hall, in particular for boarding the floor, for hangings, and for glazing the windows. Nele's name was duly inscribed in the glass inserted at the upper end of the hall in 1517.[2]

All this work at Merton from 1483 to 1517 can be seen to have a certain coherence, first enhancing the splendour of the chapel and its services, then making more comfortable other major parts of the college, warden's lodging, library and hall; even if practically no structural work to the college buildings was involved. It can probably be assumed that the major new works at other colleges undertaken in the early sixteenth century were less isolated than they now appear.

At Queen's Robert Langton, a fellow whose uncle had been pro-vost of the college and in 1501 died as bishop of Winchester, added, in memory of his uncle, a two-storeyed bay window to the provost's lodging and paid for the enlargement and refitting of the chapel in 1516–18.[3] At Balliol William Bell (master *c* 1484–95) seems to have been a moving spirit. His arms were on the south range of the cloisters, and at his death he left ten marks towards the building of a new chapel. Money was slow to come in, however, so that the chapel was not replaced until the 1520s.[4] The other main building works in the early sixteenth century were merely the drawn-out completion of primary campaigns: the cloister quadrangle and lowest stage of the abortive bell tower at All Souls 1491–1510; and the final phases of Magdalen College—accounts survive recording payments in 1507–8 towards the building between the chapel and the tower, and in 1508–9 a total of £25 17s spent on the chaplains' building.[5] The Cistercian St Bernard's College was encour-

[1] Information from Dr Roger Highfield. Compare also the inventory of 1507 with that of 1483 in *Reg. ann. mert. 1483–1521*, 344–5 and 12–13 respectively.

[2] Ibid., 421; 'Oxford church notes 1643–4', ed R. Graham, *Collectanea* iv (OHS xlvii 1905), 122.

[3] J. R. Magrath, *The Queen's College, Oxford* (2 vols 1921) i. 165–70.

[4] *VCH Oxon.* iii. 90; L. F. Salzman, *Building in England down to 1540* (Oxford 1952, 2nd edn. 1967), 573–4.

[5] Magdalen College MS e ii 4. 3.

aged towards completion in 1502–17 by the abbot of Fountains, after decades of disgraceful stagnation. The chapel was erected, glazed and provided with plate, books and vestments, as was a small hall, probably intended to be replaced by a larger one later; and the walls of the north range were erected, making provision for the library in the upper storey. The chapel was tardily consecrated in 1530, but then building was once more delayed, leaving an incomplete quadrangle for Sir Thomas White to take over for his new foundation in 1557.[1]

The story of St Mary's College for Austin Canons, in what is now New Inn Hall Street, seems to have been similar. Building dragged on slowly from the foundation of the college in 1435 until in 1518 Cardinal Wolsey energetically urged it on. Although in this case the buildings did not long survive the dissolution, recent research has shown that St Mary's was architecturally important; it seems to have had a cloistered quadrangle predating Cardinal College, presumably inspired by Magdalen, and the chapel roof, which survives reused in the mid-seventeenth century chapel at Brasenose, is almost identical with the roof of the hall at Corpus and clearly the work of the same carpenter, Robert Carow, and the same designer, Humfrey Cooke, who went on to produce a more elaborate version of the same design for the hall at Cardinal College. Both features suggest the importance of Wolsey's intervention at St Mary's.[2]

Brasenose College

The first of the three new colleges to be begun was Brasenose.[3] The founders, William Smith, bishop of Lincoln and chancellor of the university, and Sir Richard Sutton, a layman and steward of Syon nunnery, acquired the lease of a quarry at Headington in late June 1509, the month in which the foundation stone was laid (at the entrance to what is now staircase 1); the final phase of building is represented by the only other documentary evidence about the construction process, a bill for £14 14s for lead for the tower roof, paid on 10 June 1518 by the college bursar to William Thomas, plumber. The college was founded for a society to consist of a principal and sixty scholars or more, according to the foundation charter of 1512, drawn up three years after the laying of the foundation stone. The later statutes provided for twelve scholars only, but clearly envisaged additional endowment, and allowed also for six

[1] H. M. Colvin, 'The building of St. Bernard's College', *Oxoniensia* xxiv (1959), 37–48.

[2] J. Blair, 'Frewin Hall, Oxford: a Norman mansion and a monastic college', *Oxoniensia* xliii (1978), 48–99.

[3] See *VCH Oxon*. iii. 214–15; E. W. Allfrey, 'The architectural history of the College', *Brasenose College Quatercentenary Monographs* (2 vols in 3 OHS lii–liv 1909) i. 5.

sons of noblemen. Since the first scholarships were endowed only in 1538, the building, which would house some eighty occupants, was only partly occupied.[1] It consisted of a single two-storeyed quadrangle, the hall and first-floor chapel occupying the south range, the library part of the upper storey of the north range, and the principal's lodging being over the entrance gateway in the centre of the east range with the treasury in the tower over it. Only the kitchen projected from the courtyard ranges, and it is generally accepted that this was taken over from one of the halls already standing on the site. The disposition of the chambers in the remainder of the quadrangle ranges is not entirely clear, since so much of the fenestration and internal partitioning has been altered; but a likely arrangement would have been eight in the west range, four lower and two upper in the north range, perhaps four in the east range, one under the chapel and two west of the hall in the south range, where it is known that the six sons of noblemen were assigned chambers. According to the statutes as revised by the co-founder, Sir Richard Sutton, the upper chambers were to have three occupants, the lower four, in accordance, that is to say, with what had been laid down for the fellows of New College in 1379 and practised there and at other late medieval colleges.

Whether the chambers were ever occupied in this way is not known; but from its earliest years the college had at its disposal other accommodation besides its new quadrangle. The founders had acquired besides the two academic halls, Brasenose Hall and Little University Hall, which provided the site for the new college, other halls extending southwards as far as the High Street. According to Anthony Wood, Little St Edmund Hall was used as 'lodging rooms' for students of the college until the chapel was put up in the middle of the following century, and Staple Hall on the opposite side of Schools Street was leased at 40s per annum to provide further chambers.[2]

The purchase of property south of the site of the quadrangle itself suggests furthermore that the founders intended that the college buildings should grow in the way they eventually did. Both the original chapel and the original library were seriously undersized and must have been considered temporary expedients from the outset. The ante-chapel nevertheless was given traceried windows of a sort unsuitable except in hall or chapel.

In the design and decoration of the early sixteenth-century

---

[1] See J. McConica, 'The rise of the undergraduate college', above, p. 11.

[2] A. Wood, *Survey of the Antiquities of the City of Oxford*, ed. A. Clark (3 vols OHS xv, xvii, xxxvii 1889–99) i. 85.

buildings, the most striking piece of display is the blind panel tracery applied to the inner and outer faces of the gatehouse tower at the level of the principal's lodging which is surmounted by battlements and angle pinnacles, behind which the tower climbs on for a further two storeys with a bay window awkwardly butting into the panelled battlements. This is clearly at attempt, perhaps an afterthought, to emulate or even outdo the two-storeyed, panelled bay windows on the founder's tower at Magdalen College, built to William Orchard's design in the 1480s. The four bay windows, on the other hand, distributed with rough symmetry on the entrance front of the college to left and right of the gate-tower are, to judge by their simplified mouldings, an Elizabethan improvement, connected with the extension of the principal's lodging across the upper storey of the front range. The other conspicuous features of the front range which were presumably original, visible in Loggan's print, but almost entirely masked when the range was heightened by a third storey, were the moulded brick chimneystacks, at least four groups of stacks rising from the front wall of the range, and others carried up the end gables to north and south. Inside what is now the History Library south of the gate-tower the lower parts of two shafts of one of these survive. The shafts are entirely of brick, cylindrical, one decorated with a bold spiral, the other with a lozenge pattern. No other similar chimneystack survives in Oxford, where such a use of brick is a surprise.

The only other part of the fabric of the Tudor college which had any architectural pretension was the timber roof of the hall, erected with the intention that it should be seen, but hidden from view since 1754 by a plaster ceiling. It is nevertheless handled more simply than the roofs of most college halls, having its main and subsidiary collar-beam trusses merely chamfered, and wind-braces between the purlins but no arched braces under the collar beams. One may therefore sum up the architectural effect of Brasenose College by saying that it had showy elements in the front range but consistently modest arrangements behind.

Corpus Christi College

The buildings of Corpus Christi College are almost contemporary with those of Brasenose. The site, on which five academic halls had stood, was acquired from the priory of St Frideswide, Oseney Abbey and Merton College. Negotiations with Merton were under way already in November 1511.[1] The first intention of the founder, Richard Fox, bishop of Winchester, was to provide a college where

[1] *Reg. ann. mert. 1483–1521*, 419.

monks of St Swithun's Priory, Winchester, could study at Oxford, along the lines of existing monastic colleges such as Canterbury and Durham. Fox managed things better than the Cistercians at St Bernard's or the Austin Canons at St Mary's.[1] An indenture dated 30 June 1513 states that building had already begun, to house a society which would consist of a warden, eight monks, two readers, two clerks and nine college servants; by March 1517 the quadrangle was ready for occupation. By that time, however, Fox had changed his mind, and the statutes of that year established a college of the normal type training men for the secular priesthood. There were to be a president, twenty fellows and twenty scholars ('discipuli' to be aged between 12 and 17), two chaplains, two clerks, two choristers, three readers (who might be fellows), four to six sons of noblemen or lawyers and eight college servants. This much enlarged society was furthermore to be distributed in the chambers less densely than had been envisaged in the statutes of earlier colleges from New College to Brasenose. Instead of three or four occupants to each chamber, there were to be only two, a fellow and the discipulus allotted to his supervision. The effect of this was to make the quadrangle too small as soon as it was occupied, and the surviving building accounts which start on 2 March 1517 record (among other things) the erection of additional chambers in the cloister quadrangle south-east of the main quadrangle. Whether the contract design in accordance with which the monastic college was being erected in June 1513 was modified in other important ways after Fox changed his intention cannot be known. There are, however, some interesting comparisons to be made with Brasenose. At Brasenose neither library nor chapel received adequate space, and the hall is treated semi-independently, being wider than the range in which it stands. At Corpus, however, where the setting out of the ranges is unaffected by pre-existing structures, the ranges are of different widths; the east (hall) range is 24 feet wide internally, the south (library) 21 feet (continued eastwards to give a chapel of the same width), whereas the west and north ranges are 18 feet, the standard width for chamber ranges from New College onwards. A further feature of the north range which suggests that it was set out to accommodate the maximum number of chambers, is the position of the gate-tower slightly off-centre, giving room on each floor for one chamber to the east of it and two to the west. It is in fact probable that twenty chambers would have been available in the main quadrangle for the twenty fellows and twenty discipuli, leaving the cloister quadrangle primarily for the other college personnel, and it is there that for instance

[1] Thomas Fowler, *The History of Corpus Christi College* (OHS xxv 1893), 60 ff.

Ludovicus Vives, the first Greek lecturer, is said to have had his chamber.

Bishop Fox secured first-rate craftsmen to design and supervise the erection of his college. His master-masons were William Vertue and William East. Vertue was one of the king's master masons and had in the preceding decade been involved in the design of Bath Abbey and the construction of the vault of St George's Chapel, Windsor.[1] In the indenture of June 1513 in which the erection of the college is referred to 'after the manner of a double platt made for the over and the nether lodginge' Vertue is named as one of the two 'Masters of the workes'. East is not so named, for the other master of the works was Humfrey Cooke, the master carpenter.[2] East may, however, have been in charge of works on site. He is named as master of the works with Vertue and Cooke in university proceedings in August 1514 which resulted from an affray led by a fellow of Brasenose College in which East was wounded and the others threatened. East came from Abingdon and in 1495–1501 had worked for the king on Woodstock Palace. He had been employed at Magdalen in 1505, but the building of Corpus was his first major job in the city. Later, however, he went on to act as master mason for the antechapel at Queen's, and in 1522 contracted for the south side of the new chapel at Balliol.[3] The work at Queen's overlapped with the later phases of building at Corpus, for which detailed accounts survive covering the period from March 1517 to November 1518.[4] During that time Vertue received a payment for eight days' attendance in June 1517 and another, of 10s, for six days in October/November of that year which included a visit to Taynton quarry. East on the other hand was employed on a contract basis, undertaking on 22 June 1517 to supply 760 foot of 'cresse table and severall table' (moulded string courses?) of Taynton stone at 4d the foot. Of the £13 owed to him under this contract he received instalments totalling only £10 during the eighteen months covered by the account. A similar contract was made with John Ward of Little Barrington for the windows of the cloister and chambers.

In view of the division of responsibility for mason's work at Corpus it is worth relating the design to Oxford college tradition. Not surprisingly perhaps, considering Bishop Fox's original intentions, the closest parallel is with the Cistercian St Bernard's College (still incomplete in 1513). Both have the hall and chapel in the range left of the gatehouse, the chambers mainly concentrated on the right

---

[1] E. A. Gee, 'Oxford masons, 1370–1530', *Archaeological Journal* cix (1952), 89–90.
[2] Fowler, 64–5; Reg. Chanc. 1506–14, fo 231.   [3] Gee, 88–9.
[4] Corpus Christi College Archives H/1/4/1.

and the library between the two occupying the upper storey in the range facing the gatehouse. Such an arrangement is a simplification of what was built in the late fourteenth century at New College. The way the gable-ends of the cross ranges are expressed at the ends of the street front is another direct link between St Bernard's and Corpus. The gate-tower itself is handled very similarly to the recent towers at St Bernard's and Balliol, with niches flanking an oriel and in the top storey a reverse arrangement of central niche flanked by windows. The vault supporting the tower, however, may be Vertue's contribution, for it is the earliest fan-vault under an Oxford gate-tower and started a fashion which did not die out until the early eighteenth century (Radcliffe gateway, University College, 1719). The other parts of the college do not lend themselves to such analysis; but it must be noted that the college walls were not of ashlar, as in all other recent colleges, but of rough rubbly stone, wholly or largely roughcast over.[1] The surviving account indicates how great a financial saving this made: John Franklin of Headington supplied freestone at a shilling the load, and ragstone at 13s 4d per hundred loads. Payments to Nicholas Herne and William Brytton for digging the foundations of the cloisters were made in May 1517, and John Ward, mason, was engaged in making windows for the cloister and chambers from August 1517 to February 1518. The windows were set up by Richard Parker, who also erected five freestone chimneys in the chambers over the cloister. The front quadrangle and the kitchen yard were both paved by John Townsend in 1517, and during the period of the account Richard Leyowse (Lewis) was employed building the boundary walls round the college, which varied greatly in height, only six feet high for a considerable stretch towards St Frideswide's but 18 or 19 feet in several other places.

The master carpenter at Corpus, Humfrey Cooke, was a London craftsman in royal employment comparable in standing with Vertue.[2] The hammerbeam roof of the hall, the most impressive piece of carpentry in the college, was completed before Bishop Fox's change of mind, for one of the corbels on which the wall pieces rest is carved with the words 'Sancti Swithini'. Much, however, still remained to be done in the primary buildings at the date, March 1517, when the surviving account begins, and Cooke's close involvement in the work

---

[1] This is clear from Loggan's print and Hegge's view of the sundial in the main quadrangle, reproduced as the frontispiece to Fowler. In 1801 it was resolved 'to substitute a facing of stone to the Walls, instead of following the late practice of Rough Cast'. The refacing was put in hand three years later: Fowler, 78. Original walling can still be seen on the south side of the south range.

[2] E. A. Gee, 'Oxford carpenters, 1370–1530', *Oxoniensia* xvii/xviii (1952–3), 134–6.

is clear. He received money with Vertue in June and November 1517, when they presumably came down from London together; but earlier that year, from 28 February to 13 March and again from 13 April to 2 May he received a daily wage of 1s 8d. It was Cooke who made the contracts with the joiners; on his visit to the college in November he received money with which to pay Thomas Russell of Westminster the carver of the bosses for the chapel ceiling; the contract, also datable to November 1517, for the roof and floor of the cloister chambers specifies that all is to be 'accordyng to a platt made by humfray Cooke'.

The executant carpenter was Robert Carow, the most active master carpenter resident in Oxford at this period, his major previous job being the carpentry of the bell tower at Magdalen.[1] He had already done work to the value of £93 13s 4d at Corpus before the surviving account opens. In May 1517 he received 40s for making twenty beds, presumably for the twenty fellows, at two shillings apiece. In November 1517 he contracted to make the roof and floor of the cloister chambers to Cooke's design.[2]

Joiner's work on the other hand was distributed among several different craftsmen. Roger Morwent made the woodwork (wainscot and furniture) of the president's lodging. The chapel and library wainscot were executed by Robert More and Roger Gryffyth respectively. In March 1517 Cornett Clerke contracted to make the sixteen library desks 'after the maner and fforme as they be in Magdaleyn College except the popie heeds off the seites'.

Ironwork, for window frames and locks of all sorts, is frequently mentioned in the accounts; but, oddly, there is only one payment for glass, of 23s 8d for 57 feet to Robert Glasyar in December 1517. Payments made during the period of the surviving account total £670.

Corpus then, in spite of the high quality of the master craftsmen employed by Fox, was a relatively modest and unostentatious building standing firmly in the tradition of Oxford collegiate building which went back at least to All Souls College of the mid-fifteenth century. Although Fox had close links with Magdalen, and John Claymond, the first president, migrated from there, the influence of Magdalen's buildings did not extend far at Corpus.

Cardinal College

The third and last of the new foundations in the early Tudor period, Wolsey's Cardinal College, was begun in January 1525 and left

---

[1] Ibid. 129-33.

[2] Corpus Christi College Archives H/1/4/1 fos 30^V and 55. Gee, 'Oxford carpenters', 131, wrongly associates this contract with the library.

unfinished at his fall in 1529.[1] This was an undertaking unprecedented in scale and ambition. The college was to be a society of 176
persons. To supply an income of £2,000 per year numerous monastic
houses were suppressed, besides the great Augustinian priory of
St Frideswide which provided Wolsey with a site. The total cost of
building the incomplete college is unknown, but from 16 January
1525 to 29 December 1527 expenditure on labour and materials
amounted to no less than £8,882.[2] Craftsmen were diverted from
Wolsey's own palace-buildings, York House in Whitehall, and
Hampton Court; at periods of greatest activity there were about 500
workmen on site. By the time work stopped hall and kitchen were
complete, the chambers in the rest of the south range and in two-
thirds of the west range were habitable, as was the south-west tower.
The gate-tower was half up and the walls of the chapel had risen
7 feet.

Like Bishop Fox at Corpus, Wolsey could employ senior royal
craftsmen to oversee his works. The master carpenters were the same
as Fox's. Humfrey Cooke with Robert Carow of Oxford as Warden
of the carpenters, i.e. chief executant. A vivid way of appreciating
the difference in conception between the two colleges is to compare
their hall roofs, the great rich mouldings of Cardinal College and the
plain sturdy timbers of Corpus, designed and executed by the same
craftsmen to the same basic pattern.[3] There were three master
masons, Henry Redman, who had been one of Wolsey's master
masons at York Place and Hampton Court, and who had collaborated
with William Vertue and Humfrey Cooke on the design of Lupton's
Tower at Eton College; John Lubyns, another royal craftsman of
twenty years' standing; and William Johnson, warden of the masons.
All three visited Oxford in February 1525 to compare a plan they
had made with the site for the college. Lubyns seems to have been
resident during building works, receiving a fee of £10 per annum,
and in 1528 he and Johnson undertook the second contract for
Balliol College chapel.

The college can best be assessed, however, if it is seen as a conscious

[1] The building of Cardinal College has been thoroughly discussed by John Harvey in
'The building works and architects of Cardinal Wolsey', *Journal of the British Archaeological Association*, 3rd ser. viii (1943), 48–59, and 'The building of Cardinal College,
Oxford', *Oxoniensia* viii, ix (1943–4), 145–53. Dean Higdon's daybook covering 28 January–
1 July 1525, analysed by J. G. Milne in ibid. 137–44, and four other summary building
accounts in the Public Record Office, SP 1/55, fos 221–38, E 101/479/9–11, together
cover the greater part of the building period. The detailed accounts for one fortnight in
November 1528, are transcribed in Bodl. MS Twyne 21, fos 350–6.

[2] PRO E 101/479/11.

[3] See *City of Oxford* (Royal Commission on Historical Monuments 1939), plates 81,
110.

attempt to exceed the scale and spendour of Magdalen, even though the college, like Wolsey's two great houses, was conceived on such a princely scale that any model was inevitably far transcended. Already in April 1528 Thomas Cromwell wrote to Wolsey: 'Every man thinks the like was never seen for largeness, beauty, sumptuous, curious and substantial building.'[1] Even in its incomplete state, lacking chapel and cloister, it is as regards size and elaboration quite without parallel in English collegiate building, and its great gateway is rich to a degree unrivalled by any Tudor palace before Nonsuch. The almshouses, on the other hand, which Wolsey erected across St Aldate's facing the college were quite modest. They partly survive in the street range of Pembroke College.

Wolsey had been bursar at Magdalen while it was still under construction. In financing his own foundation by the suppression of religious houses he followed where William of Waynflete had led, though on a daringly increased scale. Architecturally the links between the two colleges are fundamental. At both a cloister walk was to surround the main quadrangle. But whereas at Magdalen the upper chambers extended over the cloisters (as they do for instance in the vicars choral quadrangle at Hereford Cathedral), the cloisters at Cardinal College were to be attached to the inner face of each range, a broader (c 16 feet as against 10 feet) and a more open and airy arrangement, derived from monastic cloisters. At Magdalen the upper chambers extending over the cloister could be 27 feet deep, instead of the standard width of 18 feet. At Wolsey's college the ranges themselves were 27 feet wide internally excluding the cloister, giving both upper and lower chambers the spaciousness achieved only in the upper storey at Magdalen. This extra width gave room for a longer flight of stairs to the upper storey, so the chambers at Cardinal College are also of unprecedented height. This in its turn is expressed in the fenestration. Both the two-light chamber windows and those with single lights for the studies are lofty enough to have transoms. The south-west tower is besprinkled with the college rebus, a cardinal's hat, and the bay window soffit bears a remarkable piece of early renaissance decoration in the shape of putti carved practically in the round and flanking panels of arabesques and urns. As at Magdalen the hall at Cardinal College is raised on an undercroft. But in spite of the convenient orientation and great size of the quadrangle, hall and chapel were not set end to end in the same range as in the New College plan followed also at Magdalen. The hall was placed in the south range, the chapel set out on the north range facing the hall across the quadrangle. Its foundations were laid

[1] *L & P Henry VIII* iv. no. 4135.

and 7 feet of the side walls had been erected before work stopped in 1529; but although they survived until the 1660s and John Aubrey sketched the basement moulding and decorative band before the walls were swept away for Dean Fell's north range, the plan of the chapel is not known, and in particular it is not clear how long it was intended to be.[1]

Whatever its length, the chapel, and any intended ante-chapel, would doubtless have been laid out so as to preserve the overall symmetry of the west front of the college. The conception of this front is the clearest evidence of a new approach to collegiate design, for it is the first college to have a façade contrived at the expense of practical arrangements. During the 1520s only two-thirds of the entrance range was put in hand, the range of chambers north of the great gateway being finished off with a cross-wall halfway along. The lop-sided appearance this gave can be seen in Bereblock's view of 1566. But one can feel certain that a completion of the range along the lines adopted in the present building of the 1660s was intended from the start; the great gateway and the south 'tower' projecting from the south-west angle of the quadrangle, both with mighty polygonal angle-turrets, are proportioned to read as the major accents of a façade 300 feet long. In the chamber ranges between, the tremendous array of large, if irregularly spaced, windows was made possible by siting the fireplaces, and thus the chimneybreasts, not in the external wall, as was the case in the south and east ranges and as had been the universal medieval practice, but in the wall towards the quadrangle. The further visual advantage of displacing the chimneys in this way was to leave the skyline of the street front free for a display of armorial beasts bearing banners, as Bereblock's view shows.

The intended layout of Wolsey's college is not clear in all its details. Presumably the south-west tower was to have housed the dean, though the lodging of the dean of Christ Church from 1546 was transferred to the east range to be nearer the church of St Frideswide, which would not under Wolsey's scheme have been spared. Wolsey's major omission was adequate space for a library. It is inconceivable that he did not intend one; but even in the early years of Christ Church there seems to have been no proper library, for it was not until 1563 that second-hand stalls and desks were acquired from the library of the theology school and placed in the former

---

[1] A wooden roof for the chapel was constructed down-river at Sonning in 1528-9. Sir Alfred Clapham made the attractive suggestion that Henry VIII appropriated this roof and made use of it in his chapel at Hampton Court: see J. Harvey, 'Building works and architects', 151. If the suggestion is correct, the chapel at Cardinal College will have been set out with a width of 33 feet, but its length cannot validly be deduced from the length of the Hampton Court chapel.

monastic refectory.[1] Wolsey may have intended to erect a library on the site of Peckwater's Inn, which he had acquired, and where masons were lodged during the building process.[2]

The fall of Wolsey in 1529, followed by the suppression of monastic colleges in the mid-1540s, left Oxford with a surplus of collegiate buildings; for Henry VIII's college, which had taken over the buildings of Cardinal College, and the monastic foundations, Canterbury College, Durham College, Gloucester College and the colleges of St Bernard and St Mary all became redundant. The new foundations of the mid-sixteenth century merely took over existing buildings with the minimum of adaptation; thus in 1546 Henry VIII's new foundation of Christ Church reoccupied Wolsey's buildings, together with a considerably extended site which included the quadrangle of Canterbury College; Durham College, suppressed in 1544, provided the buildings for Sir Thomas Pope's Trinity College, founded in 1555–6; similarly, Sir Thomas White in 1555 acquired the buildings of St Bernard's College for his new foundation, St John's College; and in 1560 Gloucester Hall was founded, taking over the somewhat dilapidated buildings of the Benedictine Gloucester College. Only the buildings of St Mary's College fell into the hands of a townsman and were largely demolished.

That exhausted the usable monastic structures. Jesus College, founded in 1571, was established in what had been two academic halls, Great and Little White Hall, just inside the north wall of the city in Somenor's Lane and Cheyney Lane (Market Street). To the south and west the founder, Dr Hugh Price, seems to have erected c 1571–4 an L-shaped block of chambers.[3]

Between 1530 and the end of the century little new building of architectural significance was put in hand at any of the established colleges. At Oriel the hall was rebuilt c 1534–5; at New College the warden's lodging was heightened by an extra storey in 1540–1; at All Souls the unfinished steeple in the cloister was converted in 1572 into a block of four chambers; at St John's the east range of the unfinished quadrangle of St Bernard's College was completed, giving lodging for the president where the library was to have been, and in 1596–1601 a new freestanding range of chambers with a library over was erected beyond the south-east corner of the college. Only in the

[1] W. G. Hiscock, *A Christ Church Miscellany* (Oxford 1946), 1–3.
[2] Bodl. MS Twyne 21, fo 351.
[3] *VCH Oxon.* iii. 271, and see Loggan's print.

first decades of the seventeenth century did a new building boom begin in the Oxford colleges; but it was a boom which had been prepared for in the Elizabethan years, and which can only be explained by a consideration of the major changes in college life which had taken place before the turn of the century and which had produced many minor modifications to the structure and fittings of every college. These changes had two main causes, the greater privacy and comfort demanded in institutions of learning during the Tudor period just as they were being demanded in domestic accommodation at every level of society; and the pressure of rapidly increasing numbers of undergraduate members of colleges during the second half of the century, especially in the years after the matriculation statutes of 1565 and 1581.

In order to appreciate the changes most vividly it will be best to consider individually the various elements of the typical college, hall, chapel, library, lodging of the head and chambers of the other college members.

The Hall

The function of the hall as the place where members of the college ate together day by day did not change during the Tudor period—any more than it has done since. In some, perhaps most, colleges it was put to other uses too. The lectures which were ordered to be given at Merton, Queen's, New College and All Souls from 1535 were probably delivered in college halls. At Merton, for instance, fellows were ordered to lecture on set texts 'in alta aula' in 1537, 1539, 1548 and 1566.[1] Bachelors' disputations were also held in hall at Merton so regularly that in 1565 a fixed seating pattern was agreed.[2] Formal meetings of the governing body of the college for elections and scrutinies seem also as a general rule to have been held in hall. At Oriel on the contrary, the other college where the appropriate information has been preserved from the beginning of the sixteenth century, no formal meeting of the fellows is recorded as having taken place in hall until 1545; meetings took place usually in the chapel or 'cipharia' but occasionally in the provost's chamber. Financial matters were naturally discussed in the treasury, or audit chamber. But in 1565 it suddenly became usual to meet in the hall.[3] Practice no doubt varied from college to college, as it clearly varied from time to time within one college.

There is evidence that at some, but by no means all, colleges the

---

[1] See *Reg. ann. mert. 1521–67*, 68, 77, 140, 264.
[2] Ibid. 254.
[3] *Dean's Register of Oriel*, passim.

open hearth or brazier sending smoke through the hall and out of a louvre on the roof ridge was early abandoned in favour of an enclosed fireplace and chimney; by 1500 this had taken place at Queen's, Magdalen and New College.[1] Yet the new-built colleges of the Tudor period were provided with hall louvres and open hearths, and the same is true of the halls rebuilt in the seventeenth century; for fires were lit in college halls only on special occasions.

Draughts in hall, on the other hand, were considered in the early sixteenth century to be no longer endurable, and a panelled dado or 'ceiling' came to be fixed round the lower parts of the walls and across the screen. Until then walls had been generally covered with hangings of some sort. Entries in the treasurer's accounts at Oriel illustrate this, in 1493-4 for washing the hangings in the hall, and in 1516-17 for their cords.[2] Some of these hangings must have been highly decorative: the series of inventories of the monastic Canterbury College extending from 1443 to 1534 records various patterned hangings in the hall, and in the early 1520s the prior of Christ Church, Canterbury, donated a particularly spendid one decorated with angels and figures of the prophets and patriarchs.[3]

The following decades seem to have been the period of change. Money had been left in 1512 for hangings and other improvements to Merton hall, and Warden Chambre (1525-44) gave a set of 'clothes of Arras' to hang round the hall, but a mid-seventeenth-century visitor to the. college noted the date 1540 carved in wood on wainscot at the upper end of the hall.[4] The earliest datable panelling to survive is at New College, of 1533-5.[5] Here the complete scheme is preserved, linenfold panelling 12 feet high covering the screen at the lower end and its doors and the side-walls of the hall between the windows, and similar panelling rising higher on the three sides of the dais, where it is crowned by a shallow vaulted canopy. Cresting runs round the whole, carved with foliage and shield-bearing putti of a renaissance character and heads in roundels, and punctuated by undersized obelisk-like pinnacles.[6] At the same time the roof was ceiled—bosses survive bearing the monogram of John London, warden 1526-42. The next surviving scheme is at Magdalen and bears

[1] E. A. Gee, 'A history of Oxford collegiate architecture from 1370 to 1530' (Oxford DPhil thesis 1953), 315, 343, 295.

[2] Oriel College Archives Provost Shadwell's transcripts, vols vi, ix.

[3] *Canterbury College*, ed. W. A. Pantin (3 vols OHS new ser. vi–viii 1941–4) i. esp. 69.

[4] *Reg. ann. mert. 1483–1521*, 421; *Reg. ann. mert. 1567–1603* (*sub* 1586); *Collectanea* iv. 123.

[5] *VCH Oxon.* iii. 147.

[6] *City of Oxford*, plate 153; G. Jackson-Stops, 'Gains and losses: the college buildings, 1404–1750', in John Buxton and Penry Williams (eds), *New College, Oxford, 1379–1979* (Oxford 1979), 197.

the date 1541. Previously there had been hangings, and the roof was ceiled at the same time as the walls were wainscotted.[1] Here the design is less advanced, having an almost wholly gothic feeling, but in the centre of the dais end there is an impressive set of nine carved panels, with scenes of the life of St Mary Magdalen above and royal armorial devices and a demi-figure of Henry VIII below.[2]

Both the New College and the Magdalen sets of panelling incorporate armorial shields of benefactors. During the sixteenth century, however, it continued to be the practice to place the arms of benefactors in the glass of hall windows. A small part survives, much restored, of the spectacular display of Wolsey's arms and motto supplied for the hall at Cardinal College in 1528 by the leading London glazier, James Nicholson—forty-seven armorial panels at 6s 8d each and 246 panes at 12d each bearing the Cardinal's motto, *Dominus mihi adiutor*.[3] Much more humbly, the benefaction at Merton mentioned above was in part at least put towards the insertion in 1517 of glass at the dais end of the hall bearing the arms of Walter de Merton.[4] At Exeter one of the ways in which the benefactions of Sir William Petre were recorded was by paying 42s 8d in 1566–7 to a London glazier for glass bearing Petre's arms and inserting it in the hall windows.[5] At New College shields of arms— Archbishop Warham, Edward prince of Wales—were added to the series of fourteenth-century shields: Warham's cost 6s 8d in 1527 and in 1534 'sex pecys off Armys' for the hall cost 17s 4d.[6]

Plate

Towards the end of the century colleges began to build up their holdings of plate once more, but now most of the plate was secular, for the buttery and the head's lodging rather than for the chapel. Certain colleges received bequests of secular plate, Corpus in 1558, Brasenose in 1587;[7] but plate collections normally grew by gifts from scholars, probationary fellows or fellow commoners. In 1571 Warden Hovenden of All Souls decreed that each probationer should present to the college a piece of plate or 20s in lieu, and by the 1590s a new pot or two was coming in each year. Similarly at Exeter,

[1] Macray, *Reg. Magdalen* ii. 19–20. However, Dr Gee notes heavy expenditure on carpenters' work in the hall in 1520–1, and concludes that this was a first phase of wainscotting.

[2] *City of Oxford*, plates 50, 127, 137

[3] Bodl. MS Twyne 21, fo 352.

[4] *Collectanea* iv. 122.

[5] Exeter College Archives A II 9, volume of rector's accounts, 1566–1639.

[6] What survived was in 1865 reset in the windows of the hall staircase. C. Woodforde, *The Stained Glass of New College, Oxford* (Oxford 1951) 10, 62, 93–4.

[7] Fowler, *Corpus Christi College*, 100: A. J. Butler, 'The college plate', *Brasenose Monographs* i. no. 5, 21.

Rector Glasier in 1578 began the practice of taking 10s from each fellow at his first admission for the purchase of plate.[1] The dean's register at Oriel records the decision in 1588 that scholars were to present pieces of plate to the college on election, and that in 1599 the minimum value of such pieces was set at 50s.[2] At Balliol the practice was delayed until as late as 1609, with the first admission of fellow commoners.[3] At many colleges, however, notably Christ Church, Magdalen, Oriel and St John's, pieces of such plate, engraved with the names or arms of the donors, were being received by the 1590s.[4]

The Chapel

The chapel was the other main venue for official college meetings, besides its daily use for the saying of the offices. Disputations sometimes took place there too. These varied uses had, since the building of New College, made it fashionable to preface the chapel with an ante-chapel at right angles, about as large in ground area as the chapel itself, and divided longitudinally by an arcade on slender piers. This never became a standard feature. At Queen's the ante-chapel added in 1516–18 measured 33 feet by 48 feet internally, larger than the chapel itself, which was only 42 feet long and 22 feet wide. At Balliol, on the other hand, the chapel rebuilt in 1522–9 had only a small ante-chapel no wider than the chapel itself; and the other new full-sized sixteenth-century chapel, at Corpus, has a similar, if slightly larger, ante-chapel. The T-plan arrangement recurs in the seventeenth century, at Wadham, 1610–13, at Oriel, in truncated form, 1637–42, and finally at Brasenose, 1656–9, where it is possible that the intention to build a chapel of this form goes back to the foundation of the college in the early sixteenth century.

A number of college heads and fellows were buried in chapels during the Tudor period. Monuments were rare until the end of the century, being confined to founders and special benefactors. Thus the donor of the ante-chapel at Queen's was commemorated by a large brass at its centre; the remarkable, if artistically undistinguished, shroud brass to John Claymond, first president of Corpus, was laid down in the 1530s in the centre of the chapel itself; and for the founder of Trinity, Sir Thomas Pope (died 1559) and his wife a fine freestone monument was set up in the chapel in 1566–7. In

[1] All Souls Vellum Inventory fo 44; plate list at the beginning of Exeter College Rector's Accounts 1566–1639.

[2] *Dean's Register of Oriel*, 213.

[3] Balliol College Plate Book 1607–88.

[4] Hiscock, *Christ Church Miscellany*, 135; Macray, *Reg. Magdalen* iii. 197–9; Oriel College Muniments ETC 8, 1–3; St John's College MS Acc vi A 1, F3. 16.

1568, soon after the virtual refoundation of Exeter College, a monument to Walter de Stapledon was erected there, the gift of Bishop Alley. At St John's, however, piety towards the founder was not expressed in this way, in spite of a legacy of 100 marks as late as 1606 'given to the buildinge of a Tombe for our founder'.[1]

Some idea has already been given of the wealth of fittings which a college could attract for the embellishment of its chapel in the decades immediately before the reformation.[2] The tradition of filling the windows with stained glass continued also. At both Queen's and Balliol a substantial amount of early sixteenth-century chapel glass survives. At Queen's fifteen figures and shields of arms, some dated 1518, have been reset in later backgrounds in the late seventeenth-century chapel. At Balliol the glass, much restored, has been reset in something resembling its original arrangement in the chapel. The east window, given by Lawrence Stubbs, brother of the Master, in 1529, has scenes of the passion and ascension of Christ; the eastern-most window on the south side has six scenes from the legend of St Catherine, dated 1529, given by the master, Richard Stubbs, and his brother Lawrence. In the other side-windows are figures of saints under canopies, and arms and inscriptions dated 1530 and recording various benefactions towards the glass. In both these sets of glass renaissance influence is discernible, at Queen's in the excessive modelling of the faces, and at Balliol in the derivation of two of the passion scenes in the east window from the prints by Dürer, the Agony in the Garden and Ecce Homo of his 'Engraved Passion'.

With the reformation the embellishment of chapels and their equipment with a superabundance of plate, vestments and fittings came to an abrupt halt, and widespread destruction and defacement ensued. The reign of the catholic Mary saw a beginning of reparation but it was too short to restore all that had been laid waste under Henry VIII and his son; and by the 1570s even the most prudent colleges saw that under Elizabeth's ecclesiastical policy they could safely realize the cash value of their remaining church goods.[3]

The Library

One might have expected much enlargement of library buildings in the century which followed the invention of printing. Dr Neil Ker has shown that, on the contrary, a sharp reduction in book bequests, and stringent policies against the retention of duplicates or the in-

[1] VCH Oxon. iii. 137; Fowler, Corpus Christi College, 83; City of Oxford, 111; Reg. Univ. ed. Boase, p. v; St John's College MS Acc vi. A. 2/F3. 17, p. 25.

[2] See too the heavy expenditure at Magdalen on the chapel and its goods as late as 1534, 1538 and 1541, Macray, Reg. Magdalen ii. 13.

[3] See chapter 6 for a more detailed account of this subject.

discriminate chaining of books, kept the size of college libraries in bounds during this period. Only at New College was any increase made in usable library space. There a new room for law books had been constructed over the chequer *c* 1480, and a century later, *c* 1585, the roof space of the main library was ceiled over and the attic thus formed devoted to a manuscript library.[1] No other college made use of this expedient, for from the mid-1580s a new method of storing books came into fashion, and so dramatic was the resultant saving in space that in less than a quarter of a century it was almost universally adopted in Oxford.

Medieval libraries were equipped with cases with sloping lectern-tops on which the chained books lay both when they were shut and when open and in use by readers. More books could be stored, probably lying on their sides, on the shelf or shelves which seem to have been provided below the lectern top. The shelving of books in the manner familiar today (but with their fore-edges outwards to allow for chaining) was first employed in Oxford when the present stalls were erected in the west library of Merton in 1589–90. These had two shelves for folio volumes above the reading shelf and were placed where the lecterns had been, projecting into the library at right angles to the side walls, the readers' benches (aligned on the windows of each bay) being retained. In 1596–7 stalls three shelves high were fitted at All Souls, increasing the shelf-space there ten fold. By 1610 the change from lecterns to stalls had been made at Queen's, St John's, Duke Humphrey (1598–1600), New College (1602–6), Corpus (1604), Magdalen and Christ Church (both 1610–11). Stalls, being higher and bulkier than lecterns, must have made the medieval library rooms appear dark and oppressive. At Merton lighting was soon improved, as dormer windows were inserted in the roof in the 1590s. At All Souls however, where the splendidly enriched plaster vault bears the date 1598, recent investigation suggests that the library had previously had a plain plaster barrel-vault and not an open timber roof.

The great new library of St John's, erected and fitted up in 1595–1601, was the first in Oxford to be designed for the new stall system. In fact the bay-width there, of 10 feet, proved to be excessive, for, although the stalls at St John's were made deeper than the depth required by two folio volumes back-to-back, the space between stalls was still too great for the comfort of readers seated at fixed benches. General illumination was provided by a large mullioned and transomed bay window in the east wall.[2]

[1] *VCH Oxon.* iii. 148.

[2] J. Newman, 'Oxford libraries before 1800', *Archaeological Journal* cxxxv (1978), 248–57 with bibliography.

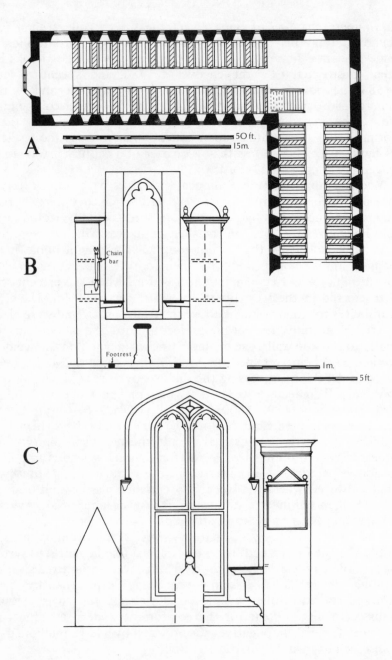

Library furniture: A–B, *Merton College Library*, as fitted with stalls from 1589: A, plan (after Clark), B, end bay in south range; and C, *Duke Humfrey's Library*, showing (left) medieval lectern, and (right) Bodley's stalls of 1598–9.

Common Rooms and Common Spaces

There is evidence that during the sixteenth century the need was first felt for common rooms. While monastic traditions continued to influence college life common rooms were inevitably frowned upon. In 1547 the senior fellows of New College were ordered to desist from using the chequer as a private dining room. The earliest neutral reference to anything approaching a fellows' common room seems to be at St John's, where Sir Thomas White in his statutes of 1556 designated the upper storey of the south half of the east range as a 'superius ambulacrum' reserved for the use of fellows.[1] But the common room in the modern sense of the term is at Oxford an innovation of the mid-seventeenth century.

The other communal spaces within colleges were outdoor, gardens and ball-courts (mentioned in accounts at Queen's in 1583, at Exeter in 1590), where the fellows, most of whom were under thirty, and the scholars, almost all under twenty, could take more or less strenuous exercise. Other sports were pursued outside the college confines, particularly archery: bows and arrows occur regularly in inventories throughout the sixteenth century. In the 1590s James Whitelocke when fellow of St John's hunted the hare 'as his only exercise of the body', and an inventory of 1602 includes for the first time '2 birdinge pices'.[2]

The Lodging of the Head

The residential parts of the colleges comprised two separate elements, the lodging of the head of the house and the fellows' and scholars' chambers. It was here more than anywhere else in the colleges that fundamental developments took place during the Tudor period. The changes resulted primarily from an expectation of increased comfort and privacy, an expectation largely offset for the ordinary members of colleges by the great expansion in numbers during the second half of the sixteenth century.

Heads of houses of course were not directly affected by the expanding numbers in colleges, at least as far as their living-quarters were concerned. It is possible to distinguish two types of accommodation for heads of houses in the late medieval period, types which reflect the two contrasting functions of the head of house. In the first place, he was the custodian of the college valuables, and

---

[1] A. H. Smith, *New College, Oxford, and its Buildings* (1952), 73–4; W. H. Stevenson and H. E. Salter, *The Early History of St. John's College* (OHS new ser. i. 1939), 106.

[2] *The Liber Famelicus of Sir James Whitelocke*, ed. John Bruce (Camden Society lxx 1858), 14; Chanc. Court Inv., inventory of John Bayle.

responsible for the safety and discipline of the other members of the college; so his lodging was naturally over the entrance gateway and under the treasury, which could only be reached by passing through his chamber. The fifteenth-century gate-towers of All Souls, Balliol and St Bernard's reflect this conception of the head's duties, and Brasenose and Corpus repeat it in the early sixteenth century. In all these gate-towers the head's chamber is lit by an outward-facing oriel window and, generally, by a second oriel facing into the college quadrangle. At All Souls, it seems, the warden never occupied this chamber as his lodgings. Inventories of the monastic Canterbury College show the warden's chamber to have been in use in the early sixteenth century only as a treasury and office. In the early 1520s the prior of Christ Church, Canterbury, allowed a bed and hangings to be installed there, but by 1534 these had disappeared again.[1]

At New College, however, William of Wykeham had made provision for a head of a different sort.[2] The warden, although he had to reside in college for ten months of the year, and although his lodging was situated over the entrance gateway, was forbidden to dine in hall with the fellows except at gaudies and even then had to sit alone and be served with food from his own kitchen. This allowed him to carry out more effectively the second major role of the head of house, which required him to act as a sort of patron of the college, negotiating for its welfare with influential ecclesiastics and statesmen. The lodging with which he was provided allowed him to entertain sumptuously, and the college treasury came to be segregated from his quarters in a separate muniment tower.

At some of the early colleges, where by about 1500 the head had his lodging adjacent to the upper end of the hall, one may suspect that this latter conception of the head's duties prevailed, as at Merton under Fitzjames, and at Queen's and Lincoln Colleges. But this position never became the norm at Oxford in the way that it was at Cambridge. At Balliol the two types of accommodation appear to have been combined, for besides the oriel-windowed gate-tower the master had a lodging adjoining the upper end of the hall, and it too was given a handsome oriel window in the late fifteenth-century (bearing the arms of William Grey, bishop of Ely, who died in 1478). What Wolsey intended at Cardinal College is not clear, but it may well have followed the pattern of New College, already repeated at Magdalen, since the dean's lodging occupied the

[1] *VCH Oxon.* iii. 187; *Canterbury College*, ed. Pantin i. esp. 68. 75.

[2] For the enlargement of the warden's lodging at New College see Jackson-Stops in *New College, Oxford*, 198–200.

southwest 'tower' with its oriel window to the street, and a muniment tower stood over the staircase to the hall.

During the sixteenth century college heads showed a clear preference for the lordly rather than the custodial type of lodging. There was a tendency for the larger lodgings to expand. Warden Fitzjames's additions at Merton in the first decade of the century have been mentioned already. But the warden's lodging there further increased from five to eleven rooms between 1508 and 1525, as inventories show. At New College the substantial sum of £134 3s 10¾d was spent in 1540-1 on enlarging the warden's lodging.[1] At Magdalen the president's lodging, which had begun in the founder's tower, grew quickly westwards. Additions or improvements were made in 1485, 1530 (at a cost of £65), 1557, 1562-3 (for a married president whose wife was at the same time provided with a seat in chapel) and 1568.[2] Similar developments took place at some, but not all, of the poorer colleges. The master of University College was first allotted a lodging of his own as a result of the new statutes of 1476-8. This was in the gate-tower. In 1531, however, Little University Hall, a house standing on the High Street immediately east of the college, was appropriated as the master's lodging and he surrendered the tower room for the use of a fellow. The lodging was 'restored and beautified' by Master Key in 1564, and inventories of 1572 and 1587 list nine rooms, hall, upper hall, gallery, parlour and five bedchambers.[3]

A similar migration took place at All Souls, where new lodgings were built east of the High Street front in 1553 for £36 16s 8d. The warden then surrendered the tower room (but kept the south-east corner chamber in the quadrangle). His new quarters had a first-floor hall with a kitchen under it, a parlour, two chambers and a gallery running over the whole lodging.[4]

Developments at Corpus were more elaborate. There the statutes ordained that the president should take the two main meals in the college hall each day. His chamber was in the tower. From 1572, however, President Cole, the first married head of the college, became a semi-absentee, living with his family in Lower Heyford. In 1599 his successor, the unmarried President Rainolds, enlarged the lodging in the street range of the main quadrangle, adding a gallery, parlour and kitchen, with a two-storey porch in the corner of the quadrangle and a kitchen chimneybreast which encroached awkwardly on the street.

[1] VCH Oxon. iii. 149.
[2] Macray, Reg. Magdalen ii. 35.
[3] VCH Oxon. iii. 64, 73; Chanc. Court Inv., University College MS HH Fasc. 5 no. 2.
[4] VCH Oxon. iii. 188.

In 1607, however, Rainolds was succeeded by another married president, for whom the college spent about £300 in that year on a new freestanding house, set immediately south-west of the college precinct, where he could live with his family. Rainolds's enlarged lodging was also retained for the president's use until it was finally surrendered in 1689.[1]

At St John's the founder, Sir Thomas White, placed the president's lodging not in the tower, as the builder of St Bernard's College had intended, but in the east range of the quadrangle, thus giving his president spacious accommodation at the expense of adequate room for the college library.

By 1600 perhaps only the provost of Oriel and the principal of Brasenose inhabited chambers in the gate-tower. Rector Prideaux's early seventeenth-century account of the rector's lodging at Exeter, however, suggests that the treasury in the tower there could not be reached except through the lodging.

The lodgings of heads were naturally fitted to a higher standard than were fellows' chambers. At Corpus for instance in 1517 joinery in the president's parlour consisted of a bench 18 foot long, wainscot beneath and above the windows, a draught-excluding portal (and another in the chamber above), two cupboards and a ceiling 'with panys glued and ffrett with well ynbowed batons of a yard square'.[2] That is half a century before the wainscotting of fellows' chambers is heard of and a full century before it became normal. Then some time between 1556 and 1571 the president's chamber at Corpus was enriched with a splendid plaster ceiling, still surviving, with arms of the colleges in the frieze below.

At Merton, on the other hand, the series of inventories of the warden's lodging, which extends from 1507 to 1586, makes no mention of wainscot but refers to hangings in most of the rooms. That wainscot was something special throughout most of the period is suggested by the name 'wainscot chamber' still attaching to one of the rooms in the master's lodging at University College as late as 1587, by which time all his rooms were at least partly wainscotted.

The Merton inventories give a good impression of the furnishing of a head's lodging.[3] Naturally they list only the college property found there. The hall contained nothing but a long table with trestles and one or two forms and cupboards. Each chamber was dominated by a bedstead with its hangings of red or green say or silk and various

[1] *The Pelican Record* (Corpus Christi College, Oxford) xxxii (1959), 123–9.

[2] Corpus Christi College Archives H/1/4/1 fo 3.

[3] See *Reg. ann. mert. 1483–1521*, for inventories of 1507 and 1508; *Reg. ann. mert. 1521–1567*, for those of 1525, 1544 and 1586, and Merton College MSS 3112 (1561) and 3366 (1568).

plain and patterned coverlets; chests and cupboards are listed there, and very occasionally a table and chair. In some chambers a form or two stood by the bed. In the parlour, first listed as such in 1525, was a long table, four or so forms, three or so stools, one spruce chair (replaced by seven chairs in 1586). Other rooms were the chapel (until 1544), kitchen and buttery (both from 1525 onwards). The furniture of the whole lodging remained strikingly constant over the years, with a gradual increase in the number of such items as cupboards, coverlets and cushions. College property in the master's lodging at University College in 1587 was very similarly distributed through the various rooms. In the gallery, however, was a table and three forms, mats on the floor and a fine display of fifteen maps and pictures of the seven liberal arts.

But that gives only half the picture. The exceptionally full and vivid inventory of the lodgings at University College taken when Master Key died in May 1572 lists besides these items a great deal more which must have been Key's personal property.[1] In his own chamber besides the bed, bedding and hangings, four chairs are listed (one of them being a close-stool) and fourteen cushions, a looking glass, a desk covered with red velvet and matching hangings and carpet. In the two halls and the gallery Key had a collection of pictures of exceptional size and variety for its date. In the lower hall there normally stood a pair of virginals on a pillared table. The rector's lodgings at Exeter College in the time of Thomas Glasier (died 1592) were smaller and more modestly furnished. He was married, had a house 'in Bocardo', i.e. by the North Gate, and may have been non-resident. Of his four chambers only two contained beds. There were virginals in the dining chamber and in the hall four chairs and six stools as well as three pictures.[2]

Fellows' Chambers

The other college members lodged in chambers throughout the remainder of the college buildings. Before the sixteenth century no college building was more than two storeys high. Chambers on the upper floor were preferable to the lower chambers, which generally had earth floors and no hearths. The upper chambers may well have been uncomfortably draughty too, for they were normally open to the roof and it is doubtful whether chamber windows, which were universally of two lights, had begun to be glazed before the early sixteenth century. The chamber walls were normally of plaster and given a periodic whitewash. Panelling in fellows' chambers was rare before the end of the century (for example, Christ Church 1578–9,

[1] Chanc. Court. Inv. Hyp. B. 15 and 12.   [2] See pp. 634–40 below.

University 1587, All Souls 1590) and at All Souls it was forbidden for a time by an injunction of 1602. In each chamber a timber-framed study was provided for each occupant, roughly 8 foot square and lit by a single-light window. One survives at St John's (staircase 4.2), set under the stairs, with a stud and panel wall crowned by a moulded cornice about one foot below the ceiling of the chamber. In the studies, which were lockable, the fellows and other inmates worked, the chamber forming a communal bedroom. This, the standard late medieval arrangement, had been established at New College, the upper chambers being fitted for four occupants, the lower for three. The upper chambers were allocated to senior fellows.[1] The statutes of Magdalen and Brasenose allocated members similarly. It became common in the sixteenth century for a fellow to share his chamber with a scholar whom he tutored and who acted as his personal servant. This is clearly what is envisaged by the provisions in the statutes of Magdalen College, that in the upper chambers there shall be two chief and two truckle beds, and two chief and one truckle bed in the lower.

At Corpus, however, Bishop Fox laid down that each chamber should be occupied by only one fellow and one scholar. In this he may have been affected by the practice in the monastic colleges, Canterbury, Durham and St Bernard's, where the average age of students was considerably higher. Detailed descriptions of the latter two drawn up in 1546 show that no chamber had more than one study,[2] although the chambers in St Bernard's were given four single-light windows each, so a denser population could have been accommodated if required. At Merton early in the century, when the number of fellows was somewhat depleted, we find from inventories in 1509 and 1512 that senior fellows were occupying two chambers apiece, one having a study in each chamber, the other a chamber with a study and a chamber lacking a study but having a bed for his 'boy'.[3] To judge from the evidence of college accounts, fellows rarely seem to have shared chambers with one another in the sixteenth century.

The physical evidence at St John's of the chambers under the library built in 1596, revealed in 1975, showed that, unlike the fifteenth-century chambers, each was provided with only two single-light windows, presumably to light studies for one fellow and one pupil. And in this instance the study windows were widened into

[1] See A. H. M. Jones's accounts of the chambers at New College and All Souls in *VCH Oxon.* iii. 150–1 and 187–9.

[2] This is pointed out in Stevenson and Salter, *Early History of St. John's*, 54.

[3] *Reg. ann. mert. 1483–1521*, 396, 425.

two-lighters before long.[1] At the end of the sixteenth century fellows in at least some colleges did not have pupils living in their chambers. This was the case at Christ Church, where Broadgates Hall served as an annexe, and only the senior students living in the prebendal houses had resident pupils.[2]

The improvement of chambers in the direction of greater comfort began in the early sixteenth century. At Magdalen, for instance, the lower chambers seem originally to have had earth floors, but in 1515–16 the college undertook a campaign of boarding them.[3] The lower chambers at New College were boarded in 1536.[4] But at other colleges earth floors persisted until the latter part of the century. At Brasenose Alexander Nowell, dean of St Paul's, paid £40 in 1572 to lay floorboards throughout the lower chambers, which were 'dampeshe and unholsome beyng unboorded'.[5] At Christ Church the buildings of Peckwater Inn were greatly improved at the end of the century and this included in 1598–9 'scruyng up the timber worke of vi chambers . . . whereof the lower chambers were lower, then was fit for the helth of students'.[6]

The lower chambers of the medieval colleges generally had no fire-places. Sixteenth-century college building accounts contain many references to work on chamber chimneys and hearths, but rarely in terms which make it clear that they were being newly inserted. It is possible that well after the Tudor period some lower chambers still lacked hearths. Loggan's meticulous engravings suggest that as late as the early 1670s there were hearthless chambers in the south range at St John's, below the library at Corpus, and on the street front at Lincoln.[7]

The glazing of chamber windows is also hard to be definite about, for at first glazed windows were often movable and thus might be the personal property of fellows; so the evidence of college accounts may well give a misleading impression. The early sixteenth-century inventories of fellows' chambers at Merton list window glazing as part of the fittings: in 1509 Mr Walker moved into lodgings of which the lower chamber had two north windows entirely glazed and one south window half glazed, and a study with a half-glazed window,

[1] Mr H. M. Colvin kindly pointed this out to the writer when the building was stripped of panelling.

[2] See *Memorials of Father Augustine Baker*, ed. J. McCann and H. Connolly (Catholic Record Society 1933), 40, and *VCH Oxon*. iii. 235.

[3] Gee, 'Oxford collegiate architecture', 634.

[4] *VCH Oxon*. iii. 150.

[5] R. W. Jeffery, 'History of the College, 1547–1603', *Brasenose Monographs* ii. no. 10, 31.

[6] Christ Church MS xii b. 20, 2nd term of 1598–9.

[7] For St John's, see Stevenson and Salter, 54.

and another chamber listed in 1512 had one window wholly and one window half glazed.[1] At Oriel during the same period (surviving college accounts run from 1482 to 1526) no payment at all is recorded for glazing the windows of fellows' chambers.[2] By contrast the accounts of Trinity from 1561 and of Exeter from 1566 are full from the beginning of references to repairs to glazing in fellows' chambers. It is possible that the unprecedentedly large windows of Cardinal College, which must have been glazed throughout from the start, popularized this amenity in other colleges.

When space in the colleges began to seem intolerably restricted, the first expedient was to ceil over the upper chambers and form a third storey in the roofspace, lighting the attics or 'cocklofts' thus formed by dormer windows in the roof slopes. The earliest reference noted to the construction of a cockloft is at New College in 1539, where a complete upper chamber (*superius cubiculum*) was built. They became common only from the 1570s. In 1567 at Merton for instance the college took responsibility for tiling 'a new window made in the roof of the chamber' of a fellow;[3] and the first reference to overlofting chambers at Trinity, where the accounts are complete from 1561, is in 1573. By 1587 five of the ten upper chambers at University College had cocklofts (each with a standing bedstead besides the bedstead in the chamber). At All Souls three of the eleven upper chambers had 'lofts' by 1588, although as many as seven had studies distinguished as 'upper' and 'lower', implying a more limited use of the roof space.[4]

Most colleges pushed out dormer windows at random, indeed individual fellows might take the initiative in doing this. But at St John's as early as 1573 an orderly sequence of windows was built on the outer slope of the roofs of the south and west ranges, for, as the college wrote to the Merchant Taylors that year, 'We are also, partly through coldnes, partly for wante of roome, constrained to overloft all the chambers in the whole coledge, which ariseth to no small some of money'.[5]

Regular dormer windows lighting cocklofts were erected perhaps at the same time in Hugh Price's new range at Jesus. Merton rebuilt St Alban's Hall in 1599 with similarly orderly dormers. By pushing out dormer windows and creating habitable cocklofts in the roof-space it was also possible to make provision for the vastly increased

[1] *Reg. ann. mert. 1483–1521*, 396, 425.

[2] Oriel College Archives Bursar's Accounts, Shadwell transcripts vols. v–x.

[3] *Reg. ann. mert. 1521–67*, 274.

[4] University College MS HH Fasc. 5 no. 2; All Souls College MS D.D. c. 369. For Corpus see James McConica, 'Elizabethan Oxford: the collegiate society', p. 675 below.

[5] Stevenson and Salter, 100.

numbers of students who inhabited many colleges after the matriculation statutes of 1565 and 1581. This had little effect on well-
endowed foundations such as New College, Magdalen and All Souls;
but other colleges, Balliol, Brasenose, and most notoriously Exeter,
experienced great overcrowding.

Considerable evidence exists of the furnishing of fellows' chambers.
Normally the college provided the basic furniture, bedsteads, tables
and forms.[1] Soft furnishings and, normally, hangings were provided
by the occupants. The numerous inventories in the university
archives give a detailed impression, particularly for the second half
of the century. Only a few generalizations can be made here.[2] The
bed was clearly the most prominent object in a chamber, and, apart
from a fellow's gowns, the featherbed and bolster or pillows
normally constituted the most valuable item, ranging from £2 to
5s, with 6s 8d or 10s being the norm in the early part of the century,
but the valuation later becoming extremely variable. A flock bed was
also itemized in many chambers, but a second featherbed only rarely.
Up to about 1560 it was normal for a tester to the bed to be listed
(17:7); thereafter it was unusual (16:51). Hangings to the bed or to
the chamber, or to both, are generally listed. In the early part of the
century these are frequently specified as painted cloths or painted
papers, but such items disappear after 1581, and hangings or cur-
tains, normally of say, first listed in 1529 occur frequently from
about 1570. Coverlets are commonly listed throughout the century.
Occasionally they are specified as being of tapestry or otherwise
decorated; but the bed coverings of William Gryce, the vice-president
of Magdalen who died in 1528, are exceptional, one 'with bestes',
one 'with flowres', one 'with ymagry' and one 'with a hert yn the
mydds'. Carpets, for tables or cupboards rather than as floor covering, are occasionally mentioned, with increasing frequency after
about 1570. The mention of mats is extremely rare.

Many, but not all, fellows owned tables, forms or stools in their
chambers or studies besides those provided for them. One in three

[1] For beds at Corpus see p. 627 above. For inventories of furniture belonging to University College in 1587 and All Souls College in 1588 see p. 629 n. 4 above. See too the
undated joiner's bill c 1600, All Souls College MS D.D. c. 255 no. 4 for making beds, tables
and a settle for specific fellows' chambers; items in Exeter College Archives Rector's
Accounts 1566 onwards, A ii (9).

[2] Four inventories of college heads, fifty inventories of fellows, twenty-three of other
inhabitants of college chambers and sixteen of heads or other inhabitants of academic halls
between 1507 and 1602 have been examined in the Reg. Canc. 1506–14, 1527–43, 1545–
1661 and Chanc. Court. Inv., and in Mr Walter Mitchell's typed transcripts of them. See
also St John's College Archives x. 19, inventory of Henry Price, fellow, died 1601, and
p. 622 n. 2 above. The inventory of Edward Beaumont, BA, has been printed in Reg.
Univ. ed. Boase, xx–xxi.

inventories includes cushions, which are specified occasionally as being window cushions. Desks, where listed, were it seems portable, lockable and of very little value. Of over eighty inhabitants of chambers whose inventories survive for the sixteenth century only twenty-two owned poker and shovel or other items which would suggest that they had fires to warm them. Presumably such things were often college property. Eating utensils hardly ever occur.

There is little to indicate the individual tastes of these, normally young, scholars. Only four images are noted in the nineteen inventories up to 1537, and these are valued at only a few pence each. About one in four inventories, on the other hand, lists gold rings or other pieces of plate. Musical instruments appear occasionally, lutes in 1508, 1553, 1570, 1577 (three times) and 1578; gitterns in 1553, 1561 and 1578; and a larke in 1578. Besides the heads of houses mentioned above a few fellows also had virginals in their chambers, Thomas Palmer (died 1566) and Robert Hert (died 1570) of St John's College, William Smallwood of Gloucester Hall (1572) who also had a pair of 'clarecolles', James Raynoldes, fellow of Exeter College, in 1577, George Holland, fellow of Balliol College, in 1596,[1] and John Baylie, late fellow of New College, but at the time of his death in 1601 a medical practitioner in the city. Eleven inventories list maps or globes, eleven list pictures, which are invariably valued very cheaply, two list bird cages and three playing tables, one together with a chess board and men (1566).

It was normal for members of a college to put necessary work in hand in their own chambers, pay for it and claim reimbursement from the college.[2] By an extension of this practice fellows, heads or even college servants occasionally built extra chambers and studies at their own expense, rented them out during their lifetimes and bequeathed them to the college. At Exeter John Bentley, college butler in Rector Holland's time (1592–1612), built a two-storeyed structure of timber-framing over the old library, providing six chambers and nineteen studies. Rector Prideaux in his description of the college (1631) compared unfavourably the flimsiness of this 'nest' with the solid stone range of 'mansions' built as a free gift to the college in 1618 by John Peryam. Yet Prideaux himself in the early seventeenth century built at his own expense some chambers to accommodate four prestigious gentleman-commoners under his care; and Richard Carpenter (fellow 1596–1606) added to his room a cockloft containing eight studies.[3] At Balliol, Hammond's Lodging of about 1593, replaced in 1769 by Fisher's Building, though

[1] See pp. 632–3 below.   [2] See, for example, Macray, *Reg. Magdalen* iii. 22, 33.
[3] *VCH Oxon.* iii. 116.

probably paid for by the college, served a similar function; and in 1607 the master and fellows granted the second cook of the college a lease without fine 'in consideration that he has been at some charges of building of a tenement in the backside of the College . . . being part of the storehouse of the College'.[1] At St John's in 1612 the senior cook built a kitchen with four chambers which he rented to commoners. At his death the building reverted to the college and became the nucleus of Cook's Building.[2]

At the end of the Tudor period Oxford was a much busier and more densely populated place than it had been a hundred years earlier. In terms of new building, however, the townsmen had done a great deal more than the academic bodies. As we have seen, increased demand for living space in the colleges had made little visible impact on them, just an irregular eruption of dormer windows in the roofs; while increased book-holdings were being absorbed without alteration to the fabric of libraries. Since the new foundations of Henry VIII's reign virtually no new college buildings had been raised, and in 1605 the young Prince Henry could still commend Magdalen 'for the most absolute building of Oxford'.[3]

Nevertheless, there had been sown the seeds of the early Stuart flowering of new buildings in the university. Sir Thomas Bodley was soon to improve dramatically the university library and its schools, and the new quadrangles of Merton, Wadham, Oriel and University College, all built three storeys high and with a flourish of gables on the skyline, finally provided the extra living accommodation so badly needed by colleges. These demonstrated, moreover, that a pride in regular buildings was now felt throughout the university and was not merely expressed in those colleges where an episcopal founder had determined to leave behind him a visual reminder of his patronage of scholarship.

APPENDIX: THE GOODS OF GEORGE HOLLAND AND THOMAS KEY

George Holland

A trew Inventorie of all the goodes of Mr George Holland m[r] of the artes and fellowe of Baliall College in Oxford, decessed the 27th of Maye 1596. Sene and praysed.

---

[1] *The Oxford Deeds of Balliol College*, ed. H. E. Salter (OHS lxiv 1913) 31, 361, 89–90.

[2] *VCH Oxon.* iii. 261.

[3] Macray, *Reg. Magdalen* iii. 39.

In primis a standing bedsteed and bedding iii^{li}
Item a faire wenscot chest viii^{s}
Item a table with a frame, 2 formes iii ioyned stooles viii^{s}
Item 2 carpets $\text{ii}^{\text{s}}\ \text{vi}^{\text{d}}$
Item a backe of wenscot with a benche and wenscot
    about the chimney $\text{vi}^{\text{s}}\ \text{viii}^{\text{d}}$
Itm a paier of virginals x^{s}
Itm an iron and a bason x^{d}
Itm mattes rounde about the chamber $\text{xiii}^{\text{s}}\ \text{iiii}^{\text{d}}$
Itm 2 iron dogges a fiershowle and paier of tongues ii^{s}
Itm two chaires and two quissions $\text{ii}^{\text{s}}\ \text{vi}^{\text{d}}$
Itm a window quission xx^{d}
Itm a candle boxe ii^{d}
Itm a great mappe of the world with curteans $\text{vi}^{\text{s}}\ \text{viii}^{\text{d}}$
Itm seven lesser maps and 2 tables of armes vi^{s}
Itm an instrument for the mathematicall iewell with
    the quadrant belonginge $\text{ii}^{\text{s}}\ \text{vi}^{\text{d}}$

In his studye

In primis wenscot presses rounde about with shelves
    for bookes viii^{s}
Item a table with carpet, & a ioyned stole $\text{iii}^{\text{s}}\ \text{iiii}^{\text{d}}$
Itm a deske with locke and key & boxes in it iii^{s}
Itm a bigge boxe with locke and keye xx^{d}
Itm a case with boxes xvi^{d}
Item two small deskes viii^{d}
Item 8 pictures vi^{d}
Itm wood and cooles v^{s}

In the upper studies

Im primis a square table & a presse xv^{s}
Itm a deske covered with greene clothe vi^{d}
Itm a curteon, a rodde and 4 pictures xii^{d}
Itm small formes and wenscot $\text{ii}^{\text{s}}\ \text{vi}^{\text{d}}$
Item his bookes $\text{iiii}^{\text{li}}\ \text{vii}^{\text{s}}\ \text{vii}^{\text{d}}$

        sum̄a $\text{xiii}^{\text{li}}\text{xi}^{\text{d}}$
Henry Mylward stationer
Jemes Willims bidle

Thomas Key

An Inventorie of all suche goods as are in the Lodginge of Mr Thomas Key Maister of the Universitie College the nynth day of May Ao dni 1572.

In primis in the Uppermost chamber nexte unto Widowe Manckesmans howse these things folowinge

Ffirst a wenscot bedstede wthoute a teaster wt a mat thrombd
Itm a square table standing in the windowe
Itm an owld fether bed
Itm a litle blanket
Itm ii pillowes and a cosion of white silke
Itm a wenscot cobberd with a grene clothe uppon it
Itm a picture of Erasmus hanginge over the table
Itm a pillowe
Itm a curteine of buckeram hanginge before the windowe
Itm Bristowe mattes uppon the floer
Itm a frame wth ii steps to stand on under the windowe

In ii^d chamber under neath that

Itm a wenscot bedstedd wth a tester of gren sey fringed & iii curteins to the same bed belonging of sey
Itm a new fetherbed with newe grete bolster to the sam bed
Itm a wenscot trocle bed under the same
Itm a square table of wenscot wth ii joyned stooles wth torned pillars
Itm ii joyned fowrmes of wenscot wth like worthe
Itm a wensco cubbord
Itm ii carpettes of yelow, red, and grene vewed worke on for the table another for the cubborde
Itm Irons of the bed for curtens
Itm a pillerd chaire
Itm vi coshions
Itm a paire of Andirons and a paire of bellows
Itm ii sey curteins in the windowe
Itm hangings of grene sey throughowte the whole chamber wth a written border
Itm a paire of snaffers
Itm ii thrommed mattes in the trockle bed and the highe bed wth cordes for bothe.

In the chamber where Mr Key him self lyethe

Inprimis a bedsted with pillered postes

Itm a paned tester of grene & red sattyn wth fringe of like diver-
sitie of silke

Itm iiii curteines of grene and red sasnet to the same

Itm a newe bed of downe wth a greate bowlster of downe new

Itm a mattres to the same

Itm a red blancket, wth ii rogged blancketes

Itm a faire large coverlet for the sam bed

Itm a matte

Itm iii three pillowes

Itm a troclebed wth a matte and cordes for both beddes

Itm a flocke bed wth a greate fetherbolster

Itm a blancket of whight

Itm a close rounde cobberd of wenscot

Itm a gren cloth and a coshion of silke and blewe velvet uppon the
same

Itm a nother cubbord of carved wenscot toward the streateside
wth a grene cloth uppon it

Itm a bason and a yewer

Itm v coshions of nedle worke of divers colors as yelowe and
grene wth a rose in the middest

Itm a coshion grene silke lined wth red lyinge in the great windowe

Itm v grene coshions of branched worke for the benche lyned wth
red

Itm a longe table of wenscot wth a doble frame wth a carpet a
dise worke

Itm ii chaires lined wth grene cloth and frenged the on wherof
is a stole of ease

Itm ii wenscot chaires wth ii torned pillers on everie side

Itm an Iron cheaste wth King Phillips Armes

Itm iii longe goundes on of grogeram faced wth budge and ii of
cloth faced wth the same

Itm ii short clokes the on furred throughout wth lambe the other
lined wth cotten

Itm a cloth coate, a wosted cote and a frise Casocke

Itm iiii shertes

Itm a loking glasse wth ii leaves to shut

Itm hangingings for parte of the chamber of like coloure as the
carpet is wth a border

Itm a paire of snoffers and an Iron shewinge horne

Itm a brosse of pecockes tailes wth a long handle
Itm a brosse
Itm a litle bason to washe in
Itm vii candelsticks, iiii of pewter, iii of brasse
Itm iii grene windowe clothes
Itm a pare of Andyrons a fire showle, a paire of bellowes and a paire of tonges
Itm vi joyned stoles a piller worke
Itm a deske covered wth red velvet
Itm ii coshions in ii chaires
Itm a pewter panne in the stoole of easment
Itm a water pot of pewter
Itm iiii flowre pottes of pewter

In the upper hawle next the strete

In primis table wth a pillerd fram & turners worke
Itm a fowrme of the same worke
Itm a carpet of blewe red & grene worke of vewed worke for the same table
Itm vi greate coshions of grene with a red rose in the middes[t] lyned with leather for the bynche
Itm ii grene sattin coshions lyned wth red
Itm ii windowe clothes of grene
Itm ii picturs in the windowe next the streate on of the greate Turke another of his daughter
Itm a cubbord wth a cloth of thicke thrommed worke of divers colors
Itm a picture over the table in blewe of a gentle woman playing on the lute and a gentleman by hir
Itm a picture in the litle windowe of a gentleman having death in his breaste
Itm a picture of the King of Mores and his wife over the portall
Itm ii pictures in the great windowe of ii faire nonnes
Itm ii curteins of grene for the sam windowe
Itm a cansticke of brasse wth a brode brasen backe by the litle windowe
Itm a faire grene chaire
Itm a nother wenscot cheire wth litle pillors in the side
Itm a coshion for the same chere
Itm newe grene hangings of sey hanged round aboute the hawle wth a border of like worke as the hangings of his other chambers
Itm a paire of Andirons

In the lower hawle

In primis ii windowe clothes of grene sey
Itm a table for the virginalls to stand on wth pillers
Itm a close cubbord wth pillers
Itm a stillytarie
Itm a cubbord clothe of grene sey
Itm iii square pillered cheares
Itm ye picture of James y iiii[th] King of Scotts
Itm ye picture of the Quenis Armes
Itm the picture of John Babtist baptysing Christe
Itm the picture of a douche woman
Itm a picture a gentlewoman having a luite in her hande
Itm a nother picture of Christe and the woman at the well

In Merickes Chamber

Imp̄mi a bedsted wth cordes
Itm a cheste
Itm a matte

In Mr Sherborns chamber otherwise called the [grene hawle *erased*]
parler

In primis a large a newe fetherbed
Itm a mattres
Itm a bolster
Itm a matte
Itm ii pillowes
Itm a newe coverlet
Itm a pillowebeare
Itm a paire of shetes
Itm ii grene coshions lyned with red
Itm a bedsted of wenscot wth pillers and a wenscot tester
Itm frenge off grene & red aboute the valance
Itm cordes for the sam bedsted
Itm a troklebed wth mat & cordes
Itm a red coshion
Itm a paire of Andyrons
Itm a close cubbord
Itm a square table
Itm a grete cypres cheast
Itm in the saide iiii coshions of copes lyned wth whyte satten
Itm a grene carpet

Itm ii Grene courtens for the sowth window
Itm another curteine for another windowe
Itm hangings of Grene wth a border
Itm iii joyned fourmes
Itm ii ioyned stoles
Itm a fire showle
Itm Irons of the bed for curtens

In the Galerie

Itm a sqare table wth a frame of pillers with a grene clothe of sey
Itm ii curteins of Sey
Itm iii joyned formes i wth a frame of pillers
Itm a rowle of the pictures of fowrtene of the first emperours of
   Rome
Itm a rowle of All the Kings of England from Brute to or soveraign
   ladie Quene Elizabeth
Itm a mappe of the whole world of Mercators
Itm a mappe Europe of Mercators
Itm a Mappe of Germanie
Itm a Mappe of Spaine
Itm a Mappe of ffraunce
Itm a Mappe of Hungarie
Itm a Mappe of Grycia
Itm a mappe of the peregrination of paule
Itm a mapp of Islandia
Itm a mappe of Aegypte
Itm a mappe of Helvetia
Itm a mappe of the world wth Armes
Itm a mappe of the world of Ortelius
Itm a Mappe of the lowe contries of Germanie
Itm a mappe of the world Globewise wth a sprede Egle
Itm a mappe of Italie
Itm ii rounde pictures of heds sed at everie end of the Galerie like
   a buckler
Itm the picture of Calvin
Itm the picture of Beza
Itm ii picturs of ii Doctors
Itm a picture of ii Twins
Itm a picture of Quene Elizabeth
Item a picture of the Kinge of Suenlande
Item vii picturs of the seven sciences
Item ii picturs of iiii philosophers
Item mappe on the flore

Itm ii Grene windowe clothes
Itm an Iron rod for ye window
Itm a picture of Plato & Aristotele
Itm pop pius picture

In Mr hopkins chamber

In primis an Iron bownd cheste with lynnen
v paire of shetes iii lockeram and ii hollen in all
Item v pillowbearers of wch som are in on place som in an other
Item xi diaper napkens
Item xiiii other napkens
Item ii yewer clothes of fine hollen
Itm iii cubberd clothes of fine hollen
Itm a diaper tableclothe
Itm ii drap towelles
Itm ii table clothes of hollen
Itm ii towells of hollen
Itm a paire of fustian blancketes
Itm nyntene peces of Copes
Itm a carpet of grene and blacke
Itm a picture of King phillip and the Duke of Savoy
Itm a picture of the Emperors sister with another
Itm a grene curten for the window
Itm an odd sheete of hollen
Itm hangings of red sey and grene wth border on the west side &
    the southe
Itm a cubbord of wenscot with a cubbord cloth of divers colors
Itm a bedsted of wenscot colored wth red
Itm a coverlet
Itm valance of red velvet wth sylke fringe of yelo & red
Itm a newe greate fether bed
Itm a grene chere colored
Itm a grete new bolster
Itm ii wollen blanckets
Itm a coshion in the chare
Itm a picture of ii Gentlewomen
Itm a waterpot
Itm a matres and a matte
Itm mattes uppon the floor
Itm a gren windowe clothe
Itm a paire of andirons
Itm a curtein of red and grene sey for ye bede

Itm a perfewmynge panne
Itm Irons of the bed for Curtens

In the stable

Itm a bay nagge
Itm ii saddelles
Itm a bridell

A note of all suche stuffe or goodes of Mr. Keyes as either is myssyng
oute of his lodginge or lyeth in other mens handes

In primis a paire of virginalles at Mr Garbrandes
Itm a coverlet that Mr Dewhurst hathe in his chamber
Itm iiii curtaines of grene & red sey, wch Mr. Vahann hathe
Itm iiii curtaines wch Gawen the bedell hathe of grene & red
Itm a faire grene stole of ease wch the said Gawen hathe
Itm a joyned stoole wch Mericke set to mendinge xii moneth agon
    to Holton[s]
Itm a litle cheste, wch Mericke toke owte of the chamber over the
    parler
Item that wheras there should be xii candelstickes in the whole
    there are but vii lefte
Itm wheras there was vii paire of shetes, there was but v[ ]
Itm wheras ther was xi pillowes, there are but eight
Itm that Mr Dudley for ii pillowes and pillowbear or mo must
    accompt
Itm a water pote a paire of shetes wth other things
Itm that Sir Medford being burser toke an Inventorie aboute
    half a yere past, he must make a compte for certayne thinges,
    wch he kepeth back, as mericke saieth
Item that William the northen man, then being Mr. Keyes servaunt
    was at the doing of this and knoweth Somwhat as Mericke
    saieth
Itm hangings in Mericks his chamber are gonne
Itm Mr Chewe hath a wendscot trockle bed wth cords
Itm Mr Dewhurst hath iiii coshions
Itm Mr Dobson hath a stole of easment of grene cloth before and
    a water pot
Itm mericke hath a chaire
Itm a newe fine hollen sheete at Jerome Mayes at pledge for iii[s]
    iiii[d]
Itm a nother fine hollen sheete at Randalls for iii[s] iiii[d]
Itm that Mr Dudley oweth Mr Key x[s] wch he lent him.

Oxford in 1578 (after Ralph Aga's diagramm

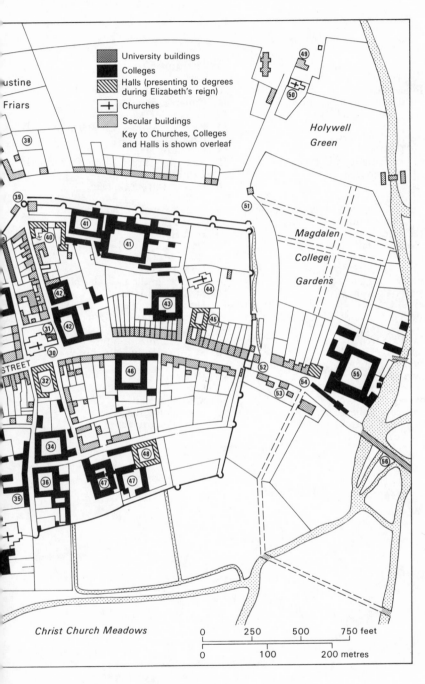

University buildings
Colleges
Halls (presenting to degrees
during Elizabeth's reign)
+ Churches
Secular buildings
Key to Churches, Colleges
and Halls is shown overleaf

ustine

Friars

Holywell
Green

Magdalen

College

Gardens

STREET

Christ Church Meadows

0   250   500   750 feet

0   100   200 metres

re-drawn to a true scale by John Blair).

Key to the map of Oxford in 1578

1	Gloucester Hall.	30	St Mary the Virgin church.
2	Site of Whitefriars.	31	Congregation house.
3	Castle and prison.	32	St Mary's Hall.
4	West gate.	33	Part of Christ Church (formerly Peckwater Inn).
5	Site of Blackfriars.		
6	New Inn Hall.	34	Oriel College.
7	St Peter-le-Bailey Church	35	Part of Christ Church (formerly Canterbury College).
8	St Ebbe's church.		
9	Little gate.	36	Corpus Christi College.
10	Site of Greyfriars.	37	Cathedral.
11	Bridewell (site of St Mary's College).	38	Site of Austin Friars.
12	St Martin's church.	39	Smith gate and bastion chapel.
13	St Aldate's church.	40	Hart Hall.
14	Broadgate Hall.	41	New College.
15	Christ Church almhouses.	42	All Souls College.
16	St John's College.	43	Queen's College.
17	St Mary Magdalen church.	44	St Peter-in-the-East church.
18	Trinity College.	45	St Edmund Hall.
19	Balliol College.	46	University College.
20	North gate and St Michael's church.	47	Merton College.
21	Jesus College.	48	St Alban Hall.
22	Christ Church.	49	Holywell manor-house.
23	South gate.	50	St Cross (Holywell) church.
24	Exeter College.	51	Holywell.
25	Divinity School.	52	East gate.
26	University Schools.	53	Site of Trinity Hall.
27	Lincoln College.	54	Magdalen Hall.
28	Brasenose College.	55	Magdalen College.
29	All Saints' church.	56	Magdalen bridge.

IO

Elizabethan Oxford:
The Collegiate Society

JAMES McCONICA

COLLEGIATE society was intimate and it centred on the college hall where lectures and disputations, entertainments, college business and formal discipline took place, as well as all the meals. The hall at Corpus Christi College, like all others during the Tudor period, was without a fireplace.[1] On the rare occasions when they were provided fires were lit in a central hearth whence the smoke rose through the hall and out of a louvre in the roof. Trestle tables, with seating on forms, were arranged laterally around the hearth. Unlike their modern successors they were covered with cloths, of qualities befitting the rank of those who sat there. For everywhere the seating arrangements reflected the strict distinctions of status which pervaded the life of Elizabethan Oxford: the high table where the president sat with the theologians, the table of the masters of arts where the readers in Greek and Latin sat, tables for the scholars, the vice-president and the bursars.[2] Throughout the century the walls of the Corpus hall were whitewashed and decked with painted hangings, although panelling was introduced in halls and chapels at New College (1533) and Magdalen (1541) as a step towards elegance and comfort. In 1559, at the beginning of the new reign, the hall at Corpus was paved and the paving was covered with a carpet; a lectern was bought in 1578 for the use of readers and lecturers. Apart from the hangings the chief decoration came from the glass,

[1] On what follows see John Newman, 'The physical setting: new building and adaptation', pp. 597–632 above; G. D. Duncan, 'Tudor Corpus: the hall and the chapel', in *The Pelican 1981-2* (Corpus Christi College Oxford 1982), 56–7; Thomas Fowler, *The History of Corpus Christi College* (OHS xxv 1893), 50–1.

[2] Remarked on by the German traveller Paul Hentzner in 1598 who described three tables in the Oxford college: the 'mensa sociorum' where earls, barons, nobles, doctors and a few MAs would sit with the fellows; a second table for MAs, BAs, gentlemen and prominent citizens; and a third for plebeians and those of low condition: *Itinerarium germaniae, galliae, angliae, italiae: scriptum a Paulo Hentznero* . . . (Nuremberg 1612), 143–4. It is not known exactly where Hentzner was entertained. Also Vivian Green, *The Commonwealth of Lincoln College 1427-1977* (Oxford 1979), 229–30.

whose blazonings and painted inscriptions commemorated the sovereign, the college's founder and benefactors, and the society's religious purposes. The finest feature was the hammer-beam roof which, like the fan vault in the tower at the entrance to Corpus, was a real mark of distinction. Apart from those two features, the lack of ostentation in the buildings and the fact that construction was uninterrupted makes Fox's provision a fairly useful index to ordinary accommodation; we may think of the Corpus man's lodging as a sign of the times.

It was certainly such in the reduction of numbers in each chamber from the usual three or four to two, a fellow and his 'disciple'. This was undoubtedly a feature of Fox's emphasis on training and dis-cipline; inadvertently, it anticipated the taste for greater privacy which is noticeable by the end of the century. On the other hand, these chambers were generally draughty and almost certainly damp.[1] Thomas Cogan, a former fellow of Oriel,[2] advised the undergraduate, 'Let your lodging be in an upper chamber, yet severed from the roufe with some false flower [floor]; let the bedsteed be large and long, and no higher than a man may easily fall into it standing uppon the chamber flower. Let the bed be soft, wel shaken, and made rising up towards the feete, so that the bulke or chist of the bodie may be lowest. . . . I pray God sende all good studentes soft lodging.'[3] Soft, and warm; although the addition of cocklofts later in the century by ceiling over existing upper chambers had the added benefit of making both rooms easier to heat, there is little doubt that throughout our period many an undergraduate could echo the plaintive phrase which survives from Magdalen College school in the late fifteenth century: 'The moste part of this wynter my hands wer so swellynge with colde that I could nother holde my penn for to wrytt nother my knyff for to cutt my mete at the table, and my fete also their wer so arayde with kybblayns [chilblains] that it grevyde me to go enywhere.'[4] In an appeal of 1550 to the merchants of London for support for the universities, Thomas Lever of St John's College, Cambridge, alleged that Cambridge students 'are fayne to walk or runne up and downe halfe an houre to gette a heate on their feete whan they go to bed'.[5]

---

[1] See Newman, p. 626.

[2] From 1563 until 1575 when he took his BM with licence to practise.

[3] *The Haven of Health: chiefely gathered for the comfort of students . . . by Thomas Coghan master of artes & bacheloer of phisicke* (Henry Middleton for William Norton 1584), ch. 241 'Of sleepe' pp. 240-1. A summary of his views is found in C. S. Emden, *Oriel Papers* (Oxford 1948), ch. 3. See also P. A Slack, 'Mirrors of health and treasures of poor men: the uses of the vernacular medical literature of Tudor England', in C. Webster (ed.), *Health, Medicine and Mortality in the Sixteenth Century* (Cambridge 1979), 237-73.

[4] *A Fifteenth Century School Book*, ed. William Nelson (Oxford 1956), p. 6 no. 20.

[5] *A sermon preached at Pauls Crosse the xiii. day of December by Thomas Lever. Anno*

What of the diet? It was substantial, if limited and monotonous. There were two meals a day. The chief was dinner at about 11 a.m. with the main dish, a piece of meat, carved in the hall into portions for each table. Bread, butter, cheese and beer were the staples otherwise. Supper, eaten at five or six in the evening, was informal, and might offer cold meats from the buttery in addition to the staples. Oatmeal steeped in the liquor left from parboiling meat before roasting made a pottage to supplement this diet.[1] Beef and mutton were probably the regular fare at most colleges: Cogan recalled that, 'At Oxford in my time they used commonly at dinner, boyled beefe with pottage, bread & beere and no more.' The quantity he reckoned at 'an halfepenie for one man', and thought it beneficial that but one variety of meat should be taken at a meal, the quantity not such as to provide 'fulness of bellie'.[2]

For a contrast we might turn to a well-endowed college of graduates: a long run of weekly stewards' accounts at All Souls College shows an unusually detailed record of food purchases.[3] Throughout the century at least two varieties of meat—usually beef and mutton —were available at each meal, with stockfish, whitings, 'saltfish' or fresh salmon on days of abstinence. During the week of the college's principal feast, All Souls' Day,[4] the menu included in addition, baked eels, pickerel, 'pyggs', geese, rabbits, capons, woodcocks, larks, blackbirds, pigeons and chickens, and to accompany these, wine, ale, cream, butter and fruit. This was in 1544. During Lent no meat was consumed but the long fast was broken by a solemn observance of the feast of St Gregory which fell on 12 March 1545, conveniently in the middle of the penitential season. Gregory the Great was also one of the patrons of the chapel, and his feast was the only one in the year to receive a special allowance of 30s, equal to All Souls' Day itself. Abstinence was faithfully kept, but the manciple seems to have exerted his every effort to make up in variety of fish for the meatless menu. To the salt salmon, plaice, stockfish, whitings and herrings purchased regularly during Lent with 'lykes

---

mdl. (John Day 1550), sig. E ii.ᵛ. Lever, born in 1521, had been an undergraduate at St John's and became a fellow in 1548; in 1551 he was elected master.

[1] Green, *Commonwealth*, 230–1.

[2] Cogan, *Haven of Health*, ch. 211 'Of Dinner', p. 187.

[3] All Souls College Archives on deposit in Bodl. MS DD All Souls College b.31; Charles Trice Martin, *Catalogue of the Archives in the Muniment Room of All Souls' College* (1877), p. 411 item 19 (*recte* 18); wrongly described as 'bursars' books'.

[4] The feast of All Saints was supplemented separately to a total allowance of 50s. Easter Day was allotted 20s. Here as elsewhere fresh fruit and vegetables in season might have been supplied from the college gardens, escaping mention in the accounts, but Cogan's remarks do not reflect it, at least as a feature of undergraduate diet.

and oynyons' we see added in that festive week, salt eels, baked eels, roast eels, pike, tench, perch, carp and oysters. There was also 'almon butter', and 'fyggs, almons and appels in Mr Wardens chamber'. A plaintive voice is heard from Magdalen College school: 'Thou wyll not beleve how wery I am off fysshe, and how moch I desir that flesch were cum in ageyn, for I have ete non other but salt fysh this lent, and it hathe engendyrde so much flewme within me that it stoppith my pypys [so] that I can unneth speke nother brethe.'[1]

When we consider the plight of an undergraduate similarly afflicted rising at four in the darkness of a February morning to attend mass and morning prayers in an unheated chapel, then turning to two or three hours of work prior to lectures, the constant mortality is less surprising.[2] Things were no different after the reformation. Thomas Lever described the day of the ordinary Cambridge student as beginning between four and five in the morning, with common prayer and 'exhortacion of god's worde' in the chapel. From six to ten there was private study or attendance at lectures, and dinner at ten, when they would be content with a penny piece of beef among four, pottage, 'salte and otemel and nothynge els'. After dinner there would be more study until five in the evening, when they would have a supper 'not much better than theyr diner'. Immediately afterwards there followed disputations or other lessons until retiring at nine or ten o'clock.[3]

Oxford was not a healthy place, and contagion was endemic. There were regular visitations of bubonic plague as well as other epidemic and endemic diseases such as influenza, the 'sweating sickness', malaria and typhus, as in 1577.[4] Parts of the colleges and many of the houses were built on graveyards. A recurrent problem was the river, so choked with weirs and private fishing obstructions that each winter flood was an inundation—as under exceptional circumstances it may still be. A further problem was the town's characteristic industry, the trade in livestock. Local butchers were chronic offenders

---

[1] A Fifteenth Century School Book, p. 8 no. 30.

[2] Of more than 1,300 scholars admitted to New College between 1386 and 1540 one in ten died in their first four years before taking a degree; R. L. Storey, 'The foundation and the medieval college 1379-1530', in John Buxton and Penry Williams (eds), New College Oxford 1379-1979 (Oxford 1979), 17; cf Green, Commonwealth, 119 ff.

[3] Lever, A Sermon, sig. E ii^{r-v}.

[4] The 'gaol-fever' in Oxford in 1577 was caused by typhus. The low-lying meadows and chronic flooding made a hospitable environment for mosquitoes and rats, hence for malaria and for plague (from the bacterium pasteurella pestis). See P. A. Slack, 'Mortality crises and epidemic disease in England 1485-1610', in Webster, Health, Medicine and Mortality, 9-59; Leslie Clarkson, Death, Disease and Famine in pre-industrial England (1975), 44, 48, 50; J. F. D. Shrewsbury, A History of Bubonic Plague in the British Isles (Cambridge 1970), 162, 164. On the effects of plague at Lincoln College see Green, Commonwealth, 119-23.

in disposing of the refuse of their trade. On 26 June 1530 the prior of the Dominican convent and the principal of Broadgates Hall complained before the vice-chancellor's court of the stench from animal intestines left in neighbouring houses by Thomas Murday and William Clare, butchers. The butchers promised to remove the refuse and put it in the river.[1] The ordinary method of dealing with endemic pestilence was the medieval solution, although it meant serious and repeated disruption of the university year: evacuation of Oxford. Each college tried to have a country retreat, and registers are full of references to evacuation for the plague, while a contingent of fellows who had been exposed previously to the contagion was left behind.[2] Although there was general awareness of the need to improve public sanitation, Cogan's treatise shows that the effective preventive measures against plague were all variants upon the one: 'with speede to goe farre off from the place infected'.[3]

Cogan also appreciated that in these conditons it was imperative for young men to have frequent exercise, which he prescribed as a regular regimen for the Oxford scholar. Tennis was the best kind, he thought, and it was so recommended by Galen, '. . . chiefly for that it doth exercise all partes of the body alike, as the legges, armes, necke, head, eies, back and loynes, and delighteth greatly the minde, making it lusty and cheereful . . . wherefore those founders of Colleges are highly to be praysed, that have erected Tenis courtes for the exercise of their Scholers'.[4] This is some evidence of a provision for recreation of which we know otherwise only a little. In a view of frankpledge of 1508 recorded by Brian Twyne we find that a jury presented four men who kept 'tenys playes' and 'bowlinge allies'.[5] This exemplified the chronic defiance of the laws against such forms of recreation for common people: by 1530 we learn that the city authorities were themselves conspiring in the provision of two unlawful tennis courts near Smith Gate for the sake of revenue from

[1] Reg. Canc. 1527–43, fo 150. There were also regular attempts to clear the streets of pigs: Reg. Canc. 1498–1508, 97, 170, 244, 301.

[2] See Green above p. 648 n. 4; St John's College Archives St John's College Register i. fo 287 records a typical arrangement in an indenture of 1590 with the first tenant of Charlbury to provide food and lodging for twelve in time of sickness in Oxford; cf W. H. Stevenson and H. E. Salter, The Early History of St John's College, Oxford (OHS new ser i. 1939), 179. On the epidemic of 1536 see Reg. Canc. 1527–43 fo 357. Cf R. S. Gottfried, Epidemic Disease in Fifteenth Century England (Leicester 1978), 76–7 on the shortcomings of this solution.

[3] Cogan, Haven of Health, ch. 243, 'A short treatise of the plaggue, and other like contagious diseases, how they may be auoyded', p. 263.

[4] Ibid. ch. 1, 'What labour is', pp. 3–4.

[5] Bodl. MS Twyne 23, p. 388; cited in Percy Manning, 'Sport and Pastime in Stuart Oxford', H. E. Salter (ed.), Surveys and Tokens (OHS lxxv 1923), 108. Cf also Reg. Canc. 1506–14 (1 August 1514), fo 227.

enhanced rents.[1] In contrast to the world of the town it is clear that recreations in the Elizabethan university were those of the privileged in court and county. Tennis was a conspicuous example. Cardinal College owned a tennis court somewhere in the parish of St Aldates; the predecessor of the court still in use in Merton Street is mentioned in a lease of 1595. There was a court at Corpus as early as 1552; Lincoln had a court by 1566 in the north-east corner of the college next to Brasenose; Oriel's 'tennis playe' can be traced to a lease of 1572.[2] Agas's map suggests that this last was an open court where the later building for 'real' or royal tennis was built, and reminds us that the early form of tennis was played with an open, often gloved hand in place of a racket, so that it might be described as *pilae reciprocatio*, a form of recreation not far removed from 'fives'. Such games were approved in keeping with the humanist philosophy on the training of young men: Elyot, Ascham and Mulcaster all upheld the doctrines of their Italian predecessors, such as Vittorino da Feltre and Castiglione. In Oxford even the sober divine Laurence Humfrey approved, so long as sports such as tennis or even dice-play were pursued for honest pleasure, not for filthy lucre.[3] So the colleges encouraged reasonable recreation and set aside some part of their precincts for the purpose.[4] Anthony Wood said that his father Thomas, who matriculated in 1600 at Broadgates Hall, was 'tall and bigge, and in his yonger dayes verie strong, and active in manlie sports and recreations, as football, wrestling, ringing, etc.'[5] He was probably representative of many who could not afford the more artistocratic pleasures of the hunt.

[1] *Selections from the Records of the City of Oxford: Henry VIII to Elizabeth*, ed. W. H. Turner (Oxford and London 1880), 86. Tudor legislation preserved the medieval desire to maintain the skills of archery, but reflected also a concern both about public order and about the heavy gambling occasioned by many games. It also provided revenue from the licensing of authorized places of common recreation.

[2] Manning, 'Sport and Pastime', 114; J. G. Milne, *The Early History of Corpus Christi College Oxford* (Oxford 1946), 12; Green, *Commonwealth*, 218; *Oriel College Records*, eds C. L. Shadwell and H. E. Salter (Oxford 1926), 214–15, and Oriel College Archives, leases, drawer 49 (lease of 105 High Street to Henry Milward, 5 October 1572). I owe these Oriel references to Dr J. I. Catto. For evidence of tennis played by Oxford schoolboys see a different Magdalen School *vulgaria*, BL Royal MS 12.B.xx, in Nicholas Orme, 'An early-Tudor Oxford schoolbook', *Renaissance Quarterly* xxxiv no. 1 (1981) p. 27, no. 30. On courtly and upper-class enthusiasm for tennis see Dennis Brailsford, *Sport and Society Elizabeth to Anne* (1969), 30–1.

[3] Laurence Humfrey, *The Nobles or of Nobilitye* (1563), book 3; cf n. 21.

[4] Exeter College erected a 'sphaeristerium'—a ball court?—in 1590; C. W. Boase, *Register of the Rectors, Fellows, and other members of the foundation of Exeter College, Oxford* (OHS xxvii 1894), xciii, cited in Manning, 'Sport and Pastime', 109. For Corpus see note 2 above and David Sturdy, *Twelve Oxford Gardens* [n.d.], no. 6.

[5] Bodl. MS Wood Empt. 26, pp. 2–3. James Whitelocke hunted hare on foot, a 'violent exercise' by his own account, to preserve his health in Oxford: *Liber Famelicus of Sir James Whitelock*, ed. John Bruce (Camden Society 1858), 13–14.

These too could be found. The medieval statutes typically forbade the keeping of hounds or birds of prey as incongruous for those professing poverty.[1] The statutes of Magdalen College dropped the reference to those living on alms, but otherwise summarized the usual collegiate disapproval of the keeping of sporting birds and animals, of card games or other diversions where gambling could take place, and of sports that might damage the fabric of the college buildings.[2] These regulations were strict but were inspired chiefly by a concern for the domestic order and well-being of the college community, and for its reputation abroad. The statutes of the next century envisaged peaceful recreation as part of undergraduate life. Those at Corpus, while they forbade hunting with hounds or birds as such, allowed the sport when it was pursued in moderation and 'honestly'—presumably without poaching—outside the university and with permission granted. Similarly, games within the precincts that endangered the buildings and windows were forbidden as before, but ballplay was allowed in the garden for the sake of bodily exercise and general health.[3] These regulations were repeated at St John's almost word for word, with the addition of football (*pilae pedalis*) to the forbidden games; at Trinity reasonable exercise was permitted in the orchard (*in arbusto*) under the watchful supervision of the president.[4]

There is a brief account of upper-class recreation in the vivid third-person autobiography of Simon Forman, who came up to Magdalen College in 1573.[5] His patrons, both bachelors of arts, 'loved him trying welle'. Whereas Forman wished to study, their only desire as he claimed was 'to goe to scolles of defence, to the daunceing scolles, to stealle dear and connyes, and to hunte the hart and to woinge of wentches'. Forman acted as their groom on expeditions to the royal forest of Shotover which in his time began just beyond Magdalen bridge, and he was responsible for obtaining hounds from the keeper to go hunting from morning to night. As he wrote with feeling, 'And thether muste Symon rove with the bottell and the bage, erly and late.'[6]

---

[1] See, for example, New College Statutes, *SCO* i. pt 5, 48–9 and Queen's *SCO* i. pt 4, 18–19.   [2] *SCO* ii. pt 8, 42–3.

[3] *SCO* ii. pt 10, 68–9; added to the original statutes in 1528.

[4] *SCO* iii. pt 12, 66; iv. Trinity College, 61. Scholars at Trinity were allowed card games at Christmas time provided there was no gambling for money, and there were like regulations at Brasenose: *SCO* ii. pt 9, 27.

[5] Bodl. MS Ashmole 208, fos 136–42. As there is no record of him in the college it seems likely that he was maintained as a servant to his two benefactors, and he tells us that he attended the 'free scolle' for a time: fo 142.

[6] Ibid. fo 142. Cf A. L. Rowse, *Simon Forman: sex and society in Shakespeare's age* (1974), 277–8. I differ on one reading of Forman's difficult orthography.

Forman is our best witness to the availability in Elizabethan Oxford of two forms of aristocratic training, schools for dancing and fencing. Although they cannot be clearly documented before the seventeenth century, vaulting and dancing were taught in Elizabethan Oxford, and the dancing master seemingly also gave instruction in fencing—a concealment doubtless induced by the ancient university prohibitions against bearing arms.[1]

Apart from these matters, college entertainments would have continued much as they did in the previous century with occasional feasts—although there were fewer of these in keeping with the religious reform—and especially the Christmas revels.[2] Among the traditional diversions drama alone experienced a notable transformation owed largely to the new emphasis on plays for schooling in the arts of rhetoric; the humanist influence was nowhere more strongly felt than here. At Oxford the efflorescence of collegiate drama, combined with the popular if illicit visitations of travelling dramatic companies, roused a storm of controversy in which, ironically, the attack on drama was mounted by former members of Richard Fox's own college of Corpus Christi, John Rainolds and Stephen Gosson.[3]

These considerations bring us to another element in college life which has attracted much attention, the provision for discipline.[4] Undergraduates were always subject to the decrees of the university at large, but the introduction of young men into the colleges in large numbers created new problems as well as new possibilities of restraint.

[1] Manning, 'Sport and pastime', 118. In 1606 a lease of 'the Daunsing Schoole' was granted for 31 years; *Oxford Council Acts 1583-1626*, ed. H. E. Salter (OHS lxxxvii 1928), 176; cf *Oxford City Properties*, ed. H. E. Salter (OHS lxxxiii 1926), 238.

[2] See J. I. Catto, 'Citizens, scholars and masters' in J. I. Catto (ed.), *The Early Oxford Schools* (History of the University of Oxford i. 1984), pp. 151-92; C. E. Mallet, *A History of the University of Oxford* (3 vols 1924-7) ii. 142-3. On Christmas festivities see Green, *Commonwealth*, 111-12; Stevenson and Salter, *Early History*, 173, 243; Christ Church Archives MS D & C i.b.2 p. 93, a decree of the dean and chapter of 12 December, 1/2 Philip and Mary, restricting their contribution at the 'pastyme in Christmas and the plays' to two comedies at 20s apiece, and two tragedies at 40s each, with the proviso that one of each pair be in Latin and the other in Greek. Concerning halls, see James McConica, 'The rise of the undergraduate college', p. 53 ff. above.

[3] A chapter on colleges and university drama will appear in the next volume of this history. See F. S. Boas, *University Drama in the Tudor Age* (Oxford 1914); for the debate involving John Rainolds, Albericus Gentilis, Dr William Gager, and others, chapter x. See also William Ringler, *Stephen Gosson: a biographical and critical study* (Princeton 1942); A. F. Kinney, *Markets of Bawdrie: the dramatic criticism of Stephen Gosson* (Salzburg 1974).

[4] See especially Philippe Ariès, *L'Enfant et la vie familiale sous l'ancien régime* (Paris 1960), pt ii; Lawrence Stone, *The Crisis of the Aristocracy 1558-1641* (Oxford 1965), 31-3; idem, *The Family, Sex and Marriage in England 1500-1800* (1977), 165; Mark Curtis, *Oxford and Cambridge in Transition 1558-1642* (Oxford 1959), 78-80 (on the tutor as disciplinarian); Hugh Kearney, *Scholars and Gentlemen: universities and society in preindustrial Britain 1500-1700* (1970), 22, 33, 45.

The two medieval foundations in which there was a large under-graduate component therefore set the scene for Tudor practices.[1] In William of Wykeham's statutes the junior and senior members of New College were equally bound by obedience to the warden in all honest and legitimate commands, and the same deference was owed to all the designated senior officers of the college. Disobedience was punished by withdrawal of commons—in effect a monetary fine—or after eight days of obduracy by perpetual expulsion. The regulations of William of Waynflete for Magdalen College were as usual formed on the same lines.[2] Once more the ultimate penalty was perpetual expulsion; in no statute was corporal punishment envisaged.[3]

At most colleges the most solemn disciplinary occasion was the periodic scrutiny. At New College and Magdalen this was conducted by the head of the house together with one of the more discreet and judicious of the fellows. It was intended to be an unsparing and very particular examination both of the general state of the society, and of the personal conduct and scholastic performance of each of the members. It was linked with a solemn reading of the statutes to remind everyone of their undertakings and obligations. The examiners were forbidden to reveal the names of those who made disclosures, and no fellow or scholar could ask to see a copy of the depositions or to know the identity of his accusers. He was bound to reply to all accusations without appeal against the sentences. Neither could any member of the college defend another lest the process of correction be held up: as far as possible, all punishments were to be carried out within three successive days. Whenever a specific statute or regulation could be invoked it was to be read out in the presence of the person to be punished along with the penalty.[4] In addition to this the fellows and scholars were in turn held responsible for supervision of the behaviour and progress in studies of those junior to them who lodged in their chambers, the demys and choristers, and were obliged by oath to report their defaults.[5]

[1] See McConica, 'The rise of the undergraduate college', p. 2 ff.; on the university's decrees, *Statuta*, lxxviii–lxxx.

[2] *SCO* i. pt 5, 35, 60–1; ii. pt 8, 29, 45 (at Magdalen the period of eight days was extended to one month).

[3] On the subject of corporal punishment see Hastings Rashdall, *The Universities of Europe in the Middle Ages* (2 vols Oxford 1895), new edn by F. M. Powicke and A. B. Emden (3 vols Oxford 1936), iii. 370–1; Philippe Ariès, *L'Enfant et la vie familiale*, 285–9.

[4] *SCO* i. pt 5, 94–7; ii. pt 8, 31–4.

[5] *SCO* ii. pt 8, 73. Compare the provision at New College that in every chamber there should be one fellow more advanced in maturity, discretion and knowledge who would superintend the others and report to the college officers on their work and conduct; *SCO* i. pt 5, 88–9. On the scrutiny see Hastings Rashdall, *Universities of Europe* iii. 365–6 and the works cited in the notes; on delation Philippe Ariès, *L'Enfant et la vie familiale*, 282–4.

The severity of this system was only heightened by the arrangements in the new foundations of the Tudor age. At Brasenose College,
where there was no scrutiny[1] and where the obligations of obedience
to the principal were expressed in traditional terms, there were
innovations of great moment. The least of these was the substitution
of pecuniary fines for the customary deprivations of commons, a
penalty that may have been taken over from the use of the halls as
a matter of simple convenience.[2] More important was the placing
of each scholar not a fellow under the supervision of a personal
tutor. Although this was done chiefly to secure responsible control
of the young man's finances, the idea of an individual supervision
more personal than the earlier system of *informatores*[3] had a long
life before it. Finally, the introduction of the birch as a means of enforcing the rules with junior members was without real precedent. In
the statutes of Brasenose College it was sanctioned first as a discre-
tionary measure of the college lecturer to enforce discipline in the
classroom, but it was further allowed as a penalty that might be
substituted for any of the fines.[4] The verdict of Hastings Rashdall
stands as a comment on such legislation: '. . . the sixteenth century
was the flogging age *par excellence* in the English universities.'[5]

It was Bishop Fox's contribution to mould these several elements
into a collegiate society in which the principles of constant surveillance, delation erected into a principle of government, and the
extended application of corporal punishment were quite visible.[6]
The new attitude is immediately signalled in the chapter on the
office of the president: all in the college—fellows, disciples, ministers
and servants—were to be subject to him, to fear him like a prince,
honour him like a father, and obey him in all lawful commands
without a murmur—a phrase repeated in the statutes of Wolsey's
college and of those at St John's.[7] Each undergraduate 'disciple'
was lodged with a fellow or probationer, an arrangement ensuring
maximum supervision.[8] The more senior was to make it his business

---

[1] But the statutes were read to fellows at least twice, to scholars three times a year;
SCO ii. pt 9, 41.

[2] Cf the late medieval 'aularian statutes': *Statuta*, 574 ff. *passim*. On Brasenose College's
links with its aularian past see chapter 1, p. 16.

[3] See McConica, 'The rise of the undergraduate college', p. 3.   [4] *SCO* ii. pt 9, 16, 19.

[5] Rashdall, *Universities of Europe* iii. 371, 358-60; cf Stone, *Crisis of the Aristocracy*,
35. On corporal punishment in the schools see Keith Thomas, *Rule and Misrule in the
Schools of Early Modern England* (The Stenton Lecture 1975, Reading 1976), 9 ff.

[6] Ariès, op. cit., 281.

[7] 'ut eum timeant ut principem, colant ut patrem, et in licitis sine murmure parentes';
SCO ii. pt 10, 2; cf. pt 11, 14; iii. pt 12, 13. The statutes of Trinity College returned to the
milder medieval formula; *SCO* iv. Trinity 54.

[8] See on the government of Corpus, McConica, 'The rise of the undergraduate college',
p. 18 ff.

to see to the welfare of the junior by advice and example, to instruct him in his studies, confront him with his faults and correct him. If necessary he was to report any misconduct to the president, vice-president or a dean as soon as possible.[1] Grave misdemeanour —heresy, perjury, murder, adultery and the like—was punished by immediate banishment without appeal: in this there was nothing exceptional. But Fox was more explicit than his predecessors about the punishments used to correct minor faults, which 'like unheeded sparks, might kindle a fire to consume the most splendid edifice'.[2] If after a first warning an offence was repeated, and no statutory penalty was already provided, the president and one dean would decide upon an appropriate punishment: withdrawal of commons, banishment to the library 'when he would least like it'[3] to write or compose something, or a shame punishment such as dining alone in hall while the rest were at dinner, eating only bread and water. Withdrawal of commons could be used as a penalty against any member of the college or its servants, and Fox expressly provided that those so deprived should not be allowed to take their meals in town. They would eat in hall at the usual hours, masters of arts at their usual places but bachelors and undergraduates sitting with any others undergoing punishment. All such meals were paid for at the end of the term by the individual concerned who would himself enter in the dean's register the nature of the correction, the reason for it and his name.[4] Punishments like these with a careful scale of increments according to the nature and frequency of the particular offence were typical in Fox's regulations for Corpus. Junior members, however—undergraduate probationers or *discipuli* —could incur corporal punishment. Violators of the orders concerning divine service, or of the reverent decorum prescribed for meals in hall (including the stringent rules about speaking only in Latin or Greek at all times), those who failed to attend the compulsory public lectures in Latin and Greek without permission, and those who incurred the displeasure of their teachers of logic and sophistry— any of these not past his twentieth year might be flogged if such a severe punishment seemed warranted.[5]

College life was led under the supervision and most often the watchful eyes of the senior members, the president, vice-president

[1] *SCO* ii. pt 10, 81.

[2] Ibid. 98–9.

[3] 'Cum minime vellet'; ibid. 99.

[4] Ibid. 100; the sixteenth-century register, like most of its kind, has unfortunately disappeared.

[5] Ibid. 42, 48, 50, 56. In 1528 the age limit was removed, probably because it was superfluous for undergraduates; Bodl. MS Laud misc. 621, pp. 45, 50.

and deans. It was also meant to be led almost entirely within the college. Bachelors of arts who were required to attend the humanities lectures at Magdalen College were to go and return in a body.[1] It was plainly the founder's intention that no member should leave the college to venture into town alone; if he was not a graduate he was not to leave at all without the special licence of his dean or the logic lecturer.[2] No member of the college whatsoever except a servant might enter the house of a lay person within the university or the suburbs up to a distance of one mile for any reason whatsoever on pain of loss of commons for a week.[3] Even recreation abroad in the fields was to be taken in groups of three who were to remain together and return together. They were at all times to be plainly dressed as clerics easily distinguishable from laymen.[4] Leaves of absence could be granted for good reason—the statutes recognized the need for the 'bees' occasionally to be let out of the hive—but no fellow could be absent from the college for more than forty days, and no disciple or probationer for more than twenty.[5]

The scrutiny at Corpus Christi College was perhaps predictably a very solemn affair. It was held during Holy Week in the chapel immediately after the reading of the statutes.[6] The president and one of the more discreet fellows of his own choice privately examined each of the fellows beginning with those most senior, with respect to the conduct, deportment and studies of each of the members of the college. The fellows so interrogated were required in fear of perjury to tell all they knew that required correction, and the inquiry which followed procedures already described might last up to three days.[7] All punishments had to be carried out within fifteen days of Easter. Beyond this solemn investigation there was the prospect of a visitation by the bishop of Winchester at least once in five years, when the president and senior fellows would themselves be open to accusation.[8]

We must not forget in all of this that we are dealing with a society of clerics, true or potential, and that these statutes stand appro-

---

[1] SCO ii. pt 10, 54; in 1528 this rule might be waived for 'causa legitima'.

[2] Ibid. 67; for a similar provision at Magdalen College ibid. pt 8, 70.

[3] Ibid. 66.

[4] Ibid. 67; also at Magdalen ibid. 69.

[5] Ibid. 69-70; at Magdalen sixty days were allowed to both fellows and scholars ibid. 41.

[6] Ibid. 100 ff. This followed the custom at Magdalen where the statutes were read three times a year, and the scrutiny was held at the Easter reading; ibid. pt 8, 32. In 1528 the revised statutes of Corpus allowed that the scrutiny might be held in the hall.

[7] See above, p. 653. Fox's rules followed those of Magdalen closely.

[8] Appeal to the visitor was of course an ancient provision; ibid. pt 10, 103–6.

priately in a long and recognizable tradition of religious legislation.[1] None the less in comparison with those of his predecessors Fox's statutes set a new tone even within that tradition by their scrupulous attention to detail and by what can only be described as a general wariness about disorder.[2] In the characteristically rhetorical introduction to his statute on the college visitation he deplored the proclivity to evil of human kind and the mutability of all excellence.[3] In the last chapter there was a final attempt to remove any possible ambiguity from his repeated provisions for the increase of corrections according to the frequency of the offence;[4] themes of discipline and punishment ran through all the final pages like an abiding preoccupation. Yet not all was dark. Finding that members of his college were arranging private suppers in their rooms on Saturday nights he instituted a weekly Saturday supper in common. And on festivals, when the fire was lit, the fellows and probationers might remain in hall to enjoy recreations becoming to clerics, to sing, recite poems, or histories, or to discuss among themselves the wonders of the world.[5]

We are clearly in another world from that of the medieval hall or hostel, although the carefree and undisciplined life of the medieval undergraduate is more a matter of myth than of record; even the device of delation was seemingly known in the halls.[6] As for the tightly disciplined society of Corpus Christi College, its workings were like those of all living communities, less perfect than the ideals of its statutes. Although we have no trace of the dean's register of discipline which would tell us far more of what we want to know,[7] visitation records give some assistance. The visitation of Corpus in 1566 by Bishop Horne shows a charge successfully brought against Jerome Reynolds that he was partial in his punishments of scholars and for three years had failed to hear the sophisters or attend the disputations of the bachelors as all fellows were bound to do two or three times a week.[8] There is further evidence as early as 1540 that the college was experiencing difficulty especially in keeping up the arduous demands on both bachelors and undergraduates in the

[1] In 1528 Fox added the decree that all members of the college should go to confession five times a year; ibid. 115 (where the English rubric is wrong).

[2] Cf H. C. Maxwell Lyte, *A History of the University of Oxford* (1886), 410: 'The rules concerning the discipline of the college were singularly minute.'

[3] *SCO* ii. pt 10, 103.

[4] Ibid. 108.

[5] Ibid. 115 (not in 1517), 80.

[6] See J. I. Catto, 'Citizens, scholars and masters' on 'the emergence, in the fifteenth century, of a disciplined, highly organized society of colleges and halls', *HUO* i. 170 and following. On the role of the *impositor*, ibid. 181.

[7] See p. 655 n. 4 above, the earliest surviving starts in 1641.

[8] Fowler, *Corpus Christi*, 112.

teaching of Greek.[1] This is scarcely surprising, but Lawrence Humfrey's life of Jewel suggests, even allowing for its subject's exceptional character and ability, that the scholastic regime at Corpus in his day was both effective and efficient.[2]

It may be that the rule of the first president had something to do with this. John Claymond had governed Corpus for the first twenty years of its existence. He was wealthy, learned and devout with—suitably enough—a particular devotion to the holy eucharist, and his reputation as a benefactor both of the university and of the town suggests a man of unusual breadth of concern.[3] More to the point, the presidency of Magdalen College which he subsequently resigned to take on the headship of Fox's new foundation he had taken up in the wake of a visitation which was conducted by Fox's commissary, Dr John Dowman, and which revealed a state of serious disorder in Waynflete's college.[4] Fox had already shown confidence in Claymond's abilities to govern, and that confidence must have been strengthened by Claymond's successful rule at Magdalen.[5]

Magdalen's history of disorder, moreover, must be acknowledged in any account of the discipline exercised in the Tudor university.[6] Its regulations were only less strict than those of Corpus; its buildings offered a far more effective enclosure than did those of a small medieval college like Exeter. None the less successive Tudor visitations seem to reveal a fellowship that was unusually unruly and disobedient. Dowman's investigations recorded allegations of disobedience and disrespect even among the junior members; of scholars frequently spending nights out of college and even out of the town without leave; of gambling and the illegal keeping of dogs, harriers and birds of prey; of certain fellows inciting the younger bachelors and scholars to hunt by day or night; or failure by fellows to correct and report on the defects of the juniors placed in their rooms; of careless keeping of the gates by the porter.[7] While not all the allegations need be taken at the letter, it is clear that the commissary was disturbed and that there was genuine need for correction.[8] The

[1] Fowler, Corpus Christi, 92n.

[2] John Jewel entered Corpus on 19 August 1539; BA 1540, MA 1544/5; fellow 18 March 1542. Ioannis Iuelli Angli . . . vita & mors (1573); Fowler, 91 ff.; S. L. Greenslade, 'The faculty of theology', p. 318 above.

[3] Claymond's provision of gates, bridges and of a covered market in Oxford are reported in the elegiac poem of John Shepreve, Greek reader at Corpus and later regius professor of Hebrew; see Fowler, 79–81.

[4] W. D. Macray, A Register of the members of St Mary Magdalen College, Oxford from the foundation of the college (new ser. 8 vols 1894–1915), i. 35–61.

[5] Fowler, 80n; H. A. Wilson, Magdalen College (1899), 60–5.

[6] For the problems under the puritan president Laurence Humfrey see Penry Williams above, pp. 418–19.

[7] Macray i. 41–57.   [8] Ibid. 59–61.

results of another visitation by Dowman in 1520 under Claymond's successor suggest that things had improved substantially, but they also show that some difficulties were chronic: frequenting taverns, pernoctation, gambling, hunting, irreverent or disorderly conduct within the chapel and hall.[1] Like charges can be found in the visitation records of any of the other colleges, but they are particularly important in a college of relatively late foundation, where there was a large undergraduate element and a detailed code of conduct. They also form a corrective to the impression that severity of regulation implies severity of practice. On the other hand, the relative infrequency of such complaints in the visitation records at Corpus, where the struggles were much more personal and political, may suggest that in the smaller college the standards were easier to enforce.[2]

It is difficult to document the disciplining of undergraduates. Registers of discipline seem to survive for Tudor Oxford in only three colleges: Lincoln, Magdalen and Christ Church.[3] Of these the register at Magdalen College is much the most informative, and the record begins in 1547 with perhaps a dozen disciplinary actions entered for each year. Typically, however, none involves an undergraduate; all have to do with men of at least BA status. It seems likely that the misconduct of undergraduates was either thought too unimportant to record (whereas the need to judge a fellow's aptness for college positions, ecclesiastical preferment or like responsibilities would make the failings of his maturer years worth noting), or that it was preserved in books now lost, like the register bound for Magdalen College in 1530 to record the misdemeanours and accusations of the fellows and scholars.[4] We cannot of course conclude from the near silence of surviving records that correction was neglected. One of the charges brought against Claymond's successor at Magdalen, President John Higden, was excessive severity in punishing the juniors, 'whence it has been said that he has done it rather from a passion for beating than for any just cause'.[5] Like glimpses occur elsewhere. In April 1570 two undergraduates were punished

---

[1] Ibid. 71 ff. See also the Marian disciplinary decrees of 1555 and the visitation of Horne's commissary in 1566; Macray ii. 31, 36–40.

[2] Even this is uncertain. A visitation taken up with serious strife among the college officers might neglect the routine of statutory offences. There is also a difficulty about the survival of the Corpus records; see Fowler, *Corpus Christi*, 131 n. 2.

[3] Lincoln College Archives Register A.1.2 (medium registrum); Magdalen College Archives MS 730(a) (vice-president's register a); Christ Church Archives MS liii.b.1 (subdean's book 1). The last contains only leaves of absence, appointments to livings, allocations of rooms to almsmen and the like for the sixteenth century. The only penalty entered during our period in the Lincoln register (for 1600) is the punishment of a BA. Some penalties stray into other records, as will be seen.

[4] Macray ii. 5; cf. Corpus n. 68 above.

[5] Macray i. 76.

by the master and fellows of Balliol for remarks that seemed to accuse one of the fellows of perjury. The first scholar, a Dr Bell's exhibitioner named Thomas Hadden, was punished with six strokes of the whip in the presence of all the scholars. The other man, Thomas Woode, whom Hadden claimed had encouraged the offence, received the same sentence when they decided that the charge was partly proved and partly confessed. He refused to accept the penalty and was expelled.[1] At Christ Church the system of regular promotion by class made demotion a useful penalty, to judge by various entries in the chapter book. In January 1589/90 a George Gilder was demoted from among those about to proceed bachelor to the next lower form. He was also to receive from the censor in the hall 'such punishment as by us is decreed for him'; the penalty for refusal was again expulsion. A bachelor of arts accused of having encouraged Gilder in abuse of the censor was also demoted by one rank of seniority and ordered to amend his ways under penalty of expulsion —but not of public discipline.[2]

The records of the colleges and university both show that whatever the incidence of undergraduate misbehaviour, the conduct of the senior members was scarcely calculated to edify the younger men. As in the preceding centuries they were only a few years apart.[3] The gap in the Tudor registers and the irregular survival of supplementary records such as depositions rules out any attempt at statistics, but it is clear from what survives that among the serious crimes, assault and defamation ranked very high. This observation accords with other impressions of public crime in Elizabethan and seventeenth-century England, with the difference that the actors in the Oxford records were for the most part graduates and masters of arts.[4] This in turn strikingly confirms the view that recourse to violence was common throughout the social strata, for the conduct of the Oxford scholars resembles that of the more wealthy and prominent in country villages.[5] Homicides, too, when they occur seem

[1] Balliol College Archives Balliol College Register 1514–1682, p. 118.

[2] Christ Church Archives MS D & C i.b.2, p. 124. The records of the vice-chancellor's court are no more informative concerning undergraduate discipline than those surviving in the colleges. Mr Walter Mitchell tells me that in the course of calendaring those for the sixteenth century he came across no episode involving an undergraduate member of the university.

[3] J. I. Catto, 'Citizens, scholars and masters', 170.

[4] James A. Sharpe, *Crime in Seventeenth Century England: a county study* (Cambridge 1983) remarks that assault came third among the frequently indicted offences in Essex in the decades 1620–80 after grand larceny and the keeping of unlicensed alehouses; p. 115. For a study of attacks on reputation and the 'explosion' in litigation from the mid-sixteenth century onwards see idem, *Defamation and sexual slander in early modern England: the church courts at York* (Borthwick papers 58, York 1980).

[5] Sharpe, *Crime in seventeenth century England*, 118–19.

usually to have arisen from violent quarrels without premeditation.[1] A less usual case is the attack in October 1580 on one Thomas Hore, who according to one of the deponents, his companion at the time, was in Oxford to attend the quarter sessions. The accused, a master of arts named Richard Calfield, was probably a student of Christ Church who had incorporated MA in 1577. Moved 'with many great and grievous causes' he challenged Hore at Carfax in the presence of the witness. When Hore declined the challenge Calfield withdrew, only to return later armed with sword and buckler, and accompanied by perhaps a dozen supporters, some of them armed, at least one among them being also master of arts. Hore was slain with a horrifying injury, and the proctor who had come to his assistance with his man was likewise injured.[2]

While few of the cases to come before the vice-chancellor's court show the calculated malevolence of this murder, there are enough breaches of the peace to suggest that the streets of Tudor Oxford were far from tranquil. If the matter ended there one might imagine that the undergraduates at least were protected from scenes of violence within college walls. Not surprisingly, however, young men who were capable of assault and mayhem in the streets were quite likely to turn to violence anywhere. In 1559 a newly elected fellow of Merton struck the servant of another fellow with a dagger while his victim was naked and defenceless in his master's bedchamber. At Christ Church the dean and chapter found it necessary to issue decrees condemning all brawling, backbiting, intemperate and contentious speeches, insisting that if the senior at the table could not quell them the dean or subdean would intervene to impose punishments. There was also a scale of monetary fines for striking and wounding, including the drawing of blood. At Magdalen there was fighting during dinner in hall; a bachelor of arts was punished with loss of commons for a week because he stole the keys of the college from the vice-president, and a clerk was severely reprimanded because he carried round stones on his person with the intention of throwing them at the senior steward.[3]

Verbal violence and aggression were equally a feature of university and college life.[4] Sexual slanders played a predictable part. A priest

---

[1] Ibid. 131 'It seems likely . . . that small homicides were characteristically unplanned acts of violence arising spontaneously from quarrels, being simple assaults that went too far in most cases.'

[2] OUA Hyp B 2, Chancellor's court deposition book 1578–84 (unfoliated after fo 50), several depositions from 2 January 1580/1.

[3] Reg. ann. mert. 1521–67, 192; Christ Church Archives MS D & C i.b.2, pp. 233, 258; Magdalen College Archives MS 730(a), fos 89 (1594), 45^V (1584), 20 (1559).

[4] See p. 660 n. 4.

of New College in 1547 admitted having given the college butler a note reading, 'Aske Philippe [i.e. John Dodwell's wife] what tyme hir geste [a bachelor of arts of the same college] went to bede and what tyme he rose'. Three years later Garbrand Harkes, a stationer and thus a privileged servant of the university, claimed that his wife had been defamed with like abuse by a widow, Elizabeth Clare. The widow denied most of the allegations but admitted to having called her a 'buttermowthed Flemmying'.[1] Cases of libel abounded within the university community and among its servants, often culminating in blows.

When we add to these evidences the repeated charges of pernoctation, of frequenting taverns and houses of ill-fame we are forced to modify the view that collegiate enclosure entirely transformed the life of the Tudor university. Gates were not always well kept.[2] When in the last decade of the century Cecil as chancellor repeatedly tried to bring Cambridge to better order, failure to enforce enclosure was a prominent concern. In October 1601 he sent a list of articles to the vice-chancellor, among them an order that the gates were to be shut as provided in the statutes of the various colleges, 'and not to stande open most parte of the night, giving libertie to night-gaddinge in the towne and other inconveniences'.[3] Leicester's complaints about Oxford were of the same order.[4] Even without such neglect the society outside the college gates seems to have been surprisingly accessible. A careful reading of the model statutes at Corpus alone —and who can doubt that they were shrewdly examined beyond the founder's intentions?—would have revealed that any fellow, scholar, student, chaplain or servant of the college might leave unaccompanied at almost any time of the day if he could make the pretext of 'urgent attendance' at a procession, the Acts or deliberations of the university, at the schools or the library, or of being on his way to a college or hall to hear or give a lecture or attend a disputation.[5]

We must also be cautious in assuming that the disciplinary regula-

[1] Reg. Canc. 1545–1661, fos 20, 47. On Harkes or Herks see Carl I. Hammer Jr., 'Oxford town and Oxford university', p. 77 above.

[2] See p. 659 above. Even if they were, college registers reveal recurrent concern about illicit means of entry. At Lincoln College in 1589, for example, it was decided that any fellow entering the college over the walls or by other access than the gates should be punished for pernocation; Lincoln College Archives Reg. A.1.2 fo 19[v].

[3] C. H. Cooper, Annals of Cambridge (5 vols 1842–1908), ii. 614.

[4] C. E. Mallet, A History of the University ii. 118. In 1586 Sir Francis Knollys as lord lieutenant wrote to the vice-chancellor asking the university either to keep its members in order or to secure from the queen exemption from his jurisdiction. He would be ashamed 'to suffer such an outrageous disorder as was used by your universitie men laterly . . .'; Reg. Canc. 1564–82, fo 351[v].

[5] SCO ii. pt 10, 67.

tions were applied with equal force to commoners. Magdalen College, whose statutes had been first to provide for *commensales* living as members of the college, had the reputation of a staunch puritan establishment under Laurence Humfrey. Thomas Cooper's visitation as bishop of Winchester in 1585 revealed that commoners and battelars had been admitted far in excess of the number allowed, and that no regular provision had been made either for their teaching or discipline. Humfrey was responsible himself for the commoners so admitted, and benefited from their stipends; he would not allow the deans to exercise any authority over them. While these were the charges of certain of the fellows, Cooper's injunctions show that he recognized the justice of their complaints.[1] Again at St John's College, much indebted to commoners for revenue and endowment, there is no trace in the very full college registers of discipline touching them and much evidence that they were catered to lavishly; indeed, the founder himself had vainly wished the number reduced because they would not 'abide chastisement'.[2]

Another phenomenon that must have undermined collegiate discipline was the habit of migration from hall to hall and college to college. This can be discovered from even a cursory examination of the university careers of Tudor undergraduates,[3] but it is vividly illustrated by the experience of a Welsh lawyer born in 1575 into a substantial professional family in Abergavenny, county Monmouth.[4] He was David Baker, known to history as Augustine Baker, OSB, a great figure of the English Benedictine tradition and its leading spiritual writer. His autobiographical fragment, written in the third person and late in life, probably reflects the moral sensitivity of the mature contemplative, but its circumstantial details could be confirmed in many other records. He had been sent to Christ's Hospital for 'morality and civility' and to learn English as well as Latin and Greek. He came up to Oxford in May 1590 under the tutelage of a kinsman who was a student of Christ Church. Baker was lodged with most of his kind at Broadgates Hall where he fell into loose company. He and his companions ate only meat during Lent, chiefly at Baker's expense, and shortly he met with a 'far greater viciousnesse'.[5] Seeking further liberty, he left Broadgates and entered

[1] Macray, *Reg. Magdalen* iii. 11–24. Penry Williams, 'Elizabethan Oxvord: state, church and university', pp. 418–19 above.

[2] Stevenson and Salter, *Early History*, 139, 272–3.

[3] *Reg. Univ.* ed. Clark, ii–iii.

[4] *Memorials of Father Augustine Baker and other documents relating to the English Benedictines*, eds Dom Justin McCann, OSB, Dom Hugh Connolly, OSB. (Catholic Record Society xxxiii 1933), 39 ff.

[5] 'of that greatnesse that I know not how their could be greater, being of the kind

another college, not named, where he studied little, continued his former vices and acquired more, 'which was to be daily and nightly abroad, stealing some things or other, as either towards eating or fewell, . . . to serve his and their unthriftinesse and excesses'. The illicit Lenten flesh meat too was stolen, 'for mony they had not for it', their own stipends going for commons in the house. Baker's delinquencies, as is evident, cannot be attributed simply to the admittedly freer regimen of life in the halls, although since he took no degree we are unlikely ever to learn which college it was that proved so comfortable a haven for a prosperous young commoner.

Against this we should set the most detailed account of undergraduate indiscipline to survive from the Tudor period. It comes from the register of St John's College, whose statutes were copied almost verbatim from those of Corpus.[1] William Finmore was a scholar from Reading who was said to be 17 years old at his admission in June 1578. He became a fellow in June 1581 although he was still an undergraduate, being admitted BA on 4 July 1582. He kept company with another undergraduate from Merchant Taylors' School, Timothy Willis, who was apparently something of a ringleader in 'lewd life & licentious behaviour' and who had already been once expelled and readmitted.[2] Finmore was notorious for gadding and wandering in the streets, for 'haunting and frequenting tavernes, alehouses and disinge houses and other suspected places'.[3] Finally, one Sunday night the president personally searched through the college between eight and nine and found that Finmore and Willis were absent with others. On the following Monday he convened a formal disciplinary meeting in the hall with the logic reader. Finmore was unrepentant. The president condemned him and his fellow absentees to be beaten,[4] beginning with Finmore who resisted, 'and gave the President very foule words and stroke him and in the end drew his knife upon him and told him that he would thrust his knife unto him and into the best man he kept and vaunting up upon the tables of the hall he defended himself by force and violence with his naked knife, and so resisting the punishment enjoyned unto him, he ran away out of the College in his dublett and hose, crying out as

(though yet greater) of which S. Paul meant when he said *Qualia nec inter gentes auditur esse* (1 Cor. v. 1)', *Memorials*, 43.

[1] St John's College Archives Register i. fo 200; Stevenson and Salter, *Early History*, 231–2, 355–6. No register of discipline survives at St John's.

[2] Stevenson and Salter, *Early History*, 354–5.

[3] Ibid. 356.

[4] The statutes of St John's allowed flogging only of undergraduates who were not more than eighteen; *SCO* iii. pt 11, 83. It is most likely that Finmore's age was misreported on his arrival; see below, p. 676.

he went "that whosoever should lay hands on him he would kill him" '. He could not be found, but on the third day he returned and submitted, to escape expulsion simply by receiving his original punishment.[1] The following December he was elected to a law fellowship. He died in 1646 at the age of 87, a knight of the realm.

In these well-recorded events at St John's the attitude of the college is quite as interesting as the behaviour of the undergraduates. Once again we are given serious reason to doubt the effectiveness of collegiate enclosure despite the stringent rules. What is more, the fellows of St John's seem to have adopted a lenient attitude to these habitual offenders and to have resorted reluctantly to the ultimate penalties of birching and expulsion. In light of the later careers of Willis and Finmore we may perhaps assume that they were unusually able; at least with Finmore the patience of the college officers seems to have been justified. His defiance looks spectacular even by contemporary standards, and yet his threat to the president of the college brought no additional punishment on his head. We are forced to realize that we cannot know all the circumstances, nor recapture the personal understanding and estimate of each man, that must have informed the college's policy. We are again reminded of the distance between the rigid provisions of college statute and the realities as seen and acted upon by contemporaries.

Life in the Elizabethan college was undoubtedly spartan and severe, and through the vagaries of disease or other calamity it was often precarious as well. There is no reason, however, to think—contrary to accepted belief—that these Tudor collegians were actually ill-nourished, nor were the pressures unremitting since they came and went at any time throughout the university year, as the college registers recording dispensations show. Standards of official discipline reflect the full impact of the new severity even prior to the influence of protestant ideals, and we must assume that parents believed they were carried out to the letter. We have indicated our reasons for thinking they were not. We must not exaggerate the success of enclosure and internal surveillance, and we must acknowledge as well the companionable side of collegiate life as it appears in the testimony of Simon Forman, in the provisions for games and recreation, and in the vigour of festive traditions that were now enriched with the flourishing of collegiate drama.

[1] Willis, who refused to attend, was expelled for good. He became ambassador to Moscow and was made a doctor of the university by a special decree of the queen; see p. 664 n. 2, and T. S. Willan, *Early History of the Russia Company 1553–1603* (Manchester 1956), 231–3. For a possible analogue in ritual defiance see the account of 'barring-out' in Keith Thomas, *Rule and Misrule*, 20 ff.

At the same time it is clear that the triumph of cultivated manners was as slow to reach the college as it was to reach the gentry household. The savage behaviour of the propertied classes can be amply illustrated in university registers, where we find continous record of common violence, a counterpoint to the rise of corporal punishment. If renaissance urbanity finally prevailed in a later century, that achievement no doubt owed much to the humanistic ideals and sense of discipline instilled in the colleges, but David Baker's testimony to the thieving ways of well-to-do commoners living in college should not be forgotten when we reflect that most of them were reading Cicero and Castiglione—at least in translation.

Colleges took over much of the function of the family, with parental authority represented in the life of the undergraduate by his tutor. This relationship also had more to offer than repressive discipline. There were evidently strong possibilities of support in the collegiate arrangements that would make a young man's initiation into his maturity a good deal easier. If the universities had not provided some kind of effective bridge between life in the family and the adult career it would be impossible to explain the common resort to the colleges as way-stations, so to speak, in the journey. Amidst living conditions that were on the whole little more severe than those left behind, young men of 17 and 18 years of age also found a common identity among their peers, and models to consult among their youthful mentors with whom they lived in close intimacy, and who were under the same theoretical regimen, admittedly with a few additional privileges. When their tutors actually trained and disputed with them and alongside them they were more than the family paymasters and secret agents of the dean, and their office as monitors need not always have been ominous; it may be something of this that we see in the striking experience of Finmore and Willis. One result was the growth of loyalty to the college itself, bringing a rich harvest of gifts and benefactions, and the unambiguous testimony of successive generations who followed their forbears to the same collegiate home. But before anything more is said of the achievements and shortcomings of the system we must turn to the men that it served.

THE MEN OF CORPUS CHRISTI COLLEGE

The changing social composition of the post-medieval universities has long concerned historians on both sides of the Atlantic, and it forms one of the common themes of these volumes.[1] In England

[1] I have reviewed the early historiography of this question dating from the work of J. H.

the period of the sixteenth and seventeenth centuries has so far received most of the attention. It is seen as a time when the universities, on the face of it rather unlikely contenders, won out over competing schemes for the education of the sons of the well-to-do to establish themselves—clerical societies still but ever more delivered up to the bidding of the laity—in a secure, near-monopoly of higher education which was shared in part only with the inns of court. In borrowing their questions and instruments of inquiry from the social sciences, however, historians of the sixteenth and early seventeenth centuries have been frustrated by the historic deposit of record information, utterly inappropriate for the quantitative measurements that would promise some kind of assurance about the social background of entrants, or the use of the universities in promoting upward social mobility, or in enhancing or diminishing the sense of regional identity, and the like. As a result the best efforts have been made over secular intervals.[1] In the narrower but critical span of the sixteenth century the problems are little different from those facing the historian of the medieval university. Even after the establishment of the matriculation registers, the first attempt to preserve a systematic record of those who came, the university's record-keeping was fitful and at best incomplete; for long series of homogeneous and comparable data we must wait until the Stuart restoration.[2]

Faced with these difficulties it would seem that the most useful addition to the existing literature ought to come from a careful study of the social composition and relations of one particular college, and Corpus was chosen for this purpose.[3] As the example of

Hexter in 1950 in 'The prosopography of the Tudor university', *Journal of Interdisciplinary History* iii. 3 (Winter 1973), 543–54. See in particular Mark Curtis, *Oxford and Cambridge*; Hugh Kearney, *Scholars and Gentlemen*; Lawrence Stone, *Crisis of the Aristocracy*; and also by Stone, 'The educational revolution in England, 1560–1640', *Past & Present* xxvciii (1964), 41–80; 'The size and composition of the Oxford student body, 1580–1910', in Lawrence Stone (ed.), *The University in Society* (2 vols Princeton 1975), i. 3–110. In the last volume see also James McConica, 'Scholars and commoners in renaissance Oxford', pp. 151–81, and Victor Morgan, 'Cambridge university and "the country" 1560–1640', pp. 183–245. There is a preliminary account of the population of Corpus by the present writer in 'The social relations of Tudor Oxford', *Transactions of the Royal Historical Society*, 5th series vii. 115–34. See also the review articles by Joan Simon, 'The history of education in *Past and Present*', *Oxford Review of Education* iii (1977), 71–86, and Victor Morgan, 'Approaches to the history of the English universities in the sixteenth and seventeenth centuries', in G. Klingenstein, H. Lutz and G. Stourzh (eds), *Bildung, Politik und Gesellschaft* (Vienna 1978), 138–64. A recent review is found in Rosemary O'Day, *Education and Society 1500–1800* (1982), chapters 5 and 6.

[1] See especially Stone, 'The size and composition of the Oxford student body 1580–1910'.

[2] McConica, 'The prosopography of the Tudor university', 549.

[3] See the note on the collective biography of Corpus on pp. 692–3.

Brasenose indicates, the most important addition to the medieval archive in the sixteenth century came from the records of those new collegiate foundations that were in any case so closely bound up with the changes we wish to understand.[1] By using this approach we admittedly sacrifice any attempt to provide a wider look at the population of the university as a whole, but to the degree that this can be done with any kind of assurance such an account is given in the existing literature. In Corpus Christi College we have the signal foundation of the Tudor age whose idiosyncrasies are those of a plan that was widely imitated. Its story may therefore be particularly instructive.

A careful and prolonged examination of the available records suggests that from the time of foundation until the end of the reign of Elizabeth I, some 708 men were admitted to Corpus Christi College in all ranks from that of president (the admission of the first president John Claymond) to the lower servants. For members on the foundation this list seems likely to be nearly complete.[2] It shows that 20 were admitted directly as fellows[3] and another 125 as *scholares* or probationer fellows. A further 291 came in as *discipuli*.[4] Of the remaining ranks there were 22 choristers, of whom 5 are known to have taken degrees; 40 chaplains, 24 of whom qualified in arts and theology; 38 minor clerics, of whom 21 likewise took degrees, and 63 college servants. Of these last, only 5 found their way into studies. It would seem that the chapel was a more likely avenue for the advancement of the poor than was more mundane service to the college.[5]

The college recruited its members then chiefly as undergraduates or, to a lesser extent, from recent graduates eligible to become fellows. The annual intake of men in the three categories of fellow, scholar (in the statutory sense of probationer fellow) and *discipulus* moved within a fairly narrow range after the year 1522 when the full complement of twenty fellows and twenty discipuli was reached for the first time; this is scarcely surprising, since intake was dictated

---

[1] See McConica, 'The rise of the undergraduate college', 11 ff.

[2] A leaf of the *Liber admissionum* is missing for the period March 1580 to June 1581 which might have added a half-dozen *discipuli* and/or *scholares*. Admission to full fellowship above the rank of *scholaris* is recorded in the series of fellows' bonds. The *Libri magni* supply the names of 43 choristers and clerics (e.g. sacristans) and 58 servants not found in the admission register, with a further 7 *discipuli* or *scholares* (perhaps those of the missing folio).

[3] Nine before 1520 including the founder's nominees. Wolsey's readers, who were not on the foundation and only resident at Corpus are not included in the membership.

[4] Three were admitted as readers, Edward Wotton, George Rudde and John Bell.

[5] Three more were residents who seem to have taken no degrees, and there were several boy-pupils of whom two stayed to become *discipuli*.

entirely by the occurrence of vacancies according to the statutes. If the annual recruitment is plotted in five-year moving averages to smooth out short-term variations, we find that Corpus admitted four to five men a year until the 1540s, when the number rose to five or six. In 1550 the college admitted ten, an intake that ushered in a decade when the annual average peaked between seven and eight. In the sixties there is slightly more fluctuation and in the seventies a falling off, dropping further in the eighties and early nineties to four or five once more. In the last decade the annual average returns to five or six. In light of the college regulations, this would seem to point chiefly to a greater mobility for the clergy in the years between 1550 and 1570; there is no likelihood that the numbers of those on the foundation at any given moment would have wandered far from the strict statutory quota. Chaplains were recruited sporadically at the rate of four or five a decade, evidently as need arose through their promotion to other livings.

When we turn to the commoners we are on much less solid ground. From the first establishment of the college, as we have seen, the founder allowed from four to six sons of gentlemen to live there and share in its life and teaching as *commensales* or commoners who paid for the privilege. Since they do not appear in the admission registers or accounts there is small likelihood of our discovering them until the advent of the matriculation register. By chance a separate set of accounts survived at Corpus for the years 1537 to 1542,[1] and from those we glean an additional eighteen surnames suggestive of other names that have vanished from record. The registers of congregation reveal a further hundred or so names of men who matriculated or took degrees as members of Corpus but of whom there is no record on the foundation. It is to be presumed that the association was not merely casual, and the most likely explanation is that these were men who had tutorial or other teaching arrangements with the college that left no trace in the Corpus records. In due course the pressure from the university for every undergraduate to find a recognized tutor in a college or hall confirmed and enforced these once informal links.[2] These men have therefore been added to the number of commoners at Corpus, although this title may imply in some cases a far more formal association with the life of the college than was in fact the case.

[1] The *Visus*; see Milne, *Early History*, 5 and the note on p. 690 below.

[2] See McConica, 'Scholars and commoners', 159, and on matriculation, 'The rise of the undergraduate college', 48 ff. above. The Fulman manuscripts in the college archives (MS CCC 305) add the names of another thirty 'gentlemen commoners'—an anachronistic designation for the sixteenth century—from records now lost.

Fox made very precise rules about the geographical origins of those admitted to his college as he did for everything else.[1] In general the men of Corpus were to be recruited from regions associated with his career and that of Hugh Oldham, but in fact the counties and dioceses designated—eleven in all—were those in which the college also held lands and collected rents.[2] The diocese of Winchester was to supply five scholars, that of Durham one, Bath and Wells and Exeter two each. Two more were to come from the county of Lincoln where Fox had been born, one from Lancaster, Oldham's birth-place, two from Gloucester (or the diocese of Worcester), one from Wiltshire (or the diocese of Salisbury), one from Bedfordshire, two from Kent, and one from Oxfordshire. Fox did not provide for his own kin but for those of his steward, William Frost, and they were deemed to be from Hampshire in the diocese of Winchester. In practice the arrangements were much more flexible. If the designated dioceses or counties failed to produce suitable candidates the college might elect from any other, with the proviso that no such county should be represented by more than one scholar at a time. This led to an elaborate system of substitution in which additionally a candidate from a recognized county might be elected for another until a more senior man from his own vacated a place. The general result was a society made up of men chiefly from the home counties, west country and south, with a significant concentration of strength also from the west midlands.[3] This pattern persisted without much change throughout the century.

The best represented county was Hampshire (which notionally contained the kin of William Frost) followed closely by Gloucester, Lincoln, Devon and Kent. Oxford, Surrey and Somerset provided most of the balance, while the largest group from the northern counties came from Lancashire. The 112 commoners whose countries of origin can be identified with at least considerable

[1] See Fowler, *Corpus Christi*, 46–7; the alterations between the 1517 statutes and those of 1528 are complex. See also Milne, *Early History*, 3–4.

[2] *SCO* ii. pt 10, 17–18, 20–1, 32–4. Land holdings in Kent (Graveney, Sellinge, Sheldwick, Perrywood, Chilham, Ensing, Meopham and Thanet) and in Surrey (Milton, Egham, Hailsham, Chertsey, Rusham) would seem in particular to account for the recruitment to Corpus from those counties. The other principal holdings were in Oxfordshire, Berkshire, Hampshire, Lincolnshire, Bedfordshire, Gloucestershire, and to a lesser degree in Somerset, Wiltshire and Devon.

[3] The breakdown is remarkably similar whether calculated by gross recruitment, including fellows admitted from outside, chaplains and clerics, or *discipuli* and *scholares* simply, as follows: west country (Somerset, Devon, Cornwall) 17–19 per cent; home counties (Kent, Surrey, Sussex, Middlesex including London) 18–20 per cent; south (Berkshire, Hampshire, Wiltshire, Dorset) 19–20 per cent; East Anglia (Essex, Cambridgeshire, Suffolk, Norfolk) 2–3 per cent; west midlands (Oxfordshire, Gloucestershire, Warwickshire, Worcestershire, Herefordshire) 17–19 per cent; north midlands and north, 18–20 per cent.

probability alter this pattern with a notable shift to the home counties, west midlands and south at the expense of the west country and north. The largest groups of commoners came from London and Middlesex (17) followed closely by Oxford (16) and Gloucester (12). In all of this the most conspicuous omission is East Anglia, served by Cambridge, whence Corpus drew a negligible share, like Oxford in general. Indeed, the constituency from which Fox's foundation drew seems a somewhat distorted portrait of the university as a whole; the Welsh were virtually invisible at Corpus, whereas they were about 10 per cent of all Elizabethan matriculants, and Corpus drew rather more heavily on the west country, home counties and south. Its intake from East Anglia and the west midlands was almost identical with the proportion in the university from those regions, and it fell below the average from the northern counties.[1] In this respect it cannot be said to have been wholly representative of the university's general population, but it was probably as nearly so as any other given college.[2]

The commoners of course included many of the sons of the prominent and well-to-do. Little can be said of the early surnames from the *Visus* except that some agree with those of prominent Corpus families: Way or Wye, Fetiplace, Kingsmill, Lynche and Wotton are all examples. Since it is certain that family links were forged very early in the history of the new foundation there is good reason to suppose that these men, otherwise unidentifiable, came from the same families as their later namesakes.[3] To some 8 per cent of the 129 commoners who came into the college after 1570 we can attach a social status with some certainty either from their claim at matriculation or from some other clear evidence. Two-thirds of them were from the rank of gentleman and above: there were two sons of barons, nine of knights, nineteen of armigerous fathers and twenty-nine of gentlemen. To these should be added the sons of the upper clergy: John Babington whose father Gervase was

[1] Based upon the matriculants for the years 1580–90 inclusive in *Reg. Univ.* ed. Clark, ii. table D, 416–17. With a total of 3,184 matriculants (excluding privileged persons) the proportion is: Wales 10 per cent, west country 14 per cent, home counties 16 per cent, East Anglia 1 per cent, west midlands 19 per cent, northern midlands and the north, 25 per cent, enumerating the same counties as in the foregoing.

[2] Comparison is interesting with the first recruits at Christ Church whose *patriae* are recorded in Register D & C i.b. 1. Of the 90 men listed there 6 came from the west country, 23 from the home counties, 5 from the south, 3 from East Anglia, 13 from the west midlands and 31 from the north midlands and the north; 5 were from Wales, 1 from Ireland, and 1 (ab Ulmis) from Switzerland. Cf McConica, 'The rise of the undergraduate college', p. 38 n. 3.

[3] J. K. McConica and C. S. Knighton, 'Some sixteenth-century Corpus families: Kingsmills, Nappers, Lancasters and others', *The Pelican* (Corpus Christi College, Oxford 1978–9), 6–9.

bishop of Worcester, and the three sons of Edwin Sandys, archbishop of York. Samuel Sandys, the eldest, George and Henry were all commoners. The archbishop's second son Edwin was also sent to Corpus but as a scholar on the foundation: he was admitted *discipulus* on 16 September 1577 to begin a distinguished career as the most prominent of all the children. The aristocratic family of the same name also sent a son. William, third baron Sandys of the Vyne in Hampshire, was holder of the title while an undergraduate. It was his admission with a schoolmaster and a companion or servant named Bretherton that was recorded in the visitation of 1566 when President Greenway was blamed for having violated the statutory restrictions on places. Greenway pleaded discretion as president, explaining that Sandys as a nobleman was able 'to pleasure the college and pay for all'.[1]

Apart from William Sandys only two other Corpus men appear to have descended from noble families.[2] Dudley Fitzgarret (alias Fitzgerald) of Stanwell, Middlesex was the second son of the youngest son of the 9th earl of Kildare. He seemingly took no degree and went on to the inns of court three years after his matriculation in 1582. He left no further trace, or issue, but in 1629 his nephew George, the 16th earl and ancestor of the dukes of Leinster, matriculated at Christ Church. The third man was Charles Eure, second son of the 2nd Baron Eure of Heyford Warren in Oxfordshire. He was admitted as a commoner in 1586 and in 1598 was further admitted to Gray's Inn after which he too is lost to sight; a nephew Horatio followed him to Corpus in 1607.

Among these commoners of the last three decades twenty-four are known to have taken academic degrees. Some of these—six in all—can be shown to have had clerical or plebeian parentage, and two are of unknown descent and without record of matriculation. There is, however, significant evidence (in what is admittedly a very small sample) of the sons of the gentry and of successful merchants showing interest—contrary to received opinion—in the statutory curriculum. Nathanaell Taverner, who matriculated in 1600 as the son of an Oxfordshire gentleman, was admittedly the son of a successful lawyer in Sands and Nettlebed, but the claim to gentle status is borne out on closer examination. His grandfather had been high sheriff and bought the manor of Wood Eaton in Oxfordshire; he had married the daughter of a rich London goldsmith and invested

---

[1] McConica and Knighton, op. cit. 9; Hampshire Record Office Winchester Reg. Horne fo 25^v.

[2] The John Yonge of Kent who matriculated at Corpus in 1597 as 'baronis filius' has not been traced; cf Clark ii. 221. Fitzgarret entered as of armigerous rank.

some five thousand pounds in monastic lands. Nathanaell's mother was the daughter of Sir Christopher Hales. The boy supplicated for his BA in March 1602 and three years later was admitted to Gray's Inn; in 1611 he became a barrister-at-law. Since he was a younger son his academic interests are perhaps understandable, but Sir Richard Dyott who was admitted as a commoner at the very end of our period in 1604 was the eldest son of a successful lawyer and member of parliament. He too took the BA, became a barrister at the Inner Temple, and was eventually a privy councillor to Charles I, a member of the council of the north and chancellor of the county palatine of Durham.

We are still in the world of the professions. The same pattern appears among the eldest sons from landed families. Such a one was George More, whom President Cole took as a personal pupil in his own chamber about 1570, and whose letter to the boy's father, Sir William More, reveals that the college was prepared to arrange lessons in singing and other polite accomplishments for such pupils. Yet the young More took the BA and MA (admittedly within four years) before going off to the Inner Temple.[1] His son Robert came up to Corpus as a commoner in 1595 by which time George was well established as a member of parliament and courtier, and like his father Robert More took his degree in arts before going to the Inner Temple. The same could be said of Edward Goddard,[2] Robert Browne,[3] William Higford,[4] William Elkes,[5] Henry Hawker[6] and William Becher.[7] Becher was a third-generation Londoner whose grandfather, a Devonian who became a haberdasher and sheriff of London, had left a considerable fortune. His alderman son, William Becher's father, inherited extensive lands in Kent and Bedfordshire including the manor of Fotheringay. William, who was knighted in 1619, married Elizabeth, daughter of Oliver Lord St John, and the Countess of Peterborough was godmother to one of his sons.[8]

[1] VCH Oxon. iii. 222. Like other sons of gentlemen in these years he was dispensed to allow him to complete the BA in two years; Reg. Univ. ed. Clark, ii. 14. Sir William was of Loseley, co. Surrey; his wife was Margaret, heiress of the Daniels of Suffolk. For George More see also p. 709.

[2] Adm. commoner, matric. 31 January 1589 arm. f. adm. BA 1591 adm. Lincoln's Inn 1589. He inherited the whole of his father's estates in 1617.

[3] Adm. commoner, matric. 9 May 1589 gen.f.nat.max. adm. BA 1591.

[4] Adm. commoner, matric. from Oriel 14 January 1597 arm.f. adm. BA 1599.

[5] Adm. commoner, matric. from St Alban Hall 7 May 1593 gen.f. BA 1595 MA 1597. He had been a commensal at Eton.

[6] Matric. ?July 1598 gen.f. adm. BA 1601 student Gray's Inn 1601.

[7] Adm. commoner, matric. 10 October 1594 arm.f. BA 1597 adm. Inner Temple 1598; knighted 1619, sheriff of Bedfordshire 1612–13.

[8] F. A. Page Turner, 'The Becher family of Howbury', Publications of the Bedfordshire Historical Record Society v (1920), 133–60.

Among the forty commoners after 1570 who certainly ranked below the line of gentle birth were two sons of a London merchant, Francis and Henry Colthurst. Francis, the heir, was admitted a commoner of Corpus in 1594, and his younger brother at an unknown date presumably not long thereafter. Their father was a citizen and grocer of London who died in 1594 and left large charitable bequests. Francis died in turn within a decade leaving among other bequests two pounds each to twenty-five poor men of Oxford, and twenty pounds to Corpus to buy plate. His monument in the college chapel recalled him as a gentleman, citizen and merchant of London, and sometime commoner of the college, a memorial also to the shifting social designations of the urban rich.[1] There were probably more such among the thirty-two plebeians, where we also find the sons of yeomen and of the lower clergy in a few instances when we make a plausible identification.[2] For the most part, however, little more can be determined of the humbler commoners than their claim to status and the records of their career in the college and university, if such they had. For the twenty-five without such a claim the problem is even more difficult.

Among the more prominent men their claims to status seem to have accorded very closely to their true circumstances; there is only one instance, and a doubtful one at that, of a commoner who was the son of a knight matriculating as the son of a gentleman, presumably to escape the higher matriculation fee.[3] We have a fairly accurate notion of the sources from which a substantial proportion[4] drew their income, and landholding (manors and rural smallholdings) entirely predominates, although many landowners held properties also in towns, and a minority had significant income from mercantile investments and commerce.[5] These are the general lineaments of the population of commoners at Corpus Christi College, and little more can be said with certainty. Since 19 per cent (twenty-five names) of the total did not matriculate and have proved impossible to trace further, all remarks about the distribution of the

---

[1] Information drawn from Corpus Christi College Archives Fulman MSS; PRO, will registers of the Prerogative Court of Canterbury 34 Harte, 18 Scott: Wood, *History and Antiquities of the Colleges and Halls*, 404–5. On William Fulman and his collections see Fowler, *Corpus Christi*, 198–9.

[2] John and Simon Badcocke, 1587; Gabriel Honeyfold, 1592; Edward Haynes, 1602; William Webb, 1581. At least one man, James Mosan 1585, was the son of a medical doctor. Since only nine of these men professed to be the sons of clergymen it seems very likely that they commonly registered as plebeians. See below, p. 681 ff.

[3] Francis Vincent, 12 October 1582.

[4] Forty-five (35 per cent) of the commoners entered after 1570.

[5] Apart from Becher and the Colthursts, Thomas Bond, 1594; John Hooker, 1598; Humphrey Style, 1595.

various social ranks must be made with caution. It seems clear that the college received the statutory number of four to six commoners quite regularly from its early years at the rate of about two a year, and the controversy over President Greenway's admission of the young baron Sandys seems to indicate that in the late sixties the expectation in college was still that the numbers would not be increased. In the next decades the evidence suggests as we shall see that the intense concern to enrol all undergraduates in the eighties and nineties did succeed in recording a large number of informal arrangements and perhaps some that were purely a matter of convenience, but the contrast with the decade of the seventies and with the first decade of the following century indicates also that there was a substantial short-run increase in the enrolment of commoners, however they were accommodated. It must be supposed that the commoners on the college books were men living—or at least dining —in the college, but the original buildings could by no means accommodate the number reported after the second statute of matriculation. One possibility is that they were put up across the street in Beam Hall, acquired by President Morwent in 1553. This would have conformed to college custom elsewhere, but it would imply that the Beam Hall of Tudor times was more extensive than the modern structure, by no means an impossibility. Another solution was, of course, their accommodation in cocklofts built in the upper ranges of the college, and at some point such quarters were certainly built. Unfortunately no surviving record allows us to give a clear date, and the structural evidence that might assist us was obliterated by the later construction of a third storey at Corpus. The drawing on Agas's map of 1578 shows no alteration in the roofs. The *Libri magni* show large purchases of building materials in the late seventies, but the first explicit reference to a cockloft was in 1583/4 with the purchase of 3 feet of glass for the cocklofts over Mr Norton's chamber, located over the buttery. Other such references suggest that these supplementary chambers were built in stages, and cocklofts linked with the rooms of individual fellows were mentioned casually but regularly; thus in 1599/1600 2s 4d were spent on glass for a cockloft 'which the winde blows downe'.[1]

Before we turn to the members of the foundation and thereby

---

[1] Corpus Christi College Archives *Libri magni* for 1583/4, 1587/8, 1588/9, 1596/7, 1599/1600, 1601/2, 1603/4; in 1588/9 4s 4d was spent on timber 'for the staires to the cocklofts'. See also *VCH Oxon.* iii. 221, 226; Newman, 'The physical setting', p. 629 above. Beam Hall was described in 1584 as 'a stable, a decayed lymehouse and a kitchen'; see W. A. Pantin, 'The halls and schools of medieval Oxford: an attempt at reconstruction', *Oxford Studies Presented to Daniel Callus* (OHS n.s. xvi 1964), 67.

extend our survey backwards to the first years of Corpus, something more must be said about the difficulties which are already apparent in constructing a convincing account of the origins and later careers of these Tudor collegians. It is not simply that, as is well known, there is a heavy bias of information towards those who came from the upper ranks. The starting-point of each inquiry must be the records of the college itself, which provide less to go on than one might wish: from the *Liber admissionum* the man's full name, date of birth (inferentially from his age) and county of origin (whether of birth or residence is never clear). The college accounts, the *Libri magni*, record the payments of commons and stipends for individual members (although not of course for commoners) so that we can make a fairly accurate statement about the time each spent on the foundation. If the man took a degree or matriculated more information may be found about age, county of origin and status, which may help us to confirm information in the college records although inconsistencies frequently occur. But quite apart from the fact that the university records were less well kept than those of the college, we know so little about the actual procedures of matriculation in the early days that we must be very cautious in inferring too much about the nature of the bond with the college.[1] What is more, the identifications of men at various stages of their degree-taking, not to say matriculation and subscription, are inferential, although they are enshrined in the published registers of the university with perhaps more authority than their foundation in written record would warrant.

Even more difficult is the process of tracing personal identifications from the college records to the counties of origin on the one hand, or on the other to those ecclesiastical archives and secular registers where we hope to trace careers. To know a man's claim to social status is something,[2] but to be reduced as we are in most cases to a family name and county of origin is precarious indeed. Often there is little more to go on than the record of a son of the correct name who is of roughly the right age. This information will almost certainly be found among the records of the prominent, which further increases the bias of the investigation against the unrecorded local families. The same considerations apply *mutatis mutandis* in establishing the later careers of graduates. Sometimes supplementary

---

[1] See McConica, 'The rise of the undergraduate college', 49. In years like 1575 and 1581 when there was a concerted drive to record the names of undergraduates, it is conceivable that anxious junior members arranged to matriculate under whatever aegis they could find.

[2] Since the claims to status made in the matriculation registers show a high degree of reliability wherever they can be verified (see above) I have regarded them as 'probable' even if no other information about the father's social place has been found.

evidence comes to hand which will corroborate a plausible identification, most frequently in the shape of an informative will. A link by
kinship or dependency with one of the better-documented Corpus
families will serve the same purpose, and connections such as the Kingsmills, Nappers and Colthursts are associated with cousinages that also
supplied men to Corpus. Because of these problems all personal
information in this collective biographical study was flagged for
reliability as 'definite', 'probable' or 'possible' and in what follows
information drawn from the first two categories only will be used.
It must be borne in mind, however, that outside the immediate evidence of the college archives which provided the foundation of the
entire investigation, much even of the information judged as
'definite' contains an element of conjecture and represents the investi-
gator's judgement as to what is genuine and reliable.

The sons of the gentry at Corpus were by no means confined to
the class of commoners. Although they were never numerous there
was a sprinkling of the well-born on the foundation from the beginning, with Reginald Pole the outstanding example among the
founder's fellows. Among the approximately four hundred men
admitted to the foundation as *discipuli* or *scholares*[1] there were
the eldest son of a baronet, 11 sons of knights,[2] 18 of esquires
(6 of them eldest sons) and 11 of gentlemen (of whom 4 were
the eldest). In addition at least 6 were sons of urban freemen of
whom 4 were heirs. Excluding the sons of freemen and including
Edwin Sandys[3] the total on the foundation known to be from the
upper ranks is 42, of whom 11 were eldest sons.

The only one of these to enter the college as an heir was William
Huckmore of Buckland Baron, Devon. His father, a country gentleman, died the year after his son's birth in 1582 and William entered
Corpus as a *discipulus* at the age of 15, having matriculated the
year before. Although he is not credited with a degree in the
surviving records he remained in the college for twelve terms. He
became barrister at the Middle Temple in 1610 and a member of
parliament for St Mawes. On his death in October 1626 he left his
library to his third and youngest son Charles whom he wished to
attend the university; the law books, however, went to the eldest,
Gregory, who was intended for his father's chambers at the Middle
Temple. A middle son was to be apprenticed to a merchant. Two
friends of the rank of esquire were to advise his son Gregory on

[1] See p. 668. On the sons of the gentry in the early decades see McConica, 'The social
relations of Tudor Oxford', 129–30.

[2] Increased to twelve if Reginald Pole is included.

[3] See above, p. 672. There were also the eldest son of an esquire who entered as a sub-
sacristan (discussed below) and another of the rank of gentleman who entered as a chaplain.

business affairs until he reached the age of 21 Perhaps we may conclude that his experience had not led him to recommend a formal university training as particularly suitable for a man of property but that it had been gratifying enough to be recommended to his youngest son.[1]

Huckmore's fate of being left fatherless as an infant may have played a part in his decision to enter university on the foundation rather than as a commoner, as one would expect a young gentleman already entitled to his property to do.[2] Other eldest sons of gentry origins on the foundation followed careers that were virtually indistinguishable from commoners of their class, with the difference that they had studied the arts curriculum, although not always apparently to the point of taking a degree; this cannot be absolutely confirmed given the state of the university registers. Two spent only two terms in the college, one of them being the armigerous Samuel Turner who must have studied elsewhere, since he took his BA degree two years after his admission to Corpus as a sacristan in 1600. After incorporating MA in 1605 he went on to qualify as a doctor of medicine at Padua (1611) and in due course became a member of parliament for Shaftesbury in Dorset. He had an interesting political career, voted against Strafford's attainder and became a captain in the royalist army. He was excluded from the long parliament but returned to his university city as a member for Shaftesbury in the king's Oxford parliament. The other case was that of Christopher Litcott who was admitted *discipulus* in 1527 at the age of 17. His college career is in every other respect like that of a gentleman commoner, since he had already been at Corpus as a boy pupil. His father was armigerous, his mother from a prominent Berkshire family (the Barkers of Sonning and Wokingham) of the same rank. He married Katherine, daughter of Sir Robert Cheney. As a boy he had been train-bearer to Anne Boleyn, and the family link with the court was retained since he became royal bailiff of Swallowfield, Berkshire, a manor he eventually bought.[3]

Of the remaining *discipuli* who were eldest sons in landed families

[1] There was also a nephew Gregory. Will dated 4 June 1624 with revocation of 20 May 1625. PRO will registers PCC 8 Skinner: PROB 11/151, fos 59^V-60^V.

[2] One of the freemen's sons, William Fulbeck, had likewise inherited as an infant. He was the only child of a mayor of Lincoln and matriculated at St Alban Hall 20 December 1577 *plebei filius*. He was admitted to Corpus as a *discipulus* February 1580 and promoted *scholaris*, keeping a total of thirteen terms. He went from Oxford to Gray's Inn and was later ordained, becoming the author of notable legal works. See McConica, 'Social relations', 119.

[3] Information from Lady Constance Russell, *Swallowfield and Its Owners* (1901), College of Arms MSS C.2 fo 355, C. 12 fo 60^V, G.3 fo 39^V; *VCH Berks.* iii. 213, 223; *Letters of Richard Fox*, ed. P. S. Allen (1929), 84-5.

five were sons of esquires and four of gentlemen.[1] Except for Brian Twyne, who became a fellow and Greek reader in the college, they stayed in Corpus for an average of fourteen terms, ranging from eight to twenty, six of them for twelve terms or more. Five of them are known to have taken degrees, and we must regard this as a distinct probability for any man who spent as many as twelve terms in the university. Those of the rank of esquire and above clearly took on the expected responsibilities for the family property and became involved in local governement, often with some training in law at the inns of court. Two more became members of parliament like Samuel Turner. The sons of gentlemen, however, when we can trace a career at all, became barristers and clergymen.

The sons of the gentry entered the foundation with fair regularity throughout the century, supporting other evidence that the appropriation of places intended for the clergy and the poor was not new in the Elizabethan era.[2] The age at entry is also remarkably consistent.[3] The average for those who were eldest sons is 15; for the younger sons of knights, 17; of esquires, $15\frac{1}{2}$; of gentlemen, 15.[4] Their fathers were landowners or prominent in royal service, and predictably involved in local government, with the law also playing a prominent part in their careers: this is characteristic for the upper ranks. The esquires and gentlemen drew their wealth much more from the land with less involvement in law or in royal service, although two were prominent servants of noble families.

Among the younger sons there is an evident contrast between those who took degrees and those who did not. If we exclude from

[1] I include Brian Twyne the historian and antiquary among the gentlemen although he matriculated as *mediocris fortunae*, since his grandfather, John, who was headmaster of the King' School Canterbury and sometime mayor and MP for Canterbury, was descended from a prominent and armigerous family, and his grandmother was daughter and co-heiress to an alderman and freeman of Canterbury. His father Thomas, also of Corpus, was BM (Oxon), DM (Cantab.) and licentiate of the Royal College of Physicians who practised in Lewes.

[2] As the complaints of Thomas Lever and Roger Ascham had indicated; cf Curtis, *Oxford and Cambridge*, 69–70 for the later complaints of Jewel and Harrison also. Thomas Lever had connected the usurpation of places for the poor in the colleges to the decline of the hostels in Cambridge; O'Day, *Education and Society*, 88.

[3] This record of age was made at the admission of every member to the foundation, and again at promotion to the rank of *scholaris* for one who entered as a *discipulus*. Inconsistencies were decided on the basis of the widest evidence from the number of terms kept, and when possible from comparison with the matriculation register. However, the records of the college have been regarded as likely to be the more reliable and have been preferred if there is direct conflict with the age given at matriculation.

[4] The number recorded in the three categories of younger sons is respectively 11, 12 and 8. The lowest age recorded among the younger sons is 12 years, the highest 23, but that is of Reginald Pole who was already a fellow of Magdalen College and one of the founder's nominations. The range of the eldest is 13–17 years.

consideration the two men who were nominated by Fox on the original foundation,[1] three of the sons of knights and three of gentlemen apparently took no degrees, or at least no degrees are recorded for them, and they stayed in the college for periods of time ranging from less than one term (Francis Kingsmill) to sixteen terms (Edward Kingsmill). Nothing known of their later careers points to anything other than the conventional pursuits of the gentry, although this group is not well documented. The younger sons who took degrees, however, average just under fifty terms residence and with few exceptions followed clerical careers, sometimes taking senior positions in the college. The exceptions are few enough to enumerate: Thomas Twyne, the medical doctor already mentioned;[2] George Fetiplace from Bedfordshire, another son of an esquire who took his BA and was admitted *scholaris* before going on to the Middle Temple; and George Giles from Gloucestershire who went so far as to be admitted fellow, but four years later was admitted to the Inner Temple. Fetiplace, whose grandfather John, Lord Mordaunt was present at the Field of Cloth of Gold, eventually became a member of parliament for Buckingham and, having acquired a great deal of land in Gloucestershire, ended his career as a member of the council for the marches. Among the degree-taking gentry his career is highly unusual.

Nevertheless, the evidence that the landed nobility and gentry consistently took some interest in the intellectual fare of the statutory curriculum and that they did so not merely to provide clerical careers for younger sons deserves attention. Put another way, the 51 Corpus men in our period who were notable as landowners in later life (and this includes all 21 of the members of parliament) were evenly divided between those who had entered the college on the foundation (26) and those who had been at Corpus as commoners (25). Of the commoners 8 had taken degrees; of those on the foundation 9 had not. The social distinctions and career expectations of scholars and commoners can indeed be distinguished, but the distinction is not absolute.

When we try to form an impression of the social complexion of the college below the rank of gentleman our task is much more difficult. One approach is to look at all of those who claimed at matriculation to be the sons of plebeians or of clerics. This group complements that from the higher ranks just examined but is confined to the last three decades of our study. An alternative is to analyse everything that has been discovered about the occupations

---

[1] Reginald Pole, William Wye.   [2] See p. 679 n. 1.

of the fathers of all the members.[1] Each of these groups represents only a portion of the whole, and both reflect the bias of our sources towards the more substantial families. Taken together, however, they augment our knowledge of the college's social relations even if they do not provide us with the representative sampling we should prefer.

If we begin with the occupations of the fathers, we have information about two hundred and thirty-six men at Corpus, some 30 per cent of the total. To allow for the variety of occupation especially of men in the upper ranks three categories of occupation were allotted to each, with a slight weighting of the first over the second and third. On this basis it is clear that connection with the land from the ranks of gentry to the peerage is much the most common livelihood, which occasions no surprise. Royal service (including election to parliament) is the next. Rather unexpectedly, however, the third largest group (and here there were only occasionally secondary occupations in local government or local trade) is of yeomen. This must not be taken too strictly since the professions were divided between the law, medicine and church, and careers in school teaching and in university were also segregated one from another. Those from the ranks of the lower clergy, provincial traders and the law were almost as numerous as those from yeoman background. At the lowest end of the scale numerically came four who were sons of schoolmasters, six of men with careers in the universities, one who can be shown to have been the son of a husbandman, two sons of artisans and two of fathers who were musicians (at least in part). The number whose fathers had interest in London trade is half that of similar background from the provinces.[2] Allowing for the strong bias in our sources towards those who owned property, the sprinkling of sons from humbler background has some interest.

Turning to the matriculants who claimed that their fathers were plebeians or clerics we have exactly half of the total number who matriculated for Corpus from 1570 to the end of our period.[3] Only four of the clerical fathers can be plausibly identified, and we can add to those, two clergymen whose sons matriculated as 'plebei

[1] Unfortunately no college at Oxford (and no other at Cambridge) possesses a record for the sixteenth century comparable to that at Gonville and Caius College, which has been the starting point for most of the work on this topic. For each man admitted, Caius's *Liber matriculationis* gives his name, date of admission, status in college, age, birthplace, school, father's name and occupation, the room assigned in college, the name of his tutor and surety; *Admissions to Gonville and Caius in the University of Cambridge, March 1558/9 to January 1678/9*, ed. J. and S. C. Venn (1887).
[2] It should be remembered that the university men also had careers in the church, and that the schoolmasters were involved in local government, as aldermen, JP's, etc.
[3] A total of 185; there were 15 claiming clerical, 76 claiming plebeian background.

filius'.[1] In truth only fifteen plebeian fathers can be plausibly identified even with strong probability, two of them having two sons each at Corpus. One of these is Nicholas Badcocke of Boarshill in Berkshire adjacent to Oxford, whose sons John and Simon matriculated at Corpus on the same day, 28 April 1587, at the ages respectively of 18 and 14 years.[2] The second such father was Edmund Orson of Grantham, Lincolnshire. His son and namesake matriculated for Corpus on 6 July 1593 aged 17. Again assistance comes from wills. The senior Orson was seemingly a wealthy weaver in Grantham who left bequests to servants and three apprentices when he died in October 1588, and we learn from his will that he had three sons, William, Nathaniel and Edmund, and a daughter Mary. The admissions book at Corpus shows that William, the eldest, for whom no matriculation is recorded, was admitted as a probationer fellow on 21 December 1583 at the age of 20. He went on to take his BTh, was elected a fellow in 1585 and kept fifty-four terms in the college where he was eventually both dean and a bursar. Edmund, the youngest, kept twenty-seven terms to obtain his BA and MA and, although we have no record of his ordination, became rector of North Marden in Sussex in 1607. A confirming link between this family of Grantham and the college is their connection with the Colthurst family, since Edmund Orson senior was a cousin of the London grocer Henry Colthurst, the father of Francis and Henry, commoners of Corpus in 1594.[3]

Our inability more generally to penetrate to the occupation of these Corpus fathers is a disappointment and frustration since a few additional successes hint at the possible variety to be found. Of particular importance is the link with mercantile wealth which is perfectly evident in colleges such as St John's or Christ Church where there was a formal tie with urban schools.[4] Enough instances have been discovered at Corpus to show that here too the sons of townsmen were a substantial part of the whole, although it is impossible to determine the exact proportion. The Colthursts have been mentioned already, as have William Becher, William Fulbeck and others.[5] A striking example is that of the Hookers, Richard, John, Peter and Zacharias, only one of whom—John[6]—happened to matriculate.

---

[1] Thomas Cranmer, m. for the second time at Corpus 2 July 1585, became reader in humanity, and was probably the son of his namesake, registrar of Canterbury; Ralph Barlow, m. 3 May 1594 of Cheshire, was the son of the rector of Warmingham.

[2] Identification presumed from will proved 28 November 1607; Bodl. MS Berks. wills K 383.

[3] Lincolnshire Archives Office, wills 1588, ii, 57; PRO wills registers of the PCC 18 Scott; see above, p. 674.

[4] See McConica, 'Scholars and commoners', 164 f.

[5] See p. 673 and p. 678 n. 2.   [6] For Corpus 5 May 1598, gen.f. Devon.

They were related, and connected with the mercantile wealth of the city of Exeter.[1] The first at Corpus was also the most famous, Richard Hooker who was admitted 24 December 1573 (for Berkshire), the grandson of a mayor of Exeter; as the author of the *Laws of Ecclesiastical Polity* he scarcely needs to be introduced. He was the nephew of John Hooker, member of parliament and chamberlain of the city of Exeter, who was the father of the brothers John, Peter and Zacharias. Of these brothers two were *discipuli* and followed careers in the church. Their brother John, who alone matriculated and did so as the son of a gentleman, appears to have been a commoner.[2] Stephen Gosson, the sometime playwright turned enemy of drama, was another example. He was admitted *discipulus* on 4 April 1572 without matriculating and took his BA in 1576. His father was a joiner and freeman of Canterbury. Stephen's first vocation was that of an actor with a dramatic company in London which he joined in 1576, although he was ordained deacon three years later and priested in 1585.[3] We may add to this list of freemen's sons on the foundation William Weston (*scholaris* 9 August 1517), son of a London mercer who was nominated by Fox, took a BCL and became a justice of common pleas;[4] and Matthew Whythals, son of a freeman and attorney of Canterbury, who was admitted to Corpus three years later as a *scholaris* also by Fox's nomination, was a witness to the will of the first president, John Claymond, and ended his career as a canon of Peterborough, having benefited from the patronage of Sir Christopher Hales.[5] These examples give some indication of the presence of townsmen at Corpus, where it would seem that London, Canterbury and Exeter were particularly well-represented throughout the century. The comparative obscurity of so many of the plebeian fathers, however, prevents our arriving at anything like an estimate of the prominence of townsmen's sons in the college population as a whole.[6]

Since our sons of plebeians and clerics are half of those who

[1] Also of Exeter diocese were John Barcham, adm. *discipulus* 24 August 1588, the son and possibly heir of the steward of the city of Exeter, and John Berry, adm. *discipulus* 10 February 1578, whose father was a clothier at Tiverton, *DNB*; John Prince, *Damnonii orientales illustres: or The Worthies of Devon* (Exeter 1701, new edn 1810), 42, 505; College of Arms MS C.1(1), fos 181, 307; PRO wills registers PCC 6 Harte.

[2] Zacharias was the fourth, Peter the fifth, and John the seventh son.

[3] On Gosson see above, p. 652.

[4] PRO wills register PCC 26 Daper, 31 Fetiplace; *VCH Essex* iv. 199–200.

[5] Emden, *BRUO to 1540*; PRO wills register PCC 13 Dyngley; *ex inform*. Dr William Urry.

[6] A crude estimate among those whose fathers' sources of income are known would suggest they were about one-quarter of that group, which is in turn about a third of the whole in a very imperfect canvass. Only one of this group of obscure plebeians' sons at Corpus might have been a privileged person of the town, Christopher Winter, m. 22 January

matriculated for Corpus it is useful to pass with them to other questions. Ten of the fifteen clerics' sons were on the foundation and took degrees, two of them doctorates in theology.[1] They seem typically to have entered ecclesiastical careers. Among those professing plebeian origin just under half were commoners, half of whom again took degrees in arts (only). Among the forty-four who were on the foundation virtually all took degrees, seven of them rising to the doctorate in theology, one to the doctorate in medicine, while one took the BCL. We have some notion of the careers of three-quarters of these plebeian foundationers and it is clear that they were almost always clergymen, although that fact should not be thought to imply a dull uniformity. The priests among them would range from Sebastian Benefield of Prestbury, Gloucestershire, Lady Margaret professor of theology from 1613 to 1626, to Daniel Featley or Fertclough, the son of a college cook, who had been sent to Magdalen College School (his father had earlier been cook to the president of Magdalen, Laurence Humfrey) and became a doctor of theology. He rose to be chaplain to the English ambassador in Paris, Sir Thomas Edmondes, domestic chaplain to Archbishop Abbott and provost of Chelsea College. He was at one time offered the chair of theology at Leiden, but declined on account of age.[2] Henry Jacob, eldest son of a Kentish yeoman, entered the college as precentor after attending the King's School, Canterbury. He became a Brownist, formed a congregation of English exiles at Middelburg and ultimately adopted the views of John Robinson at Leiden. In 1616 he founded the first English congregational church at Southwark, and in 1622 went to Virginia to disseminate his views among the English colonists.[3] William Storr, son of a husbandman of Aisthorpe, Lincolnshire, reached Oxford on a civic exhibition of the common council. He became a fellow of the college, returned to Aisthorpe as rector, married and was murdered at Market Rasen before he reached the age of 40.[4]

1585 at 19 years. All of the other matriculants from Oxfordshire can be accounted for as genuine members of the college; see *Reg. Univ.* ed. Clark i. 386.

[1] One of these was Samuel Page, adm. *discipulus* 10 June 1587, the minor poet who was chaplain to the Cadiz expedition.

[2] *DNB*; Foster, *Alumni*. On Featley's teaching as a fellow of Corpus see p. 719.

[3] *DNB*.

[4] Adm. *discipulus* 8 December 1582, BA 1585; MA 1588, fellow 1590, ordained priest and licensed preacher by Bishop Wykeham of Lincoln; see C. W. Foster, *A History of the Villages of Aisthorpe and Thorpe in the Fallows* (Lincoln 1927); Lincolnshire Archives Office L1/1/1/3, Common council entry book fos 116, 128, 171, 214[V]. He was granted 20s. in 1580 and 1582 for books, apparel and maintenance, £5 in 1586 towards the charges of proceeding bachelor. A contemporary account of his murder is printed as appendix 1 in Foster.

If the careers of such Corpus men as these are reassuringly diverse, in other respects they show informative uniformity. The average age on admission as *discipulus* was 15½ years, ranging from 14 to 20 years.[1] Men admitted as *discipuli* spent an average of thirteen terms or slightly over three years in college before they might expect either to leave or to be promoted *scholaris*, a probationer fellow. Those who went on to become fellows remained in college some ten or eleven years before they left for a living or a like promotion; those whose college careers were rather more demanding—estimated by their having attained the senior rank of dean—averaged fourteen years on the foundation. This suggests that a senior fellow would normally leave for a new career in his late twenties, and he might have done so with the expectation of living into his mid-fifties.[2] Some 410 in all categories took the BA degree, of whom 276 are known to have incorporated as masters of arts.[3] Ninety-two bachelors of theology are recorded for the same period and 41 doctors, with 11 bachelors of medicine, 9 medical doctors, 18 bachelors and 2 doctors of civil law. In this loose way the college followed the pattern of degree-taking in the university at large.[4]

As an academic community Corpus recruited its members predominantly from its own graduates. Ninety-five who entered as *discipuli* later became fellows of Corpus, and another 20 fellows of other Oxford colleges. At the same time only 43 fellows or probationers after the original foundation were recruited from outside, including 3 of the early readers.[5] The college's powerful ethos would have been intensified by such policies, and this may help to explain the deep sense of loyalty to the founder's traditions which appeared in such an eminent figure as John Rainolds at the

---

[1] The median age is 15 years.

[2] Based on 188 cases spread quite uniformly through the century of men whose age at death is known. There is a fairly constant rise from about 50 years at the beginning of the century to about 60 years at the end. This may be compared with a life expectancy at birth in 1601 of 38.12 years, and of 60 years at the age of 30 for the second half of the sixteenth century. These figures resemble those for the life expectancy of fellows of Caius College, Cambridge, in the early seventeenth century, as conspicuously above the general average. See E. A. Wrigley and R. S. Schofield, *The Population History of England 1541-1871* (1981), tables 7.21 p. 250, A3.1 p. 528; M. Curtis, 'Alienated intellectuals of early Stuart England', *Past and Present* 23 (1962), 31; L. Stone, *The Family, Sex and Marriage in England 1500-1800* (1977), 55.

[3] It should be pointed out again that the incompleteness of the university registers makes of all these figures approximations only.

[4] See above, pp. 155-6.

[5] John Bell of Trinity Collge, Cambridge, fellow 1562-6; George Rudde also of Trinity, Cambridge, fellow 1563-72; and Edward Wotton, the fellow of Magdalen College, Oxford, whom Fox created a *socius compar* of Corpus; see chapter 1, p. 25.

end of the century.[1] Beyond the college itself four Corpus men became vice-chancellor while eight held professorships[2] but, as our earlier figures show, the vast majority of fellows left the college before the age of 30, as Fox had wished, to follow their destinies in the church.

Their careers were the background to all other achievement by those who left Corpus. In the years before the end of Elizabeth's reign the college certainly supplied 136 parish priests to the national church (some 25 of these before the reformation) and 85 members of the higher clergy—7 bishops,[3] 15 deans, 13 archdeacons, 45 canons and 4 who became head of a college or hospital. There were 6 more who ended their careers as curates, 21 chaplains,[4] and 8 recusant priests of whom the best known is the martyr George Napper (or Napier) from the family of Holywell Manor. Any attempt to trace patterns in the benefices of these men encounters an insoluble difficulty given the wide range they accumulated but it is fairly clear that the dioceses in which they chiefly found their livings represent roughly the same geographical area as that from which the college drew its membership in the first place.[5] A careful examination of the income of these men is unfortunately beyond the scope of this survey, but a crude measure may be found in the fact that about sixty of the parish priests at some time held a preferment, never of course in isolation, that had been assessed at forty pounds a year or more in the *Valor ecclesiasticus*.[6] A related profession particularly hard to trace is that of schoolmaster which must often be hidden in the listing of preferments. It is inconceivable that

---

[1] James McConica, 'Humanism and Aristotle in Tudor Oxford', *English Historical Review* xciv (1979), 308–9.

[2] Richard Marshall was vice-chancellor 1554–5; William Cole in 1557; John Williams in 1604 while he was Lady Margaret professor of theology; John Bell was vice-chancellor of Cambridge 1582–3. Sebastian Benefield succeeded Williams in the Lady Margaret chair 1613–26; John Shepreve and Richard Hooker held the regius chair in Hebrew (Hooker as deputy to Thomas Kingsmill); George Etheridge, Giles Lawrence and John Hales held the regius chair in Greek (Hales in 1612). John Rainolds was appointed to Walsingham's theology lecture in 1586. See also G. D. Duncan p. 335 ff. above.

[3] If Reginald Pole is included. The other bishops were James Brooks (Gloucester), John Jewel (Salisbury), Henry Man (Sodor and Man—Emden questions this identification), Henry Parry (Gloucester, Worcester), Richard Pates (Worcester), George Webb (Limerick).

[4] To the crown (14), archbishops (2), bishops (6), noblemen (3), privy councillors or other highly placed ministers (2), to a corporation (1) and to the college itself (38) at some point in their careers.

[5] These were chiefly: Bath and Wells (Somerset), Bristol (Bristol, Dorset, parts of Gloucestershire), Canterbury and Rochester (Kent), Chichester (Sussex), Exeter (Devon and Cornwall), Gloucester (Gloucestershire), London (London, Middlesex, Essex, Hertfordshire), York (Yorkshire, Nottinghamshire). Cf above, pp. 670–1.

[6] Not of course a reliable guide to the income actually accruing to the incumbent by the 1580s. I am particularly indebted to Dr C. S. Knighton for his painstaking work in tracing and evaluating the livings of these graduates.

among all these clergymen there were not more than the few school teachers whose existence can be demonstrated, men like Gervase Neville, a *discipulus* in 1600, who later became vicar and schoolmaster at Royston, Yorkshire, or Thomas Thackham, sometime fellow of All Souls and probationer at Corpus who became schoolmaster at Reading and vicar of St Lawrence's church there in 1551. On the other hand Corpus did produce some schoolmasters eminent in the age, such as Nicholas Udall, the headmaster of Eton, and Alexander Gill, headmaster of St Paul's school and friend of Ben Jonson. William Absolon and Nicholas Goldsborough, who were both headmasters of the King's School Canterbury in the 1560's and 1580's respectively, help to explain the high proportion of men who came thence to the college—a noticeable group at least among the few whose schools can be identified. These were Eton (3), Winchester (11), the King's School Canterbury (12), Merchant Taylors' (3) and St Paul's (1) in London, and the King's School in Worcester (3) where Thomas Bradshaw, who had been admitted to Corpus as a cleric in 1546 and became a fellow of Brasenose, was 'scholemaster of the Quene's maiesties gramer schole within the colledge of Worcester' from 1558 until 1584.[1] Undoubtedly there were others but the details of a man's schooling are difficult to come by. The most conspicuous place of recruitment for the college in surviving records was of course the college itself, where choristers and other boy pupils came for tuition before they ever sought admittance to the foundation, and some sixty of those are known. Corpus also provided masters for Magdalen College School, Tunbridge Wells, Lincoln Grammar School, the College School at Gloucester and Durham School among no doubt many others, but if these links proved important to the college the evidence of it has vanished.

Apart from the clerics the members of the foundation at Corpus seem to have divided their interests between town and country, if a rough analysis of their sources of income can form any guide.[2] Manors and rural smallholdings account for some 30 per cent, advowsons and rectories for another 50 per cent, and urban tenements including commercial investments another 20 per cent of their

---

[1] PRO wills register PCC 55 Spencer; A. F. Leach, *Early Education in Worcester 1685–1700* (Worcestershire Historical Society 1913), 186, 219. Bradshaw's stipend was £20 a year, but he married the heiress of Guthlac Edwards, MP, and died lord of the manor of Hardwick in Worcester. He left a bequest to Brasenose but not to Corpus where he spent only seven terms.

[2] We have information about 223 men, almost half of those who left the college from the foundation if we add to the 436 in the categories of fellow, *scholaris* and *discipulus* (at entrance) the 55 degree-takers from the remaining categories; see above, p. 668. The mixed background of these men has already been described.

revenues. This impression comes chiefly from analysis of wills. If we look instead at the occupations of the same group of foundationers we find without surprise that the most common by far is that of the clergy.[1] The royal service, which might include any post from that of a member of parliament to a royal bailiff claimed only 7 per cent (twenty-four) of these men, and only 4 per cent (fifteen) could be thought of as primarily concerned with proprietorship of land. The other former *discipuli* were scattered among the professions of school teaching, medicine and law, trade (one entered London trade, another four provincial trade), and music. This last was Thomas Mulliner, an organist in the college admitted in 1574 with the rank of cleric, and of whose career nothing is known except this appointment. However, he compiled the Mulliner Book, a unique collection of sixteenth-century secular and religious vocal and instrumental music.[2]

If we widen our focus to take into account secondary and tertiary occupations the general profile is scarcely altered, but we do at least acknowledge the variety of their responsibilities and the artificiality of subsuming careers under a single title. For example, Erasmus Prin was the son of a substantial merchant of Bristol. He kept twelve terms from 1542 to 1545 without record of any degree and may have been one of the many who went on to an inn of court,[3] although again there is no record. However, in later life he was an attorney in Bristol as well as a brewer of beer, and he acquired a house and lands at Aust and at Clifton.[4] Earlier in the century David Edwards from Northampton rose from *discipulus* to fellow, taking his MA in 1525 by which time he was a reader in logic and possibly also in Greek. He removed to Cambridge where he qualified as a doctor of medicine, studying also at Padua. He worked on the Aldine edition of Galen at Venice with John Clement, Thomas Lupset and William Rose,[5] but could hardly be described either as fellow of the college

[1] We can estimate occupations for 414 graduates, of whom 129 made a career directly in the lower clergy, 27 among the upper clergy. These numbers were reinforced from the ranks of those who began as college fellows (see above, p. 685), 134 in all, of whom 100 exactly are known to have gone on to end their careers in the ranks of the parochial clergy; see the discussion on p. 686. This total of 256 clerics is 70 per cent of those members of the foundation to whom a primary occupation has been assigned with the assessment at least of probability, 365 all told.

[2] BL Additional MS 30,513; ed. D. Stevens, *Musica Britannica* i. 1951. See Stanley Sadie ed., *The New Grove Dictionary of Music and Musicians* (20 vols 1980) xii. 775–6.

[3] Seventy-two are known in all; 15 at the Inner Temple, 23 at the Middle Temple, 20 at Lincoln's Inn and 12 at Gray's Inn, with 2 of an unknown inn. Thirty-six of these had taken an arts degree, 2 the DD, 1 a BCL. In most cases the later career cannot be traced.

[4] Bristol Archives Office Bristol apprentice book pp. 585, 603; *Transactions of the Bristol and Gloucestershire Archaeological Society* lxiv (1943), 140; PRO will registers PCC 71 Harrington.   [5] Emden, *BRUO 1501–40*, 185.

or as a medical doctor. Richard Edwards, a namesake from Somerset, entered as *discipulus* in 1540 and was a pupil of George Etherege, then Greek reader and future regius professor. He became a fellow and in 1550 a student of Christ Church. In 1564 he was admitted to Lincoln's Inn, was a gentleman of the chapel royal at the coronations of Mary and Elizabeth I and in due course was master of the children there, a distinguished poet, dramatist and composer.[1] At the opposite end of the social spectrum is a man much easier to classify but anomalous in his very individuality. He was Thomas Lightfoot, a simple farmer, whose older brother John was admitted *discipulus* in 1556, and became usher of the College School at Gloucester in 1563. Their father was a farmer at Maisemore, to judge by his will. Thomas was a chorister and *discipulus* in 1564-5 and died before his brother, John. Thomas's will, which was proved on 3 July 1572, reflects the circumstances of a small farmer of Down Ampney, Gloucestershire: sheep to his sister Joan Phelps and to each of her children a ewe and a lamb, farm stock to his brother-in-law. But he had some books as well which he left to his schoolmaster brother. What took either of them to Corpus we are unlikely ever to know.[2]

Limits both of time and space hinder a further account of the society at Corpus Christi College. The foregoing remarks are confined to matters where our information seems most reliable and enough has been said to explain why ambitious statistics have been avoided; Corpus accounted for only a portion of the university population, and in most questions we have only a part of that portion to discuss. Some impression has perhaps been gained of the general constitution of the collegiate world, of the mixed society it contained and of the various ambitions entertained by its members, but it must be remembered that no two colleges were alike.[3] Even from this evidence at Corpus, however, certain observations suggest themselves that bear on the wider debate.

The first has to do with the alleged influx of well-born lay students after the 1560s who came for the first time in any numbers to the universities to obtain the humanistic education now thought appropriate for their role as governors of the realm.[4] We have seen that from the first, Corpus had a mixed society of gentlemen and

---

[1] Ibid. 186-7; *New Grove Dictionary* vi. 60.

[2] Gloucester City Library probate records 174/1572, 104/1545.

[3] O'Day, *Education and Society*, 93; McConica, 'Scholars and commoners', 152 ff. concerning only the new foundations of the century in Oxford.

[4] First adumbrated by Curtis, *Oxford and Cambridge in Transition, passim*, and generally adopted, although challenged more recently by Elizabeth Russell, 'The influx of commoners into the University of Oxford before 1581: an optical illusion?', *English Historical review* xcii (1977), 721-45.

plebeians on the foundation itself in addition to the statutory allowance of commoners whose identity is largely hidden but whom Fox intended to be the sons of nobles or lawyers.[1] Moreover, the gentlemen on the foundation were not merely younger sons intended for the church but included in their number eldest sons and heirs and others who went into secular callings. These men seem to be the successors to the well-born sons we discover in the fifteenth century for whom Waynflete, Smith and Sutton also made provision, but who remain largely invisible in the records of the university.[2] How numerous were they? No general answer is possible, but it seems that at Corpus they were officially restricted to the statutory four to six of Fox's provision at least until the late 1560s. However, Corpus fellows made additional arrangements as tutors to pupils living not in college but in town. The summons of students residing in the town in 1562, the year after the Elizabethan visitation of the university, revealed four who were pupils of Corpus tutors of whom one was not a fellow but may have been a graduate commoner.[3] Within three years a survey of the colleges in response to the first matriculation statute turned up the names of five men at Corpus who are listed in none of the college records, and who must be presumed to have been residential commoners according to the founder's intention.[4] In the decade from 1570 to 1579 only one man matriculated from the college[5] and the number of commoners detectable is about what we would expect at the customary intake of two a year; it is evident from all available evidence that the enforcement of matriculation in that decade was patchy in the extreme.[6] With the second statute of matriculation in 1581 the pressure was intensified and in that single year Corpus matriculated eighteen undergraduates. In each of the next two decades the number of commoners entering the college rose to fifty, twenty of them without record of matriculation, the annual admission rising from the usual rate to five a year. However, in the first years of the

[1] See McConica, 'The rise of the undergraduate college', 28.

[2] Russell, 'The influx of commoners', 737–8.

[3] McConica, 'The rise of the undergraduate college', 49; *Reg. Univ.* ed. Clark, ii. 7. Ds Rowland appears in none of the Corpus registers. Lewis Muge (53) and Ersden were both of Kent. The former was adm. *disc.* in 1558.

[4] Ibid. 15. The names numbered 35–51 are of men below the rank of BA wherever they can be identified; Samuel Becke (46) was a *clericus* or chorister in 1564/6 and was eventually *scholaris* in December 1570. Man, Browne, Haddon, Brooks and Greneway are all unknown in the records, Greneway presumably a member of the prominent Corpus family of Basingstoke which produced the fifth president.

[5] George Lysiman of Danzig; there was also a privileged servant.

[6] All of the other Corpus men of the decade 1570–9 matriculated at another college before admission; a glance at Clark's table B, *Reg. Univ.* ii. 412–13 reveals the general state of affairs.

next century the numbers fell off again to slightly more than the traditional intake of two each year.

These figures are not easily reconciled with either of the rival theories about the influx of the well-born. On the one hand it seems evident that in the early 1580s a number of men already taught by college fellows over and above the intake of the foundation was recorded for the first time. However, the phenomenon was not so short-lived as has been thought, at least at Corpus, especially when we add to the matriculants the names of unmatriculated commoners at the college. At Corpus the high intake survives throughout the decade of the 1590s to drop off again sharply with the new century.[1] The influx of commoners, initially amplified by the university's determination to make official the informal arrangements of the years before 1580, was nevertheless a genuine phenomenon that persisted for two decades.

A second concern of social historians has been the destination of the young men who came to the universities.[2] There is no suggestion from our evidence at Corpus that the secular professions were drawing young men away from careers in the church—quite the contrary; but then Fox's college was meant to be a seminary for the nation, and in this as in other matters it seems that the Elizabethan successors of his early appointees were remarkably loyal to his intentions.[3] The commoners at Corpus took on the varied careers that their more privileged backgrounds opened to them, it would seem, but we can speak with some confidence only of those we know from the Elizabethan period. At the same time they showed more interest in the statutory curriculum in arts than historians have been willing to concede.[4] Of the men on the foundation the small proportion who did not become clergymen entered the service of the crown, nationally or locally, the professions of teaching, law and medicine (usually in combination with another vocation or employment), trade, and in a few cases the duties of the country's yeomanry and gentry. Seventy-one Corpus graduates published at least one book (a figure that for once may be stated with some confidence), more than half being religious authors, but others writing in the law, medicine,

[1] Cf Russell, 'The influx of commoners', 741–2. A survey of the social status of Corpus men from the evidence of the matriculation records alone suggests that in the period 1577/8 to 1603/4, 34 per cent of the men on the foundation were from the gentry or above compared to 50 per cent of the other matriculants; McConica, 'Scholars and commoners', 159–60.

[2] O'Day, Education and Society, 94 ff; Mark Curtis, 'The alienated intellectuals of early Stuart England', Past and Present xxiii (1962), 25–43; Lawrence Stone, 'Communication: the alienated intellectuals', ibid. xxiv (1963), 101–2; Wilfrid Prest, The Inns of Court (1972).

[3] See pp. 686–7.   [4] See p. 672.

mathematics, poetry, music and literature. The number who studied elsewhere is surprisingly small; only seventeen are known to have incorporated at Cambridge, and despite the violent religious changes, the number who went abroad for studies at some stage of their career is only twenty-six. It confirms both the nature of the college and the temper of the times that the best-known graduates of the day were great divines: John Jewel, John Rainolds and Richard Hooker.

A note on the collective biography of Corpus Christi College

A background study to the foregoing from the records of four sixteenth-century foundations (Corpus Christi, Christ Church, Trinity and St John's colleges) was published in *The University in Society* i. (see p. 666 n. 1 above). A questionnaire directing the collection of much more detailed information about the members of Corpus Christi College was drawn up somewhat earlier by me, and the initial work on the Tudor population of Corpus was done by Barbara Austin working from the college archives, chiefly in the *Liber admissionum*, which recorded admissions to the places of *discipuli* and *scholares* (probationer fellows), most choristers, chaplains and servants; the *Libri magni* (treasurers' accounts); the fellows' bonds, and the *Visus*, a set of accounts for the period 1537-42. These lists were compared with the original registers of congregation, where 107 men were discovered who had matriculated or taken degrees from Corpus but whose names were not recorded on the foundation. At the next stage, Kenneth G. Powell searched the available printed sources with special attention to ecclesiastical records, the registered wills of the prerogative court of Canterbury, local testimentary records, the registers of the inns of court and heraldic materials printed by the Harleian Society. He also searched the registers of bishops Bonner, Ridley, Thirlby and Grindal and the card index of ordinations in the Guildhall Library, as well as appropriate episcopal registers at Lambeth Palace. Through the courtesy of York Herald, Dr C. M. J. F. Swan, the manuscript sources at the College of Arms were made available. The History of Parliament Trust also very kindly gave access to the information in their unpublished files. The State Papers and, in the British Museum, manuscripts in the Royal and Harleian collections and among the Additional MSS were searched. Outside London the repositories chiefly consulted were, in Oxford (in addition to Corpus Christi College) the university archives and the Bodleian Library; the county record offices at Bristol, Durham, Chelmsford (Essex), Exeter, Kingston (Surrey), Lincoln, Maidstone (Kent), Preston and Lancaster, Taunton (Somerset) and Winchester; and the City Library and diocesan archives at Gloucester and York.

These files were then reviewed, controlled and enlarged by Dr C. S. Knighton who undertook further research at Corpus and Lambeth, and in the diocesan archives of Ely, Winchester, Lincoln, Exeter, Salisbury and Canterbury. He is chiefly responsible for the final version of the biographical files now in the offices of the History of the University in typescript, although all points of difficulty were settled by a joint decision. Dr Knighton and I together encoded the data in these files for readier access according to the computer program

FIND2. I am indebted to him and to Dr G. D. Duncan for their assistance in proof-reading these encoded files, which were intended to play the role of an index to the full biographical collections. The ICL 1906A computer for which this was prepared unfortunately was taken out of service shortly after the computerized index was completed, and the FIND2 program was inappropriate for the ICL 2988 computer which replaced it. The original program was abandoned in March 1981. A revised data model on the Data Base Management System IDMS was designed by Mr Lou Bernard of the Oxford Computing Service by April 1982 and became operable in September 1983. I wish to thank Mr Paul Salotti for his assistance in implementing the new program.

THE TEACHING OF ARTS IN COLLEGES

The great majority of undergraduates entered none of the higher faculties, reading rather some part or all of the programme in arts. What did they learn? We have shown that the evolution of undergraduate teaching in the colleges was a prominent feature of the university's life from the fifteenth century on, being developed in the first place for men on the foundation. These were expected to follow the statutory curriculum in arts beginning with the elements of logic, although college statutes might add their own requirements, as did Corpus by introducing instruction in Greek.[1] The college lectures were essential in this teaching, accompanied of course by exercises in disputation and, as the influence of humanism spread, by the art of declamation. Equally important was the tutor, about whom something more must now be said.

The principal duty of the tutor was to act as a surety for the junior members of the college to see that they paid their debts (including those owing to the college) and that they conducted themselves responsibly; Waynflete's 'creansers' were a model for the future of this institution.[2] Supervision of his pupils' studies was a natural part of the tutor's office, and with the advent of the printed book to facilitate it, his general responsibility developed naturally into some teaching done directly by himself. In the statutes given to Clare College, Cambridge in 1549 the commissioners of Edward VI insisted among other things that tutors be assiduous in 'teaching

[1] See McConica, 'The rise of the undergraduate college'; J. M. Fletcher, 'The faculty of arts', above, for the statutory curriculum. See also Curtis, *Oxford and Cambridge*, chs 4–5; K. Charlton, *Education in Renaissance England* (1965); Joan Simon, *Education and Society in Tudor England* (Cambridge 1966) chs 7, 10, 14, and the bibliographical essay by C. Webster, 'The curriculum of the grammar schools and universities 1500–1600: a critical review of the literature', *History of Education* iv (1975), 51–67.

[2] McConica, op. cit. 71; Curtis, op. cit. 78–81; Stone, 'The size and composition of the Oxford student body 1580–1910', 25; O'Day, *Education and Society*, 113–18.

what was to be taught',[1] but there was nothing to correspond to this instruction in the Oxford statutes of the time. In a chancery record of 1567 we find an actual contract whereby a tutor at Brasenose College was to have been paid a pound a year for 'reading' to his pupil—the brother as it happens of a husbandman—whose name appears neither in the registers of the college nor the university.[2] The tutor had bought the boy some thirty books, bedding and a surplice, but his pupil apparently had succumbed to Oxford's insalubrious air, and after his death his brother had ignored the debt. The tutor's fee on this occasion was to have been the same as the statutory salary of the fellow chosen to lecture to the Brasenose undergraduates in sophistry and logic, and thus a substantial addition to his income.[3] That the fee was by no means unreasonable is suggested by an entry in the chancellor's register for 1538 in which three proxies were called, among them the manciple, to prove that at Brasenose a tutor was entitled to receive twenty shillings a term for each of his pupils, a much higher rate.[4] William Vaughan, author of *The Golden Grove* (1600), who matriculated at Jesus College in 1592 at the age of 15, recommended that parents find a tutor who would himself read to his pupils, complaining that 'many Tutours now-a-dayes will not sticke to receive a marke or twentie shillinge a quarter for each of their scholers tuition, and yet not vouchsafe once to reade themselves unto them, but to substitute young Bachelors of Art, who, albeit some of them can reade tolerably, yet notwithstanding they cannot correct and provoke the sluggish, as wanting both discretion to judge, and severitie to compel'.[5]

A good tutorial fee might have compensated to some extent for the financial risks the tutor ran, which could be considerable. In the 1560s both Trinity and Queen's made tutors give bonds to the college for the debts of their pupils so that the fellows in question

---

[1] 'Tutores quae docenda sunt sedulo doceant, quaequae etiam agenda instruent atque admoneant'; *Documents relating to the University and Colleges of Cambridge published by direction of the commissioners appointed by the Queen to inquire into the state . . . of the said university and colleges* (3 vols 1852) ii. 179; Curtis, *Oxford and Cambridge*, 78. This simply repeats the Edwardine injunctions of the same year; *Statuta Academiae Cantabrigiensis* (Cambridge 1785), 67. Tutors are not mentioned in the Edwardine statutes at Oxford.

[2] The tutor, John Foster, and his father, a yeoman of Wigan in Lancashire, appealed to Sir Nicholas Bacon as lord chancellor to recover the debt, including his unpaid fee for half a year. The pupil, Richard Marckland, and his brother were of Pemberton in the same county, and 'beinge of lyttell acqaytance in the said College' had asked the Wigan man to act as tutor. See *The Brazen Nose* vi (1934–9), 168–9, incorrectly cited in *VCH Oxon.* iii. 209.

[3] *SCO* ii. pt 9, 16.

[4] Reg. Canc. 1527–43, fo 233.

[5] 'Of Tutours in the Universitie' in *The golden grove* (STC 24610) ch. 38 x4^{r-v}; I am indebted for this reference to Dr Anne L. Prescott.

were liable to prosecution.[1] On the other hand, tutors also risked displeasing the family.[2] Even if money was sent on a quarterly basis, which seems to have been the common practice, unanticipated expenses might place the tutor in an awkward position to recover the debt.[3] Tutors for the wealthy were often dispatched to Oxford with their charges, and the colleges were expected to accommodate both teacher and pupil. If the colleges expected some return by way of gratitude[4] so might the tutors, who, like Thomas Thornton, Philip Sidney's tutor, could reasonably expect their young masters to find them agreeable promotion.[5]

The studies of a well-to-do young gentleman commoner might have taken almost any form, quite evidently. It is wrong to suppose, however, that they were necessarily divorced from the statutory curriculum.[6] It should be borne in mind also that the universities in Elizabethan England were prized by the gentry often as places of what we should regard as advanced schooling rather than university study: some instruction in elementary logic and the arts of disputation were thought appropriate, along with training in the elements of classical literature and modern languages, with other arts of the gentleman. At Oxford the classic utterance on the education of the gentleman was that of Lord Herbert of Cherbury who, at the age of 14 (in May 1596) matriculated at University College. Without taking his account of his scholastic prowess at face value it is worth considering what he later thought would be valuable for his successors. In his autobiography he recommended Comenius's *Janua linguarum* (1631) as a model grammar and recalled that he had concentrated on languages 'to make myself a citizen of the world as far as it were possible', but he also recalled disputing in logic at his first arrival.[7]

---

[1] This was generally adopted; cf the entry in the Oriel register in 1586 requiring fellows to pay the battels of their pupils; *The Dean's Register of Oriel 1446–1661*, eds G. C. Richards and H. E. Salter (OHS lxxxiv 1926), 188.

[2] Curtis, *Oxford and Cambridge*, 79; H. E. D. Blakiston, *Trinity College* (1898), 83; R. H. Hodgkin, *Six Centuries of an Oxford College* (Oxford 1949), 73.

[3] OUA Reg. Canc. 1545–1661 fos 31, 53^v records an attempt in 1527 by the chancellor's court to compel the repayment of a debt owed to an undergraduate directly to his tutor.

[4] Bishop Thomas Bentham in 1561 recommended to the principal of Magdalen Hall a friend who wished to place his son and the son's tutor near to the grammar school. He pointed out that the father was 'a man of worshipp and by Gods blessyng wealthye and also . . . verye myndfull and thankfull in pleasuryng his freyndes . . .'. See 'The letterbook of Thomas Bentham bishop of Coventry and Lichfield 1560–1561', eds Rosemary O'Day and Joel Berlatsky, *Camden Miscellany* 4th ser. xxvii (1979), 202.

[5] James M. Osborne, *Young Philip Sidney 1572–1577* (New Haven 1972), 17.

[6] See McConica, 'Studies and Faculties', 152 above.

[7] The *Autobiography of Edward, Lord Herbert of Cherbury* ed. Sidney Lee (second edition revised 1906), 21, 23, 25. Richard Carew, who matriculated at Broadgates Hall in 1566 at the age of 11 recalled being called to dispute 'with the matchless Sir Ph. Sidney'

Among the languages Greek had first priority, but he had acquired this already at school. Playing on the lute and learning how 'to sing my part at first sight in music', dancing and vaulting were other attainments of this period. Although he claimed to have been almost entirely self-taught he nevertheless recommended that a young man should go to the university with a 'governor for manners' as at school. The ordinary curriculum with its concentration on 'the subtleties of logic' was definitely unsuitable for elder sons like himself, but he approved for them 'those parts of logic which teach men to deduce their proofs from firm and undoubted principles, and show men to distinguish between truth and falsehood'. With logic to serve this purpose the young gentleman should also be acquainted with 'the ground of the Platonic and Aristotelian philosophy'. He apparently felt that a year or so in these studies would suffice, after which the future man of affairs should study geography, government, the use of the celestial globe and enough of the scientific arts to be helpful in practical and military affairs.[1]

Sir Henry Wotton, on the other hand, a younger son, was among the commoners who adhered sufficiently to the statutory curriculum to qualify as bachelor of arts. He came up to New College from Winchester at the age of 16 and matriculated on 5 June 1584. Like Herbert he was armed by his schooling with a knowledge of Latin and Greek. He studied Italian and became sufficiently interested in medical science to give three lectures 'de oculo' on the physiology of the eye in his baccalaureate year, 1588. He was befriended by the Italian civilian Albericus Gentilis and by his junior, John Donne, before he 'betook himself to the useful Library of Travel'.[2] Although the two men were of similar social standing Wotton had the more scholarly bent and as a younger son, worse prospects; nevertheless both he and Herbert spent four full years at Oxford before venturing into the world of affairs.[3]

While Wotton and Edward Herbert represent commoners of

before Leicester and other dignitaries in 1569; Richard Carew, *Survey of Cornwall* (1602), fo 102[v].

[1] His enthusiasm for Paracelsian philosophy should be noted, with his interest in critics of Aristotle, Francesco Patrizi and Bernardino Telesio of Cosenza; ibid. pp. 26–7. The later stages of Herbert's curriculum seem to stray from his personal experience and resemble the generic prescriptions of seventeenth century writers.

[2] *DNB; Reliquiae Wottonianae* (1651, fourth edition 1685), life by Isaac Walton, b2[v]–b8.

[3] Wotton matriculated as the son of an esquire; Herbert, whose father was also an esquire, matriculated as the son of a knight, perhaps indicating his family's prominence in Monmouthshire and his mother's background, or perhaps simply from the vanity which permeates his reminiscences. It should also be remembered that he took a wife while up at Oxford and established a household including his bride and his recently widowed mother; *Autobiography*, 22–3.

unequal prospects within their families, both were earnest about their studies, if with rather different tastes. We find a different and perhaps more typical figure in manuscripts recently discovered and acquired by New College, Oxford.[1] These are letters and accounts by Arthur Lake, later warden of New College and bishop of Bath and Wells, to Lady Jane Townsend, mother of Robert Townsend of Rainham, Norfolk.[2] Robert had apparently been admitted at first to St John's College where, on 1 July 1593, his mother gave a white tankard in respect that her son Robert had been admitted to the table of the president as a commoner.[3] Five days later a Robert Townsend, son of a knight but described as of London, matriculated for New College. There can be no question that the Townsend at New College had arrived there from St John's since there are references in the letters to the recovery of the caution money paid at the latter college; the episode illuminates the casual and migratory allegiances of the Elizabethan collegians in a particularly clear light.[4] The surviving accounts begin in the summer term of 1593, with the payment of 3s 4d for his matriculation fee, the purchase of a psalter and psalms, and a tuition fee of 20s. In the next quarter he purchased Jewel's *Apology*, the familiar letters of Antonio de Guevara and 'a little French boke'. His tutor was again paid 20s and in the next quarter a singing instructor was added at a fee of half that amount. The following Christmas quarter the young Townsend bought Guillaume de Salluste Du Bartas' *La Semaine*, and his tutor received 33s 4d 'for my pains'. There is a break in the accounts during 1594 but we learn from those for the following Christmas quarter that he also possessed globes. The scholastic regimen sounds in principle much like that advocated by Lord Herbert, if on a considerably reduced scale.

The studies of Robert Townsend at New College in the 1590s should be compared with the well-documented regime in the diary kept by two young Cornishmen at Christ Church in the early 1570s, Richard and Matthew Carnsew.[5] The remarkable thing about the

[1] New College Archives 14, 753; I am indebted to Dr Penry Williams for informing me of these letters.

[2] Lake, born in 1569 in Southampton, had attended Winchester and became a fellow of New College in 1589; BA 1591, MA 1595, BD and DD 1605. He was elected warden in 1613. See *DNB*.

[3] Stevenson and Salter, *The Early History*, 284; she is described as the relict of Sir Roger Townsend, knight.

[4] See above, p. 663.

[5] PRO SP 46/15, fos 212–20. The two Carnsews were registered at Broadgates Hall in 1572; *Reg. Univ.* ed. Clark, ii. 31. Richard does not appear again in the university register; Matthew was admitted BA 26 March 1575, MA 1579. The diary has been discussed by A. L. Rowse, *Tudor Cornwall* (1941), 430–1, and Hugh Kearney, *Scholars and Gentlemen:*

Carnsew diaries is that they record not only much of what the boys were studying, but also how they went about it. They also take us to the teaching of the statutory curriculum. The leaves which we possess[1] begin in May of what must be 1572, since the brothers reported on 6 May that the principal of the hall 'went to the parliament'.[2] They seem always to have studied together. On 5 May the entry tells us that they 'made definitions of *homo* by the five ways'; they finished reading Sturm and began to read Sallust's account of the Jugurthine wars on 16 May. On the tenth, seventeenth and twenty-fourth days of the month they 'made exercises to Mr vice-principal'. On the twenty-sixth they finished *Jugurtha* and the next day 'read the orations following'. On 1 June they began to read 'Cicero's works to Herennius'. In the course of June they regularly reported writing epistles and 'exercises', the latter possibly of a rhetorical nature since they also mentioned practising syllogisms (and converting them 'per impossibile'). They bought Foxe's sermons and began to translate them into Latin, and on 22 June they began to read Caesar's commentary without a reader. In their accounts for this period they also recorded the purchase of 'Valerius', Melanchthon, and Caesarius's 'boocks of logic bound in one volume' for twelve pence.[3]

Mathematical sciences were a part of their curriculum; the extraction of cubes and quadrants was recorded. They also bought Realdo Colombo's *De re anatomica*.[4] They read 'the Juishe history', bought 'Dr Humphrey's book', a Latin psalter and the pseudo-Cicero's *ad Herennium*;[5] Matthew translated Cebes's *Table*, Richard, Cicero's *De amicitia*.[6] In 'October' they attended lectures in natural philosophy

universities and society in pre-industrial Britain 1500–1700 (1970), 44. The youngest Carnsew, William, came up to Broadgates Hall in 1576; see Rowse, 431–2.

[1] Folio 212^{r-v}, May and June; fo 213, August 23–31, September 1–13; fo 214, October; fo 215, November 17–30; fo 215^V, December; fo 216, September 1–30; fo 216^V, August 1574; fo 217, an unspecified month of 31 days; fo 218, April; fo 219, December. In almost every case there is an accompanying account of moneys disbursed as there is on fo 220.

[2] The opening speech of the lord keeper was on 8 May; Wallace McCaffrey, *The Shaping of the Elizabethan Regime* (Princeton 1968), 429.

[3] PRO SP 46/15, fo 212; either Valerius Maximus or the contemporary Cornelius Valerius (Cornelis Wouters). The *Dialectica* of Johannes Caesarius was first published in Cologne in 1520 and went through many editions to the end of the century; I am indebted to Charles Schmitt for this identification. A number of works by Melanchthon might have been meant: *Dialectices libri iiii* (1527) is perhaps most likely. See E. J. Ashworth, *Language and Logic in the Post-medieval Period* (Dordrecht-Boston 1974), 13–14.

[4] PRO SP 46/15, fos 212–13, 214. Colombo's treatise was published in 1560 (title-page '1559'). I am indebted for this identification to Dr R. G. Lewis.

[5] Ibid. fos 215^V, 218. This last purchase is recorded under the month of April (fo 218) but their reading of it under June 1572 (fo 212^V) as noted above.

[6] Ibid. fo 217.

and logic.[1] They read Peter Martyr's commentary on the *Nicomachean Ethics* of Aristotle; the book 'of the threefold knowledge of God'; the logic and rhetoric of Valerius; Johannes Sturm, Sleidanus and Titus Livius.[2] They also read, 'the books set forth by the purytanes to the parliament', presumably the first and second *Admonition to Parliament* of 1572.[3] Sometimes they hired a reader, sometimes worked without assistance. They spent money on food, clothing (especially shoes and shoe-repair), candles and other routine supplies including a pair of compasses.[4] On two early occasions they recorded sermons by Dr Humfrey and by Mr Kingsmill of Christ Church.[5] The blend of humanism and protestantism, the training in non-Ramist humanist logic and in the arts of eloquence is utterly characteristic of the teaching of arts throughout the later decades of the century.

Despite the great interest of this record it is not only incomplete but difficult to interpret. Thus in August 1574 (the only year-date recorded) Matthew entered into commons at Christ Church; later in the month appears the entry, 'began to read Rodolfo and turn him in[to] tables'—presumably the *De inventione dialectica* of Rudolph Agricola which was widely used as an introduction to logical topics and their use.[6] On an earlier folio we find the marginal annotation 'Rodol:' at the month of October and on the twenty-sixth following the entry, 'finis Rodo.'; two days later was added, 'wrote the tables of Rodolf, fair in a book'.[7] This is sufficient evidence that the sheets were not used in order, and recommends great caution in their interpretation. Nevertheless, since the brothers studied together we may assume that all entries, except where specified, applied to them both, and the fact that Matthew was on the way to the baccalaureate in arts makes it worthwhile to form even a general impression of their training. How did it compare with the statutory curriculum?[8]

An Oxford undergraduate during the period covered by the Carnsew diary was meant under the new statutes of 1564/5 to spend two terms on grammar using parts of Linacre, Virgil, Horace or of Cicero's letters. For four further terms he was to study rhetoric

[1] Ibid. fo 214; no other lectures are mentioned in the surviving pages.
[2] Ibid. fos 217–19; Martyr's commentary was published in 1563 by Froschauer. This Valerius would seem to be Cornelius: *Tabulae dialecticae* (Venice 1564), *In universam bene dicendi rationem tabula summam artis rhetoricae complectens* (Antwerp 1568).
[3] Ibid. fo 219.   [4] Ibid. fo 218.
[5] Ibid. fo 212^v, 22 and 29 June 1572.
[6] Ibid. fo 216^v.   [7] Ibid. fo 214.
[8] See *Statuta*, lxxxviii–cii, 378, 389–91; Fletcher, 'The Oxford faculty of arts', pp. 172–81; Charles B. Schmitt, *John Case and Aristotelianism in Renaissance England* (Kingston and Montreal 1983), 43–4; Curtis, *Oxford and Cambridge*, 86–96, 102 ff.; O'Day, *Education and Society*, 106 ff.

using Cicero or Aristotle; this was followed in turn by five terms of dialectics or logic, where the texts were Porphyry's *Institutions*, the traditional introduction, or some part of Aristotle's *Dialectics*. Then came three terms of arithmetic and two of the related science of music, using Boethius or Gemma Frisius for the former, Boethius for the latter.[1] The total was sixteen terms, or four years of study.

There is little direct evidence of grammar study in the Carnsew diaries,[2] but to the extent that they needed it, grammar may have been behind them by the time our sheets begin. What is clear from the records for May and June 1572 is that they studied dialectic and rhetoric in tandem in the month of June, beginning their study of Cicero while they also worked on syllogisms. The translations of Foxe's sermons into Latin clearly served to instruct them in both religion and literature, as their steady diet of history provided a humanistic formation not even mentioned in the statutes. Their exercises in arithmetic, on the other hand, recall the statutory provision for the fourth year of study, and while there is no mention of music we must acknowledge that the record is incomplete. The lectures on natural philosophy, which seem to have occurred in 1574,[3] were a clear anticipation of the curriculum laid down for the bachelor proceeding to inception as master of arts, as was the study of moral philosophy in Aristotle's Nicomachean ethics—and presumably also in the non-statutory *De amicitia* of Cicero.[4] While this last reflects in part the traditional idea that the baccalaureate was only a stage in the attainment of the master's degree, the true qualification in arts, we see in every aspect of their studies a like flexibility impossible to predict from the statutes. To be sure, they were taken through the formal requirements of grammar, rhetoric and dialectic, but these were taught at least in part through humanistic commentators—Rudolph Agricola, Melanchthon and Valerius—about whom the statutes were silent.[5] Great attention was given to history, which did not find its way into the statutory curriculum until the seventeenth century. There is no evidence in the

[1] *Statuta*, 389–90. The earlier list for the same date, p. 378, differs little with respect to the authorities and does not specify terms.

[2] If they were reading one of Johannes Sturm's introductory treatises like the *De literarum ludis* (1576) or *In partitiones Ciceronis dialogi duo* (1539) they were probably commencing the study of rhetoric.

[3] If my inference about the order of the folios is correct; see p. 699 above.

[4] *Statutua*, xcv–xcv, 390; see also the comment of Fletcher, 'The faculty of arts', p. 179.

[5] Fletcher, pp. 188–9. Agricola's *De inventione dialectica* was prescribed at Cambridge in 1535; see the discussion by L. Jardine, 'Humanism and dialectic in sixteenth-century Cambridge: a preliminary investigation', in R. R. Bolgar (ed.), *Classical Influences on European Culture A.D. 1500–1700* (Cambridge 1976), 141–54.

surviving leaves of their diary that they were interested in modern languages, but there is more extra-statutory material in their attention to the religious debate, with an added touch in the use of Foxe's sermons to practise Latin composition.[1] In general what we seem to find is something actually rather familiar—a broad pursuit of the statutory requirements filled out and brought up to date by the addition of authors and commentators and even of disciplines not mentioned in the statutes, but chosen by the tutor or other directors of study, who perhaps drew on teaching traditions within the college itself.

In the Carnsew diaries we seem to obtain a rare glimpse of the actual conduct and content of teaching for a man in the degree course in arts. In the absence of any like survival, or of any Tudor equivalent of the famous 'Directions for a Student in the Universitie' at Emmanuel College, Cambridge[2] we must now fall back upon two much less satisfactory classes of document, the inventories of personal libraries and student notebooks, in order to supplement this testimony.

A number of literary inventories survive from the estates of men whose wills were probated at the chancellor's court in Oxford, some 150 from 1500 to 1605. This is only a fraction of the numbers who passed through the university, of course, and is far from a statistical sampling of the whole.[3] They were distributed very unevenly throughout the century and come to an end in the mid-1580s when libraries grew too large to list. If, to try to ensure an accurate assessment of undergraduate reading, we confine ourselves only to inventories made for men who died before they had attained their MA degree the number drops to about a dozen, falling almost entirely in the decades of the 1570s and 1580s. If we were to count the most frequently recurring titles in the wider range of lists, however, there would be no significant difference from the evidence at Cambridge for the period from 1535 to 1590:[4] Latin was learned from Virgil,

---

[1] Cf Curtis, *Oxford and Cambridge*, 91–6.

[2] Emmanuel College Archives, MS 48; see Curtis, *Oxford and Cambridge*, 289–90; Kearney, *Scholars and Gentlemen*, 103–5; a transcript is printed by H. F. Fletcher, *The Intellectual Development of John Milton* (Urbana, Illinois 1961).

[3] See N. R. Ker, 'The provision of books', pp. 470–1 above. The inventory of Sears Jayne showed eighty-one containing at least fifteen separately named books for the period to 1600 in Oxford against 159 at Cambridge; see *Library Catalogues of the English Renaissance* (Berkeley and Los Angeles 1956), 47. See also, Mark H. Curtis, 'Library catalogues and Tudor Oxford and Cambridge', *Studies in the Renaissance* v (1958), 111–20; Lisa Jardine, 'The place of dialectic teaching in sixteenth-century Cambridge', *Studies in the Renaissance*, xxi (1974), 31–62; H. Smith, 'Some humanist libraries in early Tudor Cambridge', *Sixteenth Century Journal* v (1974), 15–34.

[4] Lisa Jardine, 'Humanism and the sixteenth century Cambridge arts course', *History of Education* iv (1977), 16–31.

Terence, Plautus and Ovid—authors new only in the sense that they were now studied in humanist editions; Cicero and Quintilian were the foundation of their study of rhetoric; Aristotle's *Ethics* and *Politics* taught them moral philosophy; history was imbibed from Plutarch, Sallust, Titus Livius, Caesar's *Commentaries*, Justinus Historicus and Valerius Maximus. There would be some Greek—Homer, a play of Euripides, Lucian's *Dialogues*, a work of Plato; Erasmus and Valla were the masters of style, Rudolph Agricola a standard authority on logic and dialectic. They would own the Greek grammar of Ceporinus and the dictionary of Calepinus with a Greek/Latin lexicon and a Greek New Testament, probably that of Stephanus. Peter Lombard's *Sentences* were still quite likely to turn up in private libraries: a useful work of reference is slow to disappear, even after fashions change.

At the undergraduate level all of this betrays the vast shift of emphasis away from terminist logic and speculative grammar towards the humanities and arts of persuasion. The fact that many of the old authors—Aristotle above all—were still the foundation of the curriculum should not conceal the magnitude of this cultural change. It was already under way before the injunctions of 1535 insisted on the use with Aristotle's logic of humanist commentators—Rudolph Agricola and Melanchthon—in place of the schoolmen.[1] Charles Schmitt observes that in the 1530s appeared the last of the books of logic 'still retaining strong links to the traditions of medieval Oxford'.[2] There followed a hiatus of some years until in 1545 Berthelet printed the first edition of John Seton's *Dialectica*, a work destined to become a standard introduction to logic in Britain for a century.[3]

The earliest surviving inventories, whose size indicate the expense and rarity of books in the first decades of the century, are often strictly medieval. The small libraries of John Valyn (1513) or Thomas Thomson (1514) contained the familiar classical authors— 'Tully' and Terence—along with standard texts like the logic of Thomas Bricot, *Formalitates* of Scotus, a *Liber predicamentorum* and Walter Burley's commentary on the *Ethics* of Aristotle.[4] Fifteen

---

[1] See Claire Cross, 'Oxford and the Tudor state from the accession of Henry VIII to the death of Mary', pp. 128–9 above; Mallet, *University of Oxford*, ii. 62; *Statuta Academiae Cantabrigiensis*, 134–41.

[2] *John Case*, 32; Appendix 1, 'Logic books printed in England before 1620', 225–9. This study, which appeared shortly before this book was to go to press, must be taken into account in any future work on the Tudor curriculum.

[3] 'The medieval tradition of *sophismata, insolubilia* and *obligationes* was past, and scholastic logic was being rapidly replaced by a bastardized mixture of dialectic and rhetoric', ibid. 33. See also W. S. Howell, *Logic and Rhetoric in England, 1500–1700* (Princeton 1956), ch. 2; see also note 281.

[4] Printed by A. B. Emden, *BRUO 1501–40*, appendix B, 714–42. Unless otherwise indicated I have used the typed transcripts prepared by Mr Walter Mitchell in OUA.

years later, however, a young man might own the logic of Johannes Caesarius, in which the influence of Agricola was evident.[1] In the same inventory we find a Greek dictionary, much of Erasmus, Valla and Agricola, a Hebrew alphabet and primer, Trapezuntius, the Greek grammar of Theodore of Gaza, a four-volume edition of Pliny's natural history, and at the same time, Walter Burley's commentary on the *Logic* of Aristotle. Melanchthon's *Institutiones rhetoricae* (1521) which counted the dialectical concepts of judgement and arrangement as parts of rhetoric appeared in inventories by 1531.[2]

Of private libraries in the fifth and sixth decades there is a very small and irregular record.[3] Among those that do survive, however, we seem to see at least how deep the floodtide of humanism had become, how scarce were the scholastic authors and even the texts of Aristotle. In the books owned by a 'Master Bysley', perhaps a bookseller, whose effects were listed in 1543 we find, to be sure, a *Logic* and a Greek *Rhetoric* of Aristotle but among the 120 titles there is far more of literary and religious interest: Alciati's *Emblemata*, the Hebrew grammar of Thomas Münster, a Hebrew Old Testament and a Hebrew *Genesis*, an Old and New Testament in Greek, a New Testament in Greek and Latin and several of the Fathers, while the logical works were all of the humanistic school: Clichtoveus, Caesarius, Christian Hegendorff and Erasmus Sarcerius.[4] In the largely medical library of Thomas Symonds, MA, BM, of Merton College we also find Lucian, Macrobius, Cornelius Agrippa's *De vanitate scientiarum*, the *Praise of Folly* and More's *Utopia*.[5] Five years later, in 1558, among the 228 books of William Browne, MA, of St Alban's Hall and Merton, we find Reuchlin, Ermolao Barbaro's study of Pliny, a Greek Simplicius, Diodorus Siculus, an unidentified Greek work on the rhetoric of Aristotle, the commentary of Trapezuntius, Greek texts of Euripides, Aristophanes, Hesiod, Xenophon and Dioscorides, a Greek Pentateuch, a Greek St Basil and a work of John Leland, presumably the *Assertio inclytissimi Arturii Regis* of 1544.[6]

[1] Ashworth, *Language and Logic*, 14; I presume upon the youth of William Wodrofe, about whom we know nothing more than that the inventory was made after his clandestine disappearance from his room in c 1530; *BRUO 1501–40*, 742.

[2] Thomas Cartwright of Broadgates Hall; ibid. 717, supposing that this is what is meant by *De arte dicendi*. Cf Howell, *Logic and Rhetoric*, 92.

[3] Ker, 'The provision of books', pp. 470–1.

[4] *BRUO 1501–40*, 716–17.

[5] Appraised in 1553; ibid. 738–9.

[6] Ibid. 740–1 under 'David Tolley'; see Ker, 'The provision of books', p. 471 no. 1. From the same decade the nuncupative testament of Edward Beaumont, BA of Christ Church (22 August 1552) consists of 117 items including a significant number of Greek texts: Aristotle's *Rhetoric*, Xenophon, the *Onomasticon* of Julius Pollux, the *Iliad* and *Odyssey*, Pindar, Euripides, a collection of Greek epigrams, Herodian, Demosthenes and Isocrates.

While these catalogues tell us little of the mature intellectual formation of the day they do give some notion of the widening range of antique and contemporary humanistic culture available in Oxford by the time Elizabeth came to the throne. A decade after her accession we have as it happens two personal libraries from Corpus Christi College which cast some light upon the growth of learning there. These inventories were drawn up for comparatively young fellows who died shortly after completing their bachelors' degrees. The first of them belonged to Richard Alen (Alynne) from Lincolnshire who was admitted *discipulus* in 1562 and became a probationer fellow in April 1566. He died three years later before the end of May 1569. The inventory of his goods, dated 11 July 1569,[1] was made by the bedell of law and the yeomen bedell of theology, listing his debts, creditors, simple personal effects and some hundred books.

Alen's library showed a marked interest in protestant theology, bible commentaries and church fathers; he owned Calvin's commentary on the psalms, four volumes of Luther's writings, a New Testament in Greek and Latin, scriptural commentaries by Peter Martyr, Chrysostom, Origen and Theophylact, as well as Augustine's works in six volumes. Contemporary religious literature ranged from More's *Confutation of Tyndale's Answer* to Peter Martyr on the eucharist and Nowell's catechism. There were, however, medieval authors as well: Dionysius the Carthusian, Thomas Aquinas on the method of making a confession and Walter Burley's commentary on Luke.

If we look for the books that seem to reflect his undergraduate studies we find that his early formation differed little from that of the Carnsew brothers thirty years later. A 'history of the Jews' as well as the *De bello judaico* of 'Hegisippus', Gildas's *De excidio et conquestu Britanniae*, Sallust, Agathias (in Greek and Latin) and Valerius Maximus might be said to represent the historical dimension. In Latin literature he owned Terence, two volumes of Cicero's letters, an 'epitome adagiorum', Erasmus's *Colloquies* and what would seem to have been Varro's *De lingua latina*. Greek literature was represented by Homer and a work of Demosthenes.[2] Moral philosophy began with Aristotle's *Ethics*, and apart from appropriate works

---

Some of these were printed with Latin translations and there was also an extensive collection from the Latin classics. The guides to dialectic were Agricola, Joachim Périon, Sturm, Melanchthon, Frans Titelmans and Ramus. The inventory is printed in *Reg. Univ.* ed. Boase, xx–xxi.

[1] OUA chancellor's court inventories, volume A–BO, Hyp./B/10.

[2] There was also an 'orarium grece', Chrysostom's homilies and a Theodoret in Greek and Latin. On the side of sacred oratory, he also had Andreas Hyperius' *De formandis concionibus sacris*, the English homilies and several sermon collections.

already mentioned, Isocrates' *Ad Demonicum* and an 'exempla virtutum et viciorum'. Logic interestingly showed some links with the medieval past: Jodocus Clichtoveus's *Fundamentum logicae*[1] and a *Syllogisticon* which must have emerged from the schools in Paris in the first decades of the century.[2] While we miss some standard authors such as Virgil and Rudolph Agricola, Alen's undergraduate library seems in every other respect quite conventional in its blend of dialectic, moral philosophy, history and rhetoric. In any event we cannot expect that any student would own all of the books he was expected to read as the Carnsew diaries again suggest an added difficulty in relying too much on the evidence of inventories.

The second inventory from Corpus in the same year, also recording the library of a bachelor of arts,[3] may reasonably be used to amplify the evidence from Richard Alen. This second library belonged to William Napper from Hampshire who had no detectable link with the Oxfordshire Nappers also at Corpus, and who was admitted in 1568/9 as a probationer fellow after undergraduate training at Brasenose. He died at the age of 25 within a few months of admission, leaving some 110 books and three (unidentified) maps. Here we find a rather fuller collection of undergraduate material. Frans Titelmans and Melanchthon provided introductions to dialectic with Rudolph Agricola, Cornelius Valerius and Ramus's critic, Joachim Périon. There were two unnamed 'dialectica' as well. Ambrogio Calepino's polyglot dictionary, a Greek and Latin dictionary and the Greek grammar of Ceporinus show the standard taste in that study. Latin he managed with the aid of Thomas Cooper's dictionary.[4] He owned several works of Aristotle including the *Physics*;[5] Cicero and Erasmus abounded along with Politian. There is an altogether more humanistic, less theological cast to this library than to that of Richard Alen, although they were separated in age by only three years. The obvious common ground, not surprisingly, is in their undergraduate reading. There is also some suggestion of a returning interest in the text of Aristotle: Alen owned an 'Index

---

[1] Clichtove was a disciple of Lefèvre d'Étaples and like him retained an interest in certain scholastic techniques; 'Unlike the Italians whom they admired, the Parisian humanists seem to have been clearly aware of the nature and place of semantical investigations and of formal logic'; Ashworth, *Language and Logic*, 10.

[2] For example, Lokert's *Sillogismi*, or the works of Enzinas, Juan Dolz or Coronel; Ashworth, 7.

[3] OUA c.c. invents. vol. M-O, Hyp./B/16.

[4] *Thesaurus linguae romanae et britannicae*, published by Berthelet in 1565 and in successive editions (*STC* 5686–90).

[5] 'Opera Aristotelis, physica Aristotelis cum commento, organon Aristotelis, philosophica Aristotelis.'

[ad] Aristotelem' in addition to his *Ethics*. His medieval authors serve chiefly to remind us of how rare they have become in these mid-Tudor decades.

By the 1570s, so great is the influx that it is no longer possible to single out the appearance of new works in renaissance humanism except in one important tradition conspicuous by its rarity, that of Plato and neo-Platonism. The appearance of Plato's *Opera graece* in the list of books belonging to Henry Chayney MA of Broadgates hall, among books confiscated for debt in 1580 at the behest of the man-ciple,[1] is an almost singular occurrence; references to Pico and Ficino are at least as rare. Nevertheless, Platonic and neo-Platonic strains were certainly absorbed, in part from patristic sources and early commenta-tors, perhaps also from texts available more readily in college libraries.[2] Otherwise the novel development in the later years is the revival of interest in Aristotle and to a marked degree in medieval texts.[3]

A decade after the early deaths of our two Corpus scholars a bookseller named Nicholas Clifton also died, and the inventory of his holdings was dated December 1578. Clifton had been admitted a bookseller on 28 June 1570 and was not one of those, seemingly, from whom the colleges bought their books.[4] This may account for the surprisingly small proportion of religious and theological works among the 315 titles or authors listed; there is also one disconcerting entry of 'a hundrethe and threscore unperfitt bookes'. Most of his stock in trade seems to have catered to the studies of the arts faculty. Although there were brief sections also on law and medicine, it would seem that Clifton's must have been a shop of common resort for the standard works of classical humanism and eloquence. In addition there was one work of Ramus;[5] Plato's *Laws* (apparently in Latin) and a scattering of vernacular works (apart from English) in French and Italian: Boccaccio (in French), 'sonetti' and 'canzoni', the *Heptameron*, a French 'life of the Trojans', and an Italian grammar. English works included *Piers Plowman*, 'Wiet's Rebellion'[6] and Skelton's *Merry Tales*.

[1] OUA c.c. invents. vol. BR–C, Hyp./B/11 (in alphabetical sequence under Coles, William).

[2] Schmitt, *John Case*, 47–50 on Everard Digby's 'Theorica analytica', 163–4, 189–90, 218–21. On the important issue of the relation between renaissance Aristotelianism and Platonism see also Charles Schmitt, *Aristotle and the Renaissance* (Cambridge Mass. 1983), 91 ff.   [3] Schmitt, *John Case*, 43, 63–6.

[4] The inventory is in OUA c.c. invents. vol. BR–C, Hyp./B/11; printed by Strickland Gibson, *Abstracts from the Wills and Testamentary Documents of Binders, Printers, and Stationers of Oxford, from 1493 to 1638* (1907), 11–16, although the transcription is not entirely reliable. Clifton's admission is in *Reg. Univ.* ed. Clark, i. 321. On the college book-sellers see Ker, 'The provision of books', 442–3.

[5] *Dialectica* (first published 1574).

[6] Presumably the history of John Proctor published in London in 1554; *STC* 20407–8.

The inventory is chiefly interesting, however, for the evidence of a revival of Aristotelianism in the final quarter of the century. There were Greek texts of Aristotle's *Rhetoric, Politics* and *Ethics*;[1] Latin texts of the *De anima, De coelo, Politics* and *Ethics* (two copies), as well as a work entitled simply *Philosophia*, perhaps one of the collections in translation.[2] The commentaries were provided by Leonardo Bruni,[3] Agostino Nifo and Joachim Périon among the contemporaries and among the ancients, Alexander of Aphrodisias and Ammonius Hermeae, the Alexandrian philosopher, whose presence in this list reminds us of one of the chief sources of Platonic influence among these English Aristotelians.[4] There was a full range of works by humanist logicians too: Clichtoveus, Joachim Périon once more, Johannes Caesarius, Melanchthon, Cornelius Valerius and Peter Carter's edition of Seton's *Dialectica*.[5] Accompanying these Aristotelian works and commentaries there was a stock of medieval texts reminiscent of the early decades of the century: John Major on the *Sentences* of Peter Lombard, the text of the *Sentences* itself,[6] Robert Holcot, Walter Burley, the *Questiones* of Duns Scotus and a Boethius *De philosophia cum duplici commento*. In addition to these Clifton seems to have had a copy of Thomas à Kempis.[7]

From these libraries we gain at least some idea of the kind of eclecticism that characterized both undergraduate teaching and the intellectual fare of the arts faculty as a whole by the later years of the sixteenth century. In the early decades such evidence as we have suggests that the intrusion of the new humanism among older

[1] If that is what was intended by 'Aristotles de moribus grece'.

[2] See note 256 and Schmitt, *Aristotle and the Renaissance*, 164–5 note 18. It occurs here next to Walter Burley, and throughout the inventory Clifton's topical grouping of the books seems evident. I assume that where Greek was not specified the book was in Latin; one of the appraisers was the university stationer, Henry Milward.

[3] On the *Politics*; on the importance of Bruni as the founder of the humanistic technique of interpretation see Schmitt, op. cit. 16–17, 67–8.

[4] Ibid. 135.

[5] Howell, *Logic and Rhetoric*, 50–6.

[6] Explicitly eliminated from the theology curriculum in favour of the text of Scripture by the new statutes of 1564/5; *Statuta*, 381.

[7] I owe to my colleague L. E. Boyle, OP this suggestion for 'Thomas Acapensis'. There are some half-dozen inventories from 1567 to 1578 that list books owned seemingly by young men; John Dunnet, George and Simon Digby, Tristram Farringdon, Sir Burye, Thomas Bolte. They confirm the impression left by Clifton's inventory and others about the most common textbooks: Linacre, Titelmans, Sturm, Agricola, Cornelius Valerius, Gemma Frisius, Theodore Gaza, Seton, Valerius Maximus. There is a great quantity of Cicero; Walter Burley and Robert Holcot occasionally appear. The library of Farringdon, described as a gentleman and late student of Exeter College (dec. 3 September 1577) contained several Greek authors: Thucydides, Philo Judaeus, Hermogenes, Epictetus, Johannes Grammaticus, Dionysius the Areopagite, Demosthenes, Athanasius and two homilies of Chrysostom. The stylistic and literary works of Erasmus appeared regularly as did his New Testament, especially his Latin version.

scholastic texts was also the ordinary state of affairs.[1] It was the displacement of the old logic by the new humanistic commentators more than any other single intellectual event that marked the end of the 'medieval' curriculum.[2] Outwardly the statutory curriculum remained faithful to the traditional texts, which ensured the continuing domination of the arts curriculum by Aristotle. The new Aristotle, however, was studied from Greek texts with humanistic and classical commentators in place of the medieval authorities so that the Aristotelian framework remained more or less intact and was increasingly used to support and accommodate new currents of thought. This eclectic Aristotelianism was unquestionably the characteristic intellectual culture of the Elizabethan university, by no means necessarily 'reactionary', and requiring careful investigation before the intellectual changes of the seventeenth century can truly be understood.[3]

The other occasional source of information about this Tudor scholastic culture[4] carrying its own difficulties of interpretation, is the student notebook.[5] We may begin with the letters of a fellow of Corpus Christi College, a Devonian by the name of Simon Tripp, who entered the college in 1559 and became a fellow in 1567. In the same year he succeeded the future president, John Rainolds, as reader in humanity. His letters were couched in the conventional phraseology of a humanist's familiar style, copious and intimate, but they are nevertheless informative about the state of teaching in Corpus half

[1] Evident in the well-known book list of John Dorne preserving his record of sales for the year 1520; Collectanea, i (OHS v 1885), pt 3, and Collectanea, ii (OHS xvi 1890), App. for additions and corrections. See also James McConica, English Humanists and Reformation Politics (Oxford, 1965), 88–90 for a discussion. Occasional graces are insufficient to form a reliable guide to the teaching of arts in the early decades, but such as there are show the same mixture: e.g. OUA Reg. Cong. 1518-35 fo 55 (1521), a scholar in the grammar faculty to read two books of the Georgics; fo 55^V a master of arts to read a book of Aristotle's Poetics; fo 81^V (1522) a master of arts dispensed from his necessary regency to teach at Magdalen College grammar school on condition that he read publicly in the schools Sallust's Bellum Jugurthinum.

[2] On the changes in logic see Terrence Heath, 'Logical grammar, grammatical logic, and humanism in three German universities', Studies in the Renaissance, xviii (1971), 9–64; Ashworth, Language and Logic; I. Thomas, 'Medieval aftermath: Oxford logic and logicians of the seventeenth century', Oxford Studies Presented to Daniel Callus (OHS n.s. xvi 1964), 297-311; Jardine, 'The place of dialectic teaching'.

[3] See especially Schmitt, Aristotle and the Renaissance, ch. iv.

[4] I use the term 'scholastic' here in the strict sense to describe the typical teaching of the university's schools. The tenacity of Aristotelianism was certainly due in part to its familiarity, and also to its capacity to adapt while at the same time remaining the scaffolding of the scholastic curriculum. As we see, this scholastic culture, in the above sense, was also humanistic.

[5] For the most part notes and letters additional to those already cited, none before the 1550s, most of them from the 1570s on. I count some twenty-five such records to the end of Elizabeth's reign of which perhaps one represents the work only of an undergraduate: see below, p. 710. They must be used with the greatest caution since most were compiled over a period of time, and many had more than one owner.

a century after the foundation.[1] Exhortations of obedience towards their parents and reminders of their duties to the commonweal abound in his letters to pupils and former pupils.[2] He also referred frequently to their Greek studies; Tripp himself cited Aristophanes, Xenophon and Demosthenes. He longed for a first trip to Italy.[3] He urged a pupil to immerse himself in the Latin and Greek poets and to study Cicero and Demosthenes for the arts of speech; he should read and write something daily, remembering that he came to the university as to the market-place of the arts and letters.[4] He wrote to 'G.M.', perhaps George More, the pupil of President Cole, urging him to go forward into the battle-line of his Lenten disputation having on the right hand the sword of dialectic which fells many with many words, on the left the shield of rhetoric which wards off the charges of the enemy. In the van is the Greek tongue, at the rear is Latin; moral philosophy is at the head of all. The arts curriculum of Elizabethan Oxford is seemingly epitomized.[5]

At the same time we detect in Tripp's letters some hint of the limitations of this seemingly impressive pedagogy. One of his favourites, William West, departed Oxford for London and Tripp complained in due course that for two years West had not written. So excellent a brain, Tripp felt, could not have grown dull. Was West so busy with his law that he had time only to write to family and friends? Or was it that London gentlemen did not write in Latin, so that he feared his old tutor would not like letters written in English?[6]

Interest in the changing programme of studies has tended to obscure the equally important matter of the exercises of instruction.[7] In the Carnsew diaries we have some evidence of the time spent on a single text—usually a month or six weeks—while other exercises of disputation and declamation were performed. It seems evident that the vast range of authors cited in a typical oration cannot have been assimilated in their entirety in the time available. The notebook of John Rogers, who came up to Christ Church in 1578 and ended as minister of Chalcombe in Northamptonshire

[1] BL Add. MS 6251; cf Fowler, *Corpus Christi*, 133–7. I do not construe the rhetoric of friendship as did Dr Fowler and have disputed his conclusions in 'The fate of Erasmian humanism', N. Phillipson (ed.), *Universities, Society and the Future* (Edinburgh 1983), 51–2.

[2] BL Add. MS 6251 fo 4^{r-v} to Nicholas and Humphrey Prideaux; fo 6 to William West. None of these names is otherwise known at Corpus.

[3] Ibid. fos 13, 14^v.

[4] BL Add. MS 6251 fo 20.

[5] Ibid. fo 28^v. For George More see p. 673. He determined BA 1572, MA 1574.

[6] Ibid. fo 6^v.

[7] Fletcher, 'The faculty of arts', 168 ff.

contains an unusual record of his scholastic exercises.[1] It gives some notion of the relentless pressure of disputation, at least for those in pursuit of degrees. Disputation was both a teaching instrument and the chief method of public examination; on both routine and grand public occasions the talent and skill of the graduate was thus exhibited. While the declamation, written and oral, was adopted from humanistic practice, the disputation remained the ornament of scholastic life throughout the renaissance.[2] When we consider the mass of material in the Tudor curriculum, burgeoning yearly with the output of the printing press, we may infer that collegiate instruction was shaped largely by the need to prepare for disputations, an organizing principle and a method of selection. The classical citations in two theses disputed by Rogers in Michaelmas Term 1582 seem a kind of résumé of the undergraduate reading we have been discussing: Terence, Petrarch, Justin, Suetonius, the *Iliad*, Ovid, Sallust, Cicero, Diogenes Laertius, Horace, Plutarch, Herodotus, Augustine (the *De doctrina Christiana*) Aristotle's *Ethics*, the *Odyssey*, Hesiod and Propertius.[3]

We must not lose sight of the fact that not all chose this route. Randolph Cholmondeley, the son of Sir Hugh Cholmondeley of Cheshire, matriculated at Lincoln College in 1577 at the age of 19 and he entered Lincoln's Inn three years later. His notebook, which includes evidence of his studies and a few family letters, is perhaps the only such Tudor document apart from the Carnsew diaries that can be ascribed entirely to a single undergraduate career.[4] The letters to his father would be recognizable in any age—apologies for not having written, gratitude for kindness, explanations that when he had time to spare from his studies he could think of nothing to say, a request that his father visit Oxford, the ancient home of the muses.[5] The first seventy or so folios of the manuscript consist almost entirely of annotations on various works of Cicero, the kind of collection of commonplaces recommended by all humanist pedagogues, which was certainly the quarry for their

[1] Bodl. MS Rawl. D 273 fo 153^V (reversed); cf. Schmitt, *John Case*, 55; Kearney, *Scholars and Gentlemen*, 45, 64. His questions for the baccalaureate at Austins and in quodlibetical disputation included, 'An relativa sint simul natura', 'An omnia appetant bonum', 'An ornare sit falsum', 'An iuvenis sit idoneus auditor moralis philsophiae'. On Rogers see *Reg. Univ.* ed. Clark iii. 126.

[2] See W. T. Costello, *The Scholastic Curriculum at Early Seventeenth Century Cambridge* (Cambridge Mass. 1958).

[3] Bodl. MS Rawl. D 273 fos 157–63^V; the theses were 'Concordia res parvae crescuntur' and 'Discordia res omnes crescuntur', both in November 1582.

[4] Bodl. MS Lat. misc. E 114. On Cholmondeley see *Reg. Univ.* ed. Clark, ii. 75 ('Chalmley').

[5] Ibid. fos 154–5^V; 'antiquum musarum domicilium', fo 155, a letter of 18 May 1578.

allusions in declamations and disputation.[1] There are notes on epistolary style from the letters of Paulus Manutius and some on legal matters which suggest that he might have taken this notebook on to London.[2] There are two declamations and a final postscript on the chief points to note in reading any author.[3] There is no trace of Aristotelian study or of training in disputation, and if his notebook gives a complete impression of Cholmondeley's time at Oxford we must conclude that he was one of the commoners who evaded that discipline simply to concentrate on the ornaments of style and classical learning.

At quite the opposite end of the spectrum from Cholmondeley was John Day of Oriel College, son of the protestant printer who cut the first Anglo-Saxon type used in England for Matthew Parker and who printed Foxe's *Book of Martyrs*.[4] Day's extensive commentary on the *Physics* of Aristotle showed a wide range of reading and catholicity of taste, fully conversant with the medieval tradition and continental catholic scholarship alike. He cited Franciscus Toletus, Beneto Pereira and Pedro de Fonseca as well as Aquinas, Buridan and the Coimbra commentators; Bodin, and Calvin; Andrew Willet, John Sanderson and William Temple and a host of others who testify to the new international Latin and neo-Aristotelian culture that now dominated the university's higher faculties.[5] With Day we are of course well beyond the range of undergraduate training, but we see in him how cosmopolitan the protestant graduate's academic perspective might be.

Careful study of Aristotle's *Physics* is evident in two other notebooks from the end of the century. One of these from St John's contains notes from Aulus Gellius, an analysis of the *Physics*, short notes on many ancient authors and also on Henry Cuffe, the regius professor of Greek and friend of Savile, who became involved imprudently with Essex.[6] At Corpus, Brian Twyne asked his father for a Greek text with the translation of Julius Pacius and 'an interpreter or two', namely Titelmans.[7] His notebook contains annotations on

[1] Although it is certain that they also made extensive use of collections and encyclopedias, apart from the works of Erasmus there is little evidence of this in inventories and like records. [2] Ibid. fos 129ᵛ ff., 72.

[3] Ibid. fos 150, 156, 175ᵛ: 'Cuncta cadunt crudelitate', 'Lingua continentia virtutis pars magna. Plutar. Declamatio.'

[4] Matric. St Alban's Hall 1583, BA 1587, elected fellow of Oriel 1588. I have discussed him and John Rogers also in 'Humanism and Aristotle in Tudor Oxford', *English Historical Review* xciv (1979), 314.

[5] Bodl. MS Rawl. D 274; see also Schmitt, *John Case*, 56–7; Kearney, *Scholars and Gentlemen*, 82.

[6] Mallet, *University of Oxford*, ii. 167. The notebook is Bodl. MS Rawl. D 1423; cf Kearney, 64; Schmitt, 57 n. 164.

[7] H. G. S., 'Some correspondence of Brian Twyne', *Bodleian Quarterly Record*, v

the first part of the *Physics* and a number of questions or 'suppositiones' derived from it and the *Logic*. In other pages presumably from his early career there are annotations on the *Posterior Analytics*, notes on Bede's *Ecclesiastical History* and on early British historians, and directions for the learning of Latin.[1] From this last our earlier evidence is reconfirmed: Sturm's collection was the best introduction to Cicero; the comedies of Terence and Plautus (avoiding the latter's obsolete words) were mentioned, Caesar's *Commentaries* and some of the longest speeches of Livy should all be studied with great care.[2]

The surviving records, both in the university's registers and its probate jurisdiction as in the casual survival of personal letters and notebooks are too irregular and fragmentary to support a circumstantial account of the history of undergraduate teaching of arts in Tudor Oxford. The evidence does suggest that the statutory curriculum was followed in its broad outlines although reading of texts for the *quadrivium* might have occurred in the first three years, but the crucial questions as to which supplementary texts and commentaries were used can be answered only in part. The basis of the curriculum was Aristotle still, starting with his logic, but there was a profound shift away from the sophistications of late medieval dialectic towards a concern with clarity of discourse and debate. The other Aristotelian works that appeared regularly were the *Physics, Ethics, Politics* and *Rhetoric*. Alongside this there is impressive evidence for the study of Greek, at least among the more ambitious. The range of classical literature, Latin and Greek, is wide if not always convincingly deep. Nevertheless the emphasis on a rhetorical culture and on the traditions of moral philosophy against those of speculative truth is perfectly clear.

We have already remarked on the notable absence of Platonic and neo-Platonic texts, at least in graces, private libraries and notebooks. College libraries held them, as they tended in general to contain the more expensive and less frequently used authorities of the higher faculties.[3] The library of Corpus was itself an example. By 1589 it contained a shelf of important Platonic texts including the Aldine edition of Plato's works (Venice 1513), the edition in Greek and Latin by Serranus (Paris 1578), three Greek manuscripts and the first known text in England of Ficino's Plato (Florence 1492). There

---

(1926-8), 215 (2 May 1597). Twyne was adm. discipulus 1594, made probationer fellow 1606. BA 1600, MA 1603, BD 1610.

[1] Bodl. MS Jesus Coll. 30, pp. 1–77, 82–4, 96 ff., 287.
[2] Ibid., pp. 287–8. The treatise is an epitome of accepted method.
[3] See Ker, 'Provision of books', appendices.

was also a Greek manuscript of the *Enneades* of Plotinus.[1] Yet, as we have seen, citations of such works are exceedingly rare. Corpus did produce a Platonist in Thomas Jackson who became a scholar there in 1596. He was a Laudian whose life work was a commentary on the Apostles Creed in twelve books.[2] This was unmistakably infused with Platonic thought and imagery and the tenets of natural theology. His critic William Twisse, a Wykehamist Aristotelian who became a fellow of New College in 1598, not only objected to his doctrine but to its source as well, finding it wholly uncharacteristic in an Oxford man: 'I muse not a little to see Platonicall and Plotinicall Philosophy so much advanced by an Oxonian: as if Aristotles learning left logicians perplext in a point of sophistry, and only Plotinicall Philosophy would expedite them.'[3]

The comparative rarity of Ramus is another witness to the dominance of Aristotle at Oxford. Although Ramus was certainly read and had his adherents there is no evidence that he was held generally in high esteem, and there was much criticism.[4] Robert Batt at Brasenose College, whose letters show both the literary eloquence of the practised humanist and a serious interest in Aristotelian philosophy, ridiculed Gabriel Harvey's Ramist *De restitutione logica* (1583) and looked forward to an Oxford refutation of the Ramist works of William Temple.[5] The distinguished Puritan divine John Rainolds knew Ramus much better and spoke well of his writing, but at the same time he objected to the narrowness of Ramus's perspective on the legacy of the past, and found his real intellectual master instead in Vives.[6] Rainold's mental world exactly demonstrated the flowering of the Oxford schools under Elizabeth: catholic and eclectic, sensitive to the whole of the tradition of learning in the past including the medieval achievement, widely read in contemporary continental thought, yet staunchly protestant and if anything Calvinist. It rested on the foundations erected by Fox and Wolsey, an erudite humanism in which the counsels of antiquity were dominated by the doctrines of Cicero and Quintilian on the formation of the wise and virtuous man who would strive for the common good, and by

[1] J. R. Liddell, 'The library of Corpus Christi College Oxford', *The Library* 4th ser. xiii (1938), 385–416. Items 28, 24, 25–7, 29, 32 in the catalogue, 403–16. See also Sarah Hutton, 'Thomas Jackson. Oxford Platonist, and William Twisse, Aristotelian', *Journal of the History of Ideas*, xxxix (1978), 635–52.

[2] Hutton, 'Thomas Jackson', 637 ff.

[3] Quoted by Hutton, 649.

[4] Kearney, *Scholars and Gentlemen*, 64; my own findings have tended to corroborate his views that its influence at Oxford was much less than in contemporary Cambridge; 'Humanism and Aristotle', 304 ff.

[5] Bodl. MS Rawl. D 985; cf Schmitt, *John Case*, 55.

[6] See p. 714 n. 1, and see Schmitt, *John Case*, 54–2.

the scriptural and patristic learning that looked to Augustine's *De doctrina christiana* as its fountainhead. It was well summed up by Rainolds: 'There are two parts of eloquence, the first of life, the second of the tongue . . . The latter we learn from Cicero, the former from Christ . . . truly, we read the profane authors in order that we may go forth good men.'[1]

Among Rainolds' contemporaries was a man of like views who was pre-eminently Oxford's master in the teaching of arts, John Case.[2] Case produced textbooks for most of the arts curriculum, beginning with primers for schoolboys in moral and natural philosophy.[3] His first work, the *Summa veterum interpretum in universam dialecticam Aristotelis*, was published in London in 1584 and dedicated to the university's chancellor, the earl of Leicester.[4] It was intended for the undergraduate and was entirely in the rhetorical tradition we have described, training the beginner in the logic of persuasive discourse.[5] In the following year the newly-established university press brought out Case's *Speculum moralium quaestionum in universam ethicen Aristotelis*, the first book to be printed by Joseph Barnes, who henceforth was first to publish each of Case's books.[6] These bore every appearance of official authority and were based, as he avowed, on his experience as a teacher.[7] In this instance Case dealt with moral philosophy as he did in three other works which were drawn from Aristotle's *Nicomachean ethics, Magna moralia, Politics* and *Oeconomics*.[8] His commentary on the *Politics*, the *Sphaera civitatis* of 1588, which coincided with the most critical moment of England's war with Spain, became widely popular in the protestant universities and was frequently reprinted in German.[9] Along with the *Speculum moralium* it was his most successful textbook,[10] embodying the eclectic Aristotelianism of the Tudor university.

[1] In his notes at the conclusion of the first book of Aristotle's *Rhetoric*; see McConica, 'Humanism and Aristotle', 307-8.

[2] Fortunately now the subject of a full-scale study by Charles Schmitt, *John Case*; see p. 699 n. 8. I leave to that work the account of Case's life and career.

[3] The *ABCedarium philosophiae moralis* (1596) and *Ancilla philosophiae* (1599); Schmitt, *John Case*, 83, 102.

[4] Ibid. 86, 141-2.

[5] For more advanced logicians there were two works of Griffin Powell, see Schmitt, op. cit. 141 note 4.

[6] Ibid. 86-7.

[7] McConica, 'Humanism and Aristotle', 299.

[8] Schmitt, *John Case*, 142, *Sphaera civitatis, Reflexus speculi moralis, Thesaurus oeconomiae*.

[9] Ibid. 87, 135, 143, 262. F. A. Yates, *Astraea* (1975), 64-5; R. C. Strong, *Portraits of Queen Elizabeth I* (Oxford 1963), 124-7.

[10] 'They are extended and penetrating expositions of Aristotle's two key works of moral philosophy and together provide a respectable foundation for the instruction of a sixteenth-century lad wanting a broad education in the arts'; Schmitt, *John Case*, 143, 148.

In the *Lapis philosophicus* (1599) at the end of his career he reached the height of his achievement in a commentary on the *Physics*.[1]

Case's work is not easy to characterize. He was not strictly speaking a 'humanistic' commentator; he is unusual for his interest in late medieval masters who by his day were generally forgotten.[2] His performance as a whole was uneven. Nevertheless for him Aristotle was unquestionably the master, although Case did his best to assimilate the doctrines of the peripatetic to those of Christianity while maintaining, on the whole, a critical apprehension of Aristotle's text.[3] He attacked the inimical views of Paracelsus and Machiavelli as he did those of Scotus who, by the end of the century, was beginning again to win appreciation.[4] Yet his own Aristotle was highly personal, and his interpretation was suffused with Platonic and Hermetic notions to a degree that amply demonstrates the mutability of Aristotelian tradition in the swirl and eddy of contemporary thought.[5] Above all it is important to understand that Case's intellectual world was not nostalgic. Although like other adherents to the tradition of a *prisca theologia* he spoke of lost arts and of his own as the 'age of iron', he had confidence in man's creative capacities and in new techniques.[6] He cannot be dismissed as a simple reactionary nor may his views lightly be set aside like an exotic fossil buried in the high road to modern thought.

That high road led, of course, through the endeavours of Copernicus, Francis Bacon, Galileo, Leibniz and Newton and all who came to be thought of as the architects of modern science. The debate on the place of the Tudor universities in that perspective turns inevitably upon which theories about the antecedents of modern science are upheld.[7] Without attempting to enter the slightly metaphysical quest for antecedents we must at least indicate which

---

[1] 'It is perhaps the first important exposition of the *Physics* by an Englishman since that of Burley in the fourteenth century'; Schmitt, *John Case*, 142; 101–2.

[2] Ibid. 178, 155.   [3] Ibid. 161–3.

[4] Ibid. 209 ff., 65–8.

[5] Ibid. 163–7.   [6] Ibid. 206–9.

[7] The literature on this is of course immense. For the present discussion see especially: Curtis, *Oxford and Cambridge*; R. G. Frank, Jr., 'Science, medicine and the universities of early modern England: background and sources', *History of Science*, xi (1973), 194–216, 239–69; C. Hill, *The Intellectual Origins of the English Revolution* (Oxford 1965); F. R. Johnson, *Astronomical Thought in Renaissance England* (Baltimore 1937); R. K. Merton, *Science, Technology and Society in Seventeenth Century England* (New York 1970); N. Tyacke, 'Science and religion at Oxford before the civil war', D. Pennington and K. Thomas (eds), *Puritans and Revolutionaries: essays in seventeenth-century history presented to Christopher Hill* (Oxford 1978), 73–93; R. S. Westfall, *The Construction of Modern Science: mechanisms and mechanics* (Cambridge 1977). The most searching examination of the Tudor material with reference especially to mathematics is in the recent work of M. Feingold, *The Mathematicians' Apprenticeship: science, universities and society in England 1560–1640* (Cambridge 1984).

aspects of this eclectic and neo-Aristotelian culture received most serious attention at the time.[1]

While our general impression of the programme in arts is of a highly literary and rhetorical culture, it is evident that serious scientific study was also accommodated in it. There is an informative assembly of scientific texts in a representative library predominantly of arithmetical, astronomical and medical works given to Merton College by a fellow, Robert Barnes, in November 1594.[2] Among them are several commentaries by Girolamo Cardano, Regiomontanus and Stoeffler alongside Gemma Frisius, Euclid, Ptolomy and Copernicus's *De revolutionibus orbium coelestium* in the Nuremberg edition of 1543. Nicholas Clifton, the bookseller whose stock in trade seems to have been in the art of good letters nevertheless sold the arithmetical textbooks of Tunstall and Robert Recorde, along with astronomical tables and the mathematical work of Conrad Dasypodius. In geography he stocked Pomponius Mela. The most recent work indicates that the teaching of Henry Savile, the founder of the first Oxford chairs in geometry and astronomy in 1619, was not the isolated phenomenon that it has been held to be,[3] but rather marked a high point in a broader enterprise drawing its energy from the traditional academic studies of arithmetic, geometry and astronomy with the addition of geography. Savile's lectures as regent master in 1570 called upon the most advanced authors in mathematics and astronomy including Copernicus, and show evidence of a strong disposition towards the new cosmology, this at a time when few indeed were prepared to entertain the thought of a heliocentric universe.[4] Richard Hakluyt the younger came up to Christ Church from Westminster School exactly at that time and lectured as a regent in 1577–9 in the new field of geography, which we have already discovered among the interests of Lord Herbert and Robert Townsend.[5] Almost immediately he became involved with Sir Humphrey Gilbert and his associates, and by 1580 had lent the narratives of Jacques Cartier to the Italian John Florio, whose translation, *A shorte and briefe narration of the two navigations to Newe Fraunce*, appeared in that year with financial assistance from

[1] 'We must realise that the cultural and intellectual complex of the fourteenth century (and of the fifteenth and sixteenth centuries as well) had an internal logic and structure of its own and cannot be considered only in relation to the seventeenth century'; C. Schmitt, 'Towards a reassessment of renaissance Aristotelianism', *History of Science* xi (1973), 166.

[2] *BRUO 1501–40*, appendix B, 714–15.

[3] F. A. Yates, 'Giordano Bruno's conflict with Oxford', *Journal of the Warburg and Courtauld Institutes*, ii (1938–9), 230, 231 note 1; cf Feingold, *The Mathematicians' Apprenticeship*, 4, and (on Savile) 47–50.

[4] Feingold, 47–8; on the reception of Copernicanism, ibid. 8 ff.

[5] See above, pp. 696–7.

Hakluyt and his friends.[1] Hakluyt, like Savile, was plainly a man of extraordinary ability and enthusiasm. This early effort nevertheless demonstrates that his later achievement rested upon foundations laid in his years at Christ Church. Geography and cosmography were a characteristic enthusiasm in Elizabethan Oxford and had roots that can be traced back to the early decades of the century.[2] One of the centres in the later years was Exeter College, the college of Nathanial Carpenter, whose important *Geography* appeared in 1625. He had been a pupil at Exeter of John Prideaux (rector in 1612), as had Robert Stafforde, who published a world geography in 1608.[3]

It appears that scientific interests in Tudor Oxford, which were certainly the possession of a minority, were sustained by coteries. Of these the most famous and distinguished is precisely that to which Richard Hakluyt and Henry Savile belonged. It included the Hungarian visitor Stephen Parmenius, who was shortly to perish off Cape Breton when voyaging with Gilbert. It included William Camden, Philip Sidney, Thomas Harriot, Laurence Humfrey, Alberico Gentili and Thomas Savile, the younger brother of Henry. The centre of this circle was Christ Church with its annexe, Broadgates Hall. Another such group gathered around Thomas Allen at Gloucester Hall.[4] In more than half a century in that place Allen built up an impressive collection of manuscripts, many of them from the libraries of Oxford colleges and nearby monasteries, which are an important source for the history of science in medieval Oxford.[5] His passion for collecting would seem to have provided one key to his circle of relationships, which included antiquaries like Brian Twyne and Henry Ferrers and rival collectors like Henry Savile, Miles Windsor, Robert Cotton, Selden and Camden.[6] His geniality, long life and, in part, his religious sympathies assured him of influence and a warm welcome in another circle of gentry and aristocratic

[1] See *The New Found Land of Stephen Parmenius*, eds D. B. Quinn and N. M. Cheshire (Toronto 1972), 20.

[2] Feingold, *The Mathematicians' Apprenticeship*, 39.

[3] E. G. R. Taylor, *Late Tudor and Early Stuart Geography 1583–1640* (New York 1968), 136. 'It would not be untrue to say that from about 1583 onwards, English geography entered upon a distinctly mathematical phase. The connecting link between the subjects was, of course, astronomy, which formed part of every normal course of mathematical study at the university'; ibid. 68. Also Feingold, 153.

[4] See Andrew G. Watson, 'Thomas Allen of Oxford and his manuscripts', in M. B. Parkes and A. G. Watson (eds), *Medieval Scribes, Manuscripts and Libraries: essays presented to N. R. Ker* (1978), 279–314; Michael Foster, 'Thomas Allen (1540–1632), Gloucester Hall and the survival of catholicism in post-reformation Oxford', *Oxoniensia*, xlvi (1981), 99–128; and Jennifer Loach, 'Reformation controversies', p. 382 above; Curtis, *Oxford and Cambridge*.

[5] Watson, 'Thomas Allen', 280, 284.

[6] Foster, 'Thomas Allen', 109.

families, many of them catholic.[1] But he deserves mention here as a tutor and friend of the most talented Oxford mathematicians of his day: Philip Sidney, Brian Twyne, Robert Hegge, Robert Fludd, Kenelm Digby and others who were all among his pupils and friends.[2] He seems to have known John Dee, who left him some of his manuscripts, and like Dee was in the service of the earl of Leicester.[3] Another of his patrons was Henry Percy, the ninth 'wizard' earl of Northumberland, whose second brother William came up to Oxford in 1589.[4] The two circles at Christ Church and Gloucester Hall thus touched and overlapped. They were also connected with a third focus of scientific thought in Oxford at Merton, the college of Savile, which thus honoured its distinguished medieval tradition.[5]

The wider contacts of these Oxford men with associates in Cambridge, London and abroad have been well described by others.[6] Their existence in the university creates an inference about the teaching of science in the arts faculty, but not more; what can be said about that, which is a central concern of this chapter?

The teaching of the statutory curriculum in the university at large is described elsewhere in this volume; the undergraduate was to learn arithmetic and music, a provision that seems in practice to have meant arithmetic almost entirely.[7] The statutes of the colleges, unlike those at Cambridge, tended to relegate lectures in the sciences to the summer term and to the responsibility of fellows whose chief duty, most likely, was to lecture in logic.[8] This need not mean that the subject was slighted and the Carnsew diaries support the view that it received due attention. The study of arithmetic as we have seen included astronomy and geography as well before or after reaching the degree of bachelor of arts. At the level of the baccalaureate cosmography, geometry and geography concluded the scientific instruction.[9]

---

[1] Foster, 'Thomas Allen', 118 ff.

[2] Feingold, *The Mathematicians' Apprenticeship*, 82, 157–8; Curtis, *Oxford and Cambridge*, 142–3, 238–40.

[3] Feingold, 157–8.   [4] Curtis, 236; Foster, 'Thomas Allen', 114.

[5] Merton had of course the Linacre lecturerships in medicine; see Gillian Lewis, 'The faculty of medicine', pp. 221–3 above. Others in the mathematical and cosmographical sciences were Henry Briggs, first holder of the lecturership in arithmetic founded at the college by Sir Henry Savile, Thomas Savile, Francis Mason, the astronomer, and Peter Turner (MA 1612), future Gresham professor; see Feingold, 103, 124–30 and passim.

[6] See Curtis, *Oxford and Cambridge*, and the criticism by Hill in Appendix A, 'A note on the universities' of *The Intellectual Origins*; the most extensive and recent account is by Feingold, *The Mathematicians' Apprenticeship*, chs iv and v.

[7] See Fletcher, 'The faculty of arts', p. 175.

[8] See McConica, 'The rise of the undergraduate college', and Feingold, op. cit. 36–9.

[9] In this general pattern the two universities were much alike; see Feingold, 93.

The evidence from notebooks is sparse, and some of it we have noticed already. The *Physics* seems to have been the text most often favoured from the suggested Aristotelian canon,[1] and this may have been because it had the most fundamental and mathematical application. Daniel Featley (Fertclough) of Corpus who opposed the Copernican system in a disputation for his MA (1605), wrote a compendium of physics for his pupils in Michaelmas term 1604, and his correspondence in subsequent years is very informative about the division of tutorial responsibilities between teaching and general supervision *in loco parentis*. In the former capacity it is clear that he expected to give his pupils notes and directions which represented his personal approach to the curriculum.[2] A notebook from Queen's College written largely by a contemporary of Featley, Anthony Parker, contains notes on the *Meteorologica* as well as biographical notes on Aristotle, Anacharsis the Scythian and Anaxagoras.[3] There are notes also on astronomy, on the sphere and other topics from the *De coelo*. The rest of the collection has to do with religious matters, most of it abstracts of Oxford sermons. If this notebook is indeed from Queen's College it would seem to reflect the teaching there of Richard Crakanthorpe (fellow 1598–1624), one of the very few Oxford tutors of the period whose teaching has left a trace. While Crakanthorpe followed the statutory text including the *De coelo*, he enriched this curriculum with up-to-date information and treatises including (but after Parker's time) Galileo's *Sidereus nuncius* and Kepler's commentary.[4] Of this kind of thing there is no trace in Parker's notebooks, perhaps a warning, if one were needed, that student records are at best an unreliable guide to what was taught.

There are other evidences of a like kind, none without their

[1] *Statuta*, 390.

[2] Bodl. MS Rawl. D. 47; see the useful discussion by O'Day, *Education and Society*, 115–17; also Feingold, op. cit. 102; Kearney, *Scholars and Gentlemen*, 64. Featley matriculated at Magdalen in 1590 aged 8, undoubtedly while he was attending the school; BA 1602, MA 1605, BD 1613, DD 1617. See also p. 684 above.

[3] BL MS Harl 4048, fos 1–6, 75ᵛ–8ᵛ (reversed). This notebook was attributed to Christ Church in 1576 by Kearney, 44, and this was adopted by Feingold, 99, who dated it 1581. It is signed 'Anthony Parker' repeatedly on fo 79ᵛ and facing fo 1 although several other signatures such as 'Henry Jones' and 'William Bridge' also appear. The only Anthony Parker recorded by Clark in *Reg. Univ.* matriculated at Queen's in February 1601 and determined BA in 1606. The notebook contains only one reference to Christ Church (fo 74ᵛ) to a comedy entitled 'Bellum grammaticale' enacted there on 18 December 1581. I am persuaded to accept the identification with the Parker at Queen's by the fact that the manuscript contains several references pointing to that college: a sermon by 'the Provost' at St Peter's (fo 42ᵛ) and discourses by 'Mr Provost' on Hosea (fos 50ᵛ, 54, 56). Folios 48–70 (end of text) are all reversed and there is more than one hand. Notes on a sermon by John Rainolds also appear (fo 41).

[4] Feingold 66; Queen's College Oxford MS 390. For other evidence of Crakanthorpe's influence see Frank, 'Science, medicine and the universities', 251.

difficulties. During William Camden's undergraduate years in mid-century he certainly studied mathematics, astronomy and astrology, but he was already in exceptional company.[1] The notebook of Samuel Browne, a rare matriculant at All Souls in November 1595, may have been handed on to other undergraduates for its notes on chronology, geometry and so forth as has been suggested,[2] but it may equally have been for its chief content: rules of deportment when speaking and disputing, of syntax, rhetoric and prosody, and for its elementary introductions to Greek, Hebrew and other biblical languages.[3] John Goodridge, who matriculated at Balliol in January 1598 and took his BA in February 1602, left records of his studies in mathematics and astronomy, but it is not clear whether these were undertaken as an undergraduate or bachelor of arts.[4] Such evidence is supported, however, by other kinds of testimonial[5] and questions for disputation,[6] as well as by personal library inventories. Under-graduate libraries are at a premium,[7] but a scattering of inventories in the last three decades show that, as in medicine, young Oxford bachelors and MAs kept in touch with contemporary scholarship on the continent.[8] They also confirm the blend of arithmetic, astronomy, geometry, cosmology and geography which defined the arts curriculum in science.

The account of that curriculum in recent scholarship has rightly and inevitably concentrated on the seventeenth century with the new impulse to scientific study provided in the foundation of the Savilian chairs of astronomy and geometry in 1619.[9] That impulse neverthe-less took its force and direction from the studies in Elizabethan Oxford, and in particular from the advanced thinking of certain scholarly coteries like that to which Savile himself belonged as a presiding spirit. The existence of these circles, the long careers and persistent endeavours of such men within them as Thomas Allen, Brian Twyne and Savile himself and the prestige of their wider con-nection with the rich and influential outside the world of the university

[1] Feingold, *The Mathematicians' Apprenticeship*, 101.

[2] Ibid. 99–100; Bodl. MS Jesus College 92, fos 98–111.

[3] Bodl. MS Jesus College 92, 1–96^V.

[4] Feingold, op. cit. 102.

[5] Like the *responsa scholarum* of English catholics in Rome; Feingold, 91; McConica, 'Humanism and Aristotle', 298 n. 2.

[6] Feingold, op. cit., 102–3; cf. Frank, 'Science, medicine and the universities', 205–6.

[7] Feingold cites two belonging to BAs, p. 116; those referred to earlier in this chapter contained no scientific works.

[8] Feingold, op. cit. 116–17; on medicine see Lewis, 'The faculty of medicine', 240–1.

[9] 'From the point of view of the sciences an important watershed occurred around 1620, when the institutional status of science was greatly improved at Oxford, and means were sought to promote similar developments at Cambridge.' Charles Webster, *The Great Instaura-tion: science, medicine and reform 1626–1660* (1975), 122. Cf Schmitt, *John Case*, 43–4.

provided an anchorage for efforts and investigations that were not at the focus of concern within the faculty of arts. It also seems clear, however, that most who took even the basic degree in that faculty would have had some introduction at least to the arithmetical sciences, and the statutes of Christ Church show that mathematics had a place in the humanist conception of study from the early years of the century.[1] In the last quarter of that century there is every evidence of a new surge of interest in the sciences coinciding with a revival of interest in Aristotelianism and in medieval commentators. But this remained only an element in a wider humanistic culture where the art of rhetoric with its ancillary disciplines of logic, history and modern languages prepared the university graduate for travel, government and statecraft as well as for the general discourse of cultivated society. John Rainolds would declaim 'In praise of astronomy' as a part of his MA exercises.[2] Richard Hakluyt prepared an epitome of Aristotle's *Politics* for a course of intramural lectures at Christ Church ten years later.[3] And Sir Henry Savile, the chief promoter of scientific studies in the Elizabethan university, would end his career with a monumental work of patristic scholarship.[4] A foreign visitor like Giordano Bruno might well find the ordinary representatives of the arts faculty hopelessly out of touch with the most recent scientific developments without perceiving the private interests and teaching done by some within the wider community whose connections in London, like Sidney and Greville, Bruno approved. Nor could he nor any other of the critics of Aristotle as yet provide a system of learning comprehensive enough to fill the practical needs of the faculties, or to replace that ancient structure within whose venerable and accommodating mansions the schools of a new era were already being erected.

THE COMPASS OF THE COLLEGIATE UNIVERSITY

In 1604, at the very end of our period, William Wentworth advised his son, 'Be directed in your studies by some learned judicial man of the university, methinks logic, philosophy, cosmography and especially histories yield excellent matter of instruction and judgement. Also

[1] McConica, 'The rise of the undergraduate college', pp. 34–5.

[2] Feingold, op. cit. 58; Queen's College Oxford MS 241; L. V. Ryan, 'Richard Hakluyt's voyage into Aristotle', *Sixteenth Century Journal*, xii (1981), 73–83; Schmitt, *John Case*, 57–8 n. 164; BL MSS Royal 12. G.xiii and Sloane 1982.

[3] See McConica, 'Humanism and Aristotle', 316.

[4] See S. L. Greenslade, 'The faculty of theology', 321 above; Schmitt, *John Case*, 44, 48, 58 and the bibliography therein cited.

be resolved what hours you will ordinarily keep for them. In any case have some insight in the laws, for it will be a great contentment, comfort and credit and quiet for you.'[1] Oxford could provide the first part, the inns of court the second. Our impression of the common intellectual fare at the Elizabethan university is confirmed, and the very manner of the remark suggests something more. The intellectual world of late Tudor Oxford furnished one striking advantage to the colleges: it was adaptable to almost any taste or ambition. Statutory regulations were interpreted with great flexibility even within the degree programme, as we have seen, while a commoner who eschewed a university degree might assemble almost any course of studies that he wanted and that his tutor would approve. This fact combined with the variety to be found among the colleges in regional and social character may have been decisive in the apparently quite unstudied triumph of the universities over alternative schemes for aristocratic education which were advanced throughout the sixteenth century.[2] Whatever their shortcomings they were there to be used, and it paid them to adapt.

By the last decade of the sixteenth century the social spectrum at Oxford ranged from the nobility at one extreme to the sons of husbandmen and even college cooks at the other,[3] but attempts to define the distribution of the social ranks more precisely must remain conjectural for reasons already explained in our analysis of the population at Corpus.[4] The best results rest on the records of matriculation for the last two decades of the century when the registration of undergraduates—members on the foundation and commoners alike—was most nearly complete. A simple division of the social claims of the matriculants between those who were the sons of gentlemen or men of higher ranks and those who were plebeian[5] by birth shows that the former claimed 46 per cent of the entry and the latter 50 per cent, while a further 3 per cent were the sons of clergymen.[6] This would mean that almost half of the matriculants were predominantly from landed families forming about 2 per cent of the population.[7] At the same time universities were attracting

[1] Wentworth Papers 1597–1628, ed. for the Royal Historical Society by J. P. Cooper (Camden fourth series xii 1973), 18. I have modernized the spelling.

[2] Curtis, Oxford and Cambridge, 65–8; O'Day, Education and Society, 88–9; R. M. Fisher, 'Thomas Cromwell, humanism and educational reform 1539–40', Bulletin of the Institute of Historical Research, 1 (1977), 151–63.

[3] Daniel Featley of Corpus, p. 684.   [4] See pp. 676–7.

[5] The matriculation register at Oxford did not record the rank of yeoman separately.

[6] Based on McConica, 'Scholars and commoners' table 11 for the years 1580–2, 1589–92 and 1600–2. The proportion of gentry rose from 37 to 54 per cent over the period.

[7] Stone, Crisis of the Aristocracy, 51. David Palliser, The Age of Elizabeth: England under the later Tudors 1547–1603 (1983), 71.

a higher percentage of the male age cohort than at any other time up to the First World War.[1]

The least satisfactory of these three categories is of course that of the plebeians. Among the 'gentry' there would be some sons of the higher clergy, lawyers, successful merchants and civil servants, but these would have been a small percentage of the whole. The plebeians, however, would include the sons of farmers, yeomen, townsmen and merchants of all sorts and no doubt some of the lower clergy as well.[2] Only at St John's College with its peculiar links with towns is it possible to work out the proportion of the townsmen with any accuracy, and it seems certain that the proportion there—some 48 per cent of the total intake—was the highest.[3] It is not possible at Corpus to identify enough men from an urban or mercantile background to form a comparison, or to detect any significant difference in their careers from those of other graduates. The family chronicle of Sir James Whitelocke, the scholar of Merchant Taylors' school who went on to St John's, suggests that as one might expect, the townsman's son aspired to the status of his superiors and wished to join the gentry.[4]

Among the plebeians we have noted some of genuinely humble birth, but among these were there any of the really poor? Even the husbandman could be relatively well off compared to those at the bottom, the cottager, hired labourer or servant, or even the small shopkeeper or trader. Some surplus was necessary even for men on the foundation to pay for travel, books, clothing (above the clothing allowance) and some battels, and this would have to come from the family if it did not come from a relative or other patron. Poverty was a fluctuating condition for those on the borderline and a small surplus might be reduced to want by ill health or a sudden dearth. Provision for the 'poor' then might extend to any who found themselves in need and this is perhaps the best explanation of what was understood by the poor student and poor clerk, familiar throughout the middle ages. The poor scholar was not thought of as one of a class but as one who could not support himself at the university without assistance.[5] The Lady Devorguilla intended her college expressly to help poor scholars—for 'elemosinam pauperum

---

[1] Stone, 'The size and composition of the Oxford student body 1580–1910', table 12, p. 103; his estimate is 1.18 per cent.

[2] This is discussed in McConica, 'The social relations of Tudor Oxford', 122 ff. On the issue of townsmen among the plebeians see McConica, 'Scholars and commoners', 164–7.

[3] Ibid. 166.

[4] Liber famelicus of James Whitelocke, ed. J. Bruce (Camden Society lxx 1858); cf McConica, 'The social relations of Tudor Oxford', 124–6.

[5] Rashdall, Universities of Europe ii. 405 n. 1.

scholarium'—yet these same scholars were always to maintain one poor scholar with the scraps from the common table; the ambiguity of the term is neatly demonstrated.[1]

Scholars in difficulty might be supported by their friends: in Michaelmas term 1529 Thomas Cartwright was allowed to transfer to any hall of his choice because his friends refused to maintain him any longer at White Hall as there were no lectures in civil law and few scholars.[2] A scholar might also be assisted by his local community. William Storr received payments from the corporation of Lincoln of twenty shillings a year for six years at the discretion of the common council although he was on the foundation at Corpus.[3] In 1586 he was granted five pounds toward the charges of his proceeding bachelor of arts on condition that he gave up this yearly exhibition. Employment as a servant to a college fellow or wealthy commoner was another form of aid, sometimes linked to local connection, and of course there were places in the college for servitors.[4] Personal service probably became more common as the century wore on and the life of the college became more aristocratic. Brian Twyne complained in September 1597 that while in his father's time no scholar at Corpus was allowed to take a poor scholar as a servant, now it was so much the usual thing that to perform his own menial tasks 'had bene worse than homely and beggarly: should I have carried woode and dust and emptied chamber pots and no man, no scholler so doinge but myselfe, it had been intollerable and to[o] base for my minde, yea and I had disgraced many a meane mans sonne who were fellowe schollers with me myselfe being a Gentleman'.[5]

An unusual source of aid was the remarkable benefaction of Robert Nowell, brother to Alexander, the dean of St Paul's, and like him a Brasenose man. Robert was a lawyer who rose in the royal service and prospered as a friend of Cecil. He died in February 1569 leaving a vast number of legacies and the residue of his large estate to be administered by his three executors with Alexander Nowell

---

[1] *The Oxford Deeds of Balliol College*, ed. H. E. Salter (OHS lxiv 1913), 280, 279. On the related issue of the availability of schooling to the poor see David Cressy, 'Educational opportunity in Tudor and Stuart England', *History of Education Quarterly* xvi (1976), 301–20.

[2] OUA Reg. Canc. 1527–43 fo 137[v]. Support from a scholar's friends was enshrined in the Magdalen College *vulgaria*, Royal MS 12.B.xx printed by Nicholas Orme (see p. 65 n. 2), nos 55, 60.

[3] He was admitted *discipulus* at Corpus in December 1582 but the payments began in 1580. See Lincoln AO L1/1/1/3, common council entry book fos 116, 128, 171; and p. 684.

[4] See p. 668.

[5] H. G. S. 'Some correspondence of Brian Twyne', 216.

as acting trustee.[1] The record of disbursements from this trust is a remarkable testament to Dean Nowell's fidelity in carrying out his brother's desire to help his poor kin and 'other pore folkes'. These ranged from almsmen, widows and 'poor maids' (to provide dowries) to many scholars at Oxford and Cambridge. Dean Nowell was apparently responsible for the use of the money but he sometimes acted through friends such as Laurence Humfrey at Magdalen and President Cole at Corpus, doubtless at their suggestion. Among the beneficiaries were William Whitaker, Antonio del Corro (with other protestant refugees from the continent) and Thomas Bilson. The names of Richard Hakluyt and Richard Hooker also appear, which might raise a question as to the authentic need of the Nowell beneficiaries, but an examination of the recipients at Corpus other than Hooker suggests that they were almost always from humble backgrounds: William Napper, Christopher Rawson, John Barefoot and John Seller were all sons of yeomen; Richard Turnbull and Humphrey Coles were sons of clerks; but most of the nineteen men at Corpus who benefited during the twelve years from 1569 to 1580 when the money was disbursed were from origins utterly obscure, although that need not imply of necessity that they were also very poor. They were given sums ranging from a few shillings up to a pound, although the payment might be repeated within a short time if there were need.[2]

In addition to such casual assistance as this, the university itself helped the poor scholar in two ways, by licences to beg and by loans. Both methods were established in the middle ages.[3] Licences to beg were issued by the chancellor's commissary, often for the period of the Christmas vacation, and the names of the scholars with those of their sureties for the return of the licences were entered in his register.[4] Loans were made from chests founded for the purpose on the security of books, plate or other personal property.[5] Unfortunately the few surviving records from investigations in 1510 and

---

[1] See A. B. Grosart, *The Towneley Hall MSS: The Spending of the Money of Robert Nowell of Reade Hall, Lancashire; brother of Dean Alexander Nowell, 1568–1580*. Printed for private circulation (Manchester 1877). The will and codicil, proved at the prerogative court of Canterbury 14 May 1569, by Alexander Nowell, Lawrence Nowell and John Towneley, executors, is printed pp. xliv–lii.

[2] Of the other 53 men at Corpus who are known to have been assisted by other means, one (Storr) held a civic exhibition, 6 were aided by the crown, 9 by patrons among the nobility or gentry, 2 by a cathedral foundation, one by a school, 2 by a bishop, 2 by members of their own family and 9 by the president of the college who retained them as scholar-servants.

[3] See Mallet, *University of Oxford* ii. 133.

[4] *Reg. Univ.*, ed. Clark, ii. 2–5 where a list is printed.

[5] See Graham Pollard in Appendix iii to *The Register of Congregation 1448–1463*, eds W. A. Pantin and W. T. Mitchell (OHS new ser. xxii 1972), 418–20.

and 1524 tell us mostly of the neglect of those responsible in the early decades of the sixteenth century, and the great burglary of the congregation house in 1544 not only finished the system but presumably scattered whatever records there were within the chests; at least none of these survive.[1] The chests were not refounded, perhaps in part because the endowment of colleges and of scholarships had supplanted the earlier conception of aid to students.

The expense of an Oxford education depended entirely on whether the student was a scholar or commoner. Commoners were required to pay not only for their board and room but to pay caution money, special fees to their college or hall and wages to their servants on top of the battels and other ordinary expenses that also affected the student on the foundation. By the end of the century the gentry were generally indulging in elaborate wardrobes as well, to judge from surviving accounts and the reiterations of sumptuary legislation; even Brian Twyne, whose family cannot have been rich but who (as we have seen) was very conscious of his claims to gentility, begged of his father, 'If you send me any bayes for my frocke I praye you let it be of peach colour'.[2] It is clearly impossible to guess what an average expenditure might have been even for commons although at Corpus occasional indentures for the chests of fines show commoners paying consistent sums like 2s 8d for a week's commons (1590/1), 7s for three weeks' commons (1589/90), 1s for three days (1591/2). Another, however, paid 26s 10d for fifty-two weeks (1593/4).

It is surprisingly difficult even to estimate the fees that would confront commoner and scholar alike. The matriculation statute of 1565 established a scale of fees by which the son of an esquire would pay 20d, a gentleman 12d and a plebeian 4d, but these charges might be waived or reduced for the poor scholar and were anyway altered from time to time.[3] The same uncertainty applies to the fees paid in taking degrees which might be varied by a decision of the proctors.[4] The best surviving register is that for 1601/2 giving the rates for all degrees except those in law.[5] By this scale the ordinary

    [1] Pollard, *The Register of Congregation 1448–1463*, 428–32; on the attempt to reform the chests in 1524 see *Epistolae Academicae 1508–1596*, ed. W. T. Mitchell (OHS new ser xxvi 1980), 182–6. I am grateful to Ruth F. Vyse, Assistant Archivist, Oxford University Archives for her information on the state of the records.

    [2] For the legislation see *Statuta, passim*, esp. 403–4; H. G. S., 'Some correspondence of Brian Twyne', 217; Robert Townsend's accounts include some tailor's bills that suggest a much more elegant taste than that allowed by the university.

    [3] Mallet, *University of Oxford* ii. 121; *Reg. Univ.* ed. Clark, i. 165, 387.

    [4] Clark, 217; on fees as a source of income for the university officers see G. E. Aylmer, 'The economics and finances of the colleges and the university, c.1530–1640, pp. 552–6, above.   [5] *Reg. Univ.* ed. Clark, i. 218–25.

arts undergraduate would pay 6s 6d on admission to the bachelor's degree and a further 5s 2d at determination. These payments included those to the registrar (6d adm. and 10d det.), the inferior bedells of arts (6d adm. and 8d det.), theology and law (8d adm. and 8d. det.) and (at admission) a payment of 6d toward the cost of the dinner (*pro prandio*). The corresponding fees for the MA were 8s 7d at the candidate's presentation and 14s 7d at his inception with a further 22s at incorporation. If we recall that the daily wage of a building craftsman at this time was 12d we obtain a remote index by which to estimate the accessibility of a university education, even when assisted by a scholarship, to the artisan and labourer.[1]

The much heavier fees charged to the wealthy must have been a disincentive to some in proceeding to a degree. A 'grand compounder' who had to admit under oath to have an income of £40 a year at his personal disposal would have had to pay all of the above charges at a much higher rate, including a fee of £15 10s 8d for his incorporation as a master of arts.[2] In return, his formal round of the university (*circuitus*) included the vice-chancellor and senior proctor who accompanied him back to his college, the right to wear a red gown at his presentation while the whole of his college accompanied him to the congregation house to the fanfare of a trumpet, and the privilege of wearing the same gown afterwards, a practice verified by the dispensations granted to those who asked to be relieved of it.[3]

Even if we form a very general impression of the basic cost of education in the college consisting of the fees and commons, we are further confronted by the incidentals which were billed as battels. The Carnsew brothers, who seem to have been careful, spent sums like 18s 2d in the month of June 1572, which included 8d to the cook, 3s to their laundress (paid by the quarter), 1d for ink and 1s 2d for paper. A penny was paid for a haircut for Robert ('R. was polled') whose shoes were mended at a cost of 2d, while Matthew bought a pair at 15d. Their expenses from 23 August to 13 September were 3s 7d; for the month of October were 15s.[4] As for books, Foxe's sermons cost them 8d, their catechism 7d, 'Dr Humphrey's book' 2s 1d, while Peter Martyr on the *Ethics* of Aristotle they borrowed from a bachelor of arts (Sir Matthew).[5]

---

[1] Wrigley and Schofield, *Population History of England*, table A9.1, p. 640.

[2] Clark, 63–4, 218–19.

[3] Ibid. 64–6. The distinction between ordinary candidates and compounders continued until 1853. According to Clark, p. 66, it was left to a Balliol man, Salisbury Baxendale, to bring it to an end by insisting on the full procession with vice-chancellor and proctors which had been discontinued.

[4] PRO SP 46/15, fos 212–14.

[5] Ibid. 212, 215[V], 217; a Latin psalter cost 16d, the *ad Herennium* 12d. Compare with

Fortunately, local and family archives can be more informative about the overall cost of a university education and a recent study of Kent has shown a yeoman farmer supporting a son first at St John's, Oxford and then at Corpus Christi, Cambridge at the total cost of £100, a third of his capital value. In the 1580s, however, it cost a gentleman at Emmanuel, Cambridge more than £50 a year.[1] If provision for university education in legacies can be thought to rest upon some understanding of the likely cost we may notice as well the allowance of 20 marks yearly designated by an Essex gentleman in 1579 to provide for the schooling and 'learning in one of the universities' of his younger son, and another allowance of £100 yearly in 1591.[2] But here too income and individual taste and expectations would have played a part. Some legacies were made in the clear understanding that money available would not be enough, in which case the prospective beneficiary would have to seek one of the scholarships that were becoming available in endowed schools throughout the country or were otherwise provided by benefactors like Robert Nowell, Sir Edward Boughton and Humphrey Stule.[3] Alternatively they might find help from the local gentry or, like William Storr, from the town council. The prospect of assembling enough information to piece together a general picture looks remote indeed. The wills of the Essex gentry suggest, however, that not all among them who wished to provide for such education actually had the means to meet the whole cost.

Whom did the providers for the poor really have in mind? The burden of recent scholarship is that few if any wished to disrupt society by educating the lowest orders and that access to the schools themselves was more or less restricted to precisely those whose presence in the university we have already noticed: the sons of prosperous husbandmen and yeomen, burgesses, country gentry, professional men and the lower ranks of those with title.[4] The experience of Corpus confirms this, and the benefactions from

the prices paid by Richard Madox a decade later; *An Elizabethan in 1582: the diary of Richard Madox, fellow of All Souls*, ed. E. S. Donno (Hakluyt Society 2nd ser. cxlvii 1976), 79. Although valuations abound in library inventories prices paid by the purchaser are more reliable as an index of cost.

[1] Peter Clark, *English Provincial Society from the Reformation to the Revolution: religion, politics and society in Kent 1500–1640* (Hassocks, Sussex 1977), 204–5.

[2] F. G. Emmison, *Elizabethan Life: wills of Essex gentry and merchants proved in the prerogative court of Canterbury* (Chelmsford 1978), 190, 306; cf 218 (will of William Hunte), 137 (Elizabeth Tuke).

[3] Clark, *English Provincial Society*, 204.

[4] Simon, *Education and Society*, 373–4; Cressy, 'Educational opportunity', 307: 'Most schools and scholarships were never intended for the poor, and even those that were, were swiftly appropriated by the well-born or the wealthy.'

the Nowell fund there suggest that the line of need was drawn for the most part among the sons of yeomen and husbandmen. This line would seem to have marked the effective lower limit of the university's function in Elizabethan England, allowing always for the exceptional cases whose numbers we have no reliable way of estimating; they would have come from untraceable origins to take up obscure lives in the ranks of the lower clergy. The William Storrs among them were seemingly few or we would know more of their names and careers. Yet their access to the university through the ranks of battelars and servitors remained open and was if anything enhanced by opportunities of service to the growing numbers of gentry in the collegiate population.

We therefore lack any evidence to support the famous charge of William Harrison that the sons of rich men were pushing the poor out of their places,[1] unless by this he meant the sons of the poorer gentry who may indeed have been displaced in favour of the more opulent. At Corpus, we must recall, men of gentle birth and substantial means were on the foundation from the first, presumably with the full knowledge and approval of the founder.[2] A further charge of Harrison, of the 'packing . . . used at elections'[3] can be verified at Corpus in the correspondence of Brian Twyne and at All Souls and elsewhere in visitors' injunctions.[4] Others too believed that the universities were 'in preference grown too partiall'.[5] Favouritism towards wealthier candidates for fellowship would have been in keeping with the colleges' pursuit of gentlemen commoners, as they adapted their buildings and customs to cater to the tastes of a gentry-aristocratic society. In the early years of the seventeenth century that taste completed its triumph over the rigours and simplicities of the earlier poverty and discipline.[6]

We reach the limits of this volume before the undertakings of the next century gave architectural expression to these new social distinctions and before the building of the Bodleian Library embodied its intellectual culture and aspirations.[7] To all of that the

[1] *The Description of England*, first published 1577. The 1587 text is edited by G. Edelen (Ithaca, New York 1968), 70-1.

[2] McConica, 'The social relations of Tudor Oxford', 129-30.

[3] Harrison, ed. Edelen, 71.

[4] H. G. S., 'Some correspondence of Brian Twyne', 218; Martin, *A Catalogue of the Archives . . . of All Souls' College*, 307 items 67, 70; Whitgift's injunctions of 25 October 1601, 11 November 1602; also C. Grant Robertson, *All Souls College* (1899), 79.

[5] W[illiam] C[larke], *Polimanteia or, the meanes lawfull and unlawfull, to judge of the fall of a common-wealth . . .* (1595), dedicated to the earl of Essex; reprinted by A. B. Grosart (ed.), *Occasional Issues of Unique or Very Rare Books* xv (1881), 40.

[6] The customs of Exeter College, set down in 1539 but remembered from 'still older times', preserve the pre-Elizabethan manners and collegiate atmosphere; Boase, *Register*, lxxiii-lxxiv.　　　　[7] McConica, 'Humanism and Aristotle', 316-17.

achievement of Elizabethan Oxford was in one sense a prologue. In another way, however, it displayed a spirit and genius that the Oxford of the new Bodleian, of the Savilian chairs and of William Laud would alter profoundly.

Elizabethan Oxford was the climax of the changes brought about by the reformation and by the triumph of humanism over the medieval schools. Both of those changes had their roots in the fifteenth century, and both of them are symbolized by the monarch whose portrait introduces this volume; despite its complex antecedents, Christ Church was unmistakably his creation, and the Tudor university, like all of England, lived under the spell of his successors. They established a firm hold on both the universities through parliamentary foundation, by control of senior appointments, by legislation and decrees on dress and discipline, by the imposition of a catechism, by a reorganization of government to replace the medieval meritocracy of the regents with oligarchic rule by the heads of houses and by periodic visitations to subject the whole to a vigilant scrutiny. Like its medieval predecessor Tudor Oxford trained the clergy of the realm, but a higher proportion than before, since it now shared with Cambridge a virtual monopoly of clerical education. This called for scrutiny. Unlike its medieval predecessor it contained within its society a growing proportion of highly articulate and visible laymen who now served many of the functions previously filled by their (more usually) clerical antecedents, but who were also in pursuit of a new educational ideal, one adopted from humanist insistence. It was not a new idea to serve the state and prince but the exclusive emphasis on doing so as a member of an international and latinate literary culture was indeed new. The training of these important and occasionally powerful young men also required scrutiny.

All of this has been said before. This volume has tried to add to the story the dimension of continuity, to show how the institutions that nurtured the flowering of this lay and literate society were essentially in place before the reformation and how their development was in many ways independent of that eruption, a domestic concern of the colleges whose potential as seminaries for the young was discovered in the fifteenth century and transferred to the Tudor age by men who had understood that. And so Brasenose, Corpus and Cardinal colleges were founded by powerful prelates of the previous generation before Luther had been heard of in Oxford, each foundation an advance upon its predecessor and all of them expressing a potential for widespread undergraduate education that was first enunciated at Magdalen. It was somehow appropriate that the final steps in the full conception of the undergraduate college, complete with its integral complement of undergraduate commoners, should have been taken by two catholic lay founders in the reign of Mary.

Part of this continuity has been missed because it was concealed. The growing undergraduate constituency of the colleges, which can be detected in the fifteenth century, left no trace in the archives of the university or did so without any record of the individual's collegiate attachment. It was not until the religious crisis under Elizabeth impelled the creaking machinery of the university to register as members of a college all who were taught that the full dimension of the phenomenon was exposed. At the same time the sudden rise in numbers was sustained beyond the initial burst of matriculations to confirm the widespread popularity of university training in the last decades of the century.

Essential to this popularity was the scope and flexibility of teaching arrangements in which the college tutor played a leading if not exclusive part. The members of the university seem to have been drawn from the same social spectrum as that served by the schools and to have been passed on into a wide range of public, private and professional callings. The appropriateness of the curriculum for the clergy needs no demonstration. Its usefulness to the doctor and civil lawyer is equally apparent, if there was less for them to do. Its usefulness to the layman bound to public service can doubtless also be seen but its broad appeal cannot be grasped without some inkling of the tenets of a rhetorical and humanistic culture which idealized the art of public persuasion nourished by personal convictions that were to be based upon the tested experience of Christian and pagan antiquity. It was erudite, moralistic and public spirited; it formed a perfect union with the faith and aspirations of Elizabethan England. At its best it matched mastery of style and a broad classical culture with a tested dialectical skill that was a formidable instrument in debate and exposition.

It has been held to have failed in its attitude to science—not always by such critics distinguished from science yet-to-be. Englishmen as a whole depended in medicine and science on more advanced societies abroad, but there were pioneering figures of which Oxford had its share. Hakluyt and Savile are perhaps the best known but the list includes Robert Recorde, the distinguished theorist, Thomas Harriot, Henry Briggs, Edward Brerewood and Edmund Gunter who might all be mentioned among those whose careers formed a link with the scientific community of the next generation. If we admire the evolution of the late medieval university into the new collegiate culture of the Tudor age we must equally acknowledge Oxford's lead in the endowment of scientific investigation in the early seventeenth century with (in 1619) the two Savilian chairs in geometry and astronomy and, within six more years, the Sedleian lecturership in natural philosophy, the lecturership in anatomy founded by Richard Tomlins and the endowment of the botanical garden, the earliest in England, by the earl of Danby.

Whatever its merits in the contemporary world of science Elizabethan Oxford was ideally suited to the chief intellectual concern of the day, the theory and defence of the national church. The preoccupations of humanism with philology, the biblical languages and the disciplines of textual study were all at hand for the formation of an Anglican apologetic. If relevance to contemporary public concern is a test of educational success then the eclectic and learned protestantism of the Elizabethan university was a triumph. Sidney and Savile, Rainolds, Humfrey, Bodley, Burton, Donne and Hooker together provide a measure of its achievement. Savile's edition of Chrysostom, the Oxford share in the King James version, Hooker's *Laws of Ecclesiastical Polity* are its true monuments. Above them all stands the vast and cosmopolitan quarry of erudition which is the Bodleian library, the crown and creation of that collegiate city which came into its own in the Elizabethan age.

Index

Abbotsley (Hunts.) 560, 564, 565, 566, 567, 568, 569, 570, 571, 573

Abbot, George DTh, master of University College, archbishop of Canterbury 310, 313, 333, 433, 530–1, 539–40, 545, 684

Abbott, Robert, DTh, master of Balliol College, regius professor of theology, bishop of Salisbury 313, 545

Abel, John, donor to Christ Church library 502, 513

Abergavenny (Monmouthshire) 663

Abingdon (Berks.) 67, 70, 120, 447, 609

Absolon, William, MA, fellow of Corpus Christi College 687

Abyndon, Henry, BMus 206

Adams, Andrew, MA, alumnus of Christ Church 510, 511

Adam, John, baker 101 n. 3

Admiralty, court of 266, 271

Admonition to Parliament 699

Adrianus of Castello, cardinal 174

Aesop 316

Agas, Ralph xi, 598, 675; *see also* Oxford, University of

Agathias 704

Agricola, Rudolph 44, 174, 175, 699–700, 702, 703, 705, 707 n. 7

Agrippa, Henricus Cornelius 222, 248, 703

Ailwin, Thomas, MA, student of Christ Church 506

Airey, Henry, DTh, provost of Queen's College 422, 438

Aisthorpe (Lincs.) 684

Alazard, Andrew, MD 216, 221

Albert the Great (Albertus Magnus), St 325

Alciati, Andreas 703

Alen (Alynne), Richard, BA, fellow of Corpus Christi College 704–5

Alexander de Villa Dei 158

Alexander of Aphrodisias 707

Alfred the Great, king of the English 599

Algorismus 23

Allen, P. S. 339

Allen, Richard, BA, fellow of Corpus Christi College 374

Allen, Thomas, MA, principal of Gloucester Hall 240, 278, 382, 424, 429, 717–18, 720

Allen, William, cardinal, fellow of Oriel College 320, 329, 382, 395, 409

Alley, William, DTh, bishop of Exeter 620

Allwyn, Elizabeth, widow 562

Amama, Sixtus, tutor in Hebrew 317

Ambrose, St 313, 323, 448, 450, 462, 474

Ammonius Hermeae 707

Amsterdam 416

Anacharsis the Scythian 719

Anaxagoras 719

Andrewes, Lancelot 330, 333

Anglesey 264

Antoninus, archbishop of Florence 451

Aquinas, Thomas, St 178–9, 325, 454, 704, 711

arches, court of 281, 282

Ardern, John, benefactor of Trinity College 460

Arderne, Leonard, BTh, fellow of Corpus Christi College 475

Arderne, Thomas, MA, fellow of Lincoln College 485

Argall, John, BTh 176, 178

Aristides Quintilianus 202

Aristophanes 22, 341, 469, 703, 709

Aristotle 22, 24, 30, 161–2, 172, 174, 176–9, 184, 188, 195, 214, 321, 341, 427, 446, 449, 498, 702, 703, 708, 714–15, 719
   ethics 61, 316, 699, 700, 702, 704, 706, 707, 710, 712, 714, 727
   logic and dialetic 700, 703, 712
   physics 316, 705, 711, 712, 715
   picture of 640
   politics 41, 212, 702, 707, 712, 714, 721
   rhetoric 172, 700, 703, 707, 712
Aristotelianism 177–9, 181, 323, 696, 711; revival of 706–8, 721

Aristoxenus 203

Arminianism 331, 332, 333–4, 391

Armstrong, John, MA, Greek lecturer at Magdalen College 55–6

Arnobius 449 n. 3

Arnold, abbot of Bonneval 323

Arnold, William, MA, student of Christ Church 499, 505, 506, 515

Arnolde, Francis, chaplain of Merton College 471 n. 2

Arscott, Thomas, BM 239

Arthur, prince, son of Henry VII 9

Arundel, earl of, chancellor of Oxford 401, 430, 500

Ascham, Roger 650, 679 n. 2

Ashmole, Elias 235

Aston, Hugh, BMus 207

Athanasius, St 707 n. 7

Atkins, Anthony, MA, fellow of Merton College 410

Atkinson, John, MA, fellow of Balliol College 572

Atkyns, Thomas, MA, fellow of Merton College 11

Atwater, William, DTh, fellow of Magdalen College, bishop of Lincoln 121

Atye, Arthur, DCL, fellow of Merton College 424, 428, 430–1

Aubrey, John 288, 614

Aubrey, Thomas, MA, student of Christ Church 471 n. 2, 506

Aubrey, William, DCL, regius professor of civil law, principal of New Inn Hall 233, 264, 266, 286–8, 358, 359, 360

Audley, Edmund, DTh, bishop of Hereford and Salisbury 119, 457, 483, 484, 485, 599

Audley, Sir Thomas 43, 259

augmentations, court of 43, 224, 345, 349, 351, 359

Augsburg 204

Augustine of Canterbury 386

Augustine of Hippo, St 202, 302, 313, 371, 447, 448, 449, 450, 704, 710, 714

Augustinian canons 303; at St Frideswide's 31; at Oseney Abbey 70

Augustinian friars 190, 303

Aust (Glos.) 688

Austin, John, alderman 108

Austin canons, see Augustinian canons

Aventinus, Johannes 158

Averroism 213

Avicenna 216, 220, 254, 340

Awburie, see Aubrey

Aycliffe (Co. Durham) 303

Aylworth, Anthony, MD, regius professor of medicine 226, 235, 236, 250

Baber, John, BA, fellow of Lincoln College 485

Babington, Francis, DTh, master of Balliol College, rector of Lincoln College, Lady Margaret Professor 351, 412, 428, 430, 468–9, 486

Babington, Gervase, MA, bishop of Llandaff, Exeter and Worcester 671–2

Babington, John, commoner at Corpus Christi College 673

Babington, Zachary, DCL 281 n. 4

Bache, Thomas, MA, student of Christ Church 506

Bacon, Sir Francis 563, 715

Bacon, Sir Nicholas 563, 694

Badcocke, John, commoner at Corpus Christi College 674 n. 2, 682

Badcocke, Nicholas, yeoman 682

Badcocke, Simon, commoner at Corpus Christi College 674 n. 2, 682

Bailey, William, BA 124

Bainbridge, Christopher, cardinal, archbishop of York 328

Baker, David (Augustine), scholar at Broadgates Hall 663–4, 666

Balborow, William, DCnL, DCL, fellow of All Souls College, principal of New Inn Hall 475

Baldwin, John 210

Baldwin, Justinian, MA, student of Christ Church 498, 505, 514

Bale, John, bishop of Ossory 465–6

Balguay, Nicholas, DTh, Greek lecturer at Magdalen College 56

Ball, Richard, singingman of Magdalen College 82

Ballowe, William, DTh, alumnus of Christ Church 509, 517

Banbury (Oxon.) 43

Bancroft, John, DTh, alumnus of Christ Church 510

Bancroft, Richard, archbishop of Canterbury 260, 312, 331, 530, 538–9

Banister, John, surgeon 246

Banister, William, alderman 91 n. 3

Banke, Thomas, DTh, rector of Lincoln College 467 n. 3

Bankes, John, canon of Christ Church 380

Barbaro, Ermoleo 703

Barber, Laurence, MA, fellow of All Souls College 341

Barber, Richard, MA, 412

Barber-Surgeons, Company of 245, 246

Barcham, John, DTh, fellow of Corpus Christi College 683 n. 1

Barebone, John, BTh 177

Barefoot, John, DTh, fellow of Corpus Christi College 428, 725

Barlow, Ralph, DTh, fellow of Corpus Christi College 682 n. 1

Barnard, Daniel, DTh, student of Christ Church 507

Barnard, Thomas, BTh, canon of Christ Church 380

Barnes, Joseph, Oxford bookseller 77, 430, 443, 714

Barnes, Richard, DTh, fellow of Brasenose College 11, 15

Barnes, Robert, DTh 329, 457

Barnes, Robert, MA, MD, senior Linacre lecturer 167, 221 n. 3, 222–3, 232, 243, 245, 254, 446, 453, 470, 495, 496, 497, 716

Barnes, Roger, Oxford book binder 501

Baro, Peter, DTh 390

Barrett, Richard, president of the English College, Rheims 320

Bartlett, Richard, MD, fellow of All Souls College 229, 248

Bartolus de Saxoferrato 474

Barton, Elizabeth 126

Basil, St 321, 703

Baskerville, Edmund, OFM, DTh, warden of Greyfriars 303

Basle, University of 158, 162, 237, 240, 247, 255, 321, 351

Bath Abbey 609

Bath and Wells, diocese of 670

Bathe, William 211 n. 1

Batt, Robert, BTh, scholar of Brasenose College 713

Baxendale, Salisbury, MA, commoner of Balliol College 727

Bayley, Henry, BM, fellow of New College 222, 228

Bayley, Walter, MD, regius professor of medicine 228, 233 n. 1, 234–6, 239, 243–4, 245, 250, 424

Baylie, John, MA, fellow of New College 254, 471 n. 2, 473, 632

Baylie, Thomas, city lecturer 313

Beale, Robert, clerk of the council 280

Beaufort, Lady Margaret, countess of Richmond and Derby 9, 10, 16, 18, 23, 75, 120, 137, 350
    lecturership in theology 347–52

Beaumont, Edward, BA, scholar of Christ Church, inventory of 471 n. 1, 472, 476, 631, n. 2, 703 n. 6

Beaumont Palace 69

Becher, Sir William, BA, commoner of Corpus Christi College 673, 682

Becke, Samuel, MA, fellow of Corpus Christi College 690 n. 4

Bede, St 386, 712

Bedell, Arthur, DCL, alumnus of Christ Church 511

Bedfordshire 670, 673, 680

Beeston (Beds.) 561, 571, 572

Bekynsawe, John, BTh, fellow of New College 302, 304

Bell, Gregory, MA, fellow of Queen's College 450

Bell, John, DCL, bishop of Worcester 562

Bell, John, MA, reader in humanity, Corpus Christi College 668 n. 4, 685 n. 5, 686 n. 2

Bell, William, MA, master of Balliol College 604

Bellarmine, Robert, St, cardinal 393, 454

Bellingham, Richard, BCL 101

Belson, Thomas, inventory of 471 n. 2

Belsyre, Alexander, MA, president of St John's College 406

Benefield, Sebastian, DTh, Lady Margaret Professor 318, 323, 333, 684, 686, n. 2

Bennett, Sir Simon, benefaction of 545, 550

Bennett, William, DTh, of Durham College 303

Bentham, Thomas, DTh, dean of Magdalen College, bishop of Coventry and Lichfield 139, 142, 332, 695

Bentley, John, butler of Exeter College 632

Bentley, John, MD student of Christ Church 505

Bereblock, John, MA, fellow of Exeter College 398, 600, 614, plates I–III

Bereford, John, mayor of Oxford 86 n. 1

Berkshire 678

Bernard of Clairvaux, St 454

Bernher, Augustine 134

Bernys, Richard, MA, foundation fellow of Magdalen College 108

Berry, John, DTh, fellow of Corpus Christi College 683 n. 1

Bertram, Corneille 317

Bessarion of Trebizond, cardinal, Greek manuscripts of 31

Best, John, MA, alumnus of Christ Church 509

Bettes, William, MA 124, 364

Betts, Francis, DCL, fellow of New College 282, 471 n. 2

Betts, John 453

Beza, Theodore 316, 334, 390
    picture of 639

bible, authorized version 315, 320, 333, 354, 355, 393, 732
    Bishops' Bible 315, 320
    Geneva Bible 320
    Rheims-Douay Bible 320

Bickerton, Thomas, MA, alumnus of Christ Church 511

Bickley, Thomas, DTh, fellow of Magdalen College, warden of Merton College 139, 368, 383, 452, 453

Billingsley, Henry 222

Bilson, Thomas, DTh, fellow of New College, bishop of Winchester 328, 333, 433, 438, 725

Blackborn, John, townsman 101 n. 5

Blackwell, George, MA, fellow of Trinity College 382

Blith, Edmund, pewterer 572

Blounte, Richard, BA, fellow of Trinity College 409, 437

Bluett, Humphrey, MD, Oxford medical practitioner 225

Blundell, Peter, bequest of 525, 545, 563

Boarshill (Berks.) 682

Boccaccio 706

Bodin, Jean 442, 711

Bodley, Lawrence, DTh, student of Christ Church, canon of Wells 511

Bodley, Sir Thomas, MA, fellow of Merton College 61 n. 1, 317, 551, 556, 600, 633, 732

see also Oxford, University of: libraries

Boethius 172, 174–6, 446, 700, 707

and study of music 175, 201, 204–6

Boleyn, Anne, queen of England 302

Bologna, University of 216, 247, 262, 304

Bolte, Thomas, inventory of 247, 707 n. 7

Bonaventura, St 451, 474

Bond, Nicholas, DTh, president of Magdalen College 421, 432, 433, 437, 438, 440, 453 n. 4, 454, 473

Bond, Thomas, commoner at Corpus Christi College 674 n. 5

Boniface VII, pope 340

Bonner, Edmund, bishop of London 144, 354, 357, 370, 372, 382

Boorde, Andrew, physician 255

Booth, John, MA, archdeacon of Hereford 459

Borlis, Robert, MA 194

Borrhaeus, Martin 451

Boughton, Sir Edward 728

Boulogne, siege of 264

Bourne, master, of Lincoln College 499, 505

Bourne, Sir John, principal secretary of state 515, 516

Bousfield, Bartholomew, provost of Queen's College 454

Bradshaw, Thomas, MA, scholar of Corpus Christi College, fellow of Brasenose College 687

Brandon, Charles, duke of Suffolk 92

Brattlesby (Lincs.) 561, 562

Braunch, Richard, MA, student of Christ Church 507

Brenz, Johann 314, 379

Brerewood (Brierwood), Edward, MA, professor of astronomy, Gresham College 731

Bretherton, servant to William baron Sandys 672

Braint, Alexander, of Hart Hall 381

Bricot, Thomas 702

Bridges, John, scholar of Christ Church 472 n. 3

Bridgewater, John, MA, rector of Lincoln College 428, 430

Bridgman, Edward, MA, fellow of St John's College 111

Bridgman, Mary 111

Bridgman, William, MA, fellow of St John's College 111

Briggs, Henry, MA, Savilian professor of astronomy 216, 731

Brigshaw, Christopher, of Gloucester Hall 382

Brinknell, Thomas, DTh, Wolsey's lecturer in theology 26, 329, 338

Bristol (Glos.) 46, 409, 688

Bristow, Richard, DTh, fellow of Exeter College 320

Brode, Philip, DTh, King Henry VIII lecturer in theology 344

Brograve, Sir John 538

Broke, John, esquire bedell of law and mayor 86 n. 4, 100, 101 n. 4

Broke, John MA, fellow of Merton College 410

Brooke, John 439

Brooks, Alen, commoner at Corpus Christi College 690 n. 4

Brooks, James, DTh, master of Balliol College, bishop of Gloucester 143, 146, 376, 686 n. 3

Browen, Robert 225

Brown, John, MA, student of Christ Church 506

Browne, George, DTh, archbishop of Dublin 302, 304

Browne, John, commoner at Corpus Christi College 690 n. 4

Browne, Robert, BA, commoner at Corpus Christi College 673

Browne, Samuel, MA, servitor at All Souls College 720

Browne, Thomas, alumnus of Christ Church 508

Browne, Thomas, benefactor of University College library 450, 454

Browne, Thomas, BA, scholar of Balliol College 467 n. 3

Browne, William, MA, fellow of Merton College 446, 471 n. 1, 472, 703

Bruer, Anthony 241

Bruerne (Bruarn), Richard, DTh, BM, regius professor of Hebrew 36, 316, 357, 380, 503

Brunfels, Otto 248

Bruni, Leonardo 707

Bruno, Giordano 721

Bruno the Carthusian 454

Brytton, William, builder 610

Bucer, Martin 134, 146, 314, 368, 371, 373, 447, 451

Buckeridge, John, DTh, president of St John's College, chancellor of Oxford University 357

Buckhurst, Lord, see Sackville

Buckingham (Bucks.) 608

Buckinghamshire 395

Buckland, William, OSB 469

Buckland Baron (Devon) 677

Buckler, Walter, BTh, fellow of Merton College 301, 304

Buckley, Abraham, MA, alumnus of Christ Church 510

Budden, John, DCL, regius professor of civil law 266, 278

Budé, Guillaume 449

Bugenhagen, Johann 314

Bulcombe, William, esquire bedell of law and mayor 76 n. 3, 97

Bull, John, BMus 207, 211

Bullein, William, physician 229

Bullinger, Heinrich 134, 332, 405, 452
catechism of 327, 388–9

Bunny, Edmund, BTh, fellow of Merton College 329

Burgayne, Thomas, scholar of Broadgates Hall 471 nn. 1, 3

Burges, John, MD, fellow of the College of Physicians 224

Burghley, Lord, see Cecil, William

Burghley, Lady Mildred 499, 508, 516

Burgo, see Nicholas de

Buridan, John 160, 711

Burley, Walter 199, 222, 702, 703, 704, 707, 713 n. 1, plate XIIa

Burton, Edmund, MA, inventory of 204, 475

Burton, Robert, BTh, student of Christ Church 732

Burton, Samuel, MA, alumnus of Christ Church 509

Burton Lazar's (Leics.), hospital of 9

Burye, BA, inventory of 707 n. 7

Busleiden, Jerome de, founder of the collegium trilingue at Louvain 29 n. 4, 316

Bust, Henry, MD, senior Linacre lecturer 239, 240

Bust, William, MA, student of Christ Church 507

Busterd, Richard, manciple of All Souls College 79, 110, 114 n. 4

Busterd, William, fellow of All Souls College 110

Butcher, William, BTh, fourth president of Corpus Christi College 406, 408

Bynyon, Thomas, MA, fellow of Merton College 410

Bryde, Thomas, surgeon 223 n. 1, 239, 250

Byschop, George, of London 508, 516

Bysley, master, inventory of 204, 471 n. 1, 472, 474, 476, 703

Caen 31

Caesar, Julius 702, 712

Caesarius, Johannes 698, 703, 707

Caius, John 216, 249, 341, 414

Cakebreade, Richard, bookbinder 514

Caldwell, Richard, MD, fellow of the College of Physicians 229, 233, 238, 243, 245, 511, 518

Calepino (Calepinus), Ambrogio 702

Calfhill, James, DTh, Lady Margaret Professor, bishop of Worcester 310, 330, 352, 383–4, 398, 409

Calfield, Richard, MA, student of Christ Church 661

Calphurnius, Mattheus, lecturer at Cardinal College 32, 341

Calvin, John; Calvinism 310, 313, 319, 321, 324–5, 327, 330, 331, 332, 333–4, 388, 389, 390, 395, 412, 417, 429, 451, 452, 453, 499, 704, 711, 713
picture of 639

Cambridge, University of 16, 17, 56, 68, 108, 120, 133, 141, 143, 147, 154, 172, 206, 243, 247, 251, 255, 264, 281, 299, 313, 318, 320, 324, 328, 330, 332, 333, 342, 351, 354, 367, 373, 375, 394, 397, 403, 404, 416, 422–3, 426, 431, 530, 533, 535, 538, 541–2, 557–8, 624, 662, 688, 692, 718, 725, 730
Peter Baro at 390–1
Martin Bucer at 134, 138

Cambridge, University of (*cont.*)
  centralization of authority 439
  colleges
    Buckingham College 43
    Christ's College 10, 11, 120
    Clare College 136, 693
    Corpus Christi College 414, 728
    Emmanuel College 423, 701, 728
    Godshouse 10
    Gonville and Caius College 216, 246, 414, 681 n. 1
    Jesus College 136
    King's College 135, 146, 206–7, 216, 414
    the King's Hall 3, 206
    Magdalene College 43
    Pembroke College 17, 545
    Peterhouse 216, 414
    St John's College 10, 120, 216, 221, 351, 423, 541, 646, 648
    Trinity College 42, 216
    Trinity Hall 136, 281
  Cromwell, chancellor 130
  East Anglia served by 671
  Great St Mary's 146
  Greek teaching at 21 n. 4, 67
  incorporated 402
  King Henry VIII lecture 343
  Lady Margaret professor 16, 120
  Marian exiles 144
  more protestant than Oxford 139–40, 378, 414
  numbers 152
  ordered to readopt ancient statutes 140
  Oxford theologians at 304–5
  proposed college of civil law 136, 137, 272
  regius professorships 345
  royal divorce 124–5
  visitation of 1535: 127–9
  visitation of 1549: 135–6, 693
  visitation of 1556: 145–6
  White Horse Inn 123, 363
Camden, William, scholar at Broadgates Hall 717, 720
Cameron, J. K. 353
Camney, John, barber and chandler 81 n. 4
Campion, Edmund, MA, fellow of St John's College 317, 322, 329, 378, 382, 399, 411, 414
  Decem rationes 51, 381, 383
Canterbury, archbishop of 131
  as visitor 404, 410
  court of 359
Canterbury (Kent) 683
  King's School 38, 684, 687

Canterbury, cathedral priory of 17, 301, 463, 465, 617, 624
Canterbury, province of 360
  convocation 320, 323, 324, 328
Cardano (Cardanus), Girolamo 222, 248, 469, 716
Cardiganshire 265
Carew, Christopher, MA, fellow of Balliol College 518
Carew, George, DTh, dean of Christ Church 409
Carlisle, see of 438
Carmarthen (Wales) 304
Carnarvon (Wales) 264
Carnsew, Matthew, MA, scholar at Broadgates Hall 697–701, 704, 705, 709, 727
Carnsew, Richard, scholar at Broadgates Hall 697–701, 704, 705, 709, 727
Carow, Robert, master carpenter 605, 611, 612
Carpenter, Nathaniel, DTh, fellow of Exeter College 717
Carpenter, Richard, DTh, fellow of Exeter College 632
Carpenter, Thomas, MA, fellow of All Souls College 214 n. 1
Carranza de Miranda, Fray Bartolomé 378, 379
Carter, John, BCL, scholar at Peckwater Inn 474
Carter, Peter, logician 707
Cartier, Jacques 716
Cartwright, Nicholas, DTh, fellow of Magdalen College 302, 371
Cartwright, Thomas, scholar at White Hall 724; (?) later at Broadgates Hall 703 n. 2
Casaubon, Isaac 316
Case, John, MD, sometime fellow of St John's College 55 n. 1, 109 n. 2, 211, 222, 236, 239, 241, 242, 471 n. 2, 714–15
  Apologia musices 211–12
  Lapis philosophicus 715
  Speculum moralium 430, 714, plate XVIIa
  Sphaera civitatis 211, 212, 714
  Summa veterum interpretum 714
Cassington (Oxon.) 357, 382
Cassiodorus 202
Castiglione, Baldassare 650, 666
Castleton, Lord 561
Catesby, recusant fellow of Exeter College 413
Catesby, Robert, of Gloucester Hall 382
Catherine of Aragon, queen of England 18, 67, 120, 125, 351
Cavey, Christopher ('Stoffolde'), Oxford bookseller 443–4, 468 n. 3

Cebes 698

Cecil, Robert, earl of Salisbury 433–4
  influence 435–6, 438, 544

Cecil, William, Lord Burghley 381, 397, 406,
  416, 417, 418, 429, 540 n. 2, 542–3, 662,
  724
  influence 435, 439

Celsus, Aulus Cornelius 213

Ceporinus, Johannes 316, 702, 705

Cesarius, Johannes 158

Chaderton, Laurence, puritan leader 319, 324,
  333

Chalcombe (Northants.) 709

Chambers, Richard, fellow of Magdalen
  College 406

Chambre, John, MD, junior Linacre lecturer,
  warden of Merton College 223, 224, 229,
  238, 244, 255, 617

Chancery 360

Channel Islands 392

chantries act 42

Chark, William 419

Charles I, king of England 547, 551, 557, 673

Charles V, emperor 379

Charnock, Thomas, alchemist 248–9

Charnoke, Roger, MA, inventory of 204

Chaucer, Geoffrey 64, 111

Chayney, Henry, MA, scholar of Broadgates
  Hall 706

Chedsey, William, DTh, third president of
  Corpus Christi College 131, 135, 137–8,
  302, 322, 323 n. 1, 329, 370, 372, 374–5,
  462 n. 1, plate XXIIa
  deprived 408
  disputation on the mass 143
  Greek lecturer 27
  interrogated by privy council 139

Cheke, Sir John 135

Chelle, William, BMus 204

Chelsea College 684

Chenell, John, MD 226

Cheney, Walter, MA, fellow of University
  College 442

Cherwell River 70

Cheshire 13, 710
  Oxford-trained clergy in 391

Chester school 38

Chevalier, Anthony Rudolph 316

Chichester (Sussex)
  cathedral 351
  diocese of 358

Cholmondeley, Sir Hugh 710

Cholmondeley, Randolph, commoner at
  Lincoln College 710–11, plate XVIIb

Christ's Hospital, London 663

Chrysostom, John, St 303, 313, 315, 321, 449
  n. 3, 450, 704, 707 n. 7

Churchyard, Baltazar, Oxford bookseller 444

Cicero 21, 58, 172, 179, 340, 666, 700, 702, 705,
  707 n. 7, 709, 710, 712, 713
  Ad Herennium 698
  De amicitia 698, 700
  De officiis 41, 459, 468, 470
  letters 172, 699, 704

Clare, Elizabeth, widow 662

Clare, William, butcher 649

Clark, Andrew 170, 191, 213, 282, 324, 331
  views on faculty of medicine appraised
  249–56

Clarke, Francis, BCL, fellow of All Souls
  College 282

Clarke, John, MA of Cardinal College 123, 314

Claymond, John, DTh, president of Magdalen
  College and first president of Corpus
  Christi College 15, 28, 239, 465, 599, 611,
  668, 683
  early career 658
  gift of Greek and Hebrew manuscripts to
    Corpus Christi College 67 n. 1, 458–9,
    462, plate XIV
  memorial brass to 619, plate XV a

Claymond, Thomas 214

Clayre, Robert, vicar of Flore (Northants) 518

Clayton, Thomas, MD, regius professor of
  medicine 226, 256

Clement, John, MD, Wolsey's lecturer in
  humanity, fellow of the College of Physicians 21 n. 4, 26, 68, 229, 238, 242, 247,
  248, 254, 337–8, 454 n. 6, 688

Clenardus, Nicolaus 316

Clerk, John, alderman, will of 113

Clerke, Cornett, joiner 611

Clerkenwell, London 562, 565, 572

Clichtove (Clichtoveus), Josse 703, 705, 707

Clifton, Nicolas, Oxford bookseller 205, 208
  n. 5, 706–7, 716

Clifton, (Glos.) 688

Clive, Richard, chaplain of Christ Church
  503

Clowes, William, surgeon 246

Clusius, Carolus 248

Clyff, Richard, MA, student of Christ Church
  317

Cobham, Lady 439

Cogan, Thomas, BM, fellow of Oriel College
  226, 228, 243, 244, 248, 646, 649

Coimbra commentators on Aristotle 711

Cokerel, George, baker 96

Cole, Henry, DCL, DTh, warden of New College, provost of Eton College 134, 144, 146, 376–7, 385, 418, 460, 462–3 deposed 138–9

Cole, Humphrey, BA, scholar (probably fellow) of Corpus Christi College 725

Cole, William, DTh, sixth president of Corpus Christi College 139, 320, 339, 383, 408, 416, 428, 430, 436, 625, 673, 709, 725

Colet, John 309, 313

Colfe, Abraham, BA, student of Christ Church 438

Colfe, Richard, DTh, student of Christ Church, donor 504

College of Physicians, London, see Physicians, College of

Colles, John, BTh, inventory of 474

Collinson, James, tailor 84

Collinson, Patrick 330

Cologne, University of 304

Colombo, Realdo 698

Colsell, Elizabeth 113

Colsell, William, MA 113

Colthurst, Francis, commoner of Corpus Christi College 674, 682

Colthurst, Henry, commoner of Corpus Christi College 674, 682

Colthurst, Henry, London grocer 682

Comenius, Johannes 695

confraternities of the Blessed Virgin Mary 108 n. 2

Conrad ab Ulmis 40, 134

Contarini, Gasparo, cardinal 379

Cooke, Humfrey, master carpenter 605, 609–11, 612

Cooper, Thomas, BM, DTh, dean of Christ Church, bishop of Lincoln and Winchester 110 n. 3, 233 n. 1, 332, 367–8, 416 vice-chancellor 425, 428 visitation of Magdalen College 418–19, 663, 705

Copernicus, Nicolaus; Copernican theory 222, 715, 716, 719

Copley, Peter, MA, student of Christ Church 498, 505, 514

Corbett, Richard, DTh, city lecturer, dean of Christ Church, bishop of Norwich 313

Cordell, Sir William, master of the rolls 404

Cordus, Valerius 222

Corrano (del Corro), Antonio 326, 384–5, 390, 392, 417–18, 428, 430, 440, 725

Cotes, George, DTh, master of Balliol College and bishop of Chester 343

Cottisford, John, DTh, rector of Lincoln College 108, 486

Cotton, Sir Robert, antiquary 717

council, privy 85, 92–4, 99, 132, 135, 137, 139, 142, 358, 359, 378, 434, 439 interference in Elizabethan university 404, 411, 412–13, 417, 422

council in the Marches of Wales 9, 287, 360

council of the North 673

Courthope, James, MA, canon of Christ Church 380

Coveney, Thomas, MD, president of Magdalen College 233 n. 1, 406

Coventry (War.) 46, 241

Coventry and Lichfield, diocese of 9, 13, 359

Coverdale, Martin 320

Cox, A. D. M. 549

Cox, Richard, DTh (Cantab.), dean of Christ Church, chancellor of Oxford 33, 37, 40, 124, 141, 147, 305, 316, 332, 367, 370, 371, 374, 383 destruction of university library 466 influence on Edwardine Oxford 133–9, 230, 375, 380

Coxe, William, MA, student of Christ Church 507

Cradocke, Edward, DTh, Lady Margaret Professor 301, 352

Craine, Thomas, MA, student of Christ Church 506, 515

Crakanthorpe, Richard, DTh, fellow of Queen's College 392, 719

Cranmer, George, MA, fellow of Corpus Christi College 391

Cranmer, Thomas, archbishop of Canterbury 125, 127, 131, 133–4, 145, 303, 380, 385 trial 142–4, 302, 322, 324, 325, 328, 330, 385–7, 379, 398

Cranmer, Thomas, BCL, reader in humanity, Corpus Christi College 682 n. 1

Crashall (Cressale), Robert de, MA 113 n. 3

Crato, Johann 238, 249

Crispin, Edmund, MD, fellow of Oriel College 230, 255

Croariensis, Andreas 134

Croft, Robert, MA, chaplain of New College 130, 131

Croke, Nicholas, fishmonger 108

Croke, Richard, comptroller of the hanaper 43

Croke, Richard, DTh, Greek lecturer and public orator at Cambridge, canon of King Henry VIII's College, Oxford 21 n. 4

Cromwell, Thomas, earl of Essex 90–4, 126, 131, 132, 301, 302, 307, 351, 365, 613

chancellor of Cambridge University 130, 401
'Cromwellian party' at Oxford 91
visitation of 1535: 128-9, 224
Crosse, Matthew, esquire bedell of law 554-5
Crowley, Robert, BA, fellow of Magdalen College 367
Cryse, John, BCL, BCnL 269
Cuffe, Henry, MA, regius professor of Greek 354, 355-6, 438, 711
Culmannus, Leonardus 451
Culpepper, Martin, MD, warden of New College 418, 424, 429
Cupledick, master, donor to Christ Church library 502
Curthorpe, (Curtop, Courthope), James, MA, reader in humanity at Corpus Christi College, canon of Christ Church 26, 134
Curtis, Mark H. 442, 453, 552
Curtop, see Curthorpe
Curwen (Coren), Richard, DTh, lecturer at Corpus Christi College 25
Cyprian, St 302, 323, 371
Cyril of Alexandria, St 302, 322

Dalaber, Anthony, of Gloucester College 314
Damascenus, see John of Damascus, St
da Monte (Montanus), Giovanni Battista 223, 238, 240, 249, 253, 468 n. 3
Danby, earl of, see Danvers, Henry
Daniel, John, BMus 211
Danse, Edward, MA 194
Danvers, Henry, earl of Danby 732
Darby, Edward, MA, fellow of Lincoln College 484
Darbyshire, William, scholar of Broadgates Hall 471 n. 1
Darcy, Sir Arthur 355
Dasypodius, Conrad 716
Davidson, Alan 357
Davies, Richard, DTh, bishop of St David's 320
Dawkes, Robert, MA, fellow of Merton College 410
Dawson, William, MA, fellow of Queen's College 473
Day, John, BTh, fellow of Oriel College 327 n. 5, 711
Daye, John, DCL 281 n. 5
Dayrell, William, BA, fellow of Magdalen College 473
Deale, Robert, scholar at New College 398
Decretals, see Gregory IX
Deddington (Oxon.) 43

Dedham (Essex) 330
Dee, John, mathematician and astrologer 718
Delaber, Anthony, OSB 364
Delaber, John, MD, principal of Gloucester Hall 240, 255, 429
de la Hyde, David, MA, fellow of Merton College 410
Demosthenes 22, 354, 703 n. 6, 704, 707 n. 7, 709
De motu planetarum 23
Denham, Robert, brewer 101 n. 3
Denifle, Heinrich 157
Denington, Thomas, MA, student of Christ Church 506, 515
Dennie, master, lecturer in Greek at All Souls College 63
Denys the Areopagite 454
Denys the Carthusian 454, 461, 474
De sphaera 6, 23, 35
Devereux, Robert, 2nd earl of Essex 312, 355, 401, 420, 433, 436, 711
influence in Oxford 437-8
Devon 670
Devorguilla, the Lady, wife of John of Balliol 723
Dewe, MD 239
Dewhurst, Giles, MA, student of Christ Church 208 n. 5, 473
Digby, George, inventory of 707 n. 7
Digby, Kenelm, gentleman commoner at Gloucester Hall 718
Digby, Simon, inventory of 707 n. 7
Dighton, Robert, fellow of Lincoln College 450
Dillingen, university of 379
Diogenes Laertius 469, 710
Dionysius the Areopagite 707 n. 7
Dionysius the Carthusian 704
Dioscorides Pedanius 213, 222, 235, 247, 248, 703
doctors' commons 279, 281, 287, 288, 289
Dodoens, Rembert 248
Dodonaeus, see Dodoens
Dodwell, John and Philippe, butler and wife at New College 662
Dolber, John, MA, lodger 113 n. 1
Dolet, Étienne 457
Donne, John, MA, Greek reader at Corpus Christi College 25, 27
Donne, John, poet, commoner at Hart Hall 696, 732
Dorbellus (Nicolaus de Orbellis) 177
Dorman, Thomas, BCL, fellow of All Souls College 377 n. 3, 385, 386

Dorne (Thorne), John, Oxford bookseller 76, 314, 363, 443–4, 451, 467–8, 474, 475, 708 n. 1

Dorset 12

Dotyn, John, MD, rector of Exeter College 225, 239, 248, 254

Douai, college of 332, 353, 381, 386, 395, 410, 415, 428

Dowe, Robert, BCL, musician, fellow of All Souls College 205, 208 n. 5, 210, 435, 471, 473

Dowland, John, BMus 207, 211

Dowman, John, DCL, DCnL, commissary of the bishop of Winchester 658–9

Down Ampney (Glos.) 689

Doygge, George 517

Doyley, Thomas, BM 255

Drome, Michael, BTh, Greek lecturer at Magdalen College 55–6, 364

Drury, master, donor to Christ Church library 502

Drusius, Johannes 61, 316, 317, 394

Dryander, Johann 214, 245

Du Bartas, Guillaume de Salluste 697

Duchesne (Quercetanus), Joseph 249

Dudley, John, duke of Northumberland 374, 533

Dudley, Robert, earl of Leicester, chancellor of Oxford University 51 n. 4, 61, 94, 152, 228, 235–6, 315, 351, 354, 397, 399, 401, 402, 408, 409, 415, 420, 433, 435, 714

acquisition of college leases 430–1, 438

appointments in Oxford 428–30

as chancellor 423–31, 662

attitude to puritans 430

concern with university 424–8

nominates vice-chancellors 401–2, 423

parliamentary statutes 431

patron to members of the university 240, 289, 326, 331, 384, 417–18, 428–9, 718

reputation 423–4

warns against papists 389, 393, 413, 427–8

Dugdale, James, BA, master of University College 406

Dulse, Leonard, BM 225

Dunch, Sir William 563

Dunne, Gabriel, OSB, of St Bernard's College, canon of St Paul's 394, 460, 462–3

Dunne, William, MD, fellow of Exeter College 241

Dunnet, John, inventory of 208 n. 5, 707 n. 7

Dunscomb, Thomas, MA, student of Christ Church 507

Duns Scotus, John, OFM 32, 160, 177, 178, 199, 307, 340, 474, 702, 707, 715

visitation of 1535: 128–9

Dürer, Albrecht 620

Durham, county of 12, 673

Durham, diocese of 303, 670

Durham cathedral priory 43, 303, 463

school 687

Dyer, Robert, of Crampound 102

Dymsdale, John, MA, fellow of St John's College 471 nn. 2 and 3

Dyott, Sir Richard, BA, commoner at Corpus Christi College 673

East, William, master mason 609

East Anglia 671

Eck, Johann 158

Ede, Richard, BMus 206

Edes, Richard, DTh, student of Christ Church 506, 511, 515, 518

Edmondes, Sir Thomas 684

Edmondes, James, draper 76 n. 1

Edmonds, John, MA, student of Christ Church 507

Edowe, Thomas, BM 230

Edrych, see Etheridge

Edward I, king of England 87

Edward II, king of England 87, 105

Edward III, king of England, charter of (1355) 87, 104, 132

Edward IV, king of England 104, 306, 600

Edward VI, king of England 49, 93, 133, 139, 142, 147, 224, 258, 264, 270, 301, 324, 329, 364, 387, 394–5, 446, 466, 470, 533, 557–8, 618, 620

numbers at Oxford during reign of 140

Edwards, David, MA, MD (Cantab.), lecturer at Corpus Christi College 25, 242, 244, 688–9

Edwards, Guthlac, MP 687 n. 1

Edwards, John, MD, fellow of Corpus Christi College 222, 225, 229, 233 n. 1, 239

Edwards, Richard, MA, fellow of Corpus Christi College, student of Christ Church, master of the children of the chapel royal 209, 689

Edys, William, monk of Burton-upon-Trent 469

Eedes, Richard, DTh, student of Christ Church 433

Eggecombe, John, graduate 113

Egidius (Aegidius Romanus) 177

Eley, William, BTh, president of St John's College 406

Elizabeth, princess 571

Elizabeth I, queen of England 1, 27, 49, 62, 149, 187, 190, 198, 258, 259, 263, 264, 274, 280, 281, 282, 288, 324, 329, 330, 354, 358, 392, 394, 396, 401, 404, 427, 440, 471, 477, 533, 543–4, 557, 620, 668

coronation of 689

patronage in Oxford 430–1, 434, 439

picture of 639

visit to Oxford 1566: 93, 154, 209, 397–9, 523, plates I–III

visit to Oxford 1592: 60 n. 6, 209, 227, 399–400, 523, 559

Elkes, William, MA, commoner at Corpus Christi College 673

Ely, diocese of 229

Elyot, Sir Thomas 450, 650

Emden, A. B. 106, 110, 153–4, 329, 459, 556

Emerson, John, MA, fellow of New College 131

Epictetus 707 n. 7

Epiphanius 371, 449 nn. 3 and 4, 460

Erasmus, Desiderius; Erasmianism 157, 176, 193, 309, 314, 316, 321, 322, 323, 328, 337, 380, 388, 394, 446, 449, 450, 475, 702–5, 707 n.7

approves of Corpus Christi College 66–7

client of Wolsey 30

Greek lecturer at Cambridge 21 n. 4

picture of 635

Erastus, Thomas 253

Ersden, extra-mural pupil at Corpus Christi College 690 n. 3

Essex, earl of, see Cromwell, Devereux

Essex, county of 728

Estienne, Charles 222, 245

Estienne, Henri 315

Estienne, Robert 449, 702

Eston, Robert, MA, fellow of Exeter College 11

Estwycke, John, DTh, fellow of Merton College 494

Etheridge (Edrych), George, MA, BM, regius professor of Greek 26, 36, 40, 235, 238, 242, 248, 344, 354, 355, 374–5, 686 n. 2, 689

Eton College 43, 206, 328, 357, 366, 431, 438, 535, 541, 543, 557, 558, 612, 687

Eu, Nicholas, scholar 110 n. 4

Eu, Roger, scholar 110 n. 4

Eucherius, St 449 n. 3

Euclid 161, 172, 174, 222, 231, 716

Eure, Charles, commoner at Corpus Christi College 672

Eure, Horatio, commoner at Corpus Christi College 672

Euripides 22, 341, 354, 476, 702, 703

Eusebius 321, 386, 449 n. 3, 460

Evans, Oxford bookseller 443

Evesham Abbey 305

Ewer, Richard, BTh, fellow of Merton College 444 n. 2, 451, 475

Exchequer 132

Exeter (Devon) 305, 683

Exeter, diocese of 84, 121, 265, 337, 670

bishop of, as visitor 404, 411

Faber Stapulensis, see Lefèvre d'Étaples

Fabrizio, Girolamo 238, 253

Fagius, P. B. 146

Fairford Manor (Glos.) 301

Falconer, John 247

Fallopio, Gabriele 235, 238, 253

Farnaby, Giles, BMus 207

Farre, John, DCL, fellow of New College 269

Farrington, Tristram, commoner at Exeter College 707 n. 7

Favour, John, DCL, fellow of New College 107 n. 4, 281

Fayrfax, Robert, DMus 207

Featley (Fertclough), Daniel, DTh, fellow of Corpus Christi College 684, 719

Feckenham, John, DTh, fellow of Gloucester Hall 329

Fell, John, DTh, dean of Christ Church, bishop of Oxford 614

Felton (Haresfeld), John, vicar of St Mary Magdalen 475

Fenn, James, BA, fellow of Corpus Christi College and Gloucester Hall 378, 382

Ferdinand, Philip, tutor in Hebrew 317

Fernel, Johannes 222, 248, 253

Ferrara 304

Ferrer, Robert, BTh, bishop of St David's 303

Ferrers, Henry, antiquary 717

Fetiplace, George, BA, scholar of Corpus Christi College 680

Fetiplace family 671

Ficino, Marsilio 706, 712

Field, John, (?) MA 330, 332, 392, 417, 418, 420, 437

Field, Richard, DTh, fellow of Magdalen Hall, city lecturer 107, 313, 332–3

Field of the Cloth of Gold 680

Fillingham (Lincs.) 561, 562

Finmore, William, BCL, fellow of St John's College 664–5, 666

Fisher, John, bishop of Rochester, chancellor of Cambridge University 10, 16, 18, 21 n. 4, 120–1, 131

Fissher, John, citizen and joiner of London 601

Fitzgarret (Fitzgerald), Dudley, commoner at Corpus Christi College 672

Fitzgarret, George, sixteenth earl of Kildare, commoner at Corpus Christi College 672

Fitzjames, Richard, DTh, warden of Merton College, chancellor of Oxford University, bishop of Rochester and London 119, 166, 328, 446, 599, 624–5
remodels Merton College 600–4

Flacius (Illyricus), Matthias 321, 452

Fleming, Richard, DTh, bishop of Lincoln, founder of Lincoln College 10

Flemming, William, mayor of Oxford 98

Flemyng, Robert, MA, dean of Lincoln 446

Florio, John 716

Fludd, Robert, MD, student of Christ Church 242, 718

Forman, Simon 244, 651–2, 665

Forrest, William, canon of Oseney 210, 364, 374

'Forrest-Heyther' part books 210

Forster, Edward, manciple of Christ Church 470 n. 3

Forster, Richard, MD, fellow of All Souls College, Lumleian Lecturer 238, 243, 245

Fortescue, Sir John 544

Fortey, Henry, BM, licensed to practise 225

Foster, John, MA, fellow of Brasenose College 694 n. 2

Fotheringay (Beds.) 673

Fountains Abbey 605

Foux, John, lecturer in music 205

Fowler, John, MA, fellow of New College, stationer at Louvain 386, 407

Fowler, Thomas 339, 709 n. 1

Fox, Richard, bishop of Winchester, founder of Corpus Christi College 15, 16, 25, 26, 30, 31, 57, 58, 65, 119, 120, 215, 220, 306, 313, 328, 336, 544, 545, 609, 611, 646, 652, 654–5, 657, 670, 680, 683, 686, 690, 713, plate VI
career 17
collegiate conception 17, 19, 28, 607–8, 610, 613, 628
compared to that of Wolsey 29, 612
gifts to Corpus library 67 n. 1, 458–9, 462
significance of foundation for the university 66–8

Foxe, John, MA, fellow of Magdalen College, martyrologist 139, 286, 302, 321, 329, 364, 367, 442, 451, 711
sermons of 698, 700–1, 727

Foxius, Sebastianus 457

Frampton, John, organist of Merton College 601

Francis, Thomas, MD, regius professor of medicine 40, 231–4, 411, 435

Franco of Cologne 203

Franeker, Friesland 317

Frankfurt book fair 443

Franklin, John, supplier of stone 610

Freman, William, MD, president of the College of Physicians 300–1, 304

Frere, William, alderman 91, 93

Frith, John 124, 364, 366

Froben press 321, 322

Frobysher, Anthony, MA 179

Froschover, Christopher 134, 320

Frost, William, steward to Richard Fox 670

Fryer, John, MD, fellow of College of Physicians 229, 238, 254, 364

Fuchs, Leonhard 223, 231, 235, 238, 240, 248, 249, 254, 449

Fulbeck, William, scholar of Corpus Christi College 678 n. 2, 682

Fuller, Nicholas, MA, Hart Hall 317

Fuller, Thomas 541

Furness, William, white-baker and cook 81, 82

Fusting, John, Oxford stonemason 599

Gafurius, Franchino 203

Gager, William, DCL, student of Christ Church 209, 290–1

Galeatius of St Sophia 231

Galen; Galenism 213, 214, 216, 217, 219, 221, 222, 223, 227, 228, 235, 241, 243, 249, 254, 448
Aldine edition 242, 688
recommends tennis 649

Galileo 715, 719

Garbrand, master 239

Garbrand, John, MA, fellow of New College 107, 443, 453 n. 4

Garbrand, Richard, Oxford bookseller 77, 443–4, 500, 514, 519

Garcia, see Juan de Villa Garcia

Gardiner, Stephen, chancellor of Cambridge University, bishop of Winchester 125, 126, 142, 144, 147, 258, 303, 311, 357, 377, 394

Garrett, Thomas, curate of Honey Lane, London 56, 123–4, 311, 313, 364

Garrod, H. W. 446, 488

Gascoigne, Thomas, chancellor of Oxford University 446

Gawen (Stangar), inferior bedell of law 641

Gaza, Theodorus, *see* Theodore of Gaza

Gellibrand, Edward, MA, fellow of Magdalen College 330, 392, 403
  opponent of Laurence Humfrey 419–21

Gellius, Aulus 21, 711

Gemma Frisius 152, 172, 174, 700, 707 n. 7, 716

Genebrard, Gilbert 454

Geneva 332, 384, 416

Gentilis, Albericus, DCL, regius professor of civil law 261, 265–6, 278, 279, 280, 289–93, 358, 360–1, 391, 696, 717

George of Trebizond 340, 703

German, Samuel, MA, fellow of Magdalen College 434

Gerrard, *see* Garrett

Gervase, James, DCL, warden of Merton College 410

Gesner, Conrad 235, 249, 254

Geynes, John, MD, fellow of the College of Physicians 229

Gibberd, Nicholas, BM 111, 239

Gibberd, Nicholas, draper 111

Gibbes, Richard, alderman 102

Gibson, Strickland 443–4

Gifford, Roger, MD, junior Linacre Lecturer, president of the College of Physicians 223, 233 n. 1, 254, 411, 453

Gilbert, Sir Humphrey 173, 716–17

Gilborn Thomas, MA 102

Gildas 704

Gilder, George, *discipulus* at Christ Church 660

Giles, George, MA, fellow of Corpus Christi College 680

Giles, Nathaniel, BMus 207

Gill, Alexander, MA, fellow of Corpus Christi College 687

Gillingham, William, OSB, warden of Canterbury College 464–5

Gilpin, Bernard, BTh, fellow of Queen's College 329, 372, 470

Gilys, David 102

Glareanus, Henricus 61, 203

Glasgow, university of 158, 174

Glasier, Mary neé Noble 113

Glasier, Thomas, DCL, rector of Exeter College 113, 471 n. 2, 619, 627

Glasyar, Robert, glazier 611

Gloucester, Humfrey, duke of 306

Gloucester, diocese of 354

Gloucester (Glos.) 111, 670, 671
  College School 687, 689

Gloucestershire 12

Glover, John, MA, student of Christ Church, fellow of St John's College 245, 471

Glowceter, William, OSB, BTh 305

Goddard, Edward, BA, commoner of Corpus Christi College 673

Godfrey, John, maniciple of New Inn Hall 100–1

Godwin, Francis, DTh, student of Christ Church, bishop of Llandaff and Hereford 328, 507

Godwin, Thomas, BM, DTh, dean of Christ Church, bishop of Bath and Wells 233 n. 1, 412, 416, 511, 516

Godwyn, Francis, DTh, student of Christ Church 507

Goldsborough, Nicholas, BTh, fellow of Corpus Christi College 687

Goldwell, James, DCnL, DCL, fellow of All Souls College, principal of St George Hall, bishop of Norwich 455–6

Goldwell, Thomas, BTh, bishop of St Asaph 394

Gomersall, Richard, councilman 101

Good, Hugh, of Somerset, MA, Greek lecturer at Corpus Christi College 27, plate XXIIa

Good, James, MD, fellow of the College of Physicians 233 n. 1

Goodbody, William 101 n. 3

Goodman, Christopher, MA, student of Christ Church, Lady Margaret Professor 329, 351, 380

Goodrich, Thomas, bishop of Ely 135–6

Goodridge, John, BA, scholar at Balliol College 720

Goodwyn, William, DTh, alumnus of Christ Church 511

Gore, Oxford bookseller 443

Gosson, Stephen, BA, scholar of Corpus Christi College 652, 683

Goulston, Theodore 242, 245, 249, 254

Gowre, John, MA, esquire bedell of law 471 n. 2

Grantham, Thomas, commoner of Christ Church 508

Grantham (Lincs.) 17, 682

Gratian 456

Gray, John, scholar of Oriel College 473

Gray's Inn 282, 361

Green, Bartholomew, MA 319, 372

Green, Richard, inventory of 471

Green V. H. H. 549

Greenway, Thomas, BTh, fifth president of Corpus Christi College 672, 675

Greenwood, Charles, MA, fellow and benefactor of University College 544

Gregory I, St, pope (Gregory the Great) 323, 448, 449 n. 3, 450, 474

Gregory IX, pope, *Decretals* of 340

Gregory, Christopher, BTh, bursar of Magdalen College 529

Gregory of Nazianzus, St 321, 449 n. 3

Greneway, Richard, commoner at Corpus Christi College 690 n. 4

Greneway, Robert, scholar of Gloucester Hall 114 n. 1

Greneway, Thomas, MA, fifth president of Corpus Christi College 17, 408, 459, 462

Gresham, Sir Thomas 313

Gresham College, London 211, 240, 313

Greville, Fulke 500, 502, 721

Grey, Henry, third marquis of Dorset 357

Grey, Lady Katherine 266, 287

Grey, William, DTh, fellow of Balliol College, bishop of Ely 624

Griffith, John, DCL, regius professor of civil law, principal of New Inn Hall 264, 287–8, 358, 360

Grimald, Nicholas, MA 209, 367

Grimani, cardinal Domenico 31

Grindal, Edmund, archbishop of Canterbury 287, 360, 415, 450, 537

gift of books to Queen's College 452, 453

Gris, William, wine merchant, keeper of Christ Church library 509

Grocyn, William, MA, fellow of New College, manuscripts of 458–9, plate XIVb

Gryce, William, DTh, fellow of Magdalen College 475, 631

Gryffyth, Roger, carpenter 611

Gryme, Thomas, yeoman bedell of theology 470 n. 3

Gualter, Rudolph 231, 318, 332, 451

Guarino da Verona 179

Guevara, Antonio de 697

Guido of Arezzo 203

Guildford (Surrey) 434

guild of Corpus Christi and St Mary, Cambridge 108

Guilliaud, Claude 454

Guinter (Winter), *see* Guinterius

Guinterius, Johannes 249, 254

Guiting (Glos.) 577, 578

Gunter, Edmund, BTh, student of Christ Church, professor of astronomy at Gresham College 731

Gunter, John, MA, student of Christ Church 471 n. 2

Gunter, Richard, manciple of Gloucester College 79, 80

Gwyn, Thomas, MD, fellow of the College of Physicians 224

Gwyneth, John, DMus 207

Gwynn, Matthew, MD, fellow of St John's College 238, 240, 242, 246

Hadden, Thomas, Dr Bell's exhibitioner at Balliol College 660

Haddon, Thomas, commoner at Corpus Christi College 690 n. 4

Haddon, Walter, president of Magdalen College 139, 142, 324

Hafter, John, vicar of St Mary Magdalen 459

Hakewell, George, DTh, fellow and benefactor of Exeter College 544

Hakluyt, Richard, MA, student of Christ Church 436, 716–17, 721, 725, 731

suggests lecturerships in navigation 436

Hales, Sir Christopher 673, 683

Hales, John, MA, fellow of Corpus Christi College, regius professor of Greek 686 n. 2

Hall, Humfrey, MA, fellow of All Souls College 11, 255

Hall, John, BM 233 n. 1

Hall, Thomas, MD, anatomist 246

Hall, William, MA, fellow of Merton College 410

Hambleden (Bucks.) 563

Hamden, John, DTh, alumnus of Christ Church 511

Hammond, Henry, DTh, canon of Christ Church 333

Hampshire 670, 705

Hampton Court 133, 612

Hampton Court Conference 333, 390, 393, 421

Hamsterley, Ralph, BTh, fellow of Merton College, principal of St Alban Hall, master of University College 603

Hanmer, Meredith, DTh, fellow of Corpus Christi College 321, 386, 387, 389

Hansard (Hanshart), master, of Lincoln College 484

Hanson, Richard, college rent collector 83

Harding, John, DTh, regius professor of Hebrew, president of Magdalen College 316, 356, 357–8

Harding, Thomas, DTh, regius professor of Hebrew, bishop of Winchester 36, 139, 316, 322, 345, 356, 357, 366, 368–9, 380, 407, 414

debate with Jewel 385–6

Hargrave, master 233

Harkes (Herks), Garbrand, Oxford bookseller 77, 443–4

wife defamed 662

Harley, John, MA, fellow of Magdalen College, bishop of Hereford 368

Harman, *alias* Veysey, John, DCL, DCnL, fellow of Magdalen College, bishop of Exeter 121

Harmar, John, BTh, fellow of University College, regius professor of Greek 315, 320 n. 4, 321, 354, 355, 429

Harper, Thomas, DTh, warden of Merton College 604

Harpesfield, John, DTh, fellow of New College, regius professor of Greek 324 n. 1, 345, 354–5

Harpsfield, Nichlas, DCL, fellow of New College 329, 394, 407

Harpur, Richard, of Derbyshire, benefactor of Brasenose College 15 n. 6

Harriot, Thomas, BA, scholar at St Mary's Hall 717, 731

Harrison, Robert, MA, fellow of Corpus Christi College 408

Harrison, William, MA, scholar at Christ Church 679 n. 2, 729

Hart, John, seminary priest 317, 387

Hartley, John, bailiff of Oxford 101

Hartley, William, of St John's College 381

Harvey, Gabriel 281, 713

Harvey, William 242, 247

Hastings, Sir Francis 331

Hastings, Henry, third earl of Huntingdon 331, 416, 437, 500, 502, 503

Hatley, John, chaplain of King Henry VIII College 131

Hatton, Sir Christopher, chancellor of Oxford University 292, 331, 336, 401, 420, 438

denounces disorders 432

enemy of puritans 431

Haward, Thomas, MA, donor to Christ Church library 502

Hawker, Henry, BA, commoner of Corpus Christi College 673

Hawkins, Christopher, brewer 101

Haynes, Edward, commoner at Corpus Christi College 674 n. 2

Haynes, John, mayor of Oxford 97

Heather, William 210

Hegendorff, Christian 314, 703

Hegge, Robert, MA, probationer fellow of Corpus Christi College 718

Hegisippus, reviser of Josephus (q.v) 704

Heidelberg, University of 177, 243, 395

Heidelberg Catechism 327, 388

Heiland, Samuel 175

Helyar, John, BTh, fellow of Corpus Christi College 302, 394

Hemming, John, MA, fellow of Oriel College 409

Heneage, Sir Thomas 439

Henry III, king of England 87

Henry V, king of England 84

Henry VII, king of England 9

Henry VIII, king of England (*see also* Christ Church) 42, 93, 94, 118, 124, 130, 132–3, 145, 164, 259, 263, 271, 280, 302, 307, 316, 320, 324, 325, 329, 330, 345, 365, 366, 376, 394, 533, 557–8, 615, 618, 620, 632, frontispiece

confirms university's privileges 121

interferes in choice of university's officers 149

royal divorce of and Oxford 90, 92, 125–6, 149, 154, 364

summons opinion from universities concerning Luther 123

supports Greek studies at Oxford 67

Henry, prince 571, 633

Henry, painter of Merton College chapel 602

Henry ab Ulmis 134

Henshaw, Henry, BTh, rector of Lincoln College 406

Herbert, Edward, first lord Herbert of Cherbury, gentleman commoner at University College 695–6, 697, 716

Herbert, William, third earl of Pembroke, chancellor of Oxford University 152

Hereford diocese of 204, 303, 352, 613

Herefordshire 12

Herks, Garbrand, *see* Harkes

Herleis, William, BCnL, BM 225

hermeticism 715

Hermogenes 172, 707 n. 7

Herne, Nicholas, builder 610

Herniman, John, MA, fellow of Oriel College 409

Herodian 316, 703 n. 6

Herodotus 710

Hert, Robert, MA, fellow of St John's College 208 n. 5, 632

Hesiod 22, 341, 703, 710

Hesse 301

Hethe, Michael, mayor of Oxford 98, 101, 110

Heton (Eaton), Martin, DTh, student of Christ Church 508

Heugh (Northumberland) 561

Hewes, Richard, alderman 108 n. 4

Hewes, Thomas, MD, fellow of the College of Physicians 230

Heyford ad Pontem (Oxon.) 578

Heywood, Jasper, MA, fellow of Merton College 378

Heywood, John, virginalist 210

Higden, John, DTh, president of Magdalen College, first dean of Cardinal College 88, 122, 659

Higford, William, BA, commoner at Corpus Christi College 673

Higgins, Edward, MA, fellow of Brasenose College 214 n. 1, 444 n. 2, 463, 471, 473

Highley, Robert, MA, fellow of Oriel College 471 n. 2

Hilary of Poitiers, St 313, 323, 385, 449 n. 3

Hill, John, BTh, student of Christ Church 512

Hillierd, John, MA, student of Christ Church 505, 515

Hilsey, John, OP, DTh 302

Hippocrates 213, 214, 216, 217, 220, 228, 230, 235, 241, 251, 340

Hiscock, W. G. 498

Hispanus, see Petrus Hispanus

Hodges, Thomas, inventory of 476

Hodgson, Hugh, MA, provost of Queen's College 406, 411

Holbeach, Henry, bishop of Lincon 137

Holcot, Robert 454, 707

Holdsworth, Christopher, BGramm 469

Holland, George, MA, fellow of Balliol College 632

inventory of goods of 471 n. 2, 633–4

Holland, Hugh, BCnL 268

Holland, Thomas, DTh, regius professor of theology, rector of Exeter College 315, 318, 352, 354, 632

Holm Cultram (Cumberland) 141

Holyman, John, DTh, fellow of New College, bishop of Bristol 301–2, 364

Holyngborne, Robert, OSB, warden of Canterbury College 464

Homer 22, 316, 341, 354, 449, 476, 702, 703 n. 6, 704, 710

Honeyfold, Gabriel, commoner at Corpus Christi College 674 n. 2

Hooker, John, commoner at Corpus Christi College 675 n. 5, 682–3

Hooker, John, MP, chamberlain of the city of Exeter 683

Hooker, Peter, BTh, fellow of Corpus Christi College 683

Hooker, Richard, MA, fellow of Corpus Christi College 322, 332, 333, 357, 392, 428, 430, 440, 683, 686 n. 2, 692, 725, 732

influence at Corpus Christi College 390–1

Hooker, Zacharias, BTh, fellow of Corpus Christi College 683

Hooknorton, Thomas, abbot of Oseney Abbey 599

Hooper, John, bishop of Gloucester 328, 329, 374, 376

Hoppey, Edward, MA, fellow of Lincoln College 456, 476, 484, 497

Horace 21, 61, 172, 467, 468, 699, 710

Hore, Thomas, murdered at Carfax 661

Horne, Robert, DTh, bishop of Winchester, as visitor 381, 406, 408–9, 416, 418, 657

Hothby, John 204

Hotman, Jean 289–90, 499, 505, 514

Hotomanus, see Hotman

Houllier, Jacques 222

Hovenden, Robert, DTh, warden of All Souls College 53 n. 1, 54 n. 4, 278, 389, 439, 440, 453, 539 n. 2, 618, plate XXIII

Howard, Thomas, fourth duke of Norfolk 399, 500, 502

Howberghe, William, Oxford tradesman 77

Howell, John, MD, fellow of the College of Physicians 233 n. 1

Howson, John, DTh, student of Christ Church 310 n. 1, 422, 433, 508, 511, 517

Hubbock, William, MA, fellow of Magdalen College 420

Huckmore, Charles 677

Huckmore, Gregory 677

Huckmore, William, commoner at Corpus Christi College 677

Huckvall, Robert, town clerk 84

Huggens, Thomas, master, donor to Christ Church library 502

Hugh of St Cher 313, 483

Hugh of Vienne, see Hugh of St Cher

Hughes, Thomas, clerk 517

Huick (Hicke), Robert, MD, fellow, of Merton College, fellow of the College of Physicians 131, 229, 233 n. 1, 492

Humfrey, duke of Gloucester 204, 465, 466

Humfrey, Laurence, DTh, regius professor of theology, president of Magdalen College 310 n. 1, 312, 315, 316, 317, 318, 319, 321, 322, 329, 331, 354, 384, 387, 390, 393,

404, 406, 409, 412, 430, 435, 437, 440, 451, 454, 658, 684, 698–9, 717, 725, 727, 732, plate XVIb
  approves of tennis 650
  charges against 418–19, 663
  named vice-chancellor by Leicester 425
  puritan leader in university 415–23
Hungerford, Henry, MA, fellow of Magdalen College 434
Hunsdon, Lord 439
Huntingdon, earl of, see Hastings, Henry
Hurdys, William, of Broadgates Hall, inventory of 471 n. 1, 472
Hus, John 364
Hutton, Leonard, DTh, student of Christ Church 506, 507
Hyperius, Andreas 327, 388, 704 n. 2

Iavellus, Chrysostomus, OP 177
Ibn Daud 317
Ibn Ezra 317
Ibn Husain (Johannitius) 222
Ignatius of Antioch, St 385
Illyricus, see Flacius, Matthias
Ingolstadt, university of 158, 174, 175
inns of court 667, 672, 722
  Gray's Inn 672, 673, 678 n. 2
  Inner Temple 9, 417, 673, 680
  Lincoln's Inn 234, 689, 710
  Middle Temple 417, 677, 680
Ipswich (Suffolk), Wolsey's college at 33
Ireland 360, 387
Irenaeus, St 302, 371, 449 nn. 3 and 4
Isaac, Liber februm 217
Isaac de Cardenas 316
Isidorus Hispalensis 202
Isocrates 22, 61, 316, 340, 354, 703 n. 6, 705
Ivery, Richard, fishmonger, will of 113
Ivory, John, MD, fellow of Magdalen College 434

Jackman, John, BM, fellow of Oriel College 226, 241, 254, 470, 471 n. 2
Jackman, Reginald, MA, student of Christ Church 471 n. 2
Jackson, Lionel, MA, fellow of Balliol College 474, 475
Jackson, Thomas, DTh, eleventh president of Corpus Christi College 333, 713
Jacob, Henry, MA, precentor of Corpus Christi College, sectary 684
Jakman, William, scholar at Hart Hall 53
James I, king of England 266, 326, 358, 422, 557

James IV, king of Scots 638
James, Edward, DTh, alumnus of Christ Church 510
James, Francis, BCL, regius professor nominate of civil law 265, 290, 358, 361
James, George, BM, junior Linacre lecturer 234
James, John, MA, alumnus of Christ Church 511 (see also following entry)
James, John, medical student 240
James, Thomas, DTh, fellow of New College, Bodley's first librarian 323, 446–7
James, William, DTh, dean of Christ Church, bishop of Durham 328, 423, 429, 433, 435–8, 509
Jayne, Sears 475
Jenks, Roland, Oxford bookseller 77, 413
Jerome, St 302, 303, 448, 449, 450, 462
Jessop, Thomas, MD, junior Linacre lecturer 223, 254
Jesuit Order 51 n. 4, 312, 378, 383, 387, 393, 412, 413, 420, 433, 436
Jewel, John, DTh, reader in humanity at Corpus Christi College, bishop of Salisbury 139, 141, 142, 310 n. 1, 311, 316, 318, 320, 322, 327, 329, 332, 357, 369, 371, 375, 380, 383, 384, 389, 405, 447, 658, 679 n. 2, 686 n. 3, 692, 697
  debate with Harding 385–6
  library of 451–2, 470
Joannes de Villa Garcia, see Juan
Johannes de Muris 204, 205
Johannes de Sacro Bosco, see John of Holywood
Johannes grammaticus 707 n. 7
John, duke of Bedford 306
John ab Ulmis (Johann Ulmer) 40–1, 134, 231, 232, 318
John de Coloribus, DTh, OP 304, 329
John of Damascus, St 313, 449 n. 3
John of Holywood 161, 172, 174
John of Jandun 222
Johnson, John, surgeon 225
Johnson, William, master mason 612
Jones, John, MA, fellow of St John's College 381
Jones, Leander, of St John's College 381
Jones, Richard, MA, donor to Christ Church library 507
Jones, Robert, BMus 207
Jones, Robert, sexton 470 n. 3
Jones, Roger, BCL, fellow of New College 402–3, 430
Jones, William, DCL 281 n. 5

Jonson, Ben 687
Jonys, John, BA, fellow of Lincoln College 486
Jordan, W. K. 546
Josephus, Flavius 449 n. 3, 460, 468, 698, 704
Joubert, Laurent 253
Juan de Villa Garcia, DTh, regius professor of theology 145, 325, 353, 378, 379
Juckes, Simon, DTh, alumnus of Christ Church 510
Julius II, pope 57
Julius Pacius 711
Julius Pollux 703 n. 6
Justinian 261, 292
    corpus iuris of 263, 340, 358
Justin Martyr 710
Justinus historicus 702
Juvenal 21

Kempe, Thomas, BTh, bishop of London, archbishop of Canterbury 598, 603
Kennall, John, DCL, dean of Christ Church 323 n. 1, 398, 401
Kent 12, 670, 673, 684, 728
Kepler, Johannes 719
Ker, Neil R. 620
    Lyell lecture 448
    Sandars lectures 441, 460
Ketyl, John, innkeeper 101 n. 5
Key, Thomas, MA, registrar, master of University College 555 n. 2, 625, 627
    inventory of goods 635–41
Keynsham, Robert, bedell 108 n. 4
Kiblewhyte, Roger, MA, fellow of St John's College 471
Kilbye, Richard, DTh, regius professor of Hebrew 316, 317
Kimchi, David 317
Kimchi, Moses 317
King, John, DTh, student of Christ Church 506
Kingsmill, Andrew, BA, fellow of All Souls College 384, 452
Kingsmill, Edward, scholar of Corpus Christi College 680
Kingsmill, Francis, commoner at Corpus Christi College 680
Kingsmill, Thomas, BTh, regius professor of Hebrew 56, 356, 357, 428, 430, 686 n. 2, 699
Kingston, John, OFM, DTh, praelector in theology at Magdalen College, Lady Margaret Professor 329, 350–1
Kirkham, Edward 436

Kitchen, John, manciple of Oriel College 470 n. 3
Kitson (Kytson), John, MA, fellow of Balliol College 467 n. 3
Knighton, C. S. 353, 357, 359
Knollys, Sir Francis 393, 437, 662 n. 4
Knox, John 32
Kratzer, Nicolaus, MA, lecturer in astronomy 220, 338–9
Kyghtley, Eustacius, MA, student of Christ Church 507
Kyng, John, servant 103 n. 2
Kyrton, Thomas, BTh, fellow of Corpus Christi College 462 n. 1

Lacy, Dunstan, MA, fellow of Lincoln College 476
Laguna, Andrès de 254
Lake, Arthur, DTh, warden of New College, bishop of Bath and Wells 320 n. 4, 697
Lambard, Nicholas, fellow of Magdalen College 418
Lambarde, William 500, 503, 504, 513, plate XII a
Lambert, Francis 314, 364
Lambert of Auxerre 177
Lambeth 374
Lambeth articles 331, 333
Lancashire 12, 13, 670
    Oxford-trained clergy in 391
Lancaster, duchy of 538
Lancaster (Lancs.) 670
Langbaine, Gerard, university archivist 466
Langford, John, DCL, fellow of All Souls College 259–90
Langland, William 706
Langley, John, chandler 109 n. 1
Langley, Richard, grocer 102
Langley, William 101
Langton, Robert, DCL, fellow of Queen's College 604
Lant, Bartholomew, organist of Christ Church 82
Lant, John, MA, student of Christ Church 510
Lant, Richard, singingman at Christ Church 470 n. 3
Lant, William 239
Lapworth, Michael, BM, fellow of All Souls College 239, 241
Larke, master 434
Lassellis, John, BM, licensed to practise 225
Latewarr, Richard, DTh, fellow of St John's College 313, 331

Latimer, Hugh, bishop of Worcester 279, 312
trial of 142–3, 302, 328, 330, 375, 376, 398
Latimer, William, Greek scholar 68 n. 3, 304
Laton, Thomas, scholar of White Hall 53
Laud, William, DTh, chancellor of Oxford University, archbishop of Canterbury 151–2, 307, 315, 330, 331, 333, 334, 381, 404, 530--1, 551, 730
Laurens, André du 253
Lavater 452
Lawney, Thomas 364
Lawrence, Giles, BCL, fellow of All Souls College, regius professor of Greek 36, 281, 314–15, 320, 354 n. 1, 355, 686 n. 2
Lawrence, John, scholar of Christ Church, vicar of Rainham 504, 512, 514
Lawton, David, BM 232 n. 1, 233
Layton, Richard, DCL, king's visitor to Oxford University 128, 365
Lea, William, BCL, inventory 471 n. 2
Leche, James, MA, fellow of Merton College 451, 453
Leche, Robert, lecturer in music 205
Lee, Edward, archbishop of York 328
Lee, Roland, DCL, president of the council of Wales and of the Marches 270
Lee, Thomas, BM, fellow of Magdalen College 225, 239
Leech, Humfrey, MA, chaplain of Christ Church 323
Leech, James, MA, fellow of Merton College 410, 495, 497
Lefèvre d'Étaples 61, 705 n. 1
Leibniz 715
Leicester, earl of, see Dudley
Leicester (Leics.), church library 500
Leiden, University of 255, 684
Leipzig, University of 174
Leland, John, BA, antiquary 316, 465, 703
Lence, Stephen, MA, student of Christ Church 504, 512, 518
Lever, Thomas 646, 648, 679 n. 2
Levi ben Gershon Abarbanel 317
Levins, William, apothecary 107 n. 3
Lewes, David, DCL, judge of the supreme court of admiralty 518
Lewes, Felix, DCL, principal of New Inn Hall 265, 277, 288
Lewis, John, white-baker and manciple of University College 79, 470 n. 3
Lewis, Richard, manciple of University College 470 n. 3
Lewisham (Middx.) 438
Leynham, Sir John 603

Leyowse (Lewis), Richard, builder 610
Libavius, Andreas 254
Libellus sophistarum 176
Liblerus (Lieblerus), Georgius 175
Liddell, J. R. 459
Lightfoot, John, discipulus at Corpus Christi College 689
Lightfoot, Thomas, chorister and discipulus at Corpus Christi College 689
Lilley, Edmund, DTh, master of Balliol College 423
Lily, John 435
Lily, William, master of St Paul's School 337
Limiter, Stephen, MA, fellow of All Souls College 468–9
Linacre, Thomas, MD 174, 219, 238, 242, 254, 516, 707 n. 7
grammar 172, 699
Linacre lectures, see faculty of medicine
Lincoln (Lincs.) 687, 724
bishop as visitor 404, 411–12
diocese of 9, 105, 121, 337, 599
Lincolnshire 670
Lindley (Lynley), Thomas, DTh, fellow of Merton College, lecturer in theology at Magdalen College 602
Lipomanus, Ludovicus 454
Litchfield, Richard, DCL, DCnL, principal of the civil law school, canon of Salisbury 599
Litcott, Christopher, scholar of Corpus Christi College 678
Little Barrington (Glos.) 609
Livy (Titus Livius) 44, 58, 699, 702, 712
Lloide, Richard, MA, student of Christ Church 507
Lloyd, Griffith, DCL, regius professor of civil law, principal of Jesus College 265, 266, 289, 358, 360
Llwyd, Humphrey, of Denbigh 248
Logan, F. D. 335
Loggan, David, artist and engraver 607, 629
Lollardy 395
Lombard, Peter 22, 129, 161, 296–300, 308, 314, 365, 702, 707
London, John, DTh, warden of New College 52, 91, 126, 131, 262, 363, 617
London 12, 83, 91, 92, 119, 142, 209, 226, 233, 236, 238, 242, 246, 248, 326, 336, 361, 372, 393, 417, 419, 430, 436, 438, 559, 561, 566, 568, 646, 688, 697, 709, 711, 718, 721
booksellers 442
diocese of 312, 352, 355, 359

London (cont.)
  humanists 159
  undergraduates from, at Corpus Christi College 671-4, 681, 683
  see also St Paul's, St Paul's Cross
Long Benton (Northumberland) 561, 564-7, 571, 573
Longland, John, DTh, chancellor of Oxford University, bishop of Lincoln 11, 14, 88 n. 3, 121, 125, 328, 459, 485
  death 133
  high steward of Oxford 130
  royal supremacy and 127
  succeeds Warham 126
Longolius (Christophe de Longueil) 515
Long Wittenham (Berks.) 77
Lonicerus Johannes 222
Lord, Edward 418
Lorgan, Richard, DTh, lecturer in theology at Magdalen College, Lady Margaret Professor 351
Loudell, Thomas 517
Lougher, Robert, DCL, regius professor of civil law, principal of Jesus College 264-5, 288-9, 358, 360
Louvain, University of 17, 68, 304, 322, 332, 357, 359, 381, 386, 394-5, 412, 415
  trilingual college at 29, 316, 394
Lower Heyford (Oxon.) 625
Lowthe, John, BA, fellow of New College 366
Loyseleur 326
Lubyns, John, master mason 612
Lucan 21, 179, 467
Lucian 22, 340, 702, 703
Lucy, Thomas 500, 502
Ludford, Simon, MD 232, 234
Lumleian lecturership 245
Lumley, John, baron 245, 248
Lupset, Thomas, Wolsey's reader in humanity 26, 220, 242, 254, 321, 338-9, 688
Luther, Martin; Lutheranism 31-2, 56, 123-4, 131, 149, 157, 303, 304, 310, 314, 324-5, 329, 330, 338, 350, 351, 363, 364, 374, 394, 417, 704, 730
Lye, Richard, manciple of Lincoln College 470 n. 3
Lyhart, Walter, DTh, fellow of Exeter College, bishop of Norwich 599
Lynch, Stephen, MA, fellow of All Souls College 471 n. 2
Lynche, family at Corpus Christi College 671
Lynde, Humphrey, BA, alumnus of Christ Church 509
Lyre see Nicholas of Lyra

Lysiman, George, matriculant of Danzig at Corpus Christi College 690 n. 5

Machiavelli 715
McNair, P. M. 369
Macrobius 703
Magdeburg Centuries 451, 452 and n.4
Maisemore (Glos.) 689
Major, John 707
Man, Henry, MA, scholar of Corpus Christi College, bishop of Sodor and Man 686 n. 3
Man, William, commoner at Corpus Christi College 690 n. 4
Manardus, Giovanni 248, 249, 449
Mann, John, DCL, fellow of New College, principal of White Hall 53
Mann, John, MA, fellow of New College, warden of Merton College 410-11
Manutius, Paulus 711
Marbecke, Anne née Williams 113
Marbecke, John, DMus 207
Marbecke, Roger, MD, provost of Oriel College 113, 243, 398
Marburg, University of 388
Marckland, Richard, commoner at Brasenose College 694 n. 2
Market Rasen (Lincs.) 684
Marloratus, Augustin 451
Marprelate tracts 330, 332
Marshall, Richard, DTh, dean of Christ Church 131, 144, 375, 406, 686 n. 2
  census of 1552: 49, 153
  deprived 409
Marshall, William, BCL, fellow of Merton College 241, 457 n. 5, 493, 494
Marsilius von Inghen 160
Martial, John, MA, fellow of New College 384, 386
Martial, Marcus Valerius 467, 468
Martial, William, BCL, fellow of Merton College 454, 462
Martianus Capella 202
Martin, Anthony, BA, fellow of Corpus Christi College 516-17
Martin, Edward, BTh, lecturer at Corpus Christi College 25
Martin, Gregory, MA, lecturer in Greek at St John's College 317, 320, 329, 378
Martin, Richard, MA, scholar at Broadgates Hall 507
Martin, Thomas 312
Martinius, Petrus 317
Martock, John, BM, fellow of Merton College 602

Martyn, John, *alias* Clerke, schoolmaster 109 n. 1

Martyr, Peter, regius professor of theology 36, 40, 41, 136, 145, 302, 310 n. 1, 315, 316, 322, 328, 329, 336, 352, 353, 379, 380, 383, 405, 452, 453, 699, 704, 727
  arrives in Oxford 134
  declines to return 383
  Italian teaching 134
  leaves Oxford 141
  lectures 134–5, 318–19, 369–74
  persistent opposition to 138
  wife of 147, 369, 374

Marven, Edmund, MA, dean of Corpus Christi College 131

Mary I, Tudor, queen of England 2, 42, 49, 62, 93, 117, 142, 207, 210, 264, 273, 301, 302, 303, 324, 325, 329, 349, 355, 359, 364, 365, 367, 375, 376, 394, 405, 466, 471, 620, 731
  and death of Cranmer 377
  coronation of 689
  fortunes of university revive under 140–1, 148–9, 232–3, 377–8, 396, 533, 550, 556

Mason, Francis, BTh, city lecturer 107, 313

Mason, Roger, scholar of London College 471 n. 3

Mason, Sir John, BM, chancellor of Oxford University 147, 225, 229, 231, 232, 247, 401, 423, 424, 435

Massey, John, BCL 268–9

Master, Richard, MD, fellow of the College of Physicians 229, 233

Mathew, Toby, DTh, student of Christ Church, president of St John's College 291, 399, 444, 461, 470, 499, 504, 506, 514, 516

Maxey, Emmanuel, MA, student of Christ Church 505

Mayew, Richard, president of Magdalen College 4

Maynard, Henry, secretary to Cecil 435

Maynus, Jason 474

Medford, Peter, MA, fellow of University College 641

Meibom, Marcus 204

Mela, Pomponius 172, 716

Melanchthon, Philip 157, 174, 175, 179, 314, 363, 364, 698, 700, 702, 703 n. 6, 705, 707
  Dialectics 41
  Institutiones rhetoricae 703

Mercator, Gerardus, maps of 639

Mercers' Company 313

Merchant Adventurers 416

Merchant Taylors 45, 46, 630
  school of 46, 664, 687, 723

Mere, John, registrar of Cambridge University 145

Meredith, Jonas, BA, fellow of St John's College 387

Meredyth, Richard, fellow of New College 452, 453 n. 4

Merick, William, DCL 281 n. 4

Mericke, Edward, BCL, archdeacon of Bangor 276

Merton, Walter de, bishop of Rochester, founder of Merton College 618

Mervyn, George, scholar of New Inn Hall 437 n. 6, 474–5

Mesue 254

Michel, John, MA, fellow of Lincoln College 486

Middelburg, Zealand 420, 684

Middlesex 671

Millenary Petition 422

Milles, Francis, MA, fellow of Merton College 446–7

Milling, John, BA, fellow of Magdalen College 437

Millward, Henry, Oxford stationer 77, 79

Millyng, Hugh, DTh, fellow of Exeter College 475

Milton (Oxon.) 578

Mitchell, William, BTh, fellow of Queen's College, inventory of 214, 315, 471 473

Mizaldus, Antonius 248

Mollond, Simon, BTh, fellow of Merton College 603

monastries, dissolution of 129, 131

Mondino de' Luzzi 230

Mondy, George, mercer 80

Monmouthshire 696 n. 3

Montague, Richard, bishop of Norwich 333

Montanus, *see* da Monte

Montpellier, University of 216, 220, 237, 247, 249, 253, 254, 255, 256

Moorcroft, Ferdinand, MA, alumnus of Christ Church 510

Morcott, John, MA, fellow of Magdalen College 472, 474

Mordaunt, John, lord 680

More, George, MA, commoner at Corpus Christi College 673, 709

More, John, scholar at Broadgates Hall 53

More, Robert, BA, commoner at Corpus Christi College 673

More, Robert, carpenter 611

More, Sir Thomas, high steward of Oxford University, lord chancellor of England 43, 90, 131, 176, 302, 337–8, 394, 703, 704
supports Greek studies at Oxford 67, 120–1, 314

More, William, MA, rector of Exeter College 142

More, Sir William 673

Moreman, John, DTh, fellow of Exeter College 364

Moreton (Oxon.) 560, 564, 570, 571

Morey, Thomas, donor to Christ Church library 499

Morgan, see Phillips

Morley, Thomas, BMus 203, 207, 211

Morone, Giovanni, cardinal 379

Morrison, Richard 137

Mortimer, Edward, city chamberlain 83

Mortimer, William, DTh, fellow of De Vaux College, Lady Margaret Professor 351, 364

Morton, John, DCL, chancellor of Oxford University, bishop of Ely, cardinal, archbishop of Canterbury 9, 599

Morus, Horatius 243, 245

Morwent, Robert, MA, second president of Corpus Christi College 139, 146, 374, 675

Morwent, Roger, carpenter 611

Mosan, James, commoner at Corpus Christi College 674

Mosgroff, Thomas, BTh, MD, lecturer in astronomy at Merton College, Wolsey's reader in medicine 220, 224, 301, 338–9, 343

Mosse, Willaim, DCL 264, 287

Mountjoy, Charles 388

Mowsehurst, Robert, BCL, recusant at Broadgates Hall 413

Mucklestone, Richard, BA, fellow of Oriel College 409

Mugge, Lewis, discipulus and extramural pupil at Corpus Christi College 690 n. 3

Mulcaster, William 650

Mulliner, Thomas, organist, cleric at Corpus Christi College 209, 688

Munday, John 207

Mundy, William, composer 210

Munster, Sebastian 317

Munster, Thomas 703

Murday, Thomas, butcher 649

Musculus, Wolfgang 451

Mychell, John, servant to Dr Bayley 470 n. 3

Mylward, Henry, stationer at Oxford 634

Napier, Richard, commoner at Exeter College 244

Napper (Napier), George, discipulus at Corpus Christi College 686

Napper, William, BA, probationer fellow of Corpus Christi College 705–6, 725

Neale, John, MA, rector of Exeter College 411

Neale, Thomas, BTh, regius professor of Hebrew 357, 382, 414, plate I

Negose, William, MA, alumnus of Christ Church 510

Nele, William, MA, fellow of Merton College 604

Nestorius 371

Nethercot (Tackley, Oxon) 560, 564, 567, 569, 570, 571

Neville, Gervase, BTh, fellow of Corpus Christi College 687

Nevinson, Christopher 137

Newbury (Berks.) 377

Newman, G. 435

Newton, Sir Isaac 715

Newton Arlock (Cumberland) 141

Nicholas, Antidotarium 217

Nicholas de Burgo, OFM, DTh, lecturer at Cardinal College 32, 304, 341, 342

Nicholas of Lyra 313, 474

Nicholson, James 618

Nicholson, Richard, BMus 207

Nicomachus of Gerasa 201

Nifo, Agostino 707

Nipho, Fabian, MD 239–40

Noble, William, alderman 113

Nonsuch palace 613

Norfolk, duke of, see Howard, Thomas, fourth duke

Norris, master 239

Norris, Sir Henry, first baron 437

North, Roger 500, 502

North Marden (Sussex) 682

North Morton (Berks.) 563

Northampton (Northants) 111, 688

Northamptonshire, puritan ministers of 392, 419

Northumberland, duke of see Dudley, John

Norton, John, MA, fellow of Corpus Christi College 675

Norwich, diocese of 355

Nowell, Alexander, DTh, fellow of Brasenose College, dean of St Paul's 327, 328, 367, 388, 629, 704, 724–5

Nowell, Laurence, BA, scholar of Christ Church 472 n. 3, 513, plate XIIa

Nowell, Laurence, MA, dean of Lichfield 380, 383, 513
Nowell, Robert 513, 724–5, 728, 729
Nun of Kent, see Barton, Elizabeth
Nuneaton (War.) 302

Ockham, see William of Ockham
Oddington (Oxon.) 560, 564, 567, 569, 570–1
Oecolampadius 314, 364, 451
Oecumenius 450
Oglethorpe, Owen, DTh, president of Magdalen College 134, 139, 142, 375
Oldham, Hugh, bishop of Exeter 18, 19, 328, 544, 670
Olevarius, Caspar 388
Optatus, St 449 n. 3
Orchard, William, master mason 607
Orchard of Syon 9
Orientus, Finei 172, 174
Origen 303, 313, 321, 449 nn. 3 and 4, 474, 704
Ormanet, Nicholas, secretary to Reginald Pole 146, 379
Orson, Edmund, MA, fellow of Corpus Christi College 682
Orson, Mary 682
Orson, Nathaniel 682
Orson, William, BTh, fellow of Corpus Christi College 682
Ortelius, Abraham, map of the world 639
Osborne, John, MD 255
Oseney abbey 70, 105, 345, 597, 599, 607, map 1
Oseney cathedral, see Oxford, diocese of
Oseney meadow 82
Ovid 21, 467, 468, 702, 710
Owen, George, MD, fellow of Merton College, royal physician 223 n. 1, 224, 229, 238–9, 243, 247, 248
Owen, Griffin, MA, alumnus of Christ Church 509
Oxenbridge, John, MA, student of Christ Church 312, 509
Oxford, churches
  All Saints 71, 105, maps 1 and 3
  St Aldate 560, 650, maps 1 and 3
  St Cross chapel 105, maps 1 and 3
  St Ebbe 71, 560, maps 1 and 3
  St Edward 598, map 1
  St Giles 70, 71, 106, 560
  St John the Baptist 105, map 1
  St Martin 71, 107, 313, 389, maps 1 and 3
  St Mary Magdalen 70, 71, 105, 366, 475, 560, 562, maps 1 and 3

  St Mary the Virgin 70, 105, 107, 111, 118, 134, 136, 194, 350, 376, 389, 560, 599, maps 1, 2 and 3
    Austin disputations at 190
    sermons ad clerum in 296, 311
  St Michael at the north gate 71, 105, maps 1 and 3
  St Michael at the south gate 105, map 1
  St Mildred 105
  St Peter in the bailey 71, 560, maps 1 and 3
  St Peter in the east 71, 105, 124, 603, maps 1 and 3
    sermons ad clerum in 311
  St Thomas 105, map 1
Oxford, clergy of 106
Oxford, diocese of 32, 359, 360, 531
  Christ Church cathedral 33, 37, 132, 224, 345–6, 531, map 3
    sermons ad clerum in 311
  Oseney cathedral 32, 33, 210, 380
Oxford, suburbs
  Bullingdon Hundred 70
  Binsey 109
  Grandpont 70
  Headington 560, 605, 610
  Holywell 71, 107, maps 1 and 3
    Holywell Manor 70, 686, map 3; see also Napper, George
  Northgate Hundred 70
  St Clements 70
  St Thomas's 70
  Shotover, royal forest of 651
  Wolvercote 397
    chapel 105
Oxford, town and city 1, 69–116
  Blue Boar Lane 598
  booksellers and stationers 77, 443–4
  borough 69–74, 87
  Carfax 69, 313, 398, 661
  Catherine Wheel public house 395
  charter of incorporation 73
  Cheyney Lane 615
  common council 73, 82, 105, 112
  Cornmarket 70
  education 108–14
  guild merchant 73, 87
  guilds 71, 72, 77, 81–2, 95–9, 102
    and Wolsey's charter 89
  hanasters 73
  High Street 70, 606, maps 1, 2 and 3
  industrial organization 94–9
  lay subsidies 70–1, 75
  lecturerships 106–8, 313
  lodgers 2, 48, 50, 111–14

Oxford, town and city (*cont.*)
　　Magdalen Street 70
　　mayor 143
　　mayor's council 73, 74, 366
　　Merton Street tennis court 650
　　New Inn Hall Street 605
　　North Gate 627, maps 1 and 3
　　officers *see also* mayor 73
　　poll tax 70
　　population 70–1
　　prison (Bocardo) 144, map 3
　　privileged persons 74–86, 95, 105, 112, 114
　　public safety and health 103–5
　　reformatio pacis (1290) 74, 83–4
　　religious life 105–8
　　St Aldates Street 70
　　St Giles 108, map 1
　　St Mildred's Lane 70
　　Schools Street 16, 599, 606, maps 1 and 2
　　size 69–70
　　Smith Gate 649, maps 2 and 3
　　Somenor's Lane 615
　　Turl Street 70
Oxford, trades
　　barbers 81, 82, 95
　　book trade 76–7
　　brewers 72–3, 76, 79, 80, 95–6, 98, 99, 102
　　brown-bakers 72, 81, 95, 98
　　builders 72, 76, 83
　　butchers 72, 648–9
　　cappers 81, 82, 95
　　chandlers 72, 81, 97
　　collegiate rent-collectors 83, 85
　　cooks 80–2, 95, 103
　　cordwainers, *see* shoemakers
　　drapers 72, 80
　　fishmongers 72
　　fullers 71
　　glovers 72, 82, 97
　　grocers 72
　　innkeepers 72
　　mercers 72, 80
　　musicians 82
　　scholars' servants 83–6, 102
　　shoemakers 72, 97
　　skinners 95
　　tailors 72, 80, 84, 95, 96–7, 98, 99, 102, 112
　　tanners 72
　　vintners 72
　　weavers 71
　　white-bakers 72, 79, 81, 95–6, 98, 99
Oxford, University of
　　academic exercises (*see also* lectures)
　　　　circuitus 197, 727

　　comitia ('the act') 197–8, 273, 296, 310;
　　　　terrae filius at 197
　　declamation 30, 54, 60, 66, 193–4, 341,
　　　　693, 709–11
　　determinationes 170, 181–4, 727; dispen-
　　　　sations from 182, 186, 305
　　disputations, bachelors' 13, 15, 24, 58, 171,
　　　　181–3, 308–10; at royal visits 398–400;
　　　　Austins 190–1; *collectores* 191; incep-
　　　　tors 197; in colleges and halls 3, 5, 6,
　　　　13, 15, 19, 24, 34, 38, 40, 44, 54, 58, 60,
　　　　61, 64, 66, 137, 138, 693, 695, 709–11;
　　　　in parviso 23, 168–70; neglect of 427;
　　　　on the eucharist 135, 136–7, 143;
　　　　ordinary 191–3; visitation of 1556: 147
　　examinations 65, 341, 346
　　inception 6, 184, 197–8, 727
　　incorporation, fees at 727
　　reform of 426–7
　　responsions 170
　　sophista generalis 169
　　statute of 1584: 427
　　variatio 170
academic halls, general 2, 48, 50, 51–5, 66
　　academic exercises in 3, 16, 51–5, 66,
　　　　269–70
　　accommodation 2, 52–5; decline in legist
　　　　halls 277; segregation of lawyers and
　　　　artists 161
　　centres of clandestine literature 382
　　declining numbers 52–3, 55, 140, 153,
　　　　522, 598
　　discipline in 54
　　finances 556
　　Greek taught in 54–5
　　libraries 54 n. 3
　　principals 2, 48–9, 53–4, 112, 327
　　protestantism in 124
　　religious observance 54
　　visitation of 52, 54, 278
academic halls, individual
　　Alban Hall 54, 131, 216, 301, 327, 353
　　Beam Hall 675
　　Bedel Hall 350, map 2
　　Beef Hall 110
　　Black Hall 16, map 2
　　Brasenose Hall 7, 10, 16, 606, map 2
　　Broadgates Hall 40, 52, 77, 285, 287,
　　　　359, 413, 629, 649, 663, 717, map 3;
　　　　Carnsew brothers at 697–701;
　　　　Christmas plays 53
　　Burnell's Inn 54
　　Edward Hall 52 n. 5
　　Glasen Hall 16, map 2

Gloucester Hall 214, 240, 278, 326, 469, 615, map 3; recusancy at 52, 381–2, 413; scientific circle at 717–18
Great Bedell Hall 54
Great Black Hall 54
Great White Hall 615
Hart Hall 52, 53, 54, 259–60, 326, 357, maps 2 and 3; recusancy at 382, 413
Hinksey Hall 285, 359
Lawrence Hall 52 n. 5
Little St Edmund Hall 606
Little University Hall 10, 606, 625, map 2
Little White Hall 615
Magdalen Hall 52, 350, 404, 556, map 3
New Inn Hall 52, 53, 70, 101, 264, 268, 277, 288, 360, map 3; visitation of 1575: 54
Peckwater Inn 52 n. 5, 89 n. 4, 615, 629, map 3
St Alban Hall 52, 54, 630, map 3
St Edmund Hall 52, 556, map 3
St George Hall 350
St Mary Hall 52, 326, 351, maps 2 and 3
Salissury Hall 350, map 2
Staple Hall 16, 606, map 2
Trillock's Inn 54
Vine Hall 52 n. 5, 53, 54
White Hall 52, 53, 724
act of incorporation (1571) 93, 99
Agas's map xi, 598, 675, map 3
apparel of members 426–7, 433, 716
bachelors 113, 166
Blackfriars' convent (Dominican Friars) 649, maps 1 and 3
Bocardo, see Oxford town and city: prison
botanical garden 256, 551
catechists 326–7
catholics and catholicism (see also relations with the state) 51 n. 4, 52, 126, 130–1, 135, 314, 321–2, 324–5, 326, 329, 332, 387, 389, 391, 422, plate XXIb
achievements of Marian university 378–82, 393
deprivations under Edward VI: 138–9, 374
Dominican convent re-established 365, 378
Elizabethan purge of 394–5, 406–14; at New College 407–8
executions of in Oxford 51 n. 4, 381
fate of 414–15, 427–8, 440
presence in town and country 395, 718
religious census of 1577: 413

return of university to catholic allegiance 142–3, 148, 375–80
riots of 1551: 139
tutors 382–3
census of 1552: 49, 57: of 1572: 58, 59, 60
chancellor, vice-chancellor (commissary) 9, 11, 28, 40, 49, 52, 53, 67, 84, 87, 96, 98, 112, 117, 122, 124, 132–3, 140, 149, 277, 309, 310, 311, 312, 399, 421, 422, 440, 725
accounts 550–1
as justices of the peace 121
Cox 113–19
Hatton and Buckhurst 431–4
Leicester 423–31
may absolve from perjury 151
non-resident 118
office and powers 401–3
terms of commissary shortened 423
chancellor's (vice-chancellor's) court 81, 85, 95, 99, 100–3, 112, 413, 649, 661, 701–8
jurisdiction 100–1, 402, plate XXI a
library inventories 470–6, 701 ff.
colleges, general (see also monastic colleges) 1, 2, 6–7, 64–8, 105, 122, 133, 404
accommodation 548, 597–641, 645–8
accounts 524–9
battels 79
benefactions 15, 544–5
buildings 11, 18, 548, 597–641
chantry legislation 366
commoners in 7, 11, 548–9, 669–75; discipline of 663
corn rent act 431, 535–7
corporate life 168, 645–52
discipline 18, 23, 168, 652–5; see also scrutiny
elections, statute concerning 432
endowments 60 n. 6, 128, 523–4, 559; evaluated for Henry VIII: 133
entry fines 524, 527–8, 534–5
finances 521–58
heads of 49, 112, 118, 122, 124, 125, 133, 148–9, 327, 340, 346, 422, 426, 531; government interference in election 374; growing authority of 402–3, 730; lodgings of 623–7; ordered to adopt old statutes 140; pay for remodelling of schools 600; vice-chancellor chosen from 402
leases appropriated 430–1, 438–9
leases and rents 525, 534–44, plate XXIV
manciples 78–80

Oxford, University of (*cont.*)
  Colleges, general (*cont.*)
    public lectures in 5, 14–15, 21–3, 25 n. 4,
      30, 32, 34–5, 37, 55, 61, 67–8; and royal
      visitation of 1535: 128
    religious conformity enforced in 406–12,
      416
    royal visit, contributions to 523
    scrutiny 39, 653–7
    secular 1, 3, 30
    servants 77–83
    spending 545–8
    supervise degree applications 6–7, 171
    support Henry VIII's lectures 130, 342–3
    teaching arrangements (*see also* individual
      colleges) 152, 167–8, 180, 187–8, 189,
      194, 199, 215–16, 226, 278–9, 305–10,
      693–721; developments of 3–48, 188,
      199; in medieval foundations 55–64;
      relation to growth in numbers 64–8;
      tutorial teaching (*see also* under-
      graduates: tutors) 180, 529, 549
    tutors, *see* undergraduates: tutors
    undergraduates in 1–68, 666–92
    visitors 404–5
  colleges, individual
    All Souls College 4, 66, 77, 78, 79, 80,
      110, 131, 204, 205, 210, 215, 222, 229,
      260, 265, 273, 277, 280, 281, 282, 296,
      327, 342, 343, 355, 360, 404, 526, 529,
      536–40, 543, 545–6, 547, 549, 597, 604,
      611, 615, 624–5, 628, 630, 631, plates
      X, XXIII, XXIV, maps 1, 2 and 3;
      income 60 n. 6, 550; lectures in civil
      law 63; (in Greek 63; in natural philo-
      sophy 63); library 204, 230, 248, 254,
      323, 441, 443, 445–6, 447, 448, 449,
      453, 455–6, 458, 459, 468, 476, 621;
      links with Jesus College 64; numbers at
      62–3, 66, 140; proposed as college of
      civilians 137, 272; rector of theology
      63; recusants 413; successfully resists
      queen's demands 439; teaching
      arrangements 63–4; visitations of 1535
      and 1556: 128, 147; visitor's letters to
      530–1, 729; warden 327, 340
    Balliol College 59, 60, 65, 70, 143, 215,
      351, 354, 409, 415, 524, 531, 536, 545,
      549, 585, 597, 604, 609, 610, 619, 620,
      624, 660, maps 1 and 3; benefactions
      562–3; Burnell's Inn 54, 559; cheated
      by Wolsey 559; commoners 57–8, 529
      n. 2, 548–9, 556; dialectic lecture 57,
      562; Dolphin Inn 559; enforcement of

    conformity 412–13; fines 568–70;
      Greek lecture 57, 562; Hammond's
      Lodging (Fisher's Building) 632–3;
      library 445, 448, 476; location of
      properties 559–62; master 340, 404,
      561; numbers at 57, 62–3, 631; poverty
      of 525, 550, 559, 723–4; property and
      finances 559–73; rental income 564–8;
      rhetoric lecture 57, 562; statutes
      revised by Richard Fox 57, 58, 65, 66;
      tutors 57, 58
    Brasenose College 2, 7–17, 48, 52, 83,
      147, 215, 231, 245, 298, 367, 391, 404,
      597, 600, 605, 608, 609, 618, 619, 628,
      629, 650, 668, 705, 730, plate Ib, maps
      2 and 3; absorption of halls 16, 53;
      assisted by Mary Tudor 377; building
      of 605–7; discipline 654, Greek lecture
      15, 17; library 458–9, 463; numbers at
      11–12, 140, 556, 631; principal 340,
      624, 626; statutes 10; tutors 13, 694,
      plate XXIa
    Canterbury College 17, 56, 126, 301,
      304, 365, 597, 608, 615, 617, 624,
      maps 1 and 3; library 463–5; protes-
      tant opinion in 131; William Latimer
      at 68 n. 3
    Cardinal College 2, 32, 33, 34, 35, 39, 42,
      70, 78, 88–9, 105, 301, 309, 314, 316,
      320, 326–7, 329, 336, 345, 380, 523,
      559, 597, 600, 605, 615, 618, 624, 630,
      654, 730, frontispiece; building of
      611–15; choristers 209–10; creansers
      31; foundation 31, 91, 122; Greek
      teaching 30, 32; humanistic aims 30;
      inspiration for 29–30, 394; law and
      medicine 30, 32, 220, 340; library 31;
      Lutheranism at 123–4, 363–4, 367;
      public professors 30, 32, 122, 220, 307,
      339–41; statutes 220, 302; tennis court
      650
    Christ Church (*see also* Broadgates Hall)
      2, 17, 31, 32–42, 44, 48, 56, 65, 81, 82,
      86, 105, 114, 141, 142, 167, 205, 215,
      231, 245, 260, 296, 353, 355, 356, 357,
      367–8, 404, 418, 436, 438, 531, 600,
      615, 619, 660, 663, 672, 682, 730, plate
      IIb, map 3; Broadgates Hall 40, 629,
      map 3; Cardinal's Hat 562; choristers
      207–8, 211; commoners 48, 663–4,
      697–701; constitution after 1547: 35–8;
      dean 133, 144, 435, 614; disputations
      41, 138; domestic teaching 37–42,
      305–6, 697–701; endowed by Mary

Tudor 377; examinations 39–42; fellows' bonds 20; fellows' chambers 627–9; foundation 32–3; Greek teaching 32, 34, 36, 38, 41; Hebrew teaching 34–5, 36, 39; library 205, 210, 458, 461, 614, 621; gifts temp. Elizabeth I: 498–519, plate XIIa; purchase of university library desks 466; matriculation list 50; noble scholars 39; numbers at 140; protestantism 133–9, 380, 409; public lectures 41; puritan leaders 330, 419; register of discipline 659; regius professorships 132, 307, 345–7; revenues 524, 543–4, 550; royal visits 209, 398–400; scientific circle at 717; scrutiny 39; statutes 33–5, 37–9, 40, 41, 42, 346, 347, 721; tutors 39, 40; university exercises at 40

Corpus Christi College 7–8, 15, 29, 31, 39, 80, 81, 83, 131, 142, 159, 209, 215–16, 239, 248, 295, 308–9, 316, 326, 336, 355, 356, 364, 391, 404, 406, 416, 532, 536, 571, 597, 600, 605, 610, 612, 618, 619, 628, 629, 675, 730, plate IIa, map 3; accounts 526–7, 535, 545, 548–51, 574–96 (corn rents 580–3; fines 578–80; *Libri magni* 586–96, plate XXIIa; procedure 575–6); admissions 668–9, plate XXIIb (average age at 685; average time in college 685); building of 607–11; careers 684–9; commoners 28, 671–5, 726 (recruitment of 669–75); conservatives in 139, 381, 408; discipline 19, 23, 25, 651, 654–8, 662; disputations 24; foundation 17–21, 120; Greek teaching 21–2, 24, 25–8, 658, 693; humanistic aims 19, 21, 66–8, 394; library 254, 441, 442–3, 452, 458–60, plates XIII, XIV (election system 461–2, 621, 712–13); library inventories 704–5; members on foundation 677–83; numbers at 140, 690; poor scholars 728–9; president 19, 340, 346, 624–6; prosopography of 676–7, 692–3; protestants 124, 139; public lectures at Magdalen College 23, 25, 656; puritan activists 419, 421–3; readers 20–1, 25–6, 220, 306; scrutiny 39, 656; social composition 666–92; statutes 17–29 (compared to Magdalen College 28–9; compared to St John's College 45–6); tennis court 650; tutors 25, 27, 690; visitation 1535: 128; well-born scholars

689–91; Wolsey's lecturers at 26, 338–9
Durham College 17, 43, 145, 365, 597, 608, 615, map 1; library 463
Exeter College 77, 78, 79, 214, 215, 241, 280, 317, 395, 404, 597, 623, 630, 658, maps 1, 2 and 3; ball court 650 n. 4; catechist 59; commoners and battelers 58, 556, 632; fees 58; geography studied 717; Great Black Hall 54; Greek teaching 58; Hart Hall 54; library 248, 254, 445, 450, 456; numbers at 59, 62–3, 631; 'old customs' at 729 n. 6; Peryam's Mansions 632; rector 142, 340, 354, 626, 627; recusancy at 411, 413; refoundation 58, 523, 618
Gloucester College 79, 364, 365, 615, map 1; library 463
Jesus College 2, 64, 167, 265, 281, 358, 360, 404, 615, 630, 694, map 3; library 458; poverty of 524, 550, 559
King Henry VIII College 32, 33, 131, 301, 304, 342, 350, 615
Lincoln College 7. 10, 16, 59–60, 80, 105, 236, 308–9, 351, 357, 404, 597, 624, 629, maps 1, 2 and 3; lectures in Greek, logic and philosophy 60; library 317, 445, 450, 456–7, 477 (election lists 479–86, plate XIIb); rector 340, 426; register of discipline 659; rise in numbers at 62–3; tennis court 650; undergraduates 60, 549, 556, 710–11
Magdalen College 2–7, 10–12, 15–17, 21, 23, 25, 27, 31, 61, 62, 64, 78, 82, 83, 108, 111, 131, 142, 208–9, 215, 240, 246, 248, 281, 295, 342, 357, 374, 404, 406, 409, 434, 437, 439, 545, 597, 601, 604, 605, 607, 609, 611, 613, 617–19, 624–5, 628, 629, 631, 633, 645, 651, 658, 730, plate Ia, maps 1 and 3; assisted by Mary Tudor 377; choristers 207; commoners 7, 663; creansers 7, 12, 693; demies 4, 5; disorder 658–9, 661, 663; endowment valued 1546: 133; Greek teaching 55–6; Hebrew lecture 56, 61, 316–17; hospital of St John 239; income 60 n. 6, 550; library 239, 254, 386, 442, 445, 448–9, 450, 451–2, 468, 621; lectures 55; Magdalen College School 5, 55–6, 109–10, 228, 328, 646, 648, 687; numbers at 140; president 4, 6, 28, 122, 134, 139, 346, 354, 624–5; protestants and puritans 124, 329, 330, 367–8, 384; public lectures 5, 7, 23, 55, 56, 128, 128,

Oxford, University of (cont.)
Colleges, individual: Magdalen (cont.)
220, 306, 308, 336, 341, 353; puritan leadership and 391–2, 419–21, 440; register of discipline 659; rhetoric lecture 56; scrutiny 653; teaching innovations 4–7

Merton College 18, 70, 105, 118, 134, 142, 166, 215, 216, 220, 248, 298, 308, 327, 339, 342–3, 353, 355, 367, 404, 408, 597, 607, 617–18, 628, 629–30, 633, maps 1 and 3; academic exercises 60, 187, 194; accounts 526, 546; catechist 62; enforcement of conformity 410–11; Hebrew lecture 61, 188, 316; income 60 n. 6, 550; leases taken by queen 430–1; lectures in grammar, dialectic, Greek, rhetoric 60–1, 188, 616; lectures in humanity, physics and philosophy 61; library 166–7, 179, 204, 222, 223, 248, 254, 445–6, 448, 449, 450, 451–2, 453–4, 455–7, 458, 459, 468, 476, 600, 716, plate XI, plan 622 (inventory of 1556: 147, 458, 487–97; new shelving system 441–2, 460, 621; purchases 442–3); Linacre lecturerships 61, 221–3; murder at 661; numbers at 62–3, 66; portionists 62; Portionists' Hall 601; remodelling by Warden Fitzjames 600–4; response to new studies 60–2, 188; St Alban's Hall 54; scientific circle at 718; Spanish and Italian taught 188; visitation of 1535: 128; (of 1549: 136; of 1556: 147, 487); warden 340, 435, 624–7

New College 2–3, 4–7, 21, 42, 53, 61, 62, 83, 107, 109–10, 118, 130, 131, 139, 142, 167, 171, 204, 205, 208, 215, 234, 236, 265, 269, 272–3, 281, 282, 296, 302, 327, 342, 354, 355, 357, 358, 366, 374, 399, 404, 406, 414, 432, 526, 531, 536, 545–6, 606, 608, 610, 613, 615, 616–18, 619, 629, 630–1, 645, 662, plate IV, maps 1, 2 and 3; accounts 532–3; appeal to old members 523; architectural plan of 597, 628; assisted by Mary Tudor 377; catholic fellows of 381, 386 (purged 407–8, 440); choristers 207; civil law lecture 55; commoners instructed 696–7; dining room for fellows 623; discipline 653; endowment valued 1546: 133; Greek reader 55; halls connected with 53–4; income estimated 1592: 60 n. 6, informatores 3,

6; library 235, 254, 365, 445, 448, 449, 453, 456–7, 458, 621 (little spent on books 452); numbers at 140, 550; philosophy lecture 55; privy council intervenes 138–9; scrutiny 653; visitation of 1535: 128 (of 1549: 137); warden 2, 28, 340, 346, 624–5; see also Winchester College

Oriel College 7, 10, 62, 65, 70, 105, 113, 131, 194, 215, 226, 298, 314, 327, 404, 562, 597, 615, 616–17, 619, 630, 633, 711, maps 1 and 3; appeal to old members 523; awarding of degrees 65, 187, catechist 60; catholics expelled 409–10; commoners 60; Great Bedell Hall 54; Greek lecture 60; library 241, 254, 445, 448, 456, 468 n. 3; numbers at 60, 62–3; provost 138, 346, 626; tennis court 650

Pembroke College 559, 613

Queen's College 60, 62, 80, 182, 214, 215, 295, 342–3, 391, 404, 436, 527, 549, 597, 604, 609, 616–17, 619–20, 623, 624, maps 1 and 3; catechist 59; commoners 59, 556; enforcement of conformity 411, 413; Greek lecture 59; lectures in grammar, logic rhetoric and theology 59; library 442, 445–6, 450, 453–4, 476, 621 (protestant books at 452); numbers at 59, 62–3; provost 340, 435; tutors 59, 694, 719; visitation of 1535: 128

St Bernard's College 43 n. 4, 45, 145, 365, 597, 608, 609, 610, 615, 624, 626, map 1; completion of buildings 604–5

St John's College 2, 42, 45–8, 65, 70, 80, 83, 106, 111, 145, 154, 167, 211, 215–16, 237, 249, 277, 282, 295, 309, 356, 357, 377, 404, 435, 615, 619, 620, 626, 651, 654, 697, 711, 728, plate III b, map 3; canon law to be taught 378; catholics expelled 384, 411; commoners 47, 556, 663–5 (fully incorporated into college 65); Cook's Building 633; discipline 664–5; domestic lectures 46; endowment 45 n. 5, 46–7; fellows' chambers 628–9, 630, plate IX; fellows' common room 623; income 46–7, 60 n. 6, 550; leases granted to Leicester 430; library 222, 254, 256, 458, 460, 621 (election system 461–3); link with towns 45–6, 682, 723; selection of scholars 46; social distinctions 47; statutes 45, 47; tutors 47

St Mary's College 53, 303, 605, 608, 615, maps 1 and 3

Trinity College 42–5, 47–8, 65, 70, 77, 145, 154, 167, 168, 215, 278, 355, 377, 404, 406, 615, 630, 651, plate IIIa, map 3; commoners 44–5, 556 (fully incorporated into college 65); conformity imposed 409; domestic lectures 44, 47, 188; humanism 44; library 458, 460–1; recusants 413; social distinctions 44–5; statutes 43–5; tutors 45, 694

University College 10, 62, 79, 327, 404, 420, 454, 524–7, 535, 545, 547, 549–50, 559, 597, 610, 628, 630, 633, maps 1 and 3; commoners 59, 695; lectures in Greek, logic, philosophy and theology 59; library 445, 450, 452 n. 4; master 340, 625–7; numbers at 62–3; teaching arrangements 59

Wadham College 559, 619, 633

congregation 98, 111, 119, 126, 183, 197, 226, 268, 269, 310, 401, 422, 598, 669

authority of 117–18

'black congregation' of artists 164–5

development of steering committee 164, 402–3, 426, 440

Leicester and 424–7

powers of masters eroded 149, 402–3

convocation (great congregation) 105, 112, 123, 245, 258, 276, 307, 310, 313, 336, 399, 401–2, 417–18, 440

agenda of 402–3, 426

establishes levy on colleges 130

Hatton advised by 431

Leicester and 424–5

nature of 117

royal divorce and 125

diet 647–8

disorder 48, 148, 657–65

drama, see, plays and players

ecclesiastical commissions 403, 412, 419

faculties, general 157–334

regius professorships 225–38, 335–61; schools 598–600; size of 154–6; statutory curriculum 151–2

of arts 157–212, plate XVIII; bachelor's degree 171–81; European setting of 157–60, 198–9; evaluation of 198–9; exercises 168–9; master's degree 181–98; numbers of artists 162–3; powers of 163–5, 310; reformation and 160–2; regius chairs 34–5, 307–8, 314, 316, 344–7, 354–8; royal divorce and 125; statutes departed from 179–81; undergraduate studies 165–81

of canon law 154–5, 259; effect on ecclesiastical law 257–62; revival under Mary 378; statutory syllabus 267–9

of civil law 154–5, 262–93, plate XVIII; aularian instruction 269–70, 276–9; bachelor's degree 267–8, 272–3; decay of 271–2; doctor's degree 269, 273; profession of law and 279–81; recruitment and careers 270–71, 281–3; refuge for the idle 275; regency 262–3, 269; regius chair 262–7, 358–61, 554; relation to arts faculty 267, 273; syllabus 267–9; Tudor statutes 272–5

of medicine 155, 213–56, plate XVIII; evaluation of 249–56; informal studies 238–41; libraries 253–4; licences 217, 250–1; Linacre lectures (see also Merton College) 61, 221–3, 228, 232, 237; numbers 250; provision of teaching 219–38; regius chair 224–38, 361; relation to arts faculty 213–19; relation to European thought 244–9; statutory curriculum 217–19; teaching in colleges 215–16; writings of Oxford men 241–4

of theology 295–334, plates XVIII, XIX; bachelors' lectures 308; careers of graduates 327–9; city lecturerships 106–8, 313; disputations 308–10, 324; King Henry VIII College 304, 342; King Henry VIII lecturer 130, 307, 308, 343, 353, 559; Lady Margaret Professor 120, 305–7, 329, 335–6, 344, 347–52; Oxford 'Anglicanism' 329–34; regency in 305; regius chair 307–8, 310, 344–7, 352–4; relation to arts faculty 296, 326; religious orders in 298–300, 303, 305; royal divorce and 125; scholarship of 313–27; sermons 311–12; size and composition 154–6, 297–313; syllabus 296–7; use of 296, 328; Walsingham's lecture 312; Wolsey's lecture 26, 338

finances 118, 148, 550–6

assessment ordinance of 1647: 558

chests 119, 141, 551, 725–6

corn-rent act 431, 535–7, 564, 582

fees 552–6

Marian benefactions 141, 533, 550

founder's kin 46, 64

friars 130

dissolution of religious houses 1, 130, 365

Oxford, University of (*cont.*)

graces 6, 65; *see also* faculties

hebdomadal board, *see* congregation

incorporation 1571: 402, 431

Laudian code, *see* statutes

lectures 3, 5–7, 14–15, 21–3, 30, 36, 66, 141, 551

  in arts 166–8, 185–90, 196; in Latin and Greek, established 1535: 196, 342; in philosophy 343

  in law 267–70, 274–6

  in medicine 219–38

  in theology 305–10

  neglect of 427

  regius professors 34, 36, 37, 132, 224–38, 262–7, 307–8, 335–61; foundation of 224–5, 344–7; terminology of 335–6

  Wolsey's lectures, *see* Wolsey

  see also individual colleges, faculties: schools

letter-book 118

libraries, college and other

  in colleges maintained by Benedictines 463–5

  in foundations before 1500: 203–4, 445–54; election system 455–7

  in foundations after 1500: 458–61; election system 461–3

  private libraries 56, 167, 203, 208 n. 5, 214, 222–3, 230, 235, 239–41, 245, 248–9, 253–4, 278 n. 3, 315–17, 467–76, 701–8

  public library of the university 598, 599, 621; Bodleian 204, 254, 256, 317, 323, 487, 729–30, 732; destruction by Edwardine visitors 466; falls into disuse 128, 465–6, 556; use of 167

libraries, general 167, 222–54 *passim*

  and visitors of 1535: 128, 365

  and visitors of 1549: 136, 466

  and visitors of 1556: 147

  new shelving 441, 476, plan 622

loan-chest, *see* finances

masters

  accommodations 7, 11, 59–60, 62, 65, 627–41

  body of 133, 151; *see also* congregation, convocation

  careers of 685–9, 691–2

  disedifying conduct of 660–2

  regent 2, 5, 6, 7, 13, 44, 48, 117, 125–6, 133, 149, 151, 163–5, 185–7, 192, 197–8

matriculation 48–51, 428, 631

  fees 49

oath of supremacy 50, 326, 403, 406

register of 49–50, 667, 669, plate XXa

subscription 51, 171, 326–7, 413, 431, plate XXb

tutors and 51

monastic colleges 3–30, 628; *see also* Canterbury, Durham, Gloucester and St. Bernard's Colleges

closure of 1, 129–30, 153, 531, 597

Lutheranism in 124

religious orders in theology faculty 298–300, 303, 305

numbers 152–5, 598, 616, 689–91

census of 1552: 49, 140

increase under Mary Tudor 148

in early 17th century 522

inquiry in 1556: 147

officers and servants 137, 148, 553–6; *see also* chancellor, proctors bedells 74–6, 85, 86, 108, 118, 123, 127, 169, 228, 552–5, 727; of civil law 49, 75, 86 n. 4, 153, 554

  carriers 83

  keepers of chests 725–6

  stationers 74

  steward 74

  registrar 118, 555, 727

plague and epidemics 184, 648–50

plays and players 53, 209, 290–1, 367, 398, 404, 427, 652, 665, 719 n. 3

poor scholars 723–4; *see also* undergraduates: finances and poverty

  licences to beg 725

  loans 725–6

premises 598–600

  congregation house 118, 598, 726, maps 2 and 3

  public schools 169, 400, 551, 598–600, maps 2 and 3; rebuilt by Mary Tudor 141, 349, 377, 600

  St Mary the Virgin 599, maps 1, 2 and 3

printed books 167, 187, 323, 382, 386

  cost of 167, 253, 697

  Greek introduced 475

  how investigated 441, 468

  search for heretical 412–13, 417

  textbooks 467–8

  where obtained 442–4

printing press 317, 321, 430

prison 104, 144

privileged persons, *see* Oxford, town and city

privileges 86–94, 95, 119, 132, 141; *see also* incorporation

charter of Edward III: 87, 104
submission of 91, 127
Wolsey's charter 88–90, 98–9, 114, 121
proctors 87, 96, 104, 112, 164, 165, 171, 182,
191, 309, 310, 325, 421, 422, 661
accounts of 550
determine fees 726–7
election of 118–19, 122, 132, 148, 425–6
protestants and protestantism 123–4, 131,
132, 135, 314, 324–6, 376, 377, 393,
405–6, 440, 704
continental scholars 40–1, 133–5
deprivations under Mary Tudor 142, 379
fostered by Richard Cox 138–9
importance to national church 732
Marian exiles 144, 322, 330, 380, 383, 395,
408, 409
readier acceptance at Cambridge 139–40,
330
religious census of 1577: 413
trial of Cranmer, Latimer and Ridley
142–4, 375–7
puritanism 324, 330, 333, 391, 400, 415–23,
431, 433
classis 330, 392, 419
presbyterian conference 1587: 419–20
reformation (see also relations with the
state) 1, 127, 149, 153, 195–6, 257, 301,
303, 314, 730
conservatism and Erasmianism 394–6
controversies 324–5, 383–96
Jewel-Harding debate 385–6
Lutherans 31–2, 56, 123–4, 363–4
Marian Oxford 140–9
Oxford under Edward VI: 135–40, 368–74
role in Puritan movement 391–3; see also
puritanism
royal visitation 1535: 127–9, 365
regency system, see masters: regent
relations with the state 117–49, 397–440; see
also Buckhurst, Dudley, Hatton
Edwardine expulsions 138–9, 374
Elizabethan enforcement of conformity
405–15, 440
financial measures 533–6
increase in state control 132–3, 135, 149,
403, 439–40
legatine visitation 1556: 145–8
Marian benefactions and revival 141–2
persecution of protestants 142–4
puritan initiatives 415–23
royal divorce and supremacy 124–7
royal visitation 1535: 127–9
royal visitation 1549: 135–8

royal visitation 1559: 405–6
relations with the town 69–117, 121–2, 132,
149
city lecturerships 106–7, 115
confraternities 107–8
control of parishes 105–6
manipulated by Cromwell 91–4, 127
marriage of scholars 113
ownership of urban property 114
religious life and education 105–14
sanitation 104–5, 648–9
scholars, see undergraduates
scholars' servants, see Oxford: trades
schools, see premises
social relations 154, 666–92, 722–6
statutes, general 30, 68, 117–18
ancient revived under Mary Tudor 140,
273–4
codification of 119, 121
Edwardine (1549) 137–8, 159, 165, 169,
172, 185, 190–4, 196–7, 201, 217, 263,
272–3, 275, 297, 350
Laudian code (1636) 86, 88, 159, 165, 169,
170, 177, 183, 184, 186, 190–4, 197,
212, 228, 274, 308, 350, 402–3
matriculation statute (1581) 51, 326, 413
nova statuta (1565) 49, 152, 159, 169,
172–9, 190–4, 196, 201, 218–19, 274–5,
297, 311, 350, 352, 356, 424–5
Reginald Pole's (1556) 148, 378
statutory curriculum 151–2, 165
student notebooks 708–12
study of arts (see also faculty of arts)
collegiate teaching 693–721
dialectic, see logic
geography 696–7, 716–17
grammar 5, 55–6, 59–60, 109, 183, 198,
700
Greek 15, 17, 21–7, 30, 36–8, 41, 44–6,
55–6, 59–60, 63–4, 120, 196, 198,
307–8, 340, 342, 475, 655, 696, 702–13,
720; biblical and patristic studies 314–
15; in halls 54; opposition to by 'Trojans' 67; regius chair 34, 354–6;
visitation of 1549: 137; see also individual colleges
Hebrew 36–7, 39, 56, 61, 342, 475, 703,
720; in faculty of theology 316–18;
regius chair 34–5, 307–8, 316–17,
356–8; visitation of 1549: 137
humanism (see also rhetoric) 4–5, 15, 17–19,
21–3, 26, 28–9, 30, 35, 37, 41, 42, 44,
54, 58–9, 61, 120–1, 693, 720, 721, 732;
and foundation of Corpus Christi

Oxford, University of (*cont.*)
  humanism (*cont.*)
    College 66–8; and 'new learning' 128;
      resisted 175, 198; triumph of 730–1
    inception 197–8
    Italian 61, 696
    logic and dialectic 10, 14, 17, 21, 23–4,
      34–7, 41, 44, 46, 54–5, 57–9, 60, 62, 64,
      169, 176–9, 199, 324, 695–6, 699, 700;
      disparaged at Magdalen College 129;
      displacement of old logic 708
    mathematics 34–5, 37–8, 41–2, 58, 62,
      169, 698, 700, 717, 720–1
    moral philosophy 13, 24, 28, 34, 36, 41,
      47, 169, 700, 702, 712; public reader at
      Magdalen College 5, 23, 55
    music 172, 201–12, 700; degrees in 206–7;
      importance in colleges 207–9; lectures
      in 175, 187, 205; manuscript evidence
      for study of 203–5, 209–10; *musica
      speculativa* 202–3, 206; *practica musica*
      202, 206
    natural philosophy 5–6, 13, 15, 17, 24, 28,
      34, 36, 41, 47, 63, 169, 214–15, 698,
      700, 716–21, 731; physics 61; public
      reader at Magdalen College 5, 23, 55,
      56; Sedleian lecturership 732
    rhetoric (humanity) 15, 17, 19, 21–2, 30,
      35, 41, 46, 56–9, 61, 198, 324, 700, 703,
      712, 720, 731; Cardinal College 340–1;
      in halls 54; King Henry VIII College
      342; Wolsey's lecture 26–7, 337–9
    science, *see* natural philosophy
    sophister and sophistry 10, 14, 23, 41,
      169, 176
    Spanish 61
    use of 195–6, 324
  study of canon law 3, 5, 30, 340, 358
    bachelor's degree 267
    official teaching stopped 129, 153, 257,
      365
    relation to civil law 268–9
    use of 159–60, 271
  study of civil law 3, 5, 30, 40, 41, 54–6, 63–4,
    111, 340
    an easy degree 275–6, 280–3
    disputations 273, 275
    encouraged by state 135–7, 140, 155
    inception 267
    informal instruction 277–9
    length of course 268, 274–5
    proposed college of civilians 137, 230,
      272
    supplants canon law 129

  use of 271
  study of medicine 4–5, 30, 32, 34, 40, 340,
    720
    anatomy and surgery 221, 226, 228,
      244–7, 696
    botany 247–8
    disputations 226–7
    fees 219
    humane study 214
    lectures 227–9
    medical literature 240–1, 253–4
    proposed college of physicians 230, 272
    Tomlins readership in anatomy 247, 255
  study of theology 2, 5, 6, 10, 13, 19, 21–3,
    26, 28, 44, 46, 58–9, 63, 67, 111
    biblical study and languages 313–20
    catechetics 47, 49, 54, 60, 62, 326–7
    collegiate teaching 305–10, 320
    controversy 322–5
    disputations 308–9
    Marian revival of Catholic teaching 145
    patristics 320–4
    study of *Sentences* proscribed 129
  subscription to thirty-nine articles, *see*
    matriculation
  undergraduates
    accommodation in colleges 3–5, 11–13,
      18–20, 30–1, 34, 38–40, 44–5, 46–7,
      49–50, 57–60, 62–4, 608, 628–30, 645–7
    accommodation in halls 1, 2, 49–50, 52–5,
      597–8, 629
    battelers 44 n. 6, 45, 58
    chamberdeacons in town 2, 48, 50,
      111–13, 148, 153, 155
    commoners 7, 11, 17, 41, 44–5, 47–8,
      58–60, 155, 669–75; discipline of 663;
      expenses of 726–7; full incorporation
      into collegiate societies 65; gentlemen
      commoners 7, 12, 40, 47, 60, 548–9,
      695–7, 729; noble commoners 7,
      12–13, 28, 31, 45, 47
    discipline, general 17, 404, 653–66; cor-
      poral punishment 23, 653–5, 659–60,
      664–5; in colleges 14, 19, 23, 31,
      653–60, 662–4; in halls 2, 657
    disorders 404, 658–65
    expenses 45, 47, 697–9, 726–8; *see also*
      tuition fees
    finances and poverty 4, 57, 59, 723–9
    games and recreations 649–52, 665, 696
    laymen 1, 652–3, 666–92, 730
    migration 663
    numbers 49, 689–91; *see also* faculties,
      general

social origins 38, 49, 666–91, 722–9
tuition fees 47, 58, 182–3, 425, 552–4, 694–5, 726–7
tutors 3, 49, 51, 57, 153, 168, 327, 413, 666, 693–5, 719, 722; in halls 53, 54; link with rise in numbers 66, 731; *see also* individual colleges
vice-chancellor (commissary), *see* chancellor
visitations 149, 151–2, 403
   of Henry VIII (1535) 55–6, 59, 92, 127–9, 224, 252, 272, 325, 342
   of Edward VI (1549) 37, 109, 135–8, 230, 256, 272, 296, 325, 372
   legatine of Cardinal Pole (1556) 145–7, 233, 270, 325, 379
   of Elizabeth I (1559) 325, 382
   of 1647–8: 558
Oxfordshire 395, 670–1

Paddy, Sir William, MD, commoner at St John's College 216, 239, 245, 254, 255, 256
Padua, university of 25, 216, 218, 221, 223, 247, 254, 255, 301, 304, 338, 678, 688
Page, John, manciple of All Souls College 79 n. 2, 114 n. 4
Page, Samuel, DTh, fellow of Corpus Christi College 684 n. 1
Pagninus, Santes, OP 317
Palmer, Julius, MA, fellow of Magdalen College 144, 319, 377
Palmer, Thomas, MA, fellow of St John's College 471 n. 2, 632
Panormitanus 457, 474
Pantin, W. A. 463–4, 551
Pantrey, Thomas, esquire bedell of arts 75 n. 6
Pantry, John, DTh, provost of Queen's College 467 n. 3
Pantry, William, scholar of John Pantry at Queen's College 467 n. 3
Papudo, Antonio, BTh 304
Paracelsus, Paracelsians 228, 241, 249, 715
Parett, Simon, MA, fellow of Magdalen College 503
Paris, city of 256
Paris, University of 17, 68, 163, 185, 199, 206, 216, 237, 247, 254, 301, 302, 304, 332, 353, 382, 394–5; custom of Paris 151, 157
Parker, Anthony, BA, scholar of Queen's College 719
Parker, Matthew, archbishop of Canterbury 133, 145, 328, 366, 411, 415–16, 466, 711

Parker, Richard, BA, fellow of University College 330
Parker, Richard, builder 610
Parkhurst, John, DTh, fellow of Merton College, bishop of Norwich 134, 320, 332, 405
Parkynson, Edmund, MA, fellow of Brasenose College 11
Parmenius, Stephen 717
Parr, Katherine, queen of England 301
Parr, Sir William 229
Parris, Thomas, MA, donor to Christ Church library 512
Parry, Lady Blanche 439
Parry, Henry, DTh, fellow of Corpus Christi College, bishop of Gloucester and Worcester 327 n. 3, 388, 686 n. 3
Parsons, Robert, MA, fellow of Balliol College 329, 378, 381, 382, 412, 414, 415, 527 n. 1
Pascoe, tutor at Hart Hall 53
Pate, Richard, manciple of Exeter College 76 n. 1
Pates, Richard, BA, scholar of Corpus Christi College, bishop of Worcester 686 n. 3
Paul IV, pope 379
Paulet, Lady 409, 437
Paulet brothers 280
Pawe, William, BA, freeman of Oxford 113
Pawle, William, BA, inventory of 471 n. 2
Paynell, Thomas 303, 460, 462–3
Pecham, William, OSB, Canterbury College 463
Pedro de Fonseca 711
Pelling, master, lecturer in music 209
Pemberton (Lancs.) 694 n. 2
Pembroke, earl of, visitor at Jesus College 404
Pembrokeshire 265
Penry, John, MA 330
Peperell, Thomas, manciple of Gloucester Hall 79
Percy, Henry, 9th earl of Northumberland 718
Percy, Richard, DCL, student of Christ Church 260, 281 n. 4
Percy, William, commoner at Gloucester Hall 718
Pereira, Beneto 711
Periam, Lady Elizabeth (Bacon) 563
Perin, John, DTh, regius professor of Greek 354, 356, 510, 517
Perion, Joachim 703 n. 6, 705, 707
Perne, Andrew, master of Peterhouse, Cambridge 414, 542
Perrot, Robert, DMus 207

Persius 21
Pertenhall (Beds.) 577
Perugia, University of 279, 289, 360
Peryam, John, merchant of Exeter 632
Peterborough, countess of 673
Peterborough Cathedral 33, 683
Peter de Soto, public lecturer in the *Sentences* 145, 325, 347 n. 4, 379
Petrarch 710
Petre, Sir John 412, 437
Petre, Sir William, secretary of state, bene-factor of Exeter College 58, 224, 280, 450, 544, 618
Petrus Hispanus 158, 160, 177
Peurbach, George 174
Phaer, Thomas, BM 229, 234
Phelps, William, MA, logic teacher at Corpus Christi College 27
Phelps Brown-Hopkins index 546–7
Philip II of Spain, king of England 353, 636, 640
Philips, John, tailor and draper 80
Philips, Henry 394
Phillips, Morgan ('Morgan the sophister') BTh, principal of St Mary Hall 137, 370–1, 372, 394–5
Philobiblon of Richard of Bury 199
Philo Judaeus 707 n. 7
Philostratus 22, 341
Philpot, John, fellow of New College 317, 324, 329, 366
Physicians, College of 223, 224, 234, 236, 244, 245, 246, 251, 252, 255
Pico della Mirandola 706
Pighius, Albert 373
Pilkington, Francis, BMus 207
Pilkington, James, bishop of Durham 384
Pinart, Dominique, Oxford bookseller 443, 453
Pindar 22, 341, 476, 703 n. 6
Plato 20, 22, 44, 172, 222, 321, 341, 449, 469, 702, 706, 712
picture of 640
Platonism 696, 706, 707, 712–13, 715
Platter, Felix 238, 253
Plautus 21, 461, 467, 468, 702, 712
Pliny 21, 172, 176, 465, 703
Plotinus 713
Plowden, recusant fellow of Exeter College 413
Plutarch 22, 459, 702, 710
Pole, David, DCnL, fellow of All Souls College 456, 470
Pole, Reginald, chancellor of the university of Oxford, cardinal archbishop of

Canterbury 28, 141, 145, 302, 376, 379, 454 n. 6, 677, 679 n. 4, 680 n. 1, 686 n. 3
at Padua 338
elected chancellor 147, 401
legatine visitation of the universities 145–8, 233, 270, 325
Politian, *see* Poliziano
Poliziano, Angelo 21, 705
Polsted, Richard, esq., donor to Christ Church library 499, 503
Ponsonby, Thomas, fellow of New College 53
Potanus, Felix, licensed surgeon 230, 250
Pope, Thomas, Gloucester Hall 208 n. 5, 214
Pope, Sir Thomas, founder of Trinity College, Oxford 42–3, 145, 544, 615, 619
gifts to library 458, 460, 466
Porphyry 24, 44, 172, 174, 176, 184
Port, Sir John, fellow and benefactor of Brase-nose College 15
Pory, John, master of Corpus Christi College, Cambridge 414
Poston, Clement, donor to Christ Church library 502, 513
Pott, John, MA, fellow of Merton College 410
Potter, Randall, city chamberlain 86
Powell, Edward, DTh, fellow of Oriel College 123, 329
Powell, Griffin (Griffith), DCL, first principal of Jesus College 714 n. 5
Powell, Lewes, MA, fellow of St John's College 471 nn. 2 and 3
Powell, Thomas, DCL 273
Powell, William, DTh, fellow of Magdalen College 418
Pownall, Israel, MA, student of Christ Church 504
Prestbury (Glos.) 684
Preston, instructor of choristers at Magdalen College 208
Price, Henry, BTh, fellow of St John's College 631 n. 2
Price, Hugh, BCL, DCnL, founder of Jesus College 544, 615, 630
Price, John, BCL, BCnL, fellow of All Souls College 471 n. 1
Prichard, William, MA, alumnus of Christ Church 512, 518
Prideaux, John, DTh, rector of Exeter College, regius professor of theology 331, 626, 632, 717
Primasius 469
Prime, John, city lecturer 107, 110
Prin, Erasmus, *discipulus* at Corpus Christi College 688

Princes Risborough (Bucks.) 563
Priscian 172, 176
Prise, Edward, BCL 275
Proctor, John 706 n. 6
Propertius 710
Prynne, William 313
Psellus, Michael 203
Ptolemy 161, 172, 174, 201, 203, 205, 716
Pucci, Francesco, MA 384, 390
Pullan, John, MA, student of Christ Church 380
Pullen, Thomas, MA 437
Purfrey, Anthony, BCL, principal of Broadgates Hall 474
Purvyar, Robert, MA, fellow of Merton College 492, 493
Pye, John, alderman 91 n. 3
Pye, Thomas, DTh, fellow of Balliol College 318
Pym, John, commoner of Broadgates Hall plate XX
Pyper, Petrus, piper 209

Quercetanus, see Duchesne
Quintilian 21, 44, 58, 172, 176, 179, 193, 340, 461, 702, 713

Rabelais 254
Rainham (Norfolk) 697
Rainolds, Edmund, MA, fellow of Gloucester Hall 382
Rainolds, John, DTh, seventh president of Corpus Christi College 265, 310 n. 1, 312, 317, 318, 319, 320, 325, 333, 382, 387, 389, 390, 400, 436, 440, 444, 578, 580, 582, 625–6, 652, 685–6, 692, 708, 713–14, 719 n. 3, 721, 732, plate XV b
  leader of puritan party 290–2, 392–4, 419, 421–3
  library of 447
  opponent of Corro 417
Rainolds, William, MA, fellow of New College 320, 382
Raleigh, Sir Walter, gentleman commoner at Oriel College 60, 439
Ramsey, John, BTh, prior of St Mary's College 303
Ramus, Petrus; Ramism 117–18, 324, 699, 703 n. 6, 705, 706, 713
Randolph (Randall), Thomas, DCL, principal of Broadgates Hall 380
Rashdall, Hastings 114, 116, 157, 654
Rashi (rabbi Solomon ben Isaac) 317

Rastell, John, MA, fellow of New College 385, 386
Ratisbon, diet of 373, 394
Ravis, Thomas, DTh, student of Christ Church, bishop of Gloucester and London 328, 333, 433–4, 436, 438
Rawe, John, MA, fellow of Oriel College 468, 470
Rawe, Thomas, BA 460
Rawlins, Richard, DTh, warden of Merton College, bishop of St David's 496
Rawson, Christopher, MA, fellow of Corpus Christi College 725
Raynold, Thomas, DTh, warden of Merton College, bishop-elect of Hereford 496
Raynoldes, James, BA, fellow of Exeter College 208 n. 5, 632
Raynolds, John, BTh, OP 305
Reade, alias Tyler, Margaret 114 n. 1
Reade, John, MA, fellow of St John's College 471 n. 2
Reading (Berks.) 46, 687
Ream, Donatus, BCL 268
Recorde, Robert, MD, fellow of All Souls College 238, 242, 716, 731
Rede, John, councilman 101
Rede, Richard, DCL, fellow of New College, master of requests 457, 475
Redman, Henry, master mason 612
Regiomontanus 716
Renkens (Mancipull), Henry, Oxford stationer 444
requests, court of 360
Rescius, Antony 325
Reuchlin, Johann 222, 316, 317, 703
Reve, John, lecturer in music 205
Reve, William, brewer 80
Rewley Abbey 597
Reynolds, James, MA, fellow of Exeter College 214
Reynolds, Jerome, MA, theologus, medicinae deputatus, fellow of Corpus Christi College 214, 657
Reynolds, Thomas, DTh, warden of Merton College 147, 406, 410
Rhazes 254
Rheims, college of 255, 312, 332, 381, 389, 393, 409, 414
Richardson, Robert, joiner 562
Ridley, Nicholas, bishop of London 135–7
  trial of 142–3, 302, 323, 324, 328, 330, 375, 376, 398
Risdale, John 454
Risholm (Lincs.) 561, 562

Risley, George, BCL, fellow of New College 471 n. 2

Robertus de Haulo (de Handlo) 203

Robinson, Henry, DTh, provost of Queen's College, bishop of Carlisle 436, 438, 453–4, 542

Robinson, John, MA, fellow of Balliol College 474

Robinson, John, pastor at Leiden 684

Robsart, Amy 236

Rochester, diocese of 603
school at 38

Rodgers, John, maniple of Exeter College 79

Rogers, John, MA, scholar of Christ Church 709–10

Rome 247, 304, 322, 415

Rondelet, Guillaume 222, 238, 253, 254

Roper, John, DTh, fellow of Magdalen College, Lady Margaret Professor 329, 348 n. 3, 350

Roper, William, visitor of St John's College 404

Rose, William, BM, fellow of Oriel College 254, 688

Rosweld, Thomas 515

Rosweld, William 515

Roth, Cecil 317

Rotherwick (Hants) 563

Rothley, John, BCnL, BCL, student of New Inn Hall 475

Rous, John 52

Rowham, Edmund, BTh, monk of Bury St Edmund's 124

Rowland, master, extra-mural pupil at Corpus Christi College 690 n. 3

Royse, John, tailor 572

Royston (Yorks.) 687

Rudde (Roode), George, MA, reader of Greek at Corpus Christi College 668 n. 4, 685 n. 5

Ruel (Ruellius), Jean 248, 249, 254

Rupert of Deutz 449

Russell, Francis, 2nd earl of Bedford 406

Russell, J. C. 70–1

Russell, John, high steward of Oxford University, lord privy seal 93

Ruthall, Thomas, bishop of Durham 119, 328

Ryge, John 517

Sacheverell, Patrick, MA, fellow of Brasenose College 11

Sackville, Thomas, Lord Buckhurst, chancellor of Oxford University 51 n. 4, 312, 401, 420, 433–4, 436, 438, 544, plate XXIb
orders reforms 433
patronage 433–4

Sadoleto, Jacopo 175

St Andrews, University of 353

St Barbe, William, BTh, student of Christ Church 505, 512

St Catherine, confraternity of 108 n. 4

St Cuthberts, Benedictine monastery at Durham 17

St Frideswide's Priory 30, 106, 120, 122, 345, 597, 607, 610, 612, 614

St John, Elizabeth, wife of William Becher 673

St John, Oliver, third baron of Bletsoe 673

St John, hospital of, Lichfield 9–10

St John, priory of, Cambridge 10

St Just, Thomas, warden of King's Hall, Cambridge 206

St Lawrence Jewry 561, 565–7, 569–73

St Margaret Patens 561, 565, 567

St Mary Magdalen, Milk Street 570

St Mawes (Cornwall) 677

St Mildred Poultry 601

St Patrick's Cathedral, Dublin 359

St Paul's Cathedral 229, 287

St Paul's Cross sermons 302, 311–12, 331, 390, 392, 415

St Paul's School 337, 543, 687

St Quentin, siege of 264, 287

St Swithin, Benedictine priory at Winchester 17, 608

St Thomas, confraternity of 107–8, 115

Salesbury, William 320

Salisbury, diocese of 306, 670
De Vaux College 305, 351

Salisbury, Robert, DCL, fellow of Jesus College 281, 517

Sallust 21, 179, 698, 702, 704, 710

Salter, H. E. 86, 114, 313, 559, 565

Salutati, Coluccio di Piero 176

Sampoll, master, donor to Christ Church library 502

Sampson, Thomas, DTh, dean of Christ Church 311, 321, 329, 371, 374, 384, 392, 409, 423, 428, 503
puritan leader 393, 415–16, 422, 430
turned out by queen 383

Sanders, Edward, donor to Christ Church library 512, 518

Sanders, Edward, MA, scholar of Christ Church 518

Sanders, Nicholas, DTh, fellow of New College 329, 381, 386–7, 407, 414

Sanderson, John, DTh, fellow of Trinity College 711

Sanderson, Robert, DTh, fellow of Lincoln College, bishop of Lincoln 333–4

Sanderson, Thomas, DTh, fellow of Balliol College 320 n. 4

Sands and Nettlebed (Oxon.) 672

Sandys, Edwin, archbishop of York 672

Sandys, Edwin, BCL, fellow of Corpus Christi College 391, 672, 677

Sandys, George, commoner at Corpus Christi College 672

Sandys, Henry, commoner at Corpus Christi College 672

Sandys, Samuel, commoner at Corpus Christi College 672

Sandys of the Vine, William, third baron 672, 675

Sarcerius, Erasmus 703

Saunderson, BA, fellow of Lincoln College 485

Savage, Henry, DTh, master of Balliol College 561

Savile, Sir Henry, MA, warden of Merton College, provost of Eton 425–6, 438, 453, 544, 711, 716–17, 721, 731, plate XVb
editor of Chrysostom 321, 732
founds chairs 187, 720, 730, 732

Savile, Thomas, MA, fellow of Merton College 178, 223, 717

Savoy, duke of 640

Saxony 174, 301, 361

Schmitt, C. B. 702

Schmutz, Alexander 134

Schyron (Schyronius), Joannes 254

Sclater (Slater), Thomas, BTh, fellow of Corpus Christi College 462 n. 1

Scotland, universities of 173, 199

Scroope, MA, donor to Christ Church library 512

Seaver, Paul S. 107

Secoll, Richard, BA, inventory of 205

Selden, John 204, 558, 717

Seller, John, BTh, fellow of Corpus Christi College 725

Serapion 254

Serranus, Joannes 712

Servetus, Michael 417

Seton, John, DTh, logician, chancellor of Cambridge University 373, 702, 707

Severinus, Petrus 249

Seville 417

Seymour, Edward, earl of Hertford and duke of Somerset, Lord Protector 134, 136, 139, 258, 266, 272, 287, 303, 372, 380, 533

Shaftesbury (Dorset) 678

Sheffeld, MA, donor to Christ Church library 502

Sheppard, Griffin, MA, student of Christ Church 507

Sheppard, John, DMus 207

Shepreve, John, MA, regius professor of Hebrew 316, 356–7, 686 n. 2, plate XXIIa
elegiac poem of on President Claymond 658 n. 3

Sherborne, William, foundation member of New College 110

Sherbroke, David, student of medicine 101 n. 4

Sherley, Anthony, MA, fellow of All Souls College 280

Sherwin, Ralph, MA, fellow of Exeter College 381

Sherwood, John, MD 255

Shrewsbury, earl of, see Talbot

Siculus, Diodorus 703

Sidall (Siddall), Henry, BDL, BCnL, DTh, canon of Christ Church 134, 380, 503

Sidney, Sir Henry 351

Sidney, Sir Philip 695, 717–18, 721, 732

Simler, Josias 369

Simplicius 703

Sixtus IV, pope 151

Skelton, John 706

Skinner, Ralph, MA, warden of New College 139, 142, 366

Sleidan, Johann 451, 699

Slyhurst, Richard, MD, fellow of Magdalen College, Oxford medical practitioner 222, 233, 239, 241

Slyhurst, Thomas, DTh, president of Trinity College 406, 409
gifts to library 460–1

Smale, Nicholas, MA, fellow of Exeter College 456

Smallwood, William, MA, scholar of Gloucester Hall 208 n. 5, 278 n. 3, 632

Smith, Henry, BA, fellow of Lincoln College 319

Smith, John, MA, provost of Oriel College, Lady Margaret Professor 351

Smith, Matthew, BTh, principal of Brasenose Hall and first principal of Brasenose College 16, 471 n. 1, 472

Smith, Miles, DTh, chaplain of Christ Church, bishop of Gloucester 107 n. 4, 328, 508

Smith, Ralph, BTh, fellow of Magdalen College 421

Smith, Richard, DTh, regius professor of theology 14, 26, 131, 135, 307, 311, 329,

Smith, Richard (*cont.*)
  343–5,352–3, 365–6, 368, 369, 370, 373, 374, 385, 555 n. 2
  deprived of chair 134, 368
  restored 143
Smith, Thomas, public orator 428
Smith, Sir Thomas, regius professor of civil law at Cambridge 271, 431, 432, 535, 541–2, 558
Smith, William, bishop of Lincoln, co-founder of Brasenose College 7–10, 16–18, 605, 690
  and Brasenose College library 458–9
  executors of 10–14
Smith, William, BM, fellow of Merton College 233 n. 1
Smyth, Matthew, servant 12
Snape, Edmund, MA, fellow of Merton College 330, 332
Snowe, Elizabeth, will of 111
Snowe, John, brewer 111
Socinianism 391
Somerset, duke of, *see* Seymour, Edward
Somerset 670, 689
Sophocles 22, 341
Soto, Peter de, *see* Peter de Soto
Southampton, earl of, *see* Wriothesley
South Petherwyn (Cornwall) 141
Southwark (Surrey) 684
Southwick Priory (Hants) 458
Spackman, Norwicus, MA, alumnus of Christ Church 511
Spain, king of 266
Sparke, Thomas, DTh, fellow of Magdalen College 333, 389
Spensar, master, listed as regius professor of Greek 355
Spenser, John, DTh, eighth president of Corpus Christi College 391, plate XXIIb
Spenser, Richard 516
Spenser, William, MA, fellow of Trinity College 383
Spicer, Henry, chaplain of King Henry VIII College 131
Spire, William, Oxford bookseller 444
Sprint, John, MA, student of Christ Church 422
  donor to library 499
Spurway, Edward, DCL, fellow of All Souls College 282
Squier, Adam, MA, master of Balliol College 412
Stafford, Edward, third duke of Buckingham 220, 301

Stafford, Lady Jane 439, 540 n. 2
Stafforde, Robert, commoner of Exeter College 717
Stamfordham (Northumberland) 561
Standish, John, DTh, fellow of Corpus Christi College 329
Standishe, Edward, esquire bedell of law 75
Standley, Thomas, BA, fellow of Brasenose College 473
Stangar, *see* Gawen
Stanwell (Middx.) 672
Stapelford, William, foundation member of New College 110
Stapledon, Walter de, DCnL, DCL, bishop of Exeter, founder of Stapledon Hall (Exeter College) 620
Stapleton, Thomas, BA, fellow of New College 329, 378, 385, 407, 414
  edition of Bede 386
Star Chamber, court of 43, 418
Statius 468
Steeple Aston (Oxon.) 560, 564
Stempe, Thomas, DCL, fellow of New College, warden of Winchester College 457, 475
Stephanus, *see* Estienne, Robert
Stevens, John, MA, fellow of Oriel College 456
Stevens, Richard 154
Stevenson, Robert, DMus 207
Stocker, William, MA, of Broadgates Hall 278 n. 3
Stoeffler, Johann 716
'Stoffolde' (Stoffler), *see* Cavey
Stokesley, John, bishop of London 328
Stone, Lawrence 163, 552–3
Stone, Richard, OSB, Canterbury College 464
Stonyng, Gregory, fellow of Magdalen College 111
Stonyng, Oliver, fellow of Magdalen College 111
Stor, William, BA, scholar of St Edmund Hall 516–17
Storr, William, MA, fellow of Corpus Christi College 684, 724, 728, 729
Story, John, DCL, regius professor of civil law 262–4, 285–6, 345, 358, 359, 360
Strabo 172
Strafford, *see* Wentworth, Thomas, first earl
Stranchen, Edward 414
Strasbourg 380
  University of 353
Stremer, Gregory, MA, fellow of Corpus Christi College 462 n. 1
Stringer, Phillip, MA 400

Strype, John 410–11, 541–2
Stubbs, Lawrence, DTh, president of Magdalen College 620
Stubbs, Richard, DTh, master of Balliol College 620
Stule, Humphrey 728
Stumphius, John Rodolph 134, 139
Sturm, Johann 698–9, 703 n. 6, 707 n. 7, 712
Style, Humphrey, commoner at Corpus Christi College 674 n. 5
Suetonius 21, 710
Summaster, Thomas, MA, fellow of All Souls College 468–9
Sumner, Henry, MA 124, 364
supremacy, act of 259
Surrey 670
Sutton, Sir Richard, co-founder of Brasenose College 7–10, 16, 605, 606, 690
  arms of 15–16
  statutes for Brasenose College 10–14, 16, 17
Sutton, William, BTh, student of Christ Church 507
Sutton, William, MA, lector of Brasenose College 14
Sutton, Sir William 9
Swaddon, Richard, city lecturer 313
Swete, Giles, college rent collector 83, 86 n. 4
Swinburn, Ralph, MA, fellow of Trinity College 387
Swinburne, Henry, canon lawyer 259–60, 282
Swiss students 133–4
Swyft, Jasper, DTh, alumnus of Christ Church 509
Syckes, Nicholas, butler of Christ Church 470 n. 3
Sydenham, Thomas, BM 253
Sylvius, Jacobus 254
Symmynges, John, MD, fellow of the College of Physicians 233 n. 1
Symonds, Thomas, BM, fellow of Merton College, junior Linacre lecturer 221 n. 3, 232, 245, 444 n. 2, 446, 471 n. 1, 472
Syon, Brigittine monastery of 9, 605
Syston (Leics.) 141

Tabourner, John, musician 209
Tagault, Jean 245
Talbot, Francis, fifth earl of Shrewsbury 235
Tame, Sir Edward 301
Tame, Lady Katherine 301
Tappam, Christopher, MA, student of Christ Church 507
Tartaretus, Petrus 177

Tatam, John, MA, rector of Lincoln College 473, 517
Tatham, Thomas, BM, freeman of the city of Oxford 113, 233 n. 1
Tatham, Thomas, MA, fellow of Merton College, inventory of 205, 471
Tauler, John 364
Taverner, John, organist and composer 209–10, 364
Taverner, Nathanaell, BA, commoner at Corpus Christi College 672–3
Taverner, Richard 124, 320
Taylor, Robert, MA, university registrar, principal of Alban Hall 555 n. 2
Taynton (Oxon.) 609
Tehy, Robert, DTh, fellow of Magdalen College 472
Temple, William, MA, provost of Trinity College Dublin 711, 713
Tennand, Sylvester, janitor (porter) of Christ Church 506, 515
Terence 21, 467, 702, 704, 710, 712
Tertullian 302, 449 n. 3
Thackam, Thomas, BA, scholar of Corpus Christi College, fellow of All Souls College 687
Theocritus 21
Theodore of Gaza 475, 703, 707 n. 7
Theodoret 322–4, 370, 371, 703 n. 6
Theophrastus 22
Theophylact 451 n. 4, 704
Theorica planetarum 174
Thirlby, Thomas, bishop of Ely and Norwich 144
Thomas, William, plumber 605
Thomas à Kempis 707
Thompson, William, fellow of University College 474
Thomson, Thomas, MA, fellow of University College 702
Thornbury, Roland 114 n. 1
Thorne, John, *see* Dorne
Thorne, William, DTh, regius professor of Hebrew 318, 356, 358
Thornton, Richard, DTh, student of Christ Church 507
Thornton, Thomas, DTh, student and canon of Christ Church 505, 695
Thornton, Thomas, MA, alumnus of Christ Church 510, 511
Throwley, John, BTh, BM 301
Thucydides 22, 707 n. 7
Tiarda, Ezo, DCL 279
Tidyman, William 113

Tinctoris, Johannes 212

Tippyng, Thomas, BA, probationer fellow of Brasenose College 14

Titelmans, Frans 703 n. 6, 705, 707 n. 7, 711

Titus Livius, *see* Livy

Todde, Nicholas, alderman 114

Toletus, Franciscus 711

Tolley, David, MD, student of Christ Church 167, 224, 245, 471 n. 1

Tomkins, Thomas, BMus 211

Tomlins, Richard, esq., founder of anatomy lecturership 732

Tomson, Laurence, MA, fellow of Magdalen College 330, 331, 395, 418

Tonbridge school 46

Topleif, master, donor to Christ library 502

Toppyng, Ottwell 52 n. 5

Torles, Arthus, BA, fellow of St John's College 387

Torres, Jerome, SJ 454

Tostatus 454 n. 1

Totnes (Devon) 265

Townsend, Lady Jane 697

Townsend, John, builder 610

Townsend, Robert, commoner of New College 697, 716

Toye, Margaret, bookseller of London, donor to Christ Church library 503

Tragus, Heronymus 248

Trapezuntius, *see* George of Trebizond

Travers, John, MA, fellow of Magdalen College 403, 419

Travers, Walter, MA 390

Traves, John, brewer 102, 103 n. 2

Tregonwell, John, DCL, visitor to the university 128

Tremellius 317

Trenaunte (Cornwall) 141

Trent, council of 324

Tresham, Sir Thomas 460

Tresham, William, DTh, fellow of Merton College, canon of Christ Church 40, 93, 135, 137, 142–3, 322, 329, 370–1, 375, 555 n. 2
    deprived of fellowship 410
    imprisoned 374
    Longland's commissary 126
    summoned by privy council 139

Trever, Randall, MA 233 n. 1

Tripp, Simon, MA, fellow and reader in humanity of Corpus Christi College 708–9

Trivett, Christopher, MA, scholar of Broadgates Hall 508

Troutbeck, Robert, MA, fellow of Queen's College 422

Tübingen, University of 158, 304, 316

Tucke, John, MA, fellow of New College 204

Tucker, John, MD, canon of Cardinal College 230

Tunbridge Wells (Kent) 687

Tunstall, Cuthbert, bishop of London and Durham 18, 373
    De arte supputandi 172, 174, 716

Turberville, James, DTh, university registrar, bishop of Exeter 555 n. 2

Turin 304

Turnbull, Hugh, BTh, fellow of Corpus Christi College 394

Turnbull, Richard, MA, fellow and chaplain of Corpus Christi College 725

Turner, Peter, MD 243

Turner, Samuel, MA, MD (Padua), MP 678, 679

Turner, Thomas, MA, lecturer in rhetoric, Magdalen College 56

Turner, William 247, 248

Turner, William, MD, dean of Wells 138

Twisse, William, DTh, fellow of New College 713

Twyne, Brian, BTh, fellow of Corpus Christi College and antiquary 53 n. 1, 338, 649, 711, 717–18, 720, 724, 726, 729

Twyne, John 338–9

Twyne, Thomas, MD, fellow of Corpus Christi College 243, 679 n. 2, 680

Tycheborne, master of Gloucester Hall 278 n. 3

Tye, Christopher, DMus 207

Tyndale, William, MA 123, 309, 314, 317, 320, 329, 364, 394, 395

Tyrwitt, master, donor to Christ Church library 502

Udall, Nicholas, MA, fellow and lecturer in humanity at Corpus Christi College 26–7, 328, 364, 687

Ulmer, Johann, *see* John ab Ulmis

Underhill, Edmund, MA, fellow of Lincoln College 456

Underhill, John, DTh, fellow of New College, rector of Lincoln College, bishop of Oxford 107, 389, 425–6, 428–9

Upton, Isaac, DCL, fellow of New College, canon of Wells 281

Ursinus, Zacharias 388

Valerius, Cornelius 698 n. 3, 699–700, 705, 707

Valerius, Maximus 21, 61, 698 n. 3, 702, 704, 707 n. 7

Valla, Laurentius 174, 702, 703
   Elegantiae 21

Valor ecclesiasticus 11, 12, 686

Valyn, John, inventory of 475, 702

Varro, Marcus Terentius 704

Vaughan, Morris, steward of Corpus Christi College 83

Vaughan, Richard, MA, student of Christ Church 507

Vaughan, William 694

Vaux, Laurence, BTh, fellow of Corpus Christi College 379

Venice 31, 254

Vermigli *see* Martyr, Peter

Verney, Richard, BA 515

Vertue, William, master mason 609–11, 612

Versalius, Andreas 245, 248, 449, 450

Vienne, council of 22

Vigelius, Nicolaus 260–1

Villa Garcia, *see* Juan de

Villiers, Peter, minister of French church 385

Vincent, Francis, commoner of Corpus Christi College 674 n. 3

Virgil 21, 172, 467, 468, 699, 701, 705

Virginia, colony of 684

Vitellio 172, 174

Vittorino de Feltre 175, 650

Vives, Juan Luis, Wolsey's reader in humanity 26–7, 156, 220, 338–9, 609, 713

Wade, Christopher, MA, fellow of Magdalen College 434

Wadham, Nicholas and Dorothy, founders of Wadham College 544

Wake, Arthur, MA, canon of Christ Church 392

Wake, William, MA, student of Christ Church 504

Wakefield, Barnaby 439

Wakefield, Robert, BTh, lecturer in Hebrew 304, 305, 316, 342

Walby, master 232

Wales, the Welsh 12, 671

Walker, Richard, MA, fellow of Merton College 629–30

Walle, Roger, BCnL, principal of Little White Hall 486

Walley, Thomas, DCL, student of Christ Church 466

Walsh, Henry, BTh 305

Walsh, Thomas, MA, fellow of Corpus Christi College 459

Walsingham, Sir Francis 330, 395, 418–19, 540 n. 2
   influence in Oxford 436
   theology lecture 312, 389, 436–7

Walward, John, BTh, fellow of Corpus Christi College 392, 403, 419

Warcupp, Ralph, MA, student of Christ Church 384

Ward, John, stone mason 609–10

Warde, Robert, MA, praelector in philosophy 344

Warham, William, DCL, archbishop of Canterbury, chancellor of Oxford University 18, 67, 90, 141, 307, 328, 337, 363, 618
   gift to all Souls library inadequate 447–8, 456
   principal of civil law school 262–3
   rival to Wolsey 118–26

Warkin, Edward, MA, alumnus of Christ Church 511

Warner, Bartholomew, MD, regius professor of medicine 236–7

Warner, John, MD, warden of All Souls College and regius professor of medicine 224, 229–32, 343–5, 449, plate XXIII

Watkinson, William, BTh, student of Christ Church 499, 504, 506, 508, 515

Way (Wye), family at Corpus Christi College 671

Waynflete, William of, BTh, bishop of Winchester, founder of Magdalen College, Oxford 3–7, 12, 16, 17, 21, 31, 64, 109, 220, 306, 653, 690
   collegiate conception compared to that of Fox 28; of Wolsey 29, 613

Wayte, John, college rent collector 83, 86 n. 4

Webb, George, DTh, fellow of Corpus Christi College, bishop of Limerick 686 n. 3

Webb, William, commoner at Corpus Christi College 674 n. 2

Weedon (Northants) estate map plate XXIV

Weelkes, Thomas, BMus 207, 211

Wells, diocese of 206, 355, 359

Welsh, deprived fellow of Corpus Christi College 374

Weltden, Thomas, MA, student of Christ Church 504

Wendy, Thomas, MD 247

Wentworth, Thomas, first earl of Strafford 678

Wentworth, Thomas, MA, donor to Christ Church library 503

Wentworth, William 721–2

West, William, commoner at Corpus Christi College 709

Weste, John, fuller 102

Westfaling (Westphaling), Herbert, DTh, Lady Margaret Professor, bishop of Hereford 39, 306, 310 n. 1, 352, 400, 435, 512

Westminster Abbey 336, 345, 348–9, 359

Westminster Cathedral 34, 132, 224, 344–5 statutes 344

Westminster School 38, 543, 558, 716

Weston, Edward 466

Weston, Hugh, BM, DTh, rector of Lincoln College, Lady Margaret Professor 143, 324, 328, 329, 349 nn. 2 and 3, 351, 372, 375, 376, 486

Weston, Hugh, MA, fellow of Lincoln College 191, 387–8

Weston, John, yeoman bedell of theology 108

Weston, Robert, DCL, regius professor of civil law, principal of Broadgates Hall 40, 264, 285–7, 358–60

Weston, William, BCL, scholar of Corpus Christi College 683

Weston, William, MA, fellow of Lincoln College 365, 484

Wever, George, DCL 269

Whadborough (Northants) 547

Whitaker, William, BTh 382–3, 725

White, John, DTh, fellow of New College, bishop of Lincoln and Winchester 357, 376, 458

White, Sir Thomas, founder of St John's College, Oxford 43, 45, 46, 111, 145, 411, 458, 466, 544, 605, 615, 623, 626

White, William, white-baker 79

Whitehead, James, BM, junior Linacre lecturer 222, 223

Whitelocke, Sir James, BCL 277, 623, 650 n. 5, 723

Whitgift, John, archbishop of Canterbury 280, 287, 360, 392, 419–20, 423, 429, 436, 439, 540 n. 2, 544

Whitmore, Robert, DCL 282

Whitnel (Somerset) 80

Whittingham, William, DTh, fellow of All Souls College, dean of Durham 306, 320, 380, 383

Whitton, Robert, MA, fellow of Magdalen College 469

Whyte, Thomas, DCL, warden of New College 406–7

White, Thomas, DTh, prebendary of Christ Church 499, 509, 516

Whytals, Matthew, DTh, fellow of Corpus Christi College 683

Wickham, William, MA, student of Christ Church 506

Widdowes, Giles, MA, city lecturer 313

Wigan (Lancs.) 694 n. 2

Wigston hospital, Leicester 416, 428

Wilcox, Thomas 330, 417

Wilkinson, William, DCL 281 n. 4

Willet, Andrew, MA, rector of Barley 542, 711

William of Ockham 199

Williams, James, yeoman bedell of law 634

Williams, John, DTh, fellow of All Souls College, Lady Margaret Professor 352, 686 n. 2

Williams, Thomas, alderman 113

Williams, Thomas, rector of Trefriw 248

Williamson, Gerard, DTh, student of Christ Church 507

Williamson, Martin, brewer 102

Willis, Francis, MA, president of St John's College 429

Willis, Timothy, BA, fellow of St John's College 249, 664–6

Willoughby, MA, donor to Christ Church library 503

Wilson, John, citizen 366

Wiltshire 670

Winchester, city of 38

Winchester, diocese of 17, 229, 354, 670 bishop of as visitor 404, 656–8, 670

Winchester College 3, 5, 83, 107, 109–10, 302, 315, 355, 367, 376, 431, 535, 543, 557–8, 687, 696

Windsor, Miles, antiquary 717

Windsor (Berks.) 306, 535 St George's collegiate church 351–2, 357, 409, 609

Winter, Christopher 683 n. 6

Winter, Thomas 394

Winwood, Sir Ralph, BCL 282

Wisbech Castle (Camb.) 382

Withers, William 603

Withington, Oliver, MD, fellow of Brasenose College 222, 233 n. 1

Withy, William, BCL, student of Christ Church 239, 472–3, 512

Wittenberg, University of 174, 395

Wodrofe, William, MA 475, 703 n. 1

Wolfe, Reyner ('Raynarde'), London bookseller 442

Wolley, Sir John 437

Wolphe, Joachim, licensed surgeon 250

Wolsey, Thomas, DTh, fellow of Magdalen College, cardinal archbishop of York 17,

26, 32–4, 42, 56, 121–2, 141, 159, 259, 302, 328, 395, 544, 624, 713, frontispiece
Cardinal College and 29–32, 35, 37, 40, 122–4, 132, 304, 307, 336, 339–41, 605, 612–15, 618
chancellorship of Cambridge offered to 120
commissions scholars to defend orthodoxy 123
completion of St Mary's College and 605
courted by university 120
favours Greek studies 67
lectures founded by 21 n. 4, 67–8, 120–1, 137, 220, 307, 336–9, 344
privileges of university and 88–90, 98–9, 114, 132
statutes of university revised 30, 68, 121, 151
Wood, Anthony 1, 40, 141, 223, 225, 265, 312, 336, 400, 410, 424, 433, 542, 606, 650
Wood, Thomas, BCL, scholar of Broadgates Hall 650
Wood, William 323 n. 1
Woode, Thomas, scholar at Balliol College 660
Wood Eaton (Oxon.) 672
Woodson, John, singingman of Christ Church 82 n. 5, 86 n. 1
Woodstock (Oxon.) 69, 560, 562, 564, 567, 571 palace 609
Woolton, John, MD, fellow of All Souls College, bishop of Exeter 222, 239, 244
Wooton (Oxon.) 560, 564, 570
Wootton, Richard, esquire bedell of theology 75 nn. 2 and 6, 76 n. 3
Worcester, diocese of 562, 670 King's School 687
Worcestershire 12
Wormenhale, John and Thomas, scholars 110 n. 4
Worsop, P., master, donor to Christ Church library 503
Worthington, Thomas, BA, of Brasenose College, president of Douai College 317, 320
Wotton, Edward, MD, Greek reader at Corpus Christi College, president of the College of Physicians 25, 27, 238, 242, 247, 248, 254, 668 n. 4, 685 n. 5

Wotton, Henry, MD, fellow of Corpus Christi College 233 n. 1, 513
Wotton, Sir Henry, BA, commoner of New College 696
Wotton, William, organ maker of Oxford 601
Wright, Bernard, medical student 226
Wright, William, DTh, master of Balliol College 146, 233, 406, 412
Wriothesley, Thomas, first earl of Southampton 270
Wyclif, John 126, 394
Wydow, Robert, BMus 206
Wykeham, William of, bishop of Winchester, founder of New College 2–4, 6, 17, 29, 458, 624, 653
Wyllanton, Richard, fellow of Lincoln College 494
Wylleys, Richard, warden of Higham Ferrers 456
Wylliot, John de, MA, foundation of at Merton College 62
Wylsford, Edmund, DTh, provost of Oriel College, Lady Margaret Professor 350
Wysse, Thomas, scholar at White Hall 53
Wythey, William, BCL 275

Xenophon 476, 703, 709

Yakesley, Richard, OSB 366
Yeldard, Arthur, DTh, president of Trinity College 79 n. 3, 409
Yonge, John, commoner of Corpus Christi College 672 n. 2
York, ecclesiastical province of 360 archbishop of as visitor 404
York House, Whitehall 612
Yorkshire 12
Young (Yonge), John, DTh, warden of New College, bishop of Callipoli 119

Zabarella, Jacopo 178–9
Zacconi, Ludovico 203
Zarlino, Gioseffe 203
Zurich 320, 332, 353, 371, 408, 416
Zwingli, Ulrich 369

DATE DUE

OCT 0 5 1987			
GAYLORD			PRINTED IN U.S.A.